The Prophet of Nazareth
by Evan Powell Meredith

Address:
HardPress
8345 NW 66TH ST #2561
MIAMI FL 33166-2626
USA
Email: info@hardpress.net

94 93

THE

PROPHET OF NAZARETH,

OR

A CRITICAL INQUIRY INTO THE PROPHETICAL,
INTELLECTUAL, AND MORAL CHARACTER

OF

JESUS CHRIST,

AS EXEMPLIFIED IN HIS PREDICTIONS, HIS PRECEPTS, HIS
ACTIONS, HIS DISCOURSES, AND HIS SOCIAL INTERCOURSE.

BY

EVAN POWELL MEREDITH.

PRIZE ESSAY.

LONDON :
~~T. FARRAH, 282, STRAND.~~
1864.

PRINTED BY THE AUTHOR, AT MONMOUTH.

FOURTH PRIZE ESSAY.

INFIDELITY AGAINST CHRISTIANITY,

AND

CHRISTIANITY AGAINST INFIDELITY.

THE Premium for the best Essay on the above Subjects—now in the Press for *early* Publication—having been paid to MISS SARA SOPHIA HENNELL, of Ivy Cottage, Radford Road, near Coventry, after an able and ardent Competition, which, however, exacted an extent of study and research, very onerous and inconvenient to some respectable Competitors, both lay and clerical; and as it therefore now becomes desirable to *concentrate* the Discussion to one or two points, which, if demonstrated, seem to solve the momentous question of Christ's Divinity *whereon Christianity wholly rests*, the Subscriber will pay TEN SOVEREIGNS; or, in the option of the successful Competitor, will deliver to him an appropriate Medal, of equal value, for what the Subscriber shall deem the most *complete* yet *concise—truthful* yet *temperate—logical*, and *convincing*, EXPOSITION, responsive to the following two-fold question :—

Did Christ predict the Last Day of Judgment, and Destruction of the World, as events inevitable during the then existent Generation of Men ?[*] and if so, what inferences, theistical or the reverse, are fairly deducible from the non-fulfilment of that Prophecy, so dreaded by them,[†] it having been, as alleged, extensively and impressively inculcated by His apostles[‡] as promotive of Christianity in its earliest ages ?[§]

But FIRST—Each Competitor shall prefix to his Exposition, as his *accepted* Rule therein, a copy of this Advertisement, with its relative Note and References. SECOND —Each and every view of the above two-fold Question, on *both* sides, must be taken up and discussed *fully, fairly,* and *freely,* in all its aspects, *positive* and *negative,* so as to

---

[*] Matthew, Chap. x., verse 23 ; Ch. xvi., 27, 28 ; also Ch. xxiv., verses 3, 29, 30, 31, but *especially* 33 and 34, and from 35 to 42 inclusive.
Mark, Ch. ix., verse 1 ; Ch. xiii., verses 20 and 24, and onwards to the end, but *especially* verses 29, 30 ; also Ch. xiv., verse 62.
Luke, Chap. ix., verses 26 and 27 ; also Chap. xxi., verses 27 and 28, and from 30 to 36 inclusive, but especially verse 32.

[†] Thessalonians 2nd, Chap. ii., verses 1, 2, and 3.

[‡] Thessalonians 1st, Chapter iv., verses 15, 16, 17, and 18.
Timothy, 2nd, Ch. ii., verses 16, 17, and 18. James, Ch. v., verses 7 and 8.
Peter 2nd, Ch. iii., verses 2, 3, 4, and 7, and from 10 to 14, inclusive.

[§] Gibbon's Decline and Fall, Vol. 1st. Chap. xv., pages 560 to 568, inclusive.
Third Edition, Quarto, London, 1777.
Thessalonians 2nd, Chap. ii., verse 3, as to a hastening of the dreaded day by any "falling away" in the faith.

2 A

present *a complete* and *impartial* EXPOSITION of the *whole* subject, whereon SOUND convictions may repose. THIRD—All facts, arguments, and averments, must be stated with the *utmost possible regard to brevity, relevancy,* and *perspicuity,* in the form of *separate* and *distinct Propositions,* or Affirmations, *positive or negative,* as the case may be —giving to each a running number, and specifying distinctly in foot notes each authority founded on—particularly those hereto subjoined *which seem to merit special attention.* LASTLY—Each Competitor will annex his Subscription and Address to his Exposition, which must be lodged on or before the 1st day of June next (1857), with the Subscriber, who shall, within four months thereafter, notify to the successful Competitor his readiness to pay or deliver to him the said Premium; and for the further encouragement of Competitors, the Subscriber, if requested, will surrender on the *most liberal terms,* his hereby reserved Copyright to the Prize Essay, and the other Essays shall be returned to the respective Essayists, if applied for forthwith.

GEORGE BAILLIE.

37, Dalhousie Street, Garnethill, Glasgow,
　　1st January, 1857.

　　This Competition may naturally induce some serious and inquiring minds to ascertain clearly how far the Texts and Facts stated are, or are not, *in fair, legitimate,* and *grammatical, construction* of *language,* reconcileable with an opinion, that the Prophecy in question applied to the then existent generation, *solely and wholly,* with reference to the subsequent destruction of Jerusalem by the Romans under Titus, and not *in any way* to the Last Day of Judgment, and Destruction of the World. Akin to that Enquiry another of Christ's Prophecies might be adduced respecting His resurrection on the *third* day, as to which the Evangelists are, by some persons, appealed to, in proof that it took place—if at all—on a *different* and *earlier* day. Competitors, however, are left to discuss that Prophecy or not, as they incline; but if taken up—*and it seems worthy of being so* —it will fall to be treated in the manner prescribed as to the other and more prominent prophecy alluded to.

PREFACE.

THE occasion which moved the author to write the following work was the appearance in the Newspapers of the advertisement now prefixed to it, at the date which it bears. Although the prize offered was not very tempting, yet the subject proposed for discussion suited the taste of the writer, who, however, at the onset, did not intend his work to be of the size into which it has grown. But having been silent on theological matters from the time—about thirteen years previously—he had quietly withdrawn from Christianity, whose doctrine, after considerable examination and research, he had ceased to believe, and therefore could no longer conscientiously preach; and having, ever since his secédure, almost daily pursued his researches after the real origin of the Christian religion, he thought that thus to write on a given subject was an inoffensive and a favourable manner of making some of his theological views known to Christians generally, and particularly to those who had studied in the same college with him, and had taken so much pains to brand him as an infidel. With this intention, he closely applied to his task : the result has been the following work, to which the prize was awarded, and which, with some little additions, is now, after a considerable delay, about to be published.

The prefixed advertisement will show the conditions under which the work was to be written, and will explain the cause that considerable portions of it are written on the Christian side of the argument. These portions, which are strictly orthodox, are enforced with every possible fidelity and strength of reasoning that the writer could command when he was a sincere believer in the truth of the Christian religion; with the arguments in favour of which he has had ample opportunities of being acquainted. On the other hand, he must admit that, by a close study for the last twenty years, he has endeavoured to avail himself of every advantage in order to become conversant with the opposite view of the question.

The portions of the work devoted exclusively to the advocacy of Christianity are from page 9 to 50, and from 245 to 258. Should any Christian reader be so conscious of the weakness of his faith as to desire to know only what can be said in favour of his religion, he is recommended to confine himself exclusively to the perusal of these pages, and, when he has read them, to shut the book, lest his prejudice be irritated, or his mind roused to critical inquiry. But should he be one of those enlightened Christians who believe that religious truth is unchangeable and eternal; that whatever is urged against it cannot alter its nature; that the more it is assayed the brighter it shines; and that the existence of true religion does not depend upon antiquated creeds and ancient records, he may venture to read the whole of this volume, from which it is trusted he will derive some advantage.

Taught from infancy that it is sinful to read anything which calls in question the truth of their religion, there are still in Christendom, notwithstanding the rapid strides which the spirit of free inquiry has lately made, and continues to make, a great number whose predilections are shocked when they see any argument advanced against either their faith, or its founder; and whose hereditary superstitious notions have such an influence over their reflective powers that they regard Christianity as too sacred for criticism, and too solemn for argument. Such people forget that God is the author of their reasoning powers; that the *sound* dictates of reason are God's revelations to man; and that it would be as absurd to suppose that the Deity can be at variance with himself, as to imagine that any thing can be Divine which is contrary to the dictates of sound human reason.

In the following work, however, the writer has taken the utmost care not unnecessarily to wound the tender feelings of these timid Christians, by the use of any harsh language, in pointing out the imperfections of the object of their faith. Nor has he advanced many things on this point, that have not already been insinuated even by writers standing in the Christian ranks. All that he has done is to speak out a little more plainly and fearlessly than most of these have done. This is, probably, to be attributed to the fact that he is in no fear of forfeiting a rich preferment, patronage, popularity, or any of those Christian premiums which are held out to orthodoxy, are the means of existence to thousands of learned and talented men in this country, and, necessarily, regulate and guide both their tongues and pens. For men to write, shackled by the creed of a Church which they have previously sworn to defend,—to write in fear of its excommunication, or of contravening any of its Articles, has the effect of misleading truth-seekers, by such obscure suggestions of things which the writers cannot venture openly to state, as are either misunderstood by their readers, or not understood at all. This is peculiarly applicable to a great number of modern German writers of profound research, who, being connected with the Christian Church, evidently withhold much that they believe on important religious points. Having worked out a train of arguments leading inevitably to a conclusion unfavourable to Christianity, they stop short of stating that conclusion, giving the reader only dark hints as to the view they wish him to adopt. The consequence is that, thereby, they enable the advocates of orthodoxy to represent their works in a ludicrous light; whereas, if they stated their premises clearly, and drew their conclusions fearlessly and explicitly, their arguments would be unanswerable, and would have an immense weight on public opinion. The reason given by some writers for the great cautiousness they exercise in exposing religious errors, is that it is more prudent and expedient thus to proceed gradually, in proportion as the age becomes riper and riper for the change contemplated. And, indeed, when one thinks of the sad fate of almost all, in past times, who had the courage to speak plainly of what they believed to be wrong in Christianity, it must be admitted that the slow process of exposing religious error, in a country where a heretic, even in the present day, can be severely punished, possesses some advantage.

Lately, however, several of our Doctors, such as the authors of the "*Essays and Reviews*," Bishop Colenzo, and others, have broken the deep silence in which thousands of the Anglican clergy were spellbound, touching the origin of the Christian religion, and have, in comparatively plain terms, pronounced it human and erroneous. For this honest expression of their opinion, they have, of course, been denounced as heretics, infidels, and ignorant men. When these dignitaries of the Church are thus treated, the writer of these pages has no reason to expect a better fate. Orthodoxy will, doubtless, deem it a sacred duty to represent his work in the most hideous colours. It is frankly admitted that it has many imperfections. Its errata are by no means few; but these will be pardoned by the real critic, who knows the difficulty of conducting through the Press a work of this character, free from literal errors. It has, however, not the fault of *wilfully* misrepresenting a single fact. The analogical and historical proofs which it contains that Christianity has emanated from paganism—the chief element in its composition being heathen monkery—could be greatly multiplied. The question of the origin of this religion, belongs to the antiquary rather than the theologian.

CONTENTS.

CHAPTER I.

Introductory Remarks.

SECTION I.—*Importance of the subject to be discussed* 1

II.— *Definition of a prophecy.—Clearness of Christ's predictions.—Various views regarding one of them.* 4

III.—*The method of inquiry, and mode of criticism, intended to be pursued in treating the subject.* 5

CHAPTER II.

A statement of the evidences and facts which tend to prove that the prophecies of Christ, in Matthew, chap. xxiv; Mark, chap. xiii; Luke, chap. xxi, and in other passages of similar import, are predictions solely of the Destruction of Jerusalem by the Roman army, under Titus Vespasian ; and not predictions of the Last Day of Judgment and the Destruction of the World.

SECTION I.—*The language, proper interpretation, and requisite proof of the fulfilment of prophecy.— Scriptural extracts of Christ's prediction of the destruction of Jerusalem* 9

SECTION II.—*Christ's predictions explained, and shown to refer to the Destruction of Jerusalem* 14

 III.—*Historical proofs of the exact fulfilment of Christ's predictions regarding Jerusalem* 17

 IV.—*The erroneousness of the notion that Christ, in these predictions, foretold the near approach of the End of the World, and the Final Judgment* 30

 V.—*The analogy between the predictions of the ancient Prophets and those of Christ, in reference to the Destruction of Jerusalem* 35

 VI.—*The Gospel Dispensation, which followed the abolition of the Jewish Polity, not a secular dominion, meant by the expression, Kingdom of Heaven, in Christ's predictions, and elsewhere* 37

 VII.—*The Apostles, both in their writings and discourses, prove Christ's prophecy to mean, exclusively, the Destruction of Jerusalem* 41

 VIII.—*A summary of the foregoing arguments in support of the truth of Christ's predictions* 49

CHAPTER III.

A statement of the evidences and facts which tend to prove that the prophecies of Christ, in Matthew, chap. xxiv; Mark, chap. xiii; Luke, chap. xxi, and in other passages of similar import, are predictions of the Last day of Judgment and the Destruction of the World, as events which were inevitably to take place during the life-time of the generation of men who were on earth contemporary with Christ; and not predictions of the Destruction of Jerusalem by the Roman army, under Titus Vespasian.

SECTION I.—*The identity of the Jewish and Pagan prophets in name and character.—The obscurity of their predictions, and the causes of the popular belief in them.—Jesus of Nazareth a Jewish prophet, whose language, predictions, and doctrines, closely resemble those of his predecessors, and who, like them, prophesied the near approach of the End of the World and the Final Judgment* 51

SECTION II.—*Scriptural proofs that Christ predicted the End of the World and the Final Judgment, as events then close at hand; and that he represented himself as the Judge of all mankind, who, as such, was shortly to make his appearance in the clouds*.. 62

III.—*Christ taught that, at 'the End of the World, he would set up the Kingdom of Heaven; which was to be of a secular nature, and by no means, what is now called the Gospel Dispensation* 71

IV.—*Christ's prediction that Jerusalem should be encompassed with armies, evincing that he imagined the world was to be destroyed by armies of angelic soldiers* 96

V.—*The Eternal Life and Happiness promised in the Gospels.— Their nature.—The time and place at which they were to be possessed*........... 105

VI.—*Christ's prediction of the near approach of the End of the World and the Final Judgment, at variance with fact* 116

CHAPTER IV.

A review of the comparative strength and conclusiveness of the facts and arguments advanced in the two immediately preceding chapters, for and against the truth of the prophecies of Christ, so far as they have hitherto been discussed.

SECTION I.—*The strength of the historical evidence of the fulfilment of Christ's predictions considered.—The reports given of his predictions, by the Evangelists, examined* 122

II.—*The strength of the evidence adduced to show that Christ predicted the End of the World and the Final Judgment to take place within the life-time of the generation of men then living* 144

III.—*Corroborative evidence that Christ predicted the near approach of the End of the World and the Day of Judgment, afforded by the Writings of the Apostles, which are replete with assurances of the close approximation of these awful events* 150

SECTION IV.—*Corroborative evidence that Christ predicted the near approach of the End of the World and the Day of
Judgment, afforded by the Writings of the Apostolic
and other Fathers of the Church* 175

V.—*The testimony of Modern Writers that Christ, the Apostles,
and the Fathers predicted and taught the near approach of
the End of the World and the Day of Judgment* 187

CHAPTER V.

The inferences directly deducible from the foregoing established facts—that Christ predicted the Last Day of Judgment and the End of the World as near events—that his Apostles inculcated the near approach of these events, as a most important doctrine, in all their discourses and epistles—and that both the prediction of Christ and the doctrine of his Apostles have proved utterly false, as the present state of the world, and of its inhabitants, irrefutably shows.

SECTION I.—*The Prophet of Nazareth neither a Deity nor in supernatural
communication with the Deity.—Represented himself as a
Divine being.—Doubtful whether he believed he was anything more than a fallible man* 195

II.—*The Apostles rather the deceived than the deceivers, in
promulgating the erroneous doctrines of the near approach
of the End of the World.—Not necessary to suppose that,
in this and in their pretence to Divine Inspiration, they
were more under the influence of a religious mania than
other fanatics* 199

III.—*The doctrine of the approaching End of the World calculated
to excite the fear of ignorant people, and make them
embrace Christianity, in order to secure their own safety.—
The panic which this doctrine created in the tenth century.—
The Apostolic sermons and miracles created fear of the
Mundane Destruction, and thereby promoted the spread of
Christianity* 205

SECTION IV.—*The prevalent practice of the primitive Christians, in selling their possessions, and laying the produce at the Apostles' feet, under the dread and conviction of the immediate End of the World.—The powerful influence this practice must have had in promoting the spread of Christianity. — Christianity made a self-supporting system by the communism of the primitive Christians, joined to the forementioned practice.—The selling of property taught by Christ* 212

V.—*The early success of Christianity not nearly so great as that of Mormonism, and therefore no proof of its Divine origin* 235

CHAPTER VI.

An inquiry into the correctness of the alleged fulfilment of Christ's prophecies—that he would rise from the grave on the third day after his burial—that the act of the woman with the box of ointment would be mentioned wherever the Gospel was preached—and that miraculous signs would follow believers.

SECTION I.—*The course to be pursued in treating the subject.—The burden of proof.— Neutral remarks.— Jewish mode of computing time.—Commencement of a Jewish day* . . 245

II.—*Arguments advanced to show that it was on the third day, according to his prediction, Christ rose from the dead.—Extracts from Dr. Leland and Bishop Sherlock's works* 250

III.—*Mythological characters who are said to have risen from the dead.—Difference of opinion among early Christians, and their disagreement with modern Christians, as to the day of Christ's resurrection.—Proofs from the Gospel narratives that it was not on the third day from his burial Christ rose.—The notion that the Jews reckoned time inclusive confuted* 258

IV.—*Review of the comparative strength and conclusiveness of the arguments advanced in the two last sections, on each side of the question, as to whether Jesus's prophecy of his resurrection was fulfilled* 278

SECTION V.—*The prediction of Jesus regarding a woman who poured upon him a box of ointment, falsified* 291

VI.—*Christ's prophecy regarding the signs which would follow believers in Christianity, falsified* 293

CHAPTER VII.

The moral and intellectual character of the Prophet of Nazareth, as exemplified in his precepts, his discourses, his actions, and his social intercourse.

SECTION I.—*General remarks.— The criterion by which the morality of Jesus is to be tested.— His morality not a model of perfection to mankind in all ages.—No account in our Gospels of the first thirty years .of his life.— Observations on his Sermon on the Mount* 300

II.—*Many of Jesus's precepts and doctrines absurd, impracticable, and immoral in their tendency* 313

III.—*Many of Jesus's acts, and much of his conduct, of an immoral character* ......,.................... 334

IV.—*Many things which Jesus taught and said, not true*.... 365

V.—*Many of Jesus's precepts and doctrines contradictory to one another* 372

VI.—*Jesus's precepts and doctrines at variance with his practice, and of a bigoted and malevolent spirit*............ 378

VII.—*The obscurity of Jesus's teaching, and the evasive character of his answers to questions put to him, touching his doctrine and mission*............................... 386

VIII.—*Jesus deficient in knowledge of both animate and inanimate nature, and also of many things relating to human society* 399

IX.—*Most of the best things which Jesus taught, borrowed from Heathen theology*............................. 422

X.—*Both the life and doctrines of Jesus identical with the lives and doctrines of Heathen ascetics, or monks, who lived hundreds of years before his time* 443

XI.—*The alleged Divine Mission of Jesus* 553

CHAPTER VIII.

The doctrines of the Christian religion, as taught by modern divines, disproved by God's government of the universe.—Their absurdity, and utter failure in ameliorating the moral condition of mankind.—The substitute here proposed for them much more conducive to man's happiness.

SECTION I.—*The superiority of the Book of Nature over Hebrew and Greek Revelations.—Nature, which teaches the existence and the attributes of Deity, the only true Revelation given by God to man* 583

II.—*The Laws of Nature illustrated.—The punishment inflicted for their violation proportionate to the offence, and calculated to improve the offender* 586

III.—*The malevolent and vengeful character of the Christian doctrine of Eternal Punishment.—Its evil tendency.—Discountenanced and contradicted by every portion of God's work.—Increased happiness derived from increased knowledge of God's works, as displayed in Nature* 590

IV.—*The Christian doctrine of the Existence and Power of the Devil falacious, and highly pernicious to the exercise of virtue.—The absurdity of Prayer.—The doctrine of Original Sin derogatory to the character of God, and pregnant with mischief to mankind.—No traces in man's nature that he is tainted with the supposed Sin of Adam.—Death an institution of nature, for benevolent purposes* 594

V.—*The Christian doctrine of the Atonement at variance with God's work in Nature.—Denies the essential Attributes of the Deity.—Is repugnant to reason.—An atonement for sin impossible.—To know that every act must bear its own consequence the strongest possible incentive to virtue.—Man's innate desire of virtue and happiness.—The utter Failure of Christianity to ameliorate the moral condition of the human race* 604

THE

PROPHET OF NAZARETH.

CHAPTER I.

INTRODUCTORY REMARKS.

SECTION I.—IMPORTANCE OF THE SUBJECT TO BE DISCUSSED.

THE subject to be discussed in the succeeding pages is, principally, the truth of the Prophecies of Christ. A question intended to occupy a most prominent position in the inquiry is,—" Whether Christ did predict the Last Day of Judgment and Destruction of the World, as events inevitable during the then existent generation of men ; and if so, what inferences, theistical, or the reverse, are fairly deducible from the non-fulfilment of that prophecy, so dreaded by them ; it having been, as alleged, extensively and impressively inculcated by His apostles, as promotive of Christianity in its earliest ages."* The correctness of Christ's predictions also, touching his resurrection on the " third day,"—his prophecy regarding the signs which were to follow those persons who would believe in him, as recorded in the Gospels,—together with his Doctrines, Precepts, and other particulars which are alleged to affect the proofs of his Divinity,—are likewise points proposed to be examined.

The truth of the Prophecies of Christ is a question which lies at the very base of the Christian religion, and which, consequently, concerns all Christians,—nay the whole of the human race. For Christianity is proclaimed to the world as the *only* true religion—as a r.ligion from God,— and as having a Divine being, namely Christ, for its originator and founder. If, therefore, his predictions are true, the Divine character of Christianity, so far as this question can affect it, stands unimpaired. But should it be discovered that his predictions are false, this would at once be fatal alike to his claim to deity and to the notion of the Divine origin of Christianity. For although to utter *true* prophecies is no proof that the prophet is a deity, or that he has any preternatural communication with Deity ; yet, to utter *false* prophecies is, in the very nature of things, a

---

* See the subject of the Prize Essay, in the preface to this Work.

positive proof that the prophet is *not* a deity, and is not in any manner supernaturally influenced by the Supreme Being. To suppose the contrary would be to suppose God liable to mistake, or to falsify. And to imagine an imperfect, fallible deity, liable to error, or capable of misrepresentation, is to imagine an idol so mean, and so repugnant to common sense, that both the faith of the enlightened Christian and the reason of the discriminative Infidel, would alike recoil at the thought of doing it homage. If, therefore, Christ is a deity, his prophecies, as well as all other words he uttered, are true ; and every act he performed is in perfect harmony with moral virtue ;—consequently the religion, of which he is the reputed founder, is of a divine origin. But if he has uttered even one prediction which has proved false, or has spoken one word, or performed a single act which is immoral, he cannot be a deity ; nor can Christianity be a divine religion. Hence, the truth of Christ's prophecies is a question which lies at the very base of the Christian religion ; and the right decision thereof is a matter of the greatest possible importance to all Christendom. If Christianity is true, the doctrines it teaches is of endless consequence, both to the Christian and the Infidel. If, on the other hand, it is false, the injury it inflicts on men can be exceeded only by the benefit it professes to confer upon them, if true. It is, therefore, every man's most imperative duty to institute a rigid, full, and impartial inquiry into a subject of such paramount interest to him.

Some men,—more orthodox than wise,—would however persuade us it is our duty to exercise such a degree of faith in Christianity as to take its truth for granted,—without submitting it to the test of inquiry and argument ; for,—as they gravely urge,—if it is *not true* the Christian has nothing to lose, while, if it *is true*, he has all to gain, and the Infidel all to lose,* But this is by no means a correct statement of the case ; and, even if it were, it would furnish no argument against investigating the matter ; for truth shines the brighter the more it is scrutinized, but error becomes the grosser the more it is examined ;—truth teems with happy results, but error is fraught with evil consequences.—In the very nature of things, as proved by every day's experience, to embrace truth and act in conformity to it, is directly calculated to produce happiness ; but to take an erroneous course on any point is productive of misery.—To err, accordingly, with regard to Christianity,—whether by rejecting it when true, or by embracing it when false,—must entail upon man one of the greatest evils.—By rejecting it as coming from God who, as such, must be perfectly good as well as perfectly wise, he rejects a communication which must be teeming with goodness and wisdom, and calculated to introduce him into a state of perfect happiness. On the other hand, by embracing it as a revelation from God, when in reality it were but the fabulous production of man, the consequence to the individual would be very serious.—This would excite in his mind a thousand fears which had no foundation ;—make him regard

---

* The Mahomedans, the Brahmins, the Budhists, and other religionists,—by Christians considered pagan and false—may, and probably do urge precisely the same kind of argument in regard to their respective religions. But neither the Christians nor the Infidels of this country regard such reasoning of any weight. Still, if it is admissible in reference to one religion, it must be so in reference to others.—The believer in either of them *has nothing to lose*, if that religion is false ; but if *it is true*, he has all to gain, and the unbeliever all to lose.—Will Christians allow the application of such reasoning to other religions ?—If not, why ?—The case is quite parallel in every instance.

as virtuous and indispensable to happiness a vast number of useless and even injurious ceremonies ;—make him waste his time, talent, and wealth upon delusive objects ;—make him disgust the pleasures of science and all sources of real happiness, in the present life, while, full of care and anxiety, he pursues the dream of a glorious life in another world. Whatever side of the question we view, we are irresistibly driven to the conclusion that to examine the Credentials of Christianity, so as to form a correct judgment regarding their claims on our belief, is of paramount importance to our real interest. Dr. Collyer very justly observes, that " he who forbids you to reason on religious subjects, or to apply your understanding to the investigation of revealed truth, is insulting the character of God, as though his acts shrunk from scrutiny—is degrading his own powers, which are best employed when they are in pursuit of such sublime and interesting subjects."* With equal justness, also, does Mr. Rogers, the celebrated writer against Infidelity, remark, that " every *candid* mind must admit that the question of the truth of Christianity is a question of *conflicting probabilities*."† Dr. Lardner, in his *Credibility of the Gospels*, makes a similar concession. To examine the grounds of these " conflicting probabilities," and draw a true conclusion from them should, therefore, precede and dictate our adoption or rejection of Christianity.—Examination is man's security from error and its evil consequences.

In order, however, that such examination may be productive of a right decision, it should be honest, free, and fearless. Its subject should be approached with a mind divested of all pre-adopted notions,—anxious to embrace the truth, on whatever side of the question it be found. Every point should be decided—not by the bias of sentiment—but the preponderance of evidence. Whatever doctrine is supported by sufficient evidence should require no other recommendation to be embraced, and whatever dogma has not the support of evidence should not be harboured, however venerable antiquity may have rendered it, or however sacred it may have been made by the advocacy of high dignitaries. Truth alone is worthy the homage of a rational being ; and, in pursuing it, he should—as Dr. Chalmers directs—" train his mind to all the hardihood of abstract and dispassionate intelligence." But, although truth is a fixed, unchangeable, eternal principle, existing in the nature of things, and the relation which one thing bears to another, yet man—according to the constitution of his nature, and that of the external world—is able to perceive truth only by means of evidence, which, from a vast number of causes, may vary in the degree of conviction it carries with it into the minds of different individuals differently constituted and differently situated. No man can believe the truth of a proposition unless he has what *he deems* sufficient evidence ; but when he perceives sufficient evidence he feels its force irresistible—he is compelled to believe. For example, I see a book.—Of this fact I have the evidence of my senses ; and, having this evidence, I can no more avoid believing the truth it proves than I can, by a mere wish, cease to exist. Of a similar force is moral, as well as mathematical evidence. Man is more passive in believing and disbelieving than he is generally represented, or even thought to be.—He is entirely under the control of what *he* regards,—whether correctly or incorrectly,—as *sufficient evidence*.

* Lectures on Miracles, p. 149. First Ed.   † Reason and Faith, p. 95. Fourth Ed.

The sole aim of the writer, in the following chapters will, therefore, be to place, in the most impartial and simple manner, all the evidence and arguments that can be adduced, both in *favour* and *against* the truth of those prophecies of Christ proposed to be examined, before the reader ; so that having all the evidence and arguments on both sides before him, he may the more easily and accurately judge for himself, and, according to his estimate of the preponderance of proof, determine on what side of the question the *truth* lies. The utility of such a course cannot fail, at once, to recommend itself to the most cursory observer of the present state of the Christian world. While the learned of the present age, both in Britain and on the Continent, are engaged in fierce debates on the truth of the Christian religion, the masses, from want of time, and other things requisite to an investigation of their Christian creed, leave the matter almost entirely in the hands of the priests of religion, and take for granted that these are right ; instead of judging for themselves. This little work being designed to assist some of the thousands that are thus situated,— whom to mislead wilfully would be the height of cruelty,—it is trusted that the investigation of the subject in hand will be conducted with strict fidelity—free from the influence of either prejudice on the one side, or predilection on the other.

SECTION II.—DEFINITION OF A PROPHECY.—CLEARNESS OF CHRIST's PREDICTIONS.—VARIOUS VIEWS REGARDING ONE OF THEM.

Whatever was anciently the function of a Prophet—whether he was merely a poet and " a man of letters," or something higher—is foreign to our present subject. It is sufficient for our purpose that,—in the general acceptation of the term—*Prophecy* is now understood to signify the prediction of a future event, which cannot be foreseen by human sagacity, and the knowledge of which must be communicated to the prophet by some supernatural being, or be possessed by him by virtue of his inherent supernatural powers. Nor will it on any hand be denied that, to constitute a true prophet, the events which he predicts must be stated in language sufficiently clear and specific to identify them ;—that the events must come to pass precisely in the manner the prediction represents,—and that they must be such events as cannot be foreseen by any degree of sagacity, unaided by supernatural power. There is in the character of Christ's prophecies much which answers to the foregoing requisites of real predictions. Very different from many obscure, loose, and ambiguous prophecies in the Old Testament,—which are capable of being applied to various events that have happened in different countries, and different ages of the world,—those of Christ are comparatively clear, pointed, and definite in language. If, therefore, his prophecies can be proved correct, the fact of his deity, and the truth of the doctrines of Christianity—of which he is the reputed founder—will thereby, *quoad hoc*, be established ;—and no doctrine can have a higher authority than to be proved true. But it must be observed that, on the other hand, no doctrine can have a higher condemnation than to be proved false.—If Christ uttered erroneous or false predictions, this fact alone, if established, would conclusively prove that he was not a deity ; for, as already observed, it is contrary to the nature of things to suppose an erring god. It would also prove that his teaching could not be a revelation from God.—In a word, it would destroy the very foundation of Christianity, and show it to be a religion of purely human origin.

But what of that, if these inductions be the offspring of truth ?—However disastrous the consequences might seem, they could not in this, or any other case, destroy truth, which is, in its very nature unchangeable and eternal. Besides : it is always not only more honorable, but also more useful to follow truth, whithersoever it may lead, than to cling to error, on whatever downy pillow it affords rest.—The question always should be—not whether this or that doctrine lead to embarrassing and unpleasant consequences—but whether it is founded upon *truth.* Nothing can be more unphilosophic and irrational, in a person who is in pursuit of truth, than to abandon his course because the result which he foresees is not in accordance with his predilections. This is at once to pronounce the reception of truth a vice, and the retention of error a virtue—which is contrary to all sound views of morality.

The most remarkable, perhaps, of all the prophecies of Christ is that which Christians regard as a prediction of the destruction of Jerusalem, by the Roman legion, under Titus Vespasian ; but which the opponents of Christianity contend to be a prophecy of the Last Day of Judgment, and of the End of the World, as events which were to occur during the time of the generation of men then living. As already stated, it is intended in the succeeding pages to examine minutely the respective claims of these two conflicting views. There are some divines, however, who regard what they pronounce Christ's predictions of the destruction of Jerusalem as being *mixed up* with prophetical references to the Last day of Judgment ; and—as it has been very correctly observed*—considerable ingenuity has been exercised by commentators in their attempts to separate the predictions relating to the destruction of Jerusalem *from those relating to the Last Day of Judgment.* But these exertions have been neither creditable nor successful. It is, however, more consistently maintained by many,—it may be said most—of the more eminent Christian writers of the present age, that these prophecies relate *wholly* and *solely* to the destruction of Jerusalem.

SECTION III.—THE METHOD OF INQUIRY AND MODE OF CRITICISM INTENDED TO BE PURSUED IN TREATING THE SUBJECT.

In reasoning upon disputed points, it is requisite, at the onset to fix upon some common premises—some ground to which those on each side the question can agree, and which will serve the same purpose in this kind of disquisition as an axiom in mathematics, or a first principle in morals. In order, therefore, to furnish such common ground, it is deemed expedient to premise that—in this discussion of the truth of the prophecies of Christ—the following points will be taken for granted ; namely— that Christ did utter those predictions attributed to him, during the time he is said to have lived on earth, and *that* precisely in the words they are reported in the Gospels—that these Gospels were written by those whose names they respectively bear, soon after the occurrence of the events

* Greg's Creed of Christendom, p. 124.

which they relate—that the doctrines of Christianity were actually disseminated over a very large portion of the world, in the wonderfully short time which it is said they were.—In a word, the whole of the contents of the New Testament will be admitted to be genuine.

Whatever reason the Infidel may have to be dissatisfied with these concessions,— made for the sake of brevity and definiteness,—the Christian will have no cause to complain, or refuse to grant the premises from which the argument is to start.   For it would be highly detrimental to his cause to maintain that the predictions attributed to Christ were *not* uttered by him ; or that any of the events narrated in the New Testament did *not* take place in the manner we find them recorded.   Because, if these pro-prophecies, or any of the things related in the Gospels, or Epistles, were found to have been fabricated by those writers—whoever they were—either immediately after the time to which they refer, or some two or three centuries—more or less—afterwards, this very circumstance would of itself render these writings unworthy of belief—would, in short, be fatal to Christianity, of which we know utterly nothing, except what these productions teach us.   The very words of the New Testament, in their *natural* and *obvious* meaning are, therefore, the principal materials proposed to be used in the present inquiry.

It is further premised that the words of the *Authorised English Version* will be adhered to, in this disquisition, while occasional references, —principally in foot-notes,—will be made to the Greek version of the texts cited.   To adopt the Authorised English Version in this inquiry is not only fair, but highly necessary.   For, *first*, as this is an examination of a subject in which all Christians of all denominations, and all opponents of Christianity, of all shades of opinion are deeply interested, there should be one common standard to which they *all* can appeal, and by which they can *all* judge,—otherwise the result of the investigation must appear to many, if not to most of them, inconclusive.—*Secondly*, there is no other version to which the readers of this work can so aptly appeal, and no one with which the great majority of them are so well acquainted as they are with the Authorised English Version.—*Thirdly*, there is no other version which has received the express sanction of the Established Churches in the empire, and has, for the last two and a half centuries, been used and appealed to, in public and private, by almost every sect of Christians, at home and abroad.—And *finally*, there is no other version, in this country, if in any other, upon which such an accumulated amount of learning and labour has been bestowed.*   The care and erudition which have been

* When King James I., in 1603,—after repeated objections had been made to the version styled "the Bishop's Bible,"—commanded that a new translation should be made of Holy Writ, he ordered this task to be performed by fifty-four select men, who were eminent for their piety, and profound knowledge of the original tongues.   In that age, it is admitted, there were to be found better Greek and Hebrew scholars than can be found in the present age—so much better, indeed, that those of the present age rely upon the authority of those of that and the preceding age.   From death, and other causes, however, only forty-seven of the fore-mentioned number were actually engaged in the work of translating the Bible.   Ten of these met at Westminster, and translated from Genesis to the end of 2 Kings ;—eight at Cambridge translated from that to the end of the Songs of Solomon ;—seven at Oxford, from that to the end of Malachi ;—eight, also, at Oxford, from that to the end of the Acts of the Apostles, together with the Apocalypse ;—and seven, at Westminster, translated the whole of the Epistles.   Another company at Cambridge translated the whole of the Apocryphal books.   The regulations which King James ordered the translators to observe were ad-

lavished in executing this version give it a much higher claim to our preference, as a common standard, than any other which can be named. The number,—the harmony of the decision,—the high literary attainments and moral standing—of those engaged in translating and revising it, must stamp upon it such a degree of authority that cannot be claimed for any other version, and be amply sufficient to make the monoglot reader satisfied that, so far as the signification of words is concerned, this version will not greatly mislead him.

The mode intended to be adopted in examining, interpreting, and criticising the passages of the New Testament which bear on the subject to be discussed, will, it is trusted, be deemed fair and candid. The natural construction which dictates itself to common sense, and which is in accordance with *usus loquendi*, or the obvious meaning of similar passages and words in the Jewish writings, will be endeavoured to be put on each sentence cited. The meaning of one passage will be ascertained and illus-

mirably calculated to secure a correct translation. The ordinary Bible, used at the time in the Churches, was to be as little altered as the original text permitted. When any word was found to have more than one signification, that in which it had most commonly been used by the most eminent Fathers was to have the preference. No marginal notes at all were to be fixed, except for the explanation of Hebrew and Greek words, which could not, without some circumlocution, so fitly and briefly be explained in the text. Each individual, of every company of translators, was to take the same chapter or chapters, and translate them severally, by himself; and then all the company were to meet together, in order to compare their respective translations, and agree as to what portions of them should stand good. When any company had completed the translation of one book, they were to send it for examination to each of the other companies, and if any of those companies, upon a review of the work, differed, or doubted upon any part of it, they were to note the same, and send their reasons for thus differing or doubting to the company which had translated the book; and this difference, if not previously settled, was to be compounded at a general meeting, which was to consist of the chief persons in each company, and to be held at the close of the work. When any place of special obscurity was doubted, letters, by authority, were to be sent to any of the Learned in the land, for an opinion on such a place. There were to be over each company of translators, directors, who were Deans of Cathedrals and the King's Professors of Greek and Hebrew in the Universities; and, in addition to these directors, there were three or four of the most eminent and grave divines in either of the Universities, (not being employed in translating) to be assigned by the Vice-Chancellor, upon conference with the rest of the heads, to be overseers of the translations, —as well Hebrew as Greek. See Horne's Introduct. to the Study of Scriptures, vol. ii., pp. 257—259, Lond. Ed. 1821. Todd's Vindication of our Authorised Translation of the Bible, pp. 9—12, Lond. 8vo., 1819. Fuller's Church History, Book x, pp. 44—46. Thus, according to these regulations, each book passed the scrutiny of *all* the translators successively. In the first instance, each individual translated every book which was allotted to his division. In the next place, the readings to be adopted were agreed upon by the whole of the company assembled together, at which meeting each translator must have been solely occupied by his own version. The book, thus finished, was sent to each of the other companies, to be again examined and compared with the original, as well as with already existing translations in different languages. In addition to all this, the translators were empowered to call to their assistance any learned men, whose studies enabled them to be serviceable, when an urgent occasion of difficulty presented itself. The work, having occupied nearly three years, was completed, and three copies of the whole Bible, thus translated and revised, were sent to London,—one from Oxford, one from Cambridge, and the third from Westminster. Here, again, a committee of six—two being deputed by the companies at Oxford, two by those at Cambridge, and two by the company at Westminster—reviewed and perfected the work, which was finally prepared and revised by Dr. Smith (afterwards Bishop of Gloucester), and Dr. Bilson, Bishop of Winchester, and, in 1611, published in folio, in London, by Robert Barker, printer to the King. This is the present authorised version of the Bible.

trated by that of other passages, which bear resemblance to it in language and idea, but which are clear and definite as to their import. All sentiments, which can reasonably be supposed to be clothed in figurative language, will be elucidated by similar sentiments which are evidently expressed in literal terms, while due regard will be had to the contents and general tenor of the whole matter.

The order in which it is designed to treat the subject of the truth of the prophecies of Christ,—particularly the first of them to be noticed —is to adduce, in a separate chapter, first all the arguments and facts tending to substantiate the views entertained on the one side of the question ; and then, in another chapter, state all the arguments and facts calculated to support the opposite views, with equal zeal and fidelity. Finally, all the evidence, on both sides, will be summed up with the most rigorous impartiality, and regardlessly of any prepossessions of the writer, as to orthodox or heterodox views ; but accompanied with a declaration of his conviction as to which side the preponderance of evidence lies, and also a statement of his reasons for this conclusion, together with a notation of the inferences which necessarily must be drawn from such preponderance of evidence, touching the reality of Christ's deity.

Only one point more seems to require any explanation before we proceed to the question to be discussed—That is, the side on which the *onus probandi*, or the burden of proof lies. In other words—which side is to commence the argument, taking the positive view of the question, and which to follow, taking the negative, in discussing the truth of Christ's prophecies ? On a superficial view of this point, it may possibly appear to some that,—in regard to those prophecies which the Christian believes to refer to the destruction of Jerusalem, but which the Infidel contends to be predictions of the End of the World, and the final Judgment, as events considered near at hand when they were uttered,—the burden of proof lies on the side of the Infidel, because it is he that alleges that these prophecies refer to the End of the World, and it is the Christian that denies this allegation, and says they refer only to the destruction of Jerusalem. But when the true state of the case is fully and fairly considered, it will be seen that the Christian is first in the field—that it is he who first—and *that* at a comparatively remote period of the existence of his Church—has laid it down as a position—as a matter of fact—capable of demonstration, that these prophecies refer solely to the destruction of Jerusalem, and that the Infidel comes into the field after that position has been laid down, and demurs to its truth, contending that the prophecies refer to the End of the World. It must, therefore, be admitted that, according to the recognised rules of argument, the *onus probandi*, evidently, falls upon the Christian, who makes the first assertion. In treating this subject, however, the views and arguments on both sides of the question will be stated in a distinct and positive form, so that it becomes a matter of little importance which side takes the precedence.

These preliminary observations cannot be closed more properly than by urging the reader—whatever may be his preconceptions,—to peruse the succeeding pages with a mind bent upon making a free and unfettered inquiry after truth, wherever it may be found, and against whatever opinions it may militate. It is thus, and only thus, that his convictions can be justified by his own conscience, and can receive the approval of all honest and right-thinking men.

CHAPTER II.

A STATEMENT OF THE EVIDENCES AND FACTS WHICH TEND TO PROVE THAT THE PROPHECIES OF CHRIST, IN MATTHEW, CHAP. XXIV; MARK, CHAP. XIII; LUKE, CHAP. XXI, AND IN OTHER PASSAGES OF SIMILAR IMPORT, ARE PREDICTIONS SOLELY OF THE DESTRUCTION OF JERUSALEM, BY THE ROMAN ARMY, UNDER TITUS VESPASIAN; AND NOT PREDICTIONS OF THE LAST DAY OF JUDGMENT AND THE DESTRUCTION OF THE WORLD.

SECTION I.—THE LANGUAGE—PROPER INTERPRETATION—AND REQUISITE PROOF OF THE FULFILMENT OF PROPHECY.—SCRIPTURAL EXTRACTS OF CHRIST'S PREDICTION OF THE DESTRUCTION OF JERUSALEM.

To a person imperfectly acquainted with Jewish ideas and expressions, the language of the prophecies of Christ must appear much more indefinite, ambiguous, and obscure than otherwise it would. All prophetic writings, however—as may be expected—are more difficult to be understood than a plain narrative of past occurrences. For a prophecy being a representation of some future event—the insight into which is acquired in a supernatural mode—the description of such an event cannot be expected to be so precise, minute, perspicuous, and graphic as the narration of things the knowledge of which is acquired through the medium of sense. The Rev. Hartwell Horne observes that,—" in order to understand the Prophets, great attention should be paid to the prophetic style, which is highly figurative, and particularly abounds in metaphorical and hyperbolical expressions."........ " As not any prophecy of Scripture is of self-interpretation, (2 Pet. i. 20) or is its own interpreter, the sense of the prophecy is to be sought in the events of the world, and in the harmony of the prophetic writings, rather than in the bare terms of any single prediction."........ "*A prophecy is demonstrated to be fulfilled when we can prove, from unimpeachable authority, that the event has actually taken place, precisely according to the manner in which it was foretold.*"*

The prophecies of Christ respecting the destruction of Jerusalem are characterized by these qualities in a most striking manner. The sequel will show that they are clothed in the most figurative language,—that they are in harmony with the predictions of the prophets of the Old Testament, —and that history amply proves that they have been fulfilled, in the occurrence of events precisely as they had been foretold.

The principal passages in the writings of three of the Evangelists, who

* Horne's Introduction to the Study of Scriptures, Part ii, chap. viii, sec. 1—2.

have recorded these prophecies, being about to be laid before the reader, it is necessary here to remark that, in some instances, these predictions will be found to continue, in one concatenated discourse, from one chapter of the Gospels to another; so that, according to our present division of the Scriptures, part of the same prophecy will be found forming the conclusion of one chapter, and proceeding naturally through the beginning, and sometime to the end, or near the end of another chapter or two.* In the following citations, therefore, the numerals of chapters and verses will be placed between brackets, before the commencement of each; in order that, while the reader may thus turn to each in his Bible, the prophetic sayings of Christ may be presented before him in their unbroken and natural connection.

Christ having denounced several woes against the Scribes and Pharisees, who apparently in that age were the principal religious guides of

* There are, doubtless, thousands of Scripture readers who do not know that the division of the Bible into chapters and verses is a work of comparatively modern date, and that anciently no such division existed. In the year 1240 Cardinal Hugo completed the first Concordance to the Scriptures ever made. To obviate the difficulty of referring to the various passages, as he prosecuted this work, he divided his Bible into chapters. A considerable number of copies of his Concordance being transcribed, circulated, and found of great advantage in studying the Scriptures, people, therefore, in order to use this work, were obliged to divide their Bibles into chapters in the same manner as had been done by the Cardinal. Since this period all the copies of the Bible used in the Western part of the world have been divided into chapters. It was not, however, till the year 1551 that the chapters were divided into verses. This important task was performed, in a very imperfect manner, by Robert Stephens, a printer, of Lyons, in order to adapt the divisions to a Greek Concordance, which he was then preparing for the press. These divisions, being unnatural, have frequently been the cause of misunderstanding passages of the Bible. The division of the chapters is often improper, but that of the verses much more so. The English reader is frequently led to believe that every verse contains complete sense, when it is only a member of a sentence. And there are marks that some modern translators have been led astray by the present division and punctuation of the original text, even when the text itself was sufficiently clear otherwise to render such mistakes, in some cases, almost impossible. By these divisions we frequently find full periods where there should not be even the shortest pause;—nominatives separated from their verbs—adjectives from their substantives,—and even letters and syllables cruelly disjoined from the words to which they naturally belong. Thus the chain of reasoning is frequently broken,—the sentences mangled,—the eye misguided,—the attention bewildered,— and the meaning consequently lost. (See Harris's Lectures, pp. 67—69. Lond. 1820.) This improper division of texts is doubtless a great detraction from the value of our authorised version, otherwise a very excellent translation.

Michaelis on this subject remarks,—" That our chapters are only helps for the more easily finding passages quoted from the New Testament; but that whoever reads the Bible, by single chapters, will be often in the dark, and at a loss for the meaning of the Apostles, since the chapters often end abruptly in the middle of a connected discourse; for instance, Eph. v. 1, and Col. iv. 1."

" The wild and indigested invention of the learned printer (Robert Stephens) was soon introduced into all the editions of the New Testament; and it must be confessed that, in quoting and consulting the Bible, there is great use in the division into verses. But the interpretation of this Sacred Book has suffered greatly by this division. For, not to mention that Stephens often ends a verse at the wrong place, against the sense of the passage, the division itself is quite contrary to the nature of the Epistles which are connected, whereas separate verses appear to the eyes of the learned, and to the minds of the unlearned, as so many detached sentences."—Marsh's translation of Michaelis's Introduct. to the New Test. vol. ii. pp. 524—528. See also, Watson's Theological Tracts, vol. iii. pp. 290, 291, 289.—Prideaux's Connexion, vol. ii. pp. 486—491.—Simon's Hist. Crit. du Texte du N. T.—Gedes's Prospectus of a New Translation of the Holy Bible, note p. 69.—Critical Review, vol. xviii. p. 188.

the Jews, commences his predictions of the destruction of Jerusalem in the following words, as recorded by Matthew :—

(Chap. xxiii. ver. 34.)* "Wherefore behold, I send unto you prophets, and wise men, and scribes; and some of them ye shall kill and crucify; and some of them shall ye scourge in your synagogues, and persecute them from city to city; (35) that upon you may come all the righteous blood shed upon the earth, from the blood of righteous Abel unto the blood of Zacharias, son of Barachias, whom ye slew between the temple and the altar. (36) Verily, I say unto you—*all these things shall come upon this generation.* (37) O Jerusalem, Jerusalem,—thou that killest the prophets, and stonest them which are sent unto thee, how often would I have gathered thy children together, even as a hen gathereth her chickens under her wings and ye would not ! (38) Behold, your house is left unto you desolate; (39) for I say unto you, ye shall not see me henceforth till ye shall say—Blessed is he that cometh in the name of the Lord. (xxiv. 1.) And Jesus went out, and departed from the temple : and his disciples came to him, for to show him the buildings of the temple. (2) And Jesus said unto them—See ye not all these things ? Verily, I say unto you, there shall not be left here one stone upon another that shall not be thrown down. (3) And, as he sat upon the Mount of Olives, the disciples came unto him privately, saying—*Tell us when shall these things be, and what shall be the sign of thy coming, and of the end of the world.* (4) And Jesus answered and said unto them—Take heed that no man deceive you; (5) for many shall come in my name, saying,—I am Christ, and shall deceive many. (6) And ye shall hear of wars, and rumours of wars : see that ye be not troubled; for all these things must come to pass; but the end is not yet. (7) For nation shall rise against nation, and kingdom against kingdom; and there shall be famines, and pestilences, and earthquakes, in divers places. (8) All these are the beginning of sorrows. (9) Then shall they deliver you up to be afflicted, and shall kill you; and ye shall be hated of all nations for my name's sake. (10) And then shall many be offended, and shall betray one another, and shall hate one another; (11) and many false prophets shall rise, and shall deceive many; (12) and because iniquity shall abound, the love of many shall wax cold; (13) but he that shall endure unto the end the same shall be saved. (14) And this Gospel of the Kingdom shall be preached in all the world for a witness unto all nations; and then shall the *end* come. (15) When ye, therefore, shall see the abomination of desolation, spoken of by Daniel, the prophet, stand in the holy place, (whoso readeth let him understand), (16) then let them which be in Judea flee into the mountains; (17) let him which is on the housetop not come down to take any thing out of his house; (18) neither let him which is in the field return back to take his clothes. (19) And woe unto them that are with child, and to them that give suck in those days ! (20) But pray ye that your flight be not in the winter, neither on the Sabbath day; (21) for then shall be great tribulation, such as was not since the beginning of the world to this time; no, nor ever shall be. (22) And except those days should be shortened, there should no flesh be saved; but for the elect's sake those days shall be shortened. (23) Then, if any man shall say unto you,—Lo, here is Christ, or there; believe it not; (24) for there shall arise false Christs, and false prophets, and shall show great signs and wonders; in so much that, if it were possible, they shall deceive the very elect. (25) Behold I have told you before; (26) wherefore, if they shall say unto you,—Behold he is in the desert, go not forth—Behold he is in the secret chambers, believe it not. (27) For as the lightning cometh out of the east, and shineth even unto the west, so shall also the *coming of the Son of Man be;* (28) For wheresoever the carcase is, there will the eagles be gathered together. (29) *Immediately* after the tribulation of those days *shall the sun be darkened, and the moon shall not give her light, and the stars shall fall from heaven, and the powers of the heavens shall be shaken.* (30) *And then shall appear the sign of the Son of Man in heaven; and then shall all the tribes of the earth mourn, and they shall see the Son of Man coming in the clouds of heaven with power and great glory.* (31) *And he shall send his angels with a great sound of a trumpet; and they shall gather together his elect from the four winds—from one end of heaven to the other.* (32) Now learn a parable of the fig-tree—When his branch is yet tender, and putteth forth leaves, ye know that summer is nigh; (33) so likewise ye, when ye shall see all these things, know that it is *near, even at the doors.* (34). VERILY I SAY UNTO YOU, THIS GENE-

---

* Any critical reader must perceive the words cited from this chapter to be a prediction of the same event with that prophesied in the following chapter, and that the chain is broken only by the apostrophe of Matthew, for the purpose of recording that Jesus went out of the temple, and addressed himself, on the same subject, to his disciples.

NERATION SHALL NOT PASS TILL ALL THESE THINGS BE FULFILLED. (35) *Heaven and earth shall pass away, but my words shall not pass away.* (36) But of that *day* and *hour* knoweth no man—no, not the angels of heaven, but my Father only. (37) But as the days of Noe were, so shall also the coming of the Son of Man be ; (38) for as in the days that were before the flood, they were eating and drinking, marrying and giving in marriage, until the day Noe entered into the ark, (39) and knew not until the flood came and took them all away ; so shall also the *coming of the Son of Man be.* (40) Then shall two be in the field,—the one shall be taken and the other left ; (41) two women shall be grinding at the mill,—the one shall be taken and the other left. (42) Watch, there-fore, for ye know not what hour your Lord doth come ; (43) but know this, that if the goodman of the house had known in what watch the thief would come, he would have watched, and would not have suffered his house to be broken up. (44) Therefore, be ye also *ready, for in such an hour as ye think not the Son of Man cometh.* (45) Who then is a faithful and wise servant, whom his lord hath made ruler over his household, to give them meat in due season ? (46) Blessed is that servant whom his lord when he cometh shall find so doing. (47) Verily, I say unto you, that he shall make him ruler over all his goods. (48) But, and if that evil servant shall say in his heart, My lord delayeth his coming ; (49) and shall begin to smite his fellow-servants, and to eat and drink with the drunken, (50) the lord of that servant shall come in a day when he looketh not for him, and in an hour that he is not aware of, (51) and shall cut him asunder, and appoint him his portion with the hypocrites.—There shall be weeping, and gnashing of teeth.''

Such is the prophetic answer which Christ gave to the inquiry of his disciples—''When shall *these things* be ? And what shall be the sign of thy coming, and of the end of the world ?'' It may be said that in the contents of the succeeding chapter (xxv.) the same prophetic discourse ap-pears to be continued to the very close of it, and to be part of one uninterrupted answer to the same question. That chapter will not at present be cited, because it is maintained by some divines to be, as well as the foregoing chapter, from verse 29th, a descriptive prophecy of the last day of judgment. The soundness of this view will hereafter be examined. Mark, in his recital of these prophecies, varies very slightly from Matthew :—

(Mark xiii. 1.) '' And as he went out of the temple, one of his disciples saith unto him,—Master, see what manner of stones, and what buildings are here. (2) And Jesus answering, said unto him,—Seest thou these great buildings ? There shall not be left one stone upon another that shall not be thrown down. (3) And as he sat upon the Mount of Olives, over against the temple, Peter, and James, and John, and Andrew, asked him privately—(4) Tell us *when shall these things be, and what shall be the sign when all these things shall be fulfilled ?* (5) And Jesus, answering them, began to say —Take heed lest any man deceive you ; (6) for many shall come in my name, saying, I am Christ, and shall deceive many. (7) And when ye shall hear of wars and rumours of wars, be ye not troubled, for such things must needs be ; but the end shall not be yet. (8) For nation shall rise against nation, and kingdom against kingdom ; and there shall be earthquakes in divers places ; and there shall be famines and troubles. These are the beginnings of sorrows ; (9) but take heed to yourselves ; for they shall deliver you up to councils, and in the synagogues ye shall be beaten ; and ye shall be brought before rulers and kings for my sake, for a testimony against them. (10) And the Gospel must first be published among all nations. (11) But when they shall lead you, and deliver you up, take no thought beforehand what ye shall speak, neither do ye premeditate ; but whatsoever shall be given you in that hour, that speak ye ; for it is not ye that speak, but the Holy Ghost. (12) Now the brother shall betray the brother to death, and the father the son, and children shall rise against their parents, and shall cause them to be put to death. (13) And ye shall be hated of all men for my name's sake ; but he that shall endure unto the end the same shall be saved. (14) But when ye shall see the abomination of desolation, spoken of by Daniel the prophet, standing where it ought not, (let him that readeth understand) then let them that be in Judea flee to the mountains ; (15) and let him that is on the housetop not go down into the house, neither enter therein to take anything out of his house ; (16) and let him that is in the field not turn back again for to take up his garment, (17) But woe to them that are with child, and to them that give suck, in those days ! (18) And pray ye that your flight be not in the winter; (19) for in those days shall be affliction, such as was not from the beginning of the creation which God created unto this time; neither shall be. (20) And except that the Lord had shortened those days no flesh should be saved; but for the elect's sake, whom he hath chosen, he hath shortened the days. (21) And then if any man shall say to you,—Lo, here is Christ, or,—Lo, he is there, believe him not; (22) for false Christs and false prophets shall rise, and shall show signs and wonders, to seduce, if it were possible, even the elect. (23) But take ye heed:—behold, I have foretold you all things. (24) *But in those days, after that tribulation, the sun shall be darkened, and the moon shall not give her light;* (25) *and the stars of heaven shall fall, and the powers that are in heaven shall be shaken;* (26) *and then shall they see the Son of Man coming in the clouds with great power and glory;* (27) *and then shall he send his angels, and shall gather together his elect from the four winds—from the uttermost part of the earth to the uttermost part of heaven.* (28) Now learn a parable of the fig-tree.—When her branch is yet tender, and putteth forth leaves, ye know that summer is near; (29) so, ye in like manner, when ye shall see these things come to pass, know that it is NIGH, EVEN AT THE DOORS. (30) VERILY I SAY UNTO YOU, THAT THIS GENERATION SHALL NOT PASS TILL ALL THESE THINGS BE DONE. (31) *Heaven and earth shall pass away; but my words shall not pass away.* (32) But of that *day* and that *hour* knoweth no man—no, not the angels which are in heaven; neither the Son, but the Father. (33) Take ye heed; *watch* and *pray;* for ye know not when the time is. (34) For the Son of Man is as a man taking a far journey, who left his house, and gave authority to his servants, and to every man his work, and commanded the porter to watch. (35) *Watch* ye, therefore, for ye know not when the master of the house cometh,—at even, or at midnight, or at the cockcrowing, or in the morning; (36) lest coming suddenly, he find you sleeping. (37) And what I say unto you, I say unto all—*watch.*"

Luke relates the foregoing chain of remarkable predictions in words which throw much light on the narrations of the two other Evangelists, and which is thought clearly to prove that these prophecies refer to the approaching destruction of Jerusalem.—

(Luke xxi. 5.) And as some spake of the temple, how it was adorned with goodly stones and gifts, he (Jesus) said,—(6) As for these things which ye behold, the days will come in the which there shall not be left one stone upon another that shall not be thrown down (7) And they asked him, saying—Master, *but when shall these things be? And what sign will there be when these things shall come to pass?* (8) And he said—Take heed that ye be not deceived; for many shall come in my name, saying, I am Christ; and the time draweth near. Go ye not, therefore, after them. (9) But when ye shall hear of wars and commotions, be not terrified; for these things must first come to pass: but the end is not by and by. (10) Then said he unto them,—Nation shall rise against nation, and kingdom against kingdom; (11) and great earthquakes shall be in divers places, and famines, and pestilences, and fearful sights, and great signs shall there be from heaven. (12) But before all these, they shall lay their hands on you and persecute you, delivering you up to the synagogues, and into prisons, being brought before kings and rulers for my name's sake. (13) And it shall turn to you for a testimony. (14) Settle it, therefore, in your hearts not to meditate before what ye shall answer; (15) for I will give you a mouth and wisdom which all your adversaries shall not be able to gainsay nor resist. (16) And ye shall be betrayed both by parents, and brethren, and kinsfolks, and friends; and some of you shall they cause to be put to death. (17) And ye shall be hated of all men for my name's sake; (18) but there shall not an hair of your head perish. (19) In your patience possess ye your souls; (20) and when ye shall see Jerusalem compassed with armies, then know that the desolation thereof is nigh. (21) Then let them which are in Judea flee to the mountains; and let them which are in the midst of it depart out; and let not them that are in the countries enter thereinto; (22) for these be the days of vengeance, that all things which are written may be fulfilled. (23) But woe unto them that are with child, and to them that give suck, in those days! for there shall be great distress in the land, and wrath upon this people; (24) and they shall fall by the edge of the sword, and shall be led away captive into all nations; and Jerusalem shall be trodden down of the Gentiles, until the times of the Gentiles be fulfilled. (25) *And there shall be signs in the sun, and in the moon, and in the stars, and upon the earth distress of nations with perplexity; the sea and the waves roaring;* (26) men's hearts failing them for fear, and for looking after those things which are coming on the earth; *for the powers of heaven shall be shaken.* (27) *And then shall they see the Son of man coming in a cloud with power and great glory.* (28) And when these things begin to come to pass, then look up, and lift up your heads; for your redemption draweth nigh. (29) And he spake to them a parable—Behold the fig tree, and all the trees; (30) when they now shoot forth ye see and know of your own selves that summer is now nigh at hand; (31) so likewise ye, when ye see these things come to pass, know ye that the *kingdom of God is nigh at hand.* (32) VERILY I SAY UNTO YOU, THIS GENERATION SHALL NOT PASS AWAY TILL ALL BE FULFILLED. (33) *Heaven and earth shall pass away, but my words shall not pass away.* (34) And take heed to yourselves, lest at any time your hearts be overcharged with surfeiting, and drunkenness, and cares of this life, and so that day come upon you *unawares.* (35) For as a snare shall it come on all them that dwell on the face of the whole earth. (36) *Watch* ye, therefore, and pray always, that ye may be accounted worthy to escape all these things that shall come to pass, and to stand before the Son of Man."

The foregoing are the most prominent predictions of Christ on this subject, as described by three of the Evangelists. Prophetic references to the same events are found in other places in the Gospels. These shall be noticed hereafter.

SECTION II.—CHRIST'S PREDICTIONS EXPLAINED, AND SHOWN TO REFER TO THE DESTRUCTION OF JERUSALEM.

It is now proposed to show *that there is nothing in the prophetic language of the foregoing citations which does not naturally apply to the destruction of Jerusalem,—the overthrow of the Jewish polity, and the dispersion of the Jewish nation.* The subject is the Jews,—Jerusalem—their capital city,—and the temple—the material habitation of their God, and their long-established rendezvous of national worship. There is no mention made here of any other place than Jerusalem to be destroyed,—much less is the destruction of the whole world prophesied here. Jesus, at the onset of his prophetic sayings on this subject,* speaks to the Jews exclusively, but more particularly to the Scribes and Pharisees, on whom he pronounces woes. He tells them that they were the children of those who had killed the prophets, and that, by filling up the measures of their fathers, they would incur upon themselves, and the existing generation of Jews,† (not upon the world at large) " all the righteous blood shed upon the earth, from the blood of righteous Abel unto the blood of Zacharias, son of Barachias, whom" they had slain " between the temple and the altar." Then he adds—" Verily I say unto you, all these things shall come upon this generation." Having denounced this pending judgment, he bursts forth into an exclamation of pity on the holy city— " O Jerusalem! Jerusalem!—thou that killest the prophets, and stonest them which are sent unto thee, how often would I have gathered thy children together, even as a hen gathereth her chickens under her wings, and ye would not!"‡ The words,—" Jerusalem, who killest the prophets," which are metonomically used, clearly refer to the Jews exclusively, and to the calamity that was to befal them, while the words of the preceding verse define the time at which this calamity was to overtake them —" this generation."

Christ leaving the temple—within which he had uttered these predictions, with the remark that, as he, whom the Jews had rejected, now vacated it, and would no more enter it, their house—meaning the temple —was left to them desolate,—goes outside to view the buildings of this

---

* Matth. xxiii. 34, et seq.   † Luke xi. 51.   ‡ Matth. xxiii. 37.

gorgeous edifice, at the request of his disciples, whom he addresses, saying—" See ye not all these things ?   Verily, I say unto you, there shall not be left here one stone upon another that shall not be thrown down."* That this prophecy is a part, or rather, a continuation of those predictions uttered at the close of the foregoing chapter, in which so pointed a reference is made to the destruction of Jerusalem, and the judgment that was to be executed upon the Jewish nation, will appear clear to any one who will compare the citations already made from three of the Evangelists,† on the same subject, with the following passages.—" And when he was come near he beheld the city, and wept over it, saying, if thou hadst known,—even thou, at least in this thy day,—the things which belong unto thy peace ! but now they are hid from thine eyes.   For the days shall come upon thee, that thine enemies shall cast a trench about thee, and compass thee round, and keep thee in on every side ; and shall lay thee even with the ground, and thy children within thee, and they shall not leave in thee one stone upon another, because thou knewest not the time of thy visitation."‡   The same prophecy is reiterated in the following passage— " Daughters of Jerusalem, weep not for me, but weep for yourselves, and for your children ; for behold the days are coming, in the which they shall say—Blessed are the barren, and the wombs that never bare, and the paps which never gave suck.   Then shall they begin to say to the mountains,—Fall on us, and to the hills—Cover us." §   Here Christ bewails the approaching calamity of Jerusalem, as he does in Matthew xxiii., while also he uses words exactly of the same meaning here in regard to women with children, as he does in Matthew xxiv. ; —thus clearly connecting and identifying the prophetic sayings of both chapters.   The words—" They shall not leave in thee one stone upon another "—in the former of the two passages just quoted from Luke are so similar to the following, found in Matthew,∥—" There shall not be left here one stone upon another, that shall not be thrown down,"—that they forcibly prove the same thing.   In like manner does what is said in the same passage, regarding Jerusalem being surrounded by the enemy, harmonize with what occurs in another place in Luke,¶ where,—as it will be admitted on all hands,—the same series of events is recorded as that recorded in Matthew xxiv.   In the latter of the two passages in Luke, we find—" Ye shall see Jerusalem compassed with armies," and in the former,—" Thine enemies shall cast a trench about thee and compass thee round, and keep thee in on every side."   These coincidents, with several others that could be pointed out, prove, beyond a doubt, that the same chain of predictions continues, from the latter part of Matthew xxiii., where Christ pities the future fate of Jerusalem, to the close of the succeeding chapter.   This fact will be found of great importance when, in the sequel, it is shown that these prophecies were accomplished in the destruction of the holy city, and the dispersion of the Jewish nation.

Christ having warned the Scribes and Pharisees of the awful judgment which awaited them, in common with the other inhabitants of Jerusalem, and having told his disciples that the temple should be rased to the ground, the latter,—anxious to ascertain when this catastrophe would take place—

---

* Matth. xxiii. 37, 38 ; xxiv. 1, 2.   † See Sec. I. of this chapter.
‡ Luke xix. 41—44.   § Luke xxiii. 28—30.   ∥ xxiv. 2.   ¶ Chap. xxi. 43, 44.

said to Jesus—"Tell us when shall these things be, and what shall be the *sign of thy coming*, and of the *end of the world*."* Neither Mark nor Luke, in recording this inquiry of the disciples, has the words—"thy *coming*, and the *end of the world*." The latter has—"When shall these things be? and what sign will there be when these things shall come to pass?"—And the former—"When shall these things be? and what shall be the sign when all these things shall be fulfilled?"† From the expressions—"thy coming," and—"the end of the world," which occur in Matthew, one might be led to suppose that these prophecies were not uttered *exclusively* in reference to the destruction of Jerusalem,— the dispersion of the Jews, and the overthrow of the Jewish polity,—but that their fulfilment embraces a wider sphere—that they refer to the Second Coming of Christ, and the last Day of Judgment, at "the end of the world." There is here, however, no need of having recourse to this supposition, nothwithstanding that Matthew—differing from the two other Evangelists,—makes use of these words. For the expressions are not those of Christ,—they are those of his disciples. If, therefore, *they* were at the time labouring under the erroneous impression that Christ in these prophecies alluded to his Second Coming, when he should take vengeance upon his enemies,—destroy Jerusalem, in common with the rest of the world,—and establish his Messianic kingdom upon earth,—still this error, on the part of the disciples, would by no means affect the predictions of Christ.

But there are no grounds for inferring from these words that even the disciples entertained such erroneous views. As to their using the expression—"thy coming," it is well known that the Jews at large,—and, consequently, the disciples—regarded all misfortunes and calamities—all untoward events—as judgments from heaven. They,—like many Christians of the present age—whether correctly or incorrectly we shall not stop to consider—were firm believers in "temporal judgments." Such were their views of God's dealings with them, that when they were vanquished in battles by their enemies, they thought that God by this means chastised them for their sins, and that when they conquered their enemies, they were the means, in the hands of God, to punish them for their iniquities. This doctrine is so frequently advanced in Holy Writ, that to adduce passages in proof of it, is deemed wholly unnecessary. Further; the disciples unhesitatingly believed Christ to be the Son of God,—to have all authority in heaven and on earth,—to be the personage who was to judge the world in the Last Day. This was the very foundation of their faith in him. Accordingly they necessarily inferred that it was he who would execute judgment upon the Jews in destroying Jerusalem, and erasing the Temple, so as not to leave one stone upon another. Hence, they naturally asked him, *what should be the sign of his coming*. With regard to the phrase, "end of the world," it is in perfect accordance with the sense in which the Jews frequently employed the word *world*.—Tertullus, before Felix, accuses Paul of being "a mover of sedition among all the Jews throughout all the *world*"‡ (οικουμενη); but the Jews were not inhabiting the *whole world*. The word *world* is often used in the Jewish writings, as well as in those of other nations, to denote an *empire*, a *kingdom*, or a

---

* Matth. xxiv. 3.   † Luke xxi. 7.   Mark xiii. 4.
‡ Acts xxiv. 5.

province. Accordingly we find the Roman Empire called "all the world."* Isaiah calls the Babylonish empire "the world," and the Assyrian empire the earth.† It is not, however, the word *earth*, or *globe* (κοσμος), or the words *inhabitants of the globe* (οικουμενη), or any word synonimous to either, that has been used by the disciples, and translated, in our version, — "world," but a word which, in this connection, is of a much more limited signification.—It is the word αιων, which literally means *age*, or *duration of life* or *of time* ;‡ and which, in the passage under notice, may mean,—in conjunction with the word "end,"—the *end* of the Jewish age or Jewish polity. Several divines have maintained, with considerable show of reason, that the Jewish dispensation did not end until the destruction of Jerusalem, and the dispersion of the different orders of priests. Nor can it be said that, in reality, it terminated before these events. Be that as it may, there is no reason to conclude that the disciples by the words,—"end of the world"—meant the Dissolution of Nature and the Final Judgment. Nor is there any foundation for the belief that Christ, in his reply to them, where he employs the word "end," and the phrase "the coming of the Son of man"—although he speaks in highly figurative language—means any other than the destruction of Jerusalem, when the Roman army should be instruments to inflict upon the Jews the punishment awarded them.§ For he tells them that before these things—"the end" and his "coming"—shall take place, they "shall hear of wars and rumours of wars;" and that when they shall see Jerusalem compassed with armies they are to know that the dissolution of that city is nigh.‖ Such expressions as these can be intended only as predictions of the events which were to precede the temporal calamities that overcame the Jewish people. In a word, the whole tenour of this prophetic discourse is confined to Jerusalem and to the Jews. There is no mention, nor even an allusion made here to any other place or people—nothing said about the destruction of the world at large. The symbolical expressions used in reference to the darkening of the heavenly bodies shall be examined in a subsequent section.

SECTION III.—HISTORICAL PROOFS OF THE EXACT FULFILMENT OF CHRIST'S PREDICTIONS REGARDING JERUSALEM.

It is next intended to show that these prophecies have minutely been fulfilled. Thirty-six years after Christ's death, Jerusalem, by the Roman legions, under Titus Vespasian, was besieged and captured.—The inhabitants were massacred by thousands, the temple was demolished, and the Jewish polity, both in Church and State, totally subverted. Christ's prophetic description of these events accords remarkably with the manner

---

* Luke ii. 1.   See also Act. xi. 28.   We meet the word οικουμενη (world, or rather inhabitants of the earth) in profane writers, used to designate the Roman Empire, long before the time of Christ.—'Ρωμαιοι εν ολιγω χρονω πασαν εφ' εαυτους εποιησαν την οικουμενην.—Polyb. lib. vi. c. 48.   Πολλα χωρια της υπο 'Ρωμαιων οικουμενης.—Plut. Pompei p. 631 F.
 † Isa. xiii. 11 ; xiv. 17 ; xxiv. 4.   The Septuagint have here η οικουμενη ολη, and in some places η οικουμενη.
‡ Vid. Parkhurst's Lex. v. αιων.
§ Matth. xxiv. 6, 11, 27, 30.   Luke xxi. 9, 27.
‖ Matth. xxiv. 6.   Luke xxi. 20.

C

in which the events themselves actually took place, as narrated by Josephus—a Jewish historian and general, who was present at the siege of Jerusalem—whose accuracy has never been impeached,* and who could not have any motive whatever to accommodate his history of the Jewish wars to the predictions of Christ. This accordance has drawn the attention of many learned writers, in different languages, and has made some of them—owing to the harmony they perceived, even in many matters of detail, between the predictions and the narrative of the downfall of the holy city—suspect that the Evangelists wrote after that event had taken place, and moulded history into a prophetic form. But this disputed point does not concern the present argument, at the outset of which it was declared expedient to admit that these prophecies had really been uttered by Christ. And even were it relevant, it might be urged that if the three Evangelists who record these prophecies, did at all write the Gospels which pass under their respective names, it is most improbable that they deferred writing them for thirty years after the occurrence of the events they narrate, namely, until after the year 70. A.D.—when Jerusalem was destroyed, and when they were, doubtless, very old men. For as we find that one of them was an immediate companion of Christ, and the other two were associates of this companion,—and probably all three about the same age as Christ, —they would then be about seventy years of age. Besides : there is nothing in these prophecies which, in the slightest degree, suggests that they were written after the event. Very different are they in this respect from the counterfeited prophecies of the Sibyline Oracles, and those of the twelve Patriarchs, which are maintained to be transcripts of history turned into a prophetic form.†

But to proceed with the proof of the fulfilment of these prophecies.— Jesus predicted in regard to the temple—"There shall not be left here one stone upon another that shall not be thrown down."‡ According to Josephus, one of the first parts of the city that the Roman soldiers demolished was the temple, which they burnt down. So completely was it destroyed that a ploughshare was drawn over the ground upon which it had stood, as a sign of the perpetual interdiction of that once consecrated ground.|| Christ warns the Jews to take heed, because many false prophets would arise, and deceive, if possible, the very elect.§ Many of these appeared before and at the time Jerusalem was attacked. Josephus speaks of them in the following terms.—"A false prophet was the occasion of the destruction of these people, who had made a public proclamation in the city, that very day, that God commanded them to get up upon the temple, and that there they should receive miraculous signs of their deliverance. Now there was then a great number of false prophets suborned by the tyrants to impose on the people, who denounced this to them, that they should wait for the deliverance of God."¶

---

* Although some few modern interpolations have been detected in the works of Josephus, and although it must be admitted that considerable portions of them are of a very fabulous and legendary character, yet he is considered—at least by both Jews and Christians—a faithful historian on the whole. An argument, therefore, is here based upon his statements.

† See Paley's Evidence of Christianity, part II. chap. i.

‡ Matthew xxiv. 2. Mark xiii. 2. Luke xxi. 6. Jewish Wars, b. vi. c. iv. ss. 5—8.

|| Gibbon's Decline and Fall of the Roman Empire, c. xxiii. p. 338.—Cadell's Edit. Keith's Evidence of Christianity, chap. iii.

§ Matth. xxiv. 4, 5, 11, 24. ¶ Whiston's Translation of Josephus, b. vi. c. v. s. 2.

The next thing which Christ predicts is that the disciples should " hear of wars and rumours of wars," before this calamity would actually fall upon the Jews. Accordingly, we find Titus Vespasian, in addressing the Jews, tell them that when his father came into the country he acted towards them with such moderation that, notwithstanding their disloyalty, he only burnt Galilee and the neighbouring parts,—that at the time of the death of Nero (two years before) they had created civil disturbances, as well as when Vespasian himself was made Emperor,—that they had sent beyond the Euphrates for assistance to attack the Romans,—that seditions had arisen among them,—and that, one tyrant contending against another, civil war had broken out among them. These things would make the disciples hear of " wars and rumours of wars."* In addition to this it may be remarked that the circumstances which must have been concomitant with the violent deaths of the four Roman Emperors—Nero, Galba, Otho, and Vitellius—all of them within two years, and the last within a year of the destruction of Jerusalem—would, in the desperate struggle made for imperial power, cause the Jews in the distant land of Judea to hear " rumours of wars." Christ also prophesies that *nation would rise against nation, and kingdom against kingdom,* and that there should be *famines, pestilences,* and *earthquakes in divers places,* which were to be " the beginning of sorrows." Each of these particulars has been amply fulfilled.— *Nation rose against nation, and kingdom against kingdom,* when the Syrians and the Jews in Cæsarea fought for the right of the city, and 20,000 of the latter were killed. To this may be added—battles in Damascus, when 10,000 Jews were killed—in Ascalon, when 20,500 Jews lost their lives— in Scythopolis, when 13,000 of the same people were slain. Also upwards of 80,000 Jews were killed in Gadara, Alexandria in Egypt, Ptolemais, and other places, by fighting with the inhabitants of these localities ;† thus fully verifying the prediction that " nation should rise against nation, and kingdom against kingdom." *Famines* prevailed four times, in Rome, in Palestine, and in Greece, during the reign of Claudius I.—who died October 13th, A.D. 54,—to which there is reference made in the Acts of the Apostles (xi. 28.) This must be about twenty-two years after the death of Christ, and about fourteen years before the destruction of Jerusalem. Both Tacitus and Suetonius refer to these famines. There was also a most awful famine in Jerusalem soon after the commencement of the siege. Josephus tells us that " the famine widened its progress, that it devoured the people by whole houses and families. The upper rooms were full of women and children that were dying by famine, and the lanes of the city were full of the dead bodies of the aged. The children also and the young men wandered about the market-places like shadows, all swelled with the famine, and fell down dead wheresoever their misery seized them. As for burying them, those that were sick themselves were not able to do it, and those that were hearty and well were deterred from doing it by the

---

* Matth. xxiv. 6. Joseph. de Bell. Jud. lib. vi. c. vi. s. 2.

† Joseph. de Bell. Jud. lib. ii. c. xiii. s. 7 ; c. xviii. ss. 1, 3, 5 ; c. xx. 5, 2. Lib. iii. c. ii. ss. 2, 3, *et al. loc.* Although the above are not nearly all the Jews Josephus states to have been killed in war about this time, yet this number— making a total of 143,500— is an incredible number to have been slain of men whose whole nation inhabited only a paltry sterile nook of territory. This is still more wonderful when it is considered what a vast number of them was shortly after slain during the siege of Jerusalem by the Roman soldiers. Such however is the testimony of their historian.

c 2

great multitude of those dead bodies, and by the uncertainty there was how soon they should die themselves; for many died as they were burying others, and many went to their coffins before that fatal hour was come."* Well might this famine, therefore, be classed by Christ with those things which would be to the Jews "the beginning of sorrows." *Pestilences*, also, made great havoc among the Jews, both before and during the time of the siege of Jerusalem. *Earthquakes*, likewise, were felt in Rome, Laodicea, Hierapolis Colosse, Pompeii, Crete, Asia Minor, and several parts of Italy.†

The next thing in this chain of prophecies is the prediction that before the destruction of Jerusalem the Christians would have to undergo severe persecutions. They were to be cast into prisons—brought before "kings and rulers"—and even put to death, for their belief in Christ.‡ Tacitus, writing in the beginning of the second century, informs us that Nero, who was Emperor of Rome from A.D. 54 to 68, convicted and put to death a great number of Christians—some of whom he nailed on crosses, others he sewed up in the skins of wild beasts and exposed to the fury of dogs, others he smeared over with combustible materials, and used as torches to illuminate the darkness of the night. The gardens of Nero were selected for the melancholy spectacle, and honoured with the presence of the Emperor.|| Suetonius, also, who wrote a few years afterwards, refers to the same persecution, in his Life of Nero, and says that the Christians were visited with punishment.§ And in his Life of Claudius he tells us that that emperor "drove the Jews who, at the suggestion of the Chrestus, were constantly rioting, out of Rome."¶ As regards the Apostles themselves, this prophecy was verified in several of them personally. Before the destruction of Jerusalem, Peter and John were laid hold of and brought before the Council,—James and Peter were arraigned before Herod,—and Paul was seized and brought before the Roman governors—Galo, Felix, and Festus.** What has just been cited from Suetonius shows how—in accordance with this prediction—the Christians, in the short space of thirty years, became to be hated by the pagan nations. As to what Christ tells his Apostles, personally, that not a hair of *their* head should perish in the destruction of that city within which they were, we have no proof that any of them perished in that catastrophe, or even were present. Although it happened on the feast of the unleavened bread,

---

* Joseph. de Bell. Jud. lib. v. c. xii. ss. 5, 4. See also lib. vi. c. iii. ss. 3, 4. There had been another famine a few years before, in the reign of Claudius, lasting for a considerable time over the whole land of Judea. Joseph. Antiq. lib. iii. c. xv. s. 3. lib. xx. c. ii. s. 5. Acts. xi. 28.

† In order to prove the accomplishment of these particulars, compare Matth. xxiv. 7. Mark xiii. 8. Luke xxi. 10, 11, with the following authorities:—Josephus's Jewish Antiquities b. xx. c. ii. c. xviii. c. ix. s. 8. Jewish Wars b. v. c. xii. ss. 3, 4. b. vi. c. i. s. i; c. iii. ss. 3, 4, 5; c. v. s. 3; c. ix. s. 3. Tacit. Annal. lib. xii. c. 43, 58. lib. xiv. c 27. lib. xvi. c. 13. Sueton. Vit. Claud. 18.

‡ Matth. xxiv. 9. Mark xiii. 9. Luke xxi. 12.

|| "Igitur primo correpti qui fatebantur, deinde indicio eorum, multitudo ingens, haud perinde in crimine incendii, quam odio humani generis, convicti sunt. Et percuntibus addita ludibria, ut ferarum tergis contecti, laniatu canum interirent, aut crucibus affixi, aut flammandi, atque ubi defecisset dies, in usum-nocturni luminis urerentur. Hortos suos ei spectaculo Nero obtulerat" &c. Tacit Annal. xv. 44.

§ Suet. in Nero, c. xvi.

¶ Judæos impulsore Chresto, assiduè tumultuantes Româ expulit.

** Acts iv. 1—7; xii. 2, 3; xviii. 12; xxiv; xxiv; xxviii.

when thousands of strangers were within the walls of the holy city, and had no chance of escaping, yet since the Apostles, as Christians, had renounced the Jewish ceremonies, it is not probable that any of them were present for the purpose of celebrating this feast; but it is more likely that those of them who were alive were in some of the distant provinces of Judea, preaching the Gospel. Besides: we have an account of the deaths of the greater number of them, unconnected with the general massacre in Jerusalem.*

The next portion of Christ's predictions, which deserves special notice is the success which the preaching of the Gospel was to meet before the destruction of Jerusalem. There is a slight difference in the words which the two Evangelists—Matthew and Mark—employ in recording this prediction, which is not recorded at all by Luke. To apply to this apparent discrepancy the recognised sound rule of explaining one passage by another on the same point, the words of the two Evangelists are here placed before the reader. Matthew says—"And this Gospel of the kingdom shall be preached in all the world, for a witness unto all nations; and then shall the end come."† The words of Mark are,—"And the Gospel must first be published among all nations."‡ There is, however, a prediction of Christ—uttered on another occasion—which appears to be of the same import as the foregoing, and is calculated to throw some light upon it.—Christ having elected twelve Apostles, and invested them with power to preach the Gospel, tells them that they should not go over the cities of Israel before the Son of man should come.‖ The question here to be decided is—Whether the words of Christ—"all the world" and "all nations"—as recorded in Matthew and Mark—mean that the Gospel was to be preached in every part of the globe before the destruction of Jerusalem, —that is, in the short space of forty years? And if they do, was it so preached? Very few remarks will suffice to show that the words do not mean this. It has already been shown in what a loose and indefinite sense the word "world"—αιων as well as οικουμενη—was used in Jewish phraseology.§ In the generally accepted Greek version, the word οικουμενη —inhabitants, or (the word earth, γη being understood) the inhabitants of the earth—is that used in the prophecy just cited from Matthew xxiv. This word has already been shown to be employed necessarily to designate only a province, or at most an empire. The Greek words translated "all nations," in Mark, are—πάντα τὰ ἔθνη—literally all nations, or all people. But the word ἔθνος, in the New Testament, most frequently denotes the Heathen or Gentiles, as distinguished from the Jews. In this sense it is used in Luke xxi. 24—"the time of the Gentiles." In the prophetic expression under notice it is clearly employed by Christ in a hyperbolical sense—a figure of speech which occurs in the writings and orations of all nations,¶ particularly in the Hebrew prophets, where

* We find in the Acts of the Apostles, vii. 60, that Stephen was stoned to death, and we further learn from early records that Paul was beheaded; that Peter, Simeon, and Jude were crucified; and that Matthew, Mark, Luke, James, Thomas, and Matthias were put to death in different countries and in various manners. See Cave's Lives of the Apostles; Dupin; and Keith's Evidence p. 60, 10th edit. 12mo.
      † Matth. xxiv. 14.   ‡ Mark xiii. 10.
      ‖ Matth. x. 23.   § See pp. 16, 17.
¶ Such a figure is the following—"There are also many other things which Jesus did, the which, if they should be written everyone, I suppose that even the world itself could not contain the books that should be written.—John xxi. 25.

it shines forth with conspicuous lustre.   Christ here employs the figure to show the great successes which the Gospel would meet with before the destruction of Jerusalem, not to signify that before that event all the nations of the world would be converted to Christianity.   That the Gospel was proclaimed to people belonging to a great number of nations will appear from the account of the miraculous preaching of the Apostles on the day of Pentecost,* as well as from the account we have of the countries through which they afterwards travelled.†   Christ had commissioned his Apostles to preach his Gospel to the Gentiles, as well as to the Jews—to preach it to all nations.‡   Since, therefore, the Apostles were not to confine their labours to the land of Judea, the length of which was about one hundred and fifty miles, and its breadth about seventy, it is quite consistent with the fact of the great success which the Gospel met with prior to the destruction of Jerusalem, that Christ should predict, as already observed, that his Apostles would not have gone even over all the cities of Israel before that dreadful occurrence should take place.   And since he says this consistently in one place, he cannot mean in another place—by the words " all the world," and " all nations "—that all the inhabitants of the globe were to be converted to Christianity before the holy city should be destroyed.   Nor do the words in themselves—irrespectively of any circumstances—warrant such an interpretation.   The obvious meaning is, that the Apostles would, before that event, preach the Gospel in a great number of countries.

As to that declaration of Christ, that " the brother should betray brother to death, and the father the son, and children cause their parents to be put to death,"|| this was verified in innumerable instances during the persecutions of the Apostles.   The hatred evinced by Jewish as well as Pagan relatives towards a person, in the first age of Christianity, when he became a convert to the "new religion," was implacable, and rendered great aid to those in authority to convict and execute him.   A very remarkable instance of this feeling is exhibited in the story of Paul and Thecla, as related in the Apocryphal Gospels.   Thecla having been converted to Christianity, and gone to see Paul in prison, is detected ; and her mother, Theoclia, in the midst of an assembled mob cries out—" Let the unjust creature be burnt ! —let her be burnt in the midst of the theatre !"§   To say nothing of the Divine authority of these Gospels, which Cardinal Baronius, Locrinus, Archbishop Wake, Dr. Grabe, with other learned divines, consider to have been

---

* Acts ii.
† The Gospel, before the destruction of Jerusalem, had been preached—in Idumea, Syria, and Mesopotamia, by Judas,—in Egypt, Marmorica, Mauritania, and other parts of Africa by Mark, Simeon, and Judas,—in Ethiopia by the eunuch of Candace and Matthias,—in Pontus, Galatia, and the neighbouring countries of Asia by Peter,—in the territories of the Seven Churches of Asia, by John,—in Parthia by Matthew,—in Scythia by Philip and Andrew,—in the northern and western parts of Asia by Bartholomew,—in Persia by Simeon and Judas,—in Media, Armenia, and several eastern districts by Thomas,—for a great distance from Jerusalem, even so far as Illyricum by Paul,—and also by him in Italy, and, probably, in France, Spain, and Britain.   Christian Churches were planted in all the above places in less than 30 years after the death of Christ.   Thus was the Gospel preached in the most known and renowned parts of the world before the destruction of Jerusalem.—*Hughes' Commentary.*
‡ Matth. x. 5, 6 ; xxviii. 19.   Luke xxiv. 47.
|| Matth. xxiv. 10.   Mark xiii. 12.   Luke xxi. 16.
§ Paul and Thecla, chap. v. ver. 8, in Apocryphal Gospels, published by Hone, Lond. 1820

written in the apostolic age, they at least show the state of feeling at the time against Christianity. But this prediction of Christ is also verified in many of the painful incidents which happened during the siege of Jerusalem, as amply detailed by Josephus.*

Another portion of Christ's prophecies which was most remarkably and indubitably fulfilled is the following ;—" When ye, therefore, shall see the abomination of desolation, spoken of by Daniel the prophet, stand in the holy place, (whoso readeth let him understand,) then let them which be in Judea flee into the mountains."† The idea here is clothed in highly prophetical language—more so than any of Christ's predictions hitherto noticed in this chapter. The figure used is decidedly symbolical, in accordance with that of the passages in Daniel, to which Christ here alludes. But what is " the abomination of desolation " spoken of by Daniel ? There are in Daniel several passages which refer to this " abomination ;"‡ but the most striking, and that to which Christ, probably, refers more immediately is the following ;—" And *arms shall stand* on his part, and they shall pollute the sanctuary of strength, and shall take away the daily sacrifice, *and they shall place the abomination that maketh desolate.*"‖ *Abomination*, in the Scriptures, is a word used to designate idols and idolatry, and there is very little doubt that Christ, in the passage under consideration, adopted the words of Daniel to signify that the idolatrous Roman legions, with their arms, flags, and banners, would desecrate the temple§ which—together with the city, and many miles of the country around it—was considered holy ground, in a more peculiar sense than the rest of Judea. Luke solves all doubt on this point ; for he gives us the literal meaning of this prediction, divested of all its figurative character. He conveys it in the following words :—" And when ye shall see Jerusalem compassed with armies, then know that the desolation thereof is nigh. Then let them which are in Judea flee to the mountains."¶ The prediction is proved to be the same as that cited from Matthew and Mark by the identity of its contents. But what Christ prophesied on this subject on another occasion—namely, when he rode in triumph into the holy city, and foreseeing its awful fate, wept over it—sets the meaning of this passage quite at rest.

The following prophecy has already been cited in full ;** but the part of it now more particularly referred to is the following :—" For the days

---

* De Bell. Jud. lib. v. c. iv., vi, et al.
† Matth. xxiv. 15, 16. Mark xiii. 14.　　　　‡ Dan. ix. 26 ; xii. 11.
‖ Dan. xi. 31.

§ Josephus states that " the Romans, upon the flight of the seditious into the city, and upon the burning of the holy house itself, and of all the buildings round about it, *brought their ensigns to the temple*, and set them over against the eastern gate ; *and there they did offer sacrifice to them.*—B. vi. c. vi. s. 1. This is a singular fulfilment of the prediction. It should be added here that on the metal plates of the Roman standards there " were usually represented the warlike deities, Mars and Minerva." It was to the representation of these deities that the Roman soldiers offered sacrifice.—See Dr. Meyrick's " Ancient Armour." The following *figurative* language of Scripture will illustrate the Eastern Customs as to ensigns, banners, &c.—" In the name of our God I will set up our banner."—Psal. xx. 5.　" Thou hast given a banner" &c.—Psal. lx. 4.　" A root of Jesse shall stand for an ensign of the people."—Isa. xi. 10. See also xlix. 22 ; lii. 12. Tertullian says that the religion of the Roman camp almost entirely consisted in worshipping the ensigns, in swearing by the ensigns, and in preferring the ensigns to all the (other) gods.—Apolog. c. xvi. p. 162. Havercamp's.
¶ Luke xxi. 20, 21.　　　　** See p. 15.

shall come upon thee that thine enemies shall cast a trench about thee, and compass thee round, and keep thee in on every side, and shall lay thee even with the ground."* But have these things been accomplished? Has the abomination of desolation stood in the holy city?—Has Jerusalem been compassed with armies? And have the enemy cast a trench about her, compassed her round, and kept her in on every side, and laid her even with the ground? Yes:—the prophecy has been fulfilled to the very letter.—When Vespasian besieged the city he caused his soldiers to surround it on all sides, in order to keep the inhabitants within it, with a view to famish them. Having made some attacks upon the Jews, he consulted his commanders as to what future steps should be taken to reduce the city. The result of this consultation was the building of a wall round about the whole city, which was thought the only way to prevent the Jews from escaping, and make them the more willing to surrender, or the more easily conquered, when the famine had further weakened them. Having given orders to his soldiers to build this wall, it was completed in the incredibly short space of three days. Its length was forty furlongs, or nearly five miles long—embracing most of the little mounts that were about Jerusalem, and having upon it thirteen towers for garrisons. " All hope of escaping was now cut off from the Jews, together with their liberty of going out of the city. The famine now widened its progress, and devoured the people by whole houses and families."† The Romans very shortly captured the city, and so completely did they demolish it that they levelled it with the ground, excepting three towers, which were left to stand;‡ but in the reign of Julian—290 years afterwards—these also were rased to the ground. Thus was the prediction most completely fulfilled—that *not a stone of the city would be left upon another.*

The commiserative declaration of Christ in reference to the woes which would befal women with child, and those that gave " suck in those days,"‖ was most strikingly verified in several of the heart-rending incidents which took place during the siege. Of these Josephus relates one of the most horrible that can be imagined.—A woman, named Mary, of the village of Bethezub—who was of a distinguished and wealthy family —happened to be in Jerusalem when it was besieged. Being unable to escape, and suffering under the most pressing pangs of hunger, she ultimately " slew the child which was sucking at her breast, roasted it, and ate the one half, and kept the other half by her, concealed!"§ In the thousands and tens of thousands of human beings that perished within the walls of the city during these horrifying times of famine, many other circumstances, doubtless, similar to the above occurred,—although not specifically recorded by the Jewish historian, whose narrative of the siege has through all the vicissitudes of time descended to us. In the vast numbers that died from the famine, there were, undoubtedly, hundreds if not thousands of women who were with child; and, perishing from such a lingering death as this, it is only consistent with physiological fact to infer that their unborn babes lingered alive for some time after their respective mothers had expired. As there also must have been—among the

* Luke xix. 43, 44.
† Joseph. Jewish Wars, b. v. c. xii. ss. 1—3.   ‡ Ib. b. vii. c. i. s. 1.
‖ Matth. xxiv. 19.   Mark xiii. 17.   Luke xxi. 23.
§ Jewish Wars, b. vi. c. iii. s. 1.

hundreds of thousands who were at this time pent up within the walls of the city—a great number of women, with their infants at their bosoms, in many instances, unquestionably, did they witness these little ones perishing in their arms, some time before the famine put an end to their own existence. In both these cases would the prediction of woe to them be fulfilled. The following extracts from Josephus, must inferentially prove the fulfilment of this presage in a vast number of cases, both with regard to those who were with child, and who had children in their arms.— "The famine confounded all natural passions; for those who were just going to die looked upon those that were gone to their rest before them with dry eyes and open mouths. . . . The robbers were still more terrible than these miseries themselves; for they broke open those houses which were no other than graves of dead bodies, and plundered them of what they had; and, carrying off the coverings of their bodies, went out laughing, *and tried the point of their swords in their dead bodies*, and in order to prove what metal they were made of, *they thrust some of those through that still lay alive upon the ground*. . . . The famine devoured the people by whole houses and families; the upper rooms were full of women and children that were dying by famine, and the lanes of the city were full of the dead bodies of the aged. . . . . If they discovered food belonging to any one, they seized upon it, and swallowed it down, together with their blood also; . . . . and I cannot but think that, had not their destruction prevented it, their barbarity would have made them taste of even the dead bodies themselves."[*] Under such a state of things as this, the woe which Christ had prophesied would overtake women with child, or those " who gave suck," must inevitably have taken place. Luke[†] throws much light on this prediction, by recording the words—"For there shall be great distress in the land, and wrath upon this people."

Luke also adds, in the next verse,—"And they shall fall by the edge of the sword, and shall be led captive into all nations; and Jerusalem shall be trodden down of the Gentiles, until the time of the Gentiles be fulfilled." Matthew and Mark do not record this prediction in such specific terms as Luke does. Their words are—"For then shall be great tribulation, such as was not since the beginning of the world to this time; no, nor ever shall be,"[‡]—evidently, however, referring to the same things as Luke. This prophecy, in every instance, has been abundantly accomplished,—except that part of it refering to the times of the Gentiles, which is yet to be fulfilled. Josephus says that it appears to him that the misfortunes of all men, from the beginning of the world, if they were compared to those of the Jews, are not so considerable as theirs.[||] Again: in other places, he has the following expressions:—"The multitude of those that perished in Jerusalem exceeded all the destructions that men or God ever brought upon the world."[§]—"They (the Roman soldiers) ran every one through whom they met with, and obstructed the very lanes with their dead bodies, and made the whole city run down with blood, to such a degree, indeed, that the fire of many of the houses was quenched with the blood of these men."[¶]—"The number of those that perished during the whole siege was eleven hundred thousand,—the greater

---

* Jewish Wars, b. v. c. xii. s. 3. b. vi. c. vii. s. 3.   † Chap. xxi. ver. 23.
    ‡ Matth. xxiv. 21.   Mark xiii. 19. || Pref. to Jewish Wars, sec. 4.
§ Jewish Wars, b. vi. c. ix. s. 4.   ¶ Jewish Wars, b. vi. c. viii. s. 4.

part of whom were, indeed, of the same nation, but not belonging to the city itself ; for they were come up from all the country to the feast of the unleavened bread, and were, on a sudden, shut up by an army."*—" A terrible battle was fought at the entrance of the temple,.... in which battle the darts were on both sides useless, as well as the spears, and both sides drew their swords and fought it out, hand in hand..... Great slaughter was now made on both sides."†—" They went in numbers into the lanes of the city, with their swords drawn, and slew those whom they overtook without mercy."‡—" His soldiers were quite tired in killing men, and yet there appeared to be a vast multitude still remaining alive."‖ Such is the history we have of the Jews falling " by the edge of the sword."

As to their having been " led captive into all nations," we find in the same Historian that after capturing the city, Titus, while he gave orders to slay the aged and infirm, chose out of the young men the tallest and most beautiful, and reserved them for the triumph ; eleven thousand of whom, however, perished afterwards for want of food. " The rest of the multitude that were above seventeen years old he put into bonds and sent to the Egyptian mines " and the different provinces. But those under seventeen he sold as slaves § He sold also an immense number of men with their wives and children. These were sold at a very low price ; because the number was great and the buyers but few.¶ At Cæsarea Philippi, Titus wantonly exposed for sport in theatres " a great number of the captives, and caused them to be destroyed—some by being thrown to wild beasts, and others in multitudes forced to kill one another, as if they were enemies," simply to make fun for their insolent victors.** In celebrating his brother's birthday at the same place, he inflicted great cruelty upon the captive Jews in honour of him.—" The number of those that were now slain in fighting with the beasts, and were burnt, and fought with one another, exceeded two thousand five hundred."†† Shortly after at Berytus— a Phœnician city, and then a Roman colony—he destroyed an equal number in " magnificent shows " for the celebration of his father's birthday."‡‡ " The number of those that were carried captive, during the whole war, was collected to be ninety-seven thousand "!‖‖ Well might Christ, there-

---

* Jewish Wars, b. vi. c. ix. s. 3. The total number of Jews destroyed during the entire seven years before this time in Judea and the countries bordering on it, as summed up by Archbishop Usher from Lypsius out of Josephus, up to A.D. 70, amounts to one million, three hundred and thirty seven thousand, four hundred and ninety ! The number of Jews and Proselytes of Justice who usually came out of Galilee, Samaria, Judea, Berea, and other remote regions, to the Passover in Jerusalem was, according to Josephus's own reasoning, two millions five hundred and sixty five thousand, and according to his direct statement, two millions seven hundred thousand and two hundred. In some places (Jewish Wars, b. vi. c. ix. s. 3. b. ii. c. xiv. s. 3.) he makes them three millions. " In no other nation," remarks Mr. Whiston, the translator of Josephus, " could such a vast number be gotten together, and perish in the siege of any one city as now happened in Jerusalem." See Whiston's Josephus, pp. 80, 81—*note*, Tegg's edit.

† Jewish Wars, b. vi. c. i. s. 7.   ‡ Ibid. b. vi. c. viii. s. 5.
‖ Ib. b. vi. c. ix. s. 2. In another place he says—"the army had no more people to slay or plunder, because there remained none.—B. vii. c. ii. s. 1.
§ Ib. b. vi. c. ix. s. 2.
¶ Ib. b. vi. c. viii. s. 2.   ** Ib. b. vii. c. ii. s. 1.
†† Ib. b. vii. c. iii. s. 1.
‡‡ Ib. See also Cic. ad. Attic. 2, ep. 9. Flacc. 28.
‖‖ Ib. b. vi. c. ix. s. 3.

fore, prophetically declare that there should be tribulations in those days, such as had not been since the beginning of the world; and with truth did he say that the Jews should fall by the edge of the sword, and be led captive into all nations! Equally true will it prove that "Jerusalem shall be trodden down of the Gentiles, until the times of the Gentiles be fulfilled." Since her destruction she has been trodden down by the Romans, the Saracens, and the French; and she is now trodden down by the Turks. The Romans made a law that no Jew should remain in his ancient inheritance, or even come in sight of Jerusalem.

The prediction that the days, or duration of these tribulations should be shortened has been accomplished in a remarkable manner.—" And except those days should be shortened there should no flesh be saved; but for the elect's sake those days shall be shortened." * Titus had at first determined to reduce the city by famine, and therefore built a wall around it, so as to prevent either any provision from being taken in, or any of the people coming out. This, if it had been carried out to the utmost, although a tedious mode requiring a length of time, yet would make all the inhabitants fall a prey to the famine, so that "no flesh should be saved." But the banks about the upper city being finished in the short space of eighteen days, the Jews—provoked by what the Romans were doing, and seeing the danger of their city still increasing—offered battle near the walls which were being battered by the engines of the Romans, and attacked the guard guard placed on this wall. They were, however, soon overpowered by the Roman soldiers, who put them to flight, took the city by storm, and became entire masters of it. Thus was the time of these calamities shortened. "And here," as Josephus remarks, "one may chiefly reflect on the power of God exercised upon those wicked wretches, and on the good fortune of the Romans; for these tyrants (the Jews) did now wholly deprive themselves of the security they had in their own power, and came down from those very towers of their own accord, wherein they could never have been taken by force, nor indeed any other way than by famine. And thus did the Romans when they had taken such great pains about weaker walls, get, by good fortune, what they could never have gotten by their engines; for three of these towers were too strong for all mechanical engines whatever....... So they now left these towers of themselves, or rather they were ejected out of them by God himself, and fled immediately to that valley which was under Siloam."† Josephus further says‡ that when Titus had entered the city he admired the strength of its fortifications, and exclaimed,—" We have certainly had God for our assistant in this war, and it was no other than God who ejected the Jews out of these fortifications; for what could the hands of men or any machines do towards overthrowing these towers?" Hence, we at once see the reason why he determined upon reducing the city by famine—namely, because its fortifications were too strong to be taken otherwise; and hence we see that the besiegers would have to remain before and around the city for a considerable time, had not the days been thus shortened by Divine interposition, in fulfilment of

* Matth. xxiv. 22. Mark xiii. 20.

† Jewish Wars, b. vi. c. viii. ss. 4, 5. Whiston's Translation. It should be observed that Josephus here speaks of the wall built about the upper city—Mount Sion, whereas in book v. c. xii. ss. 1—3. already cited, he speaks of the wall raised about the lower city only. The former was raised in three days, but the latter in eighteen days.

‡ Ibid. b. vi. c. ix. s. 1.

Christ's prophecy, *"for the sake of the elect"**—whoever are meant by these—and in order to give an opportunity to those in the towers to flee to the valley under Siloam. Both the prediction and the history of its fulfilment recognise the hand of the Deity, throughout the melancholy event, in punishing the Jews. The Romans, apparently, were instruments in the hand of God to scatter the Jews, in order to put a stop to the cruelties—as detailed in Josephus—inflicted by the inhabitants of the city upon one another. Nor did these days of "terror" last long.—The city was taken in less than six months after it was besieged, and the whole country subjugated in less than eighteen months.

Christ having foretold that the tribulation of those days should be shortened, and having adverted to the appearance of false prophets and false Christs in those times, as already noticed, gives a caution against heeding them, notwithstanding the signs and wonders which they should pretend to show, adding his reason that—" as the lightning cometh out of the east and shineth even unto the west, so shall also the coming of the Son of man be."† This expression is clothed in highly figurative language, and the succeeding portions of this series of prophetic declarations are still more so. The appellation, "Son of man" is, unquestionably, one which Christ, in a somewhat figurative sense, applies to himself ; and which very frequently occurs in the Gospels,—used, however, only by Christ himself. The portion of Holy Writ in which we first meet with the title " Son of man " is the Prophecies of Daniel,‡ where—as supposed in all ages—it has been employed, under the guidance of Inspiration, to denote the Messiah. Daniel uses the appellation in prefiguring Christ executing judgment upon the wicked, saying—" Behold, one like the Son of man came with the clouds of heaven, and came to the Ancient of days." Christ—in conformity with the language of ancient prophecy—adopts the same figure, and almost literally the same expressions, in predicting his coming to execute temporal judgment upon the Jews, in the destruction of Jerusalem and the overthrow of the Jewish polity, both religiously and civilly. That this calamity was a temporal judgment executed by the Deity upon the Jews, is a fact both admitted by themselves and maintained by Christians. Christ, in this prediction, represents himself as the inflicter of this judgment. His immediate object, however, in using the words—" as the lightning cometh from the east " &c.—is to show the quickness and suddenness with which the judgment would fall upon the Jews. Such we find to have been the case.—The Romans who, in accordance with the language of the prediction, came " from the east," surrounded the city before the inhabitants were aware of their approach, and precluded the possibility of escape.‖

The same suddenness of destruction is also prophetically depicted by Christ when he says in the following verse, that none but the Father alone knew the day and hour this would happen,—that as they were in the days of Noe, eating and drinking, marrying and giving in marriage, until the day Noe entered into the ark, and the flood came sweeping away thousands,

---

* It is not essential to our present purpose to ascertain who are meant by " the elect " mentioned here. It may, however, be remarked that there appears no reason to believe that they were Christians, but that probably they were some of the Jews whom God would afterwards call to carry out his purposes. But there is every reason to conclude that the same are meant here, by the elect, as in verse 31 of the same chapter—Matth. xxiv.
† Matth. xxiv. 27.			‡ Dan. vii. 13.
‖ Jos. Jewish Wars, b. v. c. ii. s. 2.

so should this destruction fall upon the city of Jerusalem—that of two women found in the field, or grinding at a mill, the one should be taken and the other left.* Such must have been the case in many instances, when the Roman legion suddenly surrounded the Jewish capital.

Another particular in these prophecies, which has most strikingly been fulfilled, is the celestial signs that were to appear before the destruction of the city. In Matthew† we find the following expression:—"Then shall appear the sign of the Son of man in heaven;" and in Luke—"There shall be signs in the sun, and in the moon, and in the stars, and upon the earth distress of nations with perplexity, the sea and the waves roaring."‡ Now, Josephus who was a Jew and who, therefore, could have no motive in writing a history to prove the truth of Christianity, records the appearance of some of these signs. He writes that "the Jews did not attend nor give credit to the signs that were so evident, and did so plainly foretell their future desolation; but like men infatuated—without either eyes to see or minds to consider—did not regard the denunciations that God made to them. There was a star resembling a sword, which stood over the city, and a comet that continued a whole year. Thus also before the Jew's rebellion, and before those commotions which preceded the war (with the Romans) when the people were come in great crowds to the feast of unleavened bread, on the eighth day of the month Xanthicus (Nisan), and at the ninth hour of the night, so great a light shone round the altar and the holy house, that it appeared to be bright day time, which lasted for half an hour. This light seemed to be a good sign among the unskilful, but was so interpreted by the sacred Scribes as to portend those events that followed immediately upon it...... Besides these; a few days after that feast, on the one and twentieth day of the month Artemisius (Jyar), a certain prodigious and incredible phenomenon appeared. I suppose the account of it would seem to be a fable, were it not related by those that saw it, and were not the events that followed it of so considerable a nature as to deserve such signals; for before sunset, chariots and troops of soldiers in their armour, were seen running about among the clouds and surrounding of cities. Moreover, at that feast which we call *Pentecost*, as the priests were going by night into the inner court of the temple, as their custom was, to perform their sacred ministrations, they said that, in the first place, they felt a quaking and heard a great noise, and after that they heard a sound as of a multitude saying—"Let us remove hence."‖ Tacitus also writes that armies were at this time seen meeting in the clouds over Jerusalem—that arms were seen to dazzle and brandish in the air—that the temple was seen as if one mass of flames—that fire was seen to come from the clouds—that a divine voice was heard saying that the Deity had left the place—and that a great noise was heard as if it were his departure.§ It is trusted that these testimonies are sufficient to prove that the signs in

* Matth. xxiv. 36—41. † Chap xxiv. 30.
‡ Chap. xxi. 25. The expressions used in Matthew and Mark as to the falling of the heavenly bodies shall be considered in the succeeding section.
‖ Jos. Jewish Wars, b. vi. c. v. s. 3. Whiston's Translation.
§ Evenerant prodigia, quæ neque hostiis, neque votis piare fas habet gens superstitioni obnoxia religionibus adversa. Visæ per cœlum concurrere acies, rutilantia arma, et subito nubium igne collucere templum. Expassæ repente delubri fores et audita major humana vox excedere deos; simul ingens motus excedentium.—Tacit. Hist. lib. v. c. 13.

the heavens &c., predicted by Christ, took place in such a manner as cannot fail to identify the prediction with the events.

Thus have we now found that every particular, in Christ's prophecies of the destruction of Jerusalem, has clearly been accomplished. With truth, therefore, did he make the following declaration ;—" Verily I say unto you, *this generation* shall not pass away till *all these things be fulfilled.* Heaven and earth shall pass away, but my words shall not pass away."

SECTION IV.—THE ERRONEOUSNESS OF THE NOTION THAT CHRIST IN THESE PREDICTIONS FORETOLD THE NEAR APPROACH OF THE END OF THE WORLD, AND THE FINAL JUDGMENT.

The next position intended to be laid down is—that, as the foregoing prophecies have been fulfilled in the destruction of Jerusalem, they have, therefore, proved *true*,—and that no portion of them can, by a process of fair and legitimate criticism, be shown to foretell the *end of the world*, or any other events than those connected with the *capture* of the *Jewish metropolis and the destruction of the Jewish commonwealth.*

In order, simply, to substantiate the *truth* of these prophecies, not a word requires to be advanced under this proposition, with a view to effect this object.—What has been adduced in the foregoing section *should* be deemed sufficient to answer this purpose. For the rule of proof already cited* from the Rev. Hartwell Horne must be admitted, on all hands, valid— that " a prophecy is demonstrated to be fulfilled when we can prove from unimpeachable authority that the event has actually taken place precisely according to the manner in which it was foretold." Since, however, *other* views of these *prophecies* are taken, both by the friends and foes of Christianity, the subject shall be pursued somewhat further, principally with the view of anticipating any objections that may be made on the other side of the question.

It is not here forgotten that both ancient and modern divines contend that a prophecy may have a two-fold meaning,—that the Fathers, such as Jerome, Ambrose, Cassiodore, Hilary, Prosper, Chrysosotom, Theodoret and Tertullian, in the first centuries of Christianity,—that Hugo, Grotius, and John Cocceius, of the seventeenth century,—maintain that there is in the prophetic writings of Scripture, " besides the literal and obvious signification, a hidden and mysterious sense that lies concealed under the external mask of certain persons, events, and actions,"†—and that even that celebrated Biblical scholar, the Rev. Thos. Hartwell Horne of the present century, tells us that " the same prophecies frequently have a double meaning, and refer to different events, the one near and the other remote, the one temporal and the other spiritual, or perhaps eternal."‡ Nor is it *here*—on the part of Christianity—denied that a prophecy may have a two-fold meaning, or that one portion of prophetic sayings may refer to one event, and another to another ; and that both may have a mystic or spiritual application. And even were it admitted that—as some divines maintain—Christ's prophecy of the destruction of Jerusalem is connected, or mixed up with expres-

---

* Vide ante p. 9.
† See the quotation in Mosheim's Eccles. Hist. cent. xvii. sec. ii, part ii.
‡ Horne's Introduction, vol. ii. part ii. chap. vii. sec. 2.

sions which relate to the Final Judgment of the world, still this would by no means impair the truth of his predictions regarding the destruction of Jerusalem.—If he actually did utter such predictions, and such predictions have been fulfilled, the truth of such predictions remains intact—with whatever expressions they may be mixed up. All that is contended for here, however is—that, in whatever fancies ancient or modern divines have indulged regarding spiritual sense*—there is not in the language of Christ, when predicting the destruction of Jerusalem, anything which can, by fair and legitimate criticism be made to show that, in the same discourse, he alluded to *the Destruction of the world, and the Final Judgment, as events then just at hand;* or even alluded at all to them in this chain of prophecies.

The places where these events were to occur are exclusively—the *temple*, the *holy place*, *Jerusalem*, and *Judea* with its mountains and deserts. The people who were to be subject to the calamities foretold are the *Jews*—the inhabitants of Jerusalem, who *killed the prophets and stoned those that were sent to them*. The events which were to happen are—wars and commotions—nation rising against nation, and kingdom against kingdom—pestilences—famines—earthquakes—brother betraying brother to death, and father the son—falling by the edge of the sword, and led captive—Jerusalem encompassed with armies—the enemy casting a trench around her on every side, and levelling her even with the ground, leaving not a stone upon another. It must be admitted that these particulars apply only to the Jews and the destruction of their capital, and can by no fair means be construed to imply the general Dissolution of Nature and the Final Judgment. Had Christ meant the latter, it would have been the height of absurdity in him to advise the Jews—when they saw Jerusalem encompassed with armies—to flee to the top of mountains, and to caution those who, at the time, should be on the top of a house† not to descend to take anything out of it, and those who should be in the field not to return to the house to take with them their clothes.—It would have availed nothing to them to flee to the tops of mountains in case of a general Dissolution of Nature.

The portions of this prophecy however, which appear to have induced some to imagine that Christ refers to the Last Day of Judgment and the Destruction of the world, are the following.—'' Immediately after the tribulation of those days shall the sun be darkened, and the moon shall not give her light, and the stars shall fall from heaven, and the powers of the heavens shall be shaken ; and then shall appear the sign of the Son of man in heaven ; and then shall the tribes of the earth mourn, and they shall see the Son of man coming in the clouds of heaven with power and great glory. And he shall send his angels with a great sound of trumpet, and they shall gather together his elect from the four winds, from one end of heaven to the other.'' These are the words in which Matthew‡ reports this prophetic declaration of Christ. Mark|| conveys it in similar terms, but somewhat shorter. Luke—differing from the two foregoing Evangelists, in that he appears throughout his whole narrative of these prophecies, to aim, under Divine guidance, at simplifying them, and rendering their meaning clear

* See Dr. Whitby's Dissertatio de Scriptorum Interpretatione secundum Patrum Commentarios.—Lond. 8vo. 1714.

† The tops or roofs of houses in the East were and still are flat, forming a kind of terraces upon which the inhabitants can walk, and having stairs from outside to ascend them.—See Eastern Arts and Antiquities, p. 226.

‡ Chap. xxiv. verses 29—31. || Chap. xiii. verses 24—27.

to the most common understanding—gives the declaration just cited in more literal expressions, and divested of much of the prophetic style, as follows ;—"And there shall be signs in the sun, and in the moon, and in the stars ; and upon the earth, distress of nations with perplexity ; the sea and the waves roaring, men's hearts failing them for fear, and for looking after those things which are coming on the earth ; for the powers of heaven shall be shaken. And then shall they see the Son of man coming in a cloud with power and great glory."* Now, it will be admitted that the best and only sound mode of interpreting the Scriptures, particularly prophecies, is to compare one passage whose meaning is obscure or uncertain with another which resembles it in sentiment and language, but which is clearer and more intelligible in expression. Accordingly, if we apply this rule to these passages, we find that Luke throws such a flood of light on Matthew and Mark as to make them quite intelligible.—He gives us to understand that what is meant in Matthew and Mark by the darkening and falling of the celestial bodies is that there should be *signs* in them. At the close of his description he, certainly, employs the same prophetic language as the two other Evangelists, saying that the powers of heaven should be shaken and the Son of man should be seen coming in the clouds, which expressions shall be noticed anon. But now let it be observed that with regard to these signs in the heavenly bodies—as described by Luke—such signs have already, on the authority of Josephus and Tacitus,† been shown to have appeared in the firmament, prior to the destruction of Jerusalem. What is still more remarkable in Luke is that, in the context, he connects his statement of the prediction of these signs with that of men *falling by the edge of the sword, being led away captive,* and *Jerusalem being trodden down of the Gentiles.* Thus he identifies the signs in the heavenly bodies with men falling by the edge of the sword and led away captive—and both with the destruction of Jerusalem, which he says should be "trodden down of the Gentiles."

Let it be admitted that Matthew records the very words in which Christ delivered the predictions, while Luke reports them in a more simplified form, which apparently is the case ; still there is no proof that Christ here prophesied the *End of the World.* It is clear from other passages in the Scriptures, clad in similar language, that, in this part of his prophetical discourse, he enters into a highly symbolical style—at once denoting the overthrow of the Jewish polity and the heavenly signs which should precede it. Both these meanings of the predictions, Luke has been very careful to preserve, in his process of simplification ; for he not only states that there shall be signs in the sun, moon, and stars, but adds that "the *powers* of *heaven* shall be *shaken,*" which expression will hereafter be shown to refer to *those who occupied high positions in the administration of national affairs.*

That Christ should use symbolical expressions—particularly in predictions, and still more particularly in predicting the judgment that was decreed to be executed upon the Jews for their sins—is a natural consequence of his mission. For *first,* he appeared on earth in the character of a Prophet as well as that of a Saviour ; and it was, therefore, in accordance even with human reason that he should deliver his prophecies in the same strain as Divine Inspiration had infused into the ancient Hebrew prophets,

* Luke xxi. 25—27.   † Vid. ante p. 29.

who were recognised by the Jews as divinely inspired, and whose writings abound in symbolical language. Without this mark of the prophetic gift, it would have been unjust to expect the Jews to receive him as possessing such a gift.—*Secondly,* it was necessary for Christ, whose hour had not yet come, to clothe his predictions in symbolical terms, in order fully to carry out his eternal purposes on earth, and to secure the safety of his followers. Had he, in plain language, described minutely the impending temporal judgment that was to fall upon the Jews, and had told them that he himself—as the Second Person in the Godhead—would exercise a most important part in executing this judgment, in all probability they would instantly have stoned him and his disciples to death, as they did shortly after with Stephen, when he was bold enough to tell them of their wickedness in killing the prophets, and lastly in murdering the Just One.* The very cause that incited the Jews to slay so many of the ancient prophets was that the latter, too plainly to secure the safety of their lives, denounced the temporal judgments that were to overtake the former. Hence we find Christ continually having recourse to parabolical and symbolical expressions when dwelling upon anything which had a tendency to accuse the Jews of any national evil; and hence we find him so very frequently, on such occasions, using the very words of the ancient prophets—words which were recorded in the Sacred Writings of these people, and which they feigned to believe.

Accordingly, we find the symbolical language of Christ in reference to the darkening of the sun and moon, and the falling of the stars, so nearly resembling that of the ancient prophets in the following passages, *when predicting national calamities,* as to warrant the conclusion that it is, as far as language is concerned, a quotation from one of them.—" Behold, the day of the Lord cometh, cruel both with wrath and fierce anger, to lay the land desolate; and he shall destroy the sinners thereof out of it. For the *stars of heaven and the constellations thereof shall not give their light; the sun shall be darkened in his going forth, and the moon shall not cause her light to shine,*† Ezekiel, again, prophesies in the following strain.—" I will also water with thy blood the land wherein thou swimmest, even to the mountains; and the rivers shall be full of thee. And when I shall put thee out, I will *cover the heavens,* and *make the stars thereof dark; I will cover the sun with a cloud,* and the *moon shall not give her light. All the bright lights of heaven will I make dark over thee,* and set darkness upon thy land, saith the Lord God."‡ In another of the Prophets we meet with the following passages.—" They shall run to and fro in the city; they shall run upon the wall; they shall climb up upon the houses; they shall enter in at the windows like a thief. The earth shall quake before them; the heavens shall tremble. *The sun and the moon shall be dark, and the stars shall withdraw their shining.*"§ Again:—" Multitudes,

---

* Acts vii.   † Isa. xiii. 9, 10.   ‡ Ezek. xxxii. 6—8.

§ On the part of Christianity the following hypothesis, on the point at issue, may be advanced.—The cause, perhaps, that the ancient prophets, on such occasions as these, when they predicted the judgments which were to overtake the wicked, spoke so frequently of the darkening of the heavenly bodies, was that the idolatrous nations which surrounded the Jews, (and, there is reason to believe, the Jews themselves frequently, and in great numbers) worshipped these luminaries, regarded them as gods, and trusted in them for deliverance. Hence the prophets say they should be darkened—hidden;—as much as to say, their gods should—when punishment from the true God of Israel was to

D

multitudes, in the valley of decision ; for the day of the Lord is near in
the valley of decision. *The sun and the moon shall be darkened, and the
stars shall withdraw their shining.*"*

Now, it will not be denied that the foregoing passages are predictions of *temporal* national calamities, or the vanquishing of one nation by another ; nor will it be contended that they are *not* delivered in
a symbolical style, or that the prophets did intend to foretell a *literal* and
actual eclipse of the light of the heavenly bodies, or any derangement
whatever in them. What reason, then, can there be for supposing
that Christ—in a prediction expressed with very slight exception, in the
very same words as the foregoing, and when evidently in the *context* he
was treating of a *national* calamity—meant, by the darkening of the sun
and moon, *the falling of the stars*, and the *shaking of the heavenly powers*, the
actual dissolution of nature ?—the End of the World and the Final Judgment ? There is nothing more frequently met with, in the Jewish writings,
than a description of national disruptions and the downfall of men at the
head of political, as well as religious affairs, in figures—generally symbolical figures—borrowed from nature. To adduce proofs of this fact to
any one who reads the Bible is quite needless. Before Christ, therefore,
can be proved to have predicted the End of the World and the Final Judgment, in the expressions already cited, it must be proved that he neither
imitated the figurative style of the ancient prophets, nor employed any
figurative language at all. The reverse however is clearly the case. As
proofs that he used figurative language, the following expressions must
suffice.—"The leaven of the Pharisees and Sadducees"—"the temple
of his body"—"born again"—"a well of water springing up into everlasting life "—"the bread of life."† To these might be added the whole
of his numerous parables, which are entire discourses in highly figurative
language, and quite in accordance with the mode of teaching adopted
by oriental people, whose literature abounds in parables and other figurative styles of expression.

Again : that Christ, in his predictions, used *symbolical* language, similar,
even in the *very words*, to that employed by the *ancient prophets* will be
evident from the following examples. Christ, in reference to the temple,
says to the Jews—"Behold your house is left unto you desolate."—Daniel,
prophesying of the temple, says—"He shall make it desolate."‡ Christ
compares the coming of the Son of man to lightning.—Zechariah compares

---

be inflicted upon men—be hidden from them, so as to render them no assistance. And
hence these luminaries are called *the Host of heaven*, which were worshipped.--"Lest
thou lift up thine eyes unto heaven, and when thou seest the sun and the moon and the
stars, even all the host of heaven, shouldst be driven to worship them and serve them."—
Deut. iv. 19. "God turned and gave them up to worship the host of heaven."—Acts vii.
42, 43. See also Deut. xvii. 3. 2 Kings, xvii. 16 ; xxi. 3, 5 ; xxiii. 4, 5. 2 Chron.
xxxiii. 35. Neh. ix. 6. Isa. xxxiv. 4. Jer. viii. 2 ; xix. 13 ; xxxii. 22. Dan. viii.
10. Zeph. ii. v. These hosts of heaven are sometimes curiously intended to designate
angels. (See 1 Kings, xxii. 19. 2 Chron. xviii. 18.) The Jews may have been worshippers of these hosts in the time of Christ ; and he, like the ancient prophets, may have referred to this practice in saying the sun, moon, and stars would darken.
        * Joel ii. 9, 10 ; iii. 14, 15.
† Matth. xvi. 6—12. John ii. 19—21 ; iii. 3—10 ; iv. 10—14 ; vi. 32—35.
‡ Compare Matth. xxiii. 38, with Dan. x. 26, 27.

the arrow of the Lord to the same thing.* Christ says that "the sun shall be darkened, and the moon shall not give her light, and the stars shall fall from heaven, and the powers of the heavens shall be shaken."—Isaiah says that "the stars of heaven and the constellations thereof, shall not give their light; the sun shall be darkened in his going forth, and the moon shall not cause her light to shine."† Christ, in reference to the Jews, says—" and then shall all the tribes of the earth mourn."—Zechariah, in reference to the same people, says—"and the land shall mourn, every family apart."‡ Christ says—" and they shall see the Son of man coming in the clouds of heaven with power and great glory."—Daniel says—" behold one like the Son of man came with the clouds of heaven,...... and there was given him dominion, and glory, and a kingdom."§ Christ says—"he shall send his angels with a great sound of a trumpet."—Isaiah says—" that the great trumpet shall be blown."|| Christ says—" they shall gather together his elect from the four winds, from one end of the heaven to the other."—Isaiah says—" I will bring thy seed from the east, and gather thee from the west. I will say to the north—give up; and to the south—keep not back—bring my sons from far, and my daughters from the ends of the earth."¶ The identity of language, idea, and figure of speech, in these parallel passages, is so evident, that it furnishes the most glaring proof that the prophetical style of Christ closely resembled that of the ancient prophets, and that, accordingly, his prophetical language, like theirs, was highly symbolical. What then becomes of the assertion, made by certain people, that, because Christ spoke of the darkening of the celestial bodies—of the Son of man coming in the clouds of heaven—and of his angels gathering the elect from the four winds of heaven—he must have *thereby* prophesied the End of the World and the Final Judgment? By parity of argument must it be contended that, where the ancient prophets used similar symbolical expressions, they also prophesied the End of the World and the Final Judgment; whereas it is clear from the contexts that their predictions, in these figures, were intended to foretell temporal national calamities. In like manner did Christ use the same figures to designate the catastrophe that was to befall the Jews as a nation, in the destruction of Jerusalem, and the downfall of the Jewish polity.

SECTION V.—THE ANALOGY BETWEEN THE PREDICTIONS OF THE ANCIENT PROPHETS AND THOSE OF CHRIST, IN REFERENCE TO THE DESTRUCTION OF JERUSALEM.

The proofs already adduced that Christ intended the prophecies under consideration to be predictions only of the destruction of the Holy city, derive additional strength from the fact that most of the prophets, under the Old dispensation, in different ages of the world, had foretold this event,

---

* Compare Matth. xxiv. 27, with Zech. ix. 14.
† Comp. Matth. xxiv. 29, with Isa. xiii. 10.; xxiv. 23.—Ezek. xxxii. 7. 8.—Joel, ii. 10; and iii. 15. ‡ Comp. Matth. xxiv. 30, with Zech. xii. 12.
§ Comp. Matth. xxiv. 30. with Dan. vii. 13, 14.
|| Comp. Mat. xxiv. 31, with Isa. xxvii. 13. ¶ Comp Mat. xxiv. 31. with Isa. xliii. 5, 6.

distinguishing it from the previous captures of the same city, by their descriptions of the utter dispersion of the Jewish nation ; while on the other hand none of their predictions can fairly be construed to refer to the End of the World and the Final Judgment.   The analogy between the predictions of the ancient prophets and those of Christ on this point, is an argument which must be admitted to possess considerable force.   Those in the Old Testament, touching the dispersion of the Jews, and the final destruction of their capital, together with the circumstances connected therewith, are very numerous.   Only a few of them, however, can be pointed out here.   Even as early as the days of Moses it was foretold by that prophet that the Jews would be sent captive to Egypt, as bondmen and bondwomen, and that no man should buy them,* just as we are told by Josephus that they were sent to the Egyptian mines,† which is the only time on record that they were carried captive into Egypt, after they had left it under miraculous circumstances.   Hosea prophesied to the same effect.‡   Jeremiah prophesied that the enemy would scale the walls of Jerusalem, kill the Jews, but not utterly annihilate them as a people.§   Daniel foretold the destruction of the temple.‖   Again : Moses predicted—and so also did Jeremiah, Ezekiel, and Hosea—that the Jews would be wanderers among the nations,—that they would be few in number,—that they would be scattered among the heathen,—that they would be a taunt, a reproach, a proverb, and a by-word among all the nations,—that they would be put to the sword, —that their land would be made desolate, their cities waste, and that their enemies would dwell therein.¶   In a word, the prophecies in the Old Testament, foretelling the final destruction of Jerusalem, abound.   By analogy, therefore, it is only reasonable to believe that God, whose character is perfectly consistent, should pursue the same mode of dealing with his chosen people, by warning them of the consequence of their sins, until justice demanded the execution of the judgment that befell them ;—which, indeed, we find, on the authority of unimpeachable evidence, he did.—Not only did Christ predict the demolition of their city, and the downfall of their civil and religious polity, but—as we are informed by Josephus—another prophet repeated his prediction of the same catastrophe until the very day the awful event happened.   The following are the remarkable words of the Jewish historian, as translated by Whiston.—

    " But what is still more terrible, there was one Jesus" (not the Christ but**) " the son of Ananus, a plebian and an husbandman, who, four years before the war began, and at a time when the city was in very great peace and prosperity, came to that feast" (the Pentecost) " whereon it is our custom for every one to make tabernacles to God in the temple, began on a sudden to cry aloud—' A voice from the east, a voice from the west, a voice from the four winds, a voice against Jerusalem and the holy house, a voice against the bridegrooms and the brides, and a voice against this

---

* Deut. xxviii. 6, 8.   † Vide Ante, p. 26.   ‡ Hos. viii. 13; ix. 3; xi. 4, 5.
        § Jer. v. 10.   ‖ Dan. viii. 10—14.
¶ Lev. xxii. 32, 33. Deut. xxviii. 37.   Jer. xxiv. 8, 9.   Ezek. v. 13—15   Hos. ix. 17.
    ** Josephus, in different parts of his work, mentions about twelve other persons of the name of Jesus, which shows that this name was very common among the Jews. The reader will best find these names by refering to the Index of Whiston's Translation of Josephus.

whole people.' This was his cry as he went about, by day and by night, in all the lanes of the city. However, certain of the most eminent among the populace had great indignation at this dire cry of his, and took up the man and gave him a great number of severe stripes; yet did not he either say anything for himself, or anything peculiar to those that chastised him, but still went on with the same words which he cried before. Hereupon our rulers, supposing, as the case proved to be, that this was a sort of Divine fury in the man, brought him to the Roman procurator, where he was whipped till his bones were laid bare; yet did not he make any supplication for himself, nor shed any tears; but turning his voice to the most lamentable tone possible, at every stroke of the whip, his answer was—'Woe, woe to Jerusalem!' And when Albinus (for he was then our procurator) asked him who he was, and whence he came, and why he uttered such words, he made no manner of reply to what he said, but still did not leave off his melancholy ditty, till Albinus took him to be a madman, and dismissed him. Now, during all the time that passed before the war began, this man did not go near any of the citizens, nor was seen by them while he said so; but he every day uttered these lamentable words, as if it were his premeditated vow—'Woe, woe to Jerusalem!' Nor did he give ill words to any of those that beat him every day, nor good words to those that gave him food; but this was his reply to all men, and indeed, no other than a melancholy presage of what was to come. This cry of his was the loudest at the festivals; and he continued this ditty for seven years and five months, without growing hoarse, or being tired therewith, until the very time that he saw his presage in earnest fulfilled in our siege, when it ceased; for as he was going round upon the wall, he cried out with his utmost force—'Woe, woe to the city again, and to the people, and to the holy house'! and just as he added, at the last—'Woe, woe to myself also,' there came a stone out of one of the engines, and smote him, and killed him immediately; and as he was uttering the very same presage, he gave up the ghost.'*

Will we deny the truth of the foregoing narrative of this extraordinary prediction, or will we contend that the Son of God was not as likely to prophesy the destruction of Jerusalem as the obscure individual thus raised by the Deity to warn the Jews of their impending calamity?

SECTION VI.—THE GOSPEL DISPENSATION WHICH FOLLOWED THE ABOLITION OF THE JEWISH POLITY—NOT A SECULAR DOMINION—MEANT BY THE EXPRESSION—"KINGDOM OF HEAVEN," IN CHRIST'S PREDICTIONS, AND ELSEWHERE.

There is another portion of these predictions which deserves brief notice with a view further to show that—like all parts of this chain of prophecies—it refers to circumstances attending the destruction of Jerusalem. It is that which—as recorded by Luke†—occurs in the parable of the fig-tree. Christ having in this parable told his disciples that, when they saw

* Jewish Wars, b. vi. c. 5. s. 3.　　　　　　† Chap. xxi. ver. 31.

the leaves of the fig.tree and of other trees shooting forth, they knew that
the summer was nigh at hand, adds—" So likewise ye, when ye see these
things come to pass, know ye that the kingdom of God is nigh at hand."
The words *kingdom of God* do not occur in this parable as reported by
either Matthew or Mark.   The words of the latter are—" know that *it* is
nigh, even at the door ;" and of the former—" know that *it* is near, even
at the door.*"   The expression—" kingdom of God"—used in Luke, has
given occasion to the adversaries of Christianity to suppose that Christ, in
the whole of these predictions, prophesied, not only the destruction of Jerusalem, but in common with it, the destruction of all the inhabitants of
the earth who were not found his followers when, during the life of the then
existent generation of men, he would appear in the clouds of heaven,
—draw up to himself into the air all that believed in him—execute
the judgment of eternal death upon all his enemies—exterminate Jerusalem, as well as all other cities in the world—and establish on earth his
" kingdom "—a kind of universal monarchy, and an utterly new order of
things, under which men were to live eternally.

But the reader will perceive that the words—"kingdom of God"
here, by no means warrant such a supposition. What Christ meant was
that, when his disciples should see the signs he had just enumerated, they
might be assured that the destruction of Jerusalem,—the dispersion of the
Jewish nation,—the overthrow of the Jewish polity,—the end of the
Jewish economy—a theocracy instituted by God himself—were events about
to take place; and that, in lieu of this theocracy, the establishment of the
Gospel dispensation—which is here meant by "the kingdom of God," and
compared, in the parable, to the summer—was to be introduced. If we
apply to this expression that sound rule of interpretation, namely to compare it with expressions similar to it, and advert to some of the numerous
instances wherein Christ makes use of the words " kingdom of God," and
" kingdom of heaven "—which, on all hands, will be admitted identical in
import—the correctness of the foregoing exposition will fully be proved,
as well as the fact that Christ did *not* represent himself as aiming at establishing an earthly kingdom, but rather a spiritual dominion. Christ tells
the Jewish priests,—" The publicans and the harlots go into the kingdom of
God before you."† This expression cannot mean a temporal, or earthly
kingdom, to *come*; but a spiritual one *then existing ;* for it is the verb
" *go* "—not *will go*—which is here employed.‡ In verse 43 of the same
chapter he tells them that the *kingdom of God* should be taken from them.
But as the Jewish priests, it will be admitted on all hands, had not been
appointed the governors of this kingdom—whether earthly or heavenly—
this expression does not apply to a thing that did not at the time exist ;
and must therefore mean the spiritual kingdom which Christ, at the time,
was establishing. The Pharisees asked Christ " when the kingdom of God
should come," and he replied,—"The kingdom of God is within you ;"§
meaning evidently that it was a spiritual thing acting inwardly on the
heart of man, and *had already come*. The thief, on the cross, intreats
Christ to remember him when he came into his kingdom, and is told by

---

* Matth. xxiv. 33.   Mark xiii. 29.   † Matth. xxi. 31.
‡ The Greek word here is προαγουσιν—3rd pers. plu. pres. tense of προαγω.
§ Luke, xvii. 20. 21.

him—"To-day shalt thou be with me in paradise." * Although the thief may have meant an *earthly* kingdom ; yet Christ's reply points to a *spiritual* one. in a *spiritual* world. The whole of Christ's conversation with Nicodemus proves the same fact.† The expressions—" Except a man be born of water and of the Spirit, he cannot enter into the kingdom of God "— "That which is born of the flesh is flesh, and that which is born of the Spirit is spirit "—" If I have told you earthly things, and ye believe not, how shall ye believe, if I tell you of heavenly things,"—are very pointed. Christ again, in answer to Pilate says—" My kingdom is not of this world ;" as if he were to say—my government is a spiritual one over the souls of men, interfering not in any manner with the worldly affairs of the Romans and Jews. In the same manner do the Apostles represent the kingdom of the Messiah. —Paul says that " the kingdom of God is not meat and drink, but righteousness, and peace, and joy in the Holy Ghost."‡ Christ on all occasions disclaimed all pretensions to worldly dominion and sovereignty upon earth. Not only did he withdraw when the populace attempted to " take him by force to make him a king,"§ but, in order to avoid all appearance of setting up for a temporal sovereignty, when a certain person desired him to speak to his brother to divide the inheritance with him, he answered—" Man, who made me a judge or a divider over you."‖ He also severely rebuked the ambitious contentions of his disciples as to who should be greatest in his kingdom ; and, instead of enhancing their expectations of any worldly advantages, declared to them that they should " be hated and persecuted of all men for his name's sake," and that " in the world " they should have tribulation. The rewards which he promised to those that should believe and obey him, were not the riches and emoluments of the present world, but the spiritual and eternal rewards of a future state. While, however, he disclaimed all pretentions to be an earthly king, he boldly claimed to be the Messiah foretold by the prophets. Accordingly, when upon his trial before the Jewish council, and when the High-priest abjured him by the living God to tell them whether he was " the Christ, the son of the Blessed," he promptly answered, " I am." When Peter, and also Martha, declared he was the Son of God, he received their confession with approbation.¶ Such was the distinction he continually made between his earthly and and heavenly power,—clearly showing that, by " the kingdom of God," we are not to understand an earthly dominion, but the empire of " righteousness, and peace, and joy in the Holy Ghost," which he came to establish on earth, and the subjects of which are delivered from the thraldom of sin—are introduced into the glorious liberty of the children of God, and are prepared to enjoy perfect and eternal bliss in a future and spiritual state of existence !

Accordingly, in the New Testament, we meet with the expressions— "kingdom of God," and " kingdom of heaven," signifying, sometimes, the *present* state of believers in this world, and sometimes their state *after death* in a world of eternal happiness. Both these conditions of believers have reference to that Messianic kingdom touching which the angel, foretelling, in metaphorical terms, the birth of Christ, said,—" The Lord shall

---

* Luke xxiii. 42, 43. † John iii. 1—21.
‡ John xviii. 36. Rom. xiv. 17. § John vi. 15. ‖ Luke xii. 14.
¶ Matth. xvi. 17. John xi.—27.

give unto him the throne of his father David; and he shall reign over the house of Jacob for ever; and of his kingdom there shall be no end."* Hence he is called the Son of David, and described as sitting on the right hand of God, till his enemies are made his footstool; † or—as Paul expresses it—reigning "till he hath put all enemies under his feet." ‡ It is clear from the Scripture doctrines that Christ, as a mediator between God and man, has been entrusted by his Father with the government of his Church, till he shall have accomplished the design of his mediation. In this capacity, he shall " put down all rule, and all authority and power." What is meant by " all rule and authority" is, evidently, his final conquest over all his, and his Church's enemies. For the Apostle adds that " he must reign till he hath put all enemies under his feet. The last enemy that shall be destroyed is death. For he hath put all things under his feet. But when he saith all things are put under him, it is manifest that *he* is excepted, which *did* put all things under him. And when all things shall be subdued *unto* him, then shall the Son also himself be subject unto him that put all things under him, that God may be all in all."§ Before Paul gave the foregoing explanation of the nature of Christ's mediatorial reign, he had made the following statement :—" Then cometh the end, when he shall have delivered up the kingdom to God, even the Father."—The end of time—the end of all the opposition which has been made to the Church of God,—when the resurrection, as here described by the Apostle, shall take place,—when the last judgment and the second death, spoken of by John,‖ shall come to pass,—when Christ will deliver into his Father an account of the administration of his kingdom, or the economy of human redemption,—when he shall present his Church faultless before the presence of the glory of the eternal God ; and when the fulness of the Deity in Christ will become an object of worship and service for ever and ever ! At this momentous period, which the apostle terms, "the end," the economy of human redemption will cease, by Christ giving up his mediatorial kingdom ; for the administration of it will no longer be necessary, as there will be no sin to expiate and no sinner for whom to intercede. But the giving up of his mediatorial kingdom by no means implies that he will not reign for ever in heaven, as the object of the homage and adoration of all the human and angelic hosts ; so that—as the angel declared—" of his kingdom there shall be no end." The Scriptures fully sanction the doctrine that, in him God will be seen by his Church, through the countless ages of eternity, and that the administration of God's government over glorified saints will be carried on by Him, to whom " every knee should bow, of things in heaven, and things in earth, and things under the earth ; and that every tongue should confess that Jesus Christ is Lord, to the glory of God the Father."¶ For this is evidently the design of God, " that in the dispensation of the fulness of time, he might gather together in one, all things in Christ, both which are in heaven, and which are on earth, even in him."**

* Luke i. 32, 33.   † Matth. xxii. 42—45.   ‡ 1 Cor. xv. 25.
 § 1 Cor. xv. 24—28.   ‖ Rev. xx. 12—15.   ¶ Phil. ii. 10, 11.
 ** Eph. i. 10.   See Cox's Lectures on the Harmony of Scriptures, p. 119, et seq.
Lond. 1823; from which much of the above matter has been extracted.

It is trusted that the foregoing remarks will amply suffice to show that the words—" kingdom of God" and " kingdom of heaven," employed by Christ, as well as by his apostles, in whose writings they frequently occur —refer exclusively to a *spiritual* kingdom—the gracious sovereignty which Christ exercises over the souls of his saints, both while in this world and in a glorified state hereafter.

SECTION VII.—THE APOSTLES, BOTH IN THEIR WRITINGS AND DISCOURSES, PROVE CHRIST'S PROPHECY TO MEAN, EXCLUSIVELY, THE DESTRUCTION OF JERUSALEM.

Another circumstance, which materially corroborates the proofs already given, that Christ prophesied the destruction of Jerusalem, is that *the apostles, in their discourses and epistles, very frequently allude to this impending calamity, in words which can, if fairly construed, have no other meaning than that the Lord would shortly visit the Jews with punishment, abolish the Jewish economy, and fully establish a new dispensation of religion, the principles of which they were then actually engaged in disseminating.** And it is very remarkable that in those epistles which were written nearest to—in a word, only few years before—the time of the overthrow of the Jewish polity and the dispersion of the Jewish nation, that these events are the most strenuously insisted upon, as being then close at hand. It was only by one or more of the following three *means* that the apostles could acquire knowledge of the future fate of the nation to which they belonged.—Either by a direct communication from God, or by their acquaintance with the predictions of the ancient prophets on the point, or by having heard the prophecies of Christ himself on the same subject. The *last* alone of these three is, by far, the most likely, as will hereafter appear from the manner in which they express themselves on the point.

It is to be observed that, according to the most generally received chronology of the events of those times, all the epistles were written before the destruction of Jerusalem by the Roman legions. In Peter's sermon, on the day of Pentecost, (about A.D. 37) as recorded in the Acts of the Apostles,[†] we find the following words :—" And it shall come to pass in the last days, saith God, I will pour out my Spirit upon all flesh ; and your sons and your daughters shall prophesy, and your young men shall see visions, and your old men shall dream dreams. And on my servants and on my handmaidens I will pour out, in those days, of my Spirit, and they shall prophesy. And I will show wonders in heaven above, and signs in the earth beneath ; blood and fire, and vapour of smoke. The sun shall be turned into darkness, and the moon into blood, before that great and notable day of the Lord come." It is true that Peter uses these words, confessedly, as those of the prophet Joel ;[‡] but the two last verses quoted bear striking resemblance also to words used by Christ, in the predictions which form the subject of our present inquiry, and in which predictions, as already shown, Christ, for a wise purpose, imitated the symbolical style of the ancient prophets. But, what did Peter mean by the expressions—

* See Dr. Leland's Divine Authority of the Old and New Testament, part I, chap. 15, p. 260. Tegg's Edit. 1837.
  † Chap. ii. ver. 17—20.   ‡ Chap. ii. ver. 30—31.

" In the last days," and " that great and notable day of the Lord" which he says was to come ? Was it the uttermost end of time, or the end of the Jewish dispensation, that he meant by the former ? This must be ascertained by having recourse to the obvious meaning of *similar* expressions elsewhere, and by the subject treated in the *context*.—Jacob calls together his sons in order to tell them what would befall them " in the last days"[*] —meaning evidently, not the last days of the world, but of the life of his sons ; or—taking the widest possible scope—the last days of their descendants—the twelve tribes of Israel, as distinct tribes. Isaiah[†] prophesies that, " in the last days," the mountain of the Lord's house should be established in the top of the mountains. Whatever the prophet means here by the " last days," it is clear that he does not mean the end of time, or the day of judgment.—So far is he from making any allusion to either, that he predicts that all nations shall flow to the mountain of the Lord's house—that people and nations shall beat their swords into plough-shares, and their spears into pruning hooks, and shall not learn war any more. It is probable that, by the " last days," he means the end of the Jewish dispensation, and that, in the highly figurative language which follows, he refers to the influence which the Gospel of peace should have on the minds of men. Jeremiah[‡] prophesies that the Lord would " bring again the captivity of Moab, in the latter days,"—an expression which is clearly of the same import as " last days," and here means that, at the close of the Moabitish dynasty, the nation would be led into captivity. The same prophet foretells that, " in the latter days," the Lord would " bring again the captivity of Elam"[§]—signifying precisely the same thing as in the above instance of Moab. Michael, an angel, tells Daniel, in a vision, what should befall his people " in the latter days"—meaning the people of the Jewish nation, and " the latter days" of the Jewish polity, in church and state.[||] In all these instances the expressions " last" and " latter days" clearly signify the approaching end of some temporal institutions.

With regard to " the day of the Lord," the following are all the places in which the expression occurs in the ancient prophets. It will be perceived, from the connection in which the phrase is used, that, in every instance, it signifies the infliction of temporal and national punishment, having not the remotest allusion to the Last Day of Judgment. Isaiah says that " the day of the Lord" shall be upon the proud, upon the cedars of Lebanon and the oak of Bashan, upon every high tower and every fenced wall. Again, in prophesying God's threat to destroy Babylon, by the hand of the Medes, he says that there was the noise of the kingdoms of nations gathered together,—that the Lord mustered the host of the battle,—that *the day of the Lord* was at hand,—that *the day of the Lord* was coming, cruel both with wrath and fierce anger, to lay the land desolate, and destroy the sinners out of it,—that the *stars of heaven* and the constellations thereof should not give their light,—that *the sun and moon* should not give light,—and that the Lord should punish the world for their evil.[**] The same prophet,[††] in a similar strain of symbolical language, says that the fury of the Lord was upon the armies of all nations,—that

---

[*] Gen. xlix. 1.   [†] ii. 2.   [‡] xlviii. 47.
[§] Jer. xlix. 39.   [||] Dan. x. 14, et seq.   [¶] ii. 12—18.
[**] Isa. xiii. 4—11.   [††] xxxiv. 2—8.

he had utterly destroyed them,—that the mountains should be melted with their blood,—that all the *hosts of heaven* should be dissolved, and the heavens be rolled together as a scroll,—that the sword of the Lord was filled with blood,—that he had a great slaughter in the land of Idumea, —and that the land should be soaked with the blood of unicorns and bullocks. Then he adds,—" For it is the day of the Lord's vengeance." Jeremiah,* in foretelling the overthrow of Pharaoh's army, calls to battle the Ethiopians, the Lybians, and Lydians, that handled the shield and bent the bow, saying—" this is the day of the Lord God of hosts ; a day of vengeance." Again : Ezekiel† complains that the prophets had not " made up the hedge for the house of Israel, to stand in the battle, in the *day of the Lord.*" And in another place,‡ he says—" the *day of the Lord* is near ; a cloudy day it shall be for the heathen, and a sword shall come upon Egypt. Joel.§ predicting various judgments, several times uses the expression in connection with the following particulars :—" The day of the Lord is at hand, and as a destruction from the Almighty shall it come. Is not the meat cut off before our eyes ?"—" Let all the inhabitants of the land tremble, for the day of the Lord cometh,—for it is nigh at hand, —a day of darkness and gloominess,—a day of clouds and of thick dark-ness, as the morning spread upon the mountains—a great people and a strong ; there hath not been ever the like."—" The sun shall be turned into darkness, and the moon into blood before the great and terrible day of the Lord come."—" Let the heathen be wakened and come up to the valley of Jehoshaphat ; . . . . . . for the *day of the Lord* is near in the valley of decision. The sun and moon shall be darkened and the stars shall with-draw their shining. The Lord also shall roar out of Zion, and utter his voice from Jerusalem." Amos,‖ in exhorting Israel to repent, pronounces woe against those who desired " the day of the Lord," and adds that " the day of the Lord is darkness, and not light." Obadiah¶ says that " the day of the Lord is near upon all the heathen ;" but that " the house of Jacob shall possess their possessions," &c. Zephaniah** declares that " the day of the Lord was at hand," when princes and the king's children, and all that were clothed in strange apparel, should be punished. He also says that the great day of the Lord was " near"—that it was " a day of wrath—a day of trouble and distress—a day of wasteness and desolation —a day of darkness and gloominess— a day of clouds and thick darkness—a day of the trumpet and alarm against the fenced cities, and against the high towers ;" when distress should be brought upon men because they had sinned against the Lord—when their blood should be poured out as dust —and when neither their silver nor their gold should " be able to deliver them, in the day of the Lord's wrath." Malachi††—in a clear prophecy of the abolition of the Jewish economy and the introduction of the Gospel, —mentions " the coming of the great and dreadful day of the Lord,"— designative of the time when the former event should take place.

* xlvi. 1—10.   † xiii. 5.   ‡ xxx. 3, 4   § i. 15, 16 ; ii. 1, 2, 31 ; iii. 1, 2, 12—16. —Joel, after describing the darkness of the sun and moon, says, in the same prediction, that, in those days, the Lord should bring again the captivity of Judah and Jerusalem, and gather all nations into the valley of Jehoshaphat ; showing that the darkening of the sun, &c., in the great and terrible day of the Lord refers to a temporal calamity. See Joel, ii. 31 ; iii. 1, 2.
‖ v. 18—20.   ¶ Ver. 15—21.   ** i. 7, 8, 14—18 ; ii. 3.   †† iv. 1—6.

Hence we see that, in every one of the numerous instances cited, "the day of the Lord" signifies a temporal judgment, by which God punished nations and individuals for their sins. We are, therefore, fully justified in concluding that Peter, in his Pentecostal sermon, meant, by "that great and notable day of the Lord," the judgment with which God visited the Jews in the destruction of Jerusalem, and its concomitant disastrous effects; and that by the expression—"the last days"—he meant—in harmony with the usage of the phrase by the ancient prophets—the end of the Jewish dispensation; particularly since he only repeats the words of the prophet Joel, which, as we have seen, are predictions of national events. The whole tenor of the context of that portion under notice of Peter's sermon bears out this interpretation. He addresses the Jews exclusively, saying— "Ye men of Judea, and all ye that dwell at Jerusalem,"—"Ye men of Israel," and so on. He tells these Jews that they had, by wicked hands, crucified and slain Jesus of Nazareth—a man, approved of God among them, by miracles, wonders, and signs; and he applies to them the words of the prophet Joel which were calculated to impress them with three important facts.—*First*, that the time was near at hand when the Jewish nation should be slain, or scattered over the world—their temple and city levelled with the ground, and their religious and political economy abolished. *Secondly*, that the Gospel dispensation was now being introduced, when God would pour out his spirit upon all flesh. And, *thirdly*, that as many of them as would repent of their sins, believe in this Gospel, and call on the name of the Lord, should be saved.

In the same manner as their synonymies already noticed in the Acts of the Apostles do the phrases—*last day, last days, last time, last times*, and *day of the Lord*, in the Epistles also refer to the *end of the Jewish dispensation*, in the following instances. LAST DAYS:—"In the *last days* perilous times shall come."[*]—"God, who, at sundry times, and in divers manners, spake, in time past, unto the fathers, by the prophets, hath in these *last days* spoken unto us by his Son."[†]—"Ye have heaped treasure together for the *last days*," says the apostle James to the twelve tribes to whom he writes, and whom he accuses in similar language to that in which Christ accuses the Jews of killing the prophets—one of the principal causes which drew upon them the awful judgment which they suffered.[‡] LAST TIME:—"Little children, it is the *last time*; and as ye have heard that anti-christ shall come, even now are there many anti-christs, whereby we know that it *is the last time*."[§] By the word anti-christs here, John—who wrote his Epistles A.D. 68 or 69, about two years before the destruction of Jerusalem—doubtless means those who believed that Christ was not the true Messiah, but that some one of the false Christs who had appeared was the true one. There were at the time adherents, respectively, to the various false Christs, who had, in that and the preceding century, set up their claims, to Messiaship.[||] By the expression —"Ye have heard that anti-christ shall come," he evidently alludes to the expectation which the words of Jesus had raised, regarding the appear-

---

[*] 2 Tim. iii. 1.   [†] Heb. i. 1, 2.   [‡] Jam. v. 3—6.   [§] 1 John ii. 18.
[||] See Lardner's Collection of Testimonies, vol. i. p. 68. Tillotson's Sermons, vol. iii. p. 552, fol. Newton's Dissert. on Proph. Vol. ii. p. 279, et seq. 8vo. Grotius in Matth. xxiv. 5.

ance of false Christs, before Jerusalem should be "compassed with armies," and the Jews should "fall by the edge of the sword." Thus does he prove that he uses the phrase—*last time*—to designate the end of the Jewish economy. Jude employs the same expression, in the same sense:—"Remember ye the words which were spoken before of the apostles of our Lord Jesus Christ, how that they told you there should be mockers in the *last time*."* Again: Peter employs the expression—*last times* in reference to the same event.—Christ, "who verily was fore-ordained before the foundation of the world, but was manifest in *these last times*."† As to the expression—DAY OF THE LORD,—we have just seen that Peter, as well as the ancient prophets, employs it to designate temporal judgments: and what has already‡ been said upon it must suffice to show in what sense it is used by other inspired writers.

The following expressions also of the apostles will be found to refer to the punishment God inflicted upon the Jewish nation, as already described. Paul, in his Epistle to the Romans—written about A.D. 58—twelve years before Jerusalem was besieged by Vespasian—quotes the following passages almost literally.—"Esaias also crieth concerning Israel, Though the number of the children of Israel be as the sand of the sea, a remnant shall be saved; for he will finish the work, and cut it short in righteousness; because a short work will the Lord make upon the earth. And, as Esaias said before, Except the Lord of Sabaoth had left us a seed, we had been as Sodoma, and been made like unto Gomorrha."§ The apostle here, evidently, applies the words of Isaiah—which he had spoken to foretell that a remnant of the Jews should be spared from the sword of the Assyrians, and from the devastation of their own civil wars —to indicate that, in the approaching destruction of Jerusalem—when the Lord would "finish the work," "cut it short in righteousness," and make "a short work upon the earth"—a *remnant* of the Jews, nevertheless, should be saved. This is literally true, with regard to the catastrophe that befell these people. They were, before this period, exceedingly *numerous*, as it is proved by the multitudes of them slain and taken captive; and a *remnant* of them was saved and remains unto this day. God also *finished the work*, and *cut it short in righteousness*, by a total abolition of the Jewish polity. As to the expression—"a short work will the Lord make upon the earth," all that is meant by the word *earth* here is the *land of Judea*. The word γῆ is that which is used in the original, and which very frequently, in Holy Writ, denotes a particular country, or a tract of land, as—"thou Bethlehem, in the *land* (γῆ) *of Judea*,"—"the land (γῆ) of Israel,"—"the land (γῆ) of Zabulon"—"great famine was throughout all the land" (πασαν την γην).‖ There is, therefore, no ground for believing that the word *earth*, in the passage just quoted from the Romans, is intended to designate the *whole world*; and as there is nothing in the rest of the passage applicable to the End of the World, it can, consequently, refer to no other event than the destruction of Jerusalem, to which its wording most aptly applies.

Again: Paul in writing to Timothy,¶ alludes to the same event—the ter-

* Jude. 17, 18.   † 1 Pet. i. 20.   ‡ Vide ante, p. 41—44.
§ Rom. ix. 27—29.   See also Isa. x. 22; i. 9.
‖ See Matth. ii. 6, 20, 21; iv. 15; ix. 26; xxvii. 45.   Luke iv. 25.   ¶ 1 Tim. iv. 1.

mination of the Jewish polity, when he says,—"now the spirit speaketh expressly that, in the *latter times*, some shall depart from the faith, giving heed to seducing spirits." By "seducing spirits," he clearly means the same as John and Jude—already cited—mean by the *anti-christs* and *scoffers* who should make their appearance before the close of the Jewish dispensation.

Peter, in his first Epistle, written about six years before Jerusalem was besieged, to the Hebrew Christians in Asia Minor, who were suffering from persecution, with a view to support them under their afflictions, assures them that "the *end* of *all* things was *at hand*." A few sentences further on, he adds,—"The time is come that judgment must begin at the house of God; and if it first begin at us, what shall the end be of them that obey not the Gospel of God?"* As if he said—"The *end* of the Jewish polity, in Church and State, which is the chief obstacle to the propagation of the Gospel, and has been the cause of severe persecution to us followers of Christ, is now, however, at hand; for the time is coming when judgment must begin at the house of God—at the temple which, before any other part of the holy city, is to be destroyed, and all its sacrifices, rites, and ceremonies discontinued. But if judgment thus first begin at us, the Jews, what shall be the end of those of us who have refused the Gospel of God?" There is ample reason to conclude that the *Christian* Jews looked forward with considerable interest and satisfaction, if not joy, to the time when—as they had learned from Christ's predictions—the Jewish system of religion should be abolished by a judgment from heaven, executed by Christ himself, whom the priests of this religion had rejected and put to death;—and when—as they had reason to expect—the Gospel would, consequently, have a free course. Hence Paul charges Timothy to keep the commandment "until the appearance of our Lord Jesus Christ,"† and also consoles the Philippians—who were at the time suffering from the enemies of Christianity—with the assurance that *the Lord was at hand*.‡ And hence James tells the Hebrews—who had embraced Christianity, and who probably wished to see it in ascendency of the Jewish religion—*to be patient until the coming of the Lord,—to stablish their hearts; for the coming of the Lord drew nigh;*§ there being then, apparently, not more than about eight years before he would visit Jerusalem with judgment.

It must not, however, be supposed, because the foregoing expressions refer to the destruction of Jerusalem, that in all the passages in Holy Writ where mention is made of the *day, the coming, the appearing*, and so on, of the Lord, such words *always* signify his coming to inflict punishment upon the Jews, or execute any *temporal* judgment whatever. For there are therein many passages, the *contexts* of which plainly indicate that they describe his coming at the *Last Day*, with a shout, with the voice of the archangel and the trump of God, to judge the quick and the dead.—to take vengeance on those that know not God, and to be glorified in his saints,—when "the graves," "the sea," and even "hell, shall give up their dead,"—when the elements shall melt with fervent heat, the heavens be on fire, and the earth and all therein be burnt! The principal passages

---

* 1 Pet. iv. 7, 17.
† 1 Tim. vi. 14.   ‡ Phil. iv. 5.   § Jam. v. 7, 8.

which refers to this awful event will be found in the following places :—
Rom. ii. 2—16. 1 Cor. v. 5 ; xv. 20—55. Phil. iii. 20, 21. Col. iii.
4. 1 Thess. ii. 19 ; iii. 13 ; iv. 13—18. 2 Thess. i. 7—10. 2 Tim. iv.
1—8. Tit. ii. 13. Heb. ix. 27, 28. 1 Pet. iv. 5—7. 2 Pet. iii. 3—
18. Jude. 14, 15. Rev. i. 7 ; iii. 10 ; xx. 12—15.

Although these passages by no means weaken the force, or darken the
meaning of those which have been adduced to show that the apostles frequently referred to the approaching destruction of Jerusalem, and the end
of the Jewish dispensation ; yet it would appear that some of the early
Christians confounded the description given by the apostles of the coming
of the Day of the Lord, in which temporal judgment would be executed
upon the Jews, with that given by them of the coming of Christ in the
Last Day to judge the world, so as to mistake the former for the latter.
Paul, therefore, in writing to the Thessalonians, rectifies this mistake in
the following words.—" Now we beseech you, brethren, by the coming of
our Lord Jesus Christ, and by our gathering together unto him, that ye
be not soon shaken in mind, or be troubled, neither by spirit nor by word,
nor by letter as from us, as that the day of Christ is at hand. Let no
man deceive you by any means ; for *that day shall not come*, except there
come a falling away first, and that man of sin be revealed, the son of perdition, who opposeth and exalteth himself above all that is called God, or
that is worshipped, so that he as God sitteth in the temple of God, showing
himself that he is God. Remember ye not that, when I was yet with you,
I told you these things ?"* It would appear that, in the expectation that
Christ would soon appear, some of the Thessalonians had become negligent of their secular concerns ;† that there were some false teachers among
them, who pretended to have been inspired ; and that there were others
among them, who declared that they had been sent by the apostles
with a letter to the Thessalonians, apprising them that the day of Christ
was at hand, whereas this letter was a forgery. Paul, therefore, advises
them not to be shaken in mind, or troubled about these matters, but to
pay due attention to their worldly affairs,—not to be thrown into confusion,
either by any pretended revelation of the Spirit, obtruded upon them by
false teachers, or by any verbal message, as from him, or by any letter forged
in his name, importing that he believed the day of judgment was at hand ;
for nothing had fallen from him, either by speech or writing, whence they
were to infer that " the day of Christ was at hand." He further assures
them, in the most express terms, that " that day shall not come" till the
grand apostacy in religion, and other events connected with it—requiring
much intervening time for their accomplishment—first take place in the
world. He also reminds them that he had told them as much *while he
was yet with them.* He then proceeds to inform them that there was a
power at that moment existing which restrained the man of sin‡ from revealing himself, and would restrain him till it was taken away, which
things—had they recollected them—were proof sufficient that he did not
think the day of Christ was at hand§.

Besides being influenced by false teachers, the Thessalonians may have
been led into this error by misunderstanding Paul's words, in his first

---

* 2 Thes. ii. 1—5.   † See 2 Thes. ii. 2; iii. 7—15.   ‡ Ver. 6—12.
§ See Macknight's Views and Illustrations, *in loc.*

Epistle to them, written some few months before his second.—" For this we say unto you by the word of the Lord, that we which are alive and remain unto the coming of the Lord shall not prevent them which are asleep ; for the Lord himself shall descend from heaven with a shout, with the voice of the archangel, and with the trump of God, and the dead in Christ shall rise first. Then we which are alive and remain shall be caught up together with them in the clouds, to meet the Lord in the air ; and so shall we ever be with the Lord. Wherefore comfort one another with these words. But of the times and the seasons, brethren, ye have no need that I write unto you ; for yourselves know perfectly that the day of the Lord so cometh as a thief in the night. For when they shall say, Peace and safety, then sudden destruction cometh upon them, as travail upon a woman with child ; and they shall not escape. But ye, brethren, are not in darkness, that that day should overtake you as a thief."* From this language of Paul, particularly the expression—" we which are alive and remain unto the coming of the Lord"—the Thessalonians may have misapprehended him, and imagined that he had represented the Day of Judgment as an event to take place during the lives of those of them who then lived. Indeed, there are not wanting, in the *present age,* men who seem to misapprehend him, and even charge him with having, in his second epistle, contradicted what he had, on this point, written in his first.† Both this charge and the misapprehension of the Thessalonians appear to have been occasioned by the same incident ; namely, Paul's use of the first person plural—*we,* in the instance just cited. But, by the word *we* here, Paul means mankind at large,—or, at least, those Christians who will be alive when Christ shall make his second advent. He uses similar language in his first epistle to the Corinthians.—" *We* shall not all sleep, but *we* shall all be changed, in a moment, in the twinkling of an eye at the last trump."‡ But, as it has justly been remarked,§ " how common it is for us, when speaking of a society, an army, or a nation, to which we belong, to say— *we* went, or came, or did such a thing, or shall do so or so ; though *we ourselves* neither had, nor shall have any personal concern in the matter ; though the event happened before we were born, or is to happen after our decease." We find similar turns of expression in several places in the Old and New Testament.—David, in allusion to the Israelites crossing the Red Sea dry-shod, says—" they went through the flood on foot ; there did *we* rejoice in him ;"‖ but this event happened nearly 300 years before the time of David, so that, personally, neither he nor the people of his age, had any part in it. Hosea says—" Jacob found God in Bethel, and there he spake with *us* ;"¶ yet there was more than a thousand years between the time of Jacob and that of Hosea. But what is still more conclusive that Paul, by the pronoun *we,* did not mean himself and fellow Christians of that age, is that, in another place, he says—" knowing that he which raised up the Lord Jesus shall raise up us also."** Now, Paul could not, any more than another man, at the same time, believe two propositions which must, inevitably, appear to him contradictory,—he could not believe that he *should* die, and that he should *not* die. These remarks, together with Paul's

---

* 1 Thess. iv. 15—18.   † See Horne's 8th Letter, p. 37.   ‡ 1 Cor. xv. 51, 52.
  § Horne's Letters, Ib.   ‖ Psal. lxvi. 6.   ¶ Hos. xii. 4.
            ** 2 Cor. iv. 14.   See also 1 Cor. vi. 14.

reproof to the Thessalonians for believing the speedy coming of the Day of the Lord, it is trusted, will serve to convince any candid mind that the apostle neither contradicted himself, nor represented the Day of Judgment as an event which was to take place in, or near the age in which he lived. Nor is it less strongly hoped that the instances produced in this section, are sufficiently clear and pointed to prove that the apostles frequently, in their discourses and epistles, alluded to the destruction of Jerusalem as an event which was shortly to take place—thus corroborating the fact that Christ had predicted this calamity.

SECTION VIII.—A SUMMARY OF THE FOREGOING ARGUMENTS IN SUPPORT OF THE TRUTH OF CHRIST'S PREDICTIONS.

At the conclusion of this chapter it would not be amiss briefly to recapitulate all the arguments and proofs adduced to show that Christ actually prophesied—not the Destruction of the World and the Final Judgment—but solely the destruction of Jerusalem, with the concomitant calamities of its inhabitants, and that his predictions were minutely fulfilled; in order that the reader may the more advantageously, in a narrow compass, perceive therefrom how the train of reasoning pursued bears upon the subject, and to what extent it demonstrates the propositions laid down.

Three of the four Evangelists record—with very slight verbal variations—a series of prophetic sayings delivered by Christ, who, in connection with these prophetic sayings, mentions the *Jews*, *Judea*, *Jerusalem*, the *temple*, &c., as the objects upon which the events he foretold would operate. Upon minute investigation, it is found that there is nothing in the language of these predictions which does not most naturally apply to the destruction of Jerusalem, and to the incidents concomitant with that destruction, by the Roman legions under Vespasian. Authentic history proves the destruction of Jerusalem to have taken place, about forty years after these prophecies had been uttered, in such a manner, under such circumstances, and attended with such consequences, as demonstrate them to have been fulfilled most minutely. As it will be admitted on all hands, that " a prophecy is demonstrated to be fulfilled when we can prove from unimpeachable authority that the event has actually taken place precisely according to the manner in which it was foretold," and as these predictions have thus been fulfilled, in the destruction of Jerusalem, they have, therefore, *proved true*, so that there is no necessity, in order to substantiate their veracity, to look for another fulfilment of them, in the Destruction of the World, or any other event whatever; and even if there were, there is nothing in the whole tenour of them which, by any fair mode of criticism, warrants their application to the End of the World. The proofs that these prophecies are really predictions of the destruction of Jerusalem, are further corroborated by the facts that, under Divine Inspiration, the ancient prophets, in different ages of the world, had foretold the same event; and that the apostles—who were sent by Christ to promulgate the Gospel, and of whom many were present when he delivered these predictions—make

E

frequent allusions to the approaching destruction of the holy city, in their discourses and epistles, which allusions it is difficult to imagine they would make unless they had learned from Christ's predictions that Jerusalem was to be destroyed, and the Jewish polity, with all its religious rites and ceremonies, overthrown.

These are the proofs which, with full confidence in their validity, are submitted in support of the position that the prophetic sayings of Christ, as recorded in the extracts from the Gospels adduced in this work, are really and exclusively predictions regarding the destruction of Jerusalem, and the consequent calamities that befell the Jewish nation. This fact being established, although it does not, in itself, prove the deity of Christ, yet proves him to be a *true prophet*, which is the highest evidence that can be given of supernatural communication with the Deity; and which, in the case of Christ—taken in conjunction with other facts, such as the prophecies concerning his appearance in this world, his miracles, his immaculate life, and the stupendous moral influence his Gospel has had on the world—fully proves him to be "THE SON OF GOD."

What, then, becomes of the cavillous charge of falsity, made by the adversaries of Christianity, against these predictions of Christ? Since they must be fully convinced that he foretold his own sufferings, his death, and the circumstances therewith connected, with the utmost precision, a very small degree of reflection, would make them pause awhile, consider, and duly investigate the matter, before they pronounced this single prophecy false. Since they see that the inspired historians of his life describe to them a personage whose whole earthly career was perfectly free from the least spot or stain of moral guilt,—who, neither as represented by his followers, nor as attacked by his contemporary enemies, is charged with any personal vice, but who, by the former, on the contrary, is represented as exemplifying the most shining virtues, and inculcating the most sublime moral precepts,—who, in a word, is portrayed before them as possessed of moral and intellectual attributes which can belong only to the Deity,—sound philosophy, nay, the most ordinary process of thought, should dictate to them that it is absurd to imagine a being endued with Divine attributes liable to err or to falsify.*

* The writer knows of no other argument of *any weight* than what has already been advanced in proof of the fulfilment of Christ's predictions, treated of in this chapter. After making the foregoing portion of this note it is gratifying to the Essayist—now as he prepares his work for the press—to find the following remark made by the Adjudicator in regard to this part of it.—" I with pleasure confess that the author has, in this chapter, pleaded the Christian side of his subject very fully and faithfully—indeed more so than I, at present, remember to have seen from any other pen."

CHAPTER III.

A STATEMENT OF THE EVIDENCES AND FACTS WHICH TEND TO PROVE THAT THE PROPHECIES OF CHRIST, IN MATTHEW, CHAP. XXIV; MARK, CHAP. XIII; LUKE, CHAP. XXI, AND IN OTHER PASSAGES OF SIMILAR IMPORT, ARE PREDICTIONS OF THE LAST DAY OF JUDGMENT AND THE DESTRUCTION OF THE WORLD, AS EVENTS WHICH WERE INEVITABLY TO TAKE PLACE DURING THE LIFE-TIME OF THE GENERATION OF MEN WHO WERE ON EARTH CONTEMPORARY WITH CHRIST; AND NOT PREDICTIONS OF THE DESTRUCTION OF JERUSALEM BY THE ROMAN ARMY UNDER TITUS VESPASIAN.

SECTION I.—THE IDENTITY OF THE JEWISH AND PAGAN PROPHETS IN NAME AND CHARACTER.—THE OBSCURITY OF THEIR PREDICTIONS, AND THE CAUSES OF THE POPULAR BELIEF IN THEM.—JESUS OF NAZARETH A JEWISH PROPHET, WHOSE LANGUAGE, PREDICTIONS, AND DOCTRINES CLOSELY RESEMBLED THOSE OF HIS PREDECESSORS, AND WHO, LIKE THEM, PROPHESIED THE NEAR APPROACH OF THE END OF THE WORLD AND THE FINAL JUDGMENT.

The history of all ages and nations furnishes us with ample proof that there was in and among them always a goodly number of prognosticators of future events, known by the various names of prophets, seers, oracles, ovates, poets, augurs, sorcerers, magicians, diviners, conjectors, conjurors, soothsayers, and a host of other titles and appellations, too numerous to be mentioned. The mythology of every nation is replete with their sayings and doings; so that to quote authorities, in proof of this fact, would be superfluous.* The word *prophet* ($\pi\rho o\phi\eta\tau\eta s$), as therefore may be expected, is not a term confined to the language of the Septuagint translation of the Old Testament, where we find it rendered for the Hebrew word *nabia*, (נביא) nor even to the Greek version of the New Testament.—The idolatrous Greeks, as well as the worshippers of the God of Israel, having their prophets, we therefore frequently meet with the term in profane

---

* It may, however, be mentioned that the Roman Emperor, Augustus, on one occasion caused to be burnt upwards of 2,000 volumes of prophecies.—Vid. Suet. Aug. 31.

Greek writers.* Paul applies this term to a heathen poet of Crete,† whom he calls a *true* witness. It is also applied to the false prophets of Baal; to Saul, when under the influence of the *evil spirit;* and to the musicians of King David, who prophesied with *harps.* ‡ The Jews, who were the favourites of heaven—the peculiar people of God—were by no means behind other nations, either in the number of their prophets, or in the number of the predictions these prophets uttered. But as there was among the Jews, as well as among most other ancient nations, a law to punish with death those prophets whose predictions were found false, § the Jewish prophets, like those of other people, were obliged—as they loved their lives—to clothe their prophetic sayings in ambiguous and obscure language ; so that, like the answer given by the Delphic oracle to king Pyrrhus, ‖ or to Crœsus, king of Lydia, ¶ their presages could always be interpreted in several ways. The danger of being discovered to prophesy falsely, is one of the principal causes that the predictions of the Jewish prophets, which constitute such a large portion of the Old Testament, are so ambiguous, and capable of being applied almost to any national event. Hence, Hartwell Horne—sensible of the ambiguity of these prophecies—tells us, in his canons for the interpretation of prophecy, that " the words and phrases of prophecy must be explained where they are obscure ; if they be *very* intricate, every *single word* should be expounded,"—that " the prophets often change both persons and tenses, sometimes speaking in their own persons, at other times representing God, his people or their enemies, as respectively speaking, and without noticing the change of persons,"—that " the same prophecies have frequently a double meaning, and refer to different events, the one near and the other remote, the one temporal, and the other spiritual, or perhaps eternal,"—and that, " the prophets thus having several events in view, their expressions may be partly applicable to one, and partly to another.** But all that this writer says, in the many pages of

---

* Anacreon. od. 43, lin. 11.—Θερεος γλυκυς προφητης. See also a great number of Greek writers, among whom are Herodotus and Plato, quoted by Blackwall in his Sacred Classics, vol. i. p. 24, and more modern Greek writers cited by Wetstein on Matth. i. 22.
† Tit. i. 12, 13. ‡ 1 Kings xviii. 29. 1 Sam. xviii. 10. 1 Chron. xxv. 1, 2, 5.
§ Deut. xiii. 5 ; xviii. 20—22. Jer. xxvi. Suet. Tib. 14. Tac. Ann. 6, 20, 26. Dio 55, 11. Washington Irving's Life of Mahomet, pp. 183, 184. Bohn's ed. 1850.
‖ When Pyrrhus, King of Epirus, wished to assist the Tarentines against the encroaching power of Rome, he consulted the celebrated Delphic oracles, whose answer was—" Aio te, Æacida, Romanos vincere posse,"—which may be interpreted to mean, either that Pyrrhus could conquer the Romans, or that the Romans could conquer Pyrrhus. To render the answer still darker ,the name of Æacides—Pyrrhus's father—who was now dead, is used. Vid. Cic. de Divin. lib. ii.
¶ Crœsus, being on the point of invading Media, consulted the above oracles as to his future success, and was answered—Χροισος Αλυν διαβας μεγαλην αρχην διαλυσει—" If Crœsus pass over the Halys he will ruin a great empire." What empire—whether his own, or that of the enemy—he was left to conjecture. But whichever, the oracle by this language was safe. See both the above passages quoted in St. Jerome on Isaiah cap. 50, where he takes infinite pains to distinguish between the false and true prophets. See also Rollin's Ancient Hist. Pref. p. 37.
** Horne's Introduction, vol. ii, part ii, chap. vii. How is the poor illiterate inquirer after truth to understand these Jewish prophecies, and find his way to Christianity, which entirely depends upon their fulfilment, if to understand them is so difficult, and if every word of some of them requires to be expounded by some learned commentator ? Is he to consider the commentaries his revelation from heaven ?

his popular work, which are devoted to the laying down of vague rules for the interpretation of prophecy, simply amounts to this—"that if the fulfilment of the prophecy is not verified by one event, it must be applied to another ; and if it is not realized in the occurrence of any temporal event, we must look for its accomplishment in some spiritual, perhaps eternal, consummation."* By such rules as these, however, it is exceedingly easy to give the necessary colour to any historical prediction, and to distort it into conformity with the events it is supposed to foretell, which is the only thing that can really be understood to be done by *expounding every single word, where the prophecy is intricate and obscure.* This process of expounding has contributed materially to maintain the credit of prophecy from age to age. †

There are, however, other causes, which have in all ages, both in the heathen and Christian world, disposed men to give credit to prophecies, and to regard them as revelations of things future, obtained by supernatural means. One of these is the reports, either true or untrue, which are often raised that a certain prophecy has been fulfilled. For example, it is reported that Crœsus, in order to put the supernatural knowledge of the oracle of Delphi to the test, sent his ambassador to demand of her what he was doing at a specified time, and that the oracle, in Greek hexameter verse, replied to the effect that he was causing a tortoise and a lamb to be boiled in a brass pot ; which was actually the case.‡ The Emperor Trajan made a similar trial of the oracle at Heliopolis and obtained a correct answer. § Mopsus, a celebrated prophet during the Trojan war, told Amphimachus of the great disaster which would attend his arms in a war he was to undertake, while Calchas, a soothsayer of the same age,

---

* Foxton's Popular Christianity. Series No. 1. pp. 48, 49.

† The Fathers, especially Origen and Jerome, contended that Scripture had a threefold meaning, and Augustin maintained that the Jewish prophecies had a four-fold sense. See Mosh. Eccles. Hist. cent. III. chap. iii. sec. v., and works quoted by him. Tacitus (Ann. lib. II. c. 54) says that the priest who interpreted the answers of the oracle of Claros, "foretold to Germanicus his sudden death, but in dark and ambiguous terms, according to the custom of oracles." The following Pagan mode of getting up prophecies may give to a reader, unacquainted with Pagan lore, an idea of the mode in which the Jewish prophets, who, in most things, closely resembled all other prophets, produced their predictions, and will throw some light upon such expressions as—"thus saith the Lord," "saith the Lord God," "saith the Lord of Hosts," "God spoke," &c.—expressions so frequently met with in the Jewish prophecies. It will also show why the Hebrew prophecies, are in verse or poetry.—"The prophet," says Tacitus, already cited, speaking of the oracle of Claros, "after knowing the number and names of those who come to consult him, retires into a cave, and having drunk of the waters of a spring within it, he delivers answers, in verse, upon what persons have in their minds, though he is often ignorant, and knows nothing of composing in metre." Rollin, citing ancient writers, says that the oracle, Pythia, "uttered, at intervals, some words almost inarticulate, which the prophets carefully collected, and arranged with a certain degree of order and connexion.......The prophets had poets under them, who made the oracles into verses........Plutarch informs us that it was not the god who composed the verses of the oracle. He inflamed the Pythia's imagination, and kindled in her soul that living light, which unveiled all futurity to her. The words she uttered in the heat of her enthusiasm, having neither method nor connexion, and coming only by starts,......were collected with care by the prophets, who gave them afterwards to the poets to be turned into verse........The oracles were, however, often given in prose." See Rollin's Ancient Hist. vol. 1. pref. pp. 36, 37.

‡ Herodot. 1. c. 26, &c. § Macrob. lib. 1. Saturnal. c. 23.

predicted his success.   Mopsus, on being taxed by the now jealous
Calchas, prophesied that on a certain neighbouring tree, the number of
figs would be found ten thousand but one, which, upon reckoning them
proved to be the case.   He could also prophesy—when Calchas had failed
—how many young ones a particular sow would farrow.—He said that
on the morrow she would bring forth ten, of which only one would be a
male, all black, and that the females would all be known by their white
streaks.   The morrow proved the veracity of the prediction.*   Thus we
see that there were among the Gentiles, as well as the Jews, some prophets,
in whose prescience the existent age had considerable confidence.   Christians, of course, contend that the pagans prophesy—just as they work
miracles—by the agency of demons.† . The Mahomedans, from the time
of their founder till the present age, have also had a great number of
prophets whose predictions are, by thousands, believed to have been really
fulfilled.‡   Nor are the Mormons—a religious sect within our own days said
to have been divinely raised, and now in many hundreds of thousands on
the borders of the great Salt Lake—without their prophets and prophecies,
many of the latter of which are said to have been already most miraculously accomplished.§   To these may be added, the almanack prophets,
who, because they happen to be right in one out of a hundred of their
prognostications, still maintain their hold on the mind of the *credulous*.
They happen to prophesy truly some times by mere coincidence, a
most singular example of which occurred some ten or twelve years ago.
—An almanack maker, named Murphy, foretold, in the autumn of one
year the very hottest day of the following summer.   Thousands, next year,
bought his almanack, and many, doubtless, considered him a real prophet. ‖
" Of Moore's almanack not less than 40,000 are annually sold, and most
of them on the credit of 'the predictions,' which are generally ambiguous,
and sometimes notoriously false ; but because, now and then, the event
seems to correspond with the prognostication, the almanack preserves its
credit."   " Of one hundred predictions ninety-nine may miscarry ; but
these are instantly forgotten ; whereas, the single one that happens accidentally to be verified, makes a figure in the imagination, and is recorded
as a wonder."¶   There are some predictions which are the result of the
sagacious calculations of probable events.   These, although they can
seldom be more than conjectures, or inferences drawn from premises perceived by the farseeing powers of genius, yet should be distinguished from
the supernatural pretensions of empiricism.   Such, for example, was the
prediction of Bonaparte, whose deep political insight enabled him, at St.
Helena, to foresee " the destruction of the old Bourbon dynasty, the

---

* Ammian. xiv. c. 8.   Paus. vii. c. 3.   Strab. 9.   Plut. de Orac. defect.

† Tertullian, in his Apology for the Christians, has taken some pains to show that
these pagan prophets predicted truly by the influence of demons.   Others of the Fathers
were of the same opinion.   Rollin (pref. p. 38) states that Father Baltus, professor in the
university of Strasburgh, has demonstrated the same thing.   All this only proves the
credulity even in pagan prophecy.

‡ Read the Coran, or any history of Mahomedanism.

§ See the Book of Mormon, and also Hist. of the Mormons, by Pratt, Spencer, or
any other of their writers.

‖ Foxton's Popular Christianity, p. 50.

¶ Curtis's Theology Displayed, p. 41.   Lond. 1842.

succession of the Orleans branch, and the subsequent establishment of a republic—events which have literally been accomplished before our eyes."* There are men who pay attention to causes and effects, and can foretell things, as likely to take place, which appear very unlikely to *other* men. But a physician, for instance, who, from a minute knowledge of the impaired state of a particular individual's constitution, can foretell, within a few weeks, the time he will die, can hardly be said to be "among the prophets," but rather among the philosophers. Still, he has a greater claim to belief in the fulfilment of his prediction, which is only an induction from scientific facts, than the enthusiast, whose prophecy has no better foundation for its truth than the disordered impulses of his own brain, or his propensity to excite and gratify the credulity of ignorance, which superstitiously remembers one presage that is accidentally verified, while it forgets and disregards a hundred which turn out to be false.

Of the foregoing character evidently are the Jewish predictions preserved in the Old Testament.—Some few of them are the shrewd guesses of men of keener perception than their fellows, while by far the greater number are the fruits of fanaticism. They differ in nothing from the prophecies of pagan oracles. The Jewish, like the pagan prophets, before they gave forth their predictions, worked up themselves into a kind of "religious phrenzy, produced or aided by various means, especially by music and dancing." † Philo says—"the mark of true prophecy is the rapture of its utterance; in order to attain divine wisdom the soul must go out of itself, and become drunk with divine phrenzy." ‡ The same word in Hebrew (and Plato thought in Greek also) signifies to *prophesy* and to be *mad;*§ and

---

* Foxton's Popular Christianity, p. 46.

† 1 Sam. x. 5—7; xviii. 10. 2 Kings iii. 15, 16. 1 Kings xviii. 29. Jer. xxiii. 9; xxix. 26, 27. Hos. ix. 7. Ezek. iii. 14, 15.
"As soon as the divine vapour, like a penetrating fire, had diffused itself through the entrails of the priestess, her hair stood upright upon her head, her looks grew wild, she foamed at the mouth, a sudden and violent trembling seized her whole body, with all the symptoms of distraction and frenzy. She uttered, at intervals, some words almost inarticulate, which the prophets carefully collected and arranged with a certain degree of order and connexion." This is the mode in which the Pythia, in the temple of Delphi prophesied. Let it be compared with the ravings of the Jewish prophets. See Rollin and authorities, pref. p. 36.

‡ See Mackay's Progress of the Intellect, ii. 192.

§ Newman's Hebrew Monarchy, p. 34. Plato derived μαντις from μαινεσθαι. The foregoing authorities I quote, together with an extract I make, from that valuable work, the Creed of Christendom, by Mr. W. Rathbone Greg. I would add to these, that Plato appears to be perfectly correct in deriving μαντις from μαινεσθαι, the root of which is the old verb μαω—to desire ardently. Hence the following derivatives, which we frequently meet in the Greek writers—μαιμαω and μαιμαζω—to desire eagerly, to burn with rage; μαινας—a mad woman; μαινω—to make mad; μαινομαι—to become furious, frenzied, mad; μαντευομαι—to prophesy, divine; μαντεια—a prophecy, the act of consulting an oracle; μαντευω—to foretell; μαντικος—prophetic; μαντις and μαντιπολος—a prophet; μαντειον—an oracle. Thus does the very root of the word μαντις signify to be *mad*, and retain that signification in all its derivatives. I cannot meet with μαντης, and can find but few of the other derivatives of μαω, either in the LXX or in the New Testament, except μαινομαι and μανια, used in reference to maniacs. The Greek word προφημι, from προ—before, and φημι—speak—speak before (hand), is that constantly used in the Bible. This is, however, by no means a fair translation of any one of the Hebrew words used to designate the ancient Jewish prophets in the Old Testament. There is strong reason to believe that the signification of each of these has direct reference to the practice of the pagan prophets in exercising their art. The word most generally used in

even among themselves, the prophets were often regarded as madmen,* an idea to which their frequent habits of going about naked, and the performance, occasionally, of still more disgusting ceremonies, greatly contri-

the Hebrew Scriptures for *prophet* is נביא (*Nabia*), whose real meaning will best be ascertained from the signification of its root, and etymons, and from the connexions in which it occurs. Its most simple and real radix, doubtless, is יבב (ibb, or iabbib,)—to cry aloud, exclaim. See Jud. v. 28 ; and 2 Kings iii. 24. In the latter place, our translators have rendered it—*smote*. See Parkh. Heb. Lex. infra v. Some trace the root of the word to בא (ba) or בוא (booa)—to enter, to go in, as the prophets entered into the shrine of the oracle, or into a cave, in which frequently oracles made responses. (Plut. de Gen. Socr. p. 590. Pausan. lib. ix. pp. 602, 604) It is not a little remarkable, however, that באר (bar) of cognate origin, means both to *open*, such as to open a cave or a pit, and to open, to declare, by speaking. (See it as a noun in Gen. xiv. 10 ; xxi. 30.) From the root יבב (ibb), with the affix נ and other changes incidental to Hebrew letters, we find the following— נב (nab)—to put forth ; נבב (nbb); נבוב (nboob) and ביב (bib)—a hollow, a cave ; ינוב (inoob)—to speak, utter, put forth.—(" The mouth of the just one ינוב will bring forth wisdom."—Prov. x. 31) ; נבו (naboo, or Nebo)— a Babylonish oracle and idol , the confessed signification of whose name is, he that " speaks, prophesies, or produces,." It is most singular that all the derivatives, as well as the root of the word *prophet*, means to produce or fructify, as well as to utter words. נביא (nabia)—a prophet ; and נבא (naba)—to cry out, to utter extraordinary things, to prophesy. Thus is the term prophet found to be, in derivation, signification, and sound, identically the same with the name of the prophetic oracle *Nebo*. Now we know with what wild frenzy the old pagan prophets, such as those of Baal and others, exercised their calling.

Another word used a few times in the Hebrew Scriptures for a prophet is ראה (roeh), meaning a seer. (See 1 Sam. ix. 9.) As the verb ראה (roeh, or ra-ah) means to see, to look at, to look into, examine, &c., this term again points to the practice among heathen nations of prophesying by augury—by inspecting the entrails of animals, observing the flight of birds, the greediness of chickens in pecking their grain, &c.; a species of divination, or mode of foretelling future events, well known to have been generally established among the Egyptians, Assyrians, Grecians, Romans, &c. See Rollin's Ancient Hist. pref. xxxi. ; Adam's Roman Antiq. pp. 288—292. The points of similarity between the Jewish and pagan prophets are so numerous, that to do this topic justice it should be the subject of a separate work.

The word נביא (nabia), in the form of a verb, I perceive, is applied to Saul, when he prophesied, after "the evil spirit *from God* came upon him." The facts that Saul " prophesied in the midst of the house," and that he threw the javelin at David, when under the influence of prophecy, show that while thus prophesying he was, like the heathen prophets, in a divine frenzy. 1 Sam. xviii. 10, 11. The same word, as a plural noun, is used to designate the prophets of Baal, who, when under the influence of prophecy, " cried aloud, and cut themselves after their manner with knives and lancets, till the blood gushed out upon them."—1 Kings xviii. 19, 22, 26, 28.

* 2 Kings, ix. 11. Jer. xxix. 26. When Jehu had been anointed by a young prophet, under the direction of Elisha, Jehu's companions asked him why " this mad fellow" (the young prophet) had come to him. Jeremiah complains that a pretended priest, named Shemaiah, had attempted to *usurp* authority, and put in *prison, and in the stocks, every man that was mad and made himself a prophet.* So likewise with regard to the pagan prophets—mad and frantic persons were supposed to possess the faculty of presaging future events.—(Cic. Div. i. 33. Horat. Sat. ii. 3, 279. Ov. ep. iv. 49.) Plato, in speaking of such prophets, says—" they have their minds excited and inspired by the muses into enthusiastic songs and poems, and are rapt into divine ecstasy and madness, so that, being moved by divine fate, their understanding does not remain in them." He further remarks, that " the circumstance that no one in his right mind is seized with the spirit of divination is a proof that God has vouchsafed this faculty to human *madness*."—See Plato in Io. et Tim. quoted in Gale's Court of the Gentiles, part iii. b. 1. c. 3. This opinion of Plato, in regard to God enduing madmen with the gift of prophecy in the pagan world, perfectly agrees with the opinion of the Jew, Philo, already quoted (p. 55) touching the Hebrew prophets—that in order to produce a true

buted.* That many of them were splendid poets and noble-minded men there can be no doubt; but we see in conduct like this little earnest of

prophecy "the soul must go out of itself, and become drunk with divine frenzy," Potter, in his Antiquities of Greece (b. ii. c. 12) describing Heathen prophecy, says, that "few who pretended to inspiration but raged in this manner, foaming and yelling, and making a strange, terrible noise, sometimes gnashing with their teeth, shivering and trembling with a thousand antic motions." One of the pagan prophetesses, influenced by what was supposed to be "divine frenzy," while in the act of predicting, as well as the cave in which the oracle to be consulted abode, is picturesquely described by Virgil, and translated thus by Dryden :—

> "   *   *   *   * Achates came,
> And by his side the mad divining dame,
> The priestess of the god, Deiphobe her name,
> 'Time suffers not,' she said, ' to feed your eyes
> With empty pleasures : haste the sacrifice.
> Sev'n bullocks, yet unyok'd, for Phœbus choose,
> And for Diana sev'n unspotted ewes.'
> This said, the servants urge the sacred rites,
> While to the temple she the prince invites.
> A spacious cave within its farmost part
> Was hew'd and fashion'd by laborious art,
> Through the hill's hollow sides : before the place,
> A hundred doors a hundred entries graced.
> As many voices issue, and the sound
> Of Sibyl's words as many times rebound.
> Now to the mouth they come. Aloud she cries,
> ' This is the time ! inquire your destinies !
> He comes! behold the god!' Thus while she said
> (And shiv'ring at the sacred entry stayed,)
> Her colour chang'd ; her face was not the same ;
> And hollow groans from her deep spirit came.
> Her hair stood up ; convulsive rage possess'd
> Her trembling limbs, and heav'd her lab'ring breast.
> Greater than human kind she seem'd to look,
> And, with an accent more than mortal, spoke.
> Her staring eyes with sparkling fury roll ;
> When all the god came rushing on her soul.
> Swiftly she turn'd, and foaming as she spoke,
> ' Why this delay ?' she cried, ' the pow'rs invoke.' "
>   Virg. Æn. vi. 34—53. Dryd. 53—81.

* 1 Sam. xvi. 13, 14. 2 Sam. vi. 16, 20. 1 Sam. xix. 24. Isa. xx. 3. Ezek. iv. 4—15. David who, the Bible says, was a man after God's own heart, will be admitted to be a great prophet. We are told that in his Psalms he uttered many prophecies of Christ. The prophet Samuel anointed him, " and the Spirit of the Lord came upon David from that day forward ;" so that when he liked he could make the " evil spirit" depart from Saul, by playing on the harp—an instrument with which the officers of David afterwards prophesied. As a prophet, David when bringing home the ark of the Lord, played on the harp, and danced " with all his might," shouting, with all the house of Israel. But not satisfied with this demonstration of joy, he must dance in a state of *nudity*. Saul's daughter, Michal, who was one of David's wives, happening to look through the window, had her feeling of propriety and decency grievously wounded at seeing the prophet-king dancing in this state ; and on the first opportunity took the liberty to speak to him of his behaviour, saying—" How glorious was the king of Israel to-day, who uncovered himself to-day in the eyes of the handmaids of his servants, as one of the vain fellows shamelessly uncovereth himself." David incensed at this reproof, which certainly was administered in a most sarcastic manner, upbraided his royal consort that the Lord had chosen him before her father, and told her that he should be still more vile, so as to be had in honour by the maid-servants of whom she had spoken ; meaning evidently by this, that Michal, for her reflection on the character of the Lord's anointed, should by him be accursed, so

sobriety or divine inspiration, and far too much that reminds us of the
fanatics of eastern countries and ancient times."*

The Jewish prophets being of this character, and in this frantic state of
mind, when engaged in foretelling future events, it can only be expected
that they committed many egregious blunders, as already intimated. Such
precisely we find to have been the case. Many of their predictions, however, are delivered in such ambiguous and obscure language that it is
utterly impossible to decide whether they have been accomplished or not,
or even to ascertain to what event or events they refer; but all those
which are expressed in clear and specific terms, both as to the events and
dates, have proved failures. "It is, probably, not too much to affirm," as
Mr. Greg truly remarks, "that we have no instance in the prophetical
Books of the Old Testament of a (true) prediction in the case of which we
possess, at once and combined, clear and unsuspicious proof of the date,
the precise event predicted, the exact circumstance of that event, and the
inability of human sagacity to foresee.† Jeremiah, in a clear, distinct
prophecy, tells us that Jehoiakim should be buried with the burial of an
ass, drawn and cast forth beyond the gates of Jerusalem; and that his
dead body should in the day be exposed to the heat, and in the night to
the frost. But the writer of the 2nd Book of Kings assures us that
Jehoiakim "slept with his fathers."‡ Amos again prophesies that
Jeroboam, son of Joash, should die by the sword; but the Book of
Kings states that he "slept with his fathers," which, as proved by the
use of the same expression in other places, means that he died a natural
death.§ Many other such instances might be given. ‖ Jeremiah was
beaten and put in the stocks for prophesying falsely; and he again
denounces judgment upon Shemaiah for his false predictions.¶ The
king of Israel gathered the prophets together—about four hundred in
number—and inquired of them whether it was the will of the Lord
that he should, with king Jehoshaphat, engage in battle against the
Syrians. All the four hundred prophets predicted that the Lord would
make the Hebrews victorious. Jehoshaphat inquired whether there

that she should have "no child unto the day of her death"—than which no greater
disgrace was considered among the Hebrews. In like manner the Spirit of God
having come upon Saul, he also, in character with a true Jewish prophet, stripped off
his clothes, and prophesied before Samuel, "and lay down naked all that day, and all
that night." The Lord commands his prophet Isaiah to loose the sackcloth from off his
loins, put off his shoe from his foot; which the man of God does, and walks naked
and barefoot; and the Lord makes mention of this—that his "servant Isaiah hath
walked naked and barefoot three years." A great many other instances of the frantic
madness of the Jewish prophets could be added. But it is trusted that the foregoing
notes will suffice to enable the general reader to institute a comparison between them
and the pagan prophets.
    * Greg's Creed of Christendom, pp. 53, 54. This able writer, with his characteristic
candour, gives the Hebrew prophets credit for *noble-mindedness;* but it is difficult to
conceive how either a fanatic, a madman, or a knave, can be noble-minded, while
exercising either of these qualities. Some allowance should, perhaps, be made to those
prophets, owing to the religious customs of the age, and the state of civilization in
which the Jews were, at that time.
    † See Greg's Creed of Christendom, p. 58, where De Wette, ii. 357, 363, is quoted.
        ‡ Compare Jer. xxii. 18, 19; xxxvi. 30; with 2 Kings xxiv. 6.
            § Compare Amos vii. 11, with 2 Kings, xiv. 29.
                ‖ See Creed of Christendom, pp. 55, 56.
                    ¶ Jer. xx. 22; xxix. 26, 31.

was any other prophet of the Lord whom he might consult on this important undertaking, and was told that there was one named Micaiah, whom the king of Israel, although he hated him, because he always prophesied evil of him, however, ordered to be cited. When he came, he said to the Israelitish king, in the presence of the other four hundred prophets, and in the following flattering, or ironical words,—" Go, and prosper." He also added—in the obscure and ambiguous language peculiar to prophets—that he had seen all Israel scattered upon the hills, as sheep without a shepherd, and that the Lord had said,—" Let them return every man to his house." Seeing that king Ahab was dissatisfied with the seemingly unfavourable import of this prediction, he began to reflect on the character of the other prophets, declaring that the Lord had asked who should persuade Ahab to go against the enemy and be killed in battle, and that there had come forth, from among the host of heaven, a spirit who said—" I will go forth and be a lying spirit in the mouth of all the prophets." This spirit, he said, the Lord had commanded to go, and do so ; and that, therefore, the Lord had put a lying spirit in the mouth of all the king's prophets. Incensed at this calumny, one of the other prophets, named Zedekiah, accosted his opponent and struck him, at the same time, asking sarcastically,—" which way went the Spirit of the Lord from me to speak unto thee ?" Micaiah, while he persisted in the truth of his declaration, was further punished for this reflection on the veracity of the four hundred prophets, by imprisonment and low diet. The two Jewish monarchs—Ahab and Jehoshaphat—engaged in battle against the Syrians. Ahab was slain, and the Jewish armies were scattered, according to Micaiah's prophecy." * From this narrative it will clearly appear,— *first*, that while four hundred prophets predicted falsely, only *one* happened to be right—that is, right, admitting that Micaiah ever uttered the predictions attributed to him, or that these predictions were uttered before the event ; for we have ample proof that the Jewish writers habitually narrated past events as predictions of future ones, and presented history in the form of prophecy.† *Secondly*, that it was a belief among the prophets that God was capable of sending forth " a lying spirit" to deceive them,—a most low and grovelling notion of the Deity. From the foregoing remarks, and facts, the reader will be able the more fully to understand what is meant by *Jewish prophets* and *prophecies* ; and by reasoning analogically therefrom, will be the better prepared to judge of the strength of the arguments advanced in the sequel.

Now, one of these *Jewish prophets* was Jesus of Nazareth, who is said by his followers to have prophesied the destruction of Jerusalem, his own resurrection from the dead on the third day, and several other extraordinary events. Whatever higher functions and attributes are claimed for him, no one can demur to the position that he was a *prophet*, and a *Jewish prophet*. Both Peter and Stephen declare that he was the prophet of whom Moses had foretold.‡ The woman of Samaria and the multitudes that surrounded him, on different occasions, recognised him as such ;§

* Read 1 Kings xxii. 1—38.   † Creed of Christendom, p. 61.
‡ Acts iii. 22, 23 ; vii. 37.   Deut. xviii. 15, 19.
§ John iv. 19.   Luke vii. 16.   Matth xxi. 11.

and he himself rejoiced in this title, as it is clear from such expressions of his as, " a prophet is not without honour save in his own country."*   We have always been taught by divines to regard Christ in the character of a prophet, in one of his mediatorial offices, teaching his people—as it was a branch of the duties of the ancient Jewish prophets to teach the people—the will of the Lord, revealing hidden things, and working wonders. The idea of a Messiah, or a national deliverer, and that of a prophet were very closely allied—almost identical—in the Jewish mind.   A prophet was required to be anointed for his office, and the word *Messiah* means *one that is anointed.*   The idea of deliverance was inseparably connected with that of a prophet.   Moses and David were prophets, as well as Jewish deliverers or leaders ; just as Zoroaster, Confucius, Mahomed, &c., discharged the duties of this twofold office.   The Jews accepted and recognised Christ as a prophet ; but rejected him as the promised deliverer, or Messiah.   In the character of the latter he did not answer their expectations ; but with that of the former they were satisfied ; seeing he had about him much which resembled the sayings and doings of the ancient prophets. Had he claimed only the character of a prophet, and never insinuated that he was the *King* of the Jews, " he might have expected credit on the same evidence of a divine mission as that on which the other prophets had been received." †   He, however, not only frequently appealed to the ancient prophets as authority for what he said and did, but likewise closely imitated them in many things ; so that—as will hereafter be shown—his language and predictions strikingly resemble those of theirs, with the exception that they are not quite so obscure.

Christ, although like Mahomed, illiterate,‡ yet is represented as having such an insight into futurity as enabled him to predict several notable events.   These predictions, we are told, were at various times more or less distant from their delivery, recorded by four of his adherents, and among other matters, relating to his three years of public career, have descended to us in the shape of what are called Gospels.   To inquire how far these predictions are in harmony with truth—to ascertain whether the prophecies of Jesus of Nazareth, who was a Jew, as to his parentage, country, and religious training, are more in accordance with the events to which they refer, than those of his Jewish predecessors in the same art, which we have just seen to be notoriously false, is a subject replete with interest, especially to the Christian world.

The most remarkable, perhaps, of all the prophecies of Christ is that chain of predictions which evidently refer to the destruction of the present system of nature, and events concomitant therewith.   They are recorded

---

* Matth. xiii. 57.   Mark vi. 4.
† Dr. Gerard's Evidence of Religion, p. 167.
‡ Eusebius, however, in his Ecclesiastical History (lib. i. c. 14) furnishes us with letters, purported to have passed between Christ and Abgarus, which he affirms he found in Edessa, written in the Syriac language, and of which, in his above work, he gives a Greek translation.   Many divines, among whom were the learned Grabbe, Archbishop Cave, and Dr. Parker, have strenuously contended for their genuiness.   There is quite as much proof of their authenticity as there is that the four gospels were written by those apostles whose names they respectively bear.   See the letters translated into English, and published as part of the Apocryphal New Testament—a production that should be in the hands of every Biblical student.—Hone ; London, 1820.   Price only 1s.

by three of the Evangelists, at different lengths, and with slight variations. Similar prophecies have been uttered by Christ on other occasions, in a more concise form. Expressions explanatory of them pervade the four Gospels, and the events which they foretell are, in all the Epistles, together with the Acts of the Apostles and the Apocalypse, more or less dwelt upon. In a word, the subject of these predictions is a prominent doctrine in every part of the New Testament. In Matthew these predictions commence at the 34th verse of chapter xxiii. and end at the 46th verse of chapter xxv.* That the same prophetic discourse, by way of expatiation on the more pointed predictions of the foregoing chapter, is continued to the end of chapter xxv. is clear from the concatenated tenour of the whole—from the words—" then shall the kingdom of heaven, &c.," with which chapter xxv. commences—and, especially from the words—" and it came to pass when Jesus had *finished all these sayings*,"† which occur immediately after the last words of the above chapter. In addition to these proofs, it may be observed that it is the same moral lesson which is inculcated throughout chapter xxv. as in the latter portion of the previous chapter—the lesson of watchfulness—of being ready, so as to avoid punishment and obtain a reward. To the end of chapter xxiv. the lesson of the faithful and wise servant is taught ; and at the beginning of the next chapter, the lesson of the ten virgins—five wise and five foolish—is taken up, without any interruption, except the modern and arbitrary division into chapters. Then follows the lesson of a man, who, before he takes a journey into a far country, calls his servants, and gives to each the care of a portion of his goods, rewarding, on his return, each according to his merits. After all these lessons, which are in the form of parables, follows the moral—the Son of man coming in his glory,‡ &c.—which continues to the end of the chapter.§ Mark records the substance of these predictions in chapter xiii. the whole of which is taken up with them ;‖ and Luke in chapters xxi. and xvii. ver. 20—37. There are in the Gospels other passages in which predictions of the same events are found, and which, in due order, will be cited, together with the passages which show in what light the writers of the Epistles viewed the occurrence of such events.

---

* Read to the end of chap. xxiv. transcribed into this work, pp. 11, 12.
  † Chap. xxvi. ver. 1.   ‡ Ver. 31.
 § Another proof that the same subject is treated to the end of this chapter, will be found in the fact that Mark—who, in reporting these predictions, as well as in narrating almost all other matters, in his Gospel, is much briefer than the other Evangelists—relates, in a more concise form, and with slight verbal difference, in the very chapter where these prophecies are found, the parable of " a man taking a journey," which is placed by Matthew in chap. xxv.—Compare Mark xiii. 34, with Matth. xxv. 14.
  ‖ Vide Ante, pp. 12, 13.

SECTION II.—SCRIPTURAL PROOFS THAT CHRIST PREDICTED THE END OF THE WORLD AND THE FINAL JUDGMENT, AS EVENTS THEN CLOSE AT HAND; AND THAT HE REPRESENTED HIMSELF AS THE JUDGE OF ALL MANKIND, WHO, AS SUCH, WAS SHORTLY TO MAKE HIS APPEARANCE IN THE CLOUDS.

It is now proposed to show that, in uttering these prophecies, Christ *intended* to predict, and *did* predict *the Last Day of Judgment, and the Destruction of the World, as events inevitable during the then existent generation of men.* The mode in which these events were to take place, and the circumstances connected with them, shall be more fully explained in subsequent sections.

It would appear, according to Matthew, that Christ, on the occasion about to be noticed here, commenced delivering these predictions, in the temple, while addressing himself to the Scribes and Pharisees.* Having pointed out a number of things which were to take place, such as killing and crucifying some of the prophets, wise men and scribes; scourging others, and prosecuting them from city to city, so that by this cruelty, the Jews would draw upon themselves their desert of divine vengeance, he avers to them that *all these things should come to pass upon this generation;* evidently meaning the generation then living. He then deplores the fate of Jerusalem, and adds that they should not see him henceforth till they would say—" Blessed is he that cometh in the name of the Lord ;"† meaning, according to the import of similar expressions used elsewhere, that they should not see him again till he came to execute judgment, destroy the world, and establish his kingdom—" the kingdom of heaven" —as will be shown hereafter. The meaning of the words—" Blessed is he that cometh in the name of the Lord"—will best be ascertained by that of similar expressions, especially as they are evidently intended as a citation. We find precisely the same words used in one of the Psalms,‡ where it is desired that the gates of righteousness—meaning either the gates of the temple, or of the city of Jerusalem—should be opened, that the *righteous* (the king—the anointed of the Lord—probably) might enter. But let us see in what sense, in the time of Christ, the Jews, to whom these words were addressed, understood them. A short time before Christ used them, we find that the very same words, § doubtless derived

* The subject is here admitted to commence at verse 34, chap. xxiii. of Matthew, as contended for by some Christian writers.
                    † Matth. xxiii. 34—39.
    ‡ cxviii. 26. " Blessed is he that cometh in the name of the Lord."
    § Matth. xxi. 9, and Mark xi. 9, 10, have the words—" Blessed is he that cometh in the name of the Lord,"—" Blessed be the *kingdom of our father David* that cometh in the name of the Lord." Luke xix. 28, has " Blessed is the *king* that cometh in the name of the Lord." John xii. 13, has " Blessed is *the king of Israel* that cometh in the name of the Lord."

from the Psalm already cited, were used by the Jews when, in a huge, enthusiastic multitude, they hailed him by such acclamations as " Hosanna to the Son of David ! Blessed is he that cometh in the name of the Lord !" as he rode in triumph into Jerusalem, on an ass, in fulfilment, he says, of an ancient prophecy, which told the daughter of Jerusalem to rejoice because her king was coming riding upon an ass.* It is clear, therefore, that what Christ intended the Jews to understand by the expression under notice, was that they should not see him till he came as a king to establish his kingdom, the nature of which will hereafter be ascertained.† The words—" this generation"—will be explained by similar expressions which occur in subsequent portions of this chain of prophecies.‡

Jesus, having predicted the foregoing particulars, went out of the temple, and in company with his disciples, viewed that gorgeous edifice from outside.§ Gazing at this group of magnificent buildings, he said to his disciples, in reference to them,—" there shall not be left here one stone upon another that shall not be thrown down." Shortly after, the disciples—curious to know more about these momentous events—said to him :—" Tell us when shall these things be, and what shall be the sign of thy coming, and of the end of the world."‖

Here, it should be observed, the disciples connect the *coming of Christ* and the *End of the World* with " *these things*,"—the things that Christ had just enumerated. Nor is it possible to understand the passage otherwise, without the most violent perversion of language. Although Christ had not expressly mentioned his *coming* and the *End of the World*, in his predictions immediately preceding, yet it is clear that his disciples—probably from his previous predictions of the same events—understood him to mean these occurences, and that they understood the destruction of the temple and of Jerusalem at large, as included in the destruction or " End"

---

* Zech. ix. 9.

† It would not be inappropriate here, however, to observe that the fact that Christ preached throughout Judea that " the kingdom of heaven was at hand," is proved, not only by his own words, but by the testimony of his Apostles, who had often heard him announce that event, and consequently had better means of ascertaining the import of his words than have mere readers of the Gospels, who are obliged to gather his meaning from a collection—to say the least—of interpolated fragments of his discourses. Luke (xix. 11.)—as will hereafter be more fully noticed—states that " when they"—meaning the disciples—approached Jerusalem the last time, namely, the time when Jesus rode in triumph on an ass, " they thought that the kingdom of God should *immediately* appear.' It is a violent and unwarrantable assumption to suppose—as some Christian writers do— that the chosen and constant attendants of Jesus—his apostles—were *mistaken* as to the chief and most prominent topic of his discourses—one, too, which *they themselves had been sent out by him to preach, and had preached;* namely, the nature and near approach of the kingdom of heaven. We must, therefore, conclude that Christ, up to his last appearance in Jerusalem, led his apostles and followers to expect that " the kingdom of heaven was at hand," as he himself expressed it. The meaning of this expression will be illustrated hereafter. It is, however, worthy of remark here, that even Dr. Warburton admits that both ancient and modern interpreters suppose that Christ, in his prophetic announcement of the fall of Jerusalem, " interwove a direct prediction of his second coming," adding that " hence arose a current opinion, in these times" (the first ages of Christianity) " that the termination of all things was at hand."

‡ See pp. 66, 67. § Matth. xxiv. 1. Mark xiii. 1.
‖ Matth. xxiv. 2—3. Mark xiii. 4. Luke xxi. 6—7.

of the World, and the coming of Christ to judgment; and therefore that they wished to be able to ascertain, by some *sign* when *these things* were to happen. Nor does Christ attempt at correcting any error in their notions on these points, but sanctions them as being true, in the answer he gives, which is to the following effect. He tells them that before *these things* occurred, they should hear of wars and rumours of wars,—that nation should rise against nation, and kingdom against kingdom,—that there should be earthquakes, famines, pestilences, and such tribulations, as had not been seen since the beginning of the world,—that there should be persecutions, false christs, and false prophets, and " the abomination of desolation " standing in the holy place,—that the gospel of the kingdom should be preached in all the world,—and that *then should come the end.* He further says,—" *Immediately after the tribulation of those days shall the sun be darkened, and the moon shall not give her light, and the stars shall fall from heaven, and the powers of the heaven shall be shaken, and then shall appear the sign of the Son of man in heaven ; and then shall all the tribes of the earth mourn, .and they shall see the Son of man coming in the clouds of heaven, with power and great glory, and he shall send his angels with a great sound of a trumpet, and they shall gather together his elect from the four winds, from one end of heaven to the other. Now learn a parable of the fig-tree ; when his branch is yet tender, and putteth forth leaves, ye know that summer is nigh; so likewise ye, when ye shall see all these things, know that it is near, even at the doors.* VERILY I SAY UNTO YOU THIS GENERATION SHALL NOT PASS TILL ALL THESE THINGS BE FULFILLED."*

Such is part of Christ's special prophetic answer to the following special question put to him by his disciples :—" When shall these *things* be ? and what shall be the sign of thy *coming*, and of the *end of the world* ?†" Is this a prophecy of the End of the World and the Day of Judgment, as events which were to take place during the age in which Christ and his disciples lived ? The best mode to ascertain this—a mode which will be admitted to be in accordance with sound criticism—is to explain the language of these predictions by that of passages in which similar language is used, and similar sentiments conveyed, in other parts of the Gospels and Epistles, where the meaning is clear and obvious. Let us, for this purpose, first, take the words just cited from Matthew, from verse 29 till 35 inclusive, together with the next verse,—" Heaven and earth shall pass away ; but my words shall not pass away."

It will not be questioned that Peter refers to the Last Day of Judgment,

---

* Matth. xxiv. 4—34. Mark xiii. 5—30. Luke xxi. 8—32.

† Matth. xxiv. 3. The question put by the disciples here, and the answer returned to it by Christ, must stand indissolubly connected. Whatever the disciples meant by their Master's *coming*, and the *end of the world*, the same is meant by Christ in his prophetic reply, in the course of which he uses their very words—*end* and *coming*—(ver. 6, 27) ; doubtless, meaning by them the same things as his disciples meant. Indeed, the text (ver. 4) expressly states that Christ's prediction *was* a direct answer to the inquiry of his disciples,—" And Jesus *answered* and said." To assert that it was *not*, or that it did not bear directly upon it, would not only be a violation of the meaning of the plainest possible language, but likewise a reflection on the character of Christ as a teacher, by implying that when his disciples sought information upon one subject he spoke upon another, bearing no relation to it,—that when they asked one thing he answered by speaking of another thing.

in the following passage, where he describes the dissolution of nature so much like Christ, in the expressions just quoted.—" But the day of the Lord will come as a thief in the night ; in the which the heavens shall pass away with a great noise, and the elements shall melt with fervent heat ; the earth also and the works that are therein shall be burned up. Seeing then that all these things shall be dissolved, what manner of persons ought ye to be in all holy conversation and godliness, looking for, and hastening unto *the coming of the day of God*, wherein the heavens being on fire shall be dissolved, and the elements shall melt with fervent heat ? Nevertheless *we*, according to his promise, look for new heavens and a new earth." " But the heavens and the earth which are now, by the same word, are kept in store, reserved unto fire against the day of judgment."* There is still a more remarkable passage in the Book of Revelation, doubtless describing a scene at the expected End of the World and the Day of Judgment, with references to which, as will hereafter be shown, this book is replete.— " And I beheld when he had opened the sixth seal " (the last of the seals described) " and lo, there was a great earthquake, and the sun became black as sackcloth of hair, and the moon became as blood ; and the stars of heaven fell unto the earth, even as a fig-tree casteth her untimely figs, when she is shaken of a mighty wind ; and the heaven departed as a scroll when it is rolled together ; and every mountain and island were moved out of their places. And the kings of the earth and the great men, and the rich men, and the chief captains, and the mighty men, and every bondman, and every freeman, hid themselves in the dens, and in the rocks of the mountains ; and said to the mountains and rocks, Fall on us, and hide us from the face of him that sitteth on the throne, and from the wrath of the Lamb ; for the great day of his wrath is come ; and who shall be able to stand ?"† It will not be denied that this passage, and also that cited from Peter, describe events which the writers expected to take place at the end of the world,—in fact, describe *the* End of the World itself. Nor can the dullest mind fail to perceive their similarity, in language and description, to Christ's words in Matthew, where he speaks of the darkening of the sun and moon, the falling of the stars, and the passing away of heaven and earth. So striking is the identity, in language and sentiment, that the conclusion that they all describe the same events—the End of the World—is irresistible.

Another portion of the passage under consideration, uttered prophetically by Christ, as quoted already, is the following.—" And they shall see the Son of man coming in the clouds of heaven, with power and great glory ; and he shall send his angels with a great sound of a trumpet, and they shall gather together his elect from the four winds, from one end of heaven to the other." What do these words mean ? Do they refer to events which are to take place at the end of the world ? Christ and his Apostles shall explain them. That he means himself by the appellation

---

* 2 Pet. iii. 10—13, 7.

† Rev. vi. 12—17. There is a striking resemblance between the last words in the above passage from Revelation and those of Christ in Luke xxiii. 30, where, after using words precisely the same in meaning as those in Matthew xxiv. regarding women with children, he says—" Then shall they begin to say to the mountains, Fall on us, and to the hills, Cover us."

F

—*Son of man*, is evident from his own words on a vast number of occasions, such as—" until the *Son of man* be risen again from the dead."* He says, therefore, of *himself*—" the *Son of man* shall come in the glory of his Father with his angels ; and then he shall reward every man according to his works."† When the high priest asked Jesus if he was the Christ, the Son of God, he answered—" Hereafter shall ye see the Son of man sitting on the right hand of power, and coming in the clouds of heaven."‡ " So shall it be in the *end* of this world :—The *Son of man* shall send forth his angels, and they shall gather out of his kingdom all things that offend, and them which do iniquity, and shall cast them into a furnace of fire."§ Let us again attend to his *Apostles* on this point.—" We shall all be changed, in a moment, in the twinkling of an eye, at the last trump ; for the trumpet shall sound, and the dead shall be raised."‖ " The Lord himself shall descend from heaven, with a shout, with the voice of the archangel, and with the trump of God, and the dead in Christ shall rise first."¶ " Behold, he cometh with clouds, and every eye shall see him."** One passage more, which is composed of words from Christ's own mouth, and like all the foregoing, will, by Christians, readily be admitted to refer to the End of the World and the Last Day of Judgment, must suffice on this head.—" When the Son of man shall come in his glory, and all the holy angels with him, then shall he sit upon the throne of his glory ; and before him shall be gathered all nations ; and he shall separate them one from another, as a shepherd divideth his sheep from the goats."†† Now, as there can be nothing clearer than that all these passages directly refer to the Final Judgment and the End of the World, by parity of reasoning, founded upon the analogy of language, the passage with which they are compared, is, by them, proved most conclusively to refer to the same events. In the present stage of the argument, no other proofs are deemed necessary to demonstrate that Christ *did* prophesy the End of the World, and the Last Day of Judgment.

The next point to be ascertained is the *time* at which, according to Christ's predictions, these momentous events were to take place. His language on this head is as lucid and definite as we could wish.‡‡ His words are—" Verily I say unto you, this generation shall not pass till all these things be fulfilled."§§ The word translated *generation* here is γενεα, which signifies a generation, or race of men, living at the same time, or in the same age, and leaves no room whatever for philological criticism

---

* Matth. xvii. 9.   † xvi. 27.   ‡ xxvi. 64. Mark xiv. 62.
  § Matth. xiii. 40—42.   ‖ 1 Cor. xv. 51—53.
  ¶ 1 Thess. iv. 16.   ** Rev. i. 7.

†† Matth. xxv. 31, 32. The identity of language and ideas in this passage and that in ver. 30 and 31 of the preceding chapter, furnishes an additional and most conclusive proof that the same prophecy is continued throughout to the end of chap. xxv.

‡‡ Indeed, there is not to be found in the whole Bible a single prediction so definite and precise as this is, in point of *time* for its fulfilment. The day and hour thereof, *alone*, are unfixed.

§§ Matth. xxiv. 34. Whitby translates this text thus,—" The men of this age shall not pass." There is no resisting of the Greek of this passage. The criticism of Christian writers on it rests wholly on the accommodatory nature of the English word " generation ; but this position is quite untenable in the Greek of the New Testament, upon which so much stress is laid by these writers, on some occasions, when it suits them.

on the correctness of the translation.* The meaning of the expression, obviously, is that the people—or at least some of the people—who lived contemporarily with Christ, should not die before the predictions which he had uttered—and which we have seen to be those regarding the End of the World and the Final Judgment—should be accomplished. In other words —that these events would take place before all the men then living should die. That Christ positively meant this is fully borne out by other passages. Throughout the whole of this chain of prophecies, indeed, he speaks to his disciples in a manner that warrants the inference that *they, personally,* were to witness the End of the World and the Last Judgment; such as— " *Ye* shall hear of wars,"—" They shall deliver *you* up to be afflicted,"— " When *ye* shall see the abomination, let them that be in Judea flee,"— " Pray *ye* that *your* flight be not in the winter,"—" When *ye* shall see all these things, know that it is near, even at the doors,"—" Watch, therefore, for *ye* know not the hour *your* Lord doth come,"—" When these things begin to come to pass, then look up, and lift up *your* heads, for *your* redemption draweth nigh,"—" When *ye* see these things come to pass know *ye* that the kingdom of God is at hand."† But let Christ explain his own words in the following passages, where he evidently treats on the same subject.—" The Son of man shall come in the glory of his Father, with his angels; and then he shall reward every man according to his works. Verily I say unto you, there be some standing here which shall not taste of death till they see the Son of man coming in his kingdom."‡ Here Christ positively declares that he would come to judge the world and reward every man according to his desert, and that there were some (of his disciples) *then present who should not die till this would take place.* The same expression is also recorded by Mark § and by Luke.‖

Again : besides the evidence furnished by the parallel sentences just adduced, and the obvious meaning of the very words of Christ in the prophetic passage under consideration, touching the near approach of the *time* the End of the World was to take place; the context also—further than has already been pointed out—proves that he meant to convey to his hearers that they were to expect this to take place during their lifetime. Immediately after stating that the heavenly bodies should darken and fall— that the Son of man should come in the clouds of heaven—and that his angels, with a great sound of trumpet, should be sent to gather together the elect, he tells his disciples, by way of a parable, that just as when they saw a fig-tree, puting forth leaves, they knew the summer was near, so when they should see the signs he had enumerated, they would be able to know that the events he had predicted to succeed them were "near, even at the doors." And then he adds the remarkable words,—" Verily I say unto you, *this generation* shall not pass till all these things be fulfilled. Heaven and earth shall pass away, but my words shall not pass away." He, however, excuses himself for not predicting the very " day and hour,"

---

* In this sense the word γενεα is employed by Herodotus;—Αρξαντες επι δυο και ειχοσι γενεας—" Governing for two and twenty generations."—Lib. i. c. 7. See also c. 3, and Homer's Il. i. lin. 250. In the same sense the word is used in the New Test. See Matth. xi. 16, and other places cited in Parkh. Greek Lex.
        † Carefully read Matth. xxiv. Mark xiii. and Luke xxi.
    ‡ Matth, xvi. 27, 28.   § viii. 38 ; ix. 1.   ‖ ix. 26. 27.

                                                                    2 F

on which " all these things " should be fulfilled, by assuring his disciples that this was not known even to the Son, nor to the angels in heaven,—in short, was known to none but to the Father alone.* But, at the same time, he tells them that this day and this hour would come suddenly— would come *as a snare on all that dwelt on the face of the whole earth.*†

If any more evidence be required corroborative of the fact that Christ predicted the End of the World and the Last Judgment, as being then just at hand, it is to be found in almost all the Epistles, as well as the Acts of the Apostles, and the Book of Revelation, the writers of which inculcate the very same doctrine. Paul, in treating of the resurrection, writes to the Corinthians;—" *We* shall not *all* sleep, but *we* shall *all* be changed, in a moment, in the twinkling of an eye, at the last trump ; for the trumpet shall sound, and the dead shall be raised incorruptible, and *we* shall be changed."‡ In writing to the Philippians this Apostle teaches the same doctrine :—" Christ who shall change *our* vile body."§ And in writing to the Thessalonians, he holds forth the same views most prominently :—" For this we say unto you, by the word of the Lord, *that we which are alive and remain unto the coming of the Lord*, shall not prevent them which are asleep. For the Lord himself shall descend from heaven, with a shout, with the voice of the archangel, and with the trump of God, and the dead in Christ shall rise first. Then *we which are alive and remain*, shall be caught up together with them in the clouds, to meet the Lord in the air."‖ In the first and last of these passages, Paul not only makes a clear distinction between the dead who should be raised, and the living who should be on earth at the coming of Christ in Judgment, but he classes *himself with the survivors :*—" We which are alive and remain." The language is here clear and explicit, affording no room whatever for cavil ; and is in striking accordance with that of Christ on the same subject. Both Paul and Christ's language forcibly proves that they regarded the End of the World and the Final Judgment as occurrences which were to take place during the lifetime of their contemporaries. It is trusted, therefore, that —irrespectively of what shall be advanced hereafter—the proofs furnished in *this* section alone, will, by any impartial reader, be deemed irrefragable evidence that Christ predicted the Last Day of Judgment, and the Destruction of the World, as events inevitable during the then existent generation

---

* Christ himself here denies his Divinity, by denying that he possessed one of the essential attributes of Deity—Omniscience. He makes his prescience limited by saying that he did not know " the day and hour " the events he had predicted would occur. Some commentators, seeing the awkward position in which Jesus here places himself, try to help him out of it, by imagining a distinction between his predictive power as God, and his mere foresight as man ; but it is difficult to conceive how Jesus could positively and emphatically predict his final advent, during the then existent generation of men, and still could not predict the day or hour he should come. Divine omniscience and prescience, as hitherto represented in all Christian Creeds, do not countenance this finely spun distinction, evidently made to meet a difficulty.

† Matth. xxiv. 26, 27, 36—51. Luke xxi. 35. ‡ 1 Cor. xv. 51, 52. § Phil. iii. 21.

‖ 1 Thess. iv. 15—17. Read to the end of ver. 9th in chapter 5th. The writer makes no apology for transcribing some of these passages twice, for they are very remarkable and prove several points of his subject. See p. 66. There is a great number of such passages—more or less pointed—in the Epistles, which will hereafter be cited. At present the foregoing must suffice.

of men.* Several predictions of things which were to attend these events, to take place simultaneously with them, and resulting therefrom, remain to be noticed.

According to Christ's predictions, he was to make his first appearance, as a judge of the world, and a dispenser of rewards and punishments to mankind " *in the clouds,*" *or the air.* This was to be the only foundation —the *solus fundamentum*—upon which he was to stand or sit, while he caused the destruction of universal nature, and while his angels gathered, from one end of the heaven to the other, all the elect, who were to meet him in the air, prior to their being received to his kingdom; and also gathered the wicked, and " cast them into a furnace of fire." Thus, it would appear, that these are the first things which Christ at his coming would do; by which he would—as a judge of the world— separate the whole of mankind, both living and dead, into two distinct multitudes. In proof of this construction put upon his predictions, no evidence can be so unobjectionable and conclusive as the words of the predictions themselves, explained, where they are obscure, by the inspired words of Christ's Apostles, which, as such, must be correct, and to which all Christians must be so far from having any objection, that they will feel themselves in duty bound to obey, and implicitly believe them. In the expressions cited in the preceding section, Christ says,—" They shall see the Son of man coming in the clouds of heaven." And again,—" Hereafter shall ye see the Son of man sitting on the right hand of power, and coming in the clouds of heaven," The former of these citations he uttered in immediate connection with his prediction of the disruption of the heavenly bodies.† The latter forms part of his answer to the Jewish high-priest,‡ who, after Christ's apprehension, interrogated him regarding his arrogation of Deity, and pronounced these words blasphemy. But be their blasphemy—with which we have now nothing to do—what it may, the expression—" *sitting* on the right hand of power," would seem to indicate that Christ was to appear in the clouds in a *sitting posture,* as if it were in a kind of locomotive throne.§ " Behold he cometh with clouds; and every eye shall see him," says the Apocalypse." In the clouds were the saints, or the elect, to meet him; and here, apparently, they were to be preserved, while the earth was being burnt, and a new heaven and earth created for them :— " We which are alive and remain shall be caught up together with them," (the elect that had before died, and were now to be raised from the dead,) " *in the clouds to meet the Lord in the air,* and so shall we ever be with the Lord." While this passage does not warrant the conclusion that the saints were to be for ever with the Lord *in the air,*—but simply that they were to be always *with the Lord,* wherever he might be—it throws

---

* The xxvth chapter of Matthew furnishes several proofs, not mentioned, that Christ continues his predictions of the Day of Judgment throughout that chapter. These shall be noticed hereafter.

† Matth. xxiv. 29, 30.   ‡ Matth. xxvi. 64.

§ To make their appearance in the air, gliding with the clouds, which they used as a kind of ærial chariot, or balloon, is a very common description of the heathen deities also. The God Mercury is frequently described as thus moving.—Volat ille per aera magnum remigio alarum.—Virg. Æn. i. lin. 300. The God Prometheus could climb the heavens, and steal fire from the chariot of the sun.—Hesiod. Theog. 510, 580.

considerable light on Christ's prediction, touching his appearance " in the clouds of heaven," and shows that the saints were to be caught up to their Lord into the air.   This—as well as the work of driving the wicked into a furnace of fire—was to be done by the ministration of angels ; for we read, in reference to the one, that they were to " gather together his elect from the four winds," and with regard to the other, that the Son of man should send forth his angels, and that they should gather out of his kingdom all things that offended, and them that did iniquity, and should cast them into a furnace of fire.*

It would, however, appear from Christs words that all men—both good and bad—were to be brought formally before him as a judge, in order to have their fate decided, and to be classed, either with those who were to suffer eternal punishment, or with those who were to enjoy eternal life, in the universal kingdom which he was now about to establish ; and that after the wicked had their doom-pronounced, the angels were to cast them into a fiery furnace—perhaps hurl them from before the seat of judgment, in some of the upper regions of the skies, down to the earth, which was then to be one mass of flames !   For we have, from Christ himself, the follow-ing description of the manner in which he, as judge of the world, should discharge the functions of his office :—" When the Son of man shall come in his glory, and the holy angels with him, then shall he sit upon the throne of his glory ; and before him shall be gathered all nations ; and he shall separate them one from another, as a shepherd divideth his sheep from the goats.   And he shall set the sheep on his right hand ; but the goats on the left.   Then shall the King say unto them on the right hand, —Come ye blessed of my Father, inherit the kingdom prepared for you from the foundation of the world."   After stating his reasons for this favourable reception of the " blessed," he addresses those on his left hand thus :—" Depart from me, ye cursed, into everlasting fire, prepared for the devil and his angels."   Having shown the grounds of this doom, he adds,—" These shall go away into everlasting punishment; but the righteous into eternal life."†   There is here clearly described a separation of those judged into two distinct classes—the one to be the subjects of Christ's kingdom, and to live eternally—the other to be eternally punished in an everlasting fire,—the fire, probably, which would be kindled by the burning of the earth,—a process supposed to last for ever, (or literally, for ages of ages) while the new earth and the new heaven to be created for Christ's kingdom were to be above it, or at least far apart from it.‡

The same doctrine of the two classes—the one admitted into, and the other excluded from the kingdom,—is inculcated throughout the former

* Matth. xiii. 41, 42.   † Matth. xxv. 31—46.
‡ This would appear to be most in accordance with Christ's view of hell.   See his notion in Luke xvi. 23—26.   John the Baptist also preached the doctrine of unquench-able fire which was to burn the chaff ; (Matth. iii. 12. Luke iii. 17) and Christ speaks of fire which shall never be quenched, and which he calls hell-fire. (Matth. v. 22; xx. 43—48.) He appears to allude to this fire which was to burn the earth when he says,—" I am come to send fire on earth ; and what will I, if it be already kindled ?" (Luke xii. 49.) For throughout the chapter in which this passage occurs, there are evident allusions to the end of the world.   Paul alludes to the same fire which should try every man's work. (1 Cor. iii. 12—15.)   Christ also in describing the last judgment, uses the term " ever-lasting fire."—Matth. xxv. 41.

part of the chapter from which the above citations are made. In the parable of the ten virgins—referrible as it is to ancient Eastern customs*—the five wise go in with the bridegroom, while the five foolish are shut out. In the parable which follows of a man going abroad, and entrusting his property to his servants, the faithful servant is invited to the joy of his lord on his return, but the unprofitable servant is cast into outer darkness to weep, wail, and gnash his teeth. The moral, after the former of these parables, is,—" Watch, therefore, for *ye* know neither the day nor the hour wherein the Son of man cometh." And the instruction, drawn from the latter, is that already noticed,—that " when the Son of man shall come in his glory, and all the holy angels with him, then shall he sit upon the throne of his glory." Again : the words in which both parables are introduced are—" Then shall the kingdom of heaven be likened" &c. ; and " The kingdom of heaven is as a man travelling" &c.† These are facts which, not only show that Christ was to divide the population of the world into two classes—the point now under immediate consideration—but also indubitably prove that the contents of this chapter are a continuation of the prophetical discourse of the foregoing, in which it has been demonstrated that Christ predicts the End of the World and the Last Day of Judgment, as events inevitable during the then existent generation of men.

Section III.—Christ taught that, at the end of the world, he would set up the Kingdom of Heaven, which was to be of a Secular nature, and, by no means, what is now called the Gospel Dispensation.

Christ prophesied that at the end of the world he should establish a universal kingdom, in which he should reign eternally over what he calls " the elect." Indeed, he represents this as the chief object of his coming on the clouds of heaven. For this purpose the world was to be destroyed, and a new one created. These facts, as already intimated, are evident from the words of Christ himself on a great number of occasions. Nor is it less clear, from the Acts and the Epistles, that, after his death, the Christians, in the Apostolic age, lived in daily expectation of his coming to destroy the world, and establish this kingdom, into which they were to be received, and thus saved from the catastrophe that would befall mankind generally, when the earth would be in flames. Before this event, however, they were, as we have seen, to be " caught up into the air to meet the Lord." In order to demonstrate the fact that Christ foretold that, when he should come to destroy the world, he should also establish a kingdom of this kind, no better or fairer mode can be pursued than to lay before the reader all the principal passages in the Gospels, wherein Christ is represented to have used the expressions " kingdom of heaven," " kingdom of

---

* See Ward's View of the Hindoos, vol. ii. pp. 171, 173. Forbes's Oriental Memoirs, vol. iii. p. 53. Clarke's Travels, vol. iii. p. 200. Agreement of Customs between East Indians and Jews, Art. xvii. p. 78.
† Matth. xxv. 1—30.

God," and the like, in the order they occur, but classified, and accompanied with necessary explanations. Thus will Christ be made to speak for himself, and the reader placed in a position to judge of his veracity as a prophet, and his wisdom as a God, so as to decide whether he has any claim whatever either to the former or the latter. Antecedently, however, a few remarks on the meaning of the word *kingdom*, as used by Christ, may not be amiss.

The word "kingdom" (βασιλεια) is from the word "king" (βασιλευς) and signifies the dominion or territory of a king; royalty,—royal power. It is used, in Matthew, to denote "all the kingdoms of the world" (πασας τας βασιλειας του κοσμου) which, it is said the devil, conditionally, offered Christ, within a few sentences to that in which he himself uses it, in connection with the word "heaven" (βασιλεια των ουρανων).* It is also used by Christ himself for the kingdom a certain nobleman had gone to receive.† In both the above instances, the word "kingdom" clearly means an earthly dominion. In this sense, doubtless, the Jews understood the word; for we *have no proof* that they had any notion of any other than an *earthly* kingdom before the time of Christ. On the contrary, *we have*, throughout the Gospels, *ample proof* that they had no idea of any other kingdom. Is it reasonable, then, to suppose that Christ so far departed from the *usus loquendi* of the time, as to employ the word in an unknown sense? Can Christians judge him to have been so cruel as to have spoken to his hearers in words which they did not understand, and therefore could not obey? Neither the word *empire*, nor any other word synonymous with it was then in use, as signifying a greater extent of territory than a kingdom, as at present. *Kingdom* was the word then most extensive in meaning, with regard to territorial domains. The term "heaven" (ουρανος) did not, in ancient times, signify a spiritual world; but rather the aerial regions,‡ where the clouds, the birds, &c. are seen, and where the heathen thought the sun, moon, stars, and the Gods resided. In this sense it is also used in the New Testament; nor is there any conclusive proof that it is there, even once used to denote a world or state of existence purely spiritual. In the same sense precisely as the heathen used it, is the word employed in the New Testament. Christ speaks of the "birds of heaven," (πετεινα του ουρανου) which words are

---

* Matth. iv. 8, 17.   † Luke xix. 12, 15.

‡ Ουρανος is clearly derived from ουρα, which is again from ορα,—a boundary, or extremity. Aristotle (De Mundo) says—Ουρανον ετυμως καλουμεν απο του ουρον ειναι των ανω. It is remarkable that Peter, in preaching at the Pentecostal feast, says, —"David is not ascended into the heavens."—ου γαρ Δαβιδ ανεβη εις τους ουρανους —(Acts ii. 34) by which he evidently means that he had not, like Enoch, Elias, and Christ, ascended into the air—the heaven of the hero-gods,—but "slept with his fathers and was buried in the city of David"; (1 Kings ii. 10. Acts ii. 29) for he speaks of his *non-ascension* in direct contra-distinction with Christ's *ascension.* Hence, we never hear of David, after his death, making his appearance, like Elias, Moses, (whom the Lord buried) and Christ. Peter speaks of Christ's resurrection and ascension, as a recompense to David for not having been taken bodily into heaven. He says that David, who was a prophet, was buried; but that God made a promise to him that of the fruit of his loins he would raise up Christ to sit on his throne. (ver. 29, 30.) As already intimated, it is questionable whether the Hebrews had any distinct notion of the existence of a soul separate from the body. (See Eccl. iii. 19—21.) Like other nations, they imagined a Tophet and an Elysium,—a kind of underground abodes for the spirits of the dead.

translated in our version, "the fowls of the air."* Again, in reference to the weather, he speaks of discerning the face of *heaven*, the last of which words, (ουρανος) in the English version, is rendered *sky*.† In like manner, speaking of himself, he says, in several places, that the Son of man should be seen coming in the clouds of heaven, in immediate connection with his predictions of the end of the world.‡ So also, James says, the heaven (ουρανος) gave rain and the earth produced fruit.§ These instances leave no doubt that Christ and his apostles, by the word "heaven" meant,—not a spiritual world,—but, in common with the heathens, the aerial regions. Accordingly, Paul expected that, at the appearance of Christ, he and others of his contemporaries would be caught up in the clouds to meet him in the *air*.|| The more ancient Hebrews entertained the same notion of a material heaven. We read that God placed the sun and moon in the firmament of the heaven; (ם׳מש) and we learn that all creation was supposed to be included in "the heaven and the earth."¶ In this heaven of clouds, air, stars, moon, and sun, God·and the holy angels were supposed to reside.†† From this heaven Christ had descended, and hither he ascended, after his resurrection from the dead.‡‡ Such is the heaven of the Bible, and such the heaven spoken of by Christ. His kingdom he frequently called "the kingdom of heaven," either because he was to come from the aerial regions to establish it, or because the new heaven and the new earth which— in imitation of the present earth, with its circumambient expanse and visible celestial luminaries—he was to create, were to be *fixed* in space— which he regarded as the then existing heaven—and were to be the terri- tories in which he was to reign. Be this as it may, it is clear that the same thing is meant in the New Testament, by *the kingdom of heaven*, as by *the kingdom of God*. (βασιλεια του Θεου) The phrase *kingdom of heaven* is, with few exceptions, peculiar to the gospel of Matthew. In the other gospels we almost invariably meet with "the kingdom of God." But since one evangelist uses the phrase, "kingdom of God," and another "the kingdom of heaven," in narrating precisely the same parables, and other discourses of Christ, in a vast number of instances,§§ it is beyond doubt that both expressions are designed to signify exactly the same thing.

The following is the first mention we find made in the Gospels of the kingdom of heaven.—John the Baptist preaches in the wilderness of Judea that "the kingdom of heaven is at hand."|||| That John meant the kingdom that Christ was to establish at the end of the world will appear, not only from the import of parallel passages hereafter to be adduced, but likewise from his own words—that Christ, who was to come after him, would baptise with *fire*, gather the wheat into the garner, and *burn* the chaff with unquenchable fire.¶¶ Again: Christ makes his *debut* as a public teacher, proclaiming the near approach of the same event.—Matthew tells us that "Jesus began to preach and to say—Repent, for the kingdom

---

* Matth. vi. 26 ; viii. 20.   † Luke xii. 56.
‡ Matth. xxiv. 30 ; xxvi. 64.   § James v. 18. || 1 Thess. iv. 17.
¶ Gen. i. 15—17 ; 1.   †† Matth. vi. 1. Mark xiii. 32.
‡‡ John vi. 38. Luke xxiv. 51.
§§ The passages about to be cited will enable the reader to compare the Evangelists on this point.
|||| Matth. iii. 2.   ¶¶ ver. 11, 12.

of *heaven* is at hand." Mark informs us "that after John was put in prison, Jesus came into Galilee, preaching the gospel of the kingdom of *God*, and saying,—The time is fulfilled, and the kingdom of *God* is at hand."* Jesus, like John, begins his public career by preaching that this kingdom is at hand. This appears to be the burden—the very essence— of the mission of each. But if this kingdom had by Christ been understood to be spiritual; in other words, to be the Dispensation of the Gospel, as Christian divines tell us it was, he could not, in any possible sense, *after* it had been preached by John, and *when* it was then being preached by himself, say that it was *at hand*, or *to come*; for in that case it would then *have* actually come. Such expression, however, naturally applied to the kingdom which he would make his hearers believe he was going to establish. Of *this* he might say that it was *at hand*. It is not here forgotten that the word εγγιζω which, in the above passages is fairly rendered—"is at hand"—signifies the nearness of a place, as well as of time; as,—"he was come nigh (εγγιζειν) unto Jericho."† But in the instances cited of the word employed in connexion with *kingdom*, the idea of proximity to a *place* can, by no means, be supposed to be implied. It would be highly absurd to say, or write that a *kingdom travelled* about, and *approached a place*. The meaning of the words under notice evidently is that the *time* for establishing the kingdom of heaven *was at hand*.

Christ's sermon on the mount is replete with the doctrine of his *reign*, and the treatment of those who should be admitted into his kingdom. It commences with blessing the poor in spirit whose was "the kingdom of heaven."‡—The persecuted were to be admitted into "the kingdom of heaven."—Whoever broke the least of the commandments was to be called "the least in the kingdom of heaven,"§—Righteousness exceeding that of the Scribes and Pharisees was required to entitle admission into "the kingdom of heaven;"¶ and instruction is given to pray that this kingdom should come;—"Thy kingom come."†† This injunction to pray for its coming shows it was a thing to be expected, and utterly destroys the idea that this kingdom is the *gospel* dispensation, under which we are now said to live. The words "thine is the kingdom, the power, and the glory," in this formale of prayer, carry in them the same idea. In this sermon also, it is inculcated to take no thought of the necessaries of life, but to seek first "the kingdom of God." We are told that not every one who should say to Christ, "Lord, Lord," should enter "the kingdom of heaven;" for many would say unto him *in that day*, "Lord, Lord," we have prophesied, cast out devils, and done many wonderful works in thy name; but then he would profess unto them he never knew them, and would tell those that worked iniquity to depart from him.‡‡ Such is a sample of the doctrine of this *kingdom*, which pervades Christ's sermon. The last passage cited, proves most conclusively that the phrase "kingdom of heaven" does not mean the Gospel Dispensation, but that it points to the

---

* Matth. iv. 17. Mark i. 14, 15.
† Luke xviii. 35.—The adverb εγγυς however, is most frequently employed with an applicable verb, in the Gospels, to denote proximity of space. See John iii. 23; vi. 19, 23; xi. 18, 54. Acts xi. 38; xxvii. 8; *et al. loc.*
‡ Matth. v. 3. Luke vi. 20.   § Matth. v. 10, 19.   ¶ ver. 20. Luke xi. 2.
†† Matth. vi. 10—13 and ver. 25—34.   ‡‡ Matth. vii. 21—23.

expected Day of Judgment and the End of the World, when Christ was to establish this kingdom, which in this passage, as well as in a great many other places in the Gospels, is represented as having an entrance that could be closed up, the keys of which entrance were to be given to Peter.* The expression—" many *will* say to me *in that day*"—in the passage just cited, one would think must be sufficiently clear and pointed to convince the most obtuse that, at a *future period*, application was to be made for admission into this kingdom; and that, therefore, Christ did not mean by it, what is now understood by the *Gospel Dispensation*.

Jesus, in commenting upon the faith of the centurion, says—" Many shall come from the east, and west, and shall sit down with Abraham, Isaac, and Jacob, in the kingdom of heaven : but the children of the kingdom shall be cast into outer darkness."† We have words precisely of the same import in Luke, apparently spoken by Christ on another occasion. The context of these throws much light upon the meaning of the passage just cited from Matthew, and puts the import of the " kingdom of heaven" in a very clear light.—" Then said one unto him, Lord, are there few that be saved ?‡ And he said unto them, Strive to enter in at the strait gate, for many, I say unto you, will seek to enter in, and shall not be able. When once the master of the house is risen up, and hath shut to the door, and ye begin to stand without, and to knock at the door, saying, Lord, Lord, open unto us ; and he shall answer and say unto you, I know you not whence ye are ; then shall ye begin to say, We have eaten and drunk in thy presence, and thou hast taught in our streets. But he shall say, I tell you I know you not whence ye are ; depart from me, all ye workers of iniquity. There shall be weeping, and gnashing of teeth ; when ye shall see Abraham, and Isaac, and Jacob, and all the prophets in the *kingdom of God,* and you yourselves thrust out. And they shall come from the east, and from the west, and from the north, and from the south, and shall sit down in *the kingdom of God.* And, behold, there are last which shall be first, and there are first which shall be last."§ In both the foregoing passages Christ insinuates that those Jews who—although, in common with the rest of the nation, believed that the end of the world would soon take place, and a universal kingdom of bliss (a kind of golden age) be established, yet did not believe that Christ was the personage who was to establish this kingdom—would be excluded and left to perish in the universal destruction of the inhabitants of the earth. These, although the children of the kingdom—the descendants of Abraham— were to be shut out, and cast into outer darkness ; while, however, others from the four quarters of the world were to be admitted.‖

This description is not that of a partial or local kingdom, nor of one which *then* existed, but of a universal one which was to " come." The

---

* In passages hereafter cited, this notion will be more clearly seen to be entertained by Christ. See the strait gate.—Matth. vii. 13, 14 ; but particularly, Luke xiii. 23—30. Matth. xvi. 19.　　† Matth. viii. 11, 12.

‡ " Save" " salvation" &c. will, in the sequel, be seen to mean nothing else than being received into Christ's kingdom, instead of being left to perish in the general conflagration of the world when being destroyed.

§ Luke xiii. 23—30.

‖ Agreeably to this he says, in another place, that the kingdom of God should be taken from the Jews, and given to another nation that brought forth fruit.—Matth. xxi. 43.

enumeration of the four quarters of the globe identifies the whole with what Christ, in another place,* when positively predicting the end of the world, says about gathering the elect from the four winds. Abram, Isaac, Jacob, and the prophets were to be in this kingdom ; which would indicate that, before it was to be established, there was to be a resurrection,—just as we have shown in preceding sections.

Jesus, having chosen his twelve apostles, tells them to go and preach that *the kingdom of heaven was at hand;* and in the charge he delivers them, he says that " in the day of judgment" it should be more tolerable for the land of Sodom and Gomorrha than for that city that would not receive and hear them. To this he adds that they should not go over all the cities of Israel before the Son of man came.† In like manner, when he sends forth seventy other apostles, he tells them to go their ways, heal-ing the sick, and saying to them—"The kingdom of God is come nigh unto you."‡ When we find that he sends his apostles thus to preach that " the kingdom of heaven is at hand," and, at the same time, avers to them both that those who would not receive them should, " in the day of judgment" be visited with punishment, and that, before they were gone over all the cities of Israel, the Son of man should *come,* what can we make of such expressions as these? We have already ascertained what is meant by the *coming* of the Son of man, and have also seen that the day of judgment was to arrive during the *then existent* generation of men. The conclusion, therefore, is inevitable,—that, in saying that *the kingdom of heaven was at hand,* Christ meant that he should very shortly set up a kingdom in which he was to reign.

Of John the Baptist, Christ says that, although a greater prophet than he had never risen, yet that the least in the kingdom of heaven was greater than John.§ The meaning of this passage which has baffled the ingenuity of all commentators, whose views of it are as conflicting as they are numerous, is clear, if we apply it to the idea of the kingdom that Christ was then about to establish. Jesus, having pronounced John " a prophet" —" yea much more than a prophet," adds,—" among those that are born of women there is not a greater prophet than John the Baptist ; *but he that is least in the kingdom of God is greater than he.*"—That is, although John is great, yet his greatness is comparatively nothing to the greatness of those who are to be admitted into the kingdom of heaven. The *least,* in greatness of those in that kingdom will be greater than John is in this world. It is by no means meant, in this passage, that the degree of great-ness possessed by the least in the kingdom of heaven, would be higher than that possessed by John, in the same kingdom ; but what is meant is, that the least eminent individual subject of that kingdom would be more eminent than John was, as a prophet among the inhabitants of Judea. Nor is there an intimation here that John was not to be admitted into that kingdom, and even to occupy a much higher position, not only than he occupied in the deserts of Palestine, as proclaimer of the *coming* of this kingdom, but higher than many of the subjects of this kingdom. Christ, as it is clear from his words on several occasions, would make his hearers

* Matth. xxiv. 31. † Matth. x. 1—23. ‡ Luke x. 1—9.
§ Matth. xi. 11. Luke vii. 28.

believe that there should be degrees, in rank and dignity, in *his* kingdom, like those in other kingdoms. Hence, he speaks of the "*least* in the kingdom of heaven." It might, possibly, be objected that the present tense of the verb—*to be* is employed in the passage under consideration, and that the words are—"*is* least," not *will be* least; and therefore cannot have been intended to have a future reference, but must mean the present Dispensation of the Gospel, which had begun when Christ spoke these words. But it is to be observed that the Greek verb, rendered *is*, in our version, does not warrant this conclusion.* In the New Testament, as

---

* As Christians have failed to explain this passage themselves, and as several of their most learned commentators, after writing pages upon it, admit—not so much from their inability as scholars, as from their attempts to make it prove what they wish it to mean—that is difficult to be interpreted, it is worth while, on the part of Freethought, to take some pains in explaining it for them. The Greek text of the difficult part, as it is found in Wetstein, the most generally received version, is as follows:—Ο δε μικροτερος εν τη βασιλεια των ουρανων μειζων αυτου εστιν. Much has been said by commentators about μικροτερος being in the comparative degree instead of the superlative, into which it is translated. But there is no great obstacle raised by this. The idiom of the Greek language is such that an adjective can be used, elliptically, in the comparative degree with greater elegance than in the superlative, while the sense of the latter is fully conveyed. Such can be rendered into English in either the comparative or superlative degree. For example—μικροτερος εστι παντων των σπερματων can be rendered either *smallest of* all the seeds, or *smaller than* all (or any of) the seeds.—(Matth. xiii. 32.) Hence the English translators, while in this place they translate the words just cited, *the least of all seeds*, and—μειζον των λαχανων—*the greatest among herbs*; still in another place, (Mark iv. 31, 32) render the same words—μικροτερος παντων των σπερματων and παντων των λαχανων μειζων into *less than all the seeds*, and *greater than all herbs*. In like manner, τις αρα μειζων εστιν εν τη βασιλεια των ουρανων;—who is greater; that is, greater *than* others, or greater than *all* others, in the kingdom of heaven?—(Matt. xviii. 1.) or if it is wished, who is *the greatest?* The writers of the New Testament very frequently use the comparative degree of the adjective where an English writer would use the superlative.—See John x. 29. 1 Cor. xiii. 13; xv. 19; *et alia* So also did the classic writers. —Χαλεπωτερον δε παντων, which may be translated either "the hardest of all," or "harder than all."—Anac. od 46, line 3. See also Herodotus. lib. 1. c. 26. So the expression of Christ, just cited, regarding John may be rendered, either "he that is less" (than all others understood) or "he that is the least (of all others) is greater than he." As to the verb ειμι, (*I am*) in this expression, being in the present tense, εστιν (*is*) there are numerous instances of this verb, as well as many other Greek verbs, used in the present tense, when futurity is understood and clearly meant. There is evidently reference to the future in the verbs of the following passages, both in the Greek and English, although the *aorist* is employed in most of those of the former language.—"Except ye be converted and become as little children, ye shall not enter into the kingdom of heaven. Whosoever, therefore, shall humble himself as this little child, the same is greatest in the kingdom of heaven.—Matth. xviii, 3, 4.—Ειμι here clearly has a future signification. So has γινομαι in the following passage—"In the resurrection, whose wife is she of them?" Luke xx. 33. Besides, ειμι in the passage under notice is influenced by the genitive case of the pronoun αυτος,—μειζων αυτου εστιν—which gives it a possessive signification. Parkhurst, on the verb ειμι, makes the following remarks.—"With a genitive case, it denotes possession or property—Matth. vi. 13—σου εστιν, of thee is; i. e. thine. So with a dative—Luke ix. 13—ουκ εισιν ημιν, there are not to us." Parkhurst produces several other instances, which see.

We have most remarkable instances of the verb ειμι denoting possession when with the word τοιουτος in the genitive case; such as—των τοιουτων εστιν η βασιλεια των ουρανων—translated into English, "of such is the kingdom of heaven."—Matth. xix. 14. Mark x. 14. Luke xviii. 16. Here, for want of a word implying possession, there is in the English no sense. Expositors, in a very far-fetched manner, have attempted an explanation. In the Welsh version of the Bible, admitted to be the best of all translations, owing to the similarity of construction between that language and the

well as in other Greek productions, it is frequently employed indefinitely as to time, and even sometimes in reference to the future. Besides: the verb *to be*, in this passage, is connected with a genitive case, which makes it have an idea of possession. These facts utterly destroy the notion that here, the form of the present tense, in connexion with the words "kingdom of heaven," shows this kingdom to be the Dispensation of the Gospel, which, at the time the expression was uttered, is said to exist.

This kingdom is further mentioned in connection with the Baptist. It is said, that "from the days of John the Baptist until now the kingdom of heaven suffereth violence, and the violent take it by force." According to Luke, the expression is—"Since that time (of John) the kingdom of heaven is preached, and every man presseth into it.* The same word is

Hebrew and Greek, the above passage is rendered—"eiddo y cyfryw rai yw teyrnas nefoedd." Literally translated—"the possession of such as they, is the kingdom of heaven." But there is no word in the English language which, precisely conveying the meaning of "eiddo," can be used with any degree of smoothness of composition immediately before "such." The English words into which lexicographers render it, are "one's own, possession, chattels." The words *mine*, *thine*, *his*, &c., if they were, like it, substantives, would take its place in a translation. Probably the translators of the English version felt this difficulty, and, for want of a better word, substituted "of," which by no means conveys the meaning of the idiomatic sentence just cited. Nor is the Latin "talis" a much better word.

In the following passage the verb and the pronoun are exactly in the same relative position as in that where John is said to be least in the kingdom of heaven.—Οτι αυτων εστιν η βασιλεια των ουρανων—translated "*theirs* is the kingdom of heaven." But there is no word synonymous to "theirs" here, any more than in the passage regarding John. The pronoun αυτος is in both, not σφετερος (their or theirs.) Αυτος in itself, when not connected with ειμι, is not a possessive pronoun, and has no possessive signification. It means simply, *he*, *she*, *it*, or *himself*, &c.; or with a prepositive article, *the same*. When used in the possessive case, it means only *of him*, &c. Why then is the one phrase translated "*than he*" (Matth. xi. 11.) and the other "*theirs*" ? (Matth. v. 3.) A far better translation of the latter passage would be—"to them belongs the kingdom of heaven," or "they are possessed of the kingdom of heaven." Much more in analogy with similar idiomatic expressions would even be "of them is the kingdom of heaven." All these would, more or less, permit the verb ειμι to retain the idea of possession. It is true that in the latter passage, cited from Matthew, this sense is retained by the pronoun theirs, and that a similar sense is given by the translators to almost all other passages where ειμι with a noun or pronoun in the possessive case occurs, agreeably to the meaning given to verbs in this position by Parkhurst and most other lexicographers. But the question still revolves,—why not have given it this sense in the passage which relates to the position of John in the kingdom of heaven? In order that the candid reader may perceive the idiomatic similarity of the two passages, now compared, they are here placed side by side—

Οτι αυτων εστιν η βασιλεια των ουρανων—Matth. v. 3.

Ο δε μικροτερος εν τη βασιλεια των ουρανων, μειζων αυτου εστιν—Matth. xi. 11.

Now it will be seen that the verb ειμι and the relative pronoun αυτος are in the same relative position in both the above expressions. It is not very clear, however, what induced the translators to refuse the latter the idea of possession, to which the verb ειμι was entitled in both instances.

Granting to the verb ειμι here a future reference and a sense of possession, both which it has been shown to have, then the passage reads,—the least in the kingdom of heaven shall be possessed of more greatness than John is possessed of. This clears the expression of all the theological difficulties which are usually imagined to surround it.

* Compare Matth. xi. 12; and Luke xvi. 16. The words—"From the days of John the Baptist until now," furnish one of the many proofs which exist of the comparatively late origin of the Gospels. Jesus cannot have uttered these words. They are put in his mouth by the writers of these Gospels. For in the same chapter as these occur, we

used, in the Greek text, for "suffereth violence," as for "presseth"; namely, the noun βιαιος and its derivative verb βιαζω, meaning *force*, and *to force :* and, for "take it by force," in the former passage, we have in the original the verb αρπαζω,* which means *to seize upon, snatch, take by force, invade.* But giving the English version its full meaning, to what can the words—in accordance with common sense—refer, but to a kingdom to which there belonged a king and subjects? Supposing the Gospel Dispensation was meant here, how could that be taken by force, or pressed into? These expressions are quite applicable, however, to an earthly kingdom, which is often said to be taken by force by one person from another, who is its monarch. The obvious meaning of the words is, that there were persons who tried to usurp the kingdom of which Christ was to be the king; and this idea is borne out by the words of Christ on a great number of occasions. The foregoing passages, being usually adduced by Christians to show that the kingdom of heaven means the Gospel Dispensation, or the Church upon earth, have been dwelt upon more largely than they otherwise would, and than their real merits are entitled to.

The next place where we meet with the *kingdom of heaven* in the Gospels, is in some of Christ's parables. In the parable of the sower,† if while we examine it, we put off our "theological spectacles," we shall see that Christ's comparison of the kingdom of heaven does by no means imply the idea of a spiritual kingdom. As a reason for teaching in parables, he tells his disciples that it was given only to them "to know the mysteries of the kingdom of heaven"; and in his explanation of the same parable, he speaks of "the word (λογος) of the kingdom," meaning nothing more than the doctrine of, or discourses about the kingdom of heaven. In the next parable—that of the tares—just as in the foregoing, he describes the difference in those who believed the doctrine of the kingdom, which was to be established in connection with the last judgment and the destruction of the world, saying—"the kingdom of heaven is likened unto a man which sowed good seed in his field," &c.‡ In his explanation of this parable he says that the sower is the Son of man; the good seed is the children of the kingdom; the tares, the children of the wicked; the harvest, the end of the world; the reapers, the angels. "The tares are gathered and burned in the fire; so shall it be in the end of this world. The Son of man shall send forth his angels and they shall gather out of his kingdom all things that offend, and them which do iniquity; and shall cast them into a furnace of fire. There shall be wailing and gnashing of teeth. Then shall the righteous shine forth as the sun in the kingdom of their Father."§ This parable cannot, by any fair mode of criticism, be

read that John was now alive, and sending his disciples to Jesus. Jesus, therefore, would never have said,—"From the days of John the Baptist until *now*," when John's days had not terminated. Before these words can have any meaning, they must be admitted to have been used many years (perhaps some centuries) after the death of John.
* The same verb is employed to designate the intention of the multitude to take Jesus by force and make him a king.—John vi. 15. See also Matth. xiii. 19. John x. 12, 28, 29. Acts viii. 39; xxiii. 10. 2 Cor. xii. 2. Jude 23.
† Matth. xiii. 3—30. Mark iv. Luke viii.
‡ Matth. xiii. 24—30, 36—43. Read the parable and its striking explanation by Christ himself.
§ Matt. xiii. 40—43.

made to signify a spiritual kingdom. Here is precisely the same description given of the end of the world, as that given in other places, already noticed, where it has been shown that the last judgment and the end of the world were to take place during the life-time of the generation of men contemporary with Christ. Here, as in chapters xxiv and xxv of Matthew, are described the two classes into which mankind were to be divided—the one to be admitted into the kingdom to be established, the other to be cast into a furnace of fire ; here are the angels to gather mankind together ; and here is the end of the world mentioned as to take place before the righteous should "shine forth in the kingdom." There cannot be more conclusive evidence than is afforded by this parable, that the kingdom of heaven was regarded as a thing to be established at the end of the world.

Again : the parables which, in the same chapter, compare the kingdom of heaven to a grain of mustard seed, leaven, hidden treasure, a merchant-man, a net—all of them convey the idea of a secular kingdom to be set up at the end of the present system of nature.* Of the " net cast into the sea, and gathered of every kind," Christ says,—" which when it was full they drew to the shore, and sat down and gathered the good into vessels, but cast the bad away." Then he adds,—" so shall it be at the end of the world ; the angels shall come forth and sever the wicked from among the just, and shall cast them into the furnace of fire. There shall be wailing and gnashing of teeth." The idea set forth here, as well as in the parables of the sower and of the tares, is that all sorts of men, good and bad, came forward, now that he was proclaiming the news of the blissful kingdom to be set up, and were anxious to have a guarantee for admission into it ; but that not all these should enter into it ; for the angels would separate those that were worthy from those that were not. The parables of the mustard seed and of the leaven are intended simply to show the greatness in number, of those to be admitted into this kingdom : that of the merchant and his pearl which he sells to buy a field, has reference to the custom, then and long afterwards prevalent, for people who became candidates for admission into to the kingdom of heaven to sell their property, and give the produce to the leaders in the Christian cause, such as the Apostles and others.† The comparison of the kingdom of heaven to a king reckoning with his servants,‡ is evidently intended to persuade the disciples to agree with, and forgive one another. This is inculcated by an intimation that if they did not do so they should, like the unforgiving servant of the king in the parable, be *delivered to the tormentors*, instead of being admitted into the kingdom of heaven.

The disciples of Jesus, whose words show that they had understood him to mean a secular kingdom, on one occasion asked him,—" Who is the the greatest in the kingdom of heaven ?" Jesus calling to him a little child, tells them,—" Except ye be converted, and become as little children, ye

---

* Matth. xiii. 31 —33, 44—50. See also Mark iv. Luke xiii.

† Just as Joses did. Ananias and Sapphira managed their affair badly.—Acts iv. 34 —37; vi. 11. This subject will be treated in the sequel. Did the restrictions under which this Essay is written permit, to show the late date at which these parables were written would render their meaning more lucid.

‡ Matth. xviii. 23—35.

shall not enter the kingdom of heaven."* Without insisting here upon the fact that, in the question of the disciples, the word *is*—translated from *εστιν*—although in the present tense in the English version, yet in the original is with a dative case, and therefore has (as we have seen it has with a genitive case) a future and possessive meaning,† and here implies possession of the kingdom :—without insisting upon this, we say, Christ's answer evidently proves that the kingdom of heaven was a thing to be entered into *in future*. He tells them—" ye *shall* not *enter* the kingdom of heaven." Here it is clearly implied, that, although the disciples, nearly since the commencement of Christ's ministry, had been under what Christians call the Gospel Dispensation, yet when Christ spoke these words they had not entered the kingdom of heaven. This was a state afterwards to be entered. Luke, apparently relating the same words of Christ, throws much light upon them, and settles the question, beyond a doubt, that Christ meant a secular kingdom. After a few words, touching the strife among his disciples as to who should be accounted greatest, Christ adds,—" I appoint unto you a kingdom, as my Father hath appointed unto me, that ye may eat and drink at my table in my kingdom, and sit on thrones judging the twelve tribes of Israel."‡

Christ has a very singular expression regarding eunuchs. But singular as it is, it proves his kingdom to be secular, as strongly as anything that could be said. In enumerating the several sorts, he says—" there be eunuchs which have made themselves eunuchs for the kingdom of heaven's sake."§ An eunuch is a man either naturally or made *impotent*. Such in ancient times were, and indeed are to this day, among oriental nations, usually advanced to the highest offices in the palaces and courts of kings. They were a kind of lords-chamberlain or lords of the bed-chamber. The meaning of the word is one deprived of cohabitation—(*ευνουχος,*—*ευνις* deprived ; and *οχειας,* cohabitation.) Hence eunuchs had anciently, in eastern countries, the charge of the bed-chamber and the care of the women in the palaces of princes, as they have to this day. The Turkish grand-seignior still employs eunuchs to attend his harem. ‖ As such, they had

---

* Matth. xviii. 1—3. † Vide Note, pp. 77, 78, and Parkhurst Greek Lex. infra *ειμι*.

‡ Luke xxii. 24—29. Jesus does not attempt at correcting any misconception of his disciples regarding the nature of his kingdom,—does not utter a word here to teach them that it was a spiritual one—that it was the gospel dispensation—that it had already been established on earth—and that they were already within that kingdom ; but takes up the notion of his disciples as perfectly correct, and promises to them that, in due time, they should (even Judas apparently included) have admission into his kingdom, and in this kingdom should eat and drink and sit on thrones ! Nor is it likely that his disciples who had so frequently heard him describing the kingdom of heaven—the principal topic of his discourses—who, of all people, had the best possible opportunity of ascertaining the precise meaning of the words he used, and who themselves were to preach the near approach of this kingdom, should have misunderstood what he meant by the phrase—*kingdom of heaven.* Besides, the language which he repeatedly uses in describing this kingdom is so positive, precise, and clear, that even a stranger to him and his doctrines could not fail to understand him. The apology that the disciples were mistaken is a shift of Christian divines to meet a desperate case.

§ Matth. xix. 12.

‖ "Eunuchu vocari quód testes quidem fuissent castrati, sed non nervus." Consequently, it would seem that eunuchs were sometimes allowed to marry; for it would appear that Potiphar had a wife who fell in love with Joseph. (Gen. xxxix. 7—20.) So also in more

other high offices and great authority in eastern states. Such was occupied by Potiphar, an officer of Pharaoh, as the meaning of the Hebrew word סריס (sairis) which is rendered ευνουχος by the LXX clearly shows.[*] Such were the seven chamberlains of king Ahasuerus;[†] such the sons of Hezekiah in the palace of the king of Babylon;[‡] such the eunuchs which Isaiah calls blessed;[§] such the eunuchs in king Zedekiah's house;[||] such those in the house of Nebuchadnezzar;[¶] and such the eunuch under Queen Candace, whom Philip baptized.[††] All these eunuchs occupied the highest positions in the courts and palaces of their respective princes. Hence it will be seen why eunuchs, as Christ says, had "made themselves eunuchs for the kingdom of heaven's sake." They had made themselves eunuchs in expectation, thereby, to obtain offices of rank in the present life, and in the secular kingdom that Christ was to establish. Than this nothing can be more obvious. Christ, here, in his discourse on adultery, does not, however, say one word in disapprobation of this inhuman practice, but the tenour of his remarks goes to sanction it rather than otherwise [‡‡]

When little children were brought to Christ, he said—"Of such is the

---

modern times. In Tonquin they had wives. (Dampier's Voyages; Salmon's Geograph. Gram. p. 461.) Dow, in his History of Hindostan, says that Caffoor, although an eunuch, had married one of the Sultanas. (Crit. Rev. Oct. 1768. p. 243.) Niebuhr, in his Description de l'Arabie, p. 71, speaks of an eunuch who had made a voyage with him and his companions from Suez to Jambo, as having several female slaves destined to his pleasures, one of whom was treated like a great lady. He also mentions a rich eunuch at Basra who had his harem. Habesci, in his State of the Ottoman Empire, says, that the eunuchs among the Turks are allowed to marry, and that some of them have several wives. (p. 106.) See Parkhurst's Heb. Lex. infra סריס, whence much of the foregoing matter about eunuchs is abstracted.

Should any delicate Christians complain that their sense of decency is wounded by the language used here to describe eunuchs, they are reminded that it is only the language of Holy Writ, which, according to their own belief, cannot in any manner be at fault, and which they are commanded to read, or rather to *search*. It is further submitted as an apology, that the language of Scripture in regard to eunuchs, here commented upon, is not nearly so indelicate as that of Divine Inspiration in many other places; such for example as the following:—Gen. ix. 21, 22; xxx. 1—5; xxxi. 33—35; xxxv. 22; xxxix. 7—20; xxxviii. 1—3, 13—30; xix. 30—36; xxxiv. 1—5. 2 Sam. xiii. 10—14; xvi. 21, 22. Ruth iii. 3—11. Ezek. iv. 12—15; xvi. 15, 16; xxiii. 3—23; and many others, which *wicked* infidels point out in the holy book, and of which they say that if our legislators, who are now-a-day making laws against obscene prints, were to enact a law, prohibiting youths and females to read such passages as these found in the Bible, which they say are more obscene than any prints exhibited in London, or elsewhere, they would thereby materially ameliorate the moral condition of the age. It is true, that no Christian of common decency ever presumes to read the above and the like portions of Scripture to his wife, sons, or daughters, however strong his faith may be that the *whole* Bible is a Divine Book.

[*] Gen. xxxvi. 36; xxxix. 1; xl. 2.   [†] Esth. i. 10; ii. 3, 14.   [‡] 2 Kings xx. 18.

[§] Lvi. 3—5.   [||] Jer. xxxviii. 7.   [¶] Dan. i. 3.   [††] Acts viii. 27—39.

[‡‡] However revolting it may be to the feeling of this more enlightened age, bodily mutilation was evidently considered an act of piety among the early Christians as among the Jews who circumcised. Christ himself openly preached this doctrine. Hence his precepts —"If thy right eye offend thee, pluck it out;"—"If thy right hand offend thee, cut it off," &c. (Matth. v. 29, 30.),—precepts which there is not the slightest ground to allege that they were intended to be understood in any other sense than literal. Accordingly, we find it the practice of the Ascetics, in the second century, to mortify their flesh or bodies. (Mosh. Eccl. Hist. p. 310.) See much curious matter on this point in Gibbon's Decline and Fall, chap. xv. notes 91—100, and text.

kingdom of heaven."* It has already been observed† that in this instance, where the substantive verb εμι in connection with the pronoun τοιουτος is employed, a word denoting property or possession is to be understood. There is here evidently an ellipsis, which is of frequent occurrence in the New Testament writings; as for example in the case of the word παν, after which almost always such a word as χρημα, εργον, πραγμα, or some term of similar import, is understood, and is indeed supplied by the English translators by the word *thing*. But here they have not supplied the deficiency. If they had, the expression just cited, would read,—the *possession* of such is the kingdom of heaven. As already observed, the omission is supplied in the Welsh translation, and the phrase reads as just rendered.‡ What Christ means is, that the possession or heritage of such people as these little children were in harmlessness, was the kingdom of heaven. In other words, that people who were harmless, like these little children, should be admitted into the kingdom of heaven. But this by no means shows what commentators tell us, namely, that the claim of children was here shown by Christ to be in the church under the Gospel Dispensation, as they were under the Jewish economy. Should any one doubt that the words refer to a kingdom to be entered into in future, let him attend to Christ's own declaration, as reported by two of the evangelists just cited :—" Whosoever *shall* not receive the kingdom of God as a little child, *shall* not enter therein."

Again : in the parable of the vineyard,§ the comparison made of the kingdom of heaven shows that, in the time of Christ, it was a thing to " come." This is evidently implied in the equality with which the man who had only laboured one hour, and he who had laboured twelve, are treated ;—at the end of the world all were to be at once admitted into this kingdom. Besides, there is in the moral of this parable that doctrine which pervades almost all the discourses of Christ, namely,—that those who wished to be the highest or *first*, in this kingdom, should be the lowest or *last*. Such an expression as this can have no real meaning in reference to what is termed the *gospel dispensation ;* for Christ utters it touching the reward to be received by his followers. He further intimates that those whom he called to join him in his kingdom were many,—still that few of them would he choose‖—" many be called, but few chosen."†† How, therefore, can such an expression as this apply to the present Dispensation of the Gospel, without the most violent perversion of language ? Apply it to Christ choosing officers for the government of his kingdom, and the language is natural and proper.

The next mention of this kingdom occurs in connection with the aspiring request of Salome, the mother of Zebedee's children. This

---

* Matth. xix. 14. Mark x. 14. Luke xviii. 16.   † Vide Note, pp. 77, 78.   ‡ Ibid.
§ Matth. xx. 1—16.

‖ The literal and real meaning of the word—chosen (εκλεκτος) here, is to be elected out of many to some office or dignity. The LXX use the same word for *picked* or *chosen* soldiers. (Jud. xx. 16, 34. 1 Sam. xxiv. 2.) See also Josephus De Bell. Jud. lib. ii. cap. xvi. sec. 4. In this sense the Jews used the word in derisively calling Christ " the chosen of God"—chosen of God to be the king and deliverer of the Jews.—Luke xxiii. 35. And in the passage under notice, the word means those who should be chosen by Christ to posts of honour in his kingdom.

†† Matth. xx. 16.

venerable dame whose husband, apparently, was now dead, and whose two
sons, James and John, were disciples of Christ, came to him, making her
obeisance,—or according to the words of the evangelist, worshipping,—
and asking him the following favour :—" Grant that these my two sons
may sit, the one on thy right hand, and the other on the left in thy
kingdom."*   Mark, differing a little from Matthew, says that it was the
two young men themselves who made this very modest request.   However
about this, Jesus attempted to be spared the disagreeableness of giving a
directly negative answer, by asking the two aspirants to regal glory, if
they could drink the cup he should drink, and be baptized with the baptism
in the which he was baptized.   This, however, they boldly engaged to do,
saying—" we can."   Christ rejoiced by a promise that they should drink
of his cup, and be baptized with his baptism, but excused himself for not
promising them seats on each side of his throne, by saying that this distinction was not in his power to confer upon them,—that his Father retained
this honour to be bestowed upon those whom he thought proper.   The
other disciples, to whom thrones in the kingdom of heaven† had just been
promised, became jealous of this application, and " were moved with indignation against the two brethren."   Jesus, however, calls them to him, and to
allay their anger, tells them that princes and mighty men among the
Gentiles exercised undue authority and dominion over their subjects.
Among his disciples it should not be so ; but whoever attempted to be great
among them should have to be their servant.   Now, although it is beyond
all doubt that James, John, and their mother, as well as the other ten
disciples who had been promised thrones, thought that Christ's kingdom
was to be a *secular* one, yet Christ *does not by a single word correct their
mistake,* but simply refuses the preference which the two sons of Zebedee
wished to be given them.   Although one would think that since he wished
some pretext to put off the request of these two brothers, and since he
actually spoke of the difference between the *Gentile* kingdoms and the
one which he should establish, he could hardly avoid saying that his
kingdom was not of a *secular* nature, but that it consisted in having a
sanctifying power over men's souls in this world, and in being the source
of their bliss and the object of their homage and adoration in a spiritual
world, into which all would enter at death.   But *not a word* to this effect,
or in any manner which shows that his kingdom was not of a secular
nature, falls from his lips !   He, as a Jew, only shows the difference which
should exist in his kingdom from the kingdoms of the Gentiles.   In his,
there was not to be the tyranny and oppression which prevailed in their
kingdoms.   What are we to think of Christ's silence on this important
point, and on this remarkable occasion ?   Are we not fully entitled to
conclude that his views as to the *secularity* of his kingdom perfectly harmonised with those of his disciples and the wife of Zebedee ?

Jesus tells the elders of the Jews that the publicans and harlots go
into the kingdom of God—or rather led the way, προαγουσιν—before them,
because these characters believed John's proclamations of this kingdom ;

---

* Matth. xx. 20—28; x, 2 ; xix. 28. Mark x. 35—45.   In the courts of the Jewish
kings, an officer called the *Nasi,* and also *Ab Beth Din,* sat on the right hand of the king,
and another called the *Cacham* on his left.   Hence the *rationale* of Salome's request.
                                    † Luke xxii. 30.

and then, in a parable about a vineyard, he suggests that the Jews should be punished and the kingdom of God taken from them,* or rather, raised up (*αρθησεται*) from among them. Again : Christ, in comparing the kingdom of heaven to a marriage of the king's son, teaches the doctrine of the end of the world and the punishment of the wicked, in connection with the coming of this kingdom. The burning of the city and the casting into outer darkness, are expressions shown, in other places, to refer to the day of judgment.

But the parables which liken the "kingdom of heaven unto ten virgins," and to "a man travelling unto a far country," as already noticed,† perhaps, of all, furnish the most irrefragable evidence that Christ represented his kingdom as a thing to be set up at the End of the World and the Day of Judgment. Here, the kingdom of heaven is treated of in immediate connection with these occurrences, and a whole chapter details the circumstances of the final doom of mankind.‡ Having, in the foregoing chapter, said that the sun and moon should be darkened ; that the stars should fall ; that the Son of man should come in the clouds of heaven with power and great glory, as the lightning cometh out of the east and shineth even unto the west ; that he should send his angels, with a great sound of a trumpet, to gather the elect from the four winds ; that heaven and earth should pass away, and that all these awful things should happen before the then living generation should be extinct ; but that no one except the Father knew the exact hour the Son of man should come; and that therefore all should watch, lest like the unfaithful servant, they should be cut asunder.—Having foretold these awful events with many others, he says in the first words of the next chapter ;—" *Then* shall the kingdom of heaven be likened unto ten virgins."§ Five of these are excluded, and five enter into the marriage with the bridegroom. The moral is—" Watch therefore, for ye know neither the day nor the hour the Son of man cometh." The clear meaning of this parable is that the kingdom of heaven is to be entered into when the Son of man cometh, just as the five wise virgins, compared to it, entered in with the bridegroom when he came.

The next parable compares the kingdom of heaven to a man travelling into a far country, leaving his slaves at home to take care of his goods. On his return, he commends some of these, invites them to the joy of their lord, and makes them rulers over many things ; while he disapproves of others, and casts them into outer darkness to weep and gnash their teeth. But what is the moral of this parable of the kingdom of heaven ? It is to the following most striking effect ;—that *when the Son of man shall come in his glory, and the holy angels with him, he shall sit on the throne of his glory, and before him shall be gathered all nations, and he shall separate them one from another, as a shepherd divideth his sheep from the goats. The King* (that is, the Son of man) *shall say unto them on his right hand,—" Come, ye blessed of my Father, inherit the kingdom prepared for you from the foundation of the world."* Now we perceive that it is at the *end of the*

---

* Matth. xxi. 31—43.   † Ante, pp. 71, 72.   ‡ Matth. xxv.
§ This parable and the following one are so well known, that they do not require now to be transcribed here at large. Bearing in mind what has been stated in p. 10, as to the arbitrary division of chapters, it should be observed that the same subject precisely is here continued.

world, this *kingdom* which is compared to ten virgins, to a man going abroad, and to many other things, as we have seen by tracing it through the Gospels ; we perceive, we repeat, that *it is at the end of the world this kingdom* is to be inherited ; that *the final judgment is to take place, as described in this parable*, before the kingdom of heaven is entered ; and that this judgment and this end of the world are said by Christ to take place during the *life-time of those to whom he speaks*. We would, therefore, simply and emphatically ask any honest searcher for truth ;—Is this true ? Did it happen so ? Was Christ correct in these prophetical sayings ? These are simple yet very serious questions, over which Christians should ponder ;—questions which lie at the very base of their religion ;—questions whose truthful answers place Christianity on a level with the religion of the Mussulman, or of the Brahmin.

The frequent mention which is made of eating bread and drinking wine in the kingdom of heaven, in expressions as literal as ever were uttered, having nothing in them to indicate that they are in the least degree figurative, is another proof of the secularity of this kingdom. Luke* has these words ;—" Blessed is he that shall eat bread in the kingdom of God." Some commentators imagine them to be words spoken by one of the men who sat at meat in the house of one of the chief Pharisees into which Christ had, by invitation, gone to dinner. But the whole construction of the narrative rather sanctions the opinion that Christ spoke these words to a man present,—not this man to Christ. The latter having advised the Pharisee, whose guest he was, to invite the poor, maimed, lame, and blind, when he made a dinner or supper, instead of his rich friends, the Evangelist tells us that " when one of them that sat at meat with him" heard these things, *he* said unto him, Blessed is he that shall eat bread in the kingdom of God." But whether Christ or one of the men who sat with him said this,—or which of them is to be understood by *he*,—is not easily determined, owing to the abrupt and sudden transitions which the writer here makes. But admitting that it was another than Christ who spoke these words, still it must be granted, that it was the foregoing expressions of Christ suggested them, and that those who sat with him regarded his kingdom as secular. For so far is he from contradicting, or even discountenancing this notion, that, from these words, he appears to embrace the opportunity of speaking the parable of " the great supper," which must be admitted to be a simile in illustration of the terms of admission into his kingdom, and to be in reference to what had already been said of it. But whether Christ or his companion uttered the foregoing words, there is no doubt that Christ himself, when eating the passover with his disciples, gave utterance to the following expression, which carries with it the same notion of a secular kingdom :—" I will not drink henceforth of this fruit of the vine until that day when I drink it new with you in my Father's kingdom."† Luke, after recording the above expression with slight variations, has the following words, as uttered by Christ, a little further on, and in such a connection that no ground whatever is left to suppose that they are metaphorical. They were spoken in reference to the dispute which had arisen between his disciples as to which of them should be

* xiv. 15.   † Matth. xxvi. 29. Mark xiv. 25. Luke xxii. 16, 18, 29, 30.

accounted greatest in the kingdom of heaven. Christ, with a view to reconcile them, speaks thus.—"Whether is greater, he that sitteth at meat, or he that serveth? Is not he that sitteth at meat? But I am among you as he that serveth. Ye are they which have continued with me in my temptations; and I appoint unto you a kingdom, as my Father hath appointed unto me, that ye may eat and drink at my table in my kingdom, and sit on thrones judging the twelve tribes of Israel."[*] It must either be contended that the whole of the above passage is metaphorical, or be admitted that the whole is literal. To contend for the former would be to contend that the terms *disciples, Christ, Father, the eating of the passover*, and the whole of the transaction referred to are metaphorical, allegorical, imaginary! To admit the latter is to admit that the kingdom spoken of was secular—worldly, requiring food and drink in it—and that this kingdom (although Christ had now been nearly three years proclaiming it) had not yet been received even by the disciples,—had as yet only been appointed to them, just as the Father had appointed the same kingdom to Christ. Both these positions are clearly proved by the passage.

Another remarkable instance where reference is made to this kingdom is the following. While one of the two malefactors, between whom Christ was crucified, joined the spectators in reviling him for having set himself up as the king and saviour of the Jews, whereas it now turned out that he could not even save himself,[†] the other, having more faith in his pretensions, said to him,—"Lord, remember me when thou comest into thy kingdom;"—the kingdom, evidently, that Christ had before repeatedly told his hearers he was going to set up. This request of the thief on the cross is very remarkable, as showing that the kingdom of Christ was to come after the resurrection of the dead. The spectators revile Christ as *king* of the Jews, and this thief, at the same time, and doubtless when hearing others call him *king* of the Jews, speaks of his *kingdom*, asking to be remembered when Christ should come into this kingdom. What he asks for, clearly, is to be favoured with admission into this kingdom, after death,—at the resurrection, when "Christ should come in judgment"; for death now stares him in the face, the pangs of crucifixion tell him that few minutes will terminate his life. He, therefore, looks "beyond the grave," and implores Christ to admit him into his kingdom at the resurrection. But what is Christ's answer? An answer which is more favourable than the thief could have expected, and which promised more than he had asked.— "Verily I say unto thee, To day shalt thou be with me in Paradise."[‡] But let us inquire what Christ meant by this expression, and how he regarded it a direct answer acceding to the request of the thief, who wished to be remembered when he came into his kingdom. Did Christ mean the same by "Paradise," as the thief by Christ's "kingdom?" The word translated "*verily*" is αμην—*amen*, conveying the idea of affirmation, and here affirming that it should be as the thief had desired. This affirmation identifies Paradise with Christ's kingdom. Another instance is here furnished of ειμι with a genitive implying the idea of possession, or of obtaining; so that the passage would not be translated amiss if it were rendered

* Luke xxii. 27—30.

† Luke xxiii. 35, 37, 39. Mark xv. 29—32. Matth. xxvii. 29, 38—44. John xix. 14, 15, 21.

‡ Luke xxiii. 43.—Αμην λεγω σοι, σημερον μετ' εμου εση εν τω Παραδεισω.

—To day shalt thou be with me in *possession* of Paradise. If it be contended that, contrary to what is advanced in a succeeding section of this work, there is here implied a notion of the separate existence of the soul between death and the resurrection, the answer is, that although the heathen believed the souls of the good to enter Elysium—the same place as Paradise, this is the only passage in the Gospels, from which it can hardly be conceived that Christ entertained any such idea; and further, that here there is no mention made of the soul or life. ($\psi\nu\chi\eta$) It is, therefore, not improbable that Christ here said "To day shalt thou be with me in Paradise," from his notion, in common with the pagan world, that heroes, after death, were raised to the skies or heaven, both body and soul or life.* But what is meant by the word Paradise, ($\pi\alpha\rho\alpha\delta\epsilon\iota\sigma\sigma$) a word not frequently met with in the Bible? To define its meaning, Parkhurst shall here be cited in an abridged form.—"This is without controversy an oriental word. The Greeks borrowed it from the Persians. among whom it signified a *garden*, a *park*, or inclosure, full of all the valuable products of of the earth. In this sense the word is used by Xenophon, Herodotus. and Diodorus Siculus. The original word פרדם pardes. occurs in Neh. ii. 8. Eccl. ii. 5; and Cant. iv. 13. The LXX have rendered the word by $\pi\alpha\rho\alpha\delta\epsilon\iota\sigma\sigma$ in all the three passages just cited; and have constantly rendered גן (garden) when it relates to the garden of Eden by the same word. Hence $\pi\alpha\rho\alpha\delta\epsilon\iota\sigma\sigma$ in the New Testament is applied to the state of faithful souls between death and the resurrection. It may, perhaps, be worth observing that the Jews likewise used פרדם, or פרדיסא. paradise, and גן עדן (garden of Eden) for the intermediate state of holy departed souls."† But is not this, by another name, the Elysium of the Greeks and Romans. where the souls of the virtuous were placed after death;—where pleasures and innocent refinement were enjoyed in a degree of perfection;—where meadows were ever decked with the gayest flowers;—bowers, for ever green; —groves, in which birds most melodiously warbled;—air, the most salubrious;—living streams, the most refreshing;—where the inhabitants of this place of bliss, supposed by some to be near the moon, were blessed with a sun and stars the most serene, for themselves exclusively; and

---

* It is remarkable that only Luke mentions this conversation between the thief and Christ. Nor is it less remarkable that only he records the parable of Lazarus and the rich man, which states that the latter was, after death, in torments, and the former in the bosom of Abraham; from which expression some might infer the doctrine of the separate existence of the soul after death, as taught by Christ. But here again there is no mention made of soul. Nor is there anything said from which it can be decided whether this is intended to describe a state of things after or before the resurrection, which was to be at the coming of Christ. There are evident marks, however, in the Gospels thro (to say the least) their respective writers tinged them with their personal mythological notions. Hence, both the heaven and hell of Luke differ from those of Matthew and Mark. We cannot therefore, *ceteris paribus*, know exactly what to attribute to Christ.

† Park. Greek Lex. sub $\pi\alpha\rho\alpha\delta\epsilon\iota\sigma\sigma$. Mr. Parkhurst, however, does not tell us that not only this word, which means *garden*, but that the whole tale about the garden of Eden, as well as most of the cosmogony, &c. in the book of Genesis, has been borrowed from the Persic mythology, and written, as we now find it in the Hebrew Bible, some time after the Babylonish Captivity,—some 500 years, not 1,500, as we are taught, before the Christian era. He, however, gives us a broad hint that this garden or paradise of the Jews was the same with the pagan Elysium. See further on $\pi\alpha\rho\alpha\delta\epsilon\iota\sigma\sigma\nu$—Jul. Pollux Onomast. lib. ix. c. 13. Xenophon's Œconomics, cited by Parkhurst.

where they exercised themselves in pursuit of all the enjoyment they could desire or imagine?* Lexicographers explain Elysium by Paradise, and Paradise by Elysium. Let us see the description usually given of Paradise, in order that we may the better form an opinion of the place where the robber was to be with Christ. There were in the garden of Eden, which in the Septuagint is translated Paradise, every tree that was pleasant to the sight, and in the midst of it the tree of life, and the tree of knowledge.— There was also in this garden a river which parted into four streams ; the whole very much like the Persian paradise ; and its very name, Eden— *pleasure, delight*—is very significant. In addition to all this, the term "Eden" is used as a comparison to describe joy and gladness, praise and melody,† such as were to be in the Elysian fields. Again : in the New Testament we have a similar description of the same place under the name of the "Paradise of God," in the midst of which it is said the tree of life grew. The same writer, a little further on in his curious production, describes the same place, although not by name, as having a pure river of the water of life, like crystal, on each side of which grew the tree of life, bearing twelve sorts of fruit, yielding its fruit every month, and clad in such precious foliage that its leaves healed the nations. In this place there was no night, and no need of the light of a candle, or even of the sun, for the Lord God lighted the inhabitants by his face, and they were to reign for ever and ever.‡ This last description precisely answers to the Elysium of the heathen.

But let us see whether we can ascertain *where the Jewish Paradise lay*, better than the poets could agree as to where the Elysium was situated, which was thought by some to be near the moon, while others described it as being in the centre of the earth. We shall, doubtless, have some difficulty in finding out the Jewish Paradise or heaven ; for the Bible does not tell us where it is. Dr. Samuel Clarke§ and others think that Paradise was "Hades or hell, or rather part of it." And indeed the parable of Lazarus and the rich man rather countenances this opinion ; for the rich man, from his position, could see Lazarus in the bosom of Abraham. The great gulf, mentioned in the parable, is very remarkable if we think of the rivers Styx and Acheron.‖ There is another circumstance that favours this view :—Christ says to Peter that he should give him the keys of the kingdom of heaven ; and Pluto, the king of Hades, (hell) is represented as having "the key of his kingdom in his hand."¶ Christ further says, that "on this rock" he would build his church, and that the gates of Hades (that is—the gates, the key of which Pluto is represented as having in his hand) should not prevail against it."** Hence it would appear, that Hades or hell was to be near Christ's kingdom. The Creed of the Church of England tells us that Christ descended into hell, but neither Christ nor

---

* Virg. Æn. vi. Herodot. lib. x. c. 129. Homer. Od. iv. xv. xi. Juv. ii. 149. Tibull. i, el. 3, v. 57. Plut. De Consol. Pindar. Lucian. &c.
† Gen. ii. 9, 10. Is. li. 3. ‡ Rev. ii. 7 ; xxii. 1—5.
§ See Clarke's Paraphrase, p. 233—Note on Luke xxiii. 43.
‖ Read of the Lake Styx, Charon's boat, &c., in Diod. ii. Senec. in Her. Fur. Act. 3, v. 765. Virg. Æn. vi. 298, &c.
¶ Homer. Il. ix. lin. 312 et al. Hesiod. Theog. 311. Apollod. ii.
** Matth. xvi. 17, 18.

this Creed tells us where it is.   Let us, therefore, consult Paul on this
point.   He says he has been to Paradise or heaven.   As an open and frank
man, he will possibly inform us where it is.   It was nothing in ancient
times to go to heaven or hell and return to the earth.   The musician and
bard Orpheus once went to hell to fetch his wife from thence, and brought
her back part of the way ; and Ulysses went thither to consult the prophet
Tiresias.   Paul once took a trip to the third heaven or Paradise, which he
thus describes.—" I knew a man in Christ above fourteen years ago,—
whether in the body, I cannot tell, or whether out of the body, I cannot
tell, God knoweth ;—such an one caught up to *the third heaven*.   And I
knew such a man, whether in the body or out of the body I cannot tell,
God knoweth,—how that he was caught up into *Paradise*, and heard
unspeakable words which is not lawful for a man to utter.   Of such an one
will I glory ; yet of myself I will not glory, but in mine infirmities.   For
though I would desire to glory, I shall not *be a fool ;* for I will say the
truth."*   Although Paul here says much about the matter, yet he does not
tell us exactly, where this Paradise is.   All we can gather is, that he was
caught up,—that is, to the air,—caught up to the third heaven, and caught
up into Paradise ; but he does not tell us whether the third heaven is the
highest or lowest of the three ; nor does he inform us whether Paradise
is below, or above, or in the third heaven.   We must, therefore, proceed by
analogy.—We are told that Christ after his resurrection ascended into
heaven, and that he was to appear again in the clouds.   It would consequently seem that Paradise was imagined to be somewhere beyond the
clouds.   But wherever it was supposed to be situated, it is clear that it was
believed to be the same place as the Elysium of the heathen.   Hence we
see that the Heaven or Paradise of Christ is, like his Hell, made up of the
mythological notions afloat at the time; and that it was in this Paradise
the robber was to be with him on the day he was crucified.   The main
object of the foregoing inquiry into the situation of Paradise was to ascertain
where the kingdom of Christ was to be ; for it would seem from his answer
to the robber, that the former and the latter were the same, unless it be
contended that the meaning is, that Christ, with the thief, was to be in a
kind of intermediate state (limbo) until the time of his appearance as a
judge to destroy the world, which is by no means improbable.   Since,
however, this is not a point of vital importance to our main inquiry, it is
scarcely expedient now to pursue it any further.
   There are other very strong proofs that Christ fostered the belief of
the vulgar that he was to be the king of a secular but blissful kingdom, in
his pretence to a lineal descent from King David, the grounds of which
pretence we will not stop now to consider.†   He asked the Pharisees what
they thought of Christ,—whether he was the son of David, and how it
was that David called him his Lord.‡   He quotes David as an authority
for violating the Sabbath, giving the Pharisees to understand that as David,
being king, could faultlessly do this in the case of the shew-bread, so he,
being king, could do the same in reference to the ears of corn.§   The

* 2 Cor. xii. 2—6.
† The reader, however, may at his leisure compare the Genealogy of Christ given by
Matth. i. with that given by Luke iii. 23—38.
‡ Matth. xxii. 42—45. Mark xii. 35—37. Luke xx. 41—44.   § Luke vi. 3, 4.

same thing is proved by the narrative which we have of Jesus making his triumphal entry, at the time of a national feast, into Jerusalem—the Jewish capital, in which had resided so many of the Jewish kings—riding on an ass, attended by a vast convention of mob, who spread their garments before him, and vociferously hailed him with such flattering epithets as— "Hosanna to the son of David"—"Blessed be the kingdom of our father David"—"Blessed be the King that cometh in the name of the Lord"— "Blessed is the King of Israel" &c. ; while he so far from discouraging these proceedings, actually defended them. For when the authorities spoke to him of the disloyalty and illegality of such conduct. he said,—"If these should hold their peace, the stones would immediately cry out ;"— "Out of the mouth of babes and sucklings, thou hast perfected praise."* His conduct also, on that occasion, in going into the temple, overthrowing the stalls of the merchants, scattering their money and dispersing their cattle, was, besides being exceedingly outrageous, directly calculated and evidently intended, like that of his riding into Jerusalem, to show his regal authority as monarch of the kingdom he intended to set up.† His expression in regard to paying tribute shows that he aspired to being a secular king. When Peter is about paying the tax-collector, Christ asks him— "What thinkest thou, Simon? of whom do the kings of the earth take custom, or tribute? of their own children, or of strangers?" Peter replies,—"Of strangers." Christ rejoins,—"Then are the children free." Here, he clearly intimates that. as he is a prince—the heir-apparent to the throne—he is free. He, however, says that, lest he should give offence, he would pay.‡ When Pilate asked him,—"Art thou the king of the Jews?" his reply was,—"thou sayest it ;" which is a form of affirmation, as proved by the explanatory manner in which Mark records the same form of expression when Christ made answer to the question whether he was the Son of God. Matthew tells us that the high-priest asked Jesus whether he was the Christ, the Son of God, and adds that Jesus answered "thou hast said," which is the same *form* of expression as that in which the answer is made to Pilate. Mark, recording the same question of the high-priest, says that Jesus replied,—"I am."§ In this sense the Jews understood such an answer, for Luke tells us (infra) that they asked Jesus,— "Art thou the Son of God? And he said unto them, Ye say that I am. And they said, what need we any further witness? for we ourselves have heard of his own mouth." Having thus persisted in asserting his claim to be king of the Jews, that nation crucified him as such.‖ It is true that, after much hesitation, he said to Pilate that his kingdom was not of this world ; but it is equally true that, when he made this admission, he had been apprehended ; and then saw the horrible death of crucifixion staring him in the face,—a death which, when he knew there was a conspiracy against him, even within the circle of his own apostles, he feared was inevitable, and from which he fervently prayed to be delivered.¶ It is not at all wonderful, therefore, that, although the whole tenour of his life,

---

* Matth. xxi. 1—16. Mark xi. 2—19. Luke xix. 30—40. John xii. 12—19.
  † See foregoing citations. ‡ Matth. xvii. 25—27. Luke xxiii. 1.
  § Luke xxiii. 38, 39.. Matth. xxvi. 64. Mark xiv. 61, 62. Compare with the above,
Matth. xiv. Luke xxii. 70, 71. John xviii. 33—39; xix. 9, 10. et al.
  ‖ John xviii. 33 ; xix. 3, 12, 14, 15, 19, 21. ¶ Matth. xxvi. 24, 25, 36, 42.

both in words and actions, contradicted him,—although the three other evangelists state that he avowed himself the king of the Jews, yet that, according to John, (whose testimony alone, and that only in one solitary instance, is against the other three evangelists,) Jesus should make the concession that his kingdom was *not* of this world. But observe how unwillingly, even under the existing aggravatingly distressing circumstances, he makes this concession. After the question has been put to him, he asks another, namely, who had instructed the Roman governor, who was then on the seat of justice, to interrogate him as to whether he was, or was not the king of the Jews. Pilate retorts, saying,—" Am I a Jew ? Thine own nation and chief priests have delivered thee unto me ; what hast thou done ?" Jesus does not answer the question, nor has he answered it to this day ; any more than he has answered another question then put to him, namely,—" what is truth ?" Evading a direct answer, he says,—" My kingdom is not of this world ; if my kingdom were of this world, then would my servants fight that I should not be delivered to the Jews ; but now is my kingdom not from hence." To say nothing of the facts that one of his servants, namely Peter, actually had fought, and that he himself had ordered the rest to be provided with swords, let us observe that Pilate, upon obtaining this answer, asked Jesus,—" Art thou a king then ?" Christ replied in the affirmative,—" Thou sayest that I am a king. To this end was I born, and for this cause came I into the world, that I should bear witness unto the truth."* This answer, in a great measure, was in accordance with the doctrine of the kingdom of heaven, which Christ had been proclaiming. He was a king, and a king of the Jews. This he did not deny ; but he denied that his kingdom was of this world. Nor had he ever said that it was. He had always taught that this world was to be burned before he should establish his kingdom ; and that his first appearance, for this purpose, would be in the clouds, where, probably, the new earth was to be *fixed*, while *this world* was to be eternally burning. This answer of Christ to Pilate, therefore, by no means proves that his kingdom was to be a spiritual one, or that it was not to be of a secular character ; much less that it was the Gospel Dispensation.

Notwithstanding Christ's declaration, Nathaniel, as if prompted by Inspiration, calls Christ, the very first time he sees him, " the King of Israel ;"† and even the angel, in predicting his birth, announces that " the Lord God shall give him the throne of his father David, that he shall reign over the house of Jacob for ever, and that of his kingdom there shall be no end ;"‡—a description of his kingdom quite conformable to that which he himself gives of it. He calls himself a king, when speaking of himself as judge of mankind,—the office of judge§ in ancient times, and still in some countries, being discharged by the king ; and he calls his dominions a kingdom, in quite as literal a sense as either of the kings and kingdoms of Judah or Israel is spoken of, without ever giving the least intimation that we should understand him otherwise than literally. If, therefore, the kings and kingdoms of Judah and Israel were literally so, Christ is literally a king, and his kingdom literally a kingdom. Nathaniel says to him,—

---

* John xviii. 33—37.   † John i. 49.   ‡ Luke i. 32, 33.
                § Matth. xxv. 40.

" Thou art the Son of God ; thou art the King of Israel."* Would it not be absurd to suppose that, in this instance, he is literally called the Son of God ; but figuratively, the King of Israel ?†

As the King of Israel, who was to establish an everlasting kingdom, after conquering all his enemies, in the destruction of this world and the creation of a new one ; (or perhaps a remodification of the old materials, purified by fire,—a very ancient notion,) the pious Simeon waited for him, whom he terms " the consolation of Israel."‡ And in expectation of the same event, the ever-memorable Joseph of Arimathea "waited for the kingdom of God."§ This would be a most singular expression, if by the kingdom of heaven and the kingdom of God were meant the Dispensation of the Gospel Here has Christ been on earth ; has established his kingdom ; has promulgated its doctrines through the length and breadth of Palestine ; has sent apostles by twelve and by seventy to preach it to all the world ; has made thousands of converts to the new religion—the Gospel Dispensation ; (?) has just died on the cross to atone for the sins of the world ; and is now being buried by this very Joseph of Arimathea, " an honourable counsellor," and therefore a man neither of low position, mean intellect, scanty education, nor slight acquaintance with Christ and his doctrines, but a man who still *waits for the kingdom of God*,—waits for this kingdom to come or be established ; whereas it has long ago come, and has made considerable progress in the world, by working thousands of stupendous miracles, the fame of which has resounded throughout the whole land ; nay whereas the very essence, the Alpha and Omega of this kingdom is conveyed into the tomb, perhaps between the arms of this very Joseph, who, notwithstanding, waits still for the *kingdom of God*. Can this mean the Gospel Dispensation ? Would not Joseph of Arimathea have known, —would not Christ or some of the disciples have told him,—would not the wonderful works, and the still more wonderful words of Christ, who always drew after him great multitudes of people, have convinced him that the marvellous three years which Christ spent as a public teacher, at the close of which period rocks rent, the earth quaked, the sun darkened, the graves opened, and the dead rose and walked about, was the commencement of the Gospel Dispensation ? Must not Joseph, who was a disciple of Christ and resided within a short distance of Jerusalem, have known all these things ? Why then did he wait for the kingdom of God ? Obviously, because he, in common with all others of his age, and many ages after, firmly believed, from the teaching of Christ and his apostles, that the kingdom of God meant the End of the World, the Final Judgment, and after these events, an eternal age of bliss in what was called the kingdom of heaven or of God. The notion that the kingdom of heaven means the Dispensation of the Gospel is a figment of the brains of men of comparatively modern times, to which the first ages of Christianity were entire strangers. Joseph of Arimathea, who it is said was a good and just man, and a disciple of Christ, waited *also himself*,—waited with many others for the

---

* John i. 49.

† Peter also, in his Pentecostal Sermon (Acts ii. 29, 30) makes Christ to descend from David, and claims his right to the throne of David (the fruit of whose loins he was) in as literal a sense as ever words were uttered.

‡ Luke ii. 25, 34. § Mark xv. 43. Luke xxiii. 51. Matth. xxviii. 57.

kingdom of God,—waited in daily expectation of seeing the Judge appear in the clouds of heaven, and of being "caught up into the air, so as to be for ever with the Lord."

A few more instances of the sense in which the phrase "kingdom of heaven" is employed, must suffice on this head.   Christ having told Zaccheus, a little man in stature but great in riches,* that he was going to abide at his house, adding as he entered in, and after he had heard the vaunts of his host as to his liberality to the poor, that *that day* salvation had come to this house, because Zaccheus also was a son of Abraham, and because the Son of man was come to seek and to save that which was lost, the multitude who followed Christ, and heard these words, "thought that *the kingdom of God should immediately appear.*"   The words of the Evangelist are.—"And as they heard these things, he added and spake a parable, because he was nigh to Jerusalem, and because they thought that the kingdom of God should *immediately* appear."†   These words clearly show that the writer meant to indicate that the kingdom of God had *not appeared* when Christ spoke to Zaccheus.   Therefore, the appearance and preaching of Christ on earth was not the kingdom of heaven, as understood by the Evangelist, who wrote, as we are told, under Divine guidance, and than whom none, it will be admitted by all Christians, could know better.   *That* kingdom was a thing yet to come.   The people then *expected* it "*immediately*," because the supposed king of this supposed kingdom had intimated his intention to take his abode with one of the sons of Abraham, the celebrated ancestor of the Jews ; and because he had said, —"*this day is salvation come* to this house."   But it will be observed that they only *expected* this kingdom,—"thought that the kingdom of God should *immediately* appear."

Jesus, in order to correct their mistake as to the *instant* appearance of this kingdom, and to show them that a few things must yet occur before it would come, spoke a parable of a certain nobleman who went into a far country to receive a kingdom.   But the inhabitants of that kingdom hated him, and sent to tell him they would not have him to reign over them. Having, however, obtained the kingdom and returned, he called his servants, to whom at his departure he had entrusted a pound each, and he put one to reign over ten cities, and another over five, each according to the good use he had made of the money of his royal master.   To the servant, however, who had used the money improvidently he gave no power, but took from him the money, and commanded that those enemies of his, who had said they would not have him to reign over them, should be brought before him and slain in his presence.   If language has any meaning, there is certainly here depicted a secular king and a secular kingdom, *de futuro.* What is said of the servants is exactly in harmony with what is said of the faithful and unfaithful servants in the xxvth chapter of Matthew, where it is said that the Son of man shall come in his glory,—sit as a king upon his throne,—send one set of human characters to everlasting fire, and receive another into the kingdom prepared for them from the foundation of the world.   Those expressions in Matthew and those in the passage now under consideration from Luke, are uttered in reference to, and in immediate

* Luke xix. 5—27.   † Ver. 11.

connection with the same kingdom—"the kingdom of heaven," and "the kingdom of God," which clearly mean the same thing. These circumstances furnish irrefutable evidence that the passage in Luke represents the kingdom of God not only as yet to come, but as that which *was to come at the End of the World and the Last Judgment;* and which, with its concomitant events, was, at the time Christ entered Zaccheus's house, earnestly and generally expected to be just at hand. That part of the parable which represents the king as putting one of his servants, who had been faithful to him before he had obtained the kingdom, to reign over ten cities, and another, who had borne a similar character, to reign over five, has clear reference to the different degrees of power and eminence which should be given to those admitted to the kingdom of heaven;—a point referred to by Christ on a great number of occasions, so as to make his hearers deeply sensible that there were positions of different degrees of dignity to be assigned to the subjects of this kingdom, and that their claims to high stations depended upon their conduct towards him. Hence the frequent quarrels among his disciples as to who should be greatest in the kingdom of heaven, which Christ as frequently endeavoured to subdue by persuading them that the humblest then should be the highest in his kingdom; and hence the applications to Christ for being allowed to sit next to him in his kingdom.*

Additional light is thrown on the doctrine of this parable by the statement of the Evangelist that the reason why Christ spoke the parable was, not only "because they thought the kingdom of God should immediately appear," but also "because he was nigh to Jerusalem." He was about entering that royal city in triumph, which the Evangelist says he did enter, immediately after he had spoken the parable, with the greatest demonstration of regal pomp, (as already noticed) riding on a wild colt of an ass, and followed by a huge multitude who strewed their clothes on the ground before him, and shouted forth acknowledgments of his kingly authority. When he was requested by some of the Pharisees to check these disloyal proceedings, he showed his approbation of them, and afterwards prophesied that Jerusalem, either in common with, or immediately before the rest of the world, should be destroyed, saying,—"If thou hadst known, even thou, at least in this thy day, the things which belong unto thy peace; but now they are hid from thine eyes. For the days shall come upon thee that thine enemies shall cast a trench about thee, and compass thee round, and keep thee in on every side; and shall lay thee even with the ground, and thy children within thee; and they shall not leave in thee one stone upon another, because thou knewest not the time of thy visitation."†

---

* Vid. ante, pp. 83, 84.   † Luke xix. 42—44.

SECTION IV.—CHRIST'S PREDICTION THAT JERUSALEM SHOULD BE EN-
COMPASSED WITH ARMIES, EVINCING THAT HE IMAGINED THE WORLD
WAS TO BE DESTROYED BY ARMIES OF ANGELIC SOLDIERS.

Whatever Christians may think of the import of the foregoing prediction ;—however frequently it may, with that in another part of the same
Gospel,* be cited to prove that Christ thereby predicted the destruction of
Jerusalem, and did not predict the End of the World ; the numerous,
clear, and distinct passages which record his prediction of the latter, form
such a ponderous mass of irrefragable evidence of the fact that, in regard
to the meaning of the two passages in Luke, which speak about *compassing
with armies and enemies*, about *falling by the edge of the sword* and *being
led away captive*, the following alternative is inevitable :—These passages
are predictions of what would befall Jerusalem, either *immediately* BEFORE
the End of the World, or of what would befall it AT *the End of the World*,
in common with the whole earth.   Whether they mean the one or the
other is not a question which in the least alters the character of Christ as
a prophet.   Because if they mean either, they prove him to be a false
prophet.   The real question here in regard to Christ as a prophet is not,
whether he did prophesy the destruction of Jerusalem ; but whether he did
prophesy that, *during the life-time of those contemporary with him on earth,
he should come in the clouds of heaven to destroy this world, judge all mankind, establish a kingdom which he calls the kingdom of heaven, and receive
into this kingdom those whom he calls " the elect," while he punished those
whom he terms " the cursed" with everlasting fire*.   This alone is the grand
question here at issue.   That he positively prophesied the latter has already
been proved by a greater mass of evidence, adduced from his own words,
than can be found to elucidate the meaning of any other prediction ever
uttered.   Since, however, we have, in our pursuit of the import of the
phrase—" kingdom of heaven," fallen upon that passage in connection with
it, wherein Christ deplores the coming doom of Jerusalem, it would not be
amiss to digress for a moment, in order to ascertain what this passage and
others of similar language really mean ; and what relation they bear to
other passages which form their contexts, and in which Christ indisputably
predicts the End of the World.

It should at the onset be observed, that Christ does not seem to have
had any clear and definite notion of the manner in which, or the means by
which the world was to be destroyed, although he predicted its destruction.
This is evident from the different, and frequently contradictory manner in
which, at different times, he speaks of the *circumstances* connected with the
event, while *on the event itself he clearly and firmly insists*.†   Either this is

* Luke xxi. 20—24.

† To furnish proofs of this position, here, would be too tedious a task, and would
make us deviate too far from the main subject.   Any reader, at his leisure, by taking
his Testament and Concordance in hand, may amply verify the assertion.

the case, or those four Evangelists who have undertaken to furnish a narrative of Christ's words and works have done him gross injustice. The fidelity of the latter, however, we must, for the present, take for granted ; because if we do not, there will be no proof left that Christ delivered these predictions at all, either consistently or contradictorily ; or even that he himself ever had any existence. For to deny the fidelity of the Gospels is to sweep away all proof of recognised authority by Christians, not only that Jesus said and did the things attributed to him, but even that he ever existed. Christ, therefore, as indicated by these Gospels, having no definite notion of the means by which the world was to be destroyed—an event which he would have people believe to be "near at hand," even "at the doors"—may easily have supposed that large cities like Jerusalem, would be encompassed with *armies of angels*, who would pull down the building, "leaving not one stone upon another," slay the inhabitants with their swords, and put the cities on fire, with the whole of the earth. No reader of the Bible requires to be told that angels are therein often represented as having swords.—The Cherubim put to keep the garden of Eden had a sword ;—the angel who met Balaam had a sword in his hand. To say nothing of the sword with which it appears an angel threatened to destroy Jerusalem, in the time of David ; nor of the angel who, apparently with a sword, killed 4,080 men in the camp of the Assyrians ;—David is expressly said to be afraid because of the sword of an angel ; and we have an account of a war in heaven between angels. The word rendered "armies" in Luke, is στρατοπεδον—an encampment. We find mention made of "the armies" (στρατευματα—armed military forces) "which were in heaven,"* meaning the angels. In Luke,† we find στρατια ουρανιος, a heavenly army, rendered in our version, "a multitude of the heavenly host." In verse 15th of the same chapter, the same are called αγγελοι, (angels) showing that these soldiers,—this army, (for such is the very meaning of στρατια)‡ are the same "multitude of the heavenly host" as that called *angels*. In the Septuagint translation of the Old Testament, we frequently meet with στρατια του ουρανου—the army of heaven, or "the host of heaven"—as translated generally in our version, meaning really the angels of heaven, such as in the following passages :—"I saw the Lord sitting on his throne, and all the host of heaven standing by him." (1 Kings xxii. 19. 2 Chron. xviii. 18) It is true that the same expression—"host of heaven"—is used to denote the celestial bodies, such as the sun, moon, &c., which were worshipped by the ancients, and were supposed to be military beings situated in the upper regions of the sky, called the heavens. The instances in the Bible where the angels are regarded as an army, and called by that name, are very numerous.§

---

* Rev. xix. 14.　　　　　　　　† ii. 13.

‡ The words used almost invariably by the Greek writers for an army and an encampment of soldiers, are στρατος and στρατοπεδος. In Josephus (Ant. Lib. xviii. c. 7. § 6.) we find των στρατευματων ηγεμονιαν ειναι αυτω; and in his Treatise on the Maccabees, § 5. we meet with—των στρατευματων αυτω παρεστηκοτων κυκλοθεν. See the words in all their forms used in Xenophon Anab.

§ The words *armies, angels, stars, host of heaven, &c.* are used in the Bible in such a manner as clearly shows that they were considered by the writers as synonymous terms, and that a notion prevailed among the Jews, like other ancient nations, that the aerial and starry regions were inhabited by vast armies of soldiers. In accordance with this

H

And that Christ had an idea of coming to destroy the world, like a field-marshal, with legions of angelic soldiers, is strongly countenanced by

notion, was the fancy that heroes, at their death, ascended these regions, and were added to the heavenly army.   Hence heroes were so often deified, and became the gods of the ancients.   In the Bible there is frequent mention made of the *God of host* and *hosts,—the Lord of host* and *hosts,—God's hosts,—the hosts of God,—Lord God of hosts,* &c.   The word translated *host*, is צבא (Tsaba); and the phrase translated *Lord of hosts*, is יהוה צבאות (Jehovah Tsabaoth).   Now it is well known that the meaning of the word צבא as a verb, is to assemble—to meet in orderly troops, as soldiers.   As a noun, it signifies an *army*, or in the plural—צבאות (Tsabaoth) *armies;* and as already noticed, is translated *host* or *hosts*.   It is a word generally used in the Bible to designate the *army, armies, host,* or *hosts* of the different kings who fought against the Hebrews, and even to denote the Israelitish army.   It is used a great number of times in Num. ii. 4—15, for the different troops of the Israelitish army, both in the singular—צבא and in the plural—צבאות.   We read of the host—צבא of Jabin, the captain of which was the brave Sisera, who met his death at the hands of the treacherous Jael.—Jud. iv. 2.   Shobach was captain of the Syrian host—צבא.—2 Sam. x. 18.   "Uzziah had an host (צבא) of fighting men that went out to war."—2 Chron. xxvi. 11.   It is said that the host of the Lord, (צבאות יהוה) meaning the warring Hebrews, went out of Egypt.—Ex. xii. 41.   In a great number of other instances are the terms *host* and *hosts* used in the Bible to denote a *body of soldiers* or *military men ;* which, evidently, was the idea that the Jews attached to the words.   What is meant, therefore, in the Bible by the appellations—*Lord of hosts,—God of hosts,* &c., is the Lord and God of soldiers.   Lord of Sabaoth (the latter word for some doubtful purpose being left untranslated in the New Testament—Rom. ix. 29, and Jam. v. 4.) means *Lord of armies*.   Cruden very candidly says,—"Sabaoth, or rather Zabaoth, an Hebrew word that signifies *host* or *armies*."   He likewise admits that the word צבא " is also used to signify the service his ministers perform for him in the tabernacle, *because they are there as it were soldiers,* or *guards attending at the court of their Prince.*"

Having thus ascertained the meaning of the word *host* in the Bible, we are now better prepared to understand what is meant by *"the hosts of heaven,"* (צבא השמים) so often mentioned in the same book.   We read (Deut. xvii. 3. 2 Kings viii. 16; xxi. 3—5. Jer. viii. 2.) that the Israelites worshipped the *host of heaven,*—meaning thereby the soldiers, whom they imagined to be in the regions of the sky, and to make their appearance in the shape of sun, moon, stars, &c.   Cruden, Parkhurst, and all Christian writers gloss over this Biblical statement by telling us that only the apostate Israelites worshipped the *hosts of heaven,* or practised the Zabian idolatry.   But the Jewish writings, like those of the Pagans, invariably confine the habitation of the Jewish God to the region of the host of heaven—the clouds, &c., where also the angels, called *armies* and *soldiers,* were supposed to dwell.   In Job xxii. 12—14. it is asked—" Is not God in the height of heaven?   How doth God know?   Can he judge through the dark cloud?   Thick clouds are a covering to him that he seeth not; and he walketh in the circuit of heaven."   Hence he is called the *Lord of heaven,* as often as the Lord of the hosts of heaven.   A prophet says that he saw the Lord sitting on his throne, and all *the host of heaven standing by him on his right hand and on his left.* (1 Kings xxii. 19.)   Such an expression as this shows that the words—"hosts of heaven"—mean, in the Bible, something more than the sun, moon, stars, considered as inanimate bodies ; that they mean intelligent beings,—the angels who were thought to be soldiers.   From this heaven the Jewish God was supposed frequently to come down to visit the Hebrews.   In the Bible, also, he is often made to claim the hosts of heaven as his own soldiers,—said to be their commander,—to bring them out by number,—and to call them by their names. (Neh. ix. 6. Is. xl. 26; xlv. 12)   We are also told that the host of heaven worshipped Jehovah ; (Neh. ix. 6.) that he doeth according to his will in the *army of heaven;* (Dan. v. 35.) that there is no number of his *armies ;* (Job xxv. 3. Jer. xxxiii. 22) and that his chariots (of war) are twenty thousand, even thousands of angels. (Psal. lxviii. 17.)   Isaiah, (xxxiv. 4.) after predicting, in very obscene language, that the earthly armies of soldiers should be slaughtered, says that the *host* or *army* of heaven should also be dissolved, or rather disbanded.   Daniel (viii. 10, 11.) speaks of the *Prince* or leader of the *host of heaven.*   Jacob, after the *angels, ambassadors,* or soldiers of the Gods (אלהים) met him, calls them (not exactly *God's host,* as translated) but the encampment of the Gods—מחנה אלהים

the following words he spoke to one of his disciples when he was being taken into custody.—" Put up again thy sword into his place ; for all they that take the sword shall perish with the sword. Thinkest thou that I cannot pray to my Father, *aud he shall presently send me more than twelve legions of angels ?*"* These words at least prove that Christ regarded the angels as celestial soldiers. The circumstances also under which the words were spoken afford additional strength to this fact.—There were men under arms at the time surrounding Christ, and military operations at the time performed. One of the disciples, Peter, as we learn from John,† drew his sword, and with it cut off the ear of the high-priest's servant; aiming, probably, at his head, but his blow being warded off by the sword of his adversary. All the disciples of Christ, apparently, carried swords ; for Christ had just told them to be provided with them, even if they sold their clothes to buy them.‡ To show the harmony of this combative conduct with what Christ says afterwards against using a sword, and with his precept in his sermon on the mount regarding the non-resistance of evil, is one of the tasks of impossibility in which Christians are so frequently engaged touching the contradictory statements found in the Bible. It is sufficient for our present purpose to show that Christ told his disciples to buy swords ; that

and in commemoration of them, calls the place, the Encampers—מחנים (Mahanaim)— Gen. xxxii. 1, 2. In like manner does the Psalmist speak about the angel of the Lord encamping. (Psal. xxxiv. 7.) Similar inferences are to be drawn from the expression— אלהי צבאות—the God of hosts.—See 2 Sam. v. 10. Psal. lix. 5; lxxx. 4, 7, 14, 19. (where the God of host was the sun whose face *shone.*) Psal. lxxxiv. 8—12. Amos iii. 13; v. 14—16, 27; vi. 8. Parkhurst, under the word *host*, (Heb. Lex.) admits that the hosts of heaven seem to denote the spiritual, created angels; the Hebrew phrase—host of heaven, in 1 Kings xxii. 19, and 2 Chron. xviii. 18. exactly answering to the heavenly host of Luke, which are called angels, and, as already shown, mean soldiers. To this it may be added, that the Hebrew word לאך, translated angel, means a soldier, or a military officer sent on an embassy.

In perfect accordance with this notion of a heavenly *army*, or a host of heavenly soldiers, Deborah says :—" They fought from heaven,—The stars in their courses fought against Sisera." (Jud. v. 20.) But how did the stars, these inanimate bodies, fight? By causing rains, says Parkhurst, to overflow the river Kishon, and to drown Sisera's soldiers. In the text, however, there is no mention made of rain. Further, we know that the word מכסלותם, translated here, courses, whose root is סל, has—with all its cognates—the signification of a *military mount*, or bank cast up in besieging a city, and for other warlike purposes.—See Job xix. 12. 2 Chron. xi. 11. Jer. xxxii. 24; xxxiii. 4; vi. 6. 2 Sam. xx. 15. Again, the word כוכבים (cochabim) rendered *stars* in the passage, often means living objects.—See Amos v. 20. Is. xiv. 13, 14. and compare with Job. xxxviii. 7. where Parkhurst admits (Heb. Lex. ver. כבב) that the morning stars coupled with the sons of God mean angels. Cruden makes a similar admission under the word *star*, and further assures us that the idolatrous Israelites called the sun and moon, the king and queen of heaven, and the stars were, as it were their *armies* or *militia*. The Scriptures generally ascribe life, knowledge, &c. to the stars, moon, and sun.—Psal. xix. 5 ; civ. 19; clxviii. 3. Job. x. 12. Eccl. i. 5. The Jews worshipped an idol in the form of a star.— Amos v. 26. Acts vii. 43. The host of heaven and the host of the stars were considered to be the same, and to have a prince or captain over them.—Dan. viii. 9—12. Indeed there is abundant evidence in the Bible, that the Jews thought there were armies of soldiers above them in the skies. Hence their dreams of wars in heaven and a thousand other idle tales. Precisely in accordance with the notion of his countrymen does Christ imagine the End of the World to be brought about, and a new kingdom established on the ruins of the present world, by the instrumentality of these heavenly soldiers.

* Matth. xxvi. 52, 53.
† Compare John xviii. 3—13. with xxvi. 50—57. Mark xiv. 43—53. Luke xxii. 47—54.
‡ Luke xxii. 36.

they asked Jesus should they draw and use them; and that one of them did use a sword, and cut off a man's ear with it.   We are further told by Mark, that a *great multitude*, with swords and staves,—but by John, that a *band* of men and *officers* with lanterns, and torches, and weapons—came to apprehend Christ.   Moreover; that they were armed men is shown by the following words of Jesus—" Are ye come out as against a thief, with swords and staves for to take me ?"*   It is to be observed that the word in John translated " band of men," is σπειρα, meaning a *band of soldiers*,—supposed to consist of the same number as a Roman cohort,—the tenth part of a legion.†   We are likewise told, in the passage already referred to in John, that the *band* and *captains* and *officers* of the Jews took Jesus and bound him.   Now, it was under these circumstances—being surrounded by a number of soldiers, and military officers,—that Jesus, who had on several occasions affected the authority of a king,—who had repeatedly uttered words which intimated that he *was* a king; and who was believed by some to be the King of the Jews, and apprehended on the charge of having made that pretension :—it was under these circumstances, that he said he could have more than twelve legions of angels.   Can there be the shadow of a doubt that he meant he could have these legions of angels as *soldiers* to combat with, and defeat a portion of the Roman army which then surrounded him and his followers ?   He said this, at the same time that he enjoined Peter to put his sword in its scabbard ; meaning, evidently, that he would not resist being taken into custody, but would surrender. Otherwise, if he wished to resist, he could have of his Father more than twelve legions of angels ; which would, of course, soon put all the Roman legions *hors de combat*.‡   Is it, therefore, at all wonderful that we find Christ—who professedly was to destroy the world, in order to avenge his enemies, and reward his friends—speaking of Jerusalem being surrounded with armies ; having a trench cast about it ; having its inhabitants put to the sword, and led away captive ; together with other things which constitute the horrors of war ?   There can, indeed, be little doubt that he meant to destroy the world by the aid of angels, whom he regarded as soldiers.

In confirmation of this view, we have already seen that it was those *angels* who were to come and destroy the world ;—Christ was to make his appearance with his holy *angels*, and with power and great glory ;—the *angels* were to be sent with a great sound of a trumpet, (an instrument used in war) to gather the elect together ; and the *angels* were to be sent to gather out of the kingdom all things that offended.   We have also just seen that the very writer§ who reports Christ to have thus spoken of the *angels*, calls an aggregate number of those beings, both by the terms *angels* and *army*.   We have likewise pointed out other instances in which these supposed heavenly beings are called an *army*, and have shown that

---

* See passages just cited.
† See Parkhurst and his authorities under the word σπειρα.
‡ The word "legion" appears to be a Latin military term, from *lego*, to elect, or choose ; although used by Polybius (says Parkhurst) in his History of the Roman Wars, lib. vi. pp. 468—472. Paris Edit. 1616. written 150 years before Christ.   A legion of soldiers is thought to be 7000 men ; so that 12 legions of angelic soldiers would number 84,000 ;—a formidable army, when it is recollected that only one individual of this force killed so many thousands in the Assyrian camp.
§ Luke ii. 13, 15.

they are represented frequently as having swords,—instruments indispensable to soldiers. The question, therefore, which presents itself, but which, with the mass of evidence already adduced, presents no difficulty of decision, is;—Did Christ mean an *army* of these supposed celestial beings, or of human beings, when he said "Ye shall see Jerusalem compassed with armies"?

It is very remarkable that it is only Luke who states that Jesus predicted that Jerusalem should be compassed with armies;—that the enemy should cast a trench about it ;—that not one stone of it should be left upon another ;—that some of its inhabitants should be put to the edge of the sword, and some be carried away captive. Neither Matthew nor Mark—both of whom record the same predictions of Christ on this occasion as Luke—has any of these words, although all three have nearly the same words preceding and succeeding those which Luke alone records. Instead of the words—" when ye shall see Jerusalem compassed with armies, then know that the desolation thereof is nigh," both Matthew and Mark have —" when ye, therefore, see the abomination of desolation, spoken of by Daniel the prophet, stand in the holy place."* Instead of the words of Luke—" There shall be great distress in the land, and wrath upon this people, and they shall fall by the edge of the sword, and shall be led away captive into all nations ; and Jerusalem shall be trodden down of the Gentiles, until the time of the Gentiles be fulfilled," Matthew and Mark merely state that " there shall be great tribulation in those days."† Still here is so close a resemblance between the contexts, and indeed the whole chain of predictions narrated by the three Evangelists respectively, as to leave no doubt on the mind of any one who reads them that the three versions are narrations of the very same prophecies. As to the passage, already cited from Luke,‡ regarding the prediction, that not one stone of the city of Jerusalem should be left upon another, and that its enemies should cast a trench about it, this occurs, in his Gospel, between the account of Jesus riding in triumph into the holy city, and that of his entering the temple, and overthrowing the tables of the money-changers. Matthew and Mark, in closely similar terms, relate both these occurrences consecutively ; and John relates the latter ; but in neither of these three Evangelists is the passage we find in Luke.§ It is for Christians to show the harmony of these four Gospels. All that concerns us now is the preponderance of evidence against Luke as to whether Christ uttered the passages here under notice. In the one case, he has three Evangelists against him, and two in the other ; so that supposing all the Evangelists equally truthful, the preponderance of evidence goes to show that Christ *did not* utter those passages. For it cannot be supposed that such an important prediction as Christians say it contains—that of the abolition of the Jewish Polity, instituted by God himself—should intentionally be left unrecorded by three out of the four Evangelists ; especially, as they all four

* Compare Matth. xxiv. 15. Mark xiii. 14. with Luke xxi. 20 ; and also compare the contexts of each.

† Compare Matth. xxiv. 21, 22. Mark xiii. 19, 20. with Luke xxi. 24 ; and observe the similarity of the contexts.

‡ Vid. ante, p. 95.

§ Compare Matth. xxi. 1—16. Mark xi. 1—18, and John ii. 12—18. with Luke xix. 28—48.

alike record incidents of the most trivial character. But waiving this objection, and admitting that Christ *did* deliver these predictions as Luke records them, still they furnish no conclusive evidence that they are predictions of the destruction of Jerusalem apart from that of the world, nor that they are predictions of the destruction of that city, under any circumstances, by an army of human beings;—much less by a Roman army, to which there is not the slightest reference. For the passage in the xixth chapter occurs *shortly after* that in which it is said that the multitude who followed Christ believed that the kingdom of God (which we have seen to be connected with the End of the World) was "immediately to appear;"* and still *closer* to the parable in which Christ indisputably describes the conditions which gave persons a title of admission into, and of a position of dignity in this kingdom. Nor does it appear that a long period of time had elapsed between the utterance of the one and the other. The whole of the proceedings narrated here, clearly took place on the same day, and the account of them is obviously a narration of one unbroken chain of occurrences. As to the passage in chapter xxi. Luke, in the very same concatenated series of predictions as that in which he says that Jerusalem should be compassed with armies, the inhabitants fall by the edge of the sword and be led away captive, represents Christ to have said that *the Son of man should be seen coming with the clouds of heaven ;*—that when the signs he enumerates should be visible, *the kingdom of God was nigh at hand ;*— and that men *should stand before the Son of man.* These are expressions of which there are the most conclusive proofs that they are descriptive, solely, of the End of the World and the Last Judgment. If we apply to the passages under consideration that sound rule of criticism which explains one passage of doubtful meaning by another of clear import, we shall find in this case overwhelming evidence that those in Luke are predictions of the End of the World, which, like the other Evangelist, he states Christ said would occur before the generation then living should pass away. In the other Gospels, where, as admitted on all hands, are recorded the same prophecies as in Luke, we have the very mention of the End of the World, —the Son of man coming in the clouds with his angels and a great sound of trumpet, as the lightning cometh out of the east and shineth even unto the west,—the sun and moon darkening, and the stars falling from heaven. In a word, there is no comparison between the amount of evidence which is against, and that which is in favour of the view that Christ, as reported by Luke, as well as by the other Evangelists, predicted the End of the World and the Final Judgment, as events to take place during the age of those then living.

The only thing here, about which there can be any question, is that which, as already stated, is of no vital importance, namely—whether, according to Luke, Jerusalem was to be compassed with armies,—made level with the ground,—the inhabitants to be put to the sword and carried away captive,—together with the other events enumerated, *immediately before* or *simultaneously with* the destruction of the World. It would appear that Christ meant that the following calamities,—wars and commotions; nation rising against nation, and kingdom against kingdom; perse-

* See p. 94.

cutions of the disciples; earthquakes and pestilences,—should take place a short time before the End of the World. For in immediate connection with these he says,—" but the END is not by and by ;" meaning—the end is not immediately or instantly. (ουκ ευθεως το τελος) The word "end" here is very remarkable, as furnishing a strong proof that the prediction is that of the End of the World ; for, differently from the narrative in Matthew and Mark, the *End* of nothing had been mentioned by Luke ; nor had the circumstance of Jerusalem being compassed with armies been intimated. The *End* of nothing can be meant here, therefore, but that of the *World ;* the prediction of which Luke knew he was recording. Besides, the words— *not immediately* (ουκ ευθεως) show that, although the event would not occur *instantly,* yet it would before a long time elapsed. Jerusalem to be compassed with armies, appears, however, to be an event which was to take place *immediately* before the End of the World, and to be a precursory portion of its destruction. For when this should be seen, it is said —" Then know that the desolation thereof is *nigh.*"* The word *desolation* (ερημωσις) however, does not exactly mean the destruction of the city, but rather its privation of inhabitants, by flight, slaughter, and captivity. Accordingly, when the city is seen to be encompassed with armies, the inhabitants within it are admonished to flee to the mountains; those who are in the middle of it to depart from it, and those who are outside, not to enter it. Then, the events to happen are enumerated in the following order :—woe to those with child, or who give suck,—great distress in the land,—the people falling by the edge of the sword, and led away captive, —Jerusalem trodden down by the Gentiles,—signs in the sun, moon, and stars,—distress and perplexity of nations upon the earth,—the sea and waves roaring,—men's hearts failing them, for fear, and for looking after those things which are coming on the earth,—and the powers of heaven shaken. There are several of these particulars which cannot, with any degree even of plausibility, be applied to the destruction of Jerusalem alone. "Great distress in the land," is an expression not confined to Jerusalem, but regards at least the land of Palestine at large. "Distress of *nations* upon the *earth"* is another expression which must be much more extensive in its signification than to be confined to the distress of the inhabitants of Jerusalem, or even the inhabitants of the whole of Palestine,— must, in a word, refer to all the nations of the earth. "The sea and the waves roaring" cannot apply to Jerusalem, which is nearly an hundred miles from any sea, except the Lake of Asphaltites, which is more than twenty miles from it, and that part of it which is nearest the city is not more than two miles wide. The expression,—" looking after those things which are coming on the *earth"* is of much too extensive a signification to be confined to Jerusalem. After enumerating the foregoing particulars, Christ says,—" And then shall they see the Son of man coming in a cloud, with power and great glory. And when these things *begin* to come to pass, then look up, and lift up your heads, for your redemption draweth nigh." This passage is conclusive. Not only does its language, as to " the Son of man coming in a cloud," correspond with the other Gospels, where there is clear evidence of the prediction being that of the End of the

---

* ηγγικεν—approached, or came near. See p. 74.

World; but it tells the disciples, when they see these things, to lift up their heads, because their redemption is near. This cannot, by any means, apply to the destruction of Jerusalem; for, first, not one, according to Josephus, was allowed to escape from it, after it was besieged by the Romans; secondly, if any were allowed, the apostles,—or disciples according to Matthew,—but according to Mark only *Peter, James,* and *John,* who had come to Christ to inquire the time when these predictions should be fulfilled, were put to death before the destruction of the Jewish capital by the Roman legions; so that, at any rate, *their* redemption could not be said to be drawing near. But this expression most emphatically applies to the destruction of the World; for at the time of Christ's coming in the clouds, with power and great glory, when it is here said the redemption of the disciples "drew near," they were, according to the declaration of Paul, to be "caught up in the clouds, to meet the Lord in the air." And Christ's own words, immediately after, in explaining what he had just said, by an illustrative comparison of a fig-tree putting forth its leaves at the approach of summer, most strongly corroborate this, especially his concluding words of the elucidation,—" So likewise ye, when ye see these things come to pass, know ye that *the kingdom of God is at hand.*" It cannot, by any distortion of words, be said that the same thing is meant by the destruction of Jerusalem by the Roman army, as by *the kingdom of God being at hand.* The latter has been amply proved to mean a kingdom which Christ was to set up after destroying this world and creating another. The fact however, that Christ, after saying that the Son of man should be seen coming in a cloud, states that *when these things should come to pass,* it might be known that the kingdom of God was *nigh at hand,* furnishes one of the strongest proofs that this kingdom was to be established *immediately* upon the destruction of the world. Christ, having affirmed that *that* generation should not pass away till all be fulfilled, further says, that heaven and earth should pass away, and that *that day* should come as a snare *on all them that dwelt on the face of the whole earth.* What day is meant here? Evidently, the Day of Judgment, which was to come, not only on the inhabitants of Jerusalem, but on them that dwelt on the face of the *whole earth,* when heaven and earth should pass away. There is, therefore, no room for any rational doubt that what Luke records throughout this chapter, are the predictions of Christ regarding the End of the World.

It is true that Christ, as already intimated, had by no means very precise or sublime conceptions of the mode in which the End of the World was to be effected. But these conceptions, low as they are, probably were shared by that age in general. Having, by means of their external senses, obtained ideas of burning cities, encompassing them with armies, casting a trench about them, and pulling down the houses, so as not to leave one stone upon another;—having understood that when an enemy besieged a city, many of the inhabitants, if they were able, fled, while others were put to the sword, led away captive, devoured by famine, pestilence, and so on;—having found that there always attended these events, great troubles and perplexities; great hardship to females, especially those with child, or having the care of young children; great commotions;—great rumours of wars, and rising of nation against nation and kingdom against kingdom;—

having experienced the terrible effects of earthquakes, which, in eastern countries, frequently happened, and have contributed richly to the idea of the destruction of the World, in a measure indeed effected by them ;— having learned, from traditionary lore, the notion of signs in the heavens, the sun and moon darkened, the stars falling, and hero-gods appearing in the clouds ;—having acquired imaginary ideas of all these things, we say, the ancients, out of these crude materials were, by analogy, just as we at present imagine similar things, enabled to concoct them into what they deemed a system of the End of the World.   By the same process of analogy, drawn from kings and judges of earthly courts, they were also enabled to imagine a Day of Final Judgment.   Now, such exactly we find to be the materials out of which Christ had formed his notions of the End of the World, the Last Day of Judgment, and so on. With such prophecies, in abundance, the world has, in every age even to the present year been favoured.

SECTION V.—THE ETERNAL LIFE AND HAPPINESS PROMISED IN THE GOSPELS,—THEIR NATURE, WITH THE TIME AND PLACE AT WHICH THEY WERE TO BE POSSESSED.

Having, in preceding sections, amply shown that, at the End of the World, Christ had promised to establish a universal kingdom, which he described as of a secular character, calling it the " kingdom of heaven," and into which he promised to receive those of mankind whom, at the day of judgment, he should deem worthy, while he consigned the rest into everlasting fire, it is now proposed to lay before the reader those passages in the Gospels, where Christ promises to those who should be admitted into his kingdom, *Eternal Life and Eternal Happiness.*   To substantiate the fact that Christ held forth such promises requires very little labour ; for it will be admitted by all Christians that he promised Eternal Life and Happiness to his followers.   The *time*, however, at which, and the circumstances under which, he promised they should be admitted to the enjoyment of this boon make the fact of the utmost importance.   If he solemnly declared, that before the death of all those who were contemporary with him on earth, he should come, in the clouds of heaven, to raise the dead, take those that were good, of the living, up into the air, judge the quick and the dead, destroy the world, create a new one, and establish a kingdom, in which he and his were to dwell for ever, in the enjoyment of unsullied bliss, and has *not yet come,*—not yet done any one of all these things,—it becomes a question of the greatest doubt, if not of more than doubt, whether he will ever come,—whether he will ever raise the dead, whether he will ever judge all mankind, and take those he called the " *blessed of his Father*" to the kingdom he promised them.   Seeing that now nearly two thousand years have rolled away since this positive promise was to be fulfilled, it is difficult to see how human reason can possibly imagine any ground for believing that it ever will be fulfilled ; and still more difficult is it to see how the character of Christ,—if he be viewed as a god, who knew all things, and could do all things, so that nothing could prevent him from accomplishing his designs,—can be free from the charge of circumvention, which for a deity to be capable of is revolting to reason; or if viewed even as a mere man, it is equally difficult to clear him from the charge of either craft, or mental delusion.   Christians, however, from age to age, trust in the promise of his coming, and as already observed, now and then raise the cry that he is to appear in a particular year,—on a particular day and hour named by them.   And when this point of time is past, and they see they are deceived, and hear scoffers, now, as in ancient times, ask them in derision,—" Where is the promise of his coming ? for since the fathers fell asleep, all things continue as they were from the beginning of the creation ;"* still Christians, as if they were in a kind of reverie or trance, trust that he *is* coming, and live from age to age in daily expectation of the event, at the expense of making themselves miserable, and those around them more or less unhappy.   It is feared, therefore, that upon many of this class, arguments,—substantial proofs,— tangible evidences,—have no more effect than arrows have, when shot at the firmament.   Happily, however, there is in these days another class in the Christian world,—a class who think for themselves, who are in a great measure free from prejudice and bigotry, who scrutinize their creed, who " prove all things and hold fast that which is good," and who, therefore, are able to give " a reason of the hope that is in them."   These are they who are likely to derive some benefit from the investigation of the present subject ; and to the consideration of these, principally, are dedicated the following expressions of Christ regarding Eternal Life.

It will be recollected that it has already been shown that the kingdom of heaven was to be established simultaneously with, or immediately after the Day of Judgment and the Destruction of the World ; and that we have Christ's own words, at divers times and places, for proofs that he positively predicted these events would come to pass before the generation of men then existing should be extinct.   On one occasion, some of those who stood near him were pointedly told by him, that *they should not taste of death till they saw the Son of man coming in his kingdom, and in the glory of his Father with his holy angels, to reward every man according to his works.*†   Matthew informs us that, on another occasion, a rich young man came to Christ, and, addressing him, said,—" Good Master, what good thing shall I do that I may have eternal life ?"   Jesus said to him,—" If thou wilt enter into life, keep the commandments."   The young man replied that all these he had kept, from his youth up, and wished to know what more was required.   Christ rejoined ;—" Go and sell that thou hast, and give to the poor, and thou shalt have a treasure in heaven."   The young man, however, upon being commanded to do this, turned " sorrowful away, for he had great possessions."   Jesus, on observing this conduct, turned to his disciples and said ;—" Verily, I say unto you, that a rich man shall hardly enter into the kingdom of heaven.   And again I say unto you, it is easier for a camel to go through the eye of a needle, than for a rich man to enter into the kingdom of God."   The disciples, exceedingly amazed at this, exclaimed,

---

* 2 Pet. iii. 4.

† Matth. xvi. 27, 28. Mark ix. 1. Luke ix. 27.—A prediction which leaves not the least ground to suppose it refers to Jerusalem.

—" Who then can be saved !" Jesus consoled them by promising to them, that *they* who had followed him in the regeneration, should, when the Son of man sat on the throne of his glory, sit also upon twelve thrones, judging the twelve tribes of Israel ; and that every one who had forsaken possessions or friends for his sake, should receive an hundred-fold, and should inherit *everlasting life.** Here is a train of conversation which clearly connects *Eternal Life* with entering the *kingdom of God*, or the *kingdom of heaven*, both which are used by Christ in this passage indiscriminately. Indeed, he uses the phrase *Eternal Life* in a sense which is identical with that of the *kingdom of heaven* and *kingdom of God*, and which shows that he meant the same thing by all these three expressions. He says to the rich man, who wished Eternal Life ;—" If thou wilt enter into life, keep the commandments ;" and in reference to the same individual, " that a rich man shall hardly enter into the kingdom of heaven." Eternal Life, therefore, was evidently a life to be enjoyed in the kingdom of heaven. Nor is there any reason to believe that the language is, in the least, figurative. This passage also furnishes an explanation of the meaning of the words—*save, to be saved, salvation, Saviour*, and so on ;—words frequently met with in the New Testament. The disciples amazed at Christ saying that a rich man should hardly enter the kingdom of heaven, exclaimed ;—" Who then can be saved !" obviously meaning who could enter the kingdom of heaven, or be saved from the destruction which was to befall men at the End of the World. The reply of Christ, again, in substance, shows that to be saved was the same as to be admitted into the kingdom of heaven, at the End of the World. For he tells his disciples that when he should sit on the throne of his glory, they also should sit on thrones. It is true that Christians, to this day, regard " to be saved," the same as to be admitted into the kingdom of heaven ; but what a different gloss, by the polishing of our interested Christian guides for the past eighteen centuries, is put upon the doctrine now, from the unrefined yet urgent aspect it wore, as delivered by Christ, when it clearly meant to be saved from being burnt in the fire which was to destroy the world in the Day of Judgment, and to be received into a secular kingdom, where people were never to die; and when also he intended it to apply only to the then existing generation ! There is ample reason to conclude that Christ little thought that a doctrine which he meant to apply only to that generation should be applied to a generation of men living nearly two thousand years to come.

But let us inquire into the real import of the words *Eternal* and *Everlasting Life*. Do they mean endless duration of time, in the same sense as we now use the word *Eternity ?* The same expression, precisely, is that translated *Eternal Life* as that rendered *Everlasting Life*, namely, —ζωη αιωνιος, which (except αιδιος be substituted for αιων) may be the best expression found in the Greek tongue to convey the idea of Eternal Life. The primary† signification of αιων appears to be an *age*, or *period*. Hence we find the expressions—εις τους αιωνας των αιωνων—for ages of ages ;‡ υιοι του

---

* Matth. xix. 16—29. Luke x. 25—37 ; xviii. 18—30. Mark x. 17—31.
† Our words—Eternal and Eternity, from ætas and æternitas, (*Lat.*) mean literally nothing but age.
‡ Gal. i. 5. Rev. v. 14. et al.

αιωνος τουτου—the children of this age ;* προ των αιωνων—before the ages;†
εν τω αιωνι τω ερχομενω ζωην αιωνιον—in the age to come Eternal Life or
Eternal Age ;‡ translated in the English version, " in the *world* to come
Eternal Life." This is a remarkable instance, being one of those in which
the same word is employed to denote the duration of the age of the world
to come, and to denote the duration of the life to be enjoyed in it. It is to
be observed that the word *αιων*, in our version is repeatedly translated
world, when in connection with τελος (end) so as to make—the " End of the
World," the meaning literally being the " End of the Age."§   But Paul
uses the word κοσμος—the earth‖ most frequently. John uses the same
word throughout his Gospel. The word *αιων*, however, is used by Paul,¶
and other writers of the New Testament, to denote the created and material
world, so as to leave no doubt that, when it is connected with the word
τελος, it means not only *the End of the Age*, as has been asserted, but also
the End or Destruction of the Globe upon which we live.   The word
οικουμενη—*the inhabitants of the earth*, is used sometimes for the material
world,†† by way of metonymy, where the cause instead of the effect, or the
container instead of the things contained, is mentioned. That this word
was used in this extensive signification is proved by the fact that it is used
for the " world to come,"—the world which Christ was to create after
destroying the present.‡‡ There is, therefore, no foundation for the supposition that, because the above words are sometimes used in a more limited
sense to denote only part of the earth, or a certain region of it, they do
not mean the *End* or *Destruction* of the habitable Globe by Christ, at his
coming, when they are employed in connection with τελος or some other
word of similar import ; the context clearly defining the meaning.   But to
return to the adjective of *αιων*, (age) namely, *αιωνιος*. This word is used
quite as frequently to designate *an indefinite time*, or time of very long
duration, the end of which cannot be fixed or foreseen, as it is used to
denote *infinite time*.   Hence it becomes a question whether the phrase—
ζωη αιωνιος, as used by Christ, was designed to mean *Endless Life*, or life
of very long and indefinite duration.   At all events, the Greek words
translated " Eternal Life," in themselves do not necessarily imply the
former. Christ's words in another place, however, are much stronger than
these, in favour of the view that those who entered the kingdom of heaven
were to have Endless Life :—" If a man keep my sayings, he shall never
see death."§§   But the *literal* translation here again weakens the passage,
and makes it mean,—*he shall not see death for ages*.   Not, however, to
insist on this point, so as to found any argument upon it,‖‖ but giving

---

* Luke xx. 34.
† I Cor. ii. 7.   The word עולם is used in the same various modes precisely.
‡ Mark x. 30. Luke xviii. 30.   § See Matth. xii. 32 ; xxiv. 3. Rom. xii. 2.
    ‖ 1 Tim. vi. 7.   Heb. xi. 38.   ¶ Heb. i. 2 ; xi. 3.
        †† Acts xvii. 6, 31. Rom. x. 18.   ‡‡ Heb. ii. 5.
    §§ John viii. 51.   Θαναταν ου μη θεωρηση εις των αιωνα.
‖‖ There is, however, ample proof that αιων and αιωνιος do not mean what we now
understand by *Eternity*, and *Eternal*. Many passages could be cited from the Septuagint
where the very contexts prove that only some distant time is meant, such as—" I have
considered the year of *ancient* (αιωνιος) time."—Ps. lxxvi. 5.—" He remembered the
days of old." (αιωνις)—Is. lxiii. 11. The word αιδιος, *ever, alway, without beginning or
end*, would certainly convey an idea of the eternal duration of time, but this is used only

Christians full credit for their promise of a life of endless duration, let us point out a few more of the passages upon which they build their hope of this boon.

Christ, in indoctrinating Nicodemus on this point, said that except a man was born of *water* and of the *spirit* he could not enter the kingdom of God ; and shortly afterwards told him that whosoever *believed* on the Son of man should not perish, but have Everlasting Life. These three things were essential pre-requisites to obtain admission into this kingdom ;—to believe that Christ was to be the king of the kingdom, to be baptized by immersion, and to receive the Holy Ghost, so as to be able to perform miracles. When we consider that, at the time Christ is said to have been on earth, there was a general belief among the Jews that the End of the World was at hand, and also that they were taught to regard baptism—the ancient καθαρισμος (purification by water,) of the Jews remodified—as one of the essential conditions to enter the future kingdom of Christ, we find no difficulty in understanding why such multitudes flocked to John and the apostles to be baptized. But what chiefly concerns us at present to notice is the fact that Christ, in his conversation with Nicodemus, identifies, as usually, the kingdom of God with Eternal Life.* Another passage which proves this identity, and to which for another purpose recourse has been had already, is the following :—Jesus having promised Peter the keys of the kingdom of heaven, as a reward for pronouncing him the Son of the living God ; and having, almost immediately afterwards, had an altercation with him, under the influence of which he calls him, "Satan," addresses the other disciples thus ;—"Whosoever will save his life shall lose it ; and whosoever will lose his life for my sake shall find it. For what is a man profited if he shall gain the whole world and lose his own soul ? or what shall a man give in exchange for his soul ? For the Son of man shall come in the glory of his Father with his angels ; and then he shall reward every man according to his works ? Verily I say unto you, *there be some standing here, which shall not taste of death till they see the Son of man coming in his kingdom.*† This short passage contains the whole of Christ's doctrine. It may aptly be called his "body of Divinity." It includes the salvation of men, the coming of Christ to judge the world, and his reception of the saints into his kingdom,—the whole "scheme of redemption." Let us examine its contents. In the first place, it is observable that the same word is translated *soul* in verse 26, as is translated *life* in verse 25. It is the word ψυχη. Now, it is of importance to our subject to ascertain the meaning of this word, and to know whether it means that life possessed by the brute creation in common with man, or the immaterial principle designated by the word *soul*. Rather than that the author's *ipse dixit* should be taken for authority on the meaning of this important word, the definition of that pious Christian and celebrated Greek and Hebrew scholar—Mr. Parkhurst, in his Greek Lexicon, (a standard authority by divines on questions of this kind) is here given in a condensed

---

in two places in the Bible ; the one in an instance not connected with Eternal Life, and the other in reference to the everlasting chains of the fallen angels. In the next sentence, however, the word αιωνιος is used in regard to the *eternal fire* of Sodoma and Gomorrha. (See Rom. i. 20. Jude 6, 7.) See *Note* on αιων in chapter IV. sec. I.

* John iii. 3, 5, 16, 36.   † Matth. xvi. 25—28. Mark viii. 27—38.

form.—Ψυχη (from ψυχω, to refresh with cool air, also to breathe.)—
1. *Breath.* 2. *Animal life.* 3. *A living animal, a creature or animal that lives by breathing.* 4. *The human body though dead.* 5. *The human soul or spirit.* 6. The human *animal soul,* as distinguished from both man's body and from his πνευμα, or spirit, breathed into him immediately by God.—
7. *The mind or disposition,* particularly as denoting the *affections.* 8. *A human person.* 9. The *souls* of those who had been *slain* for the Word of God, and for the testimony which they held, are represented as being *under the altar,* in allusion to the *blood* of the *sacrifices,* which, according to the Levitical Law, used *to be poured out upon the altar* of the burnt-offerings, (Lev. i. 5. Deut. xii. 27.) and part of which, consequently, *ran under the altar.* The blood is likewise called the ψυχη in the LXX, where it is used in a great number of passages, and most commonly answers to the Hebrew noun שׁבֶנ, derived from the same word, as a verb, *to breathe.* Such, according to Parkhurst, and other lexicographers, who are perfectly correct, is the meaning of the word translated in our Bible into that term which designates a thing of which there is nothing in nature bearing any analogy to it,—an immaterial principle,—*a soul.* The word for which this stands, as we have seen, means almost everything of which man is composed, but *a soul.* To any one that will consult Parkhurst under the word ψυχη, it will be clear that the only reason given under sec. 5. for making it denote " *the human soul or spirit,*" is that it is *translated soul* in our version of the Bible. But it must strike the meanest capacity as being very surprising that a word said to denote man's immaterial principle,—his immortal soul, should, under the guidance of *Inspiration,* be used to denote the *blood* of brutes, the *life* and *breath* of brutes, and so on. The monoglot reader, however, may rest assured that the true meaning of ψυχη, in the words of Christ just quoted, is *life,* or *breath.* Man breathing as long as there is life in him, *breath* and *life* are thus identical in their meaning. *Wherever the word soul is met with in the New Testament it is a translation of the word* ψυχη, *which means breath.* Precisely similar remarks may be made regarding πνευμα, (spirit) which Parkhurst derives from a verb of the same signification, meaning *breath, wind,* or *air.* This word is translated *spirit* in the English version of the Bible. The translators must have found it very hard to be obliged to translate this word *wind,* in the same verse as they have translated it *spirit.*—" The *wind* (πνευμα) bloweth where it listeth,"......
" so is every one that is born of the *spirit.*"* (πνευμα.) Nor does the word רוח (rooach) from which the words *soul* and *spirit* are translated in the Old Testament mean anything, according to its primary signification, but *breath, air, air in motion, wind, life,* &c. It is a remarkable fact, that while the metaphysical notion of the immortality of the soul, apart from the body, was at a very early period taught in India, Assyria, Egypt, and Gaul, there is no reference made to it in the Old Testament,—not so much as a term used to denote an immaterial and immortal spirit;† and such exactly is the case in the New Testament. Thus Christ seems to have had no idea of the

---

* John iii. 8.

† Accordingly, in the conjuring tale of the Witch of Endor bringing up Samuel, the latter is represented to have come from the *invisible* world in a *visible* and *material* form, with his power of speech and all the other properties of the human body.—1 Sam. xxviii. A great many other instances of this notion might be added.

possible existence of a soul in a separate state from the body. He made no promises of rewards and punishments* till after the resurrection, when the former were to be dispensed in his kingdom, and the latter inflicted on those excluded, by plunging them into the universal conflagration of the world.†

With these facts before us, we are better prepared to inquire what Christ meant by the word ψυχη, in the expression already cited, where it occurs not less than four times. That he meant the same thing in every instance here, where the word is used, is clear from the close contiguity of one to another, and from the drift of the discourse; whatever may be thought of the motive which induced the translators of the English version to render the word "soul" in the two last instances. But did Christ mean an immaterial and immortal principle, by the word—soul? No. The very sense of the passage prohibits such an opinion. It should be observed, that by the words—*will lose* is meant *wish* or desire *to lose*. (θελη σωσαι). Therefore verse 25. would read thus;—For whosoever wishes to save his life shall lose it, and whosoever will lose his life for my sake shall find it. In the next verse, also, it should be observed that the meaning of ζημιοω is to damage, injure, or suffer loss; and that of ανταλλαγμα is compensation or ransom; and that the verse reads thus;—For what is a man profited if he shall gain the whole world, and suffer the loss of his life? or what shall a man give as a ransom for his life. There is here no reference whatever to a soul; Christ means simply life. The context further proves this.— Christ having told his disciples that, although he should be put to death by the Jews, he would again rise from the dead on the third day, Peter, with commendable feeling and affection, tells him he hoped these sufferings would not befall him. But Christ, untouched by these loving sentiments, turns upon Peter, and exclaims;—"Get thee behind me, Satan; thou art an offence unto me." He then says to the other disciples;—"If any man

---

* In the Pentateuch, like the rest of the Old Testament, there is no clear allusion to a future state of rewards and punishments, or to the soul's immortality and separate existence from the body after death; but on the contrary, a man's sins were to be punished in this world, on himself personally, or in the persons of his posterity, "unto the third and fourth generation." (See the meaning of the word Paradise, pp. 87—90.) Indeed some portions of the Bible, such as Eccl. ii. 15, 16; iii. 19—21; ix. 4, 5. positively deny future rewards and punishments, and even the conscious existence of man after death, describing his end like that of the beast, in such words as—"There is no remembrance of the wise more than of the fool *for ever*."—"That which befalleth the sons of men befalleth beasts; even one thing befalleth them; as the one dieth, so dieth the other; yea they have all one *breath*; so that *a man hath no pre-eminence above a beast*; for all is vanity. All go unto one place; all are of the dust, and all turn to dust again. Who knoweth the *spirit of man* that goeth upward, and the *spirit of the beast* that goeth downward to the earth?"—"The dead *know not any thing*; neither have *they any more* a reward." Such is the Scripture notions of man with regard to a future state, rewards and punishments, &c. That there are contradictory doctrines in other parts of the book, only proves its imperfect character. What honest motive could induce the English translators to render the word רוח *breath* in one place, but *spirit* in another place, in the above citations? (Compare Eccl. iii. 19. with ver. 21.) The translation is otherwise very bad here. For the words—רוח בני האדם (rooach beni headim,) *the spirit of the sons of men*, we have "the spirit of man." In the immediately preceding verses, the same words are rendered "the sons of men."

† See further on this point, Greg's Creed of Christendom, pp. 282—286. Dr. Priestley's Hist. Cor. Christianity, vol. i. p. 401. Taylor's Diegesis, p. 28.

will (wishes to—θελει) come after me, let him deny himself, and take up his cross and follow me."* Then come the words which we have already

---

* Precisely the same views will be found set forth in the following places.—Luke ix. 23—27; xiv. 26, 27; xvii. 33. John xii. 25, 26. There is, however, one passage of this class which requires a word of explanation.—Matth. x. 28.—" Fear not them which kill the body, but are not able to kill the soul; but rather fear him which is able to destroy both body and soul in hell." (See also Luke xii. 4, 5.) It has been thought that this passage proves the *immateriality* and *immortality* of the soul; and that by "him which is able to destroy both body and soul in hell," we are to understand the devil. Very different things, however, are meant here. There is in the passage no reference at all to an *immaterial* principle. The verb, translated *kill*, is αποκτεινω, meaning to *slaughter*, or *massacre*, and the other, translated *destroy*, απολλυω, meaning to *destroy, kill, perish, die*, &c. The word translated *soul* here, again is ψυχη, and that for which the word *body* stands, is σωμα; so that thus far the passage is translated very fairly. The word rendered *hell* is γεεννα, a word composed, or rather corrupted from γη, *land, earth*, and Hinnon; or the Hebrew words גי (valley,) and Hinnom; the latter being the name of a person who once possessed the Valley of Hinnom, which was situated near Jerusalem, and in which there were furnaces, particularly in that spot of it called *Tophet*, (which word appears to signify a furnace) where human beings were burnt alive to Moloch and other gods. See Josh. xv. 8. 2 Kings xxiii. 10. 2 Chron. xxviii. 3; xxxiii. 6. Jer. xix. 2; xxxii. 35. In all these passages the Valley of Hinnom is in Hebrew called *Gehenna*, גי־הנם or uncontracted גיא בן־הנם) the Christian hell. In reference to this place Christ says—that whosoever should call his brother a fool should be in danger of the fire of Gehenna, or rather *of a Gehenna of fire*, (γεεννα του πυρος,) translated in our version *hell-fire*. (Matth. v. 22.) The same *Gehenna* or hell he means where, in the same chapter, he exhorts people to pull out their right eye, and cut off their right hand, in order to avoid it. (ver. 29, 30; xviii. 8, 9. Mark ix. 43—47.) Also the same when he tells the Pharisees that they made their proselytes twofold more the children of hell (γεεννα) than themselves; and when he calls this religious sect, serpents, and a generation of vipers who could not escape the damnation of hell. (chap. xxiii. 15, 33.) The hell of Jesus Christ, therefore, was in the Valley of Hinnom, where human beings, particularly children, were burnt alive to Moloch. (See Park. Greek Lex. infra γεεννα.) Christ mentions Hades but in few instances; and only in one instance he connects the idea of fire with it. Hades, in Grecian and other ancient mythologies, means a dark place where the dead were supposed to be shut up, and where there was a gate to let them in, —a deep pit, a cavern, the grave. Accordingly we find Christ saying that Capernaum should be reduced to *Hades*, (Matth. xi. 23. Luke x. 15.) that the gates of *Hades* should not prevail against the rock upon which he was building his church, (chap. xvi. 18.) and that in *Hades* the rich man lifted up his eyes, (Luke xvi. 23.) in which last instance only is the least allusion made to fire. The hell, however, in which Christ says the body and life should be destroyed was not Hades, but Gehenna, or rather the furnace Tophet, in the Valley of Hinnom. But it is questionable, whether in any of the foregoing passages, which are the whole to be found in the Gospels where hell is mentioned, he means the punishment to be inflicted on those who were to be burnt at the End of the World.— The furnace of fire, however, in which he says the wicked should be burnt at the End of the World, would seem to indicate that he thought his enemies should then be burned in some such place as Tophet.

In corroboration of the correctness of these explanations of Christ's pagan or mythological hell, it may render some degree of satisfaction, if not solace to the Christian reader, smarting under the loss of his *Tophet*, of which the foregoing facts have just deprived him, to cite a few passages from some standard and orthodox writers on the point. Parkhurst, in his Greek Lexicon to the New Testament, under the word γεεννα writes, *inter alia*,—" *Gehenna* of the New Testament, is in like manner a corruption of the two Hebrew words גי *a valley*, and הנם the name of a person........ ..... "*A Gehenna of fire*, Matth. v. 22. does, I apprehend, in its *outward* and *primary* sense, relate to that dreadful doom of being *burnt alive in the Valley of Hinnom*............" And in ix. 43, 44, &c. our Lord seems to allude to the *worms* which continually preyed on the dead carcases that were cast out into the Valley of Hinnom—*Gehenna*, and to the perpetual fire kept up there to consume them." Under the word Moloch he says, that this fiery idol worshipped by the apostate Israelites, means a *king* or *ruler*. He also, under

examined. The whole is to the following effect :—Christ tells his disciples that the Jews would put him to death by crucifixion. Peter entreats him to

Tophet, in his Hebrew Lexicon, defines the word—*a furnace,* which was in the *Valley of Hinnom.* The pious and learned Cruden, in his Concordance, under the same word, says ;—" It is thought that *Tophet* was the butchery, or the place of slaughter, at Jerusalem, lying on the south of the city, in the Valley of the children of Hinnom.".......
Others think that the name of *Tophet* is given to the Valley of Hinnom, because of the sacrifices that were offered there to the god Moloch, by beat of drums, which in Hebrew is called *Toph.*....... They lighted a great fire within the statue, and another before it. They put upon its arms the child they intended to sacrifice, which soon fell into the fire at the foot of the statue, putting forth cries, as may easily be imagined. To stifle the noise of these cries and howlings, they made a great rattling of drums and other instruments, that the spectators might not be moved with compassion at the clamours of these miserable victims." Such is the account these two divines give of *Gehenna.*
Of course both of them spiritualize this pagan and material hell a little, and apply it to the prevalent Christian notion of Tophet. It is, however, indisputable that this pagan fire-worship in the Valley of Hinnom was the hell described by Christ. Moreover, we have positive proof in the Old Testament, not only that the Jews offered human sacrifices in the Valley of Hinnom, but that they believed that *Jehovah* was the *Moloch,* or statue-king of this Gehenna. Isaiah, (xxx. 27—33.) in his description of the rites of *Tophet,* after stating that there would be *song, tabrets, drums,* and *harps,* when Jehovah, (or the statue Moloch) would show *the lighting* down of his arm, with *the flame of devouring fire,* in the destruction of the Assyrians, adds ;—" Tophet is ordained of old ; yea for the *king* (קלם—Moloch) it is prepared ; he hath made it *deep* and *large :* the pile thereof is *fire* and much wood ; the breath of the Lord (יהוה—Jehovah) like a *stream of brimstone doth kindle it.*" There is not the least room to doubt that the same personage is meant, in one part of this passage, by *Moloch* or king, as in another part of it by *Jehovah.* Hence, it is clear, that the Jewish and pagan *Gehenna* were the same, and both the same as Christ's *Gehenna* or hell. Jehovah was the king of the Gehenna of the ancient Jews ; and we shall have reason hereafter to see that Jehovah—"the Father," was the king of Christ's Gehenna, whom he says was to be *feared,* because he was able to destroy both body and soul in this Gehenna, by casting a person from his arms down to the deep pit of fire at his feet, till he was annihilated, just as the custom was in the Valley of Hinnom to place the victim on the arms of the idol—Moloch, which held it in a half-bending posture in his fiery arms, and which, being thought to possess life, &c., was supposed, presently, to throw the unfortunate individual into the pit of fire at its feet, so as to be seen no more ; whereas, in reality, the victim rolled off itself to this pit when half burnt.—Εκτετακως τας χειρας υπτιας της γης, ωστε τον εντιθεντα των παιδων αποκυλιεσθαι και πιπτειν εις τι χασμα πληρες πυρος.—*Diodor. Sic.* lib. xx. This was the Jehovah, who had his *fire* in Zion, and his *furnace* in Jerusalem, (Isa. xxxi. 9.)—the same furnace of fire as that into which Christ says his enemies should be cast at the End of the World, to wail and gnash their teeth. (Matth. xiii. 42, 50.)—
Having thus explained Christ's confused and mythological notion of hell, let us see what he means by killing the *body* and *life,* destroying both in hell, and so on. He encourages his disciples to brave persecutions, and even death ; he tells them, that as he was persecuted and his life sought, such treatment they might expect ; for a disciple could not expect better treatment than his master ; he further gives them to understand that all that would be done to them should be revealed,—should be made known to him, whether present or absent ; and then he tells them, therefore, not to fear those persecutors who might be able to put them to death,—to *slaughter, destroy,* or *kill* their bodies, —but who would not be able to put an ultimate end to their lives, as he was going to give them *Eternal Life,* even if they were dead and buried ; but to fear *him* who was able to destroy both soul and body in hell. (Gehenna.) But who is meant by " *him*" ? The Father ;—from whom Jesus continually says he received the Eternal Life he promises to his followers. The same is meant by *him* here, as is meant in the passage just cited from Isaiah ;—*Jehovah,* or the *king,* who had power to burn into ashes in the fire of *Moloch,*—the furnace *Tophet,*—the *Gehenna* of Christ,—and the *Hell* of the English translators of the Bible ;—so that, after this process of supposed annihilation in the fire of Gehenna, resurrection would, as supposed by Christ, be impossible, and therefore, the Eternal Life he promised would be lost. That Christ means the Father,

I

abandon such apprehensions.   Christ tells Peter that he hindered him in
fulfilling the purposes of his mission ; and adds that, instead of displaying
the cowardly spirit of Peter, any one that wished to be a disciple of his
should be ready to take up his cross with him, and carry it to the place of
execution, (a thing which those who were put to death, anciently, were
made to do,) for whoever, like Peter, wished then to save his life, would
lose it when the Son of man should come to destroy the world ; but whoever would at the time being lose his life in the cause of Christ should find
it thereafter, by being raised at his coming into the enjoyment of Life
Eternal.   Then the following words expatiate on the folly of any one trying
to save his life under these circumstances.—For what is a man profited if
now he shall gain the whole world, and at the coming of the Son of man

here, by *him*, is proved by the context.   In verse 20, he says that the breath or spirit of
his Father spoke in his apostles.   In the verses immediately following the passage under
examination, he says that not a sparrow fell to the ground without the *Father ;* that the
very hairs of the apostles' heads were numbered ; that they should, therefore, *not fear,*
for they were more valuable than sparrows ; and that he should confess some, and deny
others, before his *Father* in heaven.   The whole context proves that the *Father* is
meant here, as having power to annihilate, in the fire of Gehenna, both the body and
soul, or rather life.   There is nothing more frequently inculcated in the Gospels, particularly in the Gospel of John, as well as throughout the Epistles, than that the lives of
Christ's followers were safe, whatever happened to their bodies ;—meaning, the Eternal
Life he was to give them.   Paul forcibly expresses this when he tells the Colossians
(iii. 3.) that their life was hid with Christ in God.   Any one, on taking his Concordance
and referring to the quotations under the word—*life,* will have ample proof that the life
of the saints,—meaning, the Eternal Life Christ was to give them,—was hid in him.
The only way to lose this life, was by forsaking him ; in which case, life was to be
irrevocably destroyed with the body in the fire of Gehenna.
    It may further be remarked that the verb—απολλυω, in the passage under considera-
tion, translated *destroy,*—namely, " destroy both soul and body in hell,"—not less than
the foregoing verb—αποκτεινω, translated *kill,* means, *taking away life,* in the ordinary
acceptation of the phrase, so as utterly to invalidate any argument for the immateriality
or indestructibility of the soul that may be built upon the words,—" Fear not them
which *kill* the body, but are not able to kill the soul."   Besides : the remainder of the
verse refers to a power able to *destroy* or *kill* both *soul* and *body* in hell.   The verb—
απολλυω, translated *destroy* (soul and body in hell,) here, is used, in a great number of
instances, to denote, simply, the taking away of life, such as—to destroy the child Jesus ;
(Matth. ii. 13.)—to crucify Christ ; (Matth. xxvii. 20.)—to die by the sword ; (Matth.
xxvi. 52.)—to be drowned ; (Mark iv. 38.)—to be massacred ; (Luke xi. 51.)—in short,
to lose one's life in any manner. (Matth. x. 39 ; xvi. 25.)   So also in profane authors,—
Απολεσει την ψυχην—will lose his life.—Herodot. lib. I. c. 112.   The *soul,* therefore,
as well as the body, was to be *killed* or *destroyed* in Christ's Gehenna or hell.   His meaning, however, as already stated, is, that if a person lost his life in his cause by means of
persecution, he should be raised afterwards to Eternal Life ; but that if a person renounced
him, his Father would annihilate him in the fire of Gehenna.   This notion is continually
held forth by him in different words, such as ;—" He that findeth his life shall lose it ;
and he that loseth his life for my sake shall find it."—" Whosoever will save his life shall
lose it ; and whosoever will lose his life for my sake shall find it."
    There is nothing clearer than that neither in the New Testament nor in the Old is
the present Christian notion of Hell entertained.   Nor is there in the Bible so much as
a name for a place of torment for the souls of the dead.   The Hebrew word—שאול
(Shaol) often translated *Hell* in the English, and *Hades* in the Greek version of the Old
Testament, means nothing more than—*the grave, a pit, a great depth, a cave* or *cavern,*
where anciently they buried the dead.   And, indeed, the very Saxon word—*hell* is of
the same import :—*hillon* or *helon, hol,* to be concealed ; hence *hole, hollow, &c.*   See the
Hebrew word—*Shaol* in Gen. xxxvii. 35 ; xlii. 38. Deut. xxxii. 22. and a great many
other places.   The whole of this investigation irresistibly leads to the conclusion that
the Christian Hell, like the Christian Heaven, is clearly of a pagan origin.

lose his own life ? or what shall a man then give as a ransom for his life ?* That this is the real meaning, is clearly shown by the words which immediately follow.—"For the Son of man shall come in the glory of his Father with his angels ; and then he shall reward every man according to his works. Verily I say unto you, There be some standing here, which shall not taste of death, till they see the Son of man coming in his kingdom."† These words are evidently uttered as a reason for saying that it would profit nothing for a man to gain the whole world and lose his life, and that he could find nothing that would be accepted as a ransom for his life.— The passage, therefore, implies the following points :—that there was what is called Eternal Life, (ζωη αιωνιος) to be given to those who were to be the subjects of Christ's kingdom, while those who did not merit this favour, were to lose their lives in the destruction of the world, at the coming of Christ with his angels ;—that those who should lose their lives, were to be overtaken by this calamity, and those who should obtain Life Eternal, were to receive this boon, *at the same period of time ;* namely, when the Son of man should come to reward every man according to his works ;—and lastly, that these things were to take place *before some of those* who were then present hearing Christ uttering these words *should die :*—" There be some *standing here,* which shall not *taste of death,* till they see the Son of man coming in his kingdom." This very passage, in itself, conclusively proves that the coming of Christ with his angels,—the end of the world,— the day of judgment,—the establishing of Christ's kingdom,—the reward of eternal life and the punishment of eternal death, were, all of them, to take place *during the lifetime of the generation of men existing at the time Christ spoke these words.* But the passage does not contain one syllable about man's *soul ;* although a thousand times has it been taken as a text to prove the existence of an *immaterial* entity. To ascertain the real existence of such, however, is not the object of our present inquiry.

The following passages, like the foregoing, identify the act of entering into life with that of entering into the kingdom of heaven.—" If thy hand offend thee, cut it off : it is better for thee to enter into life maimed, than having two hands to go into hell ; (γεεννα) into the fire that never shall be quenched ; where their worm dieth not, and the fire is not quenched.— And if thy foot offend thee, cut it off : it is better for thee to enter halt into life, than having two feet to be cast into hell ; into the fire that never shall be quenched ; where their worm dieth not, and the fire is not quenched. And if thine eye offend thee, pluck it out : it is better for thee to enter into the kingdom of God with one eye, than having two eyes to be cast into hell fire ; where their worm dieth not, and the fire is not quenched."‡ Here, *entering the kingdom of God* and *entering life,* are phrases used precisely in the same connection, and evidently mean the same thing. Nor is there anything in this passage, any more than in the preceding passages, which suggests that the language is figurative. The injunction to pluck out an eye, amputate a leg, or lop off an arm, together with many other self-inflicted cruelties, in order to secure Eternal Life,

---

* See the preceding Note which, properly, should be attached to this sentence. The mistake of the Compositor was not discovered till it was too late to correct it.

† Matth. xvi. 27, 28.   ‡ Mark ix. 43—47. Matth. v. 28, 29 ; xviii. 8, 9.

doubtless, in ancient times, was literally carried out by Thyestean Christians, who frequently were convicted of feasting on the flesh of murdered infants.[*]

The same *Life* is again connected with the kingdom of God in the following instance.—The Pharisees demanded of Christ " when the kingdom of God should come." He replied to them, that it did not come with observation ; meaning that it would come suddenly, when they little expected it ; and he added ;—" The kingdom of God is within you ;" that is, within your reach, or within your possession. Supposing the kingdom of heaven to mean the Gospel Dispensation, as Christians tell us, still Christ could not, in this passage, (which the advocates of the Christian religion claim for themselves to show that Christ's kingdom was spiritual,) mean that the kingdom of God, if he meant the Gospel Dispensation, was *within* the Pharisees, who were open enemies to its doctrines, and who now, apparently in derision, asked when it would come. The words are— H βασιλεια του Θεου εντος υμων εστιν. Here is another instance of the verb ειμι, as already noticed, with a genitive case,—the genitive υμων, and the adverb εντος, which always governs the genitive,—elliptically signifying possession ; and, in this instance, meaning, *within your possession, or reach.* Overlooking this peculiarity of ειμι, Biblical critics have been much puzzled by this expression.[†] Christ proceeds to give utterance to predictions, precisely like those in Matth. chap. xxiv. relating to the End of the World ; and among other things, says that the Son of man should come as lightning, and that whosoever should seek to save his life should lose it ; but whosoever should lose his life should preserve it.[‡] We have already seen what is meant by losing and finding life, and now it remains only to observe that here, again, this "life" is connected with the "kingdom of God," and that the striking similarity of the language of the whole passage, just pointed out, to that in Matth. chap. xxiv. which is a series of predictions of the End of the World, proves both to bear relation, as to time and other particulars, to the coming of Christ in Judgment.

SECTION VI.—CHRIST'S PREDICTION OF THE NEAR APPROACH OF THE END OF THE WORLD AND THE FINAL JUDGMENT AT VARIANCE WITH FACT.

The next question to be decided, is ;—*Was Christ a true prophet, in predicting what, in the foregoing sections, he has been shown to have predicted?* What the Evangelists state that he uttered, with regard to his coming in the clouds with his angels and a great sound of a trumpet, while the heavenly bodies were being disrupted,—his sitting in judgment to reward every man according to his works, punishing some in unquenchable fire, and receiving others into the kingdom of heaven, in which he was to

---

* Euseb. Hist. Eccles. lib. v. c. 1. Agreeably to this Christian doctrine and practice, Paul exhorts his brethren to mortify their members, (Col. iii. 5. Rom. viii. 13.) and Origen undergoes a most painful and inhuman operation, (Euseb. Hist. Eccles. lib. vi. c. 8.) which Christ sanctions in Matth. xix. 12. The Christian monk, Ammon, even as late as the fourth century, cut off his ear in order to avoid being made a bishop.—Sozom. Hist. Eccles. lib. vi. c. 30. Evagrius also appears to have cut off his tongue in order to preserve silence.—Socrat. Hist. Eccles. lib. iv. c. 23.
† Vid. Park. infra εντος.   ‡ Luke xvii. 20.—37.

reign for ever; and all to happen during the lifetime of the generation
of men then living,—cannot be denied to be prophecies, or predictions of
future events, uttered in a most clear and unequivocal language. Whether
Christ, as a Jewish prophet, imitated his predecessors in that religious
frenzy, under the influence of which, as already described,* they delivered
their presages, is not known to us.   Nor can we at this period gather
much information on this point, since there is nothing on record, concerning
him, written by any of his contemporaries, if we except what is attributed
to his own illiterate apostles.   To these we give the credit of having
written nothing that would lead to that conclusion, with the following
exceptions however; namely,—that, like the prophet Jeremiah, Christ
wept now and then, and went into a furious rage against the Pharisees and
Scribes, before he uttered predictions, calling them by all sorts of opprobrious names,—that his apostles record that the Jews said he had a devil,
and was mad,—and that the same apostles also record that, on one occasion
at least, his relations laid hold on him, and pronounced him beside himself.†
But, upon the whole, the Evangelists represent him as of a more temperate
disposition than the old prophets even describe themselves.   And further;
he differs certainly from them in that his predictions are uttered in clearer
and more distinct terms, so as to leave little doubt, either as to their being
real predictions, or as to the events which they are intended to foretell.—
The question which remains, however, is whether they are *true predictions*.
The fact that he prophesied the day of judgment,—the end of the world,
—the coming of the kingdom of heaven, and the everlasting life to be
enjoyed in it,—is supported by such a mass of clear evidence, furnished by
his own words, as can scarcely be adduced in proof of any other fact, either
in history, science, or morals.   Indeed, the whole burden—the " very pith
and marrow" of the Gospel doctrines, is the *kingdom of heaven*, and the
events concomitant with its coming.   The most prominent and important
doctrines of Christianity, as insisted upon by Christians of the *present age*,
are scarcely alluded to in the Gospels; and some of them have no place
whatever in them.   The doctrines of the Trinity,—of the Fall of man and
Original Sin,—of the Atonement, Mediation, and Intercession of Christ,—
of Sanctification and other " works of the Spirit;" together with a vast
number of other fundamental doctrines now taught by Christians of all
denominations, are not anywhere inculcated by Christ.   He predicts that
he should be put to death, and that he should rise from the dead on the
third day; but he does not even intimate that he was to die in order to
make an atonement to Divine justice for the sins of men; and that he was
to rise from the dead and ascend to heaven, in order that he should there
intercede on behalf of sinners, who supplicated the throne of his Father.
Nor does he give any instruction as to how Christian churches were to be
formed and managed; or even intimate that any churches at all were to
be formed.   All he does, is to send his disciples to preach that the *kingdom
of heaven* (meaning what we have seen,) was at hand.   All his discourses,
whether in parables or otherwise, directly refer to the proximity of the End
of the World, the Last Judgment, and the kingdom of heaven.   Again:
his language, in fixing the time when these events were to occur, is such as

* pp. 55—58.   † John x. 20.   Mark iii. 21.

to admit of no rational doubt that they were to come to pass within the *lifetime* of those who listened to him ; or at least the generation of men *then living*.   His words on this point, on one occasion, are—" Verily I say unto you, This generation shall not pass, till all these things be fulfilled ;"* and on another occasion,—" Verily I say unto you, there be some standing here which shall not taste of death till they see the Son of man coming in his kingdom."†   These expressions, it will be observed, are uttered by Christ in immediate connection with clear predictions of the Day of Judgment, the End of the World, and the coming of his kingdom ; and there can be nothing more certain than that it is the occurrence of these events he means, in the one passage, by the words—" all these things" ; and in the other, by—" the Son of man coming in his kingdom." In the one passage, he says that " *this* generation,"—meaning, indisputably, the generation then existing,—should not pass till " all these things be fulfilled ;" and in the other, that some of those who then stood by him should " not taste of death" till they saw these things.   No human language can be clearer and more definite than that which Christ has used on these occasions.

But perhaps some Pyrrhonean may demand a proof of the length of time a *generation* of men existed in the age of Christ, as well as of the length of time men then lived without *tasting of death;* intimating, of course, that *that generation* to which Christ referred has not yet passed, or that those men, who at the time stood by him, have not yet tasted of death ; and, therefore, that his prophecies *may* still be fulfilled in due time.— Although this would be a very far-fetched objection, and would show that any one who raised it felt the desperate state of his case ; yet it must be admitted that instances are on record of Christian writers having had recourse to objections and modes of argument quite as extreme, and as contrary to common sense, when, in the heat of controversy, they endeavoured to uphold their favourite tenets.   It would, however, be very easy to prove, from authentic history, that, notwithstanding the accounts we have of antedeluvian personages living nearly a thousand years,‡ the age of man at the time of Christ was not longer than it is now.   Augustus Cæsar died a natural death, at the age of 76, A.D. 14.   Flavius Josephus died A.D. 96, aged 56 years ; and John the Evangelist is said by Christian chronologists to have died A.D. 100, whatever was his age.   Hence we may safely conclude that none of the human beings, who were contemporary with Christ, are now living.

That *generation*, therefore, having *passed*,—in other words, the men who composed it having *tasted of death,* were Christ's predictions fulfilled *before they tasted of death ?* or have they been fulfilled even to this day ? Has the Son of man come in the glory of his Father with his angels ?—

---

* Matth. xxiv. 34.   † Matth. xvi. 28.

‡ We frequently meet with accounts of fabulous longevity in Greek and Roman authors, such as seven or eight hundred years.   Josephus mentions several heathen writers, ancient even in his time, who had indulged in this romance.   Hesiod, who lived about a thousand, according to some, and according to all, nine hundred years before the Christian era, says that, during the *Silver Age*, men remained with their mothers, in a state of infancy, for the first century of their existence !· Hesiod. Εργ. και Ημα. v. 129. Josephus. Antiq. Jud. lib. ι. c. 3.

come in the clouds of heaven with power and great glory; and sent his angels with a great sound of a trumpet to gather his elect from the four winds;—from one end of the heaven to the other ? Has he come as the lightning cometh out of the east and shineth even unto the west,—while the sun darkened, the moon refused her light, and the stars were falling from heaven,—to reward every man according to his works ? Has he, in his glory, and the holy angels with him, sat upon the throne of his glory; and, having caused all nations to be gathered before him, " separated one from another,"—setting the sheep on his right hand, and the goats on the left,—saying to those on the right hand,—Come, ye blessed of my Father, inherit the kingdom prepared for you from the foundation of the world; and to those on the left,—Depart from me, ye cursed, into everlasting fire ? Has he sent his angels to gather out of his kingdom all that offended and did iniquity, as he had promised to do with the tares "at the end of the world" ? Has he sent the one set of men into everlasting punishment, and the other into eternal life ? Have heaven and earth passed away, and verified his words ?* These are grave questions,—questions, to all of which truth sternly demands negative answers,—and questions which thus answered, must determine the character of the Nazarean prophet,—must pronounce his predictions false;—and consequently infer, however reluctantly, that the popular notion of his Divine origin is not founded in fact, —that Christianity has no better foundation than the countless varieties of other religions, past and present, which,—while all claiming a Divine origin,—are based only upon the credulous tales and fabulous notions of benighted ages, and fostered by the knavery of some, and the enthusiasm of others of their adherents. Eighteen centuries have rolled away since the prophet of Nazareth predicted that all the events, just enumerated, should take place *during the lifetime of men then living;* still not even one of them has occurred, as the present state of things abundantly proves. Generation after generation, and age after age have passed, and no Son of man, with angels and trumpets, appears in the clouds;—no heaven and earth pass away;—no elements, according to the words of the apostles, melt with fervent heat;—no earth and the works that are therein burned up;—no new heavens and new earth, wherein dwelleth righteousness, created;†—no Son of man gathering all nations before him;—no "Lord himself" descending "from heaven with a shout, with the voice of the archangel, and with the trump of God," first raising "the dead in Christ," and lifting them up with the living into "the clouds, to meet the Lord in the air." Time, the great revealer of truth and exposer of falsity, has, after the lapse of eighteen centuries, surely given abundant proof that these prophecies were utterly false! and that, consequently, whoever uttered them was a false prophet! That he *was* such has been told Christians a thousand times, from the days of Celsus, Porphyry, Julian, and Hierocles,‡ to the present age, in which, owing to its advancement in

* See all the above prophetic expressions in Matth. xiii. xvi. xxiv. xxv. already cited verbally in preceding pages.
    † 2 Pet. iii. 10—13. 1 Thess. iv. 15—17.
    ‡ Celsus wrote against Christianity, exposing its pagan origin, in the second century; Porphyry and Hierocles in the third; and Julian in the fourth. As Christians obtained edicts from Theodosius, Dioclesian, and other Roman emperors to have the books of these

knowledge and *liberty of expression*, it has been told them, perhaps more frequently, plainly, and forcibly, than in any other. Still there are thousands of men and women to be found,—owing to the influence that their interested religious guides have over them, and other circumstances,—who believe the Nazarite a true prophet ;—nay a *God:* just as the Mussulman believes in Mahomet, or the Mormons (called also Latter-Day Saints) believe in *Joe Smith,*—a man of the present age, who had the arrogance to assert that he was a prophet influenced by the Supreme Being ; and that he had received a revelation from Him, called the Book of Mormon, in which now nearly a million of people, *from Christian countries*, believe ! The votaries of the last-named religion, in a thousand years hence will, doubtless, be much more numerous than even at present ; and the difficulty to persuade them that their creed is false will increase with its age ; so that as much time will be required to erradicate it as it will take to reach its acme. Such, exactly, has been, and still is, the case with Christianity.

For human reason, however, to prostrate itself so far as to believe in such religions is the greatest blasphemy (if in any case such a thing can exist,) against the Supreme Being,—the true, and only God ; and is idolatry of the worst kind. To convince men of the abject mental slavery to which they thus reduce themselves, instead of raising their thoughts to the God of Nature,—the originator and governor of the universe, whose works, throughout all creation, are calculated to call forth their wonder, love, and adoration, is the sole purpose of thus setting before them the true character of the prophecies under consideration.

Instead of living in continual fear of the near approach of the end of the world, and of being cast into unquenchable fire,—a feeling which must chill and deaden the noblest emotions and faculties of the mind,—let man seek a higher and more powerful incentive to virtue. Let him pursue virtue for its own intrinsic value,—not in order to gain heaven ; and let him shun vice because of its inherent hurtful nature,—not in order to escape hell. Let him contemplate his God,—not as a being whose arbitrary will has inclined him to prepare a lake of fire and brimstone for some of his creatures, and a paradise of pleasure for others,—but as that infinite Being whose power is manifested in the immensity of creation, and in the force which keeps every portion of it in continual motion ;—his wisdom, in the variety of combinations, perfect harmony, and exquisite beauty, which the universe presents ;—his goodness, in the abundant provision made for the innumerably varied wants and gratifications of all living and organised beings ;—and his justice, in the fact that he governs the whole world by those universal and invariable laws, the observance of which, on the part of man, produces its own reward—happiness,—and the infraction of which carries with it its own proportionate punishment—misery ; thus, at once, demonstrating to man the justice and benevolence of the Supreme Ruler.

writers committed to the flames, and as all their works were then, of course, in manuscripts, and consequently only few copies in circulation, they are apparently all destroyed. Except some of Julian's works, none others of them have descended to us than fragments inserted in the works of Origen, Eusebius, and Lactantius,—the Christian writers who defended their religion from the charges brought against it, by the above heathen philosophers. See Origen contr. Celsus. Julian apud Cyrill. lib. ii. Lactantii Instit. lib. iii. Tertull. Apolog. Euseb. Hist. Eccles. lib. iii. iv. Dr. Lardner's Credibility, Jewish and Heathen Testimonies, &c.

Let man,—instead of poring over fables which teach him to look for God coming in the clouds, after the form of a human being,—study the *Book of Nature*, in every atom of which,—from the sun in the firmament down to the smallest grain of sand on the sea shore,—from the largest being in the animal kingdom down to the most imperceptible animalcule,—he will be able to perceive His existence, and ascertain His attributes. Let him read this *Book*, in which the very will and laws of his Creator are inscribed in characters which require no comment,—no translation from Greek or Hebrew,—no priest to inculcate the doctrines they set forth. Soon will he find out the advantage of the exchange ;—soon will he feel that his happiness proceeds from the observance, and his misery from the violation of the laws of nature ;—soon will he feel that to infringe the physical law of gravitation, for instance, by falling from the height of a few yards, he will be punished by the pain he suffers ; while another man who has observed the same law is proportionately happy. The same thing could be said of the organic, moral, social, and all other laws of nature. The infraction of either of them makes man more or less miserable ; and the observance of *all of them* makes him *perfectly* happy. If man, therefore, loves happiness, this is the book for him to study. To abandon the Jewish writings would neither deprive him of God, nor leave him destitute of most refined intellectual enjoyments,—much more suitable to his advancing mind than those of which he now participates.

CHAPTER IV.

A REVIEW OF THE COMPARATIVE STRENGTH AND CONCLUSIVENELSS OF
THE FACTS AND ARGUMENTS ADVANCED IN THE TWO IMMEDIATELY PRE-
CEDING CHAPTERS, FOR AND AGAINST THE TRUTH OF THE PROPHECIES
OF CHRIST, SO FAR AS THEY HAVE HITHERTO BEEN DISCUSSED.

SECTION I.—THE STRENGTH OF THE HISTORICAL EVIDENCE OF THE FUL-
FILMENT OF CHRIST'S PREDICTIONS CONSIDERED.   THE REPORTS GIVEN
OF HIS PREDICTIONS BY THE EVANGELISTS EXAMINED.

In the chapter just closed, the writer is not conscious of having
omitted any fact or argument tending to confirm the views therein taken
of Christ's prophecies, any more than he is sensible of having done so in
the preceding chapter, which maintains opposite views on the same subject.
But he thinks, on cool reflection, that he has argued each side of the
question with all the ability and zeal that *he* could command.   It becomes
now his duty to fulfil what—in Section III. of his introductory remarks—
he promised to do; namely, to sum up the evidence on both sides, with
the most rigorous impartiality, and regardlessly of any prepossessions of
his own,—determine the side on which the preponderance of evidence lies,
—state the reasons leading to this determination,—and point out the
inferences deducible from such a conclusion, touching the reality of Christ's
Deity.   The important duties he has now to perform are similar to those
of a judge, in summing up the evidence he has heard on both sides of a
case, civil or criminal; and then to those of a jury, in deciding on what
side the preponderance of evidence lies.   The inferences promised to be
drawn from the *conclusion* to which the evidence given will lead, shall,
probably, form the subject of a separate chapter.
     Now, the evidence on both sides having been given, it remains, at
present, only to determine, from that evidence, whether Christ—in uttering
the predictions in question—intended to foretell only the Destruction of
Jerusalem, or the Destruction and End of the World at large, and the
Final Judgment, together with their concomitant events; and also to state
the reasons which influence the determination to which the preponderance
of evidence will lead.   On several considerations, this is by no means a
post to be envied.   It is no other than that of sitting as judge, or umpire,

to decide between the Christian and Deistical world; and the writer must say that,—did his love of truth, as well as the prescribed conditions of this work permit,—he would rather let both sides of the question remain as they are, leaving the reader to judge for himself, and draw his own conclusions; especially as he perceives the strength of evidence so unequal. The wording of the given subject of this Essay, however, being in an interrogative form,* and requiring a decisive answer—either negative or affirmative—to the question it propounds, the task must not be eschewed.

The explanations given of the prophecies of Christ,†—as applicable to the Destruction of Jerusalem,—although plausible, are by no means conclusive. As to the argument built upon the signification of the word— αιων, translated *world*, in connection with *end*,‡ where it is maintained that αιων means only *age* or *time*, and here means the *end of the time* of the Jewish Dispensation, it must be admitted that this word is frequently used in the New Testament to designate not only the *physical world*, but also "the world to come," and *eternity*, wherein it must, on all hands, be granted that it signifies, literally, *a world*. The connection in which it occurs, in the passage here in question, shows that it means *the end of time*, or of the present system of nature; and the arguments advanced to show that it means this, undoubtedly, are incomparably stronger than those adduced to show that it means the " end of the Jewish Dispensation."§—

---

* See the Advertisement prefixed to the Preface of this work.
† See chap. II. s. 2.   ‡ pp. 16, 17.

§ See p. 63. et seq. In however varied a sense the word—αιων may be used, it is clear that the disciples, in their enquiries as to the time that Christ's prophecies should be accomplished, used it in reference to his coming, which *coming* must mean his second advent. "What shall be the sign of *thy coming* and of *the end of the world?*" are the *ipsissima verba* of the question put by the disciples to Christ, as reported by Matth. xxiv. 3. And it is to this question, Christ, evidently, addresses himself, in the whole of the discourse which follows, and extends to the *end* of chapter xxv. The questions put by the disciples and the answers rendered to them, *must* be considered in connection with one another. To imagine that the answers do not bear upon the questions, or are not intended to bear upon them, and to serve as *direct* answers to them, is to suppose what the Gospel narrative does not warrant;—is indeed absurd, and derogative to the mental and moral character of Christ. That the word—αιων, when connected with the word— τελος *(end)* or συντελεια, *(the very end)* is repeatedly rendered into English by the word— *world*, furnishes a strong presumptive proof that it means *world;* and is a positive proof, at least, that the English translators believed it to possess this meaning. But the contexts, in many of the places where these words are so rendered, preclude the shadow of a doubt that they actually mean the *end* of the present system of nature, or of the physical world. Take for example the following passages.—" The harvest is the *end of the world*, (συντελεια του αιωνος) and the reapers are the angels."—" And burned in the fire. So shall it be in the *end of this world.*" (συντελεια του αιωνος τουτου.)—"So shall it be at the *end of the world*: (συντελεια του αιωνος) the angels shall come forth, and sever the wicked from among the just, and shall cast them into the furnace of fire: there shall be wailing and gnashing of teeth."—Matth. xiii. 39, 40, 49, 50. These are the words of the same writer as those in question,—found in the same Gospel; and are clearly used to designate the *end* of the physical world. It is, therefore, beyond the power of any kind of criticism to show that the words of the disciples, in their questions to Jesus, did not mean the end of the physical world; but that they meant the end of the Jewish Dispensation. Quite as clearly do the following expressions show that the word—αιων means the physical world, and the inhabitants in the world.—" By whom also he made the worlds." (αιωνας)—" The worlds (αιωνας) were framed by the word of God."— Heb. i. 2; xi. 3. Hence it would be quite as reasonable to contend that it is not the physical world, but the Jewish Dispensation is meant in Genesis, where the account of

If wars and rumours of wars—earthquakes—famines—pestilences—and persecutions—took place, before the destruction of Jerusalem by Titus Vespasian ;* still, as these things, in those times, were of frequent occurrence in the East, they are not events of sufficient singularity to identify, conclusively, the predictions of Christ, in their *entirety*, with the destruction of Jerusalem. Nor is the inference sound, that, because the apostles had become Christians, they had renounced the Jewish ritual and were not likely to be in Jerusalem with the rest of the Jewish nation, assembled from all parts of Judea and other countries, at the feast of the unleavened bread, when, suddenly, the Roman legions besieged the city ;—for we are informed that Christ himself did eat the Passover the day before he was crucified ; and the Acts and the Epistles prove that Christians, and even the apostles themselves, practised the Jewish ceremonies for a considerable period afterwards. The argument built upon this supposition, therefore, when scrutinized, must be felt untenable.†

The principal proof, however, is drawn from an alleged similarity between Josephus's narration of the destruction of Jerusalem and the

---

the creation is given, as to assert that this is meant by αιων in Matthew. The same word is also used for the *world to come.*—Matth. xii. 32. Eph. i. 21. Luke xx. 35. In the last place Christ says, in reference to a question put to him by the Sadducees, about the possession of a wife in the resurrection, that "they which shall be accounted worthy to obtain that *world,* (αιωνος) and the *resurrection* from the dead," do not marry, but are equal to the angels. In such instances as these there can be *no Jewish Dispensation meant* by the word—αιων. The same may be said of such an expression as the following.— "The powers of the *world to come.*" (Heb. vi. 5.)—αιων μελλων. It is worthy of remark, that the same writer connects οικουμενη with μελλων, showing that both αιων and οικουμενη are used in the same sense,—to denote a world.—Οικουμενην την μελλουσαν —the world to come. (Heb. ii. 5.) See the various applications of αιων,—*ante* pp. 107, 108. The writer is fully aware of the secondary or metonymical sense in which αιων is used in the works of the Greek philosophers, particularly of the Platonic school, to denote, apparently, imaginary beings, whose nature was supposed to be unchangeable or of immense duration, lasting for ages and ages; such as was supposed to be that of angels and demons. It acquired this sense also among the Gnostics and other Christians of the first three centuries of the Christian era. But there is no reason for even imagining that it is used in this sense in the New Testament, except, perhaps, in the following places—Eph. ii. 2. Heb. i. 2.

* p. 19. et seq.

† Indeed there is ample evidence in the New Testament that both Christ and his apostles adhered scrupulously to all the ritual of the Jewish religion, throughout their lives. Christ declares that he had not come to destroy the law, and that it was easier for heaven and earth to pass than one tittle of the law to fail. (Matth. v. 7. Luke xvi. 17.) He countenances circumcision,—a rite which he himself underwent. (John vii. 2.) He justifies an unlawful act of his disciples, by a reference to David eating the shew-bread. (Matth. xii. 4.) It was his custom to frequent the Jewish synagogues; (Luke iv. 16.) and he attended the Jewish feasts. (John ii. 23; vii. 10. et al. loc.) The apostles, in like manner, attended these feasts. (Acts ii. 1; xviii. 21.) Although the rite of circumcision was a subject of much debate among them, and at length became an open question; yet, *it was practised.* Paul circumcised Timothy because of the Jews, and gloried in the fact that he himself had been circumcised. (Acts xv. 5—35; xxi. 21; xvi. 3. Phil. iii. 5.) The apostles made a practise of preaching in the Jewish synagogues. (Acts xiii. 5, 14; xiv. 1; xvii. 1, 2.) Paul so minutely adhered to the Jewish customs, that he shore his head at Cenchrea, because of his Jewish vow. (Acts xviii. 18.) As we read in the following verses, that he sailed from Ephesus to Jerusalem to be present at a feast, saying, as he departed, that he *must by all means keep this feast,* the natural inference is,—not that the apostles would be absent,—but that they would be very likely to be present at the feast, during which Jerusalem was captured.

predictions of Christ,—especially as to Jerusalem being encompassed with armies, surrounded by a trench, and levelled with the ground.* Here it should first be observed, that—if what Josephus says of the destruction of Jerusalem came up to the criterion which Horne lays down for proving the fulfilment of a prophecy; namely, that "a prophecy is demonstrated to be fulfilled when we can prove, from unimpeachable authority, that the event has actually taken place, *precisely* according to the manner in which it was foretold"—then the prophecies of Christ could be proved to be predictions of the destruction of Jerusalem *exclusively.* But there is a great difference between what Josephus narrates and what Christ prophesies. Granting that these predictions refer, exclusively, to the destruction of Jerusalem, still, *the event,* according to Josephus, has *not* taken place *precisely according to the manner in which it was foretold.* Christ says that the enemy should cast a *trench* (χαραξ) about Jerusalem,—a very common thing done when besieging a city,—but Josephus says that the Roman soldiers built a *wall* (τειχος) about it,—which is a very uncommon thing to be done in besieging a city;—such a wall as was about Damascus as a fortification, or such as the walls of Jericho, for which the same word (τειχος) is used.† That this was a stone wall, appears from the use which Josephus elsewhere makes of the same word.‡ Besides: before the Romans built this wall they had raised banks, or made trenches, in *some* parts.— Moreover, the Roman soldiers did not *compass* Jerusalem,—they only "guarded the known passages out of the place."§ These are important differences, when it is considered that the modes of besieging all cities are very similar. It is true that there is a similarity between what Christ predicts regarding the Jews falling by the edge of the sword, carried away captive, and so on, and what Josephus relates to have befallen these people. But it must be borne in mind that these are things which would happen in the capture of any large city, like Jerusalem. Nor must this important difference be overlooked;—that Josephus narrates these things as having happened *after* the city was captured; but that Christ predicts them as things to take place before the *end,* of which he speaks, should come. When the disciples should see these things, they were to *know that their redemption drew nigh, and the kingdom of God was at hand.* Further than in the apparent similarity of the above points, Josephus and Christ do not at all accord. The former does not record that remarkable phenomenon,—the Son of man making his appearance in the clouds of heaven. He,—himself a Jew,—must have been well acquainted with the term, and supposed meaning of the " Son of man," as used in the prophecies of Daniel; for the whole of his writings,—supposing them to have descended genuinely to us,—prove that he was well versed in the sacred books of the Jews;‖ from which, indeed, he has drawn a considerable portion of the

---

* See pp. 23—29. † See Acts ix. 25. Heb. xi. 30.

‡ Compare Jos. Bell. Jud. lib. v. c. 12. s. 1. with lib. vi. c. iv. s. 1.

§ Jos. Bell. Jud. lib. v. c. 12. s. 1. Indeed, whoever has seen Jerusalem must know that the Roman army *could not* do otherwise, owing to the steep ascents and deep valleys —of Jehosaphat and Hinnom—which encompass it on every side, except the north, close to the city walls.

‖ It is, however, not a little remarkable that Josephus is frequently made to say that he had already treated of certain things, about which there is not a syllable to be found in his works, as they descend to us. Josephus's works, in the Hebrew or Chaldee,

materials with which he has compiled his Antiquities. Nor does Josephus say a word even of "the sign of the Son of man in heaven" appearing. It is true that he says that there stood over the city a comet for a whole year. But it is difficult to ascertain how much knowledge of comets he had,—in common with the Jews, and indeed the whole world in that age,*—to enable him to judge whether that phenomenon stood still for a year, or whether there was anything at all miraculous about it; or indeed whether it was a comet or a star. It is, however, certain that very little is known of comets, even in the present age; notwithstanding the rapid strides science has made, particularly in that noble and sublime

as well as his Greek History of the Jewish Wars, have long been lost; so that according to a Note made by his translator—Mr. Whiston, there is not implicit reliance to be placed on what we now have of his. (*Note* on sec. 1. c. 5. book III.) Besides : there are evident marks, pervading the works of Josephus, that he was very prone to exaggeration. The Jews generally,—as their books amply prove,—were much given to exaggerate facts ; and Josephus, as a writer, appears to form no exception. For example, the number of men he gives, in relating many occurrences, such as the slaughter and captivity when Jerusalem was taken, is incredibly great ;—is, in a word, evidently exaggerated. His statement regarding a wall of nearly five miles in length and of adequate height and strength to its intended purpose, with its thirteen towers, which he tells us was built around Jerusalem by the Roman soldiers in the short space of three days, (Jewish Wars, b. v. c. 12.) is a relation which is enough, *per se*, to throw discredit on his history in its most salient points. His statement, also, that Jerusalem was so completely demolished by the Roman army that it was levelled with the ground, except three towers, which, however, in 290 years afterwards were rased to the ground, (b. VII. c. 1.) is another exaggeration. Travellers in oriental countries,* who are still living, state that they have seen portions of the ancient walls of Jerusalem, especially along those parts which skirt the Valley of Jehoshaphat, and near the site of the ancient temple, where the stones at the base of the wall are exceedingly large. Portions of the walls still remaining, Jerusalem therefore was not completely destroyed, as Josephus says. This fact is of the utmost importance, as it shows that Christ's prediction—that *not one stone of the city should be left upon another*—has not yet been verified. But there is another way of accounting for the exaggerations and the many incredible statements found in the works of Josephus, than by supposing him to have personally penned them; —a way which, if proved to be founded in fact, makes the passages cited from the writings that pass under his name to be of little value in proving the fulfilment of Christ's predictions. His works, like most other ancient writings which have descended to us through the hands of the Christian Fathers, have, unfortunately, undergone the ordeal of *pious fraud*. They are known, and now admitted by the most learned Christian writers of the age, to contain *forged passages*, especially passages which tend to prove the divine origin of Christianity. The most remarkable of these is a passage in reference to Jesus Christ, (Antiq. b. xviii c. 3. s. 3.) not found in any transcripts from the works of Josephus older than the time of Eusebius. This is declared by Dr. Lardner, Bishop Warburton, Le Clerc, Vandale, and a host of other Christian writers of note, to be a forgery. Since, therefore, there are in the works of Josephus forged passages, intended to prove the existence of Christ, what guarantee have we that the same works do not contain forged passages, intended, likewise, to prove the fulfilment of his predictions? At all events, a work of such character has very little weight, especially when uncorroborated by any other proof, in showing that Christ's predictions have been fulfilled in the destruction of Jerusalem ; even if it contained historical passages narrating the occurrence of events exactly corresponding to these predictions. The historical details of the Jewish wars found in Josephus cannot, therefore, be received as *positive* proofs of the fulfilment of Christ's predictions.

    * The ancients, for the greater number, thought comets to be real stars, and their appearance to portend some national calamity. Hence Virgil calls them *diri* and *sanguinei*. —Geo. I. 488. Æn. x. 272. See also the ancient notions of comets in Suet. Ner. 36. Plin. II. 25. ss. 22, 23. Cic. de Nat. Dei. II. 5. Lucan. I. 529. Senec. Nat. Quæst. VII. 2, 22. Sil. VIII. 638.

branch—astronomy, within the last two centuries.   It is also admitted that Josephus says there was a star,* resembling a sword, standing over the city for a whole year; and that, on the night of the feast of unleavened bread, there appeared a light as bright as day around the altar, for half an hour in the holy house;—at least it is admitted that the priests told Josephus,—probably after the destruction of Jerusalem, and before he wrote his history,—that they had seen such things; for he does not pretend to have seen them himself.† Nor is it denied that it was related to him that chariots and troops of soldiers in armour were seen running among the clouds, and surrounding the city.   But no one professes to have seen "the sign of the Son of man," or the Son of man himself in the clouds; no one professes to have seen the *sun being dark,—the moon refusing to give her light,—the stars falling from heaven,—or the powers of heaven being shaken.* We have no evidence that these, the most important and remarkable portions of Christ's predictions were fulfilled, any more than we have that the *heaven and earth passed away,* at the destruction of Jerusalem.   These are the most extraordinary things which Christ prophesied should take place at the time the event he foretold should occur.   If Josephus does not say that these things took place, all the other things he states do not apply, and therefore must go for nothing.   The signs urged to have been seen, and recorded by Josephus, not only prove too little on the one hand, but on the other prove too much.   They prove, not only the reality of the gift of prophecy, but also the reality of miracles, which, indeed, appear to have gone hand in hand in every age, and to have been supported by similar testimony.   In this case, however, it is attempted to make them afford a kind of reciprocal strength;—miracles are made to prove prophecy, and prophecy thereby is made to prove miracles.   But supposing what Josephus says, and also what Tacitus narrates, did really appear before the destruction of Jerusalem, still their statements do not prove that Christ prophesied these events; for there is a great difference between what these historians relate to have miraculously appeared, and what Christ foretold would appear.‡

It is also not a little singular that Josephus and Tacitus, who were contemporaries, and both patronised by Vespasian, differ so materially from each other in the accounts they give of what was seen in the air, just before the destruction of the Jewish capital; especially as there is every reason to believe that Tacitus had seen the Jewish history of Josephus before he wrote his Annals.   While Josephus states that a *star* and a *comet,*

---

* Mr. Whiston has the following *Note* on Josephus in this place:—" Whether Josephus means that this star was different from that *comet* which lasted a whole year, I cannot certainly determine.   His words most favour their being different one from another."— See Note on Jewish Wars, book v. c. v. s. Whiston's trans.

† Bell. Jud. lib. vi. c. 5. s. 1.

‡ Considered apart from the question of the truth of Christ's prophecies, the miraculous appearances related both by Josephus and Tacitus should be received, as facts, with considerable caution.   In the age of Josephus and Tacitus the belief in miracles was rife,—had arrived at its acme,—had enlisted all men in its favour; even grave divines (magicians are not meant here,) and profound philosophers.   The works of both the above writers prove them to be firm believers in miracles.   What they affirm of miraculous events should, therefore, be taken at least with great caution and discrimination.   Nature was then governed by the same invariable laws as it is at present.

chariots and *troops of soldiers*, were seen in the air over Jerusalem, and that a light as bright as day was seen shining about the altar ; Tacitus says that *armies* were seen *meeting in the clouds*, over Jerusalem,—*arms dazzling and brandishing* in the air,—the *temple as in one mass of flames*,—*fire coming out of the clouds*, and a *divine voice* heard, saying that the *Deity had left* the place.* Tacitus does not mention either the *comet, star,* or *chariots,* enumerated by Josephus ; nor does Josephus say anything about fire coming out of the clouds, and a Divine voice saying that the Deity had left the place ; together with other things mentioned by Tacitus. Thus, not only are the two historians at variance with the prophet, but also at variance with each other. What Tacitus states is not much nearer to what Josephus states than it is to what Christ has prophesied. Supposing the historians to be of equal authority, then the question arises ;—to which of their conflicting narratives are we to give the preference ? But were this question decided, still, neither narrative agrees with the predictions of Christ, and therefore neither affords them support. The argument built upon what these historians state, therefore fails. For so far are they from rendering any support to the truth of Christ's predictions, that they render no support to each other. It is true that, by the exercise of a little ingenuity, the predictions of Christ on this head, may, on some points, be made to *appear* similar in import to what Josephus and Tacitus narrate.— For instance, the signs predicted by Christ were to be seen *in the clouds ;* and several of the signs these historians state to have been seen were *in the clouds ;* but they were not the *same,* or *similar* signs. What Christ and Josephus says of warriors and armies surrounding Jerusalem, as already noticed,—of the *city* being levelled with the ground,—of men falling by the sword and being led away captive,—are also points of similarity. But the evidence that these points afford, in establishing the position that Christ predicted the destruction of Jerusalem, is very slight when compared with the evidence adduced to show that, by uttering these predictions, he meant to foretell the *Destruction of the World and the Final Judgment.*— The latter is corroborated by passages dispersed, here and there, over the whole of the Gospels, bearing internal marks that they are direct predictions of the End of the World and the Last Day of Judgment, as events to happen during the lifetime of the men who were contemporary with Christ. Such, for example, is the corroboration afforded by that remarkable prediction in Matthew (xvi. 27, 28.),—where it cannot be imagined there is *any* reference, or even the *slightest allusion, made* to the destruction of Jerusalem by the Romans,—and yet where it is expressly foretold that the *Son of man should come in the glory of his Father with his angels, to reward every man according to his works ; and that there were some then present who should not taste of death till they saw the Son of man thus coming in his kingdom.* On the other hand, the passages in Luke (xix. 42—44 ; xxi. 20, 24.) which predict that Jerusalem should be encompassed with a trench and armies,—that her inhabitants should fall by the edge of the sword, and be led away captive ; and which, be it observed, contain the strongest evidence that has been, or can be adduced from Scripture, that Christ's predictions referred to the destruction of the Jewish captital,—are

* Tacit. Hist. lib. v. c. 13.

unsupported by any other passages. The expressions just referred to are not found in either of the other two evangelists,—Matthew and Mark,—who evidently relate, more fully and emphatically, the same series of prophetic sayings as Luke. Further: there are in the narrative given of these predictions by Luke himself, expressions, which identify it, as to subject, with the narrations of Matthew and Mark; such as,—"They shall see the Son of man coming in a cloud with power and great glory;"—"Heaven and earth shall pass away;"—"As a snare shall it come on all them that *dwell on the face of the whole earth;*"—"Watch ye therefore, and pray always, that ye may be accounted worthy to escape all these things that shall come to pass, and to stand before the Son of man."—Now, according to the report of Luke himself, these expressions said to have been uttered by Christ, even when considered by themselves, can be made to refer to no other events than the End of the World, and the things which, as represented in the New Testament, were expected to attend it. But when they are compared with similar words of Christ and his apostles, found in other places, the conclusion that they refer to the End of the World becomes irresistible. What Luke says, using Christ's words, namely, that the calamity predicted should *come as a snare on all them that dwelt on the face of the whole earth,* is a complete refutation of the argument that the disaster, in the predictions, is confined to the Jews and Judea; and accords with the report of the other evangelists, that all the tribes of the earth should mourn at the appearance of the Son of man, before whom should be gathered all nations. It is also very remarkable that all the three evangelists—Matthew, Mark, and Luke,—in their respective reports of these predictions, and about the same parts of their narratives, have the following emphatic averment of Christ's, in precisely the same words:—"Verily I say unto you, *this* generation shall *not* pass, till *all* these things be fulfilled."

With regard to the argument that,—were it admitted that the prophecies of Christ, respecting the destruction of Jerusalem, are mixed up with expressions relative to the Final Judgment, their being so mixed by no means impairs the truth of his predictions of the destruction of Jerusalem;*—it must be granted it does not. But if it is proved that these expressions are distinct predictions of the Day of Judgment, as an event to take place *within the lifetime of the generation of men then living,* and that that event *has not yet come to pass;* such a deficiency in foreknowledge nullifies Christ's divinity, and utterly disentitles him to the character of a true prophet. It proves that while he was right in predicting the Destruction of Jerusalem, he was wrong in his prediction of the Day of Judgment. For it cannot be shown, by any mode of criticism capable of standing the test of reason, that, instead of belonging to those portions of the prophecies which are admitted to relate to the Day of Judgment, the words—"This generation shall not pass till all these things be fulfilled," belong to what is contended to be a prediction of the Destruction of Jerusalem. Because they *immediately follow* the most clear predictions that Christ uttered of the *former,* while they are found in each of the three evangelists who record them, at a *distance from,* and *disconnected with* the

---

* See pp. 30, 31.

K

predictions which are supposed to foretell the *latter*. The *double meaning* of prophecy, pleaded as an apology, is indeed scarcely worth a serious thought; for it would be defamatory to the character of God to suppose that he speaks to his creatures in ambiguous words of "a hidden meaning," while at the same time these words are intended to direct their conduct.— The true state of the case appears to be, that Christ predicted the destruction of Jerusalem to take place in no other manner than with the rest of the world. That he foretold the destruction of Jerusalem, however, is not the point at issue;—this is admitted on all hands. For the destruction of the world involved the destruction of Jerusalem. If Christ predicted the former, he necessarily predicted the latter. It should, therefore, constantly be borne in mind that the whole and sole question here at issue, is— *whether he predicted the Final Judgment and the End of the World to take place during the lifetime of his contemporaries on earth;*—and that, if he did so predict, such a prediction inevitably *implied the destruction of Jerusalem.* There is, however, no ground for saying that the predictions of the destruction of Jerusalem have been "mixed up" with those which refer to the End of the World, any further than the destruction of the former was involved in that of the latter. And indeed, to suppose them thus mixed reflects great discredit either upon Christ or upon the Evangelists. If Christ mixed them in delivery, it shows imperfection in him;—it shows either that he could not prophesy so clearly and distinctly as to be understood; or if he could, that he wished not to do so, but wished to keep his creatures in suspense and even ignorance as to the meaning of his words; —a conduct contrary to any right moral principle, and seriously affecting Christ's character, not only as a divine being, or an inspired prophet, but even simply as a moral being,—a mere man! If, on the other hand, these predictions have been huddled together, or mixed up by the evangelists in recording them, this shows how little reliance can be placed on the accuracy of the Gospels;—in a word, that these productions are invalid as proofs of anything Christ either said or did. Thus the plea of *mixture*, by no means, serves the cause of Christianity.

　　The following passage, found only in Luke, goes further than any other, perhaps, in the estimation of some, to prove that Christ predicted the destruction of Jerusalem. It stands preceded by a prediction that the Jews would fall by the edge of the sword, and be led away captive into all nations, as already noticed; and it is followed by a declaration that there would be signs in the sun, moon, and stars; and that upon the earth there would be distress of nations; and it runs thus;—"Jerusalem shall be trodden down of the Gentiles, until the times of the Gentiles be fulfilled."* The language of this passage is very much after the style of the ancient prophets,† and probably is a modified quotation from one of them. Let us give all possible attention to its import. The *natural* meaning would appear to be—that between the time when some of the Jews should perish by the sword and others be led away captive,—between *this time* and *that when* there should be signs in the sun, moon, and stars, Jerusalem would be trodden down of the Gentiles, until the time of the Gentiles was fulfilled. Now, this expression cannot be understood in any other sense than that

---

* Luke xxi. 24. See p. 32.　　　　　　† See Isa. v. 5; lxiii. 18.

the holy city was to be trodden down by the Gentiles during the time that would elapse between the two classes of events just mentioned;—the latter class of which is evidently connected with the *Destruction of the World.*— But there would appear to be an intimation in the passage that, after the time of the Gentiles was fulfilled, Jerusalem,—as had been the case after previous destructions,—was to be restored to the Jews. And in this very point lies the strength of the argument. The expression does not enable us to conjecture how long the Jewish capital was to be thus trodden down. There is, however, a passage in the Book of Revelation calculated to throw some light upon the matter. and even to explain the whole meaning of the expression. In the prophecies which precede that passage, a mighty angel appears to John, having in his hand a book, which John ultimately eats.— This angel swears there shall be no more time. Then he commands John to measure the temple, but tells him,—" The court which is without the temple, leave out, and measure it not, for it is given *unto the Gentiles, and the holy city shall they tread under foot forty and two months.*"* The angel afterwards proceeds to say, that he would give power to his two witnesses (μαρτυσι—*martyrs*) to prophesy for a thousand two hundred and threescore days. In the sequel he says, among other things, that these witnesses should have power to turn the heaven and the waters into blood, and smite the earth with plagues;—that when they should have finished their testimony, the beast, from the bottomless pit, would kill them;—that their bodies should remain for three days in the great city, *where our Lord was crucified ;*—that, at the expiration of this time, the spirit of life should enter their bodies, and they should stand upon their feet, and should hear a great voice from heaven, saying,—" Come up hither,"—whereupon they ascend up to heaven in a cloud. In " the same hour" that John, in his vision, saw all these things, there was " a great earthquake, and the tenth part of the city fell, and in the earthquake were slain of men seven thousand." This, he intimates, was the second woe which was now past. But he tells us—" the third woe cometh quickly";—the seventh angel sounds, and there are great voices in heaven saying,—" The kingdoms of this world are become the kingdoms of our Lord, and of his Christ; and he shall reign for ever and ever." Further : the twenty elders give thanks to the Lord, because he has reigned ; and because his wrath has come, and the time of the dead, that they should be judged, and the prophets rewarded. Now, not only is the doctrine of the End of the World and the Final Judgment taught here, but precisely the same doctrine as Christ teaches throughout the Gospels ; only clothed in much more bombast. Here is the resurrection taught in what is said of those that are reanimated;—here those who are reanimated ascend up in a cloud to heaven ;—here is the kingdom of Christ coming ;—and here he reigns for ever and ever.— Here also are seen, in this vision of John, the earthquakes, the persecutions and pestilences, or plagues, mentioned by Christ. The Book of Revelation is replete with the doctrines of the End of the World, the Final Judgment, and the kingdom of heaven, in which there was to be eternal life, as taught in the Gospels. But our business, at present, is with the passage which states that the holy city should be *trodden down for forty and two months.*

* Rev. xi. 2. Read chapters x. xi.

2 K

There is no reason for believing that, by this space of time, John means more than, literally, forty-two months, or three years and a half. This is the time he allots the Gentiles to tread down Jerusalem. Accordingly, the witnesses were to prophesy for the same length of time, namely, a thousand two hundred and threescore days. Shortly after the end of the three years and a half, John, evidently, thought the End of the World would take place. Seeing that there is such a close resemblance between John's doctrine and that of Christ, on other important points, it is natural to infer that Christ thought that the same period as that mentioned by John was to elapse before the time assigned for the Gentiles to tread down Jerusalem would be fulfilled; and that near the close of this period the End of the World was to take place. Or, if we make allowance for the time between the supposed date of the Book of Revelation and that at which Christ is thought to have delivered his prophecies; then about sixty years, according to Christ, would elapse before the *time of the Gentiles should be fulfilled*. Still this calculation would lead us to infer,—even from the prophecy regarding the Gentiles treading down the holy city, which has been thought to favour an opposite view,—that Christ here referred to the End of the World; and that, therefore, the prophecy has not proved true. But let us see how this prediction would apply to the destruction of Jerusalem by the Gentile Romans. When is the *time of the Gentiles to be fulfilled*, and Jerusalem restored to the Jews? Since the time of the Gentile Romans, it has been trodden down by the Gentile Saracens, the Gentile Franks, and is, at present, trodden down by the Gentile Turks.— It has now been trodden down by the Gentiles for about eighteen centuries; and there is very little reason to hope that the Jews will ever again possess it, as a nation; or indeed that they will ever again have a national exist-ence; for they are now intermixed with almost every nation on the face of the earth, so as to cease,—nationally considered,—to be a distinct Hebrew race. Analogy, or the history of all the ancient nations of the world, proclaims it absurd to imagine that the Jews will ever again live under a monarch of their own, with their barbarous laws, customs, and religion, in the land of Palestine.* Therefore, on this view again, the prophecy is not likely ever to be fulfilled.

The argument adduced to show that the mention made by Christ of the darkening of the sun and moon, and the falling of the stars, are meta-phorical or symbolical expressions, is liable to grave objections.† For in the first place, supposing these prophecies to have been enunciated either

---

* Notwithstanding the many volumes written with the view to show that, in confor-mity to certain prophecies in the Old Testament, the Jews, in twelve distinct tribes, will be restored, as a nation, to their former possession of the Land of Canaan, having Jeru-salem as their capital; the very idea, when soberly entertained, is most preposterous;—implies a wide-spread national insanity, to which there is nothing in the history of any nation bearing the slightest resemblance. It implies that a people, the most selfish in the world, and also exceedingly sagacious, will some day, all at once, abandon their thriving traffics in the richest countries of Europe, Asia, Africa, and America, and march towards Jerusalem, in order to establish themselves under a despotism of the most brutal kind, in a paltry nook of the earth, which,—as testified by modern travellers, who have minutely surveyed it,—is remarkable only for its extreme sterility, scanty population, mercantile and manufacturing destitution, and the grossly superstitious practices of its present inhabitants.

† See pp. 32—40.

by, or under the influence of Deity, it would appear inconsistent with any sound and proper idea of God to think that he would use, or sanction the use of metaphors, symbols, or parables to represent things to his creatures different from what they are. Reason would expect that God,—if he wished to inform his creatures what was to happen hereafter,—would represent things as they *were* to happen,—not in a manner in which they were *not* to happen. It can hardly be supposed of him that when he meant one thing, and wished his creatures to understand that one thing, he should say another thing;—that when he meant the downfall of the Jewish Polity in church and state, he should not say a word about this Polity, but speak of the darkening of the sun and moon, and the falling of the stars;—or that when he spoke of the *latter* he *meant* any other. For God,—in revealing things, either present, past, or future,—to use a dark and enigmatic style of speaking to his creatures, the meaning of which is not clear to them, is not only not to reveal anything at all to them, but is a proof that either he did not wish them to understand, or was unable to make them understand what he meant. Either of these suppositions would be derogatory to the character of God. But we are told by divines that Christ, in his predictions, as well as all other expressions, accommodated his language to human modes of thinking and speaking, so that the great things he revealed might be adapted to the weak capacity of human understanding. Here, however, it is forgotten that the inability of understanding Christ's words to mean what *divines say* they mean, is the very point complained of. In such a case as the prediction of the destruction of Jerusalem, which occurrence had been seen taking place, over and over again, and for the description of which, in intelligible terms, copious language existed at the time, it is absurd to allege that if Christ had spoken of such a calamity as it really was to happen he would not have been understood. If his words conveyed ideas of things as they were *not* to be, it is certain that he could not be understood as speaking of things as they *were* to be. If, without the least intimation of a figure, he mentioned the sun, moon, and stars, he could not expect to be understood to mean men. It would have been much better not to be understood at all, than to be understood falsely, or than to speak so as to mislead. Why speak at all, if not so as to be understood, and so as *not* to mislead? To be misunderstood, to speak falsely, and to mislead, are faults incident to fallible man, —not to the all-perfect Deity. Such, when applied to God, are a blasphemous reflection on his character as a perfect being, implying that he speaks like ignorant, erring, falsifying man,—speaks falsely, when he well knows the truth!*

Besides: the argument of symbolical language not only blasphemously represents God like fallible and deceptive man, but it necessarily implies that Christ *meant* what he said of the heavenly bodies to be understood in a symbolical sense. Even supposing that Divine Inspiration was not claimed for the passage, but that it was found in the writings of some profane author; still it would, by no means, be deemed clad in symbolical language. For there is nothing about it, any more than there is about the rest of Christ's prophetical sayings, or his ordinary mode of speaking,

* See Berg and Barker's Great Discussion on the Bible, p. 54. Turner's Edit,

which in the least indicates a symbolical style. If, therefore, it be contended that the darkening of the sun and moon, the falling of the stars, and the shaking of the powers of heaven, are *symbols ;* then, by parity of argument, it must be admitted that the Son of man—the mourning of the tribes of the earth—the clouds of heaven—angels—trumpet—elect—four winds—heaven and earth ;—all expressions in immediate connection,— are also *symbols.* Further: if such words were symbols here, it would inevitably follow that they are symbols in other places in the New Testament where they are employed, precisely for similar purposes. To make this concession, however, would not be very convenient ; for it would sweep away every notion of the second advent of Christ,—of the last judgment, —in a word, it would overthrow the entire system of the Christian religion ; making the whole history of Christ, from the prediction of his birth by an angel, to his ascension in a cloud to heaven, as told in the Gospels, a fable, —a wild romance. To such a conclusion leads the argument of symbolical language,—where there is not the faintest mark to distinguish such language from that which is literal. For, to imagine that the same word, exactly in the same connection, is used symbolically in one place, and literally in another, is, in point of argument, arbitrary, futile, and capricious ; besides being, in the present case, an attempted interpretation of a supposed communication from God to his creatures quite unworthy of that great God and perfect Being ;—quite revolting to his attributes, even as they are described by Christians.

It is, however, maintained that Christ used these expressions, said to be symbolical, in imitation of similar expressions of the ancient prophets, proved to be symbolical by the connections in which they occur. And it is thence argued, that similar expressions used by Christ are also in the same style. In other words, it is maintained that the ancient prophets, whilst guided by Divine Inspiration, described national calamities by the disruption of the celestial bodies, or the darkening of the sun and moon ; and that the similarity of Christ's language to that of these prophets, proves him also to have predicted the destruction of Jerusalem in a symbolical style, without any reference to the destruction of the world and the final judgment. This part of the argument would possess some weight towards proving that Christ predicted the destruction of Jerusalem,—not the end of the world, —if the premises were admissible ; that is, if it were, or could be demonstrated, that it was simply national calamities which the ancient prophets had in view when using similar terms to those used by Christ, as to the heavenly bodies. The same remarks apply to the arguments adduced to prove that such expressions as—" the day of the Lord"—"the latter days" —" last days," &c., used by the apostles, do not refer to the end of the world ; but are employed in the same sense as parallel expressions found in the ancient prophets. These, therefore, may here be reviewed together. Now, there is no reason to doubt that the ancient prophets had, in common with most people of their times, very vague and limited notions of the extent of the world, and of its probable destruction by fire or water.— Their notions on the latter point were naturally and necessarily founded partly on traditionary lore, and partly on observation and experience, derived from the effects of volcanoes and other commotions in the earth, as well as from frequent and sudden outbursts of the watery element, anciently in the East, sweeping away multitudes of human beings from the stage of existence. Such visitations as these were recorded as destructions of the world ; and as they frequently destroyed nearly as much of the world as was known to exist, they were always considered as a judgment from God ; and were viewed as "the day of the Lord"—"the day of his wrath," and so on. Nor has there been any lack of predictions of such destructions as these, among any nation, or in any age ; as all ancient mythologies testify. Such predictions, accordingly, we find in the sacred books of the Jews, in common with those of other ancient nations. Even the very last of the Jewish prophets—Malachi ;—supposed to have flourished about four centuries before Christ,—thus predicted such a destruction, as— *the day—the great and dreadful* day of the Lord coming and *burning as an oven.* Nor did the predictors of the end of the world cease with the dispersion of the Jews. We find the early Christians predicting the same event to be preceded by internal commotions ;—wars, pestilence, and famine, which were to visit the Roman empire,—the country of the Scipios and the Cæsars, where the profession of idolatry was persisted in ; and hence was it with the city of Rome called "Babylon." These things, together with comets, eclipses, and inundations, were to be as so many signs before Rome and her territories should—with the rest of the world, —be consumed by fire from heaven, and made into an immense lake of fire and brimstone.* "In the opinion of a general conflagration," remarks Mr. Gibbon, "the faith of the Christian very happily coincided with the traditions of the East, the philosophy of the Stoics, and the analogy of nature ; and even the country which, from religious motives, had been chosen for the origin and principal scene of the conflagration, was best adapted for the purpose by natural and physical causes, by its deep caverns, beds of sulphur, and numerous volcanoes, of which those of Ætna, of Vesuvius, and of Liprandi, exhibit a very imperfect representation."†— Such have suggested the idea of the end of the world, in every age ; and have prompted those pretending to the prophetic gift to predict the event as just at hand.

But let those predictions of the Jewish prophets, which enunciate a disruption in the celestial bodies, be examined ; in order to ascertain whether they bear any marks of a symbolical style, or afford any reason whatever for believing that they are not, literally, predictions of the destruction of the world. Thus it may the better be determined what reason exists for believing that the prophetic sayings of Christ—expressed in similar terms — are to be regarded as arrayed in *symbolical* language.— Isaiah‡ speaks of "the day of the Lord," and "the day of his fierce anger;" when he would "punish the *world* for their evil, and the wicked for their iniquity,"—destroy the sinners out of the land ; cause the earth to remove out of her place; shake the heavens ; cause the stars and constellations, together with the sun and moon, not to give light ; and make man more precious than fine gold. There is no reason whatever to believe that *sun, moon, stars,* and *constellations,* in this prediction, are symbolical words, any

* Lactantius Inst. Div. vii. 16. Burnet's Sacred Theory, part iii. c. 5.
† Gibbon's Decline and Fall of the Roman Empire, chap. xv. p. 177. Cadell's Edit.
‡ Chap. xiii. 9—14. The passage, with others of similar language, has already been cited, pp. 42, 43.

more than *the day of the Lord, world, man, fine gold, sinners, wicked,* and
iniquity. The whole of the passage is as clear a prediction of the destruction of the world as any in the Bible. It is true that the prophet differs,
in his notion of the *manner* in which the world was to be destroyed, from
the present notions generally entertained of its destruction; so that, in the
course of his predictions, he has many expressions which do not coincide
with them; and it is equally true that, like all other prognosticators of this
event, he speaks of *war* in connection with it. It would appear also that
his object, in uttering these predictions, was to show that Babylon, in
particular, was to be destroyed, just as the early Christians predicted that
Rome should be destroyed at the end of the world. This city—Babylon,
was to be destroyed, so as to be like Sodom and Gomorrah, and never to
be inhabited. To say the least of this prophecy, there is no proof in it
that the names of the heavenly bodies are used as symbols. Ezekiel uses
similar words in reference to the darkening of the celestial bodies.* Here,
in the context, there is a metaphor, or rather a simile employed; but the
form of expression used,—"thou art *like* a young lion,"—clearly denotes it
to be such a figure. The names of the heavenly bodies, however, even in
this instance, are not symbols—any more than the words—" hearts of
many nations," which immediately follow them:—they are words, used
only in their ordinary acceptation, to convey an idea, in carrying out the
simile, according to the notion of the writer. Much less are they symbols,
or types, representing the fall of any great personages, at the head of the
affairs of any nation, as is thought of such words in Christ's predictions.
Indeed, they appear to mean, literally, that the Lord would cover the
luminaries of heaven in order to prevent Pharaoh, king of Egypt, from
having light, when fighting with his enemies, and would "set darkness on his
land" similar to the plague of darkness† which Moses had brought upon
the land of Egypt, to which apparently the words allude. Nor is there
any better ground for supposing that the darkness prognosticated by
Ezekiel had anything symbolical about it any more than that described by
Moses.

The prophet Joel, also, in several passages predicts a disruption of the
celestial bodies; but his predictions like those already noticed in Isaiah,
foretell the destruction of the world, and the day of judgment, according
to the notions he entertained of these events.‡ For in connection with his
predictions of the darkening of the heavenly luminaries he has such expressions as,—"Alas for the day! for the day of the Lord is at hand, and as a
destruction from the Almighty shall it come."—" The day of the Lord
cometh, for it is nigh at hand;—a day of darkness and of gloominess,—a
day of clouds and of thick darkness."—" A fire devoureth before them,
and behind them a flame burneth."—" All faces shall gather blackness."—
" The day of the Lord is great and very terrible, and who can abide it?"—
" Let the heathen be wakened, and come up to the valley of Jehoshaphat;
for there *will I sit to judge* all the heathen round about."—" *The day of
the Lord is near* in the valley of decision." Such expressions as these

---

* Ezek. xxxii. 1—10.   † Exod. x. 21—23.

‡ Joel i. 15; ii. 1, 2, 3, 6, 10, 11, 31; iii. 12, 14, 15. See all these passages, already
cited, p. 43; and read the contexts.

evidently show that the prophet represents the day of judgment as close at hand. Then there is here an apparent reference to wars, just as we find in predictions of the same event by Isaiah and Christ. But such expressions as—" The Lord shall utter his voice before his *army ;* for his *camp* is very great," if closely examined, would be found not to mean exactly an *army* and a *camp* of *human,* but rather *angelic* soldiers ; such as are, throughout the Bible, represented as constituting the army, and the host of Jehovah, and of the *Aleihim ;* (Gods) and such also as are represented as coming to destroy the world.* Throughout the prophecies of Joel, there are points, regarding the destruction of the world and the circumstances which were to attend it, that bear striking resemblance to the same doctrines taught in the New Testament ;—such as exhortations to repent, (ii. 12, 13) and promises (like that of the kingdom of heaven) that " Judah shall dwell for ever, and Jerusalem from generation to generation." (iii. 20.) But the most remarkable is the following passage, proving both that Joel prophesied the end of the world, and that his notions of it were identical with those of Christ and his apostles.—" And it shall come to pass afterward, that I will pour out my spirit upon all flesh ; and your sons and your daughters shall prophesy, your old men shall dream dreams, your young men shall see visions : and also upon the servants and upon the handmaids in those days will I pour out my spirit. And I will shew wonders in the heavens and in the earth, blood and fire, and pillars of smoke. The sun shall be turned into darkness, and the moon into blood, before the great and terrible day of the Lord come. And it shall come to pass, that whosoever shall call on the name of the Lord shall be delivered : for in mount Zion and in Jerusalem shall be deliverance, as the Lord hath said, and in the remnant whom the Lord shall call "† The prophet then proceeds to say that the Lord would gather all nations, and bring them down into the valley of Jehoshaphat, where he commands the heathen to be assembled. There is nothing more meant by the *valley of Jehoshaphat,*‡ (יהושפט—*Jehovah the*

---

* See p. 98. et seq. The word translated *army* in the above passage is חיל, which may mean *riches, virtue, strength, a host, a band, a train, a company, an army, bulwark, rampart,* or almost any thing involving either mental, moral, or physical strength.—Accordingly, the same word in verse 22. is, in connection with trees, translated *strength* (of trees) ; but there are reasons to believe that, in the passage under notice, it means the angelic forces—the army of Jehovah. Numerous are the references in Scripture to these heavenly soldiers, hosts, or armies. The writer of the book of Job (xxv. 3.) speaks of the armies—גדודים of God, in connection with the light or the luminaries of the sky, where these armies were thought to be quartered. The word rendered *camp* is—מחנה. The same word is used to denote the encampment of the angel of the Lord. (Psal. xxxiv. 7.) and also the camp of the angels of the Gods. (*Aleihim.*) See Note, pp. 98, 99.

† Joel ii. 28—32.

‡ There is no reason whatever for supposing that the word—יהושפט here stands for the name of king Jehoshaphat, or any other man of that name. It is composed of יה or יהו—the root of the word *Jehovah,* and ש.פ.ט - *a judge, or judgment* All that can be made of it is *the judgment of the Lord* It is not wonderful that it is only one word, instead of two, and that it has been mistaken, by our translators and others, for the name of a man ; not only because there was a name of this signification, but also because the Hebrew Scriptures were originally written without any division of words, without capital letters, without periods, and without vowels ; thus :—

נעירווועלוהנריומאלעמקיהושפטכישראבשלשפטאתכלהנרימהנסביבשלחומגלכיבשלקצירבאורריכימלאהנת
" Let the heathen be wakened and come up to the valley of Jehoshaphat,"&c.—Joel iii. 12.

Judge, or " Lord Judge") than the valley where the Lord was to sit in judgment; for the prophet declares that the Lord said—" there will I sit to judge all the heathen round about." This appears to be given as a reason for calling the place to which Joel alludes,—*the valley of Judgment.* In the context he calls it " the valley of decision."* Now, in passages just cited, Joel predicts the following things :—wonders in heaven and earth, blood, fire, and darkness of the heavenly bodies, which were to take place before the great and terrible day of the Lord came. This is precisely what is predicted by Christ and his apostles to take place before the end of the world and the day of judgment came. He further says that those who would call upon the name of the Lord should be delivered, as well as the remnant whom the Lord should call. Here is precisely the doctrine of Christ concerning those who were to be admitted into the kingdom of heaven. He also says, that this deliverance should be in mount Zion and in Jerusalem. It was a belief among the early Christians that upon mount Zion Christ would take his seat as a judge, at the end of the world,† which they daily expected. And on one occasion, as we shall hereafter notice more at large, thousands of them, believing the end of the world would come in few months, took a pilgrimage, from all parts, to mount Zion, in order to be there to meet the judge in time, and to beseech him to deal leniently with them. Another thing the prophet declares is, that all nations were to be gathered together and be judged in the valley of decision. The whole of these predictions look very much like a prophecy of the end of the world and the final judgment. And indeed those divines —who, at considerable pains, have so much assisted the weak-minded Christian to understand the Bible, by heading each chapter with what is termed " contents," thus prefixing to each a kind of creed,—appear to be in great doubt whether Joel here did not prophesy the *end of the world,* as an event *just at hand.* For they do not attempt at applying these predictions to temporal judgments on any *particular nation,* or to the *appearance of the Messiah in the flesh,* to which almost all prophecies are made to apply : but here they content themselves with heading the chapters with such intimations as—" sundry judgments of God"—" the terribleness of God's judgments"—" God will be known in his judgment," and so on.

But let us inquire in what light the Jews themselves viewed these

---

* Joel iii. 2, 12, 14. It is singular that all the proper names in the Old Testament are designative of the principal trait or quality in the objects for which they are given. The names of men are frequently indices of what they did *at the close of their lives.* Does this bespeak the narratives to be mythological ?

† A similar notion is retained, even to the present day, by the superstitious inhabitants of Jerusalem. A friend of the author, who has minutely examined the ruins of this ancient city, writes :—" Near the top part of the north wall of Jerusalem, facing the valley of Jehoshaphat, and consequently facing the mosque of Omar, which stands on the site of the ancient Jewish temple, I was shown a small aperture. Near it stood a Turkish sentinel or soldier ; and I was told that upon this *precise spot* Christ was expected to sit in judgment on the whole assembled nations of the earth,—all human beings that have existed since the creation." According to this traditional notion, all mankind were to be gathered into the valley of Jehoshaphat, and the Judge was to sit opposite to them on the south side of mount Olives. When it is recollected that judicial courts were, anciently, held in the open air, not only in the East but also in this country, such an idea of the Final Judgment would naturally be conceived in a superstitious and benighted age.

predictions of their prophet Joel.   Peter, in his Pentecostal sermon,*
recites the passage just quoted from Joel almost literally.   In the first
place, it is observable that Peter cannot, by any show of reason, be said to
regard the disruption of the heavenly bodies predicted by Joel as symbols
of national calamity; for he quotes the predictions expressly for the purpose
of showing that those on whom the Holy Ghost had descended, and who
spoke in strange tongues, were not drunk, but acted in conformity to the
predictions of Joel.   There is no national calamity whatever,—no downfall
of great men in national affairs,—implied in the view taken by Peter of these
predictions touching the heavenly bodies.   Nor would Christians be very
consistent in supposing that these are symbolical expressions of national
calamities.   For here they occur in the very prediction which they continually
cite as foretelling the success which should attend the preaching of the
Gospel, when the Spirit,—the Comforter that Christ should send,—was to
be poured on all flesh.   Further : neither the prediction nor this interpretation of it, given by Christians, and partly sanctioned by Peter, can apply to
the destruction of Jerusalem, which did not happen till about forty years after
this period ; and, consequently, after the prophecy, according to the view
taken of it by Peter, in common with succeeding Christians, had been
fulfilled.   The national calamity which befell the Jews, in the destruction
of their capital, cannot, therefore, be portrayed here by the darkening of
the celestial bodies, and the mention of " the great and terrible day of the
Lord,"—which Joel says was " nigh at hand,"—when all nations should
be judged.   There is, however, positive proof that Peter understood Joel,
in this prophecy, to predict the end of the world, and that he regarded
those particulars, implied in the passage he cites, as to occur before that
event should take place.   For he alters the words of Joel so as to make
them more clearly express that.   Instead of—" it shall come to pass afterward," Peter has—" it shall come to pass in the *last days.*"†   That the
apostles meant by—" last days," and " latter days," the *last days* of time,
or of the duration of the world, there is the most positive proof that
language can afford ; as will hereafter be shown.   Hence Peter, and probably the Jews at large, understood Joel, in the predictions under notice,
to refer to the end of the world.   We must therefore conclude that this
prophet, and others already cited, were so far from using the expressions
which convey an idea of the darkening of the heavenly bodies as *symbols*
that, by such expressions, they intended, *literally*, to predict the end of the
world.   There is not the slightest ground for doubting that the Jewish
prophets, like those of other ancient nations, frequently predicted the end
of the world to be at hand, and a new heaven and a new earth to be
created, in which there was endless bliss to be enjoyed.   Isaiah makes
Jehovah to say ;—" Behold, I create new heavens and a new earth : and
the former shall not be remembered, nor come into mind.   But be ye glad
and rejoice for ever in that which I create : for, behold, I create Jerusalem
a rejoicing, and her people a joy.   And I will rejoice in Jerusalem, and
joy in my people : and the voice of weeping shall be no more heard in her
nor the voice of crying."   These are the new heavens and earth, and the
new Jerusalem, mentioned in the Epistles and Apocalypse, in connection

---

* Acts ii. 17—21.   † Compare Joel ii. 28. with Acts ii. 17.

with the last judgment and the end of the world, where the inhabitants should never die, neither weep nor cry, and feel neither pain nor sorrow; but reign for ever and ever.*

The fact, therefore, that the ancient Jewish prophets have predicted the end of the world utterly destroys the course of argument pursued to show that these prophets, *symbolically*, described the calamities, or the utter destruction of potentates and kingdoms, by such figures as the darkening and falling of the sun, moon, and stars,—in the passages cited for this purpose,—and that, consequently, Christ made use of the same figure to foretell the downfall of the Jewish Polity, in church and state, without at all referring to the destruction of the world and the last day of judgment. Nay, the analogical proof it furnishes further strengthens the evidence already adduced that Christ predicted the destruction of the world. And even if there were no proof that these prophets predicted the end of the world, still the argument that Christ used the expressions which occur in his predictions, regarding the celestial luminaries, as symbols of national calamities, *in imitation of the ancient* prophets, would, by no means, be conclusive. For admitting that the eastern prophets and poets symbolised their rulers,—which certainly was, and, even to this day, is the custom in the East,—still it would be absurd to suppose that whenever mention is made, in their works, of the darkening of one or more of the luminaries of the sky, this is a prediction of the downfall of potentates or kingdoms.— Thus, even upon the admission that the ancient prophets make use of the names of these bodies as symbols, it would be too difficult to draw a line of distinction between the instances in which they use them as such, and those in which they do not, so as to be able therefrom to adduce a sound argument; seeing the instances in which it is contended that the names of these luminaries are used as symbols bear no marks whatever of their being used as such. What reason can there be for understanding Joel to speak *literally*, when he says,—"They shall run upon the wall; they shall climb up upon the houses; they shall enter at the windows like a thief;" but *symbolically* when he continues in the same strain,—"the earth shall quake before them; the heavens shall tremble; the sun and moon shall be dark, and the stars shall withdraw their shining"? Are we to believe that he speaks *literally* when he says,—"upon the servants and upon the handmaids, in those days, will I pour out my spirit;" but *symbolically*, when, in the immediately following words, he says,—"And I will show wonders in the heavens and in the earth,—blood, and fire, and pillars of smoke.— The sun shall be turned into darkness and the moon into blood, before the terrible day of the Lord come"? Are the words,—"The day of the Lord is near in the valley of decision," to be understood *literally*, but the next words,—"the sun and moon shall be darkened, and the stars shall withdraw their shining," *symbolically*?† Do the Scriptures not speak *literally* of earthquakes,—*literally* of the falling of stars,—*literally* of darkening the sun, and moon, and so on? How then are we to know that, in the passages already referred to, the prophets use such expressions as *symbols*? Of this

---

* Compare Isa. lxv. 17—20; lxvi. 22. with 2 Pet. iii. 12, 13. Rev. xxi. 1—26; xxii. 3—5.

† See passages already cited, p. 137. et seq.

there must be given an indubitable proof, before they can be admitted as evidence of the symbolical character of the predictions of Christ, in which they occur. Indeed were this species of evidence admitted, it could be used to prove *too much* for the interests of Christianity. The Evangelists relate that Jesus walked upon the sea,—turned water into wine,—fed five thousand with five loaves and two fishes, augmenting the fragments into twelve baskets full,—raised men and women from the dead,—transfigured himself so as to shine like the sun ;—also that he was crucified, and hung on the cross, a dying and dead Divinity,—that while he was thus suspended, darkness came over all the land for three hours, the earth quaked, the graves opened, the dead rose up alive, and Christ himself, having been buried, sprang up into life, and broke out of the grave. But alas! all such expressions may be nothing but *symbols !*   There is quite as much reason to maintain that these are *symbols*, as that the disruption of the celestial bodies, in Christ's prophecies, are such figures. The argument of *symbols*, therefore, in the present case, cannot, in conformity with sound criticism, be admitted as proof that Christ predicted the destruction of Jerusalem, and did not predict the end of the world.

Again : the argument adduced, in various parts of Chapter II. to show that Christ means, in the predictions in question, only the *destruction of the Jewish capital*, and the *downfall of the Jewish Polity in church and state*, are equally inconclusive. Nor is this a matter to be overlooked. It is of the utmost importance ; for it involves the very essence of the point at issue,—the very nucleus of the dispute.   If *the overthrow of the Jewish commonwealth—the Jewish Polity—civil and religious—a theocracy established by God himself*—* implies the total abolition of the Jewish religion, either in its ritual, moral, or theocratic aspects ; then, the prophecy, even on this view, has not been fulfilled. For the Jewish religion was not abolished, at the time Jerusalem was destroyed ;—is not abolished even to this day. Indeed, Christ himself distinctly declared that he came not to abrogate the Jewish Law, but to fulfil it. No reasonable doubt can exist as to the sense in which he used this expression, if we examine his conduct, and that of his father, mother, brothers, and sisters,—all of them, so far as Scripture indicates, conformed to the Jewish ritual.†   Christ, to his very death, adhered to the Mosaic religion. His last act—of keeping the feast of unleavened bread, or eating the passover,—was in compliance with the Mosaic institution, both on his own part and that of the whole of his apostles. Moreover, the Jewish religion has never been abolished, either in its ritual, moral, or theocratic aspects. On the contrary, wherever, in any nation on earth commerce flourished, Jews were found enriching themselves ; and yet adhering, under every persecution, to the faith of their forefathers. True, the temple erected by Solomon had perished, but the Mosaic Law was not of stone and mortar to perish with it. Long before that event, the ark of the covenant had ceased to exist ; but the religion itself still subsisted. In fact, there is every reason to believe that, at this moment, there are more Jews following the faith of their fathers,

---

* See pp. 14, 17, 30, 35, 36, 38, 40, &c.

† Luke ii. 21—24; xxii. 8—15. John iv. 45; v. 1 ; vii. 2, 8—11, 14, 37. Matth. xxvi. 17—19.

than ever existed at any previous period of the Jewish nationality. There-fore, the only true sense in which total abolition can be said to have been effected, is the Roman conquest of the Jews, as a separate, distinct, and independent nation. But that event took place *previously*—not *subsequently* —to the prophecy of Christ, here under investigation ; and, therefore, yields no support to the plea that, in any degree, it verified the prediction. To urge the contrary is to apply Christ's prophecy to an event past before such a prophecy had been delivered. Still, this is the only event to which the terms—*total abolition of the Jewish Polity*—can be applied with any show of reason.

As to the argument built upon the similarity said to exist between expressions used by the ancient prophets and expressions which occur in Christ's predictions, now under notice,* it should be observed that each of the passages cited from the former has a meaning and tendency peculiar to itself ; and not generic, as contended ; and that the special predictions of the latter, in order truly to ascertain their meaning, should be judged of as they appear on the whole *scope* and *intendment* of the chapters to which they belong ; and also as they were understood by Christ's apostles— Matthew, Mark, Peter, James, John, and Paul ;—all of whom, except Paul, were eye and ear witnesses of the predictions themselves, as well as of the tone and manner of their utterance. This is indispensable in order to determine the real meaning of these predictions. Further : in instituting a comparison between these predictions and any expressions of the ancient prophets, it should be noticed that, *first*, those uttered by Christ receive a precise and definite signification, by their being an answer to a special question put to him by his assembled apostles ; thus :—" What shall be the sign of thy *coming*, and of the *end of the world ?*"—*Secondly*, that all his statements must, in fairness, be held to bear upon those terrible events to which the question refers.—*Thirdly*, that they do obviously bear upon them, and cannot be made to refer to anything else, without doing violence to the language in which these statements are made.—*Lastly*, that none of the passages, cited from the ancient prophets, contain anything corre-spondent to many passages in Christ's predictions respecting stars falling from heaven,—the gathering of the elect from the four winds of heaven,— the occurrence of these events during the generation then existing,—and the repeated injunction to watch and pray. Besides : the *whole* of the argument built upon the similarity of the expressions used by Christ, in this prediction, to expressions employed by the ancient prophets, is founded upon the *supposition* that the latter did not prophesy the near approach of the end of the world and the day of judgment ;—a supposition, the correct-ness of which is neither borne out by evidence, nor admitted by those who contend that Christ prophesied the near approach of these events. The premises, therefore, not being granted, the conclusions drawn from them cannot be admitted as sound.

Again : the explanation given of the following remarkable portion of Christ's prophecy is, by no means satisfactory, when closely examined.— " As the lightning cometh out of the east, and shineth even unto the west, *so shall the coming of the Son of man be.*" To imagine that here he means

* pp. 34, 35.

his coming simply " to execute temporal judgment upon the Jews, in the destruction of Jerusalem and the overthrow of the Jewish Polity, both religious and civil,"* is not only quite gratuitous, but contrary to the whole tenour of the prophecy.   If Christ, in his prediction, means that he himself was to *come* to execute temporal judgment upon the Jews, he must come to execute it in the manner he predicts ; otherwise the prediction is not verified. He must come himself with angels and trumpet-sounding ;— the elect must be gathered ;—the sun and moon must darken ;—the stars must fall from heaven.   A prophecy must be taken as it stands,—in all its length and breadth of expression, and according to its natural and obvious meaning :—not in detached and mangled portions.   Still, it is in the latter manner that Christian writers, most generally, attempt at showing the truth of the Jewish predictions.   It is wonderful to observe how much more freedom they take with a Book which they profess to consider of Divine Inspiration than they would dare take with any other book, ancient or modern.

The evidence adduced from the writings of the apostles† to show that Christ's predictions refer solely to the destruction of Jerusalem, is also liable to grave objections.   The argument advanced here is founded on the assumption that all the Epistles were written before the destruction of Jerusalem.   But the dates, as well as the authorship, of these productions are quite uncertain.   We have nothing like a positive proof as to when, or by whom they were written.   The *pious frauds* of ancient times, when whole books on Christian subjects were forged, have made these matters entirely conjectural.   The dates usually assigned to them, by Christian writers, wholly depend upon popish tradition ;—a foundation too sandy, upon which to build an argument, and draw conclusions therefrom.— Besides : the admission made‡ that many passages, in the apostolic writings, refer to the last day of judgment, nullifies much of the argument built upon the writings of the apostles.   For the similarity of the passages *admitted* to refer to the end of the world, to those *denied* to refer to the near approach of this event, is so striking as to furnish, at least, a strong pre- sumptive proof that all of them refer to it.   Such for example are,—1 Cor. xv. 51, 52. 1 Thess. iv. 15 — 17.   The explanation given of the use of the pronoun—*we*, in these passages, is by no means sufficient.§   Nor is the argument used therein conclusive—that Paul did not expect to see the end of the world in his lifetime.   In the last passage, just cited, he uses the *first person plural* four times ; and the second person plural—*ye* or *you* —six times.   To place, beyond doubt, Paul's intention to confine his obser- vations to the then existing Thessalonian believers, he uses the emphatic pronoun—*yourselves* (αυτοι) in the context.|| He tells them to " comfort one another with these words ;" namely, the words he had just written to them ; and he appeals to their own perfect knowledge of Christ's sudden coming in judgment,—" as a thief in the night."   Hence all the efforts made here, with the aid of the ingenious passage from Horne, utterly fail to divest these expressions of their pointed personality to then existing believers.   Surely, those who received these Epistles, and for whose comfort they were written and sent,—who knew Paul personally, and had often

---

* See pp. 28, 46.   † p. 41, et seq.   ‡ pp. 46, 47.   § p. 48. || 1 Thess. v. 2.

heard from his lips the enforcement of his Epistles, behoved to know the import thereof infinitely better than people of a distant nation, living nearly two thousand years afterwards.   Surely the Thessalonians were better judges than people of the present age are, whether Paul, in his first Epistle to them, taught that the end of the world and the final judgment were close at hand.   They understood him so to teach.   Nor does Paul, in his second Epistle, say that he had not so represented these events.   He only tells them not to be shaken in mind or troubled.   And as a reason for not to be so troubled, he assures them that *the day of Christ was at hand.**

It may, by some, be regretted that the evidence adduced to show that Christ's predictions now under notice refer solely to the destruction of Jerusalem is thus found liable to so many important exceptions.   But the observant reader will perceive that no pains have been spared to bring forward the best evidence obtainable, with a view to establish that point; and will, in candour, admit that its weakness does not proceed from any want of honest dealing on the part of the writer.

SECTION II.—THE STRENGTH OF THE EVIDENCE ADDUCED TO SHOW THAT CHRIST PREDICTED THE END OF THE WORLD AND THE FINAL JUDGMENT TO TAKE PLACE WITHIN THE LIFETIME OF THE GENERATION OF MEN THEN LIVING.

It is now proposed to examine the validity of the arguments adduced in proof that Christ predicted the end of the world and the day of judgment as events then just at hand.   With regard to the frantic mood into which it is said the ancient Jewish prophets wrought themselves when prophesying,† this does not cast any reflection upon Christ as a prophet.   He was, it is true, a Jewish prophet, but no proof has been adduced that he indulged in the "divine frenzy" in which other prophets did, so as to identify himself with them on this point.   In delivering his predictions, he appears to have been much more temperate than the old school of prophets.

Again : as to the remarks made with the view to show that the Hebrews were not acquainted with the heathen notion that the soul, or what the Greeks called $\psi v \chi \eta$, existed *separately* after death, it can scarcely be said that the arguments advanced on this topic are sufficiently conclusive to establish the point in question.‡   For although the Hebrews and Greeks

---

* 2 Thess. ii. 2.   † See pp. 55—58.

‡ Dr. Priestley, however, remarks that the doctrine of the distinction between soul and body as two different substances, which he says was of oriental origin, " does not appear to have ever been adopted by the generality of the Jews, and perhaps not even by the more learned and philosophical of them, such as Josephus, *till after the time of our Saviour;* though Philo, and some others, who resided in Egypt, might have adopted that tenet in an earlier period.   Though a distinction is made in Scripture between the principle or seat of thought in men, and the parts which are destined to other functions; and in the New Testament that principle may sometimes be signified by the term *soul,* yet there is no instance, either in the Old or New Testament of this *soul* being supposed to be in one place and the body in another.   They are always conceived to go together, so that the perceptive and thinking power could not, in fact, be considered by the sacred writers as any other than *a property* of a living man, and therefore, as what ceased, of course, when the man was dead, and could not be revived but with the revival of the

had no name for a soul or spirit but that which signified *wind* or *life ;* and although the doctrine of the existence of a soul is not taught in the Old

body. Accordingly, we have no promise of any reward, or any threatening of punishment after death, but that which is represented as taking place at the general resurrection.— And it is observable that this is never, in the Scriptures, called, as with us, the resurrection of *the body*, (as if the soul, in the meantime, was in some other place,) but always the resurrection of *the dead*, that is, of the man."—*Hist. Corruption of Christianity, vol.* i. *part* v. *Introduction.*

"In the second and third centuries those who believed that there was a soul distinct from the body supposed that after death it went to some place under ground." We are however informed that the Christians in Arabia, as late as the third century, "maintained that the soul perishes with the body, but that it will be raised to life again, by the power of God, at the resurrection. It is said, however, that they were induced to abandon this opinion by the arguments and influence of Origen." (Euseb. Hist. Eccles. lib. vi. c. 37.) .... "Whenever the Jews received the opinion of the separate existence of the soul, it was in the imperfect manner above mentioned For they held that there was a place below the earth which they called *Paradise*, where the souls of good men remained ; and they distinguished this from the *upper Paradise*, where they were to be after the resurrection. The Christians borrowed their opinions from the Jews, and supposed that *Hades*, or the place of the souls, was divided into two mansions, in one of which the wicked were in grief and torment, and in the other the godly were in joy and happiness, both of them expecting the general resurrection. (Hist. Apostles' Creed, p. 198, &c.)— Into this general receptacle of souls it was the opinion of the early Fathers that Christ descended to preach ; they supposing these to be the *spirits in prison* mentioned by the apostle Peter. (1 Pet. iii. 19.) .... Others, however, thought that our Saviour preached so effectually as to empty the whole of the *limbus patrum*, (for so also they called the precincts within which these ancient patriarchs were confined,) and carried all the souls with him into heaven. (Burnet on the Articles, p. 71.) But this must have been a late opinion, because it was not supposed in the time of the Fathers that the souls of good men in general would be with Christ, and enjoy what was called then *the beatific vision of God*, till the resurrection. This opinion is clearly stated by Novatian, for he says, —' Nor are the regions below the earth void of powers *(potestatibus)* regularly disposed and arranged ; for there is a place whither the souls of the righteous and of the wicked are led, expecting the sentence of a future judgment.' (De Trinitate, cap. 1. p. 5.) This was evidently the uniform opinion of Christian writers for many centuries after this time. The article concerning *the descent of Christ into hell*, in what we call the *Apostles' Creed*, is not mentioned by any writer before Ruñnus, who found it in his own church at Aquileia, but it was not then known at Rome, or in the East. At first, also, the expression was καταχθωνια, but in the Creed of Athanasius, made in the sixth or seventh century, it was changed into *Hades*. And even then, it seems to have been put for *burial*, there being no other word expressing the burial of Christ in that Creed. (Burnet on the Articles, p. 69.) In the declension of the Greek, and chiefly in the Latin tongue, the term *Hades* or *Hell* began to be applied to the *mansion* of wicked souls; some of the Fathers imagining *Hades* to be in the centre of the earth, others under the earth, and some being uncertain about its situation."—*Dr. Priestley's History of the Corruption of Christianity, vol.* 1. *part* v. *sec.* 1.

It is difficult to ascertain to what particular part of Josephus's works Dr. Priestley alludes, as stated at the commencement of this Note, since he cites none. It may not be amiss, however, just to mention here that the writer is well acquainted with the views advanced of *Hades*, the soul, judgment, &c., in that ingenious forgery called— *Josephus's Discourse to the Greeks concerning Hades ;*—a production fabricated, apparently, some time between the third and seventh century, replete with touches of Christian doctrines, and containing such expressions as—" God the *Word*,"—" to whom the Father hath committed all judgment," and " whom we call Christ ;"—" unquenchable fire ;"—" eternal punishment ;"—" a worm that never dieth ;"—" eternal life ;"—" incorruptible and never-fading kingdom ;"—" heavenly kingdom ;"—" neither eye hath seen, nor ear hath heard, nor hath it entered into the heart of man, the things that God hath prepared for them that love him ;" (compare 1 Cor. ii. 9.)—" in whatsoever ways I shall find you, in them shall I judge you entirely ; so cries the *end*," &c. Several other Christian phrases might be added. When such a production is found to be attributed to

L

Testament at all, while it is but very seldom and faintly alluded to,—and that in very questionable language,—in the New Testament, yet the Hebrews, in common with other nations, had their *Hades*, in which it was thought the souls (or some things which they called ψυχαι) of both good and bad men were shut up. The Jews also had their *Paradise*, in common with the Persians and other nations, apparently for the abode of the ψυχαι (souls) of the blessed. This, however, by no means affects the main argument, in which it is only collaterally used.

The mass of evidence adduced to show that Christ predicted the End of the World and the Day of the Last Judgment, as events which were positively to take place during the then existent generation of men,* is, however, of a most conclusive character. So numerous, clear, and definite are the proofs on this point, and so strongly do the many passages cited corroborate one another, that they can leave no doubt in the mind of any one who will candidly examine them, that *Christ predicted these events in the most distinct and unequivocal terms that language can furnish.* The overwhelming evidence advanced on this side of the argument, both as to the number of proofs and their individual strength, dwarfs into insignificance the arguments advanced to show that it was only the destruction of Jerusalem that Christ prophesied. The latter derive their principal strength from words found in Luke, which are not corroborated by any other passages; but the former is supported by the whole tenour of the Gospels and Epistles. Further: those words in Luke have been clearly shown to mean events which were to befall Jerusalem, either immediately *before*, or *at* the destruction of the world.† The near approach of the end of the world and the day of judgment, with their supposed consequent effects, were evidently the grand theme of Christ and his apostles. These formed the very substance of their discourses. We find them, therefore, things not accidentally mentioned, but treated upon deliberately, frequently, and pointedly, throughout whole chapters. The doctrines based upon them pervade the whole of the New Testament,—a fact which shows that they were events firmly believed by the vulgar, and universally inculcated by

---

Josephus, it makes one suspect that some of the other productions which pass under his name are forgeries, and makes all the works attributed to him unreliable. How fruitful of device must *Pious Fraud* have been, to use such Gospel expressions as the foregoing, and yet at the same time pretend, in the name of Josephus—a Jew, not a Christian—to write to the pagan Greeks, speaking of *transmigration*, of the doctrines of Plato, of philosophy, of the inspired Jewish prophets, &c., by way of disguise. This forgery, doubtless, proved very useful when quoted to show that Josephus—a renowned character —bore testimony to the truth of the Christian doctrines; and the forger must have largely imbibed the spirit of Paul, who asks—"If the *truth of God* hath more abounded through MY LIE *unto his glory*, why yet am I also judged as a sinner?" (Rom. iii. 7.) If any one wishes to know the real meaning of this apostolic avowal, let him ask the pious and learned Casaubon, who says (as quoted in Lardner, vol. IV. p. 524.)—"It greatly affects me to see the numbers who, in the *earliest* times of the church, considered it an excellent thing to lend to heavenly truth the help of their own inventions, in order that the *new doctrine* might be more readily allowed by the *wise* among the Gentiles.— These officious lies (officiosa hæc mendacia) they said, were invented for a *good* end.— From this source, doubtless, sprang nearly innumerable books." Or let him consult Mosheim, (Eccles. Hist. vol. I. p. 189.) who says, that "it was an almost universally adopted maxim that it was an act of virtue to deceive and lie, when, by such means, the interests of the church might be promoted."

* See p. 64, et seq.   † pp. 96—116.

Christ and his apostles. It is clear that the Evangelists thought more of
the prophecy of the End of the World and the Day of Judgment, than of
any other sayings of Christ; for *there are not two chapters in the whole of
the Gospels so much alike* as those in which Matthew and Mark respectively
record these predictions. And even the chapter in which Luke records
them does not differ much from the narratives of Matthew and Mark.

The evidence which the Gospels afford that the kingdom of heaven,
or the kingdom of God, spoken of by Christ, was a secular kingdom to be
set up at the end of the world, and had no reference to what is called
the Gospel Dispensation of the present age, is so abundant and positive
that it firmly establishes this position. The passages adduced to show that
it was a *spiritual* kingdom are not only few, but lose all their apparent force
and seem distorted when compared with their contexts and parallel passages;
which, however, is the only sound mode of interpretation. But as to those,
on the other hand, cited to prove the contrary, they are not only *ten times
the number*, but the construction put upon them is obvious, natural, and in
harmony with the whole drift of the Gospel narrative.* To suppose that
the expressions used regarding the kingdom of heaven are intended to be
understood in a spiritual sense,—metaphorical sense,—or any other sense
than a literal one, is, in effect, to suppose the whole of the Gospels, and
much of the Epistles, to consist only of allegories, enigmas, and riddles!
This supposition would be quite as fatal to the Divine origin of Christianity,
as the fact that its founder predicted the End of the World and the Day of
Judgment to be just at hand, in his time. An attentive perusal of the
discourses of Christ, as reported in the Gospels, must satisfy any one of
very ordinary mental acumen that, in all of them, he refers, more or less
pointedly, to the kingdom of heaven. Indeed, every one of his numerous
parables is obviously delivered in order to illustrate something appertaining
to this kingdom. When he says "the kingdom of heaven is like unto"
this, or that, he intends, of course, the phrase "kingdom of heaven" to be
understood literally. It is the figures he uses in his parables, by way of
comparison to that kingdom, which he intends to be understood metaphorically. For example, in the parable of the tares,—the good seed,—the field,
—the wheat,—the enemy,—the tares, and so on, are obviously metaphorical
figures; but the phrase "kingdom of heaven" is evidently literal.† This
is fully proved in Christ's own interpretation of the parable. The plea,
therefore, that the phrase "kingdom of heaven" is to be understood in a
metaphorical or spiritual sense is not supported by the shadow of a proof.
If ever Christ uttered a literal expression, the following words are intended
by him to be understood literally, — " I appoint unto you a kingdom, as my
Father hath appointed unto me, that ye may eat and drink at my table in
my kingdom, and sit on thrones, judging the twelve tribes of Israel."‡—
" I will not drink henceforth of this fruit of the vine, until that day when
I drink it new with you in my Father's kingdom."§ No evidence that
Christ meant his kingdom to be *secular*,—*worldly*,—or whatever is diametrically opposed to *spiritual*, can be more unexceptionable and conclusive
than that furnished by these and other passages already cited. It is true

---

* Compare Sec. vi. of Chap. ii. with Sec. iii. of Chap. iii.

† Matth. xv. 24—30, 37—43.   ‡ Luke xxii. 29, 30.   § Matth. xxvi. 29.

that many of Christ's notions are borrowed from the mythological lore of
the times in which he lived, and are enunciated in a modified form. None
of his doctrines, when compared with heathen mythology, are found to
contain much originality.   The bliss to be enjoyed in his kingdom closely
resembles that of the Elysium and Paradise of the ancients.   And the
notion of the very kingdom itself appears to be no other than the Jewish
idea of the *Golden Age* which is depicted in the mythology of various nations,
according to their respective wants and circumstances.   The Jews were a
declining and an oppressed nation, groaning for a Deliverer, or *Saviour*.—
Their prophets had repeatedly prophesied that such a Deliverer would
come,—that there would be a destruction of this world with its population,
—that new heavens and a new earth would be created,—that in this new
world there would be but one kingdom and one king, under whose reign
there would be universal and eternal peace and bliss.* This is the kingdom
of heaven, which is the grand theme of the Gospels. The king who was to
reign in this blessed kingdom, is in the Jewish books, called the *Messiah*,
which epithet simply means "the anointed," because the Jewish kings
and prophets were anointed or rubbed with oil, as a ceremonial indication
of their office. The Jews, even to this day, believe and say they understand
the prophecies of Daniel to mean that, in the days of the Messiah, there
should be on earth one kingdom, one king, and that king the Messiah.
They likewise maintain that Isaiah, Jeremiah, and Ezekiel, prophesied an
endless age of peace and happiness.   Such were and still are the notions
of the Jews of a Golden Age, or a universal kingdom. But they say Christ
did not answer their expectations.   The more the Jews were oppressed
by their conquerors, the more earnestly they expected their heavenly king
and kingdom ; and many were those who, from time to time, set up themselves as Messianic pretenders, until the Jews were dispersed and their
capital razed to the ground by the Roman legions.   Josephus informs us
that these Messiahs pretended to divine inspiration,—led away vast multitudes of people,—and raised their enthusiasm to a degree of madness.†—
The *kingdom of heaven*, long before the time Christ is said to have appeared,
was a phrase in common use among the Jews,‡ to denote the dominion
which the Messiah was to establish on earth. Christ, therefore, by no
means originated the idea of the kingdom of heaven. He only modified it,
and placed it in rather a different position with regard to its relation to the
end of the world, the day of judgment, and eternal life, together with
other details of secondary importance.   It is, however, difficult—very
difficult—to determine, from the Gospels and Epistles, whether Christ
was to be on the *present* earth, after it had been destroyed and remodelled
into a new world ; or upon *another* earth, which was to be made of entirely
new materials. This, however, is a question, the decision of which is not
essential to our present object.
      Lastly, the evidence deduced from the Gospels to establish the position
that Christ promised eternal life to those who were to be admitted into

---

* See p. 139.

† Josephus also says that the notion of the Messiah was a vulgar error which obtained
credence among some of his nation, in consequence of one prophecy found in their
sacred books.—De Bell. Jud. lib. vi. c. 5. et al.   See also Tacit. Annal. lib. v. c. 13.

‡ See Bloomfield's Lectures, p. 278. and Human Origin of Christianity, Lond. 1831.

his kingdom, and that he pronounced eternal punishment upon those who were to be excluded, is of a very determinate nature. This eternal life was incessantly held forth as an incentive to continue faithful to the principles of the new religion. He that endured to the end was to be saved.—— Whatever befell the disciples, eternal life was ensured to them.* Although they should be hated of all men,—persecuted, and even put to death, yet so sure were they of eternal life that not a hair of their heads would be left to perish. Nor is the proof less conclusive that this eternal life and the admission into the kingdom of heaven, were to be obtained at the end of the world and the day of judgment; and that the whole was to take place during the lifetime of the generation of men contemporary with Christ; nay, during the lifetime of the disciples themselves.—"Verily I say unto you, there be some standing here, which shall not taste of death, till they see the Son of man coming in his kingdom."† The conclusion, therefore, is irresistible *that Christ did predict the Last Day of Judgment and the Destruction of the World as events inevitable during the then existent generation of men.* The proofs which go to establish this fact are so numerous,—so consistent,—so powerful, and so overwhelming, that they cannot fail to convince any mind which has the least capacity to appreciate evidence and love truth; or is not engrossed with the most inveterate prejudice. Such massive evidence has forced the writer, after a minute, full, and impartial investigation of the matter, thus to declare his honest conviction that Christ *did* predict the forementioned dread events as being just at hand. There are, however, a great many other corroborative proofs of these facts, which shall be enumerated in the next section, and are intended to serve as additional reasons for coming to the conclusion just declared;—a conclusion which, it must be admitted, pronounces Christ's predictions to have proved untrue, and therefore divests Christianity of every possible pretence to Divine origin.

---

* As already noticed, (p. 81.) Judas Iscariot, and the eleven other apostles were promised thrones, wherein they were to sit in judgment on the twelve tribes of Israel.— But if such sovereign honour awaited these twelve, poor, illiterate fishermen, it is not very easy to imagine what positions of high rank were reserved for the rest of their countrymen,—many of them far their superiors in all that dignifies humanity. For what have we recorded respecting the virtues, or acquirements, or distinctions of these twelve men so worshipped by enthusiastic Christians? Not a single word or action, worthy of notice, except that one of them betrayed his master for a few pieces of silver; another denied him three times, though specially warned thereof a few minutes before; and all of them deserted him in the hour of danger, showing no sympathy with him in his sufferings. To reward such characters with thrones to reign over their fellow-citizens, seems very much like holding forth a premium to ignorance, cowardice, falsehood, and treachery.

† Matth. xvi. 27, 28.

The apostles of Christ, throughout the whole of their Epistles, and even in the Apocalypse, inculcate the doctrine that the Last Day of Judgment and the End of the World were at hand, when Christ should establish his kingdom, and endue those admitted into it with eternal life, while he punished those who should be excluded with unquenchable fire. That the apostles taught these doctrines has already been intimated, and some of their words have been cited. But here it is intended to quote the principal passages in which they are prominently held forth, in the order in which they occur ; and, for the sake of brevity, with very little comment. Let it, however, first be observed that these men—the apostles, having been commissioned by Christ, and invested with authority and power of a miraculous nature, to preach the doctrines he had taught them—called "the Gospel"—the fact that they continually *did* inculcate the near approach of the End of the World and the Day of Judgment, with their concomitant effects, is a strong corroborative proof that Christ, in the prophecies which have already been examined, *did* actually predict these events ; and that it was of him they learned them, and received a command to promulgate them.* Indeed, unless this be admitted, not only will it be difficult to imagine whence the apostles derived these doctrines, but their very connection with Christ, the divine inspiration of their teaching, and the heavenly origin of their Gospels, must, in that case, be ignored and denied by every devotee of Christianity. Every effect must have a cause. Hence, the predictions of Jesus and the preaching of his apostles possess

---

* Should it be objected that the same doctrines were preached by Paul, who was not a disciple of Christ, and who could not, therefore, have learned them of him, this would serve only to show how general, at the time, the belief was in the near approach of these stupendous events, and thereby furnish a presumptive proof that Christ, in accordance with the notions and expectations of the age, prognosticated the near approach of these things. It was, indeed, quite a trait in Christ's character not to oppose the prevailing Jewish prejudices, not only of the people at large, but even those of his own disciples. He appears to have always aimed at maintaining a perfect accordance with the religious feelings of the nation, while only opposing a few of the religious guides, such as the Pharisees, who were a mere faction. But even here it is to be observed that the ill-feeling and opposition was more on the part of these religious guides than on the part of Christ. It is not he, but they who appear to have commenced the quarrel, and to have given him occasion to speak of them in hard terms. He appears to have won the regard of the masses, and to have attacked only the priests and their dependents, whom he knew to be his enemies. Such, however, is the representation of the case given in the Gospels ; which, as it has been premised at the onset, are in the whole of this work taken as a genuine history of what they narrate, *independently of the writer's private thoughts of these documents.*

all the features and resemblances of cause and effect, furnishing a body of internal evidence which no craft can counterfeit, and no sophistry can confute.

Within a few days after Christ's ascension to heaven we find Peter preaching the same doctrines as his master had taught, and alluding to the events he had foretold. Quoting the words of the prophet Joel, which, probably, he thought more palatable then to the Jews than those of Christ whom they had just put to death as a malefactor, he says that the display of strange tongues then witnessed was what had been foretold should take place *in the last days*, when *wonders* and *signs* should be shown in heaven and earth,—when the *sun should be turned into darkness*, and the *moon into blood, before that great and notable day of the Lord came*,—and when whoever called upon the name of the Lord should be *saved*.* The words—*last days*, taken in connection with what is said of *signs* and *wonders*, and of the *heavenly bodies*, show that Peter then regarded the End of the World as an event just at hand. The meaning of the same words in passages already cited, renders this a positive fact. Reference is here likewise made to the admission into the kingdom of heaven, in the words that—those who called upon the name of the Lord should be saved.

Peter, in his next sermon, dwells upon the same points. He tells the people,—'' Repent ye therefore, and be converted, that your sins may be blotted out, when the *times of refreshing shall come* from the presence of the Lord ; and he shall send Jesus Christ, which before was preached unto you ; whom the heaven must receive *until the times of restitution of all things*.''† Like John and Christ, who preached repentance and the near

---

* See the passage cited at large in p. 139. et seq.

† Acts iii. 19—21. The meaning of this passage has greatly puzzled all the commentators. They find much difficulty in straining the words so as to make their signification accord with orthodox theological views. Nor can the singularity of the apparent idea which the passage conveys have failed to arrest the attention of the general reader, who must often have been inclined to ask,—'' How is to *refresh from the presence of the Lord?*'' Is not the Lord everywhere, so that it is impossible to be out of his presence ? And besides, are all things to be restituted or restored ? I thought all the present things were to be annihilated.'' Such are the ideas which strike the general reader in meditating upon this passage. Besides, the passage has been translated into some languages by words which convey the idea of *resting from the sight of the Lord.* This makes the reader think that there is reference here to the period the body *rests* in the grave, from death to the time of the general resurrection, and as a consequence, to suppose that it is here taught that God cannot *see* into the grave. The passage, however, means quite another thing. The word translated ''*times*'' here, in connection with ''*refreshing*'' is καιροι—*seasons*. It is used by Josephus to signify the solemn Jewish feasts observed at *certain times*. See Parkhurst Greek Lex. infra v. καιρος. The word is also used in a similar sense in Gal. iv. 10. The word καιρος was evidently used by the writers of the New Testament to signify *a fixed, or determined time or season, when anything was to take place.* See Luke xx. 10. Rom. v. 6. Here it means the determined *time* for Christ to appear, and more particularly the *times of enjoying* what is implied in the meaning of the next word,—αναψυξις. This word can scarcely be said to mean *refreshing*. It is composed of ανα—*again,* and ψυχω—*breathe, cool ;* or rather the noun ψυχη—*breath, life ;*— the word we have already seen to be translated *soul,*—but to mean, simply, *life* or *breath.* The literal meaning of the word—αναψυξις is *breathing again,* or *living again.* In its secondary meaning it signifies *cooling,* or *refrigerating ;* because a person, after striving hard, cools by breathing again and again. There are some writers who trace ψυχη or ψυχω—*life,* or *to breathe,* to ψυξις—*cooling,* or *refrigeration.* Thus they trace the cause to the effect, instead of the effect to the cause.—In other words, they put the effect for

approach of the kingdom of heaven, Peter preaches repentance, and also clearly alludes to the kingdom of heaven, in the words—" the times of refreshing," and "the times of restitution of all things." Christ was to be in heaven until the times of the restitution of all things ;—that is, until he should come in the clouds to give a second life to those whose sins were blotted out, destroy those who refused to repent, in the general conflagration of the world ; and then create a new heaven and a new earth, establish his kingdom, and reconstitute all things.*

Should the citation of clearer passages be demanded in proof that the apostles taught the near approach of the End of the World and the Day of Judgment, they are easily found.   Paul, in his remarkable treatise on the resurrection, writes thus :—" Behold, I show you a mystery : *we shall not all sleep*, but we shall all be changed, in a moment, in the twinkling of an eye, at the last trump ; for the trumpet shall sound, and the dead shall be raised incorruptible, and we shall be changed."† It is unnecessary to remark that Paul here means, by the expression—" the trumpet shall sound," the same thing as Christ, when he says that the Son of man " shall send his angels with a great sound of a trumpet" to gather the elect ;‡ or the same as he himself means, in another place, by the " trump of God." It deserves particular notice, however, that, in the passage just cited, Paul expected this trump to sound *during his lifetime;* that is,—he expected the End of the World and the Day of Judgment to take place before he and some of his contemporaries should close their eyes in death ; for he emphatically declares—" *we* shall not all sleep, but *we* shall all be changed ;" that is,—they should not all die, in order to

---

the cause, and vice versa.   Plutarch gives the following curious mode of accounting for the origin of the word—ψυχη. as the opinion of Chrysippus, a Stoic philosopher.—Το βρεφος εν τη γαστρι φυσει τρεφεσθαι καθαπερ φυτον. Οταν δε τεχθη, ψυχομενον υπο του αερος, και στρομουμενον, το πνευμα μεταβαλλειν, και γινεσθαι ζωον οθεν ουκ απο προπου την ψυχην ωνομασθαι παρα την ψυξιν.—"The child, in the womb, is fed by nature, as a plant.   But when born, being cooled and invigorated by this air, respiration is repeated, and it is made a living creature.   Wherefore, it is not unlikely that ψυχη has been so named from ψυξις."—*Plut. de Stoic. Repug.*   The primary meaning of χυχη, is *breath*, or *life;* and the whole analogy of the Greek language shows that ψυξις is derived from this word.   It must, therefore, be admitted that the most direct signification of αναψυξις is *breathing again,—living again,—receiving life again,—being reanimated, &c.*, being synonymous with αναζαω and αναβιοω.   The meaning of the words under notice;—οπως αν ελθωσι καιροι αναψυξεως απο προσωπου του Κυριου, is—*when the appointed time of living again shall come from the Lord*;—that is, the *time* when life eternal was to be given to those who repented.   For it is said (ver. 23.) that every life or breath—ψυχη—that should not repent, or hear the prophet, should *be destroyed.*   The future lives of the saints are continually represented in the New Testament as being with God.   And life is represented as coming from the *breathing* of God. He breathed into man's nostrils the *breath of life.* (Gen. ii. 7.)   Elihu says to Job, (xxxiii. 4.) "the *breath* of the Almighty hath given me *life.*"   And it was no other than this life, or *living again*, that was to come from the Lord in the passage under consideration.   In this passage also, Christ is represented as abiding in heaven, of which it is said it behoved it (δει) to contain him, (δεχομαι) *until the times of restitution of all things ;* by which, Parkhurst, under the word—αποκαταστασις. candidly admits, is to be " understood *the Day of Judgment and the End of the World.*"

* *Restitution*, in the text cited, is a translation of αποκαταστασις, from απο—*back again*, and καθιστημι—*to constitute, make, give existence.*   The word, therefore, means— *reconstitution.*

† 1 Cor. xv. 51, 52.   ‡ Matth. xxiv. 31.

undergo the process of having the incorruptible and immortal bodies of which he treats, but all of them, whether, at the time, alive or dead,—both the dead and the living,—should "be changed, in a moment, in the twinkling of an eye," so as not to have, apparently, a body of flesh, but of some more durable material. For he expressly says that flesh and blood could not inherit the kingdom of God, thus proving that this change, whether of living or of dead bodies, was to take place in order to enter this kingdom; which, as we have had abundant proof, was to be set up by Christ at the end of the world. In the first place, it is clear that Paul intended the words—"we shall not all sleep," to apply exclusively to himself and his contemporaries; and in the next place, it is equally clear that he believed some of them would be alive when the trump should sound. He therefore wished the Corinthians to understand that the end of the world would take place *during that age;* that is,—some eighteen centuries ago!

But let Paul's following words to the Thessalonians explain those of his to the Corinthians.—"I would not have you to be ignorant, brethren, concerning them which are *asleep,* that ye sorrow not, even as others which have no hope. For if we believe that Jesus died and rose again, even so *them also which sleep* in Jesus will God bring with him. For this we say unto you, by the word of the Lord, that WE WHICH ARE ALIVE *and remain unto the coming of the Lord shall not prevent them which are asleep.* For the Lord himself shall descend from heaven with a shout, with the voice of the archangel, and with the trump of God; and the dead in Christ shall rise first; *then we which are alive and remain shall be caught up together with them* in the clouds, to meet the Lord in the air; and so shall we ever be with the Lord. Wherefore comfort one another with these words.— But of the *times* and the *seasons,* brethren, ye have no need that I write unto you; for yourselves know perfectly that *the day of the Lord so cometh as a thief in the night.* For when they shall say,—peace and safety, then sudden destruction cometh upon them, as travail upon a woman with child; and they shall not escape. But *ye,* brethren, are not in darkness, that *that day should overtake you as a thief.* Ye are all the children of light, and the children of the day; we are not of the night, nor of darkness. Therefore let us not sleep as do others; but let us *watch and be sober.*"* The apostle proceeds at some length, exhorting the Thessalonians to be sober, watchful, and so on, and praying that their "whole spirit and soul and body" should "be preserved blameless *unto the coming of our Lord Jesus Christ.*"† The above passage throws considerable light upon that just cited from the Epistle to the Corinthians, and teaches, in the most clear and positive language, that Paul and his Thessalonian disciples were to be *alive till the Day of Judgment.* The main object of the apostle here is to dissuade the Thessalonians from being anxious about their deceased friends, and to persuade them that those who had already died, as well as those who would remain alive till the coming of Christ, should *be caught up together in the clouds.* The dead were first to rise, and then they were to be mounted up with the living into the air, to meet the Lord. He tells them, —"*we which are alive and remain unto the coming of the Lord* shall not

---

* 1 Thess. iv. 13—18; v. 1—6.　　　　† Ib. ver. 23.

prevent them which are asleep,"—that is, prevent those who were asleep in death from meeting the Lord in the air. That Paul thought that he and the Thessalonians, to whom he was writing, should remain alive till the coming of Christ to judge the world, is clear from the following conspicuous points in this passage.—*First*, some of these Christians were apprehensive that their deceased friends would not be as likely to be caught up in the clouds to meet the Lord, as they themselves who should be alive at the time of Christ's coming.—*Secondly*, Paul classes himself with those who should be alive at the time :—although he speaks of the dead also, and makes a distinction between them and those who should be alive, yet he does not class himself with those who should then be dead, and should be raised from the grave. One would naturally suppose that if he believed that, at least, eighteen centuries would elapse before the end of the world, he would have classed himself with the dead, and have said, —*they* which *shall be* alive and *shall* remain unto the coming of the Lord shall not prevent *us* which *shall be asleep* ;—*we*, the dead in Christ, shall rise first, then *they* which *shall be* alive and *shall* remain shall be caught up together with them in the clouds. The reverse, however, is the case ;—he classes himself with the *living*, not with the *dead*, at the time of Christ's coming. The supposed case, therefore,—adduced by Horne[*]—of a person speaking of an army, a society, or a nation, to which he belongs, and saying *we* went, came, did, or shall do such a thing, though the person himself neither had nor shall have any concern in the matter, is by no means parallel with the case of Paul speaking of himself and the Thessalonians in the first person—*we ;* because he speaks of them as being alive in contradistinction to those who were dead at the time, whereas there is no such contradistinction implied in the case of a person speaking as just described. Similar remarks apply to the instances cited from the Hebrew Scriptures ; —" they went through the flood ; there did we rejoice."—" Jacob found God in Bethel ; there he spake with us." And as to Paul, in another place,[†] saying,—" God will also raise *us* by his own power," there is no positive proof that here he means to raise from the grave, but rather raise to the clouds, to meet the Lord in the air.—*Thirdly*, Paul, in the passage under consideration, exhorts the Thessalonians *to watch* and *be sober*, so as to be prepared to meet the Lord whose day, he says, would come suddenly, like *a thief in the night ;* and he further prays that their whole spirit, soul, and body[‡] be preserved blameless unto the coming of our Lord Jesus Christ ;—expressions which plainly indicate that he would have them understand that they were to expect Christ's advent *in their lifetime*. The exhortations to watch, which he gives, bear a striking similarity to those in the Gospels, given by Christ to his disciples when predicting the approach of the day of judgment.[§] The manner in which the apostle expresses himself regarding the time of Christ's advent, also shows that the Thessalonians were well acquainted with the subject, and that they, personally, were to expect to see Christ coming suddenly.—" Of the times and the seasons, brethren, ye have no need that I write unto you, for yourselves

---

[*]   Vid. ant. p. 48.   [†] 1 Cor. vi. 14.

[‡] Πνευμα, ψυχη και σωμα—breath, life, and body.

[§] Compare 1 Thess. v. 2, 3, 7.   Matth. xxiv. 42, 43.   Luke xxi. 34—36.

know perfectly that the day of the Lord so cometh as a thief in the night." In a word, the whole tenour of Paul's discourse on this topic, proves beyond a doubt that he viewed the Day of Judgment as an event to happen during that age.

Philip, in preaching to the Samaritans, inculcates the same doctrine; —" the things concerning the kingdom of God."* Saul, when he becomes a Christian, begins to preach in the same strain,—" expounding and testifying the kingdom of God,"—" preaching the kingdom of God,"—" disputing and persuading the things concerning the kingdom of God,"— " that we must through much tribulation enter into the kingdom of God," —that God had appointed a day in which he should judge the world by that man whom he had raised from the dead,—discoursing about salvation and eternal life, telling his hearers and those to whom he wrote epistles, that knowing *the time*, it was high time to awake out of sleep, for *now* their *salvation* was nearer than when they believed, and the *day was at hand*.†— The very gist of the apostolical preaching and writing was the near approach of the end of the world,—the day of judgment,—the admission into the kingdom of heaven,—and the eternal life to be enjoyed in it.— Nothing more is meant by the words—*save, saviour*, and *salvation*, which so frequently occur, than what is implied in being *saved* from the punishment which was to be inflicted on those who should be excluded from the kingdom which Christ was to set up.

Paul's epistle to the Romans gives prominence to the same notions, in such expressions as—" the end" is " everlasting life ;"—" the gift of God is eternal life ;"—" joint-heirs with Christ ;"—" liberty of the children of God ;"—" short work will the Lord make upon the earth ;"—and so on.‡ His epistles to the Corinthians are of the same character. He tells these poor people ;—" Ye come behind in no gift ; *waiting for the coming* of our Lord Jesus Christ ; who shall also confirm you unto the *end*, that ye may be blameless *in the day of our Lord Jesus Christ*."—" Judge nothing *before the time*, until *the Lord come*."§ He advises them to deliver unto Satan such a fornicator as had taken his father's wife, (his mother, or stepmother, or one of those who constituted his father's harem ? or whom ?) " for the destruction of the flesh, that the *spirit* (breath or life) may be saved *in the day of the Lord Jesus*." This cannot apply to the present notions of the resurrection. Divines, now-a-day, would say " that the *body* may be saved *in the day of the Lord Jesus*," and would think that the *spirit* of a man dying in the apostolic age, nearly two thousand years ago, would long have had its doom fixed, either in heaven or in hell.‖ The word πνευμα is here translated *spirit*,¶ meaning *breath*, which breath Paul, in the expression

---

* Acts viii 12.
† Acts xxviii. 23, 31 ; xx. 25; xix. 8; xiv. 22 ; xiii. 46—48; xvii. 31. Rom. xiii. 12, 13.
‡ Rom. vi. 22, 23; viii. 17—22; ix. 28.   § 1 Cor. i. 7, 8; iv. 5.
‖ 1 Cor. v. 1—5. Those Christians, however, who believe in purgatories, as well as those who maintain restitution from punishment, may claim an exemption on this point.
¶ The word πνευμα is identical in its primary meaning with ψυχη—*breath* or *life*,— although the apostles, sometimes, in their writings, use both together, and appear to make a distinction between them. It is derived from πνεω—to breathe. Parkhurst defines it—" the material spirit, wind or air in motion ;" and under the word, remarks that the leading sense of the old English—*ghost* is breath. We have now the word— *gust* (of wind,) and the Saxons have still *gost* for ghost. The word—spirit (from *spiro*— to breathe, to blow) has precisely the same meaning.

under notice, wishes to "be saved in the day of the Lord Jesus." In other words, he wishes such an individual to be received into the kingdom of heaven, instead of being destroyed at the coming of Christ. Repeated references to the same events are made throughout this chapter and the rest of the book. Paul tells the Corinthians that they, as saints, were to judge the world,—judge even angels,—the angels, probably, that Jude informs us, were reserved "unto the judgment of the great day."* He also reminds them that the unrighteous should not inherit the kingdom of God, and enumerates other classes, such as—fornicators—idolaters—adulterers—the effeminate—abusers of *themselves with mankind*†—thieves—those that coveted—drunkards—revilers—and extortioners ; such as some of them, he says, had been. These were not to inherit the kingdom of God. This expression shows that this kingdom—so far from being the Dispensation of the Gospel—was a thing to be inherited by the Corinthians after the time Paul writes thus to them. He tells them that they had been sanctified and justified,— two important operations, as now regarded, to be performed under the Dispensation of the Gospel,—but his words imply that they had not as yet inherited this kingdom ;—this was a thing to be obtained in future.‡ In prescribing rules for them touching conjugal matters, and discussing the question—whether it was better for them, under the then existing circumstances, to be married or remain single, he emphatically tells them that *the time was short*, and that *the fashion of this world was passing away ;*§ evidently meaning, that the time for them to be in a married state, before the *end of the world* should come, *was short ;* for in the world that was to come, as Christ had declared, they neither married nor gave in marriage.‖ There is room for very little doubt that Paul here alludes to the end of the world ; for it is precisely the same matter he has in hand, where he says, "the time is short," as where he says, that "the fashion of this world passeth away." By the word *fashion* ($\sigma\chi\eta\mu\alpha$—Eng. *scheme*,) he means habit, manner, condition in life, disposition, shape, or state of one thing in reference to another. Paul uses the word in reference to what he had already said of the propriety of being married. Having advised those who were single, and those who were married, to remain in their then respective conditions, and added that if those who were single, married, it would be no sin, he says—"the time is short ;"¶ or, more

---

* 1 Cor. vi. 2.   Jude 6.

† Although $\varepsilon\upsilon\nu\upsilon\upsilon\chi\upsilon\iota$ were, apparently, to be admitted into the kingdom of heaven, (Matth. xix. 12.) yet $\mu\upsilon\iota\chi\upsilon\iota$ and $\mu\alpha\lambda\alpha\kappa\upsilon\iota$ were to be excluded. The Corinthians, who were to judge the world,—who were justified and sanctified by the Spirit, (ver. 2, 11.) were a set of bright saints, if they required the admonitions Paul gives them in ver. 9—18. Nor is Paul himself very cautious in avoiding what, now-a-day, would be termed obscene language. (See ver. 16.) But we may be told that he had the license of Inspiration. Besides, moral vice and moral virtue are not, *perhaps*, in the estimation of some people, unchangeable in their nature. What was virtue yesterday *may* be vice to-morrow! notwithstanding that such a notion is diametrically opposed to the moral axiom—that virtue and vice are unchangeable in their nature,—are such independently of any circumstance whatever.

‡ 1 Cor. vi. 9—11.   § 1 Cor. vii. 29—31.   ‖ Matth. xxii. 23.

¶ The translation is here exceedingly bad. The passage would read much more intelligibly, and more in accordance with the original, thus—" But this I say, brethren, that the time having been shortened, during what remaineth, those having wives should be as if having none." Or, if a smoother translation be aimed at, thus—"The time being

properly,—"the time being short," it behoves those who have wives, during what remains of *it*,—namely, of *the time*,—to live as if they had no wives ; those that weep as if they did not weep ; those that rejoice as if they did not rejoice ; those that buy as if they did not possess ;[*] and those that use this world as not abusing it,[†] "for the fashion of this world passeth away."[‡] The reason he gives for advising the Corinthians to be thus indifferent, on the points he enumerates, is because the *fashion of this world*, or the present condition of life passeth away,—is just at an end.

Having already noticed Paul's treatise on the resurrection in this epistle,[§] where he enters at large into the subject of the day of judgment and the coming of Christ, which in his lifetime he expected to see, we shall now pass on to some of his other epistles. We find him again, in writing to the Galatians, enumerating certain bad characters who, he declares, should "not inherit the kingdom of God," and thereby showing that this kingdom was prospective.[||] In similar terms, also, he writes about this kingdom to the Ephesians, and further reminds them that God had made known to them the mystery of his will, "that in the dispensation of the fulness of times he might gather together in one all things in Christ, both which are in heaven, and which are on earth, even in him ; in whom also" he adds, "we have obtained an inheritance."[¶] Here, again, is the *reign* and *kingdom* of Christ taught. Likewise, in writing to the Philippians, he expresses his confidence that God would carry on the good work he had begun in them, *even until the day of Jesus Christ ;* and hopes that they would continue sincere and without offence *till the day of Christ*.[††] Such expressions plainly show that Paul believed *the day of Christ* would arrive in the lifetime of these Philippians ; otherwise, he would not, in this connection, have used the words—*day of Christ,* but would, like a divine of the present age addressing Christians on such a subject, have written,—*until the day of*

short, those who have wives should live during what remaineth as if they had none."— To λοιπον is an expression meaning—*the remainder, the rest, henceforth, &c.* ; not "it remaineth," as if it were an impersonal *verb.* And συστελλω means—*to shorten, wind up, contract.* Ο καιρος συνεσταλμενος literally means—the season having been contracted or shortened.

[*] Κατεχω *here* means not exactly *to possess.* The idea is—to buy freely, as if at the price asked, and as if not wishful to retain any money they had ; but to give it for what they bought ;—to be indifferent about the things of this world. The verb means—*to hold, retain, withhold.*

[†] The sense of χραωμαι and καταχραομαι, as applied here, is not given by—"*use and not abuse*" : the context proves that the meaning of the writer is,—"they that deal with the world as not overdealing with it, or not dealing *much* with it. What is here throughout recommended is a kind of indifferent conduct towards the *world,* which is said to be *passing away.* There is no reference here to what is generally understood by *abusing the world.* The passage, however, has been made the basis of many a pathetic sermon, in which this notion has been inculcated.—See Blair's Sermons, serm. XLVI.

[‡] The verb translated "passeth away" is παραγω,—from παρα—*transition,* and αγω —*to go.* The word signifies *to vanish, to disappear.* Parkhurst, citing several authorities, says that the apostle borrowed the phrase—το σχημα παραγει—from the theatre, where it meant the change of scene, and the introduction of an entirely new appearance. The same form of expression, however, is used by John in such a connection as to explain clearly the meaning of the phrase, as used by Paul. "The world passeth away, and the lust thereof ; but he that doeth the will of God abideth for ever." (1 John ii. 17.) Here is the expression used without the perplexing word—*fashion,* and evidently implies the actual vanishing of the terrestrial globe.

[§] 1 Cor. xv. See p. 152. et seq. [||] Gal. v. 20, 21. [¶] Eph. i. 10; v 5. [††] Phil. i. 6, 10.

death, or *until death*. Without supposing he meant this, it is impossible to
attach any idea to his words ; but taking them in this sense their meaning
is clear : and this remark applies to a vast number of expressions both in
the Epistles and the Gospels.   A little further on, in this epistle, he has
the following passage :—"Our conversation is in heaven, from whence
also we look for the Saviour, the Lord Jesus Christ, who shall change our
vile body that it might be fashioned like unto his glorious body."*   Now,
we have already seen when and in what manner this change of body was
to be effected :—" We shall not all sleep, but we shall all be changed, in a
moment, in the twinkling of an eye, at the last trump "†   And it is to be
observed, that he does not tell the Philippians that they were to be raised
from the grave, but that he and they were to be *changed* by Christ at his
coming.   Hence, it is obvious that he was to come before they died ; and
therefore Paul says that they *looked* for the Saviour coming from heaven ;
from which it is clear that they were then in daily expectation of Christ's
coming.   Accordingly the apostle, a few sentences further on, assures
them that *the Lord was at hand*.   He says to those whose names were in
the book of life,—" Rejoice in the Lord alway ; and again I say, rejoice.
Let your moderation be known unto all men.   *The Lord is at hand.*   Be
careful for nothing."‡   What can afford a clearer proof than these passages
that Paul taught those Christians to whom he wrote that the day of judgment, and, consequently, the end of the world, were *close at hand ?*   The
word translated—*at hand*, is εγγυς—*near, approaching;* a word which,
truly, is used to denote proximity to a place, as well as proximity of time ;
but here no *place* is either mentioned or implied.   If, however, this were
the only passage in the New Testament where the notion is supposed to be
entertained, this expression *alone* would be entitled, comparatively, to little
weight.   But the Epistles and the Gospels abound with passages conveying
similar sentiments, more or less pointed in language.   Accordingly, we find
Paul again, in writing to another community of Christians—the Colossians,
using the following words :—" The Father which hath made us meet to be
partakers of the inheritance of the saints in light ;—who hath delivered us
from the power of darkness, and hath translated us into the *kingdom* of his
dear Son."—" When Christ, who is our life, *shall appear*, then shall *ye*
also appear with him in glory."—" My fellow-workers unto the *kingdom of
God*."§   Again : he teaches the same doctrine to the Thessalonians.—" Ye
turned to God from idols, to serve the living and true God ; and to *wait
for his Son from heaven*."—" Are not even ye in the presence of our Lord
Jesus Christ *at his coming ?*"—" To the end he may stablish your hearts
unblameable in holiness before God, even our Father, *at the coming of our
Lord Jesus Christ with all his saints*."‖   We have already cited large
portions of the two next chapters, in which Paul describes the day of
judgment at some length, and tells his " brethren" that he and they who
should *remain alive till the coming of the Lord*, should be caught up in the
clouds, when Christ should descend from heaven with a shout, the voice of
the archangel, and the trump of God.¶

---

* Phil. iii. 20, 21.   † 1 Cor. xv. 51, 52,   ‡ Phil. iv. 4—6.
§ Col. i. 12, 13; iii. 4; iv. 11.   In the first of these passages the verb—μεθιστημι—
to turn, *translate*, is in the first aorist, and therefore indefinite as to time.
   ‖ 1 Thess. i. 9, 10; ii. 19; iii. 13.   ¶ See p. 153. et seq.

Let us, therefore, now glance at Paul's second epistle to the Thessalonican church. The first chapter in this again is replete with the same doctrine.—" So that we ourselves glory in you in the churches of God for your patience and faith in all your persecutions and tribulations that ye endure ; which is a manifest token of the righteous judgment of God, that ye may be counted *worthy of the kingdom of God*, for which ye also suffer ; seeing it is a righteous thing with God to recompense tribulation to them that trouble you ; and to you who are troubled *rest with us, when the Lord Jesus shall be revealed from heaven with his mighty angels, in flaming fire taking vengeance* on them that know not God, and that obey not the gospel of our Lord Jesus Christ, who shall be punished with *everlasting destruction from the presence of the Lord*, and from the glory of his power ; when he shall come to be glorified in his saints, and to be admired in all them that believe (because our testimony among you was believed) *in that day*."*— Now, it is manifest from this extract that, when Christ should be revealed from heaven in flaming fire to take vengeance, the persecuted Thessalonians *were to be admitted into the kingdom of God and to have rest with the apostles*. It is worthy of remark also, that the everlasting destruction was to come from the *presence of the Lord*, just as the seasons of refreshing, or rather living again was to come from the face of the Lord. The forms of expression are the same.† Paul continues the same subject from the place just cited till the commencement of the next chapter,‡ which begins thus :— " Now we beseech you, brethren, by the coming of our Lord Jesus Christ, and by our gathering together unto him, that ye be not *soon shaken in mind, or be troubled, neither by spirit, nor by word, nor by letter as from us, as that the day of Christ is at hand.* Let no man deceive you by any means ; for *that day shall not come, except there come a falling away first,* and that man of sin be revealed, the son of perdition, who opposeth and exalteth himself above all that is called God, or that is worshipped ; so that he as God sitteth in the temple of God, shewing himself that he is God.— Remember ye not that, when I was yet with you, I told you these things ? And now ye know what *withholdeth* that he might be revealed in his time." The apostle proceeds to describe the mystery of iniquity which already worked, and the Wicked who should be revealed at the Lord's coming, consumed with the spirit of his mouth, and destroyed with the brightness of his coming. And then, by reminding the Thessalonians of the prospect of salvation and glory, he exhorts them to stand fast, and hold the traditions which had been taught them, whether by word of mouth, or by epistle.§

The foregoing expressions of Paul have caused perhaps more contention than any others which, in the New Testament, hold forth an expectation of the near approach of the day of judgment. On the one hand, those who disbelieve in the divine origin of the Scriptures, maintain that Paul, in this passage, contradicts what he had previously written ;—

---

* 2 Thess. i. 4—10.   † See p. 151. et seq.
‡ 2 Thess. ii. 1—8. It should never be forgotten that the chapters and verses are not made by the apostles and evangelists, but by us in modern times. (See p. 10) What an obstacle in the way of the general reader to understand the drift of Paul's discourse is the division of chapters in this place !
§ 2 Thess. ii. 8—15.

that in his first epistle to the Thessalonians he describes the day of judgment and the end of the world as near events, in such terms as—" The Lord is at hand,"—" We which are alive and *remain unto the coming* of the Lord," and so on ; but that, in his second epistle to them,—particularly in the passage just cited,—he tells them not to be disturbed as if the day of the Lord *was* at hand, and adds that some time must elapse before the event takes place.   The advocates of the Christian religion, on the other hand, contend that Paul did not in his first epistle give any grounds to the Thessalonians for believing that he thought the day of judgment was close at hand, but that they misunderstood the meaning of his words ; and that, in his second epistle to them, he corrects the mistake under which they laboured regarding the near approach of that event, telling them that that day should not come until Antichrist should first acquire considerable influence ; and reminding them that he had told them so before.   There is nothing, however, clearer than that Paul in the first of these epistles represented the day of judgment as an event to happen even *during his own lifetime.* This has already been amply illustrated.*   As to what he says in his second epistle, he appears, even in the very passage in dispute, to use language which conveys the same meaning.—" We beseech you, brethren, by the coming of our Lord Jesus Christ, and by *our gathering together unto him."*   These last words, taken in comparison with those evidently of a similar import in his first epistle, would irresistibly lead to the conclusion that he meant that those Thessalonians to whom he was writing should, during their lifetime, as well as his own, *gather together unto Christ* at his coming.   There is no allusion in these words to being raised from the dead, or being gathered by angels, or by any other means ; but they appear to be words of the same import as the following he had already written :—" We which are alive and remain shall be caught up together with them in the clouds, to meet the Lord in the air."   Also, in the passage already cited from the first chapter of the same epistle, he would seem to represent the kingdom of heaven as a thing into which the Thessalonians were to enter during their lifetime, and where they were to have rest with the apostles.   Further, he prays, near the conclusion of his last epistle, that their hearts might be directed " into the patient *waiting* for Christ."   But taking the passage in which it is contended that he says the day of the Lord was *not* at hand, as we find it in the English translation, Paul does not even then, exactly say that it was *not* at hand.   The whole drift of his words goes no further than to dissuade the Thessalonians from allowing their continual apprehension that that day was close at hand, to engross their minds so entirely as to throw them into anxiety and confusion, and thus cause them to neglect all the duties of life.   For a community of people firmly to believe that the day of judgment was fast approaching, and to act accordingly, must throw them into terrible disorder, and cause a total stagnation in all worldly pursuits.   Under these circumstances such an advice as that given by the apostle must be of the greatest utility ; of which we may have some idea from the panics into which the people of this country, labouring under a similar delusion, have repeatedly been thrown, both in ancient and *very* modern times.   A slight proof of this

* See pp. 153, 154.

was experienced on the continent of Europe, and indeed some parts of England, even this very summer, (1857,) when the end of the world was by thousands believed to be close at hand.

But the Greek text *does not* imply that Paul attempted at thus dissuading the Thessalonians from continually thinking of the circumstance that the day of the Lord was at hand. The words,—"*that day shall not come,*" which are in italics in the English version, *do not occur at all, and are not even implied in the Greek text*, of which, from verse 1st to the 8th, the following is a correct and comparatively close translation :—" But, concerning* the coming of our Lord Jesus Christ, and our gathering together unto him, we entreat you, brethren, not to be quickly disturbed in mind, or be put into tumult, either by spirit, word, or epistle, as from us ; FOR† THE DAY OF CHRIST IS AT HAND. May any one seduce you ? By no means ; except that first there should come an apostacy, and there should be revealed the man of sin, the son of perdition who opposes and exalts himself over everything called God, or object of worship, so that in the temple of God he sits as God, showing himself that he is God. Do you not remember that, being yet with you, I spoke to you of these things ? And now you have known what restrains so that he may be revealed in his own time. For the mystery of iniquity already works ; only that as yet he who restrains is not taken out of the way. Then also shall be discovered the transgressor whom the Lord will consume with the breath of his mouth, and annihilate with the splendour of his presence."‡ Paul requests the Thessalonians not to be turbulent and raise tumults about Christ's coming ; and as a reason for thus remaining quietly for a short time, and for no outcry against the heretic, of whom he is about speaking, he tells them—" For the day of Christ is at hand." He has not a word in the text to the effect that the day of Christ was *not* at hand. Having, in allusive language, advanced several things concerning the heretic and the heresy to which he adverts as being well known to the Thessalonians, he exhorts them thus :—" Stand fast, and hold the traditions which ye have been taught, whether by word or our epistle." By *epistle*, he apparently means his first epistle to them. But if what is urged by some were true, namely, that they had *misunderstood* his first epistle to mean that the day of Christ was at hand, whereas he had not so represented it, he would not have exhorted them to " stand fast and hold the traditions" they had been taught in that epistle. If this were the case, we might expect him to have referred in some other manner to his former epistle, and the cause of their misapprehension of it, instead of dwelling at great length upon the heresy that had crept in among them. But he does not even allude to their having misunderstood his former epistle. He asks them whether they remembered that he had previously told them,—not that the day of Christ was *not* at hand, but that the heresy he describes should arise. Besides : his words

* Ὑπερ.—Parkhurst, citing Whitby, Wetstein, Macknight, Newton, and Raphelius, says that this word should here have been translated—*concerning*, or *of*.

† 'Ως ὁτι.—The direct meaning of ὁτι, as a conjunction, is *for, because, wherefore, &c.* And as to ὡς, when connected with ὁτι, as in this instance, it is *redundant*.—See Parkhurst in loc., also Kypke on 2 Cor. xi. 21.

‡ It is difficult to imagine what induced the Translators to insert in verse 3. the words in italics, —" *that day shall not come.*" It is clear that οτι εαν μη ελθη refer to μητις υμας εξαπατηση κατα μηδενα τροπον, not to ως οτι ενεστηκεν η ημερα του Χριστου.

imply that no sooner should the heretic make his appearance openly, than that the Lord should consume him with the breath of his mouth, and destroy him *with the brightness of his coming;* thus making the day of the Lord immediately to succeed the appearance of the heretic. Accordingly, in the next chapter (verse 5.) he prays God to direct the hearts of the Thessalonians " into the *patient waiting for Christ.*" There is nothing in the whole of this epistle but what perfectly accords with the notion which Paul had so prominently advanced in the foregoing,—that the day of judgment was close at hand.*

Passing on to Paul's epistles to Timothy, we find these also abounding with the same representations, such as :—" The Spirit speaketh expressly, that in the *latter times* some shall depart from the faith, giving heed to seducing spirits."—" Lay hold on *eternal life.*"—" Keep this commandment without spot, unrebukeable, until the *appearing of our Lord Jesus Christ.*" —" A good foundation against the time to come, that they may lay hold on *eternal life.*"—" If we suffer, we shall also *reign* with him."—" Hymeneus and Philetus, who concerning the truth have erred, saying that the *resurrection* is past already; and overthrow the faith of some."—" This know also, that in the *last days* perilous times shall come; for men shall be lovers of their own selves,........ from such turn away."—" I charge thee therefore before God, and *the Lord Jesus Christ, who shall judge the quick and the dead at his appearing and his kingdom;* preach the word."— " There is laid up for me a crown of righteousness which the Lord, the righteous judge shall give me at that day, and not to me only, but unto all them also that love his *appearing.*"—" The Lord shall deliver me from every evil work, and will *preserve me unto his heavenly kingdom.*"† Such are some of the references to the coming of Christ,—his kingdom,—and his eternal life, made in these two short epistles. All these expressions regard Christ's coming as in that age. Timothy was to keep the commandment *until the appearing* of Christ. The " latter times" and " last days" were evidently the times and days *in which Paul lived;* for he tells Timothy to " turn away" from the wicked men of these days, clearly connecting the times of which he speaks with the age of Timothy. So prevalent, at these times, seems to have been the doctrine of the nearness of the world's end, that there were numerous theories afloat regarding it : some contended even *that the resurrection was already past.* And so far was Paul from regarding the *kingdom of heaven* as the Gospel Dispensation that, although he had for years been preaching the Gospel, he had not been admitted into this

---

* But even supposing that the Thessalonians had *misunderstood* Paul in his first epistle to them to represent the Day of Judgment as close at hand, still this would prove the following important points.—*First*, that a strong apprehension of the near approach of the advent of Christ to execute judgment existed, *de facto*, in the minds of Christians at the time.—*Secondly*, that that strange and wide-spread dread must have had a cause of corresponding power before it could be produced.—*Thirdly*, that Paul's first epistle to the Thessalonians contained expressions which,—whether rightly or wrongly understood,—were calculated to inspire that dread of the supposed approaching mundane destruction. If no expectation already existed of the near approach of this event, it is scarcely possible that Paul's words regarding it could have been misunderstood. But all these inferences only furnish additional evidence that Christ and his apostles inculcated the near approach of the Day of Judgment.

† 1 Tim. iv. 1; vi. 12, 14, 19. 2 Tim. ii. 12, 17, 18; iii. 1, 2, 5; iv. 1, 2, 8, 18.

kingdom. This had yet to take place;—He was to be *preserved unto this heavenly kingdom.* When he wrote his second epistle to Timothy he appears to be in prison at Rome, and to be in daily expectation of being put to death. Hence he says :—" I am now ready to be offered, and the time of my departure is at hand." He seems, therefore, in these epistles, to have relinquished the hope of being alive at Christ's coming. But he expects to be raised from the dead, and to have a crown of righteousness, from the righteous judge at that day. He writes, however, concerning the same things in better spirits to Titus, speaking of the "hope of eternal life," and the " heirs according to the hope of eternal life," who were " looking for that *blessed hope, and the glorious appearing of the great God and our Saviour Jesus Christ."* It is remarkable that we can glance scarcely at any portion of these epistles which does not contain clear reference to the *near approach* of the Day of Judgment.

The epistolary discourse to the Hebrews opens with the same doctrine. —" God, who at sundry times and in divers manners spake in time past unto the fathers by the prophets, hath *in these last days* spoken unto us by his Son."† And throughout the epistle we find such expressions as,— " Hold the beginning of our confidence stedfast unto *the end,"*—The "resurrection of the dead, and of eternal judgment," "and the powers of the *world to come."*—"The full assurance of hope unto *the end;"*—"Once in *the end of the world* hath he appeared to put away sin."—"And unto them that look for him shall he *appear a second time* without sin unto salvation." —"Yet a *little while,* and he that *shall come will come."*—"Ye are come unto mount Sion, and unto the city of the living God, the *heavenly Jerusalem,* and to an innumerable company of *angels;* to the general assembly and church of the first born, which are written in *heaven,* and to God the Judge of all, and to the spirits of just men made perfect, and to Jesus the mediator of the new covenant."—"Wherefore we receiving *a kingdom* which cannot be moved, let us have grace."‡ From the manner in which the apostle expresses himself in his references to Christ's near approach, it is evident that the Hebrews were already conversant with the doctrine.— And, indeed, this remark applies to all others to whom Paul's epistles are addressed.

Having thus seen that the great apostle of the Gentiles makes the near approach of the end of the world and the speedy coming of Christ the grand theme of all his discourses, let us inquire whether *other* apostles of somewhat less celebrity give any prominence to these doctrines. That production which is ascribed to James is the next we meet in the canonical epistles. This, likewise, is addressed to the Hebrews, or, as it expresses, " to the twelve tribes which are scattered abroad," and in it also we find the same notions most earnestly inculcated.—" Be patient therefore, brethren, *unto the coming of the Lord.* Behold, the husbandman waiteth for the precious fruit of the earth, and hath long patience for it, until he receive the early and latter rain. Be ye also patient ; stablish your hearts : *for the coming of the Lord draweth nigh.* Grudge not one against another, brethren, lest ye be condemned: *behold, the judge standeth before the door."*§

* Tit. i. 2 ; iii. 7; ii. 13. † Heb. i. 1, 2.
‡ Heb. ii. 14 ; vi. 2, 5, 11; ix. 26, 28; x. 37; xii. 22—28. § James v. 7—9.

Such words as these require no comment. We have heard Peter as an apostolical preacher on these topics; let us now attend to him as an epistolary writer.—" An inheritance incorruptible, and undefiled, and that fadeth not away, reserved in heaven for you, who are kept by the power of God through faith unto *salvation*, ready to be revealed in the *last time*."—" Hope to *the end* for the grace that is to be brought unto you at *the revelation of Jesus Christ*."—" Who verily was foreordained before the foundation of the world, but was manifest *in these last times*."—" The *end of all things is at hand*."—" Give account to him that is *ready to judge the quick and the dead*."—" The time *is come* that judgment must begin at the house of God."—" A partaker of the glory that shall be revealed."—" Ye shall receive a crown of glory that fadeth not away."—" An entrance shall be ministered unto you abundantly into the *everlasting kingdom* of our Lord."* Should those who are accustomed to take the old theological views of these expressions of Peter unaffectedly object that they are not sufficiently clear and conclusive to establish the point in question, it is trusted that the following extract will satisfy them, as being an illustration of what he means in the preceding citations. Here is a whole chapter announcing, in the most lucid manner, the proximity of the end of the world and the day of judgment.—" This second epistle, beloved, I now write unto you; in both which I stir up your pure minds *by way of remembrance: that ye may be mindful of the words which were spoken before by the holy prophets*, and of the commandment of us the apostles of the Lord and Saviour : knowing this first, that there shall come *in the last days* scoffers, walking after their own lusts, and saying,— *Where is the promise of his coming? for since the fathers fell asleep all things continue* as they were from the beginning of the creation. For this they willingly are ignorant of, that by the word of God the heavens were of old, and the earth standing out of the water and in the water; whereby the world that then was, being overflowed with water, perished. *But the heavens and the earth which are now, by the same word are kept in store, reserved unto fire against the day of judgment and perdition of ungodly men*. But, beloved, be not ignorant of this one thing, that one day is with the Lord as a thousand years, and a thousand years as one day. The Lord is not slack concerning his promise, as some men count slackness; but is longsuffering to us-ward, not willing that any should perish, but that all should come to repentance. But *the day of the Lord will come* as a thief in the night, in the which the heavens shall pass away with a great noise, and the elements shall melt with fervent heat; the earth also and the works that are therein shall be burned up. Seeing then that all these things shall be dissolved, what manner of persons ought *ye* to be in all holy conversation and godliness, *looking for and hasting unto the coming of the day of God*, wherein the heavens being on fire shall be dissolved, and the elements shall melt with fervent heat? Nevertheless, *we, according to his promise, look for new heavens and a new earth*, wherein dwelleth righteousness. Wherefore, beloved, seeing that *ye look for such things, be diligent that ye may be found of him in peace, without spot and blameless*; and account that the longsuffering of our Lord is salvation; even as our beloved brother Paul also

---

* 1 Pet. i. 4, 5, 13, 20; iv. 5—7, 17; v. 1, 4.   2 Pet. i. 11.

according to the wisdom given unto him *hath written unto you* ; *as also in all his epistles, speaking in them of these things ;* in which are some things hard to be understood, which they that are unlearned and unstable wrest, as they do also the other scriptures, unto their own destruction. Ye therefore, beloved, seeing ye know these things before, beware lest ye also, being led away with the error of the wicked, fall from your own stedfast-ness. But grow in grace, and in the knowledge of our Lord and Saviour Jesus Christ. To him be glory both now and for ever. Amen."[*]

In the laborious description of the day of judgment and the destruc-tion of the world given in this chapter, it is observable :—*First ;* That there are here expressions which prove that Peter thought these events would occur *during the lifetime* of those to whom he writes. He tells them that they ought to be *looking for and hasting unto the coming of the day of God ;* and that *he* and *they* looked *for new heavens and a new earth.* He also calls the *time* in which he lives and writes, *the last days,*—the meaning of which phrase we have seen to signify the *end of time.* Further : the expressions he uses, such as—" The day of the Lord will come as a thief in the night ; in the which the heavens shall pass away," bear so striking a resemblance to those used by Paul and Christ,[†] where they respectively, in the most positive terms, describe these events as close at hand, that they furnish the strongest proof that Peter also viewed them precisely in the same light.[‡]

---

[*] 2 Pet. iii. 1—18.

[†] See 1 Thess. iv. 14—18 ; but more particularly v. 1—3 ; and Matth. xxiv. 35—43. Luke xxi. 33—35.

[‡] It is a most remarkable fact that in none of the Epistles is there any mention made of the various wonderful things narrated in the Gospels, as having been said and done by Christ. Indeed, there is scarcely an allusion made in them to those astounding details with which every page of the Gospels is replete. No mention is made in them of what the Gospels state that Christ declared *regarding the Day of Judgment.*—Nothing about Christ's preternatural birth, his baptism, his Satanic temptation, his denunciations of the different existing sects, his precepts, his parables, his intimate acquaintance with publi-cans, with Magdalene, with Mary and other women.—Not one of his miracles is detailed, and nothing is said of the marvellous circumstances which attended his crucifixion and death, such as the sun darkening, the earth quaking, the temple rending, rocks cleaving asunder, graves opening, the dead rising and walking the streets of Jerusalem. These are matters which, one would imagine, should occupy a very prominent position in all the Epistles ;—should be relied upon by the writers respectively, as facts with which to attest and establish the truth of Christianity, and which would, *of themselves,* suffice to convince and convert the most incredulous and obdurate mind. In the Epistles ascribed to Peter, James, and John, who are said to have been eye and ear-witnesses of what Christ did and said, one would expect, certainly, to find frequent details of the marvellous things said of Jesus in the Gospels. But Peter does not so much as allude to the keys of heaven and hell which the Gospels say were given him to keep ; nor even to the fact that Jesus, walking on the sea, enabled him also to do so, and saved him from drowning. Neither does he tell those to whom he writes that Jesus conferred his blessing upon him when he pronounced him—" The Christ, the Son of the living God ;" nor that Jesus, after he had suspiciously asked him three times whether he loved him, and had as often received affirmative answers, charged him to *feed his flock.* Of course we cannot expect him to have recorded in his Epistles that Jesus graced him with the epithet—" Satan ;" or that he denied the same Jesus thrice. If it was the son of Zebedee who wrote "the general epistle of James," (about the authorship of which Christians have not as yet agreed,) it would not seem too great a tribute to his *Divine Master,* for him to refer to some of his mighty words and deeds which he must have witnessed. Or if the author is the brother of Jesus, (which is not very likely, since all his relatives except his mother shunned him,) he could deplore the fact that he and his brothers—Joses, Simon, and

This argument derives additional force from the fact that he *refers to what Paul had written on the subject.* Moreover : what Peter says of "scoffers" proves, not only that he himself believed that Christ's advent and the end of the world were very shortly to take place, but likewise that the approximation of these events had for a considerable period been inculcated and extensively propagated ; otherwise *scoffers* would not have ridiculed this notion, " saying, where is the promise of his coming ?" for since the fathers fell asleep all things continue as they were from the beginning of the creation." As if these scoffers said :—" We have now for many years heard it preached that the coming of Christ and the end of the world were at hand ; but there is no more sign of these events coming to pass now than when we first heard they were speedily to happen ;—all things continue the same as they were when the fathers (probably the prophets) predicted these events. What has become of the promise of your God ? We fear he has broken or forgotten it." Peter disposes of the derision of these scoffers by assuring the Christians that it was destined that, in the *last days*, such characters should appear—that they were wilfully ignorant of the cosmogony of the world—that the cause the day of the Lord had not *as yet* arrived was the longsuffering of God, with whom one day was as a thousand years—but that the dread day of the Lord would be sure to come, unexpectedly, as a thief in the night. Thus does Peter, like Paul, who on more than one occasion refers to similar characters,* dexterously make the non-appearance of Christ to destroy the world the very means of promoting the faith of the Christians, by showing them that the appearance of these scoffers, who had attempted to seduce them, was of itself a sure sign that the day of judgment *was* close at hand.—*Secondly ;* Peter here confirms what has already been advanced in this work regarding the Jewish prophets, namely, that they predicted the proximity of the end of the world ; and that he, in his Pentecostal sermon, quoting Joel, regarded these predictions in that light. Here he tells the Christians to whom he writes that his object is *to remind them of the words spoken before by the holy prophets* regarding the day of judgment. By the " holy prophets" he can mean no other than the Jewish prophets.—*Thirdly ;* he says that Paul, " in all his

---

Judas—*did not believe* in the pretensions of their Divine brother—Jesus. But the very name of Jesus is mentioned—and that casually—only thrice in the whole epistle. John, " the beloved disciple," could, in one of his Epistles, or at least in that which it is agreed he wrote,—to the confirmation of the genuineness of Matthew, Mark, and Luke's Gospels, —have adverted to that curious incident of his mother asking Jesus to allow him and his brother James to sit on each side of him in his kingdom ;—or could, with a mixture of joy and sorrow, ruminate on the pleasure he had felt in accompanying Peter to prepare the last Passover which they had eaten with their divine Master, and bemoan the fatal disaster which, shortly after, overtook his Lord. But he writes not one word about these remarkable events, or about anything that occurred personally between him and Jesus. Indeed the writers of the Epistles totally ignore the contents of the Gospels. How, then, is this fact to be accounted for ? Did the writers of the Epistles—whoever they were—know anything at all about the contents of the present Gospels ? Are we not entitled to infer that either the churches, &c. to which these Epistles were addressed were much older than the date of the Gospels, and even than the time at which the Christ of the Gospels was born ? or that,—if the present Gospels then existed,—the authors of the Epistles knew nothing of them ? This is, however, a question which requires much more space for its proper examination than can, conveniently, be afforded thus in a Note.

* See 2 Thess. ii. 4—12. 2 Tim. ii. 16—19; iii. 6—9. 1 John ii. 18. Jude.

epistles" speaks "of these things," namely, the near approach of the day of judgment and the events concomitant with it. Thus he confirms our *construction* of Paul's words, and shows his views to be identical with his own.

The three epistles of John and the epistle of Jude, short as they are, teem with expressions which show that the writers wished it to be believed that *the day of the Lord was at hand.*—"The world passeth away."— "Little children, it *is* the *last time;* and as ye have heard that Antichrist shall come, even now *are* there many Antichrists; whereby we know that *it is the last time.*"—"Abide in him, that, when *he shall appear,* we may have confidence, and not be ashamed before him *at his coming.*"—"No murderer hath *eternal life.*"—"Behold, *the Lord cometh* with ten thousands of his saints, to execute *judgment* upon all."—"They told you there should be mockers in *the last time.*"*

But of all portions of what is called "Holy Writ," that part most replete with predictions of the near approach of the day of judgment and the end of the world is the Apocalypse. These are, doubtless, the grand subjects upon which this curious Riddle-book exclusively treats. The coming of Christ,—the destruction of the world,—the day of judgment,— the new heavens and new earth which were to be created,—the kingdom which Christ was to set up therein,—the torments he was to inflict on some, and the bliss he was to confer on others of mankind,—together with a great number of circumstances connected therewith, are described by the author of the Book of Revelation, in the most wild and flighty phantasms ever conceived by the human mind.† These topics are, evidently, the theme of

---

* 1 John ii. 17, 18, 28; iii. 2, 15. Jude 14, 15, 18.

† It is true that in many of the fabulous writings of ancient times we find unnatural descriptions of animals and things bearing some similarity to those in the Book of Revelation given of locusts, for example, in the shape of horses, with human faces, lions' teeth, women's hair, scorpions' tails, &c. (Rev. ix. 3—10); but none of them exceeds those of "the beloved disciple" in revolting phantasm. The following specimens, however, closely approximate his production in boldness of fancy, and show that the writer of the Apocalypse was not unique in the exercise of this species of genius.—"In the first year there made its appearance, from a part of the Erythræan sea, which bordered upon Babylonia, an animal endowed with reason, who was called Oannes. According to the account of Apollodorus, the whole body of the animal was like that of a fish, and had under a fish's head another head, and also feet below, similar to those of man, subjoined to the fish's tail. His voice too and language were articulate and human, and *a representation of him is preserved even to this day.*........After this there appeared other animals like Oannes, of which Berosus promises to give an account when he comes to the history of the kings. ....Men (then) appeared with two wings, some with four, and with two faces; they had one body but two hands,—the one of a man, the other of a woman. There were likewise in them several organs, both male and female. Other human figures were to be seen with the legs and horns of goats; some had horses' feet; others had the limbs of a horse behind, but before were fashioned like men, resembling hippo-centaurs. Bulls likewise were bred then with the hands of men, and dogs with fourfold bodies, and tails of fishes; also horses with the heads of dogs; men too and other animals with the heads and bodies of horses, and the tails of fishes; in short there were creatures with the limbs of every species of animals. Add to these fishes, reptiles, serpents, with other wonderful animals which assumed each other's shape and countenance. *Of all these were preserved delineations* in the temple of Belus, at Babylon.—*Cory's Translation of the Fragments of Berosus, taken from Polyhistor,* pp. 25—27. The foregoing extracts show, *first,* with what great caution we should receive the statements of ancient history, as facts. And, *secondly,* how easy and natural it was for the writer of the Apocalypse to make use of the fantastic figures we find in his work, when the notion of such animals as those just described having existed, was rife in his time.

Makay, however, produces proofs to show that much of the imagery of the Book of

his whole thoughts. At the *commencement* and *conclusion* of his production *he mentions them in open terms*, and throughout he refers to them enigmatically. In some places he describes the destruction of the nations and kingdoms, exclusively, upon which he wished the vengeance of heaven more particularly to be wreaked. This is a peculiar characteristic of all those who have predicted the end of the world. Although to us, at this distant time, some of these references to nations and kingdoms are more or less obscure; yet at the time they were put forth they were, probably, more intelligible to the people of that age; just as the predictions of the

Revelation is borrowed from the Book of Daniel, and, *inter alia*, makes the following remarks.—"In symbolical language, borrowed from Daniel, it describes a beast rising out of the sea, having seven heads and ten horns, with feet like those of a bear. (Rev. xiii. 1, 2.) In chapter xvii. the description is repeated; but here a woman sits upon the beast, arrayed in scarlet and gold, drunken with the blood of the saints and martyrs of Jesus. The woman is there explained to be the city of Rome; and the beast she rides the Roman empire; the seven heads are the seven hills of Rome. (ver. 18, 9.) They are also seven successive kings or emperors, five of whom are fallen, the sixth still is, and the seventh yet to come. (ver. 10.) This is a remarkable coincidence with the state of the Roman empire at the time. The beast that *was* and *is not*, and yet *is*, is placed eighth in the list of kings; still he is one of the forementioned seven. (ver. 11.) Nero, the fifth king in the list of the Cæsars, corresponds exactly with the fifth king of the Apocalypse; and Sulpicius Severus expressly refers to him the enigmatical attribute of simultaneous existence and non-existence. (Hist. ii. 29.) Lactantius applies the Sibylline oracles to Nero, in which he is called "the great Italian king, the runaway, the dire serpent, the murderer of his mother, who for a time would be preserved unseen, but, soon reappearing with the pretensions of a god, would cross the Euphrates with many myriads of men, ravage Judea, burn the temple, &c." .. ..A strange notion had prevailed about this time in Rome, Achaia, and Asia, that Nero was not dead, but concealed beyond the Euphrates, among the Parthians, whence he would return with the assembled forces of the barbarians to plunder Rome. He was now prefigured as the great public enemy of Christianity,—the Antichrist, who was to reappear before the second coming of the Messiah. The time allowed for the continuance of the *beast*, or the Roman monarchy, is forty two months. This again is the period of woe assigned in Daniel. It is the same "time, times, and half a time," or 1260 days, during which the Gentiles are to tread under foot the holy city; and the woman, representing the Christian church, to take refuge in the wilderness. (Rev. xii. 6, 14.) The καιροι, or unexpired terms of calamity, are dated from the Messiah's translation to God's throne; (Rev. xii. 5, 6.) i. e. from the death of Jesus. The last oppression of the holy city, as well as the Christian church, would probably, in the view of the writer, end about A.D. 70, and, supposing the death of Jesus to have been about A.D. 33—35, would consist of 35 years. As Daniel, in his construction of a *time* or καιρος, changes each individual year of Jeremiah's period into seven years, so the writer of the Revelation in order to adapt Daniel's phraseology to the case before him, may have divided the years elapsed since the Nativity into seven decades of years, half of which will be three decades and a half, or 35 years. In order to complete the sacred number of seven kings (answering to seven hills) from Augustus, under whom Rome began an impious rivalry with Divine power, (Rev. xiii. 4.) he requires only one more short reign, after which the Millenium and End of the World take place *immediately*. The writer clearly places us at the extreme verge of earthly things. One short reign, and then Messiah's instant arrival, and the hurrying of Antichrist to destruction. There is here absolutely no room for postponement; and orthodox interpreters, finding it impossible, with any plausibility, to substitute *papal* for *heathen* Rome, are obliged, in order to keep the prophetic interest still in suspense, to sever the horns from the beast to which they belong, to make them allies to the Lamb, instead of enemies; and, there being no one left for them to conquer, to make them conquer themselves. In spite of the precision with which the writer of the Revelation carefully limits the time and scene, every one now thinks himself at liberty to give to vaticinations, *long ago falsified*, a chance of fulfilment, by appropriating them to actual circumstances.—*Extracted from M. IV. Makay's Sketch of the Rise and Progress of Christianity*, pp. 65—67.

early Christians were intelligible to their contemporaries that Rome, because they hated it, would, at the approaching end of the world, be burnt with hotter fire than any other part of the globe. The whole of the Book of Revelation, as to matter, language, and figures, is in perfect accordance with the Jewish lore and Jewish notions of the time. What the writer says of *angels, trumpets, beasts, elders, crowns, thrones, tribes, seals, plagues, Lamb, sun, moon, Babylon,* and so on, are mere fancies, most extravagantly carried out, from notions of these things which already existed among the Jews.

Mr. Makay, in the work cited in the accompanying Note, justly remarks that "the tone and feeling of the Book of Revelation, its imagery and language are unmistakeably Jewish,—are a reflex of Judæo-Christianity. Its Christianity may be a *new song,* but the rhythm is Jewish,........and instead of the Christian liberality and charity of the Gospel ascribed to John, we find in it all the petty partiality and bitter vindictiveness of the Old Testament........ Almost all the Apocalyptic imagery may be traced either in the Old Testament or the Jewish writings, such as the Targums and the New Testament Apocrypha; or to familiar types and ideas which the writer has skilfully adapted and combined. Thus the beast, representing the worldly power of Rome, is a compound of the four beasts or monarchies of Daniel, carrying, in happy correspondence with the seven-hilled city, their aggregate amount of heads." The term "Babylon,"— which also indicates that the writer dealt in the imagery of Daniel,—will, however, be found in the Book of Revelation to be an epithet applied to the Roman empire, which had persecuted the Christians. Although the book professes to be the production of John, yet it is scarcely possible that this can have emanated from the pen that wrote the Gospel and Epistles which pass under the name of John. The date at which it was written is also purely inferential. Touching this point, Mr. Makay makes the following observations. "An eager expectation of Christ's coming to judge the world and vindicate his elect was a great moral lever of early Christianity. We find it expressed in every varying tone of hope, impatience, and disappointment; and we may form a near estimate of the date of a given composition from the degree of assurance or despondency assumed on this subject....... When these expectations were at the highest, the dreadful persecution under Nero produced a profound and lasting impression on the Christians....... The Book of Revelation is generally allowed to have been written about this time (A.D. 70). Its apparent date seems to coincide with the short reign of Galba; (chap. xvii. 10.) and it must at all events have been composed soon afterwards." If we apply Mr. Makay's criterion to ascertain the date of the Book of Revelation, we must conclude that it was written at a very early period of the Christian era; for no production is more confident and replete in its assurances of the *immediate* coming of Christ in judgment. But waiving, for the nonce, the question of the date and authorship of the book, and admitting with Christian divines that it was written by John, as the book itself implies, when he had been exiled to the Isle of Patmos by one of the Roman emperors, it would follow that he must have been much incensed against the Roman government; which would account for the dreadful doom he pronounces upon it,—a doom much more terrible than even that which awaited the rest of the world.

Although the Book of Revelation has baffled the ingenuity of all Christian commentators, and to this moment, remains *to them* a book of mysteries—enigmas—riddles; yet to any one who will view it as a chain of predictions of the End of the World, and its accompanying events,—expected to be at hand in the time John is said to have lived,—the whole book becomes at least as intelligible as most other parts of the Bible. In the first century of the Christian era this book was held in the most profound reverence,—indeed rather more so than any other portion of the present New Testament,—and it was commented upon most favourably by the earliest Christians,* doubtless, because it was a book which so ably described the near approach of the end of the world. " It is a remarkable circumstance" observes Mr. Hartwell Horne, " that the authenticity of this book was very generally, if not universally, acknowledged during the two first centuries, and yet in the third century it began to be questioned. This seemed to be occasioned by *some* absurd notions *concerning the Millenium,* which a few well-meaning but fanciful expositors grounded on this book, which notions their opponents injudiciously and presumptuously endeavoured to discredit, by denying the authority of the book itself."† The very cause of this change, however, was the change which took place in public opinion as to the *End of the World.* In the first century the end of the world was daily expected; and therefore the Book of Revelation, which predicts the event, was highly esteemed. In the third, and more particulary the fourth century, people, not seeing the end of the world coming, began to question whether it would come at all, and therefore disregarded the Book of Revelation as their belief in the near approach of the end of the world weakened, so that at last they excluded it altogether from amongst their sacred books, as a string of false prophecies. Accordingly, we do not find it named in the catalogues of the books of the New Testament by the following writers.— The catalogue of Cyril, bishop of Jerusalem, who flourished about A.D. 340; the catalogue made at the Council of Laodicea, 364; the catalogue of Gregory Nazianzen, 375, and that of Philastrius, bishop of Brixa, 380. But we find it inserted in the catalogue of Origen, A.D. 210; (probably the first catalogue ever written) that of Eusebius, 315; and that of Athanasius, 315.‡ The Book of Revelation, however, in the fifth century, began to regain confidence, owing to the new explanations given of its contents by the advocates of Christianity.§   But let us examine the book itself.

* See Horsley's Edition of Sir Isaac Newton's works, vol. v.

† Horne's Comp. Introd. part IV. book ii. chap. 4.

‡ See Apocryphal Gospels, Hone's Edit. table II. at the end of the vol.

§ Mr. Gibbon observes that "in the Council of Laodicea (about the year 360,) the Apocalypse was tacitly excluded from the sacred Canon, by the same churches of Asia, to which it is addressed; and we may learn from the complaint of Sulpicius Severus that their sentence had been ratified by the greater number of Christians of his time. From what causes then is the Apocalypse now so generally received by the Greek, the Roman, and the Protestant churches? The following ones may be assigned :—1. The Greeks were subdued by the authority of an impostor, who, in the sixth century, assumed the character of Dionysius, the Areopagite.—2. A just apprehension that the Grammarians might become more important than the theologians, engaged in the Council of Trent to fix the seal of infallibility on all the books of Scripture contained in the Latin Vulgate, in the number of which the Apocalypse was fortunately included. (Fr. Paulo Istoria del Concilio Tridentino, lib. II.)—3. The advantage of turning those mysterious prophecies

It professes to be " the Revelation of Jesus Christ, which God gave unto him, to show unto his servants *things which must shortly come to pass,*" and adds that "*the time is at hand.*"[*] This may be considered as the intended title of the book. The writer then dedicates his work to the seven churches in Asia. He speaks of himself as being " in the isle that is called Patmos," "in tribulation, and in the *kingdom* and patience of Jesus Christ," of whom he says, that he is " the prince of the kings of the earth," and that—" Behold, he *cometh with clouds ;* and *every eye* shall *see him.*"[†]— Then, among other expressions, he has the following :—" Hold fast *till I come.* And he that overcometh, and keepeth my works unto the *end*, to him will I give power over the nations."—" I will *come on thee as a thief.*" —" I also will keep thee from the hour of temptation, which *shall come upon all the world.*"—" Behold, I *come quickly ;* hold that fast which thou hast, that no man take thy crown."—" Behold, I *stand at the door and knock.*"[‡] The contents of this book from chapter v. to xii. as well as the following chapters are a description of what the *new* kingdom would be, and throw much light on the prophecies of Christ on the same subject in the Gospels. The description given here also strongly countenances the notion that Christ's kingdom was to be on *earth,* whence, probably, the dream of the Millenium emanated in succeeding ages :—" We shall *reign on the earth.*"[§] The descriptions repeatedly given in this book of angels destroying portions of the world also favour the opinion already advanced, that Christ intended to destroy the world by the agency of angels. The following description of the end of the world bears a striking similarity to that given by Christ on several occasions.—" And, lo, there was a great earthquake ; and the sun became black as sackcloth of hair, and the moon became as blood, and the stars of heaven fell unto the earth, even as a fig-tree casteth her untimely figs, when she is shaken of a mighty wind. And the heaven departed as a scroll when it is rolled together ; and every mountain and island were moved out of their places. And the kings of the earth, and the great men, and the rich men, and the chief captains, and the mighty men, and every bondman, and every free man, hid themselves in the dens and in the rocks of the mountains ; and said *to the mountains and rocks,—Fall on us, and hide us* from the face of him that sitteth on the throne, and from the wrath of the Lamb ; *for the great day of his wrath is come ; and who shall be able to stand ?*"[||] There can be little doubt in any mind capable of ordinary thought that this is a description of the end of the world, and that it is very much alike that given by Christ and the apostles of the same event. The expression that the angel swore "that there should be time no longer,"[¶] is very significant, especially as it occurs after the description given of an angel killing the third and last portion of mankind ; and also after John's declaration, at the onset, that the things he was about prophesying " must shortly come to pass." This can therefore

against the See of Rome inspired the Protestants with uncommon veneration for so use-ful an ally. See the ingenious and elegant discourses of the present bishop of Litchfield on that unpromising subject."—*Gibbon's Decline and Fall of the Roman Empire*, chap. xv. note 67.
[*] Rev. i. 1, 3.   [†] Ver. 5—9.   [‡] ii. 25, 26 ; iii. 3, 10, 11, 20.   [§] Rev. v. 10.
[||] Rev. vi. 12—17. and compare Luke xxiii. 29, 30. Matth. xxiv. 7, 29, 35. 2 Pet. iii. 9.
[¶] Rev. x. 6.

be no other than a prediction of the destruction of the world as being then just at hand. It is further said that after the seventh angel had sounded—"there were great voices in heaven, saying, The kingdoms of this world are become the kingdoms of our Lord, and of his Christ; and he shall reign for ever and ever."* It scarcely requires to be remarked that here the kingdom which Christ was to establish at the end of the world is meant. Chapters xii. to xix., inclusive, are taken up in describing the punishments which should be inflicted upon the Roman empire, when the vengeance of God should be poured upon it, for persecuting the Christians. Intermixed with these are descriptions of the victory which Christ should obtain over Satan, with allusions to the inmates of cloisters, and sundry other things, conceived and delineated in the most fantastic manner that a mind labouring under the maddest fanaticism can possibly devise.

There is one peculiarity in the description of the End of the World, given in the Apocalypse, which distinguishes it from all other predictions of the same event, as recorded in the Bible.—It predicts two resurrections of the dead,—a thousand years to elapse between the first and the second. The prediction, or rather the vision, is as follows :—" And I saw an angel come down from heaven, having the key of the bottomless pit† and a great chain in his hand. And he *laid hold on the dragon*, that old serpent, which is the Devil, and Satan, and bound him a thousand years, and *cast him into the bottomless pit*, and shut him up, and set a seal upon him, that he should deceive the nations no more, till the thousand years should be fulfilled ; and after that he must be loosed a little season. And I saw thrones, and they sat upon them, and judgment was given unto them. And I saw the souls of them that were beheaded for the witness of Jesus, and for the word of God, and which had not worshipped the beast, neither his image, neither had received his mark upon their foreheads, or in their hands ; and they *lived and reigned with Christ a thousand years. But the rest of the dead lived not again until the thousand years were finished. This is the first resurrection.* Blessed and holy is he that hath part in *the first resurrection ;* on such the *second death* hath no power, but they shall be priests of God and of Christ,

---

* Rev. xi. 15.

† The *bottomless pit* does not appear to be so deep as one would imagine. The Greek word here is αβυσσος—*deep, very deep, an abyss.* It is composed of α—signifying intensity, and βυσσος—deep. In the Septuagint it answers, generally, to the Hebrew—תהום, signifying *deep waters.* Homer uses it to signify the bottom of the sea.— Η δε, μολυβδαινη ικελη ες βυσσον ορουσεν. (Il. xxiv. lin. 80.) Herodotus has—Χωρεειν ες βυσσον, in a similar sense. (Lib. iii. c. 23.) And in Luke viii. 31. the word αβυσσος is used, in connection with the legion of devils and the Gadarenish pigs, to signify, apparently, the *deep* waters of the sea. In Rom. x. 7. it is translated—*deep*, meaning the abode of the dead ;—the same place, it would seem, is called *lower parts of the earth*, in Eph. iv. 9. ; and *the heart of the earth*, in Matth. xii. 40. It is difficult to imagine what made the English translators render the word—*bottomless pit.* The strongest construction that can be put upon it is—*very deep pit.* A witty writer remarks on the bottomless pit ; very properly, that it is difficult to imagine a pit any more than a well without a bottom, and adds that if the writer of the Apocalypse and his interpreters had the sense that men have in general, they would have perceived the folly of imagining the devil to be confined in a *bottomless* pit ; for if the angel cast this "dragon, that old serpent," bound or not bound, into the pit *at the top*, it would escape at the *other* end, if the pit had *no bottom*, or, in other words, was bottomless.

and *shall reign with him a thousand years.* And when the thousand years are expired, Satan shall be loosed out of his prison, and shall go out to deceive the nations which are in the four quarters of the earth, Gog and Magog, to gather them together in battle ; the number of whom is as the sand of the sea. And they went up on the breadth of the earth, and compassed the camp of the saints about, and the beloved city : and fire came down from God out of heaven, and devoured them. And the devil that deceived them was cast into the lake of fire and brimstone, where the beast and the false prophet are, and shall be tormented day and night for ever and ever. And I saw a great white throne, and him that sat on it, from whose face the earth and the heaven fled away ; and there was found no place for them. And I saw the dead, small and great, stand before God ; and the books were opened : and another book was opened, which is the book of life : and the dead were judged out of those things which were written in the books, according to their works. And the sea gave up the dead which were in it ; and death and hell delivered up the dead which were in them : and they were judged every man according to his works. And death and hell were cast into the lake of fire. *This* is the *second death.* And whosoever was not found written in the book of life was cast into the lake of fire."* After this follows a glowing description of the new Jerusalem erected of gold and precious stones, where Christ and the blessed were to reside. It is probable that it was the foregoing prediction that gave rise to the doctrine of the Millenium, which was firmly believed by most of the primitive Christians, and is believed even by many Christians of the present age ;—modified, however, in every age, from that of the apostles, according to the whims and fancies of leading theologians.

Of this tenet, the acute and learned Mr. Gibbon writes as follows :— " The ancient and popular doctrine of the Millenium was intimately connected with the second coming of Christ. As the works of creation had been finished in six days, their duration in their present state, according to a tradition which was attributed to the prophet Elijah, was fixed to six thousand years. By the same analogy it was inferred that this long period of labour and contention, which was now almost elapsed, would be succeeded by a joyful sabbath of a thousand years ; and that Christ, with the triumphant band of the saints and the elect, who had escaped death, or who had been miraculously revived, would reign upon earth till the time appointed for the last and general resurrection. So pleasing was this hope to the minds of believers that the *New Jerusalem,* the seat of the blissful kingdom, was quickly adorned with all the gayest colours of the imagination. A felicity consisting only of pure and spiritual pleasure would have appeared too refined for its inhabitants, who were still supposed to possess their human nature and senses. A garden of Eden, with the amusements of the pastoral life, was no longer suited to the advanced state of society which prevailed under the Roman empire."† According to the extract just cited from the Apocalypse, John expected that those who had suffered martyrdom, and those who had refused to conform to the heathen worship, were to have preference over others who should be dead, at the end of the world,—they

---

* Rev. xx. 1—15.

† See Gibbon and his authorities,—Decline and Fall of the Roman Empire, chap. xv.

were to come to life before the rest, and to reign with Christ for a thousand
years. Then, at the expiration of this period, the others were to be raised
into life, and also Satan was to be let loose. But John describes the
destruction of the world as a thing which was *to take place before all this.*
It is difficult, truly, to arrange the events here prophesied by John, in regard
to the order in which they were to come to pass. But there are two things
here stated in the most clear manner; and these are amply sufficient to
determine the present question.—Christ was to come in a very short time
to raise the dead of "the first resurrection;" for his coming is here continually represented as just at hand; and he was to reign with these saints in
the new kingdom for a thousand years. About seventeen centuries have
rolled away since John is said to have delivered these predictions; and
Christ is not yet come, even to begin this reign of a thousand years. The
predictions, therefore, have proved utterly false. Whatever view be taken
of John's predictions of what is called the Millenium, the conclusion that
they are not true is irresistible. Whether Christ was to reign on this earth
or in a new world,—whether he was to destroy the world and punish the
wicked in a lake of fire and brimstone *after* or *before* his reign of a thousand
years, makes no difference on this point. It may be observed, however,
that John appears to suppose that the dead were confined not only in hell,
or Hades, as they are, in ancient mythology, described to be waiting the
last judgment, but that some of them were in the sea, and some in another
place he calls *death*, (θανατος); for he says that the *sea, death,* and *hell*
delivered up the dead which were in them, to be judged every man according to his work; and that *death* and *hell* were cast into the lake of fire.
(ver. 13, 14.)

    The next scene John saw was a new heaven and a new earth; the
first heaven and earth, as well as the sea, having passed away. Nor does
there appear to be any sea in the new world. As to the new Jerusalem,
John saw this coming down from God out of heaven, *en masse*, surrounded
by a high wall, having twelve gates, guarded by twelve angels.* Having
finished his description of the new Jerusalem, he adds,—"The Lord God
of the holy prophets sent his angel to shew unto his servants *the things
which must shortly be done. Behold I come quickly;* blessed is he that
keepeth the sayings of the prophecy of this book."—"Seal not the sayings
of the prophecy of this book; for *the time is at hand.* He that is unjust,
let him be unjust still; and he which is filthy, let him be filthy still; and
he that is righteous, let him be righteous still; and he that is holy, let him
be holy still. And, behold, *I come quickly;* and my *reward is with me,* to
give *every man according as his work shall be.*"—"The Spirit and the bride
say, *come;* and let him that heareth say, *come;* and let him that is athirst,
come."—"He which testifieth these things saith, *Surely I come quickly.*
Amen. Even so, *come, Lord Jesus.*"† Thus ends the Apocalypse, as it
begins, testifying that *Christ comes quickly.* At the commencement and
the close, this book expressly professes to be a description of what was to
come to pass within a very short time to that in which it was written.—At
the commencement, it states that it is a *Revelation of things which must
shortly come to pass,*—that *the time was at hand;* and *at the close,* it makes

---

* Rev. xxi. 1—27; xxii. 1—6.   † xxii. 6, 7, 10—20.

similar declarations—that *the Lord had sent his angel to show unto his servants the things which must shortly be done*, and that *the time was at hand*. Now, that the *things* which are described throughout this book, are the *destruction of the world*, the *creation of a new world*, the *judging of mankind*, the *punishing of some*, and the *rewarding of others*, together with similar things, are points which cannot be denied. The conclusion, therefore, is inevitable,—that the book is professedly a series of predictions regarding the *coming of Christ, the end of the world*, and *the final judgment, as events close at hand;* and that its predictions, upon the whole, are in harmony with those found in the Gospels and Epistles. It is therefore trusted that the copious evidence adduced in this section cannot fail to convince any serious thinker that the apostles inculcated the above doctrines in strict conformity to the previous predictions of their Lord and Master.

SECTION III.—CORROBORATIVE EVIDENCE THAT CHRIST PREDICTED THE NEAR APPROACH OF THE END OF THE WORLD AND THE DAY OF JUDGMENT, AFFORDED BY THE WRITINGS OF THE APOSTOLIC AND OTHER FATHERS OF THE CHURCH.

The same doctrines were inculcated by all the apostolic Fathers, and Fathers of the following centuries from Barnabas, the companion of Paul, and Clement, a disciple of Peter, down to Lactantius, the preceptor of the son of Constantine. The following citations from the Fathers are given from the Apocryphal New Testament, the general accuracy of the translation of which may be relied upon by the English reader. Barnabas is frequently mentioned in the Acts of the Apostles[*] as a companion and fellow-preacher of Paul. There is extant an epistle which goes by his name, and at the close of it there are the following words :—"The end of the epistle of Barnabas, the apostle, and fellow-traveller of St. Paul the apostle." This epistle has as much claim to be deemed genuine as any of the canonical epistles. It has been cited by Clemens, Origen, Eusebius, Jerome, and many other ancient Fathers. Dr. Bernard, Savilian Professor at Oxford, not only believed it to be genuine, but states that it was read throughout, in the churches at Alexandria, as the canonical Scriptures were. Vossius, Dupuis, Dr. Cane, Dr. Mill, Dr. Samuel Clarke, Whiston, and Archbishop Wake, also believed it to be genuine.[†] Although some learned men think it was written before the epistle of Jude and the writings of John, yet it bears internal marks of having been written some time time after the destruction of Jerusalem ;[‡] still it is evidently of a very ancient date, written perhaps about A.D. 75. Like the canonical epistles, it abounds with the doctrine of Christ's second advent. The following passage throws considerable light on the views of the approaching end of the world entertained so generally in that age.—" God made in six days the works of his hands ; and he finished them on the seventh day ; and he rested the seventh day and sanctified it. Consider, my children, what that

---

* iv. 36, 37 ; xi. 25, 30 ; xii. 25 ; xiii. 12, 50 ; xiv. 12 ; xv. 2, 12, et al.
† Apocryphal New Testament, Hone's Edit. ‡ Barn. xii. 14, 15.

signifies, he finished them in six days. The meaning of it is. this :—that *in six thousand years the Lord God will bring all things to an end.** For with him one day is a thousand years, as himself testifieth, saying ; Behold, this day shall be as a thousand years. Therefore, children, in six days, that is in six thousand years, *shall all things be accomplished.* And what is it that he saith,—And he rested the seventh day : he meaneth this ;— that *when his Son shall come, and abolish the season of the Wicked One, and judge the ungodly ; and shall change the sun and the moon, and the stars ;* then he shall gloriously rest in that seventh day.". . . . . " When resting from all things, I shall begin the eighth day, that is the beginning of the other world."† Thus it was thought by the primitive Christians that *then* nearly 6000 years had elapsed since the creation of the world, and that, as the world had been created in six days, it was to remain in its present condition only for 6000 years, allowing a thousand years for each day it had been in process of creation. At the expiration of this period—6000 years, Christ was to make his appearance, in order to put an end to this world and create a new one ; or—to use the words of the apostle Barnabas just cited—to *bring all things to an end,* abolish the season of the Wicked One, judge *the ungodly,* change the sun, moon, and stars, and *begin the other world.* "The primitive church of Antioch" as Mr. Gibbon very justly remarks, " computed almost 6000 years from the creation of the world to the birth of Christ. Africanus, Lactantius, and the Greek Church have reduced that number to 5500, and Eusebius has contented himself with 5200 years. These calculations were formed on the Septuagint, which was universally received during the six first centuries. The authority of the Vulgate and of the Hebrew text has determined the moderns, Protestant as well as Catholics, to prefer a period of about 4000 years ; though in the study of profane antiquity, they often find themselves straitened by those narrow limits."‡ However erroneous all these computations may be regarding the lapse of time since this world came into existence, it is to be observed that Barnabas, in the foregoing extract, furnishes an explanation of what Peter means when, writing of the near approach of the end of the world, he complains of scoffers taunting Christians that there was no sign of this event, and urges, as an apology, the certainty of one thing ; namely, that one day was with the Lord as a thousand years, and a thousand years as one day.§ Both Peter and Barnabas will be found, on comparison, in perfect harmony as to their views of the near approach of the end of the world. The following citations will further show that Barnabas held, on this point, precisely the same tenets as those found in the canonical Scriptures.—" For this end the Lord hath *shortened the times* and the days, that his beloved might *hasten his coming* to his inheritance."—" Let us give heed unto the last times."—" God will *judge the world* without respect of persons."—" Take heed lest (the wicked one) shut us out of *the kingdom*

---

* The notion that this world was to be destroyed and a new one created at the expiration of six thousand years from its creation, and that this period was about expiring, was very general at the commencement of the Christian era.—See Coteler. Annot. in loc. Edit. Oxon. p. 90. and Dr. Bernard Annot. p. 127. Ed. Oxon. as cited by the Editor of the Apoc. New Test.

† Apocryphal New Testament, Barnabas xii. 3—6, 9.

‡ Decline and Fall, chap. xv. *note* 62.　　§ 2 Pet. iii. 8.　Vid. ante pp. 161—166.

of the Lord."—" So they, says Christ, that will see me, and come to *my kingdom,* must through many afflictions and troubles attain unto me."— " He who does such things shall be glorified in *the kingdom of God."*— " Ye may be *saved in the day of judgment."* —" The Scripture saith—And it shall come to pass *in the last days* that the Lord will deliver up the sheep of his pasture, and their fold, and their tower unto destruction; and it came to pass as the Lord hath spoken."[*] The last cited expression has been spoken in reference to the destruction of Jerusalem, which Barnabas says had taken place; but he does not apply the phrase—*last days*—to the *end* of the Jewish dispensation, but to the *end* of the world, thereby furnishing a proof that so the phrase is to be understood in the canonical Scriptures.

The Epistles of Clement to the Corinthians are other very ancient productions where the same doctrines are taught. Clement, called Clemens Romanus, was a disciple of Peter and afterwards bishop of Rome. Some of the Fathers call him an apostle. His first Epistle is included in one of the ancient collections of the Canon of Scripture. The translation given of both in the Apocryphal Gospels, is that of archbishop Wake. That of the first is made by the worthy primate from the ancient Greek copy of the Epistle which is at the end of the celebrated Alexandrian MS. of the Septuagint and New Testament, presented by Cyril, patriarch of Alexandria, to king Charles I., now in the British Museum. The archbishop, in his preface to the translation, esteems it a great blessing that this Epistle was at last so happily found out for the increase and confirmation both of our faith and charity.[†] In the Epistles of Clement we find the following

---

[*] Barn. iii. 4, 10, 13, 15; vi. 15; xv. 7, 18; xii. 15.

[†] Apocryphal New Testament—Heading to the Epistle of Clement. The most Reverend Father in God—William (Wake) was Lord Bishop of Lincoln, and afterwards Lord Archbishop of Canterbury. This erudite and honest primate translated all the Apocryphal Epistles into English. His translation, in 1817, was published by Mr. Baxster, Paternoster Row, under the title of " Apostolical Fathers." The general reader, however, would doubtless wish to know something more ot the production from which we quote under the name of the Apocryphal New Testament. For some 300 years after the time Christ is said to have lived, no New Testament existed in its present collected form. There was, however, then atlıat a vast number of Gospels and Epistles, purporting to have been written by the different saints whose names they respectively bore; some of which were rejected by one person or by a certain sect of Christians, while they were received as divine by others. About the year 327, a council of 318 bishops was convened at Nice, to determine, among other things, how many and which of the vast number of Gospels and Epistles then in circulation should be considered canonical. The Council was presided over by the Emperor Constantine. The mode of deciding which productions were inspired and which were spurious appears to have been by a majority of votes. The first thing, however, the bishops did was to quarrel, and present accusations to the Emperor one against another; so that it is difficult to determine from the scanty history we have of the proceedings, whether, before they separated, they decided which books were and which were not inspired. Pappus, in his Synodicon, tells us that, having put all the books referred to the Council for determination under the communion table in a church, they besought that the inspired writings might get upon the table while the spurious ones remained underneath, and *that it happened accordingly.* This certainly would have been more rational than voting books inspired by majority. Whether the Canon of the New Testament was fixed at this, or at some future Council, there are, however, grounds for believing that, shortly after, the Catalogue of the Canonical Books was very much the same as it is at present. But one would ask—What became of the numerous Gospels and Epistles that were rejected at the time when those that have descended to us were made canonical? A great proportion of them, doubtless in process of time, were destroyed

N

expressions :—" Of a truth yet *a little while* and his will shall *suddenly* be accomplished; the Holy Scripture itself bearing witness that he *shall quickly come* and *not tarry*, and that *the Lord shall suddenly* come to his temple, even the holy ones, whom ye *look for*. Let us consider, beloved, how the Lord does continually show us that there shall be a *future resurrection*."— " And thus he foretels us ; *behold the Lord cometh*, and his *reward is with him*, even *before his face*, to render to every one according to his work."— " Eye hath not seen, nor ear heard, neither have entered into the heart of man, the things which God has prepared for them that *wait for him*."— " Let us therefore strive with all earnestness that we may be found in the number of those that *wait* for him, that so we may *receive the reward* which he has promised."*—" The promise of Christ is great and wonderful, even the rest of *the kingdom that is to come*, and of *everlasting life*."—" How can we hope to enter into *the kingdom of God*, except we keep our baptism holy and undefiled ?"—" As ye were called in the flesh, ye shall also *come to judgment* in the flesh."—" Wherefore, my brethren, let us not doubt in our minds, but let us *expect with hope*, that we may receive our reward, for he is faithful who has promised that he will render to every one a reward according to his works. If therefore we shall do what is just in the sight of God, we shall *enter into his kingdom*, and shall receive the promises ; which neither eye has seen, nor ear heard, nor have entered into the heart of man. Wherefore, let us *every hour expect the kingdom of God*, in love and righteousness, because we know *not the day of God's appearing*."†

In the Epistles of Ignatius, bishop of Antioch, who lived in the *first* century, we find *numerous* passages conveying similar sentiments ; such as, —" The *last times are come upon us ;* let us therefore be very reverent, and fear the longsuffering of God, that it be not to us unto condemnation."— " If any one follows him that makes a schism in the Church, he shall not inherit *the kingdom of God*."—" Neither fornicators, nor *effeminate*, nor *abusers of themselves with mankind*, shall inherit *the kingdom of God*."‡ The Visions and Similitudes of Hermas, brother to Pius, bishop of Rome, a production of the Apostolic age, quoted by Irenæus, under the very name of *Scripture*, and thought by Origen to be *divinely inspired*, are of a similar

---

by different means. Those that have been preserved form the contents of the *Apocryphal New Testament*, which consists of the Gospel of the Birth of the Virgin Mary,—the Protevangelion, or an account of the birth of Christ and the perpetual virginity of his mother, —the Gospels of the Infancy of Jesus Christ,—Epistolary Correspondence between Jesus Christ and Abgarus,—the Gospel of Nicodemus,—Epistolary Correspondence between Paul and Seneca,—Epistle of Paul to the Laodiceans,—the Acts of Paul and Thecla,— Epistles of Clement, of Barnabas, and of Ignatius to different Christian churches and individuals,—and the Visions or Revelations of Hermas. These are the principal contents of the Apocryphal New Testament, as being all those rejected writings preserved from the ravages of time. There are, however, some sixty other Gospels, Acts, and Epistles, mentioned by writers of the four first centuries of the Christian era, which are not now extant. Let the reader, therefore, not imagine that the Gospels, Acts, and Epistles which constitute our Canonical New Testament are the only productions of the kind that ever existed. These are only a very small number selected from those that were afloat at the time, all claiming divine origin. For further information on this topic the reader is referred to the Apocryphal New Testament, from which much of this Note has been extracted.

* 1 Clem. xi. 14—16 ; xvi. 3, 8 ; xvii. 4, 6.   † 2 Clem. iii. 3, 9 ; iv. 2, 13—15.

‡ Ignatius to the Ephesians, iii. 5.   Philadelphians i. 9.   Philippians ii. 12.

character.—" The gate is therefore new, because he appeared in the fulness of time, that they who shall attain unto salvation, may, by it enter the kingdom of God."—" No man shall enter into the kingdom of God, but he who shall take upon him the name of the Son of God."* A great many other references to the same things may be found on consulting these ancient writings. The works of all the Fathers of the three first centuries abound in discussions on the coming of Christ and the end of the world.

Pantænus, a convert to Christianity from Stoicism,—who was at the head of the celebrated Alexandrian school, whence almost all the Christian romances have emanated,—is said to have gone to India, about A.D. 180. where he found that the apostle Bartholomew had, some time previously, been preaching the *coming of Christ* according to the Gospel of *St. Matthew,* which he found there *written in Hebrew,*† and brought back with him to his own country.‡ Having resumed his duties as preceptor of the school he, apparently, propagated *the same* doctrines. Papias, bishop of Hierapolis, at the commencement of the same century, also propagated these views.§ Irenæus, bishop of Lyons, in the second century, and a disciple of Papias, who had seen the apostle John, describes, in the most fantastic way conceivable, the coming of Christ and the new world to be created.‖

Hegesippus, who lived in the Apostolic age, as cited by Eusebius, makes James the brother of Christ to have said, when about suffering martyrdom,—" Why ask me concerning Jesus the Son of man? He is now sitting in the heavens, on the right hand of great power, *and is about to come on the clouds of heaven.*"¶ Montanus, the founder of a numerous Christian sect, and his female companion—Maximilla, about the middle of the second century, in the reign of Marcus Aurelius, predicted and taught that the End of the World and the Day of Judgment were close at hand; and would be preceded by wars, plagues, famines, the coming of Anti-Christ, the destruction of the city of Rome, and other things, such as we

---

* III. Herm. Sim. ix. ver. 111, 113.

† St. Jerome De Viv. Ill. c. 36. Euseb. Hist. Eccles. lib. v. c. 10. Orig. Epist. lib. vi. c. 19.—Le Clerc, (vol. i. p. 757.) fixes the date of Pantænus's return from India about A.D. 179; but Lardner (part ii. c. 21.) about A.D. 192. See Waddington's Ecclesiastical Hist. pp. 16, 40. Edit. Library of Useful Knowledge, Lond. 1833. Mosheim's Eccles. Hist. cent. ii. c. 1.

‡ A little sound criticism would demonstrate that this Hebrew Gospel mentioned by so many ancient writers,—was that which gave origin to the other Gospels, written afterwards, from time to time, in Greek, by different Alexandrian monks who, in common with all the Christian Fathers, (see Note pp. 145, 146, 386. and Gibbon's Decline and Fall, chap. xvi.) believed that it redounded to the glory of God to deceive in order to promote the cause of Christianity. But to discuss the question of the origin of the Gospels, although the writer intends this to form the subject of a future work, yet is not within the scope of our present enquiry.

§ Euseb. Hist. Eccles. lib. iii. c. 39. ‖ Iren. adv. Hæres. lib. v. c. 25. p. 445.

¶ Euseb. Eccles. Hist. lib. ii. 23. Supposing James to have really made this avowal of his belief in the divinity of his brother Jesus, he must have wonderfully changed his opinion since the time to which John refers in his Gospel. For the evangelist states,— " Neither did his brethren believe in him." (John vii. 5.) We have no reason to infer that his four brothers—James, Joses, Simon, and Judas,—were not included in the word —" brethren," by John. The traditional or mythological passage purported to be cited from Hegesippus, however, shows that *the end of the world* was expected in the early age to which it belongs.

find mentioned in connection with the same subject in the Gospels, Epistles, and the Apocalypse.* Cerinthus, the founder of another large sect of

---

* Dr. Mosheim, in order to account for the implacable enmity of other Christian sects against the Montanists makes the following note, much of which directly bears upon our subject.—"At the time when Montanus prophesied, namely, under the reign of the emperor Marcus Aurelius the philosopher, the affairs of the Christians were everywhere, as we have above shewn, involved in the utmost peril. It became, therefore, a matter of the very first importance to them to be strictly on their guard, lest, in any thing which they might say, teach, or do, they might lay themselves open to misrepresentation, or furnish the Romans with any pretext for accusation or complaint. But that imprudent, or rather insane man, Montanus, predicted, without reserve, a variety of things in the highest degree obnoxious to the Romans; such, for instance, as *the overthrow of their city and empire; the destruction that awaited the world; wars, plagues, and calamities of divers kinds, that might speedily be expected, as well as the tremendous advent of Antichrist;* concerning which things, whoever dared to utter any prophecies, were always considered by the Romans as enemies to the state, and consequently made to undergo capital punishment. Tertullian, in his apology for Montanus, a work that unfortunately has perished, reduces the whole matter in dispute between his master and other Christians under two general heads, namely, "second marriages," and "the future judgment." His words are preserved in the ancient work edited by J. Sirmond, Paris, 1645, 8vo. that goes under the title of *Prædestinatus*, lib. i. cap. xxv. p. 30. *Hoc solum discrepamus, quod secundas nuptias non recipimus, et prophetiam Montani de futuro judicio non recusamus.* It is to be observed that Tertullian here makes light of the controversy between Montanus and the church, as was customary with him whenever he conceived that it might tend to promote his purpose; but on this we shall not stay at present to make any remark. All that we would wish to impress on the reader's attention is, that it is clear from these words that Montanus had, amongst other things, *predicted somewhat respecting a future judgment, and that this prophecy of his was held most sacred, and had more than ordinary weight attached to it by his followers;* but that it was marked with the most decided disapprobation by the catholic Christians. It would be idle in any one to pretend to refer this prediction to the last general judgment of the world and the human race; *for as to this there was the most perfect accordance between Montanus and all other Christians.* Indeed it was impossible that the Christians should make it a matter of accusation against Montanus, *that he predicted the near approach of the last judgment; for it was at that time a point of common belief with the whole church, that the final consummation of all things was at hand.* We are bound to conclude, therefore, that Montanus predicted the approach of some particular judgment (*i. e.* some calamities and evils not far remote) of which the Christians knew that they could not join with him in prophesying without involving themselves in the utmost peril. But what else could this be than the judgment that awaited the Roman empire? The temerity of this man, unless I am altogether deceived, was such, that he announced the most signal punishments as about to fall on the Romans, the enemies of the Christian faith, and predicted, at no very distant period, the final overthrow of the whole empire. *That other Christians, as to this, entertained a belief similar to his, namely, that our blessed Saviour would speedily avenge the blood of his slaughtered servants on the Romans, and overturn their government, is what I very well know.* But of this their belief they made a secret, referring it to the *Disciplina Arcani,* or that kind of knowledge which it was deemed expedient to cherish in silence, and entrust only to a few of approved stability and faith, inasmuch as they were well assured that any disclosure or promulgation of it could not be made without exposing their fortunes to the utmost jeopardy and hazard. And in this place I will content myself with referring merely to those prophecies respecting the dreadful calamities which awaited the Roman empire, that are set down as received from the mouths of the Christians by the author of *Philopatris,* (a work commonly ascribed to Lucian): vid. *Luciani Opera,* tom. iii. p. 613 et seq. edit. Reizian.— Hence we are furnished with an easy interpretation of the words of an ancient writer cited by Eusebius, *Hist. Eccles.* lib. v. cap. xvi. p. 180, and of which the learned have hitherto confessed themselves utterly unable to elicit the meaning. He says that Montanus foretold things that were to come, παρα το κατα παραδοσιν και κατα διαδοχην αρωθεν της εκκλησιας εθος, *præter morem atque institutum Ecclesiæ a majoribus traditum et continua deinceps successione propagatum;* which is as much as to say that it was the ancient and invariable usage of the church cautiously to abstain from divulging or making

Christians, inculcated the same doctrine, in a modified form, regarding the *speedy* coming of Christ to establish his kingdom and reign upon earth.*

Tertullian, who lived in the same century, thus exults in the prospect of the near approach of the destruction of the world :—" You are fond of spectacles; expect the greatest of all spectacles, the last and eternal judgment of the universe. How shall I admire, how laugh, how rejoice, how exult when I behold so many proud monarchs and fancied Gods groaning in the lowest abyss of darkness; so many magistrates, who persecuted the name of the Lord, liquifying in fiercer fires than ever they kindled against the Christians; so many sage philosophers blushing in red-hot flames, with their deluded scholars; so many celebrated poets trembling before that tribunal, not of Minos, but of Christ; so many tragedians, more tuneful in the expression of their own sufferings; so many dancers !" &c. In another place, he tells us that the Christians prayed for the Roman empire because they knew that its continuance retarded the Day of Judgment, which he means by—"the greatest calamity that hung over the world." In his work against Marcion he avows his belief in the speedy establishment of the kingdom promised to the saints upon earth, the resurrection of the dead in Christ, and their living with him in the New Jerusalem, enjoying most exquisite pleasures, for a thousand years, at the expiration of which the general judgment and the end of the world was to take place.† Here it should be particularly observed that it is evidently the same thing which is meant in the writings of the Fathers and other early Christians by the *Millenium*,—the kingdom which Christ was to establish on earth, and in which he was to reign for a thousand years,—as that which is in the Gospels, the Epistles, in a word, the whole of the New Testament, called the *kingdom* of heaven and the kingdom of God. It is true that the views held of many circumstantial things touching this kingdom, by different

public mention of any tenets or prophecies that might tend to excite animosity against the Christians, or bring them into danger; such, for instance, as those which respected the coming of Antichrist, the overthrow of the Roman empire, or any other impending evils or calamities. But Montanus broke through this custom, and proclaimed to the world what had never before been communicated to any except confidential ears. And in this most hazardous line of conduct the females, who had espoused the cause of Montanus, should seem to have been by no means backward in following the example of their master; for Maximilla predicted πολεμυς και ακαταϲαϲιας, "wars and tumults" as awaiting the Roman empire, (Euseb. l. c. p. 182.) and that, after her death, no more prophetesses would arise, but people might look for ϲυντελεια τε αιωνος, "the consummation of all things." These prophecies, supposing that nothing else offensive or objectionable had been brought forward by Montanus and his associates, must surely, of themselves, have justified all such Christians as had the welfare of the church at heart, in excluding these bold and incautious men from their society. The sect of the Montanists, as they themselves boast, and the ancient fathers do not pretend to deny, abounded in martyrs. It should seem, however, not at all improbable that most of these might have fallen martyrs to their own imprudence and temerity, rather than in the cause of Christ, and been put to death by the Roman magistrates, as conspirators against the commonwealth."—*Mosheim's Commentaries on the Affairs of the Christians*, cent. II. vol. ii. pp. 352—355.

How exactly this interpretation of the prophecy of Montanus accords with that already given of the prophecy of Christ in the Gospels regarding the end of the world and its accompanying effects !

* Theodoret. Fabul. Hæret. lib. ii. c. 3.

† Tertullian. De Spectaculis. c. 30. De Resurrect. Carnis. c. 24. Apol. c. 32. Contra Marcion. c. 24.

persons, in different ages, and even in the same age vary; but the main idea is always the same. Justin Martyr, also a Father of the second century, had likewise great faith in the speedy occurrence of the same events. In speaking of "the last times" as immediately preceding the day of judgment and the end of the world, he says :—" As for me, and the rest of us that are orthodox Christians, we know that there shall be a resurrection of the flesh, and that the saints shall spend a thousand years in Jerusalem, which shall be rebuilt and enlarged."* With regard to the manner in which this New Jerusalem was to be prepared for the saints, he certainly differs slightly from Tertullian, who thought that this holy city, built of precious stones, was to descend miraculously from heaven upon earth,—that men's souls were shut up in some subterraneous place till the day of judgment, —that heaven was not to be opened to the faithful till the end of the world,—that Paradise, which he supposed to be a place beneath the heavens, was open only to martyrs, whose blood was the key to this blissful region; and that the resurrection of the faithful was to be accomplished by degrees, according to merit.† Methodius, another Christian bishop and writer, that lived at the close of the second century, in expectation of the speedy coming of Christ, informs his readers that after the resurrection and the final judgment he and they should dwell for ever upon earth, and exercise themselves in all good things."‡

Lactantius, another Father, who flourished about the beginning of the fourth century, and who accounts for the existence of devils upon the reasonable hypothesis that angels defiled themselves with women, the result of which gave origin to this supposed infernal tribe, also presents us with the following views of the coming of Christ and the day of judgment: —" Our Saviour Christ shall come again upon the earth, before the last and final resurrection; and those who shall be found alive shall not die at all but shall be preserved alive, and shall *beget an infinite number of children*, during the space of a thousand years, living all of them peaceably together, in a most happy city, which shall abound with all good things, under the reign of our Saviour Jesus Christ, and of some of the saints who shall be raised from the dead.".......... " Because all the works of God were finished in six days, it was necessary that the world should remain in this state six ages; that is, six thousand years.".......".For, having finished the works, he rested on the seventh day and blessed it; it is therefore necessary that at the end of the six thousandth year all wickedness should be abolished out of the earth, and justice should reign for a thousand years.".........." The prince of devils shall be bound in chains, and shall be in custody for the thousand years of the *heavenly kingdom*.".......... " When the thousand years of *the kingdom* shall be completed, then shall be that second and public resurrection of all, wherein the unjust shall be raised to everlasting torments,"......." The world shall then be renewed, the heavens folded up, and the earth changed. God shall transform men into the appearance of angels, and they shall be white as snow, and shall always hold communion with the Almighty.".......".This is the doctrine

     * Justin. Mart. Dial. cum Tryph. pars II.
     † Tertull. advers. Marc. c. 24, 55, &c.
     ‡ Method. apud Epiphan. in Panar. Hær. 54.

of the holy prophets, which we Christians follow ; this is our wisdom."*
Augustin, about the end of the fourth century, in a similar strain tells us
that the judgment having been finished, this heaven and this earth should
cease, and a new heaven and a new earth be introduced ; adding, that it
was by a change of things, and not by an utter annihilation, this world
would pass away.† Jerome, Chrysostom, and indeed almost all the Christian
teachers and sects, whether orthodox or heterodox, during the four first
centuries, believed and inculcated the fanciful notion of the speedy coming
of Christ in judgment and the near approach of the end of the world, as a
fundamental principle of their religion, differing from one another only in
details of minor importance.

Neither Christ, nor his Apostles, nor the Fathers, however, originated
this notion. Like almost all other things in the Gospels, there is very
little originality in the predictions regarding the end of the world attributed
to Christ by the Evangelists. They are borrowed from traditions many
centuries older than the time of the Prophet of Nazareth. How entirely
the notions of John in his pretended Revelation ; of Barnabas in his
Epistle ; and even of the writers of the Gospels in the predictions they
attribute to Jesus, are based upon a wild fancy which had been prevalent
among the Jews,—to say nothing of other nations,—many hundreds of
years before the son of Mary and Joseph had been born, will be seen from
the following account.—Rabbi Ketina, as cited in the Gemara,—a kind of
a comment upon the Jewish Talmud,—had said :—"The world endures for
six thousand years ; and one thousand it shall be laid waste, of which it is
said—*The Lord alone shall be exalted in that day.* Tradition assents to
Rabbi Ketina ; as out of seven years every seventh is the year of remission,
so out of seven thousand years of the world the seventh millenary shall
be the millenary of remission, that God alone may *be exalted in that
day.*‡ Dr. Burnet, citing authorities, says it was a tradition of the house
of Elias, that—"the world endures six thousand years ; two thousand
before the Law, two thousand under the Law, and two thousand under the
Messiah.§ Another tradition of the house of Elias was that—"the just

---

* Lactant. Instit. Div. lib. vii. c. 14, 15, 24, 26. This holy Father, although he agrees
with Christ in the main, yet slightly differs from him regarding human procreation
after the second advent of the latter. (Matth. xxii. 30.) What a vast number must be
the progeny of only a thousand human pairs in a thousand years ! To what an infinite
number must they multiply, in this incomprehensible space of time—a thousand years—
especially since there was to be no death during that time ! How could Jerusalem, even
if it were enlarged as Justin thought,—nay, how could the whole of that paltry nook of
land called Judea, hold such an innumerable multitude ? Well might Lactantius say,—
" This is our wisdom." It is singular, however, that he calls this absurdity "the doctrine
of the holy prophets," and that he does not intimate that the same doctrine had been
prophetically taught by Christ, and John the exile of Patmos, as well as inculcated by the
Apostles in their discourses and epistles. In perfect harmony with other Fathers he
ignores the New Testament, just as the Apostles ignore the Gospels.
    † August. de Civ. Dei. lib. xix. c. 14. Vid. lib. xx. c. 19.
    ‡ Dixit Rabbi Ketina, sex annorum millibus stat mundus, et uno millenario vastabitur;
de quo dicitur—*Et exaltibitur Dominus solus die illo.* Traditio adstipulatur R. Ketinæ :
sicut ex septennis annis septimus quisque annus remissionis est, ita ex septem millibus
annorum mundi septimus millenarius millenarius remissionis erit, ut Dominus solus
exaltatur in die illo.—*Mede Placita Doctorum Hebræorum* de Magno Die Judicii. lib v. c. 3.
    § "Traditio domus Eliæ : sex mille annos durat mundus : bis mille annis inanitas;
bis mille annis Lex ; deinque bis mille annis dies Christi."—Burnett's Sacred Theory,
pars iii. c. 5. apud Mede. pp. 536, 894.

whom God shall raise up shall not be turned again into dust.   Now if you inquire how it shall be with the just in those thousand years during which the holy blessed God shall renew his world, whereof it is said,—*And the Lord alone shall be exalted in that day;* you must know that the holy blessed God will give them the wings as it were of eagles, that they may fly upon the face of the waters; whence it is said (Psal. xlvi. 2.)—*Therefore will we not fear, when the earth shall be changed.*"*   Hence it is clear that the notion of the approaching end of the world originated neither with Jesus of the Gospels, nor any of the writers of the New Testament, nor the Christian Fathers.   These only modified it, particularly in regard to the final judgment, and the judge, whom they made to be Jesus of Nazareth.

The doctrine of the near approach of the end of the world with its accompanying tenets, however, became less popular during the third, and more especially the fourth century.   Seeing that the predictions of these events did not prove true as to time, people gradually began to lose faith in them.   But thousands of the more enthusiastic still believed in them, and, for centuries afterwards, daily expected their accomplishment, while now and then a certain master-spirit in divine knowledge rose up and declared that *the day of the Lord was at hand,* and that, at a certain time named, it would arrive; thereby creating great alarm and confusion in society.   Origen, in the third century, is the first, of whom we have any account, that set his face against this doctrine. He opposed it (as Mosheim tells us, calling it the Millenium) " with the greatest warmth, because it was incompatible with some of his favourite sentiments.   Nepos, an Egyptian bishop, endeavoured to restore this opinion to its former credit, in a book written against the *Allegorists;* for so he called, by way of contempt, the adversaries of the Millenium system.   This work, and the hypothesis it defended, were extremely well received by great numbers in the canton of Arsinoe, and, among others, by Coracion, a presbyter of no mean influence and reputation.   But Dionysius of Alexandria, a disciple of Origen, stopped the growing progress of this doctrine by his private discourse, and also by two learned and judicious dissertations concerning the divine promise."†
It would appear, however, that *before* the time of Origen there were *some* who denied the doctrine of the coming of Christ and the end of the world, regarding as allegories the prophecies which, in the sacred books of the time, referred to these events; whence Nepos, the Egyptian bishop, just mentioned, calls such *the Allegorists.*   And Irenæus, who lived nearly fifty years before Origen, complains,—" there are some in the church, in divers nations, and by various works, who believing, do consent with the just, who do yet endeavour to turn these things *into metaphors.*"‡   Eusebius,

* Traditio domus Eliæ: Justi quos resuscitabit Deus non redigentur iterum in pulverum.   Si quæras autem, mille annis istis quibus Deus sanctus benedictus renovaturus est mundum suum, de quibus dicitur— *Et exaltabitur Dominus solus in die illo,*— quid justis futurum sit; sciendum quod Deus sanctus benedictus dabit illis alas quasi aquilarum ut volent super facie aquarum; unde dicitur (Psal. xlvi. 2.) *Propterea non timebimus cum mutabitur terra.*"—Mede. p. 776.

† See Whitby's Treatise on the Millenium—end of second vol. of Comment. on New Test.   Lardner's Credibility, 4th, 5th, 7th, and 9th vols.   Origen de Principiis, lib. ii. c. 9.   Euseb. Hist. Eccles. lib. vii. c. 24.   Gennadius de Dogmatibus Ecclesiast. c. 55. p. 32. Edit. Elmenh.   Mosheim's Eccles. Hist. cent. iii. part ii. c. 3.
‡ Irenæus adv. Hær. lib. v. c. 33.

in the fourth century, with his usual craft, speaks against the doctrine and attempts to account for its origin by telling us that " Papias, among certain parables and sermons of the Saviour, and other seemingly fabulous records which he professed to have received traditionally, had stated that there would be a thousand years after the resurrection of the dead, during which Christ would reign bodily upon earth.   But in this Papias had mistaken the apostolic narration, not being able to distinguish what had been mystically spoken by them ; for he appeared to be of a weak mind, as one might conjecture from his discourses."*   In the sixth century,—as there was no indication of the end of the world prophesied by Christ to be at hand even in his time, and ever since had been anxiously expected,—great doubts were entertained as to whether the awful event would at all take place.   Hence Themistius—a deacon of Alexandria, and supposed founder of the sect called the Agnoites—maintained that *Christ was ignorant of the time of the Day of Judgment.*†   Thus the doctrine of the coming of Christ to destroy and judge the world gradually fell into disrepute :—first, it began to be regarded as a profound allegory ; next to be considered as a doubtful and useless opinion ; and lastly rejected by many as the absurd invention of heresy and fanaticism.‡   It was however afterwards, in a new form, revived and firmly established, so that it is at this moment a doctrine relied on by all Christians,—a doctrine plainly taught in the VIII. and XVIII. Articles of the Church of England,— a doctrine of an essential character and of paramount importance in the creeds of all Christian denominations ! The only difference between the primitive Christians and those of the present day, is that the latter live in expectation of Christ's coming in the nineteenth century, and the former did the same during the three first centuries.§— We find the pious Erasmus in the sixteenth century. however,—like some writers of the present age when closely followed up by argument,—having recourse to the ancient method of attempting to remove the difficulty by the aid of a metaphor; and the learned Grotius. in the next century. apologising, that for *wise purposes the pious fraud of the near approach of the day of judgment* was palmed upon the world by the founder and promulgators of Christianity.‖   It would appear that from the doctrine of the end

* Euseb. Hist. Eccles. lib. iii. c. 39.

† Vid. Photius Biblioth. Cod. 230. p. 882.   Forbes Instruct. Historico-Theolog. lib. iii. c. 19.   Mich. le Quien ad Damascenum de Heresibus. tom. i p. 107.

‡ Dupin Bibliotheque Ecclesiastique. tom. i. p. 223 ; tom. ii. p. 336.   Gibbon's Decline and Fall of the Roman Empire, chap. xv. s. 2.

§ Bossuet Histoire des Variations des Eglises Protestantes, lib. ii. c. 19.

‖ This was a most strange notion of Grotius, and one contrary to all sound morality, —that the interest of *truth*, or of anything that is *good*, can be promoted by the propagation of *falsity*.   Such, however, was the notion and avowed practice of the Christian Fathers, which utterly invalidates all their statements regarding the divine origin of Christianity.   As the announcement of this fact may astound some general readers, who have never taken the pains to inquire into the origin of Christianity,—a matter studiously concealed from them by their religious teachers, who Sunday after Sunday preach Christianity to them,—the following proofs are attached.—Dr. Mosheim, who is an orthodox Christian, and an authority of the greatest weight in ecclesiastical matters, has in his history of the Church the following admissions :—" It was (thought) an act of virtue to deceive and lie when by such means the interests of the church might be promoted."........" This erroneous maxim was now of long standing ; it had been adopted for some ages past, and had produced an incredible number of ridiculous fables, fictitious prodigies, and pious frauds, to the unspeakable detriment of that glorious cause in which

of the world, in its declining state,—in the fourth and fifth centuries,—
sprang the notions of Purgatory, which proved such a fruitful source of
gain to the clergy through the succeeding ages; and, as Mosheim justly
remarks, still continues to enrich the Romish church with its nutritious

they were employed. And it must frankly be confessed that the greatest men, and most
eminent saints of this century were more or less tainted with the infection of this corrupt
principle, as will appear, evidently, to such as look with an attentive eye into their
writings and their actions."—(*Mosheim's Ecclesiastical History*, cent. IV. part ii. chap. iii.
sec. 16.)—"I am equally convinced that the greatest part of the prodigies recorded in
the histories of this age are liable to the strongest suspicions of falsehood and imposture.
The simplicity and ignorance of the generality of those times furnished the most favourable occasion for the exercise of fraud; and the impudence of impostors, in contriving
false miracles, was artfully proportioned to the credulity of the vulgar."—(*Ibid.* cent. V.
part i. chap. i. sec. 6. with a number of authorities.)—"The Platonists and Pythagoreans
held it as a maxim that it was not only lawful, but even praiseworthy to *deceive*, and even
to use the expedient of *a lie* in order to advance the cause of *truth* and *piety*. The Jews
who lived in Egypt had learned and received this maxim from them, before the coming
of Christ, as appears, incontestibly, from a multitude of ancient records; and the
Christians were infected from both these sources, with the same pernicious error, as
appears from a number of books attributed falsely to great and venerable names!"—
(*Ib.* cent. II. part ii. chap. iii. sec. 15.) Such are the admissions of this great man, and upon
the whole, faithful historian, although in some places of his work there are marks of his bias
for Christianity. Lardner, (vol. iv. p. 524.) in his Credibility, also admits that Christians
of all sects, were guilty of this fraud, and adds,—"Indeed we may say that it was one
great fault of the times." He also quotes the following words of the celebrated Casaubon,
who says,—"It mightily affects me to see how many there were in the earliest times of
the Church, who considered it as a capital exploit to lend to heavenly truth the help of
their own inventions, in order that the new doctrine might be more readily allowed by
the wise among the Gentiles. These officious lies, they were wont to say, were devised
for a good end. From which source, beyond question, sprung nearly innumerable books,
which that and the following age saw published by those who were far from being *bad
men* (for we are not speaking of the books of heretics,) under the name of the Lord Jesus
Christ, and of the Apostles, and other saints." O, no; these holy forgers were not *bad
men*, for they published their falsehoods under the name of Jesus Christ. Mosheim, however, speaks of them with the same lenity.—"Not long after Christ's ascension into
heaven, several histories of his life and doctrines, full of pious frauds and fabulous
wonders, were composed by persons, whose intentions, perhaps, were *not bad*, but whose
writings discovered the greatest superstition and ignorance. Nor was this all; productions appeared which were imposed upon the world by fraudulent men, as the writings
of the holy Apostles."—(Eccles. Hist. cent. II. part ii. chap. ii. sec. 17.) Monsieur
Daille also says,—"Neither ought we to wonder that even those of the honest, innocent,
primitive times made use of these deceits, seeing for a good end they made no scruple to
forge whole books."—(Daille de usu Patrum. lib. i c. 4.) The reader will recollect the
description already given of the Apocryphal New Testament, the very writings to which
Dr. Mosheim refers; nor will he forget that what we have now as a New Testament was voted
by majority from these so-called spurious writings. Then let him compare the Canonical
and Apocryphal New Testaments, and judge for himself whether there is the least difference in the character of their contents. The learned reader is also referred to Fabricus's
Codex Apocryphus Novi Testamenti, which is a collection of these writings, and to the
remarks made on them by the learned Beausobre in his *Histoire Critique des Dogmes de
Manichee.* livr. ii. p. 37. Eusebius, making an indirect confession of practising these
deceits, complaisantly assures us that he had written what redounded to the glory, and
suppressed whatever tended to the disgrace of religion.—(Hist. Eccles. lib. viii. c. 2;
and *De Martyr. Palestin.* c. 12.) And the great and pious Chrysostom exclaims,—
"Great is the force of deceit! provided it be not incited by a treacherous intention."—
(Comment on 1 Cor. ix. 19.) Paul also appears to entertain the same view of truth—
"If the truth of God hath more abounded through *my lie* unto *his glory*, why yet am I
also judged as a sinner?"—Rom. iii. 7. See also ver. 5. and consult 2 Thess. ii. 11, 12.
1 Cor. ix. 22. Mark iv. 12. Ezek. xiv. 9. *et al.* See likewise Taylor's Diegesis, pp.
36—53.

streams.* It seems to have been first introduced entwined with certain pagan notions already existing,—just as has been the case with all the other tenets of Christianity,—that the souls of all men should pass—from the place in which they were supposed to have been hitherto confined, namely Hades, to await the final judgment,—through a purgation of fire into final bliss. It being already the prevalent opinion that the world would be destroyed by fire, and that all men were to pass through this fire, by which the good would be purified, and the wicked consumed, the doctrine now began to be taught,—that, *immediately*, *after death*, all people, both pious and impious, even the Virgin Mary herself, were to enter this fire by which they would either be purified or destroyed.† "This opinion," says Dr. Priestley, "was the first idea of the doctrine of purgatory," which although very closely allied to that of the end of the world, we shall not here pursue any further, but recommend the reader to peruse Dr. Priestley's History of the Corruption of Christianity, part v.

It is confidently hoped that, when considered in connection with the citations made from the Gospels and the explanations thereof, the proofs given in the preceding sections that the Apostles and primitive Fathers taught the proximity of the end of the world will be deemed, even by the most bigoted adherent to what is called orthodox doctrine, sufficiently strong and numerous as collateral evidence, to justify the writer in coming to the conclusion already expressed; namely, that Christ actually did predict these events as being close at hand, and that time has pronounced his predictions utterly false. A few instances of the opinions of other writers on the subject shall close the present chapter.

Section IV.—THE TESTIMONY OF MODERN WRITERS THAT CHRIST, THE APOSTLES, AND THE FATHERS PREDICTED AND TAUGHT THE NEAR APPROACH OF THE END OF THE WORLD AND THE DAY OF JUDGMENT.

The following extracts from the works of eminent authors both in and out of the Church, wherein they admit that Christ prophesied the end of the world and the day of judgment, as being in his time just at hand; and that his apostles, and their immediate successors inculcated the near approach of the same events, will serve not only to show that the writer is not unique in maintaining the views he has advanced in this work, but will likewise materially corroborate these views.

Dr. Edwards, in a sermon delivered before the *University of Cambridge*, in 1790, classes all those prophecies of Christ and his Apostles, concerning the end of the world *in their days* with those predictions which have proved *complete failures*; and thinks that this objection ought fairly and honestly to be conceded to the adversaries of Christianity, instead of vainly attempting

---

* Eccles. Hist. cent. v. part ii. chap. iii. sec. 2.

† Augustin. Quest. ad Dulcit. lib. viii. 1b. xiii. lib. xxi. c. 28. Petrarch. vol. iii. p. 277. Burnet on the Articles, p. 269.

to remove it.* The Rev. John Macnaught, M.A. incumbent of St. Chrysostom's Church, Everton, Liverpool, in a work on the divine authority of Holy Writ, says, in reference to Christ's prophecies of the End of the World, that "unless we are prepared to think our blessed Saviour liable to err, we must believe that in this, as in other demonstrable cases, the Evangelists slightly varied the form of what the Son of God had said, and so unintentionally gave to Jesus's words a meaning which he did not intend they should bear, and in which they were not true."† But whether it was Christ that prophesied falsely, or it was the Evangelists that misrepresented him, is quite immaterial to the present subject, and as it regards the interest of Christianity, to which either would be fatal. We know nothing of Christ but from what the Evangelists and Apostles tell us in their writings. If, therefore, these writings are not reliable,—if they do not contain a

* The title of this remarkable Sermon runs thus—" A Sermon by Thomas Edwards, L.L.D. preached before the University of Cambridge, May 23, 1790, On the Predictions of the Apostles concerning the End of the World." In this sermon he observes, *inter alia*, that if the obscurity " of the Scriptures cannot be denominated a considerable error, it will be readily acknowledged to be a considerable imperfection,—an imperfection which has more deeply wounded the real interest of Christianity than the most artful machinations of its most inveterate enemies." He then proceeds to remark that "it must be added that obscurity is not the only imperfection which may justly be imputed to the authors of the New Testament. Considerable error is a charge from which they have not been rescued with that cogency of argument, and that coincidence of opinion which the nature of the case might induce us to expect." (pp. 9, 10.) A sentence or two further on, he says,—" The predictions of the Apostles concerning the End of the World, and the prophecies of the Old Testament, as they are applied in the New, will furnish examples of considerable error." (p. 11.) Here he cites a passage from Gibbon's Decline and Fall (vol. ii. chap. xv. sec. 2.) regarding the expectations of the End of the World entertained by the early Christians. Afterwards, he remarks,—" It may not be thought wonderful that Baronius and other Romanists, to avoid the application of the Man of Sin, should earnestly contend that *the speedy appearance of Christ was expected by the Apostles;* (See Mede's Works, p. 665.) but it is somewhat remarkable that the orthodox father of the celebrated prelate who translated Isaiah, in a Treatise designed to confute a supposed latitudinarian, should *assent to the validity* of our *Historian's* objection, by confessing, without reserve, that *the Apostles were mistaken.* (See Lowth's Vindication, &c. p. 52.) Grotius insinuates that for wise purposes the *pious deception was permitted* to take place. (Gibbon, vol. ii. p. 301. See Grotius de Veritat. lib. ii. sec. 6. Cleric. ad 1 Thess. v. 10.)" The Doctor next quotes Matth. xvi. 28. *showing this passage to refer to the End of the World and the coming of Christ.* In reference to the opinion that it refers to the destruction of Jerusalem, he observes,—" Christ was no more visible at the destruction of Jerusalem, than he was at the earthquake of Lisbon, or the siege of Gibraltar." He compares Acts. i. 11. and Heb. x. 28. He dwells on Matth. xxiv. Mark xiii. 4. and Luke xxi. 7. which he shows to foretel *Christ's second and speedy coming to execute judgment.* He notices 1 Thess. v. 4. &c. and observes,—" The day of Christ was not *at hand*,—would not happen within *a week, a month*, or *a year*, yet it was *not very far*," &c. He cites 1 Pet. iv. 7. by which, he says, is meant the *dissolution of the world and the appearance of Christ.* Near the conclusion of his able discourse, he says that he has now cited a sufficient number of passages to establish the justness of Mr. Locke's opinion (Vide ad 2 Cor. v. 3.) *that the Apostles, in their own time, expected the End of the World and the appearance of Christ.* (p. 35.)

Such are the principal points in Dr. Edwards's Sermon, which was indeed very remarkable considering the times and the place in which he preached it. Had he lived a few centuries earlier, when it was thought that the fire and the fagot were the best antidote against unbelief, he would have been burnt as a heretic. It is however a wonder that, even at the close of the eighteenth century, his sermon was allowed to be circulated in a typographical dress.

† Macnaught's Infallibility, Inspiration, and Authority of Holy Writ. p. 73.

correct account of the words and actions of Christ,—if their authors have given " to Jesus's words a meaning which he did not intend they should bear," then there is nothing certainly known of Christianity. Indeed Mr. Macnaught admits this when, discussing the question of the proper version of Scripture, he writes :—" This is a point which might, if it were necessary, be so worked out by itself to show the *impossibility* of ascertaining which is the infallible reading,—which is the true translation, and so the impossibility of proving any modern Bible to be infallible. But the question now is merely to what book do intelligent Englishmen refer when they speak of the infallible word of God ? And to that question the answer clearly is,— the English Authorised Version."* This version, the Rev. Mr. Macnaught thinks, is not to be relied upon. But what is more to the point of our present subject, he says,—" it *is* clear that the New Testament writings anticipated the day of the Lord and the consummation of all things as an event *which was to take place during the lifetime of many then upon earth.*— The doctrine of the *End* is *prominent* and *conspicious* in the New Testament, and its being inculcated in the sacred volume is another proof from Holy Writ itself that neither in *religion*, nor on any other subject does the Bible permit us to regard its teaching as *infallible*.† It is however with what the Bible *does say* that we have to do. It is boasted that " the Bible, and the Bible only is the religion of Protestants." If the Bible is not true, Christianity cannot be true. So far, the candour and honesty of Mr. Macnaught is exemplary. But is it not inconsistent,—is it not an anomaly in the character of any man to have the bravery to make this concession, and yet to preach Christianity ? For if the Bible is not infallible, it is not from God ; and Christianity which is confessedly taught only in the Bible, cannot therefore be from God. And not being from God, it is, like all other religions, of human invention ; consequently, all time and money spent upon it are so much time and wealth wasted ; and our anxiety respecting the rewards it promises, and the punishments it threatens is highly injurious both to ourselves and to society. This is the inevitable consequence of our reverend author's candid yet suicidal admission as a preacher of Christianity.

Even Bishop Newton makes the following concessions on this point. —" The doctrine of the Millenium (already shown to mean the coming of Christ) was generally believed in the three first and purest ages ; and this belief, as the learned Dodwell has justly observed, was one principal cause of the fortitude of the primitive Christians ; they even coveted martyrdom, in hopes of being partakers of the privileges and glories of the martyrs in the first resurrection." In commenting on " the Man of Sin" he admits almost all the passages in the Epistles, &c. already cited in this work, to refer to the coming of Christ and the day of judgment. " The phrases of 'the coming of Christ,' and 'the day of Christ,'" he remarks, " may be understood either figuratively of his coming in judgment upon the Jews, or literally of his coming in glory to judge the world. Sometimes indeed they are used in the former sense, but they are *more generally employed in the latter by the writers of the New Testament.*" In his remarks on the second epistle to the Thessalonians he combats the opinion that the destruction of Jerusalem is meant there, and asks—" What connection had

---

* Macnaught's Infallibility, &c. p. 29.   † Ibid. p. 73.

Macedonia with Judea ; or Thessalonica with Jerusalem ?" He then proceeds to show that similar expressions in other places refer to Christ's second coming. He however cautiously avoids the point,—that in these expressions Christ's coming is invariably represented as close at hand. It is amusing to observe what efforts he makes to guard against this difficulty, —an insurmountable difficulty—the truth once admitted,—to a bishop who had his *orthodoxy* to be preserved unimpeachable ! In his exposition of the Apocalypse he makes all the events predicted to be such as were soon to take place ; but the Day of Judgment—so closely interwoven with these events in that book, and which he admits to be the principal topic in the book,—he makes to be far remote in the writer's mind. What can be more inconsistent than the following passages ?—" Our Saviour's repeating so frequently in this book—' Behold, I come quickly—Behold he cometh with clouds, and every eye shall see him ; and they also who pierced him, and all kindreds of the earth shall wail because of him,' and the like expressions *cannot surely be so well understood of any other event as of the destruction of Jerusalem.''*—" Christ's second coming in power and glory is one *principal topic* of Revelation. With this it begins, (i. 7.)—' Behold he cometh with clouds, and every eye shall see him.' With this it also concludes, (xxii. 20.)—' He who testifieth these things, saith, Surely I come quickly.' "— This contradiction of Bishop Newton arises from his aim at maintaining the truthfulness of the Apocalypse, and thereby his own orthodoxy. The whole tenour of his Dissertations of Prophecy tacitly admits that the Apostles and the Fathers taught that Christ's second advent was at hand.*

Mr. Greg, in his Creed of Christendom,—a work of sterling worth, written in a style quite worthy of modern criticism,—has the following observations in his enquiry into " the fidelity of the Gospel History."— " The prophecies of the *second coming of Christ* (Matth. xxiv. Mark xiii. Luke xvii. 22—37 ; xxi. 5—36.) are mixed up with those of the destruction of Jerusalem by Titus, in a manner which has long been the perplexity and *despair* of orthodox commentators. The obvious meaning of the passages which contain these predictions,—the sense in which they were evidently understood by the *Evangelists* who wrote them down,—the sense which we know from *many* sources† they conveyed to the minds of the *early Christians,*—clearly is, that the coming of Christ to judge the world should follow *immediately* (immediately, ' in those days,') the destruction of the Holy City, and should take place during the *lifetime of the then existing generation.* —' Verily I say unto you, This generation shall not pass, till all these things be fulfilled.' Matth. xxiv. 34. Mark xiii. 30. Luke xxi. 35.)— ' There be some *standing here* which shall *not* taste of *death*, till they *see the Son of man coming in his kingdom.*' (Matth. xvi. 28.) ' Verily I say unto you, *Ye* shall not have gone over the cities of Israel, till the *Son of man be come.*' (Matth. x. 23.) ' If I will that he tarry till *I come*, what is that to thee ?' (John xxi. 23.) Now if these predictions really proceeded from Jesus, he was entirely in *error* on the subject, and the prophetic spirit was *not in him ;* for not only did his advent not follow close on the destruction

---

* Newton on the Prophecies, pp. 155, 358, 80—100. Ninth Edit. 12mo.

† Mr. Greg here, in a Note, cites a great number of passages from the Epistles, showing the near approach of the destruction of the world. They have already been dwelt upon in the present work.

of Jerusalem, but 1800 years have since elapsed, and neither he nor the preliminary signs which were to announce him, have yet appeared. If these predictions *did not* proceed from *him*, the *Evangelists* have taken the liberty of putting into the mouth of Christ, words and *announcements which Christ never uttered*."* Mr. Greg, whose object is to show that the Gospels are the fabrications of some unknown writers,† in the next paragraph proceeds to prove this point, remarking in his way that as the three Gospels in which the above predictions occur are allowed to have been written between the year 65 and 72 A.D., or *during* the war which ended in the destruction of Jerusalem, they were, therefore, written *during* and *after* the event which they predict; Vespasian entering Galilee, which was the commencement of the war, in the year A.D. 67, and taking the Jewish capital in the autumn of A.D. 70.‡ In treating of the "limits of apostolic wisdom and authority," Mr. Greg writes :—" Our second position was that the Apostles held some opinions which we know to be erroneous. It is essential not to overstate the case. They held *several* opinions which we *believe* to be erroneous, but only *one* which, as it related to a matter of *fact*, we *know* to have been erroneous. They *unanimously* and *unquestionably* believed and *taught* that the End of the World was at hand, and would *arrive in the lifetime of the then existing generation*. On this point there appears to have been no hesitation in their individual minds, nor any difference of opinion among them." The writer here cites " the passages of the apostolic writings which most strongly express, or most clearly imply, this conviction," all which passages will be found, with many others, in section v. of this chapter. Then he adds ;— "We may well conceive that this strong conviction must, in men like the Apostles, have been something far beyond a mere abstract or speculative opinion. In fact it modified their whole tone of thought and feeling ;—and could not fail to do so. The firm and living faith that a few years would bring the second coming of their Lord in his glory and the fearful termination of all earthly things,—when ' the heavens should be gathered together as a scroll, and the elements should melt with fervent heat ;'—and that many among them should be still alive, and should witness these awful occurrences, with human eyes, and should join their glorified Master without passing through the portals of the grave—could not exist in their minds without producing not only a profound contempt for all the pomps and distinctions of the world, but an utter carelessness for the future interests of mankind, for posterity, even for kindred,—without indeed distorting all the just proportions of those scenes of nature and society, in the midst of which their lot was cast.§—

---

* Creed of Christendom, pp. 123, 124.

† But if the Gospels are unreliable fabrications, attributing to Jesus words which he never uttered, this divests Christianity of its claim to Divine origin, as thoroughly as if Jesus had uttered false predictions. Both lead us inevitably to the same conclusion.

‡ This strong argument was overlooked in the second chapter of this Essay, where it should have been observed that if Christ's predictions referred to the destruction of Jerusalem, it is most strange that the Evangelists, who, according to Christian chronologers themselves, were in the act of writing them, at least during the time Jerusalem was being besieged if not after it was captured, do not say a single word about the exact fulfilment of these predictions before their eyes. They take notice of the fulfilment of Christ's prophecies regarding his death, resurrection, and other things. In the age of the Apostles it required not a little time to write a book the size of one of the Gospels.

§ See Natural History of Enthusiasm, sec. v. pp. 100, 101.

If the world and all its mighty and far-stretching interests—if the earth and its infinite and ever-varying beauties—if the sky and its myriads of midnight glories—were indeed to be finally swept away in the time and the presence of the existing actors in the busy scene of life;—where was the use of forming any new ties of kindred or affection, which must terminate so suddenly and so soon? Why give a moment's thought to the arts which embellish life, the amenities which adorn it, the sciences which smooth it or prolong it, or the knowledge which enriches and dignifies its course?—Marriage, children, wealth, power, astronomy, philosophy, poetry—what were they to men who knew that ten or twenty years would transplant, not only themselves, but the whole race of man, to a world where all would be forgotten, and would leave the earth—the scene of these things—a destroyed and blackened chaos? To this conviction may be traced St. Paul's confused and contradictory notions on the subject of marriage. And this conviction, teeming with such immense and dangerous consequences, and held by all the Apostles, was, we now know, *wholly incorrect and unfounded.* Next to the resurrection of Christ, there was probably no doctrine which they held so undoubtingly, or preached so dogmatically, as this, with regard to which they were *totally in error.* If, then, they were so misinformed, or mistaken, on a point having so immediate and powerful a bearing upon practical life, with what confidence can we trust them on matters of deeper speculation?''*

The Rev. Mr. Stanley, in his Commentary on Paul's Epistles to the Corinthians, (2 vols. Oxford) shows, that by the expression—" We shall not all sleep, but we shall all be changed," &c. (1 Cor. xv. 51, 52.) the Apostle means—we shall not all sleep the sleep of *death ;* thereby showing the expectation of Christ's advent during the *then existent generation.*— Similar extracts might be made from Professor Jowith's Commentaries on the Galatians, and others of Paul's Epistles ; the works of Dr. Donaldson, late Fellow of Trinity College, Cambridge, on Christian Orthodoxy, recently published ; the works of the Rev. Baden Powell, and of other eminent divines in the Church of England ; and still in larger proportion among the Congregational Dissenters. But we must pass on to notice others.

Mr. Gibbon, whose narration of facts—substantiated by unquestionable authorities—has not yet been detected in a single instance to be erroneous, states that " in the primitive Church, the influence of truth was very powerfully strengthened by an opinion which, however it may deserve respect for its usefulness and antiquity, has *not* been found *agreeable to experience.* It was universally believed that *the end of the world and the kingdom of heaven were at hand.* The *near approach* of this wonderful event had been predicted by the Apostles ; the tradition of it was preserved by their earliest disciples, and those who understood, in their literal sense, the discourses of Christ himself, were obliged to expect the second and glorious coming of the Son of man in the clouds before *that generation was totally extinguished,* which had beheld his humble condition upon earth, and which might still be witness of the calamities of the Jews under Vespasian or Hadrian. The revolution of seventeen centuries has instructed us not to press too closely the mysterious language of prophecy and revelation ; but

---

* Creed of Christendom, pp. 182, 183.

as long as for wise purposes this *error* was permitted to subsist in the Church, it was productive of the most *salutary* effects on the faith and practice of Christians who lived in the awful expectation of that moment, when the globe itself and all the various races of mankind should tremble at the presence of their divine Judge."* Mr. Gibbon then proceeds to notice that the doctrine of the Millenium was closely connected with the second coming of Christ. This doctrine was in fact identical with that of the end of the world, the final judgment, and the establishment of the kingdom of heaven; having been suggested, as already observed, by the ancient Jewish notion of a Golden Age.

Dr. Priestley, in his History of the Corruption of Christianity,† informs us that "it was the opinion of most of the early Fathers that the world would be destroyed by fire, and also that all men were to pass through this fire,—that the good would be purified by it, and the wicked consumed. The former part of this doctrine they might learn from the apostle Peter; but it does not clearly appear whence they derived the latter part of it." .... "The Gnostics are said to have maintained that the greatest part of mankind would be annihilated at the day of judgment; which was probably the same thing that was meant by those who said that they would be *consumed* in the fire that was to destroy the world."

Dr. Whitby and Dr. Mosheim, like others who write for the benefit of Christianity rather than for that of simple truth, find it more convenient to designate the doctrine of the near approach of the day of judgment by the palliative term "Millenium." The latter says that "long before this period (the middle of the third century,) an opinion had prevailed that Christ was to come and reign a thousand years among men, before the *entire* and *final* dissolution of the world."‡ And the former informs us that "the Fathers who adopted the doctrine of the Millenium received it from the traditions and notions of the Jews; but that this *error* will not *invalidate their authority* in any thing delivered by them, as witnesses of what they had seen, or declared to have been the practice of the Church of Christ."§ To say that they received this erroneous doctrine from the Jews is only another mode of saying that they received it from the Jewish apostles; for none but those of the Jews who were Christians would admit that Christ would have the honour to reign over them for a thousand years. A vast number of other eminent writers might be cited who, either directly or indirectly, make similar admissions. The citations already made, however, are amply sufficient to substantiate the position advanced in this section—namely, that Christ predicted the near approach of the End of the World and the Final Judgment, and that the Apostles and the Fathers, constantly taught that these dread events were close at hand, are neither newly discovered facts brought forward for the first time in this work, nor

---

* Decline and Fall of the Roman Empire, chap. xv. sec. 2.

† Vol. i. p. 411. It is difficult to conceive what could have induced such a man as Dr. Priestley to write two large octavo volumes which have the tendency to persuade the world that Christianity has been corrupted. He does not show that Christianity was ever purer than during the centuries of which he treats. He must well know that it was never so refined and pure as in the age he wrote.

‡ Mosheim's Eccles. Hist. cent. iii. part ii. chap. iii. sec. 12.

§ Whitby's Treatise on the Millenium, vol. ii. of Commentaries.

O

facts supported only by slight evidence.   It is, however, to be observed that although these facts are almost generally admitted, yet they have never had their due weight in reference to their bearing on the question of the Divine origin of Christianity.   Once they have the consideration to which they are entitled, on this point, the pretensions of the Christian religion to a heavenly origin, vanish as a necessary consequence,—a consequence never dwelt upon, but rather studiously evaded, by those divines whose candour compels them to admit the facts themselves.

CHAPTER V.

THE INFERENCES DIRECTLY DEDUCIBLE FROM THE FOREGOING ESTABLISHED
FACTS—THAT CHRIST PREDICTED THE LAST DAY OF JUDGMENT AND THE
END OF THE WORLD AS NEAR EVENTS—THAT HIS APOSTLES INCULCATED
THE NEAR APPROACH OF THESE EVENTS, AS A MOST IMPORTANT DOCTRINE,
IN ALL THEIR DISCOURSES AND EPISTLES—AND THAT BOTH THE PREDIC-
TION OF CHRIST AND THE DOCTRINE OF HIS APOSTLES, HAVE PROVED
UTTERLY FALSE, AS THE PRESENT STATE OF THE WORLD, AND OF ITS INHABI-
TANTS, IRREFUTABLY SHOWS.

SECTION I.—THE PROPHET OF NAZARETH NEITHER A DEITY NOR IN SUPER-
NATURAL COMMUNICATION WITH THE DEITY.—REPRESENTED HIMSELF AS
A DIVINE BEING.—DOUBTFUL WHETHER HE BELIEVED HE WAS ANYTHING
MORE THAN A FALLIBLE MAN.

The first inference which every thinking mind would naturally draw
from these facts is, that the Prophet of Nazareth could not be a divine
person, or be influenced by the Deity, in his words and actions, and more
especially, in the act of delivering the predictions in question. For, as
already observed, it is absurd and even blasphemous to suppose that God
was either unable to predict truly, or disposed to predict falsely. The latter
would imply that the Supreme Being is capable of an immoral act, and the
former that he is limited in knowledge. The human mind revolts against
entertaining either supposition of God. It is incompatible with any true
notion of the Deity to imagine him liable to any imperfection whatever.
Indeed, the mind of man is not capable of conceiving the existence of God
in any other manner than as a perfect Being. This will be admitted on all
hands, so that scarcely any proof is required in order to show the inevita-
bility of the inference. The Prophet of Nazareth, therefore, not being a
Divine personage,—in other words not being a God,—it becomes an important question, in reference to the character of Christianity, whether he was
influenced by God. To say that he was, is to say that God influenced one
of his creatures so as to make him impose upon the world that which was
not true, which is precisely the same as to say that *God himself* did so
impose upon the world; or in other words, upon his creatures. For, a
person thus influenced by God would be passive,—would be no other than

2 o

an instrument, while God was the active cause, or indeed the real actor in the deception. The mind recoils from supposing God to be capable of such a conduct,—a conduct which every correct notion of morality teaches us he would discountenance in any of his creatures. The conclusion, therefore, is inevitable that this prophet was neither a Deity, nor influenced by the Deity, in delivering the predictions under notice. Whether he was so influenced in saying or doing any *other* thing is a question of very little moment in the present inquiry ; for Christianity claims its superiority over all other religions on the ground that its founder was a Divine Being ; and this not being the case, it stands on a level with all other religions. But we have not the least proof that Christ was under divine influence in saying or doing *anything* that he said or did, any more than we have that he was so in uttering the predictions in question. Nor is it very easy to conceive that God would so far perplex and even deceive his creatures as to employ an agent to reveal his will at one time, and at another to leave that agent utterly uncontrolled, so as to speak falsely, and act immorally. We have no evidence whatever that God acts so inconsistently, any more than we have evidence that he *ever yet* employed any man specially to reveal his will.— Presumptive proof and ethics all conspire to confirm our convictions that he never has done and never will do either the one or the other.

Having thus arrived at the conclusion that Christ bore no more relation to God than human beings at large bear, our attention is claimed to several questions which affect his moral and mental character, considered as a mere man. Did he ever pretend that he was a Divine personage, or held supernatural communication with the Deity ? This twofold question must be answered in the affirmative. The passages in the Gospels which represent him as being in supernatural communication with God--if not a God himself—are very numerous. When Peter and others pronounce him the Son of God, he strongly approves of their declaration, and says that he and his Father are *one*. Instances of his arrogating to himself the attributes of Deity are in the Gospels exceedingly numerous, so that, for any reader of the New Testament, it is needless to cite any of them. It is true that he calls himself by the title—*Son of man*,—an appellation, apparently, borrowed from the prophet Daniel, who in a vision saw the Son of man coming in the clouds of heaven. Hence Christ, under this title, arrogates to himself the function of a Judge of all mankind, repeatedly speaking of the Son of man coming in his glory, and all nations being gathered before him. He also claims such a relationship with the Supreme Being as to say—" All things are delivered to *me* of my Father, and no man knoweth the Son but the Father; neither knoweth any man the Father save the Son, and he to whomsoever the Son will reveal him." He very frequently speaks of himself as having come from heaven—from God, and sent by the *only true God*. In a word, the testimony of the Gospels makes it quite clear and undeniable that Christ represented himself as a Divine Being. The next question, therefore, which presents itself, is,—Did he know, or was he conscious that he was *not* a Deity, and had no communication with the Deity ? or did he labour under the mental delusion that he was such a personage ? If he *did* know this, his moral character does not present itself to us in a very favourable light ; but if, like many others before and after him who have made similar claims, he believed that he was what he professed to be, this would acquit him of any motive to deceive; while, however, it would deny him the possession of any moral character at all, either good or bad; and would exonerate him of any moral responsibility to his fellow-men. Whether he was or was not conscious that he was not a Divine Being, is a question difficult to be determined, if we take for our guide the Gospel narratives, and regard them as genuine histories, as has been done throughout this work. It is true that these Gospels inform us that some of the Jews thought that he was *mad*, and laboured under what they called demoniacal possession; and further, that even his own relatives, being of a similar opinion, "went out to lay hold on him," saying, "he is beside himself."* And indeed many of his rash and injudicious acts go very far to substantiate this opinion of his mental state, such as for example, his cursing a fig-tree—an inanimate portion of matter—for having no figs *in the winter ;* his outrageous conduct in entering the temple, on a day of national gathering for religious services, upsetting the tables and seats, and beating out with a whip those who had entered for religious purposes; together with many other acts and expressions which shall be noticed in the sequel.†

Before this point, however, could be decided with any degree of certainty, we should be able to ascertain, not only what is said of Jesus in the Gospels,—not only what he *said* of himself, but also what he *thought of himself.* From many acute expressions in the Gospels, attributed to Jesus, one would infer that his mind was in a perfectly sound state. But most of the expressions in the Gospels indicating the greatest elevation of mind, and possessing the highest moral tone, are such as can be found in pagan lore, existing, with slight verbal alterations, long before the Gospels were extant. Besides: we know that many who have pretended, or perhaps rather imagined themselves to be Messiahs, prophets, deities, &c., were sane on every point but one, namely, that which inspired them with the delusion that they were such characters as they assumed; and spoke on religious matters most feelingly, wisely, and, according to the *received notions* of such religious matters, even sublimely, so as to draw crowds after them, and make many disciples.‡ In the present state of human physiology, it is most difficult to draw a line of demarcation between real, perfect, mental sanity and *insanity* ; and this difficulty increases in regard to a supposed case of insanity on a point of religion. Mahomed, Swedenborg, Joanna Southcott, the Prophet Brothers, Joseph Smith of the present age, with others that could be named of this fanatical class, whose history is well known, can hardly be said to have been insane on any other point than that of *religion*—that of the supernatural—the miraculous; for each of them has said some wise things; and some of them have accomplished tasks which display considerable mental strength. Nor is there anything like positive proof that any of these characters were impostors,—in other words, that they were conscious they were not what they pretended to be, and knew that they were deceiving their followers. That they were

---

* John x. 20.   Mark iii. 21.
† Mark xi. 13, 15.   Matth. xxi. 12.   Luke xix. 45.   John ii. 13—15.
‡ The reader is recommended the perusal of Dr. Cheyne's Essay on Mental Derangement in connection with Religion, Dublin, 1843; the Phrenological Journal, vol. ix. pp. 289, 532, 577; and Dr. A. Coombe's Work on Mental Derangement.

misleading their disciples does not admit of a doubt ; but the question is—
and a question very difficult to be determined—*whether, at the time, they
were conscious that they* were misleading them, or misrepresenting themselves, in regard to the communication they affirmed they held with the
Deity ; or whether they were, at the time, labouring under a mental delusion.
If the latter was the case, although they cannot be held accountable for
their actions, or be said even to possess properly a moral character, yet
they deserve credit for their sincerity; but if the former, they were no
other than impostors. In like manner, if Jesus believed, however erroneously, that he was the person he represented himself, he cannot be called
an impostor ; but if he did not believe this, it is impossible to regard
him either as sincere or innocent. For it would seem impossible for any
one, in a sound state of mind, to represent himself as a prophet commissioned by God to reveal his will and purposes, and to predict future events,
—when in reality he is not such a person,—without *knowing* so, and
without deceiving, or, at best, attempting to deceive. On the other hand,
it would appear impossible for a person who *believed* that he was such,
when he was not, to be in a state of mental sanity, but must be labouring
under a delusion, on this individual point. Since, however, we cannot
ascertain what Christ *thought* of himself, we cannot determine which of the
above characters he bore ; any more than we can ascertain, with precision,
whether Mahomed, Swedenborg, Southcote, Brothers, Joseph Smith, and
others of similar pretensions, really believed that they were supernaturally
influenced,—were inspired men, and were prophets, or knew that they
were impostors. Nor does it make any difference whatever in regard to
the question of the divine origin of Christianity, whether Christ did, or did
not know,—believed, or did not believe, that he was not a Deity, and had no
preternatural communication with God. For the character of the Christian
religion is positively proved to be of human origin, by the indubitable evidence we have of the fact that—whatever Jesus thought or knew of himself
—*he stood in no other relation to the Deity than men generally stand.*

However, by way of showing the inconsistency of Christians, it may
be observed that the founders of the religious sects just named, as well as
those of others who pretended to be divinely inspired prophets,—and who
as such gained the confidence of thousands,—*are believed, by all except
their respective followers, and particularly by those who call themselves
orthodox Christians,* to have been either fanatics or impostors,—to have
either laboured under mental delusion, or to have wilfully deceived. There
is, however, a difference of opinion as to which of these characters they
actually bore ;—some considering them fanatics, and others pronouncing
them impostors ; but all agreeing that they were the one or the other.—
How inconsistent then it is on the part of Christians to denounce these
founders of Faith as either fanatics or impostors, while they contend that
Jesus was neither, and maintain that he was a Divine personage ! Take the
instance of Swedenborg.—If testimony is of any authority, God made
innumerable revelations to him ; he was highly inspired ; he foretold future
events, and read men's hearts. He could tell what was taking place in
distant lands at the moment it was occurring, and could do many other
miraculous things. He was so far from being considered either insane or
deceptive—either a fanatic or an impostor by his followers—that he *was,*

and *is*, to this day, venerated as a man of profound piety, and of highly philosophic knowledge,—a man whose motives were most disinterested and philanthropic, and whose Divine revelations were of the most pure and benevolent tendency. All this, too, is attested by evidence much less objectionable than the Gospel narratives of Jesus. Still, *orthodox* Christians, while they suppose Swedenborg to have been a fanatic or an impostor, deny that Jesus was either, and contend that he was even a Divine being. It is high time for Christians to show to the world upon what grounds they inconsistently claim divinity for Jesus, while they deny that honour to the founders of all other religions, some of which are equally as moral and rational as Christianity.

SECTION II.—THE APOSTLES RATHER THE DECEIVED THAN THE DECEIVERS, IN PROMULGATING THE ERRONEOUS DOCTRINE OF THE NEAR APPROACH OF THE END OF THE WORLD.—NOT NECESSARY TO SUPPOSE THAT, IN THIS AND IN THEIR PRETENCE TO DIVINE INSPIRATION, THEY WERE MORE UNDER THE INFLUENCE OF A RELIGIOUS MANIA THAN OTHER FANATICS.

Another inference deducible from the facts already proved, in this work, as to the incorrectness of Christ's predictions of the Day of Judgment and the End of the World is, *that the Apostles, who* inculcated the near approach of these events, *were either deceivers or were themselves deceived* ; —in other words,—either they believed that the end of the world was at hand, or they imposed this notion upon others, when they did not themselves believe it. If they believed what they inculcated they were honest, although deluded ; but if they did not believe the doctrine they preached, they were what they called others ; namely,—"deceivers." However about other points of Christianity, there is no ground for supposing that the Apostles had any design to deceive, in declaring *that the end of the world was at hand*. It is most probable that they, in common with thousands of others in that age, firmly believed this to be a matter of certainty. For such was the credulity of those times that anything supernatural,—anything which participated of the new, the marvellous, and awful, was believed with avidity, and with very little investigation as to its truth.

Nor is there any necessity to suppose their minds, individually, were affected, in a *particular* manner, with a species of religious mania, before they could have *simply believed* in the near approach of the events they proclaimed, any more than there is to suppose the minds of thousands to be affected who, in the present age, believe in religious things quite as absurd. According to the account given in the New Testament, they stand in a very different light from that in which Jesus is represented, with regard to the supposition that they were either religious madmen, or religious impostors. They were not the originators* of the doctrine of the approaching End of

* The inference one would naturally draw from the Gospels, is that Christ was the originator of the doctrine of the near approach of these events,—that it was he who first predicted them. History, however, teaches us that Christ was, by no means, original on

the World, the Day of Judgment, and the coming of the kingdom of heaven, which they inculcated ;—they were only converts to it, like converts to the religion of the Mussulman, of the Mormonites, or of the Christians of the present day,—all of them creeds which are implicitly believed by millions of people. The Apostles, being persons of excited imaginations, took a leading part in promulgating this doctrine ; and so far were they from disbelieving it, that, being carried onward by circumstances tending to strengthen their faith and make them adhere to what they had already declared, many of them, possibly, died martyrs in its behalf. To account for this without supposing the Apostles to have been religious madmen, the genius of the age and the degree of civilization at which it had arrived, together with other things must be taken into consideration. In those times, a thousand tales of miracles would be circulated and firmly believed, about the Leader of every sect. These would be magnified and multiplied, and would soon become traditional,—would be collected and written down in books, which would be transcribed, improved, and circulated ; the writers, in accordance with the romancing spirit of the age, possibly, being quite unconscious of *fraud*, and having no other aim than to vie with one another in adorning the hero of their tale with every excellent quality imaginable. Hence we find the early literature of Greece, Rome, and every ancient country abounding with such fabulous tales. And hence the Apostles *might*, in regard to the near approach of the end of the world, then generally believed in the land of Judea, have been led to imagine that Jesus, whom we are told most of them had seen, would, according to his promise, quickly come to execute judgment ; and, consequently, *might have been* induced to promulgate this doctrine from purely benevolent motives ; being thus not deceivers, but deceived.

It is difficult, however, to imagine that, being *in a sane state of mind,* they could be *deceived* into the belief that they were actually *inspired men,* miraculously called and appointed by God to promulgate this doctrine, which they termed "the Gospel." On this point the same remarks apply to them as have already been made in reference to the pretended divine mission of Jesus. In the *first* place, God would not inspire them to promulgate falsity,—to proclaim that the end of the world was at hand, which eighteen centuries have proved *untrue.*—*Secondly,* they were, therefore, *not* divinely inspired men.—*Thirdly,* as they all laid claim to divine authority, and pretended to possess miraculous power, and other things calculated to make their followers believe that they held direct communication with God, the conclusion is irresistible that—either they were fully aware that they held no such communication with God, and were deceiving their followers ; or that, if they believed they held such supernatural communication with

these points—that the end of the world, the day of judgment, and the kingdom of heaven were thought close at hand long before the time he is said to have lived. It is true that these notions appear to have been revived and to have undergone some alterations, as to details, about this period. In no other sense than the foregoing can Jesus be said to be their originator, any more than his Apostles who afterwards preached them. But as the New Testament represents Christ as in more immediate connection with the Deity than the Apostles,—nay as a Deity, for whom to err it is impossible ; the Apostles, on this consideration, stood in a very different position, with reference to the manifest incorrectness of their notions touching the end of the world, and the inferences deducible from this incorrectness ; for "to err is human," &c.

the Deity, they were labouring under mental delusion ; that is, they must either have been impostors or fanatics.* They might, truly, participate of

* There are, indeed, in the Acts of the Apostles, strong proofs that both they and their converts were under the influence of a wild fanaticism, or religious frenzy. (See Notes on the Visions of Peter and Paul, page 204.) What is said to have descended on the people at the day of Pentecost, and called the " Holy Ghost," or, literally translated, the holy *wind*, or *gust*—termed " a rushing mighty wind, filling the house where they were sitting," and accompanied with the appearance of " cloven tongues like as of fire," which " sat upon each of them," so as to make them " speak with other tongues"—speak incoherent jargon that belonged to no language whatever—was nothing but an indication of religious frenzy. (Acts ii. 1—13.) It is, however, to be observed that the influence of the Holy Ghost is repeatedly described as being no other than to speak thus " with tongues."—When Peter preached to Cornelius and his company, the Holy Ghost fell on all of them, so as to make them " speak with tongues, and magnify God." (Acts x. 44—46.) When Paul laid his hands on certain disciples of John at Ephesus, " the Holy Ghost came upon them, and they spake with tongues, and prophesied." (Acts xix. 6.) Christ promises that those who believed should " speak with tongues." (Mark xvi. 17.) Paul very frequently refers to the same faculty by the phrases—" speaking with tongues"—" gift of tongues"—" unknown tongues," and so on ; (See 1 Cor. xii. 10 ; xiii. 1, 8 ; xiv. 2, 5, 9, 13 – 27.) meaning, evidently, the same as that spoken of in the Acts. It is clear from many of Paul's expressions, in his Epistle to the Corinthians, just cited, that to speak with tongues was not to preach in a foreign language, but to utter some incoherent sounds, not intelligible in any language ; and he also intimates that this practice of speaking with tongues had become a subject of ridicule to unbelievers.—For he asks;—" If the whole church be come together into one place, and all speak with tongues, and there come in unlearned men, or unbelievers, will they not say *ye are mad ?*".. ....." If any man speak in an unknown tongue, let it be by two, or at the most by three, and that by course, and let one interpret.".........." For God is not the author of *confusion*, but of peace." (1 Cor. xiv. 23, 27, 33, 39, 40.) There is very little doubt that these tongues were the unintelligible sounds which the early Christians uttered when, in an assembled state, they were under the influence of religious frenzy, similar to that into which, as already described, the ancient prophets wrought themselves. Mr. Greg, in his able criticism on " the Gift of Tongues," has the following just remarks. —" It is, we think, almost impossible to read the whole of the three chapters from which the above citations were made, (1 Cor. xii. xiii. xiv.) without coming to the conclusion that, in the early Christian church, there were a number of weak, mobile, imaginative minds, who, over-excited by the sublimity of the new doctrine expounded to them, and by the stirring eloquence of its preachers, passed the faint and undefinable line which separates enthusiasm from delirium, and gave vent to their exultation, in incoherent or inarticulate utterances, which the compassionate sympathy, or the consanguineous fancies of those around them, dignified with the description of speaking, or prophesying, in an unknown tongue. No one familiar with physiology, and medical or religious history, can be ignorant how contagious delusions of this nature always prove, and when once these incoherences became the recognised sign of the descent of the Spirit, every one would, of course, be anxious to experience, and to propagate them. We have seen the same thing precisely, in our own day, among the Irvingites. How is it, then, that the same phenomena of mental weakness and excitement which, in the one case, aroused only pity and contempt, should in the other be regarded with a mysterious reverence and awe ?.. ....That there was a vast amount of delusion and unsound enthusiasm in the Christian church at the time of the Apostles, not only seems certain, but it could not possibly have been otherwise, without such an interference with the ordinary operations of natural causes as would have amounted to an incessant miracle. Wonders, real or supposed, were of daily occurrence. The subjects habitually brought before the contemplation of believers, were of such exciting and sublime magnificence that even the strongest minds cannot too long dwell upon them without some degree of perilous emotion. The recent events which closed the life of the Founder of their Faith, and above all, the glorious truth, or the splendid fiction, of his resurrection and ascension, were depicted with all the exaggerating grandeur of oriental imagination. The expectation of an almost immediate end of the world, and the reception into glory and power of the living believer, —the hope which each one entertained, of being " caught up" to meet his Redeemer in

both these qualities. For there are, decidedly, cases on record of fanatics whose character was a compound of imposture and mental derangement.

the clouds—was of itself sufficient to overthrow all but the coldest tempers; while the constant state of mental tension in which they were kept by the antagonism and persecution of the world without, could not fail to maintain a degree of exultation very unfavourable to sobriety either of thought or feeling. All these influences, too, were brought to bear upon minds the most ignorant and unprepared, upon the poor and the oppressed, upon women and children; and to crown the whole, the most prominent doctrine of their faith was that of the immediate, special, and hourly influence of the Holy Spirit— a doctrine of all others the most liable to utter and gross misconception, and the most apt to lead to perilous mental excitement. Hence, they were constantly on the look-out for miracles. Their creed did not supply, and indeed scarcely admitted, any criterion of what was of divine origin—for who could venture to pronounce or define how the Spirit might or should manifest itself?—and thus ignorance and folly too often became the arbiters of wisdom—and the ravings of delirium were listened to as the words of inspiration, and of God.......We are driven, then, to the painful, but unavoidable conclusion, that those mysterious and unintelligible utterances which the Apostles and the early Christians generally looked upon as the effects of the Holy Ghost—the manifestations of its presence—the signs of its operation—the especial indication and criterion of its having fallen upon any one—were in fact simply the physiologically natural results of morbid and perilous cerebral exultation, induced by strong religious excitement acting on uncultivated and susceptible minds;—results which in all ages and nations have followed in similar circumstances and from similar stimuli."—*Creed of Christendom*, pp. 175—178.

Mr. Greg, in the above valuable work, has the following note on p. 175.—"Somewhat similar phenomena have manifested themselves on several occasions in the course of the last eight hundred years, and even in our own day, when religious excitement has proved too strong for weak minds or sensitive frames to bear without giving way. We find them recorded in the case of the ecstatics of Cevennes, who underwent severe persecution in France after the revocation of the Edict of Nantes, and among the *convulsionnaires* of St. Medard near the close of last century. Both these cases are examined in considerable detail in a very curious and valuable work by Bertrand, a French physician, " Sur les Vâriétés de l'Extase" (pp. 323, 359.) But our own country has presented us, within a few years, with a reproduction of precisely the same results arising from similar causes. There is extant a very remarkable and painfully-interesting pamphlet by a Mr. Baxter, who was at one time a shining light in Mr. Irving's congregation, and a great "speaker with tongues," in which he gives a detailed account of all the accompanying phenomena. It was written after he had recovered; though he never relinquished his belief in the supernatural nature of these utterances, but finally concluded them to be from Satan, on the ground of some of the speakers uttering what he thought false doctrine. The description he gives of his own state and that of others during the visitations indicate, in a manner that no physiologist can mistake, a condition of cerebral excitement verging on hysteria and madness, and by no means uncommon. Sometimes, when praying, his shrieks were so loud that he was compelled to "thrust his handkerchief into his mouth that he might not alarm the house." Others fell down "convulsed and foaming like demoniacs."— " My whole body was violently agitated ; for the space of ten minutes I was paralyzed under a shaking of my limbs, and no expression except a convulsive sigh." His friends " remarked on his excited state of mind." A servant was taken out of his house deranged, and pronounced by the tongues to be possessed by a devil. Another "speaker with tongues" did nothing but mutter inarticulate nonsense with a " most revolting expression of countenance." Mr. Baxter says that the utterances which were urged upon him by " the power," were sometimes intelligible, sometimes not, sometimes French, sometimes Latin, and sometimes in languages which he did not know, but which his wife thought to be Spanish. He says, at last, " My persuasion concerning the unknown tongue is that it is *no language whatever*, but a mere collection of words and sentences, often a mere jargon of sounds." One man seldom began to speak without the contagion seizing upon others, so that numbers spoke at once, as in Paul's time. It is clear to any one who reads Mr. Baxter's candid and unpretending narrative, that a skilful physician would at once have terminated the whole delusion by a liberal exhibition of phlebotomy and anodynes."

Amongst the various religious sects in Wales, displays of fanaticism bearing most of

Paul's vision in which he saw " a light from heaven above the brightness of the sun," and heard a voice saying, " why persecutest thou me ?" is very much like the spectral and auricular illusions of modern times, to which

the features of the foregoing have been witnessed *frequently*, even during the last thirty years ; and before that period they were of much *more frequent* occurrence. They are regarded as the effects of the outpourings of the Holy Ghost upon the churches, and called *diwigiadau*,—a word which signifies revivals. They are always the means of add-ing immense numbers to the churches ; and most generally take place, or at least are commenced, under the ministry of the most eloquent and enthusiastic preachers,—those who are capable of getting what the people, in their vernacular language, call *hwyl*, in preaching ; in other words, of carrying such an effect upon their hearers as to make them display a degree of religious enthusiasm. Welsh preaching has always been remarkable for its fiery character. This religious fanaticism is evidently contagious in its effects. If there happens to be in a congregation a person of an uncommonly excit-able temperament, and his religious feelings are powerfully addreseed by a fiery preacher, there is a fair chance of conjuring up this fanaticism into action. Once a single indi-vidual is under its influence, others are quickly affected with it, so that sometimes it runs with amazing rapidity through a whole congregation, carrying the stronger effect upon those whose cerebral developments are evidently the more susceptible of it. These mani-festations of religious madness, in general, proceed gradually, from a very low beginning, till they arrive at the highest possible pitch of frenzy. They are generally commenced by some old saint suddenly bawling out such words as—*diolch!* (praise) *bendigedig!* (blessed) or *Amen :* or by the howling and weeping of a female, during the time the preacher pours forth his sermon in thrilling eloquence. When he hears these signs that his preaching takes effect, he is thereby stimulated, and carries a much stronger influence. A second person begins to weep, or bawl out *" diolch!"* or *" bendigedig!"* then a third, a fourth, a fifth, and so on, till very soon not a word the preacher says can be heard,—all are in confusion ; some singing hymns, some throwing their arms about, clapping their hands, and uttering expressions of praise ; some jumping about and treading on one another's toes ; some weeping, and, with floods of tears flowing from their eyes, uttering expressions of despair about being saved, because their sins are so great.—Females shriek ; sometimes they lay hold of each other in endearment ; at other times, they tear their own clothes to pieces, and even pluck off the hair of their heads. They thus work themselves up into a state of frenzy, or religious hysteria, till at last they faint ; when, if any of their friends are sufficiently free from the influence of the same madness, they are carried from the chapel into the open air, foaming at the mouth, and presenting the most revolting spectacle. All those who happen to fall into these religious fits of madness are considered to be under the influence of the Holy Ghost,—to have been converted ; and, generally, at the end of the service, are received into the *" Society,"* which, at the close of these meetings, is purposely held in order to receive new converts. In this frenzy, many persons continue to repeat the same particular word for a great number of times, till their articulation becomes entirely unintelligible ; others continually mutter some words the meaning of which cannot be understood, much resembling Mr. Baxter's jargon. At these revivals, it frequently happens in a prayer meeting that some reli-giously excited member, when engaged in prayer, works himself into such a degree of madness that he can be heard at an inconceivable distance, and will infect others with his religious fury, so as to create a scene of indescribable confusion, such as these prayer meetings have produced a thousand times. Scenes similar to these the writer, some twenty years ago, witnessed in chapels then under the care of the Rev. David Williams, a most eloquent preacher, at Troed-rhiw-dalar, Llanwrtyd, and other chapels in that part of Breconshire. Perhaps that is the last revival of any note that has happened amongst the Independents. But these manifestations of religious madness occur quite as often among the other two prevalent sects in Wales—the Baptists and Calvinistic Methodists. In the time of the Rev. Howell Harris, the founder of the latter, its members were so much under the influence of religious madness, particularly that of jumping, that they were designated by some of the other sects—" the Jumpers." The writer cites no authority for the foregoing descriptions of religious frenzy in Wales. He has many times witnessed such scenes ; and every one acquainted with religion in Wales, for the last forty years, knows that much more might be said of the madness of its votaries. England, a century or two ago, in many places, bore the same character.

some people are subject when their brains are in an unsound state. Peter's vision when, in a trance, he saw a certain vessel descending from heaven, and heard a voice saying, "Arise Peter, slay and eat," was also of the same character.* Both are also similar in character to visions that persons whom Christians would call fanatics have had. Mahomed had a vision when, like Peter, he was praying; and, like Paul, saw a flood of light fall upon him, with such inconceivable splendour that he swooned away; and he also saw an angel who showed him a cloth with written characters, and said to him "Read!"† Swedenborg and Joseph Smith likewise had several visions. If these visions, therefore, are signs of a divine mission, they are by no means peculiar to the Apostles. It is, however, difficult to determine whether either Paul, Peter, Mahomed, or Joe Smith, ever really had such visions. All we know is that they are *reported* to have had them. If they had, the fact furnishes presumptive proof that such visions are peculiar to fanatics. If they never had such visions, it proves they are more addicted to knavery than subject to spectral illusions. In the case of Paul and Peter,‡ however, these visions, whether experienced or pretended to have been experienced, do not prove a call from God; for we find that, in obedience to the call they imagined or pretended to have had, they preached the kingdom of heaven, which, in other words, as we have seen, means that the End of the World was *not* then at hand, and is not even yet at hand, we may, therefore, with the greatest certainty, conclude that *God did not call upon them* to promulgate a falsehood. As in the case of Christ, it is a point of perfect indifference with regard to the character of *Christianity*, whether the Apostles were the deluded or the deluders; since it is certain they were not influenced by God in their sayings or doings. For we may rest assured that God never —either in a vision or otherwise—prompted men to deceive, alarm, and reduce to despair their poor and confiding fellow-creatures. In addition to

---

* Acts x. 10; ix.; xi.; xii. 17; xxvi.

† Irving's Life of Mahomed, p. 32. Bohn's Edit.

‡ Peter and Paul fell into a *trance*, a state of the cerebral system, which will, on all hands, be admitted to be unsound. If, therefore, in *a trance*, they must be in an unsound state of mind. In regard to Paul's vision, there is a material difference between the account we have of it by the writer of the Acts of the Apostles, where he narrates the circumstance of the conversion of Paul, (ix. 3—26.) and where he pretends to report Paul's speech, detailing the circumstances of his own conversion. (xxii. 6—19.) In the latter narrative Paul says that, some time after he had seen the first vision, he went to Jerusalem, and that while he was praying in the temple he fell into a trance. (ver. 18.) Paul's account of his own conversion must be preferable to that given by the writer of the Acts, which was only second-hand. Paul says that, upon his miraculous conversion, he retired into seclusion to meditate upon the change which had been wrought in him. He more than once speaks of trances and visions he had had; such as that which he had when he was caught up to the third heaven. It was only natural and agreeable to the known laws of physiology that Paul should be subject to these visions. A man of an ardent and excitable temperament retiring to the solitude and seclusion of an Arabian hermitage, to spend his time in fasting and meditating upon supernatural things, would, in any country, but more particularly in the East, be likely to work himself into such a state of mind, if already possessed of a cerebral development predisposed to illusions. It was very possible for Paul under these circumstances to regard these hallucinations as supernatural visions, and perhaps difficult for him to distinguish them from such. Compare Acts ix. xxii. xxvi. Gal. ii. 1, 11, 15—19. Eph. iii. 3. 2 Cor. xii. 1—7. And see Greg's Creed of Christendom, pp. 186—190.

this proof, it may be remarked that it is not very probable that the all-wise God would have chosen to communicate his will to the mind of man in a trance, or a dream,—when, unquestionably, it is in its most imperfect state, —when the phantasy is rampant and the judgment torpid and in abeyance. It is only reasonable to suppose that, if ever God wished to make the mind of man the medium of the communication of his will, he would employ it when in its most perfect state—not when "in a dream, in a vision of the night, when deep sleep falleth upon man."* Man never should imagine his Maker in action but in a manner worthy of his Divine attributes; otherwise a blasphemous and immoral result is inevitable.

SECTION III.—THE DOCTRINE OF THE APPROACHING END OF THE WORLD CALCULATED TO EXCITE THE FEAR OF IGNORANT PEOPLE AND MAKE THEM EMBRACE CHRISTIANITY IN ORDER TO SECURE THEIR OWN SAFETY.— THE PANIC WHICH THIS DOCTRINE CREATED IN THE TENTH CENTURY.— THE APOSTOLIC SERMONS AND MIRACLES CREATED FEAR OF THE MUNDANE DESTRUCTION, AND THEREBY PROMOTED THE SPREAD OF CHRISTIANITY.

Since the totality of the Gospel was, as we have seen—the End of the World—the Final Judgment—and the kingdom of heaven, with its life eternal to those admitted into it, but endless torments to those who should be excluded—were close at hand, it follows, as a necessary consequence, that people, in vast numbers, should accept with avidity the advantages held forth to them by this Gospel. Hence, not only the circumstances under which Christianity was first promulgated, but the very nature of its doctrines sufficiently accounts for the great success which we are told attended it in its primitive state, and which Christians parade as a proof of its divine origin. This great success, however—even assuming the full extent of what is said of it—is only the natural consequence of things, and —as will be shown in the sequel—is far from being without a parallel, in cases where no supernatural influence can be supposed to have existed.— Let any one picture in his mind the effect which such a doctrine as that preached by Christ and his Apostles must produce on a community of people credulous enough to believe that it was true. Then will he per- ceive that it must, in an ignorant and superstitious age, create a general panic,—strike terror into every heart, and make all anxious to secure their personal safety. Christ made his appearance as a person sent from God, —a thing in those times believed to be frequently the case.—He declared that the final judgment and the end of the world would take place during the lifetime of the generation of men then existing,—that he was the per- sonage who was to execute that judgment, and to cause the destruction of the universe,—that he was divinely commissioned to create new heavens and a new earth,—that in this new world he would establish an everlasting kingdom,—that all persons who believed in him as the prince of that

* See Greg's Creed of Christendom, p. 232,

kingdom, and would there and then join his cause, would be admitted into it, and should enjoy therein eternal life, with every imaginable bliss; but that all who opposed his claims—all his enemies should be consumed in unquenchable fire. Such was the tenour of the doctrine which Christ taught,—such also that of the doctrine taught by the Apostles after his death, who persisted in inculcating that these events were *close at hand.* Such soul-stirring doctrine, once it had begun to take hold on the minds of ignorant and credulous people, must have created a most terrific sensation,—must have excited in all who believed it the most intense anxiety, and wildest alarm for their personal safety,—an instinctive principle of self-preservation common both to man and the brute creation. In order that the reader may have a proof, *founded upon fact,* of the effect such a belief must have had upon society, the following authentic extracts are laid before him, whence he will perceive the state of a community of people under a groundless belief that the End of the World was at hand.

Mr. Waddington, a writer who cannot for a moment be supposed adverse to the interests of Christianity, in his *History of the Church,* speaking of an occurrence which took place only 897 years ago, or nearly a thousand years after Christ, says that "a very wild and extraordinary delusion arose and spread itself, and at length so far prevailed as not only to subdue the reason, but to actuate the conduct of vast multitudes. About the year 960, one Bernhard, a hermit of Thesingia, boldly promulgated (on the faith of a particular revelation from God) the certain assurance that, at the end of the thousandth year mentioned in the Book of Revelation, (xx. 2, 3.) the fetters of Satan should be broken, and after the reign of Antichrist should be terminated, the world should be consumed with a sudden conflagration. The clergy, without delay, adopted the doctrine; the pulpits loudly resounded with it; it was diffused in every direction with astonishing rapidity, and embraced with an ardour proportioned to the obscurity of the subject and the greediness of human credulity. The belief pervaded every rank, not as a cold and indifferent assent, but as a motive for the most important undertakings. Many, among whom were bishops, nobles, princes, abandoned their friends and their families, and hastened to the shores of Palestine, with the pious persuasion that Mount Sion would be the throne of Christ when he should descend to judge the world; and these, in order to secure a more partial sentence from the God of mercy and charity, usually made over their property, before they departed, to some adjacent church or monastery. Others whose pecuniary means were thought, perhaps, insufficient to bribe the justice of heaven, devoted their personal service to the same establishments, and resigned their very liberty to those holy mediators, whose pleadings, they doubted not, would find favour at the eternal judgment-seat. Others permitted their lands to lie waste and their houses to decay, or terrified by some unusual phenomenon in the heaven, betook themselves in hasty flight to the shelter of rocks and caverns, as if the temple of nature was destined to preservation, amidst the wreck of man and his works." Our historian goes on to state that " the year of terror arrived and passed away without any extraordinary convulsion,"—that the people returned to their homes,—repaired their buildings, and resumed their former occupations; and the only lasting effect of this stupendous panic was the augmentation of the temporal prosperity of the church."* Dr. Mosheim, another Christian writer of no small eminence, describes the same religious panic, somewhat more at large, as follows :— " Among these opinions, which dishonoured so frequently the Latin church, and produced from time to time such violent agitations, none occasioned such a general panic, or such dreadful impressions of terror or dismay, as a notion that now prevailed of the immediate approach of the day of judgment. This notion, which took its rise from a remarkable passage in the Revelation of John, and had been entertained by some doctors in the preceding century, was advanced publicly by many at this time, and, spreading itself with an amazing rapidity through the European provinces, it threw them into the deepest consternation and anguish; for they imagined that St. John had clearly foretold that, after a thousand years from the birth of Christ, Satan was to be let loose from his prison ; that Antichrist was to come ; and the conflagration and destruction of the world were to follow these great and terrible events. Hence prodigious numbers of people abandoned all their civil connexions and their parental relations, and, giving over to the churches or monasteries all their lands, treasures, and worldly effects, repaired with the utmost precipitation to Palestine, where they imagined Christ would descend from heaven to judge the world. Others devoted themselves by a solemn and voluntary oath to the service of the churches, convents, and priesthood, whose slaves they became, in the most rigorous sense of that word, performing daily their heavy tasks ; and all this from a notion that the supreme Judge would diminish the severity of their sentence, and look upon them with a more favourable and propitious eye, on account of their having made themselves the slaves of his ministers. When an eclipse of the sun or moon happened to be visible,† the cities were deserted, and their miserable inhabitants fled for refuge to deep caverns, and hid themselves among the craggy rocks and under the bending summits of steep mountains. The opulent attempted to bribe the Deity and the saintly tribe, by rich donations conferred upon the sacerdotal and monastic orders, who were looked upon as the immediate vicegerents of heaven. In many places, temples, palaces, and noble edifices, both public and private, were suffered to decay, and were even deliberately pulled down, from a notion that they were no longer of any use, since the final dissolution of all things approached. In a word, no language is sufficient to express the confusion and despair that tormented the minds of miserable mortals upon this occasion. This general delusion was indeed opposed and combatted by the discerning few, who endeavoured to dispel these groundless terrors, and to efface the notion from which they arose, in the minds of the people. But their attempts were ineffectual ; nor could the dreadful apprehensions of the superstitious multitude be entirely removed before the conclusion of this century. Then, when they saw that the so much dreaded period had passed without the arrival of any great calamity, they began to understand that St. John had not really foretold what they

* See Waddington's *History of the Church*, p. 260. Edit. Library of Useful Knowledge, where Hist. Litt. de la France X. Siècle, and other authorities are cited.

† This must be in consequence of their understanding Christ's words in regard to the sun, moon, and stars, in the Gospels, to refer to the end of the world ; for the passage in Revelation makes no mention of any disruption in the celestial bodies.

so much feared.* The number of saints who were looked upon as ministers of the kingdom of heaven, and whose patronage was esteemed such an unspeakable blessing, had now an extraordinary increase, and the celestial courts were filled with new legions of this species of beings, some of which, as we have had formerly occasion to observe, had no existence but in the imagination of their deluded clients and worshippers. This multiplication of saints may be easily accounted for, when we consider that superstition, the source of fear, had risen to such an enormous height, in this age, as rendered the creation of new patrons necessary to calm the anxiety of trembling mortals."†

Such were the effects of preaching the doctrine of the end of the world in Europe, in the tenth century, and such we are justified to infer were the effects of preaching the same doctrine in Judea and other Eastern countries, in the first centuries of Christianity. Men, by thousands, became converts to it *from fear*. With the exception that the diffusion of sound philosophical knowledge may make men a little less superstitious in one age than in another, human nature is the same in every age, and the report which was believed by thousands, that the end of the world was to take place last summer, might, with a little aid from the clergy, easily have been circulated to such an extent, and credited with such positiveness, as to throw society into a similar panic and terror to those of the tenth century. The picture, therefore, given in the foregoing extracts will greatly assist us, by way of analogy, in judging of the effect that the inculcation of the doctrine of the End of the World and its concomitants, by Christ and his Apostles, must have had in spreading Christianity. Let any one imagine himself firmly believing that, *positively*, *within his lifetime*, this world is to become one mass of flaming fire,—that he does not know but that the next moment this will take place,—when the judge of all the earth appears in the clouds of heaven, with an innumerable company of angels rending the air with the terrible sound of trumpets, and calling the living and the dead unto judgment,—when he, with the rest of the human race, is ushered before the heavenly tribunal,—when all the secrets of his life are laid open, and his final doom is fixed.—Let him further imagine that before this judge thus makes his appearance there is offered to him a guarantee of entrance

---

* Dr. Mosheim has the following note.—"Almost all the donations that were made to the church during this century, carry evident marks of this groundless panic that had seized all the European nations; as the reasons of these donations are generally expressed in the following words,—*Apropinquante mundi termino*, &c. i. e. *the end of the world being now at hand*, &c. Among the many undeniable testimonies that we have from ancient records of this universal delusion, that was so profitable to the sacerdotal order, we shall confine ourselves to the quotation of one very remarkable passage in the *Apologeticum* of Abbo, abbot of *Fleury*, *adversus Arnulphum*, i. e. Arnoul, bishop of *Orleans*; which apology is published by the learned Francis Pithou, in the *Codex Canonum* Ecclesiæ Romanæ, p. 401. The words of Abbo are as follows—' De fine quoque mundi coram populo sermonem in ecclesia Parisiorum adolescentulus audivi, quod statim finito mille annorum numero Antichristus adveniret, et non longo post tempore universale judicium succederet; qui predicationi ex evangeliis ac Apocalypsi, et libro Danielis, qua potui virtute restiti. Denique et errorem, qui de fine mundi inolevit, abbas meus beatæ memoriæ Richardus, sagaci animo propulit, postquam literas a Lothariensibus accepit, quibus me respondere jussit. Nam fama pæne totum mundum impleverat, quod, quando annunciatio Dominica in Parasceve contigisset absque ullo scrupulo finis sæculi esset.' "

† Mosheim's Ecclesiastical History, cent. x. part ii. chap. iii. sec. 3, 4.

into a kingdom to be established hereafter, in which there is to be enjoyed an endless life of perfect bliss, on the single and simple condition that he will now join those who proclaim the promise of such a felicity ; but that to all those who refuse this offer there is prepared eternal torments in a lake of ever-burning fire and brimstone, where the vials of the wrath of the indignant prince of the kingdom to be established, are poured down upon his enemies, without any intermission, for ever and ever ! What terror ! what consternation ! must such a belief strike into the stoutest heart ! What horror any man, labouring under such a belief, must feel coming upon him ! What shivering dread overwhelms him ! How he must shudder, and stand aghast at the idea of dwelling for ever in an ocean of fire, and of being fed with ever-burning but unconsumed sulphur ! How this awful prospect must instantly make him embrace the opportunity now offered him, not only of escaping these unequalled and interminable torments, but of securing for himself a kingdom that cannot be shaken, an unfading crown of glory, and every pleasure and happiness that he can desire, for eternal ages, by simply joining the promulgators of this doctrine ! How strongly must such a doctrine work upon the fears and the hopes of a man —especially a credulous and superstitious man—so as to make him forth-with become a Christian, even at the risk of forfeiting all other interests, however valuable, and of tearing asunder all other ties, however dear to him !

Let us further think of the influence which even but few men—once persuaded into this belief—must have upon others in a superstitious age and country, where such a doctrine is solemnly inculcated ; and how such a belief would rapidly gain ground, by the well-known secret influence which the feelings of one human being have upon those of another, so as to make the religious panic spread with the utmost rapidity ! How the influence of such a doctrine must increase ! how the converts to Christianity must daily multiply ! how a whole nation, however numerous, would be thrown into the most painful consternation, or in other words, become Christians, anxious to escape the wrath to come, and pressing with all their might to the kingdom of heaven ! How such men would cast aside and even despise all earthly enjoyments as dross,—earthly cares, as follies,—and earthly thoughts and feelings as less than vanity ! The approaching end of the world, the final judgment, the everlasting kingdom prepared for the elect, and the eternal fire in store for the wicked, would every morning be the subjects of their first waking thoughts, and every night the theme of their last slumbering contemplations. These would form their topic of conver-sation with all they met. This world, with its varied scenes of joy and grief, pleasure and pain, *which passed away*, would have no place in their minds,—their thoughts would be wholly engrossed with the things of "the world to come." To them, the society of those whom they once loved as their own lives would become valueless and even disagreeable. Their minds being concentrated upon the *delusion* that, in a very short time, the earth and the works therein would be burnt up—that the Lord would appear in the air—and that new heavens and a new earth would be created, the ties of marriage, kindred, and friendship—the strongest affections, the purest pleasures of this world, would by them be totally disregarded, and every attempt at enticing them with any earthly object must be regarded by them as outright madness ! This is the state of mind in which a

P

community of people labouring under these delusions must invariably exist. Is it therefore any wonder that the Gospel, on its first promulgation, should have met with extraordinary success?   The fear of the approaching calamity must inevitably have cast the deepest gloom over society, and thrown all persons into the greatest perplexity—a perplexity which naturally prompted them to conform to any thing they thought likely to save them from perishing in the universal catastrophe, alleged and believed to await all those who opposed themselves to the prince of the kingdom of heaven.

Accordingly, we find that when Peter, on the day of Pentecost, had preached the End of the World, speaking of the darkening of the heavenly bodies, dwelling upon Christ the Judge of the world, and exhorting his hearers to *save themselves*, not less than *three thousand* became Christians ; —*fear having come upon every soul.** The same preacher, having in the next sermon spoken of Jesus Christ whom the heavens must contain till the restitution of all things, or in other words, to the end of the world, converted not less than *five thousand*.† Mr. Gibbon, in commenting upon the early success of Christianity, justly observes that " the careless polytheist, assailed by new and unexpected terrors against which neither his priests nor his philosophers could afford him any certain protection, was very frequently terrified and subdued by the menace of eternal tortures.— His fears might assist the progress of his faith and reason ; and if he could once persuade himself to suspect that the Christian religion might possibly be true, it became an easy task to convince him that it was the safest and most prudent part that he could possibly embrace."‡ In the Gospels we have abundant proof that Christ made use of the same incentives.—Hell fire, unquenchable fire, weeping, wailing, gnashing of teeth, and outer darkness, were to be the portion of those who did not believe him; but a kingdom, thrones, eternal life, and every imaginable bliss were promised those who became his disciples.   A doctrine which held forth eternal life, with every happiness man is capable of enjoying, to all who would embrace it, and threatened everlasting punishment, with all the horrors the human mind can picture, to all who should reject it, must, in its very nature, have had the strongest possible influence upon the hopes and fears of the people to whom it was addressed. Those who *believed* this doctrine were to be *saved*, but those who *believed not* were to be *damned*. The *good*, the *watchful*, those who *continued to the end*, were to be *saved*—were to have *deliverance, salvation*, and so on. Any one that believed *should not perish* in the general conflagration of the world, but *should have everlasting life* in the kingdom of heaven.§ The whole tenour of the Gospels and the Epistles bears out the truth of Mr. Gibbon's remarks that " when the promise of eternal happiness was proposed to mankind on condition of adopting the faith and of observing the precepts of the Gospel, it is no wonder that so advantageous an offer should have been accepted by great numbers of every religion, of every rank, and of every province in the Roman empire. The ancient Christians were animated by a contempt for their present existence, and by a just confidence of immortality, of which the doubtful and imperfect faith of modern ages cannot give us any adequate notion."‖

* Acts ii.   † iii.; iv.   ‡ Decline and Fall, chap. xv. sec. 2.
§ Mark xvi. 16. John iii 15, 16, 36. Acts iv. 12. Rom. ii. 3, 10, 16. 2 Thess. i. 5—10.
‖ Decline and Fall, chap. xv. sec. 2.

In connection with the preaching of this doctrine of eternal rewards and punishments was the pretended working of miracles, which in this credulous age—wherein miracles were generally and firmly believed to be a sure sign of heavenly authority—had a most powerful effect upon the weak, mobile, and imaginative people to whom they were presented, and most materially strengthened their faith in the truth of the wonderful things which the first preachers of Christianity told them must shortly come to pass. Besides the report of the "cloven tongues like as of fire," which are said to have descended on the Apostles, and made them "speak with other tongues," and still be understood in their respective vernacular languages, by people of different, nay "of every nation under heaven" who were present, so as to cause them all to be amazed,—besides all this, we say, it was doubtless soon "noised abroad" that *life* and *death* were in Peter's hand,—that by his simple rebuke Ananias and his wife had fallen down dead,—that by his bare word Tabitha had risen from death into life, —and that also Paul, as well as Peter, had such supernatural powers at his command, that for him only to say to " a cripple from his mother's womb, who never had walked,"—" Stand upright on thy feet,"—the cripple forthwith " leaped and walked," so as to make the spectators exclaim—" The Gods are come down to us in the likeness of men."* Mr. Gibbon, in his usually inoffensive style, thus speaks of miracles in the primitive ages of Christianity.—" The supernatural gifts which even in this life were ascribed to the Christians above the rest of mankind, must have conduced to their own comfort, and very frequently to the conviction of infidels. Besides the occasional prodigies, which might sometimes be effected by the immediate interposition of the Deity, when he suspended the laws of nature for the service of religion, the Christian church, from the time of the Apostles and their first disciples, has claimed an uninterrupted succession of miraculous powers......... The expulsion of the demons from the bodies of those unhappy persons whom they had been permitted to torment, was considered as a signal though ordinary triumph of religion, and is repeatedly alleged, by the ancient apologists, as the most convincing evidence of the truth of Christianity. The awful ceremony was usually performed in a public manner, and in the presence of a great number of spectators; the patient was relieved by the power or skill of the exorcist, and the vanquished demon was heard to confess that he was one of the fabled gods of antiquity who had impiously usurped the adoration of mankind." The elegant writer, from whom we quote, having shown the groundless belief of the early Christians in miracles, proceeds to remark that " credulity performed the office of faith, fanaticism was permitted to assume the language of inspiration, and the effects of accident or contrivance were ascribed to supernatural causes. . . . . . The most curious or the most credulous among the Pagans were often persuaded to enter into a society which asserted an actual claim of miraculous powers. The primitive Christians perpetually trod on mystic ground, and their minds were exercised by the habits of believing the most extraordinary events. They felt, or they fancied, that on every side they were incessantly assaulted by demons, comforted by visions, instructed by prophecy, and surprisingly delivered from danger, sickness, and from death

---

* Acts ii. 3; v. 1—11; ix. 34—41; xiv. 10, 11.

itself, by the supplications of the church. The real or imaginary prodigies of which they so frequently conceived themselves to be the objects, the instruments, or the spectators, very happily disposed them to adopt, with the same ease, but with far greater justice, the authentic wonders of the evangelic history; and thus miracles that exceeded not the measure of their own experience, inspired them with the most lively assurance of mysteries which were acknowledged to surpass the limits of their understanding. It is this deep impression of supernatural truth, which has been so much celebrated under the name of faith; a state of mind described as the surest pledge of the Divine favour and future felicity, and recommended as the first, perhaps the only merit of a Christian."* The power of working miracles which the Apostles pretended to possess was so admirably calculated to produce faith, that, upon the occasions of performing these feats, almost invariably a great number of converts were made to Christianity.—— On one occasion there happened a contest in the art of casting out demons between Paul and certain Jewish exorcists, who took upon themselves to command the evil spirits, in the name of Jesus, to come out of men. The demons, however, would not listen to these pseudo-exorcists. In one instance of a signal failure of this kind, a demon caused the demoniac to "leap on" these quacks, overcome them, and make them run away "naked and wounded," while the demon within the demoniac exclaimed,——"Jesus I know, and Paul I know; but who are ye?" When this became known to the Jews and Greeks, "*fear* fell on them all, and the name of the Lord Jesus was magnified; and *many* that *believed* came, and *confessed*, and shewed their deeds."† So much was the power of working miracles thought of, that, when one Simon, a *sorcerer*, having *believed*, having been *baptised*, and having, with *wonder*, observed "the miracles and signs which were done," had at length perceived that one of these miracles, namely, the giving of the Holy Ghost, was performed by the imposition of hands, he, therefore, offered Peter a sum of money for endowing him with the power of performing this wonder, which he evidently thought was a clue to other miracles.‡

SECTION IV.——THE PREVALENT PRACTICE OF THE PRIMITIVE CHRISTIANS IN SELLING THEIR POSSESSIONS AND LAYING THE PRODUCE AT THE APOSTLES' FEET, UNDER THE DREAD AND CONVICTION OF THE IMMEDIATE END OF THE WORLD.——THE POWERFUL INFLUENCE THIS PRACTICE MUST HAVE HAD IN PROMOTING THE SPREAD OF CHRISTIANITY.——CHRISTIAN-ITY MADE A SELF-SUPPORTING SYSTEM BY THE COMMUNISM OF THE PRIMITIVE CHRISTIANS, JOINED TO THE FORE-MENTIONED PRACTICE.—— THE SELLING OF PROPERTY TAUGHT BY CHRIST.

Another prevalent practice of those who became Christians, which still more fully justifies the inference that a *vast number, in the first ages of the new religion, were induced to embrace it from fear of being destroyed in*

* Decline and Fall of the Roman Empire, chap. xv. sec. 3.
† Acts xix. 13—18.   ‡ viii. 13—19.

the approaching conflagration of the world, is, that of selling all their posses-
sions, and handing over the proceeds to the Apostles. Firmly believing that,
in a very short space of time, the whole of the terrestial globe would be in
a blaze, they, therefore, naturally concluded that their houses and lands
must be destroyed in the universal conflagration. Under these circumstances nothing seemed to them more prudent than to sell such possessions
to any who, being *blind* and *obstinate* unbelievers in the forthcoming catastrophe, were willing to hazard a purchase. Besides : the conditions of
securing a title to the kingdom of heaven, as we shall hereafter see,
rendered this quite imperative. Nor was it a difficult thing for any one
who had once adopted the belief that the end of the world and the final
judgment were events closely approaching, unhesitatingly to come to this
determination ; for whatever interest he felt in any of the objects of this
world must, by this belief, be entirely blighted. If he had ever thought of
securing a comfortable independence for himself against old age, he would
not now require it. If he had been laying up a competent treasure for his
children, or had been making adequate provision for the temporal wants of
his widow, they could not now enjoy it in this world ; but must like himself
prepare to enter the kingdom of heaven, or resolve to suffer eternally
the torments of unquenchable fire. Every motive that had wedded his
affections to this world was now obliterated. The only interest that he
could now feel in wife, children, parents, brothers, sisters, relatives, or
friends, was to exhort them to prepare for another, a better, and a new
world. The very belief that within a few years the world would be destroyed,
made him renounce all worldly interest in relatives, friends, and even
society at large—made him utterly despise all the objects of this world,
and become a zealous candidate for those of another—those, of the *new
heavens*—the *new earth*—and *the new Jerusalem*, where he should enjoy
immortal happiness ! Under these circumstances, and labouring under
these overpowering convictions, it was only consistent in those who
embraced Christianity to *sell all their possessions, and lay the produce at the
feet of the Apostles*, with the view, probably, that in another world, silver
and gold would answer a similar purpose to that which they answered in
this. For we have no reason to believe that they did not borrow their
notions of " the world to come" from the present ; nor that these deluded
fanatics did not think they could purchase possessions, or high positions in
the kingdom of heaven, just as they could in the land of Judea, or in any
part of the Roman empire,—which, indeed, at one time denied them the
possession of any landed property.

Accordingly, we find that after a vast number on the day of Pentecost
had become Christians from fear of the end of the world, they sold their
possessions, and divided the proceeds according to each one's need, having
all things in common.—" Then they that gladly received his word were
baptized ; and the same day there were added unto them about three
thousand souls. And they continued stedfastly in the apostles' doctrine
and fellowship, and in breaking of bread, and in prayers. And *fear came
upon every soul ;* and many wonders and signs were done by the apostles.
And all that believed were together, and had all things common ; *and sold
their possessions and their goods, and parted them to all, as every man had need.*"*

* Acts ii. 41—45.

In like manner, we learn that after a miracle and a couple of sermons more by Peter, another lot, not less in number than five thousand, was converted.—"And the multitude of them that believed were of one heart and of one soul ; neither said *any of them that ought of the things which he possessed was his own, but they had all things common.* And with great power gave the apostles witness of the resurrection of the Lord Jesus ; and great grace was upon them all. Neither was there any among them that lacked ; for *as many as were possessors* of *lands* or *houses sold them, and brought the prices of the things that were sold, and laid them down at the apostles' feet ; and distribution was made unto every man according as he had need.* And Joses, who by the apostles was surnamed Barnabas, (which is, being interpreted, The son of consolation,) a Levite, and of the country of Cyprus, *having land, sold it, and brought the money, and laid it at the apostles' feet."* *

Unfortunate Ananias and his wife Sapphira, however, very badly managed the sale of their property, which cost them their lives. Having retained in their own hands a *portion* of the proceeds, with the view, probably, of having a little money to be enjoyed, entirely by themselves, in the kingdom of heaven, instead of handing over the *whole* to the apostles, Peter, for this act of deception, with his bare word, struck them both *dead* on the spot! The narrative we have of this awful display of the miraculous powers of the apostles, and of the terror it struck into the hearts of the spectators, so as to prove a most effectual warning to all who had property, that it was of the utmost danger not to bring the price of it, when sold, to the Apostles, runs as follows.—" A certain man named Ananias, with Sapphira his wife, sold a possession, and kept back *part* of the price, his wife also being privy to it, and brought a certain part, and laid it at the apostles' feet. But Peter said, Ananias, why hath *Satan filled thine heart* to lie to the Holy Ghost, and to keep back *part* of the price of the land ? Whiles it remained, was it not thine own ? and after it was sold, was it not in thine own power ? why hast thou conceived this thing in thine heart ? thou hast not lied unto men, but unto God. And Ananias hearing these words *fell down, and gave up the ghost* ; and *great fear came on all them that heard these things.* And the young men arose, wound him up, and carried him out, and buried him. And it was about the space of three hours after, when his wife, not knowing what was done, came in. And Peter answered unto her, Tell me whether ye sold the land for so much ? And she said, Yea, for so much. Then Peter said unto her, How is it that ye have agreed together to tempt the Spirit of the Lord ? behold, the feet of them which have buried thy husband are at the door, and shall carry thee out. Then *fell she down straightway at his feet, and yielded up the ghost ;* and the young men came in, and found her *dead,* and, carrying her forth, buried her by her husband. And *great fear came upon all the church, and upon as many as heard these things."†* The narrative then

---

* Acts iv. 32—37.

† Acts v. 1—14. Taking this as a *tale,* it is a very ill-concocted story ; taking it as a *narrative of actual events,* it suggests the following observations.—1. It is not shown that Ananias had promised to devote the whole price towards the Christian cause, or that he had in any manner lied regarding the price.—2. If he had lied, Peter lays the blame to the Devil, asking—" Why hath Satan filled thine heart to lie to the Holy Ghost ?" and

proceeds to relate the signs and wonders wrought by the apostles among the people, and to inform us that "believers were the more added to the Lord, multitudes both of men and women." This account of the terrible end of Ananias and Sapphira is suggestive of many remarks, besides those made in the subjoined note; but we must confine ourselves at present to observe that the foregoing extracts regarding the selling of possessions, show that those to whom the apostles preached *were kept in continual fear*, —in a state of decided panic. It is repeatedly said that "*great fear* came upon *all*," and in the contexts it is stated that of those who were under the influence of fear a vast number believed.* Under this *fear* they sold their

yet, for this wicked act of Satan, he strikes poor Ananias dead, as if it were his duty to keep the Devil from mischief.—3. Peter admits that both the property and its price were Ananias's own, and wholly at his own disposal, so that he could do as he wished with them. Why then strike him dead for exercising his legal and moral right over his own property?—4. It is possible, nay, probable that poor Ananias was buried alive! For the moment he fell to the ground he was carried out and buried, without the least examination as to whether he was really dead, or had merely fainted. The latter appears most probably to have been the case.—5. The same indecent haste and gross ignorance were shown as to the burial of Sapphira, who most likely had merely fainted upon being told that her husband had been put to death, owing to the sale of the property, and that the same fate awaited her.—6. There is no evidence that Sapphira knew, or had been told by her husband, or any one else, except now by Peter, that any part of the proceeds of the land had been retained. And even if she knew this, there is no proof that she could have controlled her husband's disposal of the land or of the proceeds, so as to have rendered his act her own. The conclusion, therefore, is that Peter murdered Ananias when, according to his own admission, the land and the price were his own, and the real agent in the act of retaining part of the proceeds was Satan;—that he murdered Sapphira, when she was as innocent as the new-born babe of the crime attributed to her;—and that, probably, he aggravated the atrocity of this double murder by burying alive both Ananias and Sapphira. So much for Peter's zeal in the cause of his Master, and his discretion in the exercise of his miraculous power.

* Fear, as an incentive to lead a virtuous life, is one of the last means, one would think, that a wise, benevolent, and loving God would employ. Any one that has paid ordinary attention to the emotions of his own mind, must well know that he cannot possibly *love* an object which he *fears*;—in other words, that he cannot love and fear any being at the same time, or under the same circumstances. Nor can love follow as the effect of fear. The effect of the latter, wherever it exists, is hatred to the being that is feared. Let any one try the experiment of *loving* any person whom he *fears*. Let even the urchin—the child, answer whether he loves even his father when trembling under the threatening lashes of the birch. And let the father answer whether he feels the emotions of love glowing in his bosom towards his son, when on every wrinkle of his face anger and vengeance are stamped, as he resorts to the barbarous, but scriptural and orthodox practice of applying the *rod to his back*. The conscience of every reflecting and candid father must answer—No; and thereby disprove the truth of the dogma that he who "spareth his rod *hateth* his son; but he that loveth him chasteneth him betimes." (Prov. xiii. 24.) *Fear* and *love* for the same object, at the same time, are emotions which cannot exist in the human mind, any more than love and hatred. When the one enters the mind the other quits it. The Scripture is quite right where it says that " there is no *fear* in *love*, but perfect *love* casteth out *fear*." (1 John iv. 18.); but it is decidedly wrong where it contradictorily says that "the *fear* of the Lord is the beginning of wisdom." (Prov. ix. 10.) A most unworthy and despicable incentive to the exercise of virtue is to fear God because he can punish us for ever in unquenchable fire, instead of practising virtue because of its inherent good and excellency,—because it affords pleasure, and because God who loves to do good to his creatures, therefore loves virtue. This chilling fear, however, appears to have been in apostolic times the grand incentive to belief in Christianity. Nor was this by any means an unsuitable incentive to belief in an irrational doctrine which recommended itself to blind credulity, rather than to a philosophic investigation of its truth. For fear, the moment it influences the mind,

property and gave the produce of the sales to the apostles,—a practice which must have had a very powerful influence in promoting the spread of Christianity. For it not only proved to those who had not yet embraced it, that those who had been converted really believed that the *present world was to be destroyed*, so that any earthly possessions were now value-less; but also it made the new religion at once " a self-supporting system," and enabled the Christians to subsist as a separate community. When any one, against the wishes of his friends and relatives, upon whom he depended for support, joined the new sect, all his temporal wants were supplied from the general funds, so that he might at once devote himself entirely to the duties of religion. This practice made the early Christians utterly inde-pendent of the world, and did more towards *perpetuating* Christianity than, perhaps, any other thing. It was of vast utility to them when hated and persecuted by those among whom they dwelt, and, in process of time, enabled them not only to support their preachers and missionaries, but also to build places of worship. In connection with the doctrine of the near approach of the end of the world, of all others, this practice had a most powerful effect. The practice and the doctrine had a kind of reciprocal influence in promoting each other. The more, on the one hand, the doctrine of the approximation of the mundane destruction was inculcated and believed in, the more possessions were sold, and the more money placed at the disposal of the apostles; and, on the other, the more money the apostles had at their command, the more extensively and effectually could they promulgate the doctrine.

It would appear that the practice of Christian converts to sell their

prostrates reason, paralyses the noblest mental emotions, and holds spell-bound all the intellectual faculties. It is the means by which the highway robber subdues his victim. His language, to excite fear, is—" Your money, or your life !" and the language of Christianity, in order to excite the same passion, is—" Your implicit faith, or your body and soul for everlasting torments !" Hence the thousands of madlike actions that have been performed under the influence of fear; and hence the millions of human beings, under the influence of Christianity, have lost—irrecoverably lost their senses, and even their lives, owing to the deadly effect of fear. The fear of being burnt, in the supposed approaching conflagration of the world, made people, in the apostolic age, become con-verts to Christianity, so that thereby they might be securely lodged in the kingdom of heaven, and thus escape the devouring flames which were to effect the mundane destruc-tion. Such being the cause of their conversion—namely, senseless fear—it is by no means wonderful that, in this distant but enlightened age, we are inclined to question whether these early converts to Christianity in the least examined the reality of its claims to Divine origin before they embraced it; and whether the fact that they received it as such is any proof of this supposed Divine origin. *Fear*, however, even in the present age, is found to be the most effectual means of making converts to Christianity.— Accordingly, the preacher excites the selfish passions of his ignorant hearers by depicting to them the torments of Hell in the most horrifying language he can command, telling them that if they do not become Christians they will be for ever sprawling in a lake of liquid fire and brimstone, where their best companions will be hideous demons, and their choicest food will be burning sulphur ! with a thousand other such expressions.— The result is that *great fear comes upon all; and believers are the more added to the Lord, multitudes both of men and women*. At Revival Meetings they are terrified to such a degree, —in other words, *fear comes upon them* to such an extent that they fall down insensible, and in some instances, die on the spot; while in others, they linger for some time, or become permanently deranged in mind. How many cases of this kind have happened in Ireland, and other places, during the recent revivals ! All this, however, is called the work of the Holy Ghost. Those that fall down dead are said to be struck by the Deity. What blasphemy !

property and transfer the proceeds to the apostles continued, at least, during the two first centuries, unabated, and of course attended with the custom of enjoying "all things common."* For Lucian, who died at the

* Indeed it continued much longer.—Even to this day the same primitive practice exists as to all monks and nuns of the Roman Catholic faith ; as well as to the members of the Agape,—a Christian establishment of late years instituted, in England, by an enthusiast named Prince, in imitation of pristine Christianity. Similar establishments were also founded by the Moravians and Methodists about the middle of the last century. (Mosheim's Eccles. Hist. cent. xviii. vol. vi. pp. 309—316, Cadel's Edit. 8vo. Lond. 1811.) Dr. Coote, in this work, after remarking that the Agapæ or Lovefeasts of the Methodists were, by Mr. Wesley, borrowed from the Moravians, with whom he at first associated, adds, in a note, that Mr. Nightingale, the author of the "Portraiture of Methodism," whom he quotes, "does not inform us whether these meetings terminate with the *kiss of charity*, as did the Agapæ of the primitive Christians."

It would, however, be neither inexpedient nor difficult here to show that the Christian practices of selling estates and bringing the proceeds to Christian leaders, in order to enjoy a community of goods, and also of holding Lovefeasts or Agapæ, continued for many ages after the apostolic times ; nay, that they have continued with more or less regularity among Christians from that age to the present ; and further, that these Love-feasts were, in early times, one and the same with what is at present called "the Lord's Supper," or "the breaking of bread."

1. The practice of Christians to devote the proceeds of their estates to the Christian cause, and afterwards live in community, having "all things common."—We have the Latin word used to denote this life of community, even in our language to this very day, denoting participation in the Lord's Supper,—*to commune*, *communion*, *communicant*, &c. —all three, as well as others of the same etymon, directly signifying common participation, common possession, &c.; and as applied to what is now called the Eucharist— common participation in the bread and wine administered in Christian assemblies. The Latin words *communio* and *communitas* signify "mutual participation,"—"having all things common." There can be little doubt that the word *communio* is of cognate origin with κοινος, the Greek term used in the expression—*all things common*. (Acts ii. 44.) This word again implies the idea of communion, or common participation of goods, and particularly of food. Hence an ancient order "of monks were called Cœnobita, and their habitations Cœnobia, because they lived in common." (Jerom. Epist. ad Eustoc. 22. c. 15.) ; hence such words as κοινοβιαρχης, κοινοβιον, and scores of other similar words met with in Greek ecclesiastical writings ; and hence the Latin words *coco*, to assemble ; *cœna*, a supper ; and *cœnobium*, a convent ;—all implying the idea of participation, even the participation of food. There are, however, a vast number of positive statements in the works of Ecclesiastical writers that the customs under notice prevailed among Christians from the very commencement of the Christian era. Sozomen, (Hist. lib. iii. c. xiv.) speaking of ancient monks, says that "many women were deluded by them, and left their husbands ; but not being able to practice continence, they fell into adultery. Other women, under the pretext of religion, cut off their hair, and arrayed themselves in men's apparel." While some monks lived alone in desolate places such as the mountains of Nitria and Scetis, which were places of great resort, and from the latter of which, probably, they had the name—Ascetics, long before the Christian era, other monks lived in communities, enjoying all things in common. To the latter, Evagrius dedicated one of his books :—"To the monks living in communities." (Socrat. Hist. Eccles. lib. iv. c. 23.) These monks, we are assured, pretended to trace the origin of their institution, particularly the custom of the community of goods, to the first Christians of Jerusalem, and accordingly parted with their property and lived in common. (Cassian. Collat. xviii. 5.) The ascetics of the first centuries were remarkable for their extensive charity, giving up the whole of their estates to the service of God. (Jerom. de Script. Eccles. c. 76. Epiphan. Hær. 42. Orig. contra Cels. lib. vii.) Sometimes we meet with instances of a bishop and all his clergy voluntarily renouncing all their property, and enjoying all things in common ; such as Eusebius, Versellensis, and St. Austin, with all their clergy. (Abr. Epist. ad Eccles. Vercell. Aug. serm. xlix. de diversis.) So general, in ancient times, was the practice of Christians to devote all their estates to the general good, and live in common, that the Roman government was obliged to enact a law to restrain it in respect to certain subjects of the empire, who, by virtue of their landed

close of the second century, in speaking of the large sums of money which Christians had brought to one Peregrinus, an Armenian, says of them,—

property, had public duties to discharge, such as those of the *Curiales*. These were not to become monks, except on condition that, instead of parting with their estates for the common support of Christians, they transferred them to some other persons that might bear the offices of their country in their stead; it being thought unjust that men who, owing to their estates, were subject to public duties should exempt their estates from those duties under pretence of entering a religious life. (Theod. Cod. lib. xii. tit. 1.)

2. In these Christian communities, where all things were in common, there were held *Agapæ* or Lovefeasts. These were held in apostolic times; for Jude (ver. 12.) mentions them by the word—αγαπαι, translated in our version into "feasts of charity," and says that certain characters who came to these feasts and gormandised, were spots in such feasts. Paul also animadverts on the improper behaviour of Christians in such feasts (1 Cor. xi. 20—34.); and Peter, in reference to the same feasts, uses nearly the same words as Jude in denouncing unworthy partakers of them. (2 Pet. ii. 10—15.) To the same feasts, doubtless, the Christians in Bithynia referred when, according to Pliny's letter, they said in their defence before the Roman governor, that in their secret meetings held before daylight, they were accustomed only to sing a hymn, to bind themselves by an oath not to do any wrong act, and then to separate for a little, and afterwards come together to a *common and innocent repast*. Affirmabant autem, hanc fuisse summam vel culpæ suæ, vel erroris, quod essent soliti stato die ante lucem convenire; carmenque Christo, quasi Deo, dicere secum invicem; seque sacramento non in scelus aliquod obstingere, sed ne furta, ne latrocinia, ne adulteria committerent, ne *fidem fallerent*, ne *depositum appellati abnegarent :* quibus peractis morem sibi discedendi fuisse, rursusque *coeundi* ad capiendum cibum, promiscuum tamen, et *innoxium."* (Plin. Epistolar. lib. lxx. epist. 97.) It should, however, be observed that this is what the Bithynian Christians say of their Lovefeasts in their own defence, when having been apprehended, and when threatened with the punishment of death. Taking this epistle to be genuine, it is remarkable that the defence of these Christians denies in every particular, even the most insignificant, the charges brought against them. A great number of passages might be cited from ancient authors who treat of these Lovefeasts. (See Itigius Selecta Hist. Eccles. Capita. sæc. ii. cap. 3.) The supplies for these Feasts were provided by the joint oblations of the partakers. (Basnage, vol. i. p. 112.)

3. These Agapæ were originally one and the same with what is now called the *Lord's Supper*, or the *Eucharist*, or the *breaking of bread*, so frequently mentioned in the Acts of the Apostles. It should be observed that to *eat bread* in the language of the Bible means to take a meal of food, and to *break bread*, to prepare a meal. It is said of the converts to Christianity that "they, continuing daily with one accord in the temple, and *breaking bread* from house to house, *did eat their meat* with gladness." (Acts ii. 46, 42; see also Acts xx. 7, 11; xxvii. 34, 35. and other places.) In these passages, as well as others, what is meant is not to take a small morsel of bread and a drop of wine as practised now by Christians, but to take a meal—to eat at the Lovefeast. But probably Christians would place more confidence, on this point, in the words of their orthodox and learned Parkhurst, which are as follow :—" To *break bread* SOMETIMES *implies*, though it *does not strictly denote*, the celebration of the Eucharist......... Bishop Pierce, in his Note on Acts xx. 7., observes that ' in the Jewish way of speaking, to *break bread* is the *same as to make a meal;* and the *meal* here meant seems to have been *one of those* which were called αγαπαι—*Lovefeasts*. Such of the Heathens as were converts to Christianity were obliged to abstain from *meats offered to idols*, and these were the main support of the poor in the Heathen cities; απο των ιερων οι πτωχοι ζωσι, the poor are supported by the sacrifices, says the old scholiast on *Aristophanes*. (Plut. ver. 594.) The Christians, therefore, who were rich, seem *very early to have begun* the custom of those αγαπαι—*Lovefeasts*, which they made on the *first day of the week*, chiefly for the benefit of poor Christians who, by being such, had lost the benefit which they used to have for their support, of eating part of the Heathen sacrifices. It was *towards the latter end of these Feasts*, or *immediately* after them that the Christians used to take bread and wine in remembrance of Jesus Christ, which, from what attended it, was called the Eucharist or Holy Communion." (*Parkh.* Greek Lex. *infra* κλαζω.) This certainly is a liberal concession on the part of a Christian divine.—To admit that it was *towards the latter end* of this Feast what is now called the Lord's Supper took place is something; but there is ample historica

"These poor creatures are firmly persuaded that they shall one day enjoy eternal life;" meaning that they should enjoy eternal life at the end of the world, which they then expected. The practice of community of goods was, among Christians, the origin of church property, which grew to such an immense extent. Out of the common fund held by the apostles every one received according to his need. When the Christians became numerous, however, the apostles found it difficult to attend to the temporal wants of all, and some dissatisfaction arose as to the fairness of the distribution:— "There arose a murmuring of the Grecians against the Hebrews because their widows were neglected in the daily ministration." Accordingly, seven men were appointed to see that justice was done to the temporal wants of all in the community. In process of time, however, the practice of community of goods gradually relaxed; and, probably, seeing there was no sign of the end of the world, converts to the new religion were allowed to "retain the possession of their patrimony, to receive legacies and inheritances, and to increase their separate estates, by all lawful means of trade and industry. Instead of an absolute sacrifice, a moderate portion was accepted by the ministers of the Gospel; and in their weekly or monthly assemblies, every believer, according to the exigency of the occasion and the measure of his wealth and piety, presented his voluntary offering for the use of the common fund "* It was not forgotten, however, to inculcate that in the article of tithes the Mosaic law was still of divine obligation, and that it was the duty of the Christian to distinguish himself by resigning

proof that this participation of bread and wine was part and parcel of the *Lovefeast*. We are told that it was instituted for the sake of poor Christians; but we shall soon see that it was purely of a pagan origin, and not quite so humane as we might wish.— In the passages just cited from the Acts, no mention is made of the bread and wine as distinct from the Feast; and in the passage cited from Pliny's letter, the Christians do not say that they partook of bread and wine *before* or *after* the "innocent repast" they mention. *Before* it they say they took an oath (sacramentum) to be faithful and not to reveal their secrets; and probably this sacrament or oath has in later times been tortured to mean the taking of bread and wine. Mosheim, in his Commentaries on the Affairs of the Christians, (vol. I. cent. i. p. 197.) very candidly admits that we are not to consider the expression—*to break bread* as exclusively referring to the Lord's Supper, "but also as implying that *feast of love*, of which it was the customary practice of the Christians, *even from the very first, always at the same time* to partake. That these two things were thus associated together even in the very earliest infancy of Christianity is clear from what is said by St. Luke in Acts ii. 46. For, after having there told us that the brethren at Jerusalem continued daily in the breaking of bread at different houses, he immediately adds that they did eat their food together with joy and simplicity of heart." But the word—αγαλλιασις rendered "gladness" in our version, signifies that they did eat their food exulting and leaping for joy, just as the practice was in pagan feasts. That the primitive Christians were not accustomed to behave very orderly at these *Lovefeasts* is clear from Paul's reprimand to them. (1 Cor. xi. 20—34.) Basnage (vol. i. p. 112.) informs us that to these *Lovefeasts* a quantity of bread and wine and of other things was brought. In the fourth century, this Feast was very much simplified. It became customary to bring only one great cake or loaf, which was said to represent the unity of the church, and which was broken in public, and distributed to as many as communicated. All the oblations brought were limited to bread and wine only. Although the whole of the church at this time communed, yet in process of time it became the practice for the priest alone to commune, as at present in the Roman church. (Lorroche, p. 126. Suer. A.D. 963.) Thus has this Lovefeast, through many grades of superstition, descended to its present simplicity.

* Gibbon's Decline and Fall, chap. xv. who quotes Justin Martyr Apolog. major. c. 89. Tertull. Apolog. c. 39. and several other authorities.

worldly possessions which must so soon be annihilated with the world itself.* By this means the church amassed considerable wealth. Cyprian informs us that, about the close of the first century, a person from Pontus gave to the Roman church, in a single donation, the sum of two hundred thousand sesterces† (about £17,000). And about the end of the second century the bishop of Carthage was able to collect, from a comparatively poor church, the sum of one hundred thousand sesterces, on a sudden call of charity, to redeem the brethren of Numida, who had been carried away captive.‡ In the time of the Emperor Decius, it was the opinion of the magistrates that the Christians of Rome were possessed of very considerable wealth,—that vessels of gold and silver were used in their religious worship, and that many among their proselytes had sold their lands and houses to increase the public riches of the sect, at the expense, indeed, of their unfortunate children, who found themselves beggars, because their parents had been saints."§ The oblations, for the most part, were made in money, the Roman government, during the first two centuries, prohibiting the Christian church, as a body, to hold real property. About the close of the third century, however, the severity of the law was relaxed, and the Christian churches in different parts of the Roman empire became possessed of considerable estates. While part of the church revenue was applied to the maintenance of the bishops and clergy, and another part to defray the expenses of public worship, and the lovefeasts called the *Agapæ*, the greatest proportion, in the early ages of Christianity, was devoted to the relief of the poor in the Christian community, embracing widows and orphans, the lame, the sick, and the aged,—a vast number of whom, owing to the prospect thus presented to them of immediate relief and permanent support, became converts to the new religion.‖ Here it may be remarked that, in England, the tithes and other revenues of the church were originally intended partly for the support of the poor. The Mirour¶ says they were to be "sustained by parsons and rectors of the church." The "rapacious bishops and clergy" of the present age would do well to bear this in mind. The only trace of this obligation that remains in the law of England, as it stands at present, is that the churchwardens are, *ex officio*, the overseers and guardians of the poor. But to revert.

The doctrine of community of goods, however, as we have just seen, was by no means peculiar to the Christians. Plato and Pythagoras instituted similar systems, and the practice subsisted among the austere sect of the Essenes or Therapeuts,—a sect, which if not identical with Christianity, gave rise to most of its notions.†† Jesus being evidently a Therapeut,

* Irenæus ad Hær. lib. iv. c. 27, 34. Origen in Num. Hom. 11.
† Tertull. de Præscript. c. 30.   ‡ Cyprian Epistol. 62.
§ Gibbon's Decline and Fall, chap. xv. with authorities.   ‖ Ibid.
¶ C. i. s. 3. See also Stat. 12. Ric. II. c. 7. 19. Hen. VII. c. 12.

†† Josephus's Antiq. xviii. 2. Philo de Vit. Contemplat. See also Gibbon's Decline and Fall, chap. xv. where a great number of ancient authors are quoted.
The practices of religionists selling their estates and with the proceeds living in communities, and also of holding Lovefeasts are much older than the commencement of the Christian era, and all clearly of a pagan origin. Community of goods was practised among the *Essenes* or *Therapeuts*, which are only two names for the same sect of pagan religionists,—called *Therapeuts* in Greek, and *Essenes* in the language of the Egyptians. There is a striking similarity between these and Christians,—so much indeed that it

dwelling continually on the tenets of this ancient sect, taught the doctrine of community of goods,—of selling all possessions,—of giving the proceeds

appears *certain* that most of the tenets of the latter are a modification of those of the former. Michaelis and others think that the Essenes were a Jewish sect, which began to spread itself at Ephesus in the time of St. Paul, who, in his Epistles to the Ephesians, to the Colossians, and to Timothy, (which, they say, were written before either of the Gospels,) declares himself openly against them. (Introd. to New Test. vol. iv. p. 79.) The Essenes, however, were of an Egyptian origin ; although their doctrine pervades the New Testament, particularly the Gospels. Now, Eusebius, citing Philo's Book on Contemplative Life, gives the following account of these Essenes, or Ascetics of Egypt, showing their existence long before the time Christ is said to have been born.—" These persons are called Therapeutæ, and the women Therapeutrides (healers, salvers, saviours). Subjoining the reasons of such a name he (Philo) refers its origin either to the fact, that by removing the evil affections, they healed and cured the minds of those who joined them, or to their pure and sincere mode of worshipping the Deity. Whether Philo himself gave this name to them of his own accord, as well suited to their manners, or whether the founders called themselves so from the beginning, *as the name of Christians was not yet spread to every place*, is a point which needs not be accurately determined.— He bears witness, however, that they *renounced their property*, saying, that ' *as soon as they commenced a philosophical life they divested themselves of their property, giving it up to their leaders ;* afterwards, dismissing all worldly cares, they leave the city and abide in solitary fields and gardens, feeling that to be in the society of persons different from them in character is not only useless but injurious.' These persons, probably, under the influence of a lively faith, took to this mode of life, in imitation of the ancient prophets. Accordingly, we find in the Acts of the Apostles—a book well authenticated—that all the companions of the Apostles, having sold all their possessions and wealth, distributed to all according to the necessity of each, so that none suffered want. 'For as many as were possessors of lands or houses,' as this narrative says, ' sold them, and brought the prices of the things that were sold, and laid them down at the Apostles' feet, and distribution was made to every man according as he had need.' Philo, giving his testimony to facts *very much like these*, in the same narrative, adds the following statement :—' This sort of persons is every where spread over the world ; that both Greeks and barbarians may participate of so substantial a benefit. But they abound in all parts of Egypt, particularly about Alexandria. The chief men from among them emigrate to a place, slightly elevated, beyond Lake Maria, advantageously situated both as to its safety and the temperature of the air, and is as if it were the native country of the Therapeutæ.' Having thus described their dwellings, he gives the following account of the churches they have in the place.—'In every house there is a holy apartment, called by them the Semnæum or Monastery, where, retired from others, they perform the mysteries of a religious life. To this place they take with them neither drink nor food, nor any other necessary of life,—only the law, the inspired words of the prophets, hymns, and things which increase and perfect their knowledge and piety.' Having stated other things, he adds, — 'They are engaged in continual exercise between the morning and evening ; and they read the sacred writings, they argue and comment upon them, expounding the philosophy of their country in an allegorical manner. For they regard the literal interpretation as implying a secret meaning communicated in obscure intimations. They possess also commentaries of ancient men, the founders of the sect, who have left many monuments of their doctrine, in allegorical representations, which they use as certain models indicative of the manner of the original institution.' These things appear to have been narrated by a man who, at least had closely observed those that have expounded the sacred writings. But it is highly probable that *the ancient commentaries which he says they have, are the very Gospels and writings of the Apostles,* and probably some expositions of the ancient prophets, *such as are contained in the Epistle to the Hebrews, and many others of St. Paul's epistles.*"—Euseb. Hist. Eccles. lib. ii. c. xvii. Such is Philo's account of the origin of the ancient monks, according to Eusebius,—an origin which is decidedly pagan. In the same chapter also, Eusebius, in order to identify the more closely these Pagan ascetics with our Christian monks, says that the practices and doctrines of the former " are to be found among none but in the religion of Christians, according to the Gospel;"—that " their meetings, and the separate abodes of the men and women in these meetings, and the exercises performed by them, are still in use among us at the present day, especially

to the poor, and following him.   From him, it is thought by some, the apostles derived these notions which they instilled into the minds of their

at the festival of our Saviour's passion." But Philo was contemporary with Christ, and, according to Eusebius himself, wrote the work he cites, about eight years after his crucifixion. Still this Philo treats of a sect which had existed a great many years—apparently hundreds of years—before his own time; and therefore before the time Christianity is said to have had any existence.   He does not, however, mention either Christ or Christians.   Of all the works Eusebius enumerates and attributes to him, (lib. ii. c. 18) there is not one about Christ or Christians. Eusebius is very likely right when he thinks that the books of these pagan Essenes were the same as our Gospels and Apostolical writings.   He could have.gone further and have said that our present Gospels and Epistles appear to have been derived from these pagan writings.   The existence of these pagan documents, however, are much too early, to afford the shadow of a reason to suppose that *they* were drawn from *our* New Testament.   The Essenes were a numerous and influential sect in Syria, in the time of Antiochus, son of Alexander, about 143 years B.C.   Josephus says that, in contra-distinction to the Greeks and barbarians, virtue had endured *a long while* among the Essenes; and adds,—"This is demonstrated by that institution of theirs which will not suffer anything to hinder them from *having all things in common;* so that a rich man enjoys no more of his own wealth than he who had nothing at all.   There are about four thousand men that live in this way; and neither marry wives, nor are desirous to keep servants."   In another place, the same writer, in a long description of this sect—a description which fully identifies it with Christ, his apostles, and the monks—says, inter alia,—"The Essenes reject pleasures as an evil; but esteem continence and the conquest over our passions to be a virtue.   They neglect wedlock, but choose out other persons' children, ...and esteem them to be of their kindred. ....They do not absolutely deny the fitness of marriage........These men are despisers of riches.........It is a law among them that those who come to them must let what they have be common to the whole order,........so there is, as it were, one patrimony among all the brethren.........They have stewards to take care of their common affairs.........If any of their sect come from other places, what they have lies open for them just as if it were their own.........They wear white veils; and they bathe their bodies with water.........A priest says grace before and after meat....... They do nothing but according to the injunctions of their curator.........Swearing is avoided by them, and they esteem it worse than perjury.........They take great pains in studying the writings of the ancients,....... and they enquire after such roots and medical stones as may cure their distempers....... If any one wishes to come over to their sect, he is made to undergo several years of probation before he is fully admitted, during which time he wears a white garment, and a girdle; ....when he has given evidence of his worthiness, he partakes of the water of purification, and takes tremendous oaths that he will exercise piety,........show fidelity to those in authority,........ conceal nothing from those of his sect, ...discover none of the doctrines to others, though compelled on pain of his life,.......and preserve the books of the sect........ They strictly observe the seventh day as holy.........They are divided into four orders. .... They believe souls to be immortal,... .....and there are among them such as undertake to foretell things to come."—Joseph. Jud. Antiq. lib. xv. c. 10; xviii. c. 1. De Bell. Jud. lib ii. c. 8. This must suffice to show that the practice of living in common, encouraged by the Apostles, is of a pagan origin.

The apostolic Agapæ are traceable to the same pagan source.   The Eleusinian and Bacchanalian Feasts were in great renown, not only among the Greeks, but even as late as the fourth century of the Christian era also, among the subjects of the Roman empire, although as late as this, among the latter, only tolerated by Valentinian the First. (Cod. Theodos. lib. ix. tit. 16.   Annal. Eccles. A.D. 370. No. 129. et al.)   These Feasts were generally held in the night,—a great number of mysteries were connected with them; and hence they were called μυστερια.   These mysteries were not to be divulged to the uninitiated under pain of death, and all the initiated took a solemn oath to this effect. Persons of both sexes, and even children, were initiated to this solemnity. The candidate was admitted by night into the place of initiation, and having washed his hands in holy water, had the holy mysteries read to him from a large book.   It is generally agreed that the principal object of the mysterious secrecy was to prevent the disclosure of the obscene practices carried on at them. (Paus. lib. x. c. 31.   Cic. de Leg. lib. ii. c. 14,

converts, and which proved so valuable in propagating Christianity.—
The following remarks from the pen of Mr. Francis William Newman, late

Ælian. V. H. lib. xii. c. 24.) Although it appears almost incredible to a person not acquainted with the practices of the ancients, that such abominable customs were connected
with religion, yet this was the case, and it is well known that a vast number of women
subjected themselves to the basest usages in the worship of Venus. (Herodot. lib. i. c. 189.
Baruch. vi. 42.) Another thing that should be noticed here is the ancient practice of
taking an oath, or being sworn to secrecy, and to ratify that oath *by drinking human
blood* mixed with wine. The blood, generally, was that of a human victim. Sallust
says of Catiline ;—" He carried round the blood of a human victim, mixed with wine,
and when all had tasted it, after a set form of execration, (sicut in solemnibus sacris fieri
consuevit) he imparted his design." Herodotus says of the Greeks ;—" They put them
one by one to death, upon a vessel brought thither for the purpose. When they had
done this, they filled the vase which had received the blood with wine and water; having
drunk which, they engaged the enemy." (Lib. iii. c. 11.) "The ceremony of confirming
alliances is the same in this (Persian) nation as in Greece, with this addition—that both
parties wound themselves in the arm, and mutually lick the blood." (Lib. i. c. 74.) The
Scythians, he tells us, had a similar custom. So likewise have the Siamese, who if they
" wish to vow an eternal friendship, they make an incision in some part of the body till
the blood appears, which they afterwards reciprocally drink. In this manner, the ancient
Scythians and Babylonians ratified alliances; and almost all the modern nations of the
East observe the same custom." (Civil and Natural Hist. of Siam.) Human sacrifices
were also frequently offered by ancient religionists. Herodotus (lib. iv. c. 62—64.)
gives an account of the human sacrifices of the Scythians, and adds, that they drank the
blood of their enemies. Human sacrifices were offered at a very late period by the enlightened people of Greece. Porphyry informs us that, even in his time, (233 years after
the Christian era,) they were very common in Arcadia, and at Carthage. Very frequently
children were the victims sacrificed. To say nothing of such a sacrifice intended by
Abraham—supposed to be the same mythological personage—as Saturn—Herodotus
(lib. ii. c. 119; vii. 19.) tells us that Menelaus sacrificed two Egyptian children to
appease the wind. Although this kind of sacrifice was detestable to the Egyptians, it
was very common in Greece.

But what will both furnish the most perfect parallel of the Christian Agape, and
account for the persecutions of the early Christians by the Roman government, is the
following narrative of Livy, (lib. xxxix. c. 8—19.) touching the Bacchanalian religion,
in the Roman empire, (B.C. 186.) which, however, can be given here only in an abridged
form. This account and other historical facts clearly show that the Christian Agape was
an amalgamation of Bacchanalian and Ascetic rites, and was, therefore, of an entirely
pagan origin. Livy says ;—" The employment decreed to both the Consuls was to make
inquiries regarding *clandestine* meetings. A Greek of mean condition, a low *operator in
sacrifices, a soothsayer,* and a *teacher of secret mysteries,* first appeared in Etruria. These
mysterious rites, at first, were imparted only to few, but afterwards communicated to a
great number of both men and women. To the religious ceremonies of these were added
the *pleasures of wine and feasting,* in order to allure a greater number of proselytes.—
When *wine, lascivious discourse, night, and the mingling of sexes,* had *extinguished every sentiment of modesty, then debauchery* of every kind began to be *practised,* as every person
found at hand that kind of enjoyment *most congenial to his predominating passion.* Nor
were they confined to one species of vice—the promiscuous intercourse of free-born men
and women—but from this den of infamy came false-witnesses, counterfeit seals, false
evidences, and pretended discoveries. In the same place, also, were perpetrated *secret
murders,* so that, in some cases, even *the bodies could not be found* for burial. Many of
their audacious deeds were performed by treachery, but most of them by force; and this
force was concealed by long shouting, and the noise of drums and cymbals, so that none
of the cries uttered by the persons suffering *violation* or *murder* could be heard abroad.—
The infection of this mischief, like a pestilence, spread from Etruria to Rome ; where,
the size of the city affording greater room for such, and greater means of concealment,
it remained for some time undiscovered; but information of it was at length brought to the
Consul Postumius, in the following manner." Our historian here proceeds to state that
one Rutilus had a stepson named Æbutius, of whom, from interested motives, he wished
to dispose, and for that purpose prevailed upon his wife to initiate her son into the

Fellow of Baliol College, Oxford, are very appropriate.—"No precept bears on its face clearer marks of coming from the genuine Jesus than

Bacchanalian mysteries. The mother communicated her intentions to her son, who consented, and shortly after told a female, named Hispalia, with whom he was on terms of close intimacy, that he was about to be initiated into these mysteries, and "bid her not to be surprised if he separated himself from her for a *few nights*." On hearing this the woman became alarmed, and exclaimed—"May the Gods forbid ! Better for us both to die than that you should do such a thing !" The young man, ignorant of the consequence, asked her for an explanation; whereupon, after imploring the pardon of the gods for *divulging the secret she had sworn ever to keep*, she said that, when in service, she had gone into that place of worship as an attendant on her mistress, but that never since had she been near it, because she had found it to be the receptacle of every kind of debauchery. She added that, for the last two years, it was known that no one older than twenty had been initiated into it, and that when any one was introduced, he was delivered *as a victim* to the priests, who led him away to a place resounding with shouts, the sound of music, and the beating of cymbals and drums, lest his cries, while suffering forcible violation, should be heard abroad. The young man, very properly, instead of being initiated, gave information, in private, to the Consul Postumius, who, in process of time, cited Hespalia before him. Having been told that she must reveal "all that was done by the Bacchanalians in their *nocturnal* orgies," she became very much terrified, owing to the oath she had taken. After some threats and promises from the Consul, she, however, reluctantly consented to disclose some of the mysteries, saying, among other things, that she had been initiated when very young,—that *men were intermixed with women*, and, the *night* encouraging *licentious freedom*, there was nothing wicked, nothing flagitious, which had not been practised among them;—that there were more frequent pollutions of men with each other than with women;—that if any showed an uncommon degree of reluctance in submitting to dishonour, or disinclination to the commission of vice, they were held as *sacred victims*, and sacrificed;—that "to *think nothing unlawful*" was the grand maxim of their religion;—that the men, as if bereft of reason, uttered predictions with frantic contortions of their bodies;—that their number, comprising many men and women of noble families, was so great, enough almost to compose a state in themselves;—and that, during the last two years, it had been a rule not to initiate any person above the age of twenty, because they preferred persons of such age as made them more susceptible of deception and *personal abuse*.

Having secured the safety of the informers—Hispalia and Æbutius, the Consul represented the affair to the senate, the members of which were struck with consternation, not only on account of the public, lest such conspiracies and *nightly meetings* might cause secret treachery and mischief, but also on account of their own families, lest some of their relations might be involved in this infamous affair. They now passed an order that the Consuls should hold a special inquisition concerning these nocturnal orgies;—that rewards should be offered to other informers in the matter;—that those who had taken part in these rites, whether men or women, should, wherever found, be delivered over to the authorities;—that a proclamation should be made through all Italy forbidding such meetings to be held;—and that search should be made for all who had assembled at these meetings. They, further, directed the police *(curule ædiles)* to apprehend all that they could of the priests of these *mysteries*, and keep them in prison till their trials.—Other officers were commanded to place watches in order to see that these religious ceremonies were performed neither by *night*, nor *privately* by day, and that no *cities were set on fire* by these religionists. These precautions having been taken, a large assembly of the Roman people was convened, whom one of the Consuls addressed to the following effect.—He was sure that they must be aware that the Bacchanalian rites had existed in every country in Italy, and were then performed also in many parts of Rome; but he thought they were ignorant of the nature of these rites. If he told them that their votaries were thousands in number, and without order, they would necessarily be extremely terrified, unless he told them also what sort of persons they were. Now, a great proportion of these were women; and this was the source of the evil; the rest were males, but closely resembling women; actors and *pathics* in the *vilest lewdness ; night revellers*, hurried on by wine, noise of instruments, and clamours, to a degree of madness. The conspiracy, truly, was yet weak, but it was daily increasing in strength and number of supporters. And of what kind did they suppose were the meetings of these people?

that of *selling all* and *following him*. This was his original call to his disciples. It was enunciated authoritatively on various occasions. It is

They were *held in the night,* and were composed promiscuously *of men and women !* If they knew at what ages the males were initiated, not only would their compassionate feelings be roused, but their modesty shocked. Could they think that youths, initiated under such oaths as theirs, were fit to be made soldiers ?—That wretches brought out of the *temple of obscenity* could be trusted with arms ?—That those contaminated with the foul debaucheries of these meetings should be the champions for the chastity of the wives and children of the Roman people? Never was there in a state an evil so enormous ; one that extended to so many persons, and comprehended so many acts of wickedness. Whatever deeds of villany had of late been committed through lust ; whatever through fraud ; whatever through violence ; they had all proceeded from this conclave. Unless timely precautions were taken, this nightly assembly would become as large as the one now held in open day, and legally summoned. If lust, if madness had dragged any of the relations of those now present into that abyss, they should consider such a person as the relation of those with whom he had conspired for the perpetration of every vice, and not as one of their own. Indeed, he was not quite free from fear that even some then present had not even themselves erred through ignorance on this point ; for nothing was so apt to deceive, by specious appearances, as false religion."

Such is a brief sketch of the Roman Consul's eloquent speech ; from which we may infer the policy of the Roman Government towards secret assemblies whose religious practices were believed to corrupt the morals of its subjects; and from which also we may judge how far the Christian *Agapæ* resembled these Pagan Feasts ; and, by the rule that similar causes produce similar effects, learn why the Roman Government held the early Christians in such abhorrence, and *adopted measures of persecution against them exactly like those employed against the Bacchanalians.* It may further be stated, that Livy adds, that the senate promised a reward to any one who should discover any of the guilty parties, or give information against any that were absent ; – that if any person fled, and did not appear to answer the charge brought against him, he would be condemned in his absence;—that during the night succeeding the day on which the affair was made public, great numbers attempted to fly, but were overtaken and placed in custody;—that about seven thousand of both sexes had been sworn into this secret society;—that so great were the numbers that fled, that many persons thereby suffered severely;—that as the persons against whom charges were brought could not be found in Rome, it became necessary for the Consuls to make a circuit of the country towns, and there to make their inquisitions, and hold the trials;—that all those who had merely taken the prescribed imprecation, but had not themselves committed, nor compelled others to commit any of those acts to which they were bound by the oath, were left in prison ;—that all those who had forcibly committed personal defilement, or murders, or were stained with the guilt of false evidence, were put to death ;—that a greater number was executed than thrown into prison ;—and that the multitude of men and women who suffered in both ways was very considerable. (Liv. lib. xxxix. c. 17, 18.) For further information of the Bacchanalian mysteries, see Augustin de Civitate Dei, lib. vii. c 21. Arnob. advers. Gent. lib. v. Plut. in Alexandr. Eurip. Bacchant. Act I. Petron. Sat. vol. i. p. 106. Jul. Firmius. de Error. Profan. Rel. Meursus de Mysteriis Eleusiniis. Diodor. Sicul. lib. i. Strabo, lib. xvii. viii. xii.

It may, however, be added that all the Greek and Latin writers represent the most important part of the Bacchanalian feast as being held *in the night.* The women assembled and made a search for Bacchus ; but failing to find him, *they ended the ceremony with an entertainment,* part of the provisions *being human flesh.* At one of these feasts a son of Leucippe was slaughtered and served up by a daughter of Minya. Indeed, one of the names of Bacchus is *Omistes*—eater of raw flesh. (Vid. Plut. Sympos. lib. viii. Quæst. 1 ; Antonio. Quæst. Grec. et Quæst. Rom.) The Eleusinian feasts, in like manner, were held *in the night;* were denominated *Mysteries* and *Initiations ;* to divulge whose secrets was punished with death by the fraternity, who, amongst other practices much more cruel and obscene, enjoyed themselves in dancing and *singing hymns.* (Greg. Nazian. Orat. de Sacr. lam. Liv. lib. xxxi. c. 14. Hor. lib. iii. Od. 2.)

Let us now closely examine how far the Eleusinian and Bacchanalian feasts resembled the Christian *Agapæ,*—whether the latter, modified and altered a little according to the change which would take place in the taste of the age. originated from the former, or incorporated with precepts of perpetual obligation, in such a way that we cannot, without the greatest violence, pretend that he did not intend it as

were altogether from a different source. We have seen that the forementioned Pagan feasts were, throughout Italy, in a very flourishing state about 186 years before the Christian era. We have also seen that about this time they were at least partially suppressed in Italy, and those who were wont to take part in them dispersed over the world. Being zealously devoted to the religion of which these feasts were part, it is very natural to suppose that, wherever the votaries of this superstition settled, they soon established these feasts, which they were enabled to carry on secretly, and, therefore, for a considerable time, undetected. That these feasts were carried on secretly, and that those who were initiated into them were *solemnly sworn not to divulge anything done in them*, is the cause that our knowledge of their internal character is so limited and indefinite. Both Pagans and Christians, in ancient times, were particularly careful not to disclose their *mysteries ;* to do so, in violation of their oaths, would cost their lives.—— (Herodot. lib. ii. c. 171. Clem. Strom. lib. i. c. 1, 3. Philo in lib. de Sacrificiis.) Our principal and direct information of them, therefore, is derived from the testimony of persons who had once been members of these secret assemblies, whether Pagan or Christian, but had left them, and then divulged ; or had been apprehended, and had then turned informers. Although both Pagan and Christian writers often mention these mysteries, yet they never tell us what they are ;—they never confess that the abominable practices, laid to their charge by those who happened to desert their respective religions, or differ from them, were carried on *by them.* Hence, in the passage just cited, Herodotus says— " The Egyptians call them mysteries. . . . . . . Of the ceremonies in honour of Ceres, which the Greeks call Thesmophoria, *I may not venture to speak further than the obligation of my religious oath will allow me ;"*—and Philo says—" Having then, O ye initiated ! through the channel of *purified organs,* obtained a knowledge of these things, let them *sink deep* into your minds as *holy mysteries, not to be revealed to the profane."* In the Apologies and other writings of the Fathers we have abundance of *denials,* as might be expected, of the abominable practices said to be carried on in the *Agapæ* of the Christians. From these we learn that those who had either abandoned Christianity or were averse to it, asserted that in these Lovefeasts " a *new-born infant, entirely covered over with flour,* was presented like some mystic symbol of imitation to the knife of the proselyte, who unknowingly inflicted many a secret and mortal wound on the innocent victim of his error ; that as soon as the cruel deed was perpetrated, the sectaries *drank up the blood greedily, tore asunder the quivering members,* and pledged themselves to *eternal secrecy,* by a mutual consciousness of guilt. It was as confidently affirmed that this *inhuman* sacrifice was succeeded by a *suitable entertainment,* in which intemperance served as a provocative to brutal lust ; till at the appointed moment the lights were suddenly extinguished, shame was banished, nature was forgotten, and as accident might direct, the darkness of the night was polluted by the *incestuous commerce of sisters and brothers, of sons and mothers."* This description bears a *striking* resemblance to that already cited from Livy of the Bacchanalian feasts. (See Justin Martyr, Apolog. I. 35. II. 14. Athenagoras in Legation. c. 27. Tertull. Apolog. c. 7, 8, 9. Minucius Felix, c. 9, 10, 30, 31. and Gibbon's Decline and Fall, chap. xvi. where the description is cited.) This charge was brought against the Christians at a very early period ; for, in the year 141, Justin Martyr complains of it in his Apology for the Christians, addressed to the Roman Senate,—an Apology throughout which he shows the identity of Christianity and Paganism, and in which he says that the Christians " among all sorts of men are unjustly *hated and reproached."* About twenty years afterwards, as we learn from Eusebius, (Hist. Eccles. lib. v. c. 1.) the Christians at Lyons and Vienna were accused and condemned as guilty of the same charges precisely. In this instance again, as in that of the Bacchanalian devotees, persons who had been initiated, or had attended their employers as servants at these feasts, are the informers. Eusebius, citing the letter of the Gaulish Christians, says :—" Some domestics belonging to our brethren were also seized, as the Governor had publicly commanded that search should be made for us all. But these, at the instigation of Satan, through fear of the tortures which they saw the saints endure, and owing to the solicitations of the soldiers, *charged us with the feasts of Thyestes, and the incests of Œdipus,* and such crimes *as are neither lawful for us to mention nor imagine."* Thyestes, in Pagan mythology, is said to have eaten his own children in a banquet given to him by his brother Atreus, whose wife had borne those children as the fruit of her adultery and incest with

a precept to all his disciples. In Luke xii. 22—40, he addresses the disciples collectively against avarice ; and a part of the discoure is : ' Fear

her husband's brother. Thyestes also had incestuous intercourse with his daughter.— (Ovid. Trist. ii. 391. Stat. Silv. v. i. 58. Hygin. Fab. 88. Pausan. ix. 40.) Œdipus is another personage in Pagan lore, said to have committed incest with his mother, and murdered his father. (Hygin. Fab. 66. Sophocl. Œdip. Senec. in Œdip.) Hence the Christian Agapæ were called after the names of these characters; the lives of the latter indicating the supposed nature of the former. Eusebius further says ;—"These things being spread abroad among the people, all were most savage in their treatment of us..... Blandina,......while we were all trembling, and while her earthly mistress, who was herself one of the contending martyrs, was apprehensive lest, through the weakness of the flesh, she should not be able to make a bold confession,..... renewed her strength and repeated—' I am a Christian, no *wickedness* is carried on by us.'..... Sanctus,.... while the wicked tormentors hoped that, by the continuance and the greatness of the tortures, they *should hear something from him that he ought not to say*,......answered in the Roman tongue—' I am a Christian.'........The devil led forth a certain Biblias to punishment, who was one of those that *had renounced the faith*.........But she contradicted the blasphemies in her declarations. ' How,' said she, ' could such as these *devour children*, who considered it unlawful even to taste the blood of irrational animals ?'.... Those that had fallen from the faith, on the first seizure, were also themselves imprisoned, and shared in the sufferings of the rest. Their renunciation did them no good, *at this time ;* but those that confessed what they really were, were imprisoned as Christians..... At last, however, these were confined as *murderers* and guilty culprits.........Attalus, when placed on the iron scaffold, ...said to the multitude, in Latin,—' Lo, this is to *devour men ;* and you are doing it. But as to us, we neither *devour men,* nor commit any other evil.' (Hist. Eccles. lib. v. c. 1.) The same writer, in another place, tells us that a Roman commander " caused certain infamous females to be seized from the forum, and threatening to inflict torture upon them, he forced them to make a formal declaration that they *had once been Christians*, and that *they were privy to the criminal acts among them ; that in their very churches* they *committed licentious deeds.*" Hist. Eccles. lib. ix. c. 5.

Now, it is clear from all the foregoing citations that the Christians were actually *accused of murdering children and others*,—of committing *adultery, incest*, and other *flagrant crimes in their secret Lovefeasts.* The question, therefore, arises—*Were they really guilty of the barbarous crimes with which they were so often formally charged, and for the commission of which they were almost as often legally condemned, and punished with death?* Is it probable that persons *at Rome*, who had once belonged to these Lovefeasts, should tell a deliberate falsehood that the Christians perpetrated these abominable vices, and that other persons *in France*, who had also been connected with these Feasts, should falsely state that the Christians were guilty of the *very same* execrable crimes ? There was *no collusion or connexion* whatever between these parties; and in making their statements, they could have no self-interested motive. They lived in *different countries ;* they did not make their statements *within twenty years* of the same time ; and by making such statements *they rendered themselves liable to be punished with death ;* for we learn (Euseb. Hist. Eccles. lib. v. c. 1.) that those who were found to have once been Christians, but had seceded, were punished as well as those who had not seceded. The same remark applies to the disclosures made, about 150 years after, by certain females in Damascus, *far remote from either Lyons or Rome.* These make *precisely the same statement*,—that they had once been Christians ; that they were privy to criminal acts among them ; and that these Christians, in their very churches, committed licentious deeds. The Romans would never have so relentlessly persecuted the Christians had they not been guilty of some such atrocities as were laid to their charge. There are on record abundant proofs that the Romans, from the earliest account we have of them, *tolerated all harmless religions*,— all such as were not directly calculated to endanger the public peace, or vitiate public morals, or render property and life unsafe. (Vid. Cod. Theodos. lib. ix. tit. xvi. leg. 9. Mosheim's Comment. on the Affairs of the Christians, cent. i. sec. 27. Gibbon's Decline and Fall of the Roman Empire.) There were none of those religious mysteries—so common to all the Eastern nations—practised at Rome, at least with the knowledge of the Government, till about 180 years B.C. when the Eleusinian and Bacchanalian mysteries were clandestinely introduced, but soon put down by the authorities. Not until the time of Adrian (Aurel. Victor, de Cæsarib. cap. xiv.) were any such rites tolerated among the Romans ;

L Q

not, little flock, for it is your father's good pleasure to give you the kingdom. Sell that ye have, and give alms; provide yourselves bags that wax not old,

when also, for a time, the persecution of the Christians was slackened. It is absurd to suppose that men of such liberal views and enlightened minds as Marcus Aurelius, Pliny, Valerian, and others, would have caused any of the Christians to be put to death, if not guilty of some very heinous crimes. Besides: we have positive *historical proofs* that they were *regularly tried,* and *found guilty upon evidence.* When a Proconsul of one of the provinces wrote to the Emperor Adrian regarding some irregularity in the trial of Christians, the latter strictly enjoined that none of them should be put to death without an *indictment,* a *lawful accusation,* and an *examination ;* so that if "the provincials could *clearly* prove their charges, and answer before the tribunal" that the Christians had done any thing contrary to the laws, they were to be punished according to the heinousness of the crime ; but *they were not to be unjustly harassed and slandered,* and no opportunity of *malicious proceedings was to be afforded to informers,* who, if they brought a false accusation against any of the Christians—according to the mandate of Adrian just cited—were, it appears, *liable to be punished with death.* (See Gibbon's Decline and Fall, chap. xvi. Epist. Adrian. ad Minucius Fundanus, in Euseb. Hist. Eccles. lib. iv. c. 9. See also Plin. Epist. x. 98.) Again: as to the nature of the crimes of which the Christians were invariably charged, the citations already made allow no room for the shadow of a doubt, —so well known were those horrid vices to be carried on by *all* Christians in their *nocturnal and secret assemblies,* and so certain it was thought that every one who was a Christian participated in them, that for a person to be known to be a Christian was thought a strong *presumptive proof* that he was guilty of these offences. Hence, persons, in their preliminary examinations, when, on being interrogated, answered that they were Christians, were thought proper subjects for committal to prison. (Euseb. Hist. Eccles. lib. v. c. 1. et al.) It is true that very few, when further asked if they were guilty of the crimes with which they were charged, admitted their guilt. Indeed no true Christian would do so ; because of his oath—the *solemn oath,* he had taken—and the supposed awful consequences of violating it. These prohibited him from ever *divulging* any thing that was done at the Lovefeasts. All he could admit, according to his oath, was that he was *a Christian.* As Mosheim says of the Pagan mysteries, so it may be said of their offsets—the Christian mysteries,—"The votaries *were enjoined, under the peril of immediate death, to observe the most profound secrecy as to every thing that passed ;* and this sufficiently accounts for the difficulty that we find in obtaining any information respecting the nature of these recluse practices, and for the discordant and contradictory opinions concerning them." We may, however, have a tolerably correct idea of what was anciently meant by being a *Christian* from what escapes from Eusebius. (Hist. Eccles. lib. vii. c. 11.)— Æmilianus attempts at persuading Dionysius and his companions not to be Christians, but to *turn to the course of nature,* and forget those *practices which are against nature.*— Pliny, in his letter to the Emperor Trajan, says that he had been perplexed whether the *name* itself, although no *crime had been detected,* or crimes only *belonging* to the name, ought to be punished ; thereby showing that there existed the idea of certain crimes inseparably connected with the word—*Christians ;* that is,—if a person was a *Christian,* he was considered necessarily guilty of the flagrant crimes for which *Christians* had so repeatedly been condemned to die. Accordingly, Pliny says that he had accused all those brought before him simply of being *Christians,*—that he questioned them whether they were *Christians ;* and that, when they admitted they were, he threatened to punish them with death. This shows that to the word *Christian,* there was attached the idea of crime—a crime considered to deserve death, by the Roman law, which *all used the subjects to worship any gods they pleased, and to indulge in any harmless form of worship most agreeable to their tastes.* Pliny further indicates that while some brought before him, on information, refused to tell him anything as to the nature of their nocturnal meetings, others replied to his questions as far as their oath permitted them. They told him, that it was their practice, as *Christians,* to meet on a stated day—before *daylight*—to *sing hymns ;* and to bind themselves by a *solemn oath* that they would do no wrong ; that they would not steal, nor rob, nor commit any act of *unchastity ;* that they would never violate a trust ; and that they joined together in a *common and innocent repast.* (Plin. Epist. lib. x. 97.) While all these answers to the questions of the Proconsul are *suggestive of the crimes* with which the Christians were charged, still they are a *denial* of every one of them. For instance, the object of their oath was not to keep secret the obscenities,

a treasure in the heavens that faileth not." &c.   ' Let your loins be girded about, and your lights burning,' &c.   To say that he was not intending

incests, and murders committed in their Lovefeasts, but to refrain from thefts, robberies, and unchastity; their feast or repast in common, they certainly had, but it was of an innocent character, and never made up of the flesh of murdered infants; they also had sworn they would never violate a trust, but this did not mean that they would never betray their fellow-Christians by disclosing their licentiousness and villany in the *Agape*. In weighing the evidence of these witnesses, we must take into account the circumstances under which they gave it. *Death* threatened them on every side.—If they refused to make any kind of an answer to the Proconsul, they would, as persons who *had once been Christians*, be in danger of being executed; if, on the other hand, they disclosed all the horrors and obscenities of the Lovefeasts, then would they be likely to suffer death; and even if liberated by the Roman government, still their lives would be in imminent danger from the rage of their fellow-Christians, to whom they had sworn never to divulge the mysteries of their religion.   Love of life, therefore, directed these poor Christians, examined by Pliny, cautiously to "steer a middle course," whereby they got clear of rocks upon which, in those dangerous times, many had become shipwrecked.   The whole tenour of historical facts is, however, against their testimony; and the Proconsul *did not believe* them, but, in order to get at the entire truth, put some of them to the torture, and ultimately adjourned their trial.   The manner in which Greek and Latin writers mention the Christians goes far to show that they were guilty of the atrocious crimes laid to their charge.   Suetonius (in Nero) calls them " a race of men of new and villanous superstition."—Genus hominum superstitiouis novæ et maleficæ.—The Emperor Adrian, in a letter to his brother-in-law, Servianus, in the year 134, as given by Vospiscus, says—Nemo Christianorum presbyter,—non mathematicus, non aruspex, aliptes; which really means—" There is no presbyter of the Christians who is not either an astrologer, a soothsayer, or a minister of *obscene pleasures*."   Tacitus (Annal. xv. 44.) tells us that Nero inflicted exquisite punishment upon those people who, under the vulgar appellation of Christians, were held in *abhorrence for their crimes*,—quos per flagitia invisos. He also, in the same place, says they were *odious* to mankind,—odii generis humani—and calls their religion a pernicious superstition,—exitiabilis superstitio. Maximinus, likewise, in his Letter, (Euseb. Hist. Eccles. lib. ix. c. 7.) calls them votaries of execrable vanity, who had filled the world with infamy.   It would appear, however, that owing to the extreme measures taken against them by the Romans, both in Italy and in all the provinces, the Christians, by degrees, were forced to abandon, entirely, in their Agapæ, infant murders, together with every species of obscenity, retaining, nevertheless, some relics of them such as the *kiss of charity*, and the bread and wine, which they contended was transubstantiated into real flesh and blood.   Indeed the edict of Trajan, preceded by the steps taken by Nero and Domitian, seems to have considerably checked these criminal practices; and, according to Pliny's epistle already cited, even to have caused the discontinuance of the Agapæ altogether.—Quod ipsum facere desisse post edictum meum. Consequently, we find that, in succeeding years, numerous Apologics were addressed to the Roman Emperors with the view to persuade them that the Christians were not so bad as they were represented.   As soon as Trajan was dead and Adrian had taken the reins of government, we find Quadratus—only about nine years after Adrian's edict—taking the lead in the work of apologising, " because some malicious persons attempted to harass" the Christians.   (Euseb. Hist. Eccles. lib. iv. c. 3.)   In Justin Martyr's Second Apology, there are some very singular things advanced regarding the criminal charges brought against Christians; such, for instance, as the following.—In his account of his conversion from Paganism to Christianity, he says that while he admired the doctrine of Plato, and heard the Christians calumniated, while yet they courageously met death, he thought it impossible they should be devoted to vice and *voluptuousness;* or that any lover of pleasure and intemperance—any one who deemed *human flesh a delicacy* could embrace death, in order to deprive himself of the objects of his desire. (Euseb. Hist. Eccles. lib. iv. c. 9.)   A very common way of repelling these charges was for one sect of Christians, which of course denounced all other sects as heretics, to urge that *human sacrifices and incestuous festivals were not* celebrated by that sect, but that they *were* practised by other sects; such, for example, as the Marcionites and the Carpocratians. (Justin Mart. Apolog. i. 35. Iren. adv. Hær. i. 24. Clem. Alex. i 3.)—When Tertullian joined the Montanists, another sect of Christians, he divulged the

to teach a universal morality, is to admit that his precepts are a trap; for they then mix up and confound mere contingent duties with universal

criminal secrets of the church which he had so zealously defended, by saying, in his Treatise on Fasting, (c. 17.) that *in the Agape the young men lay with their sisters, and wallowed in wantonness and luxury.*—Sed majoris est Agape, quia per hunc adolescentes tui cum sororibus dormiunt, appendices scilicet galæ lascivia et luxuria. Eusebius, in like manner, perceiving it to be a fact *too glaring to be denied,* that Christians indulged in those inhuman vices with which they were charged, palliates their offences by urging that the insiduous impostors and deceivers—Saturninus and Basilides—by *assuming the name of Christians,* seduced *believers* to the *depth of destruction,*—that they boasted of pre-parations of *love potions,* and of dream-exciting demons,—that they taught that the *basest deeds should be perpetrated by those that would arrive at perfection in the mysteries,* or rather that would reach the extent of their *abominations;"*—" that no one could escape the rnlers of the world unless he performed his part of *obscenity to all;"*—that these practices "afforded abundant scope to slander the truth of God, inasmuch as the report, proceeding from them, extended with its *infamy to the whole body of the Christians;"*—that it was in this manner an impious suspicion was spread abroad respecting Christians, as that " they had *unlawful commerce with mothers and sisters,* and made use of *execrable food;"*—but that the machinations of the enemy "were almost immediately extinguished." (Hist. Eccles. lib. iv. c. 7.) In the last part of this statement, Eusebius is not quite correct. Remnants of these execrations continued for a long time; and vestiges of them exist to this very day, as well in certain words and phrases as in practices. The communion table to this very day is called *the altar,*—the name of that upon which the ancients sacrificed their victims. The word *sacrament* has a meaning, as used by Pliny already cited, which carries us back to the solemn oath of the *Agapists.* The word *mass* carries us back still further, and identifies the present *mass* with that of the Pagans. Anciently, when the service was ended, or the catechumens formally dismissed, just before the celebration of the Eucharist, the priest said—*Ita Missa est,* which, Polidore Virgil admits, were the words used in dismissing the Pagan worshippers. From the term—*Missa,* by corruption, came the English—*Mass.* (See Priestley's Hist. Cor. Christianity, with authorities, vol. ii. p. 21.) Formerly the consecrated bread was called *host,* which word signifies a *victim* offered as *sacrifice*—anciently *human* very often. This *host* or bread was elevated and worshipped as late as the fourteenth century, and there was also a festival held for it. (Ibid. pp. 26, 49.) Jerome and other Fathers called the communion bread—*little body,* and the communion table—*mystical table;* the latter, in allusion to the heathen and early Christian mysteries, and the former, in reference to the children sacrificed at the Agapæ. (Ib. pp. 4, 13, 87.) The great doctrine of transubstantiation directly points to the abominable practice of eating human flesh at the Agapæ. In by-gone times, a priest named Plecgills, as he was officiating, fell upon his knees and asked God to show him the body of Jesus in the *mystery;* whereupon an angel cried to him,—" Look at the infant !" He turned and saw upon the *altar* a *child.* (Sueur. A.D. 818.) Tertullian calls the consecrated bread the *figure* of Christ's body. In the sixth century, infant victims having apparently failed, one great loaf of a peculiar shape was substituted and broken between the communicants. (Larroche, p. 36.) All that was spare of the communion bread was burnt, in allusion to the ancient mode of burning or roasting sacrifices at the Agapæ. (Fleury, A.D. 1054.) *Lights* were, and are even to this day, used in celebrating the Eucharist, because lights were used in the nightly assemblies of the Agapists and Pagans, and, as we have seen, suddenly put out, as they are now so put out in Roman Catholic chapels. Priestley thinks " this appendage is borrowed from the heathen sacrifices." (p. 32. Larroche, p. 526.) Sacramental wine was frequently used mixed with ink, for signing writings of a peculiarly solemn nature; just as the heathen used human blood for a similar purpose. (Priestley's Hist. Cor. Christ. vol. ii. p. 27.) It was also customary to swear *by the body and blood of Christ,*—another Pagan practice.— (Euseb. Hist. Eccles. lib. vi. c. 43.) The Christian *kiss of love* or *charity* is also an im-portant relic of the *Agape.* This was formerly practised by all Christians. As people of common sense, however, taught Christians a little more decency, this custom was aban-doned. Leo III. changed it for that of kissing a plate of silver or copper. It was afterwards changed into kissing the hand of the priest, and now it is kissing the Pope's toe. (Larroche, p. 120. Hist. Ancient Ceremonies, p. 90.) In the Cyclopædia Britannica, a Christian writer, under the word *Agape,* makes the following remarks.—" These

sacred obligations, enunciating all in the same breath, and with the same solemnity. I cannot think that Jesus intended any separation. In fact,

Lovefeasts, during the first three centuries, were held in the church without scandal (?) or offence; but, in aftertimes, the heathens began to tax them with impurity. This gave occasion to a reformation of these Agapæ. The *kiss of charity*, with which the ceremony used to end, was no longer given *between different sexes*; and it was expressly forbidden to have any *beds* or couches for the convenience of those who should be disposed to eat more at their ease. (?) Notwithstanding these precautions, the abuses committed in them became so notorious that the holding of them (in churches at least) was solemnly condemned at the Council of Carthage, in the year 307." Under the following word, the same writer further says,—" *Agapetæ*, or virgins and widows who attended on ecclesiastics, who were made perhaps deaconesses, and who took up their *abode with the ministers*, and *assisted them* in their *religious functions*. In primitive times, there was nothing scandalous (?) in their societies, but they afterwards degenerated into libertinism, insomuch that St. Jerome asks with indignation—Unde Agapetorum pestis in ecclesias introiit? This gave occasion to Councils to suppress them. St. Anathius mentions a priest who, to remove all occasion of suspicion, offered to mutilate himself to preserve his beloved companion." Avoiding any remarks on these insinuating, but guarded extracts, it may be added here that the 35th Canon of the Council of Iliberis provides against the scandal which too often polluted the vigils of the Church, and disgraced the Christian name. Upon the whole, it is impossible, from the mass of evidence already adduced, to avoid the conclusion that the early Christians, in their Agapæ, were really guilty of the execrable vices with which they were so often charged, and for which they were sentenced to death. This once admitted, a reasonable and adequate cause can be assigned for the severe persecutions of the Christians by the Roman Government,—a Government which applied precisely the same laws and modes of persecution and punishment to them as to the votaries of the Bacchanalian and Eleusinian mysteries, well known to have been accustomed to offer human sacrifices, and indulge in the most obscene lasciviousness in their secret assemblies;—and a Government which tolerated all kinds of religions, except those which encouraged practices dangerous to human life, or pernicious to the morals of the subjects. Nor can the facts already advanced fail to show clearly that the Christian Agapæ were of a Pagan origin—were identically the same as those Pagan feasts which existed simultaneously with them. We have seen that both the Christian Agapæ and these Pagan feasts were held at night;—that at both solemn oaths were taken not to divulge secrets;—that the internal practices of both were called mysteries;—that both were accused of secret murders, of burning cities, and of giving false evidence;—that both had human sacrifices and wine;—that both practised revolting sexual obscenities;—that the Roman Government, consequently, dealt the same with both, proclaiming their prohibition, offering rewards for the detection of their votaries, and punishing those convicted with death. There could be enumerated a great many other points of such close resemblance as must fully establish their identity to any one who will take the pains thoroughly and impartially to investigate the subject.

This conclusion is further strengthened by the following facts which show the Pagan origin of Christianity in its entirety.—It is quite certain that the monkish institution, which we have seen to be *of a Pagan origin*, had existed in Egypt long *before the Christian era*. In the time of Pliny the elder (Hist. Nat. v. 15.) who died A.D. 79, it had long been established in the neighbourhood of Engaddi and Massada, near the Red Sea.— Mosheim, citing authorities, assures us that the Essenes and Therapeuts, or healers, had their rise in Egypt, where, principally they dwelt, long before the Christian era. (Eccles. Hist. cent. II. chap. iii. sec. 14.) Their existence at this early date is a fact which alone disproves the supposed origin of Christianity, both as to doctrines and discipline, when they are compared with the doctrines and discipline of the Essenes or Therapeuts, in whose profession the arts of curing diseases and of teaching theology were combined.— Accordingly, we find the most valuable manuscripts of the Christian Scriptures have emanated from Alexandria, in Egypt, where there was a Pagan College for teaching both medicine and divinity, and the largest library in the world. At this Pagan University almost all the Fathers of the Christian church—most of them originally Pagans—were educated. Further: Adrian's letter to Servianus, written in 134, and preserved by Vospiscus, shows that the worshippers of the god Serapis in Egypt were Christians, who called themselves the bishops of Christ. (Illi qui Serapim colunt, Christiani sunt; et

when a rich young man asked of him what he should do that he might inherit eternal life, and pleaded that he had kept the commandments, but

devoti sunt Serapi, qui se Christi episcopos dicunt.) He appears further to say that to worship Serapis and Christ meant the same thing; and to add that all worshipped but one and the same God. (Ipse ille patriarcha quum in Egyptum venerit ab aliis Serapidem adorare, ab aliis cogitur Christum......Unus illis Deus est hunc Judæi, hunc omnes venerantur et gentis.) We learn also that Constantine had his Christianity, as well as *the sign of the cross*, from pagan Egypt. After he had murdered his son, Crispus, his wife, Fausta, and his brother-in-law and colleague—the brave Lucinus, whom he had solemnly sworn to protect; but before he had murdered the pagan priest—Sopater, to whom he applied for some mode of purification from these crimes, and who told him that such enormous moral defilement admitted of no purification, he turned, on being thus refused consolation from this sect, to the Pagan Christians of Egypt—the worshippers of the god Serapis; and having met one of their bishops coming from Iberia, he was told by this dignitary that the Christian faith could purge any sin however great. Consequently, this holy Emperor—the real founder of the *present* Christianity, from this creditable motive became a Christian—one of the Pagan Christians of Egypt—the worshippers of Serapis. Vid. Zosimus Vit. Const. Pagi Ann. 324. Socrat. Scholast. lib. iii. c. 40, 41. Sozomen. Hist. Eccles. lib. i. c. 3—5. The three last make efforts to defend their Emperor, but there are much more disinterested and stronger testimonies against them. *The sign of the cross* which, it is asserted, Constantine received from heaven on his conversion, for a banner, (Euseb. Vit. Const. lib. i. c. 28—31. Sozom. Hist. Eccles. lib. i. c. 3, 4. Socrat. Hist. lib. i. c. 2.) is clearly a heathen relic. It was in the temple of Serapis long before the time of Constantine, or even the commencement of the Christian era. In Egypt, Serapis, whose devotees, we have seen, were called Christians, had been worshipped from the earliest date. It had a great number of temples, the principal one of which was at Alexandria, whence, as already intimated, both the early Fathers and the Christian Scriptures have emanated. In the worship of this god were practised obscene mysteries—mysteries so abominable that, when Antonius Pius, A.D. 146, introduced them to Rome, the senate was obliged to suppress the worship of the god. (Tacit. Hist. lib. iv. c. 83. Strab. 17. Pausan. lib. i, c. 18; lib. ii. c. 34.) Plato, who wrote upwards of 350 years before the Christian era, states that the Egyptian priests pointed out to him symbolical hieroglyphics of a religion which had existed among them upwards of ten thousand years. Now, among these people, and in one of these Egyptian temples —*that of the god Serapis, in Alexandria,*—was found *the sign of the cross*, when that magnificent edifice was destroyed by order of Theodosius in the fourth century. Socrates (Hist. Eccles. lib. v. c. 16, 17. Scholast. lib. v. c. 16.) relates that in the sanguinary resistance of the Pagan priests, some of them, and many more of the Christians were killed—that the images were broken and molten down—that the tokens of the sanguinary heathen mysteries were exposed to public view—that when *the temple of Serapis* was laid bare, there were found in it, *engraven* on stone, certain hieroglyphics *in the form of crosses*, which *both Pagans and Christians* claimed as symbols of their respective religions— that when a contention on this point had arisen, certain *heathen converts* to Christianity, who well knew the heathen signification of the symbol, declared that it denoted *life to come*—and that they thought this symbol had, for ages and generations, stood as a *Pagan prediction of Christ*. Sozomen, (Hist. Eccles. lib. vii. c. 16.) in describing how this Pagan temple was converted into a church, says, that in it were found stones on which were engraven hieroglyphics in the *form of a cross*, which, on being submitted to the learned, were interpreted to signify *the life to come*. How, then, came *the sign of the cross* —the very insignia of Constantine—which is said to have been received by him from heaven (Socr. Hist. Eccles. lib. i. c. 2.)—to have been struck on his coin, and to have been represented in pictures seen on garments, and even in the skies; (Sozom. lib. i. c. 8; lib. iv. c. 5.)—how came this, it is demanded, to have been *in the heathen temple of Serapis*, because it was *a Pagan symbol*. The Nile was worshipped as a God by those whose lands were fertilised by its inundations. Along its banks were placed crosses, or transverse beams, to indicate the height of the water, and thereby the probable fertility of the ensuing year. These crosses, therefore, would soon share the worship of that river-god.— Accordingly, one of these crosses *(elli)* was brought every year, with much religious pomp, into the temple of the god Serapis, who was believed to cause the river Nile to

felt that insufficient Jesus said unto him—' *If thou wilt be perfect*, go and sell that thou hast, and give to the poor, and thou shalt have treasure in heaven ;' so that the duty was not contingent upon the peculiarity of a man possessing apostolic gifts, but was with Jesus the normal path for all

overflow, and be the means of national prosperity. (Socrat. Schol. lib. i. c. 14.) Sozomen (lib. i. c. 8.) unblushingly tells us that, among the Egyptians, the measure used to indicate the increase of the waters of the Nile was no longer borne into *Grecian temples* but into *Christian churches*. The pious Mr. Skelton (Appeal to Common Sense, p. 45.) says that while the *fact* that the Egyptians, Arabians, and Indians, before Christ, *paid particular veneration to the sign of the cross is well known*, the *manner* in which this came to take place is to him *unknown;* and he adds that, in Egypt, it stood for the signification of *eternal life*. The *sign of the cross*, however, for ages prior to the Christian era, was in common use among the Pagans. It was the most sacred symbol of Egyptian idolatry. It is on most of the Egyptian obelisks ; and was believed to possess all the enchanting powers which have been ascribed to it by Christians. The monogram or symbol of the god Saturn was *the sign of the cross*, together with a ram's horn, in indication of *the Lamb of God*. Jupiter also bore *a cross*, with a horn ; Venus, a cross with a circle. The famous *crux ansanta* is to be seen in all the buildings of Egypt ; and the most celebrated temples of the idol Chrishna, in India, like our Gothic cathedrals, were built in *the form of crosses*. On the Phœnician medal found in the ruins of Citium, engraved in Dr. Clarke's Travels, and proved by him to be Phœnician, are inscribed, not only *the cross*, but the rosary or string of beads attached to it, together with the identical *Lamb of God*. (Taylor's Diegesis, pp. 188—189.) The Egyptian priests, even to this day, continue the practice of throwing into the Nile some beads or bits of a cross, thinking that thereby they sanctify its waters *to the mystical washing away of sin*, just as the Protestant priest, in reading the baptismal service of the Church of England to this day, says similar words, as he sprinkles the sanctified water on the child's face, and makes the sign of the cross on its forehead, accompanied with the words—" We do sign him with the sign of the cross," &c. Thus all that belongs to Christianity, when closely examined, turns out to be of a Pagan derivation. Sozomen informs us that, in Paneades, a Phœnician city, there was a celebrated statue of Christ, erected by a woman in commemoration of a cure at his hand of a flow of blood ; and that it was dragged about the city and torn by the Pagans ; but that the Christians took it into a church. Notwithstanding the fabulous tales related about this statue, still there must have been some cause for them. Probably there was a statue of Christ in the place ; but it is most unlikely that any of the followers of the Prophet of Nazareth, at this early period, should have built a statue of him. There is every reason to believe that this was a Pagan statue, built by the Phœnicians or Egyptians in honour of their God of Medicine—their *healer, salver, saviour, anointer*. (Sozom. lib. v. c. 21.) Eusebius (Hist. Eccles. lib. vii. c. 19.) has a long tale about the miraculous effects of this statue which he professes to have seen. He admits it was erected by the Gentiles, and does not produce a single proof that it was ever intended for the son of Joseph and Mary. The holy Father, Minutius Felix, in his Octavius, written about the year 211, as cited by Reeve, (Apologies of the Fathers, &c. vol. i. p. 139,) is very indignant at the supposition that *the sign of the cross* should be considered exclusively the symbol of Christianity; and, in the person of a Christian advocate, urges against his infidel antagonist, that it was *not Christians who worshipped crosses, but Pagans whose gods were wood*, whose ensigns, flags, and standards, were *beautifully gilded crosses*, whose victorious trophies *not only represented a simple cross*, but *a cross with a man upon it ;*—that almost every thing was after *the sign of a cross ;*—that when a pure worshipper adored God, with extended hands he made the sign of a cross ;—that the sign of the cross had, consequently, some foundation either in nature or in *the Pagan religion*, and therefore ought not to be taken as a ground of objection against the Christians. Indeed, the grand argument—the invariable theme of all the early Apologists for the Christians—is, *that Christianity and Paganism are identically the same*. Let the following solitary instance, however, conclude the present long note. Melito, bishop of Sardis, about A.D. 160, in his Apology to Marcus Antonius, says—"The philosophy which we profess, *flourished aforetime among the barbarous nations ;* but having been *transplanted* in the great reign of thy ancestor, Augustus, it proved to be of all things ominous of good fortune to thy kingdom."—Euseb. Hist. Eccles. lib. iv. c. 26. Christianity, in its present state, is positively nothing more than Paganism modified and refined.

who desired perfection. When the young man went away sorrowing, Jesus moralised on it, saying, ' How hardly shall a rich man enter into the kingdom of heaven;' which again shows that an abrupt renunciation of wealth was to be the general and ordinary method of entering the kingdom. Hereupon, when the disciples asked; ' Lo! we *have* forsaken all, and followed thee; what shall we have *therefore?*' Jesus, instead of rebuking their self-righteousness, promised them, as a reward, that they should sit upon twelve thrones, judging the twelve tribes of Israel. A precept thus systematically enforced is illustrated by the practice, not only of the twelve, but apparently of the seventy, and what is stronger still, by the five thousand disciples after the celebrated days of the first Pentecost. There was no longer a Jesus on earth to itinerate with, yet the disciples, in the fervour of first love, obeyed his precept; the rich sold their possessions and laid the price at the apostles' feet. The mischiefs inherent in such a precept rapidly showed themselves, and good sense corrected the error. But this very fact proves most emphatically that the precept was pre-apostolic, and came from the genuine Jesus; otherwise it could never have found its way into the Gospels. It is undeniable, that the first disciples, by whose tradition alone we have any record of what Jesus taught, understood him to deliver this precept to *all* who desired to enter into the kingdom of heaven, —all who desired to be perfect: why then are we to refuse belief, and remould the precepts of Jesus till they please our own morality? This is not the way to learn historical fact. That to inculcate religious beggary, as the *only* form and mode of spiritual perfection, is fanatical and mischievous, even the Church of Rome will admit. Protestants universally reject it as a deplorable absurdity,—not merely wealthy bishops, squires and merchants, but the poorest curate also. A man could not preach such doctrine in a Protestant pulpit without incurring deep reprobation and contempt; but when preached by Jesus, it is extolled as divine wisdom,—and disobeyed. Now I cannot look on this as a pure intellectual error, consistent with moral perfection. A deep mistake as to the nature of such perfection seems to me inherent in the precept itself; a mistake which indicates a moral unsoundness. The conduct of Jesus to the rich young man appears to me a melancholy exhibition of perverse doctrine under an ostentation of superior wisdom."*

A great number of passages could be cited from the Gospels, in addition to the foregoing pointed out by Mr. Newman, where Christ inculcates the duty of *selling all* in order to follow him. Indeed the whole tenour of his doctrines is to this effect. All objects in the present world were to be despised in order to follow him,—houses, lands, parents, children, brothers, sisters, wives, husbands, and friends were to be renounced. Accordingly, we read that he sent the twelve apostles to preach that the kingdom of heaven was at hand, and told them to take with them neither gold, silver, nor brass,—neither bread, scrip, staves, shoes, nor two coats; but, as the workman was worthy of his meat, they were to enter any house worthy of them, and remain there, eating and drinking such things as would be given to them. But if any person refused to receive them or hear their words, they were to depart, shaking off the dust of their feet as they went;

* Phases of Faith, pp. 155—156. Fourth Edition.

and it was to be more tolerable for the land of Sodom and Gomorrah in the day of judgment than for that house.* Their work was to cry that the kingdom of heaven was at hand, heal the sick, cleanse the lepers, raise the dead, and cast out devils,—none of which things have we any account they did during the lifetime of Jesus. It is, however, clear that the apostles were initiated by Christ into the doctrine of teaching people to sell their possessions when they became converts to Christianity. For we find this practice universal among the Christians of the first century. Hence, by the preaching of the near approach of the end of the world, the working of what are called miracles, and the ample funds placed at the disposal of the apostles, considerable success, naturally, followed the first promulgation of the new religion,—thousands of people, from fear, became converts to it, in order, not only to avoid being destroyed in the general conflagration of the globe, but to obtain eternal life in the kingdom of heaven, together with all the felicity that the new religion held forth.

Section V.—the early success of christianity not nearly so great as that of mormonism, and therefore no proof of its divine origin.

That great success, therefore, should have followed the first preaching of Christianity, is but what we can reasonably expect to have been the case entirely on natural grounds. Admitting the accounts we have of this success not to have been exaggerated, it is not greater than that which would follow the promulgation of any other religion of a similar character preached under similar circumstances. As similar causes always produce similar effects, this success is by no means without a parallel. To say nothing of Mahomedanism, which very rapidly spread, and which predominates over a far greater part of the earth and of its inhabitants than Christianity does, with its innumerable sects, each of which hates one another,—let us confine ourselves to a new religion of the present age, and take a glance at Mormonism which we have seen rising before our eyes,—let us compare the success of this religion with that of Christianity in its early days. In order that it may not possibly be said that, in instituting this comparison, the case has been overstated, or that facts have been tortured with the view of showing a parallel to Christianity, the following extracts have been made from a Tract, of 32 pages, published among others, by Messrs. W. and R. Chambers, called the *History of the Mormons*, in which there appears not the least intention to overstate their case. These extracts are made the more copiously because they clearly show how a religion may be established and embraced by thousands, when —as in the case of Mormonism—it will be admitted by all, except its own deluded devotees, nothing akin to *supernatural* causes has promoted its

---

* Matth. x. Luke ix. They were to go on their journey precisely in the same manner as Josephus tells us the Essenes went. The description of the Jewish historian and the instructions of Jesus are so much alike, that they fully prove the latter to be an Ascetic. Jewish Antiq. lib. ii, c. 8.

success, or in any manner whatever influenced either its founder or his adherents. The Tract commences thus :—

"The origin, growth, and present condition of the singular sect, calling themselves the 'Church of Latter-Day Saints,' form a curious and instructive chapter in the history of fanaticism. Within the space of *twenty years* since they first sprung into existence, they have gone on rapidly increasing in influence and number, and are now an established and organised society, amounting to not less than 300,000 people. They have borne the brunt of calumny and misrepresentation, endured the severest persecutions, and, in spite of every conceivable obstruction, triumphantly vindicated the earnestness and sincerity of their mistaken faith, and the practical objects which they have considered it their special mission to realise in the world. Their progress within the last ten years has been extraordinary, and is utterly unparalleled in the history of any other body of religionists........ With as much impartiality, soberness, and fair appreciation, as may be at our command, and without any disposition or temptation to speak contemptuously of their peculiarities, we will here endeavour to represent these much-derided Mormonites and their proceedings in such a way as shall seem warranted by their actual character and achievements. It is generally known that the founder and acknowledged 'prophet' of this people was a young man named Joseph Smith. Between twenty and thirty years ago, when he first attracted notice, he was living with his father on a small farm, near the town of Manchester, in the state of New York..... Very early in life he had decided impressions of the religious sort, and his mind seems from the first to have taken a fanatical and enthusiastic turn. We are told that when he was 'about fourteen or fifteen years of age, he began seriously to reflect upon the necessity of being prepared for a future state of existence.' He used to retire to a secret place in a grove, a short distance from his father's house, and there occupy himself for many hours in prayer and meditation. Once, when so engaged, he 'saw a very bright and glorious light in the heavens above, which at first seemed to be at a considerable distance,' but as he continued praying, 'the light appeared to be gradually descending towards him, and as it drew nearer, it increased in brightness and magnitude, so that by the time it reached the tops of the trees, the whole wilderness around was illuminated in a most glorious and brilliant manner.' The account of this vision, which is given by a Mormon apostle, Mr. Orson Pratt, goes on to say that the light 'continued descending slowly until it rested upon the earth, and he was enveloped in the midst of it. When it first came upon him, it produced a peculiar sensation throughout his whole system, and immediately his mind was caught away from the natural objects with which he was surrounded, and he was inwrapped in a heavenly vision, and saw two glorious personages, who exactly resembled each other in their features and likeness.' These wondrous beings informed him that his sins were forgiven; and they furthermore disclosed to him, that all the existing religious denominations were 'believing in incorrect doctrines;' and that, consequently, 'none of them was acknowledged of God as his church and kingdom.' He was expressly forbidden to attach himself to any of them, and received a promise that in due time, 'the true doctrine, the fulness of the gospel,' should be graciously revealed to him; 'after which the vision withdrew, leaving his mind in a state of calmness and peace indescribable! ... On the 21st of September, 1823, the miraculous light re-appeared, and 'it seemed as though the house was filled with consuming fire.' Its sudden appearance, as afore-time, 'occasioned a shock of sensation;' and what is more remarkable, we learn that it was '*visible* to the extremities of the body.' This time, only a single 'personage' stood before him. 'His countenance was as lightning,' yet of so 'pleasing, innocent, and glorious an appearance,' that, as the visionary beheld it, every fear was banished from his heart, and an inde-scribable serenity pervaded and possessed his soul. 'This glorious being declared himself to be the angel of God, sent forth by commandment to communicate to him that his sins were forgiven, and that his prayers were heard; and also to bring the joyful tidings that the covenant which God made with ancient Israel concerning their posterity, was at hand to be fulfilled; that the great preparatory work for the second coming of the Messiah was speedily to commence: that the time was at hand for the gospel, in its fulness, to be preached in power unto all nations; that a people might be prepared with faith and righteousness for the millenial reign of universal peace and joy.'

"The reader, doubtless, is now prepared to hear that on this occasion Joseph received an intimation that he was 'called and chosen to be an instrument in the hands of God to bring about some of his marvellous purposes in this glorious dispensation.' By way of preparing him for the work, the brilliant 'personage' gave him some verbal revelations, inform-ing him, amongst other things, that the American Indians were a remnant of Israel; that when they originally emigrated to America they were a pious and enlightened people, enjoying the peculiar favour and blessing of God; that prophets and inspired writers had been appointed to keep a sacred history of events transpiring among them; that the said history was handed down for many generations, till at length the people fell into great wicked-ness, and afterwards the records were hidden, 'to preserve them from the hands of the wicked' who were seeking to destroy them; that these records contained 'many sacred revelations pertaining to the gospel of the kingdom, as well as prophecies relating to the great events of the last days;' and that, finally, the time was come when, to accomplish the divine purposes, they were to be brought forth to the knowledge of the people. ...... The angel again appeared to him, and gave him direct instructions to go and 'view the records' (the Book of Mormon) which for many ages had been deposited in a place which was pointed out to him...... Oliver Cowdery,*

---

* Oliver Cowdery's name, together with the names of two others, is to be seen to the following testimony to the genuineness and truth of the Mormon Bible.—"Be it known unto all nations, kindreds, tongues, and people, unto whom this work shall come, that we, through the grace of God the Father and our Lord Jesus Christ, have seen the plates which contain this record." The certificate then proceeds to state that the translation of the plates is correct; that an angel laid the plates before the eyes of the subscribers and showed them the engravings. Eight other witnesses also bear testimony to having seen the plates, and that Joseph Smith had translated them, into the contents of the present book of Mormon. (See the beginning of the book of Mormon.) Thus we see that in the nineteenth century Inspired Books can be made, so as to be believed by thousands. Christians cannot say a word against the Mormonites; for the religions of both are so similar in their origin, doctrines, and other points, that whatever fraud can be charged to the one applies to the other.

a 'witness of the faith,' who visited the spot, in 1830, has favoured us with a minute description of it, mingled with various of his personal speculations concerning the position of the records at the time they were discovered...... While contemplating this extraordinary treasure with great astonishment, Joseph Smith became aware of the presence of the angel who had previously visited him, and who now, with due solemnity, called on him to 'Look!' 'And as he thus spake,' says the Mormonite apostle before quoted, 'he beheld the Prince of Darkness surrounded by his innumerable train of associates.' All this passed before him, and the heavenly messenger said; 'All this is shown, the good and the evil, the holy and impure, the glory of God and the power of darkness, that you may know hereafter the two powers, and never be influenced or overcome by the wicked one. You cannot at this time obtain this record, for the commandment of God is strict.' Joseph had to wait four years before the records were finally delivered by the angel into his hands. During that time, however, he had numerous interviews with the 'heavenly messenger,' and 'frequently received instructions' from his mouth. At length, on the morning of the 22nd of September, 1827, when he was about two-and-twenty years of age, he was formally permitted to take possession of his discovery. 'These records,' says our authority, Mr. Pratt, 'were engraved on plates which had the appearance of gold.'...... With the records was found 'a curious instrument called by the ancients the Urim and Thummim, which consisted of two transparent stones, clear as crystal, set in two rims of a bow. This was in use in ancient times by persons called seers. It was an instrument by the use of which they received revelation of things distant, or of things past or future.' Being in an unknown tongue, the book required to be translated before its contents could be intelligibly communicated to mankind; and Joseph, having now provided for himself a separate home, straightway commenced turning this ancient record into what he probably regarded as the 'American language.' It seems he translated 'by the gift and power of God, through the means of the Urim and Thummim.' ..... This is that part of Joseph's revelations which is styled the *Book of Mormon*, and which is deemed by them of equal authority with the Hebrew and Christian Scriptures, and represented to contain that 'fulness of the Gospel' which was to be revealed in the latter days...... It might strike a sceptic, as a suspicious circumstance, that the 'eight' (witnesses to the real existence of the records) with one exception, belong to two families, evidently on terms of intimacy with each other; and further, that three of them belong to the family of Joseph Smith,— being in fact his father and two brothers; but this to a genuine believer in the prophet's claims, no doubt, appears to be a consideration of no manner of moment. Certain it is that from this point Joseph rises before us as the conspicuous founder of a sect, and begins to draw after him no inconsiderable number of converts...... When unbelievers say; 'Show us the gold plates, the original records of the Book of Mormon,' the Mormonite replies: 'Show us the original manuscripts of any part of the Old or New Testaments;' and conceives that to be sufficient to silence all gainsayers. As to the book itself, the Mormons implicitly accept it; its origin and authenticity, as Smith and his associates have represented them, are matters of pure faith; no true Mormonite entertains a doubt about the genuineness or plenary inspiration of the volume.. . . . . . They believe in 'the existence of the gifts in the true church spoken of in Paul's letter to the Corinthians,' in what they describe as 'the powers and gifts of the everlasting Gospel,' and mention in particular, 'the gift of faith, discerning of spirits, prophecy, revelation, healing, tongues, and the interpretation of tongues; wisdom, charity, brotherly love,' and some indefinite ' et cetera.' They believe also 'in the literal gathering of Israel, and in the restoration of the ten tribes; that Zion will be established upon the western continent; and that Christ will reign personally upon the earth for a thousand years.' They recognise two orders of priesthood, which they call the Aaronic and the Melchisedek. The Church is governed by a prophet, whom they sometimes call president; they have twelve apostles, a number of bishops, high priests, deacons, elders, and teachers; and they assert on behalf of Joseph Smith, and many other distinguished leaders, that they had the power of working miracles, and of casting out devils. They affirm that *the end of the world is close at hand*, and that they are the saints spoken of in the Apocalypse, who will be called to *reign with Christ in a temporal kingdom on the earth.*

" In 1830, the year after he (Joseph) began to announce his visions and to speak of the discovery of the plates, his followers amounted to five persons. Among these were included his father and three brothers; but in the course of a few weeks the number increased to thirty. On the first of June, in the year just mentioned, the first conference of the sect, as an organised church, was held at Fayette, where the prophet at that time resided.. . . . . . He appears to have had many contests with the preachers and leading people of other religious sects, and to have signally exasperated them against him by the boldness of his self-sufficiency . . . . . . They had recourse to the ordinary expedient of persecution. Their animosity rose so high at last that the prophet and his followers found the place too strait for them.. . . . . . On the first Sunday after his arrival (in Jackson county) Joseph preached in the wilderness to a miscellaneous crowd of Indians, squatters, and a 'respectable company of negroes.' He made a few converts, and soon had another revelation, to the effect, chiefly, that Martin Harris should ' be an example to the church *in laying his moneys before the bishops of the church,*' the said moneys being required to purchase land for a store-house, 'and also for the house of the printing.'. . . . . . Meanwhile Joseph lost no opportunity of propagating his religion, and of planting branches of his church wherever he could find soil adapted to his doctrines. He travelled about preaching in various parts of the United States, making converts with great rapidity.. . . . . . Basing his faith upon isolated passages of the Bible; claiming direct inspiration from Heaven; promising possession of the earth, and limiting eternal blessings, to all true believers; and, moreover, announcing his mission with a courage and audacity that despised difficulty and danger; it is not surprising that ignorant and credulous people should everywhere have listened to him, and reverently credited his extravagant pretensions. Nevertheless his success, as a propagandist, was not without some drawbacks. Never, perhaps, until the enlightened nineteenth century, was it the lot of a prophet to be tarred and feathered! Such however was the ridiculous martyrdom which Mohammed Smith was called upon to suffer at the hands of lawless men. One night, in the month of March, 1832, 'a mob of Methodists, Baptists, Campbellites,' and other miscellaneous zealots, broke into his peaceable dwelling-honse, and, dragg-ing him from the wife of his bosom, stripped him naked, and, in the way just indicated, most despitefully maltreated him....... Sydney Rigdon (an apostle) was similarly handled. ... Outrages of almost every description were committed by armed mobs upon the Mormons, till at length they saw no chance or likelihood of ever being left at peace..... The history of the sect for the next three years is one of strife and contention with their enemies in Missouri.   The numbers of the Mormons increased with the numbers of their opponents ; and the warfare raged so bitterly that the whole people of the State were ranged either on one side or the other.........The Mormons to the number of 15,000 took refuge in Illinois..... Somewhere about the time at which we have now arrived (1838) the sect began to be heard of in England.   Missionaries from America appeared in Manchester, Liverpool, Leeds, Birmingham, Glasgow, and in several towns and places in South Wales.   Their preaching was attended with very considerable success, and in three or four years, the sect numbered *in this country*, upwards of 10,000 converts !...... While settled at Nauvoo, they boasted of having 100,000 persons professing their faith in the United States.— They began to be a distinct and imposing power in the country, and in various places influenced the elections.   On all political questions they were perfectly united.   So bold did they become that, in 1844, they put Joseph Smith in nomination for the presidency....... Many influential and talented persons finding themselves deceived, both in the sanctity of the prophet, and in advancing their temporal fortunes, deserted his standard. ...... It being impossible to bring the Mormon mob to justice through the Nauvoo courts, the officer who undertook to deal with them procured a county writ and attempted to enforce it in the manner resorted against ordinary offenders...... An officer was dispatched to arrest Joseph Smith, and his brother Hyrum, but to avoid the indignity, they crossed over the Mississippi into Iowa, and there stayed to watch events, keeping up by a boat a correspondence with the Mormon council.   Finding at length that their own people were incensed at their desertion, the council advised the Smiths to surrender to the governor, and to stand their trial for such a violation of the laws as they could be charged with.   They accordingly repaired to Carthage, the seat of government, and were there indicted for treason ; and in company with two of their apostles, were lodged in the county jail.   It is related that the prophet had a presentiment of evil in this affair, and said, as he surrendered, ' I am going like a lamb to the slaughter, but I am calm as a summer morning.   I have a conscience void of offence, and shall die innocent.'   As the mob still breathed vengeance against the prisoners, and as the militia sided with the people, and were not to be depended on in the way of preventing violence, the governor was requested by the citizens of Nauvoo and other Mormons to set a guard over the jail.   But the governor, seeing things apparently quiet, discharged the troops, and simply promised justice to all parties,   It now began to be rumoured that there would be no case forthcoming against the Smiths, and that the governor was anxious they should escape.   Influenced by this belief, a band of about 200 ruffians conspired to attack the jail, and take justice into their own hands.   ' If law could not reach them,' they said, ' powder and shot should.'   On the 27th of June, 1844, they assaulted the door of the room in which the prisoners were incarcerated, and having broken in, fired upon the four all at once. Hyrum Smith was instantly killed. Joseph, with a revolver, returned two shots, hitting one man in the elbow. He then threw up the window, and attempted to leap out, but was killed in the act by the balls of the assailants outside. Both were again shot after they were dead, each receiving not less than four balls.— One of the two Mormons who were with them was seriously wounded, but afterwards recovered; and the other is said to have escaped 'without a hole in his robe.' Here then ends the life and prophetic mission of Joseph Smith. Henceforth the Mormons are left to be guided by another leader. Of him (Joseph) it has been said; ' He founded a dynasty which his death rendered more secure, and sent forth principles that take fast hold on thousands in all lands; and the name of the Great Martyr of the nineteenth century, is a tower of strength to his followers. He lived fourteen years and three months after founding a society with six members, and could boast of having 150,000 ready to do his bidding when he died; all of whom regarded his voice as from Heaven. Among his disciples he bears a character for talent, uprightness, and purity, far surpassing all other men with whom they ever were acquainted, or whose biography they have read.'........ Saint or sinner, Joseph Smith must be reckoned a remarkable man in his generation; one who began and accomplished a greater work than he was aware of; and whose name, whatever he may have been while living, will take its place among the notabilities of the world.'

The narrative from which the foregoing extracts have been made proceeds, from page 24th where we have left it, to describe the success of the Mormons under the leadership of Brigham Young, the prophet who succeeded Smith; their migration to the Great Salt Lake Valley; their plurality of wives, and so on. But the reader is recommended the perusal of the pamphlet itself, which is sold for one penny; and also that of the History of the Mormons, by Lieutenant Gunnison, or by apostle Orson Pratt. Also, Chandler's Visit to Salt Lake City, just published, is worth reading. The reviewer of this last-named work remarks that " the hitherto triumphant course of the vulgar imposture called Mormonism is a significant and startling fact. Fanaticism has had many victories, but none so strange or so humiliating. Self-styled prophets and seers of all sorts the world has had, but none so unromantic and contemptible as Joe Smith and Brigham Young. Yet this heresy has taken *deep root*, and produced results of a *permanent* and *substantial* kind. On the high road from the State of California, it has founded flourishing settlements in the pathless wilderness, and reared a city which holds its place amongst the capitals of the New World. From the quiet homes of England it has lured bands of enthusiasts to its Promised Land, and, strange to say, its monstrous creed and revolting customs are sanctioned and supported by the sober zeal and stedfast faith of the Anglo-Saxon character. Never was there a sect so pretentious in its aims, or more daring and determined in action. It is at this moment doubtful whether the Central Government of the United States will be able to impose on the rebellious community the slightest check of municipal law. In the history of the world there is no instance of such stupendous power wielded by men so coarse, selfish, and sensual; such

R

potent and puerile fraud, deceiving, or appearing to deceive a multitude so greatly distinguished for energy, shrewdness, and perseverance."*

Now, the reader, who before may have known but little of the religion of the Latter-Day Saints, will be the better enabled, by the foregoing sketches of this curious Creed, to institute a comparison between the success of Mormonism and that of Christianity on their first promulgation. The similarity between the tenets of the two religions, and the circumstances under which they were set forth, must appear to him very striking. Like Christianity, Mormonism has its divine founder—a person commissioned by Heaven, who has visions, holds special communications with the Deity, has revelations made to him, is a prophet and predicts future events, works miracles, is persecuted, and dies a martyr.—It has its apostles and elders, who have the power of working miracles, the gifts of miracles, the gifts of prophecy, of casting out devils, of healing, and of speaking with strange tongues. It has its inspired records, and it believes and inculcates the *near approach of the End of the World*, the *second coming of Christ to reign on earth*, and the certainty that all who join this religion shall enjoy eternal life.—Its converts also are in the habit of *selling their possessions, and laying the price at the apostles' feet*. In a word, there are a thousand points of similarity between Mormonism and Christianity—between Joe Smith and Jesus—between the apostles of the latter and those of the former. Mormonism in its infant state, as it is yet, furnishes a perfect reflex of what Christianity was in its primitive condition, some of its more barbarous practices, however, excepted. The former supplies a real index to the history of the latter, and throws a flood of light upon the obscure and imperfect accounts which from benighted ages have descended to us, as to the causes of its early success. Human nature is the same in every age, and fanaticism, under similar circumstances, produces similar results.

But let us compare the respective successes of these two religions which we have seen so similar. Jesus preached, for about three years, and also sent his disciples to preach; but we do not read that during his lifetime he made many converts. When he was apprehended, the Christian converts did not, in thousands, come forward to his rescue. Unlike the whole people of the State of Missouri, in the case of Joe Smith, we do not find the whole people of Jerusalem, "ranged either on the one side or the other," in regard to Jesus. We do not find him with Christians "to the number of 15,000, taking refuge" in any place. He is attended only by one or two of his twelve disciples, at a crisis when one would expect that his converts by thousands, if they existed, must have "ranged" themselves on his behalf. Joseph Smith's missionaries came to England, "and in three or four years the sect numbered in this country upwards of 10,000 converts." "While settled at Nauvoo," in 1838—only ten years after the first promulgation of the doctrine—"they boasted of having 100,000 persons professing their faith in the United States." Joseph Smith lived only fourteen years to promulgate his doctrine, before he died a martyr to his religion; but in this short space we read that 150,000 of his converts "regarded his voice as from heaven." He first made his appearance as a

* Weekly Dispatch, July 5th, 1857.

prophet in 1823, and in 1853—the space of thirty years—his followers numbered not less than 300,000 people"! From that time to the present they have proportionately and gradually increased. Did such great success attend the preaching of Christianity the first *fourteen* years, or even the *thirty* years it was promulgated? We have no account of such success.— The writer of the Acts of the Apostles, who is very particular in recording the number of converts, gives us nothing like the number of the converts to Mormonism. According to Biblical Chronology, Christ was 33 years old when he began to promulgate the Gospel, and in about eight, or according to some, ten years after, Saul was converted; but we have no proof that during this period of about ten years there had been 100,000 converted to Christianity. In the case of Joe Smith, however, we have positive proof, that in ten years this vast number had been converted (most of them from Christianity) to Mormonism. In the year A.D. 64, when Christianity had been preached about thirty-one years, Paul was made prisoner at Rome; but where is the proof that there had then been 300,000 people converted to Christianity? The Mormonites are now able to show *alive* this number converted to their religion in thirty years. Where then is the proof which the early success of Christianity furnishes of its divine origin? Cannot Mormonism also boast of the same, nay, far greater proof, such as it is, that it is divine? Will Christians admit that Joe Smith and his apostles were and are true prophets, work real miracles, and are divinely inspired?—that the Book of Mormon is a revelation from God, and the religion of the Latter-Day Saints a religion from heaven? To be consistent, the only alternative for them is either to admit all this, or to admit that the early as well as the late success of Christianity is no proof of its supernatural character.

It is not denied that about the close of the first century, and during the three following centuries, very great success attended the preaching of Christianity; but it is equally true, that during these centuries not greater success, to say the least, attended it than has attended the preaching of Mormonism during the time it has as yet existed. Supposing that these fanatics will increase for four centuries at the rate they have hitherto increased,—and we have no proof that they will not do so,—they will then number about four millions. We have no proof that the Christians at the end of the fourth century amounted to this number. Although ancient authors mention a great number of provinces in which Christianity had been preached at a very early date, yet, as Mr. Gibbon very properly remarks, the number of the converts that were made, " and their proportion to the unbelieving multitude are now buried in obscurity or disguised by fiction and declamation." Although Pliny in a letter to the Emperor Trajan, at the commencement of the second century, states that in Pontus and Bithynia, owing to the number of Christians, the temples were almost deserted, and the sacred victims found scarcely any purchasers, yet the Christian religion does not appear to have taken a very deep hold of the people even there; for in the middle of the third century there were no more than seventeen believers in the extensive diocese of Neo-Cæsarea.* Even at Antioch, where the followers of Jesus were *first* greeted with the appellation of Christians, where apparently this sect was most numerous,

* See Gibbon and Authorities—Decline and Fall, c. xv. *Note* 156.

and where the population appears to have been, at least, *half-a-million*, the Christians, after they had enjoyed the sunshine of Imperial favour for sixty years, did not number more than one hundred thousand persons.— But to whatever number the Christians increased in the second, third, and following centuries, it is sufficient for our present purpose to know that within the first thirty years of the preaching of the religion of the Latter-Day Saints, Joseph Smith and his apostles have made a much greater number of converts than Jesus and his apostles made during the first thirty years that Christianity was preached to the world. This fact alone, on the ground of early progress, destroys the argument of the divine origin of Christianity, and places it on a level, at least, with Mormonism, which we know to be one of the wildest species of fanaticism that human passions ever displayed. If indeed the divine origin of a religion could be proved by its rapid progress, Mormonism, according to the success it has hitherto met, has a better claim than Christianity to such an origin. It is true that, owing to the similar character of the doctrines and pretensions of both, they have both met with considerable success, and have had a deep hold on the minds of the credulous. The inculcation of the near approach of the End of the World has proved most serviceable to both, and has been the means of intimidating thousands to flee to them for salvation. The preaching of this doctrine, in a modified form, is found very useful even among Protestants of the present day. We hear scarcely a sermon in which it is not enforced in some shape. The same terrors of the day of judgment—the same unquenchable fire—the same lake of fire and brimstone—the same worm that dieth not—the same outer darkness—the same weeping, wailing, and gnashing of teeth, descend in thundering threats from our pulpits now as were fulminated by the apostles. And, as already noticed, many are the cases on record in which persons of timid minds have been driven by these denunciations into despair—madness—irrecoverable insanity—death. As in the apostolic times, so now—*fear* is the Gospel incentive to obedience ! " The fear of the Lord"—" the fear of God"—" fear came upon all"—such is the language of the Bible; and such, consequently, is the language of the Christian preachers of the present day,—a language which, wherever it has any effect, debases and demoralises the human mind. We are not asked to become religious, or in other words, virtuous, because of the intrinsic value, happiness, and beauty of virtue, but because God is " angry with the wicked every day," and " is a jealous God, visiting the sins of the fathers upon the children, even unto the third and fourth generation"—because there is a kingdom of heaven and eternal life prepared for those that fear the Lord ! Fear is continually held forth as the motive to become a Christian. A more unmanly, poor, paltry, selfish, and mischievous incentive to action was never devised. Can man be ameliorated by no other means than by making him a coward, and his Creator a tyrant—by chilling his feelings with portraits of the pangs of hell, or exciting his selfish passions with pictures of the joys of heaven ?—a mode which during sixteen centuries of Gospel preaching has been tried, and is as far from deterring him from vice, and inspiring him with the love of virtue, now, as the very moment when the Prophet of Nazareth denounced that *whosoever should say, Thou fool ! should be in danger of hell-fire.*

CHAPTER VI.

AN INQUIRY INTO THE CORRECTNESS OF THE ALLEGED FULFILMENT OF CHRIST'S PROPHECIES—THAT HE WOULD RISE FROM THE GRAVE ON THE THIRD DAY AFTER HIS BURIAL—THAT THE ACT OF THE WOMAN WITH HER BOX OF OINTMENT WOULD BE MENTIONED WHEREVER THE GOSPEL WAS PREACHED—AND THAT MIRACULOUS SIGNS WOULD FOLLOW BELIEVERS.

SECTION I.—THE COURSE TO BE PURSUED IN TREATING THE SUBJECT.—THE BURDEN OF PROOF.—NEUTRAL REMARKS.—JEWISH MODE OF COMPUTING TIME.—COMMENCEMENT OF A JEWISH DAY.

Another of Christ's predictions, the fulfilment of which forms a matter of dispute, is that which relates to his resurrection from the dead on the third day,—a prediction recorded in the Gospels as having been uttered by Christ on various occasions, and expressed in various modes. It is proposed in this chapter to discuss the fulfilment of this prophecy in the same mode as that prediction of Christ already considered has been discussed, with the exception that, instead of devoting a whole chapter to the arguments on each side, only a section of this chapter must suffice. In one distinct section all the arguments of any strength which are usually adduced by Christians, and any others of which the writer can think, shall be stated in the fairest and strongest manner he is able, with a view to show that this prediction has been fulfilled ; in the next, the arguments adduced by the opponents of Christianity shall be stated ; and in the section following, the writer's own conviction as to the side on which the truth lies, together with any inferences that may naturally be drawn, shall be placed before the reader. As to the predictions regarding the box of ointment, and the signs which were to follow believers ; these are not so strenuously and unqualifiedly contended to have been fulfilled, and therefore will be treated in a more summary manner.

Christians maintain that Christ predicted that, after being put to death and buried, he should rise from the grave on the third day, and that he *did* rise on the *third* day, actually fulfilling this prediction. Their opponents, on the other hand, deny the correctness of this affirmation, and contend that, according to the Evangelists—whose testimony alone we have of the resurrection of Christ—he did not rise on the *third* day, but that, if he rose at all, he rose on a *different* and *earlier* day. The question of the *reality* of Christ's resurrection will, however, not be discussed here. —This, as it is clearly stated in the Gospels, will be taken for granted, and the discussion will be confined to the question of the *day he predicted* he should rise, and the day the Evangelists say that he *did* rise. The question coming before us in this shape, namely, the Christians maintaining that Christ *prophesied* he should rise on the third day, and that he *did* rise on that day; and their opponents denying these affirmations, the burden of proof, as in the case of the prediction precedently discussed, falls upon the Christian side of the argument, which, consequently, has the advantage of pre-engaging the mind of the reader, even supposing that his mind already was not occupied by the same opinion.* The dispute being a question of time, a few remarks of a neutral character, on the Jewish mode of computing time—remarks, the correctness of which, probably, will be admitted on each side of the main question—would not be inappropriate here, by way of illustrating the subject to be argued.

There is, in the Gospels, frequent mention made of *hours*, particularly in the narration of the crucifixion and burial of Christ. Let us inquire what is meant, in the Jewish writings, by this portion of time. It would appear that, according to the mode in which the Hebrews computed time, an hour was not, at all seasons of the year, of the same length. When the days were long, the hours of the day were individually long ; but when they were short, the hours, likewise, were short. In the same manner, when the nights were long, the hours of the night were individually long ; but when short the hours were also short. The Jews divided their days into twelve hours, regarding the day to begin, both in summer and winter,

* Although there can be no disadvantage whatever, but rather an advantage to the Christian, in taking the lead of the argument, and in being on the affirmative side, yet some may, perhaps, think that the *onus probandi*, or the burden of proof, falls upon the party which denies what is affirmed by another. To a sound thinker, however, it must appear that the duty of proving falls upon the party or person who affirms or asserts.— To those that would think otherwise, a perusal of Archbishop Whateley's Logic, and of Dr. Carson's Criticism (in his work on Baptism, chap. i.) on his Lordship's views, is recommended. Dr. Carson, *inter alia*, remarks,—"I entirely agree with the present Archbishop of Dublin, that, in the discussion of any question, it is of immense importance to ascertain with precision on which side lies the necessity of proof. But I utterly disagree with his Grace in his doctrine on this subject.........It is self-evident that the pre-occupation of ground does not cast the proof on the opposite side, for this might establish error rather than truth.........It is self-evident that, in every question, the *burden of proof* lies on the side of the affirmative. An affirmation is of no authority without proof. It is as if it had not been affirmed. He who denies has nothing to do till proof is advanced on the other side. Can he refute evidence till it is advanced ?.... It must be observed that, though the *burden of proof* always lies on him who holds the affirmative, yet when he has alleged his proof, the objector is bound to proof. That is, the objection must be proved before it can be admitted against the evidence. An objection can have no force till it is proved. In fact, till it is proved it does not properly exist as an objection. He who objects must affirm something to be inconsistent with that to which he objects. If he refuses to prove, his objection ceases to exist. It is perfectly the same thing as if he did not object. If a man must prove his doctrine, an objector must prove his objection. Every man must bear his own burden. He who affirms must bear the burden of proving his affirmation ; he who objects must bear the burden of proving his objection."—pp. 1—4.

at sunrise or dawn, and to end at sunset or dusk. There were in each day four quarters, or principal divisions, called the third, sixth, ninth, and twelfth hour; each quarter or division consisting of what they termed three hours. But as the end of the sixth hour was always at noon, a single hour, as well as a quarter of a day consisting of three hours, was longer when the days were long than when they were short. They further divided their nights into twelve hours, the length of which hours depended on the length of the night, according to the seasons of the year. They also divided the night into four watches of three hours each, called the first, second, third, and fourth watch ; the length of each watch depending on the length of the whole night, which was divided into four equal parts, and considered to begin at sunset and end at sunrise.

Dr. Kitto, in his Cyclopædia of Biblical Literature,[*] has the following observations.—"The ancient Hebrews were unacquainted with any other mode of noting the hours of the day but by its natural divisions of mornings, noons or midday, twilights, and night. The earliest mention of hours is in Daniel (iii. 6, 15 ; iv. 19, 33 ; v. 5). Probably it was during their residence in Babylon that the Jews became acquainted with these artificial divisions of hours. It is not until their return from captivity that we find them noting hours. In the time of Christ, the division of day and night into twelve hours each was generally established among the Jews. But the Jewish horology, in common with that of other Eastern nations, was that the hours though equal to one another were unequal in regard to the seasons, because their day was reckoned from sunrise to sunset, and not from the fixed period of noon as with us. Hence the twelve hours into which it was divided varied in duration, according to the fluctuations of summer and winter. The midday, which with us is the twelfth hour, the Jews reckoned their sixth, whilst their twelfth hour did not arrive till sunset. At the equinoxes their hours were exactly the same length as our hours ; and the time at which they began to reckon their day, at these seasons, corresponded precisely with our six a.m. Their first hour being our seven a.m. ; their third (Acts ii. 15.) our nine a.m. ; their ninth (Acts iii. 1.) our three p.m. ; and their eleventh (Matth. xx. 6.) our five p.m. This equality was, however disturbed as the season approached towards the summer or winter solstices. In midsummer, when sunrise in Judea took place at 5 a.m., and sunset at 7 p.m., the Jewish hours were longer than ours ; and the only one of their hours which corresponded exactly with ours, was the sixth, or twelve at noon, whilst in all the rest there was a considerable difference. Their third hour was a little before our nine, and their ninth hour a little after our three. In like manner, in winter, when the sun rises at seven, and sets at five, the Jewish hour was proportionably shorter than ours, their third hour not occurring till a little after our nine a.m., and their ninth a little before our three p.m." But as Judea is about 20 degrees nearer to the equinox than Great Britain the days and nights throughout the year are more equal there than they are here. Philology, however, furnishes a strong proof that not only the Hebrews, afterwards called Jews, but several other ancient nations computed their hours from sunrise to sunset, and that their *first hour* commenced at *daybreak*, or sunrise, throughout

---

[*] Vol. i. p. 871, *voc. Hours.*

the year.　For the very word *hour* means, originally, *daybreak, dawn, or the appearance of light.**

The following remarks of Mr. Horne on the Jewish hours, may further illustrate the subject.—"The Romans had two different computations of their days, and two denominations for them. The one they called the *civil*, the other the *natural* day : the first was the same as ours ; the second, which was the vulgar computation, began at six in the morning, and ended at six in the evening. The *civil* day of the Jews varied in length according to the seasons of the year. This portion of time was, at first, divided into four parts (Neh. ix. 3.) ; which, though varying in length, according to the seasons, could nevertheless be easily discerned by the position, or appearance of the sun in the horizon. Afterwards, the civil day was divided into twelve hours, which were measured either from the position of the sun,

---

* The Greek word for *hour* is ωρα ; evidently of a cognate origin with the English word, *hour*. The word translated *hour* from the Chaldee of Daniel, where, as already mentioned, we first meet with it in the English version of the Bible, is שעה (shaah) meaning to *see*, to *look*, *behold*, as we are able to do only by means of light. The word also means to set fire to any thing, by which light is produced. Hence, the word became to be employed to denote the appearance of the light of the sun, which, in the estimation of the ancients, was insepararly connected with fire. The Greek word ωρα (hour) is of a cognate origin with the Heb. אר (ar) meaning to *flow*, as light is supposed to do. Hence the participial noun אור (aur) *light*, *lightning*, the *sun*, *lustre*, *fire*, &c. See the word in its various forms occurring in Gen. i. 3. Job xxix. 24 ; xxxi. 26. Psal. iv. 7 ; xliv. 4. Prov. xvi. 15. Ezek. v. 2. *et alia ;* and always implying the idea of light. The Greek noun ωρα (now meaning *an hour)* is either from, or of the same derivation as οραω, to *behold*. Hence οραμα, a prospect, a scenery, a vision ; οριζων, boundary, limit, the horizon—the extent the light is seen ; οροθεσια, setting boundary ; ορος and οριον, a mountain,—a boundary which limits the extent the eye can see by means of light ; ορθριζω, to rise early in the morning, on the appearance of light ; ορθρος, the return of light ; and other words implying the idea of light. Hence also the Latin *aura*, brightness, and its derivatives ; and likewise *hora*, an hour. And hence the French *heure*, hour ; and the Welsh *awr*, hour, which has the same root as *gwawr*, dawn of day. The meanings of all these words concur in showing that the original signification of the word *hour* was the appearance of light, and agree with the view, already stated, that the Jews and other ancient nations computed their diurnal hours from the dawn of day. According to a well-known law in language, the word *hour*, like many other ancient words and phrases retains its original meaning, while it has long ceased to be used to designate the object of which it was originally a symbol. Such is the case with the Latin word *codex* (from cœdio) which meant originally a tree, or the stock of a tree, but when the practice of writing upon wood became prevalent among the Romans, *codex* became to signify a book. Hence we have the word *code*, such as code of laws ; and *codicil*, a little book, a little will made after the principal one. Similar observations might be made on the Greek word πιναξ, which signifies both a pine tree or a pine plank, and a book. We formerly used *sticks* to hold candles, and we still say candle-*stick* for a piece of metal. We also say sometimes "sing a stave," because songs were formerly cut on staves of wood. Many other such instances might be noticed. But to return : Ancient mythology also corroborates the view just taken of the original signification of the radix of the word *hour*. Aurora (the morning, or dawn of day) is a word derived from the same root, and the name of a goddess, in Heathen mythology, who married Astræus, (a star) by whom she had the winds and the stars,—who had intrigues also with Orion, (a famous astrologer) and whom the Poets represent as drawn in a rose-coloured chariot, while, covered with a veil, she opens with her rosy fingers the gates of the East, pouring the dew upon the earth, and making the flowers grow ; while Nox (night) and Somnus (sleep) fly before her, and the constellations of heaven disappear at her approach. Thus clearly Aurora or *Hour* is made the goddess of the Morning.—Vide Virgil. Æn. 6. lin. 533. Hom. Il. 8. Od. 10. Hymn. in Vener. Ovid Met. 3, 9, 15. Hesiod. Theog. Varro de Ling. Lat. 5. Hygin. pref. fab. &c.

or from dials constructed for that purpose.   These hours were equal to each other, but unequal with respect to the different seasons of the year; thus the twelve hours of the longest day in summer were much longer than those of the shortest day in winter.   The Jews computed their hours of the civil day from six in the morning till six in the evening; thus their *first* hour corresponded with our seven o'clock, their second with our eight, their *third** with our nine, &c.   The night was originally divided into three parts or *watches*, (Psal. lxiii. 3; xc. 4. Lam. ii. 19. Judg. vii. 19. Exod. xiv. 24.) which probably were of unequal length.   In the time of Jesus Christ, it was divided into *four* watches, a fourth watch having been introduced among the Jews from the Romans.   The *hour* is frequently used with great latitude in the Scriptures, and sometimes implies the space of time occupied by a whole watch. (Matth. xxv. 13; xxvi. 40. Mark xiv. 37. Luke xxii. 59. Rev. iii. 3.)   The Jews reckoned two evenings: the former began at the ninth hour of the natural day, or at three o'clock in the afternoon; and the latter at the eleventh hour.   Thus the Paschal lamb was required to be sacrificed between the evenings. (Exod. xii. 6. Lev. xxiii. 4.)   In common with other nations, the Jews reckoned any *part* of a period of time for the whole, as in Exod. xvi. 35.   Thus a part of the day is used for the whole, and part of a year for an entire year.   An attention to this circumstance will explain several apparent contradictions in the sacred writings; particularly the account of our Lord's resurrection, in Matth. xxvii. 63. and Mark viii. 31. *three days after*, with that of his resurrection on *the third day*, according to Matth. xvi. 21. and Luke ix. 22."†

There is only one point more which requires attention, before we proceed to discuss the main subject; that is, *the time within every twenty-four hours at which the Jewish day commenced.*   It would appear certain, and indeed it follows of necessity, that in computing a number of days they included the intervening night, allowing a night as pertaining to each day. Accordingly, Mr. Horne, in the place just cited, observes that seven nights and days constituted a Jewish *week*.   Their day, therefore, of twenty-four hours must have been considered to commence at some fixed point of these twenty-four hours, inclusive of night and day, so as to distinguish one day from another, and the transactions of one day from those of another, just as our day is considered to commence at midnight, or twelve o'clock, and everything which takes place before this point of time, as taking place on one day, but everything which takes place after it, as taking place on the next day.   The point, therefore, to be ascertained here is—when did the Jewish day of twenty-four hours *commence?*—whether at sunset, sunrise, midnight, or at any other time?   There is proof which amounts almost to positive certainty, that the Jews regarded a day as commencing at sunset. Their day of twenty-four hours, therefore, was from sunset to sunset.— Mr. Horne, in the pages of his work last cited, justly observes that " the Hebrews computed their days from evening to evening, according to the command of Moses."   The words of Moses are—" from even unto even shall ye celebrate the Sabbath."‡   The word here translated *even* is עָרֶב,

---

* Mr. Horne appears to mean that the *end* of the Jewish hour corresponded with the time he mentions.
† Horne's Compend. Introduction, part iii. book ii. chap. 4.
‡ Lev. xxiii. 32.

(arb) meaning literally a mixture, and here conveying the idea of the mixture of light and darkness, which, by the ancients, was supposed to take
place,—in the dusk, when the sun set—the evening.* It would appear,
therefore, that the Jewish Sabbath commenced at sunset. Hornet says
that "the Sabbath commenced at sunset, and closed at the same time on
the following day;" and Dr. Collyer entertains the same opinion.‡ This
is also confirmed by the fact that the Jews at present keep their Sabbath
from sunset to sunset. The Sabbath day commencing at sunset is a strong
presumptive proof that all Jewish days were considered to commence at
sunset and end at sunset. Agreeably to this view, Dr. Collyer, in the place
just cited, observes that "immediately after sunset, according to the Jewish
method of calculating time, the next day commences." The foregoing
investigation, therefore, leads us to the conclusion—that the Jews regarded
their day as commencing at sunset and closing at the following sunset, and
thus consisting of *twenty-four* of our hours;—that they divided the night
into four watches, the length of which, although always equal to that of
one another, varied in different seasons of the year, according to the length
of the night;—that the day was divided into twelve hours which, like the
watches of the night, were in length equal to one another, but all varied as
to length with the variation of the seasons, so as to be long hours when the
day was long, and short when the day was so;—and lastly, that the *first
hour of the day* commenced with the dawn, or rather *sunrise*, and the last,
or twelfth, ended with *sunset*. These are points which it is important to
bear in mind, in order to ascertain the number of days, or length of time
Christ remained in the tomb.

SECTION II.—ARGUMENTS ADVANCED TO SHOW THAT IT WAS ON THE
THIRD DAY, ACCORDING TO HIS PREDICTION, CHRIST ROSE FROM THE
DEAD.—EXTRACTS FROM DR. LELAND AND BISHOP SHERLOCK'S WORKS.

It is now intended to prove as conclusively as the writer's abilities
will permit that Christ repeatedly prophesied that he should be put to
death and be buried;—that he should rise from the grave on the third day
from that of his burial;—and that this prophecy was fulfilled by his resurrection *on the third day*, and not on any other, or *earlier* day. As Jesus,
sometime before his crucifixion, was going up to Jerusalem with his twelve
disciples, he called them apart and addressed them in the following words:
—"Behold, we go up to Jerusalem; and the Son of man shall be betrayed
unto the chief priests and unto the scribes, and they shall condemn him to
death, and shall deliver him to the Gentiles to mock, and to scourge, and
to crucify him; and the *third day* he shall rise again." Some time previously he had, when in Galilee, uttered to his disciples the same prediction,
saying—"The Son of man shall be betrayed into the hands of men, and

* See the word ערב Gen. i. 5. Exod. xii. 6; xxix. 39. Lev. xxiii. 5. Deut. xxiii. 11·
Isa. xxiv. 11.
† Compend. Introduct. part III. book iii. chap. 4.   ‡ Lectures on Miracles, p. 502.

they shall kill him, and the *third day* he shall be raised again." Still longer before the time of his sufferings, he proclaimed the same prediction to the scribes and Pharisees.—When they asked him for a sign, he answered them in the following words :—" An evil and adulterous generation seeketh after a sign ; and there shall no sign be given to it, but the sign of the prophet Jonas ; for as Jonas was *three days and three nights* in the whale's belly, so shall the Son of man be *three days and three nights* in the heart of the earth."* Now, this is a most clear and distinct prediction, announced in such definite terms, and—particularly as to the first passage cited, and others that could be cited—in such a detailed manner that its meaning cannot be misunderstood. He foretels that he should be betrayed into the hands of the chief priests and scribes,—that they should condemn him to death, and deliver him to the Gentiles to be mocked, scourged, and crucified ; but that he should rise again *the third day.* Nothing can be more pointed and minute than this prophecy. But pointed as it is, and minute as it is in its details, we learn from the Gospel narrative that its fulfilment was equally pointed and minute. Was the Son of man " betrayed unto the chief priests and unto the scribes" ? Scripture answers the question thus : —" The chief priests and the scribes sought how they might kill him.. .. Judas surnamed Iscariot.. .. communed with the chief priests and captains how he might betray him unto them.. ... And while he yet spake, behold a multitude, and he that was called Judas went before them and drew near unto Jesus to kiss him.. ... Then took they him, and led him, and brought him to the high priest's house."† Did they " condemn him to death" ?— " The chief priests and the rulers of the people.. .. cried out all at once, saying, Away with this man !"‡ Was he " delivered to the Gentiles to mock" ?—" And the soldiers also mocked him, coming to him and offering him vinegar."§ Was he " scourged" ?—" Pilate, therefore, took Jesus and scourged him."‖ Was he " crucified" ?—" They crucified him, and two others with him."¶ Did he rise again into life " the *third* day" ?—" Mary Magdalene, and Mary the mother of James and Salome, had bought sweet spices that they might come and anoint him; and very early in the morning the first day of the week, they came unto the sepulchre.. ..... And they entered in and found not the body of the Lord Jesus. And it came to pass, as they were much perplexed thereabout, behold, two men stood by them in shining garments ; and as they were afraid, and bowed down their faces to the earth, they said unto them, Why seek ye the living among the dead ? He is not here, but is risen. Remember how he spake unto you when he was yet in Galilee, saying, The Son of man must be delivered into the hands of sinful men, and be crucified, and *the third day* rise again. And they remembered his words.. ... Afterward he appeared unto the eleven as they sat at meat."†† Such is the Gospel narrative of the exact fulfilment of this prophecy. Never was a prediction in all its particulars accomplished with greater minuteness. So exact has been the fulfilment that even

---

* Matth. xx. 17—19; xvii. 22, 23; xii. 39, 40. Mark viii. 31; ix. 31 ; x. 33, 34. Luke ix. 22 ; xviii. 31. &c.

† Matth. xxvi. 47, 54. Mark xiv. 43—45. Luke xxii. 2—6, 47, 48. &c.

‡ Matth. xxvii. 20—23. Mark xv. 7—14. Luke xxiii. 13—23. John xix. 6.

§ Luke xxiii. 36. *et al.*   ‖ John xix. 1.   ¶ xix. 18.

†† Mark xvi. 1, 2, 14. Luke xxiv. 3—8.

the very words of the prediction become naturally to be used in recording its accomplishment.

But it is contended that Christ, if he rose at all, rose on an *earlier* day than he had predicted, and that therefore, contrary to the prophecy, he did not rise on the third day, and was not in the grave three days. In showing that Christ's prophecy on this point was verified, the writer shall use the words of the most eminent divines with whom he is acquainted ;— words which have been designed as answers to the opponents of Christianity on this question. By this means no suspicion can exist in the mind of the reader that any injustice has been done to the subject. But let it first be observed that, anciently, as now, the Jewish Sabbath, as we have seen, began at sunset on our present *Friday*, and ended at sunset the next day, our present *Saturday*; the length of a Jewish day, whether Sabbath or week day, including night, being from sunset to sunset. During the Sabbath, all sorts of work among the Jews were strictly prohibited, and required to be performed and completed before *sunset* on *Friday*, which was, therefore, called " the day of preparation."* Even the bodies of malefactors were not allowed to remain suspended during any part of the Sabbath ; for, according to the Mosaic Law, this was deemed a defilement of it ; nor was it right, according to this Law, to allow a body to remain suspended on a tree during the *night* of any week day.† Accordingly, in the chapters of the four Gospels just cited, we learn that the body of Christ was taken down from the cross and buried before the *commencement* of the Sabbath, which was at sunset. The reason given for burying him so hastily is that the Sabbath was approaching.‡ He was, therefore, in the grave a portion of the day before the Jewish Sabbath, namely our *Friday*,—how short a portion does not affect the present argument. He lay in the grave the *whole* of the Jewish Sabbath, namely our *Saturday*; and he rose from the grave the next day, namely our *Sunday*, or the *first* day of the week—the day after the Jewish Sabbath. The Jewish Sabbath terminating at *sunset*, the next day, namely " the first day of the week," commenced at the same point of time. Now, " early on the first day of the week" the Evangelists tell us Christ rose. This was, therefore, the *third* day from the time he had been buried. For, as it was customary with the Jews to take into their calculation of time the current day, month, or year of any transaction, the part of Friday (as we would call it) which Christ lay in the grave made *one* day, the following Saturday made a *second*, and that part of Sunday he lay in the grave before he rose made the *third day*. Thus he rose on the *third day*, according to his prediction. Dr. Leland, therefore, in writing against Woolston, remarks that " as to that part of the objection which supposes that he ought to have lain in the grave, according to his own prediction, three *whole* days and nights, it proceeds from a real or affected ignorance of the *Jewish* phraseology. This is a modern objection. The ancient enemies of Christianity did not pretend that Jesus rose before the time prefixed ; for they very well knew that, according to a way of speaking

---

* Horne's Introd. book III. part iii. chap. 4.

† Deut. xxi. 22, 23.   Mark xv. 42.   Luke xxiii. 54.   John xix. 31, 42.

‡ See the above passages in the Gospels.

usual among the Jews and other ancient nations, his rising again on any *part* of the third day was sufficient to answer the prediction."*

Dr. Sherlock also writes thus.—"Suppose, then, that we could not give a satisfactory account of the way of reckoning the time from the crucifixion to the resurrection; yet this we can say, that the resurrection happened during the time that the guards had the sepulchre in keeping, and it is impossible to imagine what opportunity this could give to fraud. Had the time been delayed, the guards removed, and then a resurrection pretended, it might with some colour of reason have been said,—Why did he not come *within* his time? Why did he choose to come *after* his time, when all witnesses, who had patiently expected the appointed hour, were withdrawn? But now, what is to be objected? You think he came too soon. But were not your guards at the door when he came? Did they not see what happened? And what other satisfaction could you have had, supposing he had come a day later? By saying of this, I do not mean to decline the gentleman's objection, which is founded on a mistake of a way of speaking common to the Jews and other people, who when they name any number of days or years, include the *first* and the *last* to make up the sum. Christ, alluding to his own resurrection, says, ' In three days I will raise it up.' The angels report his prediction thus;—' The Son of man shall be crucified, and the third day rise again.' Elsewhere it is said, ' *After*† three days;' and again, that he was to be in the bowels of the earth ' three days and three nights.' These expressions are equivalent to each other; for we always reckon the night into the day, when we reckon by so many days. If you agree to do a thing ten days hence, you stipulate for forbearance for the nights as well as days; and therefore, in reckoning, two days, and two days and two nights, are the same thing. That the expression ' after three days' means inclusive days is proved by Grotius on Matt. xxvii. 63, and by others. The prediction therefore was that he would rise on the third day. Now, he was crucified and buried on Friday; he lay in the grave all Saturday, and rose early on Sunday morning. But the gentleman thinks he ought not to have risen until Monday. Pray, try what the use of common language requires to be understood in a like case. Suppose you were told that your friend sickened on Friday, was let blood on Saturday, and the third day he died; what day would you think he died on? If you have any doubt about it, put the question to the first plain man you meet, and he will resolve it. The Jews could have no doubt in the case; for so they practised in one of the highest points of their law. Every male child was to be circumcised on the eighth day. How did they reckon the days? Why, the day of the birth was one, and the day of the circumcision another; and though the child was born towards the very end of the first

---

* Leland's View of Deistical Writers, vol. i. p. 137. Ed. Lond. 1754.

† It is but just to the author, here cited, to state that, in confirmation of his views of "after," Parkhurst, in his Greek Lexicon, under μετα, the word from which *after*, in the English version is translated, says that μετα, in reference to time, means—"Within, *intra*. Mark viii. 31; where μετα τρεις ημερας is the same as τη τριτη ημερα, on the third day, Matth. xvi. 21; and in this sense the phrase is used Matth. xxvii. 63, as is plain from ver. 64. So Josephus, Ant. lib. i. cap. xii. § 2. speaking of the circumcision of Isaac, says, Ευθυς μετ' ογδοην ημεραν περιτεμνουσι,—they circumcised him immediately, within, or on the eighth day. So the learned Hudson renders it, in his version, Die statim octavo circumcidunt."

day, he was capable of circumcision on any time of the eighth day. And, therefore, it is not new or strange that the third day, in our case, should be reckoned into the number, though Christ rose at the very beginning of it. It is more strange to reckon whole years in this manner, and yet this is the constant method observed in Ptolemy's Canon, the most valuable piece of ancient chronology next to the Bible now extant. If a king lived over the first day of a year, and died the week after, the whole year is reckoned to his reign."*

The following extract from the same learned writer is of great import- ance to the subject; since it is part of a reply to another *writer against* Christianity, who had attacked the arguments adduced by Dr. Sherlock for the reality of Christ's resurrection, in the work from which the fore- going extract is made. The following citations, therefore, give the Doctor a second chance of fortifying his position, and are of course his strongest arguments against those of his opponent.—"But the Considerer thinks the prophecy from the case of Jonas† not only dark and unintelligible at first, but, when understood and applied to the resurrection, false in fact, in two respects : I suppose he means it did not correspond to the fact foretold in two respects. Let us hear the charge.—First, 'The Son of man was to lie *three days* and *three nights* in the earth ; whereas Jesus lay but the time of *one day and a half*, that is, two nights and a day.' Secondly, ' the sign promised to be given was not given to those it was promised to' ; that is, to the evil and adulterous generation. It is somewhat strange that this great writer should be content to tread the dull road of vulgar infidels and sceptics, repeating difficulties and objections that have been a thousand times proposed, and as often confuted ; but it is still more strange that they should be such as are fully considered in the very book he professes to answer. How comes he to pass over all that is said in the *Trial* on this point ? Why such an affected silence here ? It would, by no means, have answered the Considerer's purpose to take notice how that author has explained Christ's lying *three days* in the sepulchre ; but I can promise the reader it will abundantly answer his trouble to consult him on this subject ; and if he has any doubts or scruples in the point, he may there receive satisfaction. It may be unnecessary to add any thing to what has been already said ; but that the Considerer may not think himself entirely neg- lected, I shall give a short answer to his objection, referring for the rest to the Trial itself. *It is well known that the Jews reckoned their time inclusive ;* in their computation of days, the first and the last were included in the number. *From one Sabbath to another they reckoned eight days*, and this when the computation began at the close of the first and ended at the very beginning of the second. And yet, in this case, there cannot be more than six solar days and seven nights ; and consequently, there is the very same deficiency of two days and a night, which the Considerer charges on the account given of Christ's resurrection. Three nights and three days,

---

* Dr. Sherlock's Trial of the Witnesses of the Resurrection of Jesus, p. 15. Edit. Christian Literature. First Series. Edinburgh.

† See the prophecy cited *ante* p. 251.

or three νυχθημερα were, in common language, the same as three days; they were equivalent expressions, and used the one for the other.*

"St. Luke says (ii. 21.) the child Jesus was not circumcised until eight days were accomplished; as strong an expression, one would think, as eight days and eight nights; and yet the birth might, according to the known way of reckoning in this case, be at the close of the first, and the circumcision at the beginning of the last. Again; the words 'after three days,' are very full and expressive, and how are we to understand them? The chief priests will inform us: 'Sir,' say they to Pilate, 'we remember that that deceiver said, while he was yet alive, After three days I will rise again;' and yet their demand is that the sepulchre be guarded only, 'till the third day.' He has here the authority of his own friends, the chief priests and Pharisees, that 'after three days,' and 'till the third day,' are equivalent expressions, and were so used and so understood, in the common language of the country. We have then the concurrent evidence of the chief priests, and the disciples, and that, too, in a point which neither of them could mistake; unless you can suppose them not to understand the language of their own people. How the expressions, 'three days and three nights,'—'after three days,'—'on the third day,'† are to be understood, Christ himself has expressly shown long enough before his death and resurrection : 'I do cures to-day and to-morrow, and the third day I shall be perfected,' (Luke xiii. 35.) exactly conformable to the case of a person taken ill one day, being blooded the second, and dying the third day, as

* The author has the following note.—"So forty days and forty nights, an expression often repeated in the Old Testament and the New, was the same as forty days; the first day and the last being each reckoned as a complete νυχθημερον, or night and day, though only a portion of it."

† The following note is appended to the work from which we quote.—"The Jews, it is plain, were not accurate to the letter, in their reckoning of time. I shall give the reader one instance among many to be found in the Scriptures. It is 2 Kings xviii. 9, 10. 'And it came to pass in the fourth year of king Hezekiah, (which was the seventh year of Hoshea, son of Elah, king of Israel) that Shalmaneser, king of Assyria, came up against Samaria, and besieged it, and at the end of three years they took it.' What can be stronger and more precise than this appears to be? Would the reader imagine that it could mean any thing less than three years complete? And yet, it is certainly not so to be understood; for after the words, 'and at the end of three years,' it follows, immediately, 'even in the sixth year of Hezekiah, (that is in the ninth year of Hoshea,) Samaria was taken.' Now, it is evident to sight, that if 'at the end of three years' was intended to signify three years complete, Hezekiah must have been in his seventh, and Hoshea in his tenth year, when Samaria was taken. After all, our Saviour himself is the best interpreter of his own language. In the many predictions of his resurrection the usual expression is 'the third day;' sometimes it is 'after three days;' and once, 'three days and three nights;' in which case the expression seems to be varied for no other reason than to accommodate it to the language and story of Jonas. Can it now be supposed that, speaking of the same event, he does not mean the same note of time, though the expression is a little varied? If then, one of the expressions happens to be clear, the natural and rational way is to explain the rest by it. Now this expression, 'the third day,' has nothing of obscurity in it, and consequently will help us to understand the rest. I would fain know what view our Saviour could possibly have in applying these several expressions to the same event, as implying the same note of time; or what interest the Apostles could have in publishing it to the world, had they not been the common language of the country, well known and well understood by every one, as meaning one and the same thing. Such a conduct would only have exposed both master and disciples to scorn and contempt.—See Bishop Pearson's Exposition of the Creed, and Bishop Kidder's Demonstration of the Messias, on this article."

stated in the Trial. Neither Jews nor heathens of old ever objected that the resurrection fell out too soon for the prediction, or that the language of Scripture, on this point, was not consistent. They knew very well it was the current language of the country, and the usual method of computation. The honour of starting such objections is reserved for the wise men of this age; who, knowing little of ancient usages and customs, are perpetually, from their own mistakes, raising objections against the Gospels, and such as ancient and more learned infidels would have been ashamed of.

" But the Considerer has another difficulty yet behind with regard to this history of Jonas. ' The prediction,' he says, ' was not fulfilled, because the sign promised to be given, was not given to those it was promised to ;' that is, to the evil and adulterous generation. Where does the Considerer find the promise he talks of ? I can see no such promise in the words referred to. Christ tells them no sign should be given but that of the prophet Jonas. What does he engage for here ? That he would appear to them in person after resurrection ? There is not a word about it. The promise, if you will have it a promise, was only that he would lie three days in the sepulchre. If this was not a sign to the Jews, nothing could be a sign to them ; for they had the evidence of their own eyes, and of their own guards....... The account given by St. Matthew, of guarding and sealing the sepulchre, is a very material circumstance, and was particularly so to the Jews, who had, by this means of their own contrivance, the most evident demonstration of the only sign intended them, the sign of the prophet Jonas. Our Lord told them that they should have this sign, and should know that the Son of man was three days and three nights in the heart of the earth. Had they been contented with seeing him crucified and buried, and concerned themselves no further, I know not how they would have had the evidence of his being three days in the earth. But by the secret working of providence they themselves furnished out the evidence."[*]

Very little have the two learned writers of the foregoing copious extracts left for us to say in proof that it was *on the third day* Christ rose.— They have illustrated the point that it was a custom among the Jews to include the first and last day, as well as the night of each day, of any transaction, in reckoning the number of days, and have enforced the argument drawn therefrom in a manner quite worthy of their renowned learning and talent. A few additional remarks, however, may be made to show that the expressions—"after three days," and "the third day," are intended to denote the same number of days. We read that on the day Christ rose "at evening, being *the first day of the week*, when the doors were shut where his disciples were assembled," Jesus " stood in the midst, and saith unto them, Peace be unto you;" and that " *after eight days* again his disciples were within," the doors being shut, Jesus stood in the midst, and addressed them in the same words as before. There is very little doubt that the Evangelist here means by " after eight days"—in a week's time, when the disciples were holding their weekly assembly, which they continued to do on " the first day of the week."[†] But although the word

* Sequel to the Trial of the Witnesses, pp. 48, 49, 51, 52. Edit. Christian Literature. First Series.   † Compare John xx. 19, 26.   Acts xx. 7.   1 Cor. xvi. 2.

after (μετα) is here employed, there were not eight *clear* days between the two visits of Christ.—There were only six *clear* days according to our mode of reckoning, between Sunday and Sunday, but there were *eight days* in taking into computation, according to the Jewish mode, the day of the *first*, and that of the *second* visit of Christ ; or the first Sunday and the second. Every one knows—and it is a common thing among us to say—that from Sunday to Sunday *inclusive* there are eight days.   In like manner did the Jews reckon eight days from Sabbath to Sabbath, or from any day of one week to the same day of the next ; and in speaking or writing of this *eighth* day, if it was once begun, used the word μετα (translated *after*, in the English version) in connection with it, as if the whole of the day had passed.   Μετα, however, is very indefinite in meaning, and in reference to time, is frequently used by the best Greek writers to denote *within* as well as *after*, such as—*within* eight days.   Now, just as the Evangelist, in the foregoing citation, relates that *after eight days* Christ appeared again in the midst of his disciples, whereas it was only *after six* clear *days* ; so another Evangelist,* in reporting the prediction—and probably the very words of Christ—has the expression—" And *after* three days rise again." which proved actually to be " *after* three days," according to the Jewish mode of computing time, although only *one clear* day according to ours. Consequently, it might just as well be denied that it was not *after* what the Jews called *eight days*, or in a week's time after his resurrection, that Christ made his second appearance to his disciples when assembled, as to deny that it was not on the *third day*, or on what the Jews called ' *after* the third day,' that he rose from the dead.

    This objection will appear still more cavillous when it is observed that the disciples—who must be allowed to be better judges than we of what such expressions as "after three days," "the third day," and so on, meant in their own language—believed the day on which Christ rose to be *the third*.   On the day Christ rose, one of them, as he travelled in company with another, to Emmaus, is reported by the Evangelist to have said in reference to the crucifixion of Jesus—" Hast thou not known the things which are come to pass there *in three days ?*"—" To-day is *the third day* since these things were done."†   Further : it may be noticed that the correctness of the fulfilment of his predictions on other points regarding his resurrection, discountenances the supposition that he was not correct also in precisely foretelling the day on which it should take place.   He foretold not only that he should be crucified and buried, but he further particularized.—" After I am risen I will go before you into Galilee ;" and we learn that, after he had risen, the angel at the sepulchre told the women that he *had gone to* Galilee, and that the eleven disciples, having gone thither, saw Jesus there, and worshipped him.‡   If Christ, therefore, correctly predicted his sufferings, his death, his burial, and the *fact of his* resurrection, describing the details of these events so minutely and so particularly as to foretel the very place he should go and be seen after his resurrection, surely he was fully able to foretel *the time* of his resurrection with the utmost precision.   Seeing that he has predicted the above marvellous occurrences according to the very manner in which they are narrated

---

* Mark ix. 31.   † Luke xxiv. 18, 21.   ‡ See Matth. xxvi. 32 ; xxviii. 7, 16, 17.

s

to have been realised, it is difficult to conceive any ground for charging
him with being a false prophet, because our notions of *three days* do not
accord with the Jewish mode of computing time, as spoken of in the
Gospels.   If Christ had not foretold the time of his resurrection, in terms
intelligible to his disciples and the Jews at large, the fulfilment of his prediction could not by them be seen to have taken place correctly as to time ;
and therefore the prophecy would not answer the purpose for which it was
intended.   If he had foretold, for instance, that he would rise in three
days, meaning thereby our Monday instead of Sunday, and had risen on
that day, the Jews would inevitably take that as the fourth day, and could
with propriety say that he had falsified his prediction—that he had risen
on the fourth day, whereas he had prophesied he would rise on the third.

SECTION III.—MYTHOLOGICAL CHARACTERS WHO ARE SAID TO HAVE RISEN
FROM THE DEAD.—DIFFERENCE OF OPINION AMONG EARLY CHRISTIANS,
AND THEIR DISAGREEMENT WITH MODERN CHRISTIANS, AS TO THE DAY
OF CHRIST'S RESURRECTION.—PROOFS FROM THE GOSPEL NARRATIVES
THAT IT WAS NOT ON THE THIRD DAY FROM HIS BURIAL CHRIST ROSE.
—THE NOTION THAT THE JEWS RECKONED TIME INCLUSIVE CONFUTED.

Having now carefully and candidly shown what the ablest writers on
the Christian side have adduced on the foregoing subject, this section shall
be devoted to a statement of such opposite arguments and facts as tend to
show that Christ did NOT *rise on the third day from his burial;* but that, if
he rose at all, it was on a *different and earlier day.*
In the first place it is to be observed that to rise, or be raised from the
dead was by no means considered an uncommon thing in the ancient ages
of miracles.   Æsculapius, Apollonius Thyaneus,* and others, some of them
long before the time Christ is said to have existed ; and even Irenæus, so
late as the end of the second century of the Christian era, are reported to
have raised many persons to life.   Nor was it anything new in those wonderful times for " god-men and man-gods" to die, be buried, and rise from
the dead.   Prometheus, Juno, Æsculapius, Adonis, and several others,
were once *dying* and *dead* divinities, but afterwards became alive.†   The
notion, therefore, of rising from the dead was by no means new in the time
of Christ.   Nor was there, consequently, any *originality* of conception in
the prediction that he should rise on the third day.   We have, however, at
present to confine ourselves—not to the originality of the conception, nor
even to the question whether Christ in reality rose at all, but—to the
question whether, according to his prediction, it was *on the third day* that

* See Lempriere's Classical Dictionary under the above two names, and under Hierocles.
† See Taylor's Diegesis, pp. 179—185.   Lempriere's Dict. under the names.   The
god Prometheus, who had the surname—*the Wisdom of the Father,* and—*He who died for
the people,* was punished by Jupiter for having saved the human race, when on the point
of being cast into Tartarus or Hell.   He was crucified on Caucasus, where Tertullian
says crosses have been found.   His blood had supernatural virtues.—Vid. Rondel's
De la Superstition, pp. 115—118.

he rose ; in other words, whether his prediction was verified or falsified in point of time.

This question, so far from being of modern origin—as Dr. Sherlock, already cited, twittingly tells infidels—has been one of great doubt and obscurity from a very early period of Christian history.   Even so early as the close of the first, and particularly the beginning of the second century, there was a considerable difference of opinion between the Asiatic and Western churches regarding the time which had elapsed between the crucifixion and resurrection of Christ.   In order, however, that the general reader may understand this difference, it should here be intimated that the Gospels represent Christ as having eaten the Jewish Passover, called also the "Last Supper," with his disciples at Jerusalem, on the evening or rather night of the one day, and that *on the evening or night of the following day*, as it will hereafter be more fully shown, *he was buried*,* Now, the Jewish Passover, called also the feast of the unleavened bread,† commenced to be celebrated on the fourteenth day of the first Jewish month, called Nisan or Abib, and continued for a week or seven days.‡   "But the appellation *Passover* belongs more particularly to the second day of the feast, viz. the fifteenth day of the month Nisan."§   In reference to the difference of opinion among the primitive Christians as to the celebration of the resurrection of Jesus, Mosheim remarks—"The day which was observed as the anniversary of Christ's death was called the *Paschal* day or Passover ; because it was looked upon to be the same with that on which the Jews celebrated the feast of that name.   In the manner, however, of observing this solemn day, the Christians of Asia Minor differed much from the rest, and in a more especial manner from those of *Rome*.   They both indeed fasted during the *great week*, (so that was called in which Christ died) and afterwards celebrated, like the Jews, a sacred feast, at which they distri-buted a Paschal lamb, in memory of our Saviour's last Supper.   But the Asiatic Christians kept this feast on the fourteenth day of the first Jewish month, and at the time the Jews celebrated their Passover ; and, *three days after, commemorated the resurrection* of the triumphant Redeemer.   They affirmed that they had derived this custom from the Apostles John and Philip, and pleaded, moreover, in its behalf, the example of Christ himself, who held his *Paschal feast* on the same day that the Jews celebrated their *Passover*.   The Western churches observed a different method : they celebrated their *Paschal* feast *on the night that preceded the anniversary of Christ's resurrection*, and thus connected the commemoration of the Saviour's crucifixion with that of his victory over death and the grave.   Nor did they differ thus from the Asiatics without alleging also apostolic authority for what they did, for they pleaded that of St. Peter and St. Paul as a justification of their conduct in this matter.........As they (the Asiatics) celebrated the memory of Christ's resurrection precisely on the third day after their Paschal supper, it happened, for the most part, that this great festival, which afterwards was called by the Latins, *pascha*, and to which we give the name of *Easter*, was holden on other days of the week than

---

* Matth. xxvi. xxvii.   † See Matth. xxvi. 17. and many places in the Old Test.
‡ Exod. xii. 12—28 ; xxiii. 15.
§ Horne's Compend. Introd. part III. book iii. chap. 4.

the *first*. This circumstance was extremely displeasing to the greatest part of the Christians, who thought it unlawful to celebrate the resurrection of our Lord on any day but *Sunday*, as that was the day on which the glorious event happened. Hence arose sharp and vehement contentions between the Asiatic and Western Christians."*

To say nothing of the positive proof that the above and many other facts furnish of the Jewish or rather Pagan origin of Christianity, it is to be observed that such was the uncertainty of the time of Christ's resurrection, even in the primitive age of Christianity, that one set of Christians celebrated the event the *very day after* that of the supposed "last Supper" of Christ, which day, according to the Gospel narrative, would be our Friday—two days earlier than Christians now suppose the resurrection to have taken place. Another set of Christians celebrated this event two days later, namely on our Sunday—three days from the commencement of the Paschal feast. Besides; the Jewish months being lunar months of 28 and 29 days alternately, the fourteenth of the month Nisan would not happen every year on the same day of the week, but must—supposing it to be one year on our Thursday—be the next year on Friday or Wednesday. Thus, as long as the Jewish Passover was observed by the Jews as the day enjoined by the Mosaic Law, it was impossible for them to commemorate Christ's resurrection on the *third* day from his death, or the *fourth* from his last Supper, and *that day* always to be our Sunday, or the "first day" of the Jewish week. Nor could the Western churches, whose custom has just been detailed, believe that Christ lay in his grave three days before he rose; for they celebrated his "last Supper" on one day, and on the next, his resurrection. As to the Asiatic churches, they celebrated the resurrection either on *the third day* from the fourteenth of the month Nisan, or on the seventeenth of it, on whatever day of the week, apparently, that would happen. But the time they allowed to elapse between the Paschal feast and the resurrection does not accord with the narration of the Gospels, so as to show that *they* believed that Christ rose on the *third* day from that of his burial, even according to the notions of the present Christians respecting the Jewish computation of current days. For as it was the custom of the Jews to commence the celebration of the Passover on the fourteenth of the month Nisan, and to eat the Paschal lamb on the fifteenth, Christ's last Supper, or Passover, in common with that of the whole Jewish nation, among whom he was then at Jerusalem, must be on the fifteenth. This, according to the Gospels, would be our Thursday. For we learn that the next day—which would be the sixteenth of Nisan, and our Friday—he was crucified and buried; that the day following—which would be the seventeenth of Nisan, the Jewish Sabbath, and our Saturday—a watch was set on the grave; and that the next day—which would be the eighteenth of Nisan, and our Sunday—he had risen. But as the Asiatic Christians celebrated their Paschal feast on the fourteenth of the month Nisan—supposing that to happen, as it must often have happened—on Wednesday, and, in *three days* after—which would be on Saturday—solemnized the resurrection of Christ, they thus showed that *they* believed he rose

---

* Mosheim's Eccles. Hist. cent. II. part ii. chap iv ss. 9, 10. See also Waddington's History of the Church, p. 14. Euseb. Hist. Eccles. lib. v. c. 23, 24. Tillem. vol. iii. p. 102.

on the second day, instead of *on the third,* after his burial.   For if these churches had ever seen the Gospels which *we have*—whose existence, however, in the first and even till the end of the second century, is very doubtful—they must have seen that these documents expressly state that Christ was crucified on the day before the Jewish Sabbath, (our Friday) and rose on the morning of the day succeeding it, (our Sunday) or at least was that morning seen walking about.   There is, therefore, in the practice of the primitive Christians no proof that they believed that Christ rose on the Sunday morning on which modern Christians believe he did rise.   All that can be inferred is that they believed that he had risen, but that they disagreed as to the precise time of his resurrection.

But what say the Gospels ?   " To the law and to the testimony."— First let us see what are the words of Christ's predictions as to his resurrection.   The first passage in the Gospels recording a prediction of Christ's resurrection is the following, purporting to be in his own words in answer to the scribes and Pharisees who requested him to show them a sign, or, in other words, a miracle.—" An evil and adulterous generation seeketh after a sign ; and there shall no sign be given to it, but the sign of the prophet Jonas ; for as Jonas was *three days* and *three nights* in the whale's belly, *so* shall the Son of man be *three days* and *three nights* in the heart of the earth."*   These are Christ's own words as to his predicted burial. No language can be more precise and definite as to the duration of his entombment.   It affords no just room for quibbling on the subject.— Whatever vagueness may exist in other passages recording this prediction should, according to all sound canons of criticism, be explained and cleared up by this language, which is most simple and explicit.   The next passage in which we meet the same prediction is the following.—" The Son of man shall be betrayed into the hands of men ; and they shall kill him ; and the third day he shall be raised again."†   Mark, in recording the same prediction, uses the peculiar word, *after.*—" And after three days rise again."‡   Luke, in one place, has the expression—" be *raised* the third day."§   John tells us that as the Jews asked Christ for a sign, he " answered and said unto them, Destroy this temple, and in three days I will raise it up.   Then said the Jews, Forty and six years was this temple in building, and wilt thou rear it up in three days ?   But he spake of the temple of his body.   When therefore he was risen from the dead, his disciples remembered that he had said this unto them."‖   The same prophecy occurs in a great many other places in the Gospels, and we find it recorded sometimes without any mention made of the words "three days."   Let us now inquire how this clear, distinct, and oft-repeated prediction has been fulfilled.   Supposing Christ to have risen at all, was it on *the third day* from that on which he was buried, according to the obvious meaning of his prediction, that he rose ?

In the Gospel narrative of Christ's apprehension, crucifixion, death, burial, and resurrection, there are several expressions from which we can with close exactness ascertain the length of time which elapsed between

---

* Matth. xii. 39, 40; xvi. 1—4.   Luke xi. 29, 30.   † Matth. xvii. 22, 23.
             ‡ Mark viii. 31.   § Luke ix. 22.
‖ John ii. 19—22.   The following passages also may be consulted—Matth. xvi. 21 ; xx. 17—19; xxvi. 61, 63; xxvii. 63.   Mark ix. 31; x. 33, 34.   Luke xviii. 33 ; xxiv. 7, 21, 46.

his interment and resurrection. The first *date* we shall notice is "the first day of the feast of the unleavened bread," from which to the time of the resurrection the number of days which passed is easily ascertained.— Although the four Evangelists materially differ from, and even contradict one another, on many material points regarding what was *said* and *done* by Christ and his disciples in celebrating this feast, and even regarding the place where they did eat the Passover, with none of which contradictions we have anything now to do ; yet all four perfectly agree as to *the time* when the Passover, or " the last Supper" was eaten. Matthew says— " Now, the *first day* of the *feast* of unleavened bread, the disciples came to Jesus, saying unto him, Where wilt thou that we prepare for thee to eat the Passover ?" The words of Mark are substantially the same, except that he has the expression—" when they killed the Passover."* Luke says—" Then came the day of unleavened bread when the Passover must be killed." The following words of John—" Now *before* the feast of the Passover" and so on, refer to the *same time* precisely as the words of the other Evangelists.† For, on the *first* day of the feast of unleavened bread, according to law, " the Passover" or Paschal lamb " must be killed" and " prepared," but it was not to be eaten, as already intimated,‡ till the next day, which commenced at sunset, and is emphatically called the " feast of the Passover." Hence, we perceive the agreement of the words of John— "before the feast of the Passover," namely the day before the *first* day of the feast of unleavened bread, mentioned by the other three Evangelists. It should particularly be observed here that as one Jewish day ended at sunset, and the next commenced at the same point of time,§ and as the Paschal lamb was to be killed *in the evening*, and eaten in the approaching night, it was not, according to the Jewish mode of computing time, eaten on the *same* day as it was killed,—it was killed on the fourteenth and eaten on the fifteenth of the month Nisan. In regard to the Passover, the Mosaic law expressly says—" In the tenth day of this month they shall take to them every man a lamb,"........ " and ye shall keep it until the fourteenth day of the same month,"........ " and they shall kill it *in the evening*,"...... " and they shall eat the flesh *in that night*."‖ The expression, *in the evening*—הערבים בין—means literally *between* the evenings.— The Jews reckoned *two evenings* in the same day, the former commencing at noon, says Parkhurst ; but at the ninth hour of the natural day, or three o'clock in the afternoon, says Horne ; and the latter at the eleventh hour, which was at the approach of sunset.¶ Christ, therefore, in conformity

---

* Matth. xxvi. 17. Mark xiv. 12. † Luke xxii. 7. John xiii. 1.
‡ See p. 259. § See pp. 246—250. ‖ Exod. xii. 3—8. See also Levit. xxiii. 6.
¶ Horne's Introd. book iii. part iii. chap. 4. Parkhurst, under ערב, has the following observations.—" הערבים בין, *Between the evenings*, or, more literally, between the mixtures. Occ. Exod. xii. 6 ; xvi. 12 ; xxix. 39, 41 ; xxx. 8. Lev. xxiii. 5. Num. ix. 3, 5, 11 ; xxviii. 4. The former of these ערבים commenced at noon, when the western or evening air begins to *mix* with the day ; the latter at sunset, when the cool dark air or night mixes with it. So בין הערבים will denote *between mid-day and sunset*. By a comparison of Exod. xii. 6. Num. ix. 3, 5. with Deut. xvi. 6. it appears that the expression is equivalent to בערב כבוא השמש—*In the evening when the sun is going down*, i.e. not setting, but *declining towards the west ;* and it is not improperly rendered by the LXX. προς εσπεραν, towards the evening. Exod. xii. 6 ; xvi. 2. Num. ix. 3, 11.— Accordingly, *Josephus* observes, Ant. lib. vi. cap. ix. §3. that the Jews were employed in sacrificing the Paschal lambs απο εννατης ωρας μεχρι ενδεκατης, *from the ninth to the*

to the Jewish custom, did eat the Passover, or the last Supper, with his disciples, on the night which *followed* the fourteenth day of Nisan, and which would, consequently, be regarded by the Jews as the fifteenth.*— Accordingly, Matthew says that " when the even was come he sat down with the twelve;" Mark, that "in the evening he cometh with the twelve;" and Luke, that " when the hour was come, he sat down, and the twelve apostles with him."† By the word *evening* in the above expressions, however, we are not to understand the time of sunset, but rather *a late period*. The word translated here *evening*, is οψια, from οψε, *late*, a *late hour*,‡ and conveys an idea quite in harmony with the well-known practice of the Jews to eat the Passover *at night*, in the hours of darkness—the time, we have seen, Pagan nations held their festivals. The whole of this night Christ and his disciples spent in celebrating the Passover, by eating and drinking, singing Christian songs, keeping a vigil or watch, praying, and other religious exercises—all of which strikingly resemble the practices of the Christian Agapæ.§

The next morning, apparently before daylight, he was taken into custody,‖ and ultimately brought before Pilate. On "the third hour" of the same day, according to Mark, namely a little after nine o'clock in the morning of our time ; but according to John, " about the *sixth* hour," namely about twelve o'clock at noon of our time, we find him—having been tried and condemned—now being crucified.¶ It is impossible to harmonize these two discordant statements of Mark and John as to the time of the day at which Christ was crucified. There is here a difference of three hours. Mark says—" It was the third hour, and they crucified him ;" but John states—" It was the preparation of the Passover, and about the sixth hour," when Pilate, at the request of the mob, " delivered him unto them to be crucified." It has been supposed that Mark meant to say that it was within the third hour ; that is—within the space of time

---

eleventh hour, or, according to our way of reckoning, *from about two to four o'clock in the afternoon."* There is no reason however to suppose that Josephus meant *from two to four o'clock.* From the ninth to the eleventh hour of the Jews, in the season of the year that their Passover was celebrated, would have been from a little after three till a little before six o'clock of our time.

* Dr. Giles, in his CHRISTIAN RECORDS, p. 216. calculates that the fourteenth of the month Nisan for A.D. 30, would, according to our modern calendar, be the ninth day of April.

† Matth. xxvi. 20. Mark xiv. 17. Luke xxii. 14.

‡ We shall see in the sequel that οψε is used to designate the time when the women came to the sepulchre, and that the word really means *late at night.*—Compare Matth. xxviii. 1. with Mark xvi. 1. Luke xxiv. 1. and John xx. 1.

§ Mr. Horne (Introd. article—Sacred Times and Seasons) remarks that " the later Jews made some additions to the rites prescribed by Moses respecting the Paschal sacrifice. They drank with it *four cups of wine*, of which the third was *the cup of blessing* (alluded to in 1 Cor. x. 16. Compare with Matth. xxvi. 27) ; after which they sang the hymn called the " Great Hallel," viz. Psalms cxiii—cxviii. Sometimes, when, after the fourth cup, the guests felt disposed to repeat Psalms cxx—cxxxviii. a *fifth* cup was also drunk. These ceremonies appear to have been in part imitated by Jesus Christ in the institution of the Eucharist." A very modest admission, of a practice which strongly reminds one of the Bacchanalian, the Eleusinian, and the Christian Agapæ, already described pp. 217—233.

‖ Matth. xxvii. 1. Mark xv. 1. Luke xxii. 47—66.

¶ Mark xv. 25. John xix. 14, 16.

between the third and the sixth hour, or between nine a.m. and twelve at noon of our time, and that John would be understood to mean that it was "about" the commencement of the sixth hour, or twelve o'clock of our time. The *time* of the crucifixion is not *expressly* mentioned by the two other Evangelists, but the whole tenour of their narratives, compared with those of Mark and John, goes to prove that Christ was crucified some time between the hour of *nine a.m. and twelve at noon,* or between the third and sixth Jewish hours.

As it is of much more importance to our subject to ascertain precisely when Christ died and was buried than when he was crucified, we pass on to notice that the next mention of time is the *sixth hour,* from which till *the ninth,* namely from twelve o'clock at noon till three p.m. of our time, there was preternatural "darkness over all the land." This is mentioned by three of the Evangelists, very much in the same terms.* Of course, Christ had before this time been nailed to the cross, and was now suffering, which is intimated to have been the cause of the darkness and other subsequent derangements of nature. Indeed, the mention of this hour, in this part of the narrative goes to show that Christ had been on the cross for some time before the sixth hour, and that Mark, in stating that he was crucified at *the third hour,* is more correct on this point than John who fixes the time at *the sixth hour ;* for, according to the testimony of the first three Evangelists Christ, while on the cross, had, for some time, been reviled and maltreated before the preternatural darkness at the *sixth hour* occurred. The *ninth hour,* or a little after three o'clock p.m. of our time, is another period which is mentioned, and which deserves particular attention. It would appear that about this hour Christ expired. The legendary tales of the four Gospels regarding his death, although they considerably vary in details, yet in the main, so far agree as to warrant the conclusion that Christ died some time between *three* and *six* o'clock p.m. of our time. Matthew says—" *About the ninth hour* Jesus cried with a loud voice..... Jesus, when he had cried with a loud voice, *yielded up the ghost.*" Mark says—" *At the ninth hour* Jesus cried with a loud voice," and again, three verses further on, apparently repeating the same occurrence, he says—" And Jesus cried with a loud voice and *gave up the ghost.*" Luke has the following expressions :—" And there was darkness over all the earth until *the ninth hour.*"........ "And when Jesus had cried with a loud voice, he said, Father, into thy hands I commend my spirit, and having said thus, *he gave up the ghost.*" John does not mention the preternatural darkness till the *ninth hour,* but states that Christ " said, It is finished ; and he bowed his dead, and *gave up the ghost.*"† Hence, it would appear that the four Evangelists agree, substantially, in representing Christ's death to have taken place at or immediately after the *ninth hour,* or three o'clock p.m. of our time.

The next question, and one of utmost importance in the present enquiry, is—*When was he buried ?* Malefactors who were put to death by crucifixion remained half-alive on the cross, occasionally, for a considerable time. The Romans, therefore, left the bodies of these unfortunate crea-

---

* Matth. xxvii. 45.   Mark xv. 33.   Luke xxii. 44.

† Compare Matth. xxvii. 46, 50.   Mark xv. 34, 37.   Luke xxiii. 44, 46.   John xix. 30.

tures nailed to the crosses until the flesh had wasted away, or had been eaten by birds of prey.   The Jews also were accustomed to leave the bodies on the crosses sometimes for several days, so as to be certain that death had ensued.   But in the case of Christ and the two malefactors crucified with him, this could not be done, for the Sabbath of the Passover was closely approaching, during which it was unlawful for the Jews to allow a body to remain suspended on the cross.*   The burial of Jesus and his fellow-sufferers was, therefore, in this case, hurriedly effected.   It appears from the Gospel history that they were left to remain on their crosses as long as the approaching Sabbath, which commenced *at sunset,* would permit; but that when it was perceived two of them still lingered alive, permission from Pilate was obtained to dispatch them by breaking their limbs, in order to *bury them,* if possible before *the Sabbath commenced.* The following expressions from the Gospels show that Christ was not buried at least until long after *sunset,* or the *beginning of the Jewish Sabbath.* —Matthew says that " when the *even* was come," Joseph of Arimathea went to Pilate to beg the body of Jesus.   Having obtained his request, he took the body and buried it.   Mark also says—" And now when the *even* was come, because it was the preparation, that is, the day before the Sabbath, Joseph of Arimathea . . . . . went in boldly unto Pilate and craved the body of Jesus.   And Pilate marvelled if he were *already* dead ; and calling unto him the centurion, he asked him whether he had been any while dead.   And when he knew it of the centurion, he gave the body to Joseph.   And he bought fine linen, and took him down, and wrapped him in the linen, and laid him in a sepulchre."   Luke does not mention the word *even,* but states that Joseph having obtained the body, took it down and buried it, adding that " that day was the preparation, and the Sabbath drew on."   John informs us that " the Jews, therefore, because it was the preparation, that the bodies should not remain upon the cross on the Sabbath day, (for *that* Sabbath was an *high* day) besought Pilate that their legs might be broken, and that they might be taken away.   Then came the soldiers, and brake the legs of the first, and of the other which was crucified with him ; but when they came to Jesus, and saw that he was dead already, they brake not his legs."   John proceeds to tell us that Joseph and Nicodemus, having begged Christ's body of Pilate. buried it ; in reference to which act he says—" Now, in the place where he was crucified there was a garden, and in the garden a new sepulchre, wherein was never man yet laid. There laid they Jesus, therefore, *because of the Jews' preparation* day, for the sepulchre was nigh at hand."†   Thus, it is clear from the narratives of the four Evangelists that Jesus was not buried at least *before* the Sabbath began, which was at sunset ; and would occur, in Judea, at the time of the year the Passover was held—about the tenth of April—somewhere from half-past eight to nine o'clock in the evening of our time.   The word translated *even,* in the passages just cited from Matthew and Mark, is οψια which means, late *at night,* or *at a late hour.*   Besides : it took Joseph some time, after " the *even* was come," to go to Pilate to obtain the body, to take it down from the cross, to embalm it, and other things, as John

---

* See page 252 *ante.*
† Matth. xxvii. 57—60.   Mark xv. 42—46.   Luke xxiii. 50—54.   John xix. 31—42.

says, according to the manner in which the Jews buried ; so that it must have been *very late at night* before Jesus was buried.—He could not have been in the tomb before ten o'clock on Friday night of our time. But as the_Jewish day terminated *at sunset,* and the following day began at the same *point,* there is, therefore, every reason to infer from the Gospel narrative that it was not *strictly at the end of the preparation day,* but at the *beginning of the Sabbath which followed,* that Christ *was buried.* For the word οψια, translated *even,* means late at night.—The word is used by Matthew for the time the two Marys came to the sepulchre—Οψε δε σαββατων τη επιφωσκουση εις μιαν σαββατων, translated into the English version—" In the end of the Sabbath, as it began to dawn towards the first day of the week."* It is used also by John to designate the time that the disciples held their private assemblies, which we know from many sources to be *in the night.*—" The same day *at evening,* being the first day of the week when the doors were shut where the disciples were assembled, for fear of the Jews."—Ουσης ουν οψιας τη ημερα εκεινη τη μια των σαββατων, &c.† The word οψε, in all its modifications, is always used to designate *a late hour.* Now, two of the Evangelists tell us that it was at this *late* hour, "the even," (οψια)—whether this was at sunset or when it had become dark,—that Joseph of Arimathea began to interfere in getting the body of Christ down from the cross, and in burying it ; and this he had to do by first asking Pilate's permission before he could touch it. The conclusion therefore is inevitable that, although John tells us " the sepulchre was nigh at hand," yet it must have been at least *an hour after sunset* before the body of Jesus was deposited in this sepulchre ; and therefore the *Jewish Sabbath must have commenced.* It would appear from the whole drift of the account that it was as much as Joseph could do before the Sabbath commenced to get the body down from the cross, and that, this being all the law strictly required, he laid it afterwards in the tomb. John tells us, in a passage already cited, that, in order that the bodies should not remain upon the cross on the Sabbath day, the Jews besought Pilate that their legs might be broken ; and as a reason for hurrying with the body to the sepulchre in the garden close to the place of crucifixion, he adds—" because of the Jews' preparation day." Christ therefore could not have been entombed, at the earliest, before ten o'clock on Friday evening—at least *an hour after the commencement* of the Jewish Sabbath.

The next question to be ascertained is *the time of his resurrection.*—The only mention of time between the period of Christ's entombment and the time he was found to have risen, is made by Matthew, where he says that " the *next day* that followed the day of preparation," which was the *Jewish Sabbath,* and our Saturday, the chief priests and Pharisees requested Pilate to " command therefore that the sepulchre be made sure

---

* Matth. xxviii. 1.

† John xx. 19. The writers of the New Testament had the word εσπερα which they used to denote late in the evening, or the setting of the sun ; as for example, Luke xxiv. 29.—" Abide with us ; for it is toward *evening,* and the day is far spent."—Οτι προς εσπεραν εστι, και κεκλικεν η ημερα. Acts iv. 3.—" And they laid hands on them, and put them in hold unto the next day ; for it was now *eventide.*"—ην γαρ εσπερα ηδη. The Septuagint use the word in the same sense ; see Gen. xix. 1, 2. Levit. xxiii. 5. In the last passage the word is used to designate the time the feast of the Passover was to *commence,* which we have seen, was at sunset. See note, p. 262.

until the third day, lest his (Jesus') " disciples come by night and steal him away, and say unto the people, He is risen from the dead."* This application, be it observed, was made within the same Jewish day as that on which we have just seen Christ was buried.   It is not a little remarkable, however, that it is only Matthew who mentions this application on the Sabbath for a watch to be placed on the sepulchre, and that it is only he that, in the subsequent narrative of the resurrection, mentions that this watch, at the sight of the angel who accosted the women, trembled, became as dead, and fled into the city.—In a word, he alone mentions this watch at all. It is most wonderful that Inspiration should have directed the other three Evangelists to pass in silence this remarkable guarantee against fraud, thereby affording strong proof, in addition to many others, of the fabricated character of the Gospels ; with which feature in them, at present however, we have nothing to do, but must take them as we find them. Whatever discrepance may be pointed out in the narratives of the four Evangelists regarding the time of Christ's seizure, trial, and crucifixion, we may expect them to agree precisely as to the time of his resurrection, —after the interval, of a Jewish Sabbath, or a day of rest, when, as one judicious writer remarks, no one stirred abroad, and consequently, nothing happened to embroil further the course of this history until the great event of the resurrection occurred.   The time that this marvellous thing took place Matthew states to be " In the *end* of the Sabbath as it began to dawn, the first day of the week."†   We have already seen‡ that the original words here are—Οψε δε σαββατων τη επιφωσκουση εις μιαν σαββατων ; literally,—" And *late* of the Sabbath day when beginning to dawn *towards the first from the Sabbath*,"—that is towards our first day of the week—Sunday.   The Jews, apparently, reckoned the days of the week *from* the Sabbath.   Hence we have invariably μια των σαββατων rendered into English—" upon the first day of the week,"§ that is, the first day *from* the Sabbath.   And they appear also to have called a week by the name—Sabbath.‖   In like manner, in the Hebrew version of Scripture, a week is called שבת (Shaboth) and weeks שבתות ;¶ so that for seven weeks the Hebrews would say seven Sabbaths.   Nor could, otherwise, any sense be made of the literal rendering of the passage just cited from Matthew.   He means evidently that the women went to the sepulchre at a *late* hour of, or rather *after* the *termination* of the Sabbath day, which ended at *sunset*, —so late that, at the time, it began to dawn, or the *next* day began to break.   In the middle of April, in Judea, it would *begin to dawn* about half-past three o'clock in the morning by our time.   But it will be observed that the narrative of Matthew goes on to state that when the two Marys, as it thus began to dawn, went to the sepulchre, they were told by an angel that Christ *had risen before this time*, and that as they departed from the tomb they met him, and he spoke to them.   How long *before* this early hour of the morning he had quitted the portals of the tomb we are not informed.   The words of Mark as to the time Christ rose are the following —"And when the Sabbath was *past*, Mary Magdalene, and Mary the

---

* Matth. xxvii. 62—66.   † Matth. xxviii. 11.   ‡ See p. 266.
§ See Mark xvi. 2, 9.   Luke xxiv. 1.   Acts xx. 7.   1 Cor. xvi. 2. *et al.*
‖ Luke xviii. 12.   ¶ Lev. xxiii. 15, 16.

mother of James, and Salome, had bought sweet spices that they might come and anoint him. And *very early* the *first* day of the week they came unto the sepulchre, at the rising of the sun." After detailing the circumstance of Christ's appearance, he reverts to the subject of time and says— "Now when Jesus was risen early the first day of the week."—Αναστας δε πρωι πρωτη σαββατου—*So having risen at day-break the first from the Sabbath.** Mark differs from the other three Evangelists in stating that the women came to the tomb "at the rising of the sun." But in latitudes like that of Judea, where there is not much twilight, the sun would soon give signs of its rising, in tinging the eastern horizon with its golden hue, after dawn, so that the difference of time, according to Mark, is not necessarily very great. He likewise says that Jesus had risen *before* the women arrived at the sepulchre, and that when they entered into it, they saw a young man within, who told them that Christ *had risen*, but he does not appear to have told them *how long* before they had come thither. Luke informs us that "upon the first day of the week, *very early* in the morning, they came unto the sepulchre...... and they found the stone rolled away from the sepulchre, and they entered in and found not the body of the Lord Jesus."† "Early as those good women rose," to use the sweet words of the commentators, "Jesus was up before them." The language of John on the time of the resurrection is,—"The first day of the week cometh Mary Magdalene, *early, when it was yet dark*, unto the sepulchre, and seeth the stone taken away from the sepulchre." John proceeds to narrate that she then ran to tell the disciples that "they had taken the Lord out of the sepulchre."‡ Hence we see that the accounts of the four Evangelists as to the time that the women came to the tomb agree tolerably well. Matthew, according to the words of the English version, says "it began to dawn"; Mark, that it was "very early, at the rising of the sun"; Luke, that it was "very early in the morning," or, according to the original, *in the depth of dawn;* and John, that it was "early, when it was yet dark." All four agree that the women came to the tomb at, or rather before day-break, on the first day of the week, which, according to our time, would be on Sunday morning about half-past three o'clock. The evidence of the Evangelists on this point is quite consistent and conclusive.

We are therefore now in a position to judge whether Christ, in accordance with his prediction, rose from the dead on the third day after he was buried; or, if he rose at all—a question that we are not now discussing—whether he did not rise on *an earlier and another day* than that on which he prophesied he should,—whether, "as Jonas was three days and three nights in the whale's belly," the Son of man was "three days and three nights in the heart of the earth." We have seen that he was

---

* Mark xvi. 1, 2, 9.—Και λιαν πρωι της μιας σαββατων ερχονται επι το μνημειον ανατειλαντος του ηλιου. But λιαν πρωι mean, *on the very break of day, exceedingly early.* Nor does ανατειλαντος, the participle of the first aorist, necessarily imply that the sun had risen, or was actually then coming to sight, but may take the sense—"the sun being about rising."

† Luke xxiv. 1—3. Τη μια των σαββατων, ορθρου βαθεος.—On the first from the Sabbath, in the depth of dawn. The words ορθρου βαθεος, used by Luke, convey a stronger idea of the earliness of the hour than those used by either of the other Evangelists.

‡ John xx. 1, 2. The word of John translated "early," is πρωι, break of day; and the expression rendered "when it was yet dark," is—σκοτιας ετι ουσης, being yet dark.

buried about *ten o'clock* on Friday night, and that he had risen *before half-past three* on Sunday morning.—How long before this time he had risen we have no means of ascertaining. But that he had risen at this hour we have the most clear and positive testimony of the four Evangelists. Now, this is the question—a question upon the decision of which the truth of Christ's prophecy under consideration must depend.—*Were there three days and three nights from ten o'clock Friday night till half-past three the next Sunday morning ?* Or, if he rose on that Sunday morning at half-past three o'clock, would he rise *on the third day* from his burial ? The most simple-minded child, if he had this question put before him, divested of all the theological lore and mystic verbiage in which it is always carefully shrouded, would promptly and unhesitatingly reply in the negative. From ten o'clock Friday night till half-past three on Sunday morning there are only twenty-nine hours and thirty minutes, which will not make *a day and a half*, inclusive of night. But in three days there are seventy-two hours ! The difference is vast. It will not, for a moment, be contended that we should not, like the Jews and all other nations when, reckoning three days, take into calculation the nights also. We are, however, told that the Jews always reckoned the current days,—that Christ, being a Jew, reckoned so when he prophesied his resurrection on *the third* day, and that, accordingly, he *did rise on the third day* ;—that the day on which he was buried was the *first* day, the following Jewish Sabbath the *second*, and the next day, namely our present Sunday, the *third*. But most unfortunately for those who resort to this ingenious mode of argument, the Jewish day *began at sunset*, and the whole tenour of the narrative of Christ's crucifixion and burial, as furnished by the four Evangelists, goes to prove that he was *not* buried *before* sunset,—that he was not buried till at least ten o'clock at night, and that he was, consequently, not buried until an hour of the next Jewish day had elapsed. Judging from the Gospel narratives which are our only guides, it appears almost certain that the body of Christ had not been taken down from the cross before sunset. He was buried therefore on the next Jewish day, namely the Sabbath. We have no proof when or how early he rose ; all we know is that when the women at the early hour of half-past three o'clock in the morning visited the grave he had then risen, and was walking about. Now, supposing that at this time he had just risen, and supposing that the Jews reckoned time inclusive, still he would have risen on the *second* Jewish *day* after his burial at ten o'clock the previous night, instead of *on the third*, as he had prophesied. Christ, therefore, instead of being in the heart of the earth three days and three nights, lay in the grave only one day and a night, and part of another night.

But let us inquire what grounds there are for alleging that the Jews, in calculating time, reckoned the current days, weeks, months, or years, on which a transaction began and ended, as *whole* days, weeks, months, or years, although only *parts* of them were applicable to such a transaction. We must of course draw our proofs of the Jewish practice on these points from the Jewish or Hebrew Scriptures. Let us first take the Hebrew mode of computing years. Here, however, it should first be observed that it is entirely a gratuitous assumption of Scripture chronologists, or Christian divines that, in the Old Testament, the part of the first year and the part of the last year, during which a Jewish king reigned, are taken as whole years in the number of years he is said to have reigned. The Jewish writings nowhere state that this mode of reckoning is adopted. Neither of the Jewish Talmuds anywhere contain such a statement. Nor can any *ancient* Jewish writer be pointed out who says that this was a custom.— On the contrary, many passages could be pointed out in profane Jewish writings showing that this was *not* the custom. Reference only to one writer may here suffice.—Josephus says that Aristobulus was made high priest in the seventeenth year of his age—that he lived no more in all than eighteen years—and kept the high-priesthood one year only.* It is sheer necessity which has driven our theologians to allege that the Jewish writers reckoned the current years in the reign of kings, and in other transactions. Seeing such wide chronological discrepancies in the Old Testament tales about Jewish monarchs, they find that, by admitting into the calculation of time the year of the commencement and that of the termination of the reign of a chieftain, or of some transaction, they are, in several instances, able to harmonize one account with another tolerably well ; and they therefore allege that this calculation of current years was a Jewish practice ; whereas such practice exists only in the figments of their own brains.† No argument whatever can be founded on these suppositions. Let us therefore go " to the law and the testimony," whither every Christian must willingly accompany us. With regard to the Jewish mode of reckoning *years* we read,—" The time that David was king in Hebron over the house of Judah, was *seven years* and *six months*." (2 Sam. ii. 11 ; v. 5.)— " The time that David dwelt in the country of the Philistines was a *full year* and *four* months." (1 Sam. xxvii. 7.)—" And he continued there a *year* and *six* months." (Acts xviii. 11.) Many other passages could be adduced ; but these are sufficient to show that it was not the custom of the Jews to call *part of a year* a *whole year*. In reference to *months*, we read —" *Nine* months and *twenty* days." (2 Sam. xxiv. 8.)—" The *four and twentieth* day of the *eleventh* month, (Zech. i. 7.) and so on. We never find however that *nine* months, or even *eleven* months and *twenty-four* days are called a *year*, but that the odd days are mentioned as such, and not as constituting an additional month. As to the mention of odd *days after*

---

* Antiq. lib. xv. c. iii. s. 3. also c. ii. s. 6.

† Desperate efforts have been made by many able and learned divines to harmonize the dates of the Hebrew writings; but such is their discordance that the task is hopeless. Well might Dr. Sherlock (Sequel to Trial of the Witnesses to the Resurrection, p. 49. Edition already cited—see p. 254 ante.) say that "the Jews, it is plain, were not accurate to the letter in their reckoning of time." A remarkable instance of this is to be found in the legendary tale we have of Abraham, (Gen. xvi—xxi.) where we are told that he was eighty-six years old when Ishmael was born to him,—that he circumcised Ishmael, as well as himself, when their respective ages were thirteen and ninety-nine years ; yet after a lapse of many years,—apparently after Abraham had witnessed the destruction of Sodoma and Gomorrha ; after he had "journeyed towards the south" ; after he had sojourned for some time in Gerar, and had dwelt in Kadesh, and in Shur ; after he had denied his wife, lost her, and recovered her ; after "the Lord had visited Sarah and had done unto her as he had spoken, so that Sarah conceived" ; after Sarah had borne Isaac, of course nine months hence ; and after a number of other things which required considerable time to bring them about ;—Abraham was only "an hundred years old when Isaac was born" ! only one year older than he was before all the above things occurred !

weeks, this does not occur in the Hebrew Scriptures; for the Jews appear to have counted *by days* till they came to a month; and, indeed, sometimes further; such as "*three score and six* days"—upwards of *nine* weeks. (Lev. xii. 5.) The division of time into weeks not suggested by any appearances or changes in physical nature, as it is into days, nights, months, summer, and winter, but being quite arbitrary, the Jews appear to have had no other name for a *week* than the word *Sabbath*. Such is the name given to this portion of time both in the Hebrew and Greek Scriptures*—a name which, in its original meaning, appears to signify *seven*, although some would contend that it means—*to satisfy*, and as a name for a week denotes seven days, or the seventh day. Happily, however, as to what mainly concerns our present subject, there are numerous instances, both in the Old and New Testament, of the mode in which the Jews calculated *days*, all clearly showing that it was by no means a practice amongst them "to include the first and the last day in the number," unless the first and the last day had actually been employed in the transaction narrated. Thus, we are told of a Levite, that "he abode with him (his father-in-law) *three* days," and "on the *fourth* day, when they arose early in the morning, that he rose up to depart." (Judges xix. 4, 5.) Now, if the day on which the Levite departed had been included in the number given, it would have been said that "he abode with them" *four* days; but as the day on which he rose to depart is not included, it is said that he abode *three days*, and on the *fourth day* rose to depart. Similar instances we have in the following expressions:—"They were *three days* in gathering of the spoil, it was so much; and on the *fourth day* they assembled themselves." (2 Chron. xx. 25, 26.)—"We came to Jerusalem, and abode there *three days*. Now on the *fourth day* was the silver and gold and vessels weighed." (Ezra viii. 32, 33.) Let us compare *these three days*, in each instance, with the "three days" Christ is said to have lain in the grave. Suppose the Jews began to gather the spoil on Friday morning, when would they have spent three days in gathering it? The answer is obvious—Sunday night.— Friday would be one day, Saturday another, and Sunday the third. In like manner, Christ, if he had been buried on Friday morning, should not have risen before Sunday night, in order to have been in the grave three days. But we have seen that he was buried about ten o'clock on Friday night, *when the Jewish Sabbath had begun*, and that he was found to have risen at or before three o'clock on Sunday morning, the first day of the Jewish week. This period is far from being equal in length to the three days

---

* The word שבע, or feminine שבעה—Shibaiah, is that translated *week* in the first place where the word *week* occurs in the English version. Gen. xxix. 27. The same word is also rendered *week* in English, in Levit. xii. 5. Daniel ix. 27, and indeed throughout the Hebrew Scriptures. The same word also means *seven* and *seventh*, and is so translated. This is the only word which the Hebrews appear to have had for a *week*. Nor do the Greeks and Latins seem to have possessed any other names for a week than those which denoted *seven* or *seventh*.—εβδομας and *septimana*. The Welsh, in like manner, call a week *wythnos*—*wyth* eight, and *nos* night, meaning *eight nights*, which is actually the case from the end of one Sunday to the beginning of another. The very word *week* is a modification of an old Saxon term which meant *eight*. The French word *semaine* means seven, and is of a cognate origin with this word, deriving from the Saxon seofon. It is not a little singular that in both the above languages there is only the word which signifies *seven* to denote a week.

mentioned in the two passages last cited. Suppose the Jews to have begun to gather the spoil, or weigh the gold and the silver,—for the two cases are precisely parallel as it regards time—at ten o'clock on Friday night, which at that time of the year—the month of April—would be about the commencement of a Jewish day, the night included; when would *their fourth* day arrive, of which Ezra speaks as being distinct from the other three days he mentions, thus not leaving the least ground for supposing that he reckons the inclusive days? Their first day would be from ten o'clock Friday night to the same time Saturday night; their second day from that time till ten o'clock Sunday night; their third day from that time till ten o'clock Monday night; and their fourth from that time till the same hour Tuesday night. Accordingly, Christ's third day would end at ten o'clock on Monday night. But Christ rose at or before three o'clock on Sunday morning—more than a day and a half before the expiration of *three days*. And even admitting that—as the reports of his prophecy, " the third day," are worded in some places in the Gospel—he could, consistently with the strict interpretation of this prophecy, rise *any time on the third day*, still he did *not rise on any part at all of the third day*, which would be Monday; but he rose a day sooner, namely early on Sunday morning. It is impossible, therefore, on any rational view of the case, to show that he rose *on the third day*, much less that he was *three days and three nights* in the grave, as he himself explicitly predicted.

But to proceed to give more examples of the Jewish mode of computing days.—Noah, at the time of the deluge, sent a dove out of the ark, in order that he might know from the bird's conduct whether the waters had abated. The dove returned, and the Patriarch, having waited seven days, sent it out again; and having received it back in the evening, he waited seven days more. (Gen. viii. 8—12.) The word here for *seven* is that used in the Hebrew Scriptures for a week—Shibaiath—שבעת; but if Noah reckoned the inclusive days; that is, the day on which he sent the dove out the first time, and that on which he sent it the second time, as Christian writers would have us reckon the days in the prediction of Christ regarding his resurrection, he would have an interval of eight days instead of seven. We are told that " everybody knows that from Sunday to Sunday inclusive there are eight days." Noah, however, did not reckon the inclusive time. Again we read—" He that is eight days old shall be circumcised." (Gen. xvii. 12.)—"Abraham circumcised his son Isaac, being eight days old." (Gen. xxi. 4.)—" And when eight days were accomplished for the circumcision of the child, his name was called Jesus." (Luke ii. 21.) There are no inclusive days or day reckoned here. A child that was eight days old *was* eight days old. The above passages do not furnish the least ground for supposing that the day the child was born and the day it was circumcised are included in the eight days; for it *could not* then, at most, be more than seven days old, and *might not* be much more than six days old. Neither six nor seven days would be called by the Jews eight days. They had a different name from שמנת ימים (eight days) for seven days, namely שבעת ימים Hence we read that the mother of a male child was, according to the ceremonial law, "unclean seven days" (שבעת) after the birth, and that " in the eighth day" the child was to be circumcised. (Lev. xii. 2, 3.) Here then it is expressly said that *seven* days must *elapse* before the child could be circumcised, and that it was "in the eighth day" this ceremony was to be performed upon it; so that there was no inclusive or current time reckoned. Let us see when would *we* consider a child "in the eighth day of its age. Supposing a child born on Sunday, would we not consider it in the seventh day of its age on the following Saturday, and in the eight on the next day—Sunday? Any one, however obtuse, if able to reckon the days of the week, must frankly admit this. Then, it inevitably follows that the Jews did not reckon inclusive time any more than we do so. What we consider a week they would consider a week, and what we deem *eight days*, or the *eighth day*, would be deemed so by them. But it may be contended that, if a child were born on Sunday night at twelve o'clock, it would not be *eight days* old till the following Sunday night at twelve o'clock. Granted; but it would be *in the eighth* day of its age any time after twelve o'clock on Saturday night till twelve o'clock on the following Sunday night; and it will be recollected that it was "in the eighth day" of its age that the Jewish law commanded that a child be circumcised, not *after the expiration* of eight days from its birth. And it is worthy of remark that in the passage already cited regarding the circumcision of Jesus, where the expression— "when eight days were accomplished," occurs,* it is not meant, *when the eight days were ended,* but rather when they had arrived,—when the eighth day had *fully come*. "Eight days" is an expression used here to designate the well-known time for circumcision, and is equivalent to saying—when the proper time for circumcision had come. But as the Jewish day commenced and ended at sunset, let us—to illustrate the case still further— suppose a Jewish child born *immediately after sunset* on *Sunday night;* this child, evidently, would be fully eight days old *at*, or *immediately after* sunset on the *Monday week*, according to both our calculation and that of the Jews. And their law demanded them to circumcise it in the eighth day, which would be the second Monday of its age. Now the time of the day at which the rite of circumcision would be performed on the child would be on the afternoon of Monday, according to the Jewish custom, when a number of the friends and acquaintances of the parents assembled together, in order to be present at this important rite; when also a name was given to the child. (Luke i. 58, 59; ii. 21.) A Jewish child could not therefore, at whatever time of the day it was born, be circumcised more than a few hours before it was *fully* eight days old, and even commenced its ninth day. If we suppose it born a few hours before sunset on any day, the rite of circumcision in that case could scarcely be over before it was eight days to the hour. Most probably the child, when happening to have been born about midday, was frequently a few hours more than eight days old before those who had assembled to circumcise it dispersed. At all events, as the circumcision took place during daylight on the eighth day, the child could not be more than a few hours under or over eight days

---

* Luke ii. 21. The word translated *accomplished* here is πληθω, *to fill up, be fulfilled,* or *be ended.* Parkhurst, under the word, remarks that the meaning of it in the above passage is not that *eight days were ended,* but that *the eighth day was come;* and he also states that Josephus uses συμπληρουμαι—a verb of the same origin and meaning—to denote *the time had come.* In the above passage the meaning is that the time appointed by law for circumcision had come fully and completely.

T

fully. The case, however, was very different in regard to the time of Christ's resurrection. He was entombed shortly after sunset,—that is, at the commencement of one day, namely Saturday ; and is found to have risen *before* seven hours of the *next* day had elapsed ; namely, on Sunday morning at four o'clock. This, so very different from the case of circumcision on the eighth day, can by no means be construed into three days, or the *third day ;* it being only about *thirty hours.*

There are in the Jewish writings a great many other passages which plainly show that the Jews *did not calculate time inclusive.* A few more of them, therefore, are pointed out. We are told " there was thick darkness over all the land of Egypt *three days,*" so that " they saw not one another ; neither rose any from his place for *three days.*" (Exod. x. 22, 23.) But if the Jews reckoned days *inclusive*—this darkness was only one day and two nights,—it became dark in the evening of one day about sunset, continued dark all night as usually it did, and also continued dark during the hours of the following day as well as following night, till sunrise the second morning. But the only thing unusual in this Egyptian darkness, if the Jews reckoned three days *inclusive,* namely, reckoned the evening on which the darkness *began* and that on which it *ended,* would be that there was darkness *one day,* just as Christ continued in the grave one day, added to two nights. The priest, according to the Levitical law, was to look at the plague of a leper, and if his disease appeared white, he was to shut him up " *seven days,*" and on " the seventh day" he was to look at him again ; but if the plague had not, in his estimation, stayed, he was to shut him up " seven days more." The priest was to look at the leper, the third time, " the seventh day." Accordingly, if the Jews reckoned days *inclusive,* there were in those three periods of seven days, which are called שבעת ימים or Sabbath days, twenty-three days. It is clear, however, that the priest was to visit the leper every *seventh* day, and that the three seven days just named made but twenty-one, the inclusive days not reckoned. This is made still clearer in the regulations given to the priest regarding leprous houses, which he was to shut up *seven days,* and re-examined the *seventh day.** Indeed, if the Jews reckoned days and weeks *inclusive,* they would, according to this monstrous mode of computing time, have made a lunar month of twenty-eight or twenty-nine days to consist of fifty-four or fifty-six days ; and of seven or eight Sabbaths ! This, for example, would have been their mode of computation—from Monday to Tuesday, two days ; from Tuesday to Wednesday, four ; from Wednesday to Thursday, six ; from Thursday to Friday, eight ; from Friday to Saturday, ten ; from Saturday to Sunday, twelve ; and so on. It is evident, however, that the Jews, absurd and barbarous as they were in most things, did not count time in this insane manner. To suppose that they did this would at once destroy all argument founded by Christian writers on the Chronology of the Bible, which the Rev. Thomas Hartwell Horne, in his Introduction to the study of this book, tells us " is of the greatest importance towards understanding the historical parts of" it. Hosea says—" After *two* days will he revive us ; in the third day he will raise us up."† There is no proof whatever in this expression that the time inclusive is reckoned. What the prophet

---

* Compare Lev. xii. 4—6 ; xiv. 38, 39.　　　　　† Hos. vi. 2.

means, in this poetical parallelism, is that, *within* two days, he and those of whom he speaks, should be revived, and that on the *next* or *third* day they should be raised up. He evidently does not mean that they should be raised up on the same day as that on which they should be revived. What is translated *after* here, as well as in other places, means *in, within, on,* the day spoken of; *that day* being regarded by the Jews a clear day from the time they reckoned. Accordingly, we find Christ's prediction of his resurrection on the third day from his burial translated, sometimes " *after* three days," and sometimes " *the third* day;" both expressions, it will be admitted on all hands, meaning the same thing.* It is stated that when Christ heard that his friend Lazarus was sick, he abode two days still in the same place.† But if the Jews reckoned the current days, this stay of Jesus may not have been even one day, or even half-a-day,—it may have been only a *few minutes* of one day and a few of the following. What is meant to be conveyed to us, however, is that he remained where he was during a space of time equal to what we would call two days. In reference to Herod, Jesus says—" Go ye and tell that fox, Behold I cast out devils, and I do cures *to-day*, and *to-morrow*, and *the third day* I shall be perfected. Nevertheless I must walk *to-day*, and *to-morrow*, and *the day following.*" Here Jesus himself is the exponent of what he means by *the third* day. " To-day, and to-morrow, and the day following"—three full days—is evidently an expression which Jesus intended to denote the same length of time as —" To-day, and to-morrow, and the third day"—namely, *three full days.*

* It is difficult to ascertain what made the Translators of the English version, in the passage just cited from Hosea, use the word *after*. The text is—יחיינו מימים ביום השלישי. But the formative מ prefixed to ימים does not necessarily mean *after*—it naturally takes the meaning of *in, within, at, by, near*, &c. In one of the following instances we meet with the word *after*, in our translation, although it is not easy to perceive for what word, particle, suffix, prefix, or modification whatever, it stands.—ויאמר אלהם עד שלשת ימים ושובו אלי וילך העם. This is translated in the English version:—" And he said unto them, Come again unto me *after* three days. And the people departed." (2 Chron. x. 5.) But there is nothing in the above text which justifies the use of the word *after*, —the literal translation is—" And he said unto them, again in three days return to me. And the people departed." Both the text and the very translation of the 12th verse of the same chapter prove that this is the meaning:—" So Jeroboam and all the people came to Rehoboam on the third day,—ביום השלישי—as the king bade, saying, Come again to me on the third day."—ביום השלישי. That the people came on what is called the *third* day, proves that they understood ביום השלישי—on the third day, to mean the same thing as שלשת ימים —three days; for, having been told to come in three days, they came on the third day. But it would be absurd to suppose that, for these *three days*, they allowed, as Christ did, only *one* clear day to elapse, and that, having been told by the king to stay away for *three days*—supposing the royal mandate to have been given on Friday evening —they returned on Sunday morning; which would no doubt have been considered by the king but one day; and he would have expected them not to return till Monday.— The Welsh version, which throughout is a better translation than the English, owing to the similarity of that language to the Hebrew, has for "after three days," *Yn mhen tridiau*—at the end of three days. Here also it is worthy of remark that the Greek word μετα, translated *after* in the English version, as "*after* three days," may with greater propriety be rendered *within, at, by, at the end, in,* and so on. Μετα τρεις ημερας means in or *at the end* of three days, rather than *after* three days. (Mark viii. 31.) Μετα, however, in many connexions in the New Testament, is properly translated into *after*. Its being so translated in the above instance, in connection with τρεις ημερας, only proves, like the foregoing examples, that the Jews did not reckon time inclusive, but that what they called *three days* was what we would call so.

† John xi. 6.

2 T

Here the expression—*the third day*, unquestionably means a period of three clear days, according to Jesus' own use of the phrase ; and that apparently in predicting his own resurrection on the third day,—the very point now at issue.   Here there is not the shadow of a pretence for saying that the Jews, or that even Jesus reckoned time inclusive.   A great number of other passages could be adduced in illustration of the fact that the Jews did *not* "reckon time inclusive," and consequently that the prediction of Christ that he would rise on the third day proved false, if the Gospel narrative is true ; but it is trusted that those passages already given will be deemed amply sufficient.

We now proceed to observe that the strongest expression in which we have an account that Christ prophesied his resurrection *on the third day*, is that in which he says that as Jonas was *three days and three nights* in the whale's belly, so should he be *three days and three nights in the heart of the earth.*[*]   Will we believe, in spite of the clear and forcible words of the Hebrew language in reference to Jonah, that he was only one *clear* day and two nights in the fish's belly ?[†] or will we at once admit that Christ's prediction has not proved true ?   This is the only alternative.   In order to believe the former we must believe that Nineveh was not " exceeding great"—that it was not in extent "three days' journey"[‡] but one clear day and a few hours ;—that what is meant in the statement that the Egyptian whom the Israelites found starving "had eaten no bread nor drunk any water three days and three nights," is that he had not done so from the dusk of one evening to the dawn of the next day but one—a space of about thirty hours ![§]—that what is meant by the friends of Job sitting down with him on "the ground seven days and seven nights,"[||] is that they sat with him five days and seven nights,—say from Friday evening at dusk till Friday morning at dawn,—the time inclusive being reckoned.   These, and such as these, are the absurdities which we must believe before we can consistently believe that Christ's prophecy that he would rise on the *third day*, or that he would remain in the grave *three days and three nights*, proved true.

There is, however, another important feature in Christ's prophecy of his resurrection which has not proved true.   He promised that as Jonah's preservation in the whale's belly for *three days* and *three nights* had been a *sign* or a miracle to the Ninevites, so should his resurrection, after lying *three days* and *three nights* in the grave, be a sign to the Scribes, Sadducees, and Pharisees, who wished him to perform a miracle before them.   But he did not show himself to any of these after he had risen,—he showed himself only to his immediate followers.   His resurrection was therefore no *sign* to the Scribes, Sadducees, and Pharisees ; and bore no comparison to the *sign* Jonah gave to the Ninevites, who saw and heard him after he had been three days and three nights in the fish's belly.   Most unfortunate it is to the interest of Christianity, most embarassing to the minds of Biblical students, that Christ did not allow the Scribes and Pharisees—the avowed unbelievers in his divine pretensions, the infidels of that age—to have one glimpse of him after his resurrection, during the forty days he remained on

---

[*] See the passage cited in page 261.   Matth. xii. 39, 40; xvi. 1—4.   Luke xi. 29, 30.
[†] The words are שלשה ימים ושלשה לילות—Jonah ii. 1.
[‡] Jon. iii. 3.
[§] 1 Sam. xxx. 12.   [||] Job. ii. 13.

earth before he ascended into heaven.   How this would strengthen the faith of the Christians even of the present age !   How effectual it would be to convert infidels !   But this was not permitted.   He appeared only to his disciples and followers, and that in such a manner as to render it necessary for him to reprove them for their unbelief in his resurrection.*— But the Scribes and Pharisees, to whom he had promised, in his resurrection, to be such a sign as the prophet Jonas had been to the Ninevites who had by such a sign been converted, were not favoured with a single glance at him.   It must be admitted that this prominent feature in his prophecy,— this direct promise, has not been fulfilled to this very day ; and is quite as much to be regretted as that he did not stay in the grave a day longer.— That by the expression—" an evil and adulterous generation seeketh after a sign,"—he meant the Scribes, Sadducees, and Pharisees,† who at the time conversed with him, there cannot be the shadow of a doubt ; and that, by his reference to Jonas, he gave them to understand they should see him, when risen from the dead, after remaining three days and three nights in the grave, is equally certain.   This, probably, was the reason why the chief priests and Pharisees asked Pilate for a watch to be placed on the sepulchre, saying, " We remember that that deceiver said, while he was yet alive, After three days I will rise again."‡   This sign is reported to have been referred to by Christ apparently on several occasions, and is recorded in three distinct places in the Gospels.   These passages, already cited, throw much light upon one another, and conjointly prove the correctness of the view just stated, as to the character of the sign Christ was to be to the Sadducees, Scribes, and Pharisees, or the unbelieving Jews at large.   Matthew, in one place,§ reports Christ as having briefly mentioned " the sign of the prophet Jonas" ; but in another place‖ he reports him as having explained what the sign should be :—" As Jonas was three days and three nights in the whale's belly, so shall the Son of man be three days and three nights in the heart of the earth."   Luke records similar expressions, omitting however the comparison of three days and three nights, and substituting the words—" As Jonas was a sign to the Ninevites, so also shall the Son of man be to this generation ;"¶ but evidently referring to the same thing, namely, the miracle (for such is the import of the word) of Jonah being brought alive from the fish's belly, and that of the Son of man rising from the grave after the lapse of three days and three

---

* Mark xvi. 14. Luke xxiv. 36 —42.

† The Scribes, Sadducees, and Pharisees, were the most important, learned, and influential classes of men among the Jews, in the time of Christ. The Scribes were members of the Jewish Sanhedrim, the highest council—the parliament of the nation, and were most learned in the law,—they were, in a word, the literatii of the Jews, whose office it was to make transcripts of the sacred books, publicly to interpret the most difficult passages in them, and decide in cases which arose upon the ceremonial law. The Sadducees were the followers of Sadoc—a great philosopher and pupil of Antigonus Sochœus —and were people of a most searching and philosophic turn of mind. The Pharisees were a numerous, influential, and moral Jewish sect. But the disciples of Christ were a few illiterate, destitute zealots, who could be persuaded to believe any absurdity, and be carried away by every ghost-story. What a satisfaction, therefore, to the world at large Christ would have given, if, according to his promise, he had shown himself after his resurrection to the above three influential and trustworthy classes of people, or even to a single individual of one of them !

‡ Matth. xxvii. 63.   § Matth. xvi. 4.   ‖ xii. 40.   ¶ Luke xi. 29, 30.

nights. But as this miraculous sign was not given to the wicked and adulterous generation to whom it was promised,—as no Sadducee, no Scribe, and not one Pharisee saw Christ after his resurrection, it was no sign to this wicked and adulterous generation ; and the prediction, therefore, supposing Christ to have really risen, proved as false in regard to those to whom he promised to show himself as it proved in regard to the time at which he foretold he should rise. To suppose, however, a *false* prophet to have risen or to have been raised from the dead, is a notion of so paradoxical a character, and so repugnant to common sense, that no sober mind can for a moment entertain it. Deity is incapable of dealing in falsities. Nor is it consistent with any sound and worthy notion of the Supreme Being to imagine that he ever has influenced, or ever will influence any creature of his to act so immorally as to deceive his other creatures by uttering false predictions. If, therefore, the Evangelists and Christ's disciples really believed that he rose from the dead—a question which it is not our province now to discuss—they must be labouring under a kind of cerebral aberration.—If they believed they saw him after he was buried, it must have been a spectral illusion,—they must have seen his ghost or " spirit,"* as they really thought they had ; and the story or the resurrection must be, what it seemed to the eleven apostles themselves, *who believed it not*, namely, an *idle tale.*†

SECTION IV.—REVIEW OF THE COMPARATIVE STRENGTH AND CONCLUSIVE-NESS OF THE ARGUMENTS ADVANCED IN THE TWO LAST SECTIONS, ON EACH SIDE OF THE QUESTION AS TO WHETHER JESUS'S PROPHECY OF HIS RESURRECTION WAS FULFILLED.

Having in the preceding sections stated and enforced the arguments on *both* sides of the question discussed, namely, whether Christ verified the prophecy of his resurrection, it now becomes our duty to inquire and determine on which side the preponderance of evidence lies. This, unfortunately for the cause of Christianity, is no difficult task. It would be much more pleasing to the mind of the writer, if he was sanctioned by what he deems TRUTH, to state to the reader that *he believes* that the preponderance of evidence is on the side of Christianity,—that there is stronger proof that Christ verified the prophecy of his resurrection on the *third* day, than that he falsified it. Veracity, however, compels him to declare his conscientious belief that, according to the Gospel narrative, that prophecy stands falsified ; and he humbly thinks that every one whose mind has not been warped by religious coercions and deep-rooted prejudices, must, on paying proper attention to the subject, come to the same conclusion. But the evidence, on *both* sides of the question, is now before the reader, so that he may judge for himself ; and the Gospel narrative is within his reach, so that he may pursue the subject in his own way, and

* Luke xxiv. 37.   † Luke xxiv. 11.

draw his own conclusions. Were it the practice of Christians to study that book called the Bible—to study it thinkingly, critically, and according to the rules of common sense ; not by the aid of commentaries,—not with the delusive theological spectacles of the age ; but as they would study any *other* book, according to the obvious meaning of its words and expressions, which are the true vehicles of ideas—such a treatise as this now presented to the world would not be required. The reader, therefore, is requested not to take the *ipse dixit* of the writer unconditionally, but to read the Bible, and think for himself. No expression was ever uttered more big with truth than that " the Bible is a book much more read than examined." Having been taught from infancy to regard it as a holy and inspired production, all read it and take for granted that it is so. The sincere advice of the writer of these pages, therefore, to the reader is—*Read the Bible* carefully, candidly, and impartially ; particularly the Gospels, whence the principal facts incorporated into the present Essay have been deduced.— But let us briefly review the arguments which have been advanced on each side of the question as to whether Christ rose on the *third* day.

There can be very little doubt that the same *day* is meant in the Gospels by the expression, μετα τρεις ημερας, translated into the English version—" *after* three days," as by τη τριτη ημερα, rendered " the third day." Indeed, this is admitted, and even used as an argument on *both* sides. But if the Jews did not reckon time *inclusive*, this fact by no means shows that Christ lay in the grave three days and three nights. It serves only to show that both expressions are *equivalent*, without throwing a glimpse of light upon the real meaning of the one or the other, in regard to the point of time intended to be designated. The very nucleus of the matter in dispute, therefore, is whether the Jews, and, consequently, whether Christ, in foretelling the day of his resurrection, " reckoned time inclusive,"—reckoned part of a day, however small, as a whole day ; and whether, reckoning time in this manner, Christ lay in the grave three days. The strongest evidence adduced to prove that the Jews *did* reckon time inclusive is the instance of Christ after his resurrection visiting his disciples on the " first day of the week," and in what is called—" after eight days again" visiting them. If Christ visited the disciples *the first* time—say on Sunday before sunset—and visited them the *second* time before sunset on the following Sunday, this certainly would prove that the Jews, or at least the writer of the Gospel which passes under the name of John, reckoned days inclusive ; for *otherwise*, from one Sunday before sunset to the following Sunday before sunset, there would not be *eight days*. Or if he visited his disciples the first time *before* sunset, and the second time *after* sunset, however little, there would be eight days between his two visits, without taking into calculation but one current day ; inasmuch as one Jewish day ended at sunset, and the next commenced at the same point of time. But we have no means of ascertaining that his visits were so as to time. Besides : the writer of John's Gospel does not say that it was " the first day of the week" when Jesus visited his disciples the second time.—What he says is that it was " after eight days" from his first visit.*
All that is *certain* from the Gospel narrative is that it was the first day of

* See John xx. 19, 26.

the week when he first visited them after his resurrection, and that he visited them the second time in "eight days after." That his second visit was precisely in a week's time, although called eight days, is simply *inferred* from what is said to have been the practice of the primitive Christians to assemble on the first day of the week. When, however, we read in the Acts of the Apostles that the disciples were commanded, before Christ's ascension, and probably on one of the visits already mentioned, not to depart from Jerusalem, but there to wait for the promise of the Father;—that after his ascension they went into an upper room, and there continued with one accord in prayer and supplication;—and that, for a considerable time after, the little Christian community continued to dwell together in unity, having all things in common;* these considerations considerably weaken the argument built simply upon the *supposition* that the disciples could *not* be assembled together on any other day than the *first* day of the week, and tend strongly to show that they were dwelling together *every* day of the week; so that it might be on Monday instead of Sunday that Christ visited them the second time, when they were within and the doors closed. Thus, although at first sight the inference drawn from Christ's visits appears specious, yet when closely investigated it has very little force to prove that the Jews reckoned time inclusive; especially when confronted with the strong and numerous proofs produced on the opposite side; for it needs hardly be remarked that the proofs adduced to show that the Jews *did not* reckon time thus are much more numerous, clear, and conclusive, than those adduced to show that they *did*.† While a vast

---

* Acts i. 4, 13; ii. 42—47.

† See pp. 252—257, 270—276. Even if there were proof that it was on the first day of the week that Jesus paid both his first and second visit, still this would not show that the Jews reckoned time inclusive, or in any manner differently from our present mode of reckoning. We consider that from the commencement of one Sunday to the end of another there are eight days; and therefore, in reckoning days, we say—"Sunday and Sunday are eight." But if, for example, a child is born at twelve o'clock on one Sunday, we do not say "it is eight days old" at twelve o'clock on the following Sunday; in this case, we say "it is a week old;" and even *after* twelve o'clock we do not say "it is eight days old," but rather, "it is more than a week old." It is on the *next day*, at twelve o'clock, we say "it is eight days old." When we say that a person is forty years old, we mean that his fortieth year is *ended*; but when we say that he is *in* his fortieth year, we mean that he is *between* thirty-nine and forty. We have no proof that the Jews were accustomed to reckon time otherwise; for we meet in their writings with such expressions as—"In the one and fortieth year of his reign;"—"In the twelfth year, in the twelfth month, in the first day of the month;"—"The heaven was shut up three years and six months."—Such expressions as these utterly disprove that the Jews, in calculating time, reckoned current years, months, and days, as whole years, months, and days. So particular, we find, were they on this point, that they mentioned the number of months, and even days that had elapsed over and above the years of the continuance of anything related.—Indeed, we have proof that, when they spoke in *round numbers*, they did not take into account *at all* the *fraction* of a year. For instance, we are told (2 Sam. ii. 11.) that the time David was king in Hebron was seven years and six months; but when all the years during which he reigned are summed up, the fore-mentioned *six months* are not only *not* counted as a whole year, but even *not counted at all*.—"The days that David reigned over Israel were forty years; seven years reigned he in Hebron, and thirty and three years reigned he in Jerusalem." (1 Kings ii. 11.) No Rabbinical writer,—no ancient author whatever states that the Jews reckoned part of a day, month, or year, as a whole. That they did so is not supported by a tittle of evidence; indeed there is the strongest evidence that they did not. The assertion that they did so calculate time, is on the part of modern divines purely gratuitous, and appears to have been made with a view to harmonise the contradictory dates with which the Scriptures are replete.

number of instances are cited from the Old Testament writings in confirmation of the former, the latter rests entirely upon the instance of
Christ's two visits to his disciples just noticed, and upon that of circumcision on the eighth day.   But the argument built upon the practice of
performing this rite on the eighth day, must be admitted to have been
fairly refuted.   St. Luke does not say what Bishop Sherlock asserts he
does, namely, that "the child Jesus *was not* circumcised *until* eight days
were accomplished:"* but that "when eight days were accomplished for
the circumcising of the child, his name was called Jesus."   Now, it has
been shown that, as the Jewish day commenced at sunset, and as the rite
of circumcision was usually performed in the afternoon, a child thus circumcised was fully eight days old without the necessity of reckoning parts
of days as whole days in order to make up this number.   And in confirmation of this, it is shown that the mother, after the birth of a male child
was regarded ceremonially unclean for seven days, "and in the *eighth* day"
her child was to be circumcised.   There is nothing clearer than that, in
this case, the child must be eight days old or in its " eighth day," without
reckoning any inclusive time.

With regard to the question whether Christ was buried at the end of
the preparation day, or at the beginning of the Sabbath; in other words,
before sunset on Friday evening, or after sunset, which would be the
Jewish Sabbath, we have only the term *even* or *evening*, used by the
Evangelists, for our *direct* guidance on this point ; although inferences may
be drawn from their mention of sixth and ninth hour, as well as from
their use of other expressions.   The strongest point, perhaps, upon which
the argument that Christ was buried at the close of the preparation day,
and not at the beginning of the Sabbath, is that—as Mr. Parkhurst, Mr.
Horne, and others affirm—" the Jews *reckoned two evenings*."   The former
of these, Mr. Horne tells us, " began at the ninth hour of the natural day,
or at our *three* o'clock in the afternoon ; and the latter at the eleventh
hour," which would be our *five* o'clock p.m. ; but, according to Mr. Parkhurst, the former commenced at *noon*, and the latter at *sunset*.†   Without
stopping now to attempt at reconciling the conflicting statements of these

* See page 255, and Luke ii. 21.   There are in Bishop Sherlock's defence, certainly,
some facts, but a greater number of fictions, while it contains no substantial proof that
it was on the third Jewish day Jesus rose from the dead.   It is true that from Sabbath
to Sabbath inclusive the Jews reckoned eight days; but so do we reckon.   It is likewise true that the Jews, like us, reckoned the nights into the days, when reckoning by
so many days; and that "the third day"—"after three days"—and "three days and
three nights," as used in reference to the resurrection of Jesus, are equivalent expressions.   But just as the Jews reckoned their night that preceded their day into their day,
which day commenced at sunset or *even*, and therefore comprehended the night; so do
we include the night in a day of twenty-four hours, when reckoning by so many days.—
The practice of reckoning the night into the day, or as preceding the day, has been very
prevalent from time immemorial.   So did the Germans reckon, (Tacit. de Mor. Germ.
c. 11.) also the Gauls, (Cæsar. lib. vi. c. 17.) the Saxons, and the Britons ; traces of
which remain to this day in such words as *fortnight* (fourteen nights), last Monday
sevennight (last Monday week), *wythnos*—Brit. (eight nights or a week), *pythefnos*—
Brit. (fifteen nights, or fortnight)   But none of these instances, any more than Bishop
Sherlock's νυχθημερον, proves either that the Jews reckoned time inclusive, or that
Jesus rose on the third Jewish day from his burial;—the points that the Bishop attempts
to establish.

† See pp. 248, 249.

two great theologians, we would only remark that Mr. Parkhurst's view, on this point, appears to be the correct one ; and that the two evenings or ערבים of the Jews were at *noon* and *sunset*. There is, however, a grand difficulty here in the way of any argument for the truth of Christ's prophecy being founded on the fact that the Jews had two evenings ; namely, the difficulty of proving that the *same* time of the day is meant in the Hebrew Scriptures by the term ערב translated *sometimes evening*, and the term οψε or οψια rendered also *evening* sometimes in the Greek Scriptures; while the obvious meaning of the word is *late*, or rather, *late at night*. Of this alleged identity of meaning we have no proof whatever. But admitting, for the sake of argument, that they are identical in meaning, let us see which of these two Jewish evenings,—whether that at *noon*, or that at *sunset*—is spoken of in the Gospels in connection with the crucifixion, death, and burial of Jesus. This is of importance ; for if it is the former *evening* at noon is meant, then Christ must have been buried before the commencement of the Jewish Sabbath at sunset ; but if the latter is meant, this leads inevitably to the conclusion that he was buried *after* sunset, and therefore on the Jewish Sabbath. The mention made of hours by the Evangelists, in detailing the circumstances of Christ's crucifixion, will serve at once to decide this question. Three of them state that, when Christ was on the cross, there was darkness over all the land from the sixth till the ninth hour ; that is, from twelve at noon till three o'clock p.m. of our time ; and that, at the last-named hour, namely three o'clock, Jesus cried with a loud voice.* At this time, namely three o'clock, therefore, Jesus was *alive;* and this was *after the first evening* of the Jews, if, as Mr. Parkhurst tells us, the first evening was at *noon;* or if, as Mr. Horne says, it was at *three o'clock,* then also was it the first evening when Christ cried with a loud voice. The fourth Evangelist, however, as already noticed, states that it was about the sixth hour when he was crucified,† making the time when he cried with a loud voice still later. However about this discrepancy, we are told by two of the Evangelists,‡ after mentioning the ninth hour, and after detailing several things which subsequently occurred, that " *when the even was come,*" Joseph of Arimathea applied to Pilate for leave to bury the body of Jesus. It is therefore clear that, if the Jews *did* reckon two evenings, the *latter* is meant here, namely that which occurred at *sunset.* Hence we perceive that, after thus scrutinizing this point, the result does not help us at all to arrive at the conclusion that Jesus was buried *before* the commencement of the Jewish Sabbath. When it is recollected that the very meaning of οψια (even) is *late;*§ that John

---

* Matth. xxvii. 45, 46.   Mark xv. 33, 34.   Luke xxiii. 44, 46.
† John xix. 14, 16, 30.   ‡ Matth. xxvii. 57.   Mark xv. 42.
§ From the following passages, we may judge in what sense the word *even*—οψε was used.—" When the *even* was now come, his disciples went down unto the sea towards Capernaum.   And it was now *dark*, and Jesus was not come to them."—John vi. 16, 17. Here it is clear that when the *even* was come, it was *dark*, not only *sunset.* The parable of the vineyard (Matth. xx. 8—12.) shows that *even* did not occur till the twelfth hour, which was at sunset, and at the commencement of the next day :—" When even was come" the steward called the labourers and gave them their hire, paying those who had been hired at the *eleventh hour*, and had worked only one hour, namely till the *twelfth hour*, a penny.   "*Even*," therefore, did not occur before the twelfth hour, which was at sunset.   In Mark (i. 32.) we find the expression—" At even when the sun did set"—

says the Jews would not allow the bodies to remain on the cross on the Sabbath day ;* and that considerable time after "the even was come" must have elapsed before Joseph could have obtained permission to take down the body, and made the necessary preparations for embalming, enshrouding, and depositing it, the arguments advanced to show that Christ must have been entombed *after the commencement* of the Sabbath day, or on Friday night of our time, remain invulnerable. It is impossible, therefore, to evade the conclusion—even admitting the Jews reckoned time inclusive, of which there is not the shadow of a proof—that Jesus *did not* remain in the sepulchre nearly three days—*did not* rise on the third day, and therefore *did not* verify his prediction.

There is one remarkable expression, which not only appears to have hitherto escaped the notice of Biblical critics, but strongly shows the incorrectness of the notion that the Jews reckoned time inclusive, and furnishes a strong presumptive proof that Christ was buried on the Sabbath. It is that of the Chief Priests and Pharisees, of whom it is said that the next day that followed the preparation,—that is, the Jewish Sabbath, on which Christ lay in the tomb,—they came to Pilate and said,—"Sir, we remember that that deceiver said, while he was yet alive. After three days I will rise again. Command, therefore, that the sepulchre be made sure until the third day."† Now, when we consider that it was on the Sabbath day they made this request, and that Christ rose the very next night, or early in the morning of the next day, and was found to have actually quitted the tomb at daybreak that morning, it is most singular that they should have used the expression—"until the third day," if they reckoned time inclusive and were aware that the third day would be up in a few hours after they made this application, namely, immediately after sunset *that* day—when another Jewish day commenced.‡ It is most strange that

more correctly, when the sun *had set*—οτε εδυ ο ηλιος; an expression which shows that it was not even till the sun did set. Pasor, in his Greek Lexicon, under οψε, remarks: —Idem est quod εν υστερω, in extremo.........Non vero hic primam noctis partem, quæ vespera dicitur, sed ultimam designat," etc. And the author of another Greek Lexicon, printed in 1658, and bearing the signatnre "T. C. late of C.C.C. in Oxford," defines the word thus—"Οψε, late in the evening. Mark xi. 19. Matth. xxviii. 1. In this scripture it doth not denote the first part of the night called the evening, but the last part of the night which we call the dawning of the day." At all events it is certain that the Jews did not call it *even* before the sun had set, when another day commenced. The commencement of a Jewish day, particularly a Sabbath day, may be inferred with certainty from the following words—" When the gates of Jerusalem began to be dark before the Sabbath, I commanded that the gates should be shut, and charged that they should not be opened till after the Sabbath."—Neh. xiii. 19. Hence, it is clear that the Jewish Sabbath commenced at sunset. Scarcely any twilight being in Judea after sunset, the gates of Jerusalem *began* to be dark a little before sunset.

* John xix. 31, 42. † Matth. xxvii. 62, 63.

‡ On a point of presumptive evidence like this respecting the guard demanded by the Chief Priests and Pharisees, the *onus probandi* lies on the Christian side, as that which affirms and must prove its affirmation. In all such inquiries it is a rule founded in reason and common sense that whatever is most *probable must be presumed*, or in other words, that the *probable* must be preferred to the *improbable*. Then, surely it is far more probable that the Chief Priests and Pharisees acted rationally in asking a guard for Christ's tomb, than that they acted foolishly in asking a guard for *only a few hours* instead of *for two days and nights*. To presume such silly conduct is to argue that neither the Chief Priests, nor the Pharisees, with even Pilate at their head, had among them a single person of

they should have used the expression—"until the third day" for a few hours, instead of saying—"until to-morrow," if they thought that "the third day" was up on the morrow. The obvious drift of this expression, however, shows that they believed that, at least, two days of the time were unexpired when they made this application. For they went to Pilate on the very *same* Jewish day that Christ was entombed, namely the Jewish Sabbath (our Saturday) ; and it is very natural to suppose they did so, if they expected—as they are made to say—that his disciples would come by night and steal him away. It is not likely that they would allow any time to elapse, especially a night, before they would cause the tomb to be made safe ; and the natural construction to be put on this is that, Christ having been placed in the tomb—a kind of a cave hewn in the rock—late on the Friday night,—the commencement of the Jewish Sabbath—by Joseph, who behoved to spend most, if not the whole of the night in embalming, enshrouding, and depositing the body, the Chief Priests and Pharisées the following morning (our Saturday) applied to Pilate for a guard to be placed on the sepulchre the next night and following nights, lest the disciples in the hours of darkness should come and steal the body. Accordingly, they used the expressions—"after three days" and "until the third day," which it is absurd to suppose they would use if they believed that "the third day" would be up on the very *next* night. It is on this night, however, or towards the dawn of the next morning that, we learn from the Evangelists, Christ rose. It is utterly impossible that this space of time could be three days, or that Christ rose on the third day. For it to be so would be as much of a miracle as that Christ rose at all. To believe it is to believe that one is *three ;* or that from ten o'clock Friday night till two o'clock Sunday morning is three days ! Common sense teaches that this space of time is but one day and four hours !

Another very pointed prediction of his resurrection said to have been uttered by Christ, but not hitherto noticed here, is the following.—Jesus, having gone into the temple, and, with a scourge of small cords, driven out the sheep and cattle dealers, together with their live stock, poured out the changers' money, overthrown their tables, and ordered the vendors of doves to take away these emblems of innocence, one of which not many months before, on the banks of the Jordan, had been used by the Deity to embody the Holy Ghost, and had descended upon Jesus—the Jews, not very unreasonably, asked him what *sign* he showed them for his authority thus to clear the temple. "Jesus answered and said unto them, Destroy this temple, and in three days I will raise it up. Then said the Jews, Forty and six years was this temple in building, and wilt thou rear it up in three days ? But he spake of the temple of his body. When, therefore, he had risen from the dead, his disciples remembered that he had said this."* To say nothing of the ambiguity of this expression concerning the

sufficient sagacity to perceive the folly of placing a guard at a time so useless and un-neccessary, if only few hours of risk remained. We must presume that the Chief Priests, Pharisees, and Pilate possessed some discretion,—the two former in asking, and the latter one in disposing of a guard on the occasion in question. The supposition that they considered Jesus's three days would be up in few hours, however, makes their application for a guard to be an act of the most useless and foolish character.

* John ii. 13, 22. Matth. xxvi. 60, 61 ; xxvii. 40. Mark xiv. 58 ; xv. 29.

temple, which ambiguity is characteristic of all the expressions of Jesus on any important point ; and not to stop at present to consider the moral character of the act of tumbling the merchants and their property out of the temple,—an act very unlikely to have been suffered to be done by a single individual, who shortly after, evidently against his will, was apprehended and crucified,—to say nothing, we repeat, about these things at present, let us consider whether it is likely that Christ, by saying he would rebuild the temple *in three days*, by which we are told he meant that he would rise from the grave *in three days* after he was buried, reckoned the inclusive time or not;—whether he meant for three days the time he lay in the grave—about thirty hours, or fully three days—seventy-two hours ; and whether the Jews understood him to mean the latter or the former. That by this expression, neither Jesus nor the Jews meant thirty hours or two nights and a day is, by the very drift of the ideas conveyed in the contexts, sufficiently clear to the most childish mental capacity.— Just as the Jews meant forty-six years, and not *half* this time, so did Christ mean *three* days, and so was he understood. This instance evidently shows not only that neither Jesus nor the Jews computed time inclusive, but also that Christ did not remain in the grave long enough by a day and a half, at least, to verify his prediction. To elucidate this point a little further : —Supposing a child was born at ten o'clock on Friday night, and died at three o'clock on Sunday morning, would it be said that it lived *three days* and three nights, or even that it died the *third day* from its birth ? If it would, then it follows that, if it died at three o'clock on Saturday morning, it would be said that it lived two days and two nights, when in reality it had lived but five hours ! Five hours, however, would never be called two days and two nights by any people, any more than twenty-nine hours would be called three days and three nights. Now, the case of Christ's burial and resurrection is precisely similar to the foregoing. He was entombed on Friday night about ten o'clock, and he rose Sunday morning about three—after lying in the tomb during the interval of about twenty-nine hours, or less than a day and a quarter.

If, however, we closely examine the Gospel narrative, we shall have strong reasons to infer that he was not in the tomb even twenty-nine hours. The Evangelists use the same word to denote the hour of the day at which he was buried and the time at which he was found to have risen, namely επιφοσκω,—a verb which originally signifies to dawn or shine, and in the New Testament denotes *approaching*, or *drawing on*. Luke says that, when Joseph entombed Jesus, the Sabbath was *drawing on* or *dawning* ; and Matthew says that, when the women came to the sepulchre and found Jesus had risen, it was late of the Sabbath, *drawing on* or *dawning* towards the first day from the Sabbath.* So that, whether to *dawn* or to *draw on* is meant by the verb used in these two instances, it is obvious that it is the *same time* of the Jewish day is meant in both instances. Nor is it material to our subject what part of the day is thus meant. It is sufficient that these passages warrant the inference that Jesus *rose before he had been in the tomb even twenty-four hours !* If it was *dawning* for the Jewish Monday

* Compare Luke xxiii. 54.—σαββατον επιφωσκε; and Matth. xxviii. 1.—Οψε δε σαββατων, τη επιφωσκουση εις μιαν σαββατων.

when the women found Jesus to have risen, it was *dawning* for the Jewish Sunday when Joseph placed him in the tomb. If, according to the other supposed meaning of the word used in these two places, it was *drawing towards* the beginning of the Jewish Sabbath when Joseph laid Jesus in the tomb, it was *drawing towards* the beginning of the Jewish Monday, which commenced at sunset, when Jesus was found to have risen. Not more, therefore, than twenty-fours, at the outside, can be made of the interval during which Jesus lay in the tomb. The whole of the particulars of Christ's burial and resurrection, according to the Evangelists, may be summed up thus.—At the ninth hour of the Jewish Saturday, or three o'clock on the afternoon of our Friday, Jesus was alive on the cross; (Matth. xxvii. 46. Mark xv. 34.) but he appears to have lived only a short time afterwards; for we are told that, after he had cried with a loud voice, he gave up the ghost. (Matth. xxvii. 50. Mark xv. 37.) "When *even* (or sunset) was come," which was about six o'clock, Joseph of Arimathea went to Pilate to ask permission to cut down the body and prepare it for burial, that it might not hang on the cross on the Sabbath, which was about to set in. (Matth. xxvii. 57. Mark xv. 42. Luke xxiii. 54. John xix. 31, 42.) But some time elapsed before he obtained permission to remove the body.—Pilate doubted whether Jesus was already dead; and he therefore sent a centurion to ascertain the fact. When the centurion returned, Pilate gave permission to take down the body. But considerable time again was required to prepare it for burial, (John xix. 40.) so that it could not have been entombed earlier than nine or ten o'clock that night. Although it was unlawful either to allow the bodies of malefactors to remain all night on the tree, or to bury them on the Sabbath, yet it is evident that, in order to avoid the former, in the case of Jesus, they were obliged to perform the latter. He was, unquestionably, buried long after the commencement of the Jewish Sabbath, which, like every other day, began at sunset. Having thus been entombed after the commencement of the Sabbath, he was found to have risen, according to Matthew, *in the end* of the same Sabbath, when it drew towards the next day; according to Mark, *very early* in the morning of the next day; according to Luke, the first day of the week, *very early;* and according to John, the first day of the week, *when it was yet dark.* How long before this time he had left the tomb we are not told. Matthew informs us that certain women came to the sepulchre " in the end of the Sabbath," and found that he had risen. Accordingly, we may safely conclude that he rose on the very same day as he was buried; and that he was not in the tomb fully *twenty-four hours.* Instead of being in the tomb, therefore, three days and three nights, as he had predicted, he was scarcely one day and a night,—instead of rising on the *third day* he rose on the *first;* having been entombed long after the beginning of the Sabbath, and found to have risen " in the end" of it. It is utterly impossible, by any mode of computing time, to extend this period into three days and three nights. Even admitting that the Jews reckoned days inclusive, of which there is no proof, still this mode of computation cannot, by any device, construe a day and a night into three days and nights. In supposing, therefore, that Jesus rose from the dead at all,[*]

* There are many opinions and theories regarding the origin of the tale of Christ's resurrection. One, and perhaps the most probable, is that this story, with the rest of

which is utterly incredible, and that he ever uttered this prediction, attributed to him by his biographers—the Evangelists, it is impossible to avoid

the Gospels, is only part of the fabulous productions of antiquity,—that the Gospels, in their present shape, were compiled some two hundred years after the beginning of the Christian era, from the mythological and superstitious lore that was then circulating in great abundance,—and that Christ himself is only a mythological personage who, if he ever had any existence at all, existed many centuries before the Christian era, and was very different from the Christ of the Gospels, being originally Æsculapius, or some other character of the like fame, and serving only as the basis of the Christian fable. It is certain that the primitive teachers of Christianity converted to their own purposes the writings of ancient poets and philosophers, mixing together the Oriental Gnosticism and Greek philosophy, and palming them on the world, in a new form, as things especially revealed to themselves. Accordingly, Minutius Felix, an African lawyer, who flourished about A.D. 211, in his Apology for Christianity, called *Octavius*, and written in the form of a dialogue, makes Cœcilius object thus:—" Omnia ista figmenta malesanæ opinionis, et inepta solatia, a poetis fallacibus, in dulcedine carminis lusa, a vobis nimium credulis in vestrum Deum, turpiter reformata sunt." The writer makes *Octavius* reply to this charge, not by denying, but rather admitting it. It is well known to all, and indeed confessed with sorrow, by some Christian writers of the present age, (Vid. ante, p. 185,) that the Fathers forged whole Gospels and Epistles, thinking that thereby they served the cause of truth. It is also well known that the Therapeuts of the Alexandrian School—the cradle of Christianity, where probably it was first formed into anything like a system—devoted themselves with zeal to the Eclectic philosophy, the main point of which was to collect together, in the form of written books, whatever was thought good and worthy of record in all other systems. Lactantius, Arnobius, Origen, and a host of other Christian Fathers, make a boast of this. It may further be remarked that, at a most early period of the Christian era, there appears to have been great doubts as to the real existence of Christ. The Manichees, as Augustine informs us, denied that he was a man, while others maintained that he was a man, but denied that he was a God. (August. Serm. xxxvii. c. 12.) The Fathers tell us that it was in the times of the apostles believed that Christ was a *phantom*, and that no such person as Jesus Christ had ever had any corporeal existence. —Solem negarat meridie lucere, qui docetas seu phantasiastas, hæreticos temporibus apostolorum inficiaretur erupisse. (Cotelerius ad Ignat. Epist. ad Trall. c. 10.) Apostolis adhuc in sæculo superstitibus, adhuc apud Judæum Christi sanguine recenti, phantasma Domini corpus asserebatur. (Hieron. adv. Lucif. c. iv. p. 304.) There is, therefore, considerable force in the expressions of a modern writer that the being of no other individual mentioned in history ever laboured under such a deficiency of evidence as to its reality, or ever was overset by a thousandth part of the weight of *positive proof* that it was a creation of imagination only, as that of Jesus Christ. His existence as a man, has, from the earliest day on which it can be shown to have been asserted, been earnestly and strenuously denied ; and that, not by the enemies of the Christian faith, but by the most intelligent, most learned, and most sincere of the Christian name who ever left to the world proofs of their intelligence and learning in their writings, and of their sincerity in their sufferings. The existence of no individual of the human race that was real and positive, was ever, by a like conflict of jarring evidence rendered equivocal and uncertain. Nothing, however, is more common than for some persons to assume an air of contempt, and to cry out that those who deny that such a person as Jesus of Nazareth ever existed, are utterly unworthy of being answered. It is, truly, very convenient for them thus to shelter themselves by assuming his existence as incontrovertible, instead of fairly meeting historical facts which, to say the least, render his existence very problematical. It is to no purpose to urge that it might as well be denied that no such a person as Alexander the Great, or Napoleon Bonaparte ever existed, as to set at defiance the evidence of the existence of Jesus. For the existence of neither Alexander nor Napoleon was *miraculous*, and there never was on earth one other real personage whose existence, as a *real* personage, was denied and disclaimed even as soon as ever it was asserted, as was the case with respect to the assumed personality of Christ. But the only common character that runs through the whole body of the evidence of heretics is, that they, one and all, from first to last, deny the existence of Jesus Christ as a man, and, professing their faith in him as a God and Saviour, yet uniformly and consistently hold the whole story of his life and actions to be allegorical. The very earliest Christian writings that have come down to us,

the conclusion that his attempt at foretelling what he himself would do turned out a complete failure, at least in point of time. But how absurd

are of a controversial character, and written in attempted refutation of heresies. These heresies must, therefore, have been of so much earlier date and prior prevalence; they could not have been considered of sufficient consequence to have called, (as they seem to have done) for the entire devotion and enthusiastic zeal of the orthodox party to extirpate, or keep them under, if they had not acquired deep root, and become of serious notoriety;—an inference which leads directly to the conclusion that they were of anterior origination to any date that has hitherto been ascribed to the Gospel History. (Taylor's Diegesis, pp. 350, 347.) Those who in the Apostolic age regarded the existence of Christ as fabulous, like those in the present age who entertain similar views, of course believed the tale of his resurrection also to be fabulous.

Another view taken of Christ's resurrection was that it was a *phantom* which was crucified and rose from the dead, and not a real body. Ignatius, in his time, combatted this view of the case:—Ει δε ωσπερ τινες αθεοι οντες, τουτ' εστιν απιστοι, λεγουσιν το δοκειν πεπονθεναι ουτον.—(The English reader can consult this passage in the Apocryphal New Testament—Ignatius's Epistle to the Trallians, chap. ii. ver. 13.) In accordance with the notion that Christ was a phantom, the writer of the Commentaries which are attributed to Clement of Alexandria, apparently quoting from the Gospel of Nicodemus, tells us that the apostle John attempted to touch the body of Christ, but in so doing found no hardness of flesh, and met with no resistance from it; although he thrust his hand into the inner part of it. A similar idea is conveyed by Luke where he says that Christ *vanished* out of the sight of his disciples, but yet shortly after stood in the midst of them,—a notion consistent only with that of an apparition. (Luke xxiv. 31, 36.) Similar remarks may be made on the words of Christ to Thomas, and Mary; —to the latter he says, " Touch me not, for I have not yet ascended to my Father,—that is, I am not to be felt; and to the latter he says, " Reach hither thy hand, and thrust it into my side;"—an operation which no *body* could endure. (John xx. 17, 27.) Both these expressions, contradictory as they are with regard to Jesus, still show that the writer knew something of the notion entertained that Christ was a *phantom*. Luke (xxiv. 37, 39.) also has words proving the same point, where he says that the disciples, when they saw Christ after his resurrection, thought they had seen a spirit, and that he told them to handle him. Marcion of Pontus, who flourished about A.D. 127, believed Christ not to have been born of a virgin and to have grown up gradually, but that he took the form of a man, and *appeared* as a man, without being born, and at once showed himself in Galilee, in full maturity. Manes also, according to the testimony of Socrates and others, " denied that Christ was ever really born, or had real human flesh; but asserted that he was a mere phantom." (See Lardner's Credibility, vol. ii. p. 141.) For men who entertained this notion of " the person of Christ,"—his sufferings, death, and resurrection, were of course a delusion,—were only in appearance. Apelles, who lived A.D. 160, however, was not exactly of this opinion. He maintained that Christ had real flesh, though not derived from the Virgin Mary. As he descended from the super-celestial places of this earth he collected to himself a body out of the four elements. Having thus formed a corporiety, he descended to the earth, was really crucified, and afterwards showed that very flesh in which he suffered to his disciples. But as he afterwards ascended to heaven he gave back the body he had borrowed to the elements, and sat down on the right hand of God without any body at all. Thus, according to Father Apelles, who wrote about A.D. 160, Christ was *not born*, nor was his body like ours, but consisted of aerial and etherial particles.—(Taylor's Diegesis, p. 351.) Very probably, Apelles did not think it unlikely that a body composed of such subtile matter as this should rise from the grave, and be capable of passing not only through the smallest aperture, but even through an inch-board. Barnabas, the companion of Paul, in his Gospel, which is said to be now extant in the Italian language, had another way of disposing of the question of the resurrection; namely, by denying that Christ was crucified at all, but was taken up into the third heaven by four angels,—that it was Judas Iscariot who was crucified in his stead, and that Christ will not die till the very end of the world. —(Toland's Nazarenus, letter i. chap. v. p. 17.) The *Basilidians*, about the commencement of the second century, disposed in a similar manner of the miracle of the resurrection, by asserting that it was not Christ, but Simon of Cyrene who was crucified instead of Jesus.—(See Commentar. de rebus Christian. ante Constant. p. 854, et seq. Koran, the supposition that a person who could not accurately foretell the *time* he would rise from the dead had power to rise at all! Supposing it *possible*

chap. iii. ver. 53; and chap. iv. ver. 156. of Moracci's Edit. The theory of Cerinthus, as Theodoret informs us, was that, although Christ was crucified and buried, yet he did not rise from the tomb, but that he would rise when there should be a general resurrection. Cerinthus had as good an opportunity as any to know the fact of the matter; for he lived—if not in the time assigned to Christ himself—in the apostolic age, and was contemporary with the apostle John and his followers. The writer of that ancient narrative called *Anaphora*—which is inserted in John Albert Fabricius's Codex Apocryphus Nov. Test. tom. I. and which, as well as the other pious writings found in the above work with it, had probably been intended for a Gospel or an inspired Epistle—was, however, of a different opinion of Christ's resurrection, and evidently believed that it really took place. For the *Anaphora* not only relates, like our Gospels, the miracles which were performed at Christ's death, such as the opening of graves, the rising of the bodies of saints who went into the holy city and appeared to many, (Matth. xxvii. 52, 53.) but adds that, early in the morning of the first of the Sabbath, the resurrection of Christ was announced by the most wonderful indication of divine power that ever was witnessed. At the third hour of the night, the sun broke forth into such splendour as never was seen before. (Ωφθη δε τριτης ωρας της νυκτος ηλιος ως ουδεποτε, πολλα φαιδρυνας); and the heavens became enlightened seven times more than any other day. (Ωστε τον ουρανον γενεσθαι φωταγωγον επταπλασιονα, υπερ πασας τας ημερας.) And the light ceased not to shine all that night. (Πασαν δε νυκτα εκεινην ουκ επαυσατο το φως φαινον.) This, however, was not all the miraculous manifestation of divine power on the occasion of Christ's resurrection. For the writer of the *Anaphora*, who pretends that it is a narration by Pilate to the Emperor Tiberius, of what took place, says that an instantaneous chasm occurred, and the earth opened, and swallowed all the unbelieving Jews. (Των δε Ιουδαιων πολλοι εθανον εν τω χασματι της γης καταπιωθεντες, ως μη ευρεθηναι ετι); their temple and their synagogues all vanished away, and the next morning there was not so much as one of them left in all Jerusalem. (Την αυριον το πληθος των Ιουδαιων των τα κατα του Ιησου λεγομενων. Μια συναγωγη των Ιουδαιων ουκ υπελειφθη εν αυτη τη Ιερουσαλημ.) The Roman soldiers who had kept the sepulchre, ran stark-staring mad. (Οι δε τερουντες το μνημειον στρατιωται εν εκστασει γενομενοι.) See the Codex Apocryphus, tom. ii. p. 97. and Taylor's Diegesis, p. 364. This, certainly, was something like a *sign* to the Jews; and a palpable proof of Christ's resurrection. According to the *Anaphora*, the destruction of the temple was not left to Vespasian,—it was swallowed up by the earth at the time of Christ's resurrection! It is not at all wonderful that none of the Jews told the tale of this grand display of retributive justice, and that it is not recorded by any writer of the times; for none of the unbelieving Jews, at least, were left alive to record it. It is, therefore, by no means marvellous that none of the Jews,—that none but the disciples and followers of Christ saw him after his resurrection; for none were left alive to see him,—all had been swallowed up by the earth. It is, however, most unfortunate that there is not a syllable about this grand feat of vengeance in our Gospels. But it is quite as likely that a series of miracles were performed at the resurrection of Christ, as at his death, when the sun darkened, rocks rent, graves opened, the dead rose, and the veil of the temple rent asunder. The latter is told to us by the Evangelists, but the former told to Tiberius by Pilate!

Another mode of accounting for the resurrection of Christ, resorted to by some, is that his death was more apparent than real. It is said there is a Jewish tradition that his body was quickly conveyed away by his disciples, Joseph of Arimathea and his followers, who, by means then known in Oriental countries, resuscitated it, so that Christ lived for six months afterwards, but died from the shock his system had received on the cross.—This tradition is said to be still firmly believed by the Jews, and to acquire much plausibility from the following circumstances narrated by the Evangelists themselves.—First, the short period of Christ's suspension on the cross.—Secondly, the fact of the two malefactors who suffered with him remaining alive.—Thirdly, the hastening of their death by breaking *their* bones, but *not* Christ's bones.—Fourthly, according to Mark, (xv. 44.) Pilate marvelled if Christ were already dead, and questioned the fact.—Fifthly, the Sabbath (Friday, sunset) being already begun, (the ninth hour) Jesus's body must have quickly been taken down, and hurried off.—Sixthly, it was not till the next day that a

v

to put Deity to death—to render immortality mortal—how repugnant to sound reason the idea that a person who had the divine attribute of *omnipotence*, so as to be able to become alive after he had been put to death, should not be possessed of the divine attribute of *omniscience*, so as to be able to know precisely when he would rise into life! How incredible that Jesus could foretell that he would rise at all, when he could not foretell the *time* he would rise! How unlikely that he was really endued with the prophetic gift, when he could not have a correct insight into seventy-two hours of futurity, and could not accurately foretell his own actions! How all this completely disproves that Jesus possessed either the attribute of omnipotence or of omniscience,—that he ever rose, or prophesied that he would rise! How, in a word, all this exposes the mythological character of those productions called Gospels!

It is equally evident that this prophecy was not fulfilled in regard to the *sign of the prophet Jonas*, which Christ promised he should give to the Jews, or at least to those influential sections of them—the Scribes, Sadducees, and Pharisees.* It is only an evasion of the objection to urge that Christ did not *say* he would appear to those whom he terms " an evil and adulterous generation ;"—that all he agreed to do was to lie in the grave three days and three nights, as Jonas lay in the fish's belly ; and that he did so they had the evidence of their own eyes and of their own guard.— If the words of Christ, on this point, have any meaning at all, they mean that he would appear after his resurrection to those to whom, at the time, he spoke. Applying to this question that rule of criticism admitted to be sound and adopted by all Christian writers,—namely, that of explaining one passage of Scripture by a *parallel* passage, we find in Luke the following words.—" As Jonas was a sign to the Ninevites, so shall also the Son of man be to *this* generation."† We know how Jonas was a sign to the Ninevites,—they *saw* him, and *heard* him preach, after he had been three days and three nights in the fish's belly. We are not informed that Jonas was any sign to the Ninevites, or that they knew anything whatever of him before he began to preach to them, denouncing the overthrow of their

---

watch was set on the sepulchre by the priests and Pharisees, who seem to have done so in a very silly manner, by merely sealing the great stone whereby Christ's followers had adroitly obstructed all access to the sepulchre, instead of removing it and ascertaining that the body was really within. (Matth. xxvii. 60, 62, 66.)—And lastly, the Evangelists state that Jesus was after the crucifixion, on various occasions, seen, touched, and his person examined, by his followers, with whom he ate, talked, and walked, on several occasions."

Such are some of the various opinions of the origin of the story of Christ's resurrection. They are placed before the reader that he may have a choice of theories. After matured reflection, however, he will, most probably come to the conclusion that this tale originated in the same manner as " The Gospel of the birth of Mary,"—" The Gospels of the Infancy of Christ,"—"The Gospel of Nicodemus,"—the epistolary correspondence of Christ and Abgarus, of the Virgin Mary and Ignatius, together with hundreds of other similar productions of the ages when facts were not so much appreciated as fables, in the form of books. If he arrive at this conclusion, he will see no reason to believe that such a personage as the Christ of the Gospels was ever crucified, much less raised from the dead. This will relieve him from having recourse to the unnecessary supposition that he was resuscitated. It will, however, be borne in mind, that throughout the body of this Essay, the New Testament is *taken* to be what it professes to be—a genuine production ; however far the writer is from believing this to be the case.

* See pp. 276—278.   † Compare Luke xi. 29—32. Matth. xi. 38—42.

city.   Nor have we any reason to believe that they would have heard of him, as having been in the fish's belly three days and three nights, had he not gone into their city to preach, after his miraculous deliverance.   It was in the act of Jonas going to preach to the Ninevites, after he had been in the fish's belly, that he was a sign to them.   And precisely in this manner Christ foretells he would be a sign to the " evil and adulrerous generation."—" As Jonas was a sign to the Ninevites, so shall the Son of man be to this generation."   Hence, we find him dwelling on the preaching of Jonas, saying—" The men of Nineveh repented at the preaching of Jonas, and behold a greater than Jonas is here."   The whole tenour of his comparison of Jonas's deliverance from the fish's belly and his preaching to the Ninevites, with his own resurrection and his preaching to the " evil and adulterous generation," leads inevitably to the conclusion that he would have the Jews, whom he addressed, believe that he should *appear to them*, and *preach to them after his resurrection*.   In this manner, and in this only, was he or could he be a sign to them, as Jonas had been a sign to the Ninevites.   This is clearly the true meaning of the comparison, the object of which is to show that the Ninevites, in the Day of Judgment— which was then thought close at hand, and to which Jesus had just alluded—would condemn the conduct of the Jews, because the former had believed Jonas, and the latter refused to believe Christ.   Jesus, however, was not such a sign as he foretold be should be, nor any sign at all to this "evil and adulterous generation ;"—after his resurrection he did not appear to one of *them*,—he appeared only to his own disciples.   Although he was on earth forty days before his ascent, he concealed himself from every other eye ! His prediction, therefore, in this respect again was *not* true. We must consequently arrive at the conclusion that he neither rose at the time he predicted, nor appeared to those to whom he said he should appear.   The subject having been thus far investigated, the Biblical student is left to judge for himself whether Jesus rose at all or not, and whether his disciples ever saw him after his entombment, or whether the report that they did has emanated from any other source than that which could be productive of nothing but truth.   With this remark, namely, that the prophecy of Jesus regarding these fore-mentioned points connected with his resurrection, appears to be quite as devoid of truth as his prediction of the near approach of the End of the World, the subject is left to the further consideration of the reader.

SECTION V.—THE PREDICTION OF JESUS REGARDING A WOMAN WHO POURED UPON HIM A BOX OF OINTMENT FALSIFIED.

There are recorded in the Gospels other predictions of Christ which time has proved to be equally untrue with those already noticed.   To glance at some of these would not be amiss now before we close the present chapter.   One of them is the prediction that the act of *the woman with the box of ointment* would be mentioned wheresoever the Gospel would be preached.   When Christ, on one occasion, was in Bethany, we are told

2 v

that a woman came unto him with an alabaster box of very precious ointment, and poured it on his head, as he sat at meat. When the disciples
saw this done, they indignantly made remarks on the conduct of the
woman in wasting the ointment, saying that it could have been sold for
much money and the proceeds given to the poor. Jesus reproved them,
saying, among other things,—" Verily 1 say unto you, *Whersoever* this
Gospel shall be preached in *the whole world*, *there* shall also *this* that this
woman hath done, be told for a memorial of her."* Here is as clear and
distinct a prophecy as possibly can be uttered. Wherever the Gospel was
to be preached, the tale of the woman and her box of ointment was to be
told as a memorial of her. Has this proved true ? Every one who has
heard half-a-dozen sermons preached is in a position to answer unhesitatingly that *it has not* ; for in few, perhaps in none of these sermons, could
he have heard mention made of the woman and her box of ointment. One
would naturally expect from this prophecy that either before, or after, or
at the beginning, or at the end, or in the middle of every sermon, the tale
of the box of ointment would be formally told by the preacher of the Gospel, as an indispensible part of the service, just as the Lord's prayer forms
an indispensible part of the service of the Established Church,—of the
Church of Rome, and of the Wesleyans ;—one would expect he would be
sure to find this in the Litanies and Liturgies of the fore-mentioned
churches, and in some corner, at least, of the service of every denomination
of Disssenters. Such, however, is not to be found. The Gospel has been
preached in thousands of places and on tens of thousands of occasions without any mention being made of the poor woman and her alabaster box of
very precious ointment,—and without a syllable being uttered as to what
she did "for a memorial of her." Indeed, it is very seldom that we
hear her act mentioned at all in a sermon ; and when it is mentioned, it is
only for the purpose of proving or illustrating some point the preacher has
in view, and not in order to comply with a particular command, or to
verify a pointed prediction of Jesus. Very few sermons, if any, have ever
been preached from this happy text. Thus both Christ's words and the
poor woman are *forgotten* much more frequently than *remembered*. What
then becomes of the prediction of Jesus, that "wheresoever this Gospel
shall be preached in the *whole* world, *there* shall also *this* that this woman
hath done be *told* for a memorial of her" ? It must be admitted either that
the prophecy has proved untrue, or that wherever and whenever this is
not told in a sermon, "this Gospel" is *not* preached. To admit the latter
is as fatal to Christianity as to admit the former, and is much more unreasonable and palpably at variance with truth. Very few Christians would
contend that it is only when and where the woman with her box of ointment is mentioned the Gospel is preached. Very few would not frankly
admit that there have been thousands of sermons preached without a
syllable about the ointment, quite as orthodox, evangelical, and efficacious,
as those in which frequent mention was made of it, or in which the whole tale
of it was narrated,—that Divine influence has attended sermons, and made
them the means of converting sinners, time innumerable, when not the

* Matth. xxvi. 6—13. Mark xiv. 3—9. There is here not a shadow of ground for
quibbling about the meaning of the Greek text, which is as clear and explicit as that
of the English.

slightest allusion was made to what the woman did with the ointment.— Then, if this is the case, it must be concluded that Christ's prediction is false. *The Gospel has been preached in many places in the whole world, without telling also what this woman did for a memorial of her.* Although thousands of places may be pointed out where this has been done, yet for the Gospel to be preached only in *one* place without the tale of the ointment being told, is sufficient to falsify the prediction. If we have a full and true report of Peter's Pentecostal sermon and other sermons he delivered, the prophecy was falsified in his preaching, at the outset, though attended with its alleged miraculous effects. Neither in Peter's preaching; in that of Stephen; of Paul; nor Barnabas—in neither the preaching nor the epistles of any of the Apostles have we a single word about this woman or her box of ointment. Very frequently in the streets of London, and other large cities, the Gospel is preached by "open air preachers" on a spot where, in all probability, never a sermon has been delivered before, and never, perhaps, a sermon will be delivered again, without the slightest reference to the woman and her ointment. In every such case, a fresh proof is given that this prophecy of Christ has turned out to be untrue.

SECTION VI.—CHRIST'S PROPHECY REGARDING THE SIGNS WHICH WOULD FOLLOW BELIEVERS IN CHRISTIANITY FALSIFIED.

Another, and the last that shall be noticed here, of these false prophecies is that touching the signs which Christ predicted should "follow" believers and attest their faith. In delivering his final commission to his Apostles he is reported to have said to them,—"Go ye into all the world, and preach the Gospel to every creature. He that believeth and is baptized shall be saved; but he that believeth not shall be damned. *And these signs shall follow them that believe; in my name shall they cast out devils; they shall speak with new tongues; they shall take up serpents; and if they drink any deadly thing, it shall not hurt them; they shall lay hands on the sick, and they shall recover.*"* Now the question is—Were, or are these five miraculous signs of divine power verified in believers? Did they, or do they follow a belief in Jesus? Can believers, or do they pretend that they can, cast out devils? Or do they now-a-days even believe, like the benighted followers of Christ, when he is said to have been on earth, that there is such a state of things as demoniacal possession, so as to entertain any hope of having a chance of trying their hands at casting out a devil, and thereby having a proof whether they *believe?* Do demons come out of people at the bidding of believers? Do believers now speak with new tongues? Can they, with impunity, take up poisonous serpents?— Can they handle the rattlesnake without being mortally bitten?—Can they take up "the spotted mockeson, or the deadly copper-head," without endangering their lives? Can they drink any deadly thing,† and not be

---

* Mark xvi. 15—18.

† In these words there is, doubtless, reference to the practice of heathen jugglers to drink the poison of venomous animals without receiving any injury; and the idea has

hurt?—"Can they drain the hemlock bowl, and yet escape the fate of Socrates?" Do the sick recover when they only lay their hands on them? —Do either burning typhus and scarlet fevers, or devastating plagues and cholera, or any other diseases, flee when they impose their hands on the sick?—"Do they supersede medical skill by the laying on of hands?"— All these things believers must be able to do before this prophecy can be true. And can they do them? It is positively certain that they cannot. "The poison of the death-herb, and the venom of the reptile, reach the life of him who believes as of him who believes not. Death is arrested as little by the touch of piety as of scepticism."* Natural laws are unbending, —the infringement of any of them is productive of the same result to the believer as to the unbeliever, which is proved by daily observation and experience. What, then, becomes of the truth of the prophecy of Jesus that believers would be *known* by their being able so far to violate these laws with impunity as to take up venomous reptiles, and drink deadly poisons without being hurt? The only alternative here again is that, either this prediction has proved false, or that there are no true *believers* in the present age, to say nothing of past ages. The prediction is as clear and definite as language can render it. Christ foretells that certain signs will follow those who believe,—they shall be able to do certain things; and these things are to be as signs or tests whereby people are known to be believers or not; and these signs he enumerates.† Now, these signs none of those who profess to believe in Christianity *do* exhibit, or are *able* to exhibit. The unavoidable inference, therefore, is that, either there are no believers, or Christ's prediction is not true.

The only reply that can be anticipated to this charge is the following usual quibble; namely, that Christ did not say how long these signs were to follow those who believed. If, therefore, they once followed those who believed, the prophecy is fulfilled. And that they did follow those who

---

evidently been borrowed from this wonderful feat. Lucan, (Pharsal. lib. ix. v. 614.) in reference to serpents, says,—Noxia serpentum est admisto sanguine pestis morsu virus habent et fatum dente minantur pocula morte carent. Although the poison of venomous serpents when, by means of a bite, they mix it with the blood of their victim, is certain death, if allowed to have its full effect; yet the same poison can be taken into the stomach, as a draught, unattended with any poisonous effect. After a number of experiments had been made on the most venomous serpents by Rhedi and other eminent philosophers of the age, at the command of Ferdinand II. the Grand Duke of Tuscany, Tozzi, a person who professed to charm vipers and to know all about the effect of their venom, drank, in the presence of the prince and his assembled philosophers, a considerable portion of the poison which had been extracted from the vipers experimented upon, without suffering the least injury. It is now, indeed, an established fact that the poison of reptiles is not injurious unless it mixes with the blood, and that it can be taken into the stomach with safety. This was well known to ancient Eastern conjurors, &c. Hence, the Gospel expression—"They shall take up serpents; and if they drink any deadly thing, it shall not hurt them." But if everybody can, as we have seen, drink the poison of serpents without being injured, how is this a sign to distinguish believers from infidels? Again: vegetable and mineral poisons are implied in the words —"*any* deadly thing." Can saints drink these, and not evince symptoms of approaching death? Can they long survive a strong dose of prussic acid, white arsenic, or strychnine?

* See Bachelor and Owen's Discussion on the Authenticity of the Bible, pp. 138, 161, 196.

† See Haslam's Letters to the Clergy, letter xxiv. pp. 1, 2.

believed in the early ages of the church, when miracles were performed, there is ample proof. The Apostles* and their converts did cast out devils; did speak with new tongues; did take up serpents with impunity, as in the case of Paul to whose hand fastened a viper which he shook off into the fire without receiving the least harm;† and also did lay their

---

* It is, however, very singular that the Apostles, after they had been endued with this miraculous power, failed to cast out a devil from a child the very first time apparently they put their newly received gift to the test. When Christ "ordained" his twelve apostles he gave them power to "cast out devils," or, according to Matthew, "unclean spirits," whence we infer that unclean spirits and devils are one and the same species of beings. (Compare Matth. x. 1. Mark iii. 15.) It is natural to suppose that the Apostles were anxious to try their hands now at casting out devils. Having obtained a subject, namely a child, (out of which one would be inclined to imagine it was easier to cast out the devil than out of an adult) they made the experiment; but they failed ! The power which they applied does not appear to have had any effect, either good or bad, upon the devil—whatever physical effect it had upon the poor child which was put under the operation. The father of the child, therefore, brought it to Jesus, entreating him to cure it, and saying that he had taken it to the disciples, "and they could not cure him." (See Matth. xvii. 14—21.) Jesus, however, effectually "rebuked the devil ; and he departed out of him, and the child was cured from that very hour." Now, if the power with which Christ had invested his disciples was real, it is very strange that they should have failed to cast out the devil. This the disciples themselves appear to have thought very odd. They were, doubtless, very much disappointed ; and therefore they spoke to Jesus "apart" and asked him—"Why could not we cast him out ?"—a very fair question. The answer, however, Jesus gave is even more wonderful than that the disciples failed to cast out the devil after they had been endowed with divine power to do so. He tells them—"Because of your unbelief." It is most difficult to conceive how their *unbelief* could interfere with a power which was not inherent in them. Nor does there appear any grounds for the charge of unbelief or want of faith. The disciples, doubtless, believed they could cast out the devil, otherwise they would not have attempted at such a miraculous thing; and that they had the greatest faith in Christ is clear from their coming to him to ask the cause of their failure. Christ's answer, however, like all the other answers, which the Gospels put into his mouth, is obscure and evasive. If there is any meaning at all in this answer, it means the same thing as is now-a-days impressed by charmers of the toothache and of other ills to which flesh is heir, by fortune tellers, conjurers, &c.—All tell those who are simple enough to consult them —"You must have faith."—"If you do not believe in me, I can do nothing," &c. Christ, however. prescribes prayer and fasting for the casting out of the kind of devils to which that in the child belonged. This devil was of a peculiar kind;—the cause perhaps of the failure of the disciples.

† Acts xxviii. 3—6. There is very little doubt that *Malta* is meant by *Melita*, the island in which Paul is said to have shaken a viper off his hand, notwithstanding the efforts made by some writers to show that it was another island, of the same name, on the coast of Illyricum, now called *Melede*. The situation of all the places named by the writer of the Acts, in describing Paul's dangerous voyage, indeed, clearly shows that he means *Malta*. This being certain, it is an unfortunate thing that the vipers of Malta are not, in the least, poisonous. To state, therefore, that one of these harmless vipers clung to Paul's hand, and that he shook it off without receiving any injury, does not furnish the shadow of a proof that he was endowed with preternatural power to "take up serpents" with impunity, when those serpents were of that sort whose bite causes almost instantaneous death. In Malta, as in many other islands, there are no venomous animals at all. Travellers, however, assure us that there are there *harmless* vipers ; and Linnæus and other naturalists (Philosophical Transactions, vol. lxxix.) tell us that the sorts of vipers that are not poisonous are as ten to one that are so. It is therefore very marvellous that it was on an island where vipers were not poisonous Paul shook off one of these reptiles from his hand into the fire without receiving any harm ! It is not forgotten that there is extant a priestly fable that, on this occasion, Paul cursed the venomous animals of the island, and banished them from it for ever, so that henceforth none that were even imported into it could subsist there ; and also that, on the very spot he thus

hands upon the sick so that thereby they recovered. And indeed the miraculous power which they possessed, the Apostles affirmed to be a fulfilment of this prophecy.*

But it should be recollected that Christ in the prophecy makes no such restriction. He does not, by any means, confine these signs to the apostolic age, or to any number of ages whatever. The promise of these signs to follow those that believe, according to the obvious drift of the passage, is co-extensive with the time any believers should be found in the world. Accordingly, Matthew, in reporting the same commission given by Christ, has the words—" Lo, I am with you alway, *even unto the end of the world.*"† It must, however, be admitted that Christ did not think that the End of the World would not come for eighteen centuries, as time has now proved. But that he laboured under a mistake as to the time the world would endure, by no means assists Christians in proving that his prediction of the signs which were to follow believers has not been falsified. If the promise of the signs is to be limited to the early ages of Christianity, then the threat of damnation to unbelievers, in the same commission, is by parity of argument to be limited to those ages ; in a word, the whole that is spoken of in this commission, is to be so limited.—The preaching of the Gospel to every creature was to continue only during the ages of the signs ; those who believed and were baptized in those ages only were to be saved ; and those who believed not in those ages only were to be damned. It is impossible to show that the signs were limited to any time, without inevitably admitting the same limitation to the whole of the commission. Then the argument stands thus :—either the Gospel was not intended by Christ to be preached to the people of the present age, or there are now no believers, or the prediction of the Prophet of Nazareth with regard to these signs has proved false.

The Mormonites, however, have another answer to give to this charge against Christ. The followers of Joseph Smith or Latter-Day Saints— who certainly do not disown Christ—say that they *do* cast out devils,

---

cursed the baneful animals, his statue was erected, and a church built and consecrated to him, for " the benefit of the clergy" of benighted ages. But there is the same amount of evidence that St. Patrick expelled all venomous reptiles from Ireland, where none are found, as that St. Paul did the same in regard to Malta. The absence of poisonous animals in such islands as these is accountable on causes which exist in nature, so that neither a popish nor an apostolic miracle is required to effect it. There are, however, in the writer of the Acts' narration of the viper, many touches which indicate the comparatively recent date of this book. His tale is calculated to inspire a belief that although the vipers of Malta are now not poisonous, and probably were known to him, when he wrote, not to be poisonous ; yet that they were so before Paul cursed them, as he shook one of them from his hand and consigned it to the flames. Accordingly, he tells us that the inhabitants of the island, who—he would have his readers believe—knew by experience what deadly animals these vipers were, expected to see Paul suddenly drop down dead, or, at least, to find his hand swelling. But as they perceived this natural and invariable result of a bite by a viper did not follow in this case, they deemed it a miracle, and pronounced Paul a god. Such, evidently, is the notion which this writer wished his romance of the viper to convey. This furnishes a strong presumptive proof that the fabulous tale that Paul had cursed the venomous reptiles of Malta was afloat before the book called the Acts of the Apostles was written.

* Acts v. 12, 14, 15; i. 8.   Rom. xv. 18, 19.   1 Cor. xii. 12.
† Matth. xxviii. 20.

speak with new tongues, and heal the sick by laying their hands on them; and they seriously maintain that they can, with impunity, handle venomous reptiles, and drink deadly poisons without being hurt. It must, therefore, be admitted that they are the most consistent Christians of the present age; nay, that they are the only people, according to Christ's own words, that believe; for they alone pretend to possess the miraculous powers by which true believers are to be distinguished. A slight exception, perhaps, ought to be made in favour of the Roman Catholics, who now and then work a miracle, which might, with a little torture, be construed into a sign of belief. But the Mormonites are heretics, say the rest of Christians, and the Roman Catholics are heretics say the Protestants. Christ, therefore, could not possibly by "them that believe" mean these heretics. We are, consequently, repulsed to the same ground as that already stated;— either Christ did not intend the Gospel to be preached to the people of the present age, or there are no believers in the present age, or Jesus was mistaken as to the signs which should follow those who believe, in the present day. It is true that, had it not been for the enlightened condition of the nineteenth century, the Latter-Day Saints would be in a fair way of both proving that Christ's prediction regarding the signs is not false, and that they are the only *believers* in the world. Fortunately for us, however, but unfortunately for their case, we need not spend much time in showing that their pretence to the signs of which Jesus speaks, is a pretence of the basest kind. When set forth, at least in this country, its falsity is detected on every hand, and its effrontery is regarded by all, but their own deluded and fanatical followers, as a gross insult to common sense. A retrospective glance at the history of Christianity is sufficient to convince any one of ordinary acumen that the signs which followed believers have gradually disappeared in proportion to the progress humanity has made in knowledge —particularly knowledge of the laws of nature in its various departments. They now make their appearance only where the ignorance and superstition of bygone benighted ages have not entirely been dispelled. Were Christ and his Apostles living in the present age, they would have a more difficult task to persuade people of the reality of these signs than they had to gain the confidence of even the Scribes, Pharisees, Sadducees, and the other more intelligent classes of their times,—a task which, in the case of the latter, they utterly failed to accomplish; their miracles, together with their doctrines, being believed only by comparatively few of the most ignorant and superstitious in the lower grades of society, even in that age upon the credulity of which it was so easy to impose. Various and numerous, however, were the attempts made in the apostolic age, and even up to the ninth and tenth century, to impose upon the understanding of men by the pretence to miracles, which sometimes succeeded and sometimes failed; but generally gained the confidence of only the ignorant and superstitious, while they disgusted the sober-minded philosopher. But as the illuminating beams of truth began to penetrate the intellectual horizon,—as the morning dawn of real knowledge cast its rays over man's mind, the mist of prevailing errors gradually diminished, and the clouds of gloomy superstition were scattered. Slow and tardy, indeed, was the progress of scientific knowledge, and many and strenuous were the oppositions made to it by the bigoted prejudice, and the fierce persecution of an all-grasping hierarchy ; but " onwards" was its tendency, amid the clamorous denunciations of the interested, and the yelling noise of the ignorant ; so that now, the art of printing having been in existence for many centuries, truth-fraught Philosophy shines in its meridian splendour. And what a change has thereby been effected in the minds of men regarding the *signs* which we have to consider, as well as regarding the practicability of any other miracles !   In the time of Christ and his Apostles these miraculous *signs* were the test by which it was known that men believed the religion of Jesus ; but now, were any man to exhibit such *signs* as a proof of his belief in Christ, his trickery would soon be discovered, and every right-minded Christian—so far from considering him a believer—would, with disgust, regard him either as an impostor or as a fanatic, labouring under mental delusion and suffering from a diseased brain. Indeed, such have all been pronounced who have made any pretence to such signs within the last two centuries.   If any man now, upon his conversion to any sect of Christians, (the Latter-Day Saints excepted) were to go about speaking unintelligible jargon, and understood, if understood at all, to say that persons troubled with any inveterate disease are possessed by a devil, and were to pretend to cure them by exorcisms ; or if he attempted to cure sickness by the mere laying on of hands, such is the high pitch at which sound knowledge has arrived that he would be considered, not a disciple of Jesus—not a *believer*, but either an impostor or a madman ; and if he attempted to exemplify the signs of his belief so far as to take a draught of the hemlock bowl, or any other poison ; or were he to snatch up the asp when basking in meridian sunshine, the bystanders would instantly lay hold of him, arrest his insane and suicidal effort, and make arrangements to place him in an asylum for madmen.— Such is the change which sound knowledge has wrought in men's views with regard to the *signs which follow those that believe.*

How then, in the face of these facts, are we to determine the question before us ?   Was the prophetic spirit in Jesus when he foretold the signs that would characterise believers ?   We have already brought the question into the narrow compass that—either Christ did not intend the Gospel to be preached to the people of the present age, or there are no believers in the present age, or Christ mistook the signs which should follow believers of the present age.   Now, which of these three points is the true one ?   All three are equally destructive to the interests of Christianity.—If either of them is true, Christianity cannot be of divine origin ; and one of them must be true.   Nor is it by any means difficult to decide which of them is true   That Christ intended the Gospel to be preached till the end of the world, whenever he thought that would occur, is clear from the whole tenour of the Gospels.   To adduce proofs of this obvious truth is utterly needless. Again : that there are now in the world thousands who sincerely believe in the Gospel,—or in other words, are sincere Christians, is a fact that cannot be denied.   That they believe in a false religion is no proof that they are not as sincere believers as if Christianity were divine.   For example, Mahomedanism is justly considered by Christians a false religion ; still even Christians must admit that there are thousands who sincerely believe this religion to be true.   In like manner, there are thousands now living who believe in the truth of Christianity.   Since, however, the *signs* which Christ foretold should "follow them that believe" do not follow these sincere believers in Christianity, we are led irresistibly to the conclusion that Christ's prophecy regarding these signs *is not true.* This is a conclusion which, unpleasant as it may be, it is impossible to evade; and a conclusion which precludes the possibility that Jesus is, or was a divine personage, or that he was influenced by the Deity in uttering this erroneous prediction, which is certainly highly calculated to mislead, and thereby to produce an enormous amount of evil. All the remarks which have been made touching the consequences of Christ's erroneous prophecies regarding the end of the world, the day of judgment, his own resurrection, and the box of ointment, are equally applicable to the consequences of his erroneous prognostication of the *signs* just discussed, as far as his divine or even moral character is concerned. That a false prophet cannot be a Deity, or be influenced by the Deity, is an axiom, as certain and as clear to the moralist as that " things which are equal to the same thing are equal to one another," is to the mathematician. Nor is it less certain that he who prophesies falsely in one instance is as devoid of divine perfections as if he had run the whole career of a Mahomed. And indeed, it would be difficult to show that the Koran attributes to the latter prophecies which have proved false in a greater number of instances, or to a greater degree of intensity, than those which the Bible proves imputable to Jesus, in the six particulars already considered —*First,* his second coming.—*Secondly,* his Last Day of Judgment.—*Thirdly,* his Resurrection on the Third Day. —*Fourthly,* the negative nature of his alleged Resurrection as to the " sign of the prophet Jonas," which he predicted and promised to his opponents. —*Fifthly,* the non-fulfilment of his prediction as to the incessant preaching about the Box of Ointment.—And *Sixthly,* the still more decided and glaring non-fulfilment of his marvellous prediction as to the supernatural powers whereby believers were to be known. Thus Christ's credentials, not only as a divine personage, but even as a true prophet, stand disproved ; and that not merely by an *absence* of evidence on his side, but by an accumulation of positive proof,—proof which is of such a character as must make it irresistible; since it is wholly derived from the Bible itself— that generally received canon upon which Christianity is entirely based— and from the experience and observation of a very large proportion of mankind during the last eighteen centuries.

CHAPTER VII.

THE MORAL AND INTELLECTUAL CHARACTER OF THE PROPHET OF NAZA-
RETH, AS EXEMPLIFIED IN HIS PRECEPTS, HIS DISCOURSES, HIS ACTIONS,
AND HIS SOCIAL INTERCOURSE.

SECTION I.—GENERAL REMARKS.—THE CRITERIA BY WHICH THE MORALITY
OF JESUS IS TO BE TESTED.—HIS MORALITY NOT A MODEL OF PERFECTION
TO MANKIND IN ALL AGES—NO ACCOUNT IN OUR GOSPELS OF THE FIRST
THIRTY YEARS OF HIS LIFE.—OBSERVATIONS ON HIS SERMON ON THE
MOUNT.

Having in the preceding chapters investigated the character of Jesus
as a prophet of truth, and found it " wanting," let us now glance at the
moral and intellectual character of his precepts, his discourses, his actions,
and his demeanour in society, as they are recorded in the Gospels ; with a
view to ascertain how far they are worthy of being taken by us as examples.
The manner and degree in which his erroneous predictions reflect upon his
moral character as a man have already been discussed, and shown to depend
upon the consciousness he possessed of uttering predictions, of the future
fulfilment of which he had no means of ascertaining.

We are now about entering upon points which may rather rouse the
anger of the more zealous and devoted, but the less thoughtful and discriminative Christians, than induce them to a dispassionate inquiry.   For,
having been accustomed from birth to view the Prophet of Nazareth—just
as the Musulmans have been taught to view Mahomed, or the Chinese to
view Confucius—as a personage whose infinitely moral and intellectual
perfections were unimpeachable, they are therefore not prepared for an
unbiassed perusal of any treatise which calls in question these divine qualities, considered by them too sacred to be scrutinized and too mysterious
to be submitted to the test of truth.   Accordingly, such Christians are
liable to receive—not a moral—but a nervous, and therefore a physical
shock, in attending to an inquiry which tends to show any imperfections
in the moral or intellectual character of Jesus.   In order, therefore, not
unnecessarily to wound the feelings of such Christians, the subject now
entered upon shall be treated in so reverential a manner as possibly the

statement of *assumed* truth deduced from the Gospels will permit. If, however, any Christian reader should not feel disposed to yield to the force of evidence,—if he be not prepared for a thorough investigation of the credentials of his faith,—if he be content with reading only one side of the question,—if he be determined to remain ignorant of what might be urged against the divine origin of Christianity,—let him by no means read this chapter; but, resting satisfied with his hereditary creed, peruse only such portions of this book as he may deem favourable to the heavenly origin of that religion to which, accidentally, he has become a devotee. But if, on the contrary, he should be inclined to examine the grounds upon which he has instinctively been led to regard Jesus as a model of perfection, both morally and intellectually; and if he can so far divest his mind of all pre-adopted notions as to enter upon a full and fearless inquiry after truth, it is trusted that he will ponder over the facts embodied in this disquisition with some profit. The conclusions to be drawn will be based upon statements found in the Gospels—productions which every orthodox Christian must regard as infallible; so that whatever these Gospel statements may be, by them his religion must either stand or fall.*

---

* It cannot be too often repeated that throughout this work the Gospels are taken as if they were genuine productions—as if they recorded facts which had really occurred at the times and places, and in connection with the individuals, mentioned—and as if these facts had thus been recorded shortly after their occurrence. Let it however be observed that, although this is taken for granted in order to examine the credentials of Christianity according to what they profess to be; yet, this is not the view the writer entertains of these Gospels. They appear to him to bear internal evidence that they are a collection of marvellous tales which, in more remote times, were individually applied to different mythological characters of antiquity, but which, some two hundred years after the commencement of the Christian era, were compiled in the form of our present Gospels and, for the greater number, applied to Jesus of Nazareth; having, however, for a long time previously been gradually altered and augmented by compilers and transcribers, all of whom, from a much earlier period than the beginning of the Christian era, made the Christ the hero of their romances. It requires no great amount of penetration to discover in the Gospels numerous marks that they were compiled long after the occurrence of the events they pretend to relate.—Matthew (xxvii. 8.) tells us that the chief priests, with the money Judas Iscariot returned to them, bought "the potter's field to bury strangers in;" and adds—"Wherefore that field was called the field of blood *unto this day.*" But supposing this Gospel was written shortly after Jesus's death, the writer would not then say—*unto this day.* Less than a few centuries could give no force to the expression, which in conveying a similar idea in other places in the Jewish writings is used to denote a very long space of time. The story of Judas betraying Jesus was, therefore, *very old* when Matthew's Gospel was written. The same writer (xi. 12.) makes Jesus say—"From the days of John the Baptist *until now* the kingdom of heaven suffereth violence." But the Gospels teach us that John and Jesus were contemporary, and that the former was alive in prison when the latter uttered these words. It would, therefore, be absurd in Jesus then to use such an expression as *until now;* but a writer in two or three centuries after might use it with some degree of reason. The sense in which such expressions as *until now,* and *until this day,* were employed by this very writer may be seen in the same chapter (ver. 23.) where he represents Jesus as saying of Sodom —"It would have remained *until this day.*" Here the phrase—*unto this day* imports the idea of nearly two thousand years, according to Biblical chronologers,—from the destruction of Sodom to the appearance of Christ. In Dr. Giles's Christian Records, as well as in Mr. Greg's Creed of Christendom, the reader will find most valuable and irrefragable evidence of both the legendary character and the recent date of our present Gospels. Both these learned writers point out a great number of expressions attributed to Jesus, which, owing to the immorality of some and the absurdity of others, they consider pure inventions, on the ground, chiefly, that it is utterly impossible for such to

What makes it a most imperative duty upon us to examine the moral and intellectual perfections of Jesus is not only that we may the more fully ascertain his claims upon our adoration as a divine personage, but that, under pain of eternal perdition, we are enjoined to take him as a pattern of perfection in all our words and actions. We are taught that he has " left us an example that we should follow his steps" ; and he himself says,—" I have given you an example that ye should do as I have done to you." It behoves us, therefore, as rational creatures, to inquire into the perfection of this example, and to follow it only so far as we find it consistent with wisdom and morality; by which only we can promote our own happiness and that of mankind at large. If we find in Jesus anything immoral, ignorant, or absurd, our love of justice and sense of right and wrong prohibit us, not only to bend the knee before him, but even to imitate those things which we consider wrong in him. It may be demanded—by what standard of morality and intelligence we judge the moral and intellectual character of the words and actions of Jesus, whose morality and knowledge, as those of a divine personage, may infinitely transcend our capacity to comprehend their rectitude and import, so that we may be utterly incompetent to judge whether the words he spoke and the actions he performed are virtuous or vicious—wise or foolish. To this we answer that we need no other standard for this purpose than our own sense of right and wrong—of moral virtue and moral vice. If this be denied us,—if human beings are not to exercise their reason in judging and determining what is right and what is wrong—what is virtuous and what is vicious ;- then there is an end of the matter,—an end of man's rationality,—an end of all the arguments which Christians adduce for the divine origin of their religion, for human responsibility, and for all other things connected with the entire system of Christian theology : for, by this dictum, man is adjudged unworthy to come to any conclusion respecting it, and is denied to be a being possessed of rational faculties. Such an assumption, if

have proceeded from a being whose whole career they take for granted to have been immaculate. This is a singular mode of reasoning—a mode which one can hardly believe these great writers thought to be conclusive. For as it is admitted on all hands that we know nothing of the career of Jesus but what is taught us in the Gospels, when these credentials are once proved unreliable, we have not a tittle of evidence that Jesus was *perfect.*—We have no proof of what absurdities he was capable, or of what he was not. Before this mode of reasoning can be of any value the premises must be established, —evidence must be produced from another source than the confessedly unreliable Gospels that Jesus was necessarily perfect in all that he said and did. To disprove the genuineness of the Gospels, however, is to invalidate the whole Christian system ; for if they are false in attributing to Jesus, as these writers assert, some acts and expressions of which he was not the author, we have no means of knowing how much of what they relate is really attributable to him. The most reasonable construction that can be put upon the course taken by these writers, who have certainly done great service indirectly to the cause of truth, is that, like others, they thought they would be the means of doing more good, in this superstitious and persecuting age, by giving a moderate blow to the grand error of the present as well as of ancient times, than by an apparently more crushing stroke. In this view they appear to have been right. Still it is not every lover of truth that can stoop to take this politic course. At all events, the question of the truth of Christianity, which utterly depends upon " the fidelity of the Gospel history," must sooner or later be boldly confronted by our divines. If the Gospels are not truthful and genuine productions, the Christian religion is entirely devoid of credentials. The latter is an inseparable sequence of the former.

seriously maintained, besides being self-contradictory, would prove much more disastrous to the cause of Christianity than to that of its opponents. Accordingly, it is admitted by the most enlightened advocates of the Christian religion that the proper and only available criterion by which to judge of Christ's moral character is *human virtue*, or common sense morality.* On this ground, therefore, do we find Christian writers now defending the morality of the Bible.—Thomas Hartwell Horne tells us that " nothing *false or immoral* can be taught by a God of truth ;" and that " the *moral precepts* which are contained in the Scriptures *commend them-selves to our reason*."† Our reason, therefore, is the test which we must employ to prove the moral character of the precepts and discourses, as well as acts of Jesus. There are no axioms in ethics clearer than the following : —whatever is *not* moral in man is *not* moral in a deity ;—whatever *is* moral in a deity *is* moral in man ; and whatever is moral or immoral in one *mere* man is so in another. Another fundamental principle of ethics which, it is trusted, will be admitted by any one who has in the least studied the meaning of the expression—" moral vice and moral virtue," and which is here laid-down for our future guidance is, that—whatever expression or act is *morally vicious* or *morally virtuous*, is so *in its very nature, independently* of any circumstances whatsoever. In other words, the *moral character* of an *act*, an *expression*, or a *doctrine*, is *unchangeable*, so that whatever is morally virtuous or morally vicious at *one* time must be so at all times. If this be not granted, moral vice and moral virtue are necessarily made to depend on circumstances—on the manners and customs of nations—on individual views, and a thousand other contingencies ; in a word, morality is denied to have any real and intrinsic existence in the nature of things, and is made to have no other foundation than capricious notions. Moral vice and moral virtue being necessarily of this unchangeable character, it follows that if the words and actions of Jesus were moral in his time, they must be so now ; and that if it would now be immoral in us to imitate them, it was immoral in Jesus to be the author of them. Further : since " nothing false or immoral can come from a God of truth," if we find that anything *false* or *immoral* came from Jesus, even on a single point of either practical or doctrinal teaching, we may with certainty conclude that he was not a divine teacher ; and that he is not, any more than other fallible men, to be relied upon as an absolutely perfect model for our imitation.

There are, truly, in the Gospels many wise aphorisms recorded as having been uttered by Christ. There are also in the same Gospels many acts and expressions attributed to him, which, taken alone, prove that he was a man whose bosom glowed with a high degree of benevolence. The

---

* Indeed the application of this criterion is as old as the earliest Christian Fathers who, in their controversies with the devotees of Paganism, constantly urged that the words and actions attributed to the Pagan gods were revolting to any rational view of what was morally right, and that these gods therefore were not perfect models of moral virtue ; while, on the other hand, the Pagans, like some present Christians, retorted that the gods were infinitely above human comprehension in words and deeds, speaking and acting in a manner which mortals could neither imitate nor understand. Consequently what was immoral in men was infinite morality in the gods.

† Introduct. vol. i. chap. v.

accounts we have of the many diseases he miraculously cured are of a
highly philanthropic character; and the following expressions are among
those which breathe of benevolence.—" Father, forgive them, for they
know not what they do." (Luke xxiii. 34.)—" Pray for them which despitefully use you; bless them which persecute you." (Luke vi. 28.)—" If thy
brother shall trespass against thee, go and tell him his fault between thee
and him alone; if he shall hear thee, thou hast gained thy brother."*
(Matth. xviii. 15.) Thus, his doctrine of the duty of forgiveness, of suppressing malice, and of wishing well even to enemies, is benevolent and
wise; but not more so than what we find to have been written by moral
philosophers long before the time of Jesus. The morality said in the
Gospels to have been taught by him, however, may be considered, upon
the whole, a fair specimen of that of the age which gave birth to these
productions, or of the time in which Jesus is said to have lived. He may,
therefore, have been a model in morality to the Jews among whom he
lived; he may have been considered by the age an enlightened teacher of
his own benighted nation; his doctrine may have been in advance of that
taught by his contemporaries; and, as already admitted, some of his teaching is really of an elevated moral tone, calculated to improve those who
would endeavour to reduce it to practice. Still, this by no means proves
that he is a worthy example of morality and wisdom, in *all* things, to us
in the present age; or, as it is urged, that he is a moral and intellectual
model of absolute perfection to *all* men, in *all* respects, and in *all* ages.—
Nor is it easy to conceive, even admitting him to be a divine personage,
how he can be so, according to the very nature of things. Men, whether
high or low, young or old, married or single, find themselves daily in a
thousand circumstances in reference to neither of which there is any
example of Jesus recorded in the Gospels for guidance, either directly or
indirectly. Were it granted that Jesus was a model of comparative perfection to the Jews of his own time, still this would be far from the point
that, in his personal history as found in the Gospels, he is an example of
absolute perfection to *all* men of *all* times,—to men of the present age, for
instance, who have a much higher sense of moral virtue than people had
in the time of Jesus † For although a moral act is always the same in its

---

* The word *church* (εκκλησια) which occurs in ver. 17, however, shows that, if there
were no churches, or Christian congregations, before the time indicated in the New
Testament, the whole of this doctrine regarding forgiveness, from ver. 15 to 35, was
delivered by somebody long after the time Jesus is said to have lived. For as it would
be absurd to suppose that a name for a new thing should precede that thing itself, the
word *church* was not used for a Christian congregation before the existence of such a
congregation. In the Acts of the Apostles we find the word *church* used to designate
the assemblies into which Christians formed themselves; so that, some half a century
after the time of Jesus, the word might be used as having a meaning. Similar remarks
might be made on the same word in Matth. xvi. 18, where Christ is made to say that on
Peter he would build his *church*.

† It might furnish apparent grounds of exception, in the estimation of some, to
contend that moral virtue and moral vice are unchangeable in their nature,—that the
common sense of men is the test by which to determine the moral character of an act or
an expression, and yet to say that men advance in their sense of moral virtue with the
advancement of intellect or of civilization generally. But here there is no real contradiction. For although men in one age may deem a particular act virtuous, and others,
in another, may deem it vicious; or two men in the same age may differ as to the moral

character, whether it be virtuous or vicious, yet men's sense of morality, or their standard of moral virtue, is elevated in proportion as they advance in the scale of knowledge, or in other words, in civilization ; so that the moral standard of any people who progress in knowledge, particularly knowledge of the moral laws, becomes gradually higher from age to age. Accordingly, we find that the moral standard of the British nation is now much higher than it was in the Middle Ages, when to burn infidels and supposed witches was deemed an act of profound piety,—an act which, however, the same nation now would consider grossly immoral. Much higher still is the moral standard of the English now than was that of the Jews in the time of Jesus. A person, therefore, who is an example of morality to one age might not be so to future ages; for the moral standard of such ages might be far higher than the morality he exemplified.—Consequently, to hold up such a person as a model of absolute moral perfection and teach people to conform to his morality, under the erroneous belief that it is the highest point that can be reached, arrests the moral progress of the age. Such, precisely, will be found the effect of representing Jesus as a model of consummate morality, to be imitated by all men in all ages, if it can be shown that his morality is below the moral standard of this age, or even short of absolute perfection.

Now, to a vast number of people in the present age, it appears incontestible that Jesus, like all other human beings, had glaring moral imperfections ; and that these, even as they are given by his own biographers, were neither few nor small. Contrasted with the noble feelings and wise sayings of his, to which we have just adverted, they form a decided anomaly in his character,—such an anomaly, however, as we find in all ages to be incidental even to the best of mankind. His moral and intellectual imperfections have been observed and pointed out by many of the most learned, critical, and unbiassed writers of the last and present century, in a tone and spirit which, for sobriety, earnestness, and inoffensiveness, are worthy of the present enlightened age. For example : Dr. Thomas Edwards, in a sermon preached before the University of Cambridge, in 1790, on the predictions concerning the approaching End of the World, remarks in the course of his subject, that considerable error is a charge from which the doctrines of the New Testament have not been rescued, and that Christ was no more present at the destruction of Jerusalem than he was at the earthquake of Lisbon, or the siege of Gibraltar. Professor Newman, Fellow of Balliol College, Oxford, in his Phasis of Faith, (p. 156.) after a

<hr>

character of the same act—the one deeming it virtuous and the other vicious ; yet, this difference of opinion, by no means, alters the moral character of the act. Neither vice nor virtue is a *sentiment*, but a quality arising from the very nature of things, the character of which no opinion can alter. Similar remarks may be made touching *right* and *wrong*, or truth and error. Although a thing may appear right or true to the people of one age, but wrong or erroneous to those of another age ; yet this diversity of opinion does not convert what is right to wrong, or what is wrong to right. The same may be said of two men in the same age,—their difference of opinion as to whether a certain proposition is true or false does not *make* it either true or false. Truth is eternal. What was true two thousand years ago is true now, and what is now true will always be true. It would be well to bear these remarks in mind when we hereafter examine into the truth of several of Christ's expressions ; for our guidance in which they are principally made.

W

long and masterly examination of the moral character of Jesus, writes:—
" Now I cannot look on this (Jesus inculcating poverty) as a pure intellectual error, *consistent with moral perfection.* A deep mistake as to the
nature of such perfection seems to me inherent in the precept itself; a
mistake which indicates *moral unsoundness.*"   Dr. Giles, Fellow of Christ's
College, Oxford, and Mr. Greg, both pronounce immoral, absurd, and
contradictory, a vast number of acts and expressions attributed to Christ
in the Gospels.   The former of these writers denounces them—" contradictions that cannot be reconciled, imperfections that would greatly detract
from even admitted human compositions, and erroneous principles of morality that would have hardly found a place in the most incomplete systems
of the philosophers of Greece and Rome."   Both writers, however, as
already noticed, overcome the difficulty of receiving Jesus as a model of
absolute perfection, by supposing that all the passages in the Gospels,
where these immoralities, absurdities, and contradictions occur, are spurious,
and are not a record of what the immaculate Jesus said and did.*   But
this assumption, while it sweeps away almost all the contents of the Gospels,
leaves the question of the truth of Christianity in a still more hopeless
state than by maintaining the genuineness of the whole of the New
Testament.   Nor do these writers adduce any literary proof whatever that
such portions of the Gospels as they reject as spurious are *more so* than
the parts they regard as genuine.   Taking the deeds and expressions
attributed to Jesus in these Gospels, therefore, as we find them, the immoralities, absurdities, ignorance, asceticism, bigotry, obscurity of expression,
contradictions, and other defects, which shall be pointed out in the sequel,
will abundantly show that the Prophet of Nazareth is, unfortunately, far
from being an example worthy of our constant imitation.

It is only during the short space of about three years that the Evangelists give us any account of Christ's career.   Although he lived about
thirty-three years, yet it is from what his biographers state that he did and
said during the fore-mentioned brief period that we can judge of his intellectual and moral qualities, with the exception that Luke (ii. 42—48.) mentions
that, when he was twelve years old, he ran away from his parents, and was
found in the temple among the doctors, asking and answering wonderful
questions, so as to astonish all present with his understanding.   The
Canonical Gospels give no account whatever of the manner in which he
spent thirty years out of a life of thirty-three.†   The general opinion of

* See Giles's Christian Records, pref. vii. and pp. 154—229.   Greg's Creed of
Christendom, pp. 94—160.

† Those Gospels which are termed "Apocryphal" but which, nevertheless, are supported by quite as strong evidence of their genuineness, as can be adduced for that of
the Canonical Gospels, furnish us with copious knowledge of the manner in which Jesus
spent his earlier days; particularly, " the Gospels of the Infancy of Jesus Christ." Some
of their statements may be interesting to the reader.   But before entering upon them,
let it be noticed that " The First Gospel of the Infancy of Jesus Christ" was believed to
be of a divine origin by some of the earliest Christian churches of which we have any
account.   At the end of the first, or at least early in the beginning of the second, century,
it was received as such by the Marcosians—a branch of the Gnostics—the most philosophic and intelligent sect of Christians in their time.   (Jones's Canonical Authority of
the New Test. voi. ii. pp. 226—234.)   In succeeding centuries, its narrations were
indiscriminately relied upon and referred to by Christian Fathers, such as Eusebius,

Christian divines, however, is that he spent his youth and even the most vigorous portion of his manhood, with his parents—Joseph and Mary—

Athanasius, Epiphanius, Chrysostom, &c. Sozomen, (lib. v. c. 22.) in the fifth century, relates the tales found in this Gospel of the idols of Egypt falling before Jesus, when Joseph and Mary fled with him thither; and of the well which the infant Deity caused to spring from a sycamore tree. Sir John Chardin notices Persian legends about Christ's dispute with his schoolmaster, and his miraculous lengthening of a cedar board, which are found in this Gospel. In one of these Gospels of Infancy, likewise, we find the apparent origin of the Persic notion that Jesus practised the trade of a dyer, and wrought miracles with colours; whence the Persian dyers honour him as their patron, and call a dye-house—the shop of Christ. The Nestorians—that very ancient sect of Christians who have done more towards the diffusion of the religion of Jesus than perhaps any other sect, used this Gospel as late as the sixteenth century, and most probably still continue to use it, in their divine services, among the mountains of Malabar, in India. (La Croze Hist. du Christian. de Ind. liv. v. p. 344.) Fabricius thinks that it is this, by the name of "The Gospel of Thomas," which Ocobius de Castro mentions as being read in many churches of Asia and Africa as the only rule of faith. (Hone's Preface to the Gospels of Infancy.) So general was the reception of this Gospel throughout Christendom at a very early period, that it found its way even into the Welsh language, evidently some centuries before the Canonical Gospels; for we find a very ancient transcribed translation of it, in manuscript, now in the British Museum, under the title—"*Mabinogi Jesu Grist.*" We have no account of the Canonical Gospels having been rendered into Welsh before the year 1567, whereas the MS. of the *Mabinogi* must have been written in the thirteenth or fourteenth century, at the latest. A similar remark applies to the Gospel of Infancy, as well as other Apocryphal Gospels, in the English and in the Anglo-Saxon dialects. Whatever about the truth of the opinion that a certain Anglo-Saxon translation of the Four Canonical Gospels was made as early as 721, which is very doubtful, it is clear that these Gospels were not known among the Anglo-Saxon people for more than 750 years after this date,—indeed not until they were translated by Wiclif, in 1380.— For all the ancient mysteries or Christian dramas, acted and sung as religious perform-ances, *are founded on the Apocryphal Gospels entirely.* Such are *The Birth of Mary, Her Education in the Temple, Her miraculous Espousal to Joseph, The Council of the Trinity regarding the Incarnation, Joseph's Jealousy, The Trial of Mary and Joseph,* and *The Miraculous Birth and the Midwives.* Such also are very ancient engravings still extant, among which is *The Descent into Hell;* and likewise a great number of Carols.— All these are evidently founded upon the Apocryphal Gospels, showing that they were known to the people of England long before those now termed Canonical. (See Hone's Ancient Mysteries,—a volume which entirely treats of these subjects, and contains much valuable and curious matter extracted from ancient documents.—*London,* 1823.) A translation of the Gospel of Nicodemus, one of those productions which now, curiously enough, are termed "Apocryphal," was made into Anglo-Saxon, by Ælfric, abbot of St. Albans, in 950, and published by Dr. Hicks, at Oxford, in 1698. (Lewis's Hist. of the Transl. of the Bible.) Most of the theological dogmas now cherished by Christians, such as—The doctrines of the Trinity, Incarnation, Descent into Hell, and Atonement, appear to have been preached in England at a very early period, and to have been familiar to the people long before they knew anything of the Canonical Gospels. These subjects, taught in the Apocryphal Gospels, were acted as religious plays—the divine services of the times—which show that they had taken deep root in the national feeling. The Brotherhood of the Holy Trinity—a Christian institution founded so late as the year 1373—appears to have possessed no portion of the Canonical Scriptures; for in the repeated inventories which were made, and are still extant, of *all* the property possessed by the fraternity, no mention is made of any. (Hone's Ancient Mysteries, p. 85.) Even the clergy both in Britain and on the Continent, up to the time of the Reformation, were utterly ignorant of the Canonical Gospels and our present New Testament in general.— In a Synod of Rural Deans in Switzerland few were found acquainted with the New Testament. In the sixteenth century the Doctors of Sorbonne did not know what the New Testament was. Martin Luther had never seen a Bible till he was twenty-one years old, and had taken a degree in Arts; and Carlostadt had been a Doctor of Divinity twenty-eight years before he read the Canonical Scriptures. (See Hone and Authorities —Ancient Mysteries, pp. 156, 157.) But not to digress: the foregoing facts, with many

2 w

and with his brothers—James, Joses, Judas, and Simon—and several sisters, whose names are not given in the Gospels, (Matth. xiii. 55. Mark

others which could be added, regarding the Apocryphal Gospels, show that there is quite as much evidence of the genuineness of the Gospel of Infancy as there is of that of either of the Canonical Gospels.—Indeed, we have evidence that it is of higher antiquity than either of them ; for *we have no proof that our* PRESENT *Gospels existed in the second century.*

Now this "Gospel of the Infancy of Jesus" furnishes us, *inter alia,* with the following interesting particulars of his early life.—When in his cradle, he said to his mother that he was Jesus, the Son of God. (chap. i. ver. 3. Hone's Edit.) Having been circumcised, and afterwards, in due course of time, been brought to the temple to be presented to the Lord, he shone, on this occasion, like a pillar of light, while angels stood round adoring him, and while the pious old Simeon praised him, exclaiming—" Now, O my Lord, thy servant shall depart in peace." (ii. 5—8. Compare with Luke ii. 21—29.) When the wise men from the East, who had been guided in their journey by an angel in the form of a star, visited Jesus, his mother gave them one of his swaddling clothes as a blessing. Having, like true Sabians, thrown it into the fire and worshipped it, they found that fire had no effect upon it. (iii. 1—8.) When Jesus, to avoid the rage of Herod, was taken by Joseph and Mary into Egypt, the Egyptian idols fell before him. Mary having washed his swaddling clothes and hung them to dry on a post, the son of an Egyptian priest, possessed with the devil, took down one of the clothes, and immediately devils began to come out of his mouth, flying away in the shape of crows and serpents. (iv. 1—16.)— Jesus, thus in his infancy, next comes in contact with a woman possessed with a malignant devil in the form of a young man, which instantly flies, crying—" Woe to me, because of thee, Mary, and thy Son." (vi. 1—4.) His next exploit is to restore the power of speech to a bride suddenly struck dumb by the devil as she was led to the hymeneal altar. About the same time, the water in which he had been washed cured two eases of leprosy. (vi.) He was next introduced to a gentleman who had, by witchcraft, been turned into a mule, which, when Jesus was put on its back, returned into a man. (vii.) Jesus and his parents pass through a country infested with robbers, of two of whom he prophesies that they shall be crucified with him, and that one of them shall go before him into Paradise. "Hence they went to that sycamore tree which is now called Matarea; and in Matarea the Lord Jesus caused a well to spring forth in which St. Mary washed his coat; and a balsam is produced, or grows, in that country from the sweat which ran down there from the Lord Jesus." (viii. 9—11.) Having performed a great many other miracles in Egypt, and returned to Nazareth, he cured several boys of different diseases, and healed two leprous women. The next miracle he works is to cast out of a poor girl a huge devil in the shape of a dragon, which, when it only had the smell of Jesus's clothes, went out, exclaiming—" What have I to do with thee, Jesus, thou Son of Mary?" (xiii.) Jesus now comes in contact with Judas Iscariot, who was then only a little boy living with his mother in Nazareth. Young as Judas then was, he, however, had in him a devil. Jesus having gone out with his brothers—James and Joses—to play, Judas, who had come to sit at his side, attempted to bite him, but failing to do so, he struck him, so that he cried. When Jesus cried, the devil instantly went out of Judas, "and ran away like a mad dog." (xiv.) The following narration we give in the very words of the Gospel.—" When the Lord Jesus was seven years of age, he was on a certain day with other boys his companions about the same age, who when they were at play made clay into several shapes, namely, asses, oxen, birds, and other figures ; each boasting of his work, and endeavouring to exceed the rest. Then the Lord Jesus said to the boys, I will command these figures which I have made to walk. And immediately they moved ; and when he commanded them to return, they returned. He had also made figures of birds and sparrows, which, when he commanded to fly, did fly ; and when he commanded to stand still, did stand still ; and if he gave them meat and drink, they did eat and drink. When at length the boys went away and related these things to their parents, their fathers said to them, Take heed, children, for the future of his company, for he is a sorcerer ; shun and avoid him, and from henceforth never play with him. On a certain day also, when the Lord Jesus was playing with the boys, and running about, he passed a dyer's shop, whose name was Salem. And there were in the shop many pieces of cloth belonging to the people of that city, which they designed to dye of several colours. Then the Lord Jesus going into the dyer's shop, took all the cloths, and threw them into the furnace. When Salem came home, and saw the cloths spoiled, he began

vi. 3. Luke iv. 22. John i. 45 ; vi. 42.) during which time he learned of his father the trade of a carpenter, which he followed till he was inaugurated

to make a great noise, and to chide the Lord Jesus, saying, What hast thou done to me, O Son of Mary ? Thou hast injured both me and my neighbours; they all desired their cloths of a proper colour; but thou hast come, and spoiled them all. The Lord Jesus replied, I will change the colours of every cloth to what colour thou desirest. And then he presently began to take the cloths out of the furnace, and they were all dyed of those same colours which the dyer desired. And when the Jews saw this surprising miracle they praised God." (xv.) Such was Jesus's miracle of dyeing, which is also partly told in Thomas's Gospel of the Infancy of Christ. The next miracle we have on record of the boy-Deity is one relating to Joseph's trade of a carpenter. Wherever Joseph went to work, he took Jesus with him " to make gates, or milk-pails, or sieves, or boxes." And when anything was required to be made " longer or shorter, or wider, or narrower," Jesus only stretched his hand towards it and it was made. Once when Joseph had made a throne too narrow, Jesus instantly stretched it out to the proper dimensions. (xvi.) On one occasion, when certain boys saw that Jesus wished to join them in playing in the street they hid themselves in an adjacent furnace. Jesus having inquired of certain women whither the boys had gone, and having received no information, asked them to look what was in the furnace, whereupon they exclaimed that there were in it kids of three years old. " Then Jesus cried out aloud and said, Come out hither, O ye kids to your shepherd." The boys instantly came out like kids, leaping about him, to the astonishment of the women, who began to worship him, and entreat him to " restore the boys to their former state. Then Jesus said, Come hither, O boys, that we may go and play ; and immediately, in the presence of these women, the kids were changed and returned into the shape of boys." (xvii.) When Jesus was treated as king by his play-fellows, there came by certain men carrying on a couch a boy who, when taking the eggs out of a partridge's nest, had been stung by a poisonous serpent which leaped out of the nest. Jesus told the men to take the boy, who was in a dying state, back with him, that he might kill that serpent. Having arrived at the place, Jesus called the ser-pent out of its lurking-hole, and said to it, " Go and suck out all the poison which thou hast infused into that boy. So the serpent crept to the boy, and took away all its poison again. Then the Lord Jesus cursed the serpent, so that it immediately burst asunder, and died. And he touched the boy with his hand to restore him to his former health." (xviii.) On another day, Jesus and his brother James were in a wood, when the latter was bitten by a venomous viper. But Jesus " blowed upon the place where the viper had bit him, and it was instantly well." (xix. 1—3.) Jesus, in his boyhood as well as manhood, could make the dead speak. Once when he was with some boys playing on the top of a house, one of these boys fell down and was killed; whereupon all his companions, except Jesus, ran away from the house-top. The deceased boy's relations came forward and accused Jesus of the murder, saying, " Our son is dead, and this is he who killed him." Jesus indignantly denied this foul charge, and proposed to go down with them and ask the dead boy who killed him. This having been agreed upon, Jesus stood over the deceased's head, and with a loud voice said, " Zeinunus ! Zeinunus ! who threw thee down from the house-top ? Then the dead boy answered, Thou didst not, but such an one did." (xix. 4—10.) Jesus having, on one occasion, been sent by his mother for a pitcher-ful of water, broke the pitcher. But spreading out his mantle, he gathered the water in it, " and brought it to his mother who, being astonished at this wonderful thing, laid up this, and all the other things which she had seen, in her memory." (xix. 12—15. Compare with Luke ii. 51.) As he was one day with his playmates, by the side of a river, making little fish-pools, Jesus made twelve sparrows, and placed them on each side of his fish-pool. This was on the Sabbath ; and a Jew, the son of Hanani, interfered with the boys, and loosing their little pools, said, " Do ye thus make figures of clay on the Sabbath ?" Jesus perceiving the officiousness of this sanctimonious meddler, " clapped his hands over the sparrows which he had made, and they fled away chirping." As the spiteful son of Hanani came forward to destroy Jesus's fish-pool, the water that was in it vanished away, and Jesus said to his molester, —" In like manner as this water has vanished, so shall thy life vanish ; and presently the boy died." (xix. 16—21.) Thomas, the Israelite, in the *Second* Gospel of the Infancy, (i. ii.) which is evidently of a much more ancient date than even the *First*, records the same miracle, with a little variation and amplification. But there is no more difference

into his Messiahship by the baptism of John in the Jordan, at the age of thirty. Having been expressly sent from heaven into this sinful world as

between the narrations of these two Gospels, on this point, than we frequently find between two of the Canonical Gospels in narrating the same incident.—Thomas says that Jesus was five years old when he performed this miracle,—that in consequence of a shower of rain the water ran over the banks of the river, and enabled Jesus and his companions to make fish-pools,—that the water in these little pools caused by muddy flood, became clear at the word of Jesus,—and that the boy who annoyed him was the son of Anna, the scribe. He also states that when this youth scattered the water in the pool with the bough of a willow tree, "the boy Jesus, seeing what had been done, became angry, and said to him, Thou fool, what harm did the lake do to thee, that thou shouldst scatter the water? Behold now thou shalt wither as a tree, and shalt not bring forth either leaves, or branches, or fruit. And immediately he became withered all over." The parents of the withered boy, lamenting his misfortune, brought him to Joseph, asking why he left at large a son so dangerous. Jesus, however ultimately, "at the request of all who were present, did heal him, leaving only some small member to continue withered, that they might take warning." The next miracle recorded in the *First* Gospel of the Infancy (xix. 22—24.) is the following.—As Jesus was coming home, another boy violently ran against him, and threw him down. Jesus said to him, "As thou hast thrown me down, so shalt thou fall, not ever to rise. And that moment the boy fell down and died." This wreak of vengeance is told much more at large in the *Second* Gospel of Infancy. (ii. 7—20.) Here it is said that a boy, running in the street, rushed upon the shoulders of Jesus who, "being angry, said to him, Thou shalt go no further; and he instantly fell down dead." The bystanders, upon seeing this, inquired "where was this boy born," whose word, whether good or bad, was immediately fulfilled. "The parents of the dead boy" also repaired to Joseph, telling him that, as he had such a dangerous boy, he was not fit to live in their city; and that he should either depart or teach his son to bless and not curse, so as thus to kill their children. Joseph now, "calling the boy Jesus" on one side, remonstrated with him. Jesus replied that those who had just complained of him should suffer "everlasting punishment. And immediately they who had accused him became blind." Upon seeing Jesus make this extravagant use of his miraculous power, Joseph plucked him "by the ear; at which the boy was angry, and said to him, Be easy. For if they seek for us they shall not find us: thou hast done very imprudently. Dost thou not know that I am thine? Trouble me no more." Jesus is now sent to school to a person named Zaccheus, who writes out the Hebrew alphabet for him, and bids him say the letters. Jesus, after he has pronounced *Aleph*, refuses to utter *Beth* till his teacher has explained the meaning of *Aleph*. The master threatens to whip him, whereupon the pupil begins to teach his master the meaning of both *Aleph* and *Beth*, together with the signification of the vowel-points, and all other things pertaining to Hebrew orthography. The teacher now, in amazement, exclaims, "I believe this boy was born before Noah;" and, turning to Joseph, he says, "Thou hast brought a boy to me to be taught, who is more learned than any master." Jesus is sent to a more profound teacher, of whom after saying *Aleph* he demands to be told the meaning of this letter before he obeys his master in saying *Beth*. The pedagogue, irritated at such pertinacity and superciliousness in a new pupil, lifts up his hand to whip Jesus; but no sooner is his hand up than it is withered! Joseph and Mary, now, determine never again to "allow him to go out of the house;" assigning as a reason that "every one who displeases him is killed." (1 Infancy xx. 1—16. 2 Infancy iii. 1—7.) His next miraculous exploit is that which is partly related in the Canonical Gospels, namely, his learned display among the Jewish doctors in the temple. The First Gospel of Infancy states that "when he was twelve years old, they brought him to Jerusalem to the feast; and when the feast was over they returned. But the Lord Jesus continued behind in the temple among the doctors and elders, and learned men of Israel; to whom he proposed several questions of learning, and also gave them answers. For he said to them, Whose son is the Messiah? They answered the son of David.— Why then, said he, does he in the spirit call him Lord, when he saith, The Lord said to my Lord, sit thou at my right hand, till I have made thine enemies thy foot-stool?"— The Gospel proceeds to narrate the questions he asked the doctors, and the answers he gave, in his turn, to questions asked by them, in Theology, Astronomy, Mathematics, "Physic," "Natural Philosophy," "Metaphysics," Geology, Chymistry, Pathology,

a Saviour of men who were not only to obtain a title to the regions of bliss by his atonement, but were also to be morally qualified by his perfect

Physiology, Anatomy, &c. "While they were discoursing on these and such like things," Jesus's mother "came in, having been three days walking about with Joseph seeking for him. And when she saw him sitting among the doctors, and in his turn proposing questions to them, and giving answers, she said to him, My son, why hast thou done this by us? Behold I and *thy father* have been at much pains in seeking thee. He replied, Why did ye seek me? Did ye not know that I ought to be employed in my Father's house? But they understood not the words which he said to them." After the doctors had asked Mary a few questions about her wonderful son, "he returned with them to Nazareth, and obeyed them in all things. And his mother kept all these things in her mind: and the Lord Jesus grew in stature and wisdom, and favour with God and man." (I Gospel of Infancy xxi. 1—29. Compare with Luke ii. 41—52.) The Gospel goes on to state that "from this time Jesus began to conceal his miracles," and gave himself to the study of the law, till he arrived at the end of his thirtieth year, when the Father publicly owned him on the banks of the Jordan, with a voice from heaven, and in the dove-like presence of the Holy Ghost.

From these abstracts, a reader who has never perused the Gospels of Infancy may at once have an idea of their contents, and of the ancient notions entertained of the earlier days of Jesus. These Gospels where they relate the same incidents as the Canonical Gospels, in the main, agree with them. The miracles which they attribute to Jesus are quite as credible as those recorded in the Canonical Gospels. The only difference is that the former narrate the miracles he performed in his infancy and boyhood, and the latter those he wrought in his manhood. But if it is reasonable to believe that Jesus performed miracles in his manhood, it is, on the supposition that he was born a Deity, quite as reasonable to believe that he wrought miracles from infancy up to manhood; nay, it is much more reasonable to believe that he wrought miracles throughout his earthly career of thirty-three years, than to believe that he wrought miracles only during the last three years of this period. The other Apocryphal Gospels also agree with those regarded Canonical, when narrating the same particulars, the only material difference being that generally the former give a more detailed account of what they relate. Indeed the Canonical Gospels appear to be only an epitome of the contents of the vast number of elaborate Gospels which, in ancient times, existed. For example, in the Gospel of Mary, we have, among other things, Mary's espousal to Joseph, Gabriel's salutation to her, and the declaration he made to her, exactly corresponding with Luke's account. Joseph's doubts as to her fidelity, and the appearance of an angel to him in a dream, also agree with Matthew's narrative. The same may be said of the Gospel of the Birth of Christ, or the *Protevangelion*, which gives an account of the Eastern magi and the star, Herod's attempt to murder Jesus, &c. Mr. Hartwell Horne (Introd. vol. i. appendix sec. ii.) seeing the inevitable tendency of these Gospels to invalidate the divine authority of those termed inspired, makes a desperate effort to show that there are vast differences between the former and the latter. His principal arguments are.—1. That these Apocryphal writings were not acknowledged and not *much* used by the primitive Christians, —that neither Clement, Ignatius, Polycarp, nor Hermas quotes them. If, however, they were used at all by the primitive Christians,—of which there is abundant proof—this is sufficient to establish their early existence. But does not Mr. Horne well know that there is *no proof* that either of the Fathers he names *has quoted the Canonical Gospels;* that there is *positive proof* that some of them cited precisely the same words as are found in the Apocryphal Gospels; and that the writings of the greater number of them, particularly Barnabas and Hermas, are *now* abandoned by Christian divines as spurious?— 2. He urges that few of these productions *were composed before the second* century. But we have evidence that the Canonical Gospels were *not* composed *before the second century.* 3. That the fact of Origen, in one or two places, quoting an Apocryphal Gospel is no proof that he esteemed it as Canonical. But in the time of Origen the Canon of the New Testament had not been fixed;—if it had, no better proof of his approval of such a Gospel could be desired than the purpose for which he cites the Gospel according to the Hebrews. 4. That these writings contain absurdities; relate improbable and useless miracles; mention things which are later than the time in which their supposed authors lived; contain direct contradictions to authentic history; contain gross falsehoods; and support doctrines contrary to those known to be true. Now, every one of these

example of a holy life, it is most wonderful that Jesus spent thirty years of a life of thirty-three in obscurity, thus depriving mankind, at large, of the immense moral and intellectual benefit which, one would think, was to be derived from his spotless career, if he was such a model of perfection as Christians assert him to have been. It is difficult to harmonise this obscure and secluded mode of life with the alleged benevolent design of his mission. Nor is it easy to imagine, even if we suppose him a merely and an ordinarily pious man—say a missionary sent into this part of the universe to give its inhabitants " an example," and " to save that which was lost,"—how this was consistent with the emotions of a mind bent upon doing good. What would be thought of a missionary sent by the pious people of England into any remote and " dark place of the earth" who would there spend thirty years of his time without preaching, writing tracts, distributing Bibles, conversing on religious subjects, or in any manner making the way of salvation known to these perishing pagans, who " grope for the wall like the blind" ? Would they not disapprove of, nay, condemn, his unfaithfulness and inactivity ? By what rule of morality, then, is a similar conduct justifiable in Jesus ?

The first occasion on which the Evangelists bring Jesus before us, in the character of a moral teacher, is when he delivers his Sermon on the Mount. (Matth. v. vi. vii.) This sermon consists of a great number of aphorisms or maxims, occasionally illustrated by parables and apostrophes which contribute to enliven the discourse. Although the fact that parts of this sermon—given only by Matthew as a whole and complete discourse— are found interspersed throughout the Gospels of Mark and Luke,* furnishes a very strong presumptive proof that such a series of moral precepts and maxims was never delivered by Jesus at one and the same time ; yet it will here be taken for granted that he actually delivered it as reported by Matthew. This sermon, throughout Christendom, has always been considered a masterpiece of moral teaching, containing, as it is said, the heads of the moral law. It is true that it contains some good moral precepts ; but it is equally true that, being a collection of the moral sayings of antiquity which were afloat at the time the Gospels were first written, and many of which can be pointed out, with slight verbal variations, in the writings of Pagan authors, it contains, as may be expected, many things which are not strictly true and moral, and which display considerable ignorance of human nature, as well as of what really are moral vice and moral virtue. While most of the discourse, in its aim, would appear to breathe a degree of charity and benevolence, according to the simple

objections, as will be shown hereafter, most forcibly applies to the Canonical Gospels. Indeed it is singular that Mr. Horne could not perceive that what he advanced against the one most emphatically applied to the other ; so as to lead irresistibly to the conclusion that, if the Apocryphal Gospels are spurious, so are the Canonical Gospels. That they are equally spurious ; or in other words, equally the legendary and mythological productions of dark and barbarous people, is made clearer and clearer in proportion as the question, in these days of critical research, is investigated.

* Compare the following passages with parallel passages in the Sermon on the Mount. —Luke vi. 20—26. Mark ix. 50. Luke xiv. 34. Mark iv. 21. Luke viii. 16; xi. 33; xvi. 17; xii. 58, 59. Mark ix. 43—48; x. 4, 10—12. Luke xvi. 18; vi. 27—36; xi. 2—4; xii. 33, 34; xi. 34, 36; xvi. 13; xii. 22—31; xi. 9, 10; xiii. 24, 43—45; iii. 9, 46—49. Mark iv. 24; i. 2. and see Giles' Christian Records, pp. 155—164.

notions of ancient times, still several of its precepts are impracticable, and others are nonsensical, displaying great want of knowledge in the preacher. All these, in the sequel, shall be fairly and candidly considered, under the heads to which they naturally belong.

SECTION II.—MANY OF JESUS'S PRECEPTS AND DOCTRINES ABSURD, IMPRACTICABLE, AND IMMORAL IN THEIR TENDENCY.

It has already been shown that virtue and vice, truth and error, wisdom and folly, are of the same character in a being deemed supernatural as in a mere man, and to be tested by the same criteria. An infringment of the moral laws, or a breach of common sense, is as culpable, at least, in a Deity as in man. When a being, alleged to be divine, and in word and deed a perfect example for our imitation, is found to have enunciated a great number of precepts and doctrines, some of which, if reduced to practice, would be absurd, and others immoral and injurious, human reason recoils at the idea of either adoring him as God, obeying his precepts, or following his example. Such we find to be many of the precepts and doctrines said to have been delivered by Jesus. And not a few of this character are found in the Sermon on the Mount, which Christians extol as a piece of the purest wisdom and morality ever uttered.

In this sermon (Matth. v. 22.) Jesus says "that whosoever is angry with his brother without a cause shall be in danger of the judgment; and whosoever shall say to his brother, Raca, shall be in danger of the council; but whosoever shall say, Thou fool, shall be in danger of hell fire." Now, in the first place, no one can possibly be angry *without a cause*. Anger—however immoral—is the *effect* of something: and as no effect can exist without a cause, and even an adequate cause, this saying of Jesus is by no means consistent with a correct knowledge of things. If he meant—*without a just cause*, why did he not say so? Words are the vehicles of ideas; and we can judge of what Jesus meant only from the obvious meaning of the words he employed. As to *Raca*, in this denunciation, it is a Hebrew or Syriac word, meaning *vain, empty*, and used to designate a *torn garment*, or a piece of cloth cut off—a *rag*. Hence, it was, among the Jews, a term of contempt, probably applied to persons not well dressed, but in ragged clothes. The word translated "fool" is *more*, meaning simply a foolish person; or if—as supposed by some—derived from the Hebrew, meaning only "an obstinate, rebellious person." Now, can it for a moment, be supposed that—granting the existence of the Christian *hell*—a person for telling another, even his own brother, that he is a fool, or is rebellious, when he really is so, incurs the everlasting torments of "hell fire," described by Christ, on another occasion, in such strong and definite language? Can a person incur this endless and incomparably intense torment *for telling the truth*, or giving expression to what he believes? Jesus does not qualify his words, in any manner. We are therefore entitled to take them in their natural acceptation. What moral evil can there be in telling a person, in a becoming spirit, and with a view

to his improvement, that he is foolish, or vain, if he is so?   Is it not, on
the contrary, our *duty* to tell people their faults, in order that they may
avoid them?   Then, if it is so, was not this doctrine of Jesus erroneous?
Moral vice being of an unchangeable character, Jesus, in calling people
fools, as he *angrily* called the Scribes and Pharisees, according to his own
showing, would be as guilty of a hell-fire offence as any one else, if this
were sound moral philosophy. It is, however, too absurd to be entertained
for a moment, that because a man says to his brother—" Thou art a fool!"
he should be everlastingly punished in hell, "where the worm dieth not."

It is difficult to imagine a precept more absurd, and more immoral in
tendency, than the following, which three times occurs in Jesus' Sermon
on the Mount.—" Take therefore no thought for the morrow."—" Take
no thought for your life, what ye shall eat, or what ye shall drink; nor yet
for your body, what ye shall put on."—" Therefore take no thought, saying, What shall we eat? or what shall we drink? or wherewithal shall we
be clothed?"   (Matth. vi. 25, 31, 34. See also similar words in Luke xii.
22—33.)   Close and general obedience to this precept, and others of a
similar meaning, with which the Gospels abound, would soon plunge
society into general ruin: poverty, want, wretchedness, starvation would
be the inevitable consequence.   The meaning of the doctrine here taught
by Jesus being so clear and explicit, much learning and ingenuity have, in
vain, been expended by commentators on the words he used, with a view
to render them less obnoxious to common sense.   Accordingly, as it is
their custom when in similar difficulties, they would persuade us that Jesus
meant something else than what his words obviously signify.—Here they
say, the words—" take *no* thought," in the original, mean " take no *anxious*
thought,"—do not lavish inordinate care on the things of this world, and
so on.   But let us see what truth there is in this oft-repeated assertion.—
The Greek words employed here for—" take no thought," are μη ουν
μεριμνησητε, simply meaning—take *no thought* or *care,*—*be not careful.*—
There is nothing whatever in the expression which justifies the idea of
"*anxious* thought."   The verb—μεριμναω, employed here, means merely *to
care, to be careful, to heed;* and is most frequently, in the New Testament,
rendered *care;* and that in such connexions as utterly exclude the idea of
any particular *anxiety;* such as is sought to be attached to the word in the
precept under notice. The same Greek word is translated *care,* and *to care,*
in 1 Cor. vii. 32, 33, 34; xii. 15. Phil. iv. 6; ii. 20. and 1 Pet. v. 7.
In these instances the idea of anxiety is no more implied than it is ordinarily implied in the word *care.*   And, indeed, so little do commentators
mend the matter by adopting the phrase—" take no *anxious* thought," that
there is no real difference between the idea conveyed and that attached to
—" take no *care.*"   To be *careful,* and to be *thoughtful,* in this connexion,
are synonymous words.   When Paul, using the same Greek word to the
Philippians,—whom he persuades that the Lord was about to appear in
judgment—tells them to "be careful for nothing" but make all their wants
known to God by prayer, he clearly means that they should not trouble
themselves about earthly things, or even provide for their own wants.   In
like manner when Jesus says—" Labour not for the meat that perisheth,"
(John vi. 27.) he means more than—" take no *anxious* thought for your
life what ye shall eat;"—he means more than that people "should not set

their affections inordinately upon temporal things,"—he means that people should not do anything whatever towards producing food and raiment.— On this point he has not left any just ground of doubt; for he has amply illustrated his precept by references to *birds* and *lilies*. Immediately after enunciating the precept of taking no thought of life, he adds—" Behold the fowls of the air; for they sow not, neither do they reap nor gather into barns; yet your heavenly Father feedeth them."—" Consider the lilies of the field, how they grow; they toil not, neither do they spin; and yet I say unto you, that even Solomon in all his glory was not arrayed like one of these." Jesus fully explains here what he means by *taking no thought of life*, and *taking no thought for the morrow.*—Just as the fowls of the air neither sow, nor reap, nor gather into barns, in order to provide subsistence; so men should do neither of these things,—should take no thought whatever *to-day* about providing food for *the morrow;* and just as the lilies of the field neither toil nor spin, by way of manufacturing wearing apparel, so men should do nothing in order either to preserve themselves from the inclemency of the weather or to enable them to make a decent appearance,—should be quite as inactive as the lilies, and as improvident as the birds,—should take no thought whatever of their life.—" no thought for the morrow; for the morrow shall take thought for the things of itself." This, unquestionably, is what Jesus teaches, not only here, but in a vast number of other places in the Gospels. Absurd as the doctrine is, considered in itself, the mode of reasoning employed in enforcing it is equally repugnant to common sense —Because the fowls of the air neither sow, reap, nor gather into barns, man should not do so; and because the lilies neither toil nor spin, man has no need to do either. This must be confessed to be one of the grossest comparisons ever made by the most witless teacher of morality in any age. But the absurdity of both the precept and its illustration dwindles into nothing, when compared with the enormity of the evil that would ensue if the precept were reduced into general practice. Imagine this precept to be universally obeyed,—all arts, all projects which aim at the future good of mankind, all commerce, all agricultural pursuits, all secular employment whatever, must be abandoned; and the result would be inevitable wretchedness—starvation—death to all mankind! Let everybody *take no thought for the morrow;* let none either sow, reap, or gather into barns; let none *take thought of raiment*; let none *take thought for life;* and soon will all be running about naked and hungry, —soon will all die of starvation,—soon will the human race become utterly extinct! It is, certainly, not too much to say,—a more extravagant, absurd, impracticable, and immoral precept than this was never proclaimed. It teaches the most unqualified improvidence and recklessness.—It is brimful of immorality. Fortunate it is for Christians that the instincts of nature restrain them from attempting to reduce such a precept into practice, —that they content themselves with believing it as divine, as a most sublime piece of moral teaching, and as infinitely above their comprehension; while they are constrained *to disobey it.*

Another almost equally absurd and pernicious precept given by Jesus is the following.—" Resist not evil." (Matth. v. 39.) Precluding the possibility of being understood figuratively, in the immediate context he explains his meaning, thus—" But whosoever shall smite thee on thy right

cheek, turn to him the other also ; and if any man will sue thee at the law,
and take away thy coat, let him have thy cloke also. And whosoever shall
compel thee to go a mile, go with him twain.   Give to him that asketh
thee, and from him that would borrow of thee turn not thou away."   We
are not to resist any of these evils.—The evil of a blow on the cheek we
are to treat by turning the other to be dealt with in the same manner ;
the evil of having our coat taken away in an action at law, we are to deal
with by throwing our cloak also to the plaintiff; the evil of being forced
to walk a mile against our will, we are to meet by walking another ; and
the evil of being impoverished by beggars and borrowers, we are to redress
by *giving* to everybody that asks, and never turn away from any one who
wishes to borrow of us !   When we receive a blow from any ruffian in the
street, we are not to use any means of self-defence ; we are not to call for
assistance ; we are not to request a peace-officer to arrest the pommeling arm
of our assailant, and put him under restraint, lest he desist not till he has
taken away our lives ; we are not even to run away from him ; but we are
to assist him in beating us,—after he has dealt a blow on our right cheek,
we are so far to accommodate ourselves to his onslaught as to turn the
other cheek convenient to receive another blow.   When an unjust claim
is made upon us in a court of law, we are not to resist such a demand ;
but to pay not only what is thus claimed, but even more than is claimed,
so as to encourage dishonesty.   When we are wrongly forced to go a mile,
we must not complain, but go another in order to show our approbation of
the wrong thus done us.   If a thousand to day ask alms of us, and an equal
number to-morrow wish to borrow either goods or money of us, we must
comply with all these requests, notwithstanding that by such recklessness
we will be certain to reduce ourselves, and our children, to want and ruin.
Such is the evident tenor of the doctrine taught by Jesus in the series of
injunctions just cited.   But where are the Christians who practise this
doctrine which they contend to be divine, and consequently rational and
moral ?   Has it not been their practice in every age and country to resist
even what they fancied to be evil to a most cruel degree ?   Having received
a blow on the one cheek, do they turn the other for the same treatment ?
or do they fight in self-defence, and after all punish their assailant with
fine or imprisonment ?   Do they give their cloaks also to a person who
takes their coats ?   Do they relieve every beggar ? and do they lend money
oftener than other people ?   Unquestionably not : they do not attempt to
practise these precepts.   And why ?   Evidently because they are utterly
impracticable.   An attempt at practising them would be considered in any
one a mark of an unsound mind.   Such is their absurdity.   Since Christians
do not, and cannot practise these precepts,—since they continue to resist
evil as they daily do, even on an enormous scale, in the barbarous wars,
bloodshed, and carnage of Christian combatants, of which the present times
furnish signal examples in several Christian countries, —since they refuse
voluntarily to give either their coats or cloaks to persons who sue them at
law,—since they do not *give* and *lend* indiscriminately to persons who ask
of them ;—they must therefore admit that, according to their own conduct,
Jesus gave an impracticable and, consequently, a useless precept ; to say
nothing of its absurdity and immorality.   Should it be urged that Christ
did not intend his precept to convey this meaning ; then we ask why did

he not say what he meant? Why did he speak in a manner calculated to mislead and deceive? If he did so intentionally, it was an immoral act; and if he did so unintentionally, it was a sign of imperfection,—an imperfection which places him below public teachers in general, most of whom speak so as to be intelligible. But in the precept under notice there is no obscurity or ambiguity of expression,—the language is as clear as can be desired.* He explicitly and expressly enjoins—"Resist not evil," Now, although man should never revenge evil, or return evil for evil; yet there is a great difference between revenging evil and resisting it. A man resists evil from the instinctive principle of self-preservation, but he revenges it from malice. The former is a principle implanted by nature in all animals, rational and irrational; but the latter is an abuse, or an inordinate exercise of the feeling of self-preservation, and is consequently immoral in man. If a man is assailed by another, he is justified in resisting the evil or injury about to be inflicted upon him, and in using every means to defend himself and those whom it is his duty to protect; provided he uses no other means and no more violence than he thinks necessary to secure safety, and is not actuated by a feeling of revenge. The resistance of evil, the principle of which is founded in nature, pervading all animal life, is purely moral. To obey Christ's precept, therefore, if practicable, would be *immoral*,—would be contrary to nature,—would be to relinquish the principle of self-preservation,—and would be destructive to the existence of man. Further: This precept is diametrically opposed to all principles of reform.† If means are not taken to arrest *evil* in its course, no improvement,—no higher degree of moral perfection, but the reverse, is to be expected. Indeed, viewed in any light, it is impossible to avoid the conclusion that the morality taught by Christ in this precept is unsound, impracticable, and absurd, betraying lamentable ignorance both of human nature, and of what is really right or wrong.

Jesus, running from one extreme to another, is so far from teaching the non-resistance of evil, in the following doctrine, that he positively teaches *revenge*. When he sent out apostles to preach the kingdom of heaven, this was part of his charge.—"Into whatsoever city ye enter, and

---

* The Commentators here again endeavour to polish this awkward precept.—They would persuade us that all that is to be understood by "Resist not evil" is,—Revenge not evil by a malicious retaliation. But it is the word ανθιστημι which is employed here; denoting to *stand against* evil, or *resist* it. The same word is used in Acts xi. 10. to signify *resisting* wisdom; in Ephes. vi. 13. for *resisting* the evil day; and in other places where the idea of *revenging* or returning evil for evil is utterly excluded. If the word εκδικεω, τιμωρεω, or some other of similar import had been used, we might be persuaded that the precept means what the Commentators say. As it is, however, the hypothesis is entirely devoid of support.

† Justly has it been said by an able writer and speaker of the present age, that to carry out this doctrine is "to give a long lease to tyranny, to permit it to ride roughshod over the world, and to subdue, with the authority of a divine sanction, all humble and oppressed peoples, who ought to unite in resisting the oppressors, who would destroy them. If any man, desiring to keep the people in tyrannical subjection, had sought to bring the wise and noble doctrine of peace—the glorious principle, when wisely and philosophically stated, of overcoming evil, in some wise way, with good—into contempt, and to state it so impotently that no man ever could act upon it, he could not have uttered words more disastrous to liberty than Christ himself here utters."—Mr. G. J. Holyoake. Discussion with the Rev. J. H. Rutherford.—Christianity versus Secularism.

they receive you not, go your ways out into the streets of the same, and say, *Even the very dust of your city which cleaveth on us, we do wipe off against you:* notwithstanding be ye sure of this, that the kingdom of God is come nigh unto you. But I say unto you, that it shall be more tolerable in that day for Sodom, than for that city." (Luke x. 10—12. Matth. x. 14, 15. Mark vi. 11.) It scarcely needs be remarked that to shake off the dust from the feet was a well-known Jewish way of manifesting hatred and contempt,* and of imploring vengeance upon the object of one's wrath; so that whoever did this, the anger of the party to whom this national token of ill-feeling applied, was forthwith roused, and a feud thereby created. In this immoral manner, however, Jesus commands his illiterate and ignorant apostles to act. If people refused to believe their strange doctrine, they were to employ no rational means,—they were to use no argument,—in order to inspire belief in the truth of their mission; but were to excite anger by shaking the dust off their feet,—that irritating and contemptuous Jewish practice. If people did not receive these strangers into their houses, without knowing anything about their character, no attempt was to be made at teaching them the virtue of hospitality, but a feeling of hatred was to be evinced towards them, and a threat denounced that, in the day of Judgment, they would be punished more severely than even the inhabitants of Sodom. Jesus teaches the same doctrine of revenge, as well as that of injustice and cruelty, in the parable of the talents, (Matth. xxv. 14—30.) in which he consigns the unprofitable servant into outer darkness, and says that "unto every one that hath shall be given, and he shall have abundance; but from him that hath not shall be taken away even that which he hath." This doctrine pervades the whole of Christ's teaching. Its injustice is glaring. Is it to him that hath should we give? Is it our duty to take away from the poor even that which he hath? Is there a spark of either humanity or justice in such a conduct? Supposing this doctrine to be put in general practice, would not common sense denounce it as grossly unjust? Jesus teaches the same unjust doctrine in other places (Matth. xiii. 12. Mark iv. 25. Luke viii. 18.) utterly unconnected with this or any similar parable; so that it cannot be said that he has enunciated it in illustration of the parable of the talents. The *cruelty and revenge* also inculcated by this doctrine are equally prominent, in that it consigns the servant—who from fear had hidden the talent —to outer darkness, by way of *revenge*, to weep, wail, and gnash his teeth! The same spirit of revenge breathes throughout the whole of Jesus's teaching; such as—"Depart from me, ye cursed, into everlasting fire."— "Go away into everlasting punishment." Nor are those already pointed out the only instances, on record, of Jesus teaching *gross injustice*. He commends the unjust steward (Luke xvi. 5—8.) saying that he had "done wisely" in cheating his master, and advises his hearers to make "friends of the mammon of *unrighteousness*." Christian exponents of the New Testament feign not to understand this saying of "the author and finisher" of their faith. But as such a doctrine does not suit the present enlightened

---

* The same practice prevailed among other Eastern nations.—See *Light's Travels in Egypt.* The Jews used dust in several ways to indicate their hatred and rage,—one way was to throw dust into the air.—Acts xxii. 23.

age, they appear to consider it less damaging to their creed to admit that Jesus taught doctrines which cannot be understood, and which, therefore, are worthless, than openly to admit that he taught gross immorality,— taught stewards to cheat their masters. Another instance of Jesus teaching flagrant injustice is that in which he sanctions the conduct of his disciples in stealing corn. (Matth. xii. 1—8. Mark ii. 23—26. Luke vi. 3—5.)— Although the Jews, on this occasion, according to their law, accused his disciples only of Sabbath-breaking, yet the ears of corn which they plucked were not their property, but that of some other person or persons, so that —notwithstanding the liberty given by the Mosaic law, thus to plunder— they had no moral right whatever to them. Jesus, therefore, as a teacher —not of the Mosaic law but of true morality—should have known that for his disciples, even when hungry, to convert the corn to their own use, without leave or license, was an act of theft,—much more immoral in character than Jewish Sabbath-breaking. But how does he exculpate them from the charge of stealing corn on the Sabbath? By an effort, made in the most irrational manner, to justify their theft.—By urging that David and his companions had, on the Sabbath, broken into the temple, and therefrom stolen the shewbread, which belonged to the priests,—that the priests profaned the Sabbath and were blameless.—and that he, who was Lord of the Sabbath, was greater than either David or the temple. A very strange line of argument! To insist that his disciples were justified in stealing the corn because David had committed an act of the same character, was most illogical, unless he first showed that David in so doing was blameless; for "two wrongs can never make one right." Besides: David, in this act—very differently from many of his other acts—did not steal private property, and, as a king, did not steal at all. To urge that he was greater than the temple and was Lord of the Sabbath, implying that he was a God, appears equally irrational. If it is wrong in man to steal, or to profane the Sabbath, to do so would be wrong in a Deity. What would be immoral in man, would, of necessity, be immoral in God; for as moral vice and moral virtue are such in their very nature, the moral character of an act cannot depend upon the being who commits it. The argument therefore used here by Jesus to justify the conduct of his disciples is quite futile. But the consequence of his defective logic is of little moment compared with the effect which his defective moral teaching, in this instance, must have produced on the Christian world, during the eighteen centuries it has been propagated. Although the corn trampled down, plucked, and eaten by Jesus and his followers, in this act of plunder, may have been very small in pecuniary value, yet the glaring violation of a principle of justice by men whom thousands consider to have been inspired, and the defence made of this violation by Jesus who is regarded as divine and infallible, must, by way of example, be carrying continually a very powerful influence in deteriorating the morals of society.

Another most absurd and immoral doctrine frequently inculcated by Jesus was that, before a person could be his disciple, he must *hate* his own father, mother, wife, children, brothers, sisters, and even his own life.— His words on one occasion are—" If any man come to me and *hate* not his father, and mother, and wife, and children, and brethren, and sisters, yea, and his own life also, he cannot be my disciple." (Luke xiv. 26.) This must be confessed to be a most revolting doctrine. To harbour hatred towards any person is wicked; and deliberately to insist upon the exercise of such a feeling is still more wicked. But to harbour hatred, or to teach that it should be harboured towards a person's parents and nearest relatives, is one of the highest crimes of which human nature can be guilty. Were this doctrine universally practised, its evil effects upon the happiness of families and the welfare of society at large would be enormous. Happily, few Christians are so unnatural as to be able to practise this dogma thus emphatically taught them;—few of them are such faithful disciples of Jesus that they hate their loving parents, their affectionate wives, their smiling children, and their warm-hearted brothers and sisters;—few of them are so inhuman that they would not blush to feel hatred rankling in their bosoms towards their nearest relations,—their parents whose blood runs in their veins, their wives whom they have sworn to love and cherish, their children to whom they gave existence, and their brothers and sisters of the same flesh and bones! To hate these is absurd and sinful in the extreme! Jesus, however, expressly says that, before any one can be his disciple, he must do so; of which he gave us a slight example in his conduct towards his mother and brothers, as will hereafter more fully be noticed. Further, in order to become a disciple of Jesus a man must *hate his own life*. Than this doctrine nothing can be more revolting to human feeling and human reason,—nothing more impracticable. The love of life is a principle which pervades all animal nature, from the smallest animalcule up to man, in his sane state of mind. To hate life is the exercise of a grossly immoral passion, a violation of one of the first laws of nature, and a strong incentive to suicide, in which act of insanity it generally terminates. Indeed it is difficult to avoid the conclusion that Jesus did not advisedly teach the pernicious doctrine of suicide, when he repeatedly enjoined his hearers to hate their own lives, and told them that whosoever lost his life should find it, and so on. It is lamentable to find a book, considered to be divine, fraught with precepts which not only teach injustice, cruelty, and revenge, but enjoin us to hate our nearest relations, and even our own lives; and these precepts delivered by a personage held up to us as a model of moral perfection, whom we are to imitate in word and deed, if we wish to escape eternal punishment.

A very remarkable doctrine taught by Jesus was that of eating his flesh and drinking his blood. John (vi. 51—56.) reports his words as follows.—" I am the living bread which came down from heaven: if any man eat of this bread, he shall live for ever: and the bread that I will give is my flesh, which I will give for the life of the world. The Jews therefore strove among themselves, saying, How can this man give us his flesh to eat? Then Jesus said unto them, Verily, verily, I say unto you, Except ye eat the flesh of the Son of man, and drink his blood, ye have no life in you. Whoso eateth my flesh, and drinketh my blood, hath eternal life; and I will raise him up at the last day. For my flesh is meat indeed, and my blood is drink indeed. He that eateth my flesh, and drinketh my blood, dwelleth in me, and I in him." John tells us that when his disciples heard this strange doctrine, they said—" This is an hard saying, who can hear it?" and that from that time many of them " went back and walked no more with him." He also informs us that Jesus " would not walk in

Jewry, because the Jews sought to kill him." Now, if this doctrine involves the anthropophagal idea it appears to involve, it is by no means wonderful that Jesus's disciples pronounced it a *hard saying,* and walked with him no more. They apparently thought that a feast of human flesh and blood, in which early Christians are accused to have participated, would not be palatable to them, who were Jews, and who were—and are even to this day—rather squeamish as to eating the flesh of several animals, and particularly as to drinking their blood. If we bear in mind the provisions of the Mosaic law touching these things, we cannot fail to perceive that this doctrine was extremely revolting to the Jews, however acceptable to the Bacchanalians, Eleusinians, and other Pagan religionists. Nor can we fail to see why the Jews now sought to kill Jesus, who had just divulged this doctrine, or *mystery* as it is frequently termed, openly in their synagogue at Capernaum. The Christian world is very much divided as to what is meant by eating the flesh and drinking the blood of Jesus.— Roman Catholic Christians infer from the passage just cited—as well as from Jesus's words regarding the bread and the wine being his body and blood, as recorded in the three former Gospels—the doctrine of Transubstantiation, namely, the fanciful idea that the bread and the wine, in the communion, turn into the real body and blood of Christ. But Protestant Christians, rejecting this fancy, and yet cautiously evading the adoption of the broad and plain idea of cannibality conveyed by the passage, have come to the conclusion that all that is meant by *eating the flesh, and drinking the blood of Jesus, is to believe in him,* and that the expression is metaphorical.* But there is not an atom of proof here that it is metaphorical; or any other than literal. If it be contended that the word *bread* is metaphorically used for Jesus—" I am the bread of life," the answer is, that the word αρτος here rendered bread means *food;* so that, without supposing any metaphor, it is in perfect literal harmony with eating the body of Jesus. Nor did the Jews—who certainly, in their own language, could easily distinguish between a figurative and a literal expression—understand Jesus here to speak metaphorically; for after he had said that he would give his

* One eminent Protestant commentator explains the passage thus—" The real meaning of these words is that without true faith in the Lord Jesus Christ, none can have eternal life. Many have thought that Christ speaks here of eating and drinking the Lord's Supper; but this cannot be the case; for—1. That Sacrament was not established for more than two years after these words were delivered; and it is unreasonable to suppose that Christ spoke of an institution which, at the time, had no existence, so as to render it impossible for the people to understand his doctrine regarding it.—2. His words would not be true in respect to eating and drinking the Lord's Supper; for many had obtained eternal life who had never partaken of this Sacrament. Besides : to eat and drink the flesh and blood of Christ at the Lord's Supper, does not, of itself, give spiritual or eternal life to any; whereas Christ here speaks of such eating and drinking as give life eternal.—3. It is clear from ver. 29. that *to believe in Jesus* is what is meant here by eating and drinking; and it is certain that to eat and drink the Sacrament is not to believe. Although all who do so should believe, yet many, unfortunately, do it who are not believers. Those who understood Christ literally imagined that this doctrine was *absurd, and of a cannibal tendency,* and therefore forsook him; while others who understood him figuratively thought he was blaspheming."—*New Test with explanatory notes from Poole, Scott, Guyse, and Doddridge.* We shall see, in a subsequent note, how groundless the supposition is that Jesus meant *believing* in him, when speaking of eating his flesh and drinking his blood; and how it reflects upon him to suppose that he chose such a revolting metaphor.

flesh for bread or food, they asked, with astonishment, "How can this man give us his flesh to eat?" This inquiry clearly shows that his hearers, and even *many of his disciples*, who pronounced this discourse *hard*—or according to the Greek (σκληρος) *violent, shocking, impious*—understood Jesus literally; and in consequence of this revolting doctrine, "walked no more with him." If Jesus spoke metaphorically, and his hearers understood him literally, it is most reasonable to think that he would correct their mistake. Did he do so? So far was he from this that after they asked—" How can this man give us his flesh to eat?"—he confirmed the full literal meaning of his words in the most positive terms:—" Verily, verily, I say unto you, Except ye eat the flesh of the Son of man, and drink his blood, ye have no life in you. Whoso eateth my flesh and drinketh my blood, hath eternal life: and I will raise him up at the last day; for my flesh *is meat indeed*, and my blood *is drink indeed*. He that eateth my flesh and drinketh my blood dwelleth in me, and I in him." The whole drift of this part of his discourse precludes the idea of a metaphor.* Mr. Hartwell

---

* Were it not for the immorality and repulsiveness which lie on the very face of this doctrine, the hypothesis that it is to be understood metaphorically would have had no existence. It is always the practice of Scripture commentators, when any passage advances anything immoral, repugnant to common sense, or even contrary to their personal views, to assert either that it is to be understood figuratively, or that the translation is not right. Accordingly, we find the Rev. John Hayter Cox, in his Lectures on the Harmony of the Scriptures, (p. 5.) when giving rules "to distinguish metaphorical from literal language," stating that " no text can be truly rendered, which rendering contains a palpable absurdity;"—in other words, that when the literal meaning of a text conveys "a palpable absurdity," the expression must be considered metaphorical. This writer, of course, takes for granted that no passage in the Scriptures, according to its *real meaning*, contains any absurdity. While, however, thousands of such passages can be pointed out, such a rule is of no value. Metaphorical language, in the Scriptures, where certainly it abounds, is as easily distinguished as in some other writings, without having recourse to such an irrational mode as to suppose every absurdity in them to be a metaphor. Absurdities are as often involved in the metaphors as in the literal language of the Scriptures. Such, for example, are the following.—" Issachar is a strong ass" (Gen. xlix. 14.); " Thy navel a strong goblet." Indeed the whole of the Song of Solomon,— if, as Christians say, it means the Church—is a chain of the most absurd and obscene metaphors. To interpret the Scriptures by the rule of the author just cited would make them anything but what they are. So easy, however, is the metaphorical language of the Scriptures to be distinguished, that nobody of ordinary understanding can mistake it for literal expression, unless his mind is warped by religious predilection. How easy it is, for instance, to perceive the metaphorical character of the expressions just quoted, or of the following phrase,—" He only is my rock." But where is there in Jesus's words about eating his flesh and drinking his blood such a proof, or any proof at all, of a metaphor? According to John, he simply states that his followers must do what was known to be done by heathen worshippers; namely, feeding on human flesh. The Pagan idolators believed that Ceres, the goddess of corn, had given her flesh to eat, and that Bacchus, the god of wine, had given his blood to drink; and numerous are the fables in ancient lore regarding these gifts. The truth is, that that part of the chapter in John wherein is inculcated the doctrine of eating human flesh and drinking human blood has evidently been fabricated for the communion service in the Lovefeasts of the early Christians, where human flesh undoubtedly was eaten, (vide ant. pp. 226—233.) and that with a view to give this abominable practice the authority of the divine books of the Christians, as it had the authority of the divine books of the Pagans. To imitate the Pagans thus was a very general practice of early Christian writers. Accordingly, we find a vast number of the supposed miracles, ordinances, and doctrines of the Pagan deities, in the Gospels, attributed to Jesus Christ. Mosheim (Eccles. Hist. vol. i. p. 204.) is candid enough to confess that the early Christians, in imitation of the Pagans, called the Lord's Supper a *mystery*; that they " used in that sacred institution, as also

Horne very properly tells us that in a metaphor "there is some analogy between the similitude and the thing signified." Suppose then that,

in that of Baptism, several of the terms employed in the Heathen *mysteries,* and proceeded so far, at length, as even to adopt some of the *rites* and *ceremonies* of which these renowned *mysteries* consisted;" and that "a great part, therefore, of the service of the church, in this (the second) century, had a certain air of the Heathen mysteries, and resembled them considerably in many particulars." Now, we have already seen of what these abominable Heathen mysteries consisted, and this broad confession of the orthodox and chief historian of the Christian church only corroborates what we have already been forced to conclude; namely, that Christianity is entirely of a Pagan origin. Accordingly, we find that the very phrase—*Lord's Supper,* is Pagan. *Lord* was an epithet of Bacchus, and *Supper,* part of his feast celebrated at Eleusis and many other places. As he personified the sun, he was designated Adoneus—*the Lord of light;* and emphatically called *the Lord.* Hence, in invoking him, the expressions—*Io! Io! Baccoth!*—Lord! Lord! see our tears; *Io! nissi*—Lord direct us; whence the Greeks formed one of his titles— Dionysius; and one of his festivals—Dionysia. As a god identical with the sun, his *day,* even to the present time, is called *Sunday,* or the *Lord's Day.* In conformity with this notion of the worshippers of the sun, under the names—Bacchus, Dionysius, Iacchus, Ies, Osiris, Liber, and others—we find, to this day, represented the sun's rays,—called *the rays of glory,* encircling the head in portraits of Jesus Christ; and also the same *rays of glory* in churches generally over the communion table, with the letters I.H.S., the whole forming a monogram which has not a little puzzled some of the most learned even of the Christians themselves, while others of them superficially conclude that the letters are the Latin initials of *Jesus Hominum Salvator*—Jesus, the Saviour of men; and that the rays of light in the monogram represent the *glory* of that divinity. But this interpretation is as erroneous as it is devoid of proof. The *rays of glory* are found encircling the heads of the Indian gods *Brahma, Vishnu, Cueera, Varuna, Rama,* and *Chrishna;* (Sir William Jones's Works, vol. i. pp. 250—266.) also, the head of the Grecian god *Apollo,* and the heads of all gods who personified the sun. The letters in the monogram have been mistaken for, or wilfully converted into, Roman characters—I.H.S. whereas they were originally Greek letters ΥΗΣ—YES or IES. Now, Υης—in English characters, Yes or Ies,—was one of the names under which Bacchus was worshipped. (Vid. Hesych. supra Υης.) The word *Ies,* with the Latin termination *us,* would compose the name—Jesus. This monogram is unquestionably of a Pagan origin, destined to represent one of the names of Bacchus, and the rays of the sun, which he personified in the heathen *mysteries* of Eleusis—the most *mysterious* part of which was *Adoneus's* Supper— the *Lord's Supper.* The name, and many of the phrases used on the occasion, have been preserved among Christians to this day! Such is the qualification of long usage that, not only we never hear such an expression as *Christ's Supper,* or *Christ's* table, but that such would sound irreverently even in Christian ears. We therefore always, after the Pagans, say the *Lord's* Supper, the *Lord's* table, and so on. (See Taylor's Diegesis, p. 201.) Cicero, about fifty years before the beginning of the Christian era, tells us that the very term *mysteries*—by which the Lord's Supper and the rest of the proceedings of the Agape are almost invariably denominated by the early Fathers—was, in his time, almost synonymous with *abominations.* And why? Principally because it was generally believed that human flesh was eaten in them;—a practice which, although in more ancient times, was more general than some would think, yet was now by the more enlightened and civilized nations beginning to be discountenanced and opposed. Lest any ill-informed reader should doubt that such abominable practice was common, and, consequently, that Jesus's doctrine about eating his flesh and drinking his blood has no foundation in fact, and therefore cannot be understood literally, the following proofs are added. Ischenus, grandson of the god Mercury, voluntarily became a sacrifice for his country, in the time of famine. (Lycophron v. 42.) Human sacrifices were offered at Saturn's festivals. (Aristoph. Schol.) Plutarch, in Themistocles, mentions three beautiful women who were at the same time offered to Bacchus. Clement of Alexandria states that Erechtheus, king of Athens, and Marius, a Roman general, both sacrificed their own daughters. Human sacrifices, in ancient times, were general among the Gauls, the Britons, Germans, Peruvians, Scythians, Phœnicians, Egyptians, Cretans, Arabians, Persians, Carthaginians, and all the nations of the world. From Clavigero's History of the Mexicans, we learn that this nation sacrificed annually 20,000 men, and at the

2 x

according to him and other divines, Jesus here meant by eating his flesh and drinking his blood, metaphorically, *to believe in him,* what analogy or resemblance would be between the *similitude* and the *thing* signified?—— between eating Jesus's flesh and drinking his blood, and believing in him? Were there a metaphor here, it would be one of the most meaningless and ridiculous that ever could be imagined. Besides: before Jesus could have used the idea of eating human flesh and drinking human blood, even in a metaphorical sense, he must have known that such a disgusting practice existed, either among pagan worshippers, or among his own followers; otherwise, it would have been most foolish and absurd in him to make a thing which did not exist the subject of his metaphor. For the idea imported by the word or phrase used for a metaphor should always be better known than the idea attempted to be illustrated by it, before it can be of any use. Now, if Jesus used a phrase importing the idea of eating human flesh and drinking human blood, as a metaphor for believing in him, *because he knew, and because it was generally known, that such abominable practices existed* among the pagan worshippers of Ceres or Bacchus, he selected a metaphor involving the most odious acts of which humanity can be guilty. If, on the other hand, he used this phrase because he knew

dedication of their great temple not less than 70,000. The Pelasgi, in a time of scarcity, vowed the tenth of all that should be born to them for sacrifice, in order to procure plenty. Aristomenus sacrificed 300 Lacedæmonians to Jupiter. Amongst the Romans, till within about 90 years of the beginning of the Christian era, these horrid religious rites were openly celebrated, and considered legal. But about this time a law was enacted prohibiting them; and we are told by Pliny that, in his time, they were discountenanced by the state. So far, however, was this law from putting down these abominable and deep-rooted practices, that, shortly after, we find Augustus Cæsar sacrificing 300 chosen persons; and that Porphyry, at the very close of the third century, and Lactantius, still later, both mention it as a thing well known that a man was yearly sacrificed at the feast of Jupiter Latiaris. The universality of human sacrifices may further be inferred from statements in the works of Clement of Alexandria; (Protrept. p. 27.) Lactantius; (De falsa Relig. c. 21. De Justicia, lib. v. c. 10.) Cyril of Alexandria; (Adv. Jul. lib. iv.) Minutius Felix, &c. Now, it is an established fact that the worshippers—priests and people—*did eat large portions of the sacrifices offered to the Gods.*— (Hesych. v. Ύγιεια. Cic. de Nat. Deor. lib. ii. Numb. xxii. Exod. xxxiv. 15.) Accordingly we read that, after sacrificing, the ancients feasted, and thought that they thus feasted with the Gods. When human beings were the sacrifices they, unquestionably, on these occasions, *feasted on human flesh.* At the *Omaphagia,* or raw-flesh eating feast of Bacchus, where human sacrifices were offered, and also at the *Agrionian* feast to the same deity, the worshippers shared with the god in these sacrifices. (Plut. Themist.) Plutarch (Quæst. Græc.) mentions one of these feasts on which one of the name of Hippasus was feasted upon by the worshippers. Instances of feasting on human flesh abound in ancient literature. We learn from Herodotus that the Essedones made a feast of the flesh of their parents mixed with that of cattle; (Mela, ii. 1. Plin. iv. 12.) and he adds that several nations in the Indies did in the same manner. Diogenes his teacher, Chrysippus, and Zeno, followed by the whole sect of Stoics, affirmed that there was nothing unnatural in eating human flesh. (See Encycl. Brit. v. Anthropophagi.) Many other instances of eating human flesh as a religious ceremony might be added; but the subject is too disgusting for the refined feeling of the present age; and the only apology for what has already been advanced, is that the illustration of TRUTH demanded it.— Proofs of the ancient practice of drinking human blood, as a sacrament, have been given in a previous note. (p 223.) Now, when it is considered that to eat human flesh and drink human blood was a common custom, in the commencement of the Christian era, it is by no means wonderful that Jesus is reported, in the Gospel, to have inculcated the doctrine of literally eating his flesh and drinking his blood. But the generality of this abominable practice does not render the doctrine a whit the less immoral.

that eating human flesh and drinking human blood were practices secretly carried on by his followers, at their Agapæ or Lovefeasts—practices of which we have seen, they were, at least, accused, soon after his death—then, this would make the matter still worse,—would, not only identify the Christians with the Pagans in these detestable practices, but would make it still more improbable that Jesus's expressions about eating human flesh and drinking human blood were metaphorical,—would, in a word, convert this supposed metaphor into literality, or a real fact. In whatever light the question is viewed, it is impossible, by any fair mode of judging, to evade the conclusion that Jesus spoke of literally, really, and actually, eating his flesh and drinking his blood. We are therefore compelled to pronounce this doctrine horribly immoral and intolerably odious.

The following precept, although not so disgusting as the foregoing, yet is very absurd, and quite impracticable.—"Love your enemies." (Matth. v. 44. Luke vi. 27.) Jesus appears to have been utterly ignorant of the mental emotion called love; as well as of the manner in which it is roused into activity; and seems to have thought that a person can love any object at will, however unloveable or unloving that object may be. He does not appear to have known that "love is a passion which is excited at the sight of any object that appears amiable and desirable." Man, however, is so constituted that he can love only objects in which he perceives, or thinks that he perceives qualities that he likes and admires; and it is such qualities alone that do, and *can* excite his love. He cannot love a being in which he perceives none of these qualities,—cannot love a being that hates him, or one that is an open enemy to him, although a precept which he believes to be divine commands him to do so,—although the audible voice of the Deity itself were to bid him do so. Very little reflection on the emotions of his own mind is sufficient to convince any one that he cannot love another person in consequence of any command or precept to love him,—that he cannot love any one in whom he perceives no lovely qualities; and therefore that he cannot possibly love his enemies,—love those that wish him evil,—love those that hate him,—love those that would take away his life! The emotions of his own mind should have convinced Jesus that this was impossible; for his language and conduct to the Pharisees and others of his open enemies, on many occasions, show that so far was he from being able to *love* these *enemies* that his bosom rankled with *anger* against them. Mark (iii. 1—6.) indeed openly admits that when once these enemies were seeking to destroy Jesus he "looked round about on them with anger." Perhaps, if asked at that moment, he would have confessed it *impossible to love an enemy*. It is to be observed that there is a great difference between *loving* an enemy, and *refraining from doing injury to* him. The latter a man can do; and every wise and truly moral man will do. Nay, further; a noble-minded man may do good to those from whom he suffers injury. This generous sentiment; this sign of mental greatness; this moral heroism, which is not only practicable, but is of a very high moral character, has an immediate tendency to change the disposition of an enemy and make him gradually entertain friendly feelings towards the person who was once the object of his enmity. But a man by thus exalting himself so far above his enemy does not *love* him, and cannot love him, while he is an enemy. Long before the time of Jesus, we find Pagan philosophers teaching the noble doctrine of refraining from avenging evil, and of doing good to enemies. Confucius, 500 years before Christ, delivered such precepts as—" Desire not the death of thine enemy."—" Acknowledge thy benefits by the return of other benefits, but never revenge injuries."—" We may have an aversion to an enemy without desiring revenge." (Confuc. mor. 51, 53, 63.)— Pythagoras, nearly as early, enjoined—" Let men revenge themselves on their enemies only by labouring *to convert them into friends.*" Therefore, what Jesus added to his precept of loving enemies, namely—" Bless them that curse you; do good to them that hate you; and pray for them which despitefully use you, and persecute you"—had been inculcated long before his time; and there is strong reason to conclude that he borrowed this sound piece of morality from the Pagans, just as he has borrowed much of the best morality of the Gospels, as will be noticed in the sequel. For the moment Jesus goes beyond these Pagan philosophers and talks about loving enemies, he blunders, showing great ignorance of human nature, the constitution of which is to *love* only what is *lovely*. If man had been so constituted that his love would not be excited exclusively by objects he deems virtuous and beautiful—if he could be moved to love a person because that person is vicious and odious, this aberrance would form a serious barrier against the moral progress of our species; nay, would make it sink deeper and deeper in depravity—would make people love one another because of their vices; so that the more vicious a person would be the more he would be admired and loved! Happily, however, man has been so constituted as to abhor vice in another, and to admire only what he deems virtue and beauty. This leads us inevitably to the conclusion that to love a vicious person is immoral; and that, therefore, to love our enemy—who, as such, is of necessity a vicious person—would be morally wrong, even if it were possible. Then, the precept—to love an enemy involves both an absurdity and an immorality,—to do so would be wrong if possible, and impossible even if right.

In the form of prayer Jesus prescribes to us, we are to ask the Creator and Governor of the universe to " forgive us our debts, *as we forgive our debtors,*" and to " lead us not into *temptation.*" (Matth. vi. 12, 13.) But are we to entertain such a grovelling notion of the Deity as to suppose the absurdity taught in this formule; namely, that it is as we forgive our debtors, He will forgive us?—Or that unless we forgive our debtors, God will not forgive us? Is it reasonable to imagine that God acts in imitation of fallible man?—That he copies even his faults; so that when man is so wicked as to refuse to forgive the trespasses of his fellows, God imitates him in his vicious disposition? Would not this language, if found in any other production than the Gospels, be considered by Christians a blasphemy? Yet this is a doctrine repeatedly taught by Jesus.—" If ye forgive men their trespasses, your heavenly Father will also forgive you: but if ye forgive not men their trespasses, neither will your Father forgive your trespasses." (Matth. vi. 14, 15. Mark xi. 25, 26.) To inculcate this old Pagan, or rather Jewish, doctrine of forgiveness—borrowed as it is— has a good moral tendency; but to fall into the erroneous notion that *God will not be good unless man is good*, is to entertain a very low and absurd notion of the Deity. This notion robs God of the attribute of infinite mercy, claimed for him by all Christians, and makes him, at least, not more merciful than man. Indeed, as Jesus is represented by Luke, (xi. 4.) he asks the Deity to forgive because men forgive. This is the ground upon which he expects forgiveness! and therefore he implores God not to be worse than his creatures."—"Forgive us our sins; *for we* also forgive every one that is indebted to us." Also: to ask God to "lead us not into temptation," implies a supposition that it is possible for him to be so cruel and wicked as to do so. Hence arises the necessity of beseeching him not to lead his creatures into evil. Such a notion of the Deity, however, is absurd in the extreme.

"As ye would that men should do to you, do ye also to them likewise" (Luke vi. 31. Matth. vii. 12.) is a Pagan precept attributed to Christ, and by Christians considered so perfect in wisdom--so far beyond what any mind merely human could produce, that they have graced it with the distinction of "the golden rule." It is, however, far from being a perfect rule to guide men in every circumstance. To carry it out in many instances would be unreasonable and even immoral. *It makes man's erroneous wishes and evil propensities a rule of action.* Few words are sufficient to illustrate this point. For example: If I were so wicked as to wish another man to steal, rob, or murder for me, would it be my duty to do the same for him in return? Would this be morally right? Decidedly not. Still, this is *to do unto others as ye would that others should do unto you.* A far better precept would be—*Do unto others that which you judge to be right.*

But Jesus says that we are not to judge.—"Judge not, that ye be not judged; for with what judgment ye judge, ye shall be judged; and with what measure ye mete, it shall be measured to you again." (Matth. vii. 1, 2. Mark iv. 24. Luke vi. 37—39.) This, again, is a most absurd precept. Are we not to judge of men and things, and to *express* our judgment or opinion of them freely, fearlessly, and impartially, when occasion requires? If we refrain from doing so, will this exempt us from being condemned at the last judgment, which Christians expect, and which Jesus thought at hand in his time? Is it an established truth in Christian theology that with the same judgment with which we judge others —whether crooked or straight, right or wrong—that a perfect Being will judge us? Is it with the same measure of candour which we mete out in judging our fellow-men that God will judge us? This is evidently the exact meaning of Jesus. Is it true? Do Christians believe that this is the rule by which they shall be judged? If they do, and if their belief is correct, it is high time for them to begin to be charitable, or even just, in judging of others who differ from them in opinion. Hitherto, all their persecutions,—all their burning of those they call heretics,—all the human blood they have shed as the result of their harsh judgment of others,—are standing monuments against them. In this precept, again, Jesus ignores God's mercy, and makes the conduct of men individually to be that of "the Judge of all the earth."

Jesus's notion of what he calls offences is very curious and devoid of reason. He says that offences (σκανδαλα—snares, stumbling-blocks, obstacles, or hindrances) must needs come,—that it is impossible but that they will come; yet he declares that woe be unto him through whom they come; and that it were better for him that a millstone were hanged about his neck, and he be cast into the sea, than that he should offend one of his followers. (Luke xvii. 1, 2. Matth. xviii. 6, 7.) But how crooked a notion of justice to imagine that a person shall be punished for occurrences over which he has no control, and under which he is passive! If "it is impossible but that offences will come," how iniquitous it is to punish a person who is a mere instrument in their advent! How can he prevent them?—And why, therefore, should he be accountable for events which *must* come? Jesus appears to have embraced, and now to be inculcating, the Pagan doctrine of fatalism, which denies to man a moral character. His prescription, however, for avoiding the consequences of these necessary offences, namely, to lop off a hand or foot, or to pluck out an eye, is a remedy literally "worse than the disease."

Jesus, in the most direct manner, enjoins bodily mutilation.—"If thy hand offend thee, cut it off: it is better for thee to enter into life maimed, than having two hands to go into hell, into the fire that never shall be quenched; where their worm dieth not, and the fire is not quenched.—And if thy foot offend thee, cut it off: it is better for thee to enter halt into life, than having two feet to be cast into hell, into the fire that never shall be quenched; where their worm dieth not, and the fire is not quenched. And if thine eye offend thee, pluck it out: it is better for thee to enter into the kingdom of God with one eye, than having two eyes to be cast into hell-fire; where their worm dieth not, and the fire is not quenched." (Mark ix. 43—48. also Matth. v. 29, 30; xviii. 8, 9.) It has already been shown what Jesus means here and elsewhere by *life*, by the *kingdom of God*, and by *hell* and *hell-fire*. (see pp. 74—112.) It has also been demonstrated that he intended the whole of the foregoing language about mutilating members of the human body to be understood in a literal sense. (see p. 82. et al.) A few additional proofs, however, are here given of the literality of this absurd injunction.—*First*, there is nothing in the construction of the passage which furnishes the slightest ground to infer that it is to be understood metaphorically, or in any other sense than literal. In the three instances where it occurs, it is a concatenated continuation of discourses which are glaringly designed to be understood as literally as language can express.—*Secondly*, the injunction to mutilate the body is in harmony with the religious practices of the time in which Jesus is said to have lived, and of subsequent ages, as already shown.* The only difference between this injunction and the practices of those times is in degree of bodily mutilation; which difference is remarkably characteristic of all the precepts of Jesus, namely, *extremity*. This trait, which marks all his injunctions, and principally constitutes their absurdity and immorality, is a strong analogical proof that he meant the injunction under notice to be literally obeyed. For example: previous to the time of Jesus, it was taught—"Thou shalt not kill;" but Jesus taught that to be *angry*, and to say *Raca* and *fool*, deserved hell-fire.—Others taught—"Thou shalt not forswear thyself;" but Jesus taught—"Swear

---

* Vid. ante p. 82. An Egyptian monk, named Dorotheus, was asked—why he destroyed his body? His reply was—"Because it destroys me." (Sozom. Hist. Eccles. lib. vi. c. 29.)—A reply agreeing precisely with the reason that Jesus assigns for bodily mutilation. But more instances of this kind will, probably, be given in treating of the ascetic or monkish character of Jesus's doctrines.

not at all."—Others taught—" An eye for an eye, and a tooth for a tooth ;" but Jesus taught—" Resist not evil."—Others taught—" Love thy neighbour, and hate thine enemy ;" but Jesus taught—" Love your enemies."—And, precisely in the same manner, in the injunction under consideration, others taught—" Thou shalt not commit adultery ;" but Jesus taught that to look lustfully on a woman is adultery ; and hence he enjoins the bodily mutilations in the passage we have cited, in perfect harmony with the absurd extremity of all his other precepts.— *Thirdly*, this injunction, literally to mutilate the body, is in harmony with what he has taught on other occasions. We have proof that he recommended other kinds of bodily mutilation. It has already been remarked (p. 81.) that he approved of those who " made themselves eunuchs for the kingdom of heaven's sake ;" in which approval there is not the shadow of ground to suppose that he spoke figuratively.—*Fourthly*, the reason he repeatedly alleges for his proposed mutilation clearly shows that he means literal and actual deprivation of the parts of the body he names. He expressly says that it is better to forfeit an eye, a hand, or a foot, than that the whole body should be cast into hell ;—better to enter life with one eye, one hand, or one foot, than, with two eyes, two hands, and two feet, to be cast into hell-fire, which is never quenched, and in which the worm never dies. His argument is that, in order to gain life eternal, and to escape the everlasting burning of the whole body in hell, it is of a very trifling consequence, nay, a mercy to be deprived of an eye, a hand, or foot. Even if it were granted that he means by an eye, a hand, or foot, metaphorically, any *lust*, it would ill suit Christians to suppose that he means by the expression—" enter life with one eye"—to enter heaven with *one lust ;* or that any lust at all will be in heaven. Nor would it answer their purpose to imagine that by the expressions—*two eyes, two hands, two feet,* and *the whole body, be cast into hell,*—he means that it is the *lusts* of men which will be cast into hell ; not their bodies or souls,—all which they must necessarily admit in maintaining that to pluck out an eye, or to lop off a hand or foot is to be metaphorically understood. They must also, by parity of reason, conclude that *eternal life,* and *hell* are *metaphors,* not realities. For to allege capriciously that one word in the passage is metaphorical and another literal, when all represent one and the same idea, is to play fast and loose. Christians of the present age, having been refined by civilization—the effect of another cause than the doctrines taught by Jesus—perceive the barbarity of the injunction to mutilate their bodies, and therefore, rather than calling in question the wisdom of the supposed founder of their faith, resort to the supposition that such an injunction must be clad in metaphorical language ; thereby implying that Jesus either could not, or would not literally say what he meant, but that, on an important point, he said one thing while he meant another. To be consistent, however, they should not shut their eyes to the barbarity of the punishment in hell-fire, which is never quenched, and in which the worm on the tormented never dies. If they disbelieve in the literal meaning of the command—to cut off a hand or foot, they should also disbelieve in the literal meaning of burning body and soul in hell for ever. The latter is much more barbarous than the former. Why then not be consistent, and admit both either *literally* or *metaphorically* expressed ? Evidently, because the alternative would be dangerous to the

Christian faith. To maintain that the whole passage is metaphorical, would be to sweep away that cruel and repulsive Christian doctrine—eternal punishment; and, on the other hand, to grant that the whole passage is literal would be to grant that Jesus enjoined one of the most inhuman and horrible deeds of which man can be guilty. That he meant that the several acts of self-mutilation of which he speaks should be *literally* carried out, there can be no reasonable doubt. The absurdity and immorality of such foul acts are beyond description. Compared with them, in point of enormity, the crime of *offending one of his followers*, or the sin of *looking* "on a woman to lust after her"—for an antidote against each of which he prescribes these flagitious acts—dwindles into utter nothing!

Equally absurd, but not quite so barbarous, is *Jesus's doctrine of belief* or *faith* in him. He taught that it was by faith he wrought miracles; that by a sufficient degree of faith his followers, with a word, not only could uproot trees, but even remove mountains and cast them into the sea,—and that nothing would be impossible to them. (Matth. xvii. 20; xxi. 21, 22. Mark xi. 23. Luke xvii. 6.) This doctrine, which is of a pagan origin, is not only false and absurd—inasmuch as it teaches glaring impossibilities to be possible—but, even if it were true, would be extremely dangerous in practice. Supposing all Christians to have such a degree of faith as to be able, with a word, to wither fig-trees and drown pigs,—then, woe to the world from malignant saints! Jesus, however, further taught that it was by faith people were cured by him of maladies, and even saved from eternal damnation. (Matth. ix. 22. Mark v. 34; x. 52; xvi. 16. Luke vii. 50; viii. 48; x. 52; xvii. 19; xviii. 42. et al.)— Indeed, *faith* or *belief* was with Jesus the *sine qua non* to all things. The same irrational doctrine is to this very day taught throughout Christendom. Sunday after Sunday, we are urged from every pulpit to believe in Christ, and threatened with eternal damnation if we refuse, as if we could believe in the absence of evidence, or against evidence; or as if we could resist belief when sufficient evidence is presented to our minds. This, truly, is only to preach a doctrine which pervades Christ's discourses, as reported in the Gospels. He is represented to have said—" He that believeth and is baptized shall be saved; but he that believeth not shall be damned." (Mark xvi. 16.) " He that believeth on him is not condemned; but he that believeth not is condemned already, because he hath not believed in the name of the only-begotten Son of God." (John iii. 18.) Such a doctrine as this holds forth to the ignorant a most tempting inducement to deceit and hypocrisy, by making the profession of faith and submission to baptism the conditions of escaping eternal punishment and of obtaining everlasting life. It seems to be built on the erroneous assumption that man can believe just as he wishes. Its absurdity will appear the more prominent when examined in relation to a sound view of moral justice, and to man's mental constitution.

It has already been shown that man, in the exercise of faith or belief, is passive, or under the control of what he deems evidence; so that the faith he exercises in any thing is a state of mind over which his will has no power; and consequently that there is no merit due to him for believing, and no demerit attached to him for disbelieving any doctrine or statement. Here it may be more explicitly defined that the belief of every man depends upon the following conditions—The character and amount of evidence laid before him, and his reasoning capacity to draw conclusions from that evidence. If the evidence be defective, or if his reasoning capacity be defective, his belief will be defective. But as both the evidence placed before him and his own reasoning powers are beyond the control of his will, he cannot—even viewed as a free agent—be blamed for his unbelief. But if he is denied free-agency, he is not accountable at all for his unbelief, or for any other act; and therefore does not deserve damnation for unbelief, or salvation for belief and baptism. Man, however, in the act of belief, is utterly under the control of what appears *to him*, according to his mental capacity, to be sufficient evidence of the truth of what is presented to him. Let him try to believe contrary to the evidedce of his external senses,— let him try to believe that it is dark when he sees the sun shining; that it is thunder he hears when the notes of a flute strike his ear; and so on with the evidence of all his senses; and he will find that this evidence they furnish entirely controls his belief. Let him again make an experiment on the evidence of testimony.—Let him, for instance, be told by a person whom he has always found a truth-speaking man, that the Old Testament was originally written by king James I.; or that England is much larger than America; and he will find himself utterly unable to believe either of these statements, because he has evidence to the contrary; and because each of the statements is made unaccompanied by any evidence of its truth. But let even a stranger, of whose veracity he knows nothing, tell him that he has read Homer's Iliad, at the same time relating portions of it; and he is forced to believe this statement, simply because he perceives evidence of its truth. Still, in neither case has his *will* any control over his belief or disbelief. Indeed, often does evidence compel a man to believe or disbelieve *against his will*;—in many circumstances it would be his interest to believe differently; and frequently has he reason to wish that evidence were such as to enable him to believe otherwise. But let his wish be ever so strong, his belief will act independently of it, submitting only to evidence. Where then is the merit of faith, or the demerit of unbelief?*

* Mr. Greg—who is unwilling to attribute to Jesus anything irrational, and, accordingly, would imagine that the doctrine of damnation for unbelief never proceeded from him—has, on this point, some excellent remarks, from which we cannot resist the temptation of making the following extracts.—" One of the most untenable, unphilosophical, uncharitable doctrines of the orthodox creed—one most peculiarly stamped with the impress of the bad passions of humanity—is that *belief* (by which is generally signified belief in Jesus as the Son of God, the promised Messiah, a Teacher sent down from heaven on a special mission to redeem mankind) *is essential, and the one thing essential to salvation.* The source of this doctrine must, doubtless, be sought in the intolerance of opposition, unhappily so common among men, and in that tendency to ascribe bad motives to those who arrive at different conclusions for themselves, which prevails so generally among the unchastened minds of Theologians. But it cannot be denied that the Gospels contain many texts which clearly affirm and fully justify a doctrine so untenable and harsh. Let us turn to a few of these, and inquire into the authenticity to which they are probably entitled. The most specific assertion of the tenet in question, couched in that positive, terse, sententious, damnatory language, so dear to orthodox divines, is *found in the spurious portion* of the Gospel of Mark, (c. xvi. 16.) and is there by the writer, whoever he was, unscrupulously put in the mouth of Jesus after his resurrection. In the Synoptical Gospels may be found a few texts which may be wrested to *support* the doctrine, but there are none which teach it. But when we come to the fourth Gospel, we find several passages which are similar to that in Mark, proclaiming

If a person tell me that, if I believe in him, he will cure me of blindness, of lameness, or of a withered hand; or that he will give me life eternal; but furnish me with no other evidence than his bare assertion; am I to blame for my disbelief in his ability? Or if he produce proof so as to make me believe that he is able to cure me, what merit is due to me for having faith in him? Being, in common with all mankind, according to my mental constitution, utterly passive, or under the control of evidence, —whether positive or negative—in believing or disbelieving, I can no more help my belief or unbelief than I can help being short or tall. I may ardently wish to be cured of my malady, but unless I have what *I deem* evidence that the person who offers his services—on condition that I believe in him—can cure me, I can no more comply with his terms of exercising faith in him than I can get rid of my disease by a mere wish. Hence the absurdity of Christ's doctrine that people for believing in him should have everlasting life, and for not believing in him should be eternally punished. As man's belief depends upon causes over which he has

---

salvation to believers, and damnation, or something approaching it, to unbelievers.....
......The doctrine and the passages in question ascribe to 'belief' the highest degree of merit, and the sublimest conceivable reward—'eternal life;' and to 'disbelief' the deepest wickedness, and the most fearful penalty—'damnation' and 'the wrath of God.' Now, here we have a logical error, betraying a confusion of intellect which *we* scruple to ascribe to Jesus. Belief is an effect, produced by a cause. It is a condition of the mind induced by the operation of evidence presented. Being, therefore, an *effect*, and not an *act*, it cannot be, or have, a merit. The moment it becomes a voluntary act (*and therefore a thing of which merit can be predicated*) it ceases to be genuine;—it is then brought about (if it be not an abuse of language to name this state 'belief') by the will of the individual, not by the *bonâ fide* operation of evidence upon the mind;—which brings us to the *reductio ad absurdum*, that belief can only become meritorious, by ceasing to be honest. In sane and competent minds, if the evidence presented is sufficient, belief will follow as a necessary consequence;—if it does not follow, this can only arise from the evidence adduced being insufficient;—and in such case, to pretend belief, or to attempt belief, would be a forfeiture of mental integrity; and cannot therefore be meritorious, but the reverse. To disbelieve in spite of adequate proof is impossible;—to believe without adequate proof is weak or dishonest. Belief, therefore, can only become meritorious by becoming sinful—can only become a fit subject for reward by becoming a fit subject for punishment. Such is the sophism involved in the dogma we have dared to put into Christ's mouth, and to announce on his authority. But it will be urged, the disbelief which Christ blamed and menaced with punishment was (as appears from John iii. 19.) the disbelief implied in a wilful rejection of his claims, or a refusal to examine them—a love of darkness in preference to light. If so, the language employed is incorrect and deceptive, and the blame is predicated of an effect instead of a cause;—it is *meant* of a voluntary action, but is *predicated* of a specific and denounced consequence which is no natural or logical indication of that voluntary action, but may arise from independent causes. The moralist who should denounce gout as a sin, meaning the sinfulness to apply to excesses of which gout is *often, but by no means always*, a consequence and an indication, would be held to be a very confused teacher and inaccurate logician. Moreover, this is not the sense attached to the doctrine by orthodox divines in common parlance. And the fact still remains that Christ is represented as rewarding by eternal felicity a state of mind which, *if honestly attained*, is inevitable, involuntary, and therefore in no way a fitting subject for reward; and which, if not honestly attained, is hollow, fallacious, and deserving of punishment, rather than recompense. We are aware that the orthodox seek to escape the dilemma, by asserting that belief results from the state of the heart, and that if this be right, belief will inevitably follow. This is simply false in fact. How many excellent, virtuous, and humble minds, in all ages, have been *anxious*, but unable to believe—have prayed earnestly for belief, and suffered bitterly for disbelief—in vain!"—*Greg's Creed of Christendom, pp.* 153—156.

no control, a just God will never punish him for what he could not help. This would be for God to act more unjustly than any human judge. All sound jurists hold that a man is not responsible, and therefore not punishable, for acts which he cannot help, under which he is passive, or over which he has no control. If this is right in regard to finite justice—and who can prove it is not?—then why is it wrong in infinite justice? There is nothing more unreasonable than the supposition that God will attach such merit to belief, and such demerit to unbelief, as Jesus teaches. How cruel it would be on the part of the Deity to punish his creatures eternally for not being able to believe the dogmas Jesus taught! Had he furnished sufficient evidence of the truth of his doctrines, belief in them, in every age, would inevitably follow.—They would no more be *disbelieved* than the facts of Euclid, or the fundamental principles of Newton's Principia.

The doctrine of reward for belief, and punishment for unbelief, taught more or less clearly by Jesus throughout the Gospels, is of all others the sweetest to orthodox divines, while to mankind in general it has been of the greatest injury. To fulminate, incessantly, from the time of Jesus to the present, the doctrine of eternal damnation for unbelief, has driven many weak-minded and nerveless men and women into incurable madness. Besides: on the ground that belief was regarded the highest virtue, and unbelief the blackest crime, it was soon inferred that the sword, the fire, the fagot, the rack, the thumbscrew, and a thousand other engines of cruelty and death, instead of evidence, should be applied to unbelievers, by way of converting them to Christianity, or in case of failure, by way of despatching them to hell. Indeed, of all the Gospel doctrines, it is not too much to say that none has been so productive of mischief, and made a handle for the perpetration of so much cruelty, as this—" He that believeth not shall be damned." Wherever the cross has been raised, the blood of the unbeliever has been shed. In whatever country Jesus and his Gospels have been preached, human beings have fallen victims to creeds,—have been put to death because they did *not* believe *this*, or because they *did* believe *that*. Read the records of the fate of thousands, nay, millions of men and women who have suffered " martyrdom" because they *did* believe, or did *not* believe a certain dogma held by one sect of Christians and denied by another. Take a retrospect of the matchlessly barbarous deeds of Christians, and see the blaze of human bodies in Smithfield and elsewhere, illuminating the whole atmosphere; or behold the massacres and almost total extinction of the whole nation of Waldenses in Piedmont's valley; or listen to the echo of the sounds of horror which, in the dead of night, awoke the Hugenots of Paris. But instances of this kind are endless. The history of every nation among which Christianity has been introduced records the fatal results of the inculcation of the dogma—" He that believeth and is baptized shall be saved; but he that believeth not shall be damned."

When it is borne in mind that Jesus preached damnation to all who did not believe in his pretensions, his injunction—" tell no man," to almost every one whom he cured, and who at the time, generally, declared him to be the Son of God—appears exceedingly absurd. Having, in the presence of a great number of people, cured a leper, he bade him " tell no man." But as great multitudes, at the time, followed Jesus, and apparently saw the miracle, it is difficult to imagine what purpose could be answered by enjoining silence on the person cured; unless we suppose that the miracle was performed in secret, and not allowed to be scrutinized by the multitudes in attendance. It would have been of no use for the poor leper to be silent unless Jesus could tie the tongues of the numerous crowds present. But what effect had Jesus's command upon the man cured? Mark and Luke, apparently relating the same miracle, state that he "blazed abroad the matter," and that "so much the more went there a fame abroad." In like manner, when Jesus had cured two blind men, he told them to let "no man know it;" but they "spread abroad his fame in all that country." A great many other instances of the kind could be adduced.* Now, what good motive could Jesus have in endeavouring to conceal his miracles—the very means he so much insisted upon as evidence to unbelievers of his Divine mission? If he came into the world that people might believe in him and be saved, was it not most inconsistent with reason, nay, with benevolence, to aim at preventing them from *believing?* Was it not highly irrational in him, when he had wrought a miracle—such as the notions of the times regarded as evidence of his Messiahship—to caution people against making that miracle known?— Since he repeatedly charged even his own apostles, whom he sent to preach the Gospel, "that they should tell no man that he was Jesus the Christ;" and that he had, in their presence, been transfigured; (Matth. xvi. 20; xvii. 9.) to what purpose did he make his appearance in this world? Such a conduct is quite irreconcileable to the present notion Christians entertain of him as a Saviour. In the cure of the leper, it would appear from what the Evangelists say, that it was fear of the Jews which made him charge his patient not to divulge the name of the physician; for we are told that, after this ungrateful Jew blazoned abroad the benefit he had received, Jesus could not venture to go openly into the city; but was obliged to withdraw into the desert, where, notwithstanding the number of sick people who in vain sought him, he secreted himself for some time before he attempted to make his appearance in public.

A very unfeeling and irrational command Jesus gave to one of his followers, when he asked his permission to go and perform the last duties to a deceased father. In reply to this reasonable request of his disciple, Jesus imperiously said—"Follow me; and let the dead bury their dead." (Matth. viii. 22.) There is in this command, evidently, an encouragement to disregard, not only the rules of decency, but the most sacred duties of humanity; and an attempt at suppressing the purest feelings, and the most endearing emotions of the human mind. Can it be that virtue—that true religion—requires a man to refrain from paying the last debt of filial love to a father?—from shedding one parting tear upon his remains, before the portals of the tomb for ever close upon them? Can a precept be so cruel and yet be divine? Nay, can a precept be any other than extremely barbarous, which commands a man not to attend the funeral solemnities of his father, whose tender cares extended over him, from infancy to manhood, and whose wise counsels and good advice delivered him from a thousand snares? How cruel and repulsive to human feelings is this precept of

* See Matth. viii. 1—4; ix. 30, 31; xii. 16—21. Mark i. 40—44; iii. 11, 12; v. 43; vii. 36; viii. 26, 30. Luke v. 14; viii. 56.

Jesus! How injuriously it must have told upon the bereaved disciple, whose bosom already had been filled with anguish! How such a harsh prohibition must have deepened his sorrows, and aggravated his troubles! How the arrow of disappointment, intentionally shot into his already wounded heart, must have overwhelmed him with grief! Where is the Christian who will deny that Jesus, in giving such a command, was destitute even of such a degree of humanity as would teach him to respect the feelings of others under affliction? Where is the Christian who would contend that Jesus is an example to him in this particular? or that it is his duty to carry out this precept of leaving " the dead to bury their dead." Is it in accordance with sound morality, with decency, or with proper human feeling, for Christians not to concern themselves about the burial of their deceased fathers, and therefore, mothers, brothers, sisters, wives, and children, but to leave this solemn duty to be performed by some unchristian people, who may or may not perform it? If it is, why do not Christians obey this precept of Jesus? Why not sacrifice to Christianity their dearest emotions, and leave the burial of their relatives to those who are " dead in trespasses and sins"? The reason is obvious :—because such a conduct would be contrary to nature,—absurd and immoral! Accordingly, we find Christians—who generally *practise* the precepts of Jesus *only as far as they are practicable*—exercising laudable care, and observing a considerable degree of decency, in the burial of their relatives. And Christian priests—for whom every death brings a fee—show so much zeal in decent burials that, in reading the funeral obsequies, they say not a word about Jesus's precept to " let the dead bury their dead," but consign into the grave the most ungodly,—the greatest thief, and the most cold-blooded murderer, as their " dear brother here departed, in sure and certain hope of the resurrection to eternal life"; and display as much solemnity over his remains as if they were those of the brightest saint. Such is the inconsistency of Christians; and their *practical* unbelief in Christ's precepts.

Another absurd and immoral doctrine very frequently inculcated by Jesus—but *practically* disbelieved by all Christians of the present age, if we except the inferior inmates of a convent, and the dupes of the modern Agapemone—is that to be poor is a virtue, and to be rich a vice. Accordingly, he declares that the poor are blessed, and inheritors of the kingdom of heaven; but that the rich shall hardly enter that kingdom ,—that those who now hunger are blessed; but that those who are now full shall hunger, and that woe awaits the rich. This doctrine, which implies that riches are, of necessity, a curse, and poverty a blessing, is most obnoxious to common sense, and extremely injurious in tendency. Truly, it is quite in harmony with the precept of *taking no thought of the morrow*, and like that, it strikes at the root of all honest industry, frugality, and forethought. But to reduce it into practice would be to destroy the very basis of all prosperous communities, and to make whole nations mendicants. Applied to men individually, no one can fail to observe, if not to *feel*, that so far is poverty from being a blessing that it is a positive curse :—when it is not a fault, it is a great misfortune, and carries with it a thousand ills—moral, intellectual, and physical. Such, however, was the doctrine which Jesus delighted to teach. On one occasion, a young man who was rich, asked him what he should do in order to secure eternal life. Jesus told him that, if he wished to arrive at the acme of moral perfection, he must sell all that he possessed and give the proceeds to the poor ; and then follow him.   On hearing this, the young man " went away sorrowful."—— When he was gone, Jesus said to his disciples that a rich man should hardly enter the kingdom of heaven ;——that it was easier for a camel to go through the eye of a needle than for such to do so ; —and that it was profitable for a person to forsake not only houses and lands, but parents, brothers, sisters, wife and children, for the sake of the kingdom of God.—— Peter, when he heard all this, exclaimed in self-justification—" Lo, we have forsaken all, and followed thee." (Matth. xix. 16. Mark x. 17. Luke xviii. 18.)   Poor Peter! what had he to forsake, except his fishing net ? If, like the young man who came to Jesus to ask for spiritual advice, he had " great possessions" perhaps then, as similar causes produce similar effects, he would not have been so willing to forsake all.   But under the circumstances, it well suited him to *forsake all*, and to rove about the country without purse or scrip, living upon alms.   If poverty was to be the test of piety, and the enormity of a man's crime to be estimated by the length of his purse, Peter, as well as all the apostles, together with their Master, who had " not where to lay his head," would be adjudged to surpass all in point of merit.   What chance had Ananias and Sapphira with Peter to obtain the kingdom of heaven ?   Is it at all wonderful that he struck them dead for the crime of not forsaking *all ?*   But this doctrine which declares riches incompatible with piety, and poverty the pinnacle of religious devotion, will be shown hereafter to be much older than the time of Jesus;——even as old as Egyptian monachism.   St. Francis and St. Dominic, in the thirteenth century, perfectly understood the spirit of primitive Christianity, when they founded the orders of mendicant monks who lived solely on alms.   It is, however, wonderful how Christians of the present age can *pretend* to believe that all which Jesus commanded is infallibly right, and yet disregard this precept—" Sell that thou hast, and give to the poor."   As Professor Newman (Phases of Faith, p. 155.) very justly remarks, there is every proof that it was intended, to its full extent, as an injunction of perpetual obligation, extending to all Christians. It was enunciated authoritatively on various occasions, and incorporated with precepts of perpetual obligation, in such a manner that we cannot, without the greatest violence, pretend that Jesus did not intend it as a precept to *all* his disciples.   In Luke xii. the same precept—" Sell that ye have, and give alms"——occurs in immediate connection with such in-junctions as—" Take no thought for your life, what ye shall eat"——" Pro-vide yourselves bags which wax not old, a treasure in the heavens that faileth not,"——so as to leave no room for a doubt that Jesus intended to teach that it was an incumbent duty upon *all* who wished to follow him, first to sell *all* their property, and give the proceeds to the poor.   The same thing is proved by what is said to his disciples of riches, after the young man had gone away " sorrowful"; and also by Peter's declaration— " we have forsaken all and followed thee;" as well as by the general practice of the first Christians who sold all their property and laid the proceeds at the apostles's feet.   Indeed, both the manner in which Jesus always inculcated this precept, and the practice of the early Christians, prove indisputably that he would have all Christians to part with *all* wealth,—all that they possessed—so as to become the blessed poor whom he extols. Why, then, do not *all* Christians reduce this precept into practice ? Simply because they perceive its erroneousness—its moral obliquity—its fanatical and pernicious tendency—its gross absurdity.— They find it too absurd either to be practised or preached, in its intended form. Nor would such a doctrine well suit our present wealthy bishops, any more than it would have suited thousands of rich ecclesiastics in this country, prior to the age of Protestantism.

One additional instance of the grossness and immorality of the doc- trines taught by Jesus must, under this section, suffice ; namely, that in which he regards as acts of moral virtue for one man to kiss another, and to wash his feet,—for a woman, even of ill fame, to kiss a man's feet, anoint his head and feet with ointment, wash his feet with her tears, and wipe them with the hair of her head.—All these are by Jesus treated as acts of moral virtue, so high in character as to merit Divine forgiveness of sins. Having accepted an invitation to dine with a Pharisee, (Luke vii. 36—46.) as he was eating, a woman of ill fame whom Luke calls a sinner,* " stood at his feet behind him weeping, and began to wash his feet with tears, and did wipe them with the hairs of her head, and kissed his feet, and anointed them with the ointment" she had brought. The Pharisee perceiving, as he thought, the inconsistency of his guest in allow- ing such a character to take these liberties with him, remarked that if Jesus was " a prophet he would have known who and what manner of woman this" was that touched him. But here he was mistaken,—Jesus was well acquainted with this courtezan and all her relatives. John (xi. 2.) assures us that she was the sister of Martha and Lazarus, to whom Jesus was peculiarly attached, and at whose house he frequently stayed.† In reply

---

* Αμαρτωλος, a heinous sinner or a sinner of the worst kind,—a term which, when applied to a female, as the Commentators say, denotes the sin of incontinence.

† The Faculty of Theology in Paris, came to the conclusion, in 1620, that Mary the courtezan, Mary the sister of Lazarus, and Mary Magdalene—out of whom Jesus cast seven devils—were one and the same lady ; but the Doctors of the Sorbonne have since reversed this decision, and found out that these are three distinct Marys. (Bernard Nouvelles de la Repub. des Lettres, tom. 21, 32.) The Albigenses held a singular opinion of the nature of the attachment of Mary Magdalene to Jesus. (Christiade, tom. i.) Amongst the points of striking similarity between the Indian god Chrishna and Christ is that the former, like the latter, was continually followed by women. " The princesses of Hindustan, as well as the damsels of Nanda's farm, were passionately in love with Chrishna, who continues to this hour the darling god of the Indian women."—" In his early youth, he selected nine damsels as his favourites." (Sir William Jones' Works, vol. i. pp. 265, 266.) In like manner, we find Jesus going " throughout every city and village, preaching," and accompanied by Mary Magdalene, Joanna, " Susanna, and many others which ministered unto him of their substance." (Luke viii. 1, 2.) We have a long narration of his curious conversation with a woman of Samaria about the number of husbands she had had, and sundry other things, in the absence of his disciples, who wondered at him. (John iv.) We have also his conversation with Mary and Martha on several occasions. (Luke x. 39—42. John xi. 1—45 ; xii. 1—9.) Of all his followers, when he was crucified, only women were near him.—" Many women were there behold- ing afar off, which followed Jesus, ministering unto him; among which was Mary Mag- dalene, and Mary the mother of James and Joses, and the mother of Zebedee's children." (Matth. xxvii. 55, 56.) When he was buried, women—" Mary Magdalene, and the other Mary"—watched his tomb ; and afterwards, with Salome, bought spices to anoint him. When he had risen from the dead, he made his first appearance to women, who " held him by the feet and worshipped him." Indeed the figure which women cut in

Y

to the Pharisee's unkind remark he explained away the courtezan's love, together with her tears, her caresses, her kisses, and her act of anointing him; and, turning to her, he thus reproved the detractive Pharisee,—"Seest thou this woman? I entered into thine house, thou gavest me no water for my feet; but she hath washed my feet with tears, and wiped them with the hairs of her head. *Thou gavest me no kiss;* but this woman since the time I came in hath not ceased to *kiss* my feet. My head with oil thou didst not anoint; but this woman hath anointed my feet with ointment.— *Wherefore* I say unto thee, her sins, which are many, *are forgiven;* for she *loved* much." Now, without doing violence to the whole system of ethics as taught in the Gospels, it cannot be denied that there is here involved what Jesus deemed a moral principle, intended for universal application. But is it not grossly erroneous to construe the kisses and other acts of this woman into a moral virtue, and the omission of such acts, on the part of the Pharisee, into a moral vice? Is it a sin for one man to omit kissing another? Is it a moral crime for a woman to refrain from washing the feet—say of the dearest friend—with her tears, and wiping them with the hairs of her head? Common sense answers—No! and adds that it would be more vicious and far more unseemly for one man to kiss another, and for a woman to kiss a man's feet, and wash them with her tears, wiping them with the hairs of her head, than to refrain from these barbarous acts. How then can Jesus, as a moral teacher, be justified in representing such acts as virtuous?—in reflecting upon his host for not kissing him?—in praising an abandoned woman for kissing his feet, washing them with her tears, and wiping them with the hairs of her head? The Christian devotee would perhaps reply—"Aye, but this was an Oriental custom. Granted. Still this fact does not alter the moral character of either the omission or commission of the acts spoken of by Jesus. Whatever is, in itself, morally vicious in one country, must, of necessity, be so in another. Moral vice and moral virtue do not depend upon customs; but are, in their very nature, unchangeable. Still it is because a woman of bad fame has kissed his feet—like a person kissing the Pope's toe—washed them with her tears, wiped them with the hairs of her head, and anointed them with precious ointment,* that Jesus announces *her sins forgiven.*—A rare species of "good works,"—that important ingredient in the Wesleyan doctrine of justification.

This, however, is not the only instance we have of Jesus teaching the moral meritoriousness of anointing and washing feet. For the accounts given by the three other Evangelists of similar transactions differ so far from the foregoing, in regard to the time, the place, the mode in which

the whole history of Christ is most remarkable, when compared with what mythology relates of women and the Indian god—Chrishna.

* One eminent Christian writer, *inter alia*, remarks that this courtezan had been accustomed to apply her ointment to a very different purpose; namely, to decorate herself in order to entice lovers—(Prov. vii. 17.)—that her hair, before her conversion, served for alluring and wanton purposes; but now it was devoted in long tresses to wipe the weary feet of Jesus—and that her tears, which were those of love, joy, and gratitude, flowed in such abundance, as to be sufficient actually to wash his feet. All this is very natural; for it has frequently been noticed, that the temperament of debauched females, when they take to Christianity, inspires them with as much passion as they had previously displayed in their gay career.

they were performed, the persons engaged in them, and other circumstances, as to indicate three or four distinct transactions.* Admitting that Matthew and Mark refer to the same act of anointing, when a woman poured a box of ointment on Jesus's head as he sat at meat,—which act has already been noticed in treating of the prophecy he uttered on the occasion,—then this occasion would form one, although but one, additional instance in which he teaches that anointing is a morally, or rather spiritually meritorious act. We have also another instance, apparently distinct from those we have noticed, of Mary the sister of Lazarus undergoing the expense a second time of anointing Jesus's feet with very costly ointment, and wiping them with the hairs of her head, just as she had done before in the Pharisee's house. It is not said that, on this occasion, she *washed* his feet with her tears. According to the narrative (John xii. 3.) she first anointed them, and then wiped them with her hair, which must have been of beautiful length and thickness. By applying her own hair to wipe Jesus's feet, she ultimately anointed her own head, thus making double use of her costly spikenard, the odour of which, as John says, soon filled the house. This took place at a supper which this lady—who, we have seen, was, or at least had been before her conversion, a courtezan—had, in conjunction with her sister Martha, made for Jesus and, apparently, his disciples. Now, Jesus commends Mary for anointing his feet, representing her as having performed an act of great piety and moral virtue. It is not denied that to wash or anoint the feet, particularly in warm countries, is an act productive of physical virtue, and, on that account, is commendable; but it is not on the ground of physical benefit—not on account of cleanliness, that it is commended by Jesus—who was so far from having regard to the physical laws of health as not "to wash before dinner," or teach his disciples to do so, (Luke xi. 38. Matth. xv. 2. et al.)—but he evidently teaches that such an act has a moral, pious, and spiritual merit; and it is in this the obliquity of this portion of his moral teaching consists.

On the following occasion, however, Jesus teaches this doctrine in a more pointed and emphatic manner. When eating his last supper with his disciples, " he began to wash the disciples' feet, and to wipe them with the towel wherewith he was girded. Then cometh he to Simon Peter: and Peter saith unto him, Lord, dost thou wash my feet? Jesus answered and said unto him, What I do thou knowest not now, but thou shalt know hereafter. Peter saith unto him, Thou shalt never wash my feet. Jesus answered him, If I wash thee not, thou hast no part with me. Simon Peter saith unto him, Lord, not my feet only, but also my hands and my head. Jesus saith unto him, He that is washed *needeth not save to wash his feet*, but is clean every whit: and ye are clean, *but not all. For he knew who should betray him ; therefore said he, Ye are not all clean.* So after he had washed their feet, and had taken his garments, and was set down again, he said unto them, Know ye what I have done to you? Ye call me Master and Lord; and ye say well : for so I am. If I then, your Lord and Master, have washed your feet, *ye also ought to wash one another's feet.* FOR I HAVE GIVEN YOU AN EXAMPLE, THAT YE SHOULD DO AS I

---

* See Dr. Giles's Christian Records, pp. 199—203. and compare Matth. xxvi. 1—13. Mark xiv. 1—9. Luke vii. 36—50. John xii. 1—9.

HAVE DONE TO YOU." (John xiii. 5—15.) From this passage the follow-ing things are clear.—*First*, Jesus considered washing feet a moral act,—one of sanctification,—" If I wash thee not, thou hast no part with me."—*Secondly*, he considered that to wash the feet *only* was a moral act which, without washing the whole body, was sufficient to effect this sancti-fication.—" He that is washed needeth not save to wash his feet, but is clean every whit."—*Thirdly*, he washed the feet of Judas, performing this supposed act of sanctification upon this traitor, although he knew at the time that he was a traitor,—" He knew who should betray him ; therefore said he, Ye are not all clean."—*Fourthly*, he intended to establish the washing of feet as an ordinance among his followers ; and for this purpose washed the disciples' feet, by way of example, just as we are told that he was baptized, and partook of what we call the Lord's Supper, by way of example,—" Ye ought to wash one another's feet ; for I have given you an example, that ye should do as I have done." If Jesus intended any ordinance at all in his church, he certainly intended feet-washing. What-ever was the object he had in view in wishing to establish this practice—whether it was, as Christians say, to promote humility among his followers or to cultivate some other grace, is not material to the point. It is suffici-ently clear that he designed his example to be literally and permanently imitated by his followers, at least, until they entered the kingdom of heaven. If ever he taught universal morality, he did so on this occasion. His precept and practice are concurrent and definite. His words, illustrated by his actions, admit neither of the plea of a metaphor, nor of any other quibble. They afford no ground to imagine that he meant any other thing than that which he did as an example. He expressly says that his followers " ought to wash one another's feet," and that he had given them an example of this, in order that they should do as he had done. Christians might just as well say that Jesus, when he taught his followers to pray, did not mean that they should *actually* pray ;—that when he was baptized, he did not mean that his followers should *actually* undergo this ceremony ; —and that when he established what they call the Eucharist, he did not intend it a permanent institution ; as to say that he did not intend his followers permanently to practise washing one another's feet. Indeed, neither of the foregoing practices has been so explicitly taught as the obligation of feet-washing ;—neither of them enjoined in words so binding and expressive ;—neither accompanied with an example so forcible.

But what of the soundness of this doctrine and this example of Jesus, in a moral point of view ? Has the act of one Christian washing the feet of another any decided tendency to sanctify the soul ? Was it moral in Jesus, either with a view to sanctify souls, or by way of example, to wash the feet of a traitorous murderer such as Judas, making no distinction, with regard to example, so far as washing feet went, between him and the other apostles, who had not, like Judas, meditated a design upon the teacher's life ?—Was it proper in Jesus to do so, when, according to his own words, he knew Judas's foul design ? When in the act of washing his disciples' feet, and perhaps when washing the identical feet of Judas, he says, in reference to this cowardly traitor,—" Ye are clean, but not all." But as this condescending act of Jesus, in washing his disciples' feet, is performed expressly in order to give them " an example," the question arises—How is it that the Christians of the present age do not follow this example? Is Christ's example, in this particular, so unimportant, so valueless, so insignificant, as not to be worth following? Or is the practice enjoined so indecent as to be fit only for barbarous people, in a barbarous age; so that the Christians of the present age—in a more advanced stage of civilization and enlightenment than the ignorant and superstitious Jews —treat it as one that belongs to by-gone benighted ages?* If so, does not their discountenance of this custom furnish a practical proof that they do not believe either the example or command of Jesus to be Divine? Do they not show that they regard his example as unfit to be followed? And as they do not follow it, does this fact not prove that it was useless on the part of Jesus to give either the example, or the precept with which it is accompanied? How was it that his omniscience did not teach him that, as nobody would either follow his example, or obey his precept, to give them answered no good purpose? Even supposing that it is the bounden duty of all good Christians to wash one another's feet, and that, for not following the example of their Master in this instance, they will be called into account when standing before him as their Judge, is it then their duty to imitate this example so closely as to wash the feet of bad as well as good Christians,—those who are traitors as well as those who are sincere, faithful, and innocent as doves? Is it their duty to copy Jesus so exactly as to wash the feet of those whom they know to be harbouring murderous designs against them, or even against somebody else? Any right-minded man—and it is in charity trusted that many an enlightened, although exceptional, follower of Jesus—would answer that for Christians to make a practice of washing one another's feet at all, as a religious ceremony, is absurd in the extreme; but that to wash the feet of a treacherous villain, who at the moment concerts plans to effect the death—ignominious death —of one of his brethren, is an act not only revolting to all sense of morality, but an act which the nature of man, even in its most depraved state, is utterly incapable of voluntarily performing,—an act which the few remaining sparks of virtue, sense of justice, and self-preservation, left in the bosom of the most abandoned character, prohibit him to perform. Where is the moral philosopher—where is the Christian, whose nature is such that he is capable of being as kind and endearing to his deadly foe, as he is to his most attached friend? He is not to be found. Human nature is not capable of such injustice. Even Jesus was not generally able so to deport himself; for he treated his foes with great severity. Still, in the instance under notice—as if forsaken by every proper feeling of humanity —he washes the feet of a disciple whom he knows to have devised a scheme to take away his life, and he ultimately embraces and kisses this treacherous murderer. Moreover, he does this by way of an example that Christians may do the same! An example more repugnant to common sense was never given by the founder of any religion. To follow this

---

* That insignificant sect of Christians known as the Scotch Baptists are certainly an exception. They perpetuate the practice of washing one another's feet, and glory in it as a Divine injunction, as sacred and as binding as Baptism, or the Lord's Supper. They also blame other Christians for their neglect of so moral an obligation in no measured terms. This, however, is something like consistency. All other Christians should either do the same, or admit that Jesus is not a perfect example for them.

example, and wash the feet of a man bent upon taking away our lives,—wash the feet of an assassin! would be to give him the desired opportunity to plunge his dagger into our hearts! It is, therefore, by no means wonderful that Christians omit to imitate this repulsive example of the founder of their faith, and practise only a few of the less barbarous precepts and examples which are found in the New Testament, with which alone they endeavour to exhibit the few relics of Christianity found in the present enlightened age, wherein its antiquated and retrogressive character forms a perfect contrast with the nature of all other exercises of the human mind.

Such as have been given in this section, are a few out of many instances that might be adduced of the absurd and immoral doctrines taught by Jesus. It is but just, however, to observe that he taught some sound morality. To the examples already given the following may be added.—"A new commandment I give unto you, that ye love one another." (John xiii. 34.) The chief defect that Jesus evinced in enunciating this noble precept, is that, in doing so, he was too late. When he had been with his disciples, teaching them morals, as it is said, for about three years, and when he was going to die, he gave them this new commandment— "Love one another." That he had never before enunciated to them this precept is clear from his own words. This was to them "a new commandment." Nor is the precept recorded in any of the other Gospels as having been previously given. Now, one would imagine that to exhort his disciples to love one another would have been one of the first precepts of a wise, moral, or religious teacher;—that without this shining virtue, all other graces would have been wanting in lustre;—that, in a word, this would have been taught to be the very essence of a virtuous life. One would, therefore, expect to find that Jesus enjoined his disciples to love one another when he initiated them; and particularly would one expect that, in the remarkable charge which he delivered before he sent them, two by two, to preach the Gospel, he reiterated this command with strong emphasis. But in that charge there is not a word found about loving one another. Indeed, we find in it an exhortation to exercise hatred instead of love. Jesus, however, leaves the precept—"love one another"—uninculcated till within a day of his death; and then mentions it only twice or thrice in a short discourse. Wanting in love towards one another, it is by no means wonderful that his disciples so often wrangled and quarrelled about the highest position in the kingdom of heaven, and gave other signs of reciprocal unkindness. Many are the attempts which have been made by Christian writers, from the time of the Fathers to the present, to smooth down, in the morality of Jesus, what appeared to common sense absurd and destructive to society. Accordingly, we find ingenious, but fruitless efforts made to show that he never intended some of his precepts to be generally practised,—that while some of them were *positive* precepts, others were mere *counsels*, and so on. But even in his own time, Jesus was accused of both absurdity of doctrine, and immorality of conduct. The Pharisees, Scribes, and Sadducees—the most intelligent and respectable religious sections of the Jewish nation—according to the Gospels, repeatedly accused him of Sabbath breaking, of blasphemy, of uttering absurd things, and of associating with bad characters—both men and women. They charged him with eating and drinking with publicans and sinners,—men of the worst sort and of the most disreputable character among the Jewish nation, —men who were not his disciples, and whom he never made his disciples, but left in the reprobate state he found them while in their society, so that there is no ground for alleging that he associated with such vile characters for the purpose of converting them. (Luke v. 27—30.) They likewise blamed him for allowing women of ill repute to have intercourse with him. (Luke vii. 39.) The Pharisees, therefore, very properly asked his disciples—" Why eateth your master with publicans and sinners ?"—as much as to say—" Why does he associate with extortioners, and men who are odious to the community at large ? And why does he take about with him women of such fame as Mary Magdalene, Joanna, and Susanna, allowing himself to live upon what they give him ? If we are to apply to him the general rule of judging of him by the company he keeps, we cannot entertain a very high opinion of his morals." Such, doubtless, was the opinion the Pharisees held of Jesus, which opinion, however, may be utterly wrong. All that is contended for here, is that he was accused of absurdity and immorality in his own time, by the people of his own nation, who watched his career, and listened to his discourses, and therefore had a much better opportunity than we have, at this distant time and place, of forming a correct view of his moral and intellectual character. It is, how-ever, just to observe that a much higher opinion was entertained of him by people of an inferior knowledge and position in life. The poor, the wretched, and the ignorant, appear to have relished and applauded his preternatural and marvellous morality. His doctrine, in regard to the future prospects of the indigent and miserable, converted their poverty into a merit, gave them courage to endure misery, flattered their vanity, and made them proud of their abject condition, which was soon to be exchanged for an eternal kingdom, and an everlasting life of joy and plenty. (Luke vi. 20—25.)

SECTION III.—MANY OF JESUS'S ACTS, AND MUCH OF HIS CONDUCT, OF AN IMMORAL CHARACTER.

Jesus, not only delivered irrational and immoral precepts, but also performed immoral acts, and conducted himself on several occasions, both in word and deed, in a manner quite inconsistent with the impulses of a virtuous mind. One of such acts was to cause to be drowned about two thousand swine of the Gadarenes or Gergesenes. This, in its very nature, cannot be a morally virtuous act. Should it be urged that it was done in performing a miracle, and therefore justifiable, the answer is, that *no mira-cle can justify an infringement of a moral law.* This, it is hoped, will be admitted to be an axiom in both morals and religion. Supposing the possibility of a miracle, if any supernatural being performed one which involved an act of immorality, the miracle would not alter the character of the act, and the performer would be as guilty of immorality as the vilest man would be if he killed another. If, for example, a voice from heaven told me to sacrifice my son Isaac, it would be as immoral in me to do so

as if no such voice had commanded me.   If I had supernatural power so
as to be able to make a useful fig-tree wither at my word, it would be as
immoral in me to do so as if I had no such power.   It would be well to bear
in mind this truth while considering the actions and behaviour of Jesus.

Now, the tale respecting the demoniac, or demoniacs, and the pigs is
told by three of the Evangelists, (Matth. viii. 28—34. Mark v. 1—20.
Luke viii. 26—39.) varying in details, but agreeing in the main points.—
Jesus, having crossed the lake from Galilee to Gadara, just as he landed,
met with two men—according to Matthew, but one, according to Mark
and Luke—possessed with devils.   The devils immediately cried out—
" What have we to do with thee, Jesus, thou Son of God ? Art thou come
hither to torment us before the time ?"   It appears that the devils knew
Jesus much better than he knew them ; for they addressed him by name,
but he was obliged to ask their name—" What is thy name ?"   Their
spokesman replied—" My name is *Legion*;* for we are many;" that is to say,
some five or six thousand demons.   Jesus now understood his position—
perceived that he had a strong force to combat with, and, therefore, thought
it politic to enter into a treaty with the enemy.   These obstinate demons,
having no desire to return into hell, to be cast into the sea, or even to leave
that country, proposed terms of capitulation, one article of which was that
Jesus " would not send them away out of the country," but allow them to
enter the great herd of two thousand swine, then, at a distance from them,
feeding.   Jesus forthwith agreed to these terms, and the demons immediately entered into the pigs which, in consequence, ran into the sea, and
were all drowned.—" And he (one of the demons, apparently)) besought
him much that he would not send them away out of the country.   Now
there was there nigh unto the mountains a great herd of swine feeding.
And all the devils besought him saying, Send us into the swine, that we
may enter into them.   And forthwith Jesus gave them leave.   And the
unclean spirits went out, and entered into the swine ; and the herd ran
violently down a steep place into the sea, (they were about two thousand)
and were choked in the sea."†   Although some of the gay and thoughtless

* Legion is purely a Latin word—from *legio*, which is from *lego*, to choose or gather.
It is a term used expressly for a portion of the Roman army,   The number of soldiers it
contained is not quite certain.   Some writers say it was 6,000 ; others 6,200 footmen,
besides horse ; but Parkhurst thinks that, in the time of Jesus, a Roman Legion consisted only of about 4,200 foot and 300 horse—4,500.   But what is wonderful here is
that this demon made use of a Latin term, which must have been quite unintelligible to
the demoniac, to Jesus, and to his disciples, who spoke only a dialect of the Hebrew—
the language of all the people of Galilee and Perea, where this happened.   The Gospels
containing this Latin word are written in Greek.   Does not this show that these Gospels
were written when the world was subdued by the Roman arms, and the term *Legion*
generally known ?—See Giles' Christ. Records, p. 107.

† This narrative must be suggestive of a great many strange things, even to the most
devout Christian.   1. He may be puzzled to understand how it was that devils—whose
habitation exclusively is said by the orthodox to be hell—were allowed to be abroad,
and thus to make their home within human bodies.   2. As he has been taught to believe
that grace is indispensible to pray to the Deity successfully, and that this grace is not given
to demons, he may wonder that devils prayed to Jesus, and that he favourably answered
their prayer—granted their request! 3. He may be at a loss to understand why Jesus was
obliged to compromise with six thousand devils, since he could conquer this number as
well as one.   4. Since he has been taught to believe that the object of Jesus's miracles
was to establish the Divine origin of his doctrines and mission, he may find it difficult to

people of that age may have viewed the trick which Jesus served the devils—by allowing them to enter the pigs, and then making these pigs take them into the sea, where they had begged not to be sent—in a ludiludicrous light; yet this miracle afforded no fun to the herdsmen, who immediately apprized their employers of the loss of property they had sustained. These, so far from being converted to the religion of Jesus, by his miracle, told their neighbours of their loss; and, the matter being very properly thought one of public concern, the inhabitants of the city of Gadara, and of the surrounding country, having ascertained the truth of the report that Jesus had caused so many pigs to be unjustly destroyed, came in a vast multitude to meet him. Sympathising with the loss of the owners of the pigs, and, doubtless, entertaining considerable apprehension about the safety of their own property, individually, they insisted upon his immediate departure from their territory. In obedience to their order he directly entered into a ship, and, having crossed over the lake, went to his native city.

Now, upon what moral grounds could it be just to deprive these Gadarenes of their pigs? Is Jesus's example in thus destroying property worthy of being imitated? Supposing that he really exorcised this legion of demons, could he not do so without drowning a legion of pigs? Could a personage, said to be omnipotent and omniscient, not order these demons —although six thousand in number— to return to hell, their proper habitation? Was it in accordance with any right notion of justice to benefit a person or two troubled with devils "at the expense of the possessors of two thousand swine, to whom this miracle must have cost about four thousand pounds sterling?" We are not told whether the devils were drowned with the pigs. But as there is reason to conclude from the Scriptures that the *bottomless pit* and the *bottom of the sea* are of the same meaning, (vid. ant. p. 172.) it is not impossible that both the pigs and the devils went into this bottomless pit. The whole story, however, is childish and highly incredible; but childish and incredible though it is, yet since it is rendered in the Gospels as part of the history of Christ, which we must take as it stands, it does not the less reflect upon the moral character of Jesus, which is held up to us as one of unequalled grandeur, and of immaculate perfection.

An act of a like destructive, but less extensive, character was that of

---

understand why the miracle of the swine, like his other miracles, converted nobody but the demoniacs. 5. He may think it miraculous that so numerous a herd of swine was kept in a country where these animals and their flesh are held in abhorrence, and where they were of no use to their possessors—the Jews—who could not touch them without being defiled. 6. He may be inclined to infer that if, as Mark and Luke say, there was only one demoniac, either he must have been a person of great capacity to contain all the demons—about six thousand—or these demons, like all spiritual beings, although capable of physical effects on men and pigs, required very little space. 7. He may be disposed to enquire what became of the demons? Were they drowned in the sea? If they were not, of what use was it to send them thither, at the expense of drowning the pigs? If they were, then must they not have been some sort of physical creatures, or organised beings, with organs of respiration different from what Christians represent them? And if physical beings, how could so many of them enter into the man, and afterwards into the pigs? 8. He may, however, perceive that in the drowning of the pigs the cause was fully adequate to the effect—three devils having been crammed into each pig!—See Christianity Unveiled, p. 55.

cursing a fig-tree. As Jesus one morning was coming from Bethany to Jerusalem, and suffering from hunger, he saw " a fig-tree afar off having leaves." He went towards it in expectation to find fruit upon it; but " when he came to it he found nothing but leaves; for *the time of figs* was not yet;" or more correctly rendered—" it was not the time of figs."— Having been disappointed, he thus addressed the tree.—" Let no fruit grow on thee henceforward for ever. And presently the fig-tree withered away." (Matth. xxi. 18—22. Mark xi. 12—24.) This fig-tree being near Jerusalem, it is not probable that it grew on waste land, but it is far more likely that it was the private property of some person. But, as Dr Giles justly remarks, (Christ. Rec. p. 210.) " it is of no importance whether the fig-tree, which withered when Jesus cursed it, was public or private property, save that, in the latter case, the owner might justly have complained of the wrong done to him. But even if the fig-tree was growing on the waste by the road side—which is not probable, considering that Christ saw it ' afar off,' (verse 12.)—yet it was placed there by the providence of God to live its time, and to perish when its time was come, not to be cursed and to perish prematurely by a curse pronounced gratuitously upon it....... We must not omit the very extraordinary avowal of Mark that ' the time of figs was not yet.' If so, why did our Lord expect to find figs upon the tree? and why did he, as a child strikes an inaminate thing that hurts him, curse the tree for not producing fruit, when the season for fruit was not yet come?" Even if it had been the time for fruit, whose fault was it that there was none on the tree? Whose fault is it that fruit-trees do not bear every year in this country? Is it the fault of the trees, or even that of the owner? Does not the inspired book of the Christians, and did not Jesus himself, teach that all the productions of nature proceed from God? Are we not now taught from every pulpit that his finger rolls the seasons round, and impels every spring of vegetative nature? Are we not told that it is he, by the fervent heat of his sun, and the showery drops of his clouds, who makes the fertile fields stand thick with corn, and the trees bend beneath a load of fruit? On what ground then was the owner of the fig-tree which Jesus cursed to be blamed, so as to call for this act of vengeance? It is impossible to pronounce this deed to be of a morally virtuous character. Supposing it ever to have been performed, it must be considered, not only silly, but a most vicious and wanton act, totally unworthy of imitation. If any person, in the present day, were to cause the trees, or a single tree, in any orchard to wither, he would be considered too mischievous—too dangerous a character, to be left at large. Supposing Jesus divine, and this act miraculous, still this does not alter the moral character of the latter. And as to Jesus's supposed divinity this very act alone is sufficient to exclude the idea. Had he been divine, and subject to the passion of hunger—which is paradoxical—he could have miraculously satisfied his hunger in a more happy way than by cursing a fig-tree. Had he been divine—nay had he the ordinary understanding of human beings—he would have known that, even in the fertile dales about Jerusalem, fig-trees did not bear fruit in the winter. Such instances as these of Jesus employing his miraculous power to do evil are deplorable ;—they utterly disprove his divine mission.

Jesus's conduct at a marriage feast, in Cana—where he is said to have turned a large quantity of water into wine—is by no means free from moral obliquity, and is therefore not at all worthy of imitation. He and his disciples, having by invitation attended this marriage feast, at which Jesus's mother officiated, the Virgin Mary told her son, in most kind language, that the wine had run short. Jesus, however, in the most disrespectful, harsh, uncouth, and insulting manner that a son could answer his mother—a manner very far from being an example of filial veneration towards a parent, so expressly enjoined in the Mosaic law on pain of death—replied, "Woman! what have I to do with *thee* ?" That is,—of what concern was his mother to him ?—and what had he to do with her trouble about the wine being out ? What a fierce and unnatural rebuff the mother here received from her son, for nothing but her mild and casual remark about the wine ! Jesus, however, on reflection, appears to have thought better of the matter, and to have contradicted his own words—"Woman! what have I to do with thee ?"—by applying his miraculous power to the manufacture of wine, as we shall see anon. Much ingenuity has, in vain, been lavished by different Christian writers, in attempts at making Jesus's address to his mother appear faultless; but, as Mr. Greg very aptly remarks, these attempts "are, for the most part, melancholy specimens of ingenuity misapplied, and plain honesty perverted by an originally false assumption." Dr. Collyer, in his Lecture on Miracles, (p. 376.) by no means mends the matter by urging that the term—*woman*, in the East, was a most respectful epithet by which to address a female,—that "the remark of his mother produced on the part of the Saviour a reproof,"—that his mother's interference "was offensive" !—that "to the man of thirty a mother must not presume to dictate, or as much as insinuate,"—and that even at the age of twelve, in the case of Jesus, "excess of maternal solicitude received a mild rebuke." Such arguments are self-refuting. To maintain that for a mother to interfere with her son is offensive, is truly *offensive* to common sense ; and to urge that to the man of thirty a mother must not presume to dictate, is equally absurd. But Dr. Collyer admits that Jesus reproved his mother, not only on this occasion, but even when he was twelve years old. Now, this is the very conduct the propriety of which is disputed. That he reproved his mother when he was twelve years old cannot justify the repetition of this conduct when he was thirty ; any more than two wrong acts can constitute one right act. Supposing that the term—*woman*, in the East, was not one of disrespect, the expression—"What have I to do with thee ?" still remains ; and in this, principally, the insult is conveyed. We well know that it was in a disrespectful and even hateful sense this phrase was invariably employed. It is the phrase with which, repeatedly, the devils are made to address Jesus when he disturbs them.* It is impossible to exculpate Jesus from having behaved to his mother, on this occasion, in such an unkind and even contemptuous manner as constituted positive immorality. It is trusted that few would contend that his conduct is worthy of imitation by sons and daughters of

---

* Τι εμοι και σοι. Mark v. 7; i. 24. Matth. viii. 29. Luke iv. 34; viii. 28. Strenuous efforts have been made to show that the translation of this phrase is not correct, and that Jesus meant to say that the want of wine was of no concern to him and his mother,—"What to me and thee ?" But there is not the slightest foundation for such a rendering. The English translation here is admitted by the best critics to be perfectly correct.

tender parents. What dutiful son, in the present age, would address his mother—" Woman ! what have I to do with thee ?" The same may be said of Christ's behaviour to his mother and brothers who, apprehensive of his personal safety, and thinking him "beside himself" endeavoured, from the kindest motives, to have an interview with him. Having made their desire known to some of the crowd that surrounded Jesus, somebody said to him —" Behold thy mother and thy brethren stand without desiring to speak with thee." Jesus morosely said—" Who is my mother ? and who are my brethren ?" and added that his mother and brothers were his disciples. (Matth. xii. 46—49. Mark iii. 21, 31—35.) Such was the rudeness and apathy with which he treated the affectionate anxiety of his mother and brothers.

His conduct also, in going with his disciples to the marriage feast already mentioned, at which people revelled in drunkenness for many days —thus sanctioning such practices—is by no means worthy of imitation ; nor would it, on any account, be imitated by the most pious Christians of the present age.* But his miracle in turning into wine the aqueous contents of six waterpots, holding "two or three firkins" each—a quantity supposed by some divines equal to "two or three hogsheads" of intoxicating wine†—involved a still more serious point of immorality, and must have sanctioned not only revelry, but actual drunkenness. The Jewish marriage festivities generally lasted a week, and it is probable, as Dr. Collyer thinks, that Jesus intended to provide sufficient wine for the whole of the remaining portion of this period. It is, however, undeniable that the Gospel narrative implies that the guests were already drunk. The governor of the feast having tasted the wine Jesus had made and found it exceedingly strong, addressed the bridegroom thus—" Every man at the beginning doth set forth good wine ; and when men have well drunk, (according to the Greek—have been made drunk—$\mu\epsilon\theta\upsilon\sigma\theta\omega\sigma\iota$‡) then that which is worse." This naturally implies that the guests were already drunk ; but how drunk must they have been after imbibing the whole of the enormous quantity of strong wine which Jesus made ! To supply more wine to men who were already drunk, was unquestionably a grossly immoral act.

Jesus's triumphal entry into Jerusalem, his command to his disciples to take possession of an ass with her colt, and the uproar he finally created in the temple, cannot be justified on any moral principle. (Matth. xx. Mark xi. Luke xix. John ii.) The ass and colt,§ which he told his disciples to bring to him, were the private property of some person, and he had no right to them, as the bystanders intimated. For Jesus to tell his disciples to lead away these animals was positively to incite them to steal. There

---

* This conduct gave reason for people to say of Jesus what he himself admits they said ; namely, that he was " a wine-bibber ;" and it shows that he and his disciples were by no means favourable to " Total abstinence" from intoxicating liquors, the promoters of which, in the present age, have done ten thousand times more towards making men happy than all the preachers of Christianity have done during the last eighteen centuries.

† See Collyer's Lect. on Miracles, p. 394. Strauss Leben Jesu, vol. ii. p. 432.

‡ The same word occurs in Eph. v. 18.—" Be not drunk with wine" ;—and in 1 Thess. v. 7.—" They that be drunken are drunken in the night" ; and in other places, which show that it means a state of drunkenness.

§ Or, as some will have it,—the colt of an ass. Compare the passages cited above.

is no account that they ever returned them to their owner. If we suppose that his disciples acted in this matter as a press-gang—such as are employed by kings in times of war—whose acts in seizing property, if viewed in a moral light, can be called no other than robbery, notwithstanding their regal authority, and the favourable opinion, especially in times of war, held of them in this country,—still, on this supposition, it is impossible to avoid the conclusion, not only that it was an immoral act to press these beasts, but also that Jesus wished to assume the authority of a temporal king; which Christians hold to be contrary to the nature of his mission; and which, certainly, was a moral vice; for it had an immediate tendency to cause an insurrection, in which thousands of human lives might have been lost, and innumerable other crimes committed—all of them tending to create human misery, and therefore, in their very nature, vicious. That it was the intention of Jesus, on this occasion, to display regal authority will hereafter be clearly shown. But although this was his intention, yet we have no right to view his disciples, on this occasion, even in the light of a press-gang, nor the command of Jesus as that of an earthly king, so as to exculpate them from the charge of theft, on the same ground as some people would justify the taking of private property in times of war; for he was *not* an earthly king.* He had, therefore, no right to arrogate to himself the authority of an earthly king. Moreover, to assume such regal power was, on his part, an act of high treason, which forfeited his life, according to the laws of all civilized communities. Consequently, unless the laws of all nations are morally wrong, this assumption of Jesus was a highly vicious act. That he *did* assume the authority of an earthly monarch,† and that his undivided aim, on the occasion in question, was to create an insurrection and be made a king, will be clear to any one who will impartially read the narrative of his triumphal entry into the holy city —the city of the Jewish kings—the city of David—at one of the largest national feasts, when the whole Jewish nation was assembled. At his own request, he is placed upon an ass—an animal upon which Eastern kings often rode in triumph; "a very great multitude spread their garments in the way," others strew the way with triumphal or conquering branches of palm-trees—symbols of victory among the Jews and other nations,—and multitudes of people, who form the imposing procession, before and after him, shout—"Blessed is the *King* of Israel that cometh in the name of the Lord! Hosanna to the Son of David"; and so on. When the authorities

---

* He had not been chosen by the Jews as their king; unless we suppose that he was so chosen when a small faction "would come and take him by force, and make him a king." (John vi. 15.) He had not been *anointed;* unless we suppose such inauguration to royalty took place when a woman poured the contents of a box of ointment on his head. (Mark xiv. 3.) He is, however, represented as being a descendant of David, from whom all the Jewish monarchs, except Saul, derived their right to the throne; and he might thus establish some sort of a claim to monarchy. To do so was very easy, now that the oppressed Jews had no national king, and that no other person more closely related to David came forward. There is much in the Gospels which goes to substantiate this notion.

† That is, the monarch of what he termed the kingdom of heaven, of which he spoke so often, and which, as we have seen, was to be entirely of a secular nature, having Jerusalem for its capital. The notion that he was to be a king of such a kingdom was quite consistent with the triumphal entry into Jerusalem; for when this kingdom came, all other monarchies were to be destroyed.

request him to desist from these unseemly and illegal proceedings, and to restrain the multitude from uttering their disloyal and treasonable shouts, Jesus, so far from discouraging the mad conduct of this rabble, replies that, were the crowd not to shout thus the stones would cry out.— Very shortly after this display of regal pomp, Jesus was apprehended, brought before Pilate—the Roman governor of Judea—and charged with the crime of high treason—the greatest crime known to the laws of civilized communities. The particular description of high-treason, in his case, was that he had set up himself as king of the Jews—the Christ or anointed —every Jewish king being anointed as a matter of course.* He was charged with " perverting the nation, and forbidding to give tribute to Cæsar, saying that he himself was Christ a King." Hence the Roman governor asked him, " Art thou the King of the Jews ?" to which Jesus affirmatively replied—"Thou sayest." Hence Pilate asked the people, would they have him release " the king of the Jews," and they answered —" Whosoever maketh himself a king speaketh against Cæsar." Hence he told them—" Behold your King !" and asked them—" Shall I crucify your King ?" Hence, after his condemnation, the Roman soldiers, by way of ridicule, invested him with a royal robe of scarlet colour—placed a crown of thorns on his head, in allusion to the diadem which a king wore —and put a reed in his hand, in imitation of a royal sceptre. Hence, in mockery, they kneeled before him, shouting—" Hail ! King of the Jews !" Hence they cried, in derision—" If he be the King of Israel, let him come down from the cross." And hence they placed over his head on the cross the inscription—" This is the King of the Jews." From the whole drift of the four Gospels, the basis of the tale about Jesus, before it was garnished with absurd romance and interwoven with gross fictions, appears to have been simply this,—namely, that a man of the very common Jewish name— Jesus, having been tried and found guilty of an attempt to set up as a king of the Jewish people—who were now under the Roman yoke and had no king of their own—was put to death by crucifixion—the accustomed mode of execution—as a traitor to the Roman Emperor.

Jesus, having in monarchal pomp entered the Jewish capital, immediately proceeds to the temple,† and with the utmost assumption of the power of an earthly king, beats out with a whip, all the merchants, whom he designates thieves—all dealers in oxen, sheep, doves, and other animals required for religious sacrifice ; and tumbles about the tables of the money-changers, doubtless making their valuable contents roll in every direction, and affording an excellent scramble to the large multitude of mob—the rabble, the scum and off-scouring of the Jewish community—who had

---

* As a king, David was called the *anointed* of God, (2 Sam. xxiii. 1. et al.) the word *Christ* simply means anointed.—Jesus *Christ*, Jesus *the anointed ;* or Jesus the king.— Accordingly, the Jewish as well as the Roman authorities asked Jesus—" Art thou the Christ ?"—which was the same as to ask him—" Art thou the king of the Jews ?"

† Compare Matth. xxi. 1—13. Mark xi. 1—17. Luke xix. 29—46. with John ii. 13 —16. Although John places the scene which took place in the temple at the commencement of Christ's public career, while the other three Evangelists place it at the end of his life—immediately before he was arrested—and connect it with his triumphal entry, of which John says nothing ; yet, on close examination, the critical reader will perceive that the disturbance Jesus is said to have created in the temple, if it ever took place, occurred immediately after he had entered Jerusalem as a king.

formed the procession of his pompous *entree* into the royal city. John tells us—" The Jews' passover was at hand, and Jesus went up to Jerusalem, and found in the temple those that sold oxen and sheep and doves, and the changers of money sitting. And when he had made a scourge of small cords, he drove them all out of the temple, and the sheep and the oxen; and poured out the changers' money and overthrew the tables; and said unto them that sold doves, Take these things hence; make not my Father's house an house of merchandise."* Here it should be observed that the passover was now " at hand," and that on this occasion, when the whole Jewish nation assembled at Jerusalem for religious duties, all these animals —oxen, sheep, and doves—were brought thither, in order that those who attended might have animals to offer. Thousands of sheep were sacrificed at every passover; and oxen and doves were used as offerings for several ritual observances, during the week of this feast, as well as throughout the year, according to the provisions of the Levitical law. The animals, therefore, had been brought to the temple for the express purpose of the worship of the God of Israel. There were always hundreds of people in the exterior parts of the temple selling the requisite animals and other articles for sacrifices, without the least consciousness that they were doing wrong. But Jesus, all of a sudden, goes thither, and drives them out, *pouring out the money* that is being changed, and upsetting the tables upon which this money stands, to the great detriment of the owners; and all this under the pretence that he is divinely appointed king over the Jews. Even supposing that his object was simply to establish a new religion instead of that religion which the Jews had received from heaven, and which commanded them to sacrifice the animals that the traders, whom Jesus drove away, had brought to the temple, would Jesus's conduct in that case be worthy of imitation in propagating Christianity? Would it be morally right in the Christian missionaries of the present day to enter a heathen temple and drive out all whom they could find there with any articles intended for heathen worship, upsetting every table and stall as they proceeded? Supposing the most daring and fool-hardy of them to try the experiment, and make a " scourge of small cords" for the purpose.— Imagine one of them going single-handed, with a small whip, into one of the heathen or Jewish temples, in foreign countries—where he may find hundreds of people selling articles for sacrifices—and beginning to scourge them out, in imitation of Jesus;—he would be much more likely to lose his life in the attempt than he would be to effect his purpose. Or to use the words of Dr. Giles,—" Let us picture to ourselves a single man entering a throng of merchants in London or any other of our populous cities, and forcibly ejecting them from their usual haunts—some hundreds of tradesmen driven headlong away by the force of a single arm. It is inconceivable that such a scene could be real. The guards and constables of the city would have interposed, even if the traders themselves had not been firm in defending their property from destruction, and the daring assailant been speedily repulsed. It is painful to imagine such a scene as passing in reality before our eyes—the Son of God and the Saviour of men, creating

---

* According to the three other Evangelists, Jesus said that the Jewish merchants had made the temple " a den of thieves."

a tumult in the temple which he wished to purify."* With the reality of the scene we have here nothing to do; for we take the Gospels for what they say. Very likely such an occurrence never happened; but to admit or prove that it did not is to admit or prove that the Gospels are not true, which is equally as fatal to Christianity as to admit or prove that Jesus was liable to the same imperfections as other men. All that concerns us at present is—whether his conduct in the temple was consistent with moral rectitude—whether to create a disturbance, and to act with physical force, under the circumstance, was virtuous. That it was not, has been made, it is trusted, sufficiently manifest. It was to assume regal authority, not only in the most direct, but in the most unjust and tyrannical manner.— And is it wonderful that, after such a series of treasonable demonstrations, Jesus was apprehended, accused and found guilty of setting forth himself as the King of the Jews; and that, ultimately, with two other men, he was put to death by crucifixion—the accustomed penalty for such a crime?

The conduct of Jesus towards high and legally organised deputations that waited upon him, and also towards the religious sects of his time generally, is far from being fit for imitation,—is, in a word, decidedly immoral. On one occasion, at least, the chief priests and the elders of the people, or in other words, the magistrates, rulers, and heads of the Jewish nation, from the national assembly—the *Sanhedrim* or Jewish parliament, formed a deputation and waited upon Jesus, when he was indoctrinating in their temple, as if he were a duly constituted Jewish priest, having conformed with all the regulations of the Mosaic religion—a religion believed both by Jews and Christians to have been revealed by God himself. It should, therefore, be observed that Jesus was acting in violation of the institutes of this religion by assuming the office of a priest and thus teaching in the temple as well as in synagogues. Now this illustrious deputation accosted him, not with the intention of arresting him, which—having all the national power in regard to religious matters at their command—they could easily have done, but to ask him in a civil manner the following questions.—" By what authority doest thou these things? and who gave thee this authority?" (Matth. xxi. 23. Mark xi. 28. Luke xx. 2.) By "these things" they doubtless meant his treasonable proceedings on the day before, in entering Jerusalem as a king, and driving all the merchants out of the temple, thus disturbing religious worship. This being their mission, any person who has the faintest notion of preserving the safety of a state will admit that, under the circumstances, it was high time for them to interfere. Nor can he fail to perceive the mildness and the rational character of the course they adopted. But how did Jesus receive this high and noble deputation, representing both the Jewish church and state— then, truly, subject to the Roman power? And what answer gave he to their inquiries on such momentous matters as to his authority to attempt at creating an insurrection? Instead of frankly answering their reasonable questions, and clearing away any national suspicion that might be harboured against him, he attempts at puzzling his interrogators by asking them another question as to the derivation of John's baptism—a subject which bore no relation to the matter in hand. To this, the deputation candidly

* Christian Records, pp. 181, 182.

and wisely replied that they could not tell whether John's baptism was "from heaven or of men." Whereupon Jesus thinks he perceives an advantage, and rejoins—"Neither tell I you by what authority I do these things." How easily he could have said—as he had repeatedly said to ignorant and superstitious people in more benighted corners of Judea— that it was by the authority of his Father which was in heaven, whence he himself had come to this wicked world! How this would have added to his courage, his ingenuousness, and his honour, as a rational and moral being! What a lustre this would have shed upon him! How it would, in the present age, display his perfection as a Deity! How it would strengthen the faith of Christians, and not only silence, but even tend to convert disbelievers! Jesus however proceeds to utter dark and unintelligible parables, with a malignant intent to reproach the Jewish nation — Would it be considered either wise or moral in any one, at present, to treat a deputation so important in imitation of Jesus's treatment of the Jewish authorities?

His conduct to the Scribes and Pharisees was still worse. His language to these important and learned sections of the Jewish nation,* on a great many occasions, was anything but exemplary, and calculated to promote love, peace, and good-will—those nobler sentiments of the human mind. It was evidently the language of anger and enmity. Although it is not, in *every* instance wherein the violent language used by Jesus towards these people is reported, expressly stated that he was *angry* with them, yet the very reproachful terms which he employed fully establish this fact. It is however stated that, on one occasion at least, he "looked round about on them with *anger*." (Mark ii. 24; iii. 1—6.) This took place when he was holding a debate with the Pharisees as to what constituted Sabbath-breaking. Now, *anger* is a passion not only incompatible with Divinity, but quite unworthy of a great man, especially when holding a debate on a religious subject with persons of different views. Most certainly, to be excited with *anger* is not the way to convince an opponent of the truth of one's doctrines. It is said that for a controvertist to lose his temper, as Jesus did on this occasion, is a sign that he will lose his argument.— Christians, however, even to this day, are very susceptible of anger when debating on points bearing upon their religion; but it is not more immoral in them to yield to this passion than it was in Jesus to do so. Anger is unquestionably a moral evil, and has, in a thousand cases, led to the most heinous crimes of which it is possible for men to be guilty. Anger was as immoral in Jesus as in some other person; and he aggravated this evil by the frequent use of opprobrious language towards the objects of his wrath, such as—"Ye generation of vipers"—"Ye blind guides"—"Ye serpents" —"Ye hypocrites," and so on. Such terms and such fulminations as these are directly calculated to call into action the worst propensities of

* The Pharisees were the most numerous, most influential, and most religious sect among the Jews. Josephus tells us that they were more pious and devout than others, and that they interpreted the Law with greater accuracy. The Scribes, whose name signifies *men of learning*, were doctors of the law and public instructors; and they sometimes discharged the duties of civil magistrates. Such were the mental and moral qualifications of these two classes of people; and such was the high position they occupied in society.

human nature, and to produce the most atrocious deeds.   But were these
Scribes and Pharisees so bad as Jesus pronounces them ?   By no means.
They were the most moral classes of the Jewish nation—a nation under
the peculiar guidance of the Jewish Deity.   And, indeed, Jesus himself
sometimes admits that their doctrines and moral exhortations are worthy
of imitation, and enjoins his hearers to put them into practice, saying—
" Whatsoever they bid you observe, that observe and do, but do not ye
after their works." (Matth. xxiii. 3.)   Here, he recommends the doctrines
of the Scribes and Pharisees, which were those founded upon the Mosaic
Law, and the Mosaic Dispensation, and which Christians tell us Jesus
came to abolish.   On other occasions, however—quite characteristically of
his contradictory teaching—he inveighs against the doctrines of these
religious sects with unparalleled malignity of mind and scurrility of language.   But had these religious sects, or the Jews at large done anything
against Jesus, so as to cause him to avail himself of every opportunity to
malign them ?   No.   On the contrary, the heads of the Jewish religion
evinced a much kinder disposition towards him than he evinced towards
them.   We read that, almost in every place, he was allowed to preach in
their synagogues.   This shows that they entertained no ill feeling against
him.   The toleration which the Scribes and Pharisees exercised towards
the founders of Christianity was far greater than Christians have ever yet
exercised towards any that differed from them.   Even in the present
enlightened age, when this religion—having in some degree been purified
by the progress of intelligence—is much more rational than it was in its
pristine state, will such a toleration be yielded by Christians ?—Will a
Roman Catholic priest, or a Protestant clergyman permit a Dissenting
minister to preach in his church ?   Will an Episcopalian allow a Roman
Catholic priest, or will a Roman Catholic priest allow an Episcopalian, to
preach in his chapel ?   It is well known that this will by no means be
allowed.   The bigotry and prejudice of the various sects of Christians are
far too strong for such a toleration.   Such, however, was not the intolerance of the Jewish religionists,—on this point they were a better sort of
men than the Christians.   And indeed, so much kinder and more hospitable
were the Pharisees towards Jesus than he was towards them, that they
often invited him to their houses to share of their good things ; and he
readily accepted such invitations, and was frequently their guest.   On these
occasions, however, he conducted himself in a manner so improper and so
unworthy of being an example to any respectable person, that he used the
most scurrilous and reprobate language towards his hosts and the companies present, calling them by all sorts of bad names.

Once, when he had gone to dine at a Pharisee's house, the following
scene occurred. (Luke xi. 37—54.)   There were among the guests present
several persons of distinction—doctors of the law and others.   Now the
custom and law of the Jews, as well as those of many other Eastern nations,
required every person, before he sat down to dinner, to go through the
very salutary operation of washing his hands.   Jesus, however, unlike all
the other guests, sat down to eat with unwashed hands.   The host, very
naturally, " marvelled that he had not first washed before dinner."   We
are not told that he uttered a word of reproof, or cast any remark whatever, but simply that he *marvelled*.   Jesus, conscious that he had neglected

to conform to a national custom which had cleanliness for its object; and perhaps finding also that, in consequence, he was, by the very superior company present, an object, at least, of keen observation—instead of offering any apology, or justifying his deviation from this custom of the nation to which he belonged—poured forth a most bitter and exciting volley of abusive language against both the host and the guests. He told them that their "inward part was full of ravening and wickedness"—that they were "as graves"—that they had "taken away the key of knowledge" and were "fools." He repeatedly exclaimed—"Woe unto you, Pharisees!"—"Woe unto you, Scribes and Pharisees, hypocrites!"—and so on. One of the company—a doctor of the law—with the view to make him desist from using such indecent language, "said unto him, Master, thus saying, thou reproachest us also." But this attempt at pacification only excited Jesus the more, so as to make him exclaim—"Woe unto *you* also, ye lawyers!" After he had proceeded at some length, uttering woes against the doctors who sat at table with him, the company, doubtless in fun, began to urge him forward in his career of scurrility.—"And as he said these things unto them, the Scribes and Pharisees began to urge him vehemently, and to provoke him to speak many things." While all this disturbance was carried on, a vast crowd of people—apparently attracted by the noise—had assembled outside the Pharisee's house. These Jesus addressed in the following inciting language.—"Beware ye of the leaven of the Pharisees, which is hypocrisy." Such was the uproar which he created on this occasion; and such was the unprovoked insult he gave to a hospitable man, in his own house, at his own table, in the presence of his servants, his family, and his assembled friends, the last having to share with their host in the woes and the curses that were invoked, and the vile reproaches that were heaped upon all the company present without exception or distinction.

On several other occasions Jesus spoke of the Scribes and Pharisees in most opprobrious terms. Once, at least, he pronounced upon them not fewer than eight distinct woes or curses, attacking them apparently in their absence and without the shadow of provocation. (Matth. xxiii. 1—33.) Having enjoined his hearers to do whatever the Scribes and Pharisees bade them, but not to imitate their actions—because, like him, they did not practise the doctrines they preached—he very inconsistently began to utter curses against these highly religious sects, exclaiming eight times in a short oration—"Woe unto you, Scribes and Pharisees, hypocrites!" —"Woe unto you, ye blind guides!"—"Ye fools, and blind!"—"Ye serpents, ye generation of vipers!" Such are the invectives which Jesus, on this occasion, directed against the silent objects of his wrath, denouncing them, in addition to all this, as whited sepulchres, cheats, robbers, and children of murderers, and making no distinction whatever between different individuals of these numerous classes of the Jewish nation, which classes, in the aggregate, were the most pious and enlightened portions of that nation, and, according to Jesus's own admission, were not without some virtue, their teaching being such as he emphatically enjoined his hearers to reduce into practice. Wherefore then denounce them as the greatest reprobates and miscreants? Why take every opportunity, both public and private, as the Gospels show, to speak opprobriously of them ?* But, irrespectively of the merits or demerits of the Scribes and Pharisees, the language used by Jesus in reference to them had, in itself, an immoral tendency. Reproachful epithets, such as he used, serve only to inflame the passions ; and—if they do not immediately succeed in inciting to acts of vengeance—are sure to demoralise the mind. From the mouth of Jesus, they did not, any more than they would from the mouth of some other person, convert or convince the Scribes and Pharisees,—they tended only to irritate their feelings and inspire them with enmity. Such expressions, therefore, were quite as immoral from the lips of Jesus as from those of some other person, especially as there is every reason to conclude that they were dictated by a feeling of anger. Nobody, possessed of a right notion of morality, would contend that Jesus, as a public teacher, in his behaviour to those from whom he differed on points of religion, is a fit example to be followed by the Christian teachers of the present age. Even supposing the Scribes and Pharisees to be so bad as he represented them, still the language he used towards them tended only to make them worse. That it did not make them better is proved by the fact that—if we except Joseph and Nicodemus, who are not however expressly said to be either Scribes or Pharisees—he failed to make any of them his disciples. The language, especially of a public teacher, should not only be truthful but likewise expedient, having a tendency, not to offend, but to convince and instruct. Even to opponents, it must not be a string of invectives, but mild and indicative of a charitable feeling in the speaker. The language of Jesus, however, to his religious opponents, whether Scribes, Pharisees, Chief priests, Sadducees, or Herodians, was, unfortunately, coarse, abusive, extremely opprobrious, and, as such, productive of immoral results.

His conduct on that occasion when a woman was brought to him accused of adultery, is also open to grave objections, both on moral and social grounds. One morning when he was preaching in the temple, certain Scribes and Pharisees, who knew that Mary Magdalene and other females of ill repute were following him with his approval, brought before him an adultress, in order that they might have grounds of accusation against him, apparently on this point. The Gospel narrative of the affair runs thus.—"The Scribes and Pharisees brought unto him a woman taken in adultery ; and when they had set her in the midst, they say unto him, Master, this woman was taken in adultery, in the very act. Now Moses in the law commanded us, that such should be stoned ; but what sayest thou ? This they said, tempting him, *that they might have to accuse him.* But Jesus stooped down, and with his finger wrote on the ground, as though he heard them not. So when they continued asking him, he lifted up himself, and said unto them, He that is without sin among you, let him first cast a stone at her. And again he stooped down, and wrote on the ground. And they which heard it, being convicted by their own conscience, went out one by one, beginning at the eldest, even unto the last : and

---

* If he spoke of righteousness, he must hold up to ridicule the righteousness of the Scribes and Pharisees. (Matth. v. 20.) If he spoke of prayer, he must despise the mode in which the Pharisees prayed. (Luke xviii. 11.) If he spoke of bread, he must say— "Beware of the leaven of the Pharisees." (Mark viii. 15. Luke xii. 1.) Many other such instances could be added.

Jesus was left alone, 'and the woman standing in the midst. When Jesus had lifted up himself, and saw none but the woman, he said unto her, Woman, where are those thine accusers ? Hath no man condemned thee ? She said, No man, Lord. And Jesus said unto her, Neither do I condemn thee : go, and sin no more." (John viii. 3—11.) From this account we perceive that Jesus acted very strangely in regard to the woman, her accusers, and the serious crime with which she was charged. Her accusers, affirming that they had the evidence of their own eyes as to her guilt, and reminding Jesus of the severe punishment which the Mosaic Law prescribed for this heinous offence, asked him what his view was of such a breach not only of decency but of morality. Jesus, pretending not to hear what they said, stooped down and began to write on the ground, which is very strange, not only on account of his impolite behaviour to the persons who had visited him, but also because he is said by Christians to have been unable to write at all. At length, owing to their importunity, he deigned to give them the following answer.—" He that is without sin among you, let him first cast a stone at her." If these words have any meaning at all, they mean that unless there can be found men utterly free from every description of sin—perfectly immaculate—they are not to punish others for particular crimes, however heinous. According to this doctrine, our Christian courts of justice—judges, juries and all—are to be perfectly sinless before they can sit in judgment upon any one, and especially before they can inflict punishment for any crime. In other words, crime, however flagrant, however dangerous and detrimental to society, is to be tolerated and to have its full scope till sinless people can be found to punish it. Why then do not Christians reduce this doctrine of Jesus into practice, and witness the dire result of such a mad course ? Why not, in cases of the kind, in which they are personally concerned, say like Jesus— " Neither do I condemn thee : go, and sin no more," instead of repairing to courts of law for redress ? Although the punishment for this offence, among the barbarous Jews, was death, executed in the most savage manner imaginable ; namely, by a furious crowd throwing stones at the criminal until he died from the wounds which a shower of these missiles inflicted upon him, and was apparently buried under them, yet Jesus does not utter one word against the cruelty of this punishment. He does not raise his voice against taking away human life as a punishment, even under any circumstance, or for any offence however enormous. Nor does he even urge that the forfeiture of life is too heavy a penalty for the crime of adultery. But the whole that he says on this occasion, both to the woman and her accusers, shows that he wished to see crime go unpunished, at least in the present life.* The Jewish moralists, owing to the extraordinary

---

* There is very little doubt that our present system of jurisprudence, like that of all other nations, is radically and thoroughly wrong ; and that, in particular, our mode of treating offenders in prison with the view to ameliorate their moral condition is most unphilosophic and absurd ; while our practice of inflicting capital punishment " by way of example" is most repugnant to common sense. Although criminals should not be left unrestrained, yet, since the cause of crime is physical and inherent in the offenders, they should, during the time they are deprived of their liberty, whether short or long, be treated more like patients than persons undergoing a punishment—they should be morally and physically educated—not punished. Jesus, however, did not suggest that such rational means should be applied to offenders.

answer of Jesus to their question, having retired and left him alone with the adultress, he asked her—"Woman, where are those thine accusers? Hath no man condemned thee? She said, No man, Lord. And Jesus said unto her, Neither do I condemn thee: go, and sin no more." His words to this woman almost sanction her adultery. He did not *condemn* or even reprove her for this heinous offence—an offence punishable with death by the Mosaic Law which Jesus professed he had come to enforce, —an offence which destroyed all connubial happiness, and involved the injustice of entailing a spurious progeny upon the husband. For this grave offence, Jesus, when he had the most ample opportunity, did not administer a word of reproof to the woman—did not address one syllable to her touching her outrage on decency and on her matrimonial obligations; but emphatically told her that he *did not* condemn her. To say to such a reprobate character—"Go, and sin no more" was, doubtless, as transient in effect as the tract of a bark's keel on the ocean. This was far outweighed in effect by the assurance he gave her that he, before whom as her judge she had been brought, *did not* condemn her. Taking into account the whole that Jesus, on this occasion, said to the woman and to her accusers, it is impossible to avoid the conclusion that he was more inclined to sanction the woman's offence than to blame her for it. If any person, in the present age, were to express himself as Jesus did regarding adultery, he would be considered immoral. How then are we to avoid the same inference in regard to him?

On several occasions Jesus evinced a considerable degree of dissimulation entirely at variance with moral rectitude. Once, when the feast of tabernacles was approaching, Jesus's brothers, who did not believe in his pretensions, advised him to attend this feast—at which the whole male population of the Jews were required to be present—and signalize himself on account of such wonderful miracles as those which he could work in dark corners of the country. To this intimation, he replied that he did not intend to go to that feast, urging as an excuse that his time had not yet come, and exhorting his brothers to go without him. His brothers accordingly went, and Jesus, shortly after, followed them *secretly*, when he had told them *he would not go*. The narrative of this prevarication runs thus.—"Now the Jews' feast of tabernacles was at hand. His brethren therefore said unto him, Depart hence, and go into Judæa, that thy disciples also may see the works that thou doest; for there is no man that doeth any thing in secret, and he himself seeketh to be known openly. If thou do these things, shew thyself to the world. For neither did his brethren believe in him. Then Jesus said unto them, My time is not yet come; but your time is alway ready. The world cannot hate you; but me it hateth, because I testify of it, that the works thereof are evil. Go ye up unto this feast: *I go not up yet unto this feast; for my time is not yet full come*. When he had said these words unto them, he abode still in Galilee. But when his brethren were gone up, *then went he also up unto the feast, not openly, but as it were in secret*." (John vii. 2—10.) From the whole drift of this narrative, it is evident that Jesus, not only led his brethren to believe, but told them in plain terms that he would *not* be present at the feast in question. It is clear that so they understood him to say; and, under this impression they undertook the journey by themselves, leaving him in Galilee

—a distance of at least sixty miles from Jerusalem, even if Lower Galilee
is meant; but if Upper Galilee, a distance of more than a hundred miles.
It is of no avail for Christian writers to urge that what Jesus meant by the
words—" I go not up *yet* unto *this* feast, for my time is not yet full come"
—was, that it was not quite time for him yet to go to the feast—that he
did not wish to be present at the beginning of the feast—and that he
wished his brothers to be there some time before him. This is to argue as
if Jesus and his brothers were at the time only a few miles distant from
Jerusalem. It is overlooked that, in travelling from sixty to a hundred
miles on foot through the wilds of Palestine, many obstacles were to be
met with, so that the party who started last might be the first at Jerusalem. It is also forgotten that it is expressly stated that " when his
brethren were gone up, then went he also up unto the feast, not openly,
but as it were in secret." This, in the connexion it occurs, plainly shows
a design on the part of Jesus to deceive his brothers. He had told them
that he would not go to *this* feast; in consequence of which they left him
in Galilee, and went without him; but he afterwards secretly followed
them, and made his appearance publicly in the feast. It is sophistical to
contend that the words—" not openly, but as it were in secret,"—apply to
his procedure after he had entered the feast, and that his object therein
was to conceal himself from the Jews. For we read (ver. 14.) that when
he entered the feast, he went into the temple—the most public and conspicuous place in Jerusalem—delivered there a long speech, and held
some discussions with people of the Jewish faith. The next day, also,
which would appear to have been the fourth day of this feast that lasted a
week, he went into the temple to teach, when " all the people came unto
him," and the Pharisees brought to him a woman caught in adultery, as
already noticed. On this occasion also he delivered a very long oration,
and entered into warm religious disputes with Scribes, Pharisees, and other
Jews. (John vii. ix.) Indeed, the whole conduct of Jesus during this
feast, utterly precludes the supposition that it is in reference to the Jews it
is said that he went " up unto the feast, not openly, but as it were in
secret;" and the scope of the narrative clearly connects these words with
what he had but just told his brothers; namely, that he did not intend to
be present at the feast. In other words, his object in going thither "as
it were in secret" was to conceal his movements from his brothers—who
had just ridiculed his pretended miracles—at least until he entered the
feast. But it is urged that the words—" I go not up yet unto this feast,"
do not mean that he did not intend to go at all; but merely that he was
not disposed to go at the same time as his brothers; and that this construction is fully borne out by the immediate context—" My time is not
yet full come." Similar expressions to the last clause, which are very
numerous in the Gospels, however, demonstrate that Jesus, or at least the
writer of the Gospel of John, meant a very different *time* from the *time* at
which to proceed to the feast of the tabernacles; namely, *the time that
Jesus was to be crucified.* Jesus is very frequently made to say that his
time or his *hour* is, or is not come, meaning almost invariably the time of
his arrest. In the same chapter (ver. 30.) as the expression under notice
occurs, we have the words—" They sought to take him; but no man laid
hands on him, because his hour was not yet come"; which is precisely

synonymous with "his time is not yet come."* The meaning of the phrases —"my time is not yet come," and "my time is not yet full come," undoubtedly, is that the time for crucifying him had not yet arrived; implying however that, to a future feast at Jerusalem he would go, and that, his time having then arrived, he should be arrested and put to death. Accordingly, he tells his brothers to go alone to the feast that now approaches, and adds—"I go not up yet unto *this* feast," meaning that *this* feast was too soon for him to attend, because his *time* had not come. But if he wished his brothers to understand that he meant to come at all to the feast then at hand, he would not have used the expression—"*this* feast." Jesus however did go to "*this* feast," thus giving an instance of wilful prevarication, with the view of deceiving his brothers. It requires a vast degree of Christian faith to distinguish between such a prevarication and what is in the present age deemed a deliberate falsehood.

Another peculiar instance of dissimulation in Jesus was that of pretending to be another person than he was to the two disciples who travelled to Emmaus after his resurrection; and also of pretending to wish to go further than Emmaus, when at the same time it was his intention to stay there with these disciples. With these two disciples he travelled a long way, listened to their relation regarding Jesus of Nazareth, and, calling them fools, expounded to them all the scriptures concerning himself, from Moses to Malachi. All this took place without the disciples, who had familiarly lived with him, having the least suspicion that he was the personage of whom they were speaking; which is an instance of a very singular defect of memory and power of recognition. When they drew near Emmaus, Jesus "made as though he would have gone further;" that is, he *pretended* (προσεποιειτο) to be going further. Owing to the earnest invitation of the two disciples however "he went in to tarry with them." And presently "their eyes were opened, and they knew him;" but no sooner than "he vanished out of their sight." (Luke xxiv. 13—31.) But why all this disguise? Why pretend to go further than he really intended? Why dissemble himself to the two disciples, especially when they were under the distressing circumstances represented? Was it more advantageous to them to have the Scriptures expounded under the belief that it was another person than Jesus who did so, than if they had the evidence of their senses that it was he, who by his resurrection had just proved himself divine and therefore unerring, that thus expounded to them the heavenly oracles? Were they better of being thus deceived? Or could there possibly any good accrue to anybody else from this deception?— Unquestionably not. Deception, in its very nature, is a moral evil; and was not less an evil in Jesus than in some other person. Throughout the Gospel narrative of this dissimulation the writer represents Jesus as pretending to know nothing of what had just happened—his own crucifixion,

---

* Of the same meaning is the word *hour* in the following passages.—"Behold the hour is at hand, and the Son of man is betrayed." (Matth. xxvi. 45.)—"No man laid hands on him; for his hour was not yet come." (John viii. 20.)—"The hour is come, that the Son of man should be glorified." (John xii. 23.)—"Before the feast of the passover, when Jesus knew that his hour was come." (John xiii. 1.)—"Father, the hour is come; glorify thy Son." (John xvii. 1.) The word hour, in the foregoing passages and many others in the Jewish writings, denotes an appointed time.

death, and resurrection;—and in reference to these things, he is made to ask the disciples—"What things?" If he had not journeyed with them thus in disguise, what a piece of evidence of the reality of his resurrection he would have given to them and to the world! And, by this dissemblance, what an excellent opportunity he lost of giving lessons to these two disciples how to manage his church after his departure! As soon, however, as they knew him to be Jesus, he vanished; and when they afterwards had a glimpse of him, they "supposed that they had seen a spirit." How these acts of dissimulation must tend to weaken the faith of the Christians of the present distant age!

Only one instance more of Jesus's dissimulation can be noticed here. When Judas, at the head of a band of soldiers, came to Jesus to betray him—or, in other words, to point him out as the person who was to be arrested—the following scene of mutual insincerity between Jesus and Judas took place. Jesus, when in Gethsemane with his disciples, said to them—"Rise, let us be going: behold, *he is at hand that doth betray me.* And while he yet spake, lo, Judas, one of the twelve, came, and with him a great multitude with swords and staves, from the chief priests and elders of the people. Now he that betrayed him gave them a sign, saying, whomsoever I shall kiss, that same is he; hold him fast. And forthwith he came to Jesus, and said, *Hail, master; and kissed him.* And Jesus said unto him, *Friend, wherefore art thou come?*" (Matth. xxvi. 46—50.) But what a picture of deception is here displayed, not only on the part of Judas, but equally so on the part of Jesus! How inconsistent it was in Jesus to allow the murderous traitor, Judas, to embrace him! So far was he from reprimanding the foul hypocrisy of this perfidious villain that he, not only allowed him to kiss him, but called him even a *friend!* To denominate his traitor a *friend* cannot be attributed to any tendency in Jesus to use mild language, for the whole history of his life proves the contrary. Not only did he on all occasions designate the Scribes, Pharisees, and others by the coarsest terms, but he called his apostle Peter by the odious name —Satan. Still, how unjust and absurd it was in him to call the bravest and most faithful of his disciples by this detestable name, and yet to grace the execrable Judas with the endearing appellation—friend! Although he well knew that Judas had come to betray him, yet he appears to have been quite as wishful to keep on good terms with the traitor, whom he addressed as a friend, as the latter, who saluted him in the reverential language— Hail, master, seems to have been to inspire him with confidence in the harmlessness of his approach. Jesus's dissimulation, therefore, was quite as intense as that of Judas. But Jesus carried his dissimulation further than even Judas. He asked him his errand, pretending not to know it,— "Friend, *wherefore* art thou come?" whereas only a few minutes had elapsed since he had said to his disciples—"He is at hand that doth betray me." Also, when eating the passover, only a few hours before, he plainly told Judas that he was aware of his intention to betray him; and his agitated condition, as described in the Gospels, from the moment he had reason to suspect Judas's treachery, was such that made it impossible for him to have forgotten this momentous matter with which his whole mind was overwhelmed, and in reference to which he exclaimed—"My soul is exceeding sorrowful, even unto death." At the very moment, therefore, he asked Judas for what purpose he came to him with a company of armed men, he must have well known what that purpose was. To feign ignorance of it was a subterfuge which few stanch characters would wish to copy, even if martyrdom stared them in the face.

Jesus's declaration regarding the responsibility of Judas for betraying him seems very absurd, and utterly at variance with every sound notion of justice, As he was eating the Jewish passover with his disciples—having previously understood that Judas had been with the chief priests making arrangements for delivering him into their hands—he expressed his conviction that one of them was about to betray him, and added—"The Son of man goeth as it is written of him; but woe unto that man by whom the Son of man is betrayed! It had been good for that man if he had not been born. Then Judas, which betrayed him, answered and said, Master, is it I? He said unto him, Thou hast said." (Matth. xxvi. 24, 25.) On several other occasions did he announce that it was predestined that he should be betrayed; and yet pronounced woe on the betrayer. But if it was pre-ordained that Judas should betray him, why denounce woe upon him?—Why hold him responsible for an act, in the performance of which he was carrying out the decrees of Heaven? If the betrayal of Jesus by Judas was inevitable,—was done as it *had been written*, in order *that the Scriptures might be fulfilled*,—and "was determined" by an unalterable fiat, on what principle of justice was Judas responsible for this act, in which he was but a mere instrument to fulfil the purposes of a superior Being? Judas was one of the twelve chosen apostles,—who had been endued with supernatural wisdom and miraculous powers,—who had been for about three years under the divine instruction of Jesus,—who had been sent to preach the kingdom of heaven, "heal the sick, cleanse the lepers, raise the dead, and cast out devils,"—and to whom Jesus had said—"It is not ye that speak, but the Spirit of your Father which speaketh in you." Accordingly, what Christian can consistently deny that when Judas went to the chief priests and said—"What will ye give me, and I will deliver him unto you," and afterwards said—"Whomsoever I shall kiss, the same is he; *hold him fast*", it was not he that said this, but the Spirit of the Father which spoke within him? For Judas was one of those to whom Jesus had said that, when he spoke, it was not he himself that spoke, but the Spirit of the Father which was within him. How absurd then of Jesus to denounce woe against Judas for betraying him, as if he deserved some awful punishment for this act! According to John, (xiii. 21—30.) Jesus himself was the proximate cause that Judas betrayed him; and so anxious was he for this to be done that he wished it accomplished with the utmost speed. Having announced that one of his disciples would betray him, he said—"He it is to whom I shall give a sop, when I have dipped it. And when he had dipped the sop, he gave it to Judas Iscariot, the son of Simon. *And after the sop, Satan entered into him.* Then said Jesus unto him, *That thou doest, do quickly.*" Judas, having received the sop, goes immediately out, and we hear nothing of him after till he comes at the head of a band of archers, and points out Jesus to them. The idea here conveyed, evidently is, that Satan followed the sop into Judas' stomach, and that this sop was the cause of Satan thus entering into Judas.— Accordingly, the cause of Jesus's betrayal was with himself, not with

Judas,—it was this unfortunate sop.* And this view is quite in harmony with what he himself said immediately after administering this dose to Judas,—"That thou doest, do quickly." At all events, between Jesus and and Satan, Judas must have been utterly passive in the act of selling his master; and it was therefore unjust and absurd in Jesus to hold him responsible for this act, and pronounce woe upon him. It has been far too much the practice of Christians, who believe that Jesus came to the world for the express purpose of being put to death for the sins of men, to blame Judas, in unmeasured terms and most violent language, for delivering him to the very persons who had been decreed to act the part they acted in accomplishing the redemption of mankind. Judas, according to the present prevailing Christian system of theology, must be admitted to have been *merely* an instrument of the salvation of the world, or an executor of the divine decrees.† Had not he, or some one else—and it matters not who—caused Jesus to be crucified, the great doctrine of the atonement would be wanting in the Christian system, and nothing worth hearing could be preached to what is called a lost world. For Jesus himself, who, when he perceived his life in danger, exclaimed—"Father, if it be possible let this cup pass from me," evidently, would not have surrendered voluntarily to death. Such a blessing, therefore, has Judas conferred on Christians that they would be much more consistent in canonising him than they are in loading him with exprobations.

In the whole career of Jesus, perhaps there is no instance in which he has more egregiously erred, in a moral point of view, and also given a more decided proof of his unwillingness to die, than that in which he commanded his followers *to be provided with swords*. Both as a precept and as an example to Christians, this not only sanctions, but encourages bloodshed—war, with all its attendant havocs, miseries, and crimes! Perhaps that to the carrying out of this injunction of Jesus is to be attributed the fact that Christianity has been the cause of more bloodshed and cruelty than any other religion of which we have any account. The legions of armed men, now under the Pope, have Jesus's own authority for carrying their weapons of death, and are therefore, on Christian grounds, entirely exonerated from any sanguinary act they may commit. When Jesus, a very short time before he was arrested, perceived that he had been betrayed into the hands of his enemies, and every moment expected public officers to apprehend him, he meditated resistance, as the only mode of escape, and commanded his disciples to be provided with swords. Having informed them of the imminent danger in which his life stood, owing to the treachery of Judas, who had now actually gone for the soldiers, and having also advised them to secure on their persons both their money-bags and their scrips or

* According to the Apocryphal Gospels, this was not the first time for Satan to enter into Judas. When Jesus and Judas were little boys, Satan was in the latter. One day when they were playing together, Satan instigated Judas to bite Jesus, who, upon this, made Satan come out of Judas in the form of a dog, and run away for his life.—1 Gospel of Infancy, xiv.

† This rational view of Judas was maintained by some of the early Christians, who held that the plan of salvation could not possibly have been carried out, had he not done what he did. Accordingly, they held Judas in great reverence, and very naturally ascribed to him—or rather, according to the practice of those times, manufactured—a Gospel, which they named *The Gospel of Judas Iscariot.*—Iren. adv. Hær. lib. i. c. 35.

wallets, in which they carried their food, he added that if any one of them had not a sword, he must buy one, even if he sold his wearing apparel to obtain it. His disciples having assured him that there were two swords at hand, apparently over and above those which they individually had at their sides—for we learn that each of them carried a sword, and that one of them, namely Peter, made a very free use of it—he said that this number of swords would suffice.—"'He that hath no sword, let him sell his garment, and buy one."—" And they said, Lord, behold, here are two swords. And he said unto them, It is enough." (Luke xxii. 36, 38.)

If any further evidence than that afforded by these passages were required that Jesus's ¦followers carried swords, it is to be found in the fact that, when they saw themselves surrounded by armed soldiers, captains, priests, and elders, they asked their master,—" Lord, shall we smite with the sword ?" One of them however, namely Peter, who had a little while before declared that he was ready to go to prison, or even die for his master, did not wait for the word of command from his captain, but, rushing forward, cut off with his sword the ear of one Malchus, a servant of the high priest. But Jesus, although he had a short time before told his disciples to be provided with swords, yet now on perceiving that he was hopelessly encompassed by a greatly superior number of armed men, thought it prudent to alter his tactics, and to command his followers to desist from using their weapons, remarking that if they used their swords, they were likely to perish by the swords of those expert warriors who were then closing upon them, and who had by this time actually arrested Jesus, so that resistance was not only useless but productive of still greater danger to life.—" Put up again thy sword in his place; for all they that take the sword shall perish with the sword. Thinkest thou that I cannot now pray to my Father, and he shall presently give me more than twelve legions of angels." (Matth. xxvi. 51—53. Mark xiv. 47. Luke xxii. 49—51. John xviii. 10, 11.) Whoever will candidly compare the respective narratives of the four Evangelists, cannot fail to perceive clear evidence that Jesus's followers wore swords, that he himself particularly commanded all of them to have swords in readiness to defend him from being arrested, that one of them made use of his sword, and that Jesus, seeing resistance was of no avail, gave orders to refrain from using the sword, intimating that he now relied for his deliverance upon the aid of angels, one of whom, a short time before is said to have administered to him when in trouble regarding his impending danger. That he forebade the use of swords after he had been captured is no proof that he did not, a little before, order them to be prepared and used. Indeed, the manner in which Jesus addressed Peter—" Put up *thy* sword into the *sheath*," shows that his disciples habitually carried swords. Nor have we any evidence that Jesus himself was not ordinarily armed with a sword; but there is a strong probability that he was. For as his disciples were thus armed, it is unreasonable to suppose that their master was not; while it is quite in harmony with the nature of things to infer that the former wore swords in imitation of the latter. This inference derives considerable force also from the well known custom of Eastern chieftains, particularly when it is recollected that Jesus aimed at being a king.

To have recourse to swords when danger approached, suggests many

grave considerations, both in regard to Jesus and his disciples.—If Simon
Peter had really been endowed with such miraculous powers as enabled
him to raise the dead and vanquish demons, it would have been easy for
him, by means of these powers, successfully to resist a few soldiers without
having recourse to that ordinary weapon of war—the sword ; the morality
of having used which, even under the then existing circumstances, is very
questionable. Peter, however, perceived that both he and his master were
in danger ; and, utterly ignoring the possession of any miraculous power
either by himself or by Jesus, he could see no other way open to avert
this danger than by cutting down his enemies with his sword. Equally
strange it is in Jesus to say that by praying to his Father he could, if he
wished, have more than twelve legions of angels for his defence. Saying
nothing of the absurdity for one divine being to pray to another, the
question arises, why should Jesus, in order to be rescued from the hands
of his enemies, have required any aid at all from angels ? Had he not in
himself unlimited power ? Had he not all the universe under his control ?
Had he not stilled tempests ? Had he not conquered a legion of demons,
and driven them with two thousand pigs into the sea ? Why then, in this
critical juncture, refer to the power of angels instead of to his own inherent power, to deliver him from the hands of a number of mortal men ?—
His divinity, by no means shines in this momentous crisis, wherein of all
others it should shine. As to the immorality of his conduct in ordering
his disciples to provide swords for his defence, it is trusted that this
requires no comment. Those Christians who believe that this was right
in the author of their religion, to be consistent, should, in obedience to his
injunction, or in imitation of his apostles, wear swords, and defend their
faith by weapons of war, as it has, unfortunately, been defended a thousand
times since Jesus declared that he came not *to send peace on earth, but a
sword.*

Section IV.—MANY THINGS WHICH JESUS TAUGHT AND SAID, NOT TRUE.

In the Gospel narratives, there are numerous things related, as having
been said by Jesus, which, on the very face of them, are untrue. Yet, only
a few of such, which do not naturally fall under other heads, will be noticed
in this section.

Jesus, referring—according to the orthodox view of the matter—to
his ascension to heaven, said to his disciples that they knew whither he
was going, and also knew the way to that place. But this does not appear
to be a fact. Thomas, in reply to him, denies that he and his fellow-
disciples knew whither their master was about to go, and, therefore, very
reasonably, asks him how they could know the way.—" Whither I go, ye
know, and the way ye know. Thomas said unto him, Lord, we know not
whither thou goest ; and how can we know the way ?" (John xiv. 4, 5.)—
How inapplicable, irrelevant, and obscure is Jesus's rejoinder to this contradiction on the part of his disciples !—" I am the way, the truth, and the
life." That Jesus was wrong in asserting that his disciples knew whither

he was going, is further proved by the fact that Peter had previously asked him—"Lord, whither goest thou?" and that Jesus had replied—"Whither I go, thou canst not follow me now." (John xiii. 36.)   The same thing is proved by his disciples asking—"What is this that he saith, A little while? We cannot tell what he saith." (John xvi. 16—20.)   Hence, it is clear that Jesus's allegation that his disciples knew whither he was going was *not true*.   Similar remarks apply to his assertion that his disciples *knew* the Comforter—the Spirit of truth.   Judas (not the Iscariot) indirectly contradicts him, by asking how he would manifest himself to the disciples and not to the world. (John xiv. 16—26.)   The whole drift of the narrative shows that his disciples were totally ignorant of what he meant by the dark, enigmatical expressions to which he gave utterance, and proves that he was wrong in saying that they *knew* this or that.

Again : Jesus says to his disciples, in reference to his departure,— "None of you asketh me, whither goest thou?"   Yet, we read that Peter a short time before—even during the singular speech that Jesus was then delivering—had asked him, in amazement and apparent trouble,—"Lord, whither goest thou?" (John xiii. 36 ; xvi. 5.)   Now, had Jesus so treacherous a memory as not to recollect a very remarkable conversation which he had had with a very remarkable disciple only a few minutes before?   Or did he wilfully make this statement, when he knew it was not true?   Or, if neither was the case, how are we to account for this glaring contradiction?

Jesus says to his Father—"I have finished the work thou gavest me to do." (John xvii. 4.)   This expression he uttered before he was apprehended and crucified—before he had suffered, died, and risen from the tomb.   How, therefore, can Christians, according to their tenets respecting Jesus's work on earth—his sufferings, his death, his resurrection, and his atonement for sin,—reconcile with truth this declaration of the author of their faith,—that he had finished his work on earth, when, by far, the most important portions of it were not accomplished?   Was not atoning for sin by his blood,—by suffering unto death, by rising from the dead, and thereby vanquishing the last enemy, namely death—the most important part of the work which the Father had given him to do?   Few Christians, however illiterate, can fail to perceive that, even upon their own view of their religion, Jesus cannot possibly have spoken the truth when, before he was crucified, he said he had finished the work which his Father had given him to do on earth.   To smooth down this awkward expression, which is in direct opposition to the entire Christian scheme of redemption, is a task requiring the whole skill, tact, and literary quibbling of commentators, ere they can remove the objection it creates against the infallibility of the speaker.

It is difficult to perceive that Jesus's words were in strict accordance with truth when he said that he had manifested his Father's name unto the men whom his Father had given him ; evidently meaning his disciples.— (John xvii. 6.)   Certainly, *all* of them had not known the Father ; for, a short time before he had said they had, one of them made a request which proves that he knew nothing about the Father; when Jesus told him and the other disciples that, if they had known him, they would have known the Father also. (John xiv. 6—10.)   Jesus's effort, therefore, to manifest his Father's name to his disciples had been unsuccessful; and his declaration that he had accomplished this is not exactly in accordance with the facts detailed in the Gospels. He, however, on the same occasion, says that these disciples had kept the Father's word. But it must be difficult, even to the most orthodox Christian, to believe the truth of this statement. Did Peter keep the Father's word when it was necessary for Jesus to grace him with the loathsome title, Satan,—when he cut off a man's ear with his sword,—or when he denied his master, cursing, swearing, and telling a falsehood to save himself? Did ten of Jesus's disciples keep the Father's word when moved with indignation against the remaining two? Did all his disciples keep the words of the Father in cowardly deserting their master at the most critical moment of his life, and after his death, in leaving his burial to strangers? Were the lives of these disciples so immaculate as to make Jesus's declaration regarding them true? The Gospel narratives—said to have been written even by four of these disciples themselves—prove that they were not.

In his defence before the Jewish Pontiff, Jesus says, with regard to his manner of teaching—" In secret I have said nothing." (John xviii. 20.) But is this *true?* Did he not teach his disciples in secret? Was it not in secret that he explained to them his doctrines, which, in public, he delivered in ambiguous, enigmatical parables? Did he not repeatedly say that to his disciples exclusively it was given to know the mysteries of the kingdom of heaven, and that others were left to learn from obscure and mystifying parables? Have we not many instances in which he withdrew into seclusion from the reach of the vulgar ear, in order to initiate his disciples alone into these mysteries? With what semblance of truth, then, could he urge before the high priest that *in secret he had said nothing ?*

In his Sermon on the mount Jesus uttered many things which seem entirely at variance with fact, such as that the *poor,* the *mournful,* the *hungry,* and the *persecuted* were happy. (Matth. v. 3—10. Luke vi. 20— 27.) Human feeling bears testimony against the correctness of all this.— To be *poor* in pocket—as Luke reports the words of Jesus, in harmony with his continual teaching—is unfortunately too well known by thousands to be one of the chief sources of human misery; and to be *poor* in spirit is productive of neither happiness nor of any other good. Poverty of spirit, or cowardice, offers only an inducement to the *haughty* in spirit to oppress and domineer. Blind submission to every injustice imposed upon us, is so far from being a virtue that it is a positive vice. Moral courage is much more likely to produce blessedness than poverty of spirit. To *mourn* and be hungry are certainly natural results of poverty of spirit; but neither of them is productive of happiness. The poor in spirit may lament his hard fate, when hunger pinches him; but a million of moans and a river of tears will not feed him with bread; and neither his hunger nor his tears are likely to make him happy. Nor is it very probable that a man will be made happy by being reviled and persecuted. Universal experience teaches that all men when *persecuted* are more or less miserable. In a word, there is nothing in either poverty of spirit, mournfulness, hunger, or the suffering of persecution which, in the least, is productive of blessedness. There is nothing more unreasonable than to suppose that any person ever was, or ever will be blessed, *as a consequence* of being poor in spirit, mournful, hungry, and persecuted.   Such a doctrine is not only untrue but fraught with mischief.   It discountenances manly self-reliance ; it encourages melancholy and hypochondriacal feelings, which too often lead· to suicide ; it prohibits the exercise of one's mental and physical powers in order to satisfy hunger ; and it makes persons anxious to be persecuted and even to suffer martyrdom, while they dream of the consequent blessedness.

In the same sermon, Jesus said that he did not aim at abrogating the Mosaic law, but rather at fulfilling it.   He must however have well known that this statement was not correct.   For he contradicted this law, violated it, and trampled it under foot, in a vast number of instances.   It may, however, have been convenient for him, at the outset of his public career, not to denounce too harshly a law believed by his fellow-countrymen to be divine, but, while his cause was as yet weak, to persuade the people that he did not intend to sweep it away altogether, and wished only to amend it in places where it was imperfect.   Still, in a few minutes after he had declared that he had not come to destroy this law, which he said would remain intact as long as the world remained, (Matth. v. 17, 18.) he contravened it in the following manner.—This law legalised the second marriage of a divorced woman, but he pronounced such a marriage adulterous.— This law permitted oaths to be taken, but he prohibited all oaths.   This law required an eye for an eye, and a tooth for a tooth, but he enjoined the non-resistance of evil.   This law directed the Jews to hate their enemies, but he told them to love their enemies.   Surely, such teaching fully shows that Jesus had come to destroy the Mosaic law, notwithstanding his denial.   He also desecrated the Sabbath ordained by this law, and on several occasions spoke of it in a very indifferent manner.   It must, therefore, be admitted that Jesus spoke contrary to fact when he said he had not come to break the Mosaic law.   Indeed, the whole history of Christianity, together with its present state, necessitate its devotees to make this admission.   Otherwise, how can they account for Paul and his partizans making such strenuous efforts to complete the abrogation of this law, and utterly to suppress Judaism ?   How can they account for the changing of the Sabbath from Saturday to the pagan Sun-day ?   What reason can they give for having burnt so many Jews, in different Christian countries, because they observed the rites prescribed by the Mosaic law ?   Why do they not now practise circumcision ?   Why do they not now conform to the Mosaic ritual in their mode of worship, in their festivals, in their diet, and in a thousand other things ?   Even if there were no proof that Jesus came to destroy the Mosaic law, still there would be ample evidence that his followers have left very few and faint traces of it connected with the religion he established.*

After telling his hearers to do unto others as they would that others should do unto them, Jesus adds—" This is the law and the prophets ;" (Matth. vii. 12.) meaning, apparently, that this was the sum and substance of the law and the prophets.   This is, however, scarcely correct.—There is

* That portion of the Levitical law—the exaction of tithes, is certainly very jealously preserved and practised, even unto this day, by Christian priests, while, however, they have, very inconsistently, discarded the linen coat, the linen girdle, the linen breeches, and the linen mitre ; and have become eaters of the flesh of swine, hares, and rabbits.

no such doctrine or injunction taught, or even implied, in either the law or the prophets; nor is such inferrible from any particular expression in either of them. The nearest expression, in sentiment, is that found in the law—"Love thy neighbour as thyself." But if Jesus meant that the substance of the law and the prophets was contained in the injunction he then gave, he was certainly mistaken; for there are in these Jewish productions—at least as they have descended to us—a vast number of duties enjoined upon men, which have no reference to their obligations to *others*; and which therefore cannot be implied in the command—"As ye would that men should do to you, do ye also to them likewise." If Jesus meant only that this was the same doctrine as that taught in the law and the prophets, still this objection again would naturally arise, namely, that it is *not* the same. It is therefore not true, on any view of the expression, that "this is the law and the prophets;" and it will be shown hereafter that this piece of superior morality, touching our duty towards others, has been borrowed from another source than either the Law or the Prophets.

Jesus expressly teaches that if two Christians agree touching any thing they shall ask in prayer, God will be sure to grant it. He does this when giving rules for the conduct of his church generally; so as to preclude the supposition that he intended his words to apply only to his apostles. Having assured the church* that whatever it would bind on

---

* Although, in this work, all words which the Gospels attribute to Jesus are taken as if they had really been spoken by him, yet it may be here observed that the passage under notice, together with the context, particularly from ver. 15 to 23, presents strong evidence that it was written long after what is called the apostolic age. It savours of notions, at least, so late as the fourth century, and is probably from the pen of some cœnobinic monk. The word *church* (εκκλησια) used here is very remarkable. Unless it be supposed that there were Christians long before the time of Jesus—of which certainly there is some evidence (vid. ant. pp. 231, 232.)—in his time, this word could not signify an assembly of Christians; for no such assembly existed. Jesus could not, with any propriety, term his twelve disciples an assembly or church; and if he termed them so, he would not be understood to mean what is now meant by the word *church*. Still the word is here used without any explanation, and as a term which, at the time, was well understood to represent the idea which it does even in the present age. There are in the passage, however, several expressions besides which indicate that it was not written till Christian monasteries, or assemblies of Christians living in common—the earliest form of Christian churches—had become prevalent. Whatever part Jesus of Nazareth took in introducing Christianity into Judea, one thing is clear, namely, that the earliest form of Christianity, of which we have any account, was a mixture of the religious tenets of the Essenes and of the Pagan monks; and that monks did the most towards propagating this Christianity. These monks lived in huts, caves, and cells.—Hence, one of the most ancient names for a church, or the place where Christians assembled, that we find, is *casa*—a cell or cave. Even in the time of Bede, a church went by this name—*candula casa*, white church—and the building, with few exceptions, consisted only of pieces of wood placed together and covered with reeds. (Hist. Ang. lib. iii. c. 4.) A church also frequently went by the name of *cœmeterium*, and of *mensa*,—the former having reference to the monks's habits of living in caves wherein the dead were buried, and the latter to the block on which monks, in times of persecution, were beheaded.—(Concil. Elib. can. 34. Austin. Serm. 94, 237. Tertull. ad Scapul. c. 3.) Sulpitius Severus (Dial. i. c. 2.) represents the huts in which Christians held their conclaves in the deserts of Libya—about the end of the fourth century—as built with small rods interwoven together, and so low that a man could scarcely stand upright in them; and the description he gives of the men who assembled in these huts plainly shows that they were monks. It was not until after Pachomius, Eustathius, and others had succeeded in bringing the monks of different parts of the world to live in communities—about the

A A

earth should be bound in heaven, and *vice versa,* he adds—" If two of you shall agree on earth as touching any thing that they shall ask, it shall be done for them of my Father which is in heaven." (Matth. xviii. 19.) But, unquestionably, this has been falsified in innumerable instances. In thousands of cases have two Christians—as sincere Christians as ever lived— solemnly agreed to pray, and have fervently prayed for the same thing; and yet that thing was not given to them. How often have two or more true Christians, when in imminent danger of their lives—such as from shipwrecks, fires, floods, and other physical causes—been found to pray in the most ardent manner for deliverance; and yet no deliverance came;—no violation or suspension of the laws of nature was caused, in order to save their lives. When a ship, owing to a hurricane or the springing of a plank, founders and buries its human freight in the bottom of the sea, the most pious Christians—amongst whom may be a number of holy missionaries going to evangelise the heathen—are drowned like the most reprobate characters on board, notwithstanding their previously united and most fervid supplications for an escape from the awful death which every moment threatens them.. Have not Christians frequently united in prayer for fair weather when, owing to a long duration of rain, their corn was likely to

---

beginning of the fourth century—that Christians began to have any thing like churches; and these, as yet, were only monasteries. (Sozom. lib. iii. c. 14, 24. Hier. Vit. Hilar. c. 11. Pachom. Regul. c. 3.) From these habitations of the monks churches became to be called *monasteria,* and in our language *munsters* or *minsters,* which words are retained to this day in the names of such places. Eusebius (lib. ii. c. 17.) calls the churches of the Therapeuts—a class of monks who he expressly says were Christians —by the name μοναστηρια. He also, on the authority of Philo, not only identifies these Therapeuts with the monks of a later period, but assures us that they were Christians. A great mass of evidence might be collected to show that the cells of the monks, and after them their monasteries, were the places where Christians worshipped in ancient times. Indeed, the word εκκλησια—a number of people called out—derived from εκκαλεω, *to call out* or *from*—appears to have been applied to a Christian assembly owing to the ancient practice of calling the monks out of their respective cells, which were within the monastery, into that part used by them for united devotion, or for a chapel. The manner of calling them out of their cells varied in different countries. In Egypt and Palestine this was done by sounding a trumpet; in other parts by knocking with a hammer at the door of each cell, and in others by crying out "Hallelujah."— (Pachom. Reg. c. 3. Cassian. Inst. c. 17. Hieron. ep. 27. Clem. Scala. et al.) These various modes of calling were ultimately superseded by bells, which mode continues to this day. The early Christian monks were thus called out of their cells for divine worship in some monasteries, were as often as six times in the day, while in others only twice.— Hence, a Christian assembly probably had the name εκκλησια—called out; just as an assembly of Greeks—*called out* by the authority of a civil magistrate to discharge public duties—acquired the same name. It is in the time of Constantine that we find buildings beginning to be set apart for Christian worship, and denominated εκκλησιαι; namely, after he had turned all the heathen temples, within his dominions, into Christian churches—just as Hen. VIII. turned the Roman Catholic churches over to the Protestants—and after he had built several new ones. Then, we find them called εκκλησιαι, and one in particular, at Constantinople, called after his own name—*Ecclesia Constantiniana.* (Euseb. Vit. Const. lib. iii. c. 48—58; iv. 50, 58.) Indeed, it is from Constantine that the Christian church can really date its existence. Before his time it does not appear to have had any other edifices than monasteries, or any other assemblies than monks and holy virgins. And possibly, if he had never existed, or at least, if the pagan priest, Sopater, had not refused him absolution of his murderous crimes, and rendered him under the necessity of turning to the Christians of Egypt—the worshippers of the god Serapis—he would not have been the means of affording it state patronage; and it would, long ago, like many other Egyptian superstitions, have sunk into oblivion.—

be spoiled? Yet so far was their prayer from being answered that their crops rotted on their fields. Have not Christians many times—when, according to fixed laws of nature, long droughts impeded the growth of vegetation—devoutly prayed for rain? Yet no rain came—no miracle, in violation of natural laws, was performed—in order to answer their prayer. Have not pious parents often agreed to pray, and have most earnestly prayed for the conversion of a prodigal son; and yet this son was allowed to pursue his sinful career, and died in his iniquity? Indeed, we have daily proofs that, when two or more Christians agree to ask in prayer a particular thing, their request is not granted. And fortunate it is in many instances that this is the case. What awful calamities would often befall mankind, if the Governor of the universe were to act according to the request and directions of short-sighted and ignorant men! Not to enter here, however, into the folly involved in the supposition that an infinitely wise and benevolent God does any thing because one or more of his comparatively ignorant creatures asks him in prayer, let it rather be particularly noticed that there are thousands of cases which disprove the truth of Jesus's words—"If two of you shall agree on earth as touching any thing that they shall ask, it shall be done for them of my Father which is in heaven." It is of no avail to urge that this promise, prophecy, or whatever it be called, is confined to the twelve disciples of Jesus; for the word *church* is here used, showing that it was intended that the privilege of receiving what they asked in prayer should belong to the whole Christian community, so long as a church existed. His words, however, have proved untrue in countless instances.

(Vid. ant. pp. 331, 332.) Another mark of the late origin of the passage under notice, is the supreme authority it attributes to the decrees of the church.—"Whatsoever ye shall bind on earth shall be bound in heaven, and whatsoever ye shall loose on earth shall be loosed in heaven." The same inference is to be drawn from the pun which Jesus is shown to have made on the name of Peter, in which the church is both named and its supreme authority asserted —"Thou art Peter, (a rock) and upon this rock I will build my church; and the gates of hell shall not prevail against it. And I will give unto thee the keys of the kingdom of heaven: and whatsoever thou shalt bind on earth shall be bound in heaven; and whatsoever thou shalt loose on earth shall be loosed in heaven." (Matth. xvi. 18, 19.) Both this passage and that already under consideration, indicate that they had their origin when the church had become powerful, so as to make pretence to infallibility, and even when the Pope claimed to be the infallible head of this church, possessing the keys of the kingdom of heaven—which kingdom had by this time become to denote the regions of bliss—so that whatever he decreed on earth would be ratified in heaven. But it is a well ascertained fact that the Pope was not regarded as the head of the church till about the end of the fourth, or beginning of the fifth century.—(Basnage, vol. i. p. 243. Cyprian. Ep. 55, 73. Bowyer's Hist. of the Popes, vol. i. p. 180, et cet.) Nor was his authority regarded as absolute, and the opinion of the church as infallible, for nearly a century after. These passages further involve the idea of church penances and absolutions.—They imply that whatever penalties the church on earth imposed were imposed in heaven, and that whatever absolution or remission of sins it gave, the same was given in heaven. All this shows that they cannot be dated earlier than the commencement of the fourth century.

Section V.—many of jesus's precepts and doctrines contradictory to one another.

Jesus, as we have just seen, having made many statements at variance with truth, it is only to be expected that many of his precepts and doctrines contradicted one another. Truth is always consistent; and just as the orthodox and reverend Jeremiah Jones, in his standard work on the Canonical Authority of the New Testament, very justly says that a book is apocryphal which contains any contradictions, so it may be said of the teaching of Jesus—that precepts and doctrines which contradict one another cannot be all true, and may be all false. Although two contradictory expressions or assertions may be both false, yet they cannot be both true, in the same sense; and consequently many of Jesus's expressions that will now be noticed are of the same character as those pointed out in the foregoing section; namely untrue. Contradictory statements abound more in his doctrines than in those of any other public teacher of whom we have any account; and these, chiefly, have given rise to the numerous antagonistic Christian sects of both modern and ancient times, the tenets of all of which, however conflicting to those of others, are borne out by certain expressions attributed to Jesus. One would imagine that in the present age, at least, the minds of all thinking and disinterested men would shrink from receiving as truths—especially divine truths—the doctrines of a public teacher whose words were self-contradictory. This, doubtless, would inevitably be the case, were it not for the thousands of expositors and harmonisers of the words of Jesus, who write voluminous commentaries, and almost daily deliver long discourses, in order to clear up the discrepancies which common sense perceives in the moral lessons that he has bequeathed us. These, when any glaring contradiction is pointed out to them, have recourse either to a new translation, a figurative rendering, or a fresh interpretation of the contradictory passages. By thus playing fast and loose, and forgetting that words are the vehicles of ideas, they, necessarily, in all their commentaries and explanations, imply against Jesus a charge either of inability to express himself so as to be understood by his hearers and by those who now read what he said, or of an intention to mislead them. Their very commentaries on his words, are, of themselves, evidence that they think they are able to use more lucid language than Jesus either wished or was able to use. If, however, any one wishes to ascertain what Jesus really taught, let him lay aside these bewildering commentaries, and read the Gospels as he would read some other book, judging for himself whether he can find in them attributed to Jesus, doctrines and precepts which—according to the obvious meaning of the words in which they are conveyed, and the whole drift on the context—are at utter variance with others said to have been delivered by him.

Let us notice a few of these contradictions. Jesus, in defending himself from the charge of Sabbath-breaking, brought against him by the

Jews, says—" If I bear witness of myself, my witness is not true." (John v. 31.) But in answer to the accusation of praising himself, brought against him by these people, he says—"Though I bear record of myself, yet my record is true." (John viii. 14.) It should be observed that it is the same word, in the Greek, which stands for *witness* in the former passage as that translated *record* in the latter, so that there is no difference on this point.* Expressions contradicting each other more flatly than these were never uttered. It is impossible for both to be true,—as impossible as it is for a particular thing to exist and not to exist at the same time. If Jesus was right in saying that, if he bore testimony of himself, his testimony was not true, there is nothing plainer than that he was wrong in saying that, although he bore testimony of himself, yet his testimony was true. Very numerous and ingenious theories have been advanced by different writers,† in attempting to harmonise these expressions. The most plausible, perhaps, is that set up by the Rev. John Hayter Cox, in a course of lectures on the Harmony of Scripture,—which are expressly designed to meet the arguments of sceptics,—namely, that Jesus stated merely the opinion of his enemies—the Jews, when he said—" If I bear witness of myself, my witness is not true," meaning that, in the estimation of his enemies, it was not true; but that when he said—" Though I bear record of myself, yet my record is true," he stated a fact. In other words, that in the former passage he stated the opinion of others, but in the latter his own opinion. (Lect. x. p. 134.) That Jesus, in the former passage, spoke the opinion he thought the Jews held of him is, however, a gratuitous supposition, not only unsupported, but even directly contradicted by the whole drift of the discourse in which the expression occurs.— Having, on the Sabbath day, cured an infirm man, the Jews accused him of Sabbath-breaking. In justification of his act, he says to them—" My Father worketh hitherto, and I work." From this expression the Jews inferred that Jesus considered himself "equal to God," and became the more enraged against him. Jesus, with an evident design to pacify them, qualifies his expression and says—" The Son can do nothing of himself, but what he seeth the Father do." He proceeds in his explanation of the power by which he wrought his mighty works, and says—" I can of my own self do nothing: as I hear I judge; and my judgment is just; because

---

* In both passages we find Εγω μαρτυρω as the verb—I bear witness, or testify ; and μαρτυρια as the noun—witness, or testimony. It is difficult to conceive what made the translators employ *witness* in the one place and *record* in the other, unless it was to hide this contradiction, which they must have perceived. *Record* is a word which they very ill applied in several places where they used it.

† That Christians are fully sensible that there are in the Bible gross contradictions is proved by the fact that some hundreds, if not thousands of volumes, by different authors, in different ages, and different languages, have been written as *Harmonies* of such contradictions. Of these Harmonies there are now extant upwards of a hundred, in different languages, while a much larger number have sunk into oblivion. Never were so many Harmonies written on any book, and never was a book which so much required them.— Thomas Mann, in the seventeenth century, publishes a Harmony in the title of which he states there are in it 3,000 Scriptural contradictions reconciled.—London, 1662, fol. See a list of such works in Walchii Bibliotheca Selecta, vol. iv. pp. 854—900 ; Fabricii Bibliotheca Græca, vol. iv. pp. 882 —889; Pilkinton's Evangelical History and Harmony, pref. pp. 18—20. Michaelis's Introduction to the New Test. vol. iii. part i. pp. 31—36. part ii. pp. 29—49.

I seek not mine own will, but the will of the Father which hath sent me. *If I bear witness of myself, my witness is not true.* There is another that beareth witness of me; and I know that the witness which he witnesseth of me is true;" meaning here, by *another*, evidently his Father. He then tells them that they had sent to John who, certainly, had borne witness to the truth. But although John was a burning and shining light, in which the Jews for a while were willing to rejoice, yet he had a greater witness than John. Besides: he did not receive testimony from man. "And," he adds, "the Father himself, which hath sent me, hath borne witness of me." (ver. 17—37.) Such is the tenor of the discourse in which the expression occurs. There is here not the shadow of ground for supposing that Jesus in saying—"If I bear witness of myself, my witness is not true," spoke the opinion which the Jews entertained of him. What he means, and what he says is, that he did not bear witness of himself,—that it was the Father who bore witness of him; and that if he bore witness of himself, that would be a proof that such a testimony was not true. What occasioned him to utter the expression which contradicts the foregoing was this.—After he had dismissed the woman caught in adultery, as already described, he said to the Pharisees who had brought this woman to him, —" I am the light of the world;" whereupon the Pharisees being offended because Jesus thus praised himself, said to him—"Thou bearest record of thyself; thy record is not true. Jesus answered and said unto them, *Though I bear record of myself, yet my record is true.*" The Pharisees seem to have thought that—as Jesus himself on another occasion had stated—what a man said in praise of himself was not true. Jesus sets about showing them that, in his case, his testimony of himself was reliable, telling them that he knew whence he came and whither he went,—that he was not alone, but accompanied by the Father who had sent him,—that according to their own law, the testimony of two men was true,—and that, as he himself was one who bore witness, and the Father who had sent him was another, these made two, and therefore their testimony was sufficient. This is the train of argument which Jesus—in reply to the Pharisees—employs to show that although he bore record of himself, yet his record was true. Still the two expressions under notice are utterly at variance. No ingenuity—no amount of sophistry can really reconcile them. They are uttered—irrespectively of consistency—at two different times, to serve two different purposes,—the one to show that Jesus performed all his miracles by his Father's power, and the other to prove that, although he bore testimony to his own greatness, yet his testimony was true. Both assertions, however, CANNOT be in accordance with truth,—one *may* be true, but the other *must* be false.

When Jesus preached on the mount, he told his disciples—"Love your enemies, bless them that curse you, do good to them that hate you, and pray for them that despitefully use you"; but when he sent his disciples to preach the Gospel, he told them to shake off the dust from their feet as they departed from any house or city which refused to receive them; and added that it should be more tolerable for the land of Sodom and Gomorrah, in the day of judgment, than for that city; meaning, of course, the inhabitants of that city. (Matth. v. 44; x. 14, 15.) Now, these two moral precepts are quite at variance with each other. The one enjoins the disciples to return good for evil; the other bids them to evince a scornful and contemptuous feeling, diametrically opposed to love—the love even of one's enemies. If Jesus is to be followed in his precepts, how are we to know, from what he commands, whether we are to love our enemies or shake off the dust from our feet as we part with them on bad terms? This instance, like many others in the Gospels, shows that we cannot depend on Jesus as our moral guide. We must judge from the nature of things as to what is morally right and morally wrong, and can obey the Prophet of Nazareth only in those things in which common sense shows us that he was right. In this case, however, we know that even both his contradictory precepts are wrong.—The one, namely that which commands us to love our enemies is impracticable; and the other is immoral, because the practice of it is an incentive to anger, and therefore an infringement of the social law. To bless those that curse us, and do good to those that hate us, are, however, instructions of a very high moral tone, and worthy of being closely followed. But how contradictory to this doctrine is Jesus's words when he says—" Whosoever shall deny me before men, him will I also deny before my Father which is in heaven."— (Matth. x. 33.) " Those mine enemies which would not that I should reign over them, bring hither, and slay them before me." (Luke xix. 27.) The spirit of cruelty and revenge which these passages breathe is at utter variance with the humane feeling displayed in those which enjoin the returning of good for evil. The principle which Jesus teaches in these is that of returning evil for evil,—of denying a man because the man has denied him; and of killing a man because the man has spurned his authority. It is of no avail to urge that here he is speaking of the punishment of sinners in the day of judgment; for it is absurd to suppose that man is required to be less relentless than God,—that man is commanded to return good for evil, and that God will not do so,—that man is told to love his enemies, and that God will not love his enemies, but torment them for ever in a lake of burning brimstone. This is to require of man to be better than God, and to make it of no benefit for us to contemplate the goodness of our Maker, and endeavour to act in imitation of him.— Still, such is the absurdity of the Christian doctrine. To say that God is *now* so good to his creatures as to return good for evil, but that he will not be so good hereafter, is to say that he is changeable.

In a positive precept, Jesus says—" Whosoever shall smite thee on thy right cheek, turn to him the other also." (Matth. v. 39.) But, as we have seen, when he was about to be arrested, he instructed his followers to be provided with swords.—" He that hath no sword, let him sell his garment, and buy one." (Luke xxii. 36.) It is true that, shortly after when Peter used his sword, he commanded him to desist; but it is clear that he did not give this command in order to maintain the principle of non-resistance. For he already knew that his disciples carried swords; and, besides, the reason which he subjoins (ver. 37.) for ordering them to be provided with these weapons, clearly shows that he wished them to be well armed and fully prepared to prevent his arrest, which he knew would shortly be attempted. This reason evidently implies that he intended them to use their swords when an attempt would be made to arrest him. But nothing could be more inconsistent than thus to order swords to be provided, and yet to enjoin a person not to resist when a ruffian pommeled his cheeks.

Jesus said that he was the light of the world, (John viii. 12.) and that a candle should not be placed under a bushel or a bed, but on a candlestick that all might see its light; because all things should be made manifest. (Luke viii. 16, 17; xi. 33—36.) Yet he said that he delivered his doctrines in parables, in order that the uninitiated might not understand them and be converted. (Mark iv. 11, 12.) He also repeatedly told his disciples that they were the light of the world, and that their light should shine before men, that they might see their good works, and glorify the Father. (Matth. v. 14—16.) Yet he said to them—"Take heed that ye do not your alms before men, to be seen of them; otherwise, ye have no reward of your Father which is in heaven." Matth. vi. 1.) These contradictions are so manifest that no comment can make them clearer.

When a certain young man asked Jesus what he should do in order to inherit eternal life, he told him to sell all that he had, and give to the poor; (Matth. xix. 21.) but when certain followers asked him what they should do that they might work the works of God, his advice to them was to believe in him. (John vi. 28, 29.) When a woman washed, wiped, kissed, and anointed his feet, he told her that her faith had saved her; but he intimated to the publican, in whose house she was, that her works had saved her. (Luke vii. 47—50.) On one occasion he said—"By thy words thou shalt be justified, and by thy words thou shalt be condemned; (Matth. xii. 37.) but on another, he taught that man would be judged according to his works. Sometimes he declared that he who believed on the Son had everlasting life; (John iii. 36.) and at other times, he taught that to comply with the requirements of the Mosaic law gave a title to eternal life. (Luke x. 25—21.) He denounced condemnation against all that did not believe in him, (Mark xvi. 16.) and yet said that no one could come unto him except the Father drew him. (John vi. 44.) Still he exclaimed that those who believed on him *did not* believe on him, but on the Father. (John xii. 44.) His contradictions in reference to faith in him are as numerous as they are irreconcileable.

Equally self-contradictory is he in the following instances. When the Samaritans refused to receive him, because they believed him to be prejudiced against them, having his face "as though he would go to Jerusalem," two of his disciples asked him—"Wilt thou that we command fire to come down from heaven and consume them, even as Elias did?—Jesus rebuked them saying—"The Son of man is not come to destroy men's lives, but to save them." (Luke ix. 51—56.) But, in a short time afterwards, he said—"I am come to send fire on the earth; and what will I, if it be already kindled?"—"Think not that I am come to send peace on earth; I came not to send peace but a sword." (Luke xii. 49, 51—53. Matth. x. 34.) The supposition that, in the two last passages, he meant fire and sword in a figurative sense, is by no means tenable; for in the immediate context he declares that he had come to set a man at variance against his Father, and the daughter against her mother, and that from thenceforth there should be five in one house divided,—three against two, and two against three; evidently showing that he meant to create not only a civil war but even domestic battles, so that a man's foes should be those of his own household. All this is at perfect variance with his declaration that he had not come to destroy men's lives, but to save them. A great many others of his expressions, as recorded in the Gospels, show that he did not intend to save either men's natural or spiritual lives. It is true that, on the other hand, there are expressions in the same Gospels, attributed to him, which show that he wished to save the whole world. But these serve only to contradict other expressions,—show the imperfection of the speaker,—and especially enable the numerous sects of Christians now existing, and the still more numerous sects which have existed, in past ages —the very names of which are now found only in history—to produce Scriptural authority to bolster up their respective conflicting dogmas.

Jesus says, in answer to a heathen woman, who implores him to cast a devil out of her son,—" I am not sent but unto the lost sheep of the house of Israel." And when he dispatches his disciples to preach, he prohibits them to go to the Gentiles, and limits them " to the lost sheep of the house of Israel." Yet he tells the house of Israel—the Jews—" Ye are not of my sheep." (Matth. x. 6; xv. 24. John x. 26.) In like manner does he contradict himself in the following expressions.—" God sent not his son into the world to condemn (κρινη—to judge) the world; but that the world through him might be saved."—" I came not to judge the world, but to save the world."—" For judgment came I into the world." —" If the Son shall make you free, then are ye free indeed."—" The Father judgeth no man, but hath committed all judgment unto the Son." —" And hath given him authority to execute judgment also, because he is the Son of man."—" I have many things to say and to judge of you."— (Comp. John iii. 17; xii. 47. with John v. 22, 25—29; viii. 26, 36; ix. 39.) These contradictory expressions, in whatever sense they are viewed, cannot be harmonised without the utmost violence both to their language, and the evident sense of their context. Throughout the three first Gospels Jesus is made to teach that he was speedily to judge the world.

Even in the same oration he contradicts himself in the most direct manner possible. He tells his disciples—" I have yet many things to say unto you, but ye cannot bear them now;" whereas he had but just told them—" All things that I have heard of my Father I have made known unto you." And he had repeatedly declared that he spoke only the words of the Father. (John xvi. 12; xv. 15; vii. 16.)

His contradictory views and expressions regarding adultery and divorce must be very perplexing to Christians who wish to act in conformity to his doctrines and examples; especially in these days when so many of them in this country repair to the new divorce court in order to have such matters decided. Seeing that he had said, in his Sermon on the mount, that whoever looked lustfully after a woman, committed adultery in his heart,—and that he also taught that a person, in order to follow him, should *leave*, and even *hate* his wife as well as children, (Luke xiv. 26; xviii. 29. Mark x. 29. Matth. v. 28; xix. 29.) the Pharisees asked him what his views were of divorce. In reply, he said—" Whosoever shall put away his wife and marry another, committeth adultery against her; and if a woman shall put away her husband, and be married to another, she committeth adultery." On another occasion he said—" Whosoever shall put away his wife, saving for the cause of fornication, *causeth her* to commit adultery; and whosoever

shall marry her that is divorced committeth adultery. (Comp. Matth. v.
31, 32. with Mark x. 2—12. Matth. xix. 3—12. Luke xvi. 18.) Without
insisting either upon the discrepancy which is in the expressions just cited,
regarding the sin of marrying divorced persons, or upon the impiety of
Christians in contracting alliances with such persons, taking advantage of
the law of men, when the founder of their faith has declared these alliances
adulterous—it is to be observed that—notwithstanding Jesus's rigorous
definition of adultery, making it to exist in a mere desire, or in marrying
a divorced person, yet, when a woman, caught in the very commission of
this crime—a callous wretch who, when standing in the presence of her
judge, and in the awful position of a criminal to be tried for her life, does
not appear to have either expressed or felt any sorrow for her offence—is
brought before him, he, very inconsistently, tells this hardened profligate
that he does not condemn her, and dismisses her without a word of reproof!
It is also to be remarked that he expressly states that it is wrong in any
one to put away his wife, " saving for the cause of fornication,"* advancing as a reason that what God has joined no man should put asunder.—
Yet he clearly teaches that it is a man's duty to part with his wife, in order
to become his disciple. The contradiction here is of a most decided character, and the doctrine taught has a most mischievous tendency. It may
be here also remarked that to say—" Love your enemies," and yet to
declare—" If any man come to me, and hate not his father, and mother,
and wife, and children, and brethren, and sisters, yea, and his own life
also, he cannot be my disciple," is a miserably conflicting doctrine.—
Although, in the Gospels, there are attributed to Jesus, a great many more
expressions contradictory of one another, yet to enumerate them would
only weary the reader.

SECTION VI.—JESUS'S PRECEPTS AND DOCTRINES AT VARIANCE WITH
HIS PRACTICE, AND OF A BIGOTED AND MALEVOLENT SPIRIT.

That the force of example is much greater than that of precept is a
fact which observation and experience have well established. If Jesus had
himself practised the moral precepts which he delivered, he would have

---

* To restrict the grounds of divorce to adultery, however, is a very absurd precept.—
A woman may be a spendthrift, a drunkard, a thief, and a murderess ;—may be of such
a disposition and of such a dangerous character as to make it both disgraceful and unsafe
for her husband to live with her, and yet not an adultress. Still, it is for this crime
alone that Jesus allows a *man* to have a divorce against a woman. As to a *woman* he
mentions her divorcement only prohibitorily, and appears to allow her this power of
redress under no circumstance. Her lord and master may be an adulterer, may famish
her, may beat her, may half kill her, and may render her life miserable in a thousand
ways, yet on no ground does Jesus allow her to have a divorce against her husband. He
falls into the same error as all the ancient philosophers, in making a woman's virtue to
consist in one particular—continence ; and, like them, denies to her any of the rights
and liberties enjoyed by the other sex, making her the slave of her lord. Our legislators,
however, have lately, in behalf of the rights of woman enacted much wiser laws than any
suggested by the precepts of Jesus. Much might be said regarding his absurd declaration
that to marry a divorced woman is adultery.

carried much greater influence upon his disciples, his hearers, and society at large ; and his precepts, at the present distant age, would much more strongly recommend themselves to us who, under pain of eternal perdition, are told to regard him as a pattern of absolute perfection, both in word and deed. According to the Gospels, however, his precepts and doctrines —whether right or wrong—are utterly at variance with his practice or conduct, in a vast number of instances, a few of which—comparatively very few—we now intend to point out.

Jesus preached—" Be not afraid of them that kill the body, and after that have no more that they can do." But we read that, after delivering certain doctrines, unpalatable to the Jews, " he would not walk in Jewry because the Jews sought to kill him,"—that after " they took counsel together for to put him to death," he " walked no more openly among the Jews," but retired into the wilderness,—that when " they sought again to take him," he " escaped out of their hand, and went beyond Jordan,"— that when " they took up stones to cast at him," he hid himself, and went out of the temple, going through the midst of them,"—and that when even his own townsmen " were filled with wrath, and rose up, and thrust him out of the city, and led him unto the brow of the hill whereon their city was built, that they might cast him down headlong," he, " passing through the midst of them, went away." (Luke xii. 4 ; iv. 28—30. John viii. 1, 59 ; x. 39, 40 ; xi. 54.) These certainly are clear indications that he was *afraid of those who killed the body,* and that his practice or his feeling was at variance with his precepts. Of what use was it for him to preach—" Fear not them which kill the body, but are not able to kill the soul," unless he exemplified this heroic conduct ? To hide himself, or retire into a wilderness, when he knew that his enemies were about to attack him, plainly showed that he feared the loss of his life. If he had the courage which he expected others to have, and, particularly, if he had the miraculous power which he is said to have possessed, how easy it would have been for him to stand his ground, entirely fearless of the Jews, —keep them at a distance with a waive of his hand—render their feet motionless by a mere glance ;—and make the stones which they attempted to throw at him fall down at their sides, or even fall upon his own body as harmlessly as if they were feathers ! What a proof would such a course afford all spectators, not only that his precepts and practice were in harmony, but that he had supernatural power at his command ! How much more satisfactory would such a proof have been than the statement that he merely eluded the grasp of his enemies unhurt, which, in a crowd of people, many persons, when assailed, in the present age, manage to effect! Truly, it is said that, when a band of soldiers came to arrest him, they were no sooner told by him that he was the person they wanted, than they " went backward, and fell to the ground." This, however, serves only to show how contradictory the Gospel tales are about Jesus. The three first Gospels make no mention of this remarkable incident, but represent the soldiers, guided by Judas, as marching straight to Jesus and laying hands on him, which made Peter—ignoring all faith in the supernatural power of his master, as well as in that of his own—use his sword, and cut off a man's ear.

Jesus, approvingly citing the Mosaic law, told a certain young man that, in order to inherit eternal life, he must, among other things, *honour his father and mother.* (Mark x. 19.)   But Jesus himself can hardly be said to have at all times practised this precept. The dishonourable manner in which he treated his mother, on two distinct occasions—and each time before a numerous multitude of people—has already been shown. (p. 347.) He also taught that if one man was angry with another he was in danger of judgment, and if he called him a fool he exposed himself to the fire of hell; yet we have seen that, utterly regardless of this doctrine, Jesus was angry with the Scribes and Pharisees, and very often called them fools. He taught poverty of spirit and meekness ; yet he behaved to his antago- nists—the various Jewish religious sects—in a most haughty and over- bearing manner.   He taught love to enemies; but his language to the Scribes and Pharisees—his chief adversaries—amply proves that he did not love them.   He taught that if a man received a blow on the cheek he was to turn the other towards his assailant, in order to receive another blow ; but when he was struck on the face,—probably on his very cheek— for what was deemed insolence to the Jewish pontiff, we do not read that he turned the other cheek for a second blow, but that, acting much more rationally, he remonstrated with the coward who struck him, when under restraint and unable to defend himself. (Mark xxii. 64. John xviii. 19—23.) He taught—"Resist not evil" ; but, in practice, so much further did he go than merely to resist evil, or act in self defence, that he became even the aggressor—flogging out of the temple a number of inoffensive mer- chants, who had a perfectly legitimate right to the position which they occupied.   He taught—"As ye would that men should do to you, do ye also to them likewise;" but, if he had a fig tree, it is not likely that he would have wished it to be withered,—if he had two thousand swine, it is not probable that he would have wished them to be drowned,—if he had been instead of the merchants in the temple, it is doubtful whether he would have much relished the lashes of the whip, or liked to have his money scattered under the feet of a tumultuous crowd,—if he had been one of the Scribes or Pharisees, it is very questionable whether he would have liked the manner in which he used them, and the foul language with which he bespattered them.   Indeed, in a thousand instances has Jesus acted contrary to his precept of doing unto others as he would have wished them to do unto him.

Further : he taught brevity in prayer, and prohibited "vain repeti- tions," in imitation of the heathen, who thought they should be heard "for their much speaking." (Matth. vi. 7.)   But he did not himself practise this brevity.   John (xvii.) occupies a whole chapter of twenty-six long verses in giving a *verbatim et literatim* report of his prayer on one occasion, which prayer is not only very long, but contains a great number of "repetitions" or tautologies.   We find also that—in dread of the fate which awaited him, and in entreaties that it might be averted—he prayed so long that his disciples, who stood at a short distance from him, fell asleep,—prayed, apparently, for an hour, during which period he expected his disciples to keep awake.   While thus praying, it is expressly stated that, at different intervals, he "spake the same words."   But in neither of these instances did he use the words of the formula which he prescribed to his followers. (Matth. vi. 7—13; xxvi. 39—44. Mark xiv. 35—39.)

His precept is here at perfect variance with his practice, in regard to an important Christian duty. He prescribes brevity and prohibits repetitions and verbosity in prayer; yet he himself indulges in long prayers, repetitions, and verbosity, to a remarkable extent. Not to dwell on the anomaly of one divine Being supplicating another for aid, which appears very strange to human reason, it may be remarked that it would be difficult to advance any valid reason that—if Jesus gave the best possible instructions to his disciples how to succeed in praying to the Father—the same course would not have been the most successful for him to adopt in praying to the same object of worship.

Jesus further taught that people should communicate to others all the knowledge they possessed—especially knowledge of divine things. He repeatedly said to his disciples—"Ye are the light of the world : a city that is set on an hill cannot be hid. Neither do men light a candle and put it under a bushel, but on a candlestick ; and it giveth light to all that are in the house. Let your light so shine before men, that they may see your good works, and glorify your Father which is in heaven." (Matth. v. 14—16. Mark iv. 21, 22. Luke viii. 16, 17 ; xi. 33.) On some occasions, when inculcating the same duty, he taught that there was nothing hid that should not be manifested, and no secret that should not come abroad.—After evincing such a liberal spirit, in precept, who would have expected to find it the practice of Jesus to communicate his instructions in dark and unintelligible parables, avowedly that his audience might fail to understand him, "lest at any time they should be converted." (Mark iv. 12.) What influence could his precepts have even upon his disciples, when they perceived that his practice was diametrically opposed to them ? They must have thought that what he said of the Scribes and Pharisees was notoriously verified in him, namely, that they laid heavy burdens on the shoulders of others, but that they themselves would not touch such burdens with one of their fingers.

Humility was a virtue which Jesus often inculcated, both by precept and symbol, pointing out little children as emblems of this disposition, and declaring that whoever exalted himself should be abased, and whoever should humble himself should be exalted. (Matth. xviii. 1—4 ; xxii. 12. Mark x, 13—15, 43.) He also frequently disclaimed all intention of seeking his own glory, laying it down as a maxim, on one occasion, that he who spoke of himself sought his own glory. (John vii. 18.) Still the language attributed to him throughout the Gospels, when speaking of himself, or when others, in his presence, expressed their opinion of him, is brimful of egotism, self-praise, and self-glorification. He said—"I am the light of the world"—"I am the bread of life," and so on. He also said that he was greater than the temple, greater than Solomon, greater than Jonas, and that he was lord of the Sabbath, demanding that all men should honour him as they honoured the Father; yet he said he sought not his own glory, or honoured himself ! He denounced all previous prophets and patriarchs as thieves and robbers, speaking of them in the following uncharitable language—"All that *ever* came before me are thieves and robbers." (John x. 8.) On several occasions, he spoke of Abraham, Moses, and other worthies, whom the Old Testament shows to have been men under divine influence, holding daily and hourly communication with God. He frequently inveighed against the Mosaic law, which Christians say was divine, and therefore perfect. With the view of praising himself, by way of contrast, he attributed falsehood to Abraham. In a discussion with the Jews, he undertook to prove the divine origin of his misssion, advancing as an argument that he bore witness of his Father, and that his Father bore witness of him. Not satisfied with this sophistical reasoning—the substance of which was that he proved his Father, and that his Father proved him—the Jewish doctors asked him—" Where is thy Father?" and after hearing his reply, asked him—"Who art thou?" In the course of the controversy that ensued Jesus told them that they were not the children of Abraham, but the offspring of the devil, and that, as to Abraham, from whom they boasted to have sprung, he had not told the truth.*—" Ye seek to kill me, a man that hath told you the truth, which I have heard of God: *this did not Abraham.*" (John viii. 40.) If Jesus's conduct displays any meekness or humility, the notions entertained, in the present age, of these ornaments of human nature are decidedly wrong.

In his conversation with an abandoned woman of Samaria, instead of inspiring her with his greatness, by a magnanimous behaviour—glowing benevolence, transcendent wisdom, and other qualities of mental excellence, which, by means of their inherent tendency, always carry a proportionate influence on other minds, he must, in self-praise, tell her that, if she knew who asked her for water, *she* would ask *him* for a blessing. His apparent vainglory was offensive even to this low woman and made her exclaim— " Art thou greater than our father Jacob?" Jesus, however, proceeded to tell her in a vaunting strain that he could give her water that should be in her " a well of water springing up into everlasting life." (John iv. 14.)

---

* Abraham certainly did tell, at least, two notorious falsehoods; to which, perhaps, Jesus alludes. When he was very old and his wife at the advanced age of sixty-five, he took her with him into Egypt. Fearing that the Egyptians—struck with her matchless beauty even at this venerable old age—would kill him in order to obtain possession of her, he told her to pretend that she was his sister, while he also would tell the same tale. (Gen. xii. 10—20.) No sooner did the Egyptian princes glance at Sarah, than they were enchanted with her beauty. Even the king became enamoured of her, and had her brought to his harem, having been assured by Abraham that she was his sister.— The monarch, however, was soon glad to rid himself of her.—The Lord, because of Abraham's deception, punished Pharaoh and his house with severe plagues for taking Sarah; although he had done so with her own consent, with the acquiescence of her husband, and in consequence of the latter's misrepresentation! Sarah's beauty appears to have been of a wonderfully unfading sort; for in twenty-five years afterwards—when she was ninety years of age—we find that her irresistible charms were equally dangerous to the eye of man, and were again the cause that Abraham had recourse to falsehood. Alas! how human nature has degenerated! How much sooner female beauty now fades than in the time of Sarah! When, at the great age of ninety, she was pregnant, and travelling with her lord through the territories of a Phœnician king named Abimelech, her beauty had the same enchanting effect on this monarch as it had had twenty-five years before, on the Egyptian king. (Gen. xxi. 18.) It must however be admitted that Sarah's conduct was as singular as her beauty was imperishable. But to waive this point—the Lord, in a dream, threatened Abimelech with instant death, if he touched his new mistress. Yet, why was the Lord wrath with Abimelech for believing Abraham's falsehood? And even if the monarch sinned thereby, why curse all the women of his house for his fault? But as the Lord prevented him from sinning, why punish him?— Why load the real cause of all the mischief with so many gifts? These, and a thousand other questions, naturally present themselves to the meditative Christian, in reading this singular narrative.

With a remarkable degree of vanity did Jesus ask his disciples—
"Whom do men say that I the Son of man am?" Having been told that
some said he was John the Baptist, some that he was Elias, others that he
was Jeremias, or one of the prophets, he does not appear to have thought
this compliment by any means flattering; and he therefore asked his disci-
disciples—"But whom say *ye* that I am?" Whereupon Peter answered—
"Thou art the Christ, the Son of the living God." No sooner was this
said than Jesus, as if elevated by the compliment, broke out in accents of
praise to Peter, pouring upon him a profusion of blessings, attributing to
his knowledge a supernatural origin, and giving him absolute authority on
earth and in heaven.—"Blessed art thou Simon Bar-jona; for flesh and
blood hath not revealed it unto thee, but my Father which is in heaven.
And I say also unto thee, That thou art Peter, and upon this rock I will
build my church, and the gates of hell shall not prevail against it. And I
will give *unto thee* the keys of the kingdom of heaven; and whatsoever
*thou shalt bind on earth shall be bound in heaven ; and whatsoever thou shalt
loose on earth shall be loosed in heaven."* (Matth. xvi. 13—19.) So well
paid was this poor illiterate fisherman for praising his master that he was
made the *punlike* basis of the Christian church, and invested with absolute
papal power over the whole human race! Here we plainly see that Peter
complimented Jesus, and that Jesus, gratified thereby, complimented Peter
in return. Such a desire for praise of men, however, was perfectly opposite to the humiliation which Jesus so frequently inculcated. And are we
to take his conduct on this point as a pattern? If we imitated him in our
love of praise and self-glorification, would we not make ourselves odious
in the eyes of all men of sense and of proper moral feeling?

Many of the foregoing instances, like others found in the Gospels,
besides showing a disagreement between Jesus's precepts and practices,
also indicate that considerable bigotry, illiberality, bitterness of spirit, and
even a malevolent tendency, pervaded much that he said and did. It is
admitted that, likewise in the Gospels, there are attributed to him many
expressions of noble feelings; such as weeping over Jerusalem, praying
when on the cross for forgiveness for those who maltreated him, and
inviting all who laboured and were heavy laden to come to him and obtain
mental ease. But the narrow and malevolent spirit evinced by the same
person, on other occasions, ill contrasts with these touching emotions, and
exposes the fickleness and imperfection of the mind from which both could
emanate. Very limited was the benevolence which dictated such language
as—"I pray not for the world, but for them which thou hast given me,"
—"Give not that which is holy unto the dogs, neither cast ye your pearls
before swine,"—"I thank thee, O Father, Lord of heaven and earth,
because thou hast hid these things from the wise and prudent, and hast
revealed them unto babes,"—"Whosoever hath, to him shall be given,
and he shall have more abundance; but whosoever hath not, from him
shall be taken away even that he hath,"—"These twelve Jesus sent forth,
and commanded them saying, Go not into the way of the Gentiles, and
into any city of the Samaritans enter ye not; but go rather to the lost
sheep of the house of Israel,"—"I am not sent but unto the lost sheep of
the house of Israel,"—"It is not meet to take the children's bread, and
to cast it to dogs."—Such are a few of the many expressions found in the

Gospels, indicative of the narrow philanthropy of Jesus. The two passages last cited are portions of his answer to a Grecian woman, who implored him to cast a demon out of her child. (Mark vii. 26—29.) In reply to her entreaties, Jesus said—" Let the children be first filled ; for it is not meet to take the children's bread, and to cast it unto the dogs." To this insulting language the woman very deferentially, but aptly, rejoined—" Yes Lord ; yet the dogs under the table eat of the children's crumbs."— Whereupon Jesus said to her—" For this saying go thy way ; the devil is gone out of thy daughter." Now, what Jesus said to this distressed woman conveyed an exclusive, bigoted, despising idea, which could hardly come from a teacher, whose bosom glowed with benevolence towards the whole human race, and who would fain clasp the whole world in the arms of charity. Nor are such words, by any means, in accordance with a sound notion of even mere justice. To suppose that the Creator of the universe preferred the Jews to all other nations, or preferred even one of his rational creatures to another, irrespectively of any moral consideration, involves an idea of partiality and injustice. If, however, this Grecian woman had been less witty—for which she could not be blamed—if she had been less happy in her repartee about the dogs eating the crumbs, it appears that Jesus would not have driven the devil out of her daughter, because he expressly said to her—" For *this saying* go thy way ; the devil is gone out of thy daughter." Hence, it is clear that it was the *merit* of *this saying* which induced him to expel the demon ;—not the love of doing good,—not an unconditional and purely benevolent disposition to ameliorate the condition of mortals. And agreeably to this, it is repeatedly said in the Gospels, that he did this or that because of something in the person who besought his good offices. If the Syrophœnician happened to have been endowed with less sense—happened to have been a dull, spiritless woman, and yet have been a most worthy person in other respects, Jesus would not, apparently, have commanded the demon to quit her daughter. There is not only bigotry, but considerable injustice pervading the whole of this transaction.

The same narrow and malevolent spirit characterises the answer he gave to his disciples, already cited, when they demanded of him why he spoke in parables.—" Unto you it is given to know the mysteries of the kingdom of God ; but unto them *that are without*, all these things are done in parables ; that seeing they may see, and not perceive ; and hearing they may hear, and not understand ; lest at any time they should be converted, and their sins should be forgiven them." (Mark iv. 10—12. Matth. xiii. 10—17 ; xi. 25. Luke viii. 10 ; x. 21—24.) Hence it is clear that Jesus designedly kept all people, except his twelve disciples, ignorant of the true meaning of the doctrines he preached. What would be thought, in the present age, of a public instructor who would act in this malignant manner towards his audience ? But in Jesus, such a conduct was still more culpable and irrational ; for he continually endeavoured to convince people that he had been sent from God to save them from their sins. He continually exhorted his hearers to believe in him, and yet endeavoured to keep from them the evidence which was necessary for them to have, before they could believe. Such a conduct cannot be deemed either rational, wise, or benevolent, especially when it is recollected that Jesus repeatedly pronounced eternal damnation upon all who did not believe in him. How different the sentiment breathed by the passages just cited to show Jesus's bigotry and illiberal disposition, from the aspirations of many of the noble precepts attributed to him in the Gospels, such as—" bless them that curse you"—" do good to them that hate you"—" Let your light shine before men," and so on! The one class is the language of the most magnanimous disposition, the other the utterance of a vicious mind; the one glows with the noblest feelings of humanity, the other rankles with profound hatred; the one radiates with super-human benignity, the other burns with the enmity of a fiend. If both emanated from Jesus, they prove him to have been much more inconsistent and fickle than any public teacher known to history, whether ancient or modern. If only one class of these expressions came from him, how are we to know which? We have, however, no good reason for believing that both did not proceed from him, if ever one did. How then are those much abused Scribes and Pharisees—indeed all who heard him, except his twelve disciples—to be blamed for not believing in him, if he wilfully and of set purpose delivered his doctrines to them in such a manner that, hearing him, they should not understand him, lest they should be converted, and their sins be forgiven? Such a doctrine as this carries on the face of it evidence, not only that it did not proceed from the just God, who makes his sun rise on the evil and on the good, and sends rain on the just and on the unjust, but that it is not the production of either a wise or virtuous man. It has not a grain of philanthropy; nay, it strongly savours of the misanthropist; it contains an open avowal of purpose to deceive men by a system of mystification which concealed the truth from them, and led them to eternal perdition; in a word, it is more flagrant than any thing which can be attributed to Mahomed the impostor, who never thus unblushingly avowed the practice of such a system of wilful and malignant deception on the people.

This narrow spirit—this aversion to do good to mankind generally, is not a disposition occasionally evinced in incidental expressions of Jesus, but is a trait in the character of most of his parables, and pervades his general conduct; which no one can fail to see, if he read the Gospels with an unbiassed mind; notwithstanding the declaration that he went about doing good; which good, however, is shown to have consisted almost entirely in healing bodily diseases. But even when he effected a cure on any person, he displayed the same narrow spirit, in charging him not to make known the benefit he had received. He charged even his disciples not to tell any man that he was the Christ. Very frequently, when great multitudes of anxious hearers were about him, he withdrew, and left them in disappointment. (Matth. viii. 18. Mark i. 35—38; iii. 7. Luke iv. 42; v. 16.) But why thus retire? Why not impart spiritual knowledge to these multitudes who appear anxious to receive it? Why not convert them all? To deny that he had not the will, or that he had not the power to do so, is to deny his divinity. To suppose a God limited either in benevolence or power is a contradiction. But that he aimed at doing good to the human race at large—or at what is called saving the world—is flatly denied by a vast number of his own expressions, which display remarkable uncharitableness, and, in some instances, the most wretched malevolence. He delighted to dwell on the idea that *many were called, but*

BB

few chosen, and that by far the greater number of the human race would be plunged into the fire of his Gehenna, while only a select few would be received into his kingdom of heaven. (Matth. vii. 14, 22, 23 ; xiii. 1—58; xix. 25—29 ; xx. 16; xxii. 14 ; xxv. 31—46. Luke xiii. 23—30.)

SECTION VII.—THE OBSCURITY OF JESUS'S TEACHING, AND THE EVASIVE CHARACTER OF HIS ANSWERS TO QUESTIONS PUT TO HIM TOUCHING HIS DOCTRINE AND MISSION.

It was with the utmost propriety, and with noble courage—considering the position he held, and the times in which he lived—that Dr. Thomas Edwards, in a sermon preached before the University of Cambridge, in 1790, said, regarding the Scriptures, that if their obscurity "cannot be denominated a considerable error, it will readily be acknowledged to be a considerable imperfection." To no portion of them does this remark apply more forcibly than to Jesus's discourses, as reported in the Gospels. His mode of teaching—if it can be called teaching—was habitually and intentionally obscure, enigmatical, and pretentious. His answers to questions put to him were never direct, clear, and explicit ; but almost always ambiguous, dark, and often evasive. He evinced a great dislike to answer any questions in explanation of his dark sayings ; and whenever he condescended to do so, he always did it in such a manner as showed that he had a rooted aversion to be put to the test, or to enlighten those who were anxious for instruction. He loved the mystical and enigmatic, and was delighted with blind belief in his dogmas. He dreaded being known, and shunned full and free inquiry into the truth of his doctrines, and the reality of his miracles. While intolerant of the opinions of others, he expected his own to be received without any rational grounds of belief; and all who did not receive them he anathematised. It has justly been observed that truth publishes her precepts to be examined,—is mild, courteous, and tolerant of the views of others ; but that error is haughty and intolerant,—impatient of intrusion and adverse to discussion. Mr. Newman, in his Phases of Faith, (p. 157.) commenting on Jesus's reply to the rich young man, who came to him for religious instruction, very properly remarks that it appears it was not so much his aim to enlighten this youth, "as to stop his mouth, and keep up his own ostentation of omniscience. Had he desired to enlighten him, surely no mere dry dogmatic command was needed, but an intelligent guidance of a willing and trusting soul." It is clear, however, to any one who has attentively read the Gospels, that obscurity, dogmatism, and evasive replies, are the most prominent traits in the character of Jesus's teaching. Even when a child of twelve years old, obscurity was a prominent feature in the words which he uttered. In general, clearness and simplicity characterise the language of youth. But at this period of life, Jesus spoke so obscurely that even his parents could not understand him. When, coming from a national feast, they had lost him and had afterwards found him in the temple, he said, in reply to their reproof,—" Wist ye not that I must be about my Father's business? And *they understood not* the saying which he spake unto them." (Luke ii. 49, 50.)

In his conversation with the Samaritan woman, Jesus is peculiarly obscure and apparently mystical. Fatigued and thirsty in travelling from Judea to Galilee, he sat down on the brink of a well near Sychar, in the country of the Samaritans, while his disciples went into the city to purchase food. As he thus rested, a Samaritan female came to draw water from the well. Jesus asked her to allow him to drink from the pitcher she had in her hand. His Jewish countenance betraying his nation, the woman was astonished that a Jew should ask her—a Samaritan—to give him water; since the Jews and Samaritans, on religious grounds—like the different sects of Christians, in the present age, such as Protestants and Roman Catholics—profoundly hated one another, and refrained from all communication. Jesus, however, nobly surmounting his national prejudice for the nonce, said to the woman—" If thou knewest the gift of God, and who it is that saith to thee, Give me to drink, thou wouldest have asked of him, and he would have given thee living water." (John iv. 10.) But how dark and unintelligible must this expression have been to the poor benighted Samaritan, who, from the profligate life she led, appears not to have belonged to the more educated and intelligent class of society! That what Jesus said was *not* understood by her is positively proved by her rejoinder.—" Sir, thou hast nothing to draw with, and the well is deep; from whence then hast thou that living water?" Jesus does not shed a ray of light upon the question asked him—does not attempt to correct the mistaken notion of the woman—does not tell what he means by *the gift of God*, about the meaning of which the commentators to this day are puzzled—does not tell her whence he had that *living water*—does not explain to her that he did not mean, by *living water*, the same as the Orientals meant, namely, *spring water*, or water in a literal sense, such as she drew from the well; but replies to her by uttering another still more obscure sentence.—" Whosoever drinketh of this water shall thirst again; but whosoever drinketh of the water that I shall give him shall never thirst; but the water that I shall give him shall be in him a well of water springing up into everlasting life." The meaning of this language is as dark and uncertain as that of the foregoing, and has given commentators as much work to unravel it. But if it means what they say, namely *the Holy Ghost, grace*, and so on, it is unquestionable that it was far too enigmatical for this loose woman to have the faintest idea of the sense which the speaker intended to convey. For her answer was—" Sir, give me this water, that I thirst not, neither come hither to draw." Still, Jesus did not attempt to enlighten this heretic and courtezan whose conversion he had undertaken; but, when she pressed him to give her some of the wonderful water of which he had spoken, he turned the conversation, and told her to call her husband thither. Of the same dark nature, however, continued his conversation with her, till his disciples appeared and put an end to it; being much annoyed—either from their knowledge of the character of the lady, or because she was a Samaritan—that their master should thus scandalise them by his tete-a-tete with her, yet not venturing to ask him what he sought of her, or even why he talked to her. (ver. 27.) But what concerns us at present is the anomaly that, although Jesus came to preach the

2 BB

Gospel to the poor, yet he spoke so obscurely that those whom he addressed could not understand him.

Of the same mystic, ambiguous, and dogmatic character is the doctrine which he delivered to Nicodemus, a Jewish senator who came to him for instruction, but apparently received very little. He introduced himself by acknowledging Jesus's divine mission, which gave the latter an excellent opportunity to declare himself the Messiah, no Jews being now at hand to stone him. But his reply was evasive and irrelevant, as well as unintelligible to his new disciple.—"Except a man be born again, he cannot see the kingdom of God." (John iii. 3.) The Jewish ruler not being able to understand this enigmatical expression, asked with wonder—"How can a man be born when he is old? Can he enter the second time into his mother's womb and be born?" Jesus attempts to illustrate; but the unhappy mode he employs is that of explaining one obscure expression by a series of other expressions still more obscure—"Verily, verily, I say unto thee, Except a man be born of water and of the Spirit, he cannot enter the kingdom of God. That which is born of the flesh is flesh; and that which is born of the spirit is spirit. Marvel not that I said unto thee, Ye must be born again. The wind bloweth where it listeth, and thou hearest the sound thereof, but canst not tell whence it cometh and whither it goeth : so is every one that is born of the spirit."* Although the fact that Nicodemus appears to have been a man of ordinary acumen, and one whose high position in society—besides being a teacher—is a guarantee that he had received what, in that age, would be deemed liberal education, yet he utterly failed to acquire any idea of what Jesus meant, notwithstanding the pains he took to explain himself.† He therefore exclaimed —"How can these things be?" Imagining that the Jewish senator was

---

* If the English translators had not materially clarified this passage, by rendering it in harmony with their theological creed, it would be much more obscure than it is— would be as obscure in English as it is in Greek. The word πνευμα used throughout the passage, and evidently meaning the same thing in every instance, is translated in one place *spirit*, but in another *wind*. The word really means *wind* or *air*, and the passage literally and properly reads in the following absurd manner—"Except a man be born of water and *wind* (πνευμα) he cannot enter the kingdom of God. That which is born of the flesh is flesh, and that which is born of the *wind* (πνευμα) is *wind*. Marvel not that I said unto thee, Ye must be born again. The *wind* (πνευμα) bloweth where it listeth, and thou hearest the sound thereof, but canst not tell whence it cometh, nor whither it goeth : so is every one that is born of the *wind*. (πνευμα.)" There is no doubt that the writer, whoever he was, meant the same thing by πνευμα in every instance in this passage. And that he meant *wind* is clear from what he says of the wind blowing, and of its sound being heard, while itself invisible. In other places, the word may signify *breath, inspiration, life, &c.* (Vid. p. 110.)

† The doctrine of being born again is much older than the time of Jesus. As we shall hereafter have occasion to notice more fully, it was much inculcated by the Brahmin priests, and others. Moreover, it was current among the Jews at the time. It was also taught by Pythagoras, Plato, &c. (Strauss Leben Jesu. vol. ii. p. 154.) On the supposition that the Gospels are historically true, it is not a little singular therefore that Nicodemus should have been so ignorant as he appears of this doctrine. But there is ample evidence, particularly in John's Gospel, that it is not a narrative of facts which had even tradition for their basis, but that it is a composition fabricated according to the fancy of the writer. The discourses, whether dialogues or monologues, are so complete and concatenated, and also of such length, that it is absurd to imagine that the writer from memory wrote with such exactness. It has also throughout the peculiarity

very obtuse, Jesus twittingly asked him—"Art thou a master of Israel, and knowest not these things?" He then proceeded to say that he had told him only what he had known and had seen ; and that as he had told only of earthly things, and he had not believed, he would scarcely believe if be told him of heavenly things. He appears, however, to have silenced, but not to have convinced, the humble senator with the following contradictory words.—"No man hath ascended up to heaven, but he that came down from heaven, even the Son of man which is in heaven." Jesus, when he thus said that no one but himself had ascended to heaven, appears to have forgotten Enoch and Elias. But if is not very easy to understand how he had *then* ascended to heaven, seeing that he was on earth talking to Nicodemus. On the same ground it is difficult to believe that he was *then* "in heaven." Was it possible for Nicodemus, although a "teacher in Israel," to understand the ambiguous, enigmatical, and contradictory doctrine which Jesus broached to him ? Although he perceived that his disciple did not comprehend him,—although the last question which the solicitous senator asked was—"How can these things be ?" yet Jesus did not offer a word of explanation, but taunted him with being a "master," and yet unable to understand anything about being born again, and averred that he had advanced nothing to him but what was well known ; evidently expecting him to exercise blind belief in his mystic dogmas. This is a deplorable feature in the character of a public teacher, especially a missionary said to have been divinely sent to enlighten the world. If, in reality, Jesus had been thus sent, we would be driven to the conclusion that God devised means to counteract his designs ; that he thus hindered the salvation, not only of the Jews who heard the discourses of Jesus, but that of all, in the present age, who critically read the Gospels; and that he requires us, if we believe at all, to renounce and despise our own reasoning powers, and exercise a blind submissive faith in the authority of written dogmas, which are so obscurely worded that we can form no conception of their truth. This is contrary to all proper notions of an infinitely wise and just God. We may, however, rest assured that no written precepts which are obscure, mystic, or unintelligible, have been intended by the Creator of the universe for the guidance of his creatures. If he were to give us a written book for our instruction, his precepts

of putting the discourses which it attributes to Jesus into a form which enables the writer to represent those who listened to the discourses as failing to understand them, or as understanding literally that which was meant figuratively. Strauss, in page 187 of the volume just cited, comes to the conclusion that the discourses attributed to Jesus in this Gospel, are mainly free compositions of the writer. "Their gradual transitions, only occasionally rendered obscure by the mystical depth of meaning in which they lie—transitions in which one thought developes itself out of another, and a succeeding proposition is frequently but an explanatory amplification of the preceding one—are indicative of a pliable, unresisting mass, such as is never presented to a writer by the traditional sayings of another, but by such only as proceeds from the stores of his own thought, which he moulds according to his will. For this reason the contribution of tradition to these stores of thought were not so likely to have been particular independent sayings of Jesus, as rather certain ideas which formed the basis of many of his discourses, and which were modified and developed according to the bent of a mind of Greek or Alexandrian culture." For the Gospels, however, to be compositions of this nature is even more disastrous to Christianity than if the dark sayings they contain were positively known to have come from Jesus himself.—See Greg's Creed of Christendom, p. 144.

would be as clear, intelligible, and definite, in that book as they are in the book of nature.

In the Gospels, the hearers of Jesus, and particularly those termed the Jews, are repeatedly represented as failing to understand what the words he uttered really meant. In telling the Pharisees that whoever did not enter the sheepfold through the door was a thief and a robber, and that the sheep fled from him, so unintelligible were his words that even these people—whose learning and knowledge of Oriental lore were of a superior character—"understood not what things they were which he spake unto them." (John x. 6.) In like manner, when he had delivered to these people and other Jews a long oration about his heavenly descent, we are told that "they understood not that he spake to them of the Father"; and that he asked them—"why do ye not understand my speech?" (John viii. 27, 43.) Jesus having flogged the merchants out of the temple, the Jews asked him what sign—or rather miracle—he could show them, as a proof of his authority for the strange outrage he had just committed. His reply to this reasonable demand was—"Destroy this temple, and in three days I will raise it up." Upon this, the Jews—rather than pulling down that magnificent building, in order to see whether Jesus could rebuild it by a miracle—remarked—"Forty and six years was this temple in building, and wilt thou rear it up in three days?" Jesus does not utter a word to correct any mistake in their notions,—does not intimate that he did not mean the temple in which he then stood, out of which he had just driven the merchants, and concerning which he was then debating with the Jews,—does not furnish those whom he addresses with the slightest notion that his words were figurative. That they understood him to use the word *temple* in the ordinary acceptation of the term, was, under the circumstances, a natural and almost necessary consequence.— For how could they imagine that he did not use it so, seeing that he was at the time in the temple, and speaking of what he thought an abuse of the temple? Yet, singularly enough, the writer of John's Gospel tells us that "he spake of the temple of his body," and that when he had "risen from the dead, his disciples remembered that he had said this unto them." (John ii. 18—22.)—as much as to say that previously they did not understand his expression about building up the temple in three days to mean his resurrection. But why did not Jesus explain himself, when he perceived that his words were so obscure that, not only the uninitiated, but even his immediate disciples, laboured under a false notion as to their meaning? Was this not the duty of an honest teacher? If, by the word temple, he meant his own person, as he was at the time in the Jewish temple, and speaking of this temple, had he not evidently a design to mislead and deceive? How easily he could have told these Jews that he meant "the temple of his body"! When he was on his trial before the Jewish pontiff we are told that two false witnesses thus deposed—"This fellow said, I am able to destroy the temple of God, and to build it in three days." (Matth. xxvi. 61.) The high priest asked him what he had to say to the charge which these witnesses brought against him. Jesus, however, "held his peace." But were these two accusers "false witnesses"? Have we not the testimony of John's Gospel that he had given utterance to this very expression? These witnesses could not have known that he meant his own body ; for it is said that his own disciples did not know this till after his resurrection. There is no evidence that, on any other occasion, he used the word *temple* to designate his body. How then could these witnesses, the Jews at large, or even his own disciples, imagine that, by a temple, he meant a human body ? And as he had uttered the expression under notice—whatever was its intended but secret import—when, apparently, standing within the precincts of the Jewish temple, how can these two witnesses be denounced *false ?* If they are false witnesses on the ground that it was his own body which Jesus meant by the word *temple,* then how proper, how wise, how just, how honest, how charitable, it would have been in him to declare before the high priest that, by the words these witnesses attributed to him, he meant *the temple of his body !* How this would have at once shut the mouths of these witnesses ! How utterly it would have prevented scoffers, when he was on the cross, from exclaiming in derision—" Ah ! thou that destroyest the temple, and buildest it in three days, save thyself, and come down from the cross !" (Mark xv. 29.) But no : there is something in the whole tenor of Jesus's words and actions, as reported in the Gospels, which has a tendency to mislead, conceal—deceive.* A similar trait is perceptible in the delineations we have of the character of almost all the heathen deities ; as if men could not conceive of divinity apart from the notion of ambiguity, illusion, and cunning.

Not only was Jesus's teaching so obscure that he could not be understood by his general hearers who had not been initiated into the mysteries of his doctrines, but even by his chosen apostles whom he sent to teach these doctrines. A great many instances are recorded in the Gospels, either of his obscurity, or of their obtuseness. When he took them into retirement, for the express purpose of teaching them that the " Son of man" would be delivered unto the Gentiles, maltreated, put to death, and raised from the dead on the third day, " they understood none of these things ; and the saying was hid from them ; neither knew they the things which were spoken." (Luke xviii. 31—34; ix. 45. Mark ix. 10, 31, 32.) When in regal pomp he entered Jerusalem on an ass, and made remarks upon the proceedings of the cortege, " these things understood not his disciples. at the first ; but when Jesus was glorified, then remembered they that these things were written of him, and that they had done these things unto him." (John xii. 16.) When he taught them to " take heed and

* Professor Newman (Phases of Faith, p. 162.) remarks—on the accusation brought against Jesus by the two false witnesses,—" The form of imputation in Mark xv. 58. would make it possible to imagine,—if the *three days* were left out, and if his words were *not* said in demand of a sign,—that Jesus had merely avowed that though the outward Jewish temple were to be destroyed, he would erect a church of worshippers as a spiritual temple. If so, 'John' has grossly misrepresented him, and then obtruded a very far-fetched explanation. But whatever was the meaning of Jesus, if it was honest, I think he was bound to explain it ; and not leave a suspicion of imposture to rankle in men's minds." In a note on the same place, he also adds—" If the account in John is not wholly false, I think the reply in every case is very discreditable. If literal, it all but indicates wilful imposture. If mystical, it is disingenuously evasive ; and it tended, not to instruct, but to irritate, and to move suspicion and contempt. Is this the course for a religious teacher ?—to speak darkly, so as to mislead and prejudice ; and this, when he represents it as a matter of spiritual life and death to accept his teaching and his supremacy ?"

beware of the leaven of the Pharisees and of the Sadducees," so obscure
was this doctrine to them, and so far were they from understanding it,
that "they reasoned among themselves," and very naturally concluded
that—since the want of bread was the question at issue—Jesus cautioned
them against the leaven of which he spoke because they had no bread.—
He certainly intimated to them that they had mistaken his meaning, and
severely censured them for their dulness of apprehension ; but very cautiously avoided telling them plainly what he meant.   Matthew imagines
that he meant the doctrine of the Pharisees and Sadducees, and says that,
at length, the disciples so understood him.   But the evangelist must be
mistaken, for on another occasion Jesus is a little more explicit in giving
utterance to a similar expression, and says—"Beware ye of the leaven of
the Pharisees, which is *hypoçrisy.*"   Now it is scarcely credible that Jesus,
with all his ambiguity, would call a *doctrine* hypocrisy.   (Comp. Matth.
xvi. 5—12, Mark viii. 14—21. with Luke xii. 1.)   When he had uttered
a series of dark sayings about plants which his Father had not planted,
and about the blind leading the blind, Peter said—"Declare unto us this
parable."   The explanation given by Jesus was even more unintelligible
than the parable itself, and utterly irrelevant. (Matth. xv. 13—26. Mark
vii. 14—23.)   Very frequently, indeed, do we find his disciples requesting
him to explain to them his dark parables.   This was the case in regard to
the parable of the tares, of the sower, and others. (Matth. xiii. 36. Mark
iv. 10. Luke viii. 9.)   Of what use, therefore, was such teaching ?   And,
in Jesus's case, where was the justice of condemning people for not believing what they did not, and could not understand.   One of the gravest
defects in a public teacher is inability to make his audience, or even his
initiated disciples to understand him.   This utterly disqualifies him for his
office, and makes his attempt to teach quite abortive.   It is this obscurity in
Jesus's teaching which has furnished work for thousands, nay, millions of
commentators, for the last eighteen centuries, in attempting to unriddle his
enigmas.   It may be urged that Jesus employed this parabolic or allegorical
style in imitation of all Eastern teachers of ancient times.*   Granted ; but

---

* It is amusing to observe how, in ancient times, the dark, enigmatical, and allegorical style was practised, particularly in the East, by all public teachers—both Jews and
Gentiles. By this means they explained away the fabulous tales current regarding their
gods, and discoursed on every branch of knowledge known to them.   They deemed
religion a mystery not to be publicly explained, and always delivered its dogmas clothed
in dark allegories. (Cic. de Nat. Deor. lib. ii. iii.   Spencer de Legibus Heb. p. 182.
Clerici Hist. Eccles. p. 23.) The Egyptians and Chaldeans were noted for their dark
sayings. (Simon Hist. Crit. des Comment. p. 4.)   Gale (Opuscula Mythologica) gives
an account of several ancient books expressly written as instructions to interpret allegories. The Greek poets, Homer not excepted, are by their scholiasts regarded as
treating of their gods in a mystical style.   The Stoic philosophers dressed the whole
heathen theology in allegorical language. (Cic. de Nat. Deor. lib. ii.)   The Pythagorean
philosophy was taught in enigmatical expressions, the meaning of which was studiously
concealed from the vulgar mind, and revealed even to the initiated only gradually as
their years of maturity were thought to qualify them for its reception. Plato and his
followers, in the Groves of Academia, practised the same mode of teaching religion,
especially theogony.   The writings attributed to Paul the apostle are replete with mystical and enigmatical expressions.   This he confesses, saying that he spoke "the wisdom
of God in a mystery," "comparing spiritual things with spiritual." (1 Cor. ii. 7, 13.)—
Accordingly, he regards the history of Isaac and Ishmael as an allegory, (Gal. iv. 22—
25.) which he condescends to explain. The primitive Fathers of Christianity pursued

he is even more obscure and enigmatic than any of the heathen philosophers, or oracles, in his general teaching; although not so in his predictions. His parables are far inferior to the generality of Eastern parables, in elevation of thought and mental acumen. Many of them are low and vulgar, and—so far as their scope can be ascertained—are utterly inapplicable to the subjects designed to be elucidated. But a personage sent from heaven to enlighten the inhabitants of this benighted world, might reasonably be expected to have been more intelligible to mortals than pagan philosophers; and to have been able to make himself understood, at least, by Oriental people, who were accustomed to parabolic and other figurative language. It accords by no means with a proper notion of divinity to find Jesus perpetually soaring in the atmosphere of Oriental enigmas above the reach of his hearers, and endeavouring to deceive them with beclouded verbiage.— It is difficult to imagine that, if he had been sent by the Deity, he would have made it his continual study to perplex and disgust those whom he pretended to teach and to endue with saving knowledge. Such a conduct is not only unworthy of God, but even of a wise and good man.

It is, however, remarkable that it is upon the most important dogmas of the Christian religion, as now taught and believed by his followers, that he is most obscure. For example, his doctrine touching his resurrection from the dead—the sum and substance of the Christian faith—was so unintelligible to his disciples, that what he told them regarding it was of no avail whatever to them. For we read (John xx. 9.) that, even after it took place, " as yet they knew not the Scripture, that he must rise again from the dead." Indeed, the Gospels furnish a vast number of positive proofs that his disciples entertained not the slightest expectation that he would rise from the tomb, and that when he had been seen alive they did not believe in the fact. His doctrine regarding the Holy Ghost which he was to send, and which Christians say he did send, is also utterly unintelligible. (John xiv. 16, 26; xv. 26; xvi. 7, 13.) His disciples, evidently, could not understand it. They could not perceive how it was that the Holy Ghost was *then dwelling in them*,—that they then *knew him*, and yet that he was *to be sent thereafter* to them,—and that, in *guiding them into all truth, he*

the same mode of communicating instruction, and of defending their religion against the Pagans. Justin Martyr, Clement of Alexandria, Iræneus, Tertullian, Origen—all of them, were very expert in this occult system, in imitation of the heathen philosophers, by whom most of them had been educated. Eusebius (Hist. Eccles. lib. vi. c. 19.) citing what he is pleased to call the *assertions* of Porphyry, writes that Origen, having been educated in Greek literature, intermingled it with the fictions of Christianity, that he dealt in the works of Plato, Numenius, Cranius, Apollophanes, Longinus Moderatus, Nicomachus, Chæremon, and Cornutus,—and that he derived from these pagan authors the allegorical mode of interpretation usual in the mysteries of the Greeks, and applied it to the Jewish Scriptures. Thus, Origen's mode of teaching was identical with that of the Pagans—a mode commended even by the learned Dodwell, (Letters of Advice, &c. p. 208.) who says that the pagan mystical arts of concealment are of use towards understanding the Scriptures. The Jewish Rabbi also delivered their doctrines in the same obscure and mystical manner, as their Talmud, Cabbala, Gemara, and other books, besides what we call the Hebrew Scriptures, amply show. The religious teachers of all the nations of antiquity thus delighting in dark sayings, it is therefore by no means wonderful that the writers of the Gospels, whoever they were, attribute similar enigmas to Jesus. This accounts, in a measure, for the obscurity of the Gospels, while however it traces their origin to a pagan source.

should not speak what he thought, but whatever he heard of another. They had no conception how it was that—if this Holy Ghost was a deity—a god should not act independently, but should be subject to the dictation of another personage. Not only were the disciples of Jesus, after being under his supernatural tuition for about three years, devoid of any clear notion of his doctrine of the Paraclete, but its obscurity has baffled all others who have since attempted to explain it. Christian commentators stumble over this difficulty by pronouncing the doctrine an incomprehensible mystery, at which they say we should gaze with awe and wonder, rather than make an attempt to understand. They also say that only a spiritually minded person can understand the more mysterious doctrines of Jesus, and that the obscurity is in the sinful, carnal, minds of men ; not in the doctrines. But surely Jesus's own apostles, who were continually under all the divine influence with which he was capable of inspiring them, must have been as heavenly minded as grace could make them ; still we have seen that even they were utterly unable to comprehend his doctrines.* There is nothing, however, more certain than that obscurity in speaking implies an imperfection. Human reason shrinks from attributing such a defect to Deity. If God were ever to speak to men through any other medium than nature, we may rest assured that he would speak so as to be understood.

Jesus's teaching being of the obscure and enigmatic character which we have seen, it is by no means wonderful that it carried no influence.— The good effect which it had upon his own apostles was exceedingly slight. Unlike other teachers, he did not endear his disciples to him so as to make them lose their lives in his behalf. When he was apprehended "all the disciples forsook him and fled ;" (Matth. xxvi. 56. Mark xv. 50. 51.) nay, some of them actually denied that they had ever been his disciples. (Matth. xxvi. 69—74.) The moral influence he carried upon Peter—even after he had just cautioned him—had not the effect to prevent him from repeatedly uttering a glaring falsehood in his presence. (Luke xxii. 55— 61.) Nor could his teaching have had any great influence upon his hearers at large. He appears to have made but very few converts,—not one-hundredth part of what we have seen (p. 240.) that Joseph Smith made to Mormonism, within an equal space of time. This reflects very unfavourably on Jesus as a propagandist, and is certainly diametrically opposed to the effect which sound reason would expect the mission of a deity to have carried. His ill success, probably. is to be attributed chiefly to his unintelligible mode of teaching ; for many of his followers after his time, in enforcing the same doctrines—a little modified and polished, to answer the advanced state of knowledge—have been incomparably more

---

* In like manner, we are told that his words have, not only a literal sense, but also a spiritual meaning, which the carnal mind, dead in trespasses and sins, cannot understand, and which is perceived only by the *children of God* with the eye of faith. But the same fact again is an abundant refutation of this assertion.—Jesus's own disciples were utterly unable to perceive either a literal or spiritual meaning in his doctrines. The leaders of the Christian church, however, from the time of the earliest Fathers even to the present age, have found the theory of "double sense" extremely useful, as it can be applied to gloss over any absurdity."—See Horne's Introduction, vol. ii. part ii. chap. 1—12.

successful in their ministrations.* It was very unreasonable in Jesus dissatisfiedly to complain that people did not believe in him—that since he came and did such wonderful works as "none other *man*" had done, they had now "no cloak for their sin." (John xv. 22—24.) For how could he expect casual hearers to believe in him, when his own disciples, about the close of his life, confessedly, neither believed nor understood his doctrines? Their frequent practice of questioning him regarding the meaning of what he had just delivered, shows how unintelligible he was. How glad they were when, now and then, they thought they had caught a glimpse of his meaning! Having been told by him—"A little while and ye *shall not* see me; and again, a little while, and ye *shall* see me, because I go to the Father"—they could by no means understand this riddle. When they were about asking him the meaning, he furnished them with an explanation; although rather a dark and incoherent one. The disciples, however understood him better, and having obtained an inkling of his meaning, exclaimed in ecstacy—"Lo! now speakest thou plainly and speakest no proverb.† Now we are sure that thou knowest all things, and needest not that any man should ask thee. *By this* we believe that thou camest forth from God." (John xvi. 16—30) The disciples were undoubtedly right in regarding *plain speaking* as a mark that Jesus had come from God, and *vice versa*. Like us, they could not think that *enigmas came from God*, but thought that, if he spoke to them, he would make them understand his meaning.—Like us, they could not believe that of which they had no conception; and therefore held in suspense their belief in Jesus until, at least, he should speak so plainly as to enable them to understand what he said. But whether they now understood him or not, and whether they believed in him after their exultation over his plainness of speech, it is however evident that *hitherto they had not* understood him; and that on a point of doctrine about which he had been speaking to them and others for three years! This is corroborated by the deplorable instance which, only a few minutes before, Philip had given of the non-effect of his master's teaching. Jesus, having expatiated on his mysterious connection with the Father, telling his disciples that if they had known him they would have known the Father; and that as they had seen him they had therefore seen the

---

* Those of them, in the present age, have truly abandoned much, but not the whole of the dark, enigmatical, and allegorical mode of teaching. Only a few of them, now, contend for a "double sense" to Scriptural expressions; and that only when the literal sense is too absurd to be maintained. It is now considered an indispensable qualification in a public teacher to speak, not only so that he *can* be understood, but so that he *cannot* be misunderstood. So much wiser has the Christian world grown than it was in the time of Origen and other early Fathers. But if Christian teachers now maintain that they can speak of their doctrines so as to be understood by their hearers, why could not the founder of their faith have done so?

† The word which is here translated *proverb* is παροιμια which, by a well known law of spoken language, had become to signify an *obscure saying*, an *enigma*, a *riddle*. Parkhurst observes—"On account of the *obscurity* which frequently attends *proverbial* and *parabolical* expressions, παροιμια seems to mean *an obscure saying*, *not easily understood*." Hence the gladness of the disciples that Jesus, instead of uttering enigmas, as was his custom, had for once condescended to speak so that they could understand him. The transition was certainly very great and sudden, and was to them of sufficient importance to justify a joyous demonstration.

Father, Philip peremptorily demanded—"Show us the Father and it sufficeth us." Jesus is obliged to apply to Philip the same unhappy mode of persuasion as he is said to have used in his efforts to make the Pharisees, Scribes, and the Jews at large believe in his divine origin.—"Have I been so long time with you, and yet hast thou not known me, Philip? He that hath seen me hath seen the Father; and how sayest thou then, Show us the Father? Believest thou not that I am in the Father, and the Father in me? The words that I speak unto you I speak not of myself, but the Father that dwelleth in me, he doeth the works." (Comp. John xiv. 8—12. with x. 24—38.) Nor does this obscure argument seem to have had any better effect upon Philip than it had had upon the Jews. Neither Philip nor the Jews appear to have believed that Jesus was related to the Deity in any manner than all other mortals.

The evasive character of Jesus's answers to questions put to him touching his mission and doctrines, is a proof of considerable strength that his obscure mode of teaching is not to be attributed to any natural defect, or inability to explain himself; but to a deliberate design to mystify and conceal what he *thought* to be truth. It may, certainly, be urged that the evasiveness of his answers was caused by inability to speak explicitly and pointedly, resulting from the same natural defect as the obscurity of his teaching. But even if this were granted, still this natural defect would have rendered him utterly unfit for public teaching; and a very imperfect pattern to be held up by his followers for the imitation of the whole human race.

His evasive answers, however, are such as carry in themselves clear proofs that the evasion was deliberately intended, and studied in giving them. He never says "Yes" or "No" directly to any question, but either asks another question in reply, or gives an evasive answer, or delivers a circuitous oration which has no bearing upon the subject, although he tells his hearers that their communication should be *Yea* or *Nay*, and that "whatsoever is more than these cometh of evil." (Matth. v. 37.) Having told the Pharisees that his Father bore witness of him, they very reasonably asked him—"Where is thy Father?" Jesus, instead of returning a plain, unequivocal, convincing answer, said—"Ye neither know me nor my Father." After he had told them—"If ye believe not that I am he, ye shall die in your sins," they again very naturally asked him—"Who art thou?" But Jesus ambiguously replied—"Even the same that I said unto you from the beginning." (John viii. 19, 25.) But he had not at all told these Pharisees that he was the Messiah, or the Son of God. On the contrary, he had told his disciples to keep this a profound secret; and, within a sentence further on in the chapter just cited, John declares that these Pharisees "understood not that he spake to them of the Father." What would be thought of a public teacher, in the present age, who should thus evade fair questions put to him by those whom he pretended to instruct?

When the disciples of John waited upon Jesus to ask the cause that—while they and the disciples of the Pharisees often fasted—his disciples did not fast, the answer he gave them was exceedingly obscure and evasive; namely that "the children of the bridechamber" could not mourn so long as the bridegroom was with them; and that no man put a piece of new cloth upon an old garment, or new wine in old bottles. (Matth. ix. 14—17.) But even a person intimately acquainted with Eastern customs will find it a difficult task to show the bearing which sewing a piece of new cloth to an old garment, or putting new wine in old bottles, had upon the question—why Jesus's disciples did not fast. There is no analogy whatever, either literal or figurative, between the question and the answer.—The latter throws no light upon the former, and is quite irrelevant. Again, when the Scribes and Pharisees asked him why his disciples transgressed the tradition of the elders, by not washing their hands before meals, he evaded their question by asking them another—"Why do ye also transgress the commandment of God by *your* tradition?"—as if their transgression justified his transgression ; or as if "two wrongs made one right." (Matth. xv. 2, 3.) When the same people asked him what should be done to a woman they had caught in adultery, after much hesitation he rendered the evasive reply—"He that is without sin among you, let him first cast a stone at her." (John viii. 7.) But it is clear that this was a designedly evasive answer. Whatever was the motive of Jesus's religious opponents in putting the question, he did not meet it candidly, and give it a direct answer, but conducted himself as if he had been afraid to give an opinion. When the Jewish rulers asked him by whose authority he made his regal entry into their metropolis and created a disturbance in their temple, he employed a stratagem by which to elude their question ; namely by asking them whence came the baptism of John, and telling them that, if they first answered his question, he would afterwards answer theirs. (Matth. xxi. 23—25.) But the question he asked bore not the slightest relation to the subject which the Jewish deputation had expressly come to place before him ; and there is nothing clearer than that his object in asking them about John's baptism was to avoid the reply which the interrogation just put to him demanded.—When Nicodemus, also, who had purposely come to him for instruction, asked him to explain how a man could be born when he was old ; instead of throwing any light on the mysterious subject which he himself had mooted, he only repeated his previous assertion in still more obscure terms. (John iii. 3—5.)

Jesus's answers to those in authority, when on his trial, are remarkably evasive. His wariness strongly reminds one of the replies given by accused persons to questions put to them in a French court of justice, where their account of themselves has some weight in deciding their fate. Few martyrs for the Christian religion ever gave such ambiguous replies to those who questioned them regarding their supposed heresy, as did the founder of this religion return to those who interrogated him concerning the title and authority he assumed. After his apprehension, when he was before the chief priests and Scribes, they asked him—"Art thou the Christ ? tell us." His very evasive answer was—"If I tell you, ye will not believe ; and if I also ask you, ye will not answer me, nor let me go." (Luke xxii. 66—68.) If he was really the Christ, what motive could he have, now that he was going to die, in withholding an open avowal of the fact ? To conceal it from the Jews could now be of no avail; but rather to confess it would possibly answer a vast number of good purposes, besides those of truth and candour. It would, at least, give the Jews—who were still in doubt—an opportunity of knowing from Jesus's own mouth

that they were about crucifying " the Prince of life." When, however,
the Jewish pontiff asked him who were his disciples and what were his
doctrines, Jesus, instead of answering these questions in a frank and satisfactory manner, referred the high priest to those who had heard him
preach—as if the Jewish peasants who had followed him about the country,
could give a better account than he could of the dark parables he had
delivered—and he added—" Why askest thou me ? Ask them which heard
me, what I have said unto them." (John xviii. 19—21.) Some of the
Christian martyrs preoclaimed their doctrines when burning in the flames ;
but when Jesus approached death, he did not think proper even to answer
any questions touching the doctrines he had promulgated. Having been
brought before the Roman governor of Judea, on the very charge of having
set up himself as the king of the Jews, Pilate therefore asked him—" Art
thou the king of the Jews ?" But Jesus, instead of either admitting or
denying the charge,—instead of answering the question by *yea* or *nay*,
must evasively ask another question.—" Sayest thou this of thyself, or did
others tell it thee of me ?" Pilate rejoined—" Am I a Jew ?" and added
that Jesus's own nation had delivered him into his hands ; at the same
time pressing him to say what he had done. But the substance of all the
information he could obtain of Jesus was the obscure denial that his
kingdom was of this world. (John xviii. 33—38.)

On one occasion, Jesus's audience ask him the following question,
which naturally arose from his discourse.—" Who is the Son of man ?"—
One would think that an opportunity now presented itself for Jesus to tell
a multitude anxious for spiritual knowledge who he was, whence he came,
and what the object of his mission was. However, instead of returning
even an intelligible answer to the question, he said—" Yet a little while is
the light with you. Walk while ye have the light, lest darkness come
upon you ; for he that walketh in darkness knoweth not whither he goeth.
While ye have light believe in the light." (John xii. 34—36.) But is this
an answer to the question—" Who is the Son of man ?" All that he says
about light has no bearing upon it ; and is in itself remarkably dark and
unmeaning. How, for instance, is to " believe in the light" ? If a person
see light, he cannot help believing in its existence, of which he has the
direct evidence of his senses. Is not such a doctrine as this the most
sublime absurdity that can be uttered? It is not at all wonderful that
John here adds that, although Jesus " had done so many miracles before"
the people to whom he addressed the witless expressions about light, " yet
they believed not in him." John, however, gives another reason of the
most absurd kind, why these people did not believe in Jesus ; namely, that
there might be a fulfilment of the prediction of Esaias who, he intimates,
had foretold that nobody would believe in Jesus. To make the matter
worse, he adds that these people *could not* believe, because Esaias had
prophesied that Jesus would blind their eyes and harden their hearts, lest
they should be converted and be healed,—a doctrine, however repugnant
to common sense and to any proper notion of justice, precisely the same
as that taught by Jesus himself. (vid. ant. p. 384.) After all, John says
that " nevertheless among the chief rulers also many believed on him," as
if in spite of having their eyes blinded and their hearts hardened by Jesus.
To reconcile the jumbling mass of contrarieties which John has here

heaped together, is a task devolving on those Christian commentators, who seem to think that books, said to have been written under the immediate superintendence of Deity, require man's ingenuity to explain and amend them,—than which notion a greater absurdity cannot be conceived. Here, however, it may be remarked that, if any author of the present age huddled together so many contradictions as John has, in the few sentences just noticed, his work would receive the treatment it deserved.

SECTION VIII.—JESUS DEFICIENT IN KNOWLEDGE OF BOTH ANIMATE AND INANIMATE NATURE, AND ALSO OF MANY THINGS RELATING TO HUMAN SOCIETY.

Throughout the reports we have in the Gospels of the orations, precepts, doctrines, and conversations of Jesus, there is this most prominent feature; namely, an assumption on his part that he was an infallible teacher in every branch of knowledge on which he spoke, whether natural or supernatural. To no question ever put to him was he so modest as to say—" I do not know." Although he was frequently evasive and obscure in his replies, and although he sometimes maintained sullen silence in regard to questions which he could easily and candidly have answered, yet when he spoke, he always seemed to think that what he said was indubitably correct,—that his knowledge was oracular, and very far transcended that of all other teachers that ever appeared in this world. Accordingly, a dogmatic and authoritative tone pervades all his discourses. He expected, and sometimes demanded in open terms, that all other teachers should sit at his feet, and blindly receive his enunciated doctrines without the least examination. So far was he from encouraging free inquiry into the truth of his statements, and from exhorting his hearers to obtain satisfactory evidence before they gave their assent, that whenever any of them asked him a question with the view of testing the truth of what he advanced, he evinced great sourness of temper, and sometimes, as we have seen, resorted to opprobrious language. A true philosopher never behaves in this manner. Were an ignorant person to question the truth of one of his axioms, such as that " things which are equal to the same thing are equal to one another," he may fail to suppress a pitying smile, but he will not display an acrimonious temper, and refuse a clear explanation. Truth does not require this; nay it is contrary to her nature. She loves to have the rationality and soundness of her *dicta* examined. It is Error that frowns when he is accosted, and interrogated as to the correctness of his *credenda*. If so, then we may expect to find some error in the very few examples now intended to be given from Jesus's lessons on natural philosophy.

He tells Nicodemus (John iii. 8.) that " the wind bloweth where it listeth,"—that is, where it wishes—but that we cannot " tell whence it cometh, and whither it goeth." All this appears wrong, and indicates that Jesus knew nothing scientifically about wind. The wind is not exactly a *free agent*, blowing where it listeth ; but is controlled by physical causes, and, like other inanimate matter, has no volitive power. Further, we *do* know from what quarter the wind blows, or *can* tell "whence it cometh," and towards what quarter it drifts. The proximate cause of wind—of which Jesus was evidently ignorant—is the rarefaction of the atmospheric air in one region, and its condensation in another; so that—from its tendency to maintain its equilibrium—if it is more rarified or lighter in one place than another, the weightier air will rush towards that place, and thereby produce in the atmosphere an agitation which is called *wind*. The condensation and rarefaction of the air depending upon the variations of cold and heat, it is constantly carried from the polar region, where it is condensed by cold, towards the torrid zone, where it is rarified by heat. The causes that the wind blows from various other points of the heavens are accountable for on similar principles. It is therefore clear that Jesus was utterly ignorant of pneumatics.* Consequently he could not with truth say to Nicodemus—"We speak that we do know, and testify that we have seen;" for he had not, and could not have seen it was a fact what he says of the wind; nor could he *have seen* the wind. That he meant that the Jewish senator should understand literally what he said of the wind is however indisputably proved by his own words.—"If I have told you earthly things, and ye believe not, how shall ye believe if I tell you of heavenly things?" It is by no means wonderful that, in reference to this erroneous philosophy, the Jewish ruler exclaimed—"How can these things be?"—the mildest expression he could have used in denying its truth.— To a thinking Christian it must appear strange that—if Jesus made the wind, as every other part of the universe, and, like Neptune, or Oceanus, could calm a sea storm with a single word, holding the wind in the hollow of his hand—he did not know so much about it as common people did. (Mark iv. 36—41. Luke viii. 22—25.)

From the complaint made against his disciples of eating with unwashed hands—doubtless a filthy habit, very detrimental to health in a warm climate—Jesus takes occasion to speak of what really defileth man, and, in doing so, attempts to be very philosophic and precise. He says to his disciples, who had retired with him into a house expressly for the purpose of receiving correct knowledge on this point—"Whatever things from without entereth into the man, it *cannot defile him;* because it entereth *not into his heart*, but into *the belly*, and goeth out into the draught, purging all meats. And he said, That which cometh out of the man that defileth the man. For from within, *out of the heart of man*, proceed evil thoughts, adulteries, fornications, murders, thefts, covetousness, wickedness, deceit, lasciviousness, an evil eye, blasphemy, pride, foolishness: all these things come from within, and defile the man." (Mark vii. 15—23. Matth. xv. 11, 17—20.) Here we have Jesus before us both as a physiologist and as a moral philosopher. As to his language, it must be

---

* Jesus knew much less regarding this department of nature than the philosophers of the times in which he is said to have lived. Cicero says that air is a fluid surrounding the earth. (De Nat. Deor. ii. 36, 39.) Seneca (Quæst. Nat. v. 1, 5, 6.) says—Ventus est aer fluens; and describes the weight and gravity of the atmosphere. Pliny the Elder (ii. 44.) says—Ventus nihil aliud quam fluxus aeris, etc. Ctesibium had invented the common air pump, and other hydraulic instruments, more than 120 years before the time of Jesus.—Plin. vii. 37. Vetruv. de Archit. ix. 9.

observed that if any writer on human physiology, in the present age, were to imitate it, he would be branded for his coarseness and obscenity.   But this is not the worst fault in Jesus's attempt to teach physiology.   His doctrine is grossly erroneous,—is glaringly at variance with thoroughly established facts.   When he teaches something concerning things in another world—such as, for example, that spirits in heaven have some wonderful properties or qualities, or that demons in hell display very curious evil propensities,—we have no means of judging whether he is right or wrong; because we are so constituted as not to be able to have an idea of any existence or mode of existence whatever, except through the avenues of sense, which are adapted to take cognizance only of physical objects.   But when he condescends to treat of any thing in nature, then we have experience and observation for our guidance as to the truth of his doctrine.   Accordingly, when he alleges that nothing can enter into a man's stomach which has the power to defile or pollute him, we find that he is grossly in error.   To illustrate this point is quite superfluous. Every sane man well knows that there are a thousand things which, if he received them into his stomach, would not only defile his system, but soon deprive him of life.   Was there no hemlock—no henbane—no vegetable or mineral poison whatever, in Judea, or at least known as such to Jesus? The doctrine that "nothing from without a man, that entereth into him, *can* defile him," is quite as dangerous, and as incentive to suicide as that which Jesus propounded when he said that true believers would be able to drink poison and handle serpents without being injured; and is also closely akin to it. (See Mark xvi. 18. and ante p. 293.)   Again : Jesus is quite erroneous in saying that "out of the heart of men proceed evil thoughts," and the other wicked mental emotions and corporeal actions which he enumerates.   In his time, it had not been discovered that the brain is the organ of thought—the organ of every mental emotion, desire, and propensity—and that the heart has no more share in the immediate production of an idea or feeling than the lungs, or any of the other vital organs whose actions are involuntary.   There is now no fact in physiology, nor indeed in any other branch of knowledge, better ascertained and more fully established than that the brain is the organ of all mental emotions. Jesus, however, laboured under the same mistake as all the writers of the Bible—and indeed, almost all the ancient philosophers, long after the period in which he is said to have lived—in supposing that the *heart is the organ of mind;* and very frequently do we find him speak of the heart as such, in the most express terms.*   Had Jesus been omniscient—as he is thought by his followers to have been—one would think that it would not have been an act of too much benevolence on his part, especially when already treating of the physiology of the human body, to reveal to dull and erring mortals that the brain was the organ of all *thought and feeling* —that this was the organ of the *mind* or *soul,* through the medium of which it conceived "evil thoughts," and formed propensities for "adulteries, fornications, murders," and the other vices he names.   What a

---

* See Matth. v. 8, 28 ; ix. 4; xi. 29; xii. 34, 35; xviii. 35; xxiv. 48.   Mark ii. 8 ; xi. 23; xvi. 4.   Luke v. 22; vi. 45; viii. 15; ix, 47; xxiv. 25, 38.   John xiv. 1, 27 ; xvi. 6, 22.

boon he would have conferred upon science, and therefore upon the human race, by revealing that the brain was the organ of thought, instead of leaving to the labours of fallible men, who lived eighteen centuries after his time, the *full* discovery of this fact!—a fact which is now corroborated by a thousand others, and the truths which it illustrates decried by none whose opinion is of any weight! Unfortunately, however, it is as clear as meridian day that Jesus *did not know* that the brain was the organ of thought; but, in common with his contemporaries, laboured under the mistake that all thought and feeling proceeded from the heart. It is evident that on this point his knowledge was derived from the same source as that of the ignorant Jewish peasants amongst whom he moved. As they believed that the heart was the organ of mind, so did he believe. If he had been divine,—if he had had any part in creating man, he would have known the functions designed for each organ of the human body, and that the heart had not been intended to reason. Had he only incidentally mentioned the heart as the organ of mind, it could, with some show of reason, be urged that he used the term *heart*, in this connection, for the sake of speaking in popular language, and thereby be understood by his hearers. But there is not the slightest ground for this supposition.— Because, in the expressions cited, and others attributed to him by the Evangelists, he directly and with a set purpose teaches that the heart is really the organ of thought and feeling. It is difficult to imagine a clearer and stronger proof than this error affords, that he was not superior in nature or intelligence to other men with whom he mixed. To adore as God a person who, on a point of natural science, was thus in error—which error the observation and experience of mere man has been able to correct —is a task from the performance of which the reflective mind shrinks!

Another proof of deficient knowledge in human physiology was given by Jesus on the following occasion.—As he was making his escape from his hiding place in the temple, when the Jews attempted to stone him, he passed by "a man which was blind from his birth." In reference to this man his disciples asked him a very fair and philosophic question, namely— "Who did sin, this man or his parents, that he was born blind?" Jesus replied.—"Neither hath this man sinned, nor his parents; but that the works of God should be made manifest in him. I must work the works of him that sent me while it is day." (John ix. 4.) After some further remarks of the same nature, he proceeded to cure the blind man by a miracle—a thing quite inconsistent with his evident ignorance of the cause of the man's blindness. He had just told his disciples, as we have seen, that neither the sin of the man himself nor that of his parents was the cause of his having been blind from his birth, but that this miserable object had been issued into the world, deprived of sight, in order that Jesus might display what he calls "the works of God," in performing a miracle upon him. But if Jesus had the knowledge which even ordinary people, in the present age, possess of the laws of nature, he would have known that all physical deformity or bodily defect, is the result of the violation of some natural law, and—as this man was blind from birth—would have unhesitatingly answered that the cause of his blindness was a sin, or —which is the same thing—a violation of some of the laws of nature, committed either by his parents, or by one of them, or by some of his ancestors, or else by some persons whose vices had influenced his mother during her period of gestation. In the present advanced state of science, there is no truth better established than that every physical, as well as every mental defect or deformity, is caused by a violation of one or more of the laws of nature. In numerous ways—too numerous to be mentioned here—may parents infringe these laws, so as to have children born blind; and the faults and follies of even their grandfathers or grandmothers, are known sometimes to have had this effect upon their children's children.* Imminent danger from fire, shipwreck, civil war, and other things productive of fright, may have such an effect upon the mother, during her gestation, as to cause the blindness of her child. Although she may have no control over such circumstances as these, yet they are all traceable to the violation of the natural laws by somebody.† And there can exist in the mind of any intelligent and unbiassed thinker very little doubt that the blindness of the man on whom Jesus is said to have performed a miracle, was the effect of some natural cause. Jesus's disciples, however, are represented to have laboured under the old notion, prevalent to this day, that every physical defect of this kind was a direct judgment miraculously inflicted by the Deity for some particular sin. And it must be admitted that—since such corporeal defects or deformities result from a violation of the laws established by the Creator of the universe—this notion was more plausible and more easily supported than that the poor man, of whom they spoke, was ushered into the world blind, in order that Jesus might display his power of working a miracle. According to this, we must, to be consistent, believe that all the blind, lame, deaf, and dumb persons, together with all others afflicted with any bodily defects or infirmities, on whom Jesus operated, had been so afflicted for the same purpose. But, in the present instance, what a miserable doctrine to assert that this poor mortal had thus been unjustly afflicted with blindness from his birth till he had grown up to manhood, in order that Jesus might work a miracle,—a thing

---

* To such a degree, however, are the organs of sight now understood, that scientific men—not by rubbing the patient's eyes with clay and spittle, but rather by the process of couching—are able to give their sight to persons even born blind. But when the optic nerve is diseased or deformed, when the *corpora quadrigemina* are too weak or imperfectly developed—which may be the case with them as well as with any other part of the brain that causes idiocy—when there is an atrophy of the optic thalami,—or when the small fibres which diverge from them are imperfect—to give sight to a person born blind is beyond the reach of science. The human eye, at best, is weaker and more imperfect, at birth, in man than in most of the lower animals. Most of these come into the world with the perfect use of this organ; but man's eyes, for the first five or six weeks after his birth, are almost insensible to light; and even when matured, are weaker than those of most of the inferior animals.

† There is on record a vast number of such cases, in which some children were born blind, and others with various defects; such as without ears, with only one arm, or one leg, owing to the fright of the mothers. Baron Percy, a celebrated French professor, states that, after the siege of Landau, in 1793, the women, owing to a violent cannonading, were kept in constant alarm, which was enormously increased by the terrific explosion caused when the arsenal was blown up. Out of 92 children born in that district within a few months afterwards, 16 died at the instant of birth; 33 languished from eight to ten months, and then died; 8 became *idiotic*; and 2 came into the world *with numerous fractures of the bones and of the limbs caused by the cannonading and the explosion.* All this through the medium of the mother's alarm.—See Coombe's Management of Infancy, p. 79. Fifth Edit.

so generally pretended in his time by public teachers! If the man was
born blind for the purpose Jesus alleged, did not the evil, in his case, far
preponderate over the good? We do not find that even one person, except the blind man himself, believed in Jesus, owing to this miracle. Nor
does it appear (ver. 36.) that the miracle was the cause that even he
believed in him; but rather the persuasive words which Jesus, some time
afterwards, used to induce him to make a profession of his belief. But
could not Omniscience find a sufficient number of subjects for miracles,
without inflicting one of his creatures with blindness? It must be admitted
that in this instance again, Jesus not only betrays gross ignorance of
human physiology, but also inculcates a most absurd moral dogma.

The fact that Jesus, as represented in the Gospels, really believed
that he expelled devils or demons, from people imagined to be possessed
by them, is also positive evidence of his deficient knowledge of the human
constitution, or of what may be termed human pathology. Long ago has
it been ascertained beyond a reasonable doubt, that persons who, in the
age Jesus is said to have lived, were thought to be possessed by demons,
merely laboured under natural diseases, such as epilepsy, madness, and
other spasmodic and nervous maladies.* Indeed, this is now admitted by

---

* To have a full view of this point, we must examine the doctrine of demonology
amongst pagan nations long before the time of Jesus. In the religion of the heathens,
demons of different powers—always called devils or spirits in the English version of the
New Testament, but demons in the Greek version—occupied a very prominent position,
and received the homage and adoration of millions of human beings, who were quite as
sincere, if not as intelligent, as Christian worshippers of the present age. Bryant, in
his Ancient Mythology, (vol. i. p. 109.) very correctly remarks that "the whole of the
religion of the ancients consisted in the worship of demons, and that to those personages
their whole theology continually refers." Some of these they worshipped that they
might benefit them, and others that they might not injure them. Of these demons there
appears to have been regarded two distinct classes, as to their nature and origin. The
one class, according to Hesiod (Εργα και Ημερ, lib. i. 109.) were once human beings.
In describing the first or golden of the world, he says that, after this happy generation
of men died, Jupiter promoted them to be demons, (δαιμονες) guardians of mortal men,
overlookers of their good as well as bad works, and givers of their riches; and to live
in the air. Plato (De Repub. lib. v) thinks that all who bravely die in war are of
Hesiod's golden race, are made demons, and ought for ever afterwards to have their
sepulchres worshipped as those demons; and, in another place, he remarks that Hesiod
and many other poets nobly sang, in showing that when good men died they had the
great honour conferred upon them of being made demons.—Επειδαν τις αγαθος ων
τελευτηση, μεγαλην μοιραν και τιμην εχει, και γενεται δαιμων. Lucian, throughout
his Dialogues, regards these demons as having once been human beings, and, in one
place, speaks of them as "the phantoms and souls of the dead wandering upon the earth,
and appearing to whom they pleased." The other class of demons had never been
human beings. Of these, Apuleius (Deo Socrat.) says, after speaking of the former,—
"There is another higher and more august sort of demons, that have always been free
from the fetters and bonds of the body." Ammonius (in Plut. de def. Orac.) also thought
that there were not only demons who had once human bodies, but likewise those who
never had any bodies at all. Now, these demons were thought to be *mediators* and
intercessors between the gods and men.—"Every demon" says Plato, (Sympos.) "is a
mediator (μεταξυ—middle, intermediate) between God and mortals." And, a little
further on, he says that God is not to be approached immediately by man, but that all
intercourse between men and gods is carried on by the mediation of demons, who are
the interpreters and carriers from men to the gods, and from the gods to men, of the
supplications of the former and blessings of the latter. (See also Apuleius de Deo
Socratis.) Again, Plutarch (in Dion) assures us that "according to a very ancient
belief, there are certain evil and malignant demons who are invidious to good men, and

a great number of Christian writers of profound learning and knowledge, such as Dr. Lardner, Dr. Campbell, Mr. Hugh Farmer, and others.—

endeavour to prevent them from pursuing virtue, lest they should after death obtain a better lot than they themselves had." Of this disposition probably were the demons mentioned by Empedocles, of whom Plutarch (de Vit. Ære.) says that they were cast out of heaven by the gods, and fell from heaven,—like those angels mentioned in Scripture, who kept not their first estate. All those in Homer called demons and described as gods, appear to have been of the same malignant nature. Further, these heathen demons were accustomed to enter into human beings, and render them most wretched. From some passages in Æschylus, Euripides and Sophocles; and from a far greater number in later bards it is clear that the belief in demoniacal possession was rife in these early times. (Vid. Sophocl. Ajax. 244. Herodot. Erato. c. 86. Homer. Odyss. 396. Corn. Celsus lib. i. pref.) In the time of Hippocrates—about 400 years before the Christian era—the belief in demoniacal possession was so prevalent that he wrote a treatise proving that these supposed possessions were only the effects of natural causes. He however tells us (De Morbo Sacro) that the Greeks referred such possessions to their gods, especially to Neptune, Mars, Apollo, Hecate, and other hero-gods, who were known to have once been men. The prevalency of the belief, amongst the pagan Greeks, in demoniacal possession is also proved by the numerous words which we meet in early Greek writers denoting this possession or something belonging to it, such as Σεολημπτος, *inspired, possessed.* (Plutarch. de Herodot.)—Σεοφορητος, bearing a god, or demon. (Æschyl. Agamem. 1149.)—δαιμονιακος, possessed by a demon.—δαιμονιζομαι, I am possessed by a demon.—δαιμοναω, I rave, am mad, have a demon. A great many other words of similar import might be added. Among the Greeks, there were certain prophets who were thought to be possessed with demons, and therefore called δαιμονολημπτοι, and because the demons were thought to lodge and speak within their bodies, they were also called —εγαστριμαντεις. (Potter's Antiquities of Greece, vol. i. book ii. ch. 12.) Demonology formed a very prominent feature in the philosophy of Pythagoras and Plato, as well as that of all the Greek moralists. The Romans, in like manner, believed in demoniacal possessions. Their demons went under the names of Fauni, Manes, Lares, Lymphatici, and Larvæ; and those whom they possessed were called Larvati, Cerriti, &c. Pliny (Hist. Nat. lib. xxv. c. 5.) speaks of persons being agitated by the Fauni. These Fauni were among the Latins from the remotest period of their national existence. The poet Ennius, in describing what the earliest Latin bards had sung, says—Quales Fauni vatesque canebat. Both the terms *Lymphatici* and *Manes* signify madness; while *Lares* and *Larvæ* mean gods, *spirits, demons,* &c. Strabo denominates the goddess Feronia, a *demon,* and says that those who were possessed by this demon walked barefoot over burning coals. Philostratius, in his life of Apollonius Tyanæus, relates that a demon who possessed a young man, confessed himself to be the ghost of a person slain in battle. (Farmer on Demoniacs, p. 25.) The Jews also, long before the Christian era, had their demons, some of whom, like those of the heathens, were mediators between God and men; while others were of a malignant disposition, entering the bodies of mortals, and rendering them mad, until expelled by a skilful exorcist. (Maimonides de Idol. 4. Josephus Antiq. Jud. lib. viii. c. 2; lib. vii. c. 6.) The account given by Josephus is very remarkable—He tells us what demons were.—how they entered the bodies of mortals,—how Solomon, in his time, expelled them,—and how a later exorcist dispatched them in the presence of Vespasian. These are his words—"If the root *baaras* be only brought to the sick persons, it quickly drives away those called demons, which are no other than the spirits of the wicked, that enter into men, and kill them, unless they can obtain some help against them." (Antiq. lib. vii. c. 4. sec. 3.) "But as for Saul some strange and *demoniacal* disorder came upon him........The physicians could find no other remedy but this, that if any person could charm those passions by singing and playing upon the harp, they advised them to enquire for such a one, and to observe when these demons came upon him and disturbed him........He (David) charmed his passions, and was the only physician against the trouble he had from the demon whenever it came upon him, and this by reciting hymns and playing upon the harp and bringing Saul to his right mind again." (Antiq. lib. vi. c. 9. sec. 2.) This explanation throws a flood of light upon what is said in 1 Sam. xvi. 14—23. of the evil spirit from the Lord which troubled Saul but which David drove away with music. The evil spirit from the Lord, in the opinion of the Hebrew writer, was a demon, just as all the heathen demons

Jesus, however, embraced the pagan absurdity—which had existed for hundreds, if not thousands of years before his time—that a person troubled

were gods or deified heroes. Josephus, in another place, says of Solomon—"God also enabled him to learn the art of expelling demons, which is a science useful and sanative to men. He composed such incantations also by which distempers are alleviated, and left behind him the manner of using exorcisms, by which they drive away demons so that they never return. And this method of cure is of great force unto this day; for I have seen a certain man of my own country, whose name was Eleazar, releasing people that were demoniacal, in the presence of Vespasian and his sons, and his captains, and the whole multitude of his soldiers. The manner of the cure was this:—he put a ring that had a root of one of those sorts mentioned by Solomon, to the nostrils of the demoniac, after which he drew out the demon through his nostrils; and when the man fell down immediately, he adjured him to return into him no more, making still mention of Solomon, and reciting the incantations which he composed. And when Eleazar would persuade and demonstrate to the spectators that he had such a power, he set, a little way off, a cup or bason full of water, and commanded the demon, as he went out of the man to overturn it, and thereby to let the spectators know that he had left the man." (Antiq. lib. viii. c. 2. sec. 5.) Whiston, in whose translation the above extracts are given, remarks, in a note, that "some pretended fragments of Solomon's books of conjuration are still extant in Fabricius' Cod. Pseudepigr. Vet. Test. p. 1054." It may be observed also that the Delphic Pythia used roots and herbs in dealing with demons, and that the whole of the Celtic and Scandinavian enchanters did so; all of them, like Jesus, being healers of all manner of diseases, as well as expellers of demons. The Gospels also furnish evidence that, among the Jews, there was a great number of persons who cast out devils, not only before the birth of Jesus, but even at the very time in which he lived. His chief religious rivals—the Pharisees, appear to have been expert in this art. Jealous of his success as an exorcist, they attempted to defame his character by asserting that it was by the aid of Beelzebub, the prince of devils, he performed these exploits. On one occasion, at least, Jesus thus retorted.—"If I by Beelzebub cast out devils, by whom do *your children cast them out?*—meaning by *children,* the disciples of the Pharisees. (Matth. xii. 27. Luke xi. 19.) He also added that they should be judges as to whether he did not cast out devils by the same power as they themselves did, namely by the Spirit of God—the God of Abraham—not the heathen god Beelzebub. The question of dispute here evidently was—not whether Jesus did really cast out devils, nor whether the Pharisees did cast them out, which was in those times a thing very commonly done—but whether Jesus did not cast them out by the power of Beelzebub—a pagan deity who, as such, stood very low in the estimation of these Pharisees, the worshippers of Jehovah. Beelzebub was the god of Ekron, a city of the Philistines, where he had a temple, and was worshipped by the inhabitants of that large city. He was a celebrated oracle, and on that account, apparently, was called the prince of demons. To him did a Jewish king, who had met with a serious accident, send to know whether he should recover, to the great annoyance of that jealous prophet—Elijah, who thought that the Hebrew God could give information on this point, quite as correctly as Beelzebub. (2 Kings i. 1—6.) It is clear from a vast number of passages in the Bible and other writings that nothing roused the pious indignation of both the votaries of Judaism and the devotees of Christianity so much as to suspect that any person had faith in the pagan theology, or paid any adoration to the pagan gods. Both Jews and Christians entirely agreed on this point, from religious jealousy, just as the different sects of Protestants, in the present age, agree in opposing Popery, however they may differ on other points, considered by them of less importance. Although both Jews and Christians imitated the pagans in all their rites, ceremonies, and even doctrines, yet on this point—the object of worship—they mutually abhorred them. On the question of demonology, therefore, because demons were objects of worship, they were at perfect variance with the pagans. Most of the Christian Fathers, whether orthodox or heterodox, regarded the worship of these demons with great abhorrence, and thought that, as one demon was a Jupiter, another a Neptune, another an Apollo, and so on, these pagan gods had usurped the position and arrogated the attributes of the Jewish and Christian deity. Hence the repeated cautions given, not only to the Jews in the Old Testament, but to the Christian converts in the New Testament, to refrain from idolatry, and demons,—not to sacrifice, with the Gentiles, to demons, but to God,—not to have any fellowship with demons,—not to drink

with a peculiar malady was possessed by demons, and, like the pagan prophets engaged in exorcising these demons. Whether he really did so or

the cup, and be partakers of the table of demons,—and not on any account to worship demons. (1 Cor. x. 20, 21. Rev. ix. 20 ; xvi. 14. Justin. Martyr. Apol. Major. Tertull. Apol. c. 23. Athenagoras Legat. c. 22. Lactant. Inst. Div. ii. 14—19.) Hence Jesus is said to have come to expel the demons. Hence also are the demons whom Jesus is said to have expelled, frequently called by the Evangelist πνευματα ακαθαρτα—unclean spirits; the word ακαθαρτος being an epithet in a great number of places in the New Testament signifying the uncleanness which the Christians attributed to the heathen gods and heathen worship, in contradistinction to their clean or holy spirit—πνευμα αγιον. (Acts x. 14, 28. 1 Cor. vii. 14. 2 Cor. vi. 17.) Beelzebub, a heathen deity, was therefore by the Pharisees considered to be one of these unclean spirits, and to be even their prince. This was the ground of the charge which they are said to have so frequently brought against Jesus, that he cast out demons by the power of this god. Jesus, however, once in a train of argument which went to show that Beelzebub would never have thus turned against his own subjects, indignantly denied this charge ; and although he disclaimed all power of his own, yet he affirmed that he exorcised demons by the power of the God of Abraham, whom the Pharisees worshipped ; or as he expressed it, in the words of Moses—" with the finger of God,"—the same power as that by means of which they themselves cast out demons. He did not even intimate that there was any difference between his exorcism and that of the Pharisees, but expressly put both on a level. In like manner, when his disciples were piqued at seeing a person—apparently a Jew— who was a stranger to them, casting out demons, and told Jesus that this exorcist made use of his name, so far was he from entertaining the least doubt of the reality of the man's influence on the demons that he told his disciples not to molest him, and in express terms countenanced his work, (Mark xi. 38.) The generality of this practice also may be inferred from Jesus's words.—" Many will say to me in that day, Lord, Lord, have we not prophesied in thy name ? and in thy name have *cast out devils?*" (Matth. vii. 22.) The following event also will further show how common the casting out of devils was in these times—" Certain of the vagabond Jews, exorcists, took upon them" to cast out demons in the name of Jesus. Among these were no fewer than seven sons of Sceva— the sons of even a Jewish high priest. (Ιουδαιου αρχιερων.) Although they were professed exorcists, yet it is said that, by using as a charm or incantation, the name of Jesus they failed to cast out a demon in the instance recorded. Owing to this failure, the spectators lost confidence in them, and became attached to the system of miraculous power displayed by Paul. But this was not all,—so great was the influence that the Apostle of the Gentiles carried upon the multitude, that many other conjurors or exorcists publicly burned their conjuring books to the value of " fifty thousand pieces of silver," which, according to some, was £7,500 of our money, but according to others, only £1,875. (Acts xix. 13—19.) All this shows that casting out demons was very general among the Jews, so that *Jesus was not alone in the exercise of this art.* Now, were all or any of the vast number of persons amongst Greeks, Romans, Jews, and a great many other ancient nations that could be named, upon whom conjuring exorcists operated, *really possessed with demons* or evil spirits, either of human or superhuman origin? Reason would answer that they were not, and the most acute philosophers of the times believed that those indications which were thought to be signs of demoniacal possessions, were merely the effects of natural diseases, such as madness and epilepsy, and could afford to smile at the credulity of a superstitious populace deladed by a cunning hierarchy, in whose grasping hand, anciently, were both theology and the art of healing; the latter consisting of enchantments. (Porphyr. lib. iv. sec. 8. Clem. Stromat. lib. vi. c. 4. Homer. Il. i. 62. Diodor. Sicul. lib. v. 1 Kings xiv. 1—17. 2 Kings i. 2 ; viii. 7—10. Isa. xxxviii. 1, 21. Jam. v. 14.) Hippocrates—who was a man far before the age in which he lived, who is justly called the father of medicine, and from whose judicious remarks succeeding physicians have derived invaluable advantages—wrote a treatise, as already mentioned, with the view expressly to combat the error of superstitious exorcists—that what they deemed demoniacal possession was a natural disease, and no more divine or sacred than other disorders ; and many are the reasons and facts which he adduces to show that epilepsy and madness have nothing about them which is preternatural. Nobody in his time could be a better judge, and none had better opportunities of examining these cases of supposed possession, than he who lived in the age in which

not,—whether the devils, as stated, did really speak to him or not,—and whether he ever really performed a miracle, are not questions which are

thousands of them among the Greeks were supposed to occur; for he intimates (De Morbo Sacro) that it was a very common thing to attribute epilepsy and different kinds of madness to demoniacal possession. Later physicians adopted his views; for we find them applying physical remedies to such diseases, instead of charms and incantations. And our modern physicians, as Mr. Farmer, in his work on demoniacs, very properly observes, treat such disorders by bleeding, blistering, purging, and shaving. But even an orthodox Christian, would probably have some difficulty in believing that a demon could be expelled with cathartics, or extracted by a blister. Many other proofs could be added to show that the supposed demoniacal possessions of ancient times were natural diseases. But there has already been advanced ample evidence to establish the following points; namely—that, long before the time of Jesus, almost all the nations of the earth believed in demoniacal possessions, and pretended to cast out devils,—that the supposed demoniacs were afflicted merely with natural diseases—and that Jesus's knowledge of the human constitution was so imperfect as to make him share the vulgar belief, that persons thus afflicted had within them demons, or imaginary beings originated in the fancy of the pagans regarding their illustrious dead! It is most remarkable that every portion of Christianity, when investigated, proves to have been derived from the various religions of the heathens! It may further be remarked that Christians, in imitation of the heathens, continued to worship demons long after the time Jesus is said to have lived—to eat and drink at their altars, and to regard them as mediators and intercessors between men and the superior gods. Accordingly, we find Paul endeavouring to deter the Christians of Corinth from these practices. We read that he told them that the things which the Gentiles sacrificed were for *demons*—that he wished them to have no fellowship with *demons;*—that they could not drink the cup of the Lord and the cup of *demons*, nor partake of the Lord's table and of the table of *demons*—that although there were many who were called gods in heaven and on earth, yet there was to them but one God, and one Lord Jesus Christ—and that they should not sit at meat in an idol's temple. (1 Cor. viii. 1—11; x. 14, 19—21.) He thought it necessary to caution even Timothy against the doctrines of demons, and to remind him that—unlike the heathen theology which had many gods, and many demons as mediators between mortals and the celestial gods—in the Christian theology there was but one God, and but one mediator between God and men, the man Christ Jesus. (1 Tim. ii. 5; iv. 1.) The same worship he prohibits when he cautions the Colossians (ii. 18.) against worshipping angels—αγγελοι—a name frequently given to demons, as messengers or carriers between the gods and men. The term is used as often for beings who were thought to be inimical to men as it is for those supposed to be favourable to them; and of itself simply means a messenger or an agent. For a similar purpose also Paul contrasts Jesus with the angels (Heb. i. 3—8.) showing that, as a mediator, he was more worthy than these intercessors, or mediate demons. This class of demons, or αγγελοι, appears however to have been the same as the Æons of the Greeks, and afterwards of the Christian Gnostics, being superior to earthly demons or spirits of dead men. (Iren. adv. Hær. lib. ii. c. 15. Epiphan. adv. Hær. 14.) The same practice of worshipping demons or deified pagan heroes continued to flourish among Christian converts during the three or four first centuries of the Christian era, and afterwards only very slowly yielded to what became the more fashionable worship of deified saints. Most of the leaders or Fathers of the Christian faith, while they encouraged saint-worship, vehemently spoke against worshipping these heathen demons, and like Paul, urged that Jesus—who like them had ascended to heaven, and was a mediator between God and men—was much more worthy of their adoration. Like Paul and the other apostles also, these Fathers cast demons out of men and women. Justin Martyr says—" Those persons who are seized and thrown down by the spirits of deceased men, are such as all people agree in calling demoniacs and mad." In both his Apologies, he speaks against worshipping demons. Athenagoras, Lactantius, and Tertullian, are also very severe against the practice. The last named Father, who wrote a most bitter treatise against it, narrates the wonderful confessions which demons made when tormented by Christian exorcists. (See these writers in places already cited.) But it should be observed that Christians inveighed against worshipping these demons, *because they were pagan demons*—the demons of another religion than theirs; for soon did they manage to convert all these heathen practices into their own religion

now under consideration. It is sufficient for our present purpose that, on
the one hand, the Gospels represent him as believing that the men upon

and to have an amply sufficient number of demons, or the supposed spirits of dead men,
to be worshipped in their own deified saints and martyrs, in exact imitation of the
heathens, whose worship they so vehemently decried. Even at the end of the second
century, Tertullian himself could countenance acts of worship to the illustrious dead or
demons of his own religion ; and could accordingly say—" We make oblations for the
dead and for their martyrdom, on certain days yearly." The Emperor Julian sarcastically accuses the Christians of having added many new dead men to the ancient dead
man Jesus. (Cyril. lib. 10.) Anthony the monk, in his dying words, charged his disciples
to adhere to the Lord, in the first place, and next to the saints, by whom after death
they would thereby be received as friends. (Vit. Anton. c. 91.) In order to draw the
populace from the worship of heathen demons to that of deified Christians, several
" Lives of the Saints" were fabricated. (Mosheim Eccles. Hist. cent. vi. part ii. chap. 3.)
Eusebius, (Præf. Evang. lib. xiii. c. 11.) after a hearty approval of the opinions of
Hesiod and Plato, as to heathen demons, says—" The same things deserve to be done to
the favourites of God, who may truly be called the champions of the true religion.—
Consequently, we are accustomed to assemble at their tombs, and offer prayers to them,"
This Father feels no hesitation in openly admitting that Christians worshipped dead men
in imitation of the heathen. Chrysostom, however, in celebrating the wonders of the martyr
Babylas, thought that the Gentiles would laugh at him talking of the works performed
by a man after he had been consigned to the tomb and consumed to dust; but they
were not to imagine that the bodies of Christian martyrs were like those of common
men. Theodoret, (De Martyr. Serm. 8.) having like Eusebius approvingly cited Hesiod
and Plato on pagan demons, says—" If the poet has called good men after their death,
the saviours and guardians of mortals, and the best of philosophers have corroborated
the poet's words, and have declared that we should serve and worship their tombs, why
then blame us for doing these things ? For those who were eminent for their piety,
and for its sake suffered martyrdom, we likewise name our deliverers and physicians,—
not being so desperately mad as to call them demons, but rather the friends and true
servants of God." Theodoret here objects to nothing on this point of pagan theology
but *the bare name*—" demons," given to deified men. He proceeds to say, *inter alia*, that
the temples of the martyrs were eminent for their grandeur and the variety of their
ornaments,—that Christians visited them for religious worship.—that some of them
prayed to the martyrs for the recovery of health, others for the continuance of health,
and others who were childless, for children,—and that when they undertook any journey
they prayed the martyrs to be their companions and guides on the way ;—not that they
approached them as gods, but besought them as deified men to become intercessors for
them with God. He further states that the number of offerings made to these saints
was a proof that they answered the prayers of the faithful. Some offered the figure of
an eye, some of feet, some of hands, made of gold or silver, all of which were proofs of
the cure of as many distempers, and were placed there as monuments by those who had
been made whole, and as an ocular demonstration of the power of the dead. He continues:—" The martyrs have erased from men's minds the memory of those who were
called gods. For our Lord has brought his dead into the temples of your gods, (speaking
to the Greeks) whom he has entirely destroyed, giving their honours to the martyrs.—
For, instead of the feast of Jupiter and of Bacchus, there are now celebrated the feasts
of Peter, Paul, Thomas, and other martyrs. Seeing therefore, my friends, the advantage
of honouring the martyrs, flee from the error of the demons ; and, taking the martyrs
as your lights and guides, proceed in the way which directly leads to God." Precisely
in accordance with this boast of Theodoret—who, like Eusebius and other Fathers,
disagreed with the heathens only so far as that he wished to substitute his deified saints
for their demons—the pagan temples, as already noticed, with all their rites, ceremonies,
and emoluments, had actually been turned over to the Christians for the worship of dead
saints. In Rome, over the portico of the Pantheon or Rotunda—the noblest remaining
heathen temple now in the world—is an inscription to the effect that it was of old dedicated by Agrippa to Jupiter and all the gods, but that it was piously reconsecrated, by
Pope Boniface the Fourth, to the blessed Virgin and all the saints. (Dr. Middleton's
Letters from Rome, p. 161.) But thus to steal the pagan temples was not all.—In order
to accommodate *names* to the taste of prejudiced worshippers, the titles of pagan gods

whom he is said to have operated were demoniacs, and that, on the other,
we have the most ample historical evidence—as the subjoined note will

were adapted to deified saints.   St. Apollinarius was substituted for pagan Apollo; St·
Martina for Mars, and so on.   Like the pagans they accommodated places with divini-
ties, agreeably to the predilection of the inhabitants.   As there was a Jupiter Ammon, a
Jupiter Olympius, and a Jupiter Capitolinus, so the Christians had one Virgin Mary of
Loretto, another of Montserrat, &c.   (Priestley's Hist. Corrupt. Christ. vol. i. p. 368.)
Like the heathens, also, the Christians had deified saints supposed to attend to different
things, each having his proper province.   St. George was invoked in battle, but St.
Margaret in child-bearing; St. Nicholas, or St. Anthony was the deity of seamen; St.
Genevieve was invoked when rain was required. (Ib. p. 367.)   The pagan festivals were
also appropriated by the Christians, unaccompanied with any change, except in the
names of the objects of worship.   By this means, as Dr. Priestley very aptly remarks,
(Ib. p. 335.) the common people, finding the same entertainments at the usual times and
places, were more easily induced to forsake their old religion, and to adopt the new one
which so much resembled it, and especially in the very things which had kept them
attached to the old one.   Gregory Thaumaturgus, or the miracle-worker, who lived at
the commencement of the third century, is specially commended by Gregory Nyssenus
(vol. ii. p. 1006. fol. Paris.) for thus changing the pagan into Christian festivals, with a
view to draw the heathens to the new religion.   Even the very images worshipped by
the pagans were copied by the Christians, under new names, some of which apparently
are still worshipped.   Dr. Middleton, in his Letters from Rome, (p. 160.) states that he
was shown an antique statue of young Bacchus, which was worshipped in the character
of a female saint.   In imitation of the universal pagan worship of Juno, the Queen of
Heaven—who protected cleanliness, presided over marriage and childbirth, particularly
patronised the faithful and virtuous of her own sex, and severely punished lewdness in
matrons,—Christian women, at least as early as the commencement of the fifth century,
worshipped the Virgin Mary, and, on her altar, offered cakes called *collyrides*, in which
oblation no men participated.   After this period, we find the Virgin Mary a general
object of Christian worship.   It is a most remarkable fact that, upon close investigation,
the whole of the Christian religion turns out to be of a pagan origin.   Many Christian
writers, besides the Fathers, have seen and confessed this; but they do not appear to
have perceived that the fact most conclusively disproves the divine origin of Christianity.
Mosheim (Eccles. Hist. cent. v. part ii. chap. 3.) says—" The happy souls of departed
Christians were invoked by numbers, and their aid implored by assiduous and fervent
prayers; while none stood up to censure or oppose this preposterous worship.   The
question how the prayers of mortals ascended to the celestial spirits (a question which
afterwards produced much wrangling, and many idle fancies) did not yet occasion any
difficulty; for the Christians of this century did not imagine that the souls of the saints
were so entirely confined to the celestial mansions, as to be deprived of the privilege of
visiting mortals, and travelling, when they pleased, through various countries.   They
were further of opinion that the places most frequented by departed spirits were those
where the bodies which they had formerly animated were interred; and this opinion,
borrowed by the Christians from the Greeks and Romans, rendered the sepulchres of the
saints the general rendezvous of suppliant multitudes.   The images of those who, during
their lives, had acquired the reputation of uncommon sanctity, were now honoured with
a particular worship in several places; and many imagined that this worship drew down
into the images the propitious presence of the saints or celestial beings they represented;
deluded, perhaps, into this idle fancy by the crafty fictions of *the heathen priests, who had
published the same thing concerning the statues of Jupiter and Mercury*." To this passage
there are the following notes.—"See the Institutiones Divinæ of Lactantius, lib. i. p.
164. Hesiod's Op. et Dies, ver. 122.   Compare with these Sulpitius Severus, Epist. ii.
p. 371; Dial. ii. c. xiii. p. 474; Dial. iii. p. 512. Æneas Gazæus in Theophrasto, p. 65.
Macarius in Jac. Tolii Insignibus Itineris Italici, p. 197. and other writers of this age.
Clementina Homil. x. p. 697. tom. i. PP.   Apostolic. Arnobius adv. Gentes, lib. vi. p.
254.   Casp. Barthius ad Rutilium Numantian, p. 250." Bishop Newton (Dissertations
on the Prophecies, vol. ii. Dissert. 23.) in writing against what he calls Popery, makes
the following string of broad confessions.—"The promoters of this worship were sensible
that it was the same, (as the pagan worship) and that the one succeeded the other; and
as the worship is the same, so likewise is it performed with the same ceremonies;

show—that this notion was of a pagan origin, and that long before the time of Jesus, thousands of pagan exorcists had imposed upon the credulity of ignorant ages. That some of the persons mentioned in the Gospels as demoniacs were merely troubled with epilepsy, and others with different species of madness, while some of them apparently were afflicted with both these maladies which are very nearly allied, is evident from the symptoms they evinced, so far as they are described. It is said that, when the spirit seized them, they suddenly screamed—foamed at the mouth—gnashed their teeth—tore their clothes and their own bodies—fell down—received bruises—fell sometimes into water, and sometimes into fire—retired among the tombs, or into caves in the mountain rocks where the dead were buried, and where the sepulchres of demons or men deified, were supposed to be—broke asunder the cords and chains with which their friends tied

whether these ceremonies were derived from the same source of superstition common to the whole race of mankind, or were the direct copies of one another. The burning of incense or perfumes on several altars at one and the same time;—the sprinkling of holy water, or a mixture of salt and common water, at going into and coming out of places of worship;—the lighting up of a great number of lamps and wax candles in broad day-light, before the altars and statues of their deities;—the hanging up of votive offerings and rich presents as attestations of so many miraculous cures, and deliverances from dangers;—the canonization or deification of deceased worthies;—the assigning of distinct provinces or prefectures to departed heroes and saints;—the worship and adoring of the dead in their sepulchres, shrines, and relics;—the consecrating of, and the bowing down to images;—the attributing of miraculous powers and virtues to idols;—the setting up of little oratories, altars, and statues, in the street and highways, and on the top of mountains;—the carrying of images and relics in pompous processions, with numerous lights, and with music and singing;— flagellations at solemn seasons, under the notion of penance;—the making a sanctuary of temples and churches;—a great variety of religious orders and fraternities of priests;—the shaving of priests, or the tonsure, as it is called, on the crown of their heads;—the imposing of celibacy and vows of chastity on the religious of both sexes;—*all these and many more rites and ceremonies are equally parts of Pagan and Popish superstition.* Nay, the very same temples, the very same altars, the very same images, which once were consecrated to *Jupiter and the other demons*, are now consecrated to the Virgin Mary and the other saints. The very same titles and inscriptions are ascribed to both,—the very same prodigies and miracles are related of these as of those. In short, the whole almost of Paganism is converted and applied to Popery;—the one is manifestly formed upon the same plan and principle as the other; so that there is not only a conformity, but even a uniformity in the worship of ancient and modern—of Heathen and Christian—Rome." All perfectly true. But little does this worthy prelate appear to suspect that all which he has here advanced against Popery directly disproves the divine origin of the Protestantism which he advocates.— The whole that belongs to Christianity, and particularly, its chief credentials—the books of the New Testament—for the first fifteen hundred years of their existence! or until within 560 years of the present time, were in the custody of monks and priests of this Popery. What a vast length of time Christians were before any section of them discovered that their worship was of a pagan origin! Will they say there was no Christianity in the world before Luther, Calvin, and Henry the Eighth? Who came down from heaven at this period, or who on earth was inspired, to show them their mistakes, since the contents of the New Testament had been in the hands of these Papists for fifteen centuries, and since Protestants themselves admit that during this period they materially altered them? There is, however, nothing clearer than that the worship of the Roman Catholics, even at this day, is much more in harmony with the barbarous contents of the Old and New Testament than that of any other sect of Christians in this country. But not to proceed further with this lengthened note. It is trusted that enough has been advanced to place before the reader, in a sufficiently clear manner, the ancient state of demonology, which forms so prominent a feature in the Gospels, and on that account deserved the notice we have taken of it.

them down—could by no means be subdued—cut themselves with stones, and so on. All these are indications of either epilepsy or raving madness. (See Matth. iv. 24 ; xvii. 15. Mark v. 2—5 ; ix. 17—27. Luke iv. 33 ; ix. 39, 42.) Indeed, in some of the passages just cited, these unfortunate persons are expressly called *lunatics.* The father of the demoniac whom Jesus's disciples failed to cure, and who often fell into the fire and into the water, very reasonably believed his son to be *lunatic.* But Jesus, in accordance with the common delusion of the age, imagined that there was a stubborn *devil* within him, and set about expelling him. In harmony with the same popular delusion, he also imagined that every blind, deaf, or dumb person was a demoniac, and that a devil was the cause of this affliction. (Matth. ix. 32, 33. Mark ix. 17—27. Luke xi. 14.) Hence Jesus designated some devils by the epithets "dumb and deaf." The same notion prevailed in this country for a vast number of centuries, until it was —of course not by the light of the Gospel which teaches it, but by the light of scientific researches—made to flee, with the exception of few remnants, into "the dark places of the earth." All implicitly believed— as they were taught by the priests of the Christian faith, and before them, by the priests of Druidism—that when a child was born blind, deaf, or dumb, or suddenly lost the use of one of its external senses, this was the work of the devil, or in other words—witchcraft, whereby the devil had entered the child. Epilepsy, madness, paralysis, bodily deformity from birth—all were attributed to the same cause. Hence the charms, incantations, exorcisms, and witchcrafts of ancient times ; and hence the burning of wizards and witches. All this was only a modification of the doctrines of demoniacal possession and exorcism ; or—as Paul calls them—"the doctrines of devils." Now, if this notion of demoniacal possession in Europe was a delusion, under which the benighted and superstitious people of this quarter of the globe laboured, in common—as it could be shown— with *all* the nations of the earth, what valid reason can be adduced to show that there were *real* demoniacal possessions, for about three years, in that corner of Palestine where Jesus wandered ? Irrespectively of any other proof, the fact that the pagans, in his time, universally believed in demoniacal possession, is a strong presumptive proof that, if their notion on this point was erroneous, so was his. That theirs really was erroneous will be admitted by all enlightened Christians. But to be consistent, they should also admit that so meagre was Jesus's knowledge of the human constitution as to fall into the universal error of his age, in mistaking epilepsy, madness, and other maladies for demoniacal possessions; and in attributing blindness, deafness, and dumbness, to the influence of the devil or devils whom he supposed to have entered the individuals thus afflicted. How vastly superior to Jesus in knowledge of the diseases to which men are susceptible, is the most ignorant medical practitioner of the present age, in this country !

The following instance will show Jesus's deficient knowledge of the principles of political economy, which are necessarily the same in all ages and countries. A deputation of Pharisees and Herodians came to him expressly to ask the following question. Having complimented him on his superior knowledge and impartiality as a teacher, they asked him— " Is it lawful to give tribute to Cæsar or not ? Shall we give, or shall we not give?" His reply was not only characteristically evasive, and expressive of a belief that the question was put in order to entrap him, but indicative of considerable ignorance as to what gave a right of possession. —" Why tempt ye me? bring me a penny that I may see it." His mandate having been obeyed, he asked—" *Whose is this image and superscription?* And they said unto him, Cæsar's. And Jesus answering, said unto them, Render to Cæsar the things that are Cæsar's, and to God the things that are God's." (Matth. xxii. 16—21. Mark xii. 13—17.) That is—because this penny bears the image and superscription of Cæsar, it is Cæsar's property. Therefore, pay tribute to Cæsar. Or, because this penny bears Cæsar's image and superscription, it is his penny. It requires no great depth of thought to perceive that this is most fallacious reasoning. That Cæsar's image was on the coin was no reason for the justness of the tax; much less was it a proof that the coin produced was the property of Cæsar. Although coins are issued, and have their value fixed under some governing authority; yet, as a medium of commerce, every coin is the representation of so much property acquired by somebody: and is the rightful possession of the holder, if he has obtained it by honest means. If a person sells a piece of land for so much money, the coins he receives in payment are no more the property of the sovereign whose impress they bear, than the land is his property. Or if a mechanic receives a guinea for a week's work, and buys food with it for himself and his family, this guinea is no more the property of the monarch whose impress it bears, than the food which the mechanic eats. Who would contend that because the image and superscription of Queen Victoria, or one of our former monarchs, are on the coins of these realms, any tax that may be imposed by the legislature is consequently just? Who would assert that because the image of Victoria is on the coins circulated in conquered Ireland—just as the image of Cæsar was on many, not to say most of those circulated in conquered Judea—any tax levied on the Irish nation is just?—Who would argue, according to Jesus, that because the image of the Queen is on the coins which circulate in the "Emerald Isle," it is the duty of all individuals who hold these coins to hand them over to the Queen or to her ministers, rendering to "Cæsar the things that are Cæsar's"? In a word, who would be so absurd as to contend either that the image of a ruler on a coin makes him the possessor of it, or has any relation whatever to the justness of a tax? No truth is clearer than that such a coin is no more the property of the sovereign than if his image were not upon it at all.— Indeed, there are some coins which bear the image of no sovereign. Such, according to Jesus, are devoid of any proof of the justness of a tax!— There are great force and propriety in the following remarks of Professor Newman (Phases of Faith, p. 152.) on this absurd reasoning of Jesus.— " To imagine that because a coin bears Cæsar's head, therefore it is Cæsar's property, and that he may demand to have as many of such coins as he chooses paid over to him, is puerile, and notoriously false. The circulation of foreign coin of every kind was as common in the Mediterranean then as now; and everybody knew that the coin was the property of the holder, not of him whose head it bore. Thus the reply of Jesus, which pretended to be a moral decision, was unsound and absurd: yet it is uttered in a tone of dictatorial wisdom, and ushered in by a grave

rebuke—'Why tempt ye me, hypocrites?' He is generally understood to mean—'Why do you try to implicate me in a political charge?' and it is supposed that he prudently *evaded* the question. I have indeed heard this interpretation from high Trinitarians; which indicated to me how dead is their moral sense in every thing which concerns the conduct of Jesus. No reason appears why he should not have replied that Moses forbade Israel *voluntarily* to place himself under a foreign king, but did not inculcate fanatical and useless rebellion against overwhelming power. But such a reply, which would have satisfied a more common-place mind, has in it nothing brilliant and striking. I cannot but think that Jesus shows a vain conceit in the cleverness of his answer: I do not think it so likely to have been a conscious evasion. But neither does his rebuke of the questioners at all commend itself to me. How can any man assume to be an authoritative teacher, and then claim that men shall not put his wisdom to the proof? Was it not their duty to do so? And when, in result, the trial has proved the defect of his wisdom, did they not perform a useful public service? In truth, I cannot see the Model Man in his rebuke."
Mr. Rogers, in his Defence of the Eclipse of Faith (p. 125.) appears to have utterly failed in acquitting Jesus of these charges brought against him by Professor Newman. It is quite gratuitous to contend that Jesus's meaning was:—since his interrogators recognised the political authority of Cæsar in receiving the current coin which bore his image, they should render him the political allegiance which they thus acknowledged by paying tribute. Jesus's own words do not bear this interpretation. They plainly show that he thought that because Cæsar's image was on the coin, he was entitled to tribute. Besides, we have no proof that the Pharisees *did* recognise Cæsar's political authority. On the contrary, we have direct historical evidence that they rendered only passive obedience to the laws which their conquerors enforced upon them. Josephus (Antiq. Jud. lib. xvii. c. 2.) tells us that they refused the oath of allegiance to Cæsar and to Herod. And supposing they *did*, in commercial or other transactions, receive the Roman coins, in common with various others then current in Judea, still this did not imply their recognition of the political authority of Cæsar, or his right to rule them. An English merchant, in receiving the coin of a foreign country, does not thereby acknowledge himself the subject of the king of that country. Nor can it be said that the Britons, in receiving the Roman coin, as a medium of commerce, during four hundred years, thereby recognised the right of the Roman power. This position is utterly untenable. Jesus obviously meant that Cæsar's image on the coin brought to him, was a proof that he had a right to a tribute from the Jews. Whatever evil design those who questioned him had, this is no apology for the ignorance of political economy, which he displayed in his reply. In the present age, the merest tyro in this useful science, well knows that all money is the representation of property, and cannot be justly claimed by any monarch because his image and superscription is on it. How immensely more advanced on this point of knowledge, was Dr. Adam Smith, of the present century, than Jesus, who claimed supernatural wisdom!— Equally at a loss in the science of political economy was Jesus when assenting to the correctness of Peter's reply to him, that it was not of their own subjects, but of strangers, the kings of the earth demanded

tribute,* and that therefore their own subjects were exempt. (Matth. xvii. 25, 26.) This is contrary to historical fact; and even if it were true that it was only of strangers the kings of the earth took tribute, since Jesus acquiesces in the justice of this practice, it shows a miserably crooked notion of political, commercial, and international justice. It involves a principle diametrically opposed to the interest of communities, and to good government. From some of Jesus's expressions, however, one would infer that, in his political views, he was extremely *liberal*—a Republican, or almost what, in the present age, would be considered a Chartist, especially on the point of *Equality*. For he severely reflected on the rulers and aristocracy of the Gentiles, because they lorded and domineered over their subjects; and intimated that he aimed at establishing a commonwealth in which all would be equal. (Mark x. 42, 43.) And further, his opponents accused him of politically perverting the nation, forbidding to give tribute to Cæsar, and asserting that he himself was an anointed king. (Luke xxiii. 2.)

In the following instance, as well as others which could be noticed, Jesus has given us a clear proof that he was equally ignorant with his contemporaries of the operations of the laws of nature in reference to man. He tells his hearers that those whose blood Pilate mingled with their sacrifices, and also those who were killed by the falling of the tower of Siloam, did not thus come to an untimely end in consequence of their sins. (Luke xiii. 1—5.) Now, there is no fact better established in the present enlightened age than that every homicide—every bodily harm—every misfortune—every pain or sickness, is the result of the violation of some one or more of the natural laws, or in other words, the consequence of sinning against these laws. For example, when a man falls from the top of a steeple and is killed, his death is caused by the violation of the law of gravitation, and is a punishment for this violation. When he swallows prussic acid, or any other deadly poison, great pain and death ensue, because he violated one of the organic laws. When a man is slain in battle or an insurrection, and his blood—like that of the Galileans—is mingled with the blood of beasts, it is through a violation of the moral law on the part of the belligerents. When a tower—say the tower of Siloam—falls upon eighteen or more men, and kills them, it is owing to the violation of a physical law on their part, or on the part of others. So in regard to every evil that befalls man. It is because he, or some one else, violates the natural laws; and the evil that befals him is always proportionate to the degree in which these laws are violated. Jesus, however,

* Such words as κηνσος (tribute) evidently from the Latin *census*—an assessment or tax, and δηναριον (a penny) clearly from the Latin *denarius*—a Roman penny, which words occur in the passages just cited, as well as in others—furnish an additional proof of the late origin of the Gospels It is by no means credible that Jesus—a Jew, would have used the Latin word *census*, or the word *denarius* which he is said to have used in the parable of the vineyard. (Matth. xx. 2, 9, 10.) A Roman, writing in Greek, might have used such words, or a Jew might have used such, some fifty or sixty years after Vespasian had destroyed Jerusalem and established Roman colonies in Judea, by means of which many Latin words would be introduced into the spoken language of the natives. But after all, how came such words into the Greek, or how came the Evangelists to write in Greek at all, their language as Jews being Hebrew, or rather Syriac?

directly taught that it was not in consequence of sin, or the violation of these laws that evil befell men. Bishop Butler, George Coombe, and others, were infinitely before Jesus, in correct knowledge of the laws of nature, and their relation to the constitution of man.

The proofs which Jesus gave that he had very imperfect knowledge of the laws of the human mind, or of mental philosophy, are very numerous; and some of them have already been advanced in treating of his conduct towards his hearers. It was the want of knowledge on this point that made him imagine that people could believe his doctrines at will, in the absence of evidence. For instance, his hearers, on one occasion, in consequence of what he had just said, asked him—"What shall we do, that we might work the works of God?" He replied that they were to believe in him. Whereupon, they very reasonably and earnestly asked him to give them a sign or a proof that he had been sent by God; so that upon this evidence they might believe. But instead of giving them any proof at all of his heavenly mission, Jesus proceeded to speak obscurely of the bread from heaven, which he said kept away for ever the feeling of hunger. His oration, being devoid of evidence, does not appear to have had the least effect in gaining the assent of these unprejudiced and evidently *anxious enquirers ;* nay, it gave offence to another portion of the audience. (John vi. 28—40.) Never was there a public teacher whose doctrines were more unfortunate and more unadapted to convert his hearers than those which Jesus preached. It is by no means wonderful that, after labouring for three years, his disciples only numbered twelve, and that, at his apprehension and martyrdom, even these forsook and denied him.

Nearly akin to his deficient knowledge of mental philosophy—a grave defect in a public teacher—is his ignorance of the art of reasoning. Instances of this are almost innumerable in the Gospels. Only two of them, however, shall now be cited.—The first, Jesus's mode of reasoning to prove the resurrection of the dead. (Mark xii. 18—27.) He tells the Sadducees, "touching the dead that they shall rise," that God appeared to Moses, and said he was "the God of Abraham, the God of Isaac, and the God of Jacob;" and he adds—"He is not the God of the dead, but the God of the living." His argument here is that, since God told Moses, (Ex. iii. 2—15.) long after the death of the three patriarchs named, that he was still *their* God, there must be a resurrection; because God is not the God of the dead, but the God of the living. In other words, he would not have said he was the God of these patriarchs, long after they had departed this life, had they not still been alive in another world. But taking the most favourable view of the passage cited by Jesus, it cannot be made to prove a resurrection. The utmost it can be shown to prove is a state of existence after death. It is, however, a patent fact that neither a resurrection nor even a future state of existence is taught in the Hebrew Scriptures; and that the Jews, prior to the Christian era—about which period they began to become acquainted with the Platonic philosophy—had no notion of either. Nor does the passage cited by Jesus teach, or even imply, that there is to be a resurrection. The evident intention of the writer is to identify the Jewish Jehovah with the God worshipped by Moses's forefathers. Accordingly, he makes Jehovah say—I am the God of thy *fathers*, the God of Abraham, Isaac, and Jacob,—that is, the God whom these patriarchs worshipped. There is here not the slightest hint given that these patriarchs *lived* when the writer would have us believe that the words were spoken by Jehovah to Moses. The object of uttering them is clearly shown by the drift of the narrative ; namely, to inform Moses *what* God it was who had then appeared to him, and whose *name* he had not yet learned. Consequently, Moses asked Jehovah what he should say to the Israelites when—after he had told them that he was sent by the God of their fathers—they should demand to know the *name* of that God. To this, Jehovah instructed him to say that " *I am*" had sent him, and to add that the Lord God (Jehovah Elohim) of their fathers—*the God of Abraham, Isaac, and Jacob*, had sent him. Thus does the argument of Jesus utterly vanish. In the first place, he notoriously misunderstands the meaning of the passage he cites, and consequently misapplies it.— Next, were the passage really applicable, it would furnish no proof whatever of a resurrection. It is very wonderful, and exceedingly discouraging to a true believer, to find that Jesus whom he regards as omniscient, could not produce a better argument, in proof of the resurrection, to the Sadducees—a strong and learned Jewish sect, who denied that it would ever take place. Christians of the present age, being better acquainted with the subject, can furnish far stronger reasons than the " author and finisher of their faith" in support of this doctrine. The sophistical Paul argues for the resurrection much more powerfully than Jesus. The scribe, who is said to have approved of this kind of argument, thereby showed that he really belonged to the Jewish race—a race whose few writings prove them further from the principle of inductive reasoning than any other race known.

The other instance intended to be noticed of Jesus's inability to reason, is found in the controversy he held with the devil, when led into the wilderness to be tempted. (Matth. iv. 1—11. Mark i. 12, 13. Luke iv. 1—13.) It would appear that, before he entered upon the work of casting out demons, he was to prove that he was proficient in this art, by vanquishing the Prince of demons. An important part of his contest with him consisted in quoting appropriate Scriptural passages, at which the devil seems to have been the more expert ; for Jesus quoted at least one passage which could not reasonably be applied to the case. The devil having cited a passage, Jesus in reply cited—" Thou shalt not tempt the Lord thy God," clearly meaning that the devil should not tempt him. But when Jesus had gone into the wilderness expressly " to be tempted of the devil," and had, for that purpose, allowed him, apparently, to carry him bodily through the air, and place him on a pinnacle of the temple, how irrational it was in him to say—" Thou shalt not tempt the Lord thy God." Was it not for the purpose of being tempted he had gone into the wilderness, and, like Moses, had fasted for the incredible space of forty days and nights, till at last he felt hungry ? On this occasion, he not only gave a proof of his incapacity to reason, but likewise of his scanty knowledge of physical nature. If he believed that, from the " exceedingly high mountain"— whither it is said the devil took him—he could see " all the kingdoms of the world," the fact that the earth is round, or rather spherical, must have been utterly unknown to him. If he did not believe that he could see all the world from this high mountain, and knew that the earth was a globe,

DD

he should have said so, instead of incorrectly citing a passage from the Pentateuch to show that the devil was not to be worshipped. But it is clear that Jesus did *not* know that the earth was globular; for it is said that the devil actually *showed* him what he called " all the kingdoms of the world"; which implies that Jesus *looked* at them and viewed them as such. It is, however, well known that comparatively little of the world can be seen from the highest mountain in the world. If the devil took Jesus to the top of the Caucasus, the Peak of Teneriffe, or the Andes, he would not have been able to see one-tenth part of the kingdoms of the world. Let the mountain be ever so high, he could not see the kingdoms whose subjects were antipodal to him. But it is urged that only the kingdoms of the world then known is meant by " all the kingdoms of the world."— Still, Britain, France, China, and scores of other territories were then *known*; neither of which could by any possibility be seen from the highest mountain in Judea. Jesus could no more see all the kingdoms of the world from the highest mountain than a fly, standing on one side of a ball of three inches in diameter, can see the opposite side. The thing is an impossibility; and, as Dr. Giles (Christ. Rec. p. 144.) says, " is an insult to our understanding." Jesus, in supposing that, when the devil took him to the top of a high mountain, he showed him all the kingdoms of the world,—clearly laboured under the vulgar error of his times, that the earth was flat, so that from a high peak " the ends of the earth could be seen,— an error which is committed by the writers of the Bible in every expression indicating their notion of the shape of the earth.* Jesus required no Inspiration—no revelation from heaven—no divine penetration, to discover that the earth was globular; for Thales, more than six hundred years before his time, had taught this doctrine; (Diog. Laert. ii. 1.) and the fact was well known to Greek philosophers in the time of Jesus, although the barbarous Jews were ignorant of it. It may be urged that it is not Jesus, but the Evangelists who say that all the kingdoms of the world could be seen from a high mountain. Let this be granted: still it is quite as fatal to the divine origin of Christianity as if Jesus had expressly said that the earth was flat; for if the Evangelists could err, they were no more under the guidance of Deity than some other fallible mortals; and none of the supernatural things which they relate can be implicitly believed. The real state of the case, however, is that it is Jesus who is said to have been taken to the top of a high mountain and shown all the kingdoms of the world—which implies that he *saw* them; and that it is the Evangelists who narrate these wonderful things. So the matter stands precisely as already represented.

* In order to perceive this, consult the following passages where ארץ קצה, ארץ אפסי, אפסי, and πέρας της γης, are very properly translated—the *end* or *ends* of the earth, or of the world,—the words just cited as rendered *end*, clearly signifying a *termination, limit, boundary, extremity*, &c.—Deut. iv. 11, 12; xxxiii. 17. 1 Sam. ii. 10. Job xxviii. 24; xxxvii. 3; xxxviii. 4, 13, 18. Ps. ii. 8; xix. 4; xxii. 22, 27; xlviii. 10; lix. 13; lx. 8; lxv. 5; lxviii. 7; xcviii. 3; cxxxv. 7. Prov. xxx. 4. Isa. xl. 11, 28; xli. 5, 9; xliii. 6; xlv. 22; xlvi. 5; xlviii. 20; xlix. 6. Jer. xvi. 19; xxv. 31. Dan. iv. 11, 12. Mic. v. 4. Zech. ix. 10. Acts xiii. 47. Rom. x. 18. It is wonderful how Inspiration allowed all these writers to err, as to the shape of the earth. All of them regarded it as a vast platform which had *ends* or *termini*, or rather was bounded and hemmed in by a fence; while they regarded the sky or firmament above it as a canopy or a solid expanse.

Such we have found the intellectual imperfections of Jesus in almost every branch of knowledge on which he spoke. Many men have lived, both before and after him, who were vastly more intelligent than he; and thousands of such are now living; while there are very few who possess less knowledge than he possessed. On the ground of superior scientific knowledge, therefore, he has no claim upon our reverence. If in philosophical or scientific discoveries, he had been to his age what many celebrated persons who lived immediately before or after him, or were contemporary with him—whose works remain to this day, and whose discoveries in science have been of vast benefit to mankind—were to the age in which they lived; or if he had been to his age what Bacon, Newton, and others in this country have been to their age, his memory, as a person of superior genius and knowledge, would be worthy of our profound reverence. If he had written a book teaching men to avoid the millions of miseries which, through life, they endure—revealing to them the mysteries of nature—disclosing to them at once those useful arts which, since his time, have been slowly discovered and invented by the dint of human calculation and skill; such as the art of printing—the elements of matter—the circulation of the blood—the art of vaccination—the use of steam for the purpose of navigation and for sundry other purposes—the use of electricity as means of conveying knowledge to distant parts of the earth; together with a thousand other things discovered or invented by mere man within the last two centuries;—what a blessing would such a book, written in an intelligible manner, have conferred upon mankind! From how many thousands of errors it would have saved them! What a vast amount of misery it would have spared them to endure! It would not have been too much to expect Jesus, who laid a claim to superhuman wisdom, to write such a book. But he wrote nothing—made no discoveries in any branch of knowledge—revealed nothing, either physical, moral, or theological. All that he is said to have taught, had been inculcated by others before him. It is, however, questionable whether Jesus was able to write at all, or even to read correctly. It is said that, when he was interrogated as to his views on the manner in which an adultress should be dealt with, he wrote on the ground; but it would seem that the act of writing on this occasion consisted merely in making marks on the sand with his finger unconsciously, while he invented the evasive answer he gave to those who questioned him. There is also extant a letter said to have been written by Jesus to Abgarus, king of Edessa, in the Syriac language. Eusebius, who first produced it, (Hist. Eccles. lib. i. c. 13.) says he found it amongst the public records of Edessa. Some eminent Christian writers of the present age, however, contend that this letter is a forgery. If it is, then it furnishes no proof that Jesus could write. As to his ability to read, we find that he was accustomed to read in the synagogue at Nazareth, his native place. (Luke iv. 16.)· Still we are told that when he was teaching in the temple, "the Jews marvelled, saying, How knoweth this man letters, having never learned?" (John vii. 15.) It is also said that "when he was come into his own country, he taught them in their synagogue, insomuch that they were astonished, and said, Whence hath this man this wisdom, and these mighty works? Is not this the carpenter's son? is not his mother called Mary? and his brethren, James, and Joses, and Simon, and Judas? and his sisters, are they not all with us? Whence then hath this man all these things? And they were offended in him."— (Matth. xiii. 54—57.) Now, it is very difficult to reconcile the foregoing statements. One informs us that Jesus was accustomed to read the Jewish Scriptures, in the synagogues or churches of the Jews, apparently as part of their public worship; it being a practice of the Jewish doctors— like the present Christian priests—to read portions of their Scriptures, and expound them to the assembled worshippers. The other statement goes to show that, when Jesus taught in the temple, the Jews asked how he *knew letters*, saying that he *had never learned*. Although he was now at Jerusalem—comparatively far from the place of his nativity—yet, there were probably at that great feast—to which every Jew was expected to come—some persons who had known him from infancy, and therefore could from their own knowledge say that he had never learned the Hebrew letters. Be this as it may, those at the feast of tabernacles, who said that Jesus had never learned the alphabet, were confirmed in their statement by Jesus's immediate neighbours, who had known him from childhood as the *son of Joseph the carpenter*—had known his mother, his brothers, and sisters, and had had every opportunity of judging of the degree of education which he had received in early life. These, when they heard him teach in their synagogue, asked whence he had acquired any wisdom superior to what they themselves possessed, doubted the reality of his learning, and were offended with what they appear to have thought in him a pretence. It certainly does not seem very probable that Jesus, in his low social position, and in those early times, when learning was very rare, had received such a degree of education in his youth as to be able to read before the Jewish doctors in synagogues and in the temple. It is also remarkable that Luke alone says that Jesus read, or was accustomed to read in the synagogue at Nazareth. The other Evangelists, although they repeatedly state that he taught, or indoctrinated in the temple and in synagogues, yet do not once say that he ever read from a book on any occasion. Besides, if he had been taught to read in the ordinary way, when young, his neighbours in that small place—Nazareth, would have known the fact, and would not have wondered at his display of wisdom.— Indeed, Jesus's own words convey a denial that he had been taught to read in his youth, or even taught at all, in the ordinary way. When the Jews said that he had never learned letters, he replied that the doctrine he taught in the temple was not his, but that of him by whom he had been sent, meaning the Father. (John vii. 16.) Hence we are to infer that Jesus miraculously learned to read, like Alfred the Great, of whom it is said that "one day by *divine inspiration* he began to read and interpret."*

* It is curious to observe such an author as Mr. Sharon Turner devoting 115 pages of his History of the Anglo-Saxons (vol. ii. pp. 147—262.) to describe the numerous literary productions of Alfred the Great, drawing his information principally from the fallacious writings of the monks of this country. If we criticise history, we shall find evidence amounting almost to positive certainty that Alfred never wrote one of those books attributed to him. The works which bear Alfred's name were, doubtless, those of monks who, long after his death, attached his name to them in order to enhance the value and extend the sale of their manuscripts—a very common practice in ancient times. Asser, the archbishop of St. David's, who was for a considerable time in Alfred's court, as his tutor, and wrote regular annals of events in the king's life, tells us that in

Some infer from the statements of the Evangelists, that Jesus spent his time in Egypt till he began his public career, when about thirty years of age, and that it was in that country he was educated and taught the art of working miracles. But wherever, and by what means soever—whether by natural or supernatural means—he was educated, and whether he was, or was not able to read and write, one thing is clear, namely, that the education he received was very scanty and imperfect. This fact will account and apologise for the intellectual and moral imperfections which are observable in his character. To this cause, doubtless, is to be attributed the erroneous manner in which he read, cited, and applied the Hebrew Scriptures. Even on the solitary occasion on which he is said to have read in the synagogue, if Luke has reported him correctly, his lection was singularly inaccurate. The small portion that Luke (iv. 18, 19.) reports of his reading is said to be in the book of Esaias (lxi. 1—3.) But throughout the book of Esaias, neither in the Hebrew, Septuagint, nor any other version do we find the precise words which Jesus read. There are many things in the passage in Esaias which Jesus is not said to have read, and some things read by him which are not found in Esaias, such as— "recovering of sight to the blind"; while the wording in several instances is very different. The inevitable conclusion, therefore, is that either Jesus did not read correctly, or that the Hebrew Scriptures have not descended to us in the state they were in his time. When justifying the conduct of his disciples in stealing corn on the Sabbath day, and, for this purpose, referring to the Hebrew Scriptures, so little acquainted with them did he show himself that he called Ahimelech, the high priest, Abiathar. (1 Sam. xxi. 1. Mark ii. 26.) In disputing with the Jews he also appears not to have known the Scriptural account given of Enoch and Elias ascending bodily to heaven. (John iii. 13.) In a vast number of instances did he grossly misinterpret the Hebrew prophecies, and applied to himself passages which positively had not the slightest allusion to him. The most favourable construction that can be put upon these inaccuracies, is to attribute them to Jesus's scanty literary attainments. To this, perhaps, should be added the evidence presented in the Gospels that his mind, from some cause, was not in the soundest state. So thought his own relatives, who had had constant opportunities of watching all his actions, and of hearing all his words, from infancy to manhood; and who therefore, of all others, had the best possible advantages of forming an unprejudiced opinion of his mental state. Yet even they, whose natural affections would incline them to regard all that he said and did in the most favourable light—even they

A.D. 884, and in the 36th year of Alfred's life, "he could not yet understand anything of books, for he had not yet learned to read anything." Three years afterwards, as he tells us, Alfred, "by divine inspiration, began on one and the same day to read and interpret." In twelve years after, namely A.D. 900, when fifty-one years old, Alfred died. Even if he could write at all, what time had he to write half the books attributed to him? All his lifetime, and more particularly towards the end of it, he suffered from ill health, and was moreover almost continually engaged in war. A very likely king to have written many books! (See Asser's Life of Alfred. Bohn's Six Saxon Chronicles, pp. 37, 64, 70, 75, 76, 78.) A critical history of the Isle of Britain would be a boon to English readers. Those histories which we have—both ancient and modern—are replete with errors. Each historian follows the tract of his predecessor, and all depend upon uncriticised monkish legends.

thought him of unsound mind. Mark (iii. 21, 22, 31—35.) gives the following account of the opinions expressed by Jesus's relatives and others of his mental aberration.—When he was in the act of addressing a numerous crowd of people, and when " his friends heard of it, *they went out to lay hold of him ;* for they said, *He is beside himself."* The Scribes also, at the same time, expressed a similar opinion of him, saying that he was possessed with the Prince of demons, by whom he cast out demons. His kinsfolk, however, do not appear to have secured him on this occasion ; for shortly after, apparently on the same day, we find his mother and brothers—apprehensive of his personal safety—coming in search of him, and sending a messenger into the midst of the crowd with which he was surrounded to tell him that they wished to speak to him. The answer which Jesus gave to the party who told him of the wishes of his mother and brothers, however, strongly indicated that it was not without cause his relatives sought to put him under restraint. On another occasion, after he had delivered a long and most singular oration, *many* of his hearers concluded that he was *possessed with a demon,* and was *mad.* (John x. 20.) In accordance with such a state of mind, indeed, are many of his words and actions already noticed. His conduct, for example, in designating Peter—his most courageous disciple—*Satan,* and in calling Judas—the murderous traitor—his *friend,* saluting him with a kiss, cannot so rationally be accounted for on any other supposition. If the Jews, and even Jesus's own relatives were correct—the former in maintaining that he had never been taught even the rudiments of learning, and both in maintaining that he laboured under mental aberration, it is, therefore, by no means wonderful that he read imperfectly, misquoted and misapplied the Hebrew Scriptures, committed so many errors in reasoning, and displayed such lamentable want of scientific knowledge in discoursing on every branch of moral, mental, and natural philosophy.

SECTION IX.—MOST OF THE BEST THINGS WHICH JESUS TAUGHT BORROWED FROM HEATHEN THEOLOGY.

In comparing the contents of the Gospels with writings which had existed many centuries before them, we find in such writings a vast number of expressions which, in a modified form, are by the Evangelists attributed to Jesus. Taking for granted—as we have done throughout this work—that Jesus actually uttered all the expressions that are ascribed to him—which we must, or regard the so-called inspired Evangelists as guilty of forgery—we cannot therefore avoid the conclusion that he borrowed much of his ideas and expressions from the heathens. If Jesus had been too divine—if he had been omniscient—one would think that it was not too much for him to furnish us with an original system of morals,—one would think that he would have disdained the practice of adopting the old Pagan rites and expressions, and would have produced something that was not already in the world. We do not, however, find that he did so.* On the contrary, we find that the purest morality which he taught was borrowed from heathen sources. To those who are versed in pagan lore, it appears very strange that Christian writers invariably represent the scraps of morality, religious doctrines, and religious practices, taught by Jesus, as then new to the world; and that they would have us believe that before his time, there was among men no morality either taught or practised, which, in rectitude and purity, bore any comparison to that which he taught; but that all the world lay in utter moral darkness. This however was not the case. Long before his time, there were, not only individuals, but whole communities of men, quite as moral and virtuous as any that we find for at least fourteen centuries after his time. Among heathen nations, we find moral philosophers whose writings abound with moral sentiments far more elevated than any attributed to Jesus. In the history of these heathen nations also, we find that justice, benevolence, and all other moral virtues, were exercised to a very high degree. Nor could it have been otherwise; for no community of men can long exist without the exercise of virtue. To teach men that it was for their benefit, both individually and collectively, to shun vice and practise virtue, required no revelation from heaven. This they were daily taught by experience and observation —the grand sources of all their knowledge. Even if the morality which Jesus taught had not been previously inculcated, still there is nothing clearer than that every sound precept which he enunciated could be discovered by man, without any supernatural aid. If he had revealed the operations of those laws of nature—which, in his time, had not been discovered by scientific men, and many of which are still undiscovered, but the knowledge of all of which, nevertheless, is indispensable to the happiness of mankind—he would have done something towards promoting the happiness of future ages. But he neither revealed nor discovered any thing—either moral or physical. All that he taught had previously been taught by such men as Thales, Solon, Pythagoras, Confucius, Socrates, Plato, the Brahmins or Gymnosophists of India, the Peripatetics, the Stoics, and others; so that it would be no difficult task to show that every thing taught in the Gospels had been previously advanced in very similar words to those which Jesus is said to have used. A few specimens, however, must here suffice.

Confucius—the great Chinese philosopher, who flourished at least 500 years before the Christian era—in the 24th maxim of his *Ta-heo*, writes thus—" Do unto another what thou would be should do unto you; and do not unto another what you would not should be done unto you. Thou only needest this law alone; it is the foundation and principle of all the rest." Jesus, borrowing this piece of morality, says—" All things whatsoever ye would that men should do to you, do ye even so to them; for this is the law and the prophets." (Matth. vii. 12.) Irrespectively of the fact that Confucius lived more than 500 years before Jesus; if the

---

* In a great measure, this has already been shown in notes, which point out the pagan origin of Christianity. It will also be further shown in the next section, where proofs of Jesus's identity with the ancient Essenes will be produced. At present, therefore, it is not intended to cite one-hundredth part of what Jesus has borrowed from the heathens,—only a few passages by way of example.

canons of criticism which Dr. Lardner lays down for the detection of spurious writings be applied to the foregoing passages, it will be clear that it is Jesus who has borrowed from the heathen philosopher, and not the reverse; for his expression of the maxim is in a more abridged form, and more smoothly constructed. Jesus, in order to vary a little the expression of Confucius, and to apply his precept to Judaism, says—" This is the law and the prophets," instead of saying *this law alone is the substance of all the rest.* Several others of Jesus's precepts appear to have been borrowed from the *maxims* of Confucius, such as the following.—Confucius says— " Desire not the death of thine enemy ; thou wouldest desire it in vain : his life is in the hands of heaven...... Acknowledge thy benefits by the return of other benefits, but never revenge injuries....... We may have an aversion for an enemy, without desiring revenge. The motions of nature are always criminal." (Max. 51, 53, 63.)* Jesus says—" Love

* For the correctness of the translation of the passages from Confucius, the reader is referred to Josephus Tela's Translation of Confucius ; J. F. Davies's General Description of China and the Chinese, Lond. 1836. Gutzlaff's Sketch of Chinese History, &c. If it were asked how could Jesus, or rather the compilers of the Gospels, have known any thing about the contents of Confucius's moral philosophy, the answer is that not only long before we have any proof that our present Gospels existed—which was about the end of the second century of the Christian era—but long before the commencement of this era, there was in Alexandria a sect of the Therapeutic monks or Essenes, already noticed, whose sacred writings, Eusebius says, are our Gospels ; and who were professors of the *Eclectic* philosophy, which consisted principally in collecting together into one system the best tenets of morality that belonged to all the various religions of the world. These monks, therefore, who, for this purpose, travelled into all countries, would not fail to acquire knowledge of the system of morals taught by so renowned a philosopher as Confucius, and to extract from it what they thought its gems, in order to compose their moral gnomologue. A knowledge of these Eclectics and the part they played in regard to the origin of Christianity will throw a flood of light on the cause that the Gospels contain doctrines and expressions found in the morals and theology of various and widely different pagan religions. For this purpose, therefore, the following extracts are given from Dr. Mosheim's Ecclesiastical History, vol. i. pp. 37, 169—176. Cadell's Edit. 1811. Lond. This learned and orthodox Christian—after giving an account of the philosophy of Plato and other moralists, and stating that, as there were many absurd things maintained by these sects, certain men of discernment were of opinion that it was wise to extract from each sect such tenets as were good and reasonable, and to reject the rest—tells us,—" This gave rise to a new form of philosophy in *Egypt* and principally at *Alexandria,* which was called the *Eclectic,* whose founder, according to some, was Potamon, an Alexandrian, though this opinion is not without its difficulties. It manifestly appears from the testimony of Philo the Jew, who was himself one of this sect, that this philosophy was in a flourishing state at *Alexandria, when our Saviour was upon the earth.* The Eclectics *held Plato in the highest esteem,* though they *made no scruple to join with his doctrines whatever* they thought conformable to reason in the tenets and opinions of the other philosophers.—See Godof. Olearius de Philosophia Eclectica. Jac. Brucker, and others." Having, *inter alia,* made the foregoing remarks, in his history of the first century, our author, in narrating the events of the second century, would have us believe that the Eclectics of this century were a new sect, at the head of whom were Athenagoras, Pantænus, Clemens, and lastly, Ammonius, whose disciples were Origen, and Plotinus the preceptor of Porphyry, and in regard to whom modern writers have been much puzzled in deciding whether he was a heathen or a Christian. " Towards the conclusion of this (the second) century," says Dr. Mosheim, " a new sect of philosophers suddenly arose, spread with amazing rapidity through the greatest part of the Roman empire, swallowed up almost all other sects, and proved extremely detrimental to Christianity. *Alexandria,* in *Egypt,* which had been, for a long time, the seat of learning, and, as it were, the centre of all the liberal arts, gave birth to this new philosophy. Its votaries chose to be called Platonists ; though, far from adhering to all the tenets of Plato, *they*

your enemies, bless them that curse you, do good to them that hate you, and pray for them which despitefully use you, and persecute you." (Matth. v. 44.) The similarity is very striking.

collected from the different sects such doctrines as they thought conformable to truth, and formed thereof one general system. The reason then, why they distinguished themselves by the title of Platonists, was, that *they thought the sentiments of Plato*, concerning the most noble part of philosophy, which has the Deity and things invisible for its objects, much more rational and sublime than those of the other philosophers.........They professed searching after truth alone, and *were ready to adopt from all the different systems and sects such tenets as they thought agreeable to it.* Hence also they were called *Eclectics.* ....This new species of Platonism was embraced by such of the *Alexandrian Christians* as were desirous of retaining with the profession of the Gospel, the title, the dignity, and the habit of philosophers. It is also said to have had the particular approbation of Athenagoras, Pantænus, Clemens the Alexandrian, and all those who, in this century, were charged with the care of the public school which the Christians had in Alexandria. These sages were of opinion that *true philosophy*, the greatest and most salutary gift of God to mortals, was scattered in various portions through all the different sects;" (pagan sects of course included by these followers of Jesus!) "and that it was, consequently, the duty of every wise man, and more especially of *every Christian doctor*, to gather it from the several corners where it lay dispersed, and to employ it thus re-united, in the defence of religion, and in destroying the dominion of impiety and vice. *The Christian Eclectics* had this also in common with the others; that *they preferred Plato to the other philosophers*, and looked upon his opinions concerning God, the human soul, and things invisible, as conformable to the spirit and genius of the Christian doctrine. This philosophical system underwent some changes when Ammonius Saccas, who taught with the highest applause, in the Alexandrian school, about the conclusion of this century, laid the foundation of that sect which was distinguished by the name of the New Platonists. .... He attempted a general reconciliation or coalition of all sects, whether philosophical or religious, and taught a doctrine which he looked upon as proper to unite them all, *the Christians not excepted*, in perfect harmony. And herein lies the difference between this new sect and the Eclectics, who had before this time flourished in Egypt:—the Eclectics held that, in every sect there was a mixture of good and bad, of truth and falsehood, and accordingly, they chose and adopted, out of each of them, such tenets as seemed to them conformable to reason and truth, and rejected such as they thought repugnant to both. Ammonius, on the contrary, maintained that the great principles of all philosophical and religious truth were *to be found in all sects*.....that all the Gentile religions, *and even the Christian*, were to be illustrated and explained by the principles of this universal philosophy; but that, in order to this, the fables of the priests were to be removed from Paganism, and the comments and interpretations of the disciples of Jesus from Christianity.........The tenets of the philosophers, the superstitions of the heathen priests, the solemn doctrines of Christianity were all to suffer in this cause..... The *Egyptian* philosophy, which was said to be derived from Hermes, was the basis of that of Ammonius; or, as it is otherwise called, of *modern Platonism*........Ammonius therefore associated the doctrines of the Egyptians with the doctrines of Plato......... As Ammonius was born and educated among the Christians, he embellished these injunctions (which he gave his disciples) and even gave them an air of authority by expressing them in terms partly borrowed from the Sacred Scriptures... This new species of philosophy, imprudently *adopted by Origen, and many other Christians*, was extremely prejudicial to the Gospel.".......The number of learned men among the Christians, which was very small in the preceding century, increased considerably in this. Among these were few rhetoricians, sophists, or orators. *The majority were philosophers, attached to the Eclectic system.*" This description of the Eclectic Christians and heathens will amply account for the fact that some portions of the contents of the Gospels are borrowed from one heathen philosopher, and some from another; while the larger proportion is from Plato. For it is to be observed that there does not exist a tittle of evidence that *our present Gospels* existed before the end of the second century, about which time, there is every reason to conclude they were compiled from the heterogeneous collections of these Christian Eclectics at the Alexandrian college; all the moral aphorisms or gnomologues of different philosophers, thus selected, being put in the mouth of Jesus— the hero of the Christians.

The model prayer, called the *Lord's prayer*, with which Jesus furnished his followers, he evidently borrowed from Jewish literature. The few instances of verbal difference between it and the following translation of a part of the Jewish Euchologues, made by a *reverend and pious Christian*, may be the result of a little alteration effected by time, either in the Christian or the Jewish prayer, or even in both ; or may have arisen either from Jesus's imperfect recollection of the Jewish prayer, or from the imperfect manner in which his repetition of it was reported by the Evangelists. The principal difference, however, is caused by Jesus's omission of several words found in the Jewish prayer, which would indicate that he knew it but imperfectly. But even now, at this distant time, when each has undergone a translation from a dead language, they are so much alike that they furnish ample internal evidence of their identity. The Jewish prayer runs thus.—" *Our Father, which art in heaven*, be gracious to us, O Lord our God ; *hallowed be thy name*, and let the remembrance of thee be glorified *in heaven* above, and *upon earth* here below. Let *thy kingdom* reign over us, now and for ever. The holy men of old said, remit and *forgive* unto all men whatsoever they have done against me. *And lead us not into temptation, but deliver us from* the *evil* thing. *For thine is the kingdom*, and thou shalt reign in *glory, for ever* and for evermore." (The works of the Rev. John Gregorie, p. 168. Lond. 1685.) All the expressions italicised in the foregoing prayer will be found in the following.— " Our Father which art in heaven, hallowed be thy name. Thy kingdom come. Thy will be done in earth, as it is in heaven. Give us this day our daily bread. And forgive us our debts, as we forgive our debtors. And lead us not into temptation, but deliver us from evil. For thine is the kingdom, and the power, and the glory, for ever. Amen." (Matth. vi. 9—13. Luke xi. 2—4.) Well might Basnage (Hist. des Juifs, tom. vi. p. 374.) say that the Jews had an ancient prayer called the *Kadish*, precisely like Jesus's prayer ; and Wetstein remark that " it is a curious fact that the Lord's prayer may be reconstructed almost verbatim out of the Talmud." It is to be remarked that Jesus has omitted the expressions—" be gracious unto us, O Lord our God"—and " let thy kingdom reign over us now and for ever,"—that instead of " let the remembrance of thee be glorified in heaven above, and upon earth here below, he has— " thy will be done in earth as it is in heaven,"—that instead of " the holy men of old said, remit and forgive unto all men whatsoever they have done against me," he has—" forgive us our debts as we forgive our debtors," — and that instead of—" for thine is the kingdom, and thou shalt reign in glory for ever, and for evermore," he has—" for thine is the kingdom, and the power, and the glory, for ever. Amen." But as Jesus's prayer is so much shorter and smoother in expressions, while it has scarcely a word, and certainly not a single idea that is not in the Jewish prayer, much older than his time, the proof is complete that either he, or some one else, borrowed it from the Jewish Talmud—a production—like all the Jewish writings—very justly represented, even by learned Christians, as replete with the most absurd and fabulous tales that were ever penned by the religious guides of any nation. (See Drusius, in Critici Sacri, vol. vi. col. 252. Lightfoot's Horæ Hebraicæ, on Matth. vi. 9—13.) From Jewish lore also we find that Jesus borrowed the absurd doctrine—" Take no thought for your life, what ye shall eat, or what ye shall drink, nor yet for your body, what ye shall put on," &c. (Matth. vi. 25—34.) Indeed, the whole of Jesus's " Sermon on the Mount" is a collection of aphorisms taught by different nations long before his time. But to point out these aphorisms, one by one, as they existed previously to his time, and show the modifications they have individually undergone in being introduced into the Christian Scriptures, would require a distinct volume of some size.

The doctrine of being " born again" which Jesus endeavours to teach to Nicodemus, (John iii. 1—13.) and which modern Christians call regeneration, is clearly borrowed from the heathens. It is a very prominent doctrine in the religion of the Brahmins, and pervades the Institutes of Menu, of which their learned and pious translator, Sir William Jones, says, in his preface to them, that they are " really one of the oldest compositions existing;" and fixes their date " 1580 years before the birth of our Saviour," making them " older than the five books of Moses," while the Brahmins themselves make them many thousands of years older. On the subject of the second birth Jesus says—" Except a man be born again, he cannot see the kingdom of God."—" Except a man be born of water, and of the spirit, he cannot enter into the kingdom of God. That which is born of the flesh is flesh; and that which is born of the spirit is spirit. Marvel not that I said unto thee, Ye must be born again." In the Divine Laws of Menu, we find the following expressions.—" Such is the revealed law of institution for the twice born; an institution in which the second birth clearly consists."—" Let the twice-born youth, who has been girt with the sacrificial cord, collect wood for the holy fire."—" The second or divine birth ensures life to the twice-born, both in this world and hereafter eternally."—" Of him who gives natural birth, and him who gives knowledge of the *Veda*, the giver of sacred knowledge is the more venerable; since the second or divine birth ensures life to the twice born both in this world and hereafter eternally."—" The twice-born man, who shall thus without intermission have passed the time of his studentship, shall ascend after death to the most exalted regions."—" A twice-born man, void of true devotion, and not having read the *Veda*, yet eager to take a gift, sinks down together with it."—" Hear, from what sins proceeds the inclination of death to destroy the chief of the twice-born." A great many other such expressions are to be found in these ancient Institutes."[*] The same

---

* See Sir William Jones's Works, vol. iii. 4to. Edit. Lond. 1799. Laws of Menu, pp. 92, 94, 98, 103—106, 108, 111, 114, 117, 121, 187, 188, 199, 205, 284, 336, et al. It may not be improper here to enumerate some of the vast number of regulations and practices which, in these laws, resemble those we find in the Hebrew and Christian Scriptures.—The Brahmin priest had a crook or a staff, like Elisha, and like our bishops; pp. 89, 107, 166.—wore the hides of beasts, girdles of leather, and mantles, like Elijah and and John the Baptist; pp. 88, 89, 92, 107.—shaved their heads like the Nazarenes and the tonsured Christian priests; pp. 88, 92, 113.—were to have no land, like the Levites and Christian priests; pp. 393, 394.—begged like the mendicant Christian monks; pp. 108, 109, 161, 163.—and were not to be put to death for any crime, nor to pay toll, thus having the Christian " Benefit of the Clergy"; pp. 330, 332. This law also prescribed penances and expiations for sins; pp. 201, 202, 227, 239, 337, &c.—sunrise and sunset sacrifices and adorations; pp. 85, 113.—allowed plurality of wives; pp. 336, 337, 361, 363.—permitted a man to raise seed for his deceased brother; pp. 343, 344, 363.—pronounced hogs and animals with uncloven feet unclean; pp. 200, 201.—prescribed lunar days; p. 181.—sacrifices at new moons; p. 407.—water purifications; pp. 149, 207.—

doctrine is also taught by Chrishna, in his Dialogue with Arjoon, in the Bhagvat-Geeta, p. 67,—a portion of the sacred books of the Indians, translated from the Sanscrit, by Mr. Charles Wilkins, and published in 1785. " Being thus born again, he is endued with the same degree of application and advancement of his understanding, that he held in his former body ; and here he begins again to labour for perfection in devotion." It was also taught by Pythagoras, more than 500 years before the Christian era, and by all ancient moralists who believed in transmigration; and there is little doubt that it was this transmigration which Jesus meant in speaking of being *born again*, or anew.

There is in the Indian Divine book—the Bhagvat-Geeta, already mentioned, a great number of expressions identical with phrases found in the Gospels attributed to Jesus. For instance, the incarnate god Chrishna, who is said to have been on earth some thousands of years before the Christian era—who was the son of Devaci, born of a virgin—whose birth was concealed through fear of the tyrant Cansa, to whom it had been prophesied that a child, about this time, would be born, and would destroy his family—who, during the time he was hidden from Cansa when he had ordered all new-born male children to be massacred, was miraculously preserved—who performed miracles in his infancy—who when seven years old held a mountain on the top of his finger—who when a child not only bruised the head, but actually killed the serpent Caliya that was a terror to the whole country—who miraculously saved a great many lives—who raised many from the dead—who descended into hell—who was immaculately holy—who was most meek and lowly—who washed the feet of his disciples—who preached the most sublime morality—and who is represented as the Creator of all, the beginning and the end—but who was despised in human form,*—this incarnate deity, we say, expressed himself thus to his favourite disciple, Arjoon,—" They who serve me with adoration, *I am in them and they in me*." (Geeta, p. 81.) On several other occasions he uttered words of the same import. Jesus preaches precisely the same *peculiar* doctrine—so peculiar indeed that its identity with that of the incarnate god of the Hindoos cannot be attributed to chance. He tells his disciples—" Abide in me, and I in you."—" He that abideth in me, and I in him, the same bringeth forth fruit."—" I am in the Father, and ye in me, and I in you."—" He that eateth my flesh, and drinketh my blood, dwelleth in me, and I in him." (John vi. 56 ; xiv. 20 ; xv. 45.) Very frequently does Chrishna speak of the importance of having faith in him, saying—" I respect him as the most devout, who hath faith in me." —" They who put their trust in me, and labour for deliverance from decay and death, know *Brahm*." (Geeta, pp. 68, 72.) So does Christ say—

fasts and feasts; pp. 107, 108.—all of which the Jews imitated. It had a heaven and a hell; pp 172, 193.—taught the doctrine of a future state and of a resurrection; pp. 183, 456.—and had a third heaven, like the apostle Paul; p. 150. It taught that a man's sins would visit his posterity, like the Hebrew Scriptures ; p. 185. It is most singular that the Jews, who boasted that they had the Deity for their king and lawgiver, had no regulations but what other nations had practised many hundreds, if not thousands of years before they had any existence as a nation.

   * See Sir William Jones's Works, vol. i. pp. 265—279, 407—466. Wilkins's Bhagvat-Geeta, pp. 78—85.

"Whosoever liveth and believeth in me, shall never die."—"Thy faith hath saved thee," and so on. Jesus's idea of removing mountains, and casting them into the sea, is too plain to be denied that he borrowed it from the Hindoo theology. He says to his disciples—"If ye have faith, and doubt not, ye shall not only do this which is done to the fig-tree, but also if ye shall say unto this mountain, Be thou removed, and be thou cast into the sea; it shall be done. And all things whatsoever ye shall ask in prayer, believing, ye shall receive." Now, in that most ancient Indian book—the Mahabharat, (lib. i. c. 15) we find that the *Dews* or inferior gods, with faith prayed Veshnoo and Brahma to enable them to remove a high mountain called *Mandar*, and cast it into the ocean. The gods assented, and the mountain was hurled into the sea. This tale is twice as old as the Gospels. We have, further, in this tale, as well as in the Geeta, (p. 109.) the idea of the living water so often mentioned by Jesus, in such words as—"He would have given thee living water."—"The water that I shall give, shall be in him a well of water springing up into everlasting life."—" He that believeth on me, as the *Scripture* hath said, out of his belly shall flow rivers of living water." (John iv. vii.) This expression, however, is in no Jewish *Scripture* that has descended to us. Perhaps that Jesus meant the Hindoo *Scripture*. Here he would have found such words as—"When the soul has surpassed these three qualities, which are co-existent with the body, it is delivered from birth and death, old age and pain, and drinketh the water of immortality."—"Narayan drank of the living water."—"Eendra, with his immortal band, gave the water of life to Narayan to keep it for their use." (Geeta, pp. 102, 149, 151.)

Jesus was not so original, as might be supposed, in saying—"I am the good shepherd; the good shepherd giveth his life for the sheep."—"I lay down my life for the sheep."—"Therefore doth my Father love me, because I lay down my life, that I might take it again. No man taketh it from me, but I lay it down of myself I have power to lay it down, and I have power to take it again. This commandment have I received of my Father." (John x.) The following account, however, shows that the notion of such an atonement as that of which Christians say that Jesus speaks in the words just cited, is not only of a heathen origin, but also more than a thousand years older than his time. Bryant, in his remarks on the writings of Sanchoniathon—the most ancient historian in the world, of whom there are any of his works extant—says, in a very guarded manner—"The mystical sacrifice of the Phœnicians had these requisites,—that *a prince was to offer it*, and his *only son was to be the victim*. And as I have shown that this could not relate to any thing *prior*, let us consider what is said upon this subject as *future*, and attend to the consequence.— For if the sacrifice of the Phœnicians was a type of another to come, the nature of this last will be known from the representation by which it was prefigured. According to this, El, the supreme Deity, whose associates were *Elohim*, was in process of time to have a son, αγαπητον well-beloved, μονογενη his only begotten, who was to be conceived of ανωβρετ, as some render it, of grace, but according to my interpretation, of the fountain of light. He was to be called Ieoud, whatever that name may relate to, and to be *offered up as a sacrifice to his father*, λυτρον by way of satisfaction and redemption, τιμωροις δαμοσι to atone for the sins of others, and *avert the just vengeance of God*, αντι της παντων φθορας to prevent universal corruption, and at the same time, *general ruin*. And it is further remark-able, he was to make the *grand sacrifice*, βασιλικω σχηματι κεκοσμημενος invested with the emblems of royalty. These, surely, are very strong expressions, and the whole is an aggregate of circumstances highly signifi-cant, which cannot be the result of chance. All that I have requested to be allowed me in the process of this recital is the simple supposition—that *this mystical sacrifice was a type of something to come*. How truly it cor-responds to that which I imagine it alludes to, I submit to the reader's judg-ment. I think it must necessarily be esteemed as a most wonderful piece of history." Cited by Corry, in the Preface (pp. vii. viii.) to his *Ancient Fragments of Sanchoniathon, Berosus, &c.* This account is, however, by no means singular. The idea of appeasing deities with human sacrifice was very common in the heathen world. Hence the vast number of human sacrifices that was offered. Mythology informs us that the god Prome-theus also suffered to atone for the sins of men. The idea of a human, or even divine atoning sacrifice for sin was very common before the time of Jesus; and a great number of expressions used by Paul in reference to Jesus, as such a sacrifice, could be paralleled from heathen writers. Nor does Jesus represent what he says about laying down his life for men, as a new or uncommon thing.

But of all the sources whence the expressions, attributed to Jesus, in the Gospels, have been borrowed, the Platonic philosophy and those sys-tems of Theology upon which it is based, are unquestionably the principal ones. To the general reader, it may be more satisfactory here to adduce the testimonies of both ancient and modern writers, than to place before him, a long array of passages from the Gospels to which there are para-llels to be found in heathen writers. The first testimony that shall be given is that in reference to the writings of Philo Judæus, a Platonist. In a work called "The Sentiments of Philo Judæus concerning the Logos, or Word of God;" (Lond. 1797.) Mr. Bryant has collected a vast number of passages from this Greek writer and follower of Plato, regarding the views he held of the *Logos* or *Word*, which the Evangelist John tells us was made flesh. Of these passages from Philo, Dr. Adam Clarke, in his Commentary, at the end of the first chapter of John, has given thirty-five specimens, with parallel passages from the New Testament. Dr. J. Pye Smith, also, in his Scripture Testimony to the Messiah, gives a large number of the same passages from Philo. Now, since there is to be found in the writings of Philo, so much that is identical with the Gospels, it is material to inquire who and what he was; and particularly to ascertain in what age he wrote.—He was a native of pagan Alexandria, in Egypt, and of the Jewish race, being brother to the chief Jewish magistrate in that city. As to the time in which he wrote, Mr. Thomas Hartwell Horne (Introd. vol. ii. p. 309.) whose testimony will be very satisfactory to every orthodox Christian, says—"He was certainly born before the time of Jesus Christ, though the precise date has not been determined; some writers placing his birth *twenty*, and others *thirty* years before that event. *The latter opinion appears to be best supported*." In the 39th year of our era, he was sent at the head of an embassy from the Egyptian Jews to the

Roman Emperor, Caligula. (Josephus Antiq. lib. xviii. c. 8) To have been chosen for this important office, he must, at the time, have been a man of venerable age—apparently about sixty-nine. Nor does it appear that he wrote any of his works extant after this date. except a narrative of his unsuccessful Embassy. His Contemplative Life, in which so much is found identical with our Gospels, he must have written before. This being the case, Philo had written this work apparently some twenty or thirty years before Jesus had commenced his ministry, and more than 200 years before we have any proof that either of our present Gospels was written. Eusebius (Eccles. Hist. lib. ii. c, 4.) says that he was inferior to none in Alexandria, in point of birth and the learning of his country; and that, being *a zealous follower of the sect of Plato and Pythagoras*, he was well skilled in philosophy and the liberal studies of foreign countries, and was said to have surpassed all his contemporaries. Philo, however, could not have heard any of the doctrines Jesus delivered—much less have seen the Gospels—before he wrote his *Contemplative Life*. Mr. Horne, in the place just cited, very properly says—"Some eminent critics have imagined that he was a Christian; but this opinion is destitute of foundation : for we have no reason to think *that Philo visited Judea, or that he was acquainted with the important events which were there taking place.* Indeed, as the Gospel was not extensively and openly promulgated out of Judea until ten years after the resurrection of Jesus Christ, and as there is not the most distant allusion to him,—much less mention of him,—made in the New Testament, it cannot be supposed that this distinguished person was a convert to Christianity. *The striking coincidences of sentiment, and more frequently of phraseology*, which occur in the writings of Philo, with the language of St. Paul and St. John in the New Testament, are satisfactorily accounted for by his being deeply versed in the Septuagint (or Alexandrian Greek) version of the Old Testament, with which those apostles were also intimately acquainted. . . . . . . His sentiments concerning the Logos or WORD bear so close a resemblance to those of the apostle John, as to have given rise to the opinion of some eminent men that he was a Christian."*

* What acquaintance with the Greek of the Septuagint could the poor, illiterate fishermen have had, who are said to have written the Gospels, and who spoke a dialect of the Hebrew ? Mr. Horne could have said, not only that Philo is not mentioned in the Gospels, but that neither the Gospels nor Christ is mentioned by Philo; and further that neither is mentioned by Pliny the Elder, Seneca, Diogenes, Pausanias, or any profane writer of the first century. It is a dire misfortune that it is now too late to make Philo to have written *after the time of Jesus;* to have mentioned his miracles, and so on. — Eusebius, in attempting to do so, only betrays the heathen origin of the Gospels. He gives, however, a sure clue to the origin of these productions in his History (lib. ii. c. 15, 16.) when he says—" Mark is said first to have been sent *into Egypt*, and to have proclaimed there the Gospel, which he had afterwards committed to writing. There he *established the churches of Alexandria ;* and so great a multitude of men and women were collected there, at the very onset, that, owing to their extreme philosophical discipline and intense *asceticism*, Philo has thought fit to write a history of their mode of living, their assemblies, their sacred feasts, and their whole course of life." But as the Apostles, according to the Gospels themselves, were not to "have gone over the cities of Israel" till the Son of man came, and were to " go not into the way of the Gentiles ;" and as it is evident that Philo had written the work mentioned by Eusebius before the time Jesus is said to have died, if not before he had begun his ministry, he cannot, therefore, have written about any churches which Mark had planted in Alexandria. Eusebius's account, however, directs us to look for the origin of the Gospels in Alexandria. It is very probable

Eusebius (Hist. Eccles. lib. ii. c. 17.) makes a strenuous effort to show that Philo was a Christian, and contradicting himself, make him to have

that in his time, fiction had so far been entwined with the fact of a Gospel under the name of Mark having issued from Alexandria, that it was believed that Mark had been preaching this Gospel in Alexandria, after the death of Jesus. Alexandria, undoubtedly, is the place where the Gospels were compiled from materials collected in different parts of the world by the Eclectic Therapeuts. Here was the greatest library in the world, and the most renowned University, where almost all the Christian Fathers were educated. Here were written the most highly prized manuscripts of the Gospels. Here were the first Christians of whom we have any account. Here were students innumerable, learning both divinity and the therapeutic art, or the science of medicine; and after they had been duly qualified by ascetic discipline and other means, received their diploma from the College, and were sent out amongst people who imagined that almost every malady was demoniacal possession, to cast out devils, heal all manner of diseases, expound their theological dogmas, and collect, for the use of the University, religious romances from among all nations. They were called by different names, such as *Eclectics*, because they selected from every philosophy whatever they thought good; *Ascetics*, because of their austere discipline and severe self-mortification; *Monks*, because of their solitary and contemplative mode of life; and *Essenes*, by the Egyptians, but *Therapeuts* by the Greeks—both words denoting *healers*—because they pretended to cure all maladies by incantations, spells, god-spells or gospels, and *leucomancy* or *white* magic, which counteracted the baneful effects of *necromancy* or *black* magic, by means of which all diseases and evils were supposed to be effected. (Taylor's Diegesis, p. 58.) But they were one and the same religious body under all these names, and were in Egypt and other places many ages before the time Jesus is said to have lived. Were it urged that there is a considerable difference, on the point in question, between the text of Philo, as it has descended to us, and the citations made from it by Eusebius, the answer is, that even were this admitted, it by no means places the question of the Gospels in a more favourable position. For if Eusebius, upon whose testimony so much depends, as to the origin of Christianity, cannot be relied upon, in a matter in which he could have no interested motive, but the reverse, to make the statement he made, then all that he says must, in itself, be equally unreliable. But all that we contend for, at present, is that Eusebius, after comparing our Gospels with what Philo says of the ancient Scriptures of the Therapeuts, seems to be firmly of the opinion that they were the same. There is, however, nothing more probable than that the text of Philo, and particularly that portion cited by Eusebius, has been altered, like other productions unfavourable to the divine origin of the Christian religion. For we find even the text of the Gospels to have been much altered, under the pretence of emendations, so that such names as Pontius Pilate, Herod, Archelaus, and so on, have been introduced instead of others more ancient, but less suitable,—whole passages have been inserted, and evidence of the early heathen character of Christianity have been erased; and yet strenuous efforts are made to persuade us, against the most palpable proofs, that the Christian religion contracted all its heathen traits so *late* as the second, third, and following centuries. But, regarding the present purity of the text of Philo, Basnage, (Hist. des Juifs, lib. ii. c. 20—23; lib. iv. c. 5.) found it to correspond so well with what Eusebius cites, that, as a Christian, he appears to have felt himself in a dilemma touching what the Cæsarean bishop says about the identity of our present Gospels with the ancient productions of the Therapeuts. He, however, supposes that he extricates himself by proving that Philo wrote this work as early as the time of Augustus, who died when Jesus was only fourteen years old. Since, therefore, there could be no Christians then, he concludes that the Therapeuts were neither Christians nor monks. But this is on the supposition that there were no monks before the time of Christ, and that such expressions as are found in Philo could not be anterior to Christianity, or be derived from any other source than the Gospels. Little does this learned writer appear to suspect that, by proving that the religious writings of Philo existed more than twenty years before Jesus commenced his public career, he proves the heathen origin of both the Gospels and Christianity. There is, however, every reason to believe that these writings were composed long before the death, if not some time before the birth of Jesus. The moment we take for granted the correctness of Eusebius's statement, and regard the Gospels as a collection of Therapeutic and other ancient writings, and Christianity as the ancient religion of the Therapeuts—

had a familiar conversation with Peter at Rome, and that it was after this conversation he composed his Contemplative Life. The whole drift of

both modified by surrounding influences which bore upon them—the mystery which envelopes the origin of the one as well as that of the other, at once vanishes. Then we perceive how it is that early writers make it appear that the Therapeuts were the first who took active measures in propagating Christianity. Then are we able to account for the numerous forms of Christian heresies at the very dawn of the Christian era,—even before the apostles of Jesus could have had time to disseminate to any extent the principles of a new religion. Then we can account for the facts that so many learned pagans from the Alexandrian University are numbered amongst the Fathers of the Church, and that so many proud and haughty prelates, at a remarkably early period for a new religion, domineered over religious communities which appear to have existed for many centuries. Then can we understand why our Gospels were written in Greek, when, as we are told, they were intended for Hebrews, and when we lack proof, not only that their reputed authors did not understand Greek, but—like most persons in their station of life, and in that age in which literary attainments were exceedingly rare—that they could even write at all. Then can we understand the cause that none of the heathen writers, and but few Christian writers, mention the Gospels in the three first centuries of our present era. In a word, the moment the truth of the statement of Eusebius is admitted as to the origin of the Gospels, and the identity of the Christians and Therapeuts, the whole that is dark and unintelligible about Christianity becomes as clear and bright as meridian sunshine,—a flood of effulgent light being thrown upon it by heathen lore. The correctness of the Ecclesiastical Historian's opinion, that the *ancient Scriptures of the Therapeuts are the very Gospels and writings of the Apostles* is corroborated by a vast number of passages in these *very Gospels and Apostolical writings* themselves, as will be shown by the following instances; but more fully in the next section when treating of Jesus's Therapeutic or monachal character. As one example, take the two first verses in the first chapter of the Gospel which is said to be according to Luke. From some cause, or for some purpose, these verses have been grossly mistranslated into English, both as to the wording and the arrangement of the members of the sentence of which the proem consists. The relative pronoun, *which* (οἱ) in the second verse does not refer to the personal pronoun, *us*, (ημιν) but to the preceding pronoun, *they*, which has for its noun the word *many* (persons, or people being understood). Rightly rendered, the passage reads thus.—" Forasmuch as many have taken in hand to compile a narrative of the things accomplished among us, according as those who, from the beginning, were eye-witnesses and ministers of the word, have handed down to us, it seemed to me good also, having closely investigated the whole from the beginning, to write plainly to thee, most excellent Theophilus," &c. It is clear from the very words of the writer of this Gospel—whoever he was—that he did not write an original Gospel, but compiled it from documents which already existed. He does not say that he was going to give a history of *things which were most surely believed among them*, but that he was going to compile a narrative of things, works, or facts, which had been accomplished among these religionists. He does not say that he was going to relate *facts of which he or any other person then living, had been an eye-witness*, but facts which had been handed down to his time, by the writings of persons who had themselves been eye-witnesses of the things they related, and ministers of the *Logos*. Nor does he say that he had *perfect understanding of all, or* ANY *of these things;* much less does he say that he had been either an eye or ear-witness of any of them; but what he says is, that he had closely or diligently investigated the whole that had been written about them, from the beginning. There can be nothing clearer than that this writer, at the onset, openly declares that he was going to compose his narrative from pre-existing documents. Nor could such pre-existing documents have been few; for he tells us that *many*, or rather *a great many*, (πολλοι) *had taken in hand to compile* narratives of the things upon which he was going to write. But he would never have called Matthew and Mark—*many*, even if they had written before him—of which, however, we have no evidence. The word ἐπιχειρησις used by him, is also a proof of pre-existing documents; and the whole strongly countenances Eusebius's belief that our present Gospels were compiled from the ancient scriptures of the Therapeuts—the expositions of ancient prophets, and so on. Again, in the Acts of the Apostles (XX. 35.)—a production evidently written by the same hand as wrote the Gospel attributed to Luke, we have the expression—" Remember the words of the Lord

this work, however, contradicts this opinion, which certainly Eusebius gives only as a *bare opinion*, producing no proof whatever but that it was so

Jesus, how he said, It is more blessed to give than to receive." But no such words are found in either of the present Gospels. This writer, therefore, must have transcribed them, with the rest of the matter, from previously existing scriptures,—the same, probably, as those from which he had compiled his Gospel. He makes Paul, in his charge to the Elders of the Ephesian church, introduce these words as being well known to them. In composing his Gospel, which he calls his "former treatise," he appears to have reserved all matter in the documents from which he drew, that related to apostles, bishops, deacons, churches, and so on, for the purpose of compiling his next narrative, in which he arranges it, and gives what he would evidently have us believe to be verbatim reports of sermons and speeches of Paul and other apostles;—all bearing evident marks of having been collected and collated from some previously existing legends; which probably were diaries of the ancient Therapeuts or monks who, leaving their abodes in the Alexandrian University, and their monasteries in the desert of Thebais, roamed about the country, preaching their doctrines, and miraculously healing diseases. Accordingly, we read (Acts xviii. 24.) of "a certain Jew,"—who had the pagan name— *Apollo*, who had been born in the pagan city—Alexandria, who was mighty in the Scriptures—but what Scriptures is uncertain—who was instructed in the way of the Lord, who was fervent in spirit, and who taught diligently the way of the Lord, knowing only the baptism of John,—came to Ephesus, and taught in the synagogue, although not in such an accomplished manner that Aquila and his wife Priscilla—this renowned couple of Christian tent-makers, whose ecclesiastical dignity entitled them to be saluted almost in every epistle—could not make him more proficient in his avocation. Now, since this man, who turned out a mighty missionary, was a native of Alexandria—the hotbed of the Therapeuts—there is strong presumptive evidence that he belonged to that sect, and that it was on a missionary tour he visited Ephesus in common with other places. Be this as it may, it is certain that he was a preacher, "instructed in the way of the Lord," and diligently teaching the things of the Lord, before any one of the Apostles, mentioned in the Acts, can be said to have preached in the country whence he came. Well may Michaelis (Eccles. Hist. vol. iv. p. 88.) be inclined to think that the earliest members of the Christian community were Essenes. The same presumptive evidence that Christianity was a modified form of the religion of the ancient Therapeuts, and that their ancient Scriptures, as believed by Eusebius, are our Gospels and Epistles, is furnished by the following peculiar passage.—"Else what shall they do, *which are baptized for the dead*, if the dead rise not at all? *Why are they then baptized for the dead?*" (1 Cor. xv. 29.) There is here an emphatical mention made of a religious rite of which neither our Gospels nor our Epistolary Scriptures say any thing, except solely in this place,—*baptizing people for the dead* not being alluded to in any other part, either of the Jewish or Christian Scriptures, as they have descended to us. Still, it is here introduced as an important ceremony, the use of which was generally known, and thought to be of sufficient significance to base upon it so momentous an argument as that for the resurrection of the dead. Those who have written volumes of fanciful commentaries upon the Christian Scriptures are utterly bewildered as to the meaning of this passage, whose language is as explicit as any that ever was uttered. To suppose with Chrysostom—who wrote nearly four hundred years after the commencement of the Christian era, and perhaps eight hundred years after the practice of *baptizing for the dead* had been discontinued—that this expression means to be immersed so as to represent the death, burial, and resurrection of Christ, is utterly to beg the question. The words plainly say that people were literally baptized for *the dead*, which *dead* were expected as literally to be raised. There can be no allusion here either to Christ's death or resurrection. The most reasonable way of accounting for this expression is, that such a practice was in use among the ancient Therapeuts in Egypt, and other places; but that after their religion had undergone a reformation, and, in undergoing such a reformation, had acquired the new name of *Christianity*, this practice fell into disuse, and in process of time was utterly forgotten, while still the injunctions regarding it remained in the Scriptures of these ancient Therapeuts; so that in using them as materials for the compilation of our present Christian Scriptures, this passage, together with its context, was transcribed. Not only is it certain that the Christians acquired their notions of a future state, together with many fanciful tenets as to the condition of departed souls, from the heathens, particularly

said, and that it was probable to have been so. But it is clear that Philo describes religious practices and doctrines which had existed hundreds of years before his own time, as belonging to a sect of which he was a member. This religious community, as Mr. Taylor very properly observes, had parishes, churches, bishops, priests, deacons, festivals, apostolic founders, scriptures which were believed to be divinely inspired, and which were explained allegorically; missionaries and religious communities established in Rome, Corinth, Galatia, Ephesus, Philippi, Colosse, and Thessalonica,—places to the inhabitants of which, we are told, St. Paul addressed Epistles. This religious community, in the time of Philo, was in such a state of maturity, that it cannot mean the Christians, who were not thus organised for many centuries after that period. Eusebius himself tells us that Philo described the lives of *ascetics* or monks, whom he called, not Christians, but *Therapeuts*,—that the name of *Christians was not yet spread to every place*, which could not have been the case, if the churches and communities described by Philo, in various parts of the world, belonged to them,—that Philo, in his book, says—" This kind of men is *scattered everywhere over the world*, in order that both Greeks and barbarians should participate in so lasting a benefit; and they *abound in Egypt*, in each of its districts, and *especially about Alexandria*,"—that Philo describes the churches which these religionists had beyond the Lake Maria or Mœris, where they located as "the native country of the Therapeuts," —that he says, they had their laws, prophets, and hymns; that they explained the *philosophy of their country* in an allegorical manner; and that they had commentaries of ancient men who, as the founders of the sect, had left many monuments of their doctrine in allegorical representations, which they used as certain models, imitating the manner of the original institution. None of these particulars could have been applied to Christians in the time of Philo, even if he had written fifty, or a hundred years later. But Eusebius crowns the whole when he declares that— " *those Scriptures of the ancients which Philo says they* (the Therapeuts) *have, are the very Gospels and the writings of the Apostles, and probably some expositions of the ancient prophets, such as are contained in the Epistle to the Hebrews, and many others of St. Paul's Epistles.*" In this, however, there is no doubt that, in the main, he is perfectly correct. In writing,

---

the Therapeuts or Essenes, who were warm supporters of the doctrines of Pythagoras and Plato, but it is clear that, within four verses to the text in question, there is a sentence borrowed from the heathen poet Menander:—" Evil communications corrupt good manners." A great many other passages of a heathen origin could be cited from Paul's Epistles, which are said to have been written before the Gospels, but which, nevertheless, speak of churches as then well established. It is, however, not expedient to extend this note further than just to intimate that the use of the word—church, in the Gospels, (Vide note, ante p. 369,) may be owing to the fact that these Gospels are compiled from the ancient Scriptures of the Therapeuts, who had monasteries and other places of worship long prior to the Christian era; and not to the late date of these Gospels, of the existence of which, before the end of the second century, there is, however, no evidence. The grand difficulty in arriving at any definite conclusion on this point, arises from the fact that, long before the Christian era, there existed churches, or religious communities, precisely the same as the Christian churches which afterwards flourished, in every thing but the bare *name*. The question for the Ecclesiastical antiquarian, therefore, is —How came these into existence? Are our present churches modifications of these ancient establishments?

nearly three hundred years after the time of Philo, under a disposition to attribute to the Christians every thing that was deemed excellent, it was very easy for him to suppose that Philo's writings were derived from the Gospels, instead of the Gospels from his writings. For he perceived that, in his time, the Christian doctrine, discipline, and mode of worship, which were now old and well established, were precisely the same as those described by Philo. He saw that the monks, " as soon as they commenced their religious life, divested themselves of their property,"—that they had their *monasteries* in every parish,—that they were constantly engaged in reading and explaining the Sacred Scriptures, praying and singing hymns, so as to forget " to take food even for six days,"—and that they had sacred virgins, and, in short, all things mentioned by Philo. Well might he, therefore, ask—" What need is there to add to these things their meetings, the separate abodes of the men and the women in these meetings, and the exercises performed by them, which are still practised among us *at the present day*, and which, especially at the festival of our Saviour's passion, we are accustomed to observe in fasting, in watching, and in meditating upon divine discourses? All these the fore-mentioned author has accurately described in his writings, and *are the same customs that are observed by us alone, at the present day;* particularly the vigils of the great festival, and the exercises in them, and the hymns, *which are the very same as those used to be recited among us.* He states also that whilst one sang a hymn in a pleasing voice, the others, listening in silence, joined in singing the final clause of the hymn. He likewise tells us how on the fore-named days, lying on beds of straw upon the ground, to use his own words, they would taste no wine at all; nor would they eat any thing that has blood in it, but had water for their drink, and hyssop, bread, and salt for their food. Besides all this, he describes the orders of preferment among those of them who aspired to ecclesiastical ministration;—the offices of the deacons—the humbler rank—and the supreme authority of their bishops." Eusebius, thus seeing all that pertained to Christianity, in his time, exactly corresponding with the description given by Philo of the Therapeuts or Essenes, could not avoid the inference that his author had described the Christians, and that the divine books of which he had spoken were *our Gospels.* There is, however, no historical fact more certain than that Philo wrote of the Egyptian Therapeuts and their sacred writings; not of the Christians and their Gospels, which had no existence in his time. But as the writings of Philo himself which, as well as those of his sect, he describes, are identical with the Gospels, the conclusion is inevitable—that the latter have been borrowed from the former; or, in other words, that Jesus, who is said to have uttered such expressions as are found in Philo's works, borrowed them from this heathen writer.

The following summary of the doctrines of the Platonic religion, which Philo professed, shows the striking resemblance of the tenets of this religion to those of Christianity. It has been drawn up by the learned and pious M. Dacier, in his Introduction to the *Divine Dialogues of Plato,* and is cited by the Rev. F. J. Foxton, A.B. Perpetual Curate of Stoke Prior and Docklow, Herefordshire, in his *Popular Christianity,* p. 21. —" That there is but one God,—that we ought to love and serve him, and endeavour to resemble him in holiness and righteousness,—that this God *rewards humility and punishes pride.*—That the true happiness of man consists in being *united to God,* and his only misery in being *separated from him.*—That the soul is mere darkness unless it be *illuminated by God.*—That men are *incapable of praying well, unless God teaches them that prayer which alone can be useful to them.*—That there is nothing solid and substantial but piety,—that this is the source of virtue, and that it is the *gift of God.*—That it is better to die than to sin.—That we ought to be continually learning *to die and yet to endure life,* in obedience to God.—*That it is a crime to hurt our enemies, and to revenge ourselves for the injuries we have received.*—That it is better to suffer wrong than to do it.—That God is the sole cause of good, and *cannot be the cause of evil,* which always proceeds only from disobedience, and the ill use we make of our liberty.—That self-love produces that discord and division which reigns among men, and is the cause of their sins.—That *the love of our neighbours, which proceeds from the love of God,* as its principle, produces that sacred union which makes families, republics, and kingdoms happy.—That *the world is nothing but corruption,*—that we ought to fly from it, and join ourselves to God, who alone is our health and life,—that while we live in this world we are *surrounded by enemies, and have a continual combat to endure,* which requires, on our part, resistance without intermission,—and that we cannot conquer unless God or *angels come to our help.*—*That the Word* (Logos) *formed the world,* and rendered it visible.—that the knowledge of the *Word* makes us live very happily here below, and that thereby we obtain *felicity after death.*—That the soul is immortal,—that *the dead shall rise again.*—*that there shall be a final judgment, both of the righteous and of the wicked, where men shall appear only with their virtues or vices,* which shall be the *occasion of their eternal happiness or misery.*"   Although this abstract is given in other words than those of Plato, and is only the substance of his doctrine, yet there is a most striking resemblance between it and what in reality is the substance of the Gospels, and particularly the Gospel of John ; such as, for example, that the world was made by the *Word.**   But if Plato's expressions be compared with many expressions found in the Gospels, their identity will appear still more striking.   Even

---

* The doctrine of the *Word,* or *Logos,* is very conspicuous in the philosophy of Plato. St. Augustin, in his *Confessions,* (lib. vii. c. 9.) says that, in the Platonists there is to be found the whole of the beginning of the Gospel of John, which emphatically treats of the Word having been made flesh—having created the world—being the light of men, &c.   The doctrine of the *Logos,* however, is much older than even the time of Plato. It was taught, not only by Pythagoras, but by philosophers still more ancient.   Prometheus, who was both *God and man,* was designated the *Logos.* (Æschylus. Prometh.) So also was the god Mercury emphatically styled the *Logos.*   As a proof that the doctrine of the *Logos,* or *Word,* originated among the heathens,—the following language of Amelius, a pagan philosopher, is given, as cited by Eusebius, (Præp. Evang. lib. xi. c. 19.) as the testimony of a heathen to the claim of this Logos to be a deity.   In allusion to Mercury, Amelius says - " And this evidently was the Word, by whom all things were made, himself being eternal, as Heraclitus likewise would say ; and, by Jupiter, the same that the *barbarians* declare to have been in the beginning, and to have deserved a place with God, and to be God ; by whom all things were made, and in whom all things live and have their being ; and who, having been begotten, and become a body, and put on flesh, assumed the appearance of a man, although he did not reveal the glory of his nature ; but after his death was made a god again, such as he was before he took a body."

as early as about the commencement of the second century, that learned pagan, Celsus—as we are informed by Origen, in writing against him (lib. i. c. 6.)—charged Jesus with having borrowed from Plato the noblest maxims the Gospels contain; and amongst others, his exclamation that "it is easier for a camel to go through the eye of a needle, than for a rich man to enter the kingdom of God." That Plato says that the *Logos* is the light of the world, while Jesus, evidently in imitation of him, says that he himself is "the light of the world;" and that Plato calls God by the peculiar epithet—*Father*, while Jesus invariably does the same, are facts so well established that here they require only to be mentioned as proofs, in addition to those already given, that the discourses said to have been delivered by the Prophet of Nazareth are far from being original.

The following admissions of the Christian Fathers of the second, third, fourth, and fifth century, show that, in their times, it was not denied,—nay, that it was openly admitted, and adduced as an argument that the Christian Scriptures and the Christian religion, were identical with pagan lore and pagan religion. Justin Martyr, who is said to have written within half a century of the time our divines date the Gospel of John, and large portions besides of the New Testament, writes to the Emperor Adrian, an Apology for the Christian religion, in which he bases his argument on the identity of this religion with heathenism, thus.—" By declaring the *Logos* the first begotten of God, our master Jesus Christ to be born of a virgin without any human mixture, to be crucified and dead, and to have risen again into heaven ; *we say no more on this, than what you say of those whom you style the sons of Jove, &c.* As to the Son of God, called Jesus, should we allow him to be nothing more than man, yet the title of the Son of God is very justifiable on account of his wisdom, *considering that you have your Mercury in worship, under the title of* THE WORD, and *Messenger of God."*—" As to the objections of our Jesus's being crucified, I say that suffering was common to all the fore-mentioned sons of Jove, but only they suffered another kind of death. As to his being born of a virgin, you have your Perseus to balance that. And as to his curing the lame, and the paralytic, and such as were cripples from their birth, this is little *more than what you say of your Æsculapius."*—" You need not be told what a parcel of sons the writers most in vogue among you assign to Jove. There is Mercury, Jove's interpreter, *in imitation of the* Logos, in worship among you. There is Æsculapius, the physician, smitten by a bolt of thunder, and after that *ascended to heaven.* There is Bacchus torn to pieces, and Hercules burnt to get rid of his pains. There is Pollux and Castor, the sons of Jove by Leda ; and Perseus, by Danae. Not to mention others, I would fain know why you always deify the departed Emperors, and have a fellow at hand to make an affidavit that he saw Cæsar *mount to heaven* from the funeral pile."—" If then we hold some opinions *nearly akin to the poets and philosophers in greatest repute among you,* why are we unjustly hated ? For in saying that all things were made in this beautiful order by God, *what do we seem to say more than Plato ?* When we teach a *general conflagration, what do we teach more than the Stoics ?*— By opposing the worship of the work of men's hands, *we concur with Menander the comedian."* (Reeve's Apologies of the Fathers, vol. i. pp. 10, 70. and Taylor's Diegesis, p. 299.) In this strain does Justin—who, having studied the Stoic, the Peripatetic, the Pythagorean, and the Platonic philosophy, and having, for some time, been a professor of the last named, was well acquainted with every branch of heathen theology, so as to be fully qualified to institute a comparison,—in this strain, we say, does this Christian Father challenge the assent of the Roman Emperor, of his son, of the grandees of the Roman state, together with the whole of the Roman senate and the Roman people, to the truth of the Christian religion, solely on the ground that it was *identically the same with the Pagan religion!* In order to account for this sameness, and yet to show the superiority of the new religion over the old one, he advances a very curious—not to say ingenious—hypothesis—that " the devil, having heard that the prophets had foretold the coming of Christ to punish the ungodly with fire, instigated the heathen poets to bring forward *a great many characters who should be called, and were called, the sons of Jupiter ;* laying down this scheme in order to make people think that Christ's real history was like the fables and the wondrous tales of the poets."* This mode of accounting for the similarity of the history of Jesus to that of the heathen gods carries, on the very face of it, strong evidence that the resemblance was very striking in the time of Justin. Clement of Alexandria, who wrote about fifty years afterwards, in identifying the Christians with the Pagans, entertained a more favourable opinion of the latter, when he said, in his *Stromata*, that "those who lived according to the *Logos*, or WORD, were *in reality Christians*, although they were thought to be atheists, as Socrates and Heraclitus, and those that resembled them, were among the Greeks." His admission of the identity of the two religions, however, is equally complete. But Tertullian, who, like almost all the Christian Fathers, was originally a Pagan, and who wrote about the same time as Clement, namely, at the close of the second century, is not so candid in his attempt to account for the fact that the Christian writings were the same as those of the heathens, of whom he says in his *Apology* (c. 46.).—" from an acquisitive motive, they (the Pagans) put our doctrines into their writings, not having sufficient faith in their divine origin to refrain from interpolating them, and mixing that which was doubtful with that which was certain." There is nothing, however, more *certain* than that all the pagan doctrines which resemble those of the Christians, were generally taught many centuries before the time assigned to the birth of Jesus. Nor is it any the less certain that the argument of the identity of the pagan and Christian doctrines was forcibly pressed against the devotees of the new religion ; otherwise these Fathers, in their Apologies, would not have been driven to the miserable shift of alleging that the Pagans had stolen them,—not they from the Pagans. Accordingly, Minucius Felix, an African Christian, who wrote at the very commencement of the third century, in his defence of Christianity, as cited in Kortholt's Paganus Obtrectator (p. 24.) says—" You remark that the philosophers *have held exactly the same doctrines as we, the Christians ;* but this is not because we have copied

---

* His words are as follow.—Ακουσαντες γαρ παραγενησομενον τον Χριστον και κολαθησομενους δια πυρος τους ασεβεις, προεβαλλοντο πολλους λεχθηναι λεγομενους υιους τω δει, νομιζοντες ευνησεσθαι ενεργισαι τερατολογιαν ηγησασθαι τους ανθρωπους τα του Χριστου, και ομοιως τοις υπο των ποιητων λεχθεισι. —Just. Apol. ii.

from them, but because they, from the discourses of the divine prophets, have copied the shadow of truth by interpolating.   Thus have the most celebrated of their sages, *such as Pythagoras and particularly Plato*, with a corrupted and partial faith, *handed down the doctrine of regeneration.*"   But there is not a shadow of proof that the Greek philosophers knew any thing at all about the Hebrew prophets.   They are not even once mentioned by them; and they knew utterly nothing of their Scriptures, which are not pretended to have been translated into Greek until long after the death of Plato.   Besides, there is very little, if any, similarity between the Hebrew Scriptures and the contents of Plato's writings, or those of any other Greek philosopher.   Arnobius, a heathen philosopher, who had become a convert to Christianity, and wrote in its defence about the commencement of the fourth century, by no means seems to recognise this affinity, or even to know of its existence, when he says—as cited by Tindal *(Christianity as old as the Creation*, p. 397.)—that if Cicero's works had been duly read by the heathens, there would have been no need of the Christian Scriptures.   In answer to the formidable attack which Celsus, an Epicurean philosopher, in the beginning of the second century, made upon Christianity, Origen, who had been nursed in the cradle of Egyptian superstition, was a convert from heathenism to Christianity, and wrote about a hundred years after Celsus, says—"Now let us see how Celsus reproaches the *practical* part of our religion, as *containing nothing but what we have in common with the heathens,*—nothing *that is new or truly great.*   To this I answer that, they who incur the righteous judgment of God by their heinous sins would be punished by divine and unerring justice, if *all* men had not been endued with a sufficient degree of knowledge of moral virtue and vice."   Hence it is clear that one of Celsus's principal charges against the Christians was, that they had borrowed the religious notions of the heathens,—that they had no religious doctrines, or religious discipline, but what they had in common with the heathens, and consequently that Christianity and heathenism were identically the same.   Origen, who was a monk, who had mutilated himself in that inhuman and execrable manner peculiar to monks, and who had studied under that renowned Eclectic—Ammonius Saccas,—a man who taught that Christianity and Paganism, when rightly understood, were one and the same religion, and had one common origin, so that, as a true Eclectic, he collected all that was good in Paganism and added it to Christianity—does not deny Celsus's charge. Indeed, he tacitly admits it, when evasively he replies that all mankind had sufficient knowledge of good and evil, and especially when, in another part of his reply, he says that *God had revealed to the pagans whatever things they had in common with the Christians, and whatever things had been well spoken.*   Still stronger is his admission of the same charge in the following passage.—" Celsus, himself, in speaking of idolatry, adduces an argument which goes to justify, and even commend our practice.   For—in attempting to prove, in the subsequent part of his work, that our views regarding image-worship were not obtained by means of the Scriptures, but that we have them in common with the heathens—he cites a passage for this purpose from Heraclitus.   My answer to this is that—according to my previous admission touching the common knowledge of good and evil, which is innate in the minds of men—it is not wonderful that Heraclitus and others, whether Greeks or barbarians, *have proclaimed to the world the very same opinions as we hold.*" (Vid. Orig. adv. Cels. lib. ii. v. vi.) Thus, Origen does not attempt to deny that—as Celsus asserted in his book which he designated by the significant title of *The True Logos,* in contradistinction to what he would deem the *false Logos* of the Christians—the Christian doctrines were the same as, five hundred years before Christ, that renowned moral philosopher, Heraclitus, and others, had taught. This was a fact too patent to be ignored. His grand effort is, plausibly to account for this sameness, without at once admitting that the Christians had taken these doctrines from the pagans. This, as we have seen, he attempts to do by urging that, as all mankind are endowed with a common power of distinguishing between good and evil, Christians might, of themselves, have formed their religious doctrines, without having recourse to the theology and morals of the heathens. We now shift onwards ten years, and come to the testimony of that zealous Christian writer, Lactantius, who wrote about A.D. 316, and whose words show that he esteemed Paganism as highly as Christianity. For he says, that if any one had collected and systematized the truth diffused among the various sects of philosophers, there would be *no difference between such a collection and Christianity.* He accounts for this identity, however, like his predecessors, by supposing that the poets collected, from fables and obscure opinions, the predictions of the Hebrew prophets, having themselves not so much as *a letter of the divine truth* communicated to them. He consequently wonders that, when Pythagoras, and afterwards, Plato went so far as the Egyptians, the Magi, and the Persians, in quest of truth, they did not consult the Jews, with whom alone the true philosophy was to be found. (Lact. Inst. lib. iv. c. 2 ; iii. 4; vii.) The pointed testimony of Eusebius, who wrote about the same time as Lactantius, has already been given, to the effect *that the ancient commentaries of the Therapeuts are the very Gospels and writings of the Apostles.* If we advance about seventy-four years, till we come to Epiphanius, bishop of Salamis, who wrote on heresy, we shall find him confessing that all forms of Christianity, except his own, were based on heathen mythology. (Epiph. Hier. 26.) Theodoret (lib. ii. de Platone) writing about the year 420, and seeing the identity of the Christian Scriptures with the writings of Plato, charges the heathen moralist with having drawn his theological arguments from Jewish sources. The great Father Augustin, again, in the beginning of the fourth century, tells us that the Christian religion was *known to the ancients,* by another name, before Christ appeared, but that *now it received the name of Christianity.** It is, therefore, by no means wonderful that he had nothing to say against the following conclusion of the learned Christian bishop, Faustus the Manichæan ; namely, that " it is certain that the New Testament was not written by Christ himself, *nor by his Apostles,* but a long while after them, by some unknown persons who, lest they should not be credited when they wrote of affairs they were little acquainted with, affixed to their works the names of apostles, or of such as were supposed to have

---

* Christus veniret in carne, unde vera religio qua jam erat cæpit appellari Christiana. Hæc est nostris temporibus Christiana religio, non quia prioribus temporibus non fuit, sed quia posterioribus hoc nomen accepit.—Op. August. vol. i. p. 12. Basil Edit.

been their companions." (Lardner's Credibility, vol. ii. p. 221.)   Were it
urged that Faustus, being a Manichæan bishop, was considered a heretic,
the answer is, that Dr. Lardner has plainly proved that *he was a Christian;*
and, further, that Augustin himself was a Manichæan at the same time as
Faustus, until he was induced by the prospect of a bishopric, to go over to
another sect; after which we find him calumniating the Manichæan pres-
bytery, which he had left; while yet declaring that he never would have
believed the Gospel, had he not been induced by the authority of the
church, apparently meaning the church of which he had become a bishop.
But as Augustin had been a Manichæan, let us see how this sect of
Christians acquired its divine books; so that, from an acquaintance with
the genius of that age, we may be the better enabled to form a correct
opinion of the manner in which other sects, who boasted of their pure
orthodoxy, acquired their divine books.   Socrates, in his Ecclesiastical
History, (lib. i. c. 22.) tells us that Manichæus, or rather his predecessors,
introduced into Christianity the doctrine of Empedocles and Pythagoras,
and composed sacred books, thus.— A Saracen, named Scythianus, who
had married an Egyptian woman, and, on her account, resided in Egypt,
where he acquired all the learning of the Egyptians, had a disciple named
Buddas, who composed a book called the *Gospel,* together with other
books.   Buddas, dying from an accident, a woman with whom he lodged
became possessed of his books and other property.   This woman bought
a captive boy, named Cubricus, to whom she gave good education and his
freedom.   When he had grown up, she gave him also the books and
property of Buddas, with which he went to Persia; and having changed his
name into Manes or Manichæus, gave out the books of Buddas, and proclaimed their contents as Christianity.   "The contents of these books,"
says our author, "agree with Christianity in expression, but in sentiment
are thoroughly pagan."   Such was the origin of the Scriptures of that
vastly numerous and distinguished sect of Christians—the most distinguished of all that had dissented from the established church—called the
Manichees, of which bishop Augustin and bishop Faustus were members.
Nor have we any evidence that the Christian Scriptures which have
descended to us, have a more respectable origin.   These Manichees, like
most other Christians of their time, held that Paganism, Christianity, and
Judaism, were the same, which they pretended to prove from an ancient
book called the *Theosophy,* or the Wisdom of God. (Fabricius Com. i.
p. 354.)   Thus does all antiquity—all ancient religion, both orthodox
and heterodox—point to the heathen origin of Christianity, and therefore,
of our present Gospels.   This is the charge brought against it by its
earliest enemies, and the substance of the apologies made for it, by its first
advocates.   If, therefore, Jesus ever proclaimed the doctrines, and uttered
the words attributed to him in the Gospels, he must have borrowed them
from the heathens.   If, on the other hand, these Gospels attribute to him
doctrines which he never delivered, and words which he never uttered;
even then are these Gospels equally as unworthy of being taken for divine
truths as if Jesus had really borrowed their contents from pagan lore.
That either Jesus or some one else has so borrowed most that they contain,
is trusted to have been amply established by the mass of evidence given in
this section.   And inasmuch as there are in these Gospels expressions

which are clearly taken from heathen authors, who had flourished many centuries before the time assigned to his birth, the inference is quite legitimate;—that he borrowed them from these heathen authors.

SECTION X.—BOTH THE LIFE AND DOCTRINES OF JESUS IDENTICAL WITH THE LIVES AND DOCTRINES OF HEATHEN ASCETICS OR MONKS, WHO LIVED HUNDREDS OF YEARS BEFORE HIS TIME.

Having, in the last section, seen seen the identity of Jesus's doctrine with those of Philo—a Therapeut or monk—and of other heathen philosophers, we need not here be much startled, if we find his life and teaching identically the same with those of the heathen Therapeuts, monks, or Essenes at large. In order to make this clear to the general reader, it will be necessary first to show that there were heathen monks before the time Jesus is said to have lived, and that these were the same, not only as the Therapeuts and the Essenes, but also the same as the Christian monks of the four or five first centuries of our era. For this purpose, a brief sketch will here be given of monachal life and habits both among heathens and Christians, from the earliest period that we have any account of the singular institution of monkery among different nations. Some remarks have already (pp. 220, 370, et al.) been made upon monks, particularly those called Therapeuts and Essenes, from which, added to the following description, the reader will be enabled to form an adequate notion as to what is meant by the term *monk*.*

The most ancient account we have of Monachism, is among the Hindoos; where there is every reason to believe it was an established institution two thousand years before the time assigned to the birth of Jesus.— We have had already occasion to remark that the ancient inhabitants of Hindostan, or India—this source of almost all ancient superstition, if not also the cradle of civilization—had sacred books much older than the Jewish Scriptures. These ancient books,—such as the Vedas, the Laws of Menu, the Puranas, and the Angas—are replete with the principles of monkery.—For example, in the Laws of Menu we find the following injunctions to a man who would purify himself, and become a saint of the highest order.—" Let him seclude himself from the world, and gain the favour of the gods by *fasting, subduing the lusts of the flesh, and mortifying the senses.*"—" Let him crawl backwards and forwards on his belly; or let

---

* A very learned and remarkable work on Monkery, entitled "The Fathers of the Desert," was published in America, in 1850 in two volumes, from the pen of Henry Ruffner, President of Washington College, Virginia. The able work of this orthodox Christian we shall freely use in our outline of early Monkery. He, very properly, defines a monk to be a man who leads a solitary life,—who separates himself from human society that he may devote himself to sanctifying exercises,—who has renounced all worldly pursuits, property and pleasure,—who exercises himself continually in chastity, fasting, watching, prayer, and combats with evil spirits,—who macerates his body with hunger and exposure to the elements, and mortifies to the utmost all the desires of his corporeal nature.

him *stand all day long on his toes. Let him remain always sitting, or always standing.*"—"Let him, in the heat of the summer, kindle five fires about him. When it rains, let him *bare himself to the storm where it pelts the hardest.* In the winter, let him wear a wet garment. So let him *rise by degrees* in the strength of his penances." According to these laws, there were degrees of saintship. A man might become a Yogi or ordinary saint, by retiring into solitude for a term of years; but if he devoted all his life to monachism, he attained to a higher degree of sanctity, and obtained such influence with the gods that they would grant him whatever he asked in prayer. But before he arrived at such a state of perfection, he had to go through four very long and hard degrees of religious exercises. In the first degree, he had to pray much, read the Vedas, conquer his passions, by abstaining from women, from anger, revenge, and falsehood. He had to sleep very little, and that on straw, or an animal's skin, under a tree.— He was to refrain from all pleasure, to wear the coarsest dress, and to practise ablution every night and morning, by sprinkling and dipping himself, and by repetition of prayers. The second degree increased in severity. He was to spend most of the night in contemplating the heavenly bodies, so as to cultivate a desire for mounting the skies; and he was to live on charity. In the next degree, he was to renounce all worldly care, and to retire for ever from the world into some cell or grotto, in a secluded spot. If his wife wished to follow him, she might; but all intercourse was at an end for ever. Here, he wrapped his limbs in a vestment made of bark or leaves, hung down his head in grief, meditated on his sins, or silently read the Vedas. At night, he lay on the bare ground, or sat in cold water. During summer days, he sat for weeks beneath the broiling sun, with four fires around him. His food was dry grain soaked in water, a little of which he took only once a day. In the fourth, he entered the desert with a staff in one hand and a pitcher in the other, never to return; and here he subsisted on wild fruit and water, and wore no clothing, but merely a wrapper round his waist. This degree of severity enabled him to have power over all the demons in hell, and to be almost a pure spirit himself, able to drop the body at will, take an ethereal flight to the regions of bliss, and return at pleasure into his house of clay. (Fathers of the Desert, vol. i. pp. 21—29.) More than two thousand years ago, these monkish habits of the Hindoos arrested the attention of foreigners. When Alexander the Great—three hundred and thirty years before the Christian era —conquered a portion of India, he found there several sorts of monks; and some Greek scholars who followed his army, wrote a description of them. From the works of these writers, Strabo—about three hundred years after—compiled the following account of these monks, whom he calls philosophers, just as the Christian Fathers dignify the monks of their time with the same title. The Greek Geographer (lib. xv. c. 1.) tells us that Megasthenes had stated there were in India two sects of philosophers —the Brachmans, and the Garmans. The Brachmans lived in the woods, not far from cities. Their manner of life was simple; they slept on straw or skins, used no animal food, and abstained from women. They imparted instruction; but while they spoke, the hearers were not allowed to speak, cough, or spit. He also says that Aristobulus, another writer of the time of Alexander, saw two Brachmans, one of whom lay on his back, and exposed himself to the sun and the rain. The other stood upon one leg, holding in each hand a billet of wood three cubits long; when he got tired he stood upon the other leg, and he continued the whole day. This monk said he intended to persevere in his ascetic life for forty years. Strabo adds,—"Onesicritus says that he was sent by Alexander to visit some of these philosophers who, as he had heard, went naked, and were much respected. He found them two or three miles from the city. Each was naked, motionless in one position, sitting or lying the whole of the day exposed to the sun, though it was too hot for others to bear." Such were the Indian monks or Garmans, called also Sarmans or Samaneans.— We are told by the same authority that they lived in the wood upon plants and wild fruit; that they had no clothing but the leaves of trees; and abstained from women and wine. Next to them were the physicians or healers, who were simple, but not wild in their manner of life; who subsisted on rice and corn meal given them; who were hospitably entertained; who could with their medicines make women bear children; who exercised themselves in voluntary pain and sufferings; and who would continue for a whole day motionless in the same posture. We are further told that there were others who practised soothsaying and charms, and were skilled in the use of incantations for the dying. These went about the villages and cities begging. Some took women along with them to philosophize; but had no intercourse with them. Such is Strabo's account of the Indian Ascetics, whose practices and mode of life exactly correspond with those of the Christian monks. He is corroborated by Clement of Alexandria who, in his Stromata, written about two hundred years after, describes two classes of philosophers in India—the Sarmans and Brachmans—who were clothed with the bark of trees, ate acorns and wild berries, drank water with their hands, and knew nothing of marriage, or of the procreation of children. In the third book of the same work, he says that the Brachmans ate no living creature, and drank no wine,—that some of them took food daily, but others only every third day,—that they set no value on life, and despised death.—that those of the Indians called Semnoi went naked all their lives, exercised truth, predicted the future, and worshipped under a pyramid, where they believed the bones of a certain god to repose,—that neither the Gymnosophists *(naked philosophers)* nor the Semnoi *(the venerated)* used women, thinking this to be unnatural and iniquitous,—that they kept themselves chaste,—that they had virgins also called Semnai.—and that they appeared to observe celestial phenomena, from which they predicted future events. Bardesanes, who wrote before Clement, namely about the year 172 of the Christian era, recorded that persons who were admitted to their community renounced worldly goods, left their wives and children, if they had any, to the care of others; shaved all their hair from their bodies, and wore monastic gowns; had stewards to provide for their wants; assembled in the house of prayer at the ringing of bells, and were each of them, afterwards, given a dish of rice. This precisely corresponds with the discipline of the Christian Cœnobites. Still Diodorus Siculus, in his second book, before the commencement of the Christian era, relates substantially the same things of the Brachmans. (Fathers of the Desert, vol. i. pp. 39—43.)— Porphyry, writing in the third, and Ambrose in the fourth century of the

Christian era, bear similar testimony to the practices of these Indian
monks;—the whole proving that they are of a very remote origin.

Both ancient and modern travellers who have visited India, give a
similar account of these fanatics. Pinkerton, in his Collection of Voyages
and Travels, gives an account of two Arabian travellers who had visited
India. The statement of one of these about the year 850, as translated
from the Arabic by Renaudot, runs as follows.—" There are, in the Indies,
men who profess to live in the woods and mountains, and to despise what
other men most value. They abstain from every thing, but such wild herbs
and fruit as grow in the woods. They preserve their chastity with iron
buckles. Some of them are quite naked, or have only a leopard's skin
thrown over them. In this plight they keep standing with their faces
towards the sun. I formerly saw one in this posture; and when, sixteen
years afterwards, I returned to the Indies, I found him still in the same
posture, and was astonished that his eyes had not been put out by the
sun's heat." These are evidently the Gymnosophists, who had been noticed
by the writers already mentioned, in the time of Alexander—nearly twelve
centuries before. About four hundred and fifty years after, the famous
Venetian traveller, Marco Polo, found them still unchanged. Speaking of
the Hindoo Brachmans, he says,—" They are of great abstinence and long
life. There are some devotees among them called Tangui, who go altogether naked, live austerely, and rub their bodies with an ointment made
of burnt ox-bones. They neither *kill nor eat any living creature*, nor any
herb or root until it is dried, esteeming every thing to have a soul."
Bernier, a French traveller, about the year 1670, describes the same Indian
monks, who called themselves by the name *Yogi*, (united to God) the very
name by which they are designated in the Hindoo Scriptures,—but whom
Bernier calls by the general name Fakirs. Amongst the great variety of
these, he observed that a considerable number of them had *convents wherein
they maintained vows of chastity, poverty, and obedience.* They led so odd a
life that he questioned whether credit would be given to what he wrote
about them. Many of them sat stark naked, or lay days and nights upon
ashes, and very commonly under large trees near water tanks, or in the
galleries of the temples. Some of them had their hair hanging down to
the middle of their legs, and wreathed into several parcels. He had seen
some who held one arm, or both, perpetually above their heads, having at
the end of their fingers wreathed nails. Owing to the small portion of
food which they took, their arms were small and lean, and so stiff and dis-
abled that they could not use them. They had, consequently, young
novices to wait upon them as holy men with great reverence. He had
often met in fields large squadrons of these quite naked. Some held up
their arms in the posture already described, others had their terrible hair
hanging down, or else wreathed about their heads. Some had clubs in
their hands, and others had dry tiger skins over their shoulders. He had
noticed them pass through the midst of a great borough, quite naked, and
without shame. The men, women, and children, looked at them indiffer-
ently; and the women brought them alms with much devotion, esteeming
them to be very holy men, and much wiser and better than others. Some
of them were thought to work miracles, to cause thunder, and raise storms
of hail, snow, and wind. Hamilton, in his account of the West Indies,

about 1700, says that the Yogis practised great austerities and mortifications, contemned worldly riches, and went naked, except a bit of cloth about their loins. But some denied themselves that, "delighting in nastiness and holy obscenity, with a great show of sanctity." He proceeds to state by what devices they preserved their chastity, and adds, that they were much revered by young married women, who prostrated themselves before them. Papi, another traveller, describes them as being all naked except their loins, and says that he frequently saw them lying on their backs in the open street, perfectly motionless, with their eyes closed, when the sun shone with a scorching heat, and the sand under them was burning hot.— In this position they would hum through their teeth a sacred hymn, and pretend that they were so absorbed in heavenly contemplations, that they did not notice the passers by. Some of these madmen never lay down, but remained all their lives in a standing posture, and others mangled their bodies with scourges and knives. Niebuhr, in his celebrated Travels, says that one of these Yogis had lived for twenty years shut up in a cage with his arms constantly raised above his head. Dr. Fryer, in the seventeenth century, saw some of the Yogis who had vowed to keep a standing posture for sixty years ; and one who had fulfilled his term, but whose feet were dreadfully swollen and ulcerated. Purchase informs us that some of them wore heavy iron collars, and put on other irons to preserve their chastity ; others kept their fists hard shut till their nails grew through the palms of their hands ; others supported their arms above their heads by grasping the branch of a tree, standing there motionless till their arms stiffened and dried up; others lay on wooden beds bristling with spike nails ; and others tortured their bodies in diverse ways. All of them, without exception, professed total abstinence from women, wine, and delicate food. After they had signalized themselves by such achievements of bodily exercise,* torture, and privation, they were regarded as almost divine,—as beings who possessed miraculous power, and whose presence diffused blessings on all around them. (Vid. Fathers of the Desert, vol. i. pp. 44—49.) Such is the description of the Hindoo monks given by modern as well as ancient travellers. It perfectly corresponds with the religious regulations laid down in their own sacred book, long before either our present Christian or Jewish Scriptures had any existence.

Having described the Brahmin monks, it is now intended to give a brief description of the monks of Boodhism—another very ancient religion, of an Indian origin, which exists to this day, and is believed to be purely divine by upwards of three hundred and fifteen millions of people ; it being the religion of most of the inhabitants of the vast table land to the north of the Himalaya, as far as the boundary of Siberia—of the peninsula of India, beyond the Ganges—of Ceylon—of several islands of the Indian Archipelago—of the Empire of Japan—and. principally of China. (Penny Cyclop. Art. Buddha.) It is now generally agreed that Boodhism is a branch of Brahminism, and that it has been established, at least a thousand

---

* Hence, we are told, they were called by the Greeks, *Ascetics*, from ασκητης,—a word meaning one who *exercises himself*. Applied to these religious fanatics, it denoted that practice, peculiar to their religion, of exercising themselves in holding their limbs in the same position, for a number of years, or in performing some other feat, which required much exertion and endurance. Its origin is, however, doubtful and may be from *Sects*.

years before the commencement of the Christian era.* According to the Indian Scriptures, it originated under the following miraculous circumstances. Vishnu, the second god in the Hindoo trinity, having, in an

* Although most writers agree that Boodh appeared about this time, yet diverse opinions are held as to the exact year in which his religion was promulgated, and as to several other things connected with this religion. Ward, in his *View of Hindostan*, appears to think that Boodhism was the original religion of the Hindoos, and Brahminism the result of a schism in it. This would make Boodhism still older; for we have the strongest proofs that Brahminism is exceedingly ancient. The following account is collected from Sir William Jones's works on the Chronology of the Hindoos, vol. i. p. 281.—Days and nights were of two sorts among the Hindoos,—those of men and those of the gods. Forcibly reminding us of the plagiarised words of Peter, in his second Epistle, (iii. 8.) " that one day with the Lord is as a thousand years, and a thousand years as one day," we find in the Laws of Menu, that "a year is a day and night of the gods;" that a *Crita*, or age, is four thousand years of the gods; that twelve thousand such divine years is an age of the gods; and that a thousand of such divine ages is a day of Brahma, the supreme god. (Laws of Menu, chap. i. 66—73.) At the end of each of the divine ages, an incarnate deity appeared on earth, which event was called an *aratara*.— According to the Hindoos, there are to be ten *arataras*, each at an interval of four hundred thousand years, before the end of the world. Eight of these are passed; the ninth is now passing; and the tenth, named *Calci*, is yet in the womb of futurity. Sir William Jones says "These ten *arataras* are arranged by some according to the thousands of *divine* years in each of the four ages, or in an arithmetical proportion from four to one; and, if such an arrangement were universally received, we should be able to ascertain a very material point in the Hindoo Chronology; I mean the birth of Boodha, concerning which the different *Pandits*, whom I have consulted, and the same *Pandits*, at different times, have expressed a strange diversity of opinion. They all agree that *Calci* is yet to come, and that *Boodha* was the last considerable incarnation of the Deity.........The best authority, after all, is the *Bagavat* itself, in the first chapter of which it is expressly declared that ' Boodha the son of *Jina* would appear, at *Civata*, for the purpose of *confounding the demons*, just at the beginning of the *Caliyug*.........On the whole, we may safely place Boodha just at the beginning of the present (Hindoo divine) age: but what is the beginning of it? When this question was proposed to *Radhacant*, he answered,— 'of a period comprising more than four hundred thousand years, the first two or three thousand may reasonably be called the beginning.'" Our learned author, after discussing the point to some extent, and suggesting that the Hindoos had a notion that two Boodhas had appeared in the flesh in different ages, says, upon an authority he names,— "If the Ayini Achari be correctly written, that a period of 2962 years had elapsed from the birth of Boodha to the 40th year of Acbar's reign, this computation will place his birth in the 1366th year before the birth of our Saviour; but when the Chinese government admitted a new religion from *India*, in the first century of our era, they made particular inquiries concerning the age of the old Indian Boodha, whose birth, according to Couplet, they place in the 41st year of their 28th Cycle, or 1036 years before Christ, and they call him, says he, Foe, the son of Maya; but M. De Greignes, on the authority of four Chinese historians, asserts that Foe was born about the year before Christ, 1027, in the kingdom of Cashmir. Giorgi, or rather Cassiano, from whose papers his work was compiled, assures us that, by the calculation of the *Tibetians*, he appeared only 959 years before the Christian epoch; and M. Bailly, with some hesitation, places him in 1031 years before it, but inclines to think him far more ancient, confounding him, as I have done in a former tract, with the *first* Boodha, or Mercury, whom the Goths call Woden, and of whom I shall presently take particular notice. Now, whether we assume the medium of the four last mentioned dates, or implicitly rely on the authorities quoted by De Greignes, *we may conclude that Boodha was first distinguished in this country* (India) *about a thousand years before the beginning of our era.*" The vast extent over which Boodhism has been disseminated, and the different periods at which it has been introduced into different countries, are amply sufficient to account for the diversity of opinions as to the time its founder flourished; and also to account for the supposition that there were two Boodhas. It was very natural for the inhabitants of Ceylon, and of other countries where Boodhism was planted at a comparatively late period, to boast that their country gave birth to Boodh, and to imagine that Boodhism was not older than the time

immensely long course of ages, gone through eight incarnations, which the Indians call *avataras*, the ninth time he became incarnate, or appeared in the flesh, under the title of *Boonh* or *Boodha*—a word which signifies *wisdom* or virtue—in order " to effect some work of salvation on the earth." He was born of a virgin, and was of royal descent. In the vast number of very ancient legends regarding him, the following particulars of his birth, life, and death, are detailed. According to the Temoo Jetoo—a history of one of the incarnations of Boodh, translated by Carey—this incarnate god was reputed to be the son of the king of Kasheeku, by Chandradevu. The gods looking around for a proper personage to become incarnate in her womb, Boodhu-sutwa—who had fallen into hell, and had been punished for the space of eighty thousand years, after which period he had been raised to the higher heavens of the gods—volunteered the incarnation. After the young god was born, the king commanded all the Brahmin prophets to predict his destiny, which they reported to be most favourable. When a month old, he was brought before the king, who, at the time, happened to be sentencing four thieves to a very cruel punishment. The young incarnate god, remembering his own previous torments in hell, and expecting to be cast into hell again for his father's sins, was filled with horror, and, there and then, resolved to adopt a monastic life. He therefore, by fasting, made his body feeble ; and also affected to be lame, deaf, dumb, and idiotic. As he grew up, vain endeavours were made to tempt him with fruits and all sorts of luxuries, and also to excite his faculties by fright. But as all proved of no avail, the prophets were again called in ; and, after a consultation, they advised that he should be taken in a chariot to the burial ground, and buried alive. By a miracle, however, the young Divinity—who was by this time sixteen years old—caused the charioteer to drive him to a distant forest, where, the instant he arrived, he displayed his supernatural power, whirling the chariot into the air, and giving proofs of his ability to travel eight hundred miles in a day ! He influenced the mind of the charioteer to join him in leading a hermit's life in this wilderness, where he soon made a house of leaves, and a pool of water, and caused such trees to grow as bore fruit at all seasons of the

it was first introduced amongst them. It was precisely the same with regard to the Grecian and Roman deities,—several countries, for example, claimed the honour of having given birth to Jupiter, Hercules, &c. and assigned their nativity to different periods. Whatever may be said about the extravagance of the Hindoo Chronology, there is no doubt that Boodhism is at least a thousand years older than Christianity. Nor is this Chronology—when it is closely investigated, and when the recent discoveries as to the immense lapse of time since man has been an inhabitant of this globe, and especially the discoveries regarding the many millions of years that this globe itself must have existed—so extravagant as it may at first appear to a person who has been accustomed to compute the age of man, and of the world, according to the Jewish Scriptures. The Hindoos, even as early as 1181 years before the Christian era, that is, 3044 years ago—when most other nations, whose history has descended to us, were in their infancy—were great astronomers, able to observe, and even to compute with accuracy, the extent to which the vernal equinox receded yearly, and to record with precision other celestial phenomena, as Sir William Jones has indubitably proved by geometrical evidence. For further information regarding Boodhism, which is a perfect counterpart of Christianity in early times,—see Asiatic Researches, vol. i. p. 427 ; vii. 156 ; xv. 111. Hodgson's Transactions of the Royal Asiatic Society, vol. ii. p. 239. Kajiroh Nouveau Journ. Asiat. vol. xii. Remusat Melanges Asiat. vol. i. p. 116. Syme's Embassy to Ava, chap. vi. ix. xi. Bohlen das Alte Indien, c. ii. Creutzer's Religions de l'Antiquite, tom. i.

year. Casting off his royal vestments, he put on a coat made of bark,
threw over his shoulder a leopard's skin, covered his head with his long
twisted hair, laid a bamboo across his shoulder, took a staff in his hand,
and walked about his bower, quite happy. He took of the fruit of the
trees, and, having boiled it in tasteless water, without salt or acid, he fed
on it as immortal food. Having dispatched the charioteer to inform his
mother where he had settled, the queen, the king, and their numerous
retinue came to visit him, with the view of persuading him to return.
They offered him all the riches of the kingdom, and all the delights and
pleasures of the world, including the enjoyment of most lovely maidens,
and dancing girls. Boodh, not only refused to comply, but by his pathetic
orations on the transient nature of all worldly riches, pleasures, and
delights, converted them all to his own views, so that they became hermits.
The king sent a proclamation to his subjects, inviting them also to become
hermits, which they did. Shortly after, four other kings followed the
example of this monarch, so that the desert became filled with hermits,
" all of whom lived on fruit, and performed the duties of ascetics." With
whatever fables these legends may be entwined, there is no doubt that
they were written a long time before the commencement of the Christian
era, which fact is sufficient for our present purpose. All ancient accounts
regarding this supposed god, go to establish the fact that, at least a thousand years before the commencement of our era, a distinguished religious
philosopher of an ascetic life, whose proper name was Gaudama, and whose
divine title was Boodh, "appeared on the banks of the Ganges, and was
believed by the Hindoos to be an incarnation of their god Vishnu " It is
true that the numerous ancient accounts given of his origin differ in details.
Ward, in his View of Hindostan, (lib. vi. c. 2.) informs us that the Boodhu
Puranah—a portion of the sacred scriptures of India—states that Boodh
had sent his attendant gods to be born of noble families, but that he himself entered the womb of Maya-devu. Immediately after his birth, he
gave signs of divinity. At school, he showed wonderful knowledge, and
instructed thousands of his school-fellows. He fled from all his associates,
and became a monk of the highest order, practising great austerities, and
making many converts. So abstracted did he become in holy contemplation, that the boys ran sticks up his nose without awakening him to consciousness. The gods were so smitten with admiration of his sanctity, that
they came down and worshipped him. Once, a certain man censured him
so loudly for his austerities, as to rouse him to make the following reply.
—" O wicked friend! knowest thou not that I am performing *Yogu*,—
which requires the body to be purified by austerities ? Death is better
than continuance in a body so vile that meritorious actions will not proceed
from it. I will subdue my evil desires." He finally seated himself on a
rock with the vow,—" On this rock may my body, blood, and bones
become dry. Though my life depart, I will not abandon this Yogu."
The attending god, smitten with admiration at this vow, adored him.—
(Fathers of the Desert, vol. i. p. 60.)

Boodh appears to have been a religious reformer of Brahminism.
His doctrines therefore slightly differed from those of the Brahmins, and
were not quite so gross and barbarous. Owing to the difference between
his views and those upheld by the Vedas, particularly touching the

doctrine of a First Cause, not many of the Brahmins appear to have been among his followers, although they, even to this day, pay great veneration to him, and regard him as an incarnation of Vishnu. The Brahmins, however, from a very early date, were accustomed to reproach the Boodhists with being atheists; and have always shown great enmity towards them; just as the Jews have shown towards the Christians. Shortly after Boodh's death, his disciples appear to have incurred the vengeance of the old religionists, and to have been expelled from Hindostan by a bloody persecution. This necessitated them to take refuge in various parts of the East, particularly Eastern Asia. Let us now see how far these Boodhists, in the different countries where they settled, carried out the monkish principles of the founder of their religion.* After the Boodhists had been driven from Hindostan, a colony of them settled in the island of Ceylon,

---

* As Boodhism is evidently a modification of Brahminism, no great difference can be expected between their principles. The advance of civilization, however, has made monkery much less ferocious among the Boodhists, than it was 2500 years ago. Besides, the Brahmin monks do not appear to have been governed by such a strict and uniform system of monkery as the Boodhists. They appear to have had the power to relinquish their ascetic life, and return to society, and marry, if they wished. Their mode of ascetic exercise appears, also, to have been left to their own choice; and they seem not to have been governed by any superior, nor bound to any person by virtue of any vow whatever. But the Boodish monks, even to this day, are bound by vows, live in monasteries, have a regular system of government connected with the priestly office, and exercise a strict discipline over the young monks, in order to keep them from temptation, especially from women. Although the Boodhist monks are less fanatical and extravagant than the Hindoo Yogis, yet "they adopt, in great part, the same principles of ascetic severity against the body; but their practice is more sober and moderate. They depend mainly on fasting, prayer, psalmody, and the use of the whip, to keep their rebellious flesh in subjection. Like the Hindoo Sannyasis, they endeavour, by intense contemplation, to raise the soul above all earthly thoughts and cares, and to prepare themselves by divine meditations for the felicity of heaven." This is the fundamental principle of all asceticism, or monkery, particularly that of the Brahmins and Boodhists. Ascetics are thought to have a portion of the divine energy dwelling within them, and thereby to be enabled to perform their ascetic feats; and the greater the feat the greater is supposed to be the divine energy. When, therefore, an eminent saint exhibits a high control over his body, in the voluntary endurance of sufferings, and in abstraction of mind from all earthly things, he is supposed to be energized by the Deity, and to possess a portion of divinity. The ultimate effect of this divine energy, when imparted to monks, in an extraordinary degree, is to raise their souls to the rank of gods, and make them proper objects of worship after death, when they ascend to the heavens, and reign in subordination to the supreme god. The object, therefore, of ascetic habits, in torturing the body, and inflicting on it all sorts of indignities and mortifications, is to waste it away to such a degree that the monk may be comparatively all soul, and that the carnal desires of the body may not interfere with the soul in its divine contemplations, so as to retard its transformation from the human to the divine. This is the grand key to the whole mystery of the ascetic life. One of the principal tenets of both Brahmins and Boodhists is, that men raise themselves to the dignity of gods by meritorious deeds, and that the greater the merit of their works, the higher are the glory and power of their godhead after death. For, in accordance with the doctrine of transmigration which they hold, they believe, like Paul, that there are degrees in glory, and that there is above the earth a succession of heavens, differing in elevation and splendour, in which demi-gods of different degrees of merit dwell, having been absorbed into the divine nature, whence they first emanated, in a degree proportionate to the intensity of their austerities while on earth. Still, the Boodhists believe that no degree of saintship can raise an ascetic, after death, to a state of divinity coequal with that of the all-pervading Boodh, who is their chief object of worship, and whose supposed relics they regard with the most profound veneration.— *Extracted from the Fathers of the Desert,* vol. i. pp. 61—67.

long before the commencement of the Christian era. Some fix the date of
this event about 543, and others as late as 306 years B.C. It is certain,
however, that Boodhism—with its monkery in a flourishing state—is the
prevalent religion of the island to this day; and that, according to a treaty
made in the year 1815, the British government maintains and protects it,
and even appoints its priests, who are regularly educated for their office.
It is a most remarkable fact that there still exists here a class of the original monks, who are called by the significant name—*Vedas,* and who
inhabit the most secluded parts of the Island, deriving their subsistence
from the natural productions of the country, inhabiting huts in the forests,
and going about naked, except that they wear a cloth round their loins.
These are evidently a remnant of the Gymnosophists who, as already
mentioned, were noticed by the Greeks, more than two thousand years ago.
The Boodhist monks, in Ceylon, Birmah, and Siam, are very much alike,
and may be described here indiscriminately. The Boodhist priests are
required to maintain everlasting celibacy. Some of them live secluded
from the world in the rocks*—in gloomy forests and deserts, despising all
the pleasures of life. Others inhabit houses, receive gifts from the king
and his princes, and are entrusted with the education of youth. In addition
to these, there are hermits,—" a sort of wild men who are esteemed in
proportion as they are fanatic. Like the priests, they are divided into
three orders, all of whom renounce the strongest passions of our nature,
with an idea of thereby pleasing the Creator." (Pinkerton's Collection of
Voyages and Travels, vol. ix. p. 762.) The different degrees of monkery
are distinguished by the colour of the dress which each monk-priest wears.
Some monks dwell in rocky cells, which have no entrance but narrow
apertures from the top of the rock, through which food is let down to the
inmates, who never come out. (Syme's Embassy to Ava, chap. iv. & ix.)
The monk-priests of Siam generally live in cloisters about the towns;
within the walls of which cloisters there are separate cells for the inmates.

---

* To live in rocks is so strikingly characteristic of the Boodhist monks that it deserves our particular attention. Boodh himself is said to have dwelt in a rock. Hence
we find, in India, cavern temples on a gigantic scale, showing that an enormous amount
of labour and skill had been lavished on them. Such are the wonderful chambers exca-
vated in the solid rock at Elephanta, Salsette, and Ellora. Mr. Erskine remarks that
" the caves of Kanara, on the island of Salsette, and those of Carli, on the main land,
evidently belonged to the Boodhists," while others, which he names, in the same locality,
belonged to the Brahmins. In a cave at Kanara, there are boldly-carved colossal statues
of Boodh, some of them representing him with his legs folded under him, and his hands
joined as if in prayer. These appear to be of exceedingly remote antiquity; and would
suggest that Boodhism, subsequent to the incarnation of its founder, had flourished in
India for a great many centuries before its devotees were expelled. In the Brahmin
cavern, at Elephanta, there is an enormous bust of a triple-headed idol, having three
faces looking in different directions. It represents Brahma, Vishnu, and Shiva—the
Hindoo trinity. The head of Shiva incarnate is adorned with the figure of *death's skull,*
or head. In his hand the god holds a *serpent* which twists itself round his arm, and rears
its head, so as to look in his passionate face. A vast number of Indian caves in which
monks dwelt, could be mentioned. These become interesting when we recollect that
the peninsula of Mount Sinai was, at a very early period, tenanted by Christian anchorites
and other monks, whose abodes in the rock are still to be seen in this remarkable
locality. Ammonius, an Egyptian monk, who visited Sinai about A.D. 373, found these
fanatics living here then, in separate cells cut in the rock, subsisting on dates, berries,
and other fruit, and abstaining from wine, oil, and even bread.—Theodoret, Vit. Patrum.

The anchorites, however, retire into the gloomy recesses of the forests, and lead a purely contemplative life, having no other society than that of tigers, serpents, and other wild beasts. They hold, not only that marriage is sinful, but that it is sinful even to look at a woman. They believe in the doctrine of confession to a priest, the efficacy of fasting, the utility of worshipping dead saints, and of making pilgrimages to holy places. Their employment in the cloisters is studying, praying, singing, and preaching. They undergo the priestly tonsure, and practise ablutions. (Carl Ritt. Erdkunde von Asien, Band. iv. sec. 1170.)

The Empire of Japan is the eastern frontier of Boodhism, and is far beyond the utmost reach of Christianity. The precise date at which Boodhism, or Budsdo—as the Japanese call it—was introduced here, is not ascertained. According to the Japanese records, in the year 50 of our era, a Brahminical religion was introduced into Japan, bearing resemblance to Christianity, in that it had a Divine trinity, and a redeemer born of a virgin, just as Boodhism has. But, besides that it is expressly said that this religion was Brahminical, the date at which it was introduced is too early for Christians to say, with the shadow of proof, that it was theirs. There are in Japan two sovereigns—a spiritual sovereign, like the Pope, and a temporal one, like an emperor. Under the former there are religious diignitaries, priest, and a regular system of monkery, consisting of monasteries of Cœnobite monks, and wild hermits who live in desert mountains. The latter have no settled abodes, nor any regular system of exercise.— They, however, practise much bodily mortification, and make pilgrimages to certain high mountain tops, in the desolate regions of the country.— These receive the confessions of penitents, and, in doing so, subject them to much austerity and peril. (Picard. Cerem. et Cout. tom. i. des Japanais.) Kempfer, in his History of Japan, (c. xi. xvi.) remarks that, in his time, the hermits had much degenerated from the austerity of their predecessors who, according to the rules of their founder, lived upon nothing but wild plants and roots, and exposed themselves to perpetual, and very rude trials and mortifications, fasting, plunging into cold water, wandering through rocky solitudes and wild forests. The Boodhists of Japan have, in their sacred books, the following five precepts of their founder,—first, kill not; second, steal not; third, whore not; fourth, lie not; fifth, drink no strong liquors. These five commandments are multiplied into ten, called *Sikkai*, which serve for the general conduct of life; and these again into five hundred rules called *Gofiakkai*, which are intended for those who aim at moral perfection in this life, and the highest felicity in the life to come.— They are exceedingly strict, and prescribe an ascetic life of the rudest and most austere character; making mortification of the bodily senses and appetites their chief end and aim. (Kempfer c. xvi.) The Japan Boodhists have their yearly religious festivals for the dead; their monk-priests; their shaven heads; their nuns; their celibacy; their monasteries; their temples full of gilded images; their altar with images and sweet-scented candles burning before it; their sermons; their prayers in a dead language; their counting of beads; and their bowing to idols. The monks are summoned together to the convent, in which there is a large library, by the ringing of a brass bell; the prior, every evening, prescribes to his monks the theme on which they are to meditate; at midnight, a certain choir takes its turn to chant prayers at the altar; and at the dawn of day, all the monks spend an hour in private meditation. (Pinkerton's Collection, vol. vii. p. 629. Kempfer, c. xx.) It is, therefore, by no means wonderful that the Jesuit missionaries, who were the first Christians to visit Japan, expressed, in their letters, so much astonishment at finding among these remote heathens a religion so much like their own. They were, however, excessively provoked by the discovery that those whom they had come to convert were so much like themselves. This kindled their hatred towards the Japanese priests, and made them charge them with all sorts of faults, such as the *improper* sale of indulgences, the borrowing of money on a written bond for payment in the next world, and their refusal to sacrifice for the dead. (Commentaries of the Jesuits on the affairs of India and Japan, quoted by Hospinian, De Origine Monachatus.) But such was the close affinity between Boodhism and Christianity, that the Jesuits found no difficulty in making converts, and getting a strong party of adherents. They, however, pursued a policy which soon excited the suspicion of a political design, and, as they took part in a civil war that occurred in that country, they were expelled from Japan, and their followers were exterminated by persecution. Hence, the very name of Christianity has become so odious to the Japanese that Protestant missionaries will have a hard task to perform, before they remove the prejudice which has thus been created against their religion. (Abridged from the Fathers of the Desert, vol. i. pp. 91—99.)

We come next to China, where Boodhist monks have flourished from a very early period. It will be recollected that we have already had occasion to cite from Sir William Jones' works, to the effect that the Chinese regarded Boodh and Foe as the same personage, having been born about 1027 years B.C. in Hindostan. And, indeed, it is generally admitted that the words *Boodh* and *Foe* or *Fohi*, were originally the same—the latter having been modified according to the pronunciation of the Chinese.— Now, it is certain that Foe was worshipped—and, consequently, the ascetic rites peculiar to his religion were practised—in China at a very early date, even long before Confucius. Still, we are most strangely told that, in the first century of the Christian era, when the Chinese government admitted a new religion *from India*—supposed by some to have been Boodhism—they made particular enquiries concerning the age of Boodh. Although there is every reason to conclude that Boodhism was very prevalent in China long before the commencement of the Christian era, yet, as this period is sufficiently early for our purpose, we shall not stay to investigate the point further. There is no evidence that Christianity carried much influence in China before the nineteenth century. Indeed, there is strong evidence that it did not. Still, six hundred years ago, the first Jesuit Christians that appear ever to have visited it, found monkery there deeply rooted in the people's minds. Marco Polo, who visited China about that time, states that the hermits in monasteries and cells worshipped idols, honouring their gods with great abstinence of meat and drink, and observing strict chastity. They killed no living creature, and shed no blood. Two centuries after, Nieuhoff—the secretary to a Dutch embassy sent to Pekin—in describing the Chinese monks, says there was among them a tradition of an eminent monk, named Lu-zu, who had built a large monastery, who spent all his time in grinding and sifting rice for the monks, and who wore iron chains day and night on his naked body. These chains made holes in his flesh which, for want of dressing, putrefied, and bred nests of worms; yet the old monk would not suffer them to be removed; but when one dropped off, he would pick it up, and say,—"Have you not sufficient to feast yourselves left? Why then forsake my body where you are welcome to feed?" The same writer says that, a little distance from Nankin, he saw a number of monasteries built on mountains, and occupied by monks—each in a little hut or cell—where they disciplined themselves every day with lashing, which the people believed to be very meritorious in another world, for they held the transmigration of souls. "They told us (he adds) that on Quanlyu (one of these mountains) there were as many cloisters as of days in the year." The peninsula of Korea—a dependency of the Chinese empire, rarely visited by Christians—swarms with Boodhist monks. A Dutchman, named Hamel, who was shipwrecked on that coast, and wrote a very good history of the country, says—"Some of their monasteries contain five or six hundred monks, whereof there are four thousand within the liberties of some towns." In Tonquin—a country adjoining China—Boodhist monkery has been found in a most flourishing condition, having "its convents of monks and nuns; confession of sins to the priests, with priestly absolution; holy water; temples and altars lighted, and holy flambeaux; rosaries, on which to count repetitions of prayers; religious festivals and jubilees; sales of dispensations or indulgences," and so on.— Cochin China is an adjoining kingdom, noted for its ancient establishments of Boodhist monkery. Some Jesuit missionaries, who visited the country about three centuries ago, were greatly astonished at finding here a religion thoroughly heathen, so much like their own. One of these missionaries, named Bori, in his account of it, as cited in Pinkerton's Collection, (vol. ix. p. 762) says—"There is such a variety of Omsaiis in that country that it looks *as if the devil had endeavoured among the Gentiles to represent the beauty and variety of religious orders in the Catholic church.* Their several habits answering their several professions, some are clad in white, some in black, and some in blue and other colours; some live in community, others like chaplains, canons, and prebendaries. Others profess poverty, living on alms; others exercise works of mercy, administering to the sick, &c. Others, again, look to the monasteries of women, who live in community, and admit no man among them but the Onsai (priest) who looks after them, *and they are all his wives.*....... The priests have chaplets and strings of beads about their necks, and make so many processions, that they outdo the Christians, in praying to their false gods.— There are also among them persons resembling bishops, abbots, and archbishops; and they use gilt staves, not unlike our croziers, insomuch that if any man come newly into the country he might be easily persuaded there had been Christians there in former times; *so near has the devil endeavoured to imitate us.*" Bori proceeds to point out their errors regarding transmigration and other doctrines held by Boodhists. Several other parts of Northern Asia could be named, where the same sort of heathen monks have carried on their religious exercises from time immemorial.*—

* In Thibet, heathen monachism has flourished from a very remote period. Here the followers of ancient Boodh are called *Lamaists*, from the different rank of *Lamas*, both

Passing by several nations in Asia, let us proceed to Africa, and glance at Egypt. Here, again, we find ample evidence that monkery

human and divine, whom they worship. Of these, there is one Supreme Lama,—who may be termed the Pope of Northern Boodhism, and who is even higher than the Christian Pope. The Grand Lama is a god incarnate; he never dies; but merely transmigrates from an old body into a new one. No sooner does he leave one body than the priests find him again incarnate in the body of some new-born infant, which to them presents infallible marks of being a young incarnate Lama. Under the Grand Lama, there is a number of subordinate Lamas, and a vast number of monk-priests. In a word, there is here a regular hierarchy of monks, who observe all the religious duties which have already been described as observed by other monks. They live in cloisters, which they carefully shut up every evening, lest the young friars and novices should go among the female sex. When the Jesuit missionaries, a century ago, visited Thibet, for the purpose of converting the inhabitants to Christianity, they were amazed to find that here, from time immemorial, a religion had existed which they could scarcely distinguish from their own. Here they found a complete system of monachism, with monasteries, nunneries, hermitages, and monks, by thousands, and tens of thousands,—all, up to the Grand Lama himself, with shaven heads, clothed in sacerdotal robes and caps, and under vows. Here they found a holy city for the Grand Lama, inferior holy cities for the inferior dignitaries, monasteries, pilgrims from distant lands, an altar for sacrifice, a mass of bread and wine offered upon it, images of saint-gods, holy water, prayers in a dead language, and strings of beads. Here also they found, sins confessed to priests, penitents, fasting, self-whipping, and counting of prayers; the doctrine of purgatory, prayers for the dead, extreme unction, and almost every other thing practised in that very ancient branch of Christianity—Roman Catholicism; while, at the same time, these Boodhists claimed for their religion a far higher antiquity than Christians can claim for theirs. The Romish missionaries were so confounded by the similarity of the two religions, that they did not know what to think or what to do. Soon after they made their discovery known, a theory was set up that the Lamaists were a kind of bastard Christians, —that the Nestorians, about a thousand years before, had fled to this part, and planted Christian churches here. It is true that, in the fifth century, some of the followers of Nestorius, bishop of Constantinople, being persecuted by the Roman Catholics, fled into Northern Asia, and there disseminated their doctrines to some extent. But a remnant of these Christians are still in that country, particularly in the mountains of Malabar.— They are, however, very different from the Lamaists. Neither the country nor the religion of Thibet exhibits a remnant or a trace of Judaism—a feature so prominent in the Christian religion. It has none of its traditions; none of its names. All these, in Lamaism direct us to search for its origin in India. The supposition that Lamaism has borrowed from Christianity its system of monkery, is overthrown by the fact that the same conformity exists in Cochin China, in Tonquin, and in Japan,—countries far beyond the bounds of the Nestorian missions. No Christian church was ever planted within a thousand miles of them. The only Boodhists with whom the Nestorians came in contact were the Lamaists of Thibet, Tartary, and Cathay, or Northern China. But the Boodhists of Cochin China, Tonquin, and Japan, are not Lamaists. The opinion that the Lamaists were once Nestorian Christians, and retained their form of worship, when they embraced Boodhism, is as contrary to historical fact, as it is to rational probability. Besides, there is a striking resemblance between the Lamaists and the Brahminical and Boodhist monks of India, who existed hundreds, if not thousands of years before the Christian era. In the thirteenth century, Rubruquis, a French monk, visited Tartary; and Marco Polo, a Venetian merchant, visited Cathay. Both of them found Nestorian Christians in Tartary; and Polo found them in Cathay; mixed everywhere with Boodhists or Mahometans, often with both, and in a few places with Magian fire-worshippers. Both these travellers agree in representing the monastic institutions with which they met, as exclusively belonging to Boodhists. Between the Christians and these there was no fraternization or amalgamation. The line of separation was strongly drawn. Rubruquis speaking of the nations that inhabit Northern Asia, says—"They are all given to idolatry. The Nestorians *live among them as strangers*, and so do the Saracens —or Mahometans as far as Cathay. The Nestorians inhabit fifteen cities of Cathay, and have a bishop there in a city called Segin. But, if you proceed further, they are mere idolaters. The priests of the idols of those nations have all broad yellow hoods.

flourished at a very early period. Where this mode of religious life first originated, is a question which is involved in profound mystery. We find it practised among several distant nations at so early a period, that the date of its origin appears to be far beyond the most remote historical accounts that have descended to us. The people who claim a rivalship for the primitive seat of civilization and religious philosophy, as well as for the origin of the arts and sciences, with the inhabitants of the valleys of the Ganges and the Indus, are the Chaldeans on the Euphrates, and the Egyptians on the Nile. And it is not a little singular that most of these people have chronological accounts of their national existence, hundreds of thousands of years before the Jewish chronology makes the creation of the world to have taken place. The divine books of Hindostan are, however, the most ancient religious records that have come down to us. In these also we find the earliest traces of monachism. This fact, and other proofs, furnish strong reasons for referring the origin of monkery to the Hindoos; or, at least, for concluding that it came from them to the Egyptians, who, in conjunction with certain Jews* that dwelt amongst

(the very colour of the Boodhist hoods.) There are also among them certain hermits, living in woods and mountains, of an austere and strange life. The Nestorians there know nothing; for they say their service out of holy books, in the Syrian tongue, which they do not understand." In describing the rites and ceremonies common to the idol temples at Cailac, in Tartary, he says, that the priests had their heads shaven, and were clad in yellow garments, with yellow hoods or caps (the Boodhist uniform)—that after being shaven, they lived unmarried, one or two hundred together in a cloister. They also carried about with them a string of nut-shells, much like the beads of the Roman Catholics, and often repeated the same prayer. But a remarkable difference between the Nestorians and Boodhists in Asia was, that the former rejected the use of images, while the latter filled their temples with them. Indeed, there is not the shadow of a proof that the Lamaists borrowed either their monkish habits or their form of worship from the Nestorians.—*Fathers of the Desert*, vol. i. pp. 76—83.

* The Old Testament, however, furnishes abundant evidence that monkery was among the Jews, or among the people, or peoples—whoever they were—to whom the mythological tales that compose this collection of fabulous, but savage lore, originally belonged. The description given of all the Jewish prophets, as far as it goes, exactly corresponds with the accounts we have of pagan monks; and the contents of the Old Testament bear marks that they are, in their present form, the productions of people of monachal habits. To give a few instances,—these prophets wore clothes of the roughest sort, or none at all, like the Indian monks. Elijah wore a kind of a cloak, or mantle, apparently made of goat's hair, and reaching from his neck to his feet, like John the Baptist's camel hair raiment. It may be, however, that Elijah was clad in the *skin* as well as the *hair* of a goat; for we learn that the Indian hermits wore the skins of animals. He also, like the Baptist, wore over this hairy mantle a leathern girdle about his waist. So noted was Elijah's appearance that, when the messengers of Ahaziah told their sovereign what sort of a man had accosted them in their way, the king immediately knew he was Elijah. —"He was a *hairy* man, and girt with a girdle of leather about his loins. And he said, It is Elijah the Tishbite." (2 Kings i. 8.) Christian commentators, who do not wish to recognise Elijah in the habiliment of a monk, have explained this passage in various ways. They question very much whether the words "hairy man," mean that Elias was clad in a hairy garment, or had natural hair like a beast, all over his body, or had the hair of his head hanging down to his heels. The last opinion, however, would at once identify him with the Indian monks. The Hebrew words, שֵׂעָר בַּעַל אִישׁ, literally mean *a man having hair.* It is true that the word שֵׂעָר appears to be used in the Hebrew Scriptures for the hair of the head, for goat's hair, for standing barley, and for satyrs; always, however, implying the idea of *hair*. But analogy teaches that here the word is employed to denote the hairy garment of Elijah. The same word is used in the expression—"They (the prophets) wear a rough garment (שֵׂעָר) to deceive." (Zech. xiii. 4.)

them, presented it to Europe, and other parts of the world, under the name of Christianity, as we shall see anon. Indeed, it is now admitted

It is remarkable that the Septuagint translate the hairy mantle of the prophets by the word μαλωτη, a sheep-skin with the wool on it. (1 Kings xix. 13, 19. 2 Kings ii. 8, 13, 14.) It is clear from this that these Jews, who well knew the garb of their prophets, also well knew that they wore such skins, like the Indian monks. Accordingly, we read in Heb. xi. 37, that the worthies, enumerated by the writer, were attired in the skins of sheep and of goats, (εν μηλωταις, εν αιγειοις δερμασιν) and wandered in deserts, mountains, dens, and caves,—wearing the very dress, and leading the very life of the monastic fraternity. Clement, in his first Epistle to the Corinthians, (c. xvii.) leaves us in no doubt who are meant to have led this life, when he says—"We mean Elias, Eliseus, and Ezekiel, the prophets." We may, therefore, safely conclude that Elias wore either the skin and hair of a goat, or a mantle made of goat's hair. Of the latter, there was plenty at the command of the Jewish priesthood. The Mosaic Law directed that offerings of goat's hair should be made. (Ex. xxv. 4; xxxv. 6.) The Jewish women were divinely influenced to spin goats' hair, (Ex. xxv. 26.) probably to make hairy garments for their monks. Goats were often sacrificed, and the Arabians, at once, brought a Jewish monarch 7,700 of these animals. (2 Chron. xvii. 11.) Thus, were goats' skins very plentiful among the Jews. There was in the monkish mantle of Elijah a miraculous virtue, as we read there was in the mantles of later monks. When he threw it on Elisha, it put an immediate spell upon him, and when he had possession of the same precious garb, at Elijah's ascent to heaven, he performed astounding miracles. (1 Kings xix. 19. 2 Kings ii. 1—16.) It would appear that all the Jewish prophets wore such a monkish mantle. It was by his mantle that Saul knew Samuel, when the witch brought him from the regions of the dead. (1 Sam. xxviii. 14.) Some of the prophets, however, went about stark naked, like the Gymnosophists, or Indian monks. Accordingly, we find that Isaiah (xx.) threw away the bit of sackcloth which covered his loins, and went about perfectly naked, for three years; precisely like the monks already described. It is, however, clear from the narrative that he was always nearly naked, having only his shoes, and a bit of sackcloth about his loins,—exactly like the Yogis who, as already stated, Hamilton saw in the East Indies. In like manner, when the prophetic spirit fell on Saul, he stripped off all his clothes, and lay naked on the ground, like a good Indian monk. (1 Sam. xix. 24.) And because he was thus naked, he was thought to be among the prophets. Again, a cell, a den, or a cave in a desert, or on some mountain, was the abode of the Jewish prophet, or, more properly, Jewish monk. To use what is called inspired language, he "wandered in deserts and in mountains, and in dens and caves of the earth." In such a cave dwelt Elijah. It is said that, after a journey of forty days and forty nights, he reached Horeb, the mount of God; and, having entered a cave, lodged there. (1 Kings xix. 8.) The monks of the place, to this day, show the traveller a chapel consecrated to Elijah, on this hill, about half a mile above their monastery, and also the cave where they say Elijah dwelt. These Carmelites also show the fountain at which he drank, and the grotto in which he taught the sons of the prophets. The latter is a chamber in the rock, of a square shape, called the "School of Elias." In this mountain, there is a great number of caverns, to which there are repeated references in the Hebrew Scriptures. Moses went into Mount Sinai, and, evidently, into a rock, where he abode, like Elijah, for forty days. This mount, which is part of the same range as Mount Horeb, has always been noted for monks. "Their houses in the rock" are to be seen to this day. Ammonius, an Egyptian monk, who visited Sinai A.D. 373, describes them as being very old even in his time. Hence we meet with such expressions as—graving an habitation in the rock,—in the caves of the earth and in the rocks,—the holes of the rocks,—the clefts of the rocks, &c. in the connexions they occur. The disciples of Elisha, however, appear to have dwelt together in a kind of cell or monastery which, owing to their increase, became too small 'for them. (2 Kings vi.) Samuel also, at Ramah, appears to have had a cave called Naioth, for the school of the prophets, or the education of young monks, where they lived in community; and there was a similar order of men at Jericho, in the vicinity of both which places there was a vast number of caves, small and large; as well as a vast extent of mountainous desert. Another monkish feature, in the lives of these Jewish cave-dwellers, was that they subsisted on bread and water. A nameless prophet who came to Bethel—a very noted place for prophets— appears to have subsisted on this simple diet. (1 Kings xiii.) Elijah's food was a cake

by the most critical Christian writers, that monkery was imported from Egypt, into their religion. If, therefore, this monkery was brought from

and a cruse of water, except when ravens miraculously brought him flesh. It was with bread and water that Obadiah fed a hundred of his fellow-prophets, whom he had hidden in a cave from the sanguinary hand of Ahab. Other instances might be added. But let us proceed to observe that what is called the Law of Moses makes express provisions for that species of Jewish monkery, called *Nazaritism*—a word which means to be set apart, or consecrated. In the sixth chapter of the book of Numbers, we find the following regulations laid down for the guidance of the fraternity.—Whoever wished to become a Nazarite was to make a vow that he would separate himself to Jehovah, by utterly abstaining from wine and all intoxicating drink, and from eating anything made of the fruit of the vine,—by allowing neither a razor, shears, nor scissors ever to touch either his hair or beard,—and by not eating, or even touching flesh, or any dead carcase.— Women as well as men might make this vow. A person might be consecrated by his parents, even before he was born. He might also consecrate himself, either for life, or for a stated period of time. If he happened to break his vow, by touching a dead body, he was to have his hair shaved. Now, there is here a perfect picture of Hindoo mona- chism. Like the *Yogi*, the Israelite was to make a vow, was to have his long hair, was to separate himself from the world, and was to abstain from wine and flesh. Like him, also, he could become a monk of this sort, either for life, or for a definite period of time. According to the Laws of Menu, a man might become a Yogi, by withdrawing into soli- tude, at forty or fifty years of age, either for life, or for a term of years. If he began young, he might, after a certain number of years, return into the social world, and enjoy the respect and profit of his sanctity, during the remainder of his days. But he who consecrated all his remaining years to monachism, and became a forest-anchorite, attained to a higher degree of sanctity. (Fathers of the Desert, vol. i. p. 25.) Now, of those who were consecrated from the womb to Jewish monkery, or Nazaritism were,—Samson, of whom the angel declared that he should be a Nazarite from the womb, and charged his mother not to drink intoxicating liquor, or eat any unclean thing, during the period of her gestation; (Judg. xiii.) Samuel the prophet, regarding whom, before he was born, his mother vowed that he should be presented to the Lord, and that no razor should come upon his head; (1 Sam. i.) John the Baptist, of whom the angel Gabriel declared that he should drink neither wine nor strong drink, and who proved a thorough monk, by inhabiting the wilderness of Judea, attiring in camel's hair, wearing a leathern girdle about his loins, and subsisting on locusts and wild honey; and Jesus Christ, of whom, according to Matthew, the prophets predicted that he should be called a Nazarene, on which subject we shall have something more to say hereafter. Amos (ii. 11, 12.) appears to imply that some of the Jewish monks broke their vow, when he says that the young men who had been raised up for Nazarenes had had wine to drink. Dr. Jennings, in his *Jewish Antiquities*, (p. 217.) says that these Nazarenes, by their vow, "were bound to stricter sanctity, to give themselves up to reading, meditation, and prayer; and, in token of their moral purity, carefully to avoid all legal pollution, and in sign of their spiritual mortification, and as having their minds so taken up with divine contemplation, as to be negligent of external ornaments, they were to let their hair grow without trim- ming." This is a perfect picture, not only of a Jewish, but likewise of an Indian monk. Jeremiah (xxxv.) praises another section of Jewish monks—evidently *Jewish* by name and by habitation, notwithstanding what has been said to the contrary—for their stanch abstinence from wine, even when tempted to drink. We find that these monks, called Rechabites, the children of Jonadab, drank no wine, planted no vineyards, posses- sed none, sowed no seed, built no houses, but dwelt in tents; thus leading a thoroughly hermitical life. These, like the monks of all other nations, had to do with the literature of their country; they were the *scribes* of the Jews, and therefore held a very high and influential position in the nation. (1 Chron. ii. 55.) The Pharisees also, among the Jews, although not thorough monks, yet in accordance with the rest of the Pythagorean philosophy which they had embraced, practised an ascetic life to a considerable extent, and were strongly attached to the flesh-mortifying system. They macerated their bodies, by frequent fasts, by lying on rough narrow boards, and by wearing around the border of their garments a fringe of thorns, with the points projecting inwards, so as to strike upon their flesh when they moved. Some of them walked the streets with mortar-like hoods over their heads and faces, to aid their meditations.—*Fathers of the Desert.*

India into Egypt, and thence among the Christians, the identity of Indian as well as Chinese monkery, with that of the Christians, is at once accounted for, without having recourse to the supposition of the missionary Borri and others, that the devil had introduced Christianity among the heathens. (Fathers of the Desert, vol. i p. 120.) That the Egyptian system of monkery was derived from India, at some remote period of antiquity, by means of some commerce or connexion—not related in history—which existed between these two very ancient nations, is proved, to a considerable extent, by the very exact and almost unexceptional agreement of the religious philosophy of ancient Egypt with that of the Hindoos, in all fundamental principles. Both Hindoos and Egyptians had that peculiar institution of religious castes, of which the sacerdotal was the highest;—an institution, be it remarked, abolished amongst the Boodhists when they dissented from Brahminism, thus precluding the supposition that the Egyptian religion was derived from Boodhism. Again, both the Hindoo and the Egyptian religions taught transmigration of souls. These souls contracted defilement from their connexion with the flesh—even the bodies in which they were encased. This defilement was to be worked off by divine contemplations and abstinence from carnal enjoyments. If the soul, in death, was found very sinful, it was to be punished, *for a while*, in hell; but if it was so clean as not to require purgatorial torments, and yet not sufficiently pure for heaven, it was to transmigrate into another body, in order to be further prepared. (Brucker, Hist. Crit. Phil. lib. i. c. 7.— Guignaut's Creutzer Relig. de l'Egypt. lib. ii. c 5.) Both Hindoos and Egyptians believed, not only in divine emanations, but likewise in incarnations, and consequent sufferings of gods. The Hindoo Vishnu and the Egyptian Osiris, both Deities of the highest order, became incarnate on earth as men, laboured and suffered for a time, died, ascended to heaven,

---

Paul was by no means averse to monkery, not only in the doctrines he delivered—which abound in monkish expressions—but likewise in practice. Indeed, he appears to have been under the Nazarene vow, and owing to a violation of this vow, to have once had a shorn head. (Acts xviii.) Such are the traces of Jewish monachism. Almost all the early Fathers, with pride, recognised the monkery of the Jewish prophets, including that of John the Baptist. St. Jerome, in his Epistle to Paulinus, says—"Our founder, Elias, our Elisha, and our leaders the sons of the prophets, lived in fields and deserts, and made themselves tabernacles by the flowings of the Jordan." In his Epistle to Rusticus, he also says—"The sons of the prophets whom we read of as monks in the Old Testament, built themselves cells by the Jordan, away from the crowds of cities, and lived upon barley bread and herbs, having neither wives nor worldly riches." It is in these "latter times" of religious pride that Christians have learned to disdain their monkish origin. But it is most worthy of their consideration that, at the very dawn of their alleged *new* religion, John the Baptist—unquestionably, a thorough monk—was "in the deserts until the day of his showing unto Israel,"—was in that wild, mountainous, rocky, uncultivated, and thinly inhabited region, called the Hill country, extending from Jericho, southwards, along the Jordan and the Dead Sea, the very region which was swarmed with the monkish Essenes, already described,—was in this country, we say, living probably as an anchorite in some mountain cave, or some cell, until, all of a sudden, he made his appearance in the wilderness of Judea, clad in the hairy dress of a monk, subsisting on the natural productions of the forests, and preaching a most austere doctrine about the near approach of the kingdom of heaven. Is it possible that the doctrine of this man—although precisely the same as that preached by Jesus—was any other than that of the pagan monks, among whom he had spent his time "until the day of his showing unto Israel"? Still we are told that the preaching of this Essenian monk was "the beginning of the Gospel of Jesus Christ"!

and resumed their celestial glory and dominion. (Guignaut's Creutzer, &c. lib. ii. c. 5.) Both the Hindoos and the Egyptians also maintained the same doctrine regarding good and evil demons, fallen angels, and so on. Monkery, however, does not appear to have been carried out in Egypt to the same frantic degree as in Hindostan. Although, in both countries, it was the belief that the only way for a soul to purify itself, while in the body, was to mortify that body by ascetic habits, yet the mode of performing this religious duty took a milder form in Egypt. Civilization may have had something to do with this, but the physical condition of the country had doubtless much more to do with it. The difference observable between the degrees in which the ascetic principles have been developed in different countries and ages, is to be attributed to circumstances; —when these are favourable, monkery grows luxuriantly; when they are not, its growth is stunted. In Egypt, the greatest impediment to the full scope of monachism was the inundations of the Nile. These swept away the monk's hut, or filled his cave with water for several months. They disturbed him and hindered him from standing in the same position for forty years. Indeed, they interfered in a thousand ways with the life of a hermit. His only chance of security and quietude was to forego the gratification—exceedingly sweet to a monk—of being gazed at, and admired in the exercise of his piety by the people of the plains; and retire into the top of some desert mountain. Accordingly, we find very frequent mention made that the monks of Egypt were located on some eminence or mountain; but as all the cities and towns were built on mountains, each side of the Nile, and as the monks generally dwelt in, or near these cities and towns, an ample opportunity was given them to make the inhabitants at large acquainted with the privations and sufferings of their ascetic life, in which they so much delighted.

Besides the evidence afforded by the identity of the Indian and Egyptian religion, as already shown, there is other evidence that monkery flourished among the Egyptians at a very remote period. Few readers can be ignorant of that curious Egyptian structure—the labyrinth; but still fewer have imagined the probable character of its inmates. This labyrinth subsisted in the time of Pliny the Elder, (lib. xxxvi. c. 13.) and had then, as he thought, stood for 3,600 years. More than five hundred years before the time of Pliny, Herodotus (lib. ii. c. 148.) gave a glowing description of its magnificence. From him, as well as from Pliny, Strabo, Mela, and other ancient writers, we learn that this gorgeous pile consisted of twelve halls or courts, and fifteen hundred small dwellings above the ground, with an equal number of halls and small dwellings underground,— all communicating with one another; but by such innumerable windings and intricacies as made the whole very properly be called a labyrinth. Herodotus, having examined the apartments above ground, was prohibited to explore the subterranean caverns by the priests, who told him that here were kept the sacred crocodiles, and the bodies of departed kings; which shows that the place was used for religious purposes. Although both its origin and early use are involved in great mystery, and all early accounts regarding it are highly fabulous, yet the most probable opinion is that it was originally a cavern, which, according to the practice of ancient times, religious men or monks took for their abode, and, in process of time,

enlarged, improved, and embellished, building the same number of dwellings above ground as they had constructed underground. The various
tales that it was the work of a king, the work of twelve kings, and so on,
are all of them equally and utterly fabulous. (See Encyclop. Brit. Article
Labyrinth) There is very little doubt that this labyrinth, like that of
Crete, of which there are similar wondrous accounts, was originally no
more than a large cavern, and, like many others, became the abode of
religious fanatics. Such we find the cavern of Elephanta, in India, as well
as caverns in a vast number of other places,—they were subterranean temples.   Such, doubtless, was the labyrinth of Egypt, so much admired by
Herodotus, Diodorus Siculus, Pliny, Mela, and other Greek writers,—it
served both as a temple and as a congeries of dwellings for the Egyptian
monks, just as a monastery served for the Christian monks—their imitators.
This view is strongly corroborated by the history of the spot on which
this Egyptian structure is said to have stood. Herodotus (lib. ii. c. 148,
149.) tells us that this labyrinth stood near Lake Mœris. Pliny says—it
was in the Lake of Mœris. Although ancient writers slightly differ as to
its exact situation, yet the most probable opinion is that it was at the
southern extremity of Lake Mœris. Now, this spot was the chief resort
of the Egyptian monks, long before there were any Christian monks.—
Lake Mœris is, unquestionably, the same with that which Philo, as cited
by Eusebius, (Hist. lib. ii. c. 17.) calls Lake *Maria,* saying—"The principal
men among them, from every quarter emigrate to a place situated on a
moderate elevation of land *beyond the Lake Maria,* very advantageously
located both for safety and temperature of the air, as being the native
country of *the Therapeuts.*" Sozomen, (lib. i. c. 12.) however, in citing
the same author, calls the lake, *Mareotis,* saying.—"Philo, the Pythagorean, relates that, in his time, the most virtuous of the Hebrews assembled
from all parts of the world and settled in a tract of country situated on a
hill near Lake *Mareotis,* for the purpose of living as philosophers."   In
other places, he calls it *Mareota.*   Again, he says that a shepherd who
became a monk, led his flock to graze on the banks of Lake *Mareotis.*—
(lib. vi. c. 29.)   But, surely, he must have mistaken Marcotis here for
Mœris ; for he clearly describes the latter, and not the former, which was
a small island, surrounded by a lake, south of Alexandria. (Comp. Strab.
17.   Horat. Od. i. 37. Virg. Geor. ii. 91. Socrat. Hist. Eccles. lib. iv.
c. 23.)   Upon the whole, there can be very little doubt that it was the
borders of Lake Mœris which Philo meant to call "the native country of
the Therapeuts ;" where the labyrinth, already described, with its three
thousand cells—now long ago, however, all hidden by drifts of sand—
furnished dwellings for them, on a hill, secure from the floods of the Nile.
Indeed, there is every reason to conclude that, many centuries before the
Christian era, the whole range of mountains on the western side of the
Nile, from Alexandria to Ptolemais, swarmed with pagan monks.   On this
range were the mountains of Nitria and Scetis—places most noted as the
haunts of pagan and Christian monks.   Here, also, on the very border of
Lake Mœris,—"the native country of the Therapeuts"—as indicated by
the most correct maps, stood the town of Oxyrinchus. (See Rollin's Map
of Egypt.)   Indeed, this would appear to be the very spot into which
Philo says that the monks, of whom he speaks, were wont to retire—

"beyond the Lake Maria." If so, this will account for the fact that a vast number of monks resided here after the commencement of the Christian era, and considerably weaken the force of the following exclamation of Abbé Fleury.—" The great wonder of Lower Egypt was the city of Oxyrinchus, peopled with monks, both within and without, so that they were more numerous than its other inhabitants : the public edifices and idol temples had been converted into monasteries ; and these likewise were more in number than the private houses. The monks lodged even over the gates, and in the towers. The people had twelve churches to assemble in, exclusive of the oratories belonging to the monasteries. There were twenty thousand virgins, and ten thousand monks, in the city, every part of which echoed night and day with the praises of God." (Hist. Eccles. tom. v.) Hereafter, we shall have reason to see that all this was only a modification of pagan monachism.

But in order to keep within a period of time prior to the commencement of the Christian era, and yet not so early as to find Egyptian Monachism differing materially from what it was in the third and fourth century of that era, let us glance at those fanatics called Therapeuts and Essenes. These have already been described at some length. (pp. 221, 222.) Here it is necessary only to show that they existed long before the Christian era, and that the Therapeuts and Essenes are identical, not only with each other, but likewise with the Brahminical and Boodhist monks, who have already been proved to be of one and the same origin. Now, Philo,—who was older than Jesus—in his account of the Therapeuts, (vid. ant. pp. 222, 432, 435.) describes a class of monks that had existed for many ages before his time. Accordingly, he says that, in his days, such men " were everywhere over the world, to the intent that both Greeks and barbarians might share in so lasting a boon." He adds.—" They abound, however, in Egypt, in each of its districts, and particularly about Alexandria. But the principal men among them, from all parts, emigrate to a place standing on an elevation beyond the Lake Maria, (Mœris—see p. 462.) very advantageously located, both for safety and temperature of the air, as if it were the native country of the Therapeuts." He further designates their doctrine, " a philosophy derived by them from the tradition of their forefathers" ; and says, " they have commentaries of the ancients, who were the founders of the sect." Such language as this can apply only to a community of men who had existed for some hundreds of years before the time of Philo. Josephus, again, who describes the same sort of monks under the name Essenes, speaks of them as being, in his time, an ancient institution. He represents them as a numerous and influential sect of religionists in Syria, in the time of Antiochus, son of Alexander, about 143 years B.C., consisting of about four thousand men, among whom, he says, virtue had flourished for a long time. He also identifies them with the disciples of Pythagoras, showing their existence about five hundred years before the Christian era. Philo, in his *Quod Omnis Probus Liber*, gives a similar account of them. Both these Jewish writers, however, claim these fanatics—whom they highly praise—exclusively for their *own* nation. Although there is no doubt that there were amongst them many persons of Jewish extraction, in the times of Philo and Josephus, when the seed of Abraham had been scattered over the world, yet it is certain they were not exclusively Jewish, any more than the inhabitants of Egypt, or the students at the Alexandrian school, at the time of Josephus and Philo. Had they originally been a Jewish sect, it is almost certain that they would have been named somewhere in the Hebrew Scriptures. The locality in which they were found by Pliny the Elder, (Hist. Nat. lib. v. c. 17.) who was contemporary with Jesus, namely, on the western side of the Dead Sea,—comparatively near to Alexandria, the hot-bed of monkery —furnishes a presumptive proof that they had made their way thither from Egypt; and this proof is strengthened by his statement that they were constantly recruited by new comers, whom the surges of ill fortune had made weary of the world; in which manner the sect had been kept up *for several thousands of years*, without any being born among them.— Thus, there is ample historical evidence that these monks, whether they be called Essenes or Therapeuts, existed many ages before the commencement of the Christian era. Again: that the same religionists are described by different writers, under these two appellations, is proved by the identity of the meaning of their respective names, and by the sameness of their respective doctrines, modes of discipline, and life.* Whatever apparent difference there may be between those called Therapeuts by Philo,

---

* Mosheim, however, sees " nothing in the laws or manners of the Therapeutæ that should lead us to consider them as a branch of the Essenes." He further adds.—" Nor indeed has Philo asserted any such thing. There may have been, surely, many other fanatical tribes among the Jews, besides that of Essenes; nor should a resemblance of principles always induce us to make a coalition of sects. It is, however, certain that the Therapeutæ were neither Christians nor Egyptians, as some have erroneously imagined. They were undoubtedly Jews." (Eccles. Hist. vol. i. p. 46.) Whether they were Jews or Gentiles is quite immaterial to our present object. It is sufficient for us now to know that they were in Egypt, before the Christian era, and that they were monks.— That they were in Egypt before that period, Philo plainly shows; and that they were monks, Dr. Mosheim is ill prepared to deny, when he admits that the more sober Essenes were monks. His words are.—" The monks of Christianity, a description of men that first appeared in Egypt, seem to have taken for their model the manners and scheme of life of the *practical* Essenes: indeed, the account given us, by Josephus, of the latter corresponds so exactly with the institutions and habits of the early votaries of Monachism, that it is impossible for any two things more nearly to resemble each other.— Those solitary characters, who came to be distinguished by the appellation of hermits, appear to have copied after the *theoretical* Essenes or Therapeutæ." (Commentaries on the Affairs of the Christians, vol. i. p. 89.) In another place, he says that the Essenes were "a fanatical and superstitious tribe, who placed religion in a sort of seraphic indolence, and, looking upon piety to God as incompatible with any social attachment to men, dissolved, by this pernicious doctrine, all the great bonds of human society "—" They dwelt generally in a rural solitude, far removed from the view and commerce of men.— This singular sect, which spread abroad through *Syria*, *Egypt*, and the neighbouring countries, maintained that religion consisted wholly in contemplation and silence. By a rigorous abstinence also, and a variety of penitential exercises and mortifications, which they seem to have borrowed from the Egyptians, they endeavoured to arrive at still higher degrees of perfection in virtue." (Eccles. Hist. vol. i. p. 44.) It would seem, however, that, as among the present Christians, there was among these Essenes a considerable difference of opinion. While some of them considered it lawful to enter into a state of matrimony, solely for the purpose of propagating their species, others deemed it their duty to live in a state of celibacy, and to employ their time in rearing and instructing the children of others, when they could entice them into their communities, while the minds of these young ones, as Josephus tells us, were pliable and fit for learning, so that, by these means, they formed them according to their own manners, and esteemed them to be of their kindred; thus forcibly reminding us of the practices of the Jesuits in Christendom. The Syrian Essenes, like the Jews at large, thought the Deity

and the Essenes described by Josephus and others, there exists no *essential* difference. They may, truly, have been distinct sects of the *same* religion, just as, in the present age, Wesleyans and Independents are distinct sects of Christians : for there were schisms among ancient monks, just as there are among modern Christians—blades of the same tuft of grass. But the slight difference that appears between them, in matters of detail, may have arisen from the inaccurate manner in which historians describe them, or from the imperfect knowledge they possessed of the doctrines, discipline, and life of these recluse fanatics, who were under vows not to divulge the secrets of their religion to the uninitiated. The signification of both the names—*Therapeuts* and *Essenes,* however, appear to be precisely the same, —the former being Greek, and the latter Chaldaic, or rather Syro-Chaldaic. While the meaning of the word *Therapeuts*—from the Greek θεραπευται, healers, physicians, attendants—admits of no quibble, the signification of the term *Essenes* appears to have afforded Christian writers much trouble, evidently, because its true import is prejudicial to their creed, signifying the same thing precisely as *saviour, salvation,* &c. Some derive it from the name of *Jesse*—king David's father ; others, from a city called *Esse,* mentioned by Josephus. Godwin is, however, not far from the mark when he derives the term " from the Syriac word—*asa,* which signifies to *heal,* or *cure.*" The word is, evidently, either derived from, or is of a cognate origin with the Syro-Chaldaic, or Hebrew—yw', meaning *health, recovery, deliverance, remedy, salve, salvation,* and so on. As a verb it signifies to *heal, cure, deliver, serve, anoint, salve, save, &c.* Used as a name for these monks, it denoted *healers, anointers, saviours,* and so on ; the healing art, as we have already remarked, being anciently in the hands of religious fanatics. The word is to be met with in different forms, in the Hebrew Scriptures, signifying *unction, anointing, salving,* &c. And even in the English version, the meaning is preserved in such words as *Saviour* or *salver, salvation,* and others. The same may be said of the Latin *salus* (salvation), *servator* (Saviour), and so on.* Accordingly, just as the

---

was to be appeased by sacrifices; but those who wandered in the deserts of Egypt maintained that no offering was acceptable to God but that of a mind absorbed in holy contemplation. Those of them who offered sacrifices and feasted, did so, like the early Christians, in the depth of night. (Porph. de Abstin. lib. ii. c. 26) They seem to have thought that this was a more sacred season for performing their religious rites. This is, doubtless, to be attributed to the many traces of sun-worship which is observable in their practices. They thought that they should offer a sacrifice to the solar deity before he appeared. During the day, they discoursed about the things of life, but they spent most of the night in conversing and meditating upon sacred subjects; and always, before the dawn, they recited their prayers and hymns. The Phœnicians, the Egyptians, the Greeks, and other ancient nations, held the night in the same veneration. (Jablon. Panth. Ægypt. lib. i. c. 1.) These things, concerning the Essenes, are dwelt upon at such length in this note, because the Gospels, and much of the writings of the early Christians, abound in references to the doctrines of the Essenes and other pagan monks. Indeed, a knowledge of the latter is indispensable to a right interpretation of the former.

* In the Welsh version of the Bible the meaning is still clearer ; such as *Iachawdwr,* (saviour) the author of health ; *Iachawdwriaeth,* (salvation) the system of healing. In this very ancient language, which contains a vast number of oriental words, particularly such as relate to religion, we have also the very term *Essene,* in the word *asswyn,* which, like its numerous etymons, imports the idea of healing, or preserving by charms, &c.— For example, *asswyn* means medicine ; *swyn,* a preservative, a remedy, a charm; *swyna,* to collect or deal in charms and preservatives ; *swynog,* having a preserving virtue ;

Hebrews called a *healer* or *saviour*—יש׳, or rather מושיע; while the Greeks called such a person—σωτηρ;* so were the monks, under notice, called *Essenes* in the language of some nations, while, in that of others, particularly of the Greeks, they were called *Therapeuts*,—both names denoting the same religionists, or, at least, different sects of the same religionists, living in different countries. Philo, it is true, treats of the Essenes and Therapeuts as distinct sects; but not different religionists.— It is, however, very possible that he did not know of their common origin, seeing the Therapeuts were in Egypt, and the Essenes in Judea. Like Josephus, he appears to have thought the Essenes were a sect of Pythagoreans, and therefore, was led to search for the meaning of their name in the Greek language. Accordingly, he supposes it to derive from οσιος, *holy*, and to denote the piety of these men; although he admits that his derivation of the term is likely to be wrong. (Quod omnis probus Liber, ii.) The close resemblance of the Essenes to the Therapeuts, however, whether they existed in separate communities or not, will be clearly seen from the following comparative analysis of their respective doctrines and practices. The Essenes believed in the immortality of the soul; and the Therapeuts maintained the same doctrine. Both had also their inspired books; both explained these books allegorically, and spent a great proportion of their time in studying them. They both alike despised riches, and lived in monasteries, in which they had all things in common, and before entering which they parted with all their property. The Therapeuts refrained from marriage; and the Essenes, as we are told, esteemed continence, and the conquest over their passions to be virtues; and although

---

swynol, curative, tending to charm; *swynediy*, charmed, cured; *swynedigaeth*, the act of curing by charms; *swyn-gyfaredd*, an amulet, witchcraft; *swyniad*, a remedy, a charming; *swynogl*, an amulet, a charm; *swynwr* or *swynydd*, a healer, a magician; *aswyno*, to pray; *aswyniad*, a prayer; *aswynwr*, one who charms or prays. Ymswyn, to bless one's self by making a cross on the forehead with holy water, or by some other religious rite Many other forms of the word could be added. The identity of the meaning of the term *aswyn*, in its various forms, with that of *Essene* would be astounding, were it not a well known fact that the Britons received both their Druidical and Christian religion from the East. With propriety does Mr. Godfrey Higgins, in his excellent work on the *Celtic Druids*, (p. 125.) remark that " the Essenians of whom Philo has written the history, were confessedly Pythagoreans, and I think *we may see some traces of these people among the Druids*. They existed before Christianity, and lived in buildings called monasteria, or monasteries, and were called Koinoboi, or Cœnobites."

* Originally, there is little doubt, from ζωη, life, and τηρ or τηρεω, to watch, preserve,—meaning a preserver of life. It is rather singular, also, that the name Ιησους, (Jesus) in itself, means a *healer*, and is synonymous with *Essene* or *Therapeut*, and cognate with ιασις, a *cure*, a *healing*, and with יש׳, *health, healing*, or יש׳ה׳, (Joshua) a *healer*. It is for Christian writers to see that this name is not of a mythological character, and has no reference to the Essenes or Therapeuts, both which names denote healers — They should especially look into this matter, since the term Χριστος (Christ) means anointing, or rubbing with oil; and since Ιησους ὁ Χριστος may, without any great violation, be translated—the anointing healer. At all events, we are assured that it was by prayer and unction that Jesus's disciples were taught to heal people. " Is any sick among you? let him call for the elders of the church; and let them *pray* over him, *anointing him with oil* in the name of the Lord." (Jam. v. 14.) If Jesus's disciples did not learn this mode of healing from him, it would be interesting to know whence they derived it. It is precisely the same mode of healing as that practised by the Latter-Day Saints, in the present age.

they did not utterly deny the fitness of marriage, yet, most of them neglected wedlock. The Therapeuts abstained from wine and flesh; ate nothing but bread, salt, and hyssop; and drank only water. They also abstained from food often for three days, and sometimes for six days. In like manner, the Essenes ate only the coarsest food, and that very sparingly, while they drank nothing but water. Both feasted in this simple manner at night. Both were great predictors of future events, and both practised medicine; the Therapeuts *curing both bodily and mental diseases,* and the Essenes " choosing out of the writings of the ancients what they found most for the advantage of the soul and body, and inquiring after such *roots and stones as may cure distempers.*" Indeed, the resemblance between the Essenes and Therapeuts is so close in the main, as to prove that both communities had the same origin. It is true that, according to the accounts we have of them, they appear to differ in some minor points, particularly in that the Therapeuts were more extravagant in their monkish habits, while the Essenes seem to have been, of all the monkish fraternity, the most sober and rational in their practices. (Compare Philo's description of the Therapeuts with Josephus's representation of the Essenes, in places previously cited.)

In the next place, we have to compare these monks with those of India and China, already described. Between these, again, we expect to find no radical difference. Their fundamental principles appear to have been precisely the same; so as to warrant the inference that they are identical in origin. The manner in which they respectively practised these principles may, certainly, present some features of dissimilarity; but they are all of minor importance, and of such a character as would necessarily be caused by the vast length of time that these monachal communities had lived apart, by the different climate of the countries in which they were located, and by other external circumstances. In the first place, it is observable that the Therapeutic monasteries, or convents, bore the name by which the Indian monks were called. Philo says of the Therapeuts,— " In every house there is a sacred apartment which they call the Σεμνειον, where, retired from men, they perform the mysteries of a pious life."— Clement, in his Stromata, (lib. iii.) says of the Indian monks,—"Neither the Gymnosophists nor those *called Semnoi,* use women."—"They have virgins *called Semnai.*"—"Many of the Brachmans eat no living creature, and drink no wine.........Those of the Indians called *Semnoi,*—that is, venerable—go naked all their lives." In another place, (lib. i.) he plainly shows us whom he means by the *Semnoi,* when he says,—"There are two kinds of Indian philosophers, the *Sarmans* and the Brachmans. Hence, it is evident, not only that he means the same people by *Sarmans* as by *Semnoi,* but likewise that the name of the latter is the same word as the word Σεμνειον, used by Philo. Porphyry also makes a similar distinction between these two sects of Indian monks, called by Clement *Brachmans* and *Semnoi* or *Sarmans;* but he designates the latter *Samanei.* Strabo, (lib. xv. c. 1.) again, makes the following difference between them.— " Megasthenes says that there are two sects of Indian philosophers, the *Brachmans* and the *Garmans.*" He then proceeds to describe the monkish habits of each sect. Now, there is very little doubt that the same people are meant by all these ancient writers, under the names *Garmans, Sarmans*

2 GG

Samanei and *Semnoi*,* and that name of the Therapeutic convent—Σεμνειον, is of a cognate origin with them.   But even if it were admitted that
semnoi (σεμνος) is purely a Greek word—and not a word imported by
Pythagoras into the Greek language, denoting Indian asceticism, or the
exercise of veneration,—of which there is no evidence, still, to prove the
identity of the Therapeuts with the Indian monks, it is sufficient merely that
Philo uses Σεμνειον for the convent of the former, and Clement of Alexandria uses Σεμνοι for a sect of the latter.   There are, however, much
stronger proofs of their identity than the resemblance in name.   The
whole of their doctrines, discipline, and religious exercise, bears the closest
affinity.—The Therapeuts and Essenes, like the Indian monks, believed in
the immortality of the soul; and the only object of their religious exercises,
alike, was to purify this soul.   The Indian monks, like the Therapeuts
and Essenes, were called philosophers.   Josephus tells us that, before a
person was initiated to the society of the Essenes, he was obliged to take
"tremendous oaths" that he would not violate the regulations of the
fraternity; and Bernier assures us that the Indian monks took a similar
oath, and to the same effect.   As the Therapeuts and Essenes lived in
monasteries, so lived many of the Indian monks, while some of them
retired into deserts, and led a solitary life.   Among both there were grades
of dignity, and degrees among their officers.   Both had stewards to manage their monasteries.   Bardesanes and Diodorus Siculus relate that the
Samneans, as well as the Brachmins, had stewards who provided for
their wants; and Josephus says that the Essenes had "stewards appointed

---

* Although σεμνος, in Greek, now means *venerable, reverend, grave*, &c., yet there is
no proof that it was originally a Greek word; for no root can be pointed out, from which
there is any certainty, or even probability, that it has been derived.   To imagine that it
is from σεβω, is to derive it from a word which is clearly not genuine Greek.   In the
Hindoo scriptures there is ample mention made of a class of monks called *Shanyasis,
Shanyases, or Sannyas*.   It was very easy for Megasthenes—and Strabo, about three
hundred years after him—in writing names which were in a language they did not
understand, and of which they could judge of their orthography only by sound—to write
this word *Garmans*.   The same thing may be said of Clement, who writes it both *Sarmans* and *Semnoi*; of Porphyry, who writes it *Samanei*; and of Philo, who writes the
name of a convent—*Semneion*   In the Indian scriptures, *Sannyasee* means a person who
has totally renounced all worldly pursuits, and has devoted himself to religious exercises;
and *Sannyas* means the religious life of such a devotee. (See Wilkins's Bhagvat-Geeta,
pp. 81, 131.)   According to the Laws of Menu, a *Sannyasee* appears to be of a higher
sort of recluse than a *Brachmin*,—the latter seems to be only a monk-priest; but the
former a glorious anchorite.   Accordingly, it is said that, if a *Brachmin* wishes to become
a *Sannyasee*, or a forest-anchorite, he must dwell in the forest; have his passions subdued; subsist on herbs and roots; wear an antelope's hide, or a vesture of bark; suffer
the hair of his head, his beard, and his nails to grow to the utmost; eat little and
seldom; sleep on the bare ground in the haunt of pious hermits; and strictly observe
the laws ordained for hermits. (Laws of Menu, chap. vi.)   The name *Sannyasees* or
Shanyases, according to changes incidental to spoken language, may well have become
Garmans, and afterwards *Sarmans, Samneans, Semnoi*, &c.; especially in passing from
the language of one nation to that of another; just as the people of that vast African
desert, now called *Zaara*, were once named *Garamantes*, and their country was called
Garama; but afterwards *Sahara, Zopara*, and now *Zaara*.   And indeed there is some
reason to think that these *Garamantes* were originally allied to the Indian *Garmans*,
described by the followers of Alexander; for they wandered in the desert nearly naked;
lived in common; inhabited cells; subsisted on milk, barley meal, and dates; and only
adopted children.—Plin. lib. v. c. 8. Strab. 2.

to take care of their common affairs." The Indian scriptures enjoined monks to part with all worldly goods before they became cœnobites; and Josephus informs us that this was a practice among the Essenes, who lived in common. The monks of both countries also abstained from flesh, from intoxicating liquor, and from marriage. So much alike were they on the point of marriage, that we find from Josephus that some of the Essenes allowed marriage under certain conditions; and from the Hindoo scriptures, that the Brachmins had conditions under which their disciples could enter into the marriage state. As a general rule, however, they despised wedlock; and one of the most important articles of their faith was the necessity of preserving their chastity. Strabo, and also Clement, tell us that both the Brachmins and the Semnoi abstained from women, and "knew nothing of marriage, nor of the procreation of children;" and Josephus informs us that the Essenes esteemed continence, and the conquest over their passions to be virtues, and that they neglected wedlock. The monks of both countries also made a practice of taking no food for a great number of days, when in deep religious exercise; always subsisted on the coarsest and simplest diet, such as bread and water; and slept naked on the ground. The Indian monks had numerous appointed fast days, and so had the Therapeuts. The former diligently read the Vedas, and spent much time in meditation and prayer; and the latter, as well as the Essenes, studied the "writings of the ancients, and devoted much of their time to prayer and psalm-singing. They were also very much alike in their numerous ablutions, and in their remarkable notions of ceremonial uncleanness. According to the ancient Hindoo books, a person might contract a ceremonial uncleanness in a thousand ways, and could not take part in any religious worship or ceremony, until he was purified in conformity to the prescribed form; and, according to Josephus, the Essenes believed in similar pollutions and purifications. The highest degree of saintship that a Hindoo could reach was that of a *Sannyasee*, or *Semnos*, which means a monk of the most venerable order. One of the Hindoo books describes such a man as too holy to be touched by a monk of an inferior sanctity. Precisely in the same manner, Josephus says of the Essenes, that " so far were the juniors inferior to the seniors that, if the seniors should be touched by the juniors, they must wash themselves as if they had intermixed with a company of foreigners. Further, before a person could become an Indian monk, it was necessary for him to spend much time in a state of probation. The Shasters say that—if a young man—he must exercise himself in prayer, in subduing his passions of anger and revenge, in abstaining from women, in acquiring the love of truth, in learning to sleep but little and eat but little, and so on, for a period of from five to twelve years, before he could be admitted into the first degree of the fraternity's *holy orders*. He had several other degrees to go through, in a similar manner, before he could become a perfect monk. In like manner, as Josephus assures us, " if any one had a mind to join the Essenes, he was not immediately admitted, but was prescribed the same method of living which they used, for a year, while he continued excluded. When he had given evidence during that time, that he could observe their continence, he approached nearer to their way of living, and was made a partaker of the water of purification; yet he was not even then admitted to live with them ; but after this demonstration of fortitude, his temper was tried two years more, and if he appeared worthy, they might then admit him to their society." The Therapeuts, and apparently the Essenes, like the Indians, also had nuns, or holy virgins ;—devoted the night to religious meditation,—underwent severe bodily tortures and mortifications, —rejected all pleasures as the greatest evil,—delighted in suffering pain, as the soul's only salvation,—took up their abodes in solitary spots,— believed in fate,—foretold future events,—were very renowned physicians. In fine, the Therapeuts and Essenes, in every particular, were perfectly identical with the Indian monks, whose elaborate instructions for the regulation of monachism, as contained in their divine books, together with the extremely ancient origin of these books themselves, prove that it was a national institution among them, some thousands of years before the Christian era. For corroboration of all the foregoing statements the reader is referred to the writers already cited on the subject of monachism.

Having thus traced pagan monkery to the very time and place in which Jesus was born, we now come to Christian monkery, leaving, how- ever, for the present, unnoticed any indications observable that the founder of the Christian faith was a strong advocate of the principles and practice of monachism. It has been customary to attribute the origin of Christian monkery to St. Antony, Paul the Simple, Pachomius, and Hila- rion,—all in the third and fourth century of our era. Indeed, it has been the custom to regard monkery as a mode of religious life absolutely invented by these worthies ; while heathen monkery has been passed over in silence, especially by Christian writers, who could not fail to perceive that, to introduce it, would be to identify Christianity with Paganism.— *Christian monkery, however, is much older than the third century.* Irrespec- tively of the evidence deducible from what has already been advanced regarding this mode of religious life among the pagans, we have direct historical proof that it is as old as the first Christian community of which we have any account. We are scarcely told that Jesus ascended bodily into heaven, before we are furnished with evidence that Christians led a monastic life,—precisely the same as that of those pagan monks called Therapeuts and Essenes. Like these, the first Christians (vid. ante, pp. 214—223.) gave up all their property to their leaders ; lived in commu- nity, or together in a convent, having all things in common; had stewards, or deacons, to manage their common affairs, provide for their necessities, and serve their tables, so that all the rest of them might devote them- selves entirely to religious exercises. So closely did these Christians resemble the pagan monks, that Eusebius, in citing Philo's description of the Therapeuts, could not avoid pronouncing them identical with each other. Again, St. Paul's Epistles to the Christians whom he addresses throughout breathe of the spirit of monachism. He teaches bodily morti- fications, gives a decided preference to a state of celibacy over that of marriage, urges fasting and prayer, and gives frequent cautions against indulging in pleasures. He exhorts the Romans (viii. 4—11.) to walk not after the flesh, but after the spirit ; telling them that to be carnally minded is death ; but to be spiritually minded is life and peace. He tells the Colossians (iii. 5.) to mortify their members upon earth. He cautions the Galatians (v. 16, 25.) against fulfilling the lusts of the flesh, and urges them to crucify the flesh with the affections and lusts; thus teaching the same doctrine precisely as the Indian monks. He only tolerates marriage as a matter of necessity, not of propriety; and says, (1 Cor. vii.) "It is good for a man not to touch a woman."—"I say, therefore, to the unmarried and widows, it is good for them if they abide even as I."— He proceeds to teach that it is good for both male and female to remain in a state of celibacy, so as to be without worldly care, and able to devote themselves entirely to spiritual things; stating his reason,—that the unmarried man studied how to please the Lord, but the married man how to please his wife; and that the virgin cared for the things of the Lord, that she might be holy both in body and spirit, but the married woman cared for the things of the world, how she might please her husband. In these instances, like many others that could be adduced, Paul clearly teaches rank monachism. It is true that, like the Essenes, he does not absolutely prohibit marriage. Nor does he insist upon total abstinence from wine like some monkish teachers; for, while he charges bishops not to be given to wine, he allows Timothy a little wine for the benefit of his stomach, and on account of his infirmities. Timothy, however, was accustomed to observe the monkish rule of drinking only water; for Paul tells him,— "Drink no longer water." In the time of Paul, there were among Christians diverse views touching the monastic life. Some were very strict monks, utterly forbidding marriage, and insisting upon total abstinence from animal food. Against these, Paul—who appears to have been moderate in his ascetic views—bitterly inveighs. He also makes very light of the monkish *exercises* or macerations, pronouncing them to profit but little. (1 Tim. iv.) All this, however, shows that monkery was a prominent feature of Christianity at this early period. The same fact is proved by the contents of that ancient narrative—"The Acts of Paul and Thecla." (See the Apocryphal New Testament, or Fabricius's Codex Apocryphus Nov. Test. Whether this romantic production, which was in great renown among the early Christians, is genuine* or not, is immaterial to our present purpose. It is sufficient for us to know that it was in existence early in the first century of the Christian era.—It is mentioned by Tertullian, in the second century, as being then comparatively old.— He truly says it was forged by a presbyter of Asia, who confessed that he had fabricated it out of reverence to Paul. But the statement made in the narrative itself to the effect that there was a day kept sacred to Thecla's memory, shows that the tale about her sufferings was old when the narrative was written. The same thing is proved by Evagrius Scholasticus. (lib. iii. c. 8.) who informs us that the Emperor Basiliscus, erected and dedicated a noble temple to Thecla, which he says existed in his time.— Now, the tale about Thecla must be very ancient, before the former of these writers would have ventured to state that a festival was kept to her memory, and the latter that a temple had been dedicated to her. Had not such a temple and such a feast existed, the fallacy of the statement that they *did* exist in the time of the writers would soon be detected. Every

---

* Cyprian, Eusebius, Evagrius, Epiphanius, Augustin, Gregory Nazianzen, Chrysostom, and Sulpicius Severus, refer to the History of Thecla. Baronius, Locrinus, Wake, and Grabbe, consider it to have been written in the Apostolic age.—*Hone's Apocryphal New Testament.*

thing goes to show that the story of Thecla originated, at least, in the first
century. Now, in this tale, the following things are related.—That Paul
preached—" Blessed are they who keep their flesh undefiled"—" Blessed
are the chaste"—" Blessed are they who abandon their secular enjoyments"—" Blessed are they who have wives as though they had them
not"—" Blessed are the bodies and souls of virgins; for they are acceptable to God, and shall not lose the reward of their virginity."—That, in
consequence of preaching celibacy, he was accused of deluding young men
and virgins, persuading them not to marry, but continue as they were, and
telling them they should not be raised from the dead unless they remained
chaste, and avoided defiling their flesh.—That he taught that matrimony
was unlawful; perverted the minds of married women; deprived young
men of their intended wives, and virgins of their intended husbands.—
That, with other monks, who had parted with all their property, and lived
with him in a cave, he fasted and prayed for six days.—That Thecla
abandoned Thamyris, to whom she was betrothed, and, in spite of her
mother, followed Paul.—That she preserved her chastity, notwithstanding
the numerous and desperate attempts made to violate her.—That she
entered a cave in a mountain, where she was sorely tempted by the devil,
and was attended by a great number of women, who resorted to her for
religious instruction, renounced the world, and shared her monastic life.—
That, whilst in this cave, she prophesied future events, performed wonderful miracles, cast out a vast number of demons, add cured such a number
of various diseases, that the physicians of the country " lost all the profit
of their trade."—That she dwelt in this cave for seventy-two years, even
till " she was ninety years old, when the Lord translated her" to heaven.
Such is the monkish character of this tale,—told as early, at least, as the
first century of the Christian era, and bearing internal evidence that what
Christian advocates regard as being then a *new religion*, was, in its incipi-
ent state, quite as monastic as any of the pagan religions already noticed.
Of an equally monachal character is the " Shepherd of Hermas"—a production which is said to be from the pen of Hermas mentioned by St.
Paul; (Rom. xvi. 14) which was read publicly in the assemblies of the
ancient Christians; which is quoted with reverence by Origen, Eusebius,
Athanasius, and other early Fathers; and which is to this day found
attached to some of the most ancient manuscripts of the New Testament.
When Hermas is alone on a mountain, fasting and praising God, an angel
whom he describes as having a reverent appearance, clad in the habiliment
of a shepherd, and carrying a bag on his back, and a staff in his hand—
the very picture of a monk—appears to him, and teaches him what a real
fast should be. (Comp. lib. ii. Command. i. Introd. with lib. iii. Simil. v.)
This angel, whom Hermas calls a shepherd, also teaches him how to purify
his soul in fasting ; namely, by refraining from every shameful act, from
every filthy word, from every hurtful desire, and from all the vanity of the
present world ; and adds that, on the day he fasts, he is to taste nothing
but bread and water, and is to give to the poor what he saves in fasting.
The book also teaches that riches should be cast away; that people should
serve the Lord poor; that the pious should not hoard up riches; that they
should not be possessed of houses and lands; and that although marriage
is not altogether sinful, yet celibacy is much more meritorious.—" He that

marries, sins not ; howbeit, if he remain single, he shall thereby gain to himself great honour before the Lord." (Lib. ii. Com. iv.)   In a word, the very essence of the Shepherd of Hermas is monastic.   Again, in an Epistle said to be from the hand of Clement, who was a disciple of Peter, and is honourably mentioned by Paul, (Phil. iv. 3.) we find evident traces of monachism, such as—" Let him that is pure in the flesh, not grow proud of it, knowing that it was another who gave him continence ;" and so on. (xvii. 38)   Ignatius, again, another Apostolic Father, follows in the same monkish strain, saying,—" If any man can remain in a state of celibacy to the honour of the flesh of Christ, let him remain without boasting ; but if he boast, he is undone." (Epist. to Polycarp.)   The following testimony of Pliny the Younger, in his letter to Trajan, already cited, (p. 218.) shows a striking resemblance between the practices of the Christians, about the year 110, and the usages of the monkish Essenes and Therapeuts.   He informs us that those Christians whom he had caused to be arrested, told him that " they made it a practice, on a stated day, to meet together *before daylight, to sing hymns, with responses*, to Christ and God, and *to bind themselves by a solemn oath* not to do any wrong act ; but that they would not commit thefts, or robberies, or acts of *unchastity ;* that they would never violate a trust ; that when these observances were finished they separated, and afterwards came together again to a *common* and innocent repast."— In like manner, precisely, we are told by Philo and Josephus, that the Therapeuts and Essenes came together before daylight to pray and sing hymns, in the last clauses of which hymns they all joined in chorus,—that they bound themselves by " tremendous oaths," among other things, not to do harm to any one ; not to commit theft or robbery ; not to violate their chastity ; and not, for their lives, to divulge the sacred doctrines of their sect to the uninitiated ;—that, after their ceremonies of praying and singing, they dispersed, but shortly after, met again and partook of food together in the same apartment, having all things in common.   The parallel is perfect.   If we take a step onwards about thirty years, to the time of Justin Martyr, we shall find him, in his second Apology, boasting of the chastity of the Christian monks and nuns, and saying—" There are among us many men and women, sixty or seventy years old, who became disciples of Christ in their childhood, and have ever since maintained their chastity."   Tatian, his disciple—who was at the head of a community of people called Encratities, (Abstainers) who condemned marriage as an impurity, and led a thoroughly monastic life—uses still more vaunting language, when he says—" You Greeks say that we play the fool among wives and boys, virgins and old women.   But your poetess Sappho was an impudent courtezan, and sang her own wantonness.   Our women, on the contrary, are chaste, and our virgins, at the distaff, utter divine oracles much more clearly than that girl of yours."   Irenæus, (Cont. Hær. lib. iv. c. 30.) in repelling a charge made by the Marcionites—a Gnostic sect who condemned marriage, and were thorough anchorites—against the more moderate monks, namely, that they defiled themselves by commerce with their heathen neighbours, says,—" If he who makes these charges glories in his knowledge, or separates himself from the society of the unbelievers, and gets nothing from other men, but is stark naked and barefooted, living houseless in the mountains, like the animal that eats grass, shall he be excused *because he does not know the necessity that we are under of dealing with other men?*"   Here, the plea of Irenæus for not carrying monkery to so high a degree of perfection as the Marcionites was, simply, that he was prevented by circumstances, or the nature of his avocation.— About the same period, we find Athenagoras (Apol. s. 33.) saying—"Each one among us has his own wife, whom he has legally married, and whom he uses for the sole purpose of having children, and no farther.   There are also among us both men and women who have grown old in celibacy, with the hope of a closer union with God. Now, if the state of sexual absti- nence draws us near to God, the very thought and desire of carnal pleasure draws us away from him.   We therefore avoid those thoughts, and much more the acts themselves; and it is not in word, but in deed, that we carry out our principle, that each should remain in the virgin purity in which he was born, or should limit himself to one marriage ; for a second one is but decent adultery."   Although the early Christian monks, like the heathen Essenes, did not altogether deny the utility of first marriages, because, without them, they perceived they could not have *holy virgins,* yet second marriages they condemned as decidedly adulterous. Theophilus of Antioch (lib. iii.) tells us that, among the Christians of his time—as early as the middle of the second century—the exercises of bodily morti- fication* were practised, monogamy observed, and chastity sedulously

---

* Εγκρατεια ασκειται.—This was a technical expression among the monastic frater- nity, denoting the whole course of the ascetic practices.   Literally, it means to *exercise self-government* with regard to sensual pleasures.   We frequently meet with εγκρατεια in the New Testament, having reference to the monkish practices of the early Christians. But in the English version, its real meaning is concealed under the word *temperance,* into which it is generally translated.   Paul, in writing to the Galatians, (v. 16—25.) uses it in conjunction with other expressions which plainly show that his doctrine was thoroughly monastic.   Having, *inter alia,* said that the flesh lusted against the spirit, and that the work of the flesh was adultery, fornication, uncleanness, lasciviousness, &c., he adds that the fruit of the spirit was long-suffering, self-mortification or self-govern- ment (εγκρατεια), and that those who were Christ's had crucified the flesh with its affections and lusts, so as to live and walk in the spirit.—A doctrine savouring more strongly of the most austere monk was never delivered by any one of the pagan *Bonzes.* He preached the same doctrine of εγκρατεια to Felix, so as to terrify and disgust him. (Acts xxiv. 25.)   Sometimes he uses the verb, εγκρατευομαι, such as (1 Cor. vii. 5—9.) where he recommends celibacy, and says that when Christians cannot restrain them- selves by self-mortification—the very meaning of the verb εγκρατευομαι, which he uses —theyhad better marry, or, more literally, go together, "than to burn." In another place, (1 Cor. ix. 25.) where he uses this verb, he evidently refers to the monkish prac- tice of self-mortification.   For he says that every one who agonized, or strove in great pain (αγωνιζομενος) practised self-mortification (εγκρατευεται) in all things ; and in the next sentence but one, he says that he himself pommelled his body till it was black —υπωπιαζω—in order to bring it into subjection. Paul—or whoever wrote this Epistle —appears to have, in this place, borrowed a few ideas from the heathen philosopher, Epictetus : if not, both of them have drawn from the same source. Let any one com- pare 1 Cor. ix. 24—27, with the following passage from chapter xxxv. of Epictetus's *Enchiridion.*—" Would you be a winner in the Olympic games? so would I ; for it is a proud position.   But let me intreat you to consider what must precede this, and what may follow it, and then make the attempt.   You must live by rule, eat what is unpala- table, refrain from dainties, habituate yourself to constant ascetism, being at the ap- pointed time in heat and cold.   You must also abstain from wine and cold liquors ; and must, in short, be as submissive to all the directions of your master as to that of a phy- sician."   This passage throws much light upon Paul's comparison of a monachal life to a race in the Olympic games, and clearly shows the character of his doctrine.

guarded. Clement, in his Stromata, (lib. i.) although not a perfect hater of the flesh, and although an advocate of marriage in some cases, yet assures us that continence consists not only in abstaining from amorous pleasures, but in despising all earthly possessions and worldly delights; and he highly extols the virtue of celibacy and virginity. He would, however, confine these monkish practices to their original purposes, and orthodox design. For he says,—" He who, *from hatred conceived against the flesh,* abstains from conjugal intercourse and convenient food, is indocile and impious, and continent *without reason.*" We find the same sentiment in a production called the Apostolical Canons, purporting to have been written in the Apostolic age. Canon 51. prescribes that if any bishop, priest, or deacon, abstained from marriage, flesh, or wine, *not for ascetic purposes, but from abhorrence of them,* should either be corrected or deposed. If we turn to the wilds of Africa, where dwelt the earliest Latin Fathers whose works have descended to us, we shall find, at the close of the second century, at Carthage, a fiery presbyter called Tertullian, who was a zealous advocate of celibacy, virginity, corporeal macerations, nocturnal vigilance, abstinence from flesh and wine, together with all other things which good monks considered to have a tendency to weaken the body, and strengthen the soul. In his Treatise on the Resurrection, (c. 8.) he says—" Those sacrifices are acceptable to God which the flesh offers by its own suffering,—I mean those conflicts of the soul, fasting, abstinence from flesh and wine, and the filth attached to it; also virginity, widowhood, and monogamy." He had, however, reason to admire these monastic virtues, particularly virginity, with less ardour; for he found that many professed virgins did worse than entering into an honourable state of wedlock. He therefore says—" It is vanity, not piety, which induces them to profess virginity; some times their belly, their God,—they desire free maintenance; for the brethren gladly receive and support the virgins. They are publicly presented to the pastor of the church, and consecrated; their good deed is proclaimed. They are loaded by the brethren with honours and gifts. If one falls from the grace of virginity, she still appears with her head uncovered, and makes no change in her dress, lest she should betray her condition. These apostates still claim to be virgins, and will not confess, until they are betrayed by the cries of their new-born children. Virgins of this sort readily beget and bear children, which are very much like their fathers. Such are the vices which result from constrained virginity. Besides, the desire of being seen, and of pleasing the men, is not becoming to a virgin. However good her intentions may be, there is unavoidable danger in her exposing herself to the gaze of many eyes; whilst, at the same time, her vanity is tickled by the fingers that point at her,—while she is too much loved, and is warmed by the constant embraces and kisses of the brethren and sisters." He was also very much annoyed to think that the institution of virginity—so highly esteemed by Christians—was then among the heathens in a flourishing condition, and had been established, not only many centuries before the Christian era, but at a period far beyond the reach of the most ancient historical accounts then extant. In his Treatise on Monogamy, (sec. 13.) he says—" We know the virgins of Vesta, and of Juno, in a town of Achaia,—of Apollo, at Ephesus,—and of Minerva, at several places. We also know continent men, particularly those of the Egyptian god Apis. The African Ceres, likewise, has women, who, having renounced their marriage, will afterwards avoid the touch of a man, and refuse to kiss even their own sons.—See how the Devil, next to luxury, invented a destructive chastity !" In his Prescriptions, (sec. 40.) he says, the Devil " baptizes some as believers and followers of his ; promises them purification from sin, by baptism ; and if I rightly remember, the god Mithras makes the sign of the cross upon the foreheads of his worshippers. And then too, he limits his chief priest to one marriage, and has also his virgins and his male professors of continence." Origen, who was born only 185 years after the time Jesus is said to have been born, was a thorough-going monk. He carried the doctrine of bodily mortification so far into practice as to mutilate himself, according to Jesus's sanction in Matthew xix. 12. Eusebius (Hist. Eccles. lib. vi. c. 8.) tells us that Origen underwent this operation when very young, and that the bishop of Alexandria greatly admired the deed. He also, in the same book, (c. 3.) furnishes us, *inter alia*, with the following particulars of Origen's monachal career. He says—" As his doctrine, so was his life."—" He induced numbers to imitate him."—" Many years did he continue to lead the life of *philosophy*,* completely removing from him all the incentives to youthful passions ; during the whole day undergoing no trifling amount of hard exercise, and at night devoting himself, the most of the time, to the study of the Holy Scriptures, and restraining himself, to the utmost, by the most rigid and philosophical life. Sometimes he was exercised in the discipline of fasting ; then again, at night, he limited his time for sleep, which, in consequence of his great zeal, he never enjoyed on his bed, but upon the bare ground. But most of all, he thought that the evangelical precepts of our Saviour should be observed, in which he exhorts that we should not have two coats, nor make use of shoes, nor pass our time in care for the future. Indulging, also, an ardour greater than his years, he persevered in cold and nakedness ; and advancing to the greatest extremes of poverty, astonished, most of all, his nearest friends.........He is said to have walked the ground for many years without any shoes, and also to have abstained from the use of wine and other food not necessary for sustenance, many years, so that now he was in danger of subverting and destroying his stomach." Hence, we see how far from the truth is the oft-repeated assertion that monachism was a creature introduced into Christianity in the fourth or fifth century. It formed its very essence at the time we have the first account of its existence, as it will more pointedly be shown before the close of this section. In the time of Origen, monachism was as perfect and as flourishing among Christians as ever it had been among the Brachmins and Boodhists. Abstinence from wine, flesh, and sexual intercourse—with the express view of purifying the soul—was rigidly enforced. But let us hear Origen himself on this point. In his Answer to Celsus, (lib. v.) he says—" When we abstain from flesh, we do so in order to chasten the body, and bring it

---

* That is, a life of monachal self-mortification. Just as the terms *philosophers* and *philosophy* are used by the Greek writers to denote Indian monks and monkery, so are the same terms used by the Christian Fathers to signify Christian monks and monkery. —*Philosophy* here, in Eusebius, means the whole system of monachal exercise, and *philosophical life*, the life of a monk.

to submission; eradicate our earthly members—lecherous impurity, lasciviousness, depraved affections, so that we may mortify our corporeal actions." In his nineteenth Homily on Jeremiah, (sec. 4.) in recommending *pious fraud*, and "useful deceptions,"he says—"There are some who thereby exercise chastity and purity ; and others who thereby exercise monogamy ; the former believing they are lost if they marry at all; and the latter believing they are lost if they marry a second time." He proceeds to say that total abstinence from marriage is by far the most meritorious, in both male and female. Such were the monachal notions prevalent in his time. Contemporary with Origen was Cyprian, bishop of Carthage, who, when he embraced Christianity, forthwith parted with all his worldly goods, and, in order to lead a life of monkish purity, abandoned his wife. In his Treatise on the Dress of Virgins, he has written much which shows that, in his time, Christian monkery had for a long time luxuriantly flourished. Of the virgins, he says, they were the flower of the ecclesiastical tree,—the glory and ornament of spiritual grace,—the most joyful race,—the perfect and incorrupt work of praise and honour,—the image of God's holiness. His own language, however, in other parts of the same work, proves that these virgins were not so spotless as he would have them ; for he charges them with the pride of gay dress, with painting their faces and dying their hair, and with being fond of presenting themselves at marriage feasts to join in wanton sports and filthy speeches, by which lust was inflamed, and the passions of the married couple were excited. In consequence of these and similar immodest practices, he says —"The church often complains of her virgins, and groans at the infamous tales which are told of them. Thus, the beauty of the virgins is withered, the honour of continency and purity is destroyed, and all their glory and dignity are profaned." In the time of Cyprian, so old were those branches of monachism—virginity and celibacy—that it had become a practice for a monk-priest, and also for a deacon, to take one of these virgins—these brides of Christ, as they were called—out of a monastery, to live with him in his private abode ; both the priest and the virgin being under a vow to maintain their chastity. This practice frequently led to disgrace.[*] Cyprian says to Pomponius—"You ask for my opinion as to what should be done with those virgins who, after making a vow to live in a state of virginity, have been caught lying in bed with men—one of whom you say was a deacon—and who confessed they had slept with the men, but affirmed they were still pure virgins." After expressing his opinion that virgins should not be allowed even to live in the same abode as men, and that such should immediately be separated, he says—"We have seen many grievous falls resulting from this practice ; and through these illicit and dangerous connexions we have seen many virgins corrupted." Basil, bishop of Cæsarea, addresses his 55th Epistle to a priest who had kept in his house a virgin that was under vow. He gives us to understand that this practice was so general that the Council of Nice had, long before, decreed that no man should keep in his house women who were not his near relations ; and he adds—"The honour of celibacy consists in separation from women."

[*] See a great number of ancient authorities, to this effect, collected in the *Fathers of the Desert*, vol. i. pp. 208—238.

St. Jerome, St. Chrysostom, Sulpicius Severus, and others, bring similar charges against the monks and nuns of this period. We must, however, desist; as we have now traced Christian monkery up to the fourth century, in which, as admitted on all hands, it was in a flourishing condition. But in the face of the mass of historical evidence advanced, who will contend that it was in this century monachism was introduced, or even established among Christians? Who will, with St. Jerome,—a man who was himself a fiery monk, who attributed to Christianity the origin of everything he thought was good, and who, in almost all of his one hundred and fifty Epistles that have descended to us, treats of monks,—who will, with him, hazard the conjecture that his contemporaries—St. Antony and St. Paul the Simple—were the Fathers of Christian monachism? (Epist. 22. Ad Eustach. c. 16.) The same thing may be asked in regard to St. Athanasius, who wrote the life of Antony, and was only about forty-five years his senior. Surely, these men must have well known that monkery had existed, not only long before the age in which they lived, but from time immemorial. To account rationally for the motive which led Athanasius —who was by birth an Egyptian, who had lived so many years contemporarily with Antony, and who was personally acquainted with him, and with most of his disciples—to confer upon him the honour of being the founder of the monkish fraternity, is very easy. It was the same motive which induced him to attribute to him such fierce battles with the Devil, such astounding miracles, and such other things as no sober-minded person can for a moment believe. This motive was that of a desire to load with glory the hero of his tale, at the expense of truth,—a desire which has tarnished and rendered unworthy of implicit reliance, almost all the narratives of that age, in which it was believed that to falsify for the sake of promoting the interest of religion was a shining virtue.* The more sober of the early Christian writers, however, by no means attribute the origin of monkery to Antony and Paul. Sozomen (Hist. Eccles. lib. i. c. 13.) says— " Whether the Egyptians or others are to be regarded as the founders of this philosophy, it is universally admitted that it was carried to perfection by Antony, an ascetic, and a virtuous and renowned monk." Socrates (Hist. Eccles. lib. iv. c. 23.) says of the monasteries of Egypt,—" They were founded probably at a very early period, but were greatly augmented by a devout man named Ammon,"—a contemporary of Antony. Even the

---

* The Christian Fathers appear to have derived this notion, with their religion, from Egypt. Brucker, in his History of Philosophy, when speaking of the New Platonists, (sec. 16.) says that the Egyptian priests—and to some extent those of other nations— held that pious fraud and lying are justifiable, when they are useful to religion; and adds—" it was a saying of Timæus Lacrus, that as we heal bodies by certain medicines, so we may coerce minds to good by false speeches, when they are not affected by true ones. Even Plato was not averse to this principle. He allowed princes especially to deceive and lie for the public good. The New Platonists gloried in these teachers, and followed their example. What wonder then if they endeavoured to sustain a falling superstition by fables and fictions? This they did, by both feigned miracles and suppositious books. These philosophers, and the Christian teachers of these times, contended with one another in the use of these frauds."—See Fathers of the Desert, p. 224. In using the productions of the Christian Fathers and other early writers therefore, the hand of criticism must be laid hard upon every word they contain. By this means, notwithstanding their extravagance, they may be turned to a good purpose in tracing the origin of the Christian religion, and the circumstances under which it was introduced.

zealous monk, Jerome, in his Prologue to the Life of Paul of Egypt, does not appear to believe that Antony was the father of monkery. For he tells us that there *had been* much difference of opinion respecting the first monk who took his abode in the desert,—that some would go so far back as Elijah and John the Baptist,—that although there was a sense in which Antony could be termed the *first* hermit, yet *all* other monks were not led by his example,—and that Antony's own disciples affirmed that one Paul of Thebes, *in Upper Egypt*, was the first who lived a religious life in a desert; although not the originator of the name *hermit*, afterwards given to those who led this sort of life.

Let us glance at the lives of some of these Christian monks, and compare them with those of pagan monks, with the view to decide whether both are identical in origin. From St. Athanasius's Life of Antony we learn that the latter *was an Egyptian*, born 251 years after Christ. The professed object of Athanasius—another Egyptian, and bishop of Alexandria, in Egypt—in writing Antony's biography, was to acquaint *foreign* monks with his piety. When we consider that Athanasius tells us that Antony was the first who instituted monasteries,* and was only forty-five years older than his biographer, it sounds very oddly that, at that early period— only about eighty years after Antony himself had become a monk—there were *foreign monks* who were ignorant of the founder of their institution. But to pass by this inconsistency, Athanasius tells us that the monks to whom he wrote sought to emulate *the monks of Egypt*. It was not the monks of Sinai, or of any part of Judea, be it remarked, that were to be a pattern to these foreign monks; but those of Egypt, where we have seen there were pagan monks long before the Christian era. Antony, in order to become a monk, gave all his possessions to the poor. He then retired into a lonely part of the country, and devoted himself to prayer and bodily mortification. Here he found other monks whom he had reason to admire for their self-denial, their watchfulness, their fasting, their lying on the ground, and their earnestness in prayer. He had a great many severe contests with the devil, whom he always drove away by prayer and fasting. By day, the devil would endeavour to inspire him with the love of money, and by night, would make him blush, by tickling his flesh, and assuming the shape and actions of a female. Antony's prayers and fastings, and other bodily mortifications, however, made him flee. The young monk

---

* It is, however, to be observed that Athanasius does not say that Antony was the first monk,—he says only that he was the first who instituted *monasteries*, by which he means, apparently, buildings known by that name. For a little further on, he says— "Hitherto no monasteries were in Egypt or elsewhere; nor had any monk entered the pathless desert, but every one who was inclined to devote himself to asceticism, retired to some solitary place near his own village." Still, this is contrary to fact. Many monks, before his time, had lived in deserts. And as to the existence of monasteries, Athanasius contradicts himself on this point, when he says that Antony, on becoming a hermit, sent his young sister to a Virgin-house, or nunnery—παρθενων, a word clearly signifying the dwelling of holy virgins, and the name of a temple of the goddess Minerva, whose perpetual virginity, and successful resistance to the attempts made by the god Vulcan to violate her chastity, are frequently referred to by the Greek and Latin poets, who surname her Παρθενος—the virgin. A *Parthenon* was, unquestionably, a house into which virgins retired, or in which they were kept, according to a very ancient Greek custom. (Eurip. Iphigen. in Aul. 738.) Into one of these convents Athanasius evidently represents Antony as sending his sister.

watched whole nights. His food—of which he partook never oftener than
once a day—was bread and salt; his drink, water; and his bed, a mat on
the bare ground. At one time he dwelt in a cave, or sepulchre, where the
devil, with a whole troop of demons, attacked him, and beat him all over
his body, inflicting severe wounds on him, and leaving him for a dead
man. After his recovery, he removed to a mountainous desert, where the
devil, in vain, endeavoured to tempt him with silver and gold. He had
now spent fifteen years of his life as an anchorite. While in this desert,
which, apparently, was part of Upper Egypt, he found, on the eastern side
of the Nile, (Vid. Jerome Vit. Hilar. sec. 31.) the deserted ruins of an
old castle, which he converted into an abode for himself. "Having
blocked up the entrance, and laid up a store of bread for six months—
according to a frequent practice of the Thebans of Egypt, where bread
would keep for a whole year—and having a spring of water inside, he
dwelt alone, ensconced as in a sanctuary, making a monastery of the old
castle, and neither going out himself nor giving admittance to those who
visited the place. Thus he lived for a long period secluded as an ascetic,
only receiving once in six months a new supply of bread, let down to him
from above. But those of his acquaintance who came to the place, stayed
whole days and nights outside," while the anchorite within sang psalms.
Having thus exercised himself for about twenty years, within the castle,
without being seen by any one, he came out with his soul full of divine
inspiration, and began to heal diseases, exorcise demons, and preach most
eloquently. He wore next his body a hair shirt, and upon this, the skin of
an animal. These he never changed; his body he never washed; not even
his feet would he allow to touch water. He predicted future events, cast
out demons, and performed a great number of miracles. His very sight
made many an espoused damsel change her mind, and vow perpetual virginity. Having led this life for about eighty-five years, " he visited the
monks in the outer mountain," and, at his death, when 105 years old, he
gave his sheepskins to one monk, and his hair shirt to another. No one
can fail to perceive in the life of this man a perfect picture of an Indian
monk. St. Paul the Simple was a disciple of the great Antony, and an
Egyptian, who turned out an illustrious anchorite. When he sought
Antony's company, he was, like an Essenian novice, put upon his trial for
some time; but he was soon found to be proficient in all monkish austerities. He lived on bread and water, and never tasted these before sunset;
wore only sheepskins; performed stupendous miracles; healed the sick of
incurable maladies; and with a spiritual eye, saw all things past, present,
and future. (Sozomen Hist. Eccles. lib. i. c. 13. Tillemont's Mem. Eccles.
Hist. &c.) St. Paul *of Egypt* was another eminent monk. It is worthy
of observation that this recluse flourished not only before Paul the Simple,
but rather before Antony, who is regarded as the father of monkery. For
Jerome, from whose life of this saint the following particulars are extracted,
makes him contemporary with Cyprian, in the commencement of the
third century, designating him "the first hermit," and telling us that
Antony's own disciples affirmed that this Paul was the first who lived a
religious life in a desert. Although this is no proof that this Paul was
really the first hermit, yet it goes to show that he flourished at an early
date. Early, however, as it was, there were then monachal assemblies or

churches of Christians in Egypt, of an ancient date. For Jerome tells us that the storm of persecution, under Decius and Valerian, "laid waste many churches of Egypt and the Thebaid." During this persecution, Paul—a native of Lower Thebaid, who had been well educated in Greek and Egyptian literature—at the age of sixteen, fled to the desert mountains, where he found a cave, the entrance of which, at the top of a rock, was covered with a stone, and shaded by the spreading branches of a palm-tree, near which there was a spring of pure water proceeding from the cave. In this cave Paul fixed his abode, and devoted himself to prayer and seclusion, the palm-tree supplying him with both food and clothing. Jerome, anticipating that what he narrated might seem incredible, asseverates that he had seen monks in the Syrian desert, who had shut up themselves in a cell for thirty years, living on barley bread and pure water; and another monk whose dwelling was an old cistern, and whose only food was five dried figs a day. He also tells us of a young monk who—when a beautiful female, by her blandishments, endeavoured to make him violate his chastity, while his hands were tied with a cord—bit off his tongue and spat it into the fair tempter's face, in order that the pain resulting from this act might mortify his rebellious nature. "Paul having reached the one hundred and thirteenth year of his heavenly life on earth, and Antony having attained to his ninetieth year,* in another desert," the latter, directed by divine revelation, sets out on a visit to the former. Jerome embellishes this journey with a series of stupendous miracles. Antony found Paul still shut up in his cave, where he had now been for about ninety-seven years, with his hoary head uncombed, and his shrivelled body covered with a rough mat, made of the plaited fibres of the palm leaf,— precisely like an Indian monk. They feasted together on bread and water, and spent the night in singing hymns and watching. While visited by Antony, Paul died, and was buried by two lions, who had, for some time, been his faithful companions and friends in the cave. Another monk of the same name, was Paul who lived at Ferma,—a mountain of Scetis. This Egyptian lived in the fourth century, and presided over five hundred monks. He never received alms, except such food as was necessary for his subsistence, and never worked.—"He did nothing but pray; but he daily offered up to God three hundred prayers. He placed three hundred pebbles in his bosom, for fear of omitting any of these prayers; and at the conclusion of each, he took away one of the pebbles. When there were no pebbles remaining, he knew that he had gone through the whole course of his prescribed prayers." (Sozom. Hist. Eccl. lib. vi. c. 29.) We have seen precisely the same custom among the Boodhist monks. To this day, we see it modified in the rosary or bead-roll. A third monk of the name of Paul† lived about A.D. 400, and became bishop of the Novatians, in

* Here Jerome makes Paul an older monk than Antony, by twenty-three years. Sec. 7.

† It is not a little singular that there have been so many celebrated monks of the name *Paul*, almost all contemporary; especially when it is recollected—that the great Apostle of the Gentiles, in whose writings there are so many traces of gross monkery, was of this name,—that we have no data from which we can determine when the Epistles which go by his name, were written,—that, anciently, the practice of "pious fraud" was so prevalent,—that the account given of the first Christian monks is evidently fabulous, containing a vast number of things quite incredible, and directing us to look for

process of time.   Of him it is said by Socrates (Hist. Eccl. lib. vii. c. 17.) that, having abandoned his post as a teacher of Roman eloquence, he became an austere monk, founded monasteries, and "adopted a mode of life very similar to that pursued by the monks in the desert, imitating them in prolonged fastings, silence, abstinence from animal food, and a very sparing use of oil and wine." Throughout his illness, which terminated in death, he did not relax the severity of his mode of life, either as to diet or exercise. St. Hilarion, born of pagan parents, about the close of the third century, was educated in the pagan college of Alexandria; and, hearing of the fame of Antony, in the Egyptian desert, repaired thither, put on the hermitical habiliment, and became a glorious monk. But not enjoying, while with Antony, the solitude he desired, he removed to Palestine, accompanied by several other monks. Accordingly, Sozomen tells us that, about this time, monkery was "cultivated in Palestine, *whither it had been transported from Egypt*, and Hilarion the Divine acquired great celebrity." (Hist. Eccl. lib. iii. c. 24.) Indeed, all accounts, however much interwoven with fable, show that Christian monkery was imported into Judea, and other parts of Palestine, from pagan Egypt.— Having left Antony, Hilarion, at the age of fifteen, an orphan, entered a desert of Judea, near Gaza, on the coast of the Mediteranean—a spot noted for monks from time immemorial.* This desert he entered *nuked*, having given all that he possessed to the brethren and the poor. (Jerome Vit. Hilar.) He, however, afterwards covered his body with sackcloth, a coarse wrapper, and a coat of skin, while he subsisted on the juice of herbs, and a few dried figs, taken only occasionally, after three or four days' fasting. But never would he taste any thing before sunset. So

the *origin* of the tales related by them, to a time long before the Christian era, amongst heathen hermits,—and that, like many of the tales, both in the Old and New Testament, they are the result of jumbling together portions of two or more legends with which their authors were acquainted. Of this jumbling process, we have a remarkable instance in the legend about Thais, a notorious courtezan who, having been converted, became a very renowned nun.   But the story of St. Thais has every appearance of having been made up of the history of Thais, the famous courtezan of Athens, (Plut. in Alex. et al.) and the tale about Mary Magdalene.   Besides the foregoing four monks named Paul, we meet with other ecclesiastical celebrities of the same name, such as Paul the bishop of Constantinople, about the year 341.   Some have endeavoured to show that this was Paul the Simple; but the proofs they adduce are insufficient. (Vid. Sozom. Hist. Eccl. lib. iii. c. 4, 7, 24; iv. 1; vii. 10.   Socrat. Hist. lib. ii. c. 6.)   Then, we find that Paul the bishop of Tyre, about the year 335, was another important personage of the name. (Socrat. Hist. Eccl. lib. i. c. 29.)   To these may be added, Paul bishop of Emesa, Paul of Samosata, and others.   The foregoing and other circumstances render it very doubtful what Paul wrote the Epistles comprised in the New Testament.   *Paul* is not a Jewish, but a Roman name; and *Tarsus* was not a Jewish, but a Roman town.

* In Jerome's history of Hilarion's life, the fact that monks previously existed in Palestine often oozes out.   Although he says—" Hitherto there had been no monasteries in Syria before Hilarion: he was the founder and instructor of this order and mode of life in this province.   The Lord Jesus had old Antony in Egypt; and in Palestine, he had Hilarion, a younger man;" (sec. 14.) yet, in sec. 25.—29. he speaks of the innumerable monasteries that were in Palestine, and tells us that Hilarion visited the cells of the monks, at stated times, and made tours, followed by 2,000 monks, who were fed by the inhabitants of the villages through which they passed.   Besides, he speaks of the monks in Palestine as now cultivating vineyards and gardens; which shows that monachism, at this time, was there an ancient institution.

wasted he became by his frequent fastings, his bodily exercise, and laceration, that his bones scarcely hung together. His abode, for five years, was a hut covered with rushes ; and afterwards, a cell made with planks, broken tiles, and straw, so small that he could neither lie down in it at full length nor stand upright. Here he dwelt till the day of his death, his bed being rushes strewed on the bare ground. His sackcloth shirt he never washed ; and his skin coat he never changed, but left it to fall off in rags. For three years, he lived on dry bread, salt, and water. From his sixtieth "to his eightieth year, he abstained from bread with incredible fervour." He devoted much time to singing, praying, and reciting divine writings from memory. He maintained perfect chastity, and would not look at a woman. He would, however, miraculously interfere on behalf of barren women who applied to him, and by his prayers, cause them to be fruitful. Being a great physician, he cured a vast number of inveterate diseases, cast out legions of demons, and wrought numerous other Therapeutic miracles. In short, the description given of him by Jerome, in every particular, identifies him with the Indian Sannyasi. An Egyptian, named Ammon, in the time of Antony, as Socrates (Hist. Eccl. lib. iv. c. 23) tells us, the moment after he had been married, represented to his virgin bride the glories of a life of chastity and self-mortification, and both, there and then, agreed to become hermits and live as if unmarried, which they did till death, practising the most severe monastic exercises. Ammon took up his abode on the south side of Lake Mœris, in a desert—the very spot which, according to Philo, about 250 years before, was the grand rendezvous of heathen monks. It is incredible that, within this short space, the heathens should have quitted their cells or monasteries, leaving them to be occupied by Christian monks, and deserting their religious posts, which had been filled by pagans for ages untold. Ancient religious institutions are not so easily abolished, even by the harshest means. And it is to be observed that it was before Christianity was made a state religion, in the time of Constantine, that the Christian monks occupied these regions, and dwelt in other parts of Egypt. It is not a little singular that none of the Christian Fathers make mention of the heathen monks, any more than if they never had existed. The unavoidable inference from all this is, that the monks of whom they speak were, in reality, one and the same with the heathen monks. Two monks of the same name—Macarius, were both disciples of Antony ; both Egyptians ; both renowned for their chastity, ascetic exertions, and abstinence ; both the heads of monasteries at Scetis ; both exorcists, miracle-mongers, foretellers of events, and physicians. (Socrat. Hist. Eccl. lib. iv. c. 23. 24.) Pachomius, born in Thebaid of pagan parents, about the end of the third century, and educated in the Egyptian learning, was also contemporary with Antony. He is said to have become a monk after he had heard of Jesus Christ ; but it is clear from the legend that he was a monk before. For it is said that, "from his earliest youth, he cultivated chastity and the ascetic practices," and abhorred wine. Besides, when he went into the depth of the desert to the old monk Palemon, it is said that he was invested in the monastic habit, which shows that the order of monkery was then so old that the fraternity wore a peculiar uniform like the Boodhist monks. Pachomius, —having lived for some time with Palemon on bread, salt, wild herbs, and

2 H H

water, abstaining from wine, and occupied in psalm-singing, watching, and spinning hair for making sackcloth—is said to have set about reforming the Egyptian monasteries, which it is by no means likely that he should have done, had not monachism, in his time, been an old institution.— Pachomius being thus a reformer, the monks over whom he presided, as we are told, slightly differed from others. Yet, like others, they resisted lascivious pleasures, wore skins, tunics with sleeves, cowls, girdles about their middle, and sashes over their shoulders. When Pachomius was philosophising in a cave, an angel appeared, and delivered to him, inscribed on a metal plate, a code of laws by which the monks he had under him were to be governed. According to these, which were very similar to the regulations of the Essenes, the monks were to be three in a cell—to eat their food in perfect silence with covered faces—to eat, drink, fast, and exercise according to the bodily strength of each individual—to be attired in the garb just described—to sleep in a half-standing posture— to undergo probationary exercise of the hardest kind for three years before being fully initiated—to be divided into classes—to be governed by abbots and subordinate officers—to pray and sing always before meat, and a vast number of times during the day and night—and to have all things in common. Such, under Pachomius, were the regulations of the Egyptian monks, who, we are told, numbered, in the same monastery, about thirteen hundred, and soon increased to seven thousand;—the whole indicating their heathen character. (Sozom. lib. iii. c. 14. Fleury Hist. Eccles. vol. iii. p. 18.) John, a presbyter who presided over an Egyptian monastery, was a renowned monk, who foretold future events, and cured "the most desperate and inveterate diseases." Or, was another of the same time and place, who lived in solitude from his youth, ate only herbs and roots, drank only water, performed miracles, expelled demons, and healed diverse diseases. In his old age, he presided over several monasteries in Thebais. (Ibid.) Coprus led the same life, expelling demons, and healing sickness and various diseases. (Ib.) Apelles, in the same age, performed many wonderful miracles in the Egyptian monasteries, and withstood the blandishments of the devil who, in the shape of a woman, tempted him to incontinence. Dioscorus and Eulogius were famous monks, and also presbyters. We read of a vast number of monks who were either presbyters, bishops, or deacons : indeed, it appears that, in early times, these offices were filled only by monks ; a circumstance which not only identifies the Christian and Boodhist monks, but also shows that the present order of ecclesiastics is utterly of a monkish origin,—or, in other words, that our present churches are a modification of the ancient monasteries, each of which always had a portion of it set apart for the general assembly of monks to conduct divine service. Hence, that part of the church at present called the chancel. But to proceed : Apollos, an Egyptian monk, after spending forty years in the desert, shut himself up in a cave, where he performed many miracles. Dorotheus, another Egyptian, lived on bread and water, and accustomed himself to extreme abstinence, from youth to old age. Like an Indian monk, he stood for years in an erect posture, and was never seen to recline on a mat or bed, or place himself in an easy attitude for sleep. Benjamin lived in the desert of Scetis, "curing all diseases by the touch of his hand, or by means of a little oil blessed by prayer," while he neglected his own body, which he said was of no use to him. (Sozom. vi. 29) Apollonius—another monk identical with the Therapeuts—went around the monasteries at Scetis with medical drugs and food suitable to the sick, for the relief of those who suffered from disease. Moses, ultimately a *presbyter over the monks* at Scetis, prayed fifty times a day, lived upon a very small quantity of bread alone, "resorting to every means of macerating his body, inflicted upon it ten thousand ascetic mortifications." He spent the night, for six years, in an erect posture, praying, "without bending his knees, or closing his eyes in sleep." Prior, a renowned monk of Scetis, when very young, vowed to devote himself to a life of asceticism, and never again to look at any of his relatives. Fifty years of his monastic life having elapsed, one of his sisters, hearing that he was still alive, would not rest till she saw him. He would, however, not look at her, but with closed eyes said,—"I am Prior, thy brother." As with the Boodhist, so with the Christian monk, it was an inviolable rule never to look at a woman. Accordingly, Pachomius, when his sister desired an interview with him, on the business of erecting a nunnery, refused to see her, but communicated with her through the interposition of the door-keeper at the monastery. A celebrated anchorite named Peter— a native of Galatia—spent ninety-two years in constant exercise, shut up in a vault, drinking nothing but water, and eating only a small portion of bread once in two days. He wrought many miracles, and cured a vast number of diseases. (Theodoret's Philotheus, in Pet.) Theodosius lived in a hut in the wilderness, lay on the bare ground, wore a hair-cloth garment, and accustomed himself to extraordinary abstinence from food. "In addition to all this, he loaded his neck, loins, and wrists with iron. He also wore his hair all tangled and filthy, and hanging down to his feet; and as it grew still longer, he wrapped it round his middle. He spent his time in praying and singing psalms. He tamed his lust, anger, and pride, as if they had been wild beasts," and performed astounding miracles. (Theodoret in Theodosius) In all these particulars, this fanatic bears a most striking resemblance to the Indian monks. Of Romanus, who dwelt in a cell at the foot of a mountain, Theodoret says,—"Here he lived to old age, without fire or lamp, eating only bread and salt, drinking only water, and rivalling Theodosius in the length and tangles of his hair, his hair-cloth garment, and his irons. . . . . Who would not be struck with admiration at beholding the old man's wasted limbs loaded by himself with iron, his garment of rough hair, and his food barely sufficient to keep him alive. Besides his great and mighty exercises, by which he gained admiration and honour from all, he healed many dangerous and violent diseases, and procured for many barren women the gift of bearing children." James—another illustrious hermit—contemporary with his biographer, Theodoret—had in his possesion relics of John the Baptist, which he and others of the age regarded with profound veneration, just as the Boodhist monks regarded the relics of their saints. This James, like an Indian Sannyasee, lived in the open air during the severity of both heat and cold. Often was he found covered with snow for three days and nights, during which long interval he was prostrate on the ground engaged in prayer. Around his neck and waist he wore ponderous iron chains. He had also heavy chains about his arms;

and not less than four addditional chains hanging down from his neck; precisely like Lu-zu, the Chinese monk already described, and also very much like the monkish prophet Jeremiah, except that the latter had, in addition, a collar or yoke. (Jer. xxvii. 2.) Another excellent antitype of a Hindoo monk was Baradatus, who lived in a desert of Syria, within a cell so narrow that he could not lie down in it, but was always forced to stand up. Finding that, in this painful posture, he could not sufficiently "mortify the deeds of the body," he procured a large stone slab, and placed it on the low walls of this narrow hut, so as to make it impossible for him either to lie down or stand upright, and to constrain him to remain always in a stooping posture—the most painful of all. In process of time, however, a kind bishop—who certainly had more good sense than Christian faith—fearing that this saint, under his agony, would faint, ordered him to come out. The pious hermit obeyed; but afterwards, he stood upright for life, continually praising God, with his arms lifted up towards heaven, and his body so completely wrapped up in skins as to leave only a small breathing-hole at his nose and mouth. Theodoret here proceeds to show that this bodily mortification illuminated and sanctified the soul of the monk who practised it,—the very notion of the Indian mortifier of the flesh. Indeed, if Theodoret had aimed at proving the identity of the Indian and Christian monks, he could not have done so more effectually than by stating that the latter invented diverse means to make their lives painful,—that some lived in cells, huts, or caves too small for them either to lie or stand upright,—that others maintained a perpetually standing posture,—others lived in places devoid of ventilation,—while a great many disdained all shelter, and exposed themselves naked to the burning sun, the freezing cold, and the pelting storm. Thalaleus, a monk who spent ten years in such a thoroughly stooping posture that his chin touched his knees, miraculously cured many diseases, says Theodoret, in this painful attitude. Symeon Stylites, or Symon on the Pillar, endured still greater sufferings and privations. He fasted, occasionally, for forty days; took food, ordinarily, but once a week, and then only a very small quantity of the simplest kind. He wore a cord, made of the roughest palm-leaves, next the skin, so tight about his middle, that it ulcerated a circle of flesh around his body, out of which it caused the blood to ooze. Like a Hindoo Yogi, he tied the one end of an iron chain about his ancle, while the other end was fastened to a rock, on which he remained for three years, meditating upon divine things, with his eyes steadfastly looking up to heaven, and being admired by thousands of gaping spectators. When he removed to the top of a high pillar, about thirty-six feet high, but not quite a foot in diameter, he stood here for thirty-seven years, night and day, until his feet were ulcerated. Here he predicted many important events, performed astounding miracles, cured a variety of inveterate diseases, and made many a barren wife a happy mother,—in all these particulars, except the pillar, corresponding exactly to the Indian monks and the Therapeuts. (Evagrius, lib. i. c. 13. Nicephorus, lib. xiv. c. 1, 51. and Theodoret.) His resemblance to them was also very striking in that he would not kill any living thing—not even the vermin which his filthy rags and flesh bred; that he abstained from animal food; that he would not look at a female; that he spent all the night in prayer; that he preached most eloquently; and that, during many consecutive days of religious solemnity, he stood erect, from sunrise to sunset, with his hands stretched towards heaven. These were feats equal to any performed by the Indian Yogis, while the object in performing them was precisely the same; namely, " to realize in the flesh the existence of the heavenly hosts, lift man above the concerns of earth, and, overpowering the downward tendency of his nature, enable him to hold communion with God." Another Symeon, whose exploits are given by Evagrius, (lib. vi. c. 24.) as well as by Nicephorus, (lib. xviii. c. 24) was a renowned pillar-saint at a very early age, and lived so for sixty-eight years. As such, he performed the hardest exercises, wrought a vast number of miracles, predicted future events, chased away demons, and healed the sick upon the spot, by prayer and laying on of his hands. A remarkable feature in all these fanatics, which identifies them with the Therapeutic and Boodhist monks, is their power to heal the sick. A third pillar-saint,* and the last of the kind we shall notice here, was Daniel, a disciple of Symeon the first. (Nicephor. lib. xv. c. 21, 22.) Like all the fraternity, he performed most wonderful ascetic feats, cast out demons, and healed the sick. There were among Christians of the earliest times, not only holy virgins who lived in monasteries, but also holy virgins who led a thoroughly hermitical life, precisely the same with that of the male anchorites already described. Theodoret gives an account of several of them, telling us that many women chose this recluse and solitary mode of religious life, " while others preferred to associate together, living in communities of two hundred and fifty, or more, eating the same food, sleeping on bare leaves or straw, working in wool, and consecrating their tongues to sacred hymns." In his time, there were " countless numbers of such philosophic schools throughout all the East, namely, Palestine, Egypt, Asia, Pontus, Mesopotamia, and also through all Europe." In Egypt, he tells us, there were monasteries which contained five thousand monks. (Theodor. Philoth.) Of this there can be little doubt. But if monkery had originated with Antony, who had

---

* It has been thought by some as probable that it was these pillars of saints which originated the idea of Church towers, steeples, or campanili. But the correctness of this supposition is very doubtful; for both church towers and church bells are far more ancient than Christianity. They were among the Chinese and other ancient pagans, before the Christian era. It is much more likely that Christians borrowed the practice of building church towers from the pagans, just as they borrowed their very religion. However this may be, it is certain that, as already noticed, our most ancient form of churches was that of monasteries, and that, in early times, both church and steeple, or tower, were only portions of the buildings in which the monks lived in community, and were, consequently, called monasteries, munsters, or minsters. Such is the origin of the most ancient and gorgeous churches even in this country. Take, for example, Durham Cathedral. Here are found,—the hall of the monks ; the lady chapel, or chapel of the virgins ; a number of cloisters, crypts, and dormitories, for the monks. (See Penny Cyclopædia Art. Church.) The same may be said of many other cathedrals and churches, which have retained their pristine forms,—all showing that the churches which Hen. viii. stole from the Roman Catholics, and gave to the Protestants, are modified monasteries, and that our present Christianity has sprung from monkery. Accordingly, the present ancient churches, being originally the cloisters of certain monks or nuns, are called after the names of the most eminent saints who occupied these cloisters, such as St. Michael's, St. Thomas's, St. Mary's, etc. A bishop, originally, was merely an overseer, or superintendent, over a number of monastic communities, which he periodically visited ; each bishop having a particular district, or diocese, alloted to him.

died only thirty years before Theodoret was born, it would have been impossible for it to have spread over all the world in so short a time, and in an age when the means of communication between nations so far distant were very scanty. All this goes to prove that the monkery of the Fathers—which is the very essence of early Christianity—was one and the same with that of the heathens, particularly the Therapeuts and Essenes. The fact that this barbarous religious life was at this early period in the flourishing condition described by Theodoret, is corroborated by all the ecclesiastical writers of the time. Socrates speaks of the persecution under Valens, in a manner which shows that monachism was then an ancient institution; and, like other writers, identifies it with Therapeutic monkery, by stating that, when the persecutors came upon the monasteries, they found the monks engaged in their customary exercises, praying, healing diseases, and casting out demons. (Hist. Eccles. lib. iv. c. 24.) Sozomen bears abundant testimony to the same effect, telling us that some monks lived in cells, and others in monasteries, while all assembled together on the first and last day of each week. He also tells us that the Syrian monks "ate neither bread nor flesh, and drank no wine, but dwelt constantly on the mountains, and passed their time in praising God, by prayer and hymns, *according to the Canons of the church;* showing that, at this time—only about fifteen years after the death of Antony—there were Canons of the Christian church, for the regulation of monkery, which indicates that this mode of life was, at least, some centuries older than Antony. (Lib. vi. c. 31, 33.) In like manner, Sulpicius Severus (Dial. i.) in the many instances he gives of the lives of the Egyptian and other monks, describes some as living in monasteries, and others in huts. He also tells us that some of the anchorites wandered about, sleeping where night overtook them,—that they went about naked, and were all over them as hairy as wild beasts. This practice of roaming about is also mentioned by Isidore of Pelusium. (Epist. 41, 173, 314.) In describing Christian monks, Evagrius (Hist. Eccles. lib. i. c. 21.) draws a perfect picture of the Therapeuts, Essenes, and other heathen fanatics. One sort of monks he describes as living on small quantities of herbs and pulse, having in common, not only their diet, but even their scanty, course, and dirty wearing apparel, and spending most of their time in hard exercises, prayers and fastings, till they appeared "like corpses." Others, leaving the monasteries, "transported themselves into the scorching wilderness, and both men and women, covering only those parts of their bodies which nature required to be concealed, left the rest of their persons exposed both to the excessive frosts and scorching blasts, regardless alike of heat and cold. They also cast off the ordinary food of mankind, and lived upon the produce of the ground, whence they were termed Grazers. Thus, they became assimilated to the wild beasts, with their outward form disfigured, and their souls no longer fitted for intercourse with their species." Some monks, when, by their virtue, they had attained to such a degree of holiness as to be free from passion, returned into the world. Having thus conquered every natural propensity, they dwelt among men and women in a state of nudity, "it being their desire to be men among men, and women among women." In them, says our author, life and death dwelt together,—the *life* of their souls and the *death* of their passions. For, when passion entered, they were dead and entombed; but when prayer was required, they displayed vigour of body and energy of soul. "Thus, they combined the two modes of life, maintaining a constant and total renunciation of the flesh, and yet mingling with the living,—applying remedies to their bodily diseases, and also presenting to God the petitions of supplicants." Evagrius goes on to say that they fervently and frequently prayed—esteemed long fasting as a luxuriant feast—were foes to their own desires, but devoted to the requests of those arround them, in order that carnal thoughts might be expelled, and that the soul might have full dominion. Not only is this the very doctrine which Paul taught, but it is precisely the philosophy of the Hindoo monks.

It is trusted that the foregoing comparison of the monkery of the Heathen with that of the early Christians, will be found amply sufficient to enable the most unacquainted with the subject, to perceive their perfect identity.* For it has been shown that both Heathen and Christian monks gave all their property to their leaders, when they entered upon their monastic life,—that both alike had to undergo a probationary course of exercises, before they were fully admitted into the mysteries of the fraternity,—that both took oaths that they would remain faithful to the regulations of their respective communities,—that some of both had monasteries, where they lived in common, while others led a solitary life in deserts,—that both abstained from flesh and wine,—that both subsisted on the simplest diet, such as bread, salt, and water, or the natural productions of the ground,—that both abstained altogether from food, for incredibly long periods of time,—that both believed that the less they ate the more was the body subdued, and the soul purified,—that both had governors and stewards in their respective monasteries, and wore a uniform peculiar to their community,—that both were monks, and yet priests, bishops, or some order of public teachers of religon,—that both had holy virgins, or nuns,—that the males of both monks professed to live in a state of celibacy, and the females in that of virginity,—that both alike tolerated marriages in certain cases,—that both practiced most severe bodily mortifications, with the view of purifying the soul,—that both frequently went naked,—that both wore hair-clothes—if they wore anything at all—next the skin, and the hides of beasts outside,—that both wore clothing of the roughest palm-leaves,—that both loaded themselves with ponderous iron collars and chains,—that both lay—if they lay at all—on the bare ground,—that both wore the same garb unwashed till it fell from them in tatters,—that both had the most filthy habits of life,—that both wore their hair down to their

---

* Some readers, who are already well versed in the practices of the Christian and Heathen monks, may be inclined to think that the long digression made in this part of the work, is unnecessary. But such should recollect that there are thousands of English readers whose knowledge, even of Christian monkery, is exceedingly slender ; and who—without the information the preceding sketch is intended to supply—would therefore be unable to judge of its heathen origin. Besides : the subject in hand is of such importance as to justify this deviation ; for the ground that has been traversed furnishes proofs that Christianity, so called, even in its earliest state, was gross monkery,—all its advocates, in their doctrine and mode of life, being like those monks of the fourth and fifth century. It is, consequently, of the utmost importance, especially to the Christian, to ascertain whether this monkery, which is the very basis of his religion, is identical with pagan monkery. If it is, then, as a necessary consequence, Christianity is one and the same with paganism, or, to say the least, is of a pagan origin.

heels,—that some of both stood for years in an erect posture, others in a bending attitude, and others without ever sleeping,—that both made a practice of standing for years in the open air, exposed to all the severity of the weather,—that both inculcated, in the most emphatic manner, the doctrine of abstinence from all conjugal intercourse,—that both had the peculiar custom of maintaining silence for a considerable time in their assemblies,—that both preserved the relics of their respective departed saints,—that both were noted for their prayers, psalm-singing, and eloquent preaching,—that both wrought miracles,—that both predicted future events,—that both were renowned for curing all manner of diseases, —that both were endowed with the gift of causing barren women miraculously to become mothers,—that both refrained from killing any thing with life, even a fly,—that some of both were accustomed to wander about the country, nearly naked,—lastly, that both had in view the same object, in their various modes of mortifying their bodies ; namely, to purify their souls and render them too holy for this world. Surely, the foregoing numerous points of striking resemblance between the Pagan and Christian monks, must be sufficient fully to establish their identity of origin.

The reader is now, therefore, requested to judge from the following instances how far true is the proposition advanced at the commencement of this section ; namely, that the life and doctrines of Jesus were identical with those of heathen monks, who lived hundreds of years before his time. Now, in the first place, it is observable that the account we have even of Jesus's birth, contains many evident traits of monkery.* His mother is called a *virgin*—(παρθενος, not χορη, nor παιδισκη)—a word which, in the Greek language, signifies a female kept secluded from men ; (Matth. i. 23.) just as we have seen that virgins were kept in monasteries, nunneries, and in many of the heathen religious establishments, besides the *Parthenon*, dedicated to Minerva, the name of which, as already noticed, signifies *virgins*, or *of the virgins*. Few have not read of the pagan Vestal Virgins,† and of instances in which some of them, even at the cost of their

---

* This is in perfect harmony with what has long ago been demonstrated by some of the most critical writers, not only in English, but also in other languages; namely, that the New Testament has been collected by Eclectic monks—particularly Egyptian monks of Jewish extraction, connected with the Alexandrian college—from various legendary tales, and other documents then afloat, which they modified to answer their own purposes, and which, since their time, have been considerably altered to suit the requirements of different religious communities.—*Vid. Ant. pp.* 424, 432.

† The institution of the Vestal Virgins, or priestesses of the goddess Vesta, was imported from Greece into Rome at a very remote period. The Vestals, among the Romans, were to remain for thirty years in strict continence. The first ten years they spent in learning the duties of the order, the next ten in discharging them, and the remaining ten in instructing the younger virgins. When the thirty years were elapsed, they were permitted to marry; or, if they still preferred virginity, they waited upon the rest of the Vestals. As soon as a Vestal was initiated, her head was shaved; she was then free from parental authority; and at liberty to dispose of her possessions as she pleased. They all took a vow of chastity, and any one who attempted to violate a Vestal Virgin, was punished with death; while, on the other hand, if one of them proved incontinent, which was sometimes the case, she was buried alive. They wore a long white robe bordered with purple, and had a close covering on their head ; their attire thus differing, in a slight degree, from the attire of the nuns of the present age.—*See Adams's Roman Antiquities, p.* 304, *and Lempriere's Class. Dict. with their authorities.*

lives, were induced to violate their vow of chastity ; under which circumstances, they not unfrequently laid the blame on some deity. For instance, Rhea Sylvia, mother of Romulus, nearly 800 years before the Christian era, is said to have been made a Vestal Virgin by her father, Numetor. " But the Vestal," says Livy, (lib. i. c. 4.) " being defloured by force, brought forth twins, and declared that the father of her doubtful offspring was the god Mars." The Gospel writers, who furnish us with an account of the birth of Jesus, have left clear marks, in their narrations, that they were well accquainted with such pagan tales ;* and that the institution of

* The Christian apologists of the second and third century, evinced no lack of knowledge on this point. Justin Martyr, as already cited, (p. 438.) in addressing a Roman Emperor, says that the Christians, by declaring Jesus to be the Son of God, born of a Virgin, said no more than the Romans said of those whom they styled the sons of Jupiter, such as Mercury, Bacchus, Hercules, Pollux, and Castor; and as to Jesus, he repeats, having been born of a Virgin, the pagans had their Perceus, son of Jove and the virgin Danae, to balance this feature. Creusa, daughter of Erectheus, was visited by the god Apollo, and, in consequence, became the mother of the god Janus. A Chinese *virgin*, by means of the rays of the sun—regarded as a deity—became the mother of the god Foe, who acted as a mediator between his followers and another superior god. The Hindoo *virgin*, Rohini, in like miraculous manner, gave birth to a god—one of the Brachmin trinity. Another Hindoo virgin, Devaci, as already observed, having had an intercourse with the deity, Vasudeva, became the mother of an incarnate god, whose name was Chrishna,—whose birth was announced by the appearance of a new star,— whose life, when an infant, was sought in vain by the reigning tyrant of the country,— whose principal exploits were killing a terrible serpent, holding a mountain on the top of his finger, washing the feet of the Brachmins, saving multitudes by his miraculous power, raising many from the dead, dying to save the world from sin and darkness, rising from the dead, and then ascending to his heavenly seat, in Vaicontha. (Sir Wm. Jones's Asiatic Researches, vol. i. pp. 259—273.) Somonocodom, who, according to the sacred books of the Talapoins of Siam, was destined to save the world, was another personage who had a virgin mother. The followers of Plato, about 200 years after his death, but more than a century before the Christian era, reported that he had been born of a virgin. They said that Ariston, his father, on his marriage, was cautioned in a dream by the god Apollo not to have any intercourse with his wife, because she was with child by this divinity himself. Ariston obeyed, and Plato was born the son of the god Apollo. Indeed, the fabulous lore of ancient times is teeming with the amours of gods with virgins, and the results thereof. Some writers have intimated that such births were the consequences of the artful intrigues of the pagan priests with holy virgins; but Dupuis, Albert, Alphonso, Boulanger, and others, have clearly shown " that these and similar tales, which are revolting to common sense, if taken literally, were originally, in Oriental learning, astronomical and other allegories, conveying the most sublime truths then known, touching the revolutions of the heavenly bodies, and other physical and moral facts ; while their meaning, in after-ages, was gradually perverted to answer sinister purposes." The most ancient Alexandrian chronicles, which furnish ample proofs of the universal prevalence of our *Gospel religion* in Egypt, for ages before the Christian era, testify as follows :—" To this day Egypt has consecrated the pregnancy of a virgin, and the nativity of her son, whom they annually present in a cradle to the adoration of the people : and when king Ptolemy, three hundred and fifty years before our Christian era, demanded of the priests the significancy of this religious ceremony, they told him it was a mystery." (See *Christian Mythology Unveiled*, p. 94.) Probably, it was the fact that it was some of the many females, particularly young virgins, kept in the pagan temples, who almost always happened to become mothers of gods, which made ill-disposed minds to imagine that the priests were implicated in these matters. It is very remarkable, however, that most ancient records attest that the Virgin Mary herself had been in the temple from three years old till the time of her betrothal to Joseph. " The Gospel of the Birth of Mary," and the " Protevangelion," are, undoubtedly, productions which obtained general credit in the first ages of Christianity. The former, which is found preserved in the works of Jerome, and, with the latter, is translated into English

Virginity was in a flourishing state at the time in which they wrote. What is said of Joseph, as well as Mary. having angelic visions, also

in the Apocryphal Gospels, is mentioned by Epiphanius and Austin. The other professes to be from the pen of James the Lesser, brother of Jesus. The frequent allusions which are approvingly made to it in the early Fathers, show that it was held in great reverence by ancient Christians. Epiphanius, Hilary, Chrysostom, Cyril, and a host of other Fathers, believed in its genuineness. In the Eastern churches, it was publically read as canonical, and as really the production of James the brother of Jesus. Now, these Gospels state that Mary, who was the daughter of Joachim and Anna, and who was herself miraculously born, was, when three years old, brought to the temple, and devoted to divine service. Sometime afterwards, she began to receive daily visits from angels. When she was fourteen years old, the high priest ordered all virgins of that age, who had public settlements in the temple, to return home, and endeavour to be married. All the other virgins obeyed; but Mary refused, alleging that she had vowed perpetual virginity to the Lord, and was resolved never to break that vow. The high priest, having consulted others on this difficult point, assembled a great number of single men into the temple, each with a rod, telling them that when they put these rods on the altar, and one of them should blossom, and bear on its point the Spirit of the Lord, in the shape of a dove, the man that owned this rod was to be betrothed to the virgin Mary. This happened to be Joseph's rod, and, accordingly, with considerable reluctance —on the ground that he was an old widower with children,—he was betrothed to the virgin. In order to reconcile the old man to this maiden, the high priest warned him against disobedience, by reminding him of the fate of Korah, Dathan, and Abiram. Joseph, therefore, in fear, took his betrothed home; but soon afterwards left her, and went to his work of building houses, at some distance. Shortly after, however, the lot fell upon Mary to spin the material for the purple colour in a new veil for the temple, so as to give her an occasion again to visit the high priest. But before she had finished spinning her purple, an angel appeared to her, and told her that she was to be the mother of a deity. Soon afterwards, the high priest told her the same thing. She was not long before she found herself "daily growing big." "When her sixth month was come," says the Gospel of James, "Joseph returned from his building houses abroad, which was his trade, and, entering into his house, found the virgin grown big. Then, smiting on his face, he said,—With what face can I look up to the Lord my God? Or what shall I say concerning this young woman? For I received her a virgin out of the temple of the Lord my God, and have not preserved her such! Who has thus deceived me? Who has committed this evil in my house? and, seducing the virgin from me, hath defiled her?" Joseph, rising from the ground, called Mary to him, and asked her several questions in reference to her condition. "But she, with a flood of tears, replied —I am innocent, and have known no man. Then said Joseph, How comes it to pass that you are with child? Mary answered—As the Lord my God liveth, I know not by what means." Joseph turned away from her, exceedingly afraid and perplexed as to what to do with his betrothed, owing to the peril in which both her life and his stood. But that night, an angel appeared to him, and revealed the cause of Mary's critical condition. The news of her disgrace, however, soon spread abroad, and reached the ears of the officials of the temple. One of them, Annas, a scribe, made himself exceedingly busy in the matter, charging Joseph, before the high priest, with the capital crime of having defiled the virgin. Whereupon, Joseph and Mary were cited before the Jewish ecclesiastical court, and put upon their trial. Each pleaded "not guilty." Mary, when she was arraigned, in answer to the charge, said to the high priest, "with a flood of tears,—As the Lord my God liveth I am innocent in his sight, seeing I know no man." And Joseph when arraigned, in like manner, declared,—"As the Lord my God liveth I have not been concerned with her." Their plea of innocence, however, appears not to have been believed by the court; for Joseph, while "he bitterly wept," was put to the ordeal of drinking deadly water, called "the water of the Lord." But drinking this water proved harmless to Joseph; and he was therefore pronounced not guilty. Whereupon, he was discharged, and left the court with his betrothed, taking her to his own house. Some time afterwards, when both Joseph and Mary had gone to be taxed, and were far from home, Jesus was born in a cave. Such is part of the long account of the Virgin, given in these Gospels, which are well worth a perusal. The canonical Gospels scarcely on any point contradict them. The principal difference between the

savours of pagan monkery. That these writers wished to describe a monk, in their rhapsodical narrative of Jesus, is farther proved by the fact that they connect, or rather blend the history of his birth with that of the birth and career of John the Baptist, who, unquestionably, was a thorough anchorite, wearing a garb of camel's hair, and subsisting on the spontaneous production of the desert, where he remained in seclusion, and commenced preaching repentance and baptism. (Matth. iii. 1, 2. Luke i. 80.) After telling us that an angel appeared to the Baptists' father, to announce his son's miraculous birth, Luke immediately informs us that the same angel appeared to Mary and apprised her of the future birth of her son Jesus, as well as that of John. Then, the writer gives us an account of John's birth and circumcision, followed by the birth and circumcision of Jesus. He then hastens to describe John's preaching, and his administration of baptism to Jesus; and thus he proceeds, blending the history of these two personages. Matthew, in like manner, gives us a piece of Jesus's history, and then abruptly turns to treat of John, his monkish habiliment, ascetic life, and austere doctrine; turning again, however, to the history of Jesus. Mark, (i.) in same the jumbling mode, gives us to understand that the beginning of the Gospel of Jesus Christ was the history of that anchorite—John the Baptist; an outline of which he presents to us; but strangely mixed with the history of Jesus. The Gospel of John, again, begins in a platonic strain, by informing us that Jesus was the Word, and that that Word was God; but suddenly refers to John the Baptist, as a man sent from God. Throughout the remainder of the chapter, Jesus and John are spoken of alternately, in such a manner as clearly shows that the writer endeavoured to identify Jesus with the Baptist; every feature of whose character is indisputably monachal. Evidence of the same design is further seen in Matthew's Gospel, (ii. 14, 15.) where the writer makes Jesus's parents take him into Egypt, in order to fulfil the prophetic saying—" Out of Egypt have I called my son." (Hos. xi. 1.) But, unfortunately, there is in this expression no allusion to Jesus; nor does it contain even any prediction at all; it clearly refers to a historical tradition current among

apocryphal and canonical Gospels is, that the former are, almost on all matters connected with the Virgin and the birth of Jesus, much more copious in details; while the latter appear to be an abridgement of these more ancient productions. Although the canonical Gospels state that Jesus, after his birth, was placed in a *manger*, and the apocryphal Gospels say that he was born in a *cave*, yet, there is no real contradiction here. For, in many of the Eastern caves, beasts were kept and fed, and the word *manger*, $\phi\alpha\tau\nu\eta$, may properly be rendered—*a stall*. Justin Martyr, Origen, Eusebius, Jerome, Socrates, and a host of other Fathers, affirm that Jesus was born in a stable, which was a cave formed by nature. To this day, the *cave* and the *manger* are shown at Bethlehem, by persons who reap a rich harvest from this exhibition. See Parkhurst's Gr. Lex. infra $\phi\alpha\tau\nu\eta$. The whole of the tale, however, bears evident marks that it is the production of monks; probably those of Alexandria. Monks, as we have seen, being so frequently the inmates of caves, it was very natural that they should make the birth of Jesus to have occured in a cave. The importance of the institution of Holy Virgins, or nuns, is also, in this story, most conspicionsly shown. It is, likewise, curious to observe that so great was the importance attached to the institution of virginity, not only at the commencement of the Christian era, but for many centuries afterwards, that Christians believed Mary was a virgin after the birth of Jesus—*always* a virgin. (Austin, De Natura et Gracia, c. 36. Epiphan. Hæres. c. 78, 79.) Indeed, a great proportion of Christians believe this even to the present day, and many a warm controversy have some of them maintained on the subject.

the Jews, that, when they were a very weak nation, their God delivered them from Egypt, where they were in bondage. If words have any meaning, the context makes this as clear as meridian day. But the writer of Matthew's Gospel had an object in view,—he wished to represent Jesus as a monk. He well knew that Egypt, in his time, was the cradle —the hot-bed, of monkery, and that thence it had been imported into the adjacent regions of Palestine. He well knew that the monks of Egypt were now more renowned than any others; and therefore wished it to appear that the hero of his tale, although a Jew, had received his monachal training in this celebrated country. The monks of Egypt were considered a pattern of perfection, and were zealously emulated by those of Syria and Palestine. (Sozom. Hist Eccles. lib. vi. c. 33.) Into Egypt Sulpicius Severus (Dial. i.) sends his friend Postumian from Gaul, to learn monkery. The Therapeuts were in a flourishing state in Egypt, as we have seen, long before Philo wrote. (Mosheim's Commentaries, Vol. i. pp. 97, 98.) Jesus, therefore, must be made to come from Egypt. But he must also belong to the Nazarean monks, already described; and, consequently, the writer of Matthew's Gospel makes him dwell in the city of Nazareth, "that it might be fulfilled which was spoken by the prophet, —He shall be called a Nazarene." (Matth. ii. 23.) It is immaterial that no such prophecy is found in the Hebrew writings: the Evangelist— probably an Alexandrian Jew, true to the glory of his own nation—was determined to identify the hero of his tale with the *Nazarean* ascetics,*

---

* It is very remarkable that, according to the Gospels, and other ancient documents, one of the first names by which Jesus and his followers were distinguished, was *Nazarenes*. Jesus himself, in the Gospels. is frequently called a *Nazarite* and *Nazarene*. Christian writers tell us that he was called so,—first because, in his youth, he resided at Nazareth; and secondly because he was the anti-type of the ancient sect of Nazarites, who, as we have already seen, were a kind of Jewish monks. Accordingly, in order to uphold the opinion that Jesus was called a *Nazarene* because he had been brought up at Nazareth, the translators of the English version of the New Testament invariably render—Ιησους ο Ναζωραιος, and Ιησους ο Ναζαρηνος, into Jesus of Nazareth, instead of *Jesus* THE *Nazarite*, or *Nazarene*. See Mark i. 24; x. 47; xiv. 67; xvi. 6. Luke iv. 34; xviii. 37; xxiv. 19. John xviii. 5, 7; xix. 19 Acts ii. 22; iii. 6; iv. 10; vi. 14; xxii. 8; xxvi. 9. In each of these places, the Greek is clearly—*Jesus the Nazarite or Nazarene*; and should have been rendered so; just as Ιωαννης ο Βαπτιστης is rendered—John the Baptist; or Σιμων ο Καναντης—Simon the Canaanite. In the New Testament, there are found only three instances in which the Greek, with any show of propriety, could be rendered—"Jesus of Nazareth." The first is in Matth. xxi. 11:—Ιησους ο προφητης, ο απο Ναζαρετ της Γαλιλαιας. But here. απο means *from*, rather than *of*—Jesus the prophet *from* Nazareth of Galilee. The second is in John i. 46:—Ιησουν τον υιον του Ιωσηφ, τον απο Ναζαρεθ—Jesus, the son of Joseph. *from* Nazareth. The third is in the Acts x. 38, in which απο will take *from* quite as naturally as *of*. It is, however, clear that all the Evangelists believed that Jesus had resided in Nazareth until he appeared on the banks of the Jordan; and it is equally clear that they believed he belonged to that sect of ascetics called the Nazarenes. There are facts, however, which render these apparently conflicting notions quite harmonious. When the Gospels were written, there were afloat traditions, then ancient, that Jesus had been brought up at Nazareth, and belonged to the Nazarenes or Nazarites—a strong religious community which had flourished for many ages before the commencement of the Christian era. It is a remarkable fact, as showing the mythological character of the tale regarding Jesus,s early life having been spent at Nazareth, that the very name of this place implies the idea of monkery. Nazareth—if, as it is said, from the Hebrew word נזר,—means to be separated, or secluded; as a *noun*,—the state of being separated. נזיר is the Hebrew word used for a Nazarite, or one who has made a vow to separate from the several

who, by a vow, separated themselves from the world for the purpose of divine contemplation, abstained from intoxicating liquor, wore long hair,

things already enumerated, and devote himself to religion ; of which vow his long hair, like that of the Indian monks, which was never cut, was to be a sign. This long hair was also a sign that great reverence was due to the person whose head and body it covered, on account of his authority and miraculous power. Hence, the tale that Sampson, when his long hair was shaved off, lost all his strength ; (Jud. xvi. 13—20.) and hence the word נזר, figuratively denotes a crown, a diadem, the holy oil, etc. The word נזר, with a feminine plural termination נזרות, *Nazareth*, denotes the habitations of those separated from the world, and devoted to religious life, in solitude. But, Michaelis contends that Nazaritism —although injunctions are given for its regulation, in the books attributed to Moses—is of an Egyptian origin, like almost all the Mosaic religion. The name *Nazareth*, therefore, may have derived, as Godwin says, from נצר, which word, as he maintains, is the root of the name of a religious community, called *Natzarites*, or *Nazarites*, who dwelt in Nazareth. This derivation is, certainly, far the more probable ; especially, as the same word, in the plural,—frequently met with, in different forms, in the Hebrew Scriptures—signifies, *rocks, mountainous and desolate localities, caves,* and such other places as those in which people, separated from the world for religious contemplation, were wont to dwell. Precisely in such a place was Nazareth situated. It was between Mount Carmel and Mount Tabor, and within seven miles of the latter ; while Hebron was not far distant. All these places, from the earliest times to which history carries us, have been noted for the resort of monks. They were all surrounded by extensive deserts, and near the Dead Sea, where Pliny the Elder found the Essenes to have located for many centuries before his time. Although the Gospels call Nazareth a *city*, yet Epiphanius says that, in his time—the third century —it was only a village, and that, till the reign of Constantine, it was inhabited by Jews alone. Some time afterwards, however, two Churches were built there, and Christians began to exhibit the Grotto where they said the angel Gabriel appeared to Mary, the fountain at which she drank, a large stone which Jesus used as a table, and the synagogue in which he preached,—the whole, except the natural cave, now adorned as a grotto, being evidently the devices of monks. Now, in what manner soever the fact is to be accounted for—whether on the supposition that Jesus was brought up at Nazareth, or on the ground that this place was the haunt of pagan or Jewish monks, long before the Christian era—there are most indubitable proofs that the early Christians were called נזרים. (Nazarenes) Just as we have seen that Jesus was called a Nazarene, so was Paul called "a ring-leader of the sect of Nazarenes." (Acts xxiv. 5.) Like Jesus and Paul, also, all the Nazarenes, rejected the Mosaic law ; and the Jews therefore excommunicated those of their own nation who became Christians, designating them *Nazarenes.* (Jerome in Isai. et Epist. ad Jes. 8.) Even to the present day, the Jews term the Christians, *Nazerim,* or Nazarenes, while the Arabs and Persians call them *Nazeri ;* thus clearly establishing their identity with the poor and wandering Nazarenes, of much more ancient time than the commencement of the Christian era,—the mendicant heathen ascetics who, when not on their journey to preach, dwelt in mountain caves, secluded from society. These Nazarenes had a Hebrew Gospel, attributed to St. Barnabas, and sometimes called "The Gospel of the Nazarenes." Some writers say that this production differed materially from our present Gospels, and others maintain that it was very much like the Gospel of Matthew. It is mentioned, with reverence, by many of the Fathers. (Clem. Alex. Strom. i. 2. Jerome, Pref. in Comm. in Matth. Euseb. Hist. Eccles. lib iii. c. 25, 27, 29.) From these Nazarenes, early in the first century of the Christian era, there arose a sect called the Ebionites, whose separation, apparently, was caused by a difference of opinion on several points touching the Mosaic law. St. Jerome (Epist. ad Augustin) tells us that they were believers in Christ, but that other Christians considered them heretics, because they joined Jewish ceremonies to the Gospel,—just as Roman Catholics now regard other Christians as heretics, because they differ from them on some slight points. A writer in the Encyclopædia Britannica, under their name, very justly remarks,—"The Ebionites are little else than a branch of Nazarenes ; only that they altered and corrupted, in many things, the purity of the faith held among those first adherents to Christianity." Notwithstanding the distinction made between them, by some of the Fathers, it would be easy to adduce facts to show that once they were one and the same religious community. Both used the same Hebrew Gospel, and like the Indian Yogis, and were, in the fullest sense, Jewish monks. But leaving, for the present, the notion which the Evangelists entertained of Jesus, let us attend to what they have recorded as being his own words and actions.

We learn that, at the onset of his public career, his first religious act was to form an alliance with that celebrated anchorite, John the Baptist, by whom he was baptized,—baptism being a religious rite observed by *most* pagan, and by *all* Christian monks. Although it has already been shown that baptism is of a pagan origin; yet, as even the most enlightened Christians—whether dippers, pourers, or sprinklers, who alike call this rite χαρισμα κυριου, (the gift of the Lord) signaculum Domini, (the seal of the Lord) signaculum fidei, (the seal of faith) palingeuisia, (the new birth) and such names—cannot be expected to admit a fact so destructive to their own creed, unless mentally crushed by the weight of overwhelming evidence, the following proofs, therefore, are added. Most Christians maintain that John had been baptizing in the river Jordan, for about six months—during which he had administered this rite to a vast number of people—before Jesus came to him to be baptized. (Matth. iii. 5, 13. Mark i. 5, 9. Luke iii. 21.) Baptism, therefore, as a *new* rite, cannot have been introduced by Jesus. For there is no ground to infer from the Gospels that John had previously received a command from Jesus to administer baptism, or had ever had an interview with him. On the contrary, John tells us that, before Jesus came to him to be baptized, *he knew him not*. It was because he saw the Spirit descending upon Jesus, when being baptized, that John thought he was the Messiah. The person who had *sent* him to baptize had foretold him that he would know the Messiah by seeing the Spirit descending on him in baptism.—"He that sent me to baptize with water, the same said unto me," etc. (John i. 33.) But who this person was that had sent John to baptize, we are not told; probably it was some old monk, who had been his preceptor, or abbot—whose duty it would be, according to monachal custom, to send out to preach a promising young monk of thirty years, like John—and who, in a vision, may have been informed that the Spirit, in the shape of a dove, would descend upon the much-expected Messiah, when being baptized, in order to distinguish him from all the numerous crowds that rushed to undergo this rite; for it is well known that monks had frequent visions, in which marvelous revelations were made to them. At all events, there is not a shadow of proof in the

---

led the same kind of roaving life, living upon charity. The name—*Ebionites*, which is of a Hebrew or Syriac derivation, denotes *poverty, dependence, sorrow*, in its secondary sense; while, in its primary meaning, it signifies *a father, an instructor*, or *teacher*. The word אביון (*ebion*, poor) is, unquestionably, the same as אבא, or אב (father), varying only according to the genius of the language. Hence, in the Jewish monasteries named *Laura*, the head of a monastic society was called *Abbot*, which is the Syriac word for father, while the head of such a society in Egypt was called *David*, an uncle; and hence the anglicised word, *Abbot*, meaning originally both a poor man and a Christian father, or teacher. The same may be said of the word *abbey*,—the house of the poor abbot and other monks; who, in ancient times, lived on charity. (See Du Fresne's and Du Cange's Glossaries, Fosbroke's British Monachism.) All these historical facts go directly to identify our present Christianity with the monachal religion of the Nazarenes and Ebionites, and to show that "Jesus the Nazarite" even according to the Gospels—illustrated by well established fact—was a monk from his birth.

Gospels that it was Jesus who had sent John to baptize. Indeed, John, notwithstanding the praise he had previously lavished upon Jesus, became very doubtful as to his character. When in prison, he sent two of his disciples to ask him whether, in reality, he was the Messiah. (Matth. xi. 3.) Therefore, as it was not Jesus who had *sent* John to baptize, and as it was after he had seen the inhabitants of " all the land of Judea, and they of Jerusalem" hastening to the banks of the Jordan to undergo immersion, that he deigned to submit to this rite, it is clear that *he* was not the originator of it. Further : neither John himself nor the deputation of Jews, dispatched to the banks of the Jordan to demand his authority for baptizing, regarded baptism as a new thing. (John i. 19—28.) These Jews, who appear to have been sent by the supreme council of the nation, do not, by any means, regard baptism as a novelty; they do not ask what this strange practice means, but their question is,—" Why *baptizest thou* then, if thou be not that Christ, nor Elias, neither that prophet ?" Baptism, being a rite amongst them already, they expected that when the Messiah would appear, he also would baptize. They likewise thought that Elias had authority to baptize. But since John denied that he was either of these, and appeared to be only a private individual, they wished to know by what authority he administered baptism—a rite, among the Jews, allowed to be performed only by persons regularly appointed by the sacerdotal power. As to the rite itself, usage appears to have rendered it familiar to them ; so that they ask no question as to its purpose or origin. What they demand to know is,—why John, who held no sacerdotal office in the Jewish church, administered baptism—a religious ceremony allowed to be performed only by persons duly qualified and empowered by the Jewish hierarchy. This is exactly the opinion held by the learned Mosheim, on this point. (Commentaries on the Affairs of the Christians, Vol. i. p. 118.) Spencer, in his work on the Rites and Institutions of the Hebrews, says, not only that baptism was practised among the Jews prior to the time of John, but that they had borrowed it from pagan nations,—that among the Egyptians, Persians, Greeks, Romans, and other nations, it was customary to purify those who were to be initiated into the mysteries of the sacred rites, by dipping their whole body in water,—that the Jewish cup of blessing, added to the paschal supper, was of a heathen origin,—and that Jesus, in the institution of his sacraments, paid a peculiar regard to the heathens, in introducing into his religion baptism and the sacred cup, which had been borrowed from them. A writer in the Penny Cyclopædia, under the word, *Baptism*, says,—" Some early Jewish writers, whose testimony on such a subject is worthy of some regard, speak of it as a custom of their nation from very ancient times, and as having been always an accompaniment of circumcision, whether of infants or when proselytes were made."* He might have gone further, and have stated

---

* Dr. Jennings, in his Jewish Antiquities, Book. i. chap. iii. says that the Jewish proselyte, whether male or female, was " baptized by immersion of the whole body into water," in a river, fountain, or pond. This baptism, he tells us, " was a form of professing a new religion, at least new to the person professing it." The same baptism is dwelt upon in the Jerusalem Talmud. Arrian, and also Justin Martyr, refer to this Jewish baptism. Dr. Jennings, disagreeing with Godwin, thinks that the proselyting baptism of the Jews differed from John's baptism, while,

'that, even to this day, when a person is converted to Judaism, he is first circumcised, and, when healed, is baptized.   Indeed, there is abundant evidence that the rite of baptism, involving the idea of washing away moral impurity, was, at a very remote period, not only among the Jews, but among a great number of pagan nations.   The Essenes, who, as we have seen, were cœnobite monks, practised the rite of baptism daily, clothing themselves in white robes before they entered the water.* (Joseph. de Bell. lib. ii. c. 8.)   We read that early Christians in their baptism wore similar robes ; and we find that the Eastern Christians, to this day, undergo the rite, at least, once a year.   (Geddes's Church Hist. of Ethiopia, p. 33.   Priestley's Hist. Cor. Christ. vol. ii. p. 81.)   The Pharisees, precisely like the Essenes, immersed (βαπτισωνται) themselves in water, as a religious rite, which they solemnly observed always before eating ; and which was ancient at the time our Gospels were written—called the doctrine or tradition of the Presbyters.†   (παραδοσιν των πρεσβυ-τερων, Mark vii. 3—5.)   The Egyptians were immersed, as a religious rite, the moment they happened to touch a swine, which they considered

however, he tells us that the latter resembled the "diverse washings" of the Jews. He also says that the Jewish baptism "was not so very foreign to some of the heathen rites of purification." Wherefore this slight hint at the fact that heathen baptism was practised before the time of John ?   Why thus smother a fact with which the doctor's own words prove him to be well acquainted ?   Why aim at bearing the semblance of orthodoxy at the expense of truth ?

* The general custom, however, both among Pagans and Christians, was to put on white robes *after* baptism.   For the candidates were baptized in a state of nudity ; both males and females, in the presence of one another.   In the time of the Fathers, however, a canon was made that the sexes should be baptized separately.   The baptisms of both heathens and Christians formed an important feature in their festivals, such as the Pentecost, and others.   At these times vast numbers were baptized and clothed in white robes.   In the Christian Church, particularly in the second century, general baptism was administered only twice a year,—at Easter and Whitsuntide.   Hence the latter was called *White Sunday*, instead of Pentecost, owing to the vast number of Christians who were then clothed in *white* robes (Priestley's Hist. Corrupt. Christ. vol. ii. pp. 69, 81, 84, 88, and authorities.   Encyc. Brit. vol. ii. p. 793.   Mosheim's Eccles. Hist. vol. i. p. 399.)   The New Testament, particularly John's Revelation, is replete with references to these white robes.

† Most readers well know that a *presbyter* (πρεσβυτερος, a name signifying an elder, a missionary, an ambassador, a religious superintendent, etc.) was an officer among the followers of Jesus at a very early date,—even as early as the time, if not before the time, they were first called "Christians;" but comparatively few are aware that the same officer, long before the Christian era, was among the Therapeuts, Essenes, and other heathen monks.   Of this, however, there is abundant proof in the Greek works, already cited in treating of these monks.   The office of presbyter—generally translated *elder* in the English version of the New Testament—was evidently imported into Christianity from heathen monkery, like almost everything else that belongs to it.   Accordingly, we find that, in the time of James—said to be the brother of Jesus—there were, not only churches, but also over these churches, presbyters, who—identically with the Therapeutic monks already described—healed the sick.   (James v. 14.)   John the Evangelist is made to write his Epistles as a presbyter.   (2 John i.   3 John i.)   Peter, writing to the elect strangers scattered throughout Pontus, Galatia, Cappadocia, Asia, and Bithynia—regions into which Christianity, if not older than the Christian era, could not yet have penetrated—says that he, as a presbyter, exhorted the presbyters in those countries.   (1 Pet. v. 1.)   Indeed, the word presbyter, and other words denoting ecclesiastical dignitaries, in the Epistles, show that, at a period which is now deemed

morally to defile them. (Herodot. in Euterpe, 47.) They were also baptized in the Nile, as an act of worship to that sacred river. The Indians likewise baptized, by way of moral purification. Even to the present day, the Brachmins baptize expressly for the purpose of the remission of sins, at certain seasons, in the river Ganges, to the waters of which they ascribe a sanctifying quality. Hence, people flock to the banks of this divine stream, from all parts, even from Tartary, to be baptized in it, in order that their sins may be washed away by its holy waters. (Encyc. Brit. v. Bapt.) Justin Martyr, seeing baptism prevalent among the heathens, accounts for the fact by supposing that the demons had invented it in imitation of the Christians. But the former baptized long before the time we are told the latter had any existence. Justin should have recollected (Dial cum Trypho. Tertul. de Præscript. adv. Hær.) that the candidates for initiation into the pagan mysteries were wont to be baptized, *in order to wash away the stains which their souls had contracted;* whereupon, they put on new clothes all of linen, which they continued to wear until they fell from them in pieces. In reference to this heathen baptism, a very judicious and able writer, in the Encyclopædia Britannica, under the word, *mysteries,* is more suggestive than orthodox, in writing— "Whether the phrases of *washing away sin, putting on the Lord Jesus Christ,* putting off *the old man with his deeds,* putting on a *robe of righteousness, being buried in baptism,* the words *mystery, perfect, perfection,* which occur so frequently in the New Testament, especially in the writings of the apostle St. Paul, are borrowed from the pagan mysteries, or from usuages current among the Jews, we leave to our more learned readers to determine." To adduce more proof that baptism was a rite among the most ancient pagan nations is quite needless,—the fact is admitted by a vast number of Christian writers of the greatest note; so that the conclusion is inevitable, that this rite originated with neither Jesus nor John. Let us, therefore, inquire whence this John derived it; or what is the probable origin of the Gospel tale regarding John and his baptism; and whether they are not closely connected with heathen monkery.

the very dawn of Christianity, there existed a long established and perfect hierarchy. Presbyters are spoken of as being in countries where the New Testament furnishes no proof that the present Christianity had been preached. The whole tenor of the Acts and Epistles, when minutely examined, points to the conclusion that these presbyters were Therapeutic, Essenian, or some heathen monks. To make tours, in order to promulgate their doctrines in distant places; to establish new branches of their order; to superintend them; and to lay their hands on such converts as were thought worthy to receive miraculous powers, were important portions of the duties of these presbyters. Paul, Peter, Apollos, Barnabas, and others, were eminent in the discharge of these monkish duties. Throughout all the vicissitudes of Christianity, the term *presbyter,* has, even to this day, retained much of its original form and import. There is very little doubt that the word *priest* is only a slight modification of it. Mr. Mede, (Disc. i.) very properly asks—"Who can deny that our word *priest* is corrupted of *presbyter?* Our ancestors, the Saxons, first used *preoster,* whence, by a further contraction, came *preste,* and *priest.* The High and Low Dutch have *priester;* the French, *prestre;* the Italian, *preste;* but the Spaniard only speaks full *presbytero.*" Junius, (Etymol. Anglican.) after tracing the word *priest* in a similar manner, adds—"Omnia satis manifestè desumpta sunt ex πρεσβυτερος." The natural conclusion, therefore, is that the present ecclesiastical order of men called *priests,* both as to name and function, are the same as the monkish presbyters of the pagans.

2 H

From a very remote period, there has been in Persia and India a sect whose members called themselves *Mendai Ijahi, (or Iabi)* that is, the *Disciples of John.* They exist even to the present day, and are called by Europeans, "the Christians of St. John," while the Orientals, particularly the Mahommedans, call them *Sabians.* A great number of travellers and others, have minutely described them and their baptism.* Ignatius à Jesu, a Carmelite monk, who, in the first half of the seventeenth century, lived for a long time among these people, gives an elaborate account of them, in a work called, *An original Narrative of the Rites and Errors of the Christians of St John.* But there is no satisfactory proof, in any of the accounts given of these ancient Baptists, that they are, or have ever been *Christians,* according to the present meaning of the term. For they have scarcely any thing in their religious system which can be identified with what is said of Jesus by present Christians. They possess, however, some facts regarding *the Christ,* and have some religious notions which bear a faint resemblance to sentiments found in our present Gospels. They also profess themselves to be of a Jewish extraction, and maintain that their ancestors dwelt in Palestine, on the banks of the river Jordan. They assert that John was the name of the founder of their sect; but the account they give of him, while it agrees in many things with the Gospel narrative of John the Baptist, differs materially from it in some points. Their John, whom they profoundly revere, they will not admit to have been beheaded by Herod, but contend that he died a natural death in Persia, and was buried in a Persian city called Sciuster. This John delivered to them a sacred book, which they consider divine, and preserve with the utmost care.† They are baptized in the river by their priests, according to solemn forms, once a year, and they rest their hopes of the remission of sins and eternal salvation upon their repeated baptisms; believing that the oftener they are baptized, the more holy and morally refined they become. Such is the account given of these pagan Baptists, even by writers who make strenuous efforts to show that they are Christians. Now, there existed in the East, apparently many centuries before the time assigned in the Gospels to John the Baptist, a sect supposed to be Jewish, and called *Hemero-baptists,* or daily baptizers. They are mentioned by several ancient writers. According to Eusebius, (Hist. lib. iv. c. 22.) they were classed by Hegesippus, with the Jewish sects. Justin Martyr (Dial. cum Trypho.) refers to them. Epiphanius (De Hæres. Præf.) gives an account of them. In the *Indiculum Hæreseon,* said to have been written by Jerome, they are described as a Jewish sect. The author of the *Clementina* also says that this sect was founded by one John, who had a company of twelve apostles, besides seventy other select associates. Isidore, Clemens, and other ancient writers, make mention of them as one of the Jewish sects, classing them with the Essenes, the Galileans, etc., so as to furnish abundant evidence of an unsuspicious character that, about the time the Gospels make John

---

* See Thevenot and Tavernier's Travels. Fourmont, Hist. Academy of Inscriptions. Kempfer, Amœnit. Exot. Fascic. lib. ii. c. 11. Herbelot, Biblioth. Orient. v. *Sabi.* Asseman, Biblioth. Orient. Clem. Vat.

† Mosheim tells us that, in his time, a copy of this book, with copies of other books of the *Mendai Ijahi,* had been deposited in the King of the French's library.

the Baptist to have lived, there was in Judea and the adjacent countries a sect called Hemero-baptists, in a flourishing state. But they are by no means represented as being a Christian sect : on the contrary, they are described as decidedly Jewish, resembling Christians only on those points on which Christianity resembles the Jewish and Persian superstitions. It is said that they have never been accustomed to pay Jesus any adoration, or worship, whatever. There was, however, a perfect identity, on almost all essential points, between the Hemero-baptists and Persian Baptists. The authors already cited show that both believed frequent immersions in rivers indispensable to salvation. It is true that the former underwent daily immersion,* while the latter were baptized only once a year,—a cus-- tom followed to this day, in Abyssinia, by a sect of half Christians called *Kemmonts,* who also immerse at any time they happen even to touch a person of a different sect. (Geddes's Church Hist. of Ethiopia. Bruce's Travels.) But we find that, even on this point, so much alike are these *annual* and *daily* baptists, that the former are so much impressed with the utility of frequent immersions that, had it not been for the high fees charged by their priests, they would gladly enjoy a baptism every day. Again, both had a person of the name John, who had a number of disciples, for the founder of their respective sects ; both claimed a Jewish origin ; and both repeatedly underwent the ceremony of baptism with the deepest solemnity. The alternative, therefore, is, either that one of these sects, at some period before the Christian era, sprang from the other, or that both derived from a common source. Supposing that one has sprung from the other, the preponderance of circumstantial evidence would decidedly go to support the opinion that the Jews derived their notion of John and his baptism from the Persians. For, *first,* " it was from Egypt, Chaldea, and Persia," as the President of Washington College (Fathers of the Desert, vol. i. p. 120.) very properly remarks, that the Jews and Greeks derived the principles of their ascetic philosophy." The *Mendai Ijahi* of Persia are, by their countrymen, called Sabians, and con- sidered descendants of these gross idolators—the *Sabii,* or *Zabii.* Now, the ancient Sabians are known to have been fire-worshippers, as well as worshippers of the celestial luminaries. Most particularly were the Magi— another Persian sect which sprang from the Sabii—worshippers of fire. (Rollin. Book iii. chap. iv. art. iv.) Hence, we find in the Jewish religion very numerous traces of this worship. It was in " a lamp of fire " that God appeared to Abraham with a promise of Canaan. In " a flame of fire " the Lord first appeared to Moses. " In fire " he descended to give him the law. " Fire from the Lord " consumed Moses and Aaron's offer- ing. " Fire from the Lord " devoured the sons of Aaron, because they offered in their censers *strange fire*; that is, another fire than that which, according to both Jews and heathens, had originally come down from hea- ven, or from the adorable and adored sun, and which was always to be kept burning. In a " pillar of fire " the Hebrew God went before his people through the wilderness. " By fire " the monk Elijah proposed that his

---

* The Indians also baptized daily; and very minute directions are given for the celebration of the rite, in that very ancient book, considered divine—the Laws of Menu. Sir. *Wm. Jones's Works, vol. iii. pp.* 81, 107, 108.

God should answer, and convince the prophets of the god Baal. "By fire" the Lord answered his favourite David "from heaven." In "a chariot of fire and horses of fire," precisely like the heathen chariot and horse of the sun, Elijah went up to heaven. The sacred *fire of the Lord was in Zion*, as well as in the temple of Vesta. We learn that the God of the first Christians was "a consuming fire." Indeed, every part of the Bible is replete with expressions conveying direct ideas of fire-worship. Again, the Persian and Jewish creeds are precisely alike in the recognition of two omnipotent principles, or Gods,—the one good, and the other evil,—the one absorbed in light, as "God is light," and the other enveloped in darkness—"outer darkness;" being "the power of darkness." In describing these, Rollin, in the place just cited, says as follows of the Persians.—"Some held both of the two gods to have been from eternity; others contended that the good god only was eternal, and the other created. But they both agreed in this, that there will be a continual opposition between the two, till the end of the world; that then the good god shall overcome the evil god, and that, from thenceforward, each of them shall have his peculiar world; that is, the good god, his world with the good, and the evil god, his world with all the wicked." After telling us what reformation Zoroaster made in that sect of Persian religionists called the *Magi*, by making only one god to be the supreme being, independent and self-existing from all eternity; and making two angels—the one of light, the author of all good, and the other of darkness, the author of all evil—to have a continual struggle in this world, Rollin adds,—"That this struggle shall continue to the end of the world; that then there shall be a general resurrection and day of judgment, wherein all shall receive a just retribution, according to their works; after which the angel of darkness and his disciples shall go into a world of their own, where they shall suffer, in everlasting darkness, the punishment of their evil deeds; and the angel of light and his disciples shall also go into a world of their own, where they shall receive, in everlasting light, the reward due unto their good deeds; that, after this, they shall remain separate for ever, and light and darkness be no more mixed together to all eternity. And *all this the remainder of that sect, which still subsists in Persia and India, do, without any variation after so many ages, still hold even to this day*." But what a perfect picture of the essential doctrines of both the Jewish and Christian religion, is drawn by this faithful historian and orthodox divine—the president of the University of Paris! Well may he subjoin that "it is needless to inform the reader that almost *all these tenets, though altered in many circumstances, do in general agree with the doctrine of the Holy Scriptures*;" but groundless and improbable is his theory of accounting for this agreement by supposing that the Persian or Chaldean Magi borrowed their religious notions from the Jews. For there is but very slight traces of the two genii of good and evil, or God and the Devil, in the Hebrew Scriptures.—It is in the Christian Scriptures that these are treated of at any length. Besides, Zoroaster, the founder of the Magian sect, is said to have lived 2,400 years before the Christian era,* and to

* Hyde and Prideaux, writing in favour of the originality of the Jewish religion, have endeavoured to make it appear that Zoroaster flourished at a much later period

have been contemporary with Ninus. Supposing there have been two of the name, still, the latest is said to have lived nearly 600 years before our era, and, consequently, before any part of the present Bible had been written, as the ablest critics of the present day have conclusively proved. There is no point in ancient history more capable of demonstrative proof than that these doctrines originated in Chaldea, whence came the Jewish patriarch Abraham,* whose fabulous history tells us that he, with his wife and father, came from the fire-worship (*Ur* אור, fire) of the Chaldees, and is succeeded by an equally fabulous tale of the tower of Babel, or Babylon,—the whole directing us to look for the origin of much of the early history and religious notions of the Jews among the Magi of Persia and Chaldea.†

Secondly, the tale of the Magi (rendered, in the English version, *wise men* from the East) being guided by a star to the birth-place of Jesus, as told by Matthew, who, almost in the immediate context, dwells on the baptism of John, and that to a greater extent than any of the other Evangelists, indicates that, in writing this portion of his romance, he dealt in Persian lore,

and have imagined that there were, at least, two of the name,—the one the founder of the Magian religion, living about a thousand years before the Christian era; and the other, its reformer, living about five hundred years after, namely, in the time of Darius Hystaspes. But Herodotus, who was contemporary with Xerxes, son of Darius, evidently decribes the fire-worship of the Magi—which the above writers seem to regard as having been established by the latter Zoroaster—as well as their religious tenets. He also, notwithstanding the discovery of Dean Prideaux that the term *magus*, in the Persian language, means *cropped ear*—calls the Magi by name, in relating circumstances which had taken place a hundred years before the deception of the cropped ear Smerdis. (Clio, 128, 131, 140; Thal. 157—159; Polym. 191.) Indeed, Mr. Moyle, in vol. ii. of his work, refuting his uncle, Dean Prideaux, has clearly shown that the Greek writers who lived about the time of Darius, make the Magian prophet Zoroaster to have flourished about a thousand years before their own time. Plutarch (Isis and Osiris) makes him to have lived five thousand years before the Trojan War. Whatever about the correctness of this statement, Zoroaster, according to the testimony of all antiquity, flourished at a very remote period before the time of Darius. The Magi are still in Persia —with their sacred fire, their oracles, their pontiff, their elders, and their pilgrimages—subsisting under the name of Persi or Persees. They are also called Ghebers. The principles and ceremonies of their religion are contained in three books, called the Zend, Pazend, and Vestna, composed by Zerdascht, whom they make to be the same as the Jewish patriarch Abraham. But these fire-worshippers are now far in the minority, Mahomedanism being the predominant religion in that country. It is curious that the Magi were formerly classed with the Jews and Christians as the people who possessed written laws for their religion.—Reland, Dissert. tom. iii. Hottinger, Orient. p. 167.

* The Magian religion is, by the Parsees, or the modern Persian Magi, believed to be the religion of *their* patriarch Abram, received in ten books from heaven.—D'Herbelot, Biblioth. Orient. p. 701. Hyde de Relig. Vet. Pers. c. iii.

† The divine institution of the Persians, as to tithes, was remarkably similar to that of the Jews, from whom, as a nation conquered by them, it is very unlikely they borrowed it. This similarity is the more remarkable when we consider that the ancient Persians contended that the Jewish Abram was the same with their more ancient Zerdascht—the author of their sacred Scriptures, the Zend and other Holy books; and that critics of the present age maintain that Abram is from the Persian word—*Ahram*, or *Ahraman*—the name of one of the Gods of Persia. This is still more singular when we recollect that this Abram paid tithes to Melchizedek, who is represented as eternal—as a God—"having neither beginning of days, nor end of life" (Gen. xviii. Heb. vii.) If the Christian commentators were to search the Scriptures of the Persian Magi, perhaps they would no more be baffled with the question —who Melchizedek was.

and drew the history of John from the same source as his wonderful narration of these Magi.* That he meant the Persian *Magi*, of whom, in the time of Artaxerxes, there were 80,000, all priests, (Hyde de Relig. Vet. Pers.) there can be little doubt : since he makes a star to guide them, and would indicate that they had extraordinary knowledge of astronomy ; the Persian Magi being well known as the greatest astrologers in the world. Indeed, the Oriental Christians firmly maintain that these Magi were the disciples of Zoroaster, who had predicted the birth of the Messiah, and the appearance of a new star at the time. As, therefore, these Magi came from Persia, it is very reasonable, *ceteris paribus*, that John's baptism came from the same country. *Thirdly*, baptism, in Persia, had been in high repute, amongst the pagan worshippers, from the remotest period into which history carries us. In Persia and Chaldea, Mithras, the Sun—adored by means of a perpetual fire, particularly by the Magi—was one of the most ancient deities of these regions, and that whose worship was far the most prevalent. Now, when a person was a candidate for initiation into the mysteries of Mithras, the Magi made him submit to numerous immersions, or baptisms. The baptism of these candidates is mentioned by Turtullian (Præscript. adv. Hæret.) and other ancient writers. We have no reason to doubt that this rite of the Magi, which they celebrated with so much solemnity, is not so ancient as any other of their religious ceremonies, or, at least, as the time of Zoroaster. That it was among the Persians from a very remote period, is shown by the profound veneration which they paid to all rivers, and the sacredness which they attached to them. (Herodot. Clio, 138.) Connected with the rite of baptism, the Magi had several other practices precisely like those of pagan and Christian monks. For example, Zoroaster, and the other Magi, had caves for both their abodes and places of worship. In these caves, the ceremony of initiation took place ; but, before the candidates were fully admitted into the mysteries of Mithras, they had to spend seven years in a probationary state ; during which they performed a vast number of ascetic feats,—lived in a cavern, lacerated their flesh, fasted for fifty successive days and nights till they were perfect skeletons, exposed themselves to the most intense cold and heat, engaged in combats with savage beasts, subjected themselves to " fiery trials," by passing a great number of times through the sacred fire which was worshipped and " never quenched," and bound themselves by the most solemn oaths that they would never divulge "the in-

---

* At the time our present Gospels were compiled from pre-existing materials, collected by the Eclectic monks of Alexandria—as undoubtedly they were—probably there were ancient tales afloat regarding John the Baptist, just as there were about Jesus. But whether *this* John ever baptized in the river Jordan—of which there are so many wonderful Jewish things told, just as there are of Egyptian marvels told about the Nile—may be questioned. A peculiar feature in all the writers of the Gospels is, that they have altered the pagan fables as to time, places, and names, so as to identify them with persons connected with Christianity and Judea. Of this practice, a great number of examples could be given. Another feature in their writings is the tragic. They almost always contrive to make the hero of their tale suffer martyrdom, —a kind of death which the early Christians considered most praiseworthy and exemplary. Of neither of the heroes of the New Testament do we read—" He slept with his fathers." Jesus, John the Baptist, Stephen, Paul, Peter, John the Divine, James, and a host of others, are made to die the death of martyrs, either in the New Test. or in the writings of the Fathers.

effable secrets" of the *mysteries* into which they were initiated.* It would appear also that these Magi abstained from wine, drank only water, ate only the coarsest food, and were clad in the skins of animals, affording a striking type of John the Baptist.† *Fourthly,* the ancient tale about finding John the Baptist's head, has many points which direct us to look towards Persia for the origin of his baptism, or at least, its introduction among the Jews. It is said to have been found by monks who lived in a country which was over-run with this order of men, which had, for a considerable time, been under the Persian government, in which the Persian language was spoken, and the Persian religion prevalent,—found, not on the banks of the Jordan, but on the banks of the Euphrates, which formerly formed part of the boundaries of Persia,—found in the keeping of a holy virgin and a Presbyter, who were of another religion than the Christianity of the time, and one of whom—the Presbyter—it is expressly said, was a Persian.‡ Surely this tale directs us to look

* The candidate, when he had finished his probationary exercises, called *telotæ*, or "the rites of perfection," was brought out of the cave, and, with great solemnity, proclaimed the *lion*—not of Juda—but of *Mithras*, the priests of this religion being honoured with the title—Lions of Mithras. (Tertull. adv. Marc. Jul. Firmicus.) The worship of Mithras having been introduced into Rome, Lampridius very amusingly describes the initiation of the Emperor Commodus into the mysteries. Porphyry, (De autro Nymph.) makes frequent mention of the cave of Mithras, and invariably ascribes the invention of the mysteries to Zoroaster; while other writers contend that they were borrowed from India.

† Herodotus in Clio, 71. quotes the words addressed to Crœsus by a Lydian, named Sardanis, which words evidently have reference to the Magi, whose religion, at the time, was professed by the bulk of the Persian nation, and which show that these fire-worshippers were exactly like the Christian monks. He says—"You mediate, O king! an attack upon men who are clad in the skins of animals, who, inhabiting a region little cultivated, subsist, not on what they relish, but on what they can procure; who are strangers to the taste of wine; who drink only water; to whom figs are an unknown delicacy; and who are utterly unacquainted with any of our luxuries." That these words, which Herodotus cites from some unknown source, have reference exclusively to the religious portion of the Persians, is shown by his statement in other places (Clio, 133. Terps. 20.) that the Persians, generally, were immoderate drinkers of wine. Indeed, it is a well known fact that the Persians, from a very early period of their national existence, have been addicted to habits of intemperance. Chordin, Voy. de Perse, p. 344.

‡ According to Sozomen, (Hist. Eccl. lib. vii. c. 21.) who professes to relate the tale as he had heard it, this precious relic, which is to this very day exhibited, or pretended to be shown, was found, in the reign of the Roman emperor Valens, "by some monkish men of the Macedonian heresy," or sect, (ανδρασι μοναχοις της μακεδονιου αιρεσεως) who originally dwelt in Jerusalem, but afterwards fixed their abode in Cilicia. This writer does not tell us how the head of the Baptist—said in the Gospels to have been delivered to an inveterate enemy, at the time of its decapitation—was preserved for about 370 years. It is very unlikely that either Herodias, or her daughter, had it embalmed. Nor does he inform us how the *monkish men* he mentions became possessed of it. We know, however, that about this time, in imitation of the pagans, relics of saints—even saints who had never existed in the Christian Church—were pretended to have been discovered, and were almost all accumulated at Constantinople, whither John's head was brought. We also know that Cilicia—where these monkish men lived—and Persia, according to their ancient boundaries, were all but contiguous; (Herodot. Terps. 52. Euter. 34. Strabo, xiv. xv. xvi.) that Cilicia, with many other countries, from the time of Darius, was tributary to Persia, being one of its satrapes, and its governors appointed by its conquerors; (Herodot. Thal. 90—95. Terps. 49.) that, in Cilicia, the Persian government had erected, here and there, a vast number of gorgeous buildings, or inns,

towards the Persian Magi for the introduction of John's baptism among
the descendants of Abraham in Palestine. *Fifthly,* the following words,

for the accommodation of travellers, which were regarded sacred, and kept by Persians,
whose religion, as well as manners and customs, had been introduced into the country ;
(Herodot. Terps. 52.) that Cilicia abounded with mountain caves, which were the abodes
of heathen monks, bearing a very indifferent character for honesty ; that it was in Cilicia,
Tarsus was situated, at which place there was a monachal college, even superior to that
of Alexandria, a member of which college probably was Saul of Tarsus ; (Strabo, xiv.
Beaufort's *Karamania.*) and that, in Cilicia, there was manufactured a peculiar, but
celebrated sort of hair-cloth, which was worn both by heathen and Christian monk, and
which was the staple commodity of the country. (Varro, Re Rust. ii. 1, 2.) Such was
the country in which the head of the Baptist, in the time of Sozomen, was said to
have been "discovered by some monkish men of the Macedonian heresy ;" when this
country was a Roman province, but with its ancient pagan religion deeply rooted in
the minds of its inhabitants. And, unless this tale is of a pagan origin, what brought
the head of the Baptist from the banks of the Jordan, in Galilee, to the banks of the
Euphrates, on the confines of Persia ? By what means was it transferred, from among
the Christians and Jews of Palestine, into the custody of the Magian pagans of Cilicia,
where, not only the Persian religion, with its fire-worship and baptism, was predominant,
but the Persian language, in a corrupt state, spoken by all the inhabitants ? Again,
Sozomen gives us to understand that there was in attendance of the head, a holy Virgin,
who acted as a deaconess and keeper to it; (H παρθενος μεν ην ιερα ειπε· το δε αυτη
διακονος και φυλαξ.) and that there was, also, in the same sacred service, as a Therapeut and presbyter, discharging the sacerdotal functions, a Persian, named Vincent.
Here, connected with the head of the Baptist, there was a regular hierarchy, on a small
scale, before it was brought to Constantinople. But it is to be observed that, although
the holy virgin and the presbyter just mentioned, were both of the same religion, yet,
that neither of them was, at the time, of the same religion as the Roman emperor Theodosius, who was a Christian ; and that they were very reluctant to allow the Baptist's
head to be placed in a Christian church, even at the bidding of royal authority. We are
told that the holy virgin decidedly opposed this measure ; and that, even after she had
relinquished the Baptist's head—from which probably she derived some emolument—
she could by no means be prevailed upon to renounce the religion she had hitherto professed, and embrace Christianity ; although the emperor Theodosius held out promises to
her, if she did so. As to the Persian presbyter, Vincent, he was much more easily persuaded to renounce his old religion, and enter into communion with Christians, saying
that if the Baptist's head willingly followed the Roman emperor, he would do the same.
Sozomen thinks that the previous religion of both this presbyter and the holy virgin,
was the Macedonian creed, which required its devotees to take an oath never to swerve
from its doctrines. But whether he means the Macedonian religion, or that of the
followers of Macedonius, is of little importance to us, at present; for both contained an
admixture of the doctrines of the Persian Magi; and our author tells us that the presbyter Vincent was a Persian. And as to Macedonia, this country, from time immemorial,
abounded with heathen monks and holy virgins; and our author tells us that, while
Vincent was placed in the rank of the Christian clergy, and appointed a presbyter, as
amongst his former religionists, a son of his relative Abdas, who had accompanied him
from Persia, was a noted monk. In a word, the whole of Sozomen's tale regarding the
removal of the Baptist's head, drives us to the conclusion that certain pagan monks, in
Cilicia, professing the religion of the Persian Magi, exhibited a relic which they foisted
on the vulgar as the head of John the Baptist, and that the Christian emperor Theodosius,
in his zeal for accumulating all noted relics at Constantinople, hearing of the head of
this noted saint, had it conveyed thither from a territory then under his dominion. As
to any objection that might be made against the affinity of the Persian and Christian
religion, on the ground that, under Sapor, the Christians were persecuted in Persia, it
should be observed that it was not on account of their religion they were persecuted,
but because they were thought to be traitors to the government, and devoted to the interest of Rome, communicating to the latter, clandestinely, the affairs of the former, when
the two powers were at war. (Sozom. Hist. Eccl. lib. ii. c. 9—15.) Of course the
Persian priests—true to the priestly character of every age—took advantage of this circumstance, in order to rid the country of their rivals.

said to have been uttered by John himself, identify his baptism with the rites practised by the Persian Magi, in initiating candidates into the mysteries of Mithras. Refering to Jesus, he says,—"He shall baptize you with the Holy Ghost and with fire,"—literally, and properly translated—*in holy wind and fire.* (Matth. iii. 11. Luke iii. 16.) The writer of the Acts connects the operations of the holy wind and fire, in speaking of the Pentecostal feast, when two thousand people were baptized, telling us that the rushing of a mighty wind filled the house; that there appeared cloven tongues of fire; and that all were filled with holy wind.* (Acts ii. 2—4.) Now, the Magi, as already noticed, not only baptized in water the candidates for admission into the religious mysteries of the god Mithras, but also subjected them to a baptism in the sacred fire, into which they were repeatedly plunged, as a "fiery trial" before they were thought fit to be admitted into the holy mysteries. Other elements of nature, such as "holy wind," and, as Pletho, in the oracles of Zoroaster, informs us—"thunder and lightening, and fire, and everything terrible, which might be held symbolical of the divine presence," were brought to bear on the candidates. There is, therefore, every probability that the baptism by fire mentioned in the Gospels, has reference to that of the Persian Magi. This view is strongly corroborated by the fact that some of the early Christians, such as the Selucians, and Hermians, maintained that baptism was not complete without the application of fire. Valentinus administered baptism by fire to all he found to have been already baptized in water.† *Sixthly,* as the baptism of John must have derived either from the Persians or the Jews, if it had been the same baptism as the latter were wont to administer, it is most improbable that we should find in three of the Gospels the following question, with the answer said to have been given to it.—" The baptism of John, whence was it? from heaven, or of men?" (Matth. xxi. 25.) The Jews would not say that it was from heaven, lest Jesus should ask them why they did not believe in John; and, on the other hand, would not declare it to be of men, from fear of the people, all of whom regarded John as a prophet. But had this baptism been already in practice among the Jews, there would have been no force either in the question itself, or in the reasons assigned for the pretended inability of the chief priests to answer it. If it was the Jewish baptism which was continually administered, the people would know it was that, and the Jewish priests could fearlessly declare it, as their own, to be from heaven. This clearly shows that the Gospel writers thought that John's baptism was not Jewish. Indeed it is continually spoken of as in contradistinction to other baptisms, and is called emphatically *the* baptism

---

* Εν πνευματι αγιω και πυρι.—It is to be observed that the *article* is not used before the words, holy wind, any more than before the words *fire* and *water*, both of which are in the context of the passages just cited. There is nothing in the words—πνευμα αγιος, in the above instances, which indicates that either of the writers intended to personify the *holy wind* of which he speaks; but there is every thing that makes us think of the *inflatus* with which the pagan prophets were filled before they delivered their predictions. The import of the word πνευμα has already been explained.—(See pp. 110, 388.)

† Bis docuit tingi, traductoque corpore flama.—*Tertull. Carm. contr. Marc. lib.* i.

of John. (Luke vii. 29. Acts i. 22 ; xviii. 25. *et al.*) It must, therefore, be concluded that John's baptism was not Jewish, but had been derived from the pagan monks of Persia, who, about the commencement of the Christian era, had been dispersed by war, and scattered to all parts of the world. If, therefore, it be admitted that John's baptism was of a pagan origin, and he an anchorite or a monk,—facts which cannot be denied without violating truth,—then, the conclusion is inevitable, that Jesus, having lived as a monk from his birth till he was thirty years old, commenced his religious career as a monk.*

No sooner had Jesus undergone the pagan and monkish baptism of John, than he repaired to the wilderness to fast and to be tempted of the devil (Matth. iv.) In this act, there are several traits of an unquestionably

---

* Whether a person of the name John did, really, make his appearance on the banks of the Jordan, about the commencement of the Christian era, as stated in the Gospels ; or whether what is said of him in these productions is a modification of pre-existing tales regarding John the founder of the Hemero-baptists and the Mendai Ijahi, is not a question to be determined in this work, which, throughout, takes these Gospels upon their own statements. It may, however, be observed that—when it is considered that our present Gospels must have been written so late as the close of the second century, that, in the four first centuries of our era, a vast number of Christian books are positively known to have been forged, and that the exploits of John the Baptist are mentioned by no profane writer within two hundred years after the time he is said to have flourished, if we except one questionable passage in Josephus—there are reasonable grounds for doubting whether this John of the Gospels is anything more than a myth ; or, at most, the founder of the fore-mentioned pagan sects, which had existed many ages before the Christian era. It must appear very strange to a critical reader to find that there is not the slightest allusion to John the Baptist—the glorious Forerunner of the Messiah—made in any of the Epistles, although frequent mention in them is made of baptism, of the appearance of the Messiah, of circumstances preceding his appearance, and many other things which would directly lead the writer to mention John, or his baptism. But not a word is to be found,— no reference whatever to him, as the harbinger of Christ—as having been miraculously born—as having baptized Jesus and all the inhabitants of Judea in the Jordan—as having had many disciples—as having reproved Herod—as having been cast into prison and beheaded. Not a word about one of these remarkable circumstances do we find in any of the lengthy and numerous Epistles written to different Christian communities. Does this fact not indicate that the writers of these Epistles knew nothing of this renowned personage—next to Jesus himself, in Christian importance—whom the Gospel writers describe as baptizing on the banks of that sacred river—Jordan. As to the passage in Josephus, (Ant. Jud. lib. xviii. c. v. s. 2.) it is entirely at variance with the Gospels, in regard to John. Here it is said that Herod sent John to Machærus, a prisoner, because he was afraid that the great influence which the Baptist had over the people might enable and incline him to incite them to rebellion ; but, in the Gospels, it is said that Herod imprisoned John to please Herodias, who was inimical to him, because he had reflected on her illegal marriage with Herod,—that this Herod beheaded him because he promised, with an oath, to give Herodias's daughter whatever she should ask, in consequence of having been much pleased with her graceful dancing before him and a number of Galilean lords, on his birth-day,—that he was very sorry to have to order the decapitation of John, but that he did so on account of his oath and his honour, in the presence of all these great lords, who were at the banquet. The Gospels also tell us that Herod revered (εφοβειτο) and protected (συνετηρει) John, because he knew that he was a just and holy man ; and, having heard him, he contrived many things, and listened to him gladly :—a tale diametically opposed to the passage in Josephus (see Matth. xiv. 1.—11. Mark vi. 14—28. Luke iii. 19.) Further, the citadel of Machærus, where John is said to have been imprisoned, was on the borders of Arabia Petrea, in the possession of Aretas, king of Arabia, and at a distance of, at least, a hundred miles from Galilee, where Herod's seat of government lay. (Joseph. Ant. lib. xviii. c. v. De Bell. lib. vii. c. vi.) So great was the distance from Galilee to this castle, that, when

monkish character. We have seen that the Indian monks, many centuries before the Christian era, fasted for an incredibly long space of time, and

Herod's lawful wife—the daughter of Aretas—wished to leave her husband, on account of his intrigues, and be conveyed to this fort, under the protection of her father, she had to travel a great distance, and—as Josephus tells us in the first of the places just cited—had to be conveyed from one general of her father's army to another successively, till she reached the Arabian territory. But the Gospels, in the places already cited, clearly imply that John's prison was in Galilee, so that, apparently, his head was given to the damsel, at most, in few hours after she had made her sanguinary request.— "She went forth, and said unto her mother, What shall I ask ? And she said, the head of John the Baptist. And she came in straightway with haste unto the king, and asked, saying, I will that thou give me, by and by, in a charger, the head of John the Baptist. ....And immediately the king sent an executioner, and commanded his head to be brought : and he went and beheaded him in the prison, and brought his head in a charger, and gave it to the damsel ; and the damsel gave it to her mother.'' There can be nothing clearer than that, in this account, it is intended to show that John's head was brought to the damsel during the day, or rather night of the banquet. The learned reader will not, in the least, be astonished at being told that the writer of these pages thinks he sees adequate reasons to conclude that the passage in Josephus, refering to John, is a clumsy *forgery*. To find such a forgery foisted into the work of Josephus, is by no means strange, since two forged passages about Christ have already been detected in this work ; (Ant. lib. xviii. c. iii. s. 3. lib. xx. c. ix. s. 1.) both in the same part of the work as the passage about John. These have been proved to a demonstration to be forgeries, and are now admitted to be such, even by the most learned Christian writers, such as Ittigius, Vandale, Blondale, Le Clerk, Faber, Bishop Warburton, Dr. Lardner, Dr. Kippis, and others. Now, in the passage about John the Baptist, the following peculiarities appear clearly to prove its forged character. 1. There is in it such gross tautology, which is not found in any other part of Josephus's works. It begins and ends with the same words, in effect. 2. It is submitted to the learned whether the clumsy language and unnatural turns of expression, in this passage, so far as can be judged from so short an instance, are not different from the smooth, elegant style of Josephus, and very much resemble the style of the first forged passage about Jesus, and that of the Greek fathers. 3. It has justly been urged that the introduction of the first passage concerning Jesus interrupts the narration ; but in a much more decided manner does the passage about John destroy the concatenation of the facts detailed. Its introduction is glaringly unnatural.—The section before that which consists of this passage, ends with the statement that Tiberius wrote to Vitellius to make war on Aretas, and bring him before him, either dead or alive ; and the section which immediately succeeds it commences with the words,—" So Vitellius prepared to make war with Aretas," &c. Without this passage the narrative is remarkably natural and connected ; but its insertion between the above two sections (1. and 3.) entirely severs them, and the matter it contains is utterly foreign to the subject in hand. 4. If, according to the Gospels, John and Jesus were preaching at the same time, and the former declaring the latter to be the Messiah, it is very unlikely that Josephus spoke in such high terms of John who, according to the account we have of him, appeared, not as as a Judaical teacher, but as an Evangelist, and spoke most bitterly against the Pharisees, one of whom was Josephus himself. 5. Josephus, according to Christian chronology was only about thirty years older than John ; and, at the time he wrote, some of John's converts and disciples must be alive ; for, out of the many thousands he baptized, a sect must have been formed ; or, at least, a great number must, through life, have adhered to his doctrines, and been imitated by their children. Still, Josephus makes no mention of any of his adherents. Nor does he allude to the deputation of Jewish priests and Levites, sent to John, by the great council of the nation, to demand his authority for baptizing. (John I.) But what is still more singular, as evincing the spurious character of this passage, is that Josephus does not mention either John or his followers, when systematically treating of the religious sects that existed in Judea, which he does both in his Jewish Wars and Antiquities, before the passage in question occurs. If he knew any thing of John, or of his adherents ; and if John was such an important personage as he is described in the Gospels, and even in the supposed spurious passage under

we read that Jesus, immediately after his baptism, fasted even for "forty days and forty nights." Indeed, fasting was an indispensable exercise, in

notice, influencing the whole nation so as to be able at any time to persuade it to rise in rebellion; and making the governor of this nation regard him with awe, and to kill him, at last, from fear of his influence;—if, we say, the Jewish historian knew of these remarkable things—and it is impossible for them to have existed without his knowledge —he would, undoubtely, have given a detailed account of John, when treating of the other religious teachers of the Jews. Instead of this, we find only a casual notice taken of him. 6. The most direct and positive proof of the forgery of this passage is, that it makes Herod send John to the citadel of Machærus, which was, not only not within his own tetrarchy, but not within the Roman domains. It was in the possession of Aretas, the king of Arabia; so that, if Herod sent John to this castle, he would have no power over him, either to kill him, or preserve his life. To make it still more unlikely that he should have sent John to the fort of another monarch, Aretas had long ago been inimical to Herod, having had a quarrel with him about the boundaries of Gemalitus. Aretas and Herod's father, also, had always been inveterate foes. All these facts are attested by Josephus, in places already cited in this note. (See also Ant. lib. xvii. c. x. s. 9.) We may, therefore, be certain that Herod never imprisoned John in a castle which was in the possession of another king, and that a foe; and further, that Josephus, would never be so contradictory as to say that he did so. Consequently, the passage about John must be an interpolation, foisted into the text with the view of making Josephus bear testimony that John the Baptist flourished in the time and country of Herod the Tetrarch. But so clumsy is the forgery that it utterly falsifies the Gospel testimony regarding John. For Josephus, in the preceding section, states that Herod's lawful wife went to Machærus castle as soon as she discovered Herod's intention of taking to his brothers' wife; and therefore, before John could, by any possibility, have reflected on his conduct in living with her. Hence, the absurdity of the assertion, in the forged passage, that Herod sent John to the same castle as that into which his own wife had gone; and that at a time when he was at open war with her father Aretas, who held this castle. For Josephus assures us that war was declared between Aretas and Herod immediately when the former heard of the intention of the latter to abandon his lawful wife. It is difficult to ascertain the precise time at which this passage was foisted into the works of the Jewish historian His writings, at a very early period, were in the hands of Pagans, and afterwards Christians, at Alexandria and Rome. At these places, by these people—the literati of the age— numerous transcripts of them were made; so that to insert in them a few passages, here and there, was easily done, without being detected. For, in that age, the the means of comparison were few; and even if any additions were noticed, a few passages about Jesus or John, would probably be considered by many, a valuable improvement on the original work. Such were the forgeries of ancient times that it is now very difficult, in many instances, to discriminate the genuine from the spurious. Who can now precisely tell how much of what is called Josephus' work has been forged by Alexandrian Jews, in whose custody it was? If any reliance could be placed on the genuineness of the writings of Origen—a monk who flourished in the third century, who had been educated in the Alexandrian College, and who was half a heathen—we might infer that, in his time, this passage was, at least, in some manuscripts of Josephus' work. For he refers to it, (contra Celsus. lib. i. c. 25.) telling us that, although Josephus had not mentioned Jesus, yet, he had given an account of John and his baptism. But it is to be observed that, of all Christian and pagan writers, it is Origen who first mentions this passage; and that it is he who gives the first catalogue of the books of the New Testament, and does many other things to promote Christianity; so that it is imposible to determine how much of the credentials of this religion emanates from him, while we have internal evidence in his own works that he considers it a virtue to promote the interest of his creed at the expense of truth. It is very significant that—while this passage is not quoted by Justin Martyr, nor Tertullian, nor Chrysostom, nor any of the Christian Fathers who held controversies with the Jews and Pagans, before the time of Origen—he should, for the first time, cite it; and that, in the next century, Eusebius, his panegyrist, should cite it, and also, in the same work, discover another important passage regarding Christ, never quoted by anyone before. These are very suspicious circumstances, which—as all the books written against Christhe monkery of the Brachmins, Boodhists, Therapeuts, Essenes, and of all other heathens. In like manner, Jesus gives this sinful practice a con-

tianity in eary times, have been committed to the flames—we have now no means of investigating. Eusebius, (Hist. lib. i. c. 11.) in a very suspicuous manner, inveighs against certain Memoirs, or history of Jesus and John the Baptist, which existed in his time, and which, he insinuates, *had been forged*. It was a very common thing, however, at this period, for one party of Christians to accuse another of having forged religious books, palmed on the world as Divine revelations. This shows, at least, that Eusebius lived in an age and a country in which forging Divine books was not only practicable, but fashionable; so that for a man of his ability and influence to do so was a very easy matter. But to give the passage just mentioned:—Eusebius, after adducing what he calls the testimóny of Josephus respecting Jesus and John the Baptist, says,— Ταυτα του εξ αυτων Εβραιων συγγραφεων ανεκαθεν τη εαυτου γραφη, περι τε του βαπτιστου Ιωαννου και του σωτηρος ημων παραδεδωκοτος, της αν ετι λειποιτο αποφυγη, του μη αναισχυντοις απελεγχεσθαι τοις κατ' αυτων πλασαμενοις υπομνηματα. Αλλα ταυτα μεν εχετω ταυτη.—" These things having been recorded in the writings of a historian who sprang from the Hebrews themselves, regarding John the Baptist and our Saviour, can there be any farther means of escape from conviction for those impudent persons who fabricated the *Memorial* concerning them? But nevertheless, let me withold these things from this narrative." From this incidental, but guarded remark of Eusebius, it is evident that, before his time, there had existed other memorials, or records, of Jesus and John the Baptist than those which have descended to us under the title—Gospels; and that those pre-existing memorials contained statements different from what Eusebius, and other Christian Fathers of his time, wished to propagate respecting Jesus and John. Accordingly, Eusebius calls these— fabricated, or forged memorials, and is inclined to say very little about them; abruptly telling us that he wishes to keep (εχειν) these from his narrative. But why? What can be his reason for not telling us all about them,—by whom they were written, in what age, and what they contained of Jesus and John? Why not give us a full account of this matter, since he is so prolix on most other matters of much less importance? Upon what principles of honest narration can he openly declare that he suppresses this matter? unless it be upon that which, in his Martyrs of Palestine (c. xii.) he unblusingly confesses—namely, that he had thought it right to relate nothing but what would be deemed divine, (θειαν) and venerable, and of good report, (σεμνα και ευφημα), citing Scripture as an authority for this mode of writing a history (Eccles. Hist. lib. viii. c. 2.) That Eusebius denounces these Memorials as forgeries, is no proof that they were, or were not forged. For, as it has just been observed, in his time, it was a very common practice for one sect of Christians to decry the Divine books of another as forgeries; which shows that, among the various Divine books of a conflicting, but still of a Christian character, which existed, a great number of them *must*—and all of them *may*—have been forged. In the time of Eusebius, none knew more than he about these forgeries. It behoved him, therefore, to furnish us with much more substantial proofs of the genuineness of the present Gospels, than the fables and fictions found in his works. An excellent opportunity for doing so, offered itself to him, when speaking of the forged Memorials regarding Jesus and John. It should be here observed that Justin Martyr, nearly two hundred years before the time of Eusebius, makes 'mention, apparently, of the same *Memorials* in those portions of his works considered genuine. In his Apologies, and Dialogue with Trypho, he repeatedly speaks of these, calling them απομνημονευμα, and frequently, απομνημονευμα των αποστολων—Memorials of the Apostles. He says, that, on the day of the Sun, the Christians met, when either the *Memorials of the Apostles*, or the writings of the Prophets, were read to them,—that he learnt from the *Memorials* how Jesus, when on the cross, commended his Spirit to his Father's hands,—that it is shown in the *Memorials* that Jesus, with his disciples, sang a hymn,—and that it is written in the *Memorials of the Apostles* how the Magi of Arabia came to worshsp Jesus at his birth. Although the mumerous quotations made by Justin, from the *Memorials*, are, in substance, very much like portions of our present Gospels, yet, he has scarcely one quotation which perfectly agrees, in words, with these Gospels; while he has many citations not found in them at all, but detected in Gospels now considered spurious; such as his account of Jesus being born in a cavo,

spicuous place in his religion. "To be tempted of the devil," and to defeat him was another trial which candidates for admission into the mysteries of heathen monkery had to undergo ; and many a fierce battle with the devil did they fight, long before the time of Antony or even Jesus.* To retire "into the *wilderness* to be tempted" was also decidedly monachal, strikingly resembling what we read of heathen anchorites ; and the angels that administered to Jesus on this occasion, when the devil left him, strongly reminds us of the good demons that ministered to the heathen monks.

Another monkish feature in Jesus is, that—as soon as he had finished his probationary asceticism of baptism and demoniacal temptation—he went about the country, "healing all manner of sickness, and all manner of diseases among the people ;" so that "his fame went throughout all Syria, and that they brought unto him all sick people that were taken with diverse diseases and torments, and those that were possessed with devils, and those which were lunatic, and those that had the palsy ; and he healed them." (Matth. iv. 23, 24. Mark vi. 56.) Now, there is no characteris-

---

—of being thought a carpenter, when he came to be baptized; and of fire (a feature of the Magian religion) on that occasion, kindled miraculously on the waters of the Jordan,—all of which are related in the Apocryphal Gospels, already cited. To all this, it should be added, that Justin never mentions any production by the title— *Gospel*, or *Gospels*, or *Epistles ;* nor does he mention the name of one of the reputed writers of these Gospels, or Epistles, as such. The words, ἃ καλειται ευαγγελια, *which are called the Gospels*, truly, are inserted in Apol. i. c. 66. after the word *Memoirs* ; but, as several learned men have already observed, these were originally a gloss, and afterwards inserted in the text. Justin also mentions a certain man named John, as one of the apostles of Christ ; (Apol. i.) but not as if he had the slightest knowledge that this John was the author of one of the Gospels, of Epistles, and of the Book of Revelations. He likewise casually mentions Peter, telling us that Jesus changed his name. But he informs us that it was in the *Memorials* he had read all this. Indeed, he appears to have known nothing of the canonical Gospels. The natural conclusion, from what Justin and Eusebius say of these Memorials, is that, after the time of Justin, our present Gospels were compiled from pre-existing documents of various sorts ; and, in contradistinction to all other such productions then afloat, were called, ευαγγελιον, or ευαγγελια—*good news.* The emanation of these from the Alexandrian school, as productions of several hundred years old, gave them authority and influence among the credulous, as they were proclaimed, with the Epistles, by roving monks. All other *Gospels* and *Memorials* would now be denounced as forgeries, and, when found, commited to the flames. Accordingly we find Justin Martyr, in the second century, citing the *Memorials* as profound authorities ; and Eusebius, in the fourth century, *denouncing* them as impudent forgeries.

* It was the common belief, anciently, not only of heathen monks, but likewise of all Eastern nations—Jews as well as pagans—that, while the demons filled the aerial regious—their appropiate habitation—they also swarmed into dry deserts, and desolate places, not inhabited by man. Sharing in this belief, Jesus says that, "when the unclean spirit is gone out of a man he walketh through dry places (or rather regions, τοπων) seeking rest and finding none." (Matth. xii. 43. Luke xi. 24.) Both good and evil spirits were, by the Greeks and other nations, called demons ; but the Jews made a distinction, calling the good spirits, angels, and the evil spirits, demons. Now, it was believed that whoever took his abode in the desert was certain to have an encounter with evil spirits, in all shapes and forms ; and nowhere would the combat be so fierce as in this dreary solitude. But this enhanced the merits of living in such a place, and added lustre to the glory of having vanquished the devil on his own ground. Hence, we read of so many heathen anchorites having battles with demons in solitary deserts ; and hence we are told that Jesus went to the wilderness to be tempted of the devil, where, of conrse, he was victorious, and where, on the departure of the devil—the evil demon, angels, or good demons, administered to him.

tic of the heathen monks more prominent than their fame for healing
diseases. The Indian monks, as we have seen, (p. 445.) even in the time
of Alexander the Great—many centuries before the Christian era—were
renowned physicians or healers, whose medicine made the barren bear
children, and whose preternatural skill resuscitated even the dying and the
dead. The Boodhist monks, also, were wonderful healers of maladies.
The Therapeuts and Essenes—whose very names we have seen (p. 465.)
to signify physicians, or healers—were, according to the testimony of Philo
and Josephus, equally eminent in this art. In like manner, all the monks
already noticed, (p. 480, &c.) whom Christianity claims as its own, were
famous for their supernatural power to cure all manner of diseases. Indeed, the monks of every age and country have pretended to be great
physicians; and the belief that they possessed miraculous power to heal
diseases, was the principal cause of the deep reverence and awe with which
both poor and rich, high and low, regarded them. Those who dwelt in
cells, had their miserable abodes daily surrounded by persons who implored the blessing of health. As to those who lived in monasteries, some of
the most talented and renowned of them were frequently sent out as
missionaries, or preachers, to teach the vulgar, not the *mysteries*, but the
general doctrines of their religion, and to heal the sick.* On such occasions, they travelled from place to place, healing maladies and followed by
multitudes of people. Even to this day, the Indian monks—who are said
to number about two millions—thus roam about the country. So they
did two thousand years ago. Strabo, quoting the words of the Greek writers who accompanied Alexander to India, says of the Indian monks, that
they went about the villages and cities, practising the art of healing,
soothsaying, charms, and incantations for the dying; and that they preached about hell, so as to promote religion and virtue. (Strabo, lib. xv. c. 1.)
Jesus, whose name, as we have seen (p. 466.) signifies *healer*, was
throughout his whole life occupied in the same manner. All his miracles,
if we except withering the fig tree and drowning the Gadarenish pigs, are
of a Therapeutic or healing character, such as curing leprosy, plagues,
withered limbs, palsy, lunacy, dropsy, fever, female diseases, blindness,
dumbness, deafness, lameness, demoniacal possession, and so on.—Again,
his acts of reanimation, and of feeding and satisfying vast multitudes with
small quantities of food, are to be classed in the same category,—they are
all of a Therapeutic character. Now, it is narrations of these healing
miracles which form the bulk of the Gospels, and are their principal feature. Expunge these, and the first three gospels will be reduced into very

* It is by no means wonderful that the monks of all countries should have been both
physicians and divines; for it is a well known fact that, in ancient times among all
nations, medicine and divinity—which alike were thought to have been supernaturally
revealed, were connected—were both in the hands of the teachers of religion. (See
Levit. xiv. xv. 2. Kings i. 2; iv. 18—44; viii. 8. Isa. xxxviii. 1—21.) The medical
art and religious mysteries of the Egyptians were only parts of their theology. (Schol.
in Ptol. Tetrabib.) Their ancient medical books were deemed portions of their sacred
Scriptures, and were always carried about in their processions, by a religious order
called the Pastophori. (Porphyr. de Abstin. lib. iv. s. 8. Clem. Alex. Strom. lib. vi.
c. 4.) Among the Indians, the art of healing was in similar hands. (Strabo, Geog.
lib. xv.) So also among the Greeks. (Homer. Il. i. 62. xi. 512. Diodor. lib. v.) Indeed, all nations, without exception, at least till the age of Pythagoras, had their
physicians in the same persons as their religious guides.

small dimensions; and will contain scarcely anything striking. We are told, times innumerable, that great multitudes followed Jesus, from place to place, in order to be healed, and to witness cures of diseases performed. When he emerged from a desert, or when his hiding place in a wilderness was discovered, he was immediately surrounded by a vast number of people, anxious to be healed.   It was owing to his healing wonders that men and demons dignified him with the appellation—Son of God; just as Prometheus had been called so, for similar exploits. (Mark iii. 7—11; viii. 28, *et al.*)   For the same reason, he is called a prophet.   Jesus having cured the centurion's servant, and raised into life the widow's son at Nain, the people, knowing that the art of healing and reanimating belonged to a prophet, or a Therapeut, exclaimed that a great prophet had arisen among them.   This was what they expected a prophet to do, and therefore they deemed Jesus a true prophet because of his healing wonders. (Luke vii.) Among the Jews, the religious teachers, such as Elijah and Elisha, as well as the priests, had been great physicians.   Hence, Jesus so frequently told persons whom he had cured to go and show themselves to the priests. (Luke xvii. 14.) Indeed, Jesus himself openly declared that his mission was of a Therapeutic character.   Erroneously citing a passage which he thought properly applied to him, he says that he was sent to heal the broken-hearted, recover sight to the blind, liberate the bruised, and preach good news to the poor.   At the same time, he calls himself a physician and refers to the cure of the widow's son, by Elijah and that of the leper by Elisha; evidently comparing himself, in the art of healing, to these medical celebrities. (Luke iv.) In like manner does he avow his Therapeutic character, in the following instance,—John the Baptist, having been told by his disciples of the wonderful cures performed by Jesus, sent them to ask him whether he was the personage "that should come." Jesus, at the moment John's disciples arrived, being in the very act of curing many of infirmities, plagues, evil spirits, and blindness, requested the disciples of the Baptist to return, and tell their master that they had witnessed the blind made to see, the lame to walk, the lepers made clean, the deaf made to hear, and the dead to rise, while the poor had the gospel preached to them. (Luke vii. 18—22.)   These Therapeutic acts, Jesus, evidently, considered as sufficient proof to John that he was a greater monk than the Baptist.   These were his credentials; and these appear to have satisfied John, who knew as well as anybody what were the real characteristics of a Therapeutic monk.   When Jesus sends out his twelve disciples to travel about, from place to place, begging their food, like all other roving monks, he charges them to heal all manner of sickness and disease, and to cast out unclean spirits. (Matth. x. 1—8.)   When about ascending to heaven, his charge to his disciples was equally Therapeutic. His followers were to be able to cast out devils, handle serpents unhurt, drink deadly poison uninjured, and cure the sick by laying their hands on them,—all Therapeutic acts, in which pagan monks were expert.   The power of healing diseases being regarded as a supernatural gift, it was thought that the touch, or the laying of the hands* of a person so

---

* This species of enchantment, namely, to cure diseases by imposition of hands, long before the time of Jesus, was in use, not only among the Jews, but among heathen nations generally. The laying of hands upon the sick is prescribed in one of the

endowed, was sufficient to cure the most inveterate disorder. Accordingly, we find that Jesus—precisely like the heathen monks—frequently cured diseases by laying his hands on the sick. (Mark vi. 5. Luke iv. 40; xiii. 13.) And if the sick only touched the hem of his garment, it was thought sufficient to cure him. (Mark v. 23—34.) But Jesus's mode of cure was not always by the touch; like the heathen monks, he sometimes used means, and at other times used certain words. (Mark vii. 33; viii. 23; x. 52.) There is, indeed, a most striking similarity between Jesus and the Therapeutic monks, on the point of curing diseases. Hence, he has been thought by some very learned writers to have belonged either to that sect of monks called Therapeuts, or that called Essenes,—both which were renowned healers of maladies. It should, however, be observed that Jesus was very little, if any, more expert in miraculously curing diseases than the Christian monks who succeeded him, and many of whom we have already noticed. What could be more marvellous than St. Antony's cure of the "dreadful malady" of the courtier Fronto, and of the "disgusting disease of the virgin of Busiris? (Athanasius, Vit. Ant. 16.) What could be more astonishing than St. Hilarion's miraculous healing of a paralytic man, by means of bare words? (Jerome Vit. Hilar. c. 17.) Or St. Martin's feats, not only in curing a palsied maid on the point of death, in the presence of a great multitude, but even in raising into life the corpse of a man who, apparently, had been dead for three days, in the presence of a number of spectators. (Sulpicius Sever. Vit. Mart. c. 3, 5.) Many other such wonders could be cited. But enough has been advanced to show that narrations which, when criticised by an unbiased mind, appear none the less credible than the Gospels, testify that the monks who succeeded Jesus, as well as those who had preceeded him, were quite as skilful as he was in the art of healing and reanimation.

Another branch of the Therapeutic art was to cast out demons. We have already seen (pp. 404—412) that, long before the time of Jesus, heathen exorcists abounded in the East. We have now only to show that many heathen monks had a remarkable command over demons, and that another monkish characteristic in Jesus was to set about expelling imaginary devils, supposed to have entered human beings. According to Jamblicus, (Vit. Pythagor.) and Porphyry, (De Abstin. Vit. Pythagor.) who was himself a heathen monk, as well as according to the testimony of many other ancient writers, the Egyptian ascetics, long before the time of Pythagoras, were renowned exorcists. Believing in the existence of good and evil demons, they ascribed every disease to the influence of some malignant spirit, which they believed to have entered the sufferer, and which they pretended to eject, by pronouncing certain words and other enchanting means. It was the universal belief of ancient nations, and especially of the Orientals, as Mosheim, in his Notes on Cudworth's

Upavedas of the Hindoos,—one of the most ancient productions extant, which reveals the theory of diseases and medicine, together with the mode of curing every kind of malady, and is believed by millions to be a Divine Revelation. In India, at this very day, a *hand* painted or carved on anything, is considered emblematic of miraculous power conferred. When the monk Elisha resuscitated the child he had caused the barren Shunammite to bear, he laid his hands upon the child's hands, &c.—2 Kings iv. 3—37.

Intellectual System, justly observes, that certain words and sounds, for
the most part barbarous, had an effect on demons. By means of such
sounds and words, the ancient Egyptian, Persian, and Chaldean magi, were
supposed to have all demons under perfect control. The biographers of
Pythagoras inform us that, from these ancient nations, and still more ancient and monkish Gymnosophists of India, he learnt the ascetic philosophy, or, in other words, monkery, and brought it into Greece, over
which country, as well as others, he and his followers widely disseminated
it.   They also expressly tell us, not only that the Egyptian ascetics and
other pagans, cast out demons, but that Pythagoras himself and his
followers, cured patients in the same manner.   Now, that Pythagoras was
a thorough ascetic, is proved by the following particulars narrated in his
life.—He lived part of his time in a cave, abstained from flesh, killed no
living thing, subsisted on the simplest food, wore the habiliment of an
Egyptian priest, had under his charge a cœnobite college of young ascetics
in his own dwelling, which was a kind of monastery; placed these in a
probationary and silent state, like the Essenes, for a number of years; exercised his body, in order to subdue the passions of his soul, and wrought
many miracles; not the least of which was to cast out demons.   This renowned philosopher—whose biographers tell us was divine, being the son
of Jupiter, and was at his death placed among the gods—flourished, however, about five centuries before the time Jesus is said to have expelled
the first demon in Palestine. From the age of the former till that of
the latter, many an eminent monkish exorcist made his appearance in
the heathen world.   One additional instance, however, must suffice;
namely that of Apollonius of Tyana, in Cappadocia—a region remarkable
for its monkery, from the earliest period of which we have any account of
it.   This celebrated monkish exorcist of the Pythagorean religion, was
contemporary with Jesus, and must have been engaged in casting out
demons among the heathens at the very time Jesus was so engaged among
the Jews.   Philostratus, writing the life of this wonderful exorcist, about
a hundred years after his death, tells us that, at Athens, he ejected a
demon from a man by threats and menances, and that the evil spirit, in
quitting his abode, overturned a statue which stood before the porch where
the cure was performed.   On another occasion, he made a demon quit his
position in the form of a shaggy dog. Now, that he was an austere monk,
is certain from the following particulars recorded by his biographer.—He
imbued his early religious notions in a place near Tarsus, which abounded
with monks. He professed the doctrines, and practiced all the austerities
of the Pythagorean sect. He abstained from animal food and wine, lived
upon fruits and herbs, wore a course garb, walked barefoot, and, like the
Indian monks, allowed his hair and beard to grow long.   He travelled
from place to place, and from one country to another; proclaiming his
doctrines, performing miraculous cures, and visiting the ascetics of every
country into which he went; such as the Gymnosophists of India, and the
Magi of Babylon. He travelled through Asia Minor, where he performed
many miraculous cures, chased demons, and predicted future events.
With his disciples and followers, he visited Rome, where he foretold
momentous events, which were verified in a short time; and where he restored to life the dead body of a lady of high birth. Surely, Apollonius

is entitled to the name monk, if even the most renowned of the Christian ascetics of the four first centuries is worthy of that revered name; for his life and actions correspond to those of them in every essential particular, especially, such of them as travelled about.*

* Notwithstanding what Du Pin, Prideaux, Brucker, Mosheim, and others have written, with the view of showing that what Philostratus, in his Life of Apollonius, states, is much less credible than what the writers of the Gospels narrate of Jesus, still, any one, acquainted with the religious world at the time, who will critically and impartially compare them, must conclude that the former is quite as credible as the latter. Belief in the reality of such miraculous feats as those recorded to have been performed by Jesus and Apollonius, was then universal; and numerous were the actors who, from time to time, attained to great celebrity in these supposed supernatural exploits, and found writers to narrate their performances, and exaggerate their apparent supernatural character. The early Christians never thought of denying that their heathen opponents wrought miracles. All they contended for, was that their religious adversaries performed their wonders by the power of demons, but that their own were the works of the true God. The heathens, however, constantly charged the early Christians with fraud and imposture in their miracles. But now-a-days, the tables are turned,—the Christians of the present age find it convenient to urge that all the pagan miracles recorded, are juggleries, and that the accounts given of them, in many instances, are forgeries,—charges which were never made by the early apologists for Christianity, who were satisfied with having their own prodigies regarded as real as those of Æsculapius, the Saviour, and other deities. (Justin Mart. Apol. Prim. Lardner's Jewish and Heathen Testimonies, vol. iv. p. 410. Dr. Middleton's Free Inquiry, p. 144.) Now, as to the comparative claims of credibility due to the account given of Apollonius and that given of Jesus, the following particulars may be urged in behalf of the former. His biographer, Philostratus Flavius, was a person of high distinction.—He was a famous sophist, who enjoyed the patronage of the Roman Empress Julia, wife of the Emperor Septimus Severus, who was herself renowned for her literary acquirements and philosophic knowledge. She entrusted Philostratus with all the written materials which had formerly been collected by Damis concerning Apollonius, and ordered him to review them, and, out of them, to compile a history. Accordingly, this history was written within a century after the death of Apollonius. In about a century afterwards, Sotericus, the poet and historian, whose works are now lost, wrote another biography of Apollonius. (Suidas, Lex.) Some letters attributed to Apollonius are embodied in Philostratus's history of his life, and several more are preserved in the works of Cujacius. The prodigies of Apollonius are mentioned by Lucian, born A. D. 90; and also by his contemporary, Apuleius; which is more than can be said of Jesus,—no heathen writer mentions him at so early a date. In the time of the Emperor Aurelian, (Vopisc. Vit. Aurel. c. 24.) the fame of Apollonius was so high—so widely and firmly established—that temples and statues existed in honour of him. Indeed, during his life, and more particularly after his death—when he was said to have ascended to heaven—he was deemed a Divine personage. (Lamprid. Vit. Sever. c. 28.) When Hierocles, about the close of the second century, wrote against the Christians, his chief argument was that Apollonius of Tyana had performed a greater number, and more wonderful miracles than Jesus was said to have wrought,—an argument which Eusebius and Lactantius, who replied to him, appear to have found rather difficult of refutation. But we have been allowed to know very little about what Hierocles advanced against Christianity,—only what his opponents have deemed it prudent to reveal to us. Of course, his works against the religion of the Christians has been committed to the flames. It is a notorious fact that all the works of the early opponents of Christianity have been either burnt or lost; and that, generally, in a century or two after their extinction, the Christian Fathers set about refuting them. It is very wonderful that the life of Apollonius has been allowed to descend to the present age. An English translation of it, however, has been thought too detrimental to Christianity to be permitted to circulate. In 1680, Mr. Blount—a learned writer, author of the *Anima Mundi*, and other works, and a son of Sir Henry Blount—wrote and published a translation of the Life of Apollonius; but the clergy pronounced it "an attack upon revealed religion" and soon suppressed the edition, thinking this sort of argument the most effectual they could employ in defence of the Christian religion.

As to the few miracles, not exactly of a Therapeutic character, said to have been performed by Jesus,—such as withering a fig tree, walking on the surface of water, and calming a storm,—the heathen monks are said to have wrought precisely similar marvels. On the top of a mountain, in Northern India, Bernier saw a pagan monk who was thought to have nature so completely under his control that he could, at will, not only still tempests, but raise terrific storms. To adduce proofs on this point, however, is needless,—they are so numerously met with in pagan lore, that most readers must be fully acquainted with them. Equally known also, it is, that the pagan monks, as predictors of future events, were rather more renowned than Jesus. All the heathen monks, if of any fame, were great prophets. The ancient Gymnosophist of India already described, were famous for their prediction of future vents. (Clem. Strom. lib. III.) So were the Persian, Egyptian, and all heathen monks; and so they continued, down to the time of Apollonius Tyaneus, who, from Ephesus, prophesied the very moment at which the Emperor Domitian was stabbed at Rome. So, likewise, were the Christian monks. Athenasius (Vit. Anton. 17.) tells us that Antony often predicted things months before they happened; and the biographers of other Christian monks bear testimony to their prophetic wonders. Thus, were the heathen monks great prophets *before*, and *at* the time of Jesus; and the Christian monks equally great predictors *after* his time. In being a prophet, therefore, Jesus only identified himself with the monkish order of every age and country.

Again : like the anchorites in every country and in every age, Jesus, made his abode in deserts and on mountains. In these desolate places he spent his time, when not on a rambling excursion about the country, preaching his doctrine, miraculously healing diseases, and working other wonders. The Gospels are replete with proofs that such were his dwelling places. Indeed, it appears that, after being baptized and tempted of the devil, he made his fixed abode in some lonely and secret place in the wilderness, not far from the hermitage of John the Baptist; and that, for some days afterwards, he paid an occasional visit to this noted monk, who was daily engaged in baptizing, and who unquestionably made the desert his dwelling-place; sleeping on the ground, like both the heathen and Christian anchorites. (John i. 35—50.) For we read that two of John's disciples made an attempt to trace Jesus to his dwelling. Seeing that he was followed, Jesus turned to the two disciples and asked them—"What seek ye?" They replied—"Rabbi, where dwellest thou?" Jesus rejoined—"Come and see." They accordingly "came and saw where he dwelt, and abode with him that day." The whole tenour of the conversation between Jesus and these disciples, as well as others mentioned in the same narrative, shows that, at the time, his place of abode was not a house. It is curious to observe from this narrative also that, while John was alive, and baptizing, Jesus took to some of his disciples, such as Andrew; thus showing his approval of the monkish system of John. It appears further that Philip, Simon, and Nathaniel, were likewise disciples of John, before they attached themselves to Jesus. From several parts of the Gospels, it would seem that Jesus slept every night in some desert or mountain, whence he walked in the morning into some of the adjacent towns or villages. We read that, after a disputation with the Jews in the temple, "every man went unto his own house," but that "Jesus went unto the mount of Olives, and early in the next morning he came again into the temple." (John vii. 53; viii. 1.) Luke, apparently speaking of Jesus's regular practice, says that, "in the day time he was teaching in the temple, and at night he went out, and abode in the mount that is called Olives." (Luke xxi. 37.) The mount of Olives is a craggy elevation, part of which is within about a mile of Jerusalem. It must strike even a very superficial student of the Gospels, as being very strange that—if Jesus was *not* an anchorite, and was accustomed to dwell, like other people, in houses—he should at night retire into that solitary and rocky place—the mount of Olives, instead of remaining in the city, and in the houses of some of those people who had been listening to his pathetic orations, and witnessing his astounding miracles; and who, doubtless, would gladly entertain him. But we have to state that the mount of Olives, from time immemorial, has been the resorting place of monks, who, even to this day occupy it. It abounds with grottos and subterranean caverns. Even long before the time of king Josiah, these were occupied by heathen priests and monks, and had then, for ages, been the repositories of the embalmed bodies of the prophetic and monkish fraternity. (2 Kings xxiii. 6, 13—20.) That most of the Orientals deposited the bodies of their illustrious dead in caverns or subterraneous temples; and that their priests, prophets, and monks, retired into these places, for religious contemplation, are facts too well known to be insisted upon. In the time of Josiah, these caves, on the mount of Olives—which is described as being on the right hand of the mount of Corruption, and as the spot on which Solomon had established heathen worship—contained a vast quantity of "the bones of men." In a similar state has superstition preserved this mount to the present day. Modern travellers tell us that, in one part of it, are caverns shown as the sepulchres of the prophets; in another part, twelve subterranean grottos, said to have been the places where the twelve apostles composed their creed; and in another, the cave of "a departed saint," called *Pelegia*. (Encyclop. Brit. v. Olivet.) Now, in this ancient dwelling-place of anchorites, Jesus very frequently made his abode, and also performed many important things.—Here he wept over the holy city; here he sat with his disciples when he predicted the speedy end of the world; here he was when he sent them for an ass on which to ride in regal pomp into Jerusalem; here—where Dr. Clark (Travels, vol. iv.) says there are vestiges of paganism—he retired to pray, after his last paschal supper; and here he stood with his disciples when angelic beings came forward and wafted him into heaven. (Comp. Luke xxiv. 50. Acts i. 12.) He spent much of his time also in other mountains, frequently engaged for a whole night in prayer,—precisely like the pagan, as well as Christian monks. (Luke vi. 13.) In a mountain he consecrated and ordained his twelve apostles; (Mark iii. 13.) and in a mountain, while praying with three of his select disciples, he was transfigured. (Luke ix. 28.) In a mountain he delivered his noted sermon. (Matth. v. 1.) After one of his fierce altercations with the Jews, he crossed the lake of Tiberias, and "went up into a mountain, with his disciples, and there he he sat (or rather *dwelt*—εκαθητο). Having journeyed from the coast of

Tyre into Galilee, he does not seek accommodation in any dwelling house, for himself and his disciples, but goes into a mountain, and there abides. (Matth. xv. 29.) Although he frequently visited villages and towns, yet, it would appear from the Gospel narrative that he spent most of his time in mountains and deserts, and that it was in such places he performed, by far, the greatest number of his miracles. Into these secluded places he was followed by vast multitudes, who were anxious to be healed of their respective maladies, and who remained with him, sometimes, for several days; their food being miraculously provided. (Matth. xiv. xv. Mark vi. vii. viii. Luke iv. ix.) This mode of life is perfectly identical with that led by all the rambling heathen monks of the age in which Jesus is said to have lived. The answer given by him to an ardent scribe who said—"Master I will follow thee whithersoever thou goest"—plainly shows that it was this sort of life which he led;—"The foxes have holes, and the birds of the air have nests; but the Son of man hath not where to lay his head,"—has no house, and no fiixed habitation, but wanders about in deserts, like other monks; and, having neither bed nor bedding, sleeps on the bare ground, in the open air, or in some rocky cavern. Such, evidently, is the import of the words.

Like the Indian and other monks, also, Jesus took women along with him through the towns and villages which he visited in his travels. Strabo, in a passage already cited, speaking of the medical Indian monks who rambled about the country, healing diseases and preaching about hell, says—"Some take women along with them to philosophize; but they have no sexual intercourse with them." Clement, in his Stromata, refers to the same female ascetics whom he calls Semnai, and says that they lived a life of virginity. Christian monks did the same.—Jerome, in his ascetic rambles, took with him Paula and Eustochium. In like manner, Jesus, as we read, "went throughout every city and village, preaching and shewing the glad tidings of the kingdom of God: and the twelve were with him; and certain women which had been healed of evil spirits and infirmities, Mary, called Magdalene, out of whom went seven devils, and Joanna the wife of Chuza, Herod's steward, and Susanna, and *many others*, which ministered unto him of their substance." (Luke viii. 1—3.) When he was apprehended, a great company of women followed him, bewailing and lamenting his fate. When he was crucified, these women stood afar off, witnessing his death; and when he was buried, they followed him to the cave, and afterwards made preparation for embalming his body. (Mark xv. 40, 41. Luke xxiii. 27, 49; xxiv. 55, 56.) The similarity, in this instance, is very striking, especially when it is borne in mind that women in every age—whether ancient or modern—have been accustomed, not only to follow the pagan monks from place to place, and to regard them with profound reverence, but likewise to *minister unto them of their substance;* or, in other words, to supply them with the means of subsistence. Bernier, speaking of the Indian monks, says that "the women brought them alms with much devotion, taking them for very holy men, much wiser and better than others." Hamilton, Niebuhr, and other Indian travellers, bear similar testimonies.

In his diet, Jesus appears to have differed from some monks. But this difference, when closely examined, turns out to be more apparent than real. Although in the Gospels, he is called a Nazarene, yet, we are told that he drank wine and took animal food. This difference between Jesus and other monks, particularly between him and John, appears to have attracted the attention of the ascetic Pharisees. Accordingly, Jesus says to them,—" John the Baptist came neither eating bread nor drinking wine; and ye say, He hath a devil. The Son of man is come eating and drinking; and ye say, Behold a gluttonous man, and a wine-bibber, a friend of publicans and sinners." (Luke vii. 33.) Even if Jesus was so, still, he was not different from *some* of the pagan monks ; particularly those who wandered from place to place, and visited towns and villages. The Indian monks—spoken of by Strabo, in places already cited—who went about villages and cities, and were hospitably entertained in the houses they deigned to visit, appear to have taken animal food, and to have drank wine. The same thing may be said of the monks for whom the Emperor Aurengzebe is said to have prepared a banquet, and of those who dined at Alexander's table, when he invaded India. There were, also Christian monks of the highest degree of sanctity, who drank wine, ate flesh, and associated with publicans and sinners. From Evagrius and other ancient writers, we learn that some of these, in haunting cities and other places of resort, entered public houses, and ate any sort of food, and drank any sort of liquors, with any sort of people.* One of them, named Simeon—a very holy and renowned monk—who sometimes pretended madness, and rushed into taverns, devouring all food within his reach, had such an abundance of wine that he could spare some of it to a courtezan, into whose chamber he was seen to enter, with a vessel of this precious liquor " which cheereth God and man."† The same difference of practice between some monks and others, on this point, is proved by the words of Athenasius—a great admirer of monkery—who, in his Epistle to a monk named Dracontius, says,—" We have known bishops who were fasters, and monks who were eaters ;—bishops who were abstainers from wine, and monks who drank wine." But as to Jesus, the Gospels furnish no proof that he ever drank wine, except as a religious rite, or *sacrament*. We infer that, in eating the Passover with his disciples, he drank of the cup of wine as it went round ; but this Jewish as well as pagan rite, was a religious *sacrament*, or a ratification of an oath which Christians as well as heathens took to remain true to one another, and to the obligations their respective religions imposed upon them. But all monks who strictly abstained from wine at ordinary times partook of it as a sacrament, when communing at what they called the Lord's Supper. Of this fact, there is abundant proof.‡ Jesus, in taking wine at the

---

* Of these Evagrius says,—Ουτως το απαθως εσθιειν φιλοσοφουσι, και παρα καπηλοις η παλιγκαπηλοις δεησοι, ου τοπον, ου προσωπον, ουδε τι των παντων εγκαλυπτομενοι. Και βαλανειος δε συχνοις ομιλουσι, τα πολλα γυναιξι συναι λιζομενοι, και συλλουομενοι.—Hist. Eccles. lib. i. c. 21.

† Of this monk, Evagrius also says,—Και που και καπηλιο παρεισδυς εκ των προστυχοντων ησθιεν οτε πεινων....... Ουτος ποτε ες τι δωματιον εταιρας εσελη-λυθως ωφθη......κομισαι και σιτια και οινου τι αγγος.—lib. iv. c. 34.

‡ Indeed, some of the Egyptian monks appear to have daily partaken of bread and wine as a sacrament. (Palad. Hist. Lausi. c. 52.) To such a degree of extravagance was the notion of the supernatural virtue of the Eucharist carried, that bread and wine

paschal feast, did no more than any other monk would do, on a similar occasion, and for a similar purpose. On no other occasion are we told that he drank wine. Although he says that his countrymen called him a wine-bibber ; and although he was at a marriage feast, in Cana, where he went so far as to turn a large quantity of water into wine, which was to be given to persons already intoxicated, (vid. ant. p. 348.) yet, there is no evidence that he himself, or even his disciples, drank any wine at this feast, Similar remarks may be made in reference to the question— whether Jesus strictly adhered to the monkish custom of abstaining from flesh-meat. We have already seen that some monks, particularly those who, like Jesus, roamed about the country, were not very particular on this point. It is, however, to be observed that it was from the flesh of animals which have *blood* that monks appear to have abstained. It is the word κρεας or εναιμος which is generally employed to denote the meat from which they abstained. Eusebius, (Hist. lib. II. c. 17.) citing, apparently, the words of Philo Judæus, in reference to the practice of the Therapeuts, says—"They abstain entirely from wine, and from all things having blood; (των εναιμων τινος)—that is, from eating the flesh of any animal which has blood.* In the same sense is the word κρεας † (flesh-meat) used by the author of the Epistle to the Romans, (xiv. 21.) in saying—" It is good neither to eat *flesh* nor to drink wine ;" and by the writer of the first Epistle to the Corinthians, (viii. 13.) in saying,— "If meat make my brother to offend, I will eat no *flesh* while the world standeth." The same idea is couched in the frequent caution given to early Christians to abstain "from things strangled, and from blood." (Act xv. 20, 29 ; xxi. 25.) We have no proof that the monks, gene- rally, abstained from eating the flesh of what are called bloodless animals—

were placed with the monks in their coffins, when they were buried. (Bona Rer. Lit. lib. ii. c. 18.) It is true that some used wine mixed with water, which practice Cyprian and the celebrated monk Augustine, advocated, (Cypr. Ep. ad. Cæcil. Aug. de Doct. Christ. lib. iv. c. 21.) urging that this diluted wine represented the water and blood which came from Jesus' side when pierced. The Montanists, in their sacrament, mixed wine with human blood ; although on all ordinary occasions they rigidly abstained from wine, flesh-meat, marriage, &c; practising all the severities of the monkish fraternity. But the Ebionites, Encratites, and some others, communed with water, for which they were condemned by other Christians. It was, however, at the very earliest times, the custom of Christians to bring into their love-feasts, or *agapæ*, as already noticed, large quantities of bread and wine, as oblations, part of which they ate in common, in their love-feast, and part they reserved for the Eucharist. (Basnage, vol. i. p. 112.) In this, they precisely resembled both the Jews and heathens. Although they abstained from wine, and flesh-meat at all times but at their religious festivals, yet, at these seasons, they partook of both, calling them the body and blood of Christ. At the close of the love- feast, apparently, they took the oath or sacrament, which they called *a dreadful and tremendous mystery*, and which Tertullian (Apol. c. 7.) says, was "to be concealed" "like the mysteries of Ceres in Samothrace."

* Sozomen, also, referring to Philo's account of the Therapeutic monks, says,— Και οινου παμπαν και εναιμων απεχεσθαι.—They abstain altogether from wine and things having blood.—Eccles. Hist. lib. i. c. 8.

† That this word means the flesh of animals which have blood is evident from the connection in which we meet it in profane authors. This is also proved by the meaning of its numerous derivatives. Plutarch uses it in a compound form—κρεωπωλιον—to explain a word of a Latin derivation—μακελλον, (macellum) *shambles*, which is used in the same sense in 1 Cor. x. 25.

such as fish. On the contrary, we have historical evidence that both heathen and Christian monks of the most austere habits of life, *did* eat fish,—a remnant of which practice still exists in the custom of the Christians of the present day, who abstain from flesh, and eat only fish, during Lent.* Agreeably, therefore, to the practice of eating fish, which prevailed amongst the greatest number, by far, of ancient monks, we find that Jesus was a fish-eater, and that, by various means, he strongly recommended to others the same aliment. It was with two fishes and five loaves he fed to satiety upwards of five thousand hungry human beings; it was with " a few little fishes " and seven loaves, on another occasion, he satisfied the hunger of upwards of four thousand persons; and it was with five barley loaves and two small fishes, on a third occasion, apparently, that he fed about five thousand men (Matth. xiv. xv. Mark vi. Luke ix. John vi.) It was in the mouth of a fish that he told one of his disciples to look for a piece of silver to pay the Roman tribute. (Matth. xvii. 27.) It was fish that he miraculously caused his disciples to catch, so that, on one occasion, a broken net brought up, at once, as many as could be stowed in two ships, which were nearly sunk by their piscatory burdens. (Luke v.) It was on fish, miraculously caught in the same manner as that just described, that he dined with his disciples, after his resurrection; (John xxi. 1—14.†) and it was " a piece of broiled fish, and of an honeycomb " that his disciples gave him to eat, when—for the first time after he had risen—he appeared to " the eleven," and asked for food. (Luke xxiv. 42.) We have, however, no proof that Jesus ever tasted flesh-meat—that is, the meat of animals having blood—which is designated by κρεας, or εναιμος; and from which the monkish fraternity abstained. We have not the slightest reason to infer that, at any of the houses in which he is said to have " sat at meat," he ever took flesh-meat. (Matth. ix. 10; xxvi. 6. Mark ii. 15; xiv. 3. Luke v. 29; vi. 36; x. 38; xiv. 1. John xii. 36.)

* Some monks, however, appear to have totally refrained from eating even fish. The Pythagoreans held that the use of fish was equally unlawful with that of flesh. These were most austere monks, who fasted for the incredible period of forty successive days and nights, precisely like Jesus. Some of the most rigid Persian and Syrian monks also seem to have held it unlawful to eat even fish. For Sozomen, (lib. vi. c. 33.) in describing them, says—Ουτε αρτον, ουτε οψον εσθιουσιν,—they eat neither bread nor fish. If οψον here is not intended to designate fish in particular, still, it must *imply* fish, and mean that these monks did not eat any kind of meat. But although οψον—apparently from the verb οπταω, to roast, or broil—in the early ages of the Greek language, signified almost any thing eaten with bread, yet, Plutarch and his contemporary, Athenæus, assure us that, in their time, it had become exclusively to denote *fish.*

† Οψαριον is the word used here for what Jesus is said to have eaten; but it is clear that it means broiled fish. For, the same writer in ver. 6, 11, uses the word, ιχθυς evidently to denote the fish of which he treats. Where the other Gospel writers use ιχθυς, this writer uses οψαριον. (Comp. John vi. 9, 11, with Matth. xiv. 17, 19; xv. 34, 36. Mark vi. 38, 41, and Luke ix. 13, 16.) To designate fish in the sea, in the net, or in the state they are caught, he employs ιχθυς; but to denote broiled, or baked fish, he very properly employs οψαριον. (Comp. ver. 6, 8, and 11, with 9, 10, and 13, of Chap. xxi.) That he meant fish by both words, is still clearer from the connexion between the matter, in ver. 8, where ιχθυς is used, and ver. 10, where οψαριον occurs.—A net-ful of fish (ιχθυς) having been caught, Jesus is made to say—" Bring of the fish (οψαριον) which ye have *now* caught." (ων επιασατε νυν)

Although the scrutinizing and ascetic Scribes and Pharisees said he was a glutton* and a wine-bibber; accused him of eating with publicans and sinners,—of eating with unwashed hands, and of having disciples who did not fast, like the more strictly monkish disciples of John; yet, they never charged him with being a flesh-eater. Indeed, it is *bread* (αρτος) which is almost invariably mentioned as the food which he and his disciples took, whether by themselves in wildernesses, or in the houses of those who entertained them. (See Matth. xv. 2. Mark iii. 20; vi. 36; vii. 2, 5. Luke xiv. 1, 5, 15. John vi. 5, 23.) In the instances already given, truly, fish was added to bread. When Jesus was hungry, coming from Bethany, although Jerusalem, with its luxuries, was close at hand, yet, like a consistent monk, who subsisted on the spontaneous productions of the forest, he went to look for food on a fig tree, which, however, he cursed, when he saw it had no figs to break his fast. But it will be urged that, in celebrating the passover, he must have eaten flesh-meat. The answer to this is, that the Gospels do not furnish a tittle of evidence that, at this supper, called the Lord's Supper, Jesus tasted anything but bread and wine. In whatever manner, and with whatever food the Jews were accustomed to celebrate the passover, the Gospels do not afford the shadow of a proof that Jesus and his disciples had a lamb for supper on this, or any other occasion. Mark, who gives the fullest and most lucid account of this supper, tells us that, two of the disciples having been sent by Jesus to the city—apparently Jerusalem—to engage a room in an inn, and make "ready the passover," they did so. In the evening, Jesus and the rest of his disciples came thither, and sat, or rather lay down (ανεκειντο) to eat. "And as they did eat, Jesus took bread, and blessed, and brake it, and gave to them, and said, Take, eat; this is my body. And he took the cup, and when he had given thanks, he gave it to them; and they all drank of it. And he said unto them, This is my blood of the new testament, which I shed for many." After they had thus partook of the bread and wine, and "had sung a hymn, they went out into the mount of Olives." (Comp. Matth. xxvi. 17—30. Luke xxii. 7—39, with Mark xiv. 12—26.) Neither in this account, nor in the narrations of the other Evangelists—although they differ materially from one another in their statements—is there a word about eating a lamb, or a kid, or about eating any flesh-meat whatever. If Jesus had a lamb before him at this supper, it is very reasonable to suppose that he would have said something about it, just as he said about the bread and wine,— that he would have said of the lamb instead of the bread—"This is my body." The lamb, in this instance, would have been a much better subject for this supposed metaphor than the bread, especially, if—as Christians contend—the paschal lamb, eaten under the Mosaic economy, was a type of him and his sufferings, and also if John used a proper metaphor when he called him "the Lamb of God." Besides, if theological writers are correct in telling us that Jesus and his disciples did eat a

---

* Φαγος, derived from βαγος, a piece of bread. Jesus's gluttony, therefore, necessarily implied no more than that he did eat bread. Probably, he ate more freely than some of the monks of the age, who were accustomed to abstain from food for several days, and never took much when they broke their fast. Hence, the charge of the Pharisees who expected to see monkery, in its perfection, exhibited by Jesus.

lamb at what they call "the Last Supper," and that this supper was instituted for a eucharistic purpose, and intended to be of a sacrificial character, representing the sacrifice offered by Jesus on the cross,* it is

* See Dr. Johnson's *Unbloody Sacrifice;* Bishop Hoadley's *Plain Account of the Nature and End of the Lord's Supper;* Dr. Cudworth's *Discourse concerning the True Nature of the Lord's Supper;* Bishop Warburton's *Rational Account* of the same; the works of Archbishops Wake and Laud; Bishops Poynet, Bull, and Andrews; Dr. Grabe, Dr. Hickes, and a host of other writers,—all maintaining the idea—with slight differences on minor points—that the eucharist was intended to be of a sacrificial character. Scarcely any subject in Christian theology has caused more numerous and fiercer controversies than "The Lord's Supper." No disinterested and candid person who is able to trace its origin, however, can fail to perceive that it has emanated from a pagan source, as it has already been shown in describing the Christian *love-feasts,* part of which it formed. (Vid. ant. pp. 220—232, 233.) Even in the Epistles attributed to Paul, we have some proof of its pagan origin. He tells the Corinthians that the cup of blessing was the communion of the blood of Christ, and the bread broken the communion of the body of Christ,—that the things which the Gentiles sacrificed were sacrifices to devils; (δαιμονιοις) and to this he adds,—" Ye cannot drink of the cup of the Lord, and the cup of devils: Ye cannot be partakers of the Lord's table, and of the table of devils." (1 Cor. x. 16—21.) There can be nothing clearer than that, at the time this Epistle was written, the heathens, not only worshipped demons, as we have seen, (p. 404,) but, in the worship of these demons, had a communion service, or a love-feast, like the Lord's Supper; and, like the Christians of the time, had cups, from which they drank wine as a religious ceremony, and tables on which—like all ancient worshippers, and like the Christians of that age—they ate portions of the things brought as sacrifices. Had not this been the case, there would be no sense in the contrast made in the passage just cited, in which the writer, evidently and distinctly, implies that the heathens had a feast of the same kind as the Christians, and argues against the absurdity of participating in both these feasts; just as if a religious teacher of the present day were to show the absurdity of any Christian who would commune in a Roman Catholic chapel, and also in a Protestant church. The same comparison further implies that, as the heathens had offerings of flesh-meat, upon parts of which, as already observed, the worshippers always feasted, so likewise had the Christians, who, to this very day, have in their churches *altars,* and call the bread and wine—of which they partake—*the host.* The Eucharist, or the Lord's Supper, being a remnant of a pagan festival, in which there was the flesh of beasts, and even of human beings offered, and, moreover, eaten by the worshippers, there is very little doubt that—as contended for by the divines already enumerated, and by many others—this supper was anciently of a sacrificial character,—a feast of thanksgiving, at which there were flesh, bread, wine, and various other sorts of offerings made. The offerings of the Christians, however, at a comparatively early period, appear to have been principally bread and wine. Accordingly, we find that they brought to their love-feasts great quantities of these articles. But the doctrine of transubstantiation being taught by some very early Christian Fathers, such as Justin Martyr, Tertullian, Cyril, &c., there is reason to believe that, anciently, in these feasts, there were human beings offered, and feasted upon ; and that the Christians, after the fierce persecutions with which they were visited, owing to these sacred love-feasts, invented the doctrine of transubstantiation, in order to suit the predilections of the people of those barbarous ages in which human sacrifices were general. Nor is it to be forgotten that the *early Christians* were repeatedly accused of feasting on human blood and flesh, in their nocturnal assemblies, or *agapæ.* (Vid. ant. p. 226.) To broach the doctrine that the bread and wine, in these feasts, were miraculously turned into real flesh and blood, was very convenient, and still retained in the Christian love-feasts, or the communion of saints, the idea of a eucharistical sacrifice,—even a human sacrifice. Accordingly, we find all the Fathers of Christianity, nay, almost all the Christian writers, up to the time of Protestantism, representing the eucharist as a sacrifice. Nor was this ancient notion, in Britain, abandoned at this important religious epoch. We find it upheld by the writers named at the commencement of this note, who strive to identify it with the Jewish passover, for which, certainly, the Gospels furnish them with some authority. But these productions—which make almost everything Jewish, having not appeared in their

strongly inconsistent of the Christians of the present age not to celebrate the Lord's Supper with a lamb, as well as with bread and wine.   There is,

present state, before the close of the second century of our era, when flesh offerings, among Christians, had fallen into disuse—sadly blunder, when they make Jesus eat the passover without a paschal lamb—the principal feature of this feast.   Besides, there is a great difference between the mode in which the Jews are said to have celebrated the passover, and that in which the Gospel writers describe Jesus and his disciples eating the Lord's Supper.   1. The Jews did eat the passover in a standing posture, with staves in their hands, and shoes on their feet; but Jesus and his disciples lay down to eat the supper, apparently, having neither staves in their hands nor shoes on their feet.   2. The Jews ate the passover with "bitter herbs" made into a kind of sauce called charoseth; but we read of no such herbs eaten by Jesus and his disciples at the supper.   3. The Jews, washed their hands several times while they feasted on the paschal lamb; but we have no account that Jesus and his disciples, contrary to their usual practice, washed even once in eating the supper.   4. The Jews sprinkled the blood of the lamb on the door-posts ; but Jesus and his disciples had no lamb at all, and therefore no blood to sprinkle.   5. The Jews ate salad with the lamb ; but we have no account that Jesus and his adherents did eat either lamb or salad.   6. The Jews drank, at different stages of the ceremony, four cups of wine each ; but we have no account that Jesus and his disciples drank but once each, and that out of the same cup. Indeed, there is scarcely any resemblance between the description given of the Jewish passover, and that of the supper of Jesus and his followers.   The latter is evidently intended to represent the closing ceremony of a love-feast; the origin of which the Gospel writers wished to trace, not to the heathens, but to the Jews.   Accordingly, they make Jesus substitute it for a passover.   That these writers aimed at describing the close of a love-feast—at which both heathens and Christians, by the ceremony of drinking wine from the same goblet, renewed their oath to keep secret the mysteries of their respective religions, and to continue faithful to one another—is further proved by the fact, that all of them make Jesus say that Judas, who, like the rest of the disciples, drank of the cup, would break his oath, by betraying him.   Indeed, the whole tale about this passover, appears to he introduced principally for this purpose. John, (iii, 13, 23.) who only darkly alludes to the Last Supper, tells us that Jesus, with his disciples, was at a previous passover in Jerusalem, but does not inform us that he kept it with only bread and wine.   Paul's words and conduct show that he did not believe that this supper was a passover. (See Acts xviii. 21.   I. Cor. xi. 20—25.)   Christians, however, from the earliest period of their history, in celebrating their paschal feast, distributed a lamb among the initiated. (Mosheim's Eccles. Hist. vol. i. p. 207; and Commentaries on the Affairs of the Christians, vol. ii. sec. 72.)   And amongst the Coptic, the Armenian, and other Christians, the custom prevails even at this day.   Walafridus Strabo, in his *Lives of the Saints*, tells us that, in the Roman Church, a lamb was sacrificed and consecrated at the Eucharist, and its consecrated flesh eaten, by way of reverence to the Lamb of God; and Photius, in his *Nomacanon*, (De Reb. Eccles. c. 18.) informs us that this lamb was sacrificed on the altar with the *body* of Christ; the latter apparently being bread.   In the ancient *Ordo Romanus*, (Casand. in Liturg.) there is a form for the consecration of this lamb.   The Lamb of God, called by Roman Catholic Christians, *Agnus Dei*—which is a cake of wax stamped with the figure of a lamb, supporting the banner of the cross—is of a sacramental character.   Although forbidden to be brought into England, by a statute of Elizabeth, yet, in Roman Catholic countries, it is devoutly carried in religious processions, and, with great solemnity, distributed by the Pope, the Cardinals, and other prelates, to the devotees of their religion, as a sacrament, or rather a charm that will enable its possessor to have abundant faith, and even to expel demons.   The origin of all the ceremonies about this lamb—the paschal supper not excepted—can, however, be clearly traced to heathen rites, much older than Christianity.   In the pagan world, from very remote times, lamb and wine were offerings in ratification of an oath, or an agreement to perform any important engagement.   Hence, Homer, (Il. iii. 245.) in describing the treaty between the Greeks and Trojans, tells us that the heralds carried through the cities two lambs and wine as faithful oath-offerings to the gods ; and Virgil makes one of the sacrifices in ratification of the treaty between Æneas and Latinus to be a young sheep. (Æn. xii. 171.)   A lamb was a very acceptable sacrifice to Æsculapius, Apollo, and several other heathen

however, no proof that Jesus, on this occasion, did eat any flesh-meat. But even if he had eaten such meat, still this would be in perfect harmony

gods. The Jews and the Christians, therefore, in sacrificing a lamb at their paschal feasts, did no more than the heathens were accustomed to do in celebrating *their* religious rites. But we have seen (pp. 322—324.) that, even so late as the commencement of the Christian era, not only lambs, but even human beings were most frequently sacrificed to the heathen gods, and that the flesh of these human beings was eaten in celebrating festivals to these gods. When, therefore, we find such close resemblance, amounting almost to identity, between the Lord's Supper, together with the whole of the Christian *agapæ*, and heathen rites in which the flesh of human beings was feasted upon, we cannot avoid thinking that there was much truth spoken by the witnesses brought against the early Christians to prove that, in their secret *agapæ*, they—like the heathens—*feasted upon human flesh*. (Vid. ant. pp. 228—233.) When we bear in mind that the *agapæ* were secretly held in the night,—that about 96 years before the Christian era, the Roman Senate had passed a law, prohibiting any more human sacrifices, so that henceforth any person detected offering such a sacrifice, even in the Eleusinian, or Bacchanalian mysteries, was punished with death,—that no one was admitted into the *agapæ* but the initiated, who had taken a solemn oath never to divulge any of its practices, on pain of death,—that there were altars in all the ancient Christian churches, upon which Christian priests sacrificed, at least up to the time of Constantine, when the 9th and 10th canon of the council of Nice imposed upon them the penalty of degradation, if they sacrificed any more,—that the sacrament or the Lord's Supper, was deemed a sacrifice of the body of Jesus, and called an awful mystery not to be disclosed to the uninitiated,—that this sacrament, to this very day, is regarded by all theological writers, as a eucharistical sacrifice,—that early Christians were accused and convicted of offering human sacrifices in their *agapæ*, and of feasting on the bodies of infants covered over with dough and flour, when they partook of the Lord's Supper,— that the different sects of early Christians charged one another with this abominable practice,—and that, in process of time, when probably it became too dangerous any longer to offer such sacrifices in the *agapæ*, the doctrine of transubstantiation was invented, with the view of persuading the members of the secret *agapæ* that the bread and wine, which now alone were permitted to be offered, were really human flesh and blood, namely the flesh and blood of Christ;—when, we say, these facts are borne in mind, it is impossible to avoid the conclusion that *the charges brought against the early Christians of feasting on the flesh of infants, were founded in truth.* On no other ground can the strange fancy of ancient Christians be accounted for, that they feasted on the real flesh and blood of Jesus, when partaking only of bread and wine. On no other ground can the invention of the outrageous doctrine of transubstantiation, or even the necessity for such an invention, be rationally supposed. For this, like all other inventions must have had an adequate cause and a purpose. But when the facts just enumerated are once admitted, then, the cause that the celebration of the love-feasts was called a *tremendous mystery*,—that there were solemn oaths taken not to divulge what took place on the occasion,—that there were altars in churches,—that all Christians regarded the Eucharist as a sacrifice, and a thousand other things connected with the *agapæ*, become clear as meridian day. Then, the words which, in the Gospel, are attributed to Jesus, even as a monk, become full of meaning :—" Except ye eat the flesh of the Son of man, and drink his blood, ye have no life in you." But it may be asked what proof exists that the heathens ever did sacrifice infants to their gods, so as to cause the same practice to be adopted by the early Christians ? To this the answer is, that, long before the Christian era, this abominable practice was almost universal. In proof of this fact, the following extracts from the Encyclopædia Britannica, under the word *Sacrifice*, which are of undoubted authority, and cannot be supposed to have been written with a view to undermine the Christian religion, will be more satisfactory and intelligible to the general reader than citations from Greek and Latin authors—the original sources from which they are drawn.—" Among the nations of Canaan, the victims were peculiarly chosen. Their own children, and whatever was nearest and dearest to them, were deemed the most worthy offering to their god. The Carthaginians, who were a colony from Tyre, carried with them the religion of their mother-country, and instituted the same worship in the parts where they settled. It consisted in the adoration of several deities, but particularly of Kronus; to whom they

with the practice of the monkish fraternity who, in the celebration of
religious rites, did eat flesh-meat and drink wine; from both of which
they abstained at all other times.   The Indian monks, who abstained
from flesh-meat, and would not kill any thing which had life, would,
nevertheless, kill animals for religious sacrifices, and eat their flesh, as a
religious rite, or sacrament.*   In like manner did the Christian monks

offered human sacrifices, and especially the blood of children.   If the parents were not
at hand to make an immediate offer, the magistrates did not fail to make choice of
what was most fair and promising, that the god might not be defrauded of his dues.
Upon a check being received in Sicily, and other alarming circumstances happening,
Hamilcar, without any hesitation, laid hold of a boy, and offered him, on the spot, to
Kronus ; and at the same time drowned a number of priests, to appease the deity of
the sea.   The Carthaginians another time, upon a great defeat of their army by
Agathocles, imputed their miscarriages to the anger of this god, whose services had been
neglected.   Touched with this, and seeing the enemy at their gates, they seized at once
300 children of the prime nobility, and offered them in public for a sacrifice.   Three
hundred more being persons who were somehow obnoxious, yielded themselves voluntarily, and were put to death with the others.   The neglect of which they accused
themselves, consisted in sacrificing children purchased of parents among the poorer
sort, who reared them for that purpose, and not seelecting the most promising, and the
most honourable, as had been the custom of old.   In short, there were particular
children brought up for the altar, as sheep are fattened for the shambles ; and they were
bought and butchered in the same manner.   But this indiscriminate way of proceeding
was thought to have given offence.   It is remarkable that the Egyptians looked out for
the most specious and handsome person to be sacrificed.   The Albanians pitched upon
the best man of the community, and made him pay for the wickedness of the rest.   The
Carthaginians chose what they thought the most excellent, and at the same time the
most dear to them ; which made the lot fall heavily upon their children.   This is taken
notice of by Silius Italicus in his fourth book. . . . .   Besides these undeter-
mined times of bloodshed, they had particular and prescribed seasons every year, when
children were chosen out of the most noble and reputable families, as before mentioned.
If a person had an only child, it was the more liable to be put to death, as being
esteemed more acceptable to the deiety, and more efficacious for the general good.
. . . .   Those cruel rites, practiced in so many nations, made Plutarch debate
with himself—" Whether it would not have been better for the Galatæ, or the Scythians,
to have had no tradition or conception of any superior beings, than to have formed to
themselves notions of gods who delighted in the blood of men ; of gods who esteemed
human victims the most acceptable and perfect sacrifice." . . . . .   Even those
who were childless would not be exempt from this cursed tribute ; but purchased
children at a price of the poorer sort, and put them to death with as little remorse as one
would kill a lamb or a chicken.   The mother, who sacrificed her child, stood by, without any seeming sense of what she was losing, and without uttering a groan.   If a sigh
did by chance escape, she lost all the honour which she proposed to herself in the
offering, and the child was notwithstanding slain."   These instances are ample to show
how general infant sacrifices were in the heathen world, long before the Christian era,
so as to furnish early Christians with abundant precedent of this horrible practice.
That the heathen worshippers did eat of such sacrifices at their festivals, has already
been shown.—See p. 324.

    * In regulating the conduct of the highest order, but one, of the Brachmin monks,
called the " twice born men," the Laws of Menu, which we have seen to be one of the
oldest literary productions extant, decree, inter alia, with regard to the eating of flesh-
meat, thus.—" He who eats the flesh of any animal, is called the eater of the animal
itself ; and a fish-eater is an eater of all flesh ; from fish, therefore, he must diligently
abstain ; yet the two fish called pat' hina and rohita may be eaten by the guests, when
offered in repast in honour of the gods, or the manes; and so may the rajiva, the sin-
halunda, and the sasalaca of every species. . . . .   The twice-born man who has intentionally eaten a mushroom, the flesh of a tame hog, or a town cock, a leek, or an onion,
or garlick, is degraded immediately ; but having undesignedly tasted of either of these

eat sacrificial flesh-meat. Even to this very day, the Eastern monks participate of the paschal lamb. Most of the ancient monastic rules allowed flesh-eating at religious rites and festivals. All monkish writers deem what was eaten as a sacrament at the Lord's Supper, to be the flesh of Jesus, and a sacrifice ; thus implying that, anciently, there was such flesh

six things, he must perform the penance, *santapana*, or the *chandrayana*, which *anchorites practise*; for other things, he must fast a whole day. . . . . In the *primeval sacrifices* by holy men, and in oblations by the priestly and military tribes, the flesh of such beasts and birds as may be legally eaten, was *presented to the deities.* . . . . No sin is committed by him, who, *having honoured the deities and the manes,* eats flesh-meat, which he has bought, or which he has himself acquired, or which has been given him by another. Let no twice-born man, who knows the law, and is not in urgent distress, *eat flesh without observing this rule.* . . . . The sin of him who kills deer for gain, is not so heinous, with respect to the punishment in another life, as that of him who *eats flesh-meat in vain; or not previously offered as a sacrifice* : but the man who, *engaged in holy rites* according to law, refuses to eat it, shall sink in another world, for twenty-one births, to the state of a beast. Never let a priest eat the flesh of cattle unhallowed with *mantras,* but let him eat it, observing the primeval rule, when it *has been hallowed* with those texts of the *Veda.* Should he have an earnest desire to taste flesh-meat, he may gratify his fancy by forming the image of some beast with clarified butter thickened, or he may form it with dough; but never let him indulge a wish to kill any beast in vain. . . . . . On a solemn *offering* to a guest, at a *sacrifice,* and in holy rites to the manes or the gods, but on those occasions only, may cattle be slain : this law MENU enacted. . . . . . Let no twice-born man, whose mind is improved by learning, hurt animals without the sanction of Scripture, even though in pressing distress, whether he live in his own house, or in that of his preceptor, or *in a forest.* . . . . . Flesh-meat cannot be procured without injury to animals, and the slaughter of animals obstructs the path of beatitude ; from flesh-meat, therefore, let man abstain. . . . . . In *lawfully* tasting meat, in drinking fermented liquor, in caressing women, there is no turpitude ; for to such enjoyments men are naturally prone : but *a virtuous abstinence* from them produces a signal compensation.''—*Sir William Jones's Works—Translation of the Laws of Menu,* vol. iii. pp. 202—208. No one can fail to perceive the identity of the doctrine regarding flesh-meat, taught in these laws, with that taught by the Christian monks. Nor can any one fail to see that these pagan monks considered it lawful to eat flesh-meat sacrificed, or offered to the gods ; that is, eat it as a religious act, or as a sacrament. We are expressly told that no sin was committed by the man who, after he had sacrificed to the gods, did eat flesh-meat ; that is, after such flesh-meat had been offered to the gods. But we are assured that no monk or "twice born man," without observing this law, should, at all, eat flesh-meat. Indeed, there is abundant evidence that all pagan nations, about the close of their devotions, feasted on portions of the carcases of the animals offered to their gods. The Greeks and Romans did so ; of which there are a thousand proofs. Nor can any one who will read the Bible, fail to have ample evidence that the Jews, in like manner, feasted on part of the beast sacrificed. For example, the offering called the paschal lamb was thus feasted upon. Godwin, in his *Moses and Aaron,* maintains that the Christian *agapæ* were derived from the Jewish feasts *upon* the sacrifices ; and Dr. Jennings, who, in his *Jewish Antiquities,* (Book iii. chap. 2.) cites him, says that, in imitation of either the "Jewish or Gentile love-feasts, or probably of both, the primitive Christians, in each particular church, had likewise their love-feasts.'' He also adds that, "as the *agapæ* had been commonly annexed to their sacrifices, so they were now annexed to the commemoration of the sacrifice of Christ '' It is something, certainly, for the Doctor, thus far, indirectly to admit this truth. But why not openly state what he evidently believes; namely that the *Eucharist,* or the Lord's Supper, is of a pagan origin ? As already observed, Christians of every age have maintained that the Lord's Supper is a sacrifice, just as—they say—the paschal lamb, eaten at the end of a feast, was a sacrifice. That the love-feast and the celebration of the Lord's Supper was the same, among early Christians, or that the latter was part of the former, is proved by a great number of facts, some of which have already been stated. Here, it may be added, as another proof of their identity, that both ended in the same manner ; namely, with

LL

sacrificed and eaten at this Supper. (Vid. Tertul. lib. de Orat. c. 4. Cyprian. Ep. 59. *et alia.*)   If, therefore, we suppose that, at his last supper, Jesus had a lamb—of which, however, there is no evidence in the Gospels—and that he did eat of it, still, this would be no more than any other monk, either pagan or Christian, would have done, as a religious ceremony; and would be in perfect harmony with what he told his hearers,—that unless sacramentally, but literally, they did eat the flesh of the Son of man, and drink his blood, they would have no life.   But we have no evidence, that, on any occasion whatever, he even tasted such flesh-meat as that from which monks abstained.

In his habiliment, also, Jesus appears to have been much of the monk.   Although he may not always have gone about in a state of nudity, like the Indian Gymnosophists, yet, from the *original* meaning of the word that denotes the seamless coat,* woven from top to bottom, (John xix. 23.) which he wore; namely the word χιτων, which signifies a coat of mail—anciently made of cords closely platted together, and sometimes of the skins of animals, covered with shells—it would seem that his garb bore some resemblance, at least in roughness, to that of the Boodhist monks, who were clad in the rugged platted fibres of the palm-tree leaves.   Such a coat he enjoins his apostles to wear, prohibiting them to have more than one even of this rugged sort, which consequently they must have worn till it fell from them in pieces, like other monks, both Christian and pagan. (Matth. x. 10.)   Accordingly, in praising John the Baptist, who was attired in hair-cloth, he disapproves of "soft raiment;" (Matth. xi. 8.) and on another occasion inveighs against long robes, which were never worn by ancient monks. (Mark vii. 38.)   St. Chrysostom, (Homily 68, on Matth.) in praising the monks of the fourth century, says,—"The garb of these men is worthy of them.   Unlike the attire of those persons who trail their robes along the streets, they resemble the blessed angels, Elijah, Elisha, John, and the Apostles:—some are clad in goat's hair, some in camel's hair, and some in old and tattered skins."   Like both pagan and Christian monks, likewise, Jesus appears to have travelled about bare-foot; for when Mary suddenly poured a box of ointment upon his feet, they appear to have been naked. (John xii. 3.) So were the feet of his disciples, when, unexpectedly, he began to wash

---

kissing.—"The deacon cried with a loud voice,—Mutually embrace and kiss each other!" which was done. (Encyclop. Brit. v. *Eucharist.*)   This is the manner in which these rites were concluded in the fifth, sixth, and following centuries,—a manner which cannot fail to remind us of the truth of the charge brought against the more savage Christians of the preceding ages; namely, that, at the close of the love-feast, the lights were suddenly extinguished, and not only sexual obscenities engaged in, but incestuous commerce of brothers and sisters, sons and mothers. (Vid. ant. pp. 226—229. et 2 Cor. xiii. 12.   2 Pet. v. 14.)

* According to Josephus, (Antiq. lib. iii. c. vii. s. 4.) the Jewish high priest wore a garment woven throughout, which had no seam.   It is curious to observe that the name for this garment is מעיל (*mail,*—from which, possibly, the English word *mail,* in coat of *mail,* has descended) and that the goat, particularly the *Ibex,* which abounded in the rocky mountains of Palestine, is called by a name precisely of the same root and meaning—עיל.   When, in addition to this, we recollect that the Jews made offerings of vast quantities of goat's hair, and that the Jewish women spun it for religious purposes, (Vid. ant. p. 458.) it seems more than probable that the garment of the high priest was originally identical with the hairy garb of pagan monks.

them. (John xiii.) In sending them to preach, he expressly told them not to wear shoes. (Matth. x. 10.) Precisely in the same state, as we have seen, the Indian monks roved about; and also the Christian monks. Gregory Nazianzen (Orat. 12.) regards " dirty and tangled hair, *naked feet, in imitation of the Apostles*," and " a scanty mantle," as some of the principal characteristics of a monk. But the Gospels furnish some evidence that Jesus and his followers, like the Indian monks, sometimes went about perfectly naked. Of course, after his resurrection, Jesus must have travelled from place to place in a state of nudity; for he had been stripped of all his clothing by his crucifiers; (Matth. xxviii. 35.) and he left in the cave the "linen clothes " in which Joseph of Arimathea had wrapped his body. (John xx. 5—7.) He must, therefore, have come out of the grave in a state of perfect nudity, and have remained in this state till his ascension to heaven. To suppose otherwise is to suppose either that some of his disciples, to whom *only* he is said to have appeared, provided him with apparel, some time after his resurrection, or that, by a miracle, he clad himself. It is difficult even to *imagine* any other way in which he could be clad. But the Gospels—which, Christians tell us, are the only reliable authority for all things concerning him—do not warrant either supposition,—they rather discountenance each. It is, therefore, impossible to evade the conclusion that Jesus went about naked, from the time of his resurrection to that of his ascension to heaven. But even supposing that he was clothed at all, then the question arises,—what became of his clothes after his ascension? Did he take them with him, entering heaven—which is said to be a spiritual world—clad in them? We are told that, when Elijah ascended bodily into heaven, he left his hairy and monkish mantle (Vid. ant. p. 457.)—the only clothing which, apparently, he wore—to his disciple Elisha. But the mantle of Jesus is said to have fallen on nobody, not even upon Peter or John. Certainly, if Jesus after his resurrection wore any clothing, the Gospel writers would be so careful in telling us what became of it, at his ascension, as they are to tell us how his habiliment was disposed of at his crucifixion. Instead of this, we find them occasionally mentioning the state of nudity to which Jesus's followers were accustomed. Even after Jesus's resurrection, we are told that Peter was naked. A miraculous draught of fishes having been caught, this illustrious apostle, on being told that Jesus had appeared, and had wrought the piscatory miracle, " girt his fisher's coat unto him (for he was naked) and did cast himself into the sea." (John xxi. 7.) Notwithstanding all that Christians have written about επενδυτης, rendered in the English version a " fisher's coat," there is no reason to believe that it was anything more than a loose wrapper or hyke—an almost square piece of material, which, in ancient times, many of the Orientals, particularly monks, used, both for their only garment in the day, and for their bed and covering at night. Now, we are expressly told that Peter, before he wrapped himself in this hyke, was naked.* There is casual mention

* It is to no purpose that Christian writers, endeavour to persuade us that the Greek word γυμνος, the Hebrew word, ערם, and the Latin word nudus, where we meet with them in ancient writings, do not always mean stark naked, and that a person divested only of his upper garment, or of his armour, in Eastern language, is styled *naked*. It is true that, when a person puts off his armour, he is figuratively said to be naked, as it

made of another *naked* follower of Jesus.   Mark (xiv. 51, 52.) tells us that, at the time Jesus was apprehended, "there followed him a certain young man, having a linen cloth cast about his naked body; and the young men laid hold on him: and he left the linen cloth and fled from them naked." The *young men* mentioned here are, evidently, the Roman soldiers who had come to apprehend Jesus.   But had not the rest of the followers, or at least disciples of Jesus—all of whom, at the sight of the Roman soldiers, had now fled—been likewise naked, it is most improbable that these soldiers would have taken the naked young man for one of his disciples, and laid hold of him.   In this act, there is a strong presumptive proof that all his followers were naked.   At all events, the description given of this young man, who is said to have had a piece of cloth about his naked person, and the picture drawn of the Indian monks, or Gymnosophists,

regards armour; but when a person whose clothing is only a wrapper, throws that away, he is at once divested of both "upper" and "lower" garment, and is literally naked. It is contended that, although David is said to have danced *naked* in the presence of all Israel, yet, that he was not perfectly naked; because it is said he was girded with a linen ephod. (2 Sam. vi. 14, 20.)   But this ephod was only a kind of an ornament placed on the king's chest, while he shamelessly exposed the rest of his naked body, as Michal ironically told him.   In like manner, the same class of writers urge that Saul, when he prophesied, was not *perfectly* naked; although it is said that "he stripped off his clothes" and "lay down naked all that day." (1 Sam. xix. 24.)   It is, however, unfortunate for these writers that it is the same word, עֹרֹם (orm) which denotes the nakedness of Saul, and also that of Adam and Eve. (Gen. ii. 25. iii. 7.)   It is, likewise, remarkable that the word עֹרֹם, (orm) which is found in the Chaldee, as well as in the Hebrew, appears to be the root of the Greek word, $ερημος$, and the English, *hermit*; (Junius, Etymol. Anglican.) thus connecting the idea involved in it with the naked state of the ancient heathen monks.   These naked hermits, such as the Gymnosophists, being considered the fountain of all wisdom and knowledge, the same word is used to denote *wisdom, prudence, wit, understanding,* &c. (Gen. iii. 1. Sam. xxiii. 22. Prov. i. 4; viii. 5, 12; xii. 16, 23. *et al.*)   In a similar sense is the word $γυμνος$, (*naked*) in its several forms, frequently used to denote mental activity; but still more frequently to denote bodily exercise, such as the monkish fraternity performed naked; just as the champions in the Grecian games performed *their* exploits naked, in reference to both of whom the term $γυμνος$ and its derivatives are used; thereby showing that, as these champions performed their Gymnastics naked, so did the monks perform *their* ascetic exercise in a state of nudity, even before the Canonical Epistles were written.   Paul (1 Tim. iv. 7, 8.) says that bodily exercise ($σωματικη$ $γυμνασια$) profiteth little, and enjoins Timothy to exercise ($γυμναζε$) himself unto godliness.   Still, in telling us of the hardships which he underwent, he enumerates all the monkish severities, as practised by him, saying that he was "in weariness and painfulness, in watching often, in hunger and thirst, in fasting often, in cold and nakedness"—$γυμνοτητι$. (2 Cor. xi. 27.)   In another place, (1. Cor. iv. 11.) he says of himself and other ascetics, who should, as he thinks, be stewards of the *mysteries*,—"We both hunger and thirst, and are naked, ($γυμνητευομεν$.) and are buffeted, and have no certain dwelling-place,"—a very graphic description of the monkish life.   Again: after picturing the lives of those early anchorites, who, clad in the skins of sheep and goats, wandered in mountains and deserts, and inhabited dens and caves; and after dwelling on the doctrine of bodily chastisement, he adds that, although no chastening for the time being was pleasant, yet, afterwards it yielded the fruit of righteousness unto them which *are exercised* ($γεγυμνασμενοις$) thereby. (Heb. xii. 11.)   In another part of the same Epistle, (v. 14.) he says that strong food is proper only to those who, by practice, have their organs of sense "exercised ($γεγυμνασμενα$) to discern both good and evil."   Thus, we see that, among the ancient monks, the practice of performing their ascetic feats in a state of nudity was so general, that the word, *naked,* ($γυμνος$) in its various forms; even at the time the Canonical Epistles were written, had become, among Christians, as well as pagans, to denote the *exercises* of these naked monks; and, in a secondary sense, even mental exercise, especially of a religious character.

who went about with only a piece of cloth about their loins, bear a striking resemblance ; and all the facts we have been able to gather touching
the apparel of Jesus and of his apostles, furnish strong presumptive
evidence that, on this point, they closely imitated the pagan monks of that
age. Indeed, so thorough a monk was Jesus, in habiliment, in the working of wonders, in the life he led, and in the religious notions he advanced,
that he was thought to be either John the Baptist or Elias,—characters
well known to have been decided anchorites, clad in a hairy garb—when
clad at all—and living in deserts and caves. When Herod had been told:
what sort of a person Jesus was, " he was perplexed, because it was said
of some that John was risen from the dead ; and of some, that Elias had
appeared ; and of others, that one of the old prophets was risen again."
Herod, apparently, having heard more about Jesus, at length concluded—
" It is John whom I beheaded." (Comp. Matth. xiv. 1. Mark vi. 14—16,
with Luke ix. 7, 8.) In like manner, when Jesus asked his disciples
who people said that he was, they replied,—" Some say that thou art
John the Baptist ; some, Elias ; and others, Jeremias,* or one of the
prophets." (Matth. xvi. 14.) But if there had not been a striking similarity, between Jesus and these monkish men, in every point of view,
according to the notions entertained of them, he would never have been
thought to be either of them.

It is, however, in the religious notions which he taught that Jesus
perfectly identifies himself with the Pagan and Jewish monks. But the
notice taken here of this identity must be much shorter than the subject
really deserves. No doctrine was delivered by Jesus with greater emphasis, and inculcated more frequently than that if a man wished to
become religious and attain to the summit of beatitude in the world to
come, he should part with all his property and become poor, as to worldly
goods. The same doctrine was taught by the Indian monks. The Laws
of Menu, on this point, were very strict in their enactments, decreeing
that, when a man became an anchorite of the first order, he was, at the
onset, to make a " gift of all his wealth." This wealth he was to give
" to Brachmins detached from the world and learned in Scripture." †
(Laws of Menu, xi. 6.) Precisely the same doctrine Jesus taught, when

---

* It should be observed that Jeremiah participated quite as much as Elijah in the
monkish character. On close examination of the Hebrew version of the writings which
bear his name, it will be seen that he wore a wooden collar about his neck,—that he
burdened his body with chains, and that he refrained from women and wine. (Jer. xvi.
2 ; xxviii. 10—13 ; xxxv. Lam. iii. 7, 27—30.) Similar things may be said of
Isaiah, who put away the hair-cloth which he wore about his loins, as the only clothing,
and, like an Indian monk, walked about the country " naked and bare-foot three years,"
preaching his doctrines ; (Is. xx. 2.) and also of the other Jewish prophets, who were
equally monkish. Well may his fellow countrymen, therefore, have thought that Jesus
resembled the ancient prophets, as closely as he did resemble John the Baptist.

† In order that it may be seen to what perfection the system of monkery had been
brought among the Hindoos at an infinitely remote period, and how identical it was
with the monkery of the earliest Christians, even Jesus himself not excepted, the
following additional extracts are given from the Laws of Menu. They are amongst
those enactments which were designed to regulate the highest order of anchorites,
called the Sannyasis, who have already been described, and who are said, in these laws,
to exercise themselves in holiness, so as to " shake off *sin* here below, and reach the

he told the young man who had observed all the ordinary rules of morality, that, if he wished to attain to the summit of perfection, he must

Most High." This class left the monasteries, and fixed their abode in the forest, in order to undergo the utmost austerity of life. When they advanced from an inferior grade of holy orders into the highest of all, they were expected to act thus :—"Let the twice-born man, who has completed his studentship, dwell in a forest ; his faith being firm and his organs duly subdued." . . . . When the father of a family perceives his muscles become flaccid, and his hair gray, and sees the child of his child, let him seek refuge in a forest. Abandoning all food eaten in towns, and all his household utensils, let him repair to the lonely wood, committing the care of his wife to her sons, or accompanied by her, *if she choose to attend him.* Let him take up his consecrated fire, and all his domestic implements of making oblations to it ; and, departing from the town to the forest, let him dwell in it with complete power over his *organs of sense and action.* With many sorts of pure food, such as holy sages used to eat, with green herbs, roots, and fruit, let him perform the five great *sacraments* before mentioned, introducing them with due ceremonies. Let him wear a black antelope's hide, or a vesture of bark ; let him bathe evening and morning ; let him suffer the hair of his head, his beard, and his nails to grow continually. . . . . Let him, as the law directs, make oblations on the hearth with three sacred fires. . . . . He may constantly live on flowers and roots, and on fruit matured by time, which has fallen spontaneously, strictly observing the laws ordained for hermits. Let him slide backwards and forwards on the ground, or let him stand a whole day on tiptoe ; or let him continue in motion, rising and sitting alternately. . . . . . Enduring harsher and harsher mortifications, let him dry up his bodily frame. . . . . . . Not solicitous for the means of gratification, chaste as a student, sleeping on the bare earth, in the haunts of pious ;hermits, without one selfish affection, dwelling at the roots of trees. From devout Brachmins let him receive alms to support life, or from other housekeepers of twice-born classes, who dwell in the forest. Or the hermit may bring food from a town. . . . . For the purpose of uniting his soul with the *Divine Spirit,* let him study the various *upanishads,* or scripture, or chapters on *the essence and attributes of God,* which have been studied with reverence by anchorites versed in theology, and by housekeepers who dwelt afterwards in forests, for the sake of increasing their sublime knowledge and devotion, and for the *purification of their bodies.* . . . . . A Brachmin, having shuffled off his body by any of those modes which great sages practiced, and becoming void of sorrow and fear, *rises to exaltation in the Divine Essence.* Having thus performed religious acts in a forest during a third portion of his life, let him become a *Sannyasi* for the fourth portion of it, abandoning all sensual affections, and wholly reposing on the *Supreme Spirit.* . . . . Having performed the sacrifice of PRAJAPETI, accompanied with a gift of *all his wealth,* and having reposited in his mind the sacrificial fires, a Brachmin may proceed *from his house,* that is, from the second order, or he may proceed even from the first, to the condition of a Sannyasi. . . . . . Let him drink water purified by straining with a cloth, *lest he hurt some insect.* . . . . His hair, nails, and beard being clipped, bearing with him a dish, a staff, and a water-pot, his whole mind *being fixed on God,* let him *wander about continually,* without giving pain to animal or vegetable beings. . . . . . Only once a day let him demand food; let him not habituate himself to eat much at a time; for an anchorite habituated to eat much becomes inclined to sensual gratifications. . . . . By eating little, and by sitting in solitary places, let him restrain those organs, which are naturally hurried away by sensual desires. By the coercion of his members, by the absence of hate and affection, and by giving no pain to sentient rceatures, *he becomes fit for immortality.* . . . . By injuring nothing animated, by subduing all sensual appetites, by devout rites ordained in the *Veda,* and by *rigorous mortifications,* men attain, *even in this life, the state of beatitude.* . . . . . . Thus, having gradually abandoned all earthly attachments, and indifferent to all pairs of opposite things, as *honour and dishonour, and the like,* he remains absorbed in the *Divine Essence.* All that has now been declared is obtained by pious meditation ; but no man who is ignorant of the Supreme Spirit, can gather the fruit of mere ceremonial acts. . . . . The Brachmin who becomes a Sannyasi by this discipline, announced n due order, *shakes off sin here below,* and reaches the MOST HIGH."—*Laws of Menu,—Sir Wm. Jones's Works,* vol. iii. pp. 225—237. The foregoing extracts, which are only

sell all that he had ; give the produce to the poor, and follow him. This young man having turned away sorrowfully, Jesus expatiated on the same doctrine, telling his followers that, unless a man parted with all his wealth, he could not enter the kingdom of heaven ; and that, if a man forsook riches, such as houses, and land, for his sake, his happiness was thereby insured. (Matth. xix. 16—30.   Mark x. 17—31.   Luke xii. 13—48 ; xviii. 18—30.)   Accordingly, he exclaimed—" Blessed be ye poor ! (Luke vi. 20.)—" Lay up for yourselves treasures in heaven,"—" Take therefore no thought for the morrow,"—" Seek ye first the kingdom of God," and so on. (Matth. v. 12—34.)   These expressions, and a thousand others, said in the Gospels to have been uttered by Jesus, directly teach the doctrine of the community of goods, which we have seen to have been in practice among Jesus's apostles, just as it had been among the pagan monks. Indeed, there is nothing clearer from the Gospels than that—like the Brachmin monks—he taught that it was the imperative duty of a person, when he became a Christian, to hand over all his property to the leaders of the Christian religion.   His principal precepts, on this point, were such as—" Sell that ye have and give alms,"—" Whosoever be of you that forsaketh not all that he hath, he cannot be my disciple," and so on. (Luke xii. 33 ; xiv. 33.)   Hence, we see that a person could no more be a disciple of Jesus, without selling all his property, and give the proceeds towards the maintenance of his poor brethren in the faith, than he could be a Brachmin monk, an Essene, or an inmate of a Christian monastery in the fifth or sixth century.

In connexion with the doctrine of communism, Jesus, like the heathen monks, taught religious beggary.   The Laws of Menu, in reference to the first order of monks, or monachal pupils, *inter alia*, decree thus :— " Each day must a Brachmin student receive his food by begging, with due care, from the houses of persons renowned for discharging their duties. . . . . . Let him go begging through the whole district round the villages, keeping his organs in subjection, and remaining silent ; but let him turn away from such as have committed any deadly sin. . . . . . Let a student persist constantly in such begging, but let him not eat the food of one person only : the subsistence of a student by begging is held equal to fasting, in religious merit. . . . . . Yet, when he is asked on a solemn act, in honour of the gods or the manes, he may eat at his pleasure the food of a single person ; observing, however, the laws of abstinence, and the austerity of an anchorite : thus the rule of his order is kept inviolable." (Laws of Menu, ii. 183—189.)   In the extracts cited in the last note we have seen that a Sannyasi, or a monk of the highest order, was, in like manner, allowed to beg food, although only once the same day.   To this, the law adds—" At the time when the smoke of kitchen fires has ceased, when the pestle lies motionless, when the burning charcoal is extinguished, when people have eaten, and when dishes are removed, that is, late in the day, let the Sannyasi *always beg food.*   For missing it, let him not be sorrowful ; nor for gaining it, let him be glad." Precisely the same doctrine of mendicancy Jesus continually preaches

a small sample of the contents of these laws regarding monachism, will serve to show the identity of Jesus's religious notions with those of the Indian monks, on points to be hereafter advanced.

to his disciples and others.   Exhortations either to give or to beg pervade all his discourses; such as—"He that receiveth you receiveth me, and he that receiveth me receiveth him that sent me.   He that receiveth a prophet in the name of a prophet shall receive a prophet's reward."—"Whosoever shall give you a cup of water to drink in my name, because ye belong to Christ, verily I say unto you he shall not lose his reward,"—"I was an hungred, and ye gave me no meat; I was thirsty, and ye gave me no drink; I was a stranger and ye took me not in; naked and ye clothed me not."—"Inasmuch as ye did it not to one of the least of these, ye did it not to me." (Matth. x. 40—42; xxv. 35—45.   Mark ix. 41.)   The charge, which Jesus delivered on two occasions to his apostles, when he sent them to preach to the cities of Israel—in which they could not, as in the desert, live on the natural productions of the forest—indisputably shows that he intended they should subsist by begging.   When he first sent out twelve of them, he charged them to have neither bread, nor gold, nor silver, nor brass, nor wallet, nor shoes.   And the reason he gives for this injunction is,—"the workman is worthy of his meat;" clearly showing that he intended them to live upon what people would bestow upon them. (Matth. x. 5—15.   Mark iii. 7—13.)   When, afterwards, he sent out seventy apostles, he delivered to them the same charge, with slight variations, emphatically telling them, that they were to take with them none of the means of subsistence, and were therefore to live upon what they could obtain from others. (Luke x. 1—5.)   Indeed, the whole of his charge to his apostles, before he sent them to cities and villages to preach and work wonders, is throughout remarkable for its heathen monkery; and thus furnishes more positive evidence than any other as to the origin of his religious notions.   According to this charge, his apostles, as already noticed, like the heathen monks, were to travel about nearly naked—without shoes or stockings—and were to salute the people who received them with the monkish kiss of charity,—were to heal the sick, and cast out demons. Having received this charge, the apostles appear to have acted up to it, proceeding on their journey without either wallet or purse, and begging their food as they advanced.   The same mendicant life was led by their successors.   For, about the beginning of the fifth century—when strenuous efforts were being made to deter the Christian monks from roving, and to confine them to monasteries—we find the monk-priest, Isidore of Pelusium, inveighing against their begging and roving propensities.   He says that these monks were like the hare, shifting from place to place in search of a rich table.   He further tells them,—"Passing through all the cities of Israel, and all the borders of the land, with such an appetite and such a turn of mind, you will ever be a sort of Euripus, influenced by every wind of kitchen odors."   In writing to Mark, a vagrant monk, he says,—Thou art strolling from house to house, not to obtain knowledge, but from a craving desire for dainty dinners.*—Epist. 41, 173.

---

* What Josephus, already cited, p. 122, says of the monkish Essenes, throws considerable light on Jesus's charge to his apostles.   These monks, who were "despisers of riches," carried nothing at all with them when they travelled into remote parts; though still they took their weapons with them, for fear of thieves.   Hence, Jesus tells his disciples to take nothing with them, except a staff, or rather a crook, and perhaps, a

A truly monkish doctrine inculcated by Jesus was that of deserting father, mother, children, wife, husband, sister and brother, to follow him. That heathens, when they became monks, thus heartlessly deserted their nearest and dearest relatives, is proved by a great number of testimonies found in pagan lore. But as such a desertion must arise from the very nature of monkery, it is unnecessary here to adduce any of these testimonies. It may, however, be observed that the laws of Menu, on this point, were not quite so stringent as the injunctions of Jesus. The former directed that when the father of a family sought refuge in the forest, he might, not only commit the care of his wife to her sons, but might take her with him, if she chose to become a nun and follow his mode of life. A most heart-rending scene was to see Paula—a Roman lady of an illustrious family—entering upon the monachal life in the company of the monk Jerome, leaving her young afflicted family, her brothers, and other relatives, to weep, and cast a longing eye after her, while she sailed from their sight to Cyprus! In harmony with this inhuman monkish custom, Jesus delivers such as the following doctrine:—
" He that loveth father or mother more than me, is not worthy of me; and he that loveth son or daughter more than me, is not worthy of me. And he that taketh not his cross,* and followeth after me, is not worthy of me."—" Every one that hath forsaken houses, or brethren, or sisters, or

sword; for, as already observed, we find that the apostles carried swords. The Essenes were not allowed to have a change of garment, until what they had on fell from them in pieces. Hence, Jesus enjoins his apostles to take with them only one coat each. Some of these Essenes lived in every city; and if any of the sect came from other places, they went to the habitations of such of them as were quite strangers to them, as if they had been ever so long acquainted with them, and made free use of all they had. Hence, Jesus tells his apostles,—" Into whatever city or town ye shall enter, enquire who in it is worthy ; and there abide till ye go thence. And when ye come into an house, salute it,"—that is, give the kiss of charity to each of the inmates. This identity could be persued much further ; but enough has been advanced to show that Jesus's charge is of a thoroughly heathen and monkish character.—See Joseph. de Bell. lib. ii. c. 8.

* *Take his cross.*—Similar expressions occur in Matth. xvi. 24. Mark. viii. 34; x. 21. Luke ix. 23 ; xiv. 27. We are told that what Jesus meant in these passages, by the expression—taking up the cross, &c., was that, if a person wished to become his disciple, he must make up his mind to suffer affliction and persecution; and that he used the word *cross* as a metaphor, on account of the pain which a person being crucified necessarily suffered. There is, however, in these instances, no proof that the word *cross* is used metaphorically ; on the contrary, there are strong reasons for believing that it was not intended to imply the idea of an instrument upon which persons suffered death, and that it anciently signified a very different thing as to purpose, although similar in shape. This cross appears to have been the same as the staff—generally, *in the shape of a cross*—which fanatic monks and others carried as a badge, or part of the insignia of their order, representing courage, power, and authority. The word σταυρος, translated *cross*, in the New Testament, frequently, in profane authors, means no more than a staff, or a stake fixed in the ground. Bishop Pearson, on the Creed, (Arts. 4.) very justly remarks that in this sense the word is employed by the early Greek writers, particularly Homer ; and that it is thus explained by Eustathius and Hesychius. Many instances could be given in which the word is used precisely in the same sense as ραβδος—the word used for the *staff* which Jesus enjoined each of his apostles to take with him on a preaching excursion. Now, the σταυρος used by the Greeks, for the purpose of execution, as Lucian and other writers tell us, consisted of two sticks, the shortest fixed across at the top of the longest, so as to be in shape much like the letter T. The Roman cross was generally of the same form. Accordingly, Barnabas, in his Epistle (c. viii.) tells us that the letter T, in the Greek language, stands for the sign

father, or mother, or wife, or children, or lands, for my name's sake, shall
receive an hundred fold ; and shall inherit everlasting life."—" If any

of the cross of Jesus. The crosier, bishop's staff, or shepherd's crook, as it is called,
which is much more ancient than Christianity, was in early times precisely of the same
shape, having a transverse piece fixed on its top, so as to form a cross, whence—if
not from the Celtic, *croes*—the word *crosier* is derived, while the word *crook* is from the
Latin, *crux*—a cross. The shape of the ancient crosier was very much like that of a
crutch, the name of which is from the Teutonic word *krucke*, meaning a cross. Many
other etymological proofs could be given to show the identity of the cross and the crosier.
But we proceed to give other sorts of proofs, with a view, not only to show that the
cross which Jesus exhorted people to take up, was anciently one and the same with
the crosier—a staff carried as a symbol of courage and power—but that it was carried
as a similar sign by heathens, long before the time of Jesus. First, we give the
following admission from the Encyclopædia Britannica, under the word *crosier*.—"Among
the Greeks, none but the patriarchs had a right to the crosier. The crosiers were at
first no more than simple wooden staves in the form of a T, used *to rest and lean upon*.
By degrees, they were made larger ; and at length arrived to the form we now see them
of." Hence, we see that the researches of this writer have driven him to the conclusion that the *crosier*, in ancient times, was a cross, and in use among heathen nations
before the Christian era. In other words, it was a staff with a transverse piece on its
top, in order that it might be leaned upon. On the head or top of such a staff—
על-ראש המטה—Israel is said to have leaned and worshipped,—*staff* being a much
better translation than *bed*, of the Hebrew word just cited, (Comp. Gen. xlvii. 31. with
Heb. xi. 21.) every form of the root of which implies the idea of a staff of the sort just
described. Such a staff, designated by the same word, Judah carried ; (Gen. xxxviii.
18.) and such a staff was that which Moses carried, (Exod. iv.) although rendered a
rod in the English version. Other instances could be added, showing that staves of
this form, in the Hebrew Scriptures, are regarded as symbols of courage and authority.
In accordance with the practice of carrying such a staff or crosier as this, we find Jesus
repeatedly speaking about taking up the cross and following him ; and that Mark (vi. 8.)
informs us that Jesus told his disciples they were to take nothing with them on their
preaching tour but a staff. Although there is an apparent discrepance between him
and Matthew, (x. 10.) who says they were not to take even a staff, and Luke, (ix. 3.)
who says they were not to take staves ; yet, as the word ραβδος is in the plural in several
copies of Matthew's Gospel, it appears that the real meaning is that the Apostles were
not to take more than one *staff* each ; and therefore, were not to take *staves*. Unlike
some of the heathen ραβδομαντεις, who carried with them several staves for the purpose
of divination, (*Selden*, De Diis Syris, synt. i. c. 2.) they were apparently to take only
one staff each, as a symbol, in imitation of other more respectable heathen religionists,
who shall be noticed anon. The earliest Christian Fathers speak of the cross—the badge
of distinction which they carried and exhibited—as a symbol of some mystic power.
Justin Martyr, in the second century, makes a very curious apology to the heathens for
the use of this symbol. He tells them,—" The cross is the symbol of *Christ's power and
government*, and is visible in almost every thing we see ; for, look at the world, and tell
me whether commerce, or any other thing, is carried on without the representation of
the cross. Without this trophy of ours, you cannot navigate ; for navigation depends
upon sails ; and they are made in the form of a cross. There is neither ploughing, nor
digging, nor any manual labour done without instruments of this figure." After telling
them that even the body of man is in the form of a cross, he adds,—" Your banners
declare the *power of this figure*, and the trophies you use everywhere in your
public processions are *symbols of power* and *dominion*, although, in practice, you
disregard the meaning of this figure." Tertullian and Minucius Felix advance
similar sentiments as to the figure of the cross being a symbol of power, and furnish
ample grounds to infer that, in their time, crosses were carried about, by the leaders
of the Christian faith, as crosiers, and otherwise. But the *sign of the cross*, as
already remarked, (p. 232, 233.) was a symbol in general use among the heathens,
long before the time Jesus is said to have undergone the very common punishment
of crucifixion, and was employed in the worship of Jupiter, Saturn, and Venus ;
while it was in the temple of Serapis, and held in profound veneration by the
Arabians and Indians. Here, we would add that a cross forms part of an ornamental

man come to me, and hate not his father, and mother, and wife, and children, and brethren, and sisters, yea, and his own life also, he cannot

work, in the shape of a pillar, supporting the entrance into a monument lately discovered in the ruins of Pompeii, which was buried in the eruptions of Vesuvius, only about forty years after the time Jesus is said to have been crucified. But this monument had evidently been built long before he was born. (Clarke's Pompeii, vol. ii. p. 272.) On the curious remains of ancient Egyptian idolatory, brought into the British Museum, the figure of the cross is to be seen in the hands of the deities and other personages represented, and in numerous other positions. Osiris not only wears a mitre, but likewise holds in his hand the bishops *crosier*, or staff. We find that the Brachmin monks carried a similar staff, crosier, or cross. The Laws of Menu thus prescribe for its use :— " A priest ought by law to carry a staff of *Bilva* or *palasa*."—"The staff of a priest must be of such a height as to reach his hair." A young monk, having thus provided himself with a legal staff, is directed to go through the ceremony *of begging food according to law*. When he is promoted into the highest order of monkery, he is to enter the forest, as already described, taking with him his earthen waterpot and staff. (Laws of Menu, chap. ii. vi.) Hence, Boodh, as we have seen, (pp. 450, 555.) when he became a mendicant forest anchorite, took a staff ; and hence, many hundreds, if not thousands of years afterwards, Borri, found that the Boodhist monk-priests had gilt *staves*, " not unlike the Christian crosiers." It is trusted that the foregoing facts are sufficient to show, not only the pagan origin of carrying a cross, but likewise the identity of Jesus's command to his apostles to take a staff with them on their preaching excursions, with his frequent declaration that, if any one wished to follow him, he must take up the cross, crux, or crosier. But as it has been said that the cross or crosier, was an emblem of courage and power, the reader may be inclined to ask,—What courage, and what power ? The answer is—Courage to perform all the feats, and undergo all the hardships, austerities, self-mortifications and *self-mutilations* of the monkish fraternity ; and power supernatural to expel demons, and work other miracles, so as to have, not only this world, but even the invisible world under one's control. In allusion to this courage, Jesus says, in places cited at the commencement of this note—" Whosoever will come after me, let him *deny himself*, and take up his cross, and follow me." In another place, he says that if a man come to him, he must, not only hate his nearest and dearest relatives, but " hate his own life also,"—evidently meaning that his followers must have the courage to suffer such persecutions, and to undergo such austerities and mortifications of the flesh as rendered life to them, not only extremely painful, but hateful, which is the very doctrine inculcated by the Indian monks. In connexion with such expressions as these, Jesus generally says—Whosoever will save his life shall lose it, and whosoever will lose it shall save it ; and asks what advantage it would be for a man to gain the world and lose his life. The Indian doctrine of transmigration—which should be perfectly understood, in order to understand Jesus, and of which we shall hereafter give some instances—pervades these expressions, together with much that is said in other parts of the Gospels. Jesus continually speaks of losing life and of having it again in a more perfect and blissful state,—generally in the kingdom of heaven which he was to establish. In like manner is the doctrine of the repeated re-appearance of the Indian gods in the flesh, set forth when Jesus speaks of his second coming, &c. As to the power of which the cross, or crosier, spoken of by him was an emblem, he says that whosoever did not take this cross was not worthy of him,—clearly meaning that such was not worthy of the power which he conferred upon his true followers. Of this power, there is in the Gospels very frequent mention made, in such language as,—He gave them power against unclean spirits, to cast them out, to heal all manner of sickness and disease, and to tread on serpents and scorpions. As many as received him, to them gave he power to become the sons of God. The proof that people had taken up the cross and believed in Jesus was, that they had this power to cast out devils and perform other miracles. (Mark xvi. 17, 18.) When Christianity had become a state religion, and had begun to flourish under the auspices of Constantine the Great, who set up his own statue with a cross or crosier in its right hand, the courage and power conferred by this symbol became generally recognised ; especially, as this heathen—who had, in reality, received both " the sign of the cross " and his new religion from an Egyptian source (Vid. ant. p. 332.)—pretended that, in a holy vision, he had seen " the sign of the cross " in the clouds, accompanied with the inscription—" Conquer by this." Hence-

be my disciple." (Matth. x. 37, 38; xix. 29. Luke xiv. 26. *et al.*)
Precisely, in accordance with this pernicious doctrine, we find that Jesus's
disciples had left their nearest relatives to follow him. For example,
James and John suddenly left their father in a ship to the mercy of the
waves, and became the followers of Jesus. Similar acts of desertion,
attended with violation of the most solemn domestic duties, on the part of
parents, husbands, wives, and children, were almost daily committed during
the first ages of Christianity; nay, are continued to be committed to the
present day, by persons wishing to become monks and nuns. Sulpicius
Severus, (Dial. i.) a great admirer of monkery, tells us, with exultation, of
a high-born young man from Asia, who—when in Egypt engaged in war
as a tribune of the army—was inveigled by the monks, and suddenly left
his wife and child, in order to become an anchorite; which was a most
dastardly conduct. Cassian (Collat. xxi. c. 9, 10.) relates how Theonas
abandoned his wife, and entered a cell in the Egyptian desert. A vast
number of similar cases could be added. So injurious did this practice
of desertion become amongst the Romans—especially after Justinian, in
the sixth century, made a law which sanctioned this gross violation of
domestic duties—that the senate in the following century passed several
measures for its suppression; although they had very little effect.

In his notions of adultery, marriage, and the female sex, Jesus was
peculiarly monkish. It is well known that these were topics which occupied very conspicuous places in the monkish philosophy of both heathens
and Christians. The Laws of Menu were very severe against the crime of
adultery, the punishment for it being death. For, *to look at a woman*, or,
at least, talk with her, at a place of pilgrimage, in a forest, in a grove, or
at the confluence of rivers, was sufficient to incur the guilt of an adulterous
inclination. To have intrigues with a female anchorite, or a guarded
priestess, was also visited with heavy punishment. (chap. viii.) We have
already seen that the Indian monks maintained perfect celibacy, thinking it unnatural and impious to have intercourse with women. We
have also cited passages from Josephus to show that the monkish Essenes
esteemed continence to be a virtue, neglected wedlock, and guarded against
the lascivious behaviour of women, believing " that none of them preserved
their fidelity to one man." Precisely the same notion is inculcated by
Jesus, in his Sermon on the Mount, when he says,—" I say unto you that
whosoever looketh on a woman to lust after her, hath committed adultery
with her already in his heart." The Pharisees—who must have seen many
a fanatic acting upon Jesus's exhortation to abandon his wife and children,
and follow him into deserts and mountains—" came unto him, tempting
him, and saying unto him, Is it lawful for a man to put away his wife *for
every cause?*" Jesus, having made some remarks on the provisions of the

---

forth, this monogram was displayed on every thing belonging to the Roman army, from
the *Labarum* and the imperial robes down to the weapons of the private soldier. (Euseb.
Vit. Const. lib. i. c. 27—31.) The same symbol was to be seen in all the churches; and
" the sign of the cross," made with holy water, and otherwise, on the face and other
parts of the body, was regarded as a charm—a sure presevative from all accidents, and,
particularly, from the machinations of evil spirits. (Petav. Dogmat. Theol. lib. xv.
c. 9, 10.) And thus, we perceive, Christians use the heathen " sign of the cross " to this
very day.

Mosaic Law, replied :—" Whosoever shall put away his wife, except it be for fornication, and shall marry another, committeth adultery : and whoso marrieth her which is put away, doth commit adultery." (Matth. xix. 3—9.) Now, it is clear that Jesus considered that it was the second marriage which constituted the adultery in this case. It is well known how bitterly all monks, both pagan and Christian—even those who tolerated marriage once, in some circumstances—inveighed against second marriages. Athenagoras, (Apol. 33.) after praising absolute celibacy, says that " a second marriage is but decent adultery." Origen, (Hom. in Jer. s. 4.) after commending *useful deceptions*, pronounces a second marriage an impure state. Many passages, in the Epistles of Paul, are to the same effect. The Laws of Menu, (iii. 12.) and other heathen productions, in like manner, discountenance such marriages, not only in the case of a separation of the parties to the first marriage—such as that of which Jesus speaks—but even when one of these parties is dead. Jesus, sharing in the views of all the monks of that age, as well as those of preceding and subsequent ages, with regard to the duty of leading a life of celibacy, or abstinence from sexual intercourse—although he once showed no disapproval of the shameful conduct of a female really caught in an adulterous act, (Vid. ant. pp. 356—358, 377.)—yet, very frequently made a point of speaking against the adultery or debauchery ($\mu o\iota\chi\epsilon\iota a$) of the age—the grand theme of monkery. In his Sermon on the Mount, he dwelt on this subject. When the Jews asked him to favour them with a miracle, (Matth. xii. 39.) he termed them " an adulterous generation ;" and he used the same epithet in speaking of those who were ashamed of him and his words. (Mark viii. 38.)

His disciples, having heard Jesus's explanation of adultery, remarked,—" If the case of the man be so with his wife, it is not good to marry." Jesus, understanding the words of his disciples to mean—as they really do, in the Greek language—that it was a sin in a man to have intercourse with a woman, returned the following answer.—" All men cannot receive this saying, save they to whom it is given. For there are some eunuchs, which were so born from their mother's womb : and there are some eunuchs, which were made eunuchs of men : and there be eunuchs *which have made themselves eunuchs for the kingdom of heaven's sake.* He that is able to receive it, let him receive it." (Matth. xix. 10—12. Vid. ant. pp. 82, 83, 328—330.) There is nothing clearer than that, in this passage, Jesus sanctions the bodily mutilation he names, undergone, as it was, for the pious purpose of leading a life of celibacy. He told his disciples that, although everybody could not carry out what he was going to say, yet, if they could carry it out, they should do so. No other rational construction can be put on the words—" All men cannot receive this saying,"—" He that is able to receive it, let him receive it,"—words which were spoken in immediate connexion with the mentioning of men who made themselves eunuchs for the kingdom of heaven's sake. Jesus's meaning, unquestionably is, that, if his disciples, who had taken up the cross, could summon the courage which that symbol was intended to denote, they were to make themselves eunuchs, in order to be able to lead a life of purity. This, is not, however, the only instance we have of Jesus recommending bodily mutilation. In his Sermon on the

Mount, immediately after saying "that whosoever looketh on a woman to lust after her hath committed adultery with her already in his heart," he adds—by way of prescribing an antidote against this adulterous lust—that if a person's right eye ensnared him, he should pluck it out and cast it away; and if his right hand was the means of ensnaring him, he should cut it off, and cast it from him; because it was better thus to lose one member than to forfeit the whole body. Now, that the pagan as well as Christian monks of all countries and ages taught the same doctrine of self-mutilation, there are ample proofs, some of which have already been given. The following however are added. In Crete, the prophets of Jupiter "were so rigid observers of the rules of chastity, that, like the priests of the mother of the gods at Samos, they dismembered themselves. The hierophantæ at Athens, after their admission, enfeebled themselves by a draught of the juice of hemlock: in short, it was very customary for those that attended on the more sacred and mysterious rites, by using certain herbs and mendicaments, to unman themselves, that they might worship the gods with greater chastity, and purity. They also generally retired from the world, to the end that, being free from business and care, they might have the more leisure to attend to the service of the gods, and wholly devote themselves to piety and the exercise of religion." (See Archbishop Potter, with his authorities,—Antiquities of Greece, vol. i. book ii. chap. 3.) These fanatics were regular monks, who, as our author tells us, abstained from flesh-meat, and so on. The monk-priests of the mother of the gods, or Cybele, just mentioned, were all dismembered, although, in the celebration of the mysteries of the goddess, in Phrygia, we are told that they practised unbounded licentiousness—such as we are told were practised in the Christian *agapæ* by persons who are said to have been devoted to celibacy and virginity. (Lucian. in Dea Syria. Diodor. 3, 4.) The Pythagoreans, also, according to Lucian, mutilated themselves. The Laws of Menu, (Chap. xi. 105.) in language not sufficiently decent to be repeated, decree that, as a penance for a certain sin, a monk-priest of the second order, shall perform this operation upon himself. The same inhuman practice prevailed among the Christian monks. The act of Origen—the most renowned of the fathers, and a noted monk—in thus mortifying his rebellious flesh, is so well known that it requires only to be mentioned. Among the early Christians, however, he was by no means unique on this point. All the disciples of his contemporary, Valens of Barathis, made themselves eunuchs, and held that none else could lead a life of purity. Entertaining this notion, they not only dismembered those of their own persuasion, but all others on whom they could lay their hands. (Christ. Antiq. vol. i. p. 77.) So numerous, in the Christian church, at a very remote period, were those who had "made themselves eunuchs for the kingdom of heaven's sake," that, as we find from the Apostolical Constitutions, (lib. viii. c. 9, 10.) they were thought of sufficient importance to be specially mentioned in the forms of public prayers, thus:—"Let us pray for the eunuchs who walk in holiness; let us pray for those who live in the continency of virginity, and lead a pious life," and so on. Thus we see that Jesus's approval of the monstrous practice of self mutilation was in perfect harmony with the barbarous religious notions of the heathen monks who had preceded him, as well as those of the Christian fanatics who succeeded him ; and that, in preaching these absurdities, he preached only heathen monkery.

Like the Brachmin and Hindoo monks, Jesus taught the doctrine of transmigration of life or soul. That—in his conversation with Nicodemus, on the subject of being "born again"—he taught this ancient doctrine has been already shown, (p. 427.) in pointing out the extent to which he has borrowed from pagan lore. That the Indian monks taught it as one of the principle tenets of their religion, and that it is the fundamental principle of all the austerities and self-mortifications of monkery, are likewise points that have already been made clear. (p. 451.) All that requires to be noticed here is, that, as the doctrine of transmigration pervades all the teachings of the Brachmin and Boodhist monks, so does it, in a modified form, pervade all the teaching of Jesus. On no occasion, perhaps, does he teach the doctrine of transmigration so pointedly as in the conversation already detailed (p. 388.) between him and Nicodemus, in which he insists that a man must be "born again" of water and wind before he can enter the kingdom of God. The Laws of Menu, treating of transmigrations, state that water was called *Nara* because it was the production of the wind or spirit of the gods, and that a man who attained to endless felicity had a double birth,—one from his natural, and one from his spiritual mother,—and is therefore called a twice-born man.* The Gospel of John is throughout remarkable for touches

---

* In order that the general reader may have a clear idea of the Indian doctrine of transmigration, and be able to perceive how identical with it is much of Jesus's teaching, and also the teaching of Paul, whose Epistles are teeming with this doctrine, the following extracts, in addition to those found in p. 451, are here given, in an abridged form, from the Laws of Menu.—" The sole Self-existing Power, whom the mind alone can perceive, whose essence eludes the external organs, who has no visible parts, who exists from eternity; even HE, the soul of all beings, whom no being can comprehend, shone forth in person; and having willed to produce various beings from his own divine substance, first with a thought created the waters,"—" From THAT WHICH IS, the FIRST CAUSE, not the object of sense, existing everywhere in substance, not existing to our perception, without beginning or end, was produced the divine male, formed in all worlds, under the appellation of BRAHMA. From the supreme soul, he drew forth mind, existing substantially. In whatever occupation the Supreme Lord first employed any vital soul, to that occupation the same soul attaches itself spontaneously when it receives a *new body again and again*. Whatever quality, noxious or innocent, harsh or mild, unjust or just, false or true, HE conferred on any being at its creation, the same quality enters it, of course, on its *future births*."—" All transmigrations, recorded in the Sacred Books, from the state of Brahma to that of plants, happen continually in this tremendous world of beings; a world always tending to decay."—" Of created things, the most excellent are those which are animated ; of the animated, those which subsist by intelligence ; of the intelligent, mankind ; and of men, the sacerdotal class."—" The very birth of Brachmins is a constant incarnation of DHERMA, *God of Justice ;* for the Brachmin is born to promote justice, and to procure ultimate happiness. When a Brachmin springs to light, he is born above the world, the chief of all creatures."—" An action, either mental, verbal, or corporeal, bears good or evil fruit, *as itself is good or evil ;* and from the actions of men proceed their various transmigrations in the highest, the mean, and the lowest degree."—" That substance which gives motion to the body is called the vital spirit, and that body which thence derives active functions is called compound elements. Another internal spirit, the great soul, attends the birth of all creatures embodied, and thence, in all mortal forms, is conveyed a perception either pleasing or painful. Those two, the vital spirit and reasonable soul, are closely united with five elements, but connected with the Supreme Spirit, or divine essence, which pervades all beings high and low. From the substance of the Supreme Spirit are diffused, like sparks from fire,

of this doctrine; and much that is said in the other Gospels about the conditions on which people were to be admitted into Jesus's kingdom of heaven; about losing and again finding life; about regeneration, incarnation and so on, is of the same character.

Most of Jesus's parables have a decided monachal tendency. Such, for example, is the parable of the great supper, in which one of those invited is made to say that he had bought land; another that he had bought oxen; and a third that he had married a wife,—all of them acts disapproved of by the monkish fraternity, whether Christian or pagan, and evidently imported by Jesus into the parable with the view of denouncing worldy pursuits: for, in the context we are told that he said that no man could be his disciple unless he hated his nearest relatives, and even his own life,—a sentiment extremely monkish. (Luke xiv.) Such, likewise, is the parable of the rich man—clothed, not in a hairy garb, but in purple and fine linen—and the begging Lazarus, who is represented as a mendicant monk full of sores caused by ascetic feats, lying at this rich man's gate, and anxious to receive the crumbs from under the table of the epicure. The remaining part of the parable teaches the eminently monkish doctrine that people who endured want and privation in this world, thereby secured happiness in another.—"Thou in thy life-time

---

innumerable vital spirits, which perpetually give motion to creatures exalted and base. By the vital souls of those men, who have committed sin in the body reduced to ashes, another body, composed of nerves with five sensations, in order to be susceptible of torment, shall certainly be assumed after death. And being intimately united with those nervous particles, according to their distribution, they shall feel, in that new body, the pangs inflicted in each case by the sentence of YAMA. When the vital soul has gathered the fruits of sin, which arise from sensual pleasure, but must produce misery, and when its taint has thus been removed, it approaches again those two most effulgent essenses, the intellectual soul and the Divine Spirit. They two, closely conjoined, examine without remission, the virtues and vices of that sensitive soul, according to its union, with which it acquires pleasure or pain in the *present and future worlds.* If the vital spirit had practised virtue for the most part, and vice in a small degree, it enjoys delight in celestial abodes, clothed with a body formed of pure elementary particles. But if it had generally been addicted to vice, and seldom attended to virtue, then shall it be deserted by those pure elements, and, having a courser body of sensible nerves, it feels the pain to which YAMA shall doom it. Having endured those torments, according to the sentence of YAMA, and its taint being almost removed, it again reaches those five pure elements in the order of their natural distribution. Let each man, considering with his intellectual powers these migrations of the soul, according to its virtue or vice, into a region of bliss or pain, continually fix his heart on virtue."—"Such transmigrations as the soul procures in this universe by each of those qualities, I now will declare in order succintly. Souls endued with goodness attain always the state of deities; those filled with ambitious passions, the condition of men; and those immersed in darkness, the nature of beasts: this is the triple order of transmigration."—"More than once shall they lie in different wombs, and, after agonizing births, be condemned to severe captivity."—"Next, learn those acts of a Brachmin which lead to eternal bliss."—"Such is the advantageous privilege of those *who have a double birth* from their natural mother and from their spiritual mother, especially a Brachmin; since the twice-born man by performing this duty, but not otherwise, may soon acquire endless felicity."—(Sir William Jones's Translation of the Laws of Menu. Chap. i. xii.) Such is a brief sample of the doctrine of transmigration, as systematically and minutely taught in these ancient laws. Let present theologians closely study these antique productions, and say whether they cannot perceive that, in a thousand instances, the New Testament contains precisely the same religious notions. Plato and Philo Judæus teach similar things.

receivedest thy good things, and likewise Lazarus evil things; but now he is comforted, and thou art tormented." This doctrine he teaches very frequently.—"Woe unto you that are rich! for ye have received your consolation. Woe unto you that are full! for ye shall hunger. Woe unto you that laugh now! for ye shall mourn and weep." The parable of the rich man who pulled down his barns and built ones of greater size, is also expressly designed to teach one of the principal doctrines of monkery; namely, the incumbent duty of renouncing the world. In the parable of the sower also, he inculcates the same duty.—The seed which fell among thorns represented those who "are choked with cares and riches and pleasures of this life." Many other features of heathen monkery are to be met with in almost all his parables.

Another distinct mark of heathen monachism in Jesus's teaching is, that he concealed the real meaning, or mysteries of his doctrines from all but his initiated disciples. The Laws of Menu strictly enjoined conceal-ment of the mysteries of their decrees, as well as the doctrines of the Vedas, from the uninitiated.—"This transcendent system of law must be kept devoutly concealed from persons unfit to receive it."—"The primary trilateral syllable, in which the three Vedas themselves are comprised, *must be kept secret*, as another triple Veda: he knows the Veda, who distinctly knows the mystic sense of that word." (Laws of Menu, chap. xi. xii.) The Revelation of *Christna*—one of the incarnate Gods of India—made to *Arjoon*, an initiated disciple, is, even to this day, kept secret by the Hindoos. Mr. Wilkins in the preface to his translation, of this supposed divine production, known as the *Bhagvat-Geeta*, posses-sion of which he obtained with difficulty, says,—"The *Brahmans* esteem this work to contain all the grand mysteries of their religion; and are careful to conceal it from the knowledge of those of a different persuasion, and even the vulgar of their own." The Essenian monks, before they were admitted members of the fraternity, took tremendous oaths not to divulge their doctrines, or any of their mysteries, to the the uninitiated. (Jos. de Bell. Jud. lib. ii. c. 8.) Indeed, all heathen religionists, whether monks or not,* had doctrines and other mysteries which they sedulously kept secret from all but the initiated, who, on their admission, were obliged to take a solemn oath never to divulge them. To the vulgar, they spoke and wrote in obscure allegorical language. (Vid. Philo. Jud. Allegor. Legis. lib. i. iii.) So closely did Jesus follow this practice of the heathen monks and others, that, in answer to a question put to him by his disciples, in private, we find him saying,—Unto *you* it is given to know the *mysteries* of the kingdom of God; but unto them that are *without*, *all* these things are done in parables: that seeing they may see, and not perceive, and hearing they may hear, and not understand."—"With many such parables spake he the word unto them, *as they were able to hear it*. But without a parable spake he not unto them. And when *they were alone, he expounded*

---

* These mysteries have already been noticed in several portions of this work; especially in treating of the Persian Mithras, the Egyptian Osiris and Isis, the Grecian Bacchus and Ceres, &c.; in connection with the rites of whom, as well as those of the deities of the ancient Druids, and many others that could be named, there were pro-found mysteries. So well established is this point that it requires no proof.

all things to his disciples." (Mark iv. 11, 12, 33, 34. Luke viii. 10.)
The impropriety of such a conduct in public teachers has already been
noticed.* (pp. 384, 385.) The same doctrine he teaches in that collection
of monkish aphorisms—the Sermon on the Mount, (Matth. vii. 6.) where
he says—"Give not that which is holy unto the dogs ; neither cast ye
your pearls before swine." And the same doctrine had previously been
taught, in the Laws of Menu, (Chap. ii.) to "twice-born" men, or the first
order of monk-priest, in these words :—A teacher of the Vedas should
rather die with his learning, than sow it in sterile soil, even though he be
in grievous distress for subsistence. Sacred learning, having approached
a Brachmin, said to him,—"I am thy precious gem ; preserve me with
care ; deliver me not to the scorner ; (so preserved I shall become
supremely strong) but communicate me, as to a vigilant depositary of thy
gem, *to that student whom thou shalt know to be pure, to have subdued his
passions, to perform the duties of his order.*" Thus, we see that Jesus
teaches—although in a distorted form, yet in substance, the very same
doctrines as the Hindoo monk-priests. The cause of this distortion is,
that these doctrines were not imported among Christians directly from
Hindostan, where we find them, at the remotest period in which there is
any record of their existence, but were brought to Palestine through
Egypt, Persia, Greece, and other countries ; so as to be modified by the
philosophy of the Egyptians, of the Persians, of the Grecians, and, particularly, of the Jews at Alexandria. To enter, however, into the origin
and progress of these mysteries here, would cause too great a digression.

When Jesus (John xiv. 2.) says to his disciples—" In my Father's
house are many mansions," not only is he monachal both in sentiment
and language, but also shows that there existed monasteries before the
time John's Gospel was written. The word translated *mansions*, is μοναι,—
the very word from which *monastery* and *monks* derive. Besides the
meaning of the word μοναι, the very expression—many mansions, or
separate dwellings in the same house, incontestibly proves that Jesus
meant a *monastery.* We have seen (p. 461.) that, long before the reputed
time of Jesus, there were such religious houses among various pagan
nations ; and that these were afterwards copied by the Christian cœnobite
monks, and called *monasteries.* (p. 370.) In reference to no other religious house than a monastery, can we suppose that Jesus spoke—whether
literally or figuratively—of a house within which there were a large
number of seperate or single dwellings,—dwellings, each of which was
destined to be occupied by only one of the inmates, and which he therefore very properly terms—μοναι,—a word that directly signifies the state
of *dwelling alone, singly, or without company.*—" In my Father's house
there are many mansions." In allusion to the same monachal dwelling,
Jesus says, in his Sermon on the Mount,—" When thou prayest, enter into
thy closet, (ταμιειον,—secret apartment,) and when thou hast shut *thy* door,

---

* The apostolical Fathers, and all the early Christian monks, concealed their
mysteries and the contents of their sacred books from the vulgar. Accordingly, we
find that, even in England, not until after the Reformation the Bible was allowed to be
read by the commonalty ; previously, it was a sealed book to all but the priestly tribe.
Even in the time of Hen. viii. a statue was passed, forbidding workmen and women to
read it, on pain of death.

pray to thy Father which is in secret." ($\kappa\rho\upsilon\pi\tau\omega$,—a crypt.*) The crypts, or subterranean chapels and burial places of ancient monasteries, are well known. The Chaldee word *Abba*, which we have seen to have, at a very early date, signified the head of a monastery, is another expression of Jesus, suggestive of monkery.—"Abba Father, all things are possible unto thee." (Mark xiv. 33.) Christian monkery having, undoubtedly, been derived directly from Egypt, we find the word *Abba* in the Syriac, in the Ethiopic, but more particularly in the Coptic churches, as a title given to bishops, at a very early period. To one of the first Christian bishops of Alexandria, this title was given, which was corrupted into *Baba* and *Paba*, by which he was known before the bishop of Rome was so designated. Hence the title *Pope*, signifying the common father of all Christians, was, in process of time, given to the Roman Pontiff, while the head of a monastery retained the title of *Abba* or Abbot. But as there is ample evidence that the title *Abba*, given to the head of a monastery, is much more ancient than the term *Pope*, given to the bishop of Rome, in the seventh century, this is an additional proof that the present form of Christianity emanated from monkery, even heathen monkery; whence the term *Abba*—said in the Gospels to have been uttered by Jesus—explained, as it is, by the word *father*, probably, by some scholiast.

But lest it be said we play upon words, let us notice that, like the Essenian and other monks, Jesus taught it was wrong to take an oath.— "It hath been said by them of old, Thou shalt not foreswear thyself, but shalt perform unto the Lord thine oaths; but I say unto you, *Swear not at all*; neither by heaven; for it is God's throne; nor by the earth; for it is his footstool: neither by Jerusalem; for it is the city of the great King. Neither shalt thou swear by thy head; because thou canst not make one hair white or black. But let your communication be Yea, yea; Nay, nay: for whatsoever is more than these cometh of evil." (Matth. v. 33—37.) Precisely the same doctrine was taught and practised by the monkish Essenes. Josephus, (de Bel. Jud. lib. ii. c. 8.) in describing them, says,—"Whatsoever they say is firmer than an oath; *but swearing is avoided by them*, and they esteem it worse than perjury; for they say, he who cannot be believed without swearing by God, is already condemned." Whatever Jesus meant by swearing, it is clear that he meant the same as these cœnobite monks—the Essenes; which is sufficient for our present purpose.†

---

* Or if $\kappa\rho\upsilon\pi\tau\omega$ be taken as an adjective, then, some such word as $\theta\alpha\lambda\alpha\mu\omega$, or $\chi\omega\rho\omega$ must here be understood,—meaning *a hidden place*. But here, it evidently stands for a substantive, just as $\phi\alpha\nu\epsilon\rho\omega$ stands; and the passage may fairly be rendered—"Pray to thy Father who is in the crypt; and thy Father, who seeth in the crypt, will reward thee in public." To say nothing of other places, there is no doubt that, in Luke xi. 33, the word $\kappa\rho\upsilon\pi\tau\circ\varsigma$ is a substantive:—"No man when he hath lighted a candle putteth it in a crypt,—$\epsilon\iota\varsigma$ $\kappa\rho\upsilon\pi\tau\circ\nu$ $\tau\iota\vartheta\eta\sigma\iota\nu$. So also it is used in Rom. ii. 16, and 2 Cor. iv. 2. The best lexicons define the word—*fornix* subterranea,—*testudo* subterranea, etc. In these crypts, ancient monks deposited the embalmed bodies of their dead; and hither they often retired for private devotion. Accordingly, the word *crypt* often denotes a subterranean church. All this serves to show that the very words of the Gospels are monachal.

† Here, however, may be noticed the groundlessness of the opinion of most Christian writers,—that Jesus, in the words just cited, did not prohibit the taking of an oath in

Another most striking feature of heathen monkery in Jesus, was his
practice of devoting the night to eating, drinking, praying, watching, and

a court of justice, or on any occasion, as a guarantee of the truth of a statement, in a
civil or criminal matter.　Under the Mosaic Law, we are informed, there were such
oaths taken.　And in the passage just cited, it is clear that, contrary to the provisions
of that law, which prohibited only *false* oaths, Jesus says,—" Swear not at all." This he
enjoins in contradistinction to the injunction of the Mosaic Law; just as in the subsequent particulars which he names, he contravenes the same law.　It would be just as
rational to say that Jesus does *not* prohibit the exaction of " an eye for an eye, and a tooth
for a tooth ;" or that he does *not* forbid a person to hate his enemy, which he positively
does, in the immediate context, as to urge that he does not forbid *swearing at all ;* at least,
in cases pertaining to temporal matters.　The same doctrine he teaches in Matth. xxiii.
16—22, where he denounces the scribes and Pharisees, in very opprobrious language,
and derides their mode of swearing.　There is nothing clearer than that Jesus peremptorily forbids Christians to take an oath in any secular matter whatever; which is quite
in accordance with his prohibition, as well as that of his Apostles, to all Christians,
not to " go to law" with any one. (Matth. vi. 40.　1 Cor. vi. 1—8.)　The real cause
that Christian writers of the present age pervert the meaning of Jesus's prohibition to
take an oath, and endeavour to explain it away, (see Paley's Moral Philosophy, book iii.
chap. 16.) is, that it does not suit believers of modern times as well as it did those of the
first ages of Christianity, who, like Jesus himself, led the life of vagrant monks, who
had parted with any property they might once have had, who had no worldly interest
at stake, and did not, in the least, concern themselves with secular matters; but like
the Indian Yogis, lived entirely absorbed in heavenly meditations, taking no thought
whatever of the morrow, even as to what they should eat, drink, or wear.　If these
writers contended that Jesus did not prohibit oaths of fidelity to be taken in the secret
assemblies of Christians, they would have some evidence to support them.　For we find
that Christians, as early as the time of Pliny the younger, who was born A.D. 61, were
accustomed, in their midnight assemblies—like the initiated to the Bacchanalian and
Eleusinian mysteries—to bind themselves with an oath.—Seque sacramento obstrin-
gere.—Plin. lib x. epist. 97.　Josephus, in the place last cited, says a similar thing of
the Essenes.　Almost immediately after stating that they avoided oaths, he says that a
person, when initiated into the Essenian mysteries, was obliged to take tremendous
oaths that, *inter alia*, he would neither conceal anything from those of his own sect, nor
divulge any of the doctrines to others, even should he be compelled at the hazard of his
life.　In the oath which Josephus says the Essenes took, and that said by Pliny to be
in use by the Christians of his time, there is, throughout, a striking resemblance,
amounting almost to identity.　The only difference is, that the former writer gives it in
a more detailed form, while the latter appears to favour us only with the substance of it.
Now, both these communities prohibited the taking of an oath, and yet both practised
oaths respectively among themselves; and thus they closely resembled each other.　The
conclusion, therefore, is inevitable, that their prohibition to take an oath had reference
only to secular matters, or matters not within the pale of their own sacred societies, in
which alone they allowed oaths to be taken.　The Apostle James, (v. 12.) in cautioning
his brethren against taking an oath, (ομνυω,—the same verb as that used by Jesus in
prohibiting oaths, and in ridiculing the oaths of the Jews as already noticed,) clearly
advances the sentiment of the Essenes, as to the condemnation which attended the
taking of an oath, and at the same time uses words very much like those attributed to
Jesus in the Gospels.　He says,—" Above all things, my brethren, swear not, neither
by heaven, nor by the earth, neither by any other oath : but let your yea be yea; and
your nay, nay ; *lest ye fall into condemnation."*　Now, according to Christian chronology,
there could not be many years between the time that the writer of this Epistle thus
cautioned his brethren against taking an oath and the time Pliny wrote that Christians
took oaths in their sacred meetings ;—another strong presumptive proof that the oath
which Jesus, and also James, prohibit, is one of a secular character, or one enforced upon
a person by people not belonging to his own religious community.　Such an oath as
this, none of the early Christians would take.　They appear to have fully carried out
the Gospel injunction,—not to swear.　Jerome, (Com. in Matth.) after telling us that
judicial swearing was permitted to the Jews, not because it was absolutely right, but
because it was better to a ow them to swear by God than by demons, adds,—Evangelica

so on. The Essenes, as we learn from Josephus, (de Bel. Jud. lib. ii. c. 8.) chose the night, as the more sacred time, for the performance of all their religious rites and devotions, during which they spoke not a word about secular matters, and before sunrise, put up certain prayers which they had received from their forefathers. Porphyry, (de Abstin. lib. ii. s. 26.) unquestionably, referring either to the Essenes or Therapeuts, whom, after Theophrastus, he calls the Jews of Syria, says that they sacrificed in the night, and that, instead of feasting on the things offered, prepared themselves for the performance of the sacred rites by abstinence from food, all of which—as well as *philosophizing*, or rather worshiping the stars—were done in the night. The same custom prevailed among the Egyptians, long before the time of Porphyry, and even of Theophrastus. (Paul. Ern. Jablon. Panth. Ægypt. lib. i. c. 1.) Eusebius, in his Ecclesiastical History, (lib. ii. c. 17.) citing what Philo has written of the Therapeuts, says that these monks neither ate nor drank before the setting of the sun, that they kept vigils, and that, during the night, they sang hymns, and studied their sacred writings. Well might Eusebius declare,— "They are the same customs that are observed by us *alone*, at the present day;" for we find that the Christian monks, long before the time of Eusebius, spent most of the night in religious devotions, and frequently held nocturnal assemblies, or vigils.* The Egyptian monks kept perpetual vigils, in order to scare away demons, who were always ready to attack them, and were kept at bay, in the night, only by psalm singing and Scripture reading. (Cassian, Collat. vii. 23.) It is with much candour that Dr. Mosheim (Affairs of the Christians, vol. i. chap. ii. sec. 13.) makes the following admission :—" The monks of Christianity, a description of men that first appeared in Egypt, seem to have taken for their model the manners and scheme of life of the practical Essenes : indeed, the account given us by Josephus of the latter, corresponds so exactly with the institutions and habits of the early votaries of monachism, that it is

---

autem veritas non recipit juramentum. Tertullian, Eusebius, Chrysostom Basil, indeed, all the Fathers, maintained that Jesus absolutely prohibited judicial swearing. The Fathers present at the second council held at Constantinople, seem to have been unanimously of the opinion that it was a sin for a Christian to take an oath— Εντεταλται ημιν παρα του σωτηρος χριστου, μη ομοσαι.—Act. Conc. Const. act I. The only consistent Christians of the present age, on this point, are the Quakers and Moravians, who, viewing the words of Jesus in their obvious sense, refuse to take judicial oaths. It is high time for *all* Christians to be so consistent as, not only to obey the injunction of the founder of their faith in swearing not at all, but likewise to repeal those laws which they have made to prevent all persons from being witnesses of truth in a court of law, who cannot conscientiously say that they believe in the contents and divine origin of that book which says—" Swear not at all."

---

* These vigils continued in high repute long after the religious reformer, Vigilantius, in the fifth century, denounced them, together with other branches of monkery, as having been borrowed from the heathens. Jerome, the great bulwark and palladium of the monkery of his age, came to their rescue, and, in very bitter terms, (de Vigiliis et pernoctationibus Martyrum, &c.) showed that they were as old as apostolical times. The practice of all the people to stay in the church, on Easter-eve, expecting the second coming of Christ, he also says, (Com. 4. in Matth.) was equally old. He could have said that both practices were much older, having had their origin in the remote ages of heathenism.

impossible for any two things more nearly to resemble each other." But what concerns us, at present, is to show that Jesus taught and practised the same doctrine as that of both these heathen and Christian monks, regarding nocturnal devotions.——It was in the night that he went through the ceremony of eating and drinking the Passover, singing a hymn, and other religious exercises. It was in the night that he went to Gethsemane with his disciples to pray, telling them to keep a vigil, and to pray, lest they fell into temptation. (Matth. xxvi.) It was in the night that he was accustomed to engage in prayer for several hours. We read that, having gone "into a mountain to pray, he continued all night in prayer to God;" and that, when it dawned, he chose his twelve apostles. (Luke vi. 12.) The exhortations which he gave to keep vigils are very numerous. After predicting the suddenness of the end of the world, his caution was,—— "Watch therefore ; for ye know not what hour your Lord doth come." (Matth. xxiv. 42.) At the end of his parable of the ten virgins, he gives the same caution. The Gospels abound with such expressions, alleged to have been uttered by Jesus, as,——" Watch and pray."——" What I say unto you I say unto all, Watch." And wherever he is said to have used the verb " watch," ($\alpha\gamma\rho\nu\pi\nu\epsilon\omega$ or $\gamma\rho\eta\gamma\rho\rho\epsilon\omega$) it always implies the idea of night. Throughout the Epistles, the same exhortations are given to the early Christians, who, as we have seen, held their religious meetings in the night, as a sort of vigil ; who at the Lord's Supper or *agapœ*, were addressed by their leaders till daylight; (Acts xx. 7——12.) and who, at these vigils—precisely like the Therapeuts—sang psalms and hymns. (1 Cor. xiv. 26. Ephes. v. 19 ; vi. 18. Col. iii. 16.)

A vast number of other passages, in which Jesus plainly teaches heathen monkery, could be adduced ; but we must desist ; for to cite all these, would be to transcribe almost the whole of the four Gospels, which appear to consist of scarcely anything but the doctrines of heathen monachism, blended with Judaism ; or, in other words, adapted to Jewish teachings and Jewish notions.* More particularly is the Gospel of John replete with expressions attributed to Jesus, which clearly set forth the doctrines of the *Sannyasis*, or the highest order of Indian anchorites, slightly modified, however, in some places, by Egyptian and Platonic influence, in their progress from India to Palestine and Italy. Such,

---

* Mr. Greg, who, like many other writers, could not fail to see the monachism of the Gospels, is, characteristically, more suggestive than bold, in exposing it. In his *Creed of Christendom*, p. 270, after mentioning this "ascetic and depreciating view of life," he adds,——" How much of it belongs to Christ, how much to the Apostles, and how much was the accretion of a subsequent age, is not easy to determine. It appears in the Epistles as well as in the Gospels. . . . . In Christ, this asceticism assumes a mild and moderate form, being simply the doctrine of the Essenes, modified by his own exquisite judgment and general sympathies." Then, according to Mr. Greg, Jesus only improved the monkery of the Essenes. To accomplish this, no revelation, no Divine personage from heaven, was required; for it could easily be done by any person of common sense. But it is here intimated that our present Gospels are in such a corrupt state that it cannot be known how much of their asceticism belongs to Christ. Then, of what use can they be as a rule of faith ? Mr. Greg must mean much more than he says. But such hints as he gives here, serves only to perplex the general reader, who may have neither time nor ability to trace the monkery of the Gospels to its real source.

for example, are the following passages.—" I and my Father are one."—
" I am in the Father, and the Father in me."—" They are not of the
world, as I am not of the world."—" And the glory which thou gavest
me I have given them, that they may be one, even as we are one : I in
them,* and thou in me, that they may be perfect in one."—" That they
all may be one ; as thou Father art in me, and I in thee, that they also
may be one in us."—" O Father, glorify thou me in thine own self, with
the glory which I had with thee before the world was."—" Say ye of him
whom the Father hath sanctified and sent into the world, Thou blas-
phemest ? "—" I know him, for I am from him, and he hath sent me."—
" I am the light of the world."—" I proceeded forth, and came from
God."—" He that seeth me, seeth him that sent me. I am come a light
into the world. I came forth from the Father, and am come into the
world : again I leave the world and go to the Father." To these, a vast
number of such expressions, found in the same Gospel, might be added.
Any one acquainted with the ancient philosophy of the Brachmins and
Boodhists, regarding transmigrations, divine incarnations, emanations,

---

* In a dialogue, called the Bhagvat-Geeta, between the Indian incarnate God
Christna, or the Christ of the Hindoos, and his favourite disciple Arjoon—translated by
Charles Wilkins, formerly of Bengal, from the ancient language of the Brachmins—in
a letter prefixed to which translation, Mr. Warren Hastings says that the original " is
affirmed to have been written upwards of four thousand years ago,"—we find, in several
places, expressions such as the following, uttered by Christna, some of which have
already been cited. After exhorting Arjoon to adhere to " the practice of a Sannyasee,'
or an anchorite, he adds,—" They who serve me with adoration, I am in them, and they
in me." In another place he says,—" Those men who perform severe mortifications of
the flesh, not authorised by the *Sastra*, torment the spirit that is in the body, and myself also who am in them." (pp. 82, 120.) In this production, which, unquestionably,
is exceedingly ancient, are to be found the following Christian doctrines :—Regeneration, or the second birth, p. 67, note 6,—Christna, the god of love, the resurrection,
the incarnate, the beginning and the end, existing before all things, the creator and
governor of the universe, the chief of prophets, and yet despised in human form, pp. 52,
64, 78—87,—Faith in Christna required in order to obtain salvation, pp. 68, 72, 123,
132, 134,—The living water of Christna, pp. 109, 149, 151,—Perfect and eternal
happiness to be obtained by implicit reliance upon Christna, pp. 63, 64,—The heaven of
Christna, with its eternal happiness, pp. 80—82,—War of the inhabitants of this heaven,
pp. 149—157,—The radiant glory of Christna, p. 91,—The religious light, wisdom, and
divine knowledge which Christna gave his worshippers, pp. 52, 84.—The deified saints,
the prophets, the fallen angels or evil spirits, and the good angels of Christna, pp. 52,
54, 71, 83—86, 97, 130, 139, 144—152,—The anchorites of Christna, pp. 53—68,
81, 109. Indeed, all the Christian doctrines are clearly taught in this ancient document, the contents of which are said to be revelations of the incarnate deity, or *Christ*
of the Hindoos, between whom and the Christ of the Gospels we have, in foregoing
portions of this work, (pp. 337, 428,) seen so many points of identity. It is by no
means wonderful that Mr. Warren Hastings, in the letter already mentioned, pronounces it " a theology accurately corresponding with that of the Christian dispensation,
and most powerfully illustrating its fundamental doctrines." Seeing that the grand
theme of this dialogue is the monachal religion of the Hindoos, in the practice of which
the incarnate God Christna, is set forth as a pattern of perfection, Mr. Warren Hastings,
after intimating that the monkery of the Brachmins was like that of the Christians in
the Romish Church, adds :—" I myself was once a witness of a man employed in this
species of devotion, at the principal temple of Banaris. His right hand and arm were
enclosed in a loose sleeve or bag of red cloth, within which he passed *the beads of his
rosary*, one after another, through his fingers, repeating with the touch of each (as I
was informed) one of the names of God."

unions, absorptions, essences, sanctifications, and glorifications, will easily perceive the source whence they have been derived.*

Now, in taking a retrospect of what has been advanced touching Jesus's monkery, we find that, at the onset of his public career, he formed an alliance with that noted anchorite, John the Baptist,—that, like a monk, he fasted in the wilderness, where he was tempted of the devil,—that, like the Indian monks and the Therapeuts, he roamed about the country, healing diseases, casting out demons, and working other miracles,—that, like all anchorites, he made his abode in deserts and mountains,—that, like the Gymnosophists and others, he took women with him through the towns and villages which he visited,—that, in his diet and

---

* Although in this section, as well as throughout the text of this work, it has been taken for granted that the words and actions which the Gospels attribute to Jesus, were really his, and not collected by his biographers from heathen lore, and skilfully used to adorn the career of the hero of their tale, yet, the fact fully established here,—that these Gospels are composed almost entirely of heathen monachism, is one of the strongest proofs imaginable that they are—as already stated in foregoing notes—the production of the Eclectic monks of the Alexandrian college, who, in compiling them, used from the heathen materials they had already collected from various heathen sources, the tales and sentiments most congenial to their monachal taste. While the contents of the Old Testament would appear to have principally been extracted from Chaldean, Persian, Babylonian, and Egyptian lore, the contents of the New seem to have been derived chiefly from the Indian philosophy; although, apparently, not directly from India, but after this philosophy had been introduced into Egypt, Syria, Greece, and several other countries; and thereby modified by the previous religious notions of these countries, just as we find that Christianity was modified in Britain by the previous Druidism of the inhabitants. Still, we find in the New Testament many religious notions which cannot be traced to India, but must be attributed to other countries, such as Syria, Persia, and even China. In the Old Testament, also, we find purely Hindoo legends. For example, let any one compare Gen. vi. 10; ix. 18—27, with the following passages from one of the Divine books of the Hindoos, called the *Padma-Puran*, as translated by Sir Wm. Jones, in the third volume of the Asiatic Researches.—"To Satyavrata, (Noah) that sovereign of the whole earth, were born three sons; the eldest *Sherma*, (Shem) then *Charma*, (Cham) and thirdly *Jyapeti* (Japheth) by name. These were all men of good morals, excellent in virtue and virtuous deeds. . . . . But Satyavrata, being continually delighted with devout meditation, and seeing his sons fit for dominion, laid upon them the burden of government. Whilst he remained honouring and satisfying the gods, and priests, and kine, one day, by the act of destiny, the king having drank mead, became senseless, and lay asleep naked. Then was he seen by Charma ; and by him were his two brothers called, to whom he said, ' What now has befallen ? In what state is this our sire ? ' By those two was he hidden with clothes, and called to his senses again and again. Having recovered his intellect, and perfectly knowing what had passed, he cursed Charma, saying, ' Thou shalt be the servant of servants ; and since thou wast a laughter in their presence, from laughter shalt thou acquire a name.' " In the Hindoo Scriptures, which are confessedly much older than any of our sacred books, there are long tales of the deluge. Sir Wm. Jones, in his works, (vol. i. pp. 136, 287, 288.) makes the name, *Satyavrata*, the same as *Noah*, both patronymics of *Menu*, derived from *Nuh*; and tells, that " though most of the Mosaic names have been considerably altered, yet numbers of them remain unchanged." Colonel Wilford, also, in a tract on Egypt, takes notice of this passage, remarking that " it is related in the *Padma-Puran* that *Satyavrata*, whose miraculous preservation from a general deluge is told in the Matsya, had three sons, the eldest of whom was named *Jyapeti*, or lord of the earth, the others were *Charma* and *Sharma* ; in the vulgar dialect usually pronounced *Cham* and *Sham*, as we frequently hear *Crishn, Crishna*." This learned writer then proceeds, on the authority of the divine *Purans*, to describe the territories of Japheth and Sham, and the curse pronounced on Cham whose descendants inhabited the country of *Cusha* or *Cush*, making Genesis and the Hindoo Scriptures again identical. (Gen. x. 6, 7.)

habiliment, he closely resembled pagan monks,—that, like all heathen monks, he inculcated the religious duty of parting, not only with all relatives, but also with all property, and of leading a life of mendicancy,—that, not only in his notion of adultery was he like the heathen monks, but that, like them, he taught the doctrine of self-mutilation,—that, like the Brachmin and Boodhist anchorites, he taught the doctrine of transmigration,—that, like these and others, he concealed the real meaning of his doctrines from all but his initiated disciples,—that he alluded to the cells of monks, as being the "many mansions" which were in his Father's house,—that, like the monkish Essenes, he forbade his disciples to take a judicial oath,—and that, like them and other monks, he chose the night for religious devotions. It is, therefore, trusted that these points of identity fully prove the truth of the proposition laid down at the commencement of this long section ; namely, that both the life and doctrines of Jesus were identical with the lives and doctrines of heathen monks, who lived hundreds of years before his time.

SECTION XI.—THE ALLEGED DIVINE MISSION OF JESUS.

In every age, from apostolical times to the present, it has been a fundamental doctrine of the Christian religion that Jesus had a special mission in this world to fulfil,—that he was sent by his Father from heaven to work miracles, cast out demons, reveal God's will, preach new doctrines, teach men the way of salvation, and, ultimately, die on the cross, as an atoning sacrifice for their sins. Nor do Christians believe in the divine mission of Jesus, without being amply authorised by his own declarations. The Gospels abound with expressions to this effect, attributed to Jesus ; such as,—" I proceeded forth and came from God ; neither came I of myself, but he sent me."—" The Father that sent me beareth witness of me."—" My doctrine is not mine, but his that sent me."—" I must work the works of him that sent me."—" I came down from heaven, not to do mine own will, but the will of him that sent me."—" The Father which sent me, he gave me a commandment what I should say, and what I should speak."—" I must preach the kingdom of God to other cities also : for therefore am I sent."—The same works I do bear witness of me, that the Father hath sent me." A vast number of such expressions could be added. It is, however, difficult to perceive how the works which Jesus did, were any evidence that he was a divine personage sent from heaven. For, as we have seen, others who claimed no divine origin, in his time, wrought miracles, expelled demons, and did all the mighty works which Jesus is said to have done : and, doubtless, the more intelligent portion of the Jews well knew this. It is true that, before, and at the time he lived, as well as afterwards, many persons claimed a divine origin, pretended to be Messiahs, to have been sent from God, and so on. There is, however, nothing more certain than that Jesus had not—any more than these pretenders, or some other human being—been sent from heaven by the Deity ; and that God had nothing more to do with ushering him into this world, than he has to do with any other mortal man. Of this important fact, the contents of the foregoing portions of this work, as it is confidently trusted, will be deemed, by any unbiassed mind, to be one continuous proof. And here recurs the momentous question, once before touched upon,—whether Jesus knew that he was not divine, that he had not come from heaven, and that he had received no divine commission whatever. On this point the reader is left to form his own opinion, assisted by the facts already advanced, and those which follow, regarding Jesus's intellectual and moral qualities.

It is to be observed, however, that, although he repeatedly avowed himself to be the *Son* of God, and to have proceeded *from* God, which expressions are, doubtless, to be understood in the same sense as they were used in the Platonic and Hindoo theology, regarding metempsychosis and absorption,* already explained, yet he is not said to have ever expressly declared himself a deity. Indeed, he is represented, in some parts of the Gospels, as if he did not believe that he was a divine personage. On several occasions, he represented his assumed supernatural power as a thing deputed to him ; denying that he possessed any such power of himself. In an altercation with the Jews, who charged him with sabbath-breaking, and with blasphemy, (John v. vi.) he said,—"The Son *can* do nothing of himself, but what he seeth the Father do."—"I can of mine own self do nothing : as I hear I judge : and my judgement is just : because I seek not mine own will, but the will of the Father which hath sent me."—"The living Father hath sent me, and I live by the Father." On other occasions, he said,—"I do nothing of myself ; but as my Father hath taught me, I speak these things."—"Whatsoever I speak therefore, even as the Father said unto me, so I speak." Here, Jesus clearly denies that he has any power independently of the Father, and gives his hearers to understand that he makes no more pretence to deity than if he were Moses, Elias, or one of the prophets, having come down from heaven.

There, are, however, several traits in his character, and several circumstances connected with his life—not yet fully noticed in this work—which indubitably prove that he was neither a deity, nor commissioned by the Deity to do and say what he did. We read that he frequently—on some occasions whole nights—prayed to God. He prayed, before his transfiguration, till "the fashion of his countenance was altered." He told Simon that Satan had desired to have him, but that he had prayed for him that his faith failed not. But it is absurd to suppose that he was

---

* This doctrine taught that, after the human soul had undergone a great number of transmigrations, so as, at last, to become, in the body of a *Sannyasi*, or an anchorite of the first order, too holy, and to participate of too great a portion of the divine energy for this world, it was, at the death of the body, absorbed into the essence of the supreme and infinite Godhead, from which, like all other souls, both good an evil, it had emanated. In this state of absorption, it enjoyed the highest degree of felicity and glory. Still, it must be admitted that the Brachmins and Boodhists regarded such a state of absorption to be a deification ; for they believed that the same personage, thus absorbed into the essence of the supreme God, might afterwards appear on earth an incarnate God. Besides, they regarded souls thus endowed with an extraordinary portion of the divine energy, as being raised after death to the rank of Gods, and to reign in heaven, subject to the superior power of the supreme Deity. Hence, they regarded such "departed saints" as proper objects of worship.

a deity, and yet had no power to preserve Simon from Satan, without praying for help from another deity. Immediately after telling his disciples that he was in the Father, and the Father in him, Jesus says to them,—" I will pray the Father, and he shall give you another Comforter." (John xiv. 16,) If he needed to pray the Father, his disciples, whom he endeavoured to teach, could not, any more than others, consistently with reason, believe that he was in the Father, and the Father in him,—that he and the Father were one, and so on. To suppose two Gods is grossly absurd ; but to suppose one God praying to another is to carry the absurdity still further. To read that Jesus prayed to God, may not sound strange to Christians ; but what would they think if they read that God prayed to Jesus ? The fact that Jesus prayed to God, however, is a proof that he was sensible of his own inferiority,—sensible that he was not a God. Indeed, this inferiority, he acknowledged in open terms:— " My Father is greater than I." (John xiv. 28.) The same doctrine of Jesus's inferiority pervades the Gospels, utterly destroying the notion of present Christians, as to the co-equality of the Father and Son. Jesus would appear to have been sensible of his imperfection, and, consequently, of his not being a deity, when he criticised the expression of a rich young man, who, in inquiring how to secure for himself " eternal life," had addressed him by the deferential epithet—" Good Master." Jesus asked the young man,—" Why callest thou me good ? there is none good but one ; that is God." (Matth. xix. 17.) Here, Jesus evidently disclaims, not only all pretence to a divine nature; but even to moral perfection, or perfect goodness. Not to notice how very ill the stern, austere, and dogmatic tone of his subsequent answer to the humble and respectful request of the young man, accords with this modest admission of his defect in moral goodness, his reasoning, syllogistically, stands thus :—Thou shouldst not call me good ; for there is none good but God. I am not good ; therefore, I am not God. There can be nothing clearer than that Jesus here deliberately denies his divinity.

Equally conclusive evidence have we that Jesus was not a divine personage, in the many instances given in the Gospels of his finite power and knowledge. We are told that when he had proof of the centurion's great faith, he marvelled. (Matth. viii. 5—10.) If he had been omniscient, and had, consequently, known beforehand the degree of faith with which the centurion was endowed, he would not have had any cause to marvel. As proof of the same fact, we are told (John iv. 1.) that when the Lord *knew* how the Pharisees had heard that Jesus made and baptized more disciples than John, he left Judea." But the question which naturally presents itself to every believer in the divinity of Jesus, is— Did not the Lord—the omniscient Jesus—the second Person in the mysterious Trinity—*know* what the Pharisees had heard before he was made acquainted with it by natural means ? Did he not know this the very moment the Pharisees had heard it ? Evidently not : it was the reception of this piece of knowledge that made him resolve instantly to leave Judea. His limited knowledge is also evinced in his inability to foretell when the end of the world would take place. Although he could prophecy much about the awful occurrence, yet he could not tell the exact time it would take place.—" That day and that hour knoweth no man, no, not the angels which are in heaven, *neither* the Son, but the Father ;"—another admission of his inferiority to the Father. (Mark xiii. 32.)   The following is an additional instance of Jesus's finitude in knowledge, as well as in power. We are told that, when he came to his own country, he found that he could do no mighty work among his own acquaintances, and that he marvelled because of the unbelief of his countrymen. (Mark vi. 1,—6.) But had he been a deity, and therefore omniscient, he would have known beforehand that these people would have no faith in his pretensions to the power of working miracles, and would not have come amongst them with the express intention of performing his feats ; and had he been possessed of the other essential attribute of deity—omnipotence, he could have wrought miracles in his own country as well as in some other place.

The great fear of death which Jesus evinced, is likewise a proof, not only that he was not a divine personage, but that he was not sent from heaven on the mission alleged by him, or any mission at all.—This also proves that, considering the circumstances under which he died, he sadly lacked moral courage.   Supposing him to have a mission to fulfil, part of which was to die on the cross, in order to atone for the sins of men, then, he clearly showed himself unwilling to fulfil this mission ; which is incompatible with the notion that he was a deity, or a personage sent from heaven on any mission whatever.   When he had reason to believe that he had been betrayed by Judas, which betrayal consisted in pointing him out to the Jewish authorities* by the signal of a kiss, he left Jerusalem in the hours of darkness ; and—having told his disciples, who accompanied him, to arm themselves with swords, owing to the impending danger—he made his way towards his wonted cavernous abode, and the abode of anchorites

---

* It must appear very strange to any one who has read the Gospels, and observed how well known Jesus had made himself by his miracles and public teaching, in the temple, and elsewhere,—how often he is said to have come in collision with the chief priests, and scribes, and elders of the people, that when these very men came to apprehend him—after he had been for three years the most remarkable public character this world ever beheld—they did not personally know him!—that they were obliged to give money to Judas for pointing him out to them !   Still, to the glaring inconsistency of the Gospel narrative, so it is represented.   Judas asked the chief priests,—"What will ye give me, and I will deliver him unto you ? "—" He that betrayed him gave them a sign, saying, Whomsoever I shall kiss, that same is he: hold him fast "—" And forthwith he came to Jesus, and said, Hail, master, and kissed him."—" Then came they and laid hands on Jesus, and took him." (Matth. xxvi. 15, 48—50.)   From John's narrative (xviii. 2.) it may be inferred that Judas, in his agreement to betray his master, engaged also to show the place into which Jesus had retreated when he learned that his life was in danger; namely a garden beyond the brook Cedron.   John says that Judas "knew the place ; for Jesus ofttimes resorted thither with his disciples."   We have had occasion already to notice this spot. (p. 519.)   It was a garden in a deep valley, where there was a wine-press, and therefore called Gethsemane, which, according to Maundrel, lay between the brook Cedron and the foot of Mount Olivet.   Now, we have already seen that in this craggy mountain, which, to this very day, abounds with caves and grottos occupied by monks, Jesus very frequently made his abode, and slept at night.   Accordingly, we find that, after he had proof that Judas was about betraying him, he walked from Jerusalem, in the depth of night, with his disciples, who as we have seen, were armed with swords, towards this mountain, apparently with the view of seeking safety in some of its caves.   For Luke (xxii. 39.) tells us that he went, as he was *wont*, TO the mount of Olives; and John tells us that Judas *knew the place*, for Jesus ofttimes resorted thither with his disciples.   Jesus, therefore, was in this ancient haunt of anchorites when he was pointed out by Judas and apprehended.

in every age,—the Mount of Olives. When he had reached the foot of this mount, at a place called Gethsemane, where there was a garden, he "fell on his face and prayed." He "began to be very sorrowful and very heavy," and he exclaimed,—" My soul is exceeding sorrowful, even unto death,"—that is, my sorrow is so great that I am nearly heartbroken,— I am nearly dead with sorrow,—I am grieved even *to* death, (εως θανατου) not *until* death, as it is generally explained away by Christian writers. In his prayer, he thus entreats :—" Abba, Father, all things are possible unto thee ; take away this cup (meaning the death which awaited him) from me." A second, and a third time he begs,—" O my Father, if this cup may not pass away from me, except I drink it, thy will be done." When in this state of fainting fear, " there appeared an angel unto him from heaven, strengthening him." But if he was a deity, wherefore the necessity of the assistance of an inferior, a created being— an angel ? If he had, in reality, the power ascribed to him in the Gospels, so as to be able to still the tempest, calm the boisterous sea, walk on the surface of its raging billows, raise the dead, and subdue a legion of demons, why this mortal fear of death ? Why this agony owing to the conspiracy of a few of his creatures ? If he knew that, in three days afterwards, he would rise victorious from the grave, why thus, like some other mortal, shudder to meet the king of terrors ? If he had been sent from heaven to suffer for sinners, wherefore his aversion to fall into the hands of the Jews and be crucified ? Why ask his Father to deliver him from the fate that awaited him, saying, "If thou be willing remove this cup from me ? " This was quite inconsistent with divinity, and unworthy of a personage who had come from heaven to fulfil a mission on earth; for it is clear that, if Jesus had his wish, he would have avoided the death of the cross. Nor does the angel that came to his assistance seem to have allayed his fear of death, for we read that, afterwards, " being in agony, he prayed more earnestly ; and his sweat was as it were great drops of blood falling down to the ground." It cannot for a moment be rationally supposed that a deity, or a personage sent from heaven, on a mission to this world, even were he only an angel, would evince such weakness and such dire want of moral courage, in anticipation of the pangs of death. Many of the martyrs to Christianity, as well as of those to other religions, have displayed far greater courage than Jesus, when in sight of the gibbet, the scaffold, the cross, the block, the axe, the fire, the fagot, or whatever might happen to be the engine of death with which fanatics destroyed one another, in bygone benighted ages. Nor can this fact fail to appear singular to those who believe that Jesus was God as well as man. The thinking Christian must be at a loss to understand why human nature, when united to the Divine, should be weaker than when seperate from it. The same want of courage, however, is again evinced by Jesus when, on the cross, he cries twice,—" My God ! my God ! why hast thou forsaken me ? (Matth. xxvii. 46, 50.) If Jesus was a deity, it is difficult to imagine how he *could*, even now in the jaws of death, suitably use this language. Although we do not read that any martyr to any religion ever manifested such a dire want of confidence in the cause he had espoused, as to utter language so desponding, yet, it must be admitted that such language would reasonably be accounted for,

as that of a mere man ; but when uttered by a deity, it is most difficult to
reconcile it to sound common sense. If Jesus was God, why should he
have exclaimed—*my God ?* On the absurd supposition of a plurality of
gods, are some the gods of other gods, so as not to be all co-equal ? On
the other hand, supposing Christians to admit that there is but one God,
while they contend that Jesus was God, how could God *forsake* himself ?
For Jesus to exclaim that God had forsaken him, was a proof that he was
conscious he was neither God, nor commissioned by God to undergo
crucifixion.

Although it is not intended here to trace the steps which led to the
Christian deification of Jesus, who is not, any more than the marvels
attributed to him, even mentioned by any of the numerous, renowned, and
voluminous writers who flourished about the time he is said to have lived,
such as, Philo the Jew, Seneca, Pliny the elder, Diogenes Laertius,
Pausanias, Pomponius Mela, Q. Curtius Rufus, and so on, yet, it may be
observed that, according to the Gospels, it was demons and demoniacs,
or madmen, who first recognised his divine mission. We are told that
these lunatics exclaimed,—" Let us alone ; what have we to do with thee,
thou Jesus of Nazareth ? Art thou come to destroy us ? I know thee
who thou art, the Holy One of God." And also that the demons themselves, "when they saw him, fell down before him, and cried, saying,
Thou art the Son of God." (See Matth. viii. 29. Mark i. 24, 34 ;
iii. 11 ; v. 7. Luke iv. 33, 41 ; viii. 28.) While demons and demoniacs,
in spite of Jesus's prohibition, persisted in proclaiming his deity and
divine mission, the Jewish doctors—the most intelligent and learned class
of the nation, whom the Gospels make Jesus most anxious to convince—
coolly looked at what was passing for miracles, obstinately denied that he
was sent from heaven, and positively insisted that all his pretences were
wicked and deserving of punishment. In vain did he perform numberless
prodigies before their eyes ; in vain did he enter into many a warm
dispute with them, for the express purpose of convincing them of the divine
character of his mission,—this only made them openly accuse him of
blasphemy. A grave question for our decision is—whether these people
had not better opportunities than we have, in this distant age, of judging
whether Jesus had, or had not, a divine commission to execute ; and
consequently, whether they were not right in the views they entertained
of him. Even in the Gospels themselves, as we have seen, there are recorded a vast number of particulars which have a strong tendency to
corroborate their notions. Such is the account we have of Judas's betrayal of Jesus. Had he been a deity, it is utterly inconceivable that
his chosen apostle Judas—who had witnessed all his miracles—who had
heard all his discourses—who had been an eye-witness and ear-witness of
all his divine words and actions—and who, in common with the eleven
other apostles, had been promised a throne in the kingdom of heaven,
should have thus betrayed his divine master unto death. Imagine this
Judas ever so heinously wicked, still the mind of the most abandoned
wretch that ever lived, would recoil at the remotest thought of murdering
a god ! Human nature, in its most depraved state, as exemplified among
every nation, in every age of the world, held even its imaginary deities
in profound reverence, contemplating them with infinite awe, and living

in constant terror, lest it offended them. To concert plans for putting to death one of their "immortal gods" was a thing ancient heathens could no more do than think the act itself practicable.* If Judas, therefore, believed Jesus to be God—if he perceived in him the slightest sign of divinity—if, in any thing which he said or did, he discovered any proof that he had been sent from heaven, there is nothing more morally certain than that he would not, and could not betray him. The same thing may be said of all who took part in his condemnation and execution.—It was the total absence of any proof of divinity which induced and enabled the Jews to put Jesus to death. Indeed, the very fact that they crucified him, is of itself, an irrefragable proof that he was not a deity. The very mention of a deity being executed as a malefactor,—of a god dying,—is not only contradictory and absurd, but is a most grovelling expression of one's notion of the infinite, immortal, self-existent Spirit. Although we know very little by analogy, or otherwise, of what Deity is susceptible, yet, we positively know thus much,—that, if immortality is an attribute in the Deity, the notion of a deity dying is not only false, but grossly repugnant to reason. To tell us that only the human nature of Jesus died—in order to persuade us of which, thousands of volumes have, in vain, been written—is to tell us that only a man died. On the same principle might it be said, and truly said, that only a man Judas betrayed, and only a man the Jews crucified. Little do Christian writers seem to perceive that, while they—in order to avoid the absurdity of alleging that a god died—urge that only the human nature of Jesus suffered and died, they thereby abandon altogether the argument of his divinity, and admit that, in him, only a *man* suffered, died, and atoned for *man*.

That Jesus had no divine mission, is further proved by the fact that he did not secure the real and lasting love of his eleven other apostles. In this respect, he did not carry the influence which other teachers, who professed to have no divine commission, carried over the affections of their disciples, so that, from endearment, they would sacrifice their lives for them. In the last, and most trying period of his life, when he was apprehended, "all his disciples forsook him and fled;"—all, except John, left him to his fate; nay, some of them, having in disguise followed at a distance, when questioned, actually denied that they had ever been his disciples. (Matth. xxvi. 56, 69—74.) His moral influence, even over that zealous and enthusiastic disciple—Peter, was not sufficient to prevent him, after he had just been cautioned, from repeatedly uttering a glaring falsehood in his very presence. (Luke xxii. 55—61.) Indeed, his influence, not only over his disciples, but his hearers at large, appears to have grown less and less, as he approached the end of his career,—an effect quite incompatible with the notion that he had a divine mission. His very disciples, who had ample opportunities of judging for themselves, do not appear to have had any faith in his miraculous power; and therefore, must have been disbelievers in his alleged divine mission. Towards the

---

* Still, it is to be observed that, although the heathen gods were not murdered by mortals, yet they often died, in order to atone for the sins of these mortals. Bacchus died, was buried, and descended to hell. The Egyptian Osiris, who was called "*the Holy Word*" just as the dismembered god Atys was designated, "*the God our Saviour*," died, rose from the dead, and afterwards ascended into heaven.

close of his public career, namely, when he rose Lazarus from the dead, he uttered words which plainly show that he was aware his disciples did not believe in his miracles. After informing them that Lazarus was dead, he added,—'' I am glad for your sakes that I was not there, *to the intent that ye may believe;* nevertheless let us go unto him. (John xi. 15.) Hence, it appears there existed a suspicion that there was some collusion between Jesus and those he was reported to have previously raised from the dead ; or between him and their relatives. Consequently, he says to his disciples, in regard to the death and intended reanimation of Lazarus, that, for their sake, he was glad he was not present when he died, so that they might believe in the reality of the miracle of resuscitation, which he was about to perform on this body that had been in the grave for four days.—As much as to say that,—since he was not near the place when Lazarus died, no one could suspect that his death was a sham, in order that Jesus might pretend to raise him from the dead. It is, however, remarkable that his disciples had 'not yet believed in him, and that this was a mental act which he hoped would now be accomplished by the resurrection of their friend Lazarus.

In like manner, his own townsmen and nearest neighbours, who knew him from childhood, did not believe in his divine mission, or that he had any claim whatever to supernatural power. Having been preaching the kingdom of heaven and working wonders, in some distant parts, he returned to his native town, Nazareth, and entered the synagogue, like a Jewish priest, with the intention of teaching the people. His townsmen having heard him, were not slow in recognising him as the son of Joseph and Mary ; and in asking, — '' Is not this the carpenter, the son of Mary, the brother of James, and Joses, and Juda, and Simon ? And are not his sisters here with us ? '' They were, therefore, offended at his pretentions, so that here he could do very few mighty works. Others of his neighbours claimed similar acquaintance with him in his earlier days, and faithlessly asked,—'' Is not this Jesus the son of Joseph, whose father and mother we know ? How is it then that he saith, I came down from heaven.'' So unpopular, however, he became at Nazareth, that '' all they in the synagogue rose up and thrust him out of the city, and led him unto the brow of the hill whereon their city was built, that they might cast him down headlong.'' (Mark vi. 3. Luke iv. 16—30. John vi. 42.) But if his townsmen could have perceived a spark of divinity in Jesus, they would not have attempted to hurt him ; for, in all ages, and in all countries, where the bulk of the people have been trained to believe in miracles, they have, *ceteris paribus,* always been actuated by a feeling of profound fear towards workers of wonders, rather than a wish to deprive them of life. Human nature, even in the most rude state, cannot help admiring excellency. According to the very nature of things, it is always constrained to pay homage to virtue and nobleness of character, as daily seen displayed, even in the most common transactions of life. We often see persons of extraordinary moral worth revered by a whole community. If then, the moral excellencies of Deity, which must infinitely transcend the most noble qualities ever exemplified in man, had shone forth in Jesus, the inhabitants of his native town would have been constrained to pay him profound reverence, and to approach him with mingled awe and admiring amazement.   Who—except his nearest relatives, whose testimony may be liable to the charge of partiality—had better opportunities of judging whether Jesus had super-human excellencies, than these Nazarenes—his own townsmen and neighbours, who had known him from infancy?   Who—as disinterested and impartial observers—were better qualified to decide whether, on any occasion, from his birth to the time he commenced his public career, the slightest glimmer of divinity appeared in what he said or did?   So well acquainted were they with him, and with his father, mother, brothers, and sisters, that they appear never to have imagined he was the son of the Holy Ghost.   If they thought so,— if they believed that he had been sent into the world on a special mission from God, and if, during the thirty years he had lived amongst them, they had seen his transcendent virtues shining forth, in infancy, boyhood, and manhood, it would have been utterly impossible for them to treat him in the contemptuous and cruel manner described in the Gospels.   The inevitable conclusion, therefore, is, that these people did not believe in his divine pretentions.

But of all other people in the world, his own family and nearest kindred—his mother, brothers, and sisters, who were closely associated with him every moment, at least, of his earlier days, had the best opportunity of observing his private conduct, and of watching the secret emotions of his mind.   Even they, however, did not believe in his alleged divine mission.   Nor did they give him credit for working real miracles.   His brothers, therefore, on one occasion, insinuated that it was in dark and obscure corners he displayed his marvels, and exhorted him not to remain secluded in Galilee, but to go at once to the approaching feast of the Jewish nation, in Judea.   Ironically, they told him,—" Depart hence, and go into Galilee that thy disciples also may see the works that thou doest; for there is no man that doeth anything in secret, and he himself seeketh to be known.   If thou do these things, show thyself to the world.   *For neither did his brethren believe in him.*" (John vii. 1—5.)   From this statement of the beloved apostle of Jesus, it is clear that the latter's own brothers, whose natural affections would constrain them to view all his words and actions in the most favourable light possible, had, however, by their close observation of the mental qualities he had displayed from his childhood up to that time, been driven to the conclusion that he was no more divinely influenced than some other mortal.   On the contrary, they believed him to be of unsound mind,—an opinion which they had already expressed.   His mother and brothers, apprehensive of his personal safety, probably owing to what had been told them of his strange career, went in search of him.   Mark says,—" When his friends heard of it, they went out to lay hold on him; for they said, He is beside himself."   Jesus, having been told that his mother and brothers were outside the vast crowd with which he was surrounded, seeking him, returned such an answer to their affectionate intreaties as showed that their fears were, by no means, groundless. (Comp. Matth. xii. 46—50. Mark iii. 21, 31—35. Luke viii. 19—21.)   Hence, we see that so far were Jesus's mother and brothers from imagining that he had a divine mission to perform, that they attributed his strange conduct to mental derangement.   Accordingly, when he fell into the hands of the Jewish authorities, we find that, at this

NN

critical juncture, he was abandoned by all his brothers and sisters ; in a word, all his relatives, except his poor and ever affectionate mother.* Supposing that Jesus's kinsmen believed it possible for a deity to suffer and die, and also believed that Jesus was a deity, or had been sent to this world on a divine mission ; then will the apathy which they showed by abandoning him when taken to be crucified, utterly disprove that they did believe him to be such a personage. Had they regarded him as divine, they would have been his first, his most faithful, and most zealous disciples. None had stronger motives to proclaim him divine,—a thing which would shed a haloo of eternal glory upon their own obscurity. But on the other hand, none had such opportunities as they had, of judging from all his words and actions, during thirty-three years of his life, whether his claim to deity had the least foundation in truth. The fact that *they*, under the circumstances detailed, decided he had no such claim, is of the utmost weight.—That his disciples, his neighbours, and his nearest kinsmen disbelieved his doctrines, is one of the stongest possible proofs that he had no divine mission.

His own words, on one occasion, at least, while they prove that *he* thought he had a mission, also prove, indubitably, that that mission was *not* divine,—*could* not, by any possibility, have come from God. In the charge which he delivered to his apostles before he sent them about the country to preach what is called the Gospel, after dilating on the persecutions their preaching would cause, telling them that they would be delivered up to councils,—that they would be scourged,—that they would be brought before kings owing to him,—that they would be persecuted,— that they would make brothers deliver up brothers to death, and fathers their children,—and that they would cause children to rise against their parents, and be the means of putting them to death, he deliberately avows his views as to the purport of his mission, in the following terrible words :—" Think not that I am come to send peace on earth : I came not to send peace, but a sword. For I am come to set a man at variance

---

* John, (xix. 25.) certainly, says, that " there stood by the cross of Jesus his mother and his mother's sister—Mary the wife of Cleophas—and Mary Magdalene." But what the other Evangelists say, goes to contradict this statement. Matthew (xvii. 55, 56.) names " Mary Magdalene, and Mary the mother of James and Joses, and the mother of Zebedee's children." Mark (xv. 40.) mentions "Mary Magdalene, and Mary the mother of James the less, and of Joses and Salome." Luke (xxiii. 55.) gives the names of none of these women. As is the case on almost every other Gospel subject, it is impossible to reconcile the statements of these four writers on this point. It is John alone who says that " there stood by the cross of Jesus, his mother and her sister, Mary the wife of Cleophas. The other writers do not mention these women,—not even Jesus's own mother. If we grant that " the mother of Zebedee's children," mentioned by Matthew, is the same as " Salome," mentioned by Mark, still, " Mary the wife of Cleophas," mentioned by John, is the same as neither of them. In Matthew, (x. 3.) we find that James the less was the son of Alpheus, not of Cleophas ; and there is no reason for supposing that Cleophas and Alpheus were one and the same person. Again, if we imagine that " Mary the wife of Cleophas" was the same person as Jesus's mother's sister, then, we make two sisters—Jesus's mother and aunt—bear the same name— Mary—which is by no means likely to have been the case in those days, when persons bore only one proper name. From the whole of these four contradictory accounts, the evidence would show the balance of probability in favour of the opinion that Jesus's aunt was not present on the occasion.—See on these conflicting statements, Dr. Giles's Christian Records, pp. 248, 249.

against his father, and the daughter against her mother, and the daughter-in-law against her mother-in-law." (Matth. x. 34, 35,) Shocking as this denunciation is, it has been carried to the letter. Diabolical as the avowed purpose of Jesus's mission is, it has been fulfilled to a tittle. Never did he utter words more brimful of truth—melancholy truth! Never did he utter a prediction which has been so precisely and calamitously verified,—a prediction whose disastrous fulfilment has, unfortunately, lasted, without intermission, from the time of its utterance to the present day, and has overwhelmed a large proportion of the human race in heart-rending misery. From the very commencement of the Christian era, the "sword" has accompanied the cross,—a sword that has never found, and never will find a scabbard, till superstitious creeds and immoral dogmas shall be abandoned, as things invented by knaves and believed by fools, in the dark ages of the world,—as things directly calculated to sow the seeds of discord in society, create feuds between man and man, and perpetuate those animosities which turn the sweets of life into wormwood. This, Christianity has done in every age, and in every country into which it has been introduced. Wherever the cross has been raised, thither have followed fire and sword,—horrid burnings and brutal massacres. All history teems with accounts of its fierce persecutions, its savage wars, and its deluging bloodshed.

The singularly exact agreement between what Jesus promised his religion should effect and what it has actually and incessantly effected, for the eighteen centuries during which it has been exercising its influence on society, is, however, too striking, too momentous and melancholy in its consequences, to be passed over thus with a cursory remark. The importance of this prominent and deplorable feature in Christianity, calls upon us to dwell upon it at some length, and enter into the terrible particulars the point involves. To develope these fully, however, would require volumes to be written; therefore, only to a few—comparatively very few—particulars, can reference here be made. As already observed, Jesus avowed that he had come to send a sword on earth; and according to Luke, (xii. 49—53.) he declared that he had come to send "fire" on earth, as well as strife and division between the nearest and dearest relatives.—" I am come to send fire on the earth; and what will I, if it be already kindled? But I have a baptism to be baptized with; and how am I straitened till it is accomplished! Suppose ye that I am come to give peace on earth? I tell you, Nay; but rather division: for from henceforth, there shall be five in one house divided; three against two, and two against three. The father shall be divided against the son, and the son against the father; the mother against the daughter, and the daughter against the mother; the mother-in-law against her daughter-in-law, and the daughter-in-law against her mother-in-law." * A more correct de-

* These declarations, in the shape of predictions, attributed to Jesus by the writers of the Gospel, under the name of Matthew, and that under the name of Luke, whoever they were, show that these productions were compiled after Christians had begun to be persecuted; probably about the end of the second century, or the beginning of the third. Accordingly, their own observation, and, possibly, experience, would dictate to them that bold and sanguinary prediction which they put into the mouth of Jesus. Ample evidence could be adduced to show that the writers of both the Old and New

scription of what Christianity has proved to be, could not be conceived. Wherever its dogmas have been proclaimed, and have gained any influence over the minds of men, "division," "fire," "sword," and bloodshed are the fruits which it has borne in profusion. Its history is one continuous page of cruelties; its annals are written in blood. Wherever it has been believed and practised, it has filled the minds of its votaries with pernicious prejudices and blind rage; while it has enchained their intelectual faculties and nobler emotions, in the dark regions of ignorance and savage gratifications. The basest frauds, the grossest delusions, have been palmed upon the popular mind, in order to inspire belief in its tenets; and when these vile means have failed, recourse has often been had, under the pretence of divine sanction, and under the colour of serving God, to matchless cruelties, to savage tortures, to sanguinary massacres, and the destruction of human life in a thousand barbarous forms. While the advocates of Christianity professed to be the messengers of peace and bearers of mercy, the miseries they inflicted on their fellow-men, have been unparalleled. Of the truth of these grave charges, the annals of every quarter of the earth are teeming with proofs; and Ecclesiastical Histories, written even by Christians, contain abundant evidence. Jesus himself, in promulgating the Christian doctrine, engendered such strife and division, even to the unsheathing and using of the sword, that he lost his life, and fell a martyr to the strife-engendering faith of which he was the founder. Stephen advocated the same principles, and, as similar causes produce similar effects, met with the same fate. The Apostles, owing to the strife-creating doctrine they preached, were considered so turbulent that they were denominated—*those who turned the world upside down.* (Acts xvi. 6.) Paul and Barnabas—apostles of the same faith—drank so deeply into the spirit of Christianity, that they quarrelled; "and the contention was so sharp between them that they departed assunder, one from the other." (Acts xv. 39.) Allusions are also made in Paul's Epistles to the strifes and divisions of Hymeneus, Alexander, Philetus, Hermogenos, Demas, Diotrephes, and others,—all of whom were Christians, or converts to the new religion. Indeed, histories of dissensions and persecutions take up almost the whole of the Acts and the Epistles. So general were they, at the earliest date of this religion, that, as it is clear from ecclesiastical records, the sects of antagonistic Christians were exceedingly numerous, each sect designating all other Christians heretics. In the "Acts of Paul and Thecla"—a document as worthy of credit as any part of the New Testament—we have a remarkable example of the tendency of Christianity to promote strife, and a deplorable verification of Jesus's avowal that it would set "the mother against the

Testament thus made prophecies out of history. After the time of the emperors Trojan and Adrian, and perhaps Maximinus—all persecutors of the Christians—very natural it was for the writers of the Gospels—with the view of showing that the divine books of these Christians contained predictions of the treatment they had received—to put in the mouth of Jesus such words as—" I send you forth as sheep in the midst of wolves,"—" Ye shall be brought before governors and kings for my sake."—" They shall deliver you up to be afflicted, and shall kill you, and ye shall be hated of all nations, for my name's sake."—" When they persecute you in this city, flee ye into another," &c.— Read Matth. viii.; xxiv. Mark xiii. Luke xxi.

daughter, and the daughter against the mother." In this narrative, Demas and Hermogenes declare that, although they could not exactly tell who Paul was, yet, they well knew that he deprived young men of their wives, and young women of their husbands, by the divisions his doctrines incited. We have here also a full account of the strife of Thecla with her mother. Even, in the Nicene council, consisting of 318 Christian bishops, convened to settle divisions, the same spirit was so rampant that these reverend bishops would, there and then, have fought, had not the emperor Constantine restrained them by his authority. (Socrat. Hist. Eccles. lib. i. c. 8. Sozom. i. 16.)

But none ever gave stronger evidence that Jesus had come not to send peace, but strife, fire, and sword on the earth, than the zealous Constantine himself,—the first Christian emperor, and the *real* founder of the present Christian church. Almost all his wars—in some of which he killed as many as thirty thousand in one day—were waged in defence of Christianity. Such, according to early Christian writers, were his battles with his brother-in-law, Licinius, who, in addressing his army, says of Constantine,—" He is so infatuated as to honour some strange and unheard-of deity, with whose despicable standard (the sign of the cross) he now disgraces his army; and, confiding in whose aid, he has taken up arms, and is now advancing, not so much against us, as against those very gods whom he has despised." (Euseb. Vit. Const. lib. ii. c. 5.) It was in the name, and for the sake of this religion, having the cross for his standard, that he always went to war, and set to work with the *sword*, which Jesus says he had come to send on earth. Of the sign of the cross, Eusebius says (Vit. Const. lib. ii. c. 7.) that " Wherever this appeared, the enemy soon fled before his victorious troops; and the emperor, perceiving this, whenever he saw any part of his forces hard pressed, gave orders that the salutary trophy (the sign of the cross) should be moved in that direction, like some triumphant and effectual remedy against disasters: the combatants were divinely inspired, as it were, and immediate victory was the result." What zeal, throughout life, Constantine displayed in verifying Jesus's words that he came to send a sword on earth! In verification of this truth, the pious emperor caused his soldiers " to raze to the ground " an incredible number of heathen temples, among which was the temple of Æsculapius at Ægæ,—an edifice, as Eusebius tells us, which " was the object of admiration to noble philosophers," and in which, according to Sozomen, a preternatural being manifested himself by night, and " healed the diseases of the sick." In demolishing these temples, he used both fire and sword, and spilt much human blood. Of the massacres which attended their demolition, let the following instance suffice, as given in a more detailed form by Sozomen, (lib. vii. c. xv.) a writer strongly biassed in favour of the Christians.—The temple of Serapis, in Egypt, as well as others, having been given by the emperor to Christian bishops, they exposed to public gaze the statues and mysteries of the heathen priests. The latter, although they would otherwise have succumbed to the imperial robbery, yet considered this too great an insult to be borne, and, therefore, made a resolute resistance. Having converted the temple into a citadel, they slew many of the Christians, who had attacked them, and wounded several more. When the battle had lasted for some time,

and carried to a fearful pitch, the general of the Egyptian troops, with
some of the rulers of the city, hastened to the spot, and exhorted the
combatants to lay down their arms.   In vain, however, they spoke, till
the emperor himself came thither.   Sozomen goes on to tell us how other
temples were taken in a similar manner, the *sword* being used to convert
them to Christian purposes.   The more deeply Constantine drank into the
spirit of Christianity, as a matter of course, the more active he became
in the use of the sword to establishing the religion of him who had said
he had come to send fire and sword on earth, and to create dissentions
between near relatives, such as this emperor and Licinius.   Accordingly,
we find the uneducated son of the inn-keeper's daughter, Helena, was
more liberal in his religious views, and altogether a better ruler, at the
commencement of his imperial career than at its end.*   Indeed he appears
to have been a much better man *before* he became a Christian than he was
afterwards.   In the Edict of Milan, in conjunction with his colleague,
Licinius, he could enact the following liberal measure.—"As we long
since perceived that religious liberty should not be denied, but that it
should be granted to the opinion and wishes of each one to perform divine
duties according to his own determination, we had given orders that each
one, and the Christians among the rest, have the liberty to observe the
religion of his choice, and his peculiar mode of worship.   And as there
plainly appeared to be many and different sects added in that edict in
which this privilege was granted them, some of them, perhaps, after a
little while, on this account shrunk from this kind of attention and
observance.   Wherefore, as I, Constantine Augustus, and I, Licinius
Augustus, came under favourable auspices to Milan, and took under
consideration all affairs that pertained to the public benefit and welfare,
these things among the rest appeared to us to be most advantageous and
profitable to all.   We have resolved, among the first things, to ordain
those matters by which reverence and worship to the Deity might be exhibited ; that is, how we may grant likewise to the Christians, and to *all*,
(reliquis omnibus) the free choice to follow that mode of worship which
they may wish, that whatsoever divinity and celestial power may exist,
may be propitious to us and to all that live under our government."

* The fragment of the work of an anonymous historian, found at the end of Valesius's
edition of Ammianus, says of him,—"Literis minus instructus." His mother, Helena,
is said by several ancient writers to have been the daughter of a publican, at Drepanum,
in Nicomedia, while others say she was from Britain, and others, from Naissus, in
Dacia.— See Eutropius, x. 2.   Orosius, vii. 25.   Carte's Hist. of England, vol. i. p. 147.
Jul. Firm. de Astrol. lib. i. c. 4.   The country in which Constantine was born and
brought up is of some importance to any one who would ascertain whence he derived
his religious views.   It is most probable, however, that he acquired these in Persia and
Egypt, where he spent his time in military service, under Dioclesian, from the period at
which his father divorced his mother, when he was eighteen years old, till he was about
thirty-two, when, at the death of his father, he was invested with the purple.   The
beginning of his reign, although he very soon found himself one of six emperors,
gave great satisfaction ; but before its close, he had exceeded most of his predecessors
in crime.   There is very little doubt that he murdered his wife—Fausta, his own son—
Crispus, his nephew, his father-in-law, and several other relatives ; and all this, while
establishing Christian churches.   His reign has been compared to that of Nero.—
Sunt hæc gemmea, sed Neroniana.   Eusebius, a sycophantic bishop that was in his
court, extols him to the skies ; but, of course, says not a word about his heinous and
numerous crimes.

The Edict, which is of some length, goes on to decree "liberty and full freedom to the Christians to observe their own mode of worship," grant "to others to pursue that worship and religion they wish, that each may have the privilege to select and worship whatever divinity he pleases;" and, lastly, the restoration of the places of worship, whether private or public property, to the Christians forthwith, free of any payment whatever. (Euseb. Eccles. Hist. lib. x. c. 5.)   Who would have thought that the same man—about twenty years afterwards, when the sole and sovereign ruler of the Roman world, and a ripe Christian, within two years of his death—would be influenced by the bigotry and cruelty evinced in the following extracts from his Edict against Heretics.—"Forasmuch then, as it is no longer possible to bear with your pernicious errors, we give warning by this present statute, that none of you henceforth presume to assemble yourselves together. We have directed, accordingly, that you be deprived of all the houses in which you are accustomed to hold your assemblies : and our care in this respect extends so far as to forbid the holding of your superstitious and senseless meetings, not in public merely, but in any private house or place whatsoever. . . . . .   "In order that this remedy may be applied with effectual power, we have commanded, as before said, that you be positively deprived of every gathering point for your superstitious meetings; I mean all the houses of prayer (if such be worthy of the name) which belong to heretics, and that these be made over without delay, to the catholic church; that any other places be confiscated to the public service, and no facility whatever be left for any future gathering; in order that from this day forward none of your unlawful assemblies may presume to appear in any public or private place. Let this Edict be made public." (Euseb. Vit. Const. lib. iii. c. 65.)   What a deplorable change the profession of Christianity,* for a few years, made

---

* It must be admitted that it is very difficult to ascertain the exact date at which Constantine became a Christian. He retained through life the pagan title of *Pontifex Maximus*, the duties attached to which was to perform the pagan sacerdotal functions; and at his death, he was made the associate of the heathen deities. As late in his life as the year 321, he published an edict directing the regular consultation of the Aruspices; while, in the same year, he issued another edict for the observance of Sunday. When sole emperor, he enriched the temples of the gods; and his coins and medals were impressed with the figures of the principal heathen deities. His statue bore several features of the solar deity—Apollo, on whose altars he heaped offerings. It was late in life he became even a catechumen; namely, when he received the imposition of hands with prayer,—a ceremony performed on catechumens on their partial and probationary admission into the mysteries of Christianity. Nor was he baptized until within a short time of his death. All the Fathers contend that he declared himself a Christian when he had his vision of the *sign of the cross*, on the night before his last battle with Maxentius; while the Greek historian Zosimus, (lib. ii.) and others, maintain that it was after he murdered his son Crispus he joined the Christians; and that the cause of his change of religion, was that a heathen priest named Sopater, when he applied to him for absolution of his murderous crimes, told him that he could not be absolved of offences so heinous; whereupon he turned to the pagan Christians of Egypt—the worshippers of the God Serapis—who unhesitatingly purified him. (Vid. ant. p. 252.) There is no doubt, however, that Constantine's baptism—a ceremony thought by ancient Christians to effect an absolute purification from all sorts of crimes—had something to do with his past murders. Eusebius (Vit. Const. iv. 61.) must have been conscious of this, when, involving the very meaning of Zosimus's charge, he ambiguously and cautiously wrote thus :—"He felt the time was come at which he should seek to expiate the errors of his past career; firmly believing that whatever sins he had

in this emperor! How tolerant, and even liberal he was previous to his conversion! and, afterwards, how persecuting and cruel! The more he committed as a mortal man, his soul would be purified from them through the efficacy of the mysterious words, and the salutary waters, of baptism." Eusebius then proceeds to tell us that the Emperor, "now for the first time, received the imposition of hands with prayer,"—that he told the bishops to whom he applied for baptism that he had once thought to be baptized in the Jordan,—that if his life should be prolonged, and he be allowed to associate with the people of God, and unite with them in prayer as a member of his church, he would, thenceforward, devote himself to his service,—and that the prelates, having administered to him the ceremony of baptism, gave him the necessary instructions, and made him partaker of the holy mysteries. All this, in substance, is quite consistent with the statement of Zosimus. Whether it was the bishops of Serapis or others, who baptized Constantine is of little moment; for, as it has already been shown, (pp. 331—2.) these were the original Christian bishops:—Illi qui Serapim colunt, Christiani sunt; et devoti sunt Serapi, qui se Christi episcopos dicunt. Still, in a couple of centuries afterwards, or less time, when Christianity had become a religion entirely distinct in profession from all the heathen sects, this became a matter of great weight. Accordingly, we find Evagrius, (Hist. Eccl. ii. 40, 41.) and Sozomen, (i. 5.) very fierce in their denunciations against Zosimus, for asserting it was after killing his wife Fausta and his son Crispus, and having in vain applied for purification to the priests of his own religion, (that of pagan Rome) who plainly told him such crimes were too enormous for purification, that Constantine met with an Egyptian who had come from Iberia, and who assured him that the Christian faith would purge him from any sin, he embraced what was thus imparted to him, and, forsaking the religion of his fathers, was therefore initiated *by an Egyptian* into *our mysteries* —Παρα τινος Αιγυπτιον δια ταυτα των ημετερων μυστηριων μετεσχεν. The difficulty of ascertaining the precise period of his life at which Constantine can be said to be a Christian, according to what is now called Christianity, is caused principally by the following things:—1. That in his time the Christian religion, which emanated from paganism, was so closely blended with it; nay, on most points, *identical* with it, both in ceremonies and doctrines—in all but the name—so that, at this distant age, it is impossible to make a distinction. 2. That so many forgeries have been committed in works written during, and after, his time, and so many actions attributed to him, with which he had nothing to do. Witness the forgery of the decretals and donation of Constantine, with the account of his baptism at Rome, thirteen years before his death, and also of his interdiction of royal marriages with foreigners. 3. That so many works which did not suit the Christian religion have been burnt, and otherwise destroyed. 4. That the authors of those which are extant—both the pagans and Christians of these ages of religious dissensions—write with such evident bias, that their bare statement cannot be trusted, on religious points. The following dates of events in the life of Constantine, which are received as correct by the ablest critics of the present age, may assist us materially in our present enquiry.—Constantine had his vision of *the sign of the cross*, and fought his last battle with Maxentius in the autumn of the year 312; met his colleague Licinius at Milan, and issued the edict which gave equal liberty to all religionists, in the spring of 313, only about five months after he had the vision of the cross; murdered his son Crispus in the summer of 326; and issued his edict for the persecution of heretics in 331; only about two years before his death. Now, if we take for granted that, as the Fathers contend, Constantine became a Christian the day he had the vision of the cross, still this was only five months before he issued his liberal edict in conjunction with the ingenuous Licinius. During this interval, he was partly engaged in war, and partly arranging matters belonging to the empire, after the terrible battle he had won over Maxentius, so that he could not yet know much about his new religion, and, certainly, was neither baptized nor initiated into the Christian mysteries by the imposition of hands, as we have just seen. But when he enacted his law against heretics, in nineteen years afterwards, he had had ample time and opportunity to know and feel the spirit of this religion. The results were—this persecuting edict, the application of fire and sword to his Christian brethren, and the deliberate murder of his wife, his son, and several other near relations. Surely, there can be nothing clearer than that Christianity considerably altered this prince for the worse,—made him a much worse man than when he was a pagan,—made him brilliantly exemplify the persecuting spirit which the Gospels say Jesus sent on earth.

was Christianized, the more he strove to realise Jesus's words—that he had come to send strife, fire, and sword on earth—in slaughtering other religionists, destroying their books, and robbing them of their temples. The same spirit influenced his Christian son, Constantius, as shown in the following edict which bears his name:—" It is our pleasure that, in all places, and in all cities, the temples be immediately shut, and carefully guarded, that none may have the power of offending. It is likewise our pleasure that all our subjects should abstain from sacrifices. If any one should be guilty of such an act, let him feel the sword of vengeance; and after his execution, let his property be confiscated to the public." (Cod. Theodos. lib. xvi. tit. x. leg. 4.) Nor was this blood-thirsty religious feeling confined to the Emperor; it prevailed among all his Christian subjects. Not only did they slay others for their religious opinions, but they massacred one another. Socrates (Hist. Eccles. lib. ii. c. 12.) tells us that, " by the intestine war among the Christians, the city of Constantinople was kept in a state of perpetual turbulence, and the most atrocious outrages were perpetrated, whereby many lives were lost." In the next chapter, he gives us an account of a regiment of soldiers being sent to quell the disturbance the Christians created about the election of a bishop. The most prominent feature in the reign of Constantius was Christian strife, in which thousands lost their lives. The contrast between the reign of this emperor and that of his successor—the heathen emperor Julian—forcibly argues that Jesus came to send fire and sword. Julian, although professedly attached to the heathen religion, which his father and uncle had endeavoured to annihilate, yet, did not visit a single Christian with punishment on account of his religion. On the contrary, he extended to all his subjects full religious liberty, releasing from exile the bishops and other Christians who had been banished by their brethren, restoring to them their respective churches, and exhorting them to live in peace. (Ammanianus, xxii. 5, 9, 10. Libanius, Orat. Parent. c. 58.) Having no faith in the fire and the sword, as engines of conversion, the only means he used was that rational one, namely, to *write* against Christianity. He did not attempt even to restore to the pagans the temples taken from them by the Christians; he only opened those which Christian emperors had closed, affording throughout his reign a convincing proof that his religion was not so blood-thirsty as that of his predecessors.* Passing by the short reign of Jovian, we no sooner find

* Few men have been more more calumniated, by early Christian writers, than Julian. Whatever virtuous act they are forced to attribute to him, they are sure to refer it to some bad motive. Sozomen (lib. v. c. 5.) tells us that, if Julian shed less blood, and devised fewer punishments, than his predecessors, he was equally inimical to the church. His motive in recalling the priests whom Constantine had banished, was to cause division in the church. He compelled Bishop Eleusius to build a Christian church at his own expense, from hatred to Constantius. When a blind bishop, named Maris, came purposely to insult his majesty, denouncing him a reprobate, an atheist, and apostate; and, when the emperor, after telling the bishop that his Galilean deity would not cure his blindness, passed on without giving a reply to what followed, his motive for not retorting was, that he " considered paganism would be advanced by the exhibition of greater lenity and mildness towards Christians than could in ordinary circumstances be expected." (Sozom. v. 4.) It is with great caution that we can receive any unsupported statement from a historian who thus allows his prejudice to enter so deeply into his narrative. But notwithstanding the aspersions which Christians have cast upon Julian,

two Christian princes swaying their authority over the Roman world, than we discover the demon of religious persecution hovering over every province.* While the Christians, under Valens, persecuted one another in the East, those under Valentinian did the same in the West. Again, we find a still fiercer persecution of the Pagans under Gratian ; and when we come to the times of Maximus and Theodosius the Great†—two emperors renowned for their Christian piety—we are saddened to witness

on account of his religion, it is clear, not only from the testimony of heathen writers of unimpeachable veracity, but even from the admission of avowedly inimical eclesiastical writers, that he was a most impartial, liberal, and noble-minded man. Take the following few instances. A bishop, named George, had been murdered by the inhabitants of Alexandria—some say by the Christians, and others, by the pagans—under the following circumstances. Constantine having given to the Christians a ruined heathen temple of Mithras, George wished to build a church on the site. The Christians, in removing the remains of the ancient temple, discovered some of the relics of heathen worship, and, in derision, carried them through the city. This exasperated the zealous pagans, and there ensued a serious affray, in which—according to Jesus's prediction—"friends, brothers, parents and children imbrued their hands in each other's blood ;" and, among others, George, the holy bishop, who was obnoxious to both pagans and Christians, was murdered by the one or the other. Julian, hearing of this outrage, wrote to the Alexandrians, rebuking them in strong terms, and telling them that they had forgotten the universal claim of humanity and social order,—that, although this George had exasperated Constantius against them, had introduced an army into the city, and had induced the governor of Egypt to despoil their temples, yet, their duty was to impeach him before the judges,—and that, if they had thus acted, neither murder nor any other unlawful deed would have been committed, but, justice being equally dispensed, they would have been preserved from these disgraceful acts, and George would have suffered the punishment due to his impious crimes. Having told them that if they had acted thus, the insolence of their enemies would be curbed, he adds—"Your heinous misdoings utterly oppose my wishes. The people have had the audacity to tear a man in pieces, like dogs ; nor have they been subsequently ashamed of this inhuman procedure, nor desirous of purifying their hands from such polution. . . . . . . Should you say that it became you to inflict the vengeance due to this man's offences, that we could by no means acquiesce in ; for you have laws to which it is the duty of every one of you to be subject, and to evince his respect for, both publicly and in private. If any individual transgress those wise and salutary regulations, which were originally made for the well-being of the community, does that absolve the rest from obedience to them ?" This epistle, written, as it is, in the most elegant style ; against pagans for slaying a Christian, is, of itself, a sufficient proof that Julian was strongly averse to religious persecution. (Socrat. Eccles. Hist. iii. 3.) If Julian issued an edict to apprehend a Christian bishop, it was because he was thought to be concerned in the abominable mysteries in which children were sacrificed and their flesh eaten. (Socrat. iii. 13.) If he wrote a pamphlet against the Christians of Antioch, it was because they derided him, and caricatured even his beard, saying that it should be cut off and made into a rope to hang him. Few Christian emperors, under the circumstances, would have so tenderly dealt with these scoundrels. If he caused certain Christians to be apprehended and receive a few stripes, it was because they insulted him with reproachful songs ; not because they were Christians. (Socrat. iii. 18, 19.) A Christian prince would be likely to assert his dignity in a much more inhuman mode.

* About this time, two Christian Fathers, named Damasus and Ursinus, allowed their arms and those of their respective partizans to decide which of them was to be bishop of Rome. After a fierce battle, in which a great number fell on each side, Damasus's party was victorious.—Ammianus xxvii. 3. Socrat. Hist. Eccl. lib. iv. c. 29.

† This pious emperor may be considered the founder of the " Holy Office of the Inquisition," more particular notice of which will be taken anon. It is in his edict, in 382, against the Manicheans, that we find the first appointment of an Inquisition, with power of accusing, made in reference to heresy. In this edict, it is decreed that these Christian heretics be punished with death, and their property confiscated ; and the

the former assisted and encouraged by his Christian hierophants to shed the blood of the saints, for their crooked notions of religious matters, for praying stark naked in the midst of an assembly of men and women, and for other things, still more indecorous ; (Sulpicius Severus, Hist. Sacr. lib. ii. Dial. iii. 15.) while we are astonished at the severity of the fifteen edicts of the latter against heretics, and the ferocity of the armed Christians who, under the episcopal flag, marched in vast armies against the inoffensive heathens, to destroy their gorgeous temples, burn their valuable libraries, and cause innumerable lives on each side to be lost.   Nor can we forget the massacres of Antioch and Thessalonica, which were deeply tinged with religious animosity.   In the latter place, not less than six thousand were put to the sword.

But why wander so far back into the dark and barbarous ages of antiquity in search of proofs, when they abound in more modern and civilized times ?—times in which Christianity, by the progress of true knowledge and real civilization, had been divested of much of its pristine savagery.   Take, for example, the Christian massacres called the Sicilian Vespers, or the pious carnages of Jutland.   Or, come still nearer home, and hear the echo of the heart-rending groans of the French Protestants, on St. Bartholomew's horrific night, not three centuries ago, ever verifying the declaration of Jesus as to the sanguinary nature of his religion.   This terrible carnage, in an attempt to exterminate the Protestants, commenced at Paris, on the 24th of August, 1572, in the dead hour of night, and continued for three whole days, during which ten thousand defenceless persons of all ranks, of all ages, and of each sex, were indiscriminately massacred.   The streets and passages of the city resounded with the fiendish yells of the murderers, the groans of the dying, and the shrieks of those about to be slaughtered.   The courts and chambers were filled with the bodies of the slain which had been thrown out through windows and dragged along the streets.   Human blood ran in torrents down the channels into the river, and a multitude of about ten thousand men, women, and children, fell a prey to this pious destruction !—a destruction of one sect of Christians by another !—a destruction which, with equal fury, spread into the provinces, and almost throughout the whole of the French territory.   At Lyons, for example, about eight hundred persons were thus religiously butchered.—Children and parents, when in the very act of taking the last embrace of each other, were slain, and their bodies, half dead, thrown into the river.   When the news of this hydra-barbarity arrived at Rome, the head quarters of Christianity, the joy of the Christians in that city knew no bounds.—A public procession was formed ; high mass was celebrated ; a jubilee was proclaimed throughout Christendom, and other demonstrations were made, by way of expressly "thanking God for the great blessing that had thus been conferred on the

Prefect is commanded to appoint inquisitors and spies to discover heretics who should conceal themselves.   He also decreed that "all writings whatever, which Porphyry, or any one else, has written against the Christian religion, in the possession of whomsoever they may be found, *shall be committed to the fire.*"   Thus, we are deprived of what was advanced against this religion by Porphyry, a most profoundly learned man, and the ablest opponent of the Christian Fathers, who were unable to refute his arguments, and therefore obtained an imperial decree to have his work burnt.

church." But even this carnage dwindles into insignificance when compared to the blood which Christianity shed in Piedmont's valleys, when
the inoffensive Waldenses were exterminated so completely that scarcely a
a remnant of them was left "to attest the red record of their nation's
destruction." These primitive Christians were, from age to age, burnt
and massacred,—were hunted from their dwellings, and, by hundreds,
suffocated with smoke in caves; while their wives and children were put
to death in a manner too inhuman for detail. In a similar mode had Pope
Innocent III. previously destroyed his fellow-Christians in Languedoc, by
means of Crusaders,—these furiously mad fanatics, with crucifix in hand,
who, in different times, and different countries, have been roused to send
millions of victims to the slaughter. In the present case, "three hundred
thousand pilgrims, induced by the combined motives of avarice and superstition, filled the country of the Albigenses with carnage and confusion
for a number of years." Sixty thousand of the inhabitants of Baziers
were, at one time, put to death; and when a Cistercian monk, who had
the superintendence of this wholesale butchery, was asked by his myr-
midons how the heretics were to be separated from the Catholics, he
replied,—"*Kill all; God will know his own.*"

But of all the means contrived by Christians to carry out the declaration of Jesus, that Christianity was destined to produce strife,
division, sword, and fire,—of all the institutions invented to carry out the
avowed purpose of Jesus's mission, none was ever more heinous in its
machinations, and more horrible in its effects than the Inquisition, which
suddenly "dragged the suspected heretic from the embrace of affection to
a dungeon that was at once to be his dwelling and his grave!—a dwelling
whose eternal gloom was never visited by the bland light of heaven,—a
grave that yawned in secret and closed in silence!" This institution, in
which the German Christians glory, by the name of Auto-da-fé, was
within the space of one century, according to reliable authorities, the
means of destroying the lives of three millions of the inhabitants of Spain,
and of banishing a hundred and seventy thousand of them. Philip Lem-
borch, in describing this Christian institution, among other things, says—
"Not a whisper is heard, or the least hint of insecurity given, until, in
the dead hour of night, a band of savage monsters surround the dwelling;
they demand entrance:—upon the enquiry, by whom is this required?
the answer is, 'the Holy Office.' In an instant, all the ties of nature
appear as if dissolved; and, either through the complete dominion of
superstition, or the conviction that resistance would be vain, the master,
parent, husband, is resigned. From the bosom of his family, and bereft
of all domestic comforts, he enters the Inquisition house; its ponderous
doors are closed, and hope excluded—perhaps for ever. All ties of
kindred are now dissolved; his children, who are disinherited, are freed
from his control; his wife is liberated from her marriage vow, and is no
more his; he has forfeited all social rights; he has no protection from the
law, and no remedy against injustice. His friends and nearest relatives
are expected to abandon him to his fate; and the only way for his wife,
children, brothers, sisters, father, mother, to avoid his doom is to be the
first to accuse him to the *holy office* of the Inquisition." Now, this is the
very doctrine taught by Jesus, who says,—"He that loveth father or

mother more than me is not worthy of me." (Matth. x. 37.)   And numerous, doubtless, have been the cases in which the nearest relatives have thought it their imperative duty to give information to the secret emissaries of the Holy Office, touching the heresy of one another, so as to bear out the truth of Jesus's declaration that he came to set the son against the father and the daughter against her mother, and to make a persons foes be those of his own household.   Although the accuser and the accusation were kept a profound secret from the accused, and all others without the pale of the Inquisition, so that millions of charges brought by persons against their nearest kinsmen, were conducted in such a manner that their respective authors were known only to the Holy Office; yet, since the arcana of many of these temples of crime have been exposed to public gaze, several such instances have been discovered. Blaquire, the historian of the Spanish revolution, says that, one memorandum on the wall in the Inquisition in Spain, indicated that the mother of the person mentioned was his accuser.   Llorente mentions cases in which the son was the means of accusing his mother of concealing heretical books; the husband of accusing his wife of Judaism; and an illustrious lady, her sister of being a Lutherian. (Chap. 21, 33.)   Mr. Davie, in his second edition of the History of the Inquisition, (p. 68.) says,—" Many denunciations were effected through the instrumentality of confessors, who, in the exercise of their office, imposed it as a duty on such of their penitents as had heard or seen anything which was, or appeared to be, contrary to the Catholic faith, that they should communicate the fact to the Holy Office.   On such occasions, penitents seldom failed to remember some unguarded expression which had fallen from the lips of some friend or relative.   If the penitent could write, he himself drew up a declaration; if not, it was done by his confessor, who then forwarded it to the Holy Office.   As, in such cases, absolution was rigidly refused until the denunciation was effected, it frequently happened that *a wife informed against her husband, a parent against a child, or a child against a parent."*   Nor could it be otherwise, according to the very nature of the whole system of the Inquisition.   But how wonderfully this important portion of Christianity—in which indeed consisted the Christianity of the whole world for about fifteen centuries,—how wonderfully it has verified the declaration of Jesus that his religion would make the members of a person's own household be his worst enemies !   One would think that Christian persecution and the Holy Office of the Inquisition were in a flourishing state when this declaration was uttered.   But let us see what sort of fire and sword these holy men had.   Passing by their thousand modes of preliminary torture, let us come at once to the *Auto-de-fé*, (Act of faith)—the general gaol delivery of Christian persecutors—the principal part of which consisted in burning heretics, which, according to Dr. Geddes, was conducted in the following terrible manner.— The heretics who are to be burnt alive are marched to the place of execution with a Jesuit on each side of every one of these unfortunate beings, continually preaching the duty of abjuring heresy, and followed by the Inquisitor General, and other officers of the Holy Court, all mounted. Having arrived at the place of execution—a platform or amphitheatre, capable of holding about a thousand people—the person to be burnt is chained to a pole, about which there is a quantity of dry furze and fagots. Some of the furze are fastened to the end of a long stick, and, having been fired, are held to the victim's face, till it is burnt to a cinder, and presents a most horrible spectacle. Then fire is put to the pile beneath, whereupon loud shouts of joy issue from the inhuman spectators and the Jesuitical monks who officiate on the occasion. In more ancient times Christian heretics, instead of being burnt alive, in some countries, were hung; in others, beheaded; and in others, put to death by crucifixion, and by the sword. Those who have suffered death thus at the hands of the holy Christian Inquisition, are said to amount to *many millions!* Such is the *fire* which Jesus avowed he had come to bring on earth, and intimated that it had already been kindled.

Some good Christian may exclaim,—"Aye, these were great cruelties! But they were those of foreign and barbarous countries; not of civilized and Christian England." Unfortunately, their parallels are found abundantly recorded in the history of *English* Christians. Behold Thomas à Becket's sanguinary deeds; peruse the heart-rending history of the English martyrs; and read the exploits of Queen Mary of England, during whose short reign of about five years nearly three hundred persons were brought to the stake for their religion, besides many who died in prisons, were whipped, and otherwise barbarously used. "Yes, but those who acted thus were Papists,—no such charges can be brought against Protestants." Happy it were, if this were true! But to this very day, in our ears resound the words of Luther—the Great Protestant leader—in his "*State of the Popish Church,*" that "heretics should be shut up in prison, and put under restraint as madmen,"—that "the synagogues of the Jews should be levelled with the ground, their houses destroyed, their Talmud taken from them, and their Rabbis banished." Before our eyes is the following title of one of the works of an ancient Swiss reformer:—"A declaration for maintaining the true faith, held by all Christians, concerning the Trinity of Persons in one only God, by John Calvin, against the detestable errors of Michael Servetus, a Spaniard; in which it is also proved that it *is lawful to punish heretics, as this wretch was justly executed in the city of Geneva.* Printed at Geneva, 1554." Behold this Father of Protestantism, who is almost an object of worship with a large proportion of English Christians, writing, in a letter dated February, 1546,—"If Servetus come to Geneva, I will exercise my authority in such a manner as not to allow him to depart alive." See him writing to Farel concerning the same Servetus, whose arguments he could not refute, on the 20th of August, 1553,— "I hope he will be condemned to die;" and notice the same spirit of fire and sword in his subsequent letter, dated the 30th of September, 1561, to the High Chamberlain of the King of Navarre, wherein he says of heretics,—"Do not fail to rid the country of such zealous scoundrels, who stir up the people to revolt against us. Such monsters should be exterminated, as I have exterminated Michael Servetus, the Spaniard." Return now to England, and look at the additional blood-stained marks which Queen Elizabeth and other monarchs have left on Christianity. Peep into the horrible secrets of even the English Inquisition, known as the High Commission Court, and the Star Chamber. Behold these Christian institutions bringing Arch-bishop Laud, and many others, to the block, and deluging the whole nation in blood. Gaze at all Ireland pursued by its reformed Christian foes, and visited with fetters, dungeons, fire, sword, and death. See how nobly the Scottish Covenanters resist the ruthless hand of their religious oppressor, and—rather than submit—brave death, in many a mountain pass and sanguinary plain. Behold Henry VIII.— the very founder of the Protestant church, and the very image of the great Constantine, the father of the Catholic church, in the murder of relatives, and several other points—burning six persons together; three papists and three protestants; tying a protestant and a papist arm to arm; burning the papists because they do not go far enough, and the protestants because they go too far. Witness him passing that blood-shedding measure—" The Statute of Six Articles," and beheading Bishop Fisher, Sir Thomas More, and several friars and monks, for their religious opinions. Look also at his daughter, Queen Elizabeth—most of whose religious enactments, to this very day, disgrace our statute-book—imprisoning in dungeons, till death release them, all Christians who differ from her in point of belief. See her executing Copping and Thacker, for selling religious tracts; cutting off the hands of John Stubbs, and those of another man, on the scaffold at Westminster; and condemning to death eleven Dutch baptists; nine of whom, however, afterwards were only banished, while the remaining two were burnt in Smithfield. Look into her prisons, and see them filled with Non-conformists, who, as their historian tells us, die in dungeons, like rotten sheep; while many of their ministers, such as Barrow, Greenwood, Penry, and others, are executed at Tyburn, and elsewhere. During the reign of the succeeding monarch, Christianity evinced the same spirit, and pursued the same inhuman course of burning men; such as Tyndale, near Filford Castle; Bartholomew Legate, in Smithfield; Edmund Wightman, at Lichfield, and so on. In the next reign, Dr. Leighton, professor of moral philosophy in the University of Edinburgh, was, at the instigation of Christian priests, set in the pillory, had both his ears cut off, both sides of his nose ripped open, and was shut up in a dungeon to be released only by death. Prynne, Bastwich, and Burton, were treated in as brutal a manner, for similar offences, while their persecuting Christian brethren blessed God for the cruelty he thus enabled them to inflict. Even so late as the time of Charles II. only two centuries ago, the slaughter of the Scotch Covenanters was renewed; they were pursued to mountains and morasses, with fire and sword, and subjected to the horrors of the rack, the thumb-screw, the iron boot, and other engines of cruelty. Nearly eight thousand of them perished in prisons, during this reign alone, merely for dissenting from the Protestant Church. According to authentic records, sixty thousand Non-conformists suffered, by way of death, imprisonment, loss of property, and otherwise, between the restoration of Charles II. and the revolution of William III.

Such has been the real spirit of Christianity in every country where it has been proclaimed, and at all times, during nearly the whole of two thousand years,—from the very time Jesus is said to have declared he had come to send strife and division, sword and fire on earth, to the present hour. As proof of the connexion between this horrible declaration of

Jesus and the subsequent sanguinary persecutions of the Christians, it is to be observed that no other religion—that of the Jews perhaps excepted—thus carried on an uninterrupted chain of devastations for, at least, more than sixteen centuries! It is with considerable propriety that the renowned Freret makes the following observation:—" If God had designed to make himself a man, and to die in Palestine by an infamous punishment, to expiate the crimes of mankind, and to banish sin from the earth, there ought to have been no longer any sin or crime among men ; whereas religious crimes seems only to have commenced since the time when that event is said to have happened ; *and the Christians, by their holy massacres and burnings, have shown themselves more abominable monsters than all the sectaries of the other religions put together.*" He also remarks that none of the numerous nations called heathens ever spilt a drop of human blood, on the score of *theological arguments :* and in this he is corroborated by Dr. Cave, who remarks, in the preface to his " *Primitive Christianity,*" that " if an honest heathen were to estimate Christianity by the lives of its professors, he would certainly prescribe it as the vilest religion in the world ; " and also by the Rev. Simon Brown, in his Defence of Christianity, who says that, to hereticate one another is peculiar to Christians, and that the heathens never showed such mutual hatred. On this point, the Mahometans, whom we hear every day reproached with having established their religion in blood, very advantageously contrast with the Christians. For instance, when the Christian crusaders, under Godfrey of Bouillon, entered Jerusalem, *after the military force had surrendered,* they massacred all the defenceless inhabitants they found, sparing neither age nor sex, and streaming the streets with the blood of thousands of victims. But when the Mahometans, under Saladin, recovered from them the same city, *no blood was shed after the surrender ;* and the Christian captives were most mercifully treated ; the general, not only giving them their liberty without ransom, but even donations to those who were poor.*

---

* The mad exploits of the crusaders, when the influence of the Christian religion was in its full zenith, show the sanguinary spirit of this faith in a clearer manner than anything else that can be advanced. Every one of the nine crusades, was professedly made for the sake of Christianity. The first crusade was in the year 1096. We have already had occasion to observe (p. 206.) that in the tenth century it was generally believed in Christendom that the end of the world was close at hand, and that Christ would soon make his appearance in Palestine as a Judge. During this and the following century, a vast number of fanatics made pilgrimages to the Holy Land, and some of them stayed there a considerable time, in expectation to meet the Judge. Palestine being now under the dominion of the Sultan, the Christian pilgrims were much annoyed at finding all the Holy places in the possession of Mahometans, whom they called infidels, and with whom they had frequent altercations. The real cause of the first crusade, therefore, was the superstituous veneration of the Christians for these Holy places, mingled with a persecuting, blood-thirsty disposition. In the year 1095, a French hermit, named Peter, visited the Holy Sepulchre, and had a quarrel with the Patriarch of Jerusalem. When he returned home, he loudly complained of the treatment to which the Christians were subjected at Jerusalem, and enlisted the sympathy of Pope Urban II. while he himself went through the chief cities of Christendom, preaching the duty of all Christians to rescue the Holy land from infidels. Popish councils were held in open plains, and attended by a vast number of princes and nobles, 4000 ecclesiastics, and 30,000 seculars. Eloquent harangues were made in order to incite private Christians to join in the Holy war. All Christendom became anxious to engage in it ; saying that, as Christ had

Into the history of whatever country we look, we find that, if Christianity has ever had an inlet into that country, there are records of its

shed his blood for them, they were ready to take up the cross, and shed their blood for him. To defray the expenses of the expedition, opulent Christians sold both their landed and personal property, and branded all who declined taking a part in this pious enterprize with the name of impious cowards. They carried a cross on their shoulders, and had crosses on their skins stamped with hot iron. All orders of men and women, "deeming the crusade the only road to heaven, were impatient to open the way with the sword to the holy city." In the summer of 1096, about 28,300 persons of all ranks, and of every age and sex, were on their march, while there were carried before them a goose and a goat, which animals they thought divinely inspired. (Albert Aquensis, lib. i. c. 31.) On their way, they first attacked the Jews, in whatever cities they found them, for murdering the Son of God, and for refusing to believe in his name; many thousands of whom they slaughtered, pillaging their cities. (Benj. de Tudela. Voy. tom. i.) About two thirds of these fanatics having been killed by the military, for their pillage in passing through Hungary and Bulgaria, the remainder proceeded towards Palestine. But their approach being expected, the soldiers of the Sultan diverted them to the plains of Nice, where almost all of them perished in battle. Thus ended the first crusade. The second, in the following year, was both more numerous and successful. By this time, it had reached the ear of every Christian that Christ had specially taken up the cause of the crusaders; that the Virgin Mary had obtained a full pardon of all their sins; that the lance with which Jesus had been pierced in his side, had just been discovered; and that to hold up this divine lance, as an ensign in the Holy war, would make all their enemies flee. Three knights clad in white, and bearing splendid arms, had also been seen to issue from a distant hill, which was considered a sure omen of success. The crusaders, thus full of faith, rushed forward, obtained a victory over the Turks who defended Jerusalem, and entered the Holy city. When the enemy had actually surrendered, the crusaders commenced one of the most terrible slaughters on record, which lasted for three days. A Christian writer, under the word *Croisaders*, in the Encyclopædia Britannica, thus describes the indiscriminate carnage.—"The horrid cruelties they committed also were such as must have inspired the Turks with the most invincible hatred against them, and made them resist with the greatest obstinacy. They were such as could have been committed by barbarians inflamed with religious enthusiasm. When Jerusalem was taken, not only the numerous garrison were put to the sword, but the inhabitants were massacred without mercy and without distinction. No age nor sex was spared, not even suckling children. According to Voltaire, some Christians, who had been suffered by the Turks to live in that city, led the conquerors into the most private caves, where women had concealed themselves with their children, and not one of them was suffered to escape. What eminently shows the enthusiasm by which these conquerors were animated, is their behaviour after this terrible slaughter. They marched over heaps of dead bodies towards the Holy sepulchre, and, while their hands were yet polluted with the blood of so many innocent persons, sang anthems to the common Saviour of mankind." See also Gibbon, chap. 25. The Holy Land having been held by the crusaders for about 88 years, during which they often murdered one another, it was retaken by the Turks, in 1187, under the command of Saladin. But, when Jerusalem was taken and entered by the enemy, how much more humane was the conduct of the Turks than had been that of the Christians under similar circumstances! When the crusaders had lost all faith in the intercession of the Queen, the women and the monks, who, in a doleful procession, implored Jesus to save his tomb and his inheritance from the infidel, and when the enemy had opened a breach of fifteen cubits in the wall, and was pouring into the city, they intreated the mercy of the Turkish commander, to whom the general of the crusaders made the following speech.—"Know, O Sultan, that we who are exceedingly numerous, and have been restrained from fighting like men in despair only by the hopes of an honourable capitulation, will kill all our wives and children, commit all our wealth and valuable effects to the flames, massacre 5000 prisoners now in our hands, leave not a single beast of burden or animal of any kind belonging to us alive, and level to the ground the rock you esteem sacred, together with the temple of Al Aksa. After this, we will sally out upon you in a body; and doubt not that we shall cut to pieces a much greater number of you than we are, or force you to abandon the siege." The humane general, in order to prevent the threatened suicide of

sanguinary deeds,—there are proofs that it brought not peace, but strife, division, persecution, fire, and sword; and that wherever it has trodden,

these fanatics, forthwith called a council of war, at which all the general officers, from motives of humane sympathy, were for allowing the crusaders to walk out freely and securely with their wives, children, and effects. It was ultimately arranged that, on paying an acknowledgment of a small ransom, within forty days, all the Franks and Latins should evacuate Jerusalem, and be safely conducted to the seaports of Syria and Egypt; while the Greek and Oriental Christians were permitted to live under the dominion of the conqueror, who fulfilled, to the letter, *his* part of the treaty. He did more,—he excused payment of a large portion of the ransom by the poorer sort, and freely distributed alms among those who had been made orphans and widows by the fortune of war. He also, in his interview with the queen of the crusaders, evinced very deep commiseration, even by his tears. It is true that, in a previous victory over a portion of these crusaders in a distant part of the Holy land, he ordered 230 knights of the hospital to be put to death; but these were at the time in arms against him; and even in this case, as a proof of his clemency, he allowed their less ferocious brethren to continue the care of the sick, for the space of a year. Upon the whole, how humane! how admirable! is the conduct of these Turks, when compared to the savage, devastating acts of the crusaders when in the ascendant! In their subsequent crusades, the Christians displayed the same sanguinary spirit. The fourth crusade, made in 1198, although ostensibly undertaken to deliver the holy land from the hands of infidels, yet, by its ecclesiastical promoters, was really intended against the Eastern Christians, particularly those at Constantinople, on which city it poured its vengeance. This holy enterprise, again, wherein one set of Christians massacred another on an enormous scale, forcibly illustrates the dissensious spirit of the religion of these militant pilgrims. Its real cause—cleared of the mist of regal jealousy, which ecclesiastical potentates first incited, and then made a pretext for their atrocities—was the frequent quarrels of the Western and Eastern churches, which had originated in the time of Constantine. The latter reproached the former with eating things strangled, with using milk and cheese during Lent, and with allowing some of their monks to indulge in the taste of flesh. These, and other such flimsy religious matters, fanned the flame of discord between the patriarchs of Constantinople and the doctors, particularly the popes, of the Latin church, so as to make them open enemies. In the time of Manuel Comnenus, this religious hatred broke out into a most horrible slaughter.—The Greek Christians attacked the Latins who had settled at Constantinople, slaughtered them in their houses and in the streets, and burnt to ashes that part of the city which they occupied, sparing neither age nor sex, nor even their own nearest relatives; and thus singularly exemplifying the character of Christianity, in setting a man at variance with his father, mother, sisters, brothers, &c. The Latin clergy were burnt in their churches, and their sick in their hospitals. The Greek priests and monks were most active in the work of devastation; and, when the head of a Roman cardinal, the Pope's legate, was severed from his body, fastened to the tail of a dog, and dragged through the city, they chanted praises to God! About four thousand of the Latin Christians were sold in perpetual slavery to the Turks. On the other hand, the Latins were equally barbarous: those of them who had, on the first alarm, entered into ships, escaped from the scene of blood, through the Helespont; and, in their flight, burnt and ravaged two hundred miles of the sea coast, and put to death a number of Greek priests and monks. They afterwards took pains to represent to Italy the perfidy and malice of the Greek Christians. This mutual Christian massacre considerably deepened the hatred of the Latin towards the Greek church, No sooner was Innocent III. installed in the papal chair than he began to inculcate on Italy, Germany, and France, the duty of engaging in another crusade, ostensibly against the Turks at Jerusalem, in marching towards which the crusaders would pass through Constantinople. The principal agent he employed to incite the people to engage in this holy enterprise was an illiterate priest, named Fulk, who was celebrated for his sanctity and rhetorical power. When vast multitudes of crusaders, who were persuaded that they were to be marched directly to the Holy Land, had assembled together, had proceeded some distance, and had on their way massacred a considerable number of their fellow-Christians at Zara, they were told by their leaders—who were swayed by the Pope and Latin hierarchy—that, in their march, they must liberate from prison, at Constantinople, the aged father of their young prince Alexius, and overthrow the reigning usurper in that

its footmarks have been so deeply impressed in a profusion of gore, that they will be traceable for ages untold.   Such, unfortunately, has been the result of the declaration,—"I come not to send peace, but a sword;" and such that great Protestant reformer—Martin Luther, hoped it would ever continue, when he exclaimed,—"If in case, as God forbid, there should be rest and quietness, then, the Gospel is at an end; for wherever that cometh it raiseth tumults; and if not, then it is no upright Gospel. Therefore Christ says, 'I am come to kindle a fire on earth.'"   Although nearly three centuries and a half have elapsed since the time of Luther, yet, this Gospel has lost none of its real tendency to apply fire and sword to those who reject its dogmas,—all that it has lost is its former unrestrained power, which is now, at least, kept in check, by the increasing influence of knowledge and civilization upon popular opinion.   Withdraw this check, and soon will hierophants tell us that the fire and the fagot are indispensable requisites for the propagation of the Gospel.   This, indeed, many Christian writers are candid enough to admit.   The Rev. T. Finch, in his *Essays*, says,—"Though the horrible brutalities of the Smithfield burnings are now no longer allowed to terrify us, yet the different religious sects, with but few exceptions, manifest an ample

city.   Between the leaders of the crusade, who belonged to various nations, a treaty was now made, one of the stipulations of which was that an end was to be put to the long schism of the Greek Christians, and measures taken to enforce them to acknowledge the lawful supremacy of the Roman church.   It is true that many pilgrims, most renowned for valour and enthusiasm, refused to acquiesce in this proposal, and withdrew from the crusade, urging that as they had, contrary to the wish of the Pope, imbrued their hands in the blood of their fellow-Christians at Zara, they would not commit a similar offence, by avenging with the sword the schisms of the Greeks, and that the vow they had made, before they had left their families and homes, was to rescue the holy sepulchre from the infidel.   Onward, however, went the rest of the blood-thirsty crusaders: large sums of money were forthcoming to satisfy their wants and silence their importunities; and new guarantees were given to the Latin Christians that the Greek church should be subdued.   Constantinople was strongly fortified, but not stoutly defended by the Greeks against the assault of the crusaders.   The latter were soon masters of the city, for a short time; whereupon they released prince Alexius's father from the dungeon, and replaced him on his throne, when he learnt that his son's stipulations with the crusaders for his restoration were,—the submission of the Eastern empire to the Pope, the succour of the Holy Land, and a contribution of 200,000 marks of silver.   When these conditions became known in Constantinople, every convent, and every shop resounded with the danger of the church and the tyranny of the Pope.   The result of this excitement was a most savage conflict between the Greek and Latin Christians.   The latter put a vast number of their antagonists to the sword, set the city on fire, and kept it burning for eight days; during which a great number of gorgeous palaces and churches were destroyed, and merchandise, to an incalculable value, consumed in the trading streets, the buildings in which were burnt for the length of more than three miles.   The Greeks having been thus exasperated, rallied, and engaged in other battles, in which, on each side, swords, spears, and battle-axes, were used with the most appaling effect; the consequence of which was a most horrible slaughter, the blood of the Eastern and Western Christians mingling, and running in torrents along the streets.   Pope Innocent III. deplores the lust of the crusaders, who respected neither age, sex, nor religious profession; and he bitterly laments their deeds of darkness, fornication, adultery, and incest, committed in open day, telling us that noble matrons and holy nuns were polluted by the grooms and peasants of the crusaders.   But we must desist. Sufficient has been advanced to show the fearful extent to which these crusaders carried out the spirit of Christianity.   See Gibbon's Decline and Fall of the Roman Empire, with his numerous and valuable authorities, chap. 58, 59, 60, from which work the principal part of this note has been extracted.

portion of the savage spirit, and, as far as the bitterest calumnies and anathemas can have effect, endeavour to vilify and destroy one another." Dr. George Campbell, in his sermon on "The Spirit of the Gospel," preached before the Synod of Aberdeen, remarks, *inter alia*, that "nothing can equal the dogmatism and arrogance with which one sect pronounces sentence against another, except perhaps the dogmatism with which the other retaliates upon them;"—that "when sects are once formed, political causes co-operate in producing that malignity which they so commonly bear to one another;"—that religionists "hate those whom they suppose to be God's enemies, and whom he hates; and from hating to exterminating, when that is practicable, the transition, as fatal experience has shown, is not difficult." The author of *Considerations on the Dangers of the Church*, writes,—"The Catholics, in the worst ages, never showed a more intolerant spirit than these restless disturbers of neighbourhoods, the Methodists; only the former had power, which the latter have not yet obtained." Indeed, volumes of quotations could be made from modern Christian writers, fully admitting the present persecuting tendency of their religion. It is true that this tendency was begun to be checked cautiously by a few, here and there, who lived in advance of their age, in the sixteenth century, when the grey dawn of moral and scientific knowledge commenced to dispel the superstitious darkness in which the whole of Europe had been enveloped for so many ages. But, opposed by such powerful priestly influence, feeble and scarcely perceptible was this counter-check, for centuries of religious troubles. The voice of true humanity was drowned in the clamours of superstition, so as to make little progress in abating the religious cruelties of the age. Even at this very day, in the latter end of the nineteenth century, and in civilized England, that hag, Christian persecution, is still alive, and makes her shrill voice heard in a thousand ways. Although we do not at present apply the axe, the sword, the gibbet, the fire, and the fagot, to heretics, yet, now and then, we fine them, and keep them for years locked up in dreary cells, because they have given reasons for their disbelief in the divine origin of Christianity. These acts, together with the bickerings of Christians, their divisions into a thousand different sects brimful of animosity towards each other, and a multitude of other unseemly things witnessed in Christendom, ever verify Jesus's declaration that he "came not to give peace on earth, but rather division," fire, and sword. Such being his mission, not only as declared in his own words, but as proved by stubborn and deplorable facts to have been in effect, from the very hour he announced it to the present day, what think we of its origin? Was it Divine? "Whence was it? from heaven, or of men?"

Now, that we are drawing towards the close of our investigation of the mental and moral character of the Prophet of Nazareth, it would not be improper to urge the reader soberly to weigh all that has been advanced, and say whether he still sees sufficient reason to believe that this Prophet can be his spiritual Saviour,—whether he still sees sufficient moral excellence in him to constitute those qualities he would expect in the Deity,—whether he can perceive in his whole career a spark of Divinity, so as to induce him to worship him as God. We have seen that, so limited was his knowledge of futurity, that he falsely prophesied the end of the world, the time of his own resurrection, the perpetual praise of a woman who poured upon him a box of ointment, and the signs which believers in Christianity would manifest. We have also seen that a vast number of his precepts and doctrines were obscure, contradictory, bigoted, malevolent, absurd, immoral, and untrue ; and that much of his conduct was of an immoral tendency. We have further seen that he was deficient in knowledge of nature,—that he borrowed the best part of his doctrine from heathen theology,—that both his life, his teaching, and practices, were identical with those of heathen monks, who had preceded him,—that he himself made no pretence to Deity,—that, like many other human beings, he feared death,—that neither his own neighbours, kinsmen, nor even his disciples, believed that he was, either in nature or power, superior to other mortals,—and that he himself avowed that the purpose for which he had been ushered into the world was to send strife, division, fire, and sword, on earth, and to make " brother deliver up brother to death, and the father the child, and incite children to raise up against their parents, and cause them to be put to death." (Matth. x. 21.) Such has been the result of our inquiry in this work. Heartily would the writer wish it had been otherwise, and that he could see in Jesus the least glimmer of Deity. With boundless joy ! with admiring awe ! with the most profound feeling of adoration ! would he recognise in him the marvellous and mysterious union of " God in the flesh ! " Gladly would he receive and exemplify any proof found that he was even a perfect man. But facts—stubborn facts, compel him to identify him with other mortals, leading a life of alternate wisdom and folly, knowledge and ignorance, truth and error, virtue and vice. The human mind, therefore, if possessed of a proper notion of Deity, recoils at the very thought of paying adoration to an object in which it thus perceives imperfections ; and seeks a Being of infinite purity, before whom to bend the knee in an act of worship.

CHAPTER VIII.

THE DOCTRINES OF THE CHRISTIAN RELIGION, AS TAUGHT BY MODERN DIVINES, DISPROVED BY GOD'S GOVERNMENT OF THE UNIVERSE—THEIR ABSURDITY, AND UTTER FAILURE IN AMELIORATING THE MORAL CONDITION OF MANKIND.—THE SUBSTITUTE HERE PROPOSED FOR THEM MUCH MORE CONDUCIVE TO MAN'S HAPPINESS.

SECTION I.—THE SUPERIORITY OF THE BOOK OF NATURE OVER PRETENDED HEBREW AND GREEK REVELATIONS—NATURE, WHICH TEACHES THE EXISTENCE AND THE ATTRIBUTES OF DEITY, THE ONLY TRUE REVELATION GIVEN BY GOD TO MAN.

Having, in the foregoing chapters, had reason to determine that Jesus is not a Divine personage, nor even a perfect *man*, whom we can take as a pattern of life and conduct, this leads us inevitably to the conclusion that the religion of which he is the author is also not divine, and therefore, not an infallible moral guide to us, in steering our course though life. We are, consequently, left, *as far as Christianity is concerned*, without any sure moral guide in this world, and without any certain information as to the existence of another, or as to our future destiny. The same thing may be said of the aid which Judaism, Mahometanism, Brahminism, Boodism, and all other religions, which are founded on book-revelations, pretend to give on these important points. A man, therefore, who is convinced of the error which he may, for years, have cherished, and is now disposed to renounce it, must feel some doubt and perplexity as to what new course he should take. His active mind requires some subject of meditation; his perceptive powers call for a sphere of action; his intellectual faculties demand a field to survey; and his noble moral emotions, such as his feeling of veneration, his sentiment of benevolence, and his sense of justice, feel the want of objects upon which they can act congenially to their nature. In this position, the new convert from Christianity requires some guidance with regard to his future movements. Such, it is trusted, he will find in the following pages.

When thus about to forsake his old religion, a thousand things, doubtless, will be clinging to his mind,—all tending to induce him to return to his former errors,—all holding him back from proceeding on his new course. A recollection of the Christian creed of his earlier days—of his father, and of his grandfather—which he once regarded as divine and infallible, but which he now perceives to be utterly untenable; the church or chapel in which he worshipped in his merry youth, in which his relatives, friends, and acquaintances still worship, and in or near which his affectionate parents, his brothers, or sisters, or, perhaps, his wife and his children, have been interred, "in sure and certain hope of the resurrection to eternal life,"—these, and multitudes of other fond reminiscences, will now arise in his mind, and will be as so many dead weights hanging about his neck, and impeding his march in pursuit of truth. But the conscientious man, who loves truth for its own sake, will adhere to it with stern integrity, and will soon find that the benefit, the peace of mind, the pure enjoyment, resulting therefrom, far outweigh the few moments of uneasiness he feels in bidding adieu to long-cherished errors.

The enquiring reader, however, may be in haste to ask,—" If I am to renounce the Christian revelation, where am I to seek any other? If that does not teach me true religion, where am I to seek and find any revelation that does?" Cast thine eyes about thee; look at the surrounding world revealing the existence, the wisdom, the glory, the goodness of thy Creator! Open the *Book of Nature*, and read therein! Here wilt thou find and learn everything that thou canst want, or wish to know. Here canst thou contemplate the power, wisdom, and benignity—not of three Gods in one—but of one true Deity, and learn to love, adore, and glorify him. Nature's book is much easier to be understood, by the meanest capacity than the book of Christian revelation. It can be read without knowledge of Greek idioms, or Hebrew points. No portion of it has, or can be forged, counterfeited, interpolated, altered, or lost. It requires neither to be transcribed nor translated. It is an everlasting original, written in a universal language, which all mankind can read and understand. To this revelation then repair; it is the only one ever vouchsafed by God to mankind; and it reveals to man every thing that he is capable of comprehending. Wouldst thou learn the attributes of the Eternal First Cause—the Creator and Governor of the universe—from the book of nature? His power is manifested in the immensity of creation, and the force which keeps every portion of it in continual motion; his wisdom, in the variety of combinations, the designed harmony, and exquisite beauty which the universe presents; his goodness, in the abundance of provisions made for the innumerably varied wants and gratifications of all living and organised beings; his justice, in his government of the whole world by the same universal and invariable laws, the observance of which, on the part of man, produces its own reward—*pleasure and happiness*, and the infraction of which carries with it its own proportionate punishment—*pain and misery;* thus demonstrating, at once, to the subject, the benevolence and justice of the Supreme Ruler. All things around us teach that every natural law of the Creator has a benevolent purpose; and to perceive that the whole universe is thus governed on a principle in which benevolence is clearly the leading feature, is much better calculated to inspire man with love to his Creator, than the Christian doctrine which teaches that God has created, and does govern all things for the selfish purpose of his own glory.

Still, the man who has but just turned his thoughts from the perplex-ing dogmas of Christianism,—who has but just opened his eyes upon the harmony and beauty of the physical universe, may be inclined to say,—" Nature does not teach me even the existence of God as clearly as the Christian revelation enunciates it." To this it may be replied, that the Christian revelation, or in other words, the Bible, does not, by any means, prove the existence of God ; nor does it attempt to prove it. Like all other book-revelations, it takes this for granted. Blind, how-ever, is the man who cannot perceive in nature abundant evidence of the existence of an infinite, intelligent First Cause,—of an eternal God. Every thing in the universe teaches this great truth, from the most evanescent star in the remotest region of space to the meanest glow-worm on the road-side,—from the sun in the firmament down to the smallest particle of matter that floats in the air,—from the largest being in animal creation to the most imperceptible animalcule. Man himself is to himself an undeniable proof of this fact. He knows that he exists, and feels the absurdity of supposing that he made himself. He has not always existed ; and the same may be said of his father, his grandfather, and of all his ancestors, as well as of the whole human race. Convinced of the fact that he exists, and knowing that he can neither have made himself, nor can have always existed, man is irresistibly driven to the conclusion that there exists a First Cause, totally different, in its essential qualities, from any thing material ; and to this First Cause, he gives the name—God ! Every thing in the skies above, and on the earth beneath, supports him in his conclusion,—suggests to him a knowledge of the Unseen, and inspires his mind with love to him. On every part of nature, this truth is inscribed in characters that cannot be effaced, and on tablets that are always in view ;—all teach that the universe has been produced by infinite Intelligence. By analogy, we are able indubitably to ascertain what this Intelligence is, and what it is capable of producing.— We see in man instances of finite intelligence, and of its inventive powers ; and we perceive the analogy between these and things we see that exist in nature. The varied and highly finished joints, tubes, and other apparatus, in the limb of an animal, indicate a design and a designer, as clearly as do the different parts of a house, or of a steam-engine, which we know to have been designed by man, and to be evidence of his intelligence. Well has it been observed by a modern writer[*] that, in some steam-engines, the steam, after having performed its office of raising and depressing the piston, passes into the condenser and becomes cold water, which—being in this state no longer fit for the purpose of the engine—is again, by means of pipes, conveyed into the boiler to be converted into steam. That all this is the effect of design, we are so fully convinced by the very sight of it, that, were the designer to stand visibly before us, and declare it was his contrivance, we would not be more certain of the fact of design. And even if we never before had seen a steam-engine, still, if we had been in the habit of witnessing mechanical contrivances, our certainty on this point would not be less. Now, in the human body, the

---

[*] Hennell's Christian Theism, p. 23, second edit., from which able work the happy illustration now introduced is abridged.

arterial blood, after having supplied nourishment to the various glands, becomes unfit for further use, and is by a system of veins, carried back to the heart,—that very part which, by a connection with the lungs, contains a provision for re-converting it into arterial blood. Accordingly, as similar causes produce similar effects, the circumstances which compel us to infer a mental agency in the former case, do so equally powerfully in the latter. If it be objected that we can find no analogy to the universe, because, it being unique, we have no other universe with which to compare this, the answer is, that, as we can compare one part of the universe with another part, namely, ourselves with our works, the analogy arising therefrom should have as much weight as if we could compare one universe with another; so that the proof of a *design* is complete in the formation of the universe, and therefore of a *designer*—an infinite, intelligent First Cause. Such a proof of the existence of Deity is much more conclusive than any that can be found in book-revelations, which, at least, are liable to be altered and even forged,—much more conclusive than the inconsistent and absurd tale of the miraculous conception of a God, in the shape of a man; liable to all the infirmities, foibles, and follies of man; and even to the very death incident to man. Nor does Nature teach us the existence of more than one God. She does not, like the Christian faith, teach us the absurdity of paying our adorations to three distinct Divine Persons, or Gods, whose characters are diversified and contradictory; thereby distracting our minds, dividing our affections and homage, and confounding our ideas.—She does not teach us to worship God the Father as consuming fire; as a God of wrath and vengeance; as enveloped in dark clouds; as sitting morose on his terrible throne, dooming all the human race to eternal woe;—to worship God the Son as arrayed in loveliness and charming beauty; as having carried death to the regions of immortality; as having laid bare his guiltless bosom that God the Father might plunge into it his fatal dagger, in order that atoning blood might be sprinkled over his eternal throne, and the burning anger of an incensed Deity might thus be pacified; and as being continually engaged in the humiliating work of imploring God the Father to confer favours upon sinful men;—to worship God the Holy Ghost, sometimes as the father of God the Son, at other times as an emanation from the Son, and as a Deity whose office is to regenerate, sanctify, and purify the children of men, so as to render them fit to appear before God the Father, dressed in white robes, wearing crowns, and playing upon harps. No; Nature, all whose works proclaim but one God, neither demands nor suggests for her Creator such irrational worship. She points out only one God, of absolute unity, to whom to pay homage and adoration,—one Deity, whose glory fills the universe, and whose presence pervades unbounded space!—One infinite, intelligent First Cause, whose existence and attributes are much more clearly taught in his works than in a Hebrew Bible, with its *nekoodoth*, its *leshon sachar* and *leshon nekaivah*, and its *aithan moshe wechalev;*—much more intelligibly and positively than by a thousand visions and dreams, alleged to have been given to barbarous patriarchs and fanatic prophets;—much more convincingly than by a million of *Shechinahs*, or an equal number of *great lights* and *voices*, saying, "Saul! Saul!" or "Peter, arise, kill, and eat." Nature, unlike book-revelations, which address our lower propensities in proof of God, appeals to man's higher senses—his intellectual and moral faculties—and bids him draw his conclusions from the mighty work of creation; in the vastness, harmony, and beauty of which,—in the inflexible, never-varying, and beneficent laws that govern which, he feels, he hears, he sees God! Let man, therefore, read the Scripture of Nature, and cease to seek his Creator in a volume of paper or parchment, which the fallible hand of mortal has constructed. God's Word in his works;—in these he declares his existence, his character, and his will, in language which all mankind can understand, and which none can falsify.

Section II.—The laws of nature illustrated—the punishment inflicted for their violation proportionate to the offence, and calculated to improve the offender.

Having just seen that it is from nature alone God's true command-ments can be learnt,—that here they are engraven in characters which none can obliterate, and on tablets which no Moses can break; let us now point out some of these commandments, and show how obedience to them, on the part of man, insures his welfare. And here it should be premised, as a most clear and incontrovertible truth, that, in nature, whatever is productive of real pleasure and happiness, God commands us to do; and that whatever causes pain and misery, he forbids us to do. He has made our happiness the consequence of our obedience, and our misery the result of our disobedience to the laws of nature. Therefore, O thou offspring of Nature! although thou hast hitherto been accustomed to depend upon the miraculous interposition of what Christians call providence, and hast a thousand times found thy strong faith productive of misery, learn, at last—if thou lovest thine own happiness—learn to study and obey the natural laws,—the laws by which the Creator of the universe governs the world in which thou livest. In order, however, to obey these laws, thou must first know them. But do not expect to find this knowledge in a book which teaches that the earth is flat, and stands on pillars,—that the extremity of this flatness is *the end of the earth*,—that the sun revolves daily around this earth, which stands still and immoveable,—that the firmament, or the sky, is a solid substance,—that iron axes anciently swam,—that even the rivers, the seas, the sun and moon, were arrested in their course, at the bidding of man,—that the heart is the organ of thought,—that the panacea for all diseases is to lay apostolic hands on the sick, together with a thousand other absurdities. The knowledge of nature's laws is to be found in nature alone. Gaze, for a moment, at her operations, and learn some of her ways. For this purpose, thou hast been endowed with faculties admirably adapted to surrounding objects,—capable of taking cognizance of their respective properties and laws, and of turning them to thine advantage, gratification, and happiness. The soil on which thou treadest has a thousand capabilities which require only thine understanding, and thine exertion, to yield innumerable comforts. Thou hast been placed under natural laws, such as may be distinguished into *physical, organic*, and *moral*, or social laws, which thou hast only to understand and obey, in order to secure thine happiness; and for the purpose of enabling thee to understand and obey them, thou hast been pre-eminently endowed with perceptive and reflective faculties,—with a sense of right and wrong, in addition to thine animal propensities and desires. Under the physical laws, thou perceivest that the same mode of action is invariable, under the same conditions,—that, for example, water, on a level with the sea, freezes or boils at the same temperature, in every part of the world; and that a heavy body, unsupported, falls to the ground, in New Zealand as well as in England. Under the organic laws, thou perceivest that excessive heat or cold destroys organisation, and makes life extinct. Under the moral or social laws, thou perceivest that mental enjoyment proceeds from acts truly moral and good, and that mental agony is the result of immoral or vicious acts. Thou, further, perceivest that these laws are " universal, invariable, and unbending in their operations,"—that they are independent of one another; and that obedience to each of them is attended with its own reward; and *dis*obedience, with its own punishment. Under the physical and organic laws, fire, excessive heat or cold, destroys the organisation of the most pious saint, as well as that of the most impenitent sinner,—of the new-born babe, who has never trangressed any moral law, as well as of the most hardened criminal of threescore and ten years.—If either disobeys these ·laws, the immediate result is pain, misery, and, perhaps, death; all of which are punishments consequent upon disobedience to these laws. In the same manner, under the moral or social laws, vice produces its own punishment,—man suffers mental agonies from the disgrace his crimes bring upon him, as well as from the treatment which he receives at the hands of his fellow-beings, in consequence of his vice. So certain it is that obedience to each of the laws of nature is attended with its own reward, and disobedience with its own punishment, that—to borrow a very happy illustration of Mr. George Combe, in that excellent work, *the Constitution of Man*—we may frequently find the crew of a ship who obey the *physical* laws, although they rob, murder, blaspheme, and commit every species of *moral* vice on board, yet, bring their vessel in safety to its destination; while the crew of another ship, who disregard the *physical* laws in the management of their vessel, but who are, nevertheless, strictly moral, nay, most religiously disposed, and have on board, say, a cargo of pious Christians, still sink in the ocean, and are thus punished for their disregard of the *physical* laws, notwithstanding their rigorous observance of the *moral* laws. If the most saintly person, by mistake, swallows poison, and destroys the intestines of his stomach, thus violating the organic law, the result is death; or if he takes only a small portion of this poison, so as only in a slight degree to infringe this law, he is proportionately punished with sickness, pain, and langour; while another man, who cheats, lies, steals, and tramples upon all the moral laws, but who, nevertheless, obeys the organic laws, reaps the reward of health, vigour of body, and buoyancy of spirits. On the other hand, a man who disregards the moral laws,—who lies, who steals, and who murders,—suffers pain from remorse of conscience, from being shunned and despised by society, from imprisonment and its concomitant chastisements, and, sometimes, from the punishment of death itself; while another man, who scrupulously observes the moral laws, enjoys all the internal delights which spring from the due exercise of the moral faculties, and the benefits which flow from the general esteem and confidence of society. Thus does the Potentate of the universe govern men by the fixed, universal, invariable, and just laws of nature, obedience to each of which is attended with its own reward—the happiness of man; and disobedience thereto, by its own punishment—pain and misery to the transgressor. He has evidently bestowed a definite constitution on physical nature, on man, as well as on the lower animals, and has placed all of them under the regulation of fixed laws; so that every mode of action is inherent in the constitution of each being, and, under the same condition, is universal and invariable.

Nor can the punishment which God has connected with the infringement of these laws, by any means, be construed into cruelty, injustice, or caprice,—as the act of putting an apple in a garden for no other purpose than to tempt a woman to sin; or of loving Jacob and hating Esau, before either of them was born; or of killing seventy of the sons of Ahab for the sins of their father,—but is clearly perceived to be, in every instance, for the most benevolent purposes.—It is evidently designed to teach the wrong-doers, by experience, to observe these laws more strictly hereafter, in order that their happiness may, thereby, be increased. When an infant, for the first time, grasps the flame of a candle, and thereby slightly burns its hand, so as to suffer pain, the punishment thus inflicted, in consequence of violating the organic law, serves a most useful purpose. It teaches the child, henceforth, to avoid fire—which has the power, not only of causing slight pain, but of destroying life—and thus to preserve its own existence. When sickness and pain follow a debauch, the object of the suffering is to warn the individual against premature death—the inevitable consequence of continued disobedience to the organic laws; and to enable him to enjoy health—the reward of the opposite conduct. Nor is the pain, or punishment, which follows the infraction of these laws, sent immediately, or *providentially*, from God, as the Christian thinks all his afflictions, misfortunes, and calamities, are miraculously sent; but it arises from the very nature of things.—It is only the inevitable result of disobedience to the laws of nature, all of which are established for the most wise and benevolent purposes. In order that pain might not follow the infringements of the natural laws, we should, for instance, require fire which, while it burnt timber, coal, and such substances, would not burn our bodies; and water which, while it cooled and moistened the surface of the earth, quenched our thirst, and served a thousand other purposes, would, however, neither chill nor drown us. But in the institution of these laws, and in the punishment which they inflict, when transgressed, we see the power, wisdom, and goodness of God shining forth with the brightest lustre, and displaying the just and benevolent manner in which he governs the world. By the law of gravitation, for example, man preserves his equilibrium; by it, walls, when built perpendicularly, stand firmly, sheltering man from the inclemency of the weather; by it, water precipitates down its channel, turning mill-wheels, and serving a thousand other purposes for man. But if, for example, a builder, violating this law, falls from the top of an edifice which he is erecting, and is killed, this, by no means, proves that the law is not calculated to effect wise and benevolent purposes,—it proves only that the infringement of it is attended with punishment. For if this law did not exist, or if it were suspended, the builder's structure would rise up from the ground as fast as he puts it together; nay, he himself, in common with all the other portions of nature detached from the earth, would hang midway in the air; and all human operations would cease. If, however, this supposed builder, violates the law of gravitation only so far as to have a limb broken, or to bruise his body, the pain which he suffers, serves as a warning for him and others; and thus tends to enforce a closer observance of the law now slightly infringed, and therefore to secure happiness. But when the violation of this law is excessive, death ensues; and even death, under these circumstances, is of a benevolent design. For, when a man has transgressed a natural law so far that the injury he has thereby received is beyond remedy, while he suffers excruciating pain, it is a much more benevolent act of nature to cut short his life, than to protract it under the tortures of irrecoverable organic derangement. Let another illustration be given in the law of combustion.—Timber, coal, oils, and animal substances, are capable of being burnt, which quality has been bestowed upon them for many benevolent purposes to man. By means of fire, he obtains warmth in cold latitudes, light after the sun has set, and is enabled to perform countless things which administer to his wants, comforts, and happiness. But by violating the organic laws, he may be burnt to death by this fire. The utility and benevolent design of the natural laws, however, remain unaltered. To preserve men from the danger to which they are exposed by fire, " they have been endowed with nerves which communicate sensation from heat, agreeable while the temperature is such as to benefit the body, slightly uneasy when it becomes so high as to be in some measure hurtful, positively painful when the heat approaches a degree that would seriously injure the organisation of the system, and horribly agonizing whenever it becomes so elevated as to destroy the organs."* Thus has the Creator established a monitor in every sensitive nerve, whose warning increases in intensity with the degree of danger; punishing the individual only in proportion as he infringes the organic laws. Similar illustrations might be given of the punishment attending the violation of every one of the natural laws, physical, organic, and moral, by which man is governed. The punishment which attends disobedience to them is *immediate*, the effect, instantly and invariably, following its proximate cause; is *definite*, being proportionate to the degree of violation; and is *benevolent* in its design, being admirably calculated to arrest the offender in his departure from these laws, which departure, if permitted to proceed to its natural termination, would involve him in tenfold greater miseries.

* Combe's Constitution of Man,—a work in which the Laws of Nature are admirably illustrated; and from which several of the foregoing remarks have been extracted.

SECTION III.—THE MALEVOLENT AND VENGEFUL CHARACTER OF THE CHRIS-
TIAN DOCTRINE OF ETERNAL PUNISHMENT—ITS EVIL TENDENCY—DIS-
COUNTENANCED AND CONTRADICTED BY EVERY PORTION OF GOD'S
WORKS—INCREASED HAPPINESS DERIVED FROM INCREASED KNOWLEDCE
OF GOD'S WORKS AS DISPLAYED IN NATURE.

God's punishment for transgressing the laws by which he governs the
universe, whether the physical, organic, or moral laws, as we have just
seen, being prompt, definite, proportionate to the offence, and having for
its object the good of the offender, how different it is from the *eternal
punishment* which the Bible teaches, and which all Christians believe that
a merciful Father will inflict in hell upon his creatures, for transgressing
what is deemed the same God's *moral laws !* A punishment which is inflicted long after the commission of the offence, which is indefinite in
degree and duration ; nay, which is infinite and everlasting, and which
has for its object the utter destruction—the eternal damnation of the
offender—cannot, of course, be for his welfare,—cannot have any benevolent object, but must be thoroughly malevolent in its design, positively
vengeful in its character, and utterly cruel in its effect ! Can the beneficent Ruler of the universe have such an irrational punishment in store
for any of his dependent creatures ?   Can he make such an infinite difference in the punishment he inflicts for sinning against his *work*, and that
which is said he will inflict for sinning against what is called his *Word?*
Impossible ! To entertain such a notion of the Deity is the height of
impiety ! is outright blasphemy ! The doctrine of eternal punishment in
hell, however, is one on which all popular Christian preachers love to
dwell, and on which they take delight in being transcendently eloquent ;
even at the expense, not unfrequently, of driving some of their more
weak-minded hearers to madness.   The following short extracts from the
standing theological works of the age, may serve as samples of this kind
of grandiloquence.   Baxter, in his *Saints' Everlasting Rest*—a work much
revered by Christians—writes thus,—"The principal author of hell-
torments is God himself. As it was no less than God whom the sinner
had offended, so it is no less than God who will punish them for their
offences. He has prepared those torments for his enemies. His continued anger will still be devouring them. . . . . . The everlasting
flames of hell will not be thought too hot for the rebellious ; and when
they have burnt there for millions of ages, he will not repent him of the
evil which is befallen them. . . . . . The guilt of their sins will be to
damned souls like tinder to gun-powder, to make the flames of hell take
hold of them with fury. The body must also bear its part. The body
which was so carefully looked to, so tenderly cherished, so curiously
dressed ; what must it now endure ! How are its haughty looks now
taken down ! How little will those flames regard its comeliness and

beauty ! . . . . . But the greatest aggravation of these torments will be their eternity. When a thousand millions of ages are past, they are as fresh to begin as the first day ! " In that far-famed work,—*Human Nature in its Four-fold State*, by the Rev. T. Boston, we find the same horrible doctrine taught, thus :—" In hell they will find a prison they will never escape out of, a lake of fire wherein they will be for ever swimming and burning, a pit whereof they will never find a bottom. Their eyes shall be kept in blackness of darkness, without the least gleam of light ; their ears filled with the frightful yellings of the infernal crew. They shall taste nothing but the vinegar of God's wrath, the dregs of the cup of his fury. The stench of the burning lake of brimstone shall be the smell there, and they shall feel extreme pain for evermore." Thousands of such specimens could be added from the works of the most popular Christian writers, who dwell with Nero-like pleasure on the eternal punishment of the "damned." But the evils produced by such barbarous declamations can be equalled only by the absurdity of the dogma they inculcate. They have a direct tendency to create vicious, cruel, and savage habits in those who listen to them. They are, in their nature, such as address themselves to the lowest and most brutal propensities of the human mind—destructiveness and combativeness. It is a well-known law in human physiology, that the oftener and more powerfully any faculty or propensity of man's mind is addressed, the oftener it is called into activity; and that the oftener it is called into activity the stronger, the more active, and predominant it becomes. Thus are thousands of hearers, by being— from youth to old age, Sunday after Sunday, and frequently on week days—harangued on the subject of God's eternal punishment of men in hell, converted from mild, forgiving, and benevolent persons, into revengeful, cruel, and blood-thirsty fiends. Nor is it to be overlooked that this cruel disposition, when thus contracted, is transmitted by human beings to their offspring, in whom it is a natural or an innate propensity ; so that their posterity, from age to age, become more and more revengeful, cruel, brutal, murderous. This philosophical fact explains the cause that, instead of being a religion of peace, Christianity, as we have seen in the preceding chapter, has, in every age, been more sanguinary than any other faith under the sun ; and also enables us to perceive the reason that all nations, to whom this religion has been taught for a number of centuries, are peculiarly warlike ;—the national propensities of destructiveness and combativeness, being, from age to age, addressed by their religious guides with terrible lessons of God's vengeful and eternal punishment of the wicked, his wrath against the Antediluvians, the Sodomites. the Canaanites, or some other people who are depicted in our, so called, Divine books as having fallen under the vengeance of the Jewish and Christian deity. The author of *The Electrical Theory of the Universe* displays great mental penetration, when, in his Dissertation on the Being and Attributes of God, he remarks that " the history of all nations proves the great, the immense moral influence of their belief in their respective gods upon their national character ;" and when he adds,—" *Tell me the character of the gods of a nation, and I will tell you the character of that nation.* If we cast our eye over the history of ancient nations, we shall find a cruel and vindictive nation believing in a cruel and vindictive god ; a polished people, with a classic mythology; and a warlike, but magnanimous nation, worshipping a god of war, of a character corresponding to the spirit of the nation." But irrespectively of the evil influence which the doctrine of eternal damnation carries on the lower propensities of man, its effects are equally vicious on his intellectual faculties, when he contemplates this horrible dogma in conjunction with other Christian tenets. He is taught that he has been born a desperately wicked sinner, deserving to be punished, for ever, in hell,—that even the least sin he has ever committed is sufficient to ensure his everlasting damnation,—that he cannot be saved unless his salvation, personally, has been pre-ordained by God,—and that, even if it is, he can do nothing towards carrying it out, until he receives saving grace, or is influenced by the Holy Ghost; so that he can, of himself, do nothing towards escaping eternal torments. His rational conclusion, therefore, is that, if a man is to be damned for the smallest crime; nay, if he is to be tormented for ever, not only for his own sins, but even the sins of his progenitors—sins of which he is as innocent as the Deity himself—then, he can be condemned but once for the largest and most accumulated amount of crime; and he, consequently, persists in his vicious habits. Such a doctrine can make no impression, but that of disbelief, on men endowed with a high degree of moral emotions and intellectual perceptions. To any man of reflection, it must be most absurd to suppose that a just God will be so cruel as to punish eternally, by far the greater number of the human race, for having a sinful nature—a nature which, we are told, is "prone to sin," is "estranged from the womb," and "goes astray as soon as it is born, speaking lies."

Turning from these horrid dogmas to the works of God in nature, we can see nothing which indicates this eternal punishment. Here, the punishment for the violation of God's laws is temporary, and designed to reform the offender. Here, all the works of the Creator are impressed with infinite benevolence. Here, the human race, from age to age, is progressing in knowledge, virtue, and happiness. Here, the boundless scenes of grandeur and sublimity which surround us, are calculated to fill our minds with delight, and make us rapturously admire the harmonious and beautiful design of the whole scheme of the universe. Here, we can perceive that infinite wisdom has adapted every cause to the production of its proper effect; and that Almighty power has carried the design into execution. How different the effect which these works of the Creator has upon our minds, from the effect which the meditation of eternal torments has upon us! The former disposes us to adore the Deity, as the fountain of all good; the latter makes us dread him as an All-powerful tormentor. These feelings are utterly conflicting. Both cannot be right. Which is wrong? Can nature be false? Or are the beauties of the universe intended only to tantalise us? Are we intended only to have a glimpse at the splendour of nature, in order that we may the more deeply feel the degradation of our position as the children of the Devil, and the heirs of eternal damnation? Can this be? Can the infinitely benevolent Creator be so inconsistently cruel?—Can he have displayed boundless munificence in all his works, and, yet, deal with man in the most malignant manner? No! As his beneficence is manifest throughout nature, so is his goodness to man—a part of nature—displayed in all the laws of nature; admirably calculated, as they are, to ensure his happiness. Away, then, with such a barbarous doctrine as eternal damnation, which is fit only for the tyrants of the East, where it originated. In this world, the laws of nature punish man adequately, for every violation of them,—for every offence he commits. Why, then, dream of an eternal punishment in another world? Why imagine that man sins in one world, and is punished in another? Where lies the necessity of this? or where is there anything bearing the least analogy to it? Is it not clear that man is punished in the present life for every violation of the laws of his Creator? Wherefore the fancy that he will again be punished in another life? How much more in harmony with reason, with the indications of nature, with the character of God, it is that, if he has destined man to live in another world, he has also ordained that he shall therein enjoy all the good, all the pleasure and happiness, of which he is capable!

What a striking contrast there is between the teaching of Christianity and that of nature,—between the doctrine of what is supposed to be God's Word, and that of what is positively known to be his work, in regard to man's happiness! The former threatens him with eternal torments, if he does *not* exercise blind faith in unintelligible dogmas; and even if he *does*, promises him naught, in this world, but affliction, misery, and woe. The latter guarantees to him a life of happiness, if he only strive to understand and obey the natural laws. How clearly this indicates that, to study the laws nature should be the chief aim of man, and to obey them should be his religion, his virtue, his devotion! Disobedience to these is the very essence of evil; and obedience to them is actual virtue. By the former, man incurs pain and misery; by the latter, he obtains pleasure and happiness. It is true that these laws are numerous, and can be learnt by man, like all other things, only gradually. But even this gradual acquirement of knowledge, is to him an important source of happiness. If he acquired, at once, all the knowledge possible to be gained of this world, or if, at his birth, he were endued with this knowledge, his intellectual and moral faculties—the superiority of which constitutes the grand distinction between him and the lower animals—would, afterwards, be useless; having no field of exercise. On the first day of his existence, he would reach the utmost extent of his knowledge, so that, to him, every secret of nature would be familiar, and therefore devoid of interest. He would have nothing to hope for, and nothing to fear: the new and strange would no longer excite his wonder, or gratify his curiosity: the pleasure which he now experiences in making new discoveries would have no existence; and he would be as wise when born as when sevenscore years. Hence, it is clear that for man to be constituted so as to be able to understand surrounding objects and the laws which govern them, only by degrees, is much more conducive to his happiness than if he had been at once endued with intuitive knowledge of all nature. His mental faculties are thus kept in gradual activity; and this very activity constitutes pleasure. Every new discovery which he makes, is a new source of happiness. To find that he is surrounded with objects, the qualities of which, properly applied, are fitted to benefit and delight him, but improperly applied, are calculated to injure and pain him, makes him feel deeply interested in the study of nature,—the very sphere to which his capacities are adapted.

Man's gradually increased knowledge, is therefore to him, a source of gradually increased happiness.   Nor, with the most rapid strides mankind can make in acquiring knowledge, will the happiness which results from their gradual progress, diminish, even in a million of cycles.   So vast, and so varied, are the hidden treasures of nature, that man can never exhaust them, so as to know all that is to be known,—to have no more to learn, and, consequently, to have nothing more to gratify him.   If the universe is infinite, man's knowledge of it can never be complete.   But even if we suppose a period at which mankind shall have discovered all the natural laws, so that a new discovery regarding them be impossible; still the rising generation of every age, not being born with intuitive knowledge, would have to learn, or, at least, commit to memory, and, by observation, verify the recorded and communicated experience of their predecessors; in every instance of which, the knowledge thus obtained would be new to them, and productive of the pleasure inseparably connected with new philosophic discoveries.   How different, in its results, is this gradual mode of obtaining knowledge, from the alleged mode of acquiring Christian knowledge, supernaturally and suddenly, without observation or experiment, by dreams, visions, revelations, imaginary divine influence, and other miraculous means, productive, not of pleasure and happiness, but of trouble, mental distraction, and misery!   By this gradual mode of knowing God's works in nature, man's love of the strange, the new, the excellent, is continually gratified, and his exertions are rewarded.   Although the wonders of one age become the familiar things of the next; yet, the mind of man, in reflecting on the success of his predecessors, is thereby stimulated to interrogate nature more closely, and is buoyed with the hope of making some new discovery of a still superior character.   Thus, is this gradual acquisition of knowledge the very source of both the degree of happiness which mankind at present enjoy, and also of a much higher degree, to which the progress of the race tends, and to which, doubtless, it will ultimately attain, when no longer retarded by book-revelations, nor terrified by pulpit thunders of eternal torments.

SECTION IV.—THE CHRISTIAN DOCTRINE OF THE EXISTENCE AND POWER
OF THE DEVIL FALACIOUS AND HIGHLY PERNICIOUS TO THE EXERCISE
OF VIRTUE—THE ABSURDITY OF PRAYER—THE DOCTRINE OF ORIGINAL
SIN DEROGATORY TO THE CHARACTER OF GOD, AND PREGNANT WITH
MISCHIEF TO MANKIND—NO TRACES IN MAN'S NATURE THAT HE IS
TAINTED WITH THE SUPPOSED SIN OF ADAM—DEATH AN INSTITUTION
OF NATURE, FOR BENEVOLENT PURPOSES.

Scarcely less absurd and pernicious than the Christian doctrine of eternal torments is that of the existence and operations of the Devil— "the God of this world."   Christian writers, as well as the Bible, tell us that this being—often called by Jesus—"the prince of this world"—was once an inhabitant of heaven, where, *before* the creation of the universe, but *after* the production of the *eternal Son,* he conspired with other wicked spirits of that holy place, and raised the standard of rebellion against the Sovereign of the regions of bliss. In his contention for the throne of the Omnipotent, the war fiercely raged for a considerable time, and all heaven was desolated. At length, the Lord of heaven commissioned his Son to rout the enemy. This Son hurled the Devil and his army into hell. After their expulsion, the Almighty resolved to create a world, and make man. But no sooner had he done so, than the Devil entered Paradise, and ruined this man; in consequence of which, his Creator's anger was roused, not against the Devil—the cause of the mischief—but against the man, whom he condemned to suffer eternal death. To prevent this punishment from being inflicted, however, the Almighty Son promised to become incarnate and die for man, which we are told he did. But after all this, the Devil still remained unconquered,—could still triumph over Omnipotence,—is still going about, like a roaring lion,—is still leading mankind captive. Such is the description given of this terrible being by Christian writers,* and such all orthodox men believe him to be.

But as God is infinite in all his ways, no such being as the Devil can possibly exist in the universe,—as God is omnipotent, and unbounded in goodness, all the tales about the Devil are "cunningly devised fables." According to these fables, the Devil is infinite—is God—is, in the Bible, called "the God of this world." He has successfully opposed the Deity, from eternity; he has obliged him to send part of himself to this world, to suffer and die; and he will, finally, triumph over the Deity by procuring the damnation of the greater portion of the human race. To be able to do all this, clearly proves the Devil infinite. According to this doctrine, there are two infinities,—the one opposed to the other,—the one good and the other evil. The absurdity of such a doctrine can find no parallel, except in the Persian fables, whence probably it was imported into the Christian religion. Infinity being, necessarily, without limits, the supposition of two infinities is the acme of absurdity. The bare thought destroys the idea of Deity. Indeed, this doctrine implies a denial that God is God, and suggests the probability that the Devil is the Omnipotent being. For it teaches that he has frustrated God in his designs, and that, therefore, he is more powerful than God, who, if there were thus a

---

* Read Bacon's Works, vol. iv. p. 505; Boston's Fourfold State, pp. 440, 441; Paul's Epistles; the Revelation of John; Milton's Paradise Lost; Watts's Hymns, and his Preface to Lyric Poems, &c. But let it not be supposed that it is in the works of Christian writers only, the notion of a Devil is found. This doctrine, like all other Christian dogmas, is evidently of a heathen origin. It is found in productions much older than either the Jewish or Christian Scriptures. In the Divine books of the Hindoos, we have an account of several wars in heaven between gods and devils. The latter, having rebelled, were cast into a region of darkness and sorrow.—See Holwel's Feasts and Fasts of the Hindoos, p. 56, *et al.* In the Mahabharat, (lib. i. c. 15.) we have also an account of a terrific war in heaven, bearing a striking resemblance to Milton's description of the Christian Devil's war. The doctrine was also among the Egyptians, the Greeks, Romans, &c. The war of the Titans and the Giants against the sovereign god Jupiter, and against Saturn, is well known. Jupiter sent his son to defeat these rebels, whom he confined under Mount Ætna—the hell of the Greeks and Romans, which had a pit that seemed bottomless, and from the crater of which came fire, brimstone, smoke, &c.

limit to his power, would not be infinite, and, consequently, not God; while, on the other hand, the power of the Devil is not proved to be limited, and *may* therefore be infinite, and he a God.

It is impossible to conceive a story more derogatory to the character of the Almighty,— more incompatible with his power, his wisdom, and his justice, than the story about the existence and exploits of the Devil. Nor is it easy to find even a Christian dogma which has been, and continues to be, productive of more evil consequences. How many thousands of crimes have been committed, and their perpetrators screened under the pretence that they were tempted by the Devil! On the other hand, how many millions of human beings have been persecuted, and put to death, from the time Moses is said to have lived to the present day, for the supposed practices of whitchcraft and magic,—arts imagined to have been taught them by the Devil! Our own statute-books contain many enactments, which ascribe the existence of these arts to the instigations of this supposed being; and evidently imply that it was the general belief that almost every crime was produced by his agency.* The annals of various countries show that almost every evil—physical and moral—incident to man, was, formerly, by Christians attributed to the influence of the Devil, his angels, his witches, and his wizards. If a person was attacked by sudden disease, or insanity; or if he committed suicide, if his cattle died, if his house was burnt down, if a member of his family suddenly died, or met with a fatal accident,—the Devil was thought to be the cause, and the instrument supposed to be some witch or wizard, who was immediately sought for, and put to death. These witches and wizards were believed to have sold their souls to the Devil for the supernatural power he conferred upon them to work mischievous miracles. This delusion was co-extensive with Christendom; and, up to the seventeenth century, millions of human beings, as the Devil's special agents, were put to death. In Germany alone, a hundred thousand fell victims to this superstition! and in England upwards of thirty thousand were burnt for the same cause; while the masses, glorying in the punishment, sang popular airs, as they witnessed it, and the clergy preached " witch sermons." Nobody pitied the fate of witches and wizards, who had bartered their souls with the Devil. Although a relative might sympathize with a murderer, yet, if he pitied the fate of one of these agents of the Devil, however nearly related to him, he was himself suspected of witchcraft; and if he wept at seeing the victim wreathing in agony, while the flames burnt his flesh to a cinder, he was tied to the stake, to undergo the same inhuman death. So deeply rooted in the mind of Christians had this doctrine become, that all, from the king to the beggar, believed it, and that it pervaded the writings, not only of the divines, but of the historians, the poets, and philosophers. Profound theologians in their voluminous works, and popular preachers in their eloquent sermons, undertook to prove from Scripture the absolute certainty that the Devil thus employed men and women to do his work.

---

* It is curious to observe with what solemnity our legislators, only about three centuries ago, framed enactments against witchcrafts, and how stedfast was their belief, in its reality. See 33 Hen. VIII. c. 8. 2 Jac. I. c. 12. 9 Eliz. c. 16, and 9 Geo. II c. 5, by which last statute the laws against witchcraft are partially repealed.

Nor was this all; the Christian clergy of all sects taught that the world was over-run with evil spirits, who were in all places, at all times, alluring men to evil, prompting them to commit murder and suicide, and invisibly injuring their corporeal frames in a thousand modes,—that the Devil, with myriads of his angels were hovering in the atmosphere, and frequently snatching up into the air, men and women, whom they carried through the aerial regions, for thousand of miles,*—that they raised storms, caused earthquakes, and disturbed physical nature in innumerable ways,—and that they descended on the earth, assuming the forms of various living animals, such as dogs, cats, bulls, goats, lions, wolves, men, women, and children. But what a vast amount of evil must have been effected by such a doctrine! How it must have blighted and withered all the higher sentiments and emotions of the human mind! How it must have struck terror into every nerve! Imagine every human being in whole communities, night and day, shuddering with fear either that he would meet the Devil, or be ruined by the witchcraft of one of his agents, or be himself accused of witchcraft, and burnt alive! Justly does Buckle remark that, owing to such a teaching of the Scotch clergy, " reason gave way, and, under the frenzy of religious mania, the hearers of God's ministers went home and dispatched themselves." They, doubtless, thought death and the silent grave far preferable to the misery into which they had been driven by this terrible doctrine. All the good that Christianity can have the least pretension of having effected, from its first promulgation to the present hour, is not sufficient to atone for the thousandth part of the injury it has inflicted on mankind by this doctrine alone.

But even as the doctrine in its present modified and comparatively refined state—shorn of its witchcraft and other horrific things—is taught, what a discouragement to virtue must a bare belief in the existence of the Devil effect! How it must paralyze all the moral efforts of man to believe that there exists a being who is continually " suggesting evil thoughts to his mind,"—a being who " is always at his elbow inciting him to evil deeds,"—a being who has for more than six thousand years carried on, with considerable success, a rebellious war against the Sovereign Majesty of the universe,—a being who is able to baffle the designs of Infinite Wisdom, and foil the purposes of Almighty Power,—a being, from whose attacks, therefore, finite, erring, dependent man, can never be secure;

---

* No one who is accustomed to read the New Testament can fail to perceive that this doctrine pervades it. He will call to mind such phrases as—" The prince of the power of the air,"—" The prince of this world,"—" The prince of devils," &c. Indeed, all forms of the doctrine of devils, whether ancient or modern, is found in the Bible. It is true that, like every other Christian doctrine, this has, owing to the progress of civilization, been gradually refined. The early Christian monks, who had many a fierce combat with the Devil, represented him very much like the Egyptian Devil—a huge monster with horns, a long tail, cloven feet, and dragon's wings. We are told that the ancient Christian anchorites, in their battles with this preternatural being, gave him many a sore cudgelling with their clubs, till he groaned aloud, and limped away howling. They, frequently, chopped off pieces of his tail; and sometimes held him by the nose with a pair of red-hot tongs. To what a deplorable state human nature must have been reduced by superstition, before it could be susceptible of such a delusion. For more information of the Devil of the middle ages, see Buckle's *History of Civilization*, Dr. Mackay's *Popular Delusions*, &c.

and against the overwhelming strength of whose temptations it is useless
for him to struggle! How such a creed must reduce its cherisher to a
state of supine despair of ever obtaining a victory over such a mighty
monster! How it must damp all his nobler projects, and weaken all his
exertions to lead a life of virtue! How the recollection that the "God
of this world" frustrated the designs of the God of Adam and Eve, by
converting them from a state of happy immortality into one of misery and
eternal death, overwhelms him with despondency! And, above all, how
the thought strikes terror into his heart, that because "the God of this
world hath blinded his mind," and hath tempted him to sin, he shall be
punished for ever and ever!

But, O man! if thou wouldst but look at Nature, and see that, by
the harmony of design, and unity of operation, in the amazingly various
portions of the universe, she proclaims but one God, matchless in power,
boundless in goodness, and infinite in all his attributes,—that, in a thousand ways, she gives a flat contradiction to the absurd notion of two
Gods—the one infinitely good, and the other infinitely evil—thou wouldst
soon abandon the superstitious belief in the existence and works of the
Devil, and wouldst adore the Deity alone; not distracting thy mind about
another object, which is supposed to claim an equal, or a superior
reverence. Not within the whole sphere of nature wilt thou find the
slightest trace either of the existence or influence of the supposed
"prince of the power of the air," or the possibility of witchcraft. The
more closely thou dost examine Nature, who loves to be interrogated, the
more fully wilt thou be convinced of this fact. Whatever object within her
whole domains appears strange, whatever sound disagreeable, whatever
effect unaccountable, she invites thee to scrutinize, so as to satisfy thyself
it is only part of her, and of her operations. Neither in repairing to,
nor returning from her temple, at midnight or noon, wilt thou be terrified
or haunted by an angry malignant devil, a fiend, a sprite, or a hag.
Knowledge of her ways, called SCIENCE, has abundantly proved to her
students, that these phantoms have not, and never had, any existence,
except in the fancy of the superstitious and the ignorant.

Seeing, therefore, that the religion of nature is incomparably better
calculated than Christianity to make mankind virtuous and happy, and
that this religion actually rewards them with the enjoyment of a degree of
happiness the moment they reduce into practice any of her precepts, cease,
therefore, O man! to spend thy valuable time, talent, and treasure, upon
the dreams of superstition, which hold out hopes that will never be
realized, conjure up fears that have no foundation, fill thy mind with
gloomy desponding thoughts, and render thy life one of disquietude by
day and of fear by night. Cease to seek God beyond the bounds of
nature; cease to ask him to confer blessings by supernatural means, of
which thy mind can have no conception; cease from the absurd practice
of praying to the Deity to perform miracles,—to violate the laws of nature
for thy convenience; but study to know and obey these laws, by which
thou wilt learn the will of thy Creator, and obey his commands. Instead
of—with pretended humility and bended knees—finding fault with the
All-wise God, and telling him what he *should* do, and what he should *not*
do, what he *should* bestow, and what he should *not* bestow,—instead of

praying for rain when it is sunshine, and sunshine when it is rain,—instead of attempting to direct the Unerring, and persuade the Unchangeable to alter his mind, adore him for his infinite goodness displayed throughout all nature. Perceive that by the wise and eternal laws of the universe, cause and effect are indissolubly connected,—that the latter follows the former, in inevitable succession, and cannot be changed at the request of man. Learn that, if this could be done, the whole harmonious system of nature would be placed at the mercy of thy selfish desire. Relinquish the foolish and even blasphemous notion, cherished by Christians in every age, that God pours his rage upon man, by witholding rain and warmth, by causing excessive heat or incessant rain, so as to send famine on earth,—by causing earthquakes, thunder and lightening, hurricanes, plagues, disorders, accidents, sudden deaths, the loss of worldly goods, and a thousand other calamities, which superstitious people believe to be direct judgments from heaven, and to be averted by fervent prayers. But as the universe is governed by fixed laws ; or—to use the language of theology—as " all events are decreed by the wisdom of an infinite God," millions of saints cannot alter the least thing in the course of nature. Do not imagine that thou canst, by eloquent addresses to the All-pervading Spirit, move his affections, as pathetic orators move the hearts of their mortal hearers ; or arouse His compassion, by earnest intreaties, as clever beggars, by their importunities, excite the pity of charitable men.—The Deity is not susceptible of these human passions and emotions : thou canst work no change in him, or make him do aught because thou askest. To imagine that thou canst, is to entertain a most low and grovelling notion of him,—is to degrade him to a level with thyself,—is, in a word, impious ! Abandon, therefore, such a superstitious practice, and learn to adore the Sovereign Majesty of the universe in a manner more befitting thyself, as a rational being, and more worthy the reverence with which thou shouldst regard the Unchangeable, Infinite, First Cause, whose wisdom is perfect, and whose boundless benevolence shines forth in every object throughout his vast and stupendous creation.*

* It is true that some of the most enlightened Christian divines of modern times, perceiving the absurdity of the doctrine of prayer, have considerably modified it, and have spoken of it in language almost as strong as that we have just employed, reducing its use entirely to making man's mind more devotional. Dr. Blair, (Serm. 19.) after dwelling on the immutability of the Deity, and showing that " the whole system of his government is fixed, and his laws are irrevocable," asks, in anticipation of an objection,—" To what purpose, it may be urged, is homage addressed to a Being whose purpose is unalterably fixed ; 'to whom our righteousness extendeth not;' whom by no arguments we can persuade, and by no supplication we can mollify ? The objection would have weight if our religious addresses were designed to work any alteration on God ; either by giving him information of what he did not know ; or by exciting affections which he did not possess ; or by inducing him to change measures which he had previously formed. But they are only crude and imperfect notions of religion which can suggest such ideas. The change which our devotions are intended to make, is upon ourselves, not upon the Almighty. Their chief efficacy is derived from the good dispositions which they raise and cherish in the human soul." In like manner, an able theologian, in the Encyclopædia Britannica, under the word, *Prayer*, writes :—" The Being that made the world, governs it by laws that are inflexible, because they are the best ; and to suppose that he can be induced by prayers, oblations, or sacrifices, to vary his plan of government, is an impious thought, which degrades the Deity to a level with

But here, one of the orthodox school, who has, through a long Christian life, been accustomed to regard the Deity as *man*, conversing familiarly with Adam and Eve, dining on veal, butter, milk, and cake, with Abraham and Sarah, and wrestling, like a mighty giant with Jacob, would, possibly, say, —" I cannot worship God without asking him for blessings :—I must pray for his grace, from day to day, to enable me to quench the firey darts of the wicked ; and my corrupt and fallen nature, always prone to sin, requires me to pray for forgiveness through the atoning blood of the Saviour." But pause ! The doctrine of thy "corrupt and fallen nature " or of *original sin*, is not a whit less pernicious in its effects, or less revolting to reason, than are the Christian dogmas already noticed. It calls upon you to believe that two human beings had been created perfect and immortal,—that they were surrounded with every enjoyment they could possibly desire,—that they had full authority over all objects in nature, with the exception of one tree, which, they were told, possessed the strange power of imparting to them knowledge of good and evil, and of converting them almost into Gods,—that a being called the Devil tempted the female of this happy pair to eat of the forbidden fruit of this marvellous tree, and to give some of it to her mate,—that God, although he had said that, in the very day they should eat of this fruit, they should *surely* die, did not immediately inflict the threatened punishment, but commuted it into transportation from the delightful fields of Eden,—that, overlooking the crime of this disobedient couple, he sentenced the whole of their unborn progeny to all the miseries of life, to death, and the endless

---

man. One of these inflexible laws is the connexion established between certain disposition of mind and human happiness. We are enjoined to pursue a particular course of conduct under the denomination of virtue, not because our virtuous actions can in any degree be of advantage to him by whom we are created, but because they necessarily generate in our own minds those dispositions which are essential to our ultimate happiness." Lord Kames (Sketches, Book iii. sk. 3. chap. 3.) uses almost precisely the same words. Dr. Leechman, formerly the Principal of Glasgow College, advances the same views, in a sermon on *prayer* (serm. iii. p. 192.) saying—"God is not subject to those sudden passions and emotions of mind which we feel, nor to any change of his measures and conduct, by their influence : *He is not wrought upon and changed by our prayers ; for with him there is no variableness nor shadow of turning.* Prayer only works its effect upon us, as it contributes to change the temper of our minds." Such are the concessions which reason, and common sense have driven these writers, as well as many others, to make, regarding the use of prayer. It is, however, a concession made at the expense of denying, in effect, the truth of the Bible—the very foundation of their faith. No fact is more capable of demonstration than that this book, in a vast number of places, clearly teaches that men's prayers influence the deity so as to make him change his course of action. God is made to say to Abimelech that, if Abraham prayed for him, he would be kept alive. When the Lord was displeased, and his anger kindled, so that he sent fire to burn the people, Moses prayed unto the Lord, who then refrained from burning any more of them. Hannah prayed for a child, and God granted her request. Elias prayed that it might not rain, and the result was that it did not rain for three years and a half. At the end of this period he prayed for rain, and rain came. "The prayer of faith shall save the sick."—" The effectual fervent prayer of a righteous man availeth much." An angel told the old priest Zacharias that his prayer had been heard ; and also gave Cornelius a similar assurance. Jesus tells his disciples that whatever they asked in prayer, believing, they should receive.—Ask, and it shall be given you—Every one that asketh, receiveth—Whatsoever ye ask in my name, I will do it—I will pray the Father and he shall give you another comforter. That man's prayer influences the conduct of the God of the Bible, is a doctrine which pervades the whole of this book.

torments of hell,—that, instead of wreaking his vengeance upon the author of this mischief—the Devil, he poured his wrath upon the poor creature whose form the God of this world had either assumed or entered, dooming it to walk on its belly and eat dust,—and that, not satisfied with cursing the faultless serpent, he cursed the ground, because of Adam, and declared it should produce but thorns and thistles. Such is the popular, and such the Scriptural idea of what orthodox divines term *original sin ;* by which is meant that the unborn race of Adam—all mankind that ever existed, that exist, and ever will exist—were participators in his crime, which was that of " eating of one apple," and were consequently damned to all eternity, for this sin of their progenitor. A more absurd and grossly unjust doctrine could not be propounded. It ignores all proper notions, not only of benevolence, but of justice, and makes the Deity the most revengeful, and malignant being imaginable. His wrath is made to pursue men as long as one of their race is on earth, for an offence with the commission of which they had nothing whatever to do ; and after they depart this life, the same rage is made to be poured upon them incessantly, for eternal ages ! Not only is this doctrine unworthy of God ; not only is it a blasphemy against Infinite Goodness ;—it is pregnant with mischief to mankind, directly leading men to wretchedness and despair. It depreciates virtue, destroys parental love, and suppresses every benevolent feeling—every effort to ameliorate the condition of the human race. If man is condemned to eternal torments before he is born, what incentive is left him for endeavouring to be good and happy ? If it is his very nature to sin,—if he is incapable of performing a virtuous act, or entertaining a virtuous thought, as the Christian creed goes, he is only fulfilling the law of his nature when he commits the most depraved vices, and wallows in the most atrocious crimes ; and it is vain to attempt at effecting any improvement in him, till the supernatural *grace* of Christianity is shed abroad in his heart. Thus is man, who is commanded to obey God's laws, left to wander about the earth, utterly incapable of observing these laws, in consequence of an inherent sinful nature, and is, at length, consigned to everlasting punishment. How such a doctrine alienates the human affections from God ! How it makes man dread and hate his Creator as a tyrant, instead of loving him as a father ; seeing that he has condemned him to misery and death—death eternal—for the sin of his progenitor ! How it makes him fear the vengeance, and tremble at the wrath of Infinite malignity, while it withers within him every benevolent sentiment, and blasts in his bosom every pious emotion ! How strongly, by way of example, it inclines him to be revengeful, unjust, and cruel to his fellow-beings ! How it makes him despise and hate knowledge; seeing that God condemned his race to eternal misery for the supposed sin of eating of " the tree of knowledge of good and evil,"—" a tree to be desired to make one wise,"—a tree which God himself is declared to have said, had actually made man so wise as " to know good and evil,"—a tree whose qualities, consequently, had a direct tendency to make man happier and better, in every way ! How different is this doctrine from that taught in God's works ! The former declares that man's duty is to refuse knowledge—is to be ever ignorant, and content with blind faith ; and dooms him to eternal death, if he becomes wise ! But the latter daily furnishes him with additional proofs that the more knowledge he acquires the happier he becomes. How the doctrine of "the fall" makes him despise his own mental faculties and external senses—the only powers with which he has been endowed to distinguish good from evil, and truth from error — by prohibiting him to touch a tree which is good for food, and pleasant to the eyes! How it makes him distrust the righteousness of God, who is declared to have said that in the day Adam would eat of the tree of knowledge he should surely die, whereas he lived afterwards for nearly a thousand years! With what hatred it makes him regard his Maker, seeing that he is the author of his misery,—that having created him, he placed him in Eden with a disposition to sin,—that he foreknew he would sin, and wished him to sin,—that he placed before him a tree good for food, pleasant to the eye, much to be desired and calculated to make him wise,—that he brought in contact with him the most wily of his creatures, in order to tempt him to violate the arbitrary and unreasonable command he had given him,—and that, because his capricious command was thus passively broken, he sentenced him to endure everlasting torments! How this doctrine irresistibly leads its believer to reflect on the absurdity, injustice, and cruelty of his Maker! How revolting it is to the human mind! How repugnant to common sense!

But where is the proof of the truth of this horrible dogma? Where is there to be found the least indication that man has "fallen," as it is termed, and is not now as virtuous, as pure, and as sinless in his nature as the very first moment any of his race existed on this globe? Where is there within the whole range of nature a tittle of evidence that it is in consequence of "the fall" the earth produces "thorns and thistles,"— that the rose is not as sweet, the lily not as white, the pine-apple not as delicious, the sun not as bright, the lion not as tame, now as ever? Where is there aught to show that the first human being was more virtuous and intelligent than any man in the present age? Is there not abundant evidence that mankind, from age to age, in proportion as scientific knowledge dispels from their minds the gloom of superstition, increase in wisdom, virtue, and happiness? What foundation has that Christian doctrine which tends to discourage all efforts to ameliorate the moral and intellectual condition of our race, by teaching that man "is, of his own nature, inclined to evil," and has "no power to do good work," being desperately wicked, and "born unto the world deserving God's wrath and damnation?" The history of the human race, on every part of the globe, in every stage of civilization, from the most savage to the most polished, flatly contradicts the truth of this horrible dogma, and proclaims that man, naturally, loves what is truly virtuous, and hates what is really vicious; and that it requires wicked examples to make a deep impression on his mind before he loses all his innate sense of reverence for moral right. Behold how innocent! how free from moral guilt, is the smiling happy infant in the maternal arms! Does its cheerful countenance betray the curse of Eden? Do its merry eyes and affectionate gestures indicate that its "heart is deceitful above all things, and desperately wicked?" Are any traces of the poison of the forbidden fruit discoverable in its dimpled cheeks? Is there anything about the harmless babe which warrants the horrific assertion of a celebrated Calvinistic preacher of the present century, that "hell is paved with infants not a span long, for the glory of God?" Ye mothers! ye fathers! do not your feelings recoil from the very contemplation of such a horribly barbarous doctrine,—a doctrine which not only alienates your affections from your offspring, but is an outright blasphemy against God? Abandon, therefore, a creed which teaches such monstrous dogmas, and study Nature, whose operations will soon convince you that God punishes only the individual who transgresses,—punishes only in proportion to the offence, and for the express purpose of promoting the welfare of the offender. Nature will, by contrast, teach you the frivolity of a law that prohibited the eating of the fruit of a particular tree, not because it contained anything physically detrimental to the human frame, but because a command had been given not to eat it. Nature will show you that, if her laws prohibit you to feed upon hemlock, opium, and other poisonous matter, it is because that, if they are taken in undue quantities, they will cause pain, and even death; while, nevertheless, if they are taken in adequate portions, and at proper seasons, they will remove pain, and cure diseases,—their appropriate and benevolent purposes. Nature will teach you that there is no such a thing as original sin,—that all the qualities inherent in, and transmitted to man, by his progenitors, are capable of being modified; so that the bad qualities contracted by parents, through violating the natural laws, and transmitted to the offspring, can be eradicated, and all transmissible good qualities indefinitely improved. Nature will teach you that man, if he observed her laws, could live much longer and happier than he does,—that death is not the result of the sin of Adam,—that geological facts prove that, long before man existed on this globe, mortality prevailed among animals, and was one of the incidents of their life, not only by natural decay and the operation of physical forces, but by the destructive propensities of carnivorous animals, destined to prey on living beings,—that man's own constitution, which is carnivorous, is evidently destined to be terminated by death,—that, under the natural laws, even death has a benevolent tendency,—that when man has lived in accordance with the dictates of the organic laws, till he is old, and his frame fairly worn out, the pain of death is scarcely felt,—that the pain attending premature death is a punishment for infringements of the organic laws,—that the object of this punishment is to impress the living with the importance of obeying these laws,—that when death occurs during the early or middle period of life, it is the result of a departure from the physical and organic laws,—that, in premature death, even that of an infant, a benevolent principle is discernible, in releasing from misery a being whose organic disease, inherited from the errors of his progenitors, is beyond the bounds of the remedial process, and in giving a guarantee to the human race against the future transmission of his malady, by hereditary descent,—that the termination of the life of such a child, therefore, is so far in design from the cruelty of taking away the life of "infants not a span long" to pave the bottom of hell, that it is an act of the most merciful character,—that as death in the early, as well as the middle period of life, is a benevolent arrangement, so it is in old age, when an individual has been rendered, by time, incapable of either usefulness or enjoyment; and when he would feel no pain in his last moments had it not been for a violation of the natural laws on his part, or that of his progenitors, and of the society in which he moved,—that death, so far from being the consequence of original sin, is an essential part of the system of organisation, being implied in birth, growth, maturity, decay, and old age, as completely as spring and summer imply autumn and winter.—(Combe's Constitution. chap. i. et seq.)   Yes, nature will teach you all this, and much more.   But how different her lessons, regarding death, its cause, utility, and consequences, from the lore of Christian theology !   How much more rational, more in harmony with the rest of creation, and more worthy of a perfectly just, wise, and benevolent Deity are the former than is the latter, which teaches that, owing to the sin of Adam, man is capable of performing no good act acceptable to his Maker,—that all his vices are vices of his nature, which have belonged to all generations of men from the present to the first that ever lived, and which his successors will for ever inherit,—that God is his enemy, and regards his nature as not having been created by him, but as the work of the Devil !   How this makes him regard his fellow-beings as he is told that God regards him !   How it alienates his affections from both God and man !   How reckless it makes him as to his moral obligations to either !   How it makes him dread the one as an implacable foe, and hate the other as a base villain !

Section V.—THE CHRISTIAN DOCTRINE OF THE ATONEMENT AT VARIANCE WITH GOD'S WORKS IN NATURE—DENIES THE ESSENTIAL ATTRIBUTES OF THE DEITY—IS REPUGNANT TO REASON—AN ATONEMENT FOR SIN IMPOSSIBLE—TO KNOW THAT EVERY ACT MUST BEAR ITS OWN CONSEQUENCE THE STRONGEST POSSIBLE INCENTIVE TO VIRTUE—MAN'S INNATE DESIRE OF VIRTUE AND HAPPINESS—THE UTTER FAILURE OF CHRISTIANITY TO AMELIORATE THE MORAL CONDITION OF THE HUMAN RACE.

It may be urged that although the Christian theology teaches the doctrine of eternal torments and of the fall of man, yet it teaches that an atonement has been made by Christ for man's sins, so as not to leave him in the hopeless state just described.   But the doctrine of the atonement, like all other Christian dogmas, is evidently nothing more than a creation of man's fertile brain.   The very notion of an atonement is at utter variance with all the works of God in nature, wherein the infringement of each of his laws, is attended with its own punishment.   This doctrine, as taught by the most celebrated Christian divines, depicts God as a revengeful Being, who, because his mandates have been disregarded, curses creation, condemns the whole human race to endless misery, and plunges his sword into the innocent bosom of his only Son, who is also a God !   Such a notion of Deity sets man's reason at defiance, and wounds all his better feelings.   That God, in all whose works shines forth infinite benevolence, should doom all mankind to the ever-burning flames of hell, because the first man he ever created disobeyed his will in eating a certain apple,—that another God, namely, God the Son, in order to appease the wrath of God the Father, and incline him to overlook man's offence, was obliged to descend to this world, and be put to death on a cross, between two theives,—and that, after all this, only a portion of the human race, will God the Father, exempt from eternal perdition, are such a complication of blasphemy and nonsense, so widely at variance with any just notion of the perfections of Deity, that reason rejects with indignation.

Christian divines, however, gravely argue that, man having sinned against an infinite God, his sin was infinite, and therefore required an infinite atonement, which could be made only by God, who, consequently, took human nature and died on the cross. But these divines appear to forget that they have "three persons in the Godhead," equal in all attributes, and that all the attributes of each are, consequently, infinite. To say nothing of the absurd notion of more than one infinity, if the Son and the Holy Ghost are equal with the Father, man must have sinned against all three, and the *infinite justice* of each must have, thereby, been offended. Still, we hear of the Son giving satisfaction only to the justice of the Father. Did not the justice of the Holy Ghost, and even of the Son himself, alike demand satisfaction? Christian writers ignore the justice of these two Persons of the Godhead. But why? Were they not Divine Personages when man sinned? Or are God the Son and God the Holy Ghost alike destitute of the attribute of justice? The natural inference from Christian theology is, that God the Son is not possessed of the attribute of justice, that God the Father is destitute of the attribute of mercy, and that God the Holy Ghost is destitute of both these attributes. Again, who made the atonement? Christ, by his sufferings and death. Was Christ God? Yes. Then God suffered and died; which is an absurdity—an impossibility! "No," answers Christian theology, "the Godhead and manhood were joined together in one person, still only the manhood of Christ suffered and died." Then it was only the man Jesus who died; and the atonement of a man could not be infinite. On the other hand, if "the Godhead and the manhood were joined together in one person, never to be divided," then God must have died.— (See *Harris's Lectures on Trinitarianism.*) Further, if the Father, Son, and Holy Ghost be viewed as only one God, then man must have sinned against this "Triune God," and therefore against Christ as *part of the Godhead;* so that on this view of the question, again, we are driven to the same conclusion,—that either he gave satisfaction for sin committed against himself, or that man had sinned only against the Father and the Holy Ghost. But if Christ gave satisfaction for sin committed against himself, to whom gave he that satisfaction?—to himself, by dying? And if there was an *infinite* satisfaction required for the sin committed against Christ himself, as an infinite Person— a Deity, where is the satisfaction given for sin committed against the Father and the Holy Ghost,—both infinite, and both, therefore, demanding an infinite satisfaction?

The more the doctrine of the atonement is investigated, the more glaring its absurdity and impossibility appear. It represents the Deity as withholding his mercy, even from the penitent, till a full satisfaction is made to justice, and therefore precludes the idea that God is either merciful or forgiving; nay, in asserting that the Father sent his own innocent Son to be punished instead of guilty men, it denies that God is just. A doctrine which transfers the guilt from the guilty to the innocent, and makes man sin in fact and suffer by proxy, whilst it makes Christ sin by proxy and suffer in fact, is contrary to every principle of moral rectitude. The transference of guilt is not only unjust, but impossible; for an innocent person cannot feel himself guilty. If, with Christians, we imagine that only *Christ's human nature suffered* for the sins of men, still, he could never thus make an *infinite* atonement to pacify the *infinite* anger of the Father. For, if he suffered only in his human nature, he could, as man, have no terror of a guilty conscience; and could suffer nothing but the pain which ordinarily attended the death of crucifixion. Will any one dare assert that, *as God*, he *could* suffer the terrors of *a guilty conscience?* Again, if he was innocent, will any one dare assert that, *as man*, he *did* suffer the terrors of *a guilty conscience?* Such an atonement as that imagined by Christians is utterly impossible. Indeed, any atonement for sin is impossible; for every sin, or violation of God's laws, produces its own punishment. A sin, without its consequent punishment, is as impossible as a cause without an effect. The latter is, by the author of nature, made inevitably to follow the former, in order to correct the errors of man. In a word, the whole doctrine of the atonement is a tissue of the grossest absurdities that can be imagined, tending to brutalise man, and outrage the moral character of God. That the Being who pervades the universe was confined to the womb of Mary,—that the infinite Spirit, who alone possesseth immortality, was scourged, crucified, and put to death, on Mount Calvary, for the sins of men, is the climax of blasphemous nonsense, the notion of which can have originated only among barbarous people, who believed that the life of a man was a most precious oblation to deprecate a public calamity; and who, therefore, as we have seen, very frequently offered up human sacrifices, as atonements and redemptions.*

---

* That this fundamental Christian doctrine—the atonement, is of a grossly pagan origin, has already been amply shown in the course of this work.—(See pp. 223—233. 322—334, 429, 430, 527, 528.) The following additional proofs, however, are given. The Scholiast on Aristophanes (Plut. lin. 453.) says that those who were offered as expiating sacrifices to the Gods, on account of some calamity, were called, καθαρματα, *purifiers.* He also tells us that this custom prevailed among the Romans, as well as the Athenians, and that it was called καθαρισμος, *purification.* (Vid. in Equit. lin. 1133.) Dr. Dodridge says that those who were thus made expiatory sacrifices to the heathen deities, were taken from the dregs of the people, "and loaded with curses, affronts, and injuries, in the way to the altar at which they were to bleed." He also adds,—"Suidas says that these wretched victims, were called, καθαρματα, as their death was esteemed an *expiation*: and when their ashes were thrown into the sea, the very words Γινου Περιψημα, Γινου Καθαρμα, *Be thou a propitiation*, were used in the ceremony." Now, in the same manner precisely is Jesus's blood said to "cleanse (καθαριζει) us from all sin" (1 John i. 7.),—to have purged (καθαρισμον) our sins,—purged (καθαριζεται) with blood, &c. (Heb. i. 3; ix. 14, 22, 23.) The Mexicans worshipped a man for a whole year before they sacrificed him as an atonement for sin. (Bicart's Ceremonies.) The Lacedemonians frequently offered human sacrifices to their Diana, as an atonement for sin. (Pausan. iii. 16.) A Christian writer, in the Penny Cyclopædia, in a long article, under the word *Atonement*, very justly remarks that "the practice of atonement is remarkable for its antiquity and universality."—"The practice of *general* atonement, among the heathen nations, whatever may have been its origin, must have been greatly encouraged by a certain article in the popular creed."—"At the earliest date to which

Renounce, therefore, O man! this remnant of paganism, and embrace the religion which thy Creator teaches in nature, whose laws punish your sins—not as a vengeance taken for injury or insult—not because Divine justice would be impugned by pardoning the guilty, and yet would be vindicated by punishing the innocent in his stead—but because such a punishment arises from the very nature of the offence, as an inevitable sequence, and has the benevolent effect of preventing the repitition of the offence. To know that there is no pardon for violating the Creator's laws in nature,—to know that every act must produce its own consequence, is a better incentive to virtue, and a stronger motive to secure happiness than the dream of a thousand atonements for sin. Nothing can more strongly incite us to morality than to know that every act is irrevocable, and must bear its own consequences,—that every deed we commit must remain, for ever, inscribed on the tablets of Nature, and bear its own fruit—either pain and misery, or pleasure and happiness. Were all mankind actuated by this motive, the human race would soon make such strides as it has never yet made in morality and the means of happiness.

Man needs not go further than his own feelings in proof that the desire of happiness is the moving principle of his being, permeating every emotion of his nature, from birth to old age, and forsaking him only when his heart ceases to beat and his lungs to breathe. According to the very laws of his constitution, he has no power to desire misery, for its own sake; and if he thoroughly knew, beforehand, the consequence of every action, he would commit no act productive of his misery. The want of knowledge of his own constitution and of external objects, is the chief cause of man's present woe. Accordingly, we find that the progressive happiness of the human race, in past ages, has been in exact proportion to the experience acquired of new facts in the operations of nature. Prompted by his innate desire of happiness, man has at length, however, discovered much of the means of his happiness,—knowledge of the operations of external nature, and of the mode of adapting them to the wants of his own constitution. Always desiring happiness, and gradually acquiring knowledge of the manner to obtain it, man cannot fail, ultimately, to become happy; or in other words, cannot fail to become happy in proportion as knowledge of the various means of avoiding misery increases throughout the world. The admirable adaptation of everything in nature to his wants, proves that his happiness, in the present world is attainable. Every one must daily feel the falsity of the gloomy Scriptural description given of him, in common with every individual of his race,—that his nature is innately vicious, his thoughts always evil, and his heart desperately wicked. Who does not feel that he might be much better, much more virtuous, and much more happy than the present condition of the society in which he turns, and by which he is influenced, permits him to be? Who has not felt the ardour of love and the glow of

we can carry our inquiries by means of the heathen records, we meet with the same notion of atonement."—"If we pursue our inquiries through the accounts left us by the Greek and Roman writers of the barbarous nations with which they were acquainted, from India to Britain, we shall find the same notion and similar practices of atonement." So much for the heathen origin of the notion of an atonement.

benevolence thrilling his bosom ?   Who, in contemplating the fitness of
surrounding nature to satisfy his most sanguine desires, can doubt his
capability of enjoying happiness to any degree concieveable ?   And who
can put a limit to the degree of happiness which man, by a knowledge and
an observance of the laws of nature, is destined to enjoy ?   His present
misery, evidently, arises from his violation of these laws ; and the degree
of happiness he enjoys is the result of the degree of obedience he renders
to them.   General obedience to these laws, therefore, would secure to
mankind general happiness.

Now, Christianity does not, any more than other religions founded
on book-revelations, inculcate obedience to these laws ; but, on the contrary—as it has been amply shown, in foregoing portions of this work—
teaches man to disregard the world, and all within it.   It does not teach
us how to be happy in this world—does not even promise us happiness
here, but refers us for that ever desired boon to another world, of which it
gives but a very obscure and confused description.   It makes no provision
whatever for the excercise of man's intellectual faculties, with which he
has been endowed by his Maker, evidently for the purpose of studying the
works of nature :—of these it takes no cognizance.   The same may be
said of man's natural feelings or affections—the fundamental powers of
the human mind—such as conjugal, filial, and parental love, the proper
exercise of which is of more importance than any other toward securing
human happiness.   Indeed, whenever the author of Christianity referred
to the domestic affections, he invariably discountenanced their exercise,
and represented them as evil propensities.   The foregoing fact will account,
in a great measure, for the miserable state of the Christian world at the
present moment, as well as that in which it has been during the eighteen
centuries this religion has been attempting to ameliorate mankind.

There is nothing more capable of demonstrative proof than that
Christianity has utterly failed to teach man to be virtuous ; nay, there
is no fact more obvious than that much of the misery endured by the
inhabitants of Christian countries, during the last eighteen centuries, has
been the immediate result of Christianity.   The more it is spread, the
more it demoralises the world.   The following brief citation from Christian writings may serve to show its evil effects, as admitted by its own
adherents : — Wyvil, in his work on Christian Intolerance, says, in 1809,—
"The barbarities which professed Christians have committed, under the
name of wholesome severities against unbelievers, and even against their
own brethren of the same faith, exceed in horror whatever acts of sanguinary cruelty have been perpetrated by tyrants of every other species.
And such deeds of cruelty and injustice have been sometimes committed,
not by pretended believers of the Gospel, but by men sincerely attached to
it."   Chandler, in his History of Persecution, exclaims,—" What con-
fusions and calamities, what ruins and desolations, what rapines and
murders, have been introduced into the world, under the pretended authority of Christ, and of supporting and propagating Christianity ! "   In the
seventeenth century, Dr. Scott, in his *Christian Life*, says of the five
hundred Christian sects which he believed then to exist,—" It is five
hundred to one but that every one is damned ; because every one damns all
but itself ; and itself is damned by four hundred and ninety-nine."   Bogue

and Bennett (Hist. II. 362.) say that "jealousy, detraction, and persecution, are the sure attendants of a revival of religion." Dr. Claget, in one of his sermons, says,—"There are now in Christendom as monstrous errors and lewd examples, as there ever were in the world before Christianity, or as there are now where Christianity is not at all professed." The whole of Baptist Noel's large volume, on the *Union of Church and State*, goes to show that the Christianity of the Church of England, with its seventeen thousand clergymen, is effete. According to the last parliamentary returns of crime, there is now in this kingdom more immorality than has been at any past time. From the report of the Temperance Society, it appears that, in America, a truly Christian country, there were, even in the year 1829, fifty-six millions of gallons of spirits consumed, a hundred and twenty thousand habitual drunkards, and about forty-eight thousand dying annually from excessive drinking. Doyle, a priest of Arklow, in 1820, says,—"I believe that ninety in every hundred Irish Catholics, who would freely shed their blood for their faith, are living in the habit of such vices as St. Paul assures us excludes one from the kingdom of God. In London, with its four hundred places of Christian worship, the number of prostitutes, even in 1831, amounted to eighty thousand ; and in New York, to twenty thousand. M'Culloch, in his *Highlands*, says,—"I doubt much whether the immorality of Edinburgh, in proportion to its population, is not equal, perhaps greater than that of London." Thousands of additional testimonies could be adduced in proof of the fact that Christians themselves are fully sensible that their religion does not moralise the world,—(See *Curtis's Theology Displayed*.) They cannot shut their eyes at the historical fact that, in a vast number of foreign countries, where Christianity, in ancient times, was deeply rooted in the minds of the inhabitants, it has long ago been supplanted by other religions, such as Boodhism, Mahometanism, and others. Nor can they ignore the truth that, particularly in populous places, where scientific knowledge prevails, not one in twenty of the population attends places of Christian worship,—that, in London and elsewhere, they are obliged to employ Christian missionaries to visit those who live close to churches and chapels,—that, in a word, the people have known enough of Christianity to be determined not to spend their time to listen to its doctrines. In corroboration of the proofs already given that Christianity has utterly failed to moralise, or even Christianise the world,—that it is fading fast before the light of scientific knowledge—and that Christians are painfully cognizant of all this, the following grave admissions are given, in a condensed form, from a very remarkable work called, *Christianity and our Era*, written a few years ago by the Rev. George Gilfillan, a celebrated Scotch divine. This close observer of the times says that there is a profound spirit of doubt among Christians,—that many churches are visibly shaking,—that the bonds of confessions and creeds are loosening,—that a habit of examining all things, and of taking nothing on trust, is growing,—that morality is acknowledged to be among the heterodex as well as the orthodox, and sincerity not dependent on creeds or formula,—that the silent frozen seas and collossal icebergs of an ancient era of thought, are breaking up, and another era is succeeding.—that some of the defenders of the present morbid and feeble state of Christianity are abandoning as untrue, or ignoring as obsolate and unmeaning, the stupendous signs and wonders which gathered around its cradle,— and that those strange signs, so long a terror to the adversaries of Christianity, have actually become a terror to its friends. On the present influence of the Christian religion, he remarks,—that it has descended below other influences which sway our age,—that the oracular power and virtue, which once dwelt in the pulpit, have departed,—that sermons are now criticised, not obeyed,—that when our modern Pauls preach, our Felixes yawn, instead of trembling,—that the thunders of the pulpit are heard only in the agitation of despair, or where the preacher is determined to be popular,—that the private influence of the clergy, which formerly sprang from a general belief in Christianity, is lost,—that the Christian Sabbath is regarded with passive indifference, and its observance enforced by legislative enactments, and other means, which serve only to excite hatred against the day,—that those who attend public worship, in most cases, do so from another motive than to hear the Gospel preached,—that the conversions of the present age, except those of the grossly ignorant and debauched, are mockeries of solemnity,—that revivals, now-a-days, are Pentecosts without the Holy Ghost,—" that Infidelity, from a cowardly, puny thing, hiding its head under historic innuendoes, or skulking under the cloak of fiction, has become a monster of Briarean magnitude, meeting us at every point, and in every field, which is a fact openly avowed by thousands, secretly cherished by thousands more, and circulating besides through our literature, art, science, and philosophy,"—and that few intelligent and liberal-minded Christians hold their religious tenets with the sincerity and warmth of their forefathers. Of the grand army of missionaries in the field fighting the battles of the Lord, expending a vast amount of treasure, and creating a vaster amount of misery, he says that, being overpowered at home, they go to other lands, carrying to simple-minded barbarians a religion which the wisdom of the world has rejected,—that notwithstanding what is said in missionary speeches and sermons, paganism still covers the earth,—and that all the money, the toil, and the life-blood of the missionaries, are spent in vain. Our author also shows, at large, that the written documents of the churches have lost their influence, and that their study is superseded by that of ancient medals, fossil remains, and " *Combe's Constitution of Man*,"—that even the Bible has become a dead letter, has suffered from the analysis of the age, and has lost the awful reverence which once encircled its every page. Such are samples of the proofs of the failure of Christianity, adduced by Mr. Gilfillan, who says,—" Such may seem exaggerated statements ; but we are certain that the more Christians inquire dispassionately and seriously into the facts, the more convinced they must be of their truth. We have not taken them upon heresay or trust. We have no desire, and no inducement to colour the picture darkly. It is not of our device or invention at all. We have merely copied out the severe outline of what we have seen, and what has been seen by many eyes besides ours. We have simply painted a great staring fact."

This writer might have gone further than to prove that Christianity has utterly failed to have any good effect upon the human race.—He might have shown that, in every age, it has been a great barrier to man's progress in knowledge, civilization, and happiness. Its priests have always withstood every new discovery in science, and have opposed every attempt at the true amelioration of mankind. All the improvements,—all the progress that man has made in knowledge, virtue, and happiness, since the introduction of this religion, have been made under the opposition, and clamorous denunciations of a Christian hierarchy, and are to be attributed to secular science alone. The wrathful condemnation of Galileo to the gloomy dungeon; the Christian cry that Faustus's art of printing was the result of an intercourse with the Devil; the clamours against Harvey's discovery of the circulation of the blood; the denunciation against Dr. Jenner's discovered boon of vaccination, as an infidel practice; the outcry of infidelity raised against the Newtonian philosophy; and a thousand others of the kind, will, for ages untold, re-echo the opposition of Christian priests to scientific discoveries teeming with benefits to mankind. To any one who has the interest of the human race at heart, it is deplorable to contemplate that such as the foregoing has been the effect of Christianity on a country where, for nearly two thousand years, it has had the fullest and fairest trial,—where it is preached weekly, and even daily, by many thousands of paid advocates,—where millions of books and tracts are distributed in its favour,—where the Bible, which avowedly teaches it, is read every Sabbath in hundreds of thousands of pulpits; is found in every cottage, in every palace throughout the land, and in every ship that rides upon the waves,—where its contents are mingled with every prayer offered up, are introduced into much of the conversations we hear, whether in private families, in the tavern, or in the street, and form the substance of every sermon preached to us,—where they are used in christening, marrying, and burying us,—where, in a word, they pervade all the actions, and influence the conduct of men, throughout the wide domains of Christendom. Wherefore, then, should we cling to a religion which, after pouring its influence for ages, on the human mind, has made it only the more vicious and miserable; while, on the other hand, we perceive, and even daily experience that the religion revealed in Nature is admirably calculated to make us wise, virtuous, and happy?

But the child of superstition may still object that, in the religion of Nature, he can see no beauty that it should be desired—no consolation, no piety, no spiritual life, no heavenly joy, no religious feeling. What? Is there no *religious feeling* awakened in contemplating the beauty and magnificence of the universe, with its millions of living beings rejoicing in their existence, and having all their diversified wants satisfied by the contrivance of Infinite Benevolence? No *heavenly* joy experienced in gazing at the mighty orbs which roll in boundless space, displaying the almighty power and unerring wisdom of the Self-existent First Cause? No *spiritual life* but in imagining that a spiritual being called the Devil— our inveterate and most powerful foe—is every moment at our elbow, prompting us to evil deeds? No *piety* in anything but in listening to tales about the efficacy of blood,—in having hell and damnation portrayed before our eyes,—in having the burning and smoking brimstone of the bottomless pit held under our nostrils? No *consolation* in anything but the presumptuous practice of dictating to the All-wise Sovereign of the universe what he should do for us? No *beauty* in anything, but in a dying deity, with "his mantle covered o'er with streaming and with clotted gore?" Is there nothing in Nature to excite our admiration, and call forth our nobler feelings?—Nothing in this world—for the study of which we are peculiarly adapted—to engage our attention, to delight us, and make us happy? Has virtue no charm in our eyes? and can we be induced to do a good act only from fear of hell, or hope of heaven? Can we not love virtue for its own value, and hate vice on account of its intrinsic perniciousness? Can we not refrain from the latter and follow the former, not because " God is angry with the wicked every day," but because, in doing so, we *do good* to ourselves and to others? Undoubtedly, we can. There is no man, however depraved, who is not more or less strongly prompted by his own feelings to be just, from a love of justice,—to be benevolent from a spontaneously kind emotion,—and to do good, in general, from a love of virtue. The threats of hell, and the promises of heaven, as incentives to virtue, together with the whole tenour of the superstitious creeds prevalent in the world, have made man believe that he is much more immoral, and more helpless, than he really is. Free him from the trammels of book-revelations—let him study nature alone— and man will make rapid strides towards happiness. He has already discovered that his degree of enjoyment is in proportion to his moral and intellectual progress. He has learned that all his miseries arise from a violation of the natural laws—either by him, or by members of the community in which he lives—and that all his happiness is the result of obedience to these laws, in discovering which, and learning to obey them, he daily progresses, gathering a thousand facts from his own experience, as well as from that of others. When mankind, universally, will learn to obey these laws, each individual will feel intense pleasure in promoting the happiness of others, which cannot fail to secure the happiness of the whole race. Then, will knowledge and benevolence be inseperably connected in each individual, and vice and misery accidents in human life— rarely witnessed. The progress in knowledge and happiness which man has already made, by *studying nature*, warrants this conclusion, and forbids us to prescribe limits either to the high degree of knowledge he is capable of acquiring, or the intensity of happiness he is capable of enjoying.

INDEX.

ABBOT, meaning of the term, 496, *n.* 547. A title given to a bishop in ancient times, 547.

Abraham, charged by Jesus with falsity, 382. His mendacity touching his wife, 382, *n.* The unfading nature of his wife's beauty, *ib.* Its enchanting effects upon kings, *ib.* His removal from the fire-worship of the Magi, 503. Said to have composed the Divine books of the Persians, *ib. n.* His name, from a Persian word, *ib.*

Acts of the Apostles, character of, 434, *n.*

Adultery, not disapproved of by Jesus, 356—358. 378. The barbarous punishment for, among the Jews, 357. Jesus's contradictory statement concerning it, 377. 540—542. Mischievous tendency of his doctrines of, *ib.*

Agapæ, see Love Feasts.

Alexandrian College, the nursery of Christian romances, 179. Its Eclectics, 424, 425, *n.*

Alfred the Great, said to have learnt to read by Divine inspiration, 420. Mr. Sharon Turner's incredible account of, *ib. n.*

Alms, Jesus's inconsistent injunction regarding them, 376. 381.

Ammon, a monk, persuades his wife to become a nun, 483.

Ammonius Saccas, his revival of Eclectism, 425, *n.*

Angels, thought by Jesus to be the forces by which the world was to be destroyed, 97—100, *n.* 171--175. 364. Supposed in ancient times to be heavenly soldiers, 97—99, *n.* Their war in heaven, *ib.* 551, *n.* 525. Called the army, hosts, and soldiers of heaven, 97—99, *n.* Frequent mention of these angelic soldiers in the Bible, *ib.* 137, *n.* Were to be judged by saints, 156. Believed to have defiled themselves with women, 182. Their attendance upon Jesus, 557.

Anger, of Jesus, 353. 380. A passion incompatible with Divinity, *ib.* Is a moral evil, *ib.* 356.

Anomalies, (see contradictions) in Jesus's character, 385.

Antony, St. his life, 478—480. His monkery, *ib.* His prophetic gift, 518.

Apocalypse, see Revelation.

Apocryphal Gospels, (see Gospels) their narrative of Paul and Thecla, 22

Apocryphal New Testament, cited and recommended, 60, *n.* Its doctrine of the near approach of the End of the World, 175—179. Description of its contents, 177, 178, *n.* Identical in character with the canonical New Testament, 186, *n.* Its account of Jesus's earlier life, 306—311, *n.*

Apollonius Thyaneus, a native of a country remarkable for its monkery, 516. An exorcist, *ib.* A Pythagorean, *ib.* Contemporary with Jesus, *ib.* The history of his life, *ib.* 517, *n.* His command over demons, *ib.* His monkery, *ib.* His predictions, 516. 518, *n.* His disciples, *ib.* His miracle in raising into life the dead body of a female, *ib.* The credibility of his history compared with that of the history of Jesus, 517, *n.* His fame, *ib.* The temples and statues erected in honour of him, *ib.* His Divinity, *ib.* His ascension into heaven, *ib.* The assertion that he performed greater miracles than Jesus, *ib.* The behaviour of the Protestant clergy to the English translator of the history of his life, *ib.*

Apostles, the proofs which they afford that Jesus prophesied the fall of Jerusalem, 41—48. 143. Their description of the End of the World and that of temporal judgments, confounded by early Christians, 47. The proofs they afford that Jesus predicted the near approach of the End of the World, 64—66. 68. 139. 143, 144. 150—175. Their adherence to the Jewish ceremonies through life, 124. 141. Their cowardly behaviour towards their Master, 149. Inculcated the doctrine of the near approach of the End of the World, 150—175. This the substance of their teaching, 155—163. The question whether they were the deceived or the deceivers, 199. 200. Were not divinely inspired, 200, 204, 205. Were fanatical, 201—204.

Their failure to cast out a demon, 295, *n.*
Their monachal character, 498, 499, *n.*
Their garb, 530, 531.

Ass, unjustly seized by Jesus's command, 348, 349.

Athanasius, St. his motive in writing the life of St. Antony, 478.

Atonement, (see human sacrifices) often made by Pagans with human sacrifices, 223, 324, *n.* 438. 527, 528, *n.* 606, *n.* Jesus's doctrines of, borrowed from pagan lore, 429, 430. 559. The Christian doctrine of, at variance with God's work in nature, 604. Depicts God as a revengeful Being, *ib.* Sets man's reason at defiance, *ib.* 605. This doctrine at variance with a proper notion of the perfection of Deity, 605. Its absurdity, 605, 606. Precludes the idea that God is either merciful or just, *ib.* The Christian atonement impossible, 606.

Augustine, his opinion of the manner in which this world was to come to a speedy end, 183.

B.

Bagvat-Geeta, a portion of the Brahminical Scriptures, delivered by the God Chrishna, teaches the doctrine of being "born again," 428. Teaches the Gospel doctrine of faith, 428, 429. Its living water, *ib.* Its great antiquity, 551, *n.* Teaches all the Christian doctrines, *ib.*

Baptism, its pagan origin, 496—498. 500—508. Practised by all Christian, and by most heathen monks, *ib.* Its various Christian appellations, 496. 499. Origin of John's baptism, 496—508. Not instituted by either Jesus or John, 497. In use already among the Jews, *ib.* 498. The pagan origin of the ancient white robes of baptism, 498. Baptism administered to candidates in a state of nudity, 498, *n.* The two great seasons of the year for baptizing, *ib.* Egyptian and Indian baptism, 498, 499. The daily baptism of the Brahmins, 501. The origin of the Gospel baptism "with fire," 507. 512, *n.* John's baptism not Jewish, 507. This rite thought by all ancient Christians, as well as pagans, to produce regeneration and to wash away sins, 507, *n.*

Barnabas, St. on the approaching End of the World, the Millenium, and the Kingdom of Heaven, 175—179.

Beelzebub, a heathen god, 406, *n.* Jesus charged with casting out demons by the influence of, 406, 407, *n.*

Belief, (see faith) a passive act of the mind, 3. The signs of belief in Jesus, 293—299. Man controlled by evidence in the act of,

330—333. 339. The immense sacrifice of human life, caused in attempts at effecting a uniformity of, 333.

Bells, anciently used to call monks out of their cells, 370, *n.* Origin of, for religious purposes, *ib.* Used for calling together the Brahmin monks, 445. Used for convening the Boodhist monks, 453. The pagan origin of those in churches, 487, *n.*

Bible, the authorised English version of, taken as a standard in this work, 6. The pains taken in producing this version, 6, *n.* The division of, into chapters and verses of a modern date, 10. 159, *n.* The obscene language of, 82, 156, *n.* Resembles heathen lore in its account of fabulous longevity, 118, *n.* How originally written, 137, *n.* Its proper names expressive of the principal traits in their respective objects, 138. The headings of its chapters, their character, *ib.* The liberties taken by Christian writers in interpreting it, 143. Its error in exhorting parents to beat their children, 215, *n.* Its English translators, remarks on, 275, *n.* How it is to be studied, 299, *n.* More read than examined, *ib.* Obscurity of its contents, 386. 389. Bears internal marks that it is not from God, 389, *n.* None of its contents so old as the Brahminical Scriptures, 427. Many portions of it bear striking resemblance to those ancient writings, *ib. n.* Abounds with expressions referring to fire-worship, 502, *n.* Identical with the Persian theology, in its doctrine of the origin of good and evil, *ib.* Not allowed to be read in England, by the commonalty, till after the Reformation, 546, *n.* Does not prove the existence of a First Cause, 584. Many of its doctrines fraught with mischief, 590—603.

Bigotry of Jesus, 381. 383—385.

Bishop, an officer of religion among the heathens, 221. 232, *n.* 567, 568, *n.* His duties in ancient times, 487, *n.*

Blindness from birth, its cause not known to Jesus, 402, 403. Sometimes cured, in the present age, by scientific men, 403, *n.*

Blood, abstained from, by Christian and other monks, 523.

Boodh, a Hindoo god, date of the incarnation of, 448, *n.* Became incarnate for the purpose of confounding demons, *ib.* 449. The same as Foe, the Chinese god, 448, *n.* 554. Two gods of the name supposed to have been incarnate, 448, 449, *n.* Import of his name, 449. Born of a virgin, *ib.* Was of a royal descent, *ib.* Sent to this world by other gods, *ib.* Descended into hell, *ib.* Ascended to heaven, *ib.* His marvellous career predicted by the prophets, *ib.* The exploits of his youth detailed, 449, 450.

His monkery, 450. Was a religious reformer, *ib.* His disciples persecuted after his death, 451. His dwelling-place, a cave in a rock, 452, *n.* How represented in the cavern temples of India, *ib.*

Boodhism, (see monkery) a religion believed to be purely divine, by upward of three hundred and fifteen millions of people, 447. A branch of Brahminism, *ib.* 448, *n.* 450, 451, *n.* Established at a remote period of antiquity, 447, 448, *n.* Its origin and founder, 448, *n.* Its monks, 449, 450. Its introduction into several Eastern countries, 451—455.

Book of Nature, teaches the attributes of Deity, 582. Its superiority over paper and parchment revelations, *ib.* 585, 586.

Bottomless pit, signification of the phrase, 172. Where situated, *ib.* 345.

Brahmins, (see monkery) their system of asceticism, 443—447. 551, *n.* 528, 529, *n.* Their prophets, 449. Their persecution of the Boodhists, 451. Their penances, 529. Their sacrifices, *ib.* Killed no animal but for sacrifice, *ib.* Were at liberty to eat of the sacrifices, *ib.* Their abstinence from flesh-meat, intoxicating liquors, and women, *ib.* Their sublime idea of Deity, 543, *n.* Their notion of Creation, *ib.* Their transmigrations, 543, 544, *n.* Their scale of animated beings, *ib.* Their idea of a spirit, *ib.* Their metaphysics, *ib.* Their future rewards and punishments, *ib.* Mysteries of their religion, 545, 546.

Brothers of Jesus, disbelieved in him, 358. Deceived by him, 359, 360. Ridiculed his pretence to miracles, 358, 359.

Burden of proof, lies on the side which asserts, 8, 246, 283.

C.

Calvin, John, the persecuting spirit of, 574.

Canibalism, taught by Jesus, 320—325.

Carelessness, inculcated by Jesus, 314, 315.

Celibacy, (see monks) encouraged by Jesus, 81, 82. 540—542. Recommended by the Apostle Paul, 157. Practised by the Indian monks, 415, 416. Practised by Christians and pagans in every age, 540—542.

Cells of monks, the churches of early Christians, 369, 370, *n.* The manner of calling the monks out of them, 370, *n.*

Cerinthus, taught that the End of the World and the Millenium were close at hand, 180.

Chrishna, the Indian Saviour, and incarnate God of the Brahmins, his temples, 233, *n.* His striking resemblance to Jesus, 337, *n.* 428, 429. *n.* 491, Always followed by a number of women. 377, *n.* Taught the doctrine of being "born again," 428.

Mysteries of his religion, 545. His spiritual union with his disciples, 551, *n.* Inculcated all the doctrines taught in our Gospels, *ib.*

Christ, (see Jesus) statue of. 233, *n.* Meaning of the word, 350, *n.* 366, *n.*

Christianity, the importance of ascertaining whether it is of a divine origin, 2, 3. The question of its truth admitted by its advocates to be one of conflicting probabilities, 3. Its modern doctrines not inculcated by Jesus, 117. The books written against it, in early times, burnt by its advocates, 119, *n.* 511. 517, *n.* 568, *n.* 571, *n.* Few of its present doctrines taught by the Apostles, 155. Has no more claim to a divine origin than other religions, 196. 198. 243. The causes of its early success, 205—235. Many embraced it from fear, 208—214. Its original identity with the Pagan religion of the Therapeutic and Essenian monks, 220—222, *n.* Traces of its heathen origin, 223—233, *n.* 408—411, *n.* 422—452, 468, *n.* Its identity with paganism urged as a plea for its reception by its early Apologists, 233. 438—442. Its early success not so great as that of Mormonism, 235—244. Has caused more bloodshed than any other religion, 363. 576, 577—579, *n.* Its earliest form a mixture of the tenets of the Essenes and other pagan monks, 369. 432. 433, *n.* 462, 463. Its present Protestant form a reformation of Popery, 411, *n.* First promulgated by pagans, 432—435. Had existed for a long time before the Christian era, 432—435, *n.* 441. Its monachal character, in apostolic times, 470—472. 489, *n.* Its persecuting and sanguinary spirit, 563—580. Its annals one continuous page of cruelties and bloodshed, 564. Its feuds in the first century, *ib.* Its sanguinary character in the time of the first Christian emperors of Rome, 565—571. Its devastation of human life in the Middle Ages, 571—579. Its sanguinary spirit displayed by the Crusaders, 576—579, *n.* Its tendency equally persecuting in the present age, 579. Has lost merely the unrestrained power it formerly possessed, *ib.* 580. Testimony of modern Christian writers to the persecuting spirit of their religion, *ib.* The cause that it is more ferocious than any other faith, 590—592. The pernicious tendency of its modern doctrines, 590—608. Is a religion which ignores the laws of nature, 608. Makes no provision for the exercise of man's intellectual faculties, *ib.* Discourages the exercise of the chief affections and mental powers of humanity, *ib.* Has utterly failed to teach man to be virtuous, *ib.* Much of the misery, past and present, endured in Christian countries, its results, ib. Testimony of modern Christian writers to its evil effects, 608, 609. Its utter failure either to moralise or Christianise the world, 609, 610. The opposition of its priests, in every age, to scientific knowledge, 611.

Christians, in ancient times, accused of feasting on the flesh of infants, 116. 226—230, n. 321. 323. Their belief that it was on mount Zion Jesus would take his seat as Judge of the World, 138. Their community of goods, 212—235. Sold their possessions, and gave the produce to their leaders, 213—235. The unfortunate sale of Ananias and Sapphira's property, 214—215. Their Love-feasts, 217—133. Why prosecuted by the Roman Government, 225, n. 227, 228. 233, n. The odiousness anciently attached to their name, 228, 229, n. Accused of offering human sacrifices, and feasting on them, 223—230. 522. 525, Were worshippers of Serapis, 231, 232, n. 567, 568, n. Their opinion, in early times, of Jesus, 287—290, n. Those of modern times do not exhibit the signs of belief which Jesus said they would, 293—295. Do not put Jesus's precepts into practice, 316. 320. 335. 341, 342. The early Christians adopted the whole of the rites and ceremonies of the heathen worship, 322, 323, n. 392. 408—411, n. Those of the present age refined, not by their religion, but by the advance of civilization, 329. 395, n. They practically disbelieve Jesus's doctrines, 335. 337. 377, 378. n. Their susceptibility of anger, in discussing religious points, 353. Not so tolerating as the Scribes and Pharisees of old, 354. Sensible of contradictions in their Divine books, 373, n. Their hatred to one another, 387. 406. n. The essential point of difference between the early Christians and the Heathens regarding demons, 406—409, n. How in early times they acquired their Divine books, 442. Their original identity with the Nazarean monks, 495, n. Called Nazarenes, to the present day, by the Jews, Arabs, and Persians, ib.

Christians of St. John, see disciples of John.

Church, Christian, how it accumulated its wealth, 206—208. 212—235. Prohibited by the Roman law, in the first two centuries, from holding real property, 220. How in early times it applied its wealth, ib. The mention of the church in the Gospels, betrays the spuriousness of these productions, 304. 369—371, n. 435, n. The most ancient churches were cells, 369, 370, n. Were called cemeteries, 369, n. Called monasteries, or minsters, 370, n.

484. 487, n. Meaning of the word church, 370, n. Christian churches first built in the time of Constantine, ib. Were originally the dwellings and worshipping places of monks, 487, n.

Clement of Alexandria, his monkery, 475.

Clement of Rome, taught the near approach of the End of the World, and that of the Kingdom of Heaven, 178.

Collyer, Dr. cited on Jesus's insulting language to his mother, 347.

Comets, notions entertained by the ancients of their appearance, 126, n. 127.

Commentators of Scripture, how they deal with it, 318. 328—330. 366. 372. Whence arises the necessity for their works, 372. 392. 399. Their disposal of the doctrine of the Holy Ghost, 394.

Communion, (see eucharist, &c.) the same with the ancient love-feasts, 217—219. n.

Community of goods, (see monkery) among early Christians, 212—235. Its great utility in propagating Christianity, 216. Exists among Christians to the present day, 217, n. Its heathen origin, 220, 221. Existed among the Hindoo monks, long before the Christian era, 445. 470.

Confucius, his precepts borrowed by Jesus, 326, 423—425.

Constantine the Great, present at the canonisation of the New Testament, 177, n. Obtained his Christianity from pagan Egypt, 232, n. 370, n. 566—568, n. His murders, 232, n. 566—568, n. The real founder of the present Christianity, 232, n. 370, n. The pagan origin of his banner, the sign of the cross, 232, 233. 538—540, n. 565. 568, n. The first who built Christian churches, 370, n. His wars in the cause of Christianity, 566. His demolition of the heathen temples, ib. 566. His zeal for the Christian religion, ib. His massacres, ib. His parentage, 556, n. A much better man before than after he became a Christian, 566—569. His tolerant edict at Milan, before he had imbibed the spirit of Christianity, 566. His persecuting edict when a ripe Christian, 567. Remained through life half a pagan, ib. n. The date at which he made profession of Christianity, 567, 568, n. Baptized only a short time before his death, ib.

Constantius, his cruel edict against the pagans, 569.

Contradictions, abound in Jesus's precepts and doctrines, 372—378. More numerous than in the sayings of any other public teacher, 372. These, the cause of the numerous antagonistic Christian sects, ib. 377.

Cox, Rev. J. H. his rules for distinguishing a metaphor, 324, n. His theory of harmonising conflicting expressions of Jesus, 373.

Criminals, our present mode of treating them, wrong, 357, n,

Cross, sign of, utterly pagan, 232, 233, n. 539, n. Made by the the god Mithras on his worshippers, 476. Meaning of taking up the cross, 537—540, n. A staff which monks carried as part of their insignia, 534, n. 537—539, n. Its shape and construction, 537, 538, n. The same as the crosier, 538, n. A symbol of courage and authority, 537. 539, n. Used in the worship of the heathen gods, ib. Its figure found on the relics of pagan temples, 539, n. Its usage prescribed by the laws of Menu, ib. Carried by the god Boodh, ib. Its magic power, 538—540. n. The ensign of Constantine the Great, ib. Carried by each of the Crusaders, 577, n.

Crusaders, their conduct a proof that Christianity was in their time more sanguinary than Mahometanism, 576—579, n. Their nine crusades professedly made for the sake of Christianity, 576, n. Their pilgrimages to the Holy Land, ib. Their first crusade instigated by a monk, ib. Sold their lands to defray the expenses of their Holy Wars, 577. Their vast number, ib. Their ferocious attacks upon the places through which they passed, ib. Their discovery of the Holy Lance, which they converted into an ensign in their Christian battles, ib. Their entry into Jerusalem, ib. Their indiscriminate slaughter of the inhabitants, ib. Their butchery of one another, ib. Their subjugation by the Mahometans, ib. Their suicidal threat, ib. The kindness with which they were treated, in their adversity, by the Mahometans, 578, n. Their crusade against their Christian brethren at Constantinople, ib. The mutual cruelty and carnage which ensued, ib. 579, n. Their religious vow, 579, n. Their fornication and incest, ib.

Cybele, her priests dismembered, yet practised unbounded licentiousness, 542.

Cyprian, his monkery, 477. His abandonment of his wife, ib. His opinion of the state of virginity, ib.

D.

David, mad conduct of, as a prophet, 57, n. Did not at his death ascend into the heavens, 72, n. Exorcised Saul, 405, n. His state of nudity when publicly engaged in a religious dance, 532, n.

Day, Jewish, when it commenced, 247—250. 383, n. How divided, 248, 349. Included the night, 249. 253—255.

Day of Judgement, see End of the World, Jesus, and Prophecies.

Day of the Lord, and last days, import of the expressions, 41—47. 134—139. 162, 163. 165. 177, 178.

Death, not the result of Adam's sin, but a part of the system of organization, 603, 604. Its benevolent purposes, ib.

Demoniacal possession, 404—412. The belief in, rife in the heathen world, at a very remote period, 405—408, n. Jesus's belief in this pagan absurdity, 406—409. The fallacy of this belief exposed by Hippocrates, ib, 407, 408, n. Was a prevalent belief among the Jews, at a very early date, ib. Its indications believed by the most accute ancient philosophers to be the result of natural diseases, ib. Its reality believed and taught by the Christian Fathers, 408, 409, n. The symptoms given of it in the Gospels prove it to be nothing more than a disease arising from natural causes, 411, 412. The belief in it made to flee from Britain by the influence of scientific knowledge, 412.

Demons, well knew Paul who contested with the Jews in exorcism, 212. 407, n. The Apostles's failure in expelling one of them, 295. Jesus's prescription for exorcising a certain sort of, ib. Knew Jesus better than he knew them, 344. Legion of, how many, ib. The question why they are allowed to leave their proper abode, ib, n. Their petition granted by Jesus, ib. Require very little space, 345, n. Appear however to be physical beings, ib. Were believed by the heathens to vary in origin, power, and disposition, 404, 405, n. 512, n. 525, n. 551, n. Were thought to be meditators between Gods and men, 404, n. Were expelled from human beings by many besides Jesus, in his time, even among the Jews, 406, 407, n. Abhored by the Jews, and the Christian Fathers, as objects of worship, 406, 407, n, Were worshipped however by Christians long after the time of Jesus, 408, n. Were called messengers, angels, and æons, 404, n. 408, n. 512, n. Some of them originally were deified heroes, 408, n. Their worship exchanged by Christians for that of deified saints, 408—410, n. Were the chief cause of the disagreement between pagans and Christians, 408, 409, n. Were under the control of the Brahmin monks, 444. The good and evil demons of the Hindoos and Egyptians, 461. Were expelled by Christian monks, 479—489. Were thought by pagans, Jews, and Christians to fill the aerial regions, and swarm desert places, 512, n. 597, n.

Devil, to be bound for a thousand years, 172, 173. 182. The origin of him and his angels accounted for, 182. 405, *n.* His temptation of Jesus, 417, 418. Absurdity of the Christian doctrine of, 594, 595. The heathen origin of this doctrine, 595, *n.* Makes the Devil more powerful than God, 595—597. Derogatory to the character of the Deity, 596. Its direful effect on humanity, 596, 597. Paralyzes the moral efforts of man, 597, 598. Pervades the New Testament, 597, *n.* Is falsified by the whole of God's works in nature, 598.

Disciples of Jesus, received a charge from him breathing of hatred and revenge, and evincing glaring inconsistency, 318. 374, 375. 535, 536. Their abandonment of their Master, 320. 394. 559. Their quarrels about the occupation of the most honourable post in the kingdom of heaven, 342. An instance of a singular defect in the memory of two of them, 360. Carried swords, 363—365. Contradicted their Master, 365, 366. Their ignorance of his meaning, 366. 390, 391. 393—396. Did not know the Father, 366. 396. Were very slightly influenced by Jesus's teaching, 394. Their affections were not won by him, *ib.* 559. Were illiterate, 431, *n.* Did not believe in Jesus's miracles, 560.

Disciples of John, or MENDAI IJAHI, 500, 501. Have never been Christians, *ib.* Some of their religious tenets resemble those of the Gospel writers, *ib.* Have a tradition that their ancestors lived on the banks of the Jordan, *ib.* John, the founder of their sect, died in Persia, *ib.* Possess sacred writings, *ib.* Are baptized once a year, *ib.* Are the same with the Hemero-Baptists, *ib,* 501. Are called Sabians, and considered to have descended from these fire-worshippers, *ib.*

Diseases, (see monks and Therapeuts) miraculously cured by the pagan monks, 421. 445. 467. 512, 513. By the Christian monks, 479—489. 515. By Jesus, 512—515. The healing art anciently in the hands of the divines amongst every nation, 513. *n.*

Dishonesty, inculcated by Jesus, 318, 319.

Dispensation, Jewish, end of, said to have been predicted by Jesus, 16, 17. 123. Did not terminate at the destruction of Jerusalem, 141.

Dissimulation, evinced by Jesus, 358—362.

Divorce, the cause of, restricted by Jesus to adultery, 378.

Doctrines of Jesus, the meaning of, concealed by him from the uninitiated, 384, 385. 391, 392. 545. 546.

Dogmatic teaching of Jesus, 399.

E.

Earth, not known to Jesus to be globular, 417, 418. Represented by all the writers of the Bible as being flat, and having ends, 418, *n.* Known by heathen philosophers to be spheroid, long before the time of Jesus, 418.

Ebionites, (see Nazarenes) sprang from the Nazarenes, 495, *n.* Were Christian monks, *ib.* Meaning of the term, 496, *n.*

Eclectics, some account of them, 414. 425, *n.* Originated in Egypt with the Therapeutic monks, 424, *n.* 432, 433, *n.* Were in a flourishing state, in Alexandria, before the Christian era, 424, *n.* Held the writings of Plato in great esteem, *ib.* Were called Platonists, *ib.* 425, *n.* Most of the early Fathers were of their number, *ib.* Were revived by Ammonius Saccas, 425, *n.*

Egypt, (see monks and monkery) the country where Jesus is supposed to have been educated. And where Christian monkery originated, 456—463.

End of the World, Jesus's prophecies of, 1. 5. Arguments advanced, on the Christian side of the question discussed, to show that Christ did not predict the event as being near at hand, in his time, 9—50. Scriptural extracts of the predictions said to foretell the near approach of, 11—14. These predictions shown to refer to the destruction of Jerusalem, 15—17. The expression, "End of the World," explained, 16. 21. 45. 47. Historical proofs of the exact fulfilment of the supposed prophecy of the End of the World, in the destruction of Jerusalem, 17—30. Arguments advanced on the other side of the question to show that Jesus predicted the End of the World to be close at hand, 60—116. The New Testament pervaded with the doctrine of the near approach of the event, 60. 147. Was to take place during the lifetime of Jesus's contemporaries, 66, 67. Announced by the Apostles as close at hand, 68. Jesus's prophecy of it falsified by time, 86. 116—121. 129—144. 146—149. His notion of effecting the mundane destruction by means of a legion of angels, 97—102. Discrepancies of the Evangelists in narrating Jesus's prediction of, 101. No proof it was the destruction of Jerusalem only which Jesus meant in the prediction, 101—104, 124—130. The End of the World, even in the present age, predicted, now and then, to be close at hand, by Christian fanatics, 106. 208. Its near approach predicted by the Hebrew Prophets, 134—141. Their notions of it resembling those of Jesus, 137—142. The near approach of this awful event the grand theme of the Canonical Epistles, 150—167. Its approximate occurrence discredited by infidels, in apostolic times, 164. 166. The Christian mode of calculating the time the world was to last, 168. 173. 175, 176, 182. The expectation of its destruction the great moral leaver of early Christianity, 169. Its doctrine inculcated by the Fathers of the Christian church, and other writers, both orthodox and heterodox, 175—187. The prediction of, visited with punishment by the Roman Government, 180. Secretly believed by all Christians of the second century that it would take place forthwith, *ib.* The Jewish mode of ascertaining its precise time, 183, 184. Decline of the belief in its near approach, in the fourth century, 184, 185. Its refutation by Origen, 184. The doctrine of, rejected as absurd, in the sixth century, 185. Revived afterwards, and remodified, *ib.* An important doctrine, in all Christian creeds, even at the present day, *ib.* 224. Admission of modern writers that Jesus and his apostles predicted the immediate End of the World, 187—193. The general fear caused in apostolic times by the promulgation of the event, 205—235. The stupendous panic created in Europe by the promulgation of the same thing, in the tenth century, 206—208. The wealth which this panic brought into the Church, 213—223.

Enemies, love to, enjoined by Jesus, 325, 326. 341.

Epistles, canonical, replete with the doctrine of the near approach of the End of the World and the Kingdom of Heaven, 46—48. 143. 146. 155. The date and authorship of, uncertain, 148. Ignore the wonderful narrations of the Gospels concerning Jesus, 165, *n.* Were miraculously canonised, 177, 178, *n.* The same as the Divine books of the pagan Therapeutic monks, 222, *n.*

Essenes, (see Therapeuts and monks,) discipline and doctrines of, 221, 222, *n.* 403—467. Their tenets mixed with early Christianity, 339, *n.* The same as the Therapeuts, 432, *n.* 463—467. Meaning of the term, 432, *n.* 465, 466. Were the first promulgators of Christianity, 434. Differed from one another on particular religious questions, 464, 465, *n.* Some of them sacrificed in the dead of night, *ib.* Identical with the Pythagoreans, 466, *n.* Administered baptism, 497. The mysteries of their religion, 545.

Eternal life, Jesus's notion of, 105—116. To be enjoyed in the Kingdom of Heaven,

106, 107. 148, 149. Meaning of the phrase, 108. Was to be obtained only in the age in which Jesus's contemporaries lived, 115. To be poor, the means of acquiring it, 221—223. 235—237.

Eternal punishment, doctrines of, absurd, 330—333. 592. The denunciation of, has driven many to incurable madness, 333. The notion of, contradicted by God's punishment in nature for violating his laws, 590, 592, 593. Devoid of any benevolent purpose, 590. The idea of, a blasphemy against God, *ib.* The description given of, by popular preachers, 590, 591. The vicious tendency of the doctrine of, 591, 592.

Eucharist, (see human sacrifice, love-feast, oath, sacrament) placed with dead monks in their coffins, 521, 522, *n.* Both the pagan and Christian eucharists of a sacrifical character, 525, *n.* 527, *n.* 529, 530, *n.* Called the host, 525, *n.* Efforts made to show its identity with the Jewish passover. 525, 526, *n.* The lamb which among the early Christians formed part of it, 526, *n.* Why called a tremendous mystery, 527, *n.*

Eunuchs, Jesus's curious expression regarding them encourages celibacy and bodily mutilation, 81, 82. 541, 542. Those in the worship of Jupiter, 542. Those in the divine service of Cybele, *ib.* Those of the Brahmins, *ib.* Those of the early Christians, *ib.* Special prayers offered for them in the Christian church, *ib.*

Eusebius of Cæsarea, his effort to show that the doctrine of the approaching End of the World is an allegory, 184, 185. His opinion that our canonical Gospels and Epistles are the same with the Divine books of the Therapeuts, 221. His account of the writings of Philo Judæus, 431—435. His denunciation of certain forged memoirs of Jesus and John the Baptist, 511, *n.* His aversion to give an account of these productions, *ib.* His unfaithfulness as a historian, *ib.* The same memoirs mentioned by Justin Martyr, *ib.*

Evil, Jesus's doctrine of the non-resistance of, 315—317. 367. 380.

Example, more powerful than precepts, 378, 381.

F.

Faith in Jesus, doctrine of, absurd, and encourages deceit and hypocricy, 330—333. 398. No merit to be possessed of, 331—333. 395. The uncharitableness of the Christian doctrine of, 331, *n.* The irrationality of, *ib.* The sweetness of, to orthodox divines, 333. The mischief produced by, ib. Jesus's conflicting representations of, 376. 384, 385. The same doctrine as that of Chrishna, the Indian Saviour, 428, 429.

Fanaticism, of early Christians, 201, n. Of modern Christians, 202, 203, n.

Fatalism, taught by Jesus, 328. 362.

Fathers of the Christian church, believed, a prophecy to have a hidden meaning, 30. Forgeries of, 126. 143. 145, 146. 287, n. 409. 442. 478, n. 508, n. 568, n. Inculcated the near approach of the Day of Judgement and the End of the World, 135. 175—187. Their notions of the soul, heaven, and hell, 144—146. Their statement regarding the divine origin of Christianity invalid, 185, n. 568, 569, n. Most of them originally pagans, 231, n. Those of the two first centuries do not quote the canonical Gospels, 311, n. Their mysticism, 392. Their clamour against worshipping demons, 408, n. Their encouragement to worship dead saints, 408, 409, n. Exchanged the pagan, for the Christian demons, ib. Their admission that Christianity and Paganism were identical, 438—442. Their monkery described, 470—490. Their election of bishops by the decision of the sword, 570, n.

Fear, the effects of, in early Christian times, on those who expected the immediate End of the World, 205—216. A sorry incentive to virtue, 215, 216, n. The injury of, to the human constitution, ib. Excited in the present age, in order to make converts to Christianity, ib.

Feet-washing, thought by Jesus to possess spiritual merit, 337—342. Intended by him to be an ordinance in his Church, 340. Disregarded by Christians generally, ib. Practised only by the Scotch Baptist, 341, n. The inutility and absurdity of this ordinance, 341.

Fig-tree, mischievously withered by Jesus, 346. 380.

Fire-worship, traces of, in the Jewish religion, 501—504.

Fish, eaten by both heathen and Christian monks, 522, 523.

Flesh-meat, abstained from, by Christian and other monks, 522.

Forgeries, see Fathers, and pious frauds.

Free inquiry after truth, importance of, 2. 5. 8. 300, 301. Not encouraged by Jesus, 399.

G.

Gehenna, meaning of the word, 112, n. Situated in the valley of Hinnom, ib. Was the hell of Jesus, ib.

Gentiles, to tread Jerusalem under foot, 32. 130—132. 168, n.

Gethsemane, situation of, 556, n. The resorting place of Jesus and his disciples, ib. The haunt of monks, ib. Jesus repairs to, in the depth of night, ib. His prayers and shuddering fear of death in, 557.

Gibbon, Edward, cited on the End of the World, 173. 176. 192. 210. On apostolic miracles, 211.

Giles, Dr. cited on Jesus's wanton act of cursing a fig tree, 346. On the tumult he caused in the temple, 321, 352.

God, (see Jesus, mission, &c.) not liable to err, 195, 196. 313. 402. 581. The God of nature and that of the Christians contrasted, 120. Not capable of immorality, 303. 313. 343, 344. That which is immoral in man would be so in God, 319. Cannot be more relentless than man, 375. Is not partial, 384. Not limited in power, 385. His incarnation a pagan superstition, 437. 448, n. 449. 456, n. 461. His attributes taught in Nature, 583. Governs the world on principles of benevolence, 583. 588, 589. Governs man by the fixed laws of nature, 583. The description given of him in the Bible fraught with mischief, 590—593.

Gospel, early success of, 21. Dispensation of, 38. Causes of its early success, 205—235.

Gospel, Hebrew, found by Pantænus, 179. 495, n. Called the Gospel of the Nazarenes, 495, n.

Gospels, Apocryphal, some account of, 306, 307, n. Their history of Jesus's earlier life, 307—311, n. Their agreement with the canonical Gospels, 311. 492, 493, n. Their account of the birth of the Virgin Mary, and of that of Jesus, 491—493, n.

Gospels, canonical, (see New Test.) to deny the genuineness of, fatal to Christianity, 97. 302, n. 306. 310. 418. The wonderful things they narrate of Jesus, ignored by the canonical Epistles, 165, n. When and how canonised, 177, 178, n. The miracles which attended their canonisation, ib. The same as the Divine books of the pagan Therapeutic monks, 232, n. 431—435, n. Did not exist, in their present form, till the close of the second century, 261. 287, n. 311, n. 344. n. 369, n. 371, n. 415, n. 424, 425, n. 441. 512. 563, 564, n. Their conflicting statements, 263. The materials of which they are thought to have been compiled, 287, n. 301, n. 388, 389, n. 424, 425. 432, n. 504, n. 512, n. 550. 552, n. Narrate Jesus's life only for three years, 306. Their best morality borrowed from pagan lore, 326. 422—442. Their statements taken in the present work, as if true, 352. 369, *n.* 552, *n.* To be read like any other books, 372. Are the collections' of the Eclectics, 424, 425, *n.* 432, *n.* 493. Not mentioned by profane writers of the first century, 431, *n.* Their pagan origin, 431—435, *n.* 442. Their text much altered, 432, *n.* Contain internal evidence of having been compiled from pre-existing documents, 433, *n.* Much of them borrowed from Plato, 437, 438. Their jumbling history of Jesus and John the Baptist, 493. Their writers cite prophecies not extant, in order to make the hero of their tale a monk, 493, 494. Other memoirs, of Jesus, and John the Baptist, than the Gospels, mentioned by Eusebius and Justin Martyr, 511, *n.* The chief features of our Gospels are Jesus's Therapeutic miracles, 513, 514.

Greg, W. R. cited on Jesus's predictions, 5. 190. On the Hebrew prophets, 58. On the gift of tongues, 201, *n.* On the monkery of the Gospels, 550, *n.*

Grotius, believed that pious fraud answered a wise purpose, 185, *n.* 188, *n.*

H.

Hades, meaning of the term, 112, *n.* 114, *n.* Description of, 112, *n.* 187.

Happiness, see Man.

Harmonies of Scripture, the vast number of, a proof that Christians are sensible of the contradictions of the Bible, 373, *n.*

Heart, believed by Jesus to be the organ of thought, 401, 402.

Heaven, of Jesus's, 72, 73. Whither, like the heathen gods, he ascended, 438.

Hell, (see eternal torments) Jesus's heathen notion of, 112—114, *n.* Situated in the valley of Hinnom, *ib.* The same as Tophet, or the furnace of Moloch, *ib.* The modern Christian doctrine of, not in the Bible, 114, *n.* Derivation of the word, 112, *n.* 114, *n.* Notions entertained of, by the Fathers, 145, 146. Jesus believed to have descended into, like the pagan god Boodh, 145, *n.* 449. That described in the Apocalypse, 172, 173. The modern notion of, 329, 330. 590, 591.

Hemero-Baptists, existed in the East many centuries before the Christian era, 500. Said to have been founded by one John, who had twelve apostles, *ib.* Were in a flourishing state in Judea, at the commencement of the Christian era, 501. were not Christians, *ib.* Were originally identical with the Persian Baptists, *ib.* Were a Jewish sect, *ib.* Derived their baptism from the Magi of Persia, 501—507.

Hermas, his notion of the near approach of the Kingdom of God, 179. The monkish character of his work, 472, 473.

High Treason, Jesus charged with, 350. 352, *Hilarion,* his monachal career, 482, 483.

Hindoos, (see Laws of Menu, monks, &c.) their sacred writings much older than those of the Jews, 427. 443. Their Scriptures replete with the principles of monkery, 443.

Hippocrates, exposes the error of demoniacal possession, 405. 407, 408, *n.*

Holy Ghost, meaning of the name, 201, *n.* Its Pentecostal descent, *ib.* In what its influence consisted, *ib.* 507, *n.* The apostolic mode of endowing Christians with, 212. Doctrine of, not understood by Jesus's disciples, nor by modern Christians, 393, 394.

Holy water, of the Boodhists, 445.

Horne, T. H. cited on prophecy, 9. His rules for interpreting prophecy, 52, 53. His arguments against the Apocryphal Gospels, 311, 312, *n.* His definition of a metaphor, 323.

Hour, Jewish, not always the same length, 246—249. Meaning of the word, 248, *n.*

Human sacrifices, (see atonement) among the heathens, 223, 224, *n.* 527, *n.* Among the Christians, 223, *n.* 226, *n.* 230. 322—324. 525, *n.* 527, *n.* Their universality, 523, *n.* Prohibited by the Roman law, 324, *n.* Eaten by those who offered them, *ib.* Offered as an atonement for sin, at a very remote period, 429, 430. 606, *n.* Infants and children frequently offered for sacrifices, 527, 528, *n.* Such sacrifices feasted upon by the worshippers, 528, 529, *n.*

I.

Ignatius, his views of the approaching End of the World, and the Kingdom of God, 178. His doctrine of celibacy, 473.

Incarnation, of Deity, a heathen notion, 437—439. 448, *n.* 449. 456, *n.*

Infallibility, of the Pope made to be taught by Jesus, 371, *n.*

Injustice, commended by Jesus, 318, 319.

Inquisition, the Holy Office of, founded by Theodosius the Great, 570, 571, *n.* Its horrible tortures and carnages, 571—574. Description of the barbarous proceedings of its *autos-da-fe,* 572—574.

Interpretation of Scripture, the rule of, 7. 32.

Irenæus, taught that Christ was soon to appear in Judgement, and to create a new world, 179, 184.

J.

James, the Apostle, taught the speedy End of the World, 163 ; and that his brother Jesus would soon come on the clouds, 179.

James, an illustrious monk, who possessed the relics of John the Baptist, 485.

Jeremiah, his admission of the identity of madness and the art of prophesying, 56, n. His monkery, 533.

Jerusalem, Jesus's prophecy of the destruction of, 1. 5. Arguments advanced on the Christian side of the question discussed, to show that Jesus prophesied its downfall, 9 —50. Historical proofs of the fulfillment of Jesus's prediction of, 17—29. 123, 124. The prediction of the treading down of, by the Gentiles, 32. 130—132. The destruction of, predicted by another prophet named Jesus, 36. No real proof that it was the destruction of Jerusalem which Jesus of Nazareth meant in the prophecy in question, 101—104. 132—140. His alleged prophecy of the destruction of, compared with the history of its demolition, as given by Josephus and Tacitus, 125—128. The sense in which Jesus can be said to have predicted the destruction of, 130. Description of the expected New Jerusalem, as given by early Christian writers, 173. 174. 182. The pagan fire-worship of, 502.

Jesus Christ (see prophecies of the End of the World, monkery, &c.) His prediction that the End of the World and Day of Judgment were close at hand, 1. 5. 62—116. Importance of the question of the truth of his predictions, 1. 4. Arguments advanced on the Christian side of the question to show that he did not predict the End of the World and the Day of Judgment, as being in his time near at hand, 9—50. The commonness of the name, JESUS, among the Jews, 36, n. 350, n. One of the name, besides the Christ, prophesied the destruction of Jerusalem, by Titus Vespasian, 36. Jesus said to have disclaimed all secular power, 39. Was a Jewish prophet, 59, 60. 144. Said to be illiterate, 60. 310, n. 357. 419—421. His literary correspondence with Abgarus, 60. 419, n. Regarded himself as a king of the Kingdom of Heaven, 62. 90—93. Infused the same idea into his followers, 63, n. Denies his omnisciency, 68, n. His advent as a Judge, 69, 70. 152. His notion of establishing a secular Kingdom, at the End of the World, 71—95. His idea of heaven, 72, 73. Begins preaching the same doctrine, in the same words, as John the Baptist, 73, 74. Words put into his mouth by the Gospel writers, 78, n. 83. Encourages celibacy, and enjoins bodily mutilation, 81, 82. 115. 328—330. 541, 542. His conduct at dinner with a Pharisee, 86. 337. 354. Is entertained by Zaccheus, 94. His notion of destroying the world with legions of angelic soldiers, 97—101. 364. Shared with the vulgar in his views of the manner in which the mundane destruction was to be accomplished, 96. 104 105. His idea of eternal life and happiness, 105—116. His notion of a soul, 110, 141—146, n. Had no idea of an immaterial entity, 110, 111. 114, n. Made no promise of rewards and punishments till after the resurrection, 111 His heathen notion of hell, 112—114, n. Supposed a body consumed by fire, incapable of a resurrection, 113, 114, n. His false predictions of the End of the World and the Final Judgment, 117—121. 123—144. 146. 149. Adhered, through life, to the Jewish ritual, 124. 141. Resembled the Hebrew prophets, in his notion of the End of the World, 34, 35, 137. 142. His supposed symbolical style of prophesying, 134—141. Was expected to take his seat, as a Judge, on mount Zion, in Jerusalem, 138. 206. Was believed to have descended into Hell, 145, n, Not original in his doctrines, 147. Countenanced the vulgar errors of his time, 150, n. The mighty works attributed to him, in the Gospels, not alluded to in the Epistles, 165 n. Borrowed his notions of the approaching End of the World from the Jewish Rabbi, 183, 184. 199, n. Was, in the sixth century, charged with ignorance of the time of the Day of Judgment, 185. Was neither a Divine personage nor influenced by the Deity, 195, 196. 299. 393. 402. 554—581. The question whether he pretended to be a Deity 196. 554. Arrogated to himself the function of a Judge of the World, 196. The question whether he knew he was not a Deity, 196—198. 554. The question whether he laboured under mental delusion, 196—198. 421, 422. 561, 562. The incentives to belief which he used, 210. Was a decided Therapeut, 220. Taught beggary and monkery, in his reply to the rich young man, 221—234. Despised this world, 234, 235. The success of his ministry and that of the ministry of the Mormon Prophet, compared, 242—244. His prediction that he would rise from the dead, on the third day, 245, 246. Arguments showing that the prophecy was verified, 250—257. The sign of the prophet Jonas which he promised to give, 254. 256. 261. 268, 269. 276, 277. 290. Arguments to show that his prediction that he would rise on the third day, was falsified, 259—291. Difference of opinion, in the first century as to the time he rose, 259—261. Not buried till the commencement of the Jewish Sabbath, 265, 266. Had risen at the commencement of the next Jewish day, 266—268. Was in the grave only about twenty-nine hours, 268, 269. Was in error when he predicted the time of his resurrection, 276—278. 281—291. Did not appear, after his burial, to the Scribes and Pharisees, *ib.* 290, 291 Appeared only to his own disciples,' *ib.* Various opinions of early Christians, touching his resurrection, 287— 290, *n.* Denied to be a God, 287, 288. Denied to be a man, and believed to be a phantom, *ib.* His history believed by ancient Christians to be allegorical, *ib.* Denied to have been born, *ib.* Denied to have died, *ib.* The Fathers's extravagant tales of the miracles of his resurrection, 290, *n.* His false prophecy regarding a woman and her box of ointment, 291—293. His prophecy of the signs which should follow believers at variance with fact, 293—299. Is held up as an example to us, 302. The standard by which to test his morality, *ib.* 303, 304, *n.* Uttered some wise sayings, 303. 341. 383. Was frequently influenced by a benevolent feeling, 303, 304. Not a patern of moral perfection, 304. 375. His morality below that of the present age, 304, 305. Had glaring imperfections, 305, 306. 381. 419. An accouunt of only three years of his life given by the Evangelists, 306. The history of his childhood and youth, as given in the Apocryphal Gospels, 306—312, *n.* The miracles of his infancy, 308, *n.* The miracles of his boyhood, 309—311, *n.* Spent nearly thirty years of his life in obscurity, 311, 312. His Sermon on the mount not delivered all at the same time, 312. Its character, *ib.* Portions of it extracted from pagan lore, *ib.* His denouncement of saying "Raca" to a brother, 313. His absurd injunction to take no thought of the morrow, 314, 315. 427. His irrational precept, "resist not evil," 315—317. 367. 375, 376. 380. Inculcates revenge and injustice, 317—319. His immoral charge to his disciples, 318. 374, 375. 536, 537. Justifies theft, 318, 319. The deplorable effects which his unsound moral teaching carries on the world, 319, 320. His defective logic, 319. Preaches the duty of harbouring hatred towards the nearest relations, 319, 320. His conduct towards his mother and brothers, 320. Questionable

whether he taught suicide, *ib.* Enforced the doctrine of canibalism, 320—325. 527, *n.* Was forsaken by his own disciples, 320. 359-410. The cause that the Jews sought to kill him, 321. 558, 559. His notion of love, 325, 326. 341, 342. 375. Was not able to love his enemies, 325. 380. Was angry with the Pharisees, 325. 353, 354. Borrowed the moral precepts of Confucius, 326. His form of prayer, derogatory to the character of God, 326, 327. His "golden rule," 327. 380. 423, 424. His crooked notion of God's justice, 327. 333. Ignores Divine mercy, 327. Teaches fatalism, 328. 362. Extremes, a characteristic of his religious notions, 328. 329. His doctrine of faith, absurd, 330—333. 395. His inconsistency in wishing to conceal his miracles, 333, 334. 385. His fear of the Jews, 334. Prohibited the discharge of filial duties, 334, 335. Taught that poverty was a virtue, 335—337. 367, 368. 533—535. Regarded kissing an act of moral virtue, 337, 338. Considered feet-washing to have a spiritual merit, and wished to establish it as an ordinance among his followers, 337—342, Resembled the Indian incarnate God, Chrishna, 337, *n.* 428, 429. 491. Was always followed by a number of women, 337, *n.* 442. Reproves his guest for not kissing him, 338. Mary, the courtezan's attendance upon him, while at supper, *ib.* He performs an act of sanctification upon the traitor, Judas, 340, 341. Gives his new commandment of love at the end of his life, 344. Was accused of immoral acts by the Jewish religionists, 341. The cause his doctrines were more palatable to the poor than others, 342. His vicious conduct in drowning the Gadarenish swine, 343, 344. Grants the petition of demons. 344, *n.* His conduct not worthy of imitation, 345. 347, 348. 351. 353, 354. 356, 557. 383. His mischievous act of withering a fig-tree, 346. His behaviour at a marriage feast, 346—348. His rebuff to his mother, 347. 380. His rudeness to his relations, 348. His immoral miracle, in turning water into wine, *ib.* Encourages drunkenness, *ib.* Is accused of being a wine-bibber, *ib. n.* His monarchal entry into the royal city, 348—350. His unjust appropriation of an ass, 348, 349. Incites his disciples to steal, *ib.* Assumes the authority of an earthly king, 349—352. 364. 415. Aims at creating an insurrection, *ib.* Is charged with treason, 350. 353. His tumultous conduct in the temple, 350—352. 380. Employs physical force to establish his authority, 352. His behaviour to a deputation that waited upon him, 352, 353. His evasive mode of answering questions. 353. 586. 590—598. His scurrilous language to the Scribes and Pharisees, 353—356. 380. Represents them to be worse than they were, 354. Recommends their doctrines and precepts, *ib.* Was not so kind to them as they were to him, 354, 355. His outrageous conduct and opprobrious language at a dinner party, *ib.* His curses, 355. Embraces every opportunity to malign the Pharisees, 355, 356. Is not adapted for a public teacher, 356. 389. 391, *n.* 392, 393, 396. 416. Unable to convert his opponents, 557, 558. Did neither condemn nor even reprove an open adulteress, 356—358. His dissimulation, 358—362. Not believed by his brothers, 358. 560, 561. His miracles ridiculed by them, 358, 359. Deceived two of his disciples, 360. His dissimulation to Judas immediately after he had absurdly denounced him, 361—363. 422. Commanded his followers to be provided with swords, 363—465. 375. Meditated resistance to his apprehension, *ib.* Encouraged bloodshed, 363. Resistance useless, he commanded his disciples to desist from using their swords, 364. Did not believe that he possessed supernatural power, 365. Untrue statements made by him, 365—371. Wrong when he said his disciples knew whither he was going, 365, 366 Mistaken when he said he had finished his work, 366. His statement as to manifesting his Father's name, not correct, *ib.* 396, 397. His error in saying that his disciples had kept the Father's word, 367. His assertion that he had said nothing in secret, not true, *ib.* His declaration that he did not aim at abrogating the Mosaic law, contrary to fact, 368. Scarcely correct in his definition of the Law and the Prophets, 368, 369. His pun on Peter's name, 371, *n.* Was at variance with fact in saying that the united prayers of two Christians would always be answered, 369—371. His contradictory precepts and doctrines, 372—378. His conflicting statements as to bearing testimony of himself, 372, 373. His contradictory doctrines as to loving enemies, 375; as to non-resistance of evil, *ib*; as to giving alms, 376; as to faith and good works, *ib*; as to the purport of his mission, *ib*; as to the full delivery of his doctrines, 377; and as to adultery and divorce, *ib.* 378. 540. His precepts and practice at variance, 378—383. His bigotry and malevolence, 381.

383—386. His self-glorification, 381—383. His charge of falsity against Abraham, 382. His conversation with a woman of Samaria, *ib.* 387. His concealment of the meaning of his doctrines, from the uninitiated, 384, 385. 391, 392. 545, 546. The anomalies of his character, 385. The obscurity of his mode of teaching, 386—396. His love of the mystic, *ib.* His intolerance, *ib.* Was not understood by his parents, *ib.* His conversation with Nicodemus, 388, 389. 399. 427. 543, 544. His failure to make this Jewish teacher understand his meaning, *ib.* His doctrine of transmigration, 388, *n.* 427. 539, *n.* 543, 544. Was not understood by his followers, 390, 391. Is testified against by two witnesses, *ib.* His imitation of the heathen sages, in his mystical style, 392. His doctrine of his own resurrection and of the Holy Ghost not understood by his disciples, 393—396. Carried very slight moral influence upon his hearers, 394, 395. 559, 560. Made very few converts, 394. 416. The cause of his unsuccessful ministry, 394, 395. His refusal to give an account of himself and his doctrines, 397, 398. His dogmatism, 399. Was deficient in knowledge of natural things, 399—421. Was unacquainted with pneumatics, 399, 400. Knew less about air than his contemporaries, 400, *n.* His erroneous notion of the human stomach, 400, 401. Believed the heart to be the organ of thought, 401, 402. 412. Shared in the pagan error of demoniacal possession, 401—412. 512, *n.* Did not understand political economy, 412—414. Was ignorant of the laws of nature in reference to man, 415. Lacked knowledge in mental philosophy, 416. His mode of proving a resurrection, *ib.* His inability to reason, 416—418. His temptation by the Devil, 417—418. Did not know that the earth was globular, *ib.* Was not so intelligent as many who lived before and after him, 412. 416. 419. 423. Made no discovery in art or science, and revealed nothing in theology, 419. 422—442. His literary attainments, 419—421. Is supposed to have been educated in Egypt, *ib.* His erroneous reading and citing of the Hebrew Scriptures, *ib.* 514. Was said to be possessed of a demon, 406. 422. His form of prayer, borrowed from the Jewish Talmud, 426. His doctrine of being born again, borrowed from the Brahmins, 427. 528, 529. His doctrine of the atonement found in pagan lore, 429, 430. Borrowed on a large scale from Plato, 430—438. Like the pagan gods, ascended to heaven, 438.

Import of his name, 466. 513. His nativity, 490—492. His birth-place, 493—495. Was born in a cave, 492, 493, n. 511, n. His monachal life and doctrines, (see monkery) 490—552. His early history blended with that of John the Baptist, 493, 494. His alliance with the Baptist, 496—507. The doubt of the Baptist as to his character, 497. 514. The tale of the star guiding the Magi to his birth-place, 503, 504. His identity with the heathen monks, 503—552. Forged memoirs of him mentioned, 511, n. His Therapeutic marvels, 512—515. The credibility of his history compared with that of Apollonius Thyaneus, 517, n. His prohibition to take an oath, 547. The divinity of his mission the chief doctrine of Christianity, 553. His acknowledgment of his own inferiority, 555. Additional instances of his finite knowledge and power, 555, 556. His desponding fear of death, 556—558. His want of moral courage, 556, 557. Was not known personally to the Jewish priests and scribes, 556, n. Is not mentioned by writers who lived contemporarily with him. 558, His deity first recognised by madmen, ib. The opportunities enjoyed by the Jewish doctors to form an estimate of his character, 360—362. His horrible declaration of the purport of his mission, 562, 563. 572. 573. The singular fulfilment of this shocking porport, 563—580.

Jesus son of Ananus, his prediction of the destruction of Jerusalem, 36. His melancholy ditty, 37. Was thought to be a madman, ib.

Jews, offered human sacrifices to Moloch, whom they identified with Jehovah, 113, n. Their fire-worship, in Jerusalem, ib. The expected restoration of, absurd, 132, n. The religion of, to this day, in a flourishing state, 141, 142. Overthrow of their polity, whether predicted by Jesus, 141. 143. Their mode of computing time, 246—249. 255—257. 270—276. 280. The cause that they sought to kill Jesus, 321. 558—560. Were feared by him, 334. Had a better opportunity than we have of estimating his character, 342. 358. 360. Many of them burnt by Christians, 368. Could not understand Jesus's obscure teaching, 390, 391. Mysticism of their Rabbi, 393, n. Their Chronology not, by many thousands of years, so old as that of other nations, 457. Derived their baptism from the Persians, 501—507. Traces of fire-worship in their religion, 501—504. Their doctrine of good and evil, identical with that of the Persians, 502. Feasted on portions of the beasts they sacrificed,

529, n. Did not know Jesus personally after he had preached to them for three years, 556, n. Were massacred by the Crusaders for their unbelief in him, 577, n.

John, president of an Egyptian monastery, his monachal feats, 484.

John the Baptist, why the least in the Kingdom of Heaven, 77, n. Why such multitudes resorted to his baptism, 109. His monkish habiliment, and mode of life, 457. 460, n. His relics in the possession of a monk named James, 485. Was a thorough anchorite, 493. His miraculous birth, ib. His alliance with Jesus, 496—507. By whom sent to baptize, 496, 497. Becomes doubtful of the character of Jesus, 497. 514. His baptism, not new, 497. Its pagan origin, 500—508. His mythological character, ib. His baptism originally derived from Persia, 501—507. His head, a relic exhibited to this very day, found on the confines of Persia, in the keeping of a Persian monk and presbyter, 505—509. Removal of his head from Macedonia to Constantinople, 506, n. Origin of his notion of baptizing with fire, 507. Origin of his baptism made by Jesus a question with which to perplex the Jews, 507, 508. Doubtful whether such a person appeared on the banks of the Jordan about the commencement of the Christian era, 508, n. His exploits not mentioned by any profane author in the four first centuries, ib. No allusion to him or his baptism, in the canonical Epistles, ib. Reference made to him in a forged passage foisted into the works of Josephus, 508—510, n, This passage at utter variance with the Gospel narrative, 508. Was first mentioned by Origen, 510. The forged memoirs of the Baptist, 511.

John, St inculcates, in his Epistles the near approach of the End of the World, 167.

Josephus, his account of the destruction of Jerusalem by Titus Vespasian, 17—29. 124—128. His works, as they have descended to us, not to be implicitly relied upon, 125, 126, n. 145, 146. His proneness to exaggerate, ib. Forged passages found in his writings, ib. Is at variance with Tacitus, 127, 128. Furnishes no proof of the truth of Jesus's predictions, 128. Some of the writings attributed to him replete with touches of the Christian doctrines, 145, n. His account of the Essenes, 222, n. A forged passage in his works regarding John the Baptist, 508—510, n. Difficult to determine how much of the works attributed to him has been forged, 510, n.

Judas Iscariot, the act of sanctification which Jesus performed upon him, 340.

342. His dissimulation to his Master, 360. 556, n. Jesus's absurd denouncement of, 362, 363. Was passive in betraying his Master, ib. Played with Jesus, when both were boys, 363, n. Was the instrument of Christian salvation, 363. Was held in great reverence by early Christians, 363, n. Is said to have written a Gospel, ib. Could not have betrayed Jesus, had the latter been a Deity, 558.

Jude, his Epistle inculcates the doctrine of the approaching End of the World, 167.

Julian, Emperor, forms a contrast, in mildness and religious toleration, with the Christian emperors of Rome, 569. Extends full religious liberty to all his subjects, ib. Releases from prison the Christian bishops, incarcerated by their brethren, ib. Had no faith in fire and sword, ib. Is calumniated by Christians, on account of his attachment to heathenism, 569, 570, n. His humane and noble-minded letter to the Pagans, blaming their behaviour to the Christians, 570.

Justice, Jesus's notion of, 327, 328.

Justin Martyr, his opinion of the near approach of the End of the World, the resurrection, the millenium, the new Jerusalem, the state of the soul after death, and Paradise, 182. His contrast of the Holy virgins of Christianity with those of Paganism, 473. His references to certain memoirs of Jesus and his apostles, 511, n. Scarcely any of his citations perfectly agree with our Gospels, ib. Never mentions any document by the title, Gospel, or Epistle, 512, n. Appears to have known nothing of the canonical Gospels, ib.

K.

King, the title and authority of, assumed by Jesus, 90—93. 349—352. 364. 415, n.

Kingdom of Heaven, held to mean the Gospel dispensation, 38. 40. The same as the Kingdom of God, 39. 73. Regarded by Jesus, not as spiritual, but as secular, 62. 71—95. 147. The same notion infused by him into his disciples, 63, n. 19, 81, n. The sense in which he used the phrase, 72, 73. Is the burden of the preachment of Jesus and John the Baptist, 73, 74. Was a thing, in their time, not then existing, but to be established thereafter, 74—94. Its future establishment to be preached by Jesus's apostles, 76. Its subjects to have degrees of dignity, 77. 81—85. 95. 149. 208. 341. Its secular nature and future establishment proved in Jesus's parables 79, 80. 85, 86. Its subjects to eat and drink, and sit on thrones, 81. 84. 86, 87. Regarded by Jesus

as identical with Paradise, 87—90. Was therefore not the Gospel dispensation, 93, 94. 116. 162. Was to be established at the End of the World. 95. The qualification for admission into it, 109. 156. 213. Is the very essence of the Gospels, 117. 147. The notion of it borrowed from the Jews and heathens, 148. Its near approach taught by the Apostles, in their sermons and Epistles, 155—159. Is described in the Book of Revelation, 171—175. Its near approach taught by the Christian Fathers, 176—187. Its king to be Jesus, 349, n. The keys of its gates committed to the care of Peter, 371, n.

Kissing, thought by Jesus to be an act of moral virtue, 337, 338.

Kiss of charity, 230, 231, n. Affords a proof of the identity of the Love-feast and the Lord's Supper, 529, 530, n. Given at the end of the feast, ib. The lights extinguished beford it was given, 530, n. Appointed by Jesus, 536. 537, n.

Knowledge, Jesus deficient in, 399—421.

L.

Lactantius, his opinion of the origin and fate of the Devil, of human procreation during the millenium, of the second resurrection, of everlasting torments, and of the new world which was to be created, 182. His mode of calculating the time of the destruction of the world, ib. Differs from Jesus on the point of human procreation in the New Jerusalem, ib. 183, n. Ignores the predictions of Jesus, and the teaching of the Apostles, touching the End of the World, 183, n.

Lamb, not eaten by Jesus and his disciples at their Passover, 524—526, n. Eaten by early Christians at their paschal feast, 526.

Lamb of God, the pagan origin of, 233, n. 526, 527, n. 529, n.

Language of Jesus to the Scribes and Pharisees, 353—356. Its lamentable effect, 354. 356. Unfit for a public teacher, 356.

Laws of Menu, borrowed by Jesus, 427. One of the oldest compositions extant, ib. Older than the Books of Moses, ib. Teach the doctrine of being born again, ib. 528, 529, n. 543, 544, n. Contain a vast number of regulations and other things which are found in the Hebrew and Christian Scriptures, 427, n. Their doctrine of monkery, 444. 468, n. 533—535. Their decrees regarding abstinence from flesh-meat, 528, 529, n. Their definition and punishment of adultery. 540. Discountenance second marriages, 541.

Laws of Nature, (see nature) Jesus ignorant of, 402—404. 412. 415, 416. The infringement of, productive of pain and misery, and the observance of, productive of pleasure and happiness, 583. 586, 587. Man's interest to study them, and his capability to know them, 586, 587. 593. Their invariableness, 587. Their independency of each other, *ib.* The infraction of each attended with its own punishment, 587—589. Their benevolent design, *ib.* Their punishment prompt, and proportionate to the offence, *ib.* Their reward immediately follows obedience to them, 598. Observance of, calculated to prolong man's life, 603. The lesson they teach, that every act bears its own consequence, the strongest incentive to virtue, 607. Are not taught by Christianity, 608.

Legends, to be received with caution, 167, *n.*

Literary attainments of Jesus, 419—421.

Living water of Jesus, what it was, 387. The notion of, borrowed from the Hindoo Scriptures, 429. 551, *n.*

Logic, Jesus not skilled in, 416—418.

Lord's Supper, (see love-feast, lamb, eucharist, sacrament, &c.) The Pagan origin of, 323, *n.* 525, *n.* Is a remnant of the lovefeast, 525, 526, *n.* The sacrificial character of, *ib.* The controversies caused by, *ib.* Efforts made to identify it with the Jewish passover, *ib.* 526, *n.* Essentially differs from it, 426, *n.* A lamb distributed at it, by early Christians, *ib.*

Love, Jesus's idea of, 325, 326.

Love-feast of the Christians, not yet entirely extinct, 217 *n.* In early times, one and the same with the Lord's Supper, 217—219, *n.* 529, *n.* Pliny's account of, 218, *n.* Supported by the joint oblations of those who attended it, *ib.* Disorderly conduct of its partakers, *ib.* Its pagan origin, 222, 223, *n.* 322, 323, *n.* 525, *n.* 529, *n.* Compared with the Bacchanalian and Eleusinean feasts, 222—233, *n.* Its human sacrifices and other revolting rites, 226, *n.* 322, *n.* 527, *n.* 542. Its communicants, like the pagans, feasted on human flesh and blood, 226—228, *n.* 322—324, *n.* 522, *n.* 525, *n.* 527, *n.* Was secretly held in the night, *ib.* 527, *n.* None admitted to it, but those sworn to secrecy, *ib.* The licentiousness practised at it, 226, *n.* 542. Was supplied with great quantities of bread and wine, 522, *n.* 525, *n.*

Luther, Martin, his persecuting spirit, 574. His declaration that the Gospel was designed to cause persecutions, 579.

M.

Macnaught, Rev. John, cited on Jesus's prediction of the End of the World, 198,

Madness of the Pagan and Jewish prophets, 53, *n* 55—58, *n.* How far Jesus, as a prophet, displayed the same divine frenzy, 117, 144. 197. 421, 422. 561.

Magi of Persia, their religious notions borrowed by the Jews and Christians, 501—507. Their fire-worship, 501. 503. Their notion of the principle of good and evil, *ib.* The reformer of their religion, 502. Their visit to Jesus, 502, 503. The supposed origin of their name, 503, *n.* Their oracles, pontiff, elders, and pilgrimages, *ib.* Are classed with the Jews and Christians, as possessing written laws, *ib.* Their divine books, *ib.* Their patriarch Abraham, *ib.* Their number, 504. Their baptism, *ib.* Their fame as astrologers, *ib.* Their caves, *ib.* 505. Their religious ceremonies, *ib.* Their monkery, *ib.* Their religious mysteries, 506, 507. Their exorcism, 516. Their predicting talents, 518. Their abstinence from fish, 523, *n.*

Mahabharat, a portion of the Indian Scriptures, its doctrine of faith, like that of Jesus, 429. Its living water, *ib.*

Malevolence of Jesus, 381. 383—386.

Malta, or Melita, its venomous animals cursed by Paul, 395, 396.

Man, (see God, happiness, laws of nature, &c.) how he is to ensure happiness. 121. Derives all his ideas through the avenues of sense, 401. 589. 594. His gradual acquirement of knowledge, a source of happiness, 593, 594. Will always have new discoveries to make, 594. 607. His innate desire of happiness, 607, 608. Has no power to desire misery, 607. Want of knowledge the chief cause of his present woe, *ib.* His happiness, in this world, attainable, 607, 608. 612.

Marriage, discountenanced by St. Paul, 156.

Marriage feast, Jesus's conduct at, 346.

Martyrs, the only characters believed by ancient Christians to be admitted into Paradise, 182. The cause of the eagerness of early Christians to suffer as such, 189. Why put to death, 226—231, *n.* Were worshipped as mediators and Gods, by early Christians, 409, 410, *n.* Were supposed after death to cure diseases, 409, *n.* The offerings made at their tombs, *ib.* Writers of the Gospels, like the Fathers, make all their heroes die the death of Martyrs, 504, *n.* Many of them, in death, displayed greater courage than Jesus, 557, 558.

Mary, the sister of Lazarus, kissing Jesus's feet, 337. Supposed to have been a courtezan, *ib.* Thought to be the same as Mary Magdalene, *ib. n.* 342. Spoken of slightly by a Pharisee, 437. The previous purposes to which she devoted her hair and ointment, 338, *n.* Entertains Jesus at a supper, 338.

Mary, several women of the name mentioned in the Gospels, 562, *n.* Impossible to reconcile the conflicting references to them made therein, *ib.*

Mental philosophy, not known by Jesus, 416.

Menu, see Laws of Menu.

Metaphor, always seen by Christian commentators in passages too absurd for explanation, 321, *n.* 324. 329, 330. Nature of, explained, 323. 325. Often, in the Bible, involves an absurdity, 324, *n.*

Methodius, his opinion of the speedy coming of Christ, and the millenium, 182.

Millenium, notions entertained of, in Apostolical times, 168. 170—179. Was thought inseparably connected with the End of the World and the Kingdom of Heaven, 173. 181. Was to be followed by a war, 173. Early Christian notions of, falsified, 174. Origen's refutation of the doctrine of, 184, 185.

Miracles, the effect of those of the Apostles in making converts, 211, 212. Those of Jesus's infancy and boyhood, 308—311, *n.* Jesus's effort to conceal his miracles, 333, The working of, cannot justify the infringement of a moral law, 313. Are calculated to convince only demons, 345, *n.* Those of Jesus ridiculed by his own brothers, 358, 359. Almost all his of a Therapeutic character, 513. A few of them of a malevolent nature, *ib.* Jesus's Therapeutic miracles the chief features of the Gospels, 513, 514. Those of the heathens not denied by ancient Christians, 517, *n.* Those of Jesus not mentioned by writers contemporary with him, 518. Disbelieved by his disciples, 560.

Mission of Jesus, (see Jesus) his contradictory account of the purport of, 376, 377. Its divinity a fundamental doctrine of Christianity, 553. Alleged by Jesus himself to be divine, *ib.* Not proved by his works to be divine, 553, 554. The question whether he knew that he had not been sent from heaven, 554. His declaration that he had proceeded from God to be understood in a Platonic sense, *ib.* Proofs that neither the mission nor the missionary was divine, 554—562. Acknowledges his non-divinity in words and deeds, 554, 555. His divine mission first recognised by madmen, 558. His own declaration of the horrible purport of, 562, 563. The singular and melancholy fulfilment of, in every country, during the last eighteen centuries, 563—580.

Monasteries, (see monks) of the Therapeuts, 221, Of the Indian monks, 370. 446. Referred to by Jesus, 546, 547.

Monkery (see monks) of the Boodhist, some account of its founder, 448—450. More stringent than that of the Brahmins, 451, *n.* Had a divine Trinity, 452, *n.* 453. Had a Redeemer born of a Virgin, *ib.*

Monkery (see monks) of the Brahmins, the most ancient of all, 443. 457. The principles of, abound in the Hindoo Scriptures, *ib.* Description of, 444, 445. 533—535, *n.* State of, in the time of Alexander the Great, and of Clement of Alexandria, *ib.* The account given of, by European travellers, 446, 447. Was not so stringent in its laws as that of the Boodhists, 451, *n.*

Monkery of Christianity, see monks.

Monkery of the Egyptians, (see Therapeuts, and monks) 456—462. Derived from India, 457. Gave origin to Christian monkery, 458, 459. Its Indian origin proved by its identity with that of the Brahmins and Boodhists, 460, 461. Was not so highly developed as that of India, *ib.* The Egyptian Labyrinth, the dwellings of monks, 461—463. Introduced into Palestine, 494. Considered a pattern of monkish perfection, *ib.* Its devotees, renowned exorcists, 315, 316; prophets, 518; and abstainers from wine and flesh-meat, 522. The nocturnal devotions, feasts, and vigils of, 549.

Monkery of the Essenes, (see Essenes) their community of goods, 220—222, *n,* 537, *n.* Of an Egyptian origin, 221, *n.* 463, 464. The same as the Therapeuts, *ib.* Existed long before the Christian era, 222, *n.* 463, 464. Were in a flourishing state in Syria, 222. *n.* Abstained from women, *ib.* Rejected all worldly pleasures, *ib.* Led a life of celibacy, *ib.* Despised riches, *ib.* 536, *n.* Gave all their possessions to their leaders, 222, *n.* Had stewards to provide for their wants, *ib.* Wore white robes, *ib.* Practised baptism, *ib.* Said grace before and after meat *ib.* Were under the control of curators, *ib.* Swore "not at all," *ib.* 547. Cured diseases, 222. The manner in which they were initiated, *ib.* Their oaths not to disclose their mysteries, *ib.* Kept holy the Seventh day, *ib.* Predicted future events, *ib.* Were identical with the Brahminical and Boodhist monks, 463. 467—470. Resembled the Pythagoreans, 463. 466, *n.* Differed from one another on some religious points, 464, 465, *n.* Some of them sacrificed in the dead of night, *ib.* Their doctrines pervade our Gospels, *ib.* Carried arms, 536. Allowed no change of garb, *ib.* Their nocturnal devotions, feasts, and vigils, 549, 550, *n.*

Monkery of Jesus, (see Jesus) taught by him to the rich young man, 221—235.

he monachal character of the history of his birth, 490—493. His early history blended with that of John the Baptist, a thorough monk, 493. Made to have come from Egypt, the hot-bed of monkery, ib. Made to belong to the monachal Nazarenes. 459. 491. Represented as a monk, from his birth, 496, n. Commenced his religious career as a monk, 508. His forty days' fast, 508—511. Tempted of the Devil in the wilderness, 512. His miraculous cures. 512—515. His expulsion of demons, 515—517. His predictions, 518. His dwelling places, 518—520. Always accompanied by women, 520. His diet, 520—529. His habiliment, 530. 533. Travelled barefoot, 530. Went about naked, 531. His monachal doctrines, 533—551 .His monachal parables, 544. His religious mysteries, 545. His monasteries, crypts, and abbots, 516. His prohibition to take an oath, 547. His nocturnal feasts, devotions, and vigils, 548—550. His perfect identity with the pagan monks, 552.

Monkery of the ancient Jews, 457—460.

Monkery of the Nazarenes, see Nazarites.

Monkery of the Therapeuts, (see Therapeuts) their community of goods, 220, n. Their identity with the Essenes, ib. 463—467. Cured diseases, 221, n. Had holy virgins, ib. Gave up all their property to their leaders, ib. Lived in solitary places, ib. Were scattered over all parts of the world, ib. Egypt their grand rendezvous, ib. 463. Their monasteries, inspired books, and religious exercises, 221, n. Their identity with the Brahminical and Boodhist monks, 463. 467—470.

Monks of Boodhism, their founder, 448—450. Their vows, 451, n. Their monasteries, ib. 453. 455. Their strict government, 451, n. Their abstinence from women, ib. 453. Their fasts and bodily mortifications, 452. 455. Their belief in a future state, a succession of heavens, and degrees in glory, ib. Their doctrine of transmigration, ib. 456. Their relics of saints, ib. The everlasting celibacy of their priests, 452. Their dwellings deserts, rocks, cells, and cloisters, ib. 455. Their confessions to their priests, 452. 455. Their pilgrimages, tonsure, and religious devotions, 452. Their spiritual and temporal sovereigns, ib. Their hermits, sacred books, divine precepts, austere lives, future state, and festivals for the dead, ib. Their virgins, temples, images, altars, candles, sermons, prayers, beads, psalmody, bells, and vigils, 453. 455, 456, n. Their sale of indulgences,

451. Their abstinence from food, ib. Their aversion to shed blood, ib. Their baptism and holy water, 455. Their monastic habiliment, ib. 456, n. Their bishops, abbots, archbishops, crosiers, pope, prayers for the dead, purgatory, and extreme unction, 455.

Monks of Brahminism, great antiquity of, 443. Their religious exercises, 444—447. 468. Their degrees of saintship, 444. 328, n. 534. n 543, n. 554, n. Their abstinence from wine and women, 444. 417. 468. Their diet, 444. 446. 521. 528. 534, n. 543. n. 554, n. Their power over demons, 444. Their state in the time of Alexander the Great, ib. Their ancient names, ib. 446—448. Went about naked, ib. 452. Were healers of diseases. 445. 514, n. Performed miracles, 445. Were followed by holy virgins, ib. Despised life. ib. 456. Predicted the future, 445. 518. 551, n. Abandoned their families to become monks, 545. 534, n. Some shaved their heads, and others gloried in the length of their hair, 445. 453. Their habiliment, 445. 534, n. 543, n. 553. n. Had stewards to provide for their wants, 445. Were assembled by the ringing of bells, ib. The description given of them by modern travellers, 446. Their bodily mortifications, 446. 534, n. 543, n, 554. The fundamental principles of their ascetism, 451. Their penances, 529, n. Their abode, the forest, 534, n. Their sacred fire, devotion, and abstinence, 534, n. 543, n. 554, n. Their mendicant life, 535. Their crosier, 539. Their transformation into deities, 543, n. 554, n. Their absorptions, divine essences, and glorifications, 544, n. 551. 554, n. Their beads and rosaries, 551, n.

Monks of Christianity, their bodily mutilation, 116, n. 542. Their community of goods, 217, n. 445. 570—172. Their practice of enticing women, dressed in men's apparel, into their society, 217, n. Why called ascetics, ib. Existed long before the Christian era, ib. 231, n, 443. 470—479. The same with the heathen Therapeuts and Essenes, 220—222, n. 369, n. 470—490. 514. Did the most towards propagating Christianity, 369, n. Reformed by Pachomius, and others, ib. Their cells, the ancient Christian churches, ib. 370. n. Originated in Egypt, 457—460. 479—488. The names of some of the most celebrated of them, 470—489. Their identity with the Brahmin and Boodhist monks, 470—490. 514. Their bodily mortifications and celibacy, 470—472. 481. 483. 485—489.

TT

The monkery of the Christian Fathers, 473—489. Their nocturnal meetings, solemn oaths, holy virgins, and condemnation of marriage, 473—479. 485. 549. Despised earthly possessions, abstained from wine and flesh-meat, 475. 482. 486. 488. 521. 578, n. Their severe exercises, 479—487, n. 521. Their fastings, ib. 488. Their vigils, 479. 484. Their conflicts with the Devil, 479—487. 512, n. 597, n. Their food, 479—488. Their garb, ib. Their dwellings, 480—488. Were healers of diseases, 480. 483—489. 515. Were expert in expelling demons, 480. 483. 487. 488. Wrought stupendous miracles, 480—487. Predicted future events, 480. 483—487. 518. Their resistance of female blandishments, 481. 483—486. Their numerous prayers and beads, ib. Their practice of going about naked, 482. 488. 582, n. Their canons, 484. 488. Their abbots, 484. Their vast number. ib. Despised their relations, 483 540. Their long hair, ib. 488. Their chains and iron collars, 485. Their identity with the monkish men who possessed the head of John the Baptist, 505, n. Their mendicancy, 536. Their activity in the Christian crusades, 576—578.

Monks, of the Jews, 457—460. Their habiliment, 457. 533, n. Elijah's hairy mantle, ib. John the Baptist's raiment, 458, n. 530. Their habitations, 458, n. Went about naked, ib. Had monasteries, ib. Their diet, ib. 459, n. Abstained from wine and flesh-meat, ib. Despised worldly pursuits, ib. Their macerations, ib. The most celebrated of them extolled by the Christian Fathers, as glorious monks, ib. Jeremiah's chains and collar, 533, n. Isaiah's nudity, ib.

Montanus, predicted and taught that the End of the World was close at hand, 179.

Mormonism, its founder, 120. 235—244. The immense number of its votaries, 120. 242. Its success greater than that of Christianity, 235—244. Its close resemblance to Christianity, ib. Its devotees the most consistent Christians, 297. Its mode of curing diseases, 466, n.

Mosaic Law, abrogation of, attempted by Jesus, who said he came to fulfil it, 368. 548, n.

Mount of Olives, Jesus's dwelling place, 519. 556, n. Situation of, 519. The resort of monks, in all ages, ib. Abounds with grottos, ib. Its present state, ib. Its vestiges of paganism, ib.

Mutilation of the body, enjoined by Jesus, 81. 328—330.

Mysteries, of the Christians, 180, n. 545. Were of a pagan origin, 222—233, n. 323, n. 545. Disclosure of, punished with death, 226, n. Those of the Magi, 505, n. 507. The Christian sacrament called a tremendous mystery, 552, n. What these mysteries were, 527, n. The stewards over those of the Christians, 532, n. Initiation of Constantine into the Christian mysteries, 568. n.

Mysticism, of Jesus, 386—394. Of heathen sages, 392, n. Of St. Paul, ib. Of the Christian Fathers, ib. Of the Jewish Rabbi, ib.

N.

Naked state, of the Indian monks, 445—447. Of the Christian monks, 488. Persons mentioned in the Bible who went about naked, 531. Meaning of the word, ib n.

Nature, (see laws of) is unbending. 294. 587. Teaches the attributes of Deity, 583. 598. Obedience to her laws productive of pleasure and happiness, and disobedience, pain and misery, 583. 586. Teaches the existence of a First Cause, 584. Proclaims only one God, 585. 598. Contradicts book-revelations, 592. Loves to be interrogated, 598. The consolations, joys, and pleasures of her religion, 611.

Nazarenes and Nazarites, their monkish vow, 459, n. Their long hair, 495. Their abstinence from wine, ib. One of the first names given to Jesus and his followers, 494, n. Were a numerous monkish community at a very early date, ib. Import of their name, ib. Their canons, 495, n. Their Egyptian origin, ib. Paul the apostle, called the ringleader of, ib. Rejected the Mosaic Law, ib. Were identical with the first Christians, ib. Had a Hebrew Gospel, ib. Gave rise to another sect, called the Ebionites, ib.

Nazareth, the alleged place of Jesus's nativity, 494, n. The monkish signification of the name, ib. Situated amongst rocks and caves, noted for the resort of monks, 495, n. Anciently only a village, ib. The Virgin Mary's cave and fountain at, ib. Jesus's table and synagogue at, ib.

New Testament, (see Gospels) when and how canonised, 177, n. Obscurity and error imputed to its authors, 188, n. The most valuable manuscripts of, from Alexandria, 231, n. Its immoral doctrines, 320. The Christian bias of its English translators, 373. 494. n. Its contents the collection of Egyptian Eclectic monks, 424. 432. 490, n. Contains passages from the writings of Philo Judæus, 430. Written long after the time assigned to Jesus and his apostles, 441. The jumbled character of its tales, 480, n. Its contents derived originally from India, 552, n.

Newman, F. W. cited on the rich young man, 223. On Jesus's obscure language, 391, *n.*

Newton, Bishop, his inconsistency in handling predictions touching the End of the World, 189. His testimony to the pagan origin of Christianity, 410, *n.*

Nicodemus, conversation of, with Jesus, 388. 390. 427. 543 His utter failure to understand Jesus, 388.

O.

Oath, taken by ancient Christians not to divulge their secrets, of a pagan origin, 219, *n.* 221—230, *n.* 527 *n.* 548, *n.* Called a tremendous mystery, 522, *n*, Prohibited by Jesus to be taken in any secular matter, 547, *n.* Prohibited also by the apostle James, 548, *n.* Inconsistency of Christians touching oaths, 549, *n.*

Obscurity of Jesus's mode of teaching, 386—396.

Old Testament, contains no clear allusion to a future state of rewards and punishments, nor to the soul's separate existence from the body, 111. 144—146, *n.* Some portions of it deny a future state, 111, *n.* Jesus's erroneous reading and citing of, 421. 514. Its contents extracted chiefly from Indian, Chaldean, Persian, and Egyptian lore, 552, *n.* Contains purely Hindoo legends, *ib.*

Organs of sense, the medium of all man's ideas, 401.

Origen, his refutation of the doctrine of the near approach of the End of the World, 182. His mysticism, 393, *n.* Was a convert from heathenism, 440. 510, *n.* His self-mutilation, 440. 476. 542. His monkish character, 476. Rightly believed that Jesus had taught monkery, *ib.* Recommended pious fraud, 477, 510, *n.* The author of much of the credentials of Christianity, 510, *n.*

Original sin, doctrine of, absurd, 600. Represents the Deity as an unjust and malignant Being, 601. Is a doctrine pregnant with mischief to mankind, *ib.* 602—604. Neither man nor surrounding nature affords any proof of its truth, 602.

P.

Pachomius, his reformation of monkery, 369, *n.* 483. His glorious monachal career, 484. His vision, *ib.*

Pantænus, the Hebrew Gospel of, 179. Taught that Jesus's second appearance was at hand, *ib.*

Papias, taught that the Millenium was about commencing, 179.

Parables, the character of those of Jesus, 392. 544. Those of heathen sages, 393.

Paradise, Jesus's notion of, 87—90. Origin of the word, 88. The idea of, derived from the heathens. *ib.* The same as the Elysium of the Greeks and Romans, *ib.* Where situated, *ib.* Paul caught up into, 90. Jewish notion of, 145.

Parents, Jesus's prohibition to his followers touching the burial of, 334. Jesus's behaviour to his parents, 347, 348. 380. The failure of Jesus's parents to understand him, 386.

Paschal Lamb, the time at which it was to be killed, 249. 262. Eaten by Christians, long after the Apostolic age, 259. To be eaten in the night, 262. Not eaten on the same Jewish day as it was killed, *ib.* The mode of feasting on it, 263, *n.*

Passover, eaten by Jesus without a lamb, 521. 524—528. The difference between the Jewish, and that of Jesus, 526, *n.* The pagan origin of this rite, 526, *n.*

Paul, the Apostle, his notion of the End of the World and Day of Judgment, 47—49. 66. Caught up into Paradise, 90. Advocated falsehood, or pious fraud, 146, *n.* 186, *n.* Believed the world would come to an end in his life-time, 143. 152—155. 163. 192. Taught the speedy establishment of the Kingdom of Heaven, 155—159. Discountenanced marriage, 156. 192. Encouraged celibacy, 157. Taught monkery, *ib.* His two alledged contradictory expressions touching the speedy End of the World considered, 159—162. His doctrine of the approaching End of the World attested by Peter, 165. His vision, 203. The contradictory accounts of it, 204, *n.* His monkish habits, *ib.* The viper he shook off his hand not poisonous, 295, *n.* His statue at Malta, 296, *n.* His mystification, 393, *n.* His exorcising contest, 407, *n.* His efforts to deter Christians from worshipping demons, 408. *n.* His doctrine of being baptized for the dead, 434, *n.* 453, 454. 456, *n.* His monkery, 460, *n.* 470—472. 474, *n.* 532, *n.* His shaven head, 460, *n.* Was a ringleader of the Nazarean monks, 305, *n.* His birth place, Tarsus, with its college, noted for its monkery, 506, *n.* His doctrine of transmigration, 513, *n.*

Paul and Thecla, the narrative of, 22. Is a production of the first century, 471. Its monkish character, *ib.*

Paul, bishop of the Novatians, his monachal life, 481.

Paul of Ferma, was a renowned monk, 481,

Paul of Egypt, the wonders of his monachal career, 480.

Paul the Simple, an illustrious monk, 480. His diet, garb, miracles, and cures, *ib.*

Paul, a great many religious characters of this name, in the first centuries of the Christian era, 481, *n.* The probable cause of this sameness, *ib.*

Persecution of Christians by the Roman Government, its causes, 180, *n.*

Persian religion, its Magi, 501—507. Its fire-worship alluded to in the Jewish and Christian Scriptures, 501—503. Its principles of good and evil like those of our Bible, 502. Its reformation, *ib.* Its sacred books said to have been written by Abram, 502, *n.* Its divine institution of tithes like that of the Hebrew Scriptures, *ib.* Its astrology, 504. Its baptism, *ib.* Its monkery, *ib.* Its mysteries, *ib.* Conduct of its priests towards the Christians, 506,

Peter, St. taught the near approach of the End of the World, 41. 44. 139. 151. 164—166. His trance and vision, 204. Cause of the success of his preaching, 210. His murderous despatch of Ananias and Sapphira, 214, *n.* Called Satan by Jesus, 360. His free use of the sword, 364. Possessed no supernatural power, 365. His name the subject of a pun by Jesus, 371, *n.* 383. Is entrusted with the keys of the Kingdom of Heaven, *ib.* The supernatural knowledge attributed to him, 383. His mendacity, 394. 559. Went about naked, 531, *n.*

Pharisees, a numerous and influential Jewish sect, 277, *n.* 353. Were the subject of Jesus's anger, 325. 353—355. 380. Often entertained Jesus at their houses, 86. 337. 354. Accused Jesus of immoral acts, 341. Jesus's scurrilous language to, 353—356. 380. Were not so bad as Jesus represented them, 354. Their doctrines and precepts recommended by Jesus, *ib.* Exercised a more kindly feeling towards Jesus than he did towards them, *ib.* Were more tolerant than present Christians, *ib.* The curses which Jesus heaped upon them, 354—356. The cause that none of them were converted by Jesus, 356. 385. 558. Their inability to understand Jesus, 390. Taught the Pythagorean philosophy, 459. Macerated their bodies, *ib.* Were a kind of ascetics, *ib.*

Philo Judæus, makes divine frenzy the mark of true prophecy, 55. His account of the Therapeuts, 220—222, *n.* 431—435, *n.* Was an Eclectic, 424. Passages in the New Testament from his works, 430. Some account of him, 430—436. Was a Therapeut, 436.

Philosophy, the sense in which the Fathers use the word, 476, *n.*

Pious frauds, in Josephus's works, 145.

508—511. Casaubon's opinion of, 146, *n.* Advocated by St. Paul, *ib.* 186, *n.* Those of the Gospel writers, 179. Of the Christian Fathers, 186. 287, *n.* 508—512, *n.* 568, *n.* Of the New Platonists, 478. Of the Egyptians, *ib.* Of Plato, *ib.* Believed by both Pagans and Christians to be acts of moral virtue, *ib.*

Plato, his description of prophets in divine ecstacy, 56, *n.* Was held in high esteem by the Eclectics, 424, *n.* Much of the Gospels borrowed from his works, 430—438. A summary of his doctrines, 436—438. His doctrine of the Logos, 437, *n.* Jesus accused of having borrowed from him, 438. Was said to be the Son of God miraculously born of a virgin, 491, *n.*

Platonists, the same as the Eclectics, 424. Believed pious fraud to be a virtue, 478.

Poison, to be drunk with impunity by believers in Christianity, 293. 401.

Political economy, not understood by Jesus, 412—414.

Poor, why they relished the doctrines of Jesus, 342. The error of the doctrine that it is blessed to be poor. 367.

Pope, meaning of the word, 547. A title given, in the fourth century, to the head of the Christian church, *ib.*

Popery, its missionaries astonished at finding that, in the heathen countries they visited, their religion had been in a flourishing state thousands of years before their time, 454—456. 460. The human blood it has shed, 571—574. 576—579, *n.*

Poverty, taught by Jesus to be a virtue, 221—225. 335—337. This doctrine much older than his time, 336.

Prayer, Jesus's form of, a degradation to God, 326. That of a true Christian often refused, 370. Is useless and impious, *ib.* Lord's Prayer borrowed from the Jewish Euchologues, 426. Jesus praying to God a proof of inferiority, 555. 557. Prayer supposes that a miracle will be wrought at man's request, 598; that the Unchangeable will be changed, *ib*; and that the whole system of nature is subject to man's selfish desire, 559. Denies that God governs the world by fixed laws, *ib.* Degrades God to a level with man, *ib.* Its ineffectiveness admitted by modern divines, at the expense of denying the truth of the Bible, 599, *n.*

Precepts of Jesus, immoral and absurd, 313—342. Their impracticability, 316—317. Are at variance with his practice, 378—383.

Presbyter, meaning of the term, 498, *n.* The office of, among the heathen monks, *ib.* The Persian presbyter who had John the Baptist's head, 505, *n.*

Priest, heathen origin of the term, and office of, 498, *n.*

Priestley, Dr. his volumes on the Corruption of Christianity, 193, *n.*

Prophecies, two thousand volumes of, burnt by Augustus Cæsar, 51. The alleged twofold, and even fourfold meaning of, 53. Those uttered by Pagans, 51—53. The ancient mode of uttering them, 53, *n.* The causes of popular belief in them, 53. Scriptural instances of false prophecies, 58.

Prophecies of Jesus, importance of the truth of, 1. 60. Are clearer than those of his predecessors, 4. His prophecies of the Day of Judgment and the End of the World, 1. 5. 60—113. Arguments advanced, on the Christian side, to show that these refer solely to the destruction of Jerusalem, 9—50. Are clad in symbolical language, 23. 28. 32—35. 132—141. Resemble those of the ancient prophets, 36. Proofs that they foretell the End of the World and the final Judgment to take place during the life-time of Jesus's contemporaries, 62—116. Have been falsified, 117—121. 129—149. The alleged mixture of Jesus's predictions of the End of the World with those of the destruction of Jerusalem, 130. Jesus's predictions of the End of the World, like those of the Hebrew prophets, 34. 137. 142. Jesus not original in the utterance of these predictions, 183. His prophecy that he would rise from the grave on the Third Day, argued to have been verified, 245—258. Arguments to show that this prediction was falsified, 259—291. Difference of opinion, in the first century, as to the time Jesus rose, 259—261. His prediction and tumult in the temple, 284. His prophecy regarding a woman and a box of ointment, falsified, 291—293. His prediction of the signs which should follow believers, at variance with fact, 293—299. His false predictions, a disproof of his divinity, 298, 299. His prediction of the persecuting spirit of Christianity, deplorably verified, 562—580.

Prophecy, definition of, 4. How to be interpreted, 9. When demonstrated to have been fulfilled, *ib.* 143. Double meaning of, 30. 130. 221, *n.* 394, *n.* That of Jesus touching the End of the World and the Day of Judgment, definite and precise, as to the time of its fulfilment, 66, *n.* 67. Often, in the Scriptures, made out of history, 563, *n.*

Prophet, origin, meaning, and use of the term, 51. 56—58, *n.*

Prophets, the various names by which they were designated, 51. Were amongst all nations of antiquity, *ib.* Their language always ambiguous and obscure, 52. Punished with death for false predictions, *ib.* The identity of the Hebrew and Pagan prophets, 56. Their divine frenzy, 55—58. Often prophesied falsely, 58. Their notions of the near approach of the End of the World, 134—139. Their style o expression. *ib.* Testimony of Peter to their predictions of the near approach of the End of the World, 164. 166. Supposed by the heathens to be possessed of demons, 405, *n.* Those of the Jews closely resembled the pagan monks, 457—460.

Protestant Christianity, dependent on Popery, 411, *n.* Its religious massacres, 574. Its persecuting spirit, *ib.* 579.

Pun, of Jesus on Peter's name, 371, *n.*

Purgatory, its pagan origin, 186. 456. To be entered by the Virgin Mary, 187. The Indian and Egyptian doctrine of, 460.

Pythagoras, his ideas borrowed by Jesus, 326. Taught the doctrine of being "born again," 428. His exorcism, 516. His monkery, *ib.* His miracles, *ib.* His divine nature, *ib.* The age in which he flourished, *ib.* His followers, austere monks, 523, *n.* 542.

R.

Regeneration, (see transmigration) a heathen doctrine, 440.

Relations of Jesus, their opinion of him, 358. 421, 422.

Religion of Nature, its consolations, joys, and pleasures, 611.

Resurrection, general, notions of, held by early Christians, 145. 162. 182. Apostolical notions of, 151—154. Two resurrections predicted in the Apocalypse, 172—174. 182. Jesus's mode of proving it, 416. The doctrine of, not taught in the Hebrew Scriptures, *ib.*

Resurrection of Jesus, his prediction of, 245—291. Arguments showing that his prediction of, was verified, 250—258. To rise from the dead, in the time of Jesus, not an uncommon thing, 258. Heathen deities and personages who are said to have risen from the dead, *ib.* 559. *n.* Arguments showing that Jesus's prediction that he would rise on the third day was not verified, 259—291. Difference of opinion, in the first century, as to the time he rose, 259—261. Did not appear to the Scribes and Pharisees, 276—278. Appeared only to his own disciples, *ib.* The belief of early Christians that it was a phantom which rose, 288, *n.* Various opinions of early Christians touching the reality of Jesus's resurrection, 288—290. Not expected by his disciples to rise, 393.

Revelation, Book of, is replete with assurances of the near approach of the End of the World, and the Final Judgment, 65. 181. 167. 171—175. Similarity between its fantastic descriptions and others found in pagan lore, 167, n. Much of its imagery said to have been borrowed from the Book of Daniel. 168, n. Its beast with seven heads, explained, ib. All its figures in accordance with Jewish lore, 169. Its supposed date, ib. Gives Rome a more terrible doom than other cities, at the approaching End of the World, ib. Has baffled Christian Commentators, 170. Its interpreting key, ib. Was held in high esteem in the first century, ib. Its authority denied in the third century, ib. Throws much light on Jesus's prediction of his Kingdom, and the End of the World, 171. Professes to be a revelation made by God to Jesus Christ, ib. Its notion that the world was to be destroyed by the agency of angels, ib. Its predictions of the mundane destruction resemble those of Jesus, ib. Its description of the secular Kingdom of Jesus, which was forthwith to be established, ib. 172—175. Its doctrine of the Millenium, ib. Predicts two resurrections, 172. 174. The falsity of its prophecies, 174.

Revivals in religion, those of ancient times, 201, n. Those of modern date, 202, n.

Rocks, the habitations of ancient monks, 452, n. Formed the dwelling of Boodh, ib. Temples in them, ib, n. Those of mount Sinai, the habitations of Christian monks, 458. Such the dwellings of Jewish monks and prophets, ib.

Romans, why they persecuted the Christians, 180, n. Enacted a law prohibiting human sacrifices. 324, n.

Rome, its severe doom predicted by early Christians, 168, 171, 180. Prognostications of its destruction, punished with death, 180, n.

S.

Sacrament, (see human sacrifices, love-feasts, oaths, &c) meaning of the word, 219, n. Was anciently a part of the love-feast, ib. Its pagan origin, 223—231, n. Was the ratification of an oath, 521. 526, Human blood used for it, 522, n.

Saints, how canonized, 208. Worshipped by early Christians, 408—410, n. Lives of, fabricated, 409, n. Their miracles after death, ib. Relics of, 485. 505, n.

Salvation, meaning of the word, 107. 155. 465. 558, n.

Samaria, Jesus's conversation with the woman of, 382. 387.

Samaritans, Jesus's bigoted and inconsistent prohibition against preaching the Gospel to them, 383. 387.

Saul, the king, prophesied naked, under divine frenzy, 56, n. 532, n.

Saviour, meaning of the term, 465.

Scribes, (see Pharisees) their high position and importance, 277. 353 355. Did not know Jesus personally, 556.

Self-glorification of Jesus, 381—383.

Sermon on the mount, a collection of pagan aphorisms, 312. 427.

Serpents, their poison drunk with impunity, 293, n.

Signs, which were to follow believers, gradually disappeared with the increase of knowledge, 293—299. The change effected in public opinion regarding them, 297.

Son of God, (see virgins) to die for the sins of men, a very ancient pagan notion, 429.

Son of man, a title used by the prophet Daniel, and by Jesus to designate himself, 28. 35. 66. 196.

Soul, meaning of the word, 109—111. 151, n. Separate existence of, denied in the Old Testament, 110. Jesus's notion of, 111—115. 144—146, n. Opinions of the Fathers as to its state after death, 182, 187.

Speaking with tongues, in what it consisted, 201, n.

Spirit. (see soul) import of the word, 110. 155. 338, n.

Steeples, their pagan origin, 487, n.

Stomach, Jesus's notion of what defiles it, 400.

Suicide, whether encouraged by Jesus, 320.

Sunday, origin of the name, 323, n.

Swine, destroyed by Jesus, to the great loss of their possessors, 344. 380.

Swords, carried and used by Jesus's disciples, 99. 363—365. 375.

Symbolical language, derogatory to the character of God, 132—134. Its supposed use in Jesus's prediction fatal to Christianity, 140.

T.

Tarsus, St. Paul's birth-place, noted for its college and monkery, 506, n. Where Apollonius Tyaneus was educated, 516.

Temple, Jesus's tumultuous conduct in, 350—352. 380. His offer to rebuild it in three days, 390

Tertullian, his apology for Montanus's prediction of the speedy End of the World, 180. Rejoices in the belief of the near approach of the event, 181. His opinion of the New Jerusalem, heaven, paradise, and the resurrection, 182. His monkery, 475. His exposure of the Christian virgins, *ib.* His opinion of baptism, virginity, continence, and the sign of the cross, as among the heathens, 476.

Theft, justified by Jesus, 318. 348.

Theodosius the Great, founder of the Holy Office of the Inquisition, 570, *n.* His edict against the Manicheans, *ib.* His appointment of inquisitors, *ib.*

Therapeuts, (see monks) description of, 221, *n.* Their identity with the Essenes, *ib.* 463—467. Were Eclectic philosophers, 288. 424. 432, *n.* Their churches called monasteries. 370, *n.* Were identical with the early Christians, *ib.* Their sacred books the same as our Gospels. 431—436. Those of India, 445. Meaning of the term, 464. The Therapeutic art anciently in the hands of divines, 513. *n.*

Time, Jewish mode of computing, 246—249. Arguments to show that the Jews reckoned time inclusive, 249. 253—257. The Jews not very accurate in reckoning time, 255, *n.* 270. Arguments to show that the Jews did not reckon time inclusive, 270—279, 280, *n.* No terms to designate the divisions of, among ancient nations, 271, *n.* The meaning of "My time is not yet come," 359.

Translators of the English version of the New Testament, had a Christian bias, 373, *n.* 388, *n.* 433, *n.*

Transmigration, (see monks and Brahmins) doctrine of, put in the mouth of Josephus, 146. Taught by Jesus, 388, *n.* 427. 539, *n.* Taught by the Boodhist monks, 451. *n.* 455, Taught by the Egyptians, 460.

Transubstantiation, the Romish view of, 321. The doctrine of, from a pagan source, 324, *n.* The convenience of the doctrine of, to early Christians, 525, *n.* The manner in which the doctrine of, was established in Christendom, 527, *n.*

Trinity, of the Hindoos, 452, *n.* Of the Christians, 585. Supposes three Gods of diversified characters, *ib.* Perplexes the human mind. 605.

Truth, many of Jesus's sayings at variance with, 365—371.

Turner, Sharon, his incredible account of the literary productions of Alfred the Great, 420.

V.

Vestal Virgins, when defloured, laid the blame to some God, 490. One of them, proving the mother of twins, charges

Mars with the paternity, *ib.* Duties of, *ib.* Had their heads shaved, *ib.* Had power to dispose of their possessions, *ib.* Took a vow of chaststy, *ib.* Death the punishment for violating them, *ib.* Their veil and other attire. *ib.* Their history known to the Gospel writers, 491. Their sacred fire in Zion, 502.

Vipers, not all poisonous, 295, *n.*

Virgin Mary, was to enter purgatory, 187. The cakes offered to her, 410, *n.* Was in the temple three years before her betrothal, 491. *n.* The Gospel of the birth of, *ib.* Her miraculous birth, 492. *n.* Devoted to the service of the temple when three years old, *ib.* Visited by angels. *ib.* Her refusal to leave the temple, and get married, *ib.* Forced, by lot, to marry Joseph, *ib.* Her husband, a widower with children, compelled to take her home with him, *ib.* Is left at home by her husband, *ib.* Returns to the temple to spin, *ib.* Is told by an angel, and by the high priest, that she is to be the mother of a deity, *ib.* Her husband, on his return home, finds her with child, *ib.* Her protestations of her chastity, *ib.* The mystery of her state explained by an angel, *ib.* She and her husband are tried for a violation of the laws of virginity, *ib.* Both bitterly weep. *ib.* Their acquittal, *ib.* Mary gives birth to Jesus in a cave, *ib.* 493, *n.* Her cave and fountain at Nazareth, 495, *n.*

Virgins, deities born of, a very common pagan notion, 438. 491. *n.* Boodh born of a virgin, 449. 453. 491, *n.* Meaning of the word, 479, *n.* 490. A list of gods born of virgins, 491, *n.* The question of their intrigues with priests, *ib.* The Egyptian consecration of the pregnancy of a virgin, and its mystery, *ib.* Those kept in the temples became mothers of Gods, *ib.*

Virgins, holy, of Heathenism, (see monks) those of the Brahmins. 445. Those of paganism and Christianity contrasted, 473. 475, 476. Their abode, 479, *n.*

Virgins, holy, of Christianity, their character, 231, *n.* Their chastity, 471—474. Contrasted with those of paganism, 473. 475. Uttered divine oracles, 472. Their religious motives impeached, 475. Their frailty. 473—477. Their vanity, *ib.* Their depravity, *ib.* Their cohabitation with monk-priests, *ib.* Their hermitical life, 487. Their community of goods, *ib.* Went about naked, 488.

Virtue and vice, not changed by circumstances, 156. 303, *n.* 313. 319. 338. 343.

Visions, the result of cerebral disease, 203, *n.*

W.

War in heaven, a heathen idea, 595.
Wind, Jesus's erroneous notion of, 399.
Wine, a quantity of made by Jesus from water, 348. Abstained from, by the Indian mónks, 445. 482: by the Jewish monks, 459; by the Christian monks, 482, 483. 486. 488. 522. Used for sacrament, mixed with water, and with human blood, 522, *n.* 526. *n.* Abstained from, by the Therapeuts, 522.
Witchcraft, originated in the notion of demoniacal possession, 412. The appalling effect of the Christian belief in, 596. Falsified by the indications of nature, 598.
Witnesses, against Jesus, 390.
Women, a number of, always followed Jesus, 337, *n.* 342. The virtue of, made by him to consist in continence alone, 378. Are given redress by him only for the adultery of their husbands, *ib.* Are denied by him the rights and liberties enjoyed by the male sex, *ib.* Followed the Indian monks. 445.
Word, of God, an ancient phrase in heathen theology, 420. Doctrine of, or the *logos*, from pagan lore, 437. 439. 441.
World, (see End of the World) the period assigned, by early Christians, to the duration of, 168. 173. 175. 182. The new world to be created, was to have no sea, 174. The period assigned by ancient Jews to the duration of, 183.

Z.

Zaccheus, entertaining Jesus, 94.
Zoroaster, his reformation of the Persian religion, 502. The date at which he flourished, *ib.* Predicted the birth of the Messiah, and the appearance of a new star, 504.

APR 15 1915

END.

Check Out More Titles From HardPress Classics Series In this collection we are offering thousands of classic and hard to find books. This series spans a vast array of subjects – so you are bound to find something of interest to enjoy reading and learning about.

Subjects:
Architecture
Art
Biography & Autobiography
Body, Mind &Spirit
Children & Young Adult
Dramas
Education
Fiction
History
Language Arts & Disciplines
Law
Literary Collections
Music
Poetry
Psychology
Science
…and many more.

Visit us at www.hardpress.net